UNIVERSITY CASEBOOK SERIES

CASES AND MATERIALS

ESTATES AND TRUSTS

FOURTH EDITION

by

STEWART E. STERK
H. Bert and Ruth Mack Professor of Law
Benjamin Cardozo School of Law, Yeshiva University

MELANIE B. LESLIE
Professor of Law
Benjamin Cardozo School of Law, Yeshiva University

JOEL C. DOBRIS
Professor of Law
University of California, Davis

FOUNDATION PRESS
2011

1 New York Plaza, 34th Floor

New York, NY 10004

Phone Toll Free 1–877–888–1330

Fax 646–424–5201

foundation–press.com

Printed in the United States of America

ISBN 978–1–59941–928–2

Mat #40925406

PREFACE

This book is designed entirely for teaching and learning. We have assembled questions, problems, and notes to focus student attention on critical issues. We have tried to be crisp, and to present material in ways that will keep students awake and engaged. We have also tried wherever possible to use recent cases, both because recent cases highlight the issues of greatest current significance, and because recent cases demonstrate that even in areas which have supposedly been settled for decades, lawyers without the necessary skills, or lawyers who take inadequate care, can generate unwanted litigation for their clients and for the families of those clients.

Any course book dominated by appellate cases, including this one, permits and encourages teachers and students to explore legal doctrine from the perspective of policymakers and litigators. Most estates lawyers, however, are not litigators; they are lawyers who focus on drafting and planning to avoid litigation. We have designed this book to integrate drafting and planning issues with discussions of doctrine and policy. Many of the notes, questions, and problems ask students what they would do, as drafters and planners, to avoid the litigation that resulted from the planning and drafting decisions made by the lawyers in the principal cases reproduced in the book.

We seek not only to provide a thorough introduction to the doctrinal rules surrounding trusts, powers of appointment, and other wealth transmission devices, but also to show students why a client would find it advantageous to use these devices. Wherever possible, we have organized materials functionally so that students understand why a lawyer would want to use a particular technique before we consider the legal rules that govern the techniques.

Many of the clients who generate the most lucrative business for estates lawyers have one principal goal in mind: tax avoidance. The 2010 estate tax legislation significantly reduces the number of people subject to the federal estate tax, and we have reduced our treatment of the tax accordingly. At the same time, we believe that law students can more fully appreciate the importance of many of the devices they study (particularly trusts and powers of appointment) if they have at least a rudimentary understanding of the federal estate tax. We have incorporated a brief introduction to estate taxation early in the book, and we have built on that basic introduction in later chapters. The chapters that include tax issues are designed so that the teacher who does not wish to cover tax can easily exclude those materials.

At many schools, curricular pressures have reduced the number of hours available for studying estates and trusts. At the same time, we recognize the need to provide some flexibility for teachers who want to highlight different areas of the course. We believe that a teacher should be able to cover the entire book in a five-credit course. At the same time, we recognize that most schools (including our own) do not allocate five credits to a course on Estates and Trusts. The format of the book is designed to make it easily adaptable to a three or four-credit survey course, or to separate two-credit courses on "Wills" and "Trusts".

Although neither of us routinely uses power point slides in the classroom, we have found them useful for diagramming family relationships and illustrating problems related to intestate succession, the elective share and future interests. We are happy to make our (very pretty) slides available to teachers who adopt the book. To access the slides, visit our Foundation Press author website at www.sterklesliedobris.com. Once there, follow the steps to request a password.

Although we believe that most students should be able to master the material in this book without recourse to outside materials, students who are looking for additional textual material on Estates and Trusts are blessed with a number of excellent study aids. For students interested in a combination of textual material and additional problems (with solutions), we suggest Melanie B. Leslie and Stewart E. Sterk, Trusts & Estates (Concepts and Insights) (2nd ed. 2011). Other fine books include:

Roger W. Andersen, Understanding Trusts and Estates (4th ed. 2009)

Lawrence H. Averill, Averill's Black Letter Outline on Wills, Trusts, and Future Interests (3d ed. 2005).

Lawrence H. Averill and Mary F. Radford, Uniform Probate Code and Uniform Trust Code in a Nutshell (6th ed. 2010)

Gerry W. Beyer, Wills, Trusts and Estates, Examples and Explanations (4th ed. 2007)

Thomas M. Featherston, Jr., Questions and Answers: Wills, Trusts and Estates (2nd ed. 2007)

William M. McGovern, Sheldon F. Kurtz, and David English, Wills, Trusts and Estates (4th ed. 2010)

Jeffrey N. Pennell & Alan Newman, Wills, Trusts and Estates (3rd ed. 2009)

Thomas L. Shaffer, Carol Ann Mooney & Amy Jo Boettcher, The Planning and Drafting of Wills and Trusts (5th ed. 2007)

We would like to thank our students, Jenna Bernstein, Mark Bradley, Joshua Ferguson, Sara Fucci, Lindsay Gold, Eytan Goldschein, Alexandra Reimer, Nolan Robinson, Jeremy Schonfeld, Laura Tam, and Erica Thau for their assistance in preparing this edition. We also owe a debt of gratitude to a number of colleagues who have made valuable suggestions, including Ralph Brashier, James Delaney, Lynn Foster, Erica Gloger, Jim Jones, Steven Kropp, Robert Palmer, John Robinson, and Walter Schwidetzky. As always, special thanks go to Laura Cunningham, whose willingness to share both her clarity of thought and her tax expertise has made her almost a shadow co-author.

Finally, although Joel Dobris did not actively participate in the preparation of this edition, his handiwork remains evident throughout the casebook. We remain grateful for the guidance and wit he has provided during the course of this (and past) editions. Both we and the book are far richer for the contributions Joel has made over the course of numerous editions.

STEWART E. STERK
MELANIE B. LESLIE

ACKNOWLEDGMENTS

The authors wish to express appreciation for permission to reprint excerpts from the following works:

Evelyn Ginsberg Abravanel, Discretionary Support Trusts, 68 Iowa L. Rev. 273, 278–79 (1983).

Mark L. Ascher, Curtailing Inherited Wealth, 89 Mich. L. Rev. 69, 69–76 (1990).

Jane B. Baron, Intention, Interpretation, and Stories, 42 Duke L. J. 630, 638–39 (1992).

Martin D. Begleiter, Attorney Malpractice in Estate Planning—You've Got to Know When to Hold Up, Know When to Fold Up, 38 Kan. L. Rev. 193, 274–76 (1990).

Ralph C. Brashier, Children and Inheritance in the Nontraditional Family, 1996 Utah L. Rev. 93, 169–72, 222–24.

Teresa Stanton Collett, A Response to the Conference: The Ethics of Intergenerational Representation, 62 Fordham L. Rev. 1453, 1463–64 (1994).

Robert T. Danforth, Rethinking the Law of Creditors' Rights in Trusts, 53 Hastings L. J. 287, 293–94, 309 (2002).

Carolyn Dessin, Acting as Agent Under a Financial Durable Power of Attorney: An Unscripted Role, 75 Neb. L. Rev. 574, 575–76 (1996).

Joel C. Dobris, Medicaid Asset Planning by the Elderly: A Policy View of Expectations, Entitlement and Inheritance, 24 Real Prop., Prob. & T.J. 1, 5–8 (1989).

Jesse Dukeminier, Cleansing the Stables of Property: A River Found at Last, 65 Iowa L. Rev. 151, 152 (1979).

Jesse Dukeminier, Perpetuities: The Measuring Lives, 85 Colum. L. Rev. 1648, 1656 (1985). This article originally appeared at 85 Colum L. Rev. 1648 (1985).

Anne S. Emanuel, Spendthrift Trusts: It's Time to Codify the Compromise, 72 Neb. L. Rev. 179, 192–93 (1993).

Mary Louise Fellows, The Case Against Living Probate, 78 Mich. L. Rev. 1066, 1094 (1980).

Robert L. Fletcher, Perpetuities: Basic Clarity, Muddled Reform, 63 Wash. L. Rev. 791, 822 (1988).

Bradley E.S. Fogel, Back to the Future Interest: The Origin and Questionable Legal Basis of the Use of Crummey Withdrawal Powers to Obtain the Federal Gift Tax Annual Exclusion, 6 Fla. Tax Rev. 187, 211–13 (2003).

Frances H. Foster, Trust Privacy, 93 Cornell L. Rev. 555, 608 (2008).

Susan F. French, Imposing a General Survival Requirement on Beneficiaries of Future Interests: Solving the Problems Caused by the Death of a Beneficiary Before the Time Set for Distribution, 27 Ariz. L. Rev. 801, 804–05, 836 (1985). Copyright (c) 1985 by the Arizona Board of Regents.

Susan F. French, Perpetuities: Three Essays in Honor of My Father, 65 Wash. L. Rev. 323, 325, 352 (1990).

Elaine Hightower Gagliardi, Economic Substance in the Context of Federal Estate and Gift Tax: The Internal Revenue Service Has it Wrong, 64 Mont. L. Rev. 389, 419 (2003).

Susan N. Gary, The Parent–Child Relationship Under Intestacy Statutes, 32 U. Mem. L. Rev. 643, 673–74 (2002).

Iris J. Goodwin, Donor Standing to Enforce Charitable Gifts: Civil Society vs. Donor Empowerment, 58 Vand. L. Rev. 1093 (2005).

Adam J. Hirsch, Spendthrift Trusts and Public Policy: Economic and Cognitive Perspectives, 73 Wash. U. L.Q. 1, 91–92 (1995).

Adam J. Hirsch & William K.S. Wang, A Qualitative Theory of the Dead Hand, 68 Ind. L. J. 1, 6–14 (1992).

Sharona Hoffman & Andrew P. Morriss, Birth After Death: Perpetuities and the New Reproductive Technologies, 38 Ga. L. Rev. 575, 624 (2004).

Karen Kaplan, As Man Lay in Coma–Like State, His Brain Was Busy Rebuilding, Los Angeles Times, July 4, 2006.

Linda Kelly–Hill, No–Fault Death: Wedding Inheritance Rights to Family Values, 94 Ky. L. J. 319, 354–55 (2005).

Diane J. Klein, Revenge of the Disappointed Heir: Tortious Interference with Expectation of Inheritance—A Survey With Analysis of State Approaches in the Fourth Circuit, 104 W. Va. L. Rev. 259 (2002).

Sheldon F. Kurtz & Lawrence M. Waggoner, The UPC Addresses the Class–Gift and Intestacy Rights of Children of Assisted Reproductive Technologies, 35 ACTEC J. 30 (2009).

John H. Langbein, Book Review, 103 Yale L.J. 2039, 2039–40, 2045–47 (1994). Reprinted by permission of The Yale Law Journal Company and Fred B. Rothman & Company from The Yale Law Journal, vol. 103, pages 2039–48.

John H. Langbein, The Contractarian Basis of the Law of Trusts, 105 Yale L.J. 625, 629, 650–51 (1995). Reprinted by permission of The Yale Law Journal Company and Fred B. Rothman & Company from The Yale Law Journal, vol. 105, pages 625–75.

John H. Langbein, The Nonprobate Revolution and the Future of the Law of Succession, 97 Harv. L. Rev. 1108, 1132 (1984). Copyright (c) 1984 by the Harvard Law Review Association.

John H. Langbein, The Twentieth–Century Revolution in Family Wealth Transmission, 86 Mich. L. Rev. 722, 732 (1988).

John H. Langbein, The Uniform Prudent Investor Act and the Future of Trust Investing, 81 Iowa L. Rev. 641, 650–53 (1996).

W. Barton Leach, Perpetuities in Perspective: Ending the Rule's Reign of Terror, 65 Harv. L. Rev. 721, 732 (1952). Copyright (c) 1952 by the Harvard Law Review Association.

Aloysius A. Leopold & Gerry W. Beyer, Ante–Mortem Probate: A Viable Alternative, 43 Ark. L. Rev. 131, 172–74 (1990). Copyright 1990 by the Arkansas Law Review and Bar Association Journal, Inc.

Melanie Leslie, The Myth of Testamentary Freedom, 38 Ariz. L. Rev. 235, 246, 270–73 (1996). Copyright (c) 1996 by the Arizona Board of Regents.

James Lindgren, The Fall of Formalism, 55 Alb. L. Rev. 1009 (1992).

Mary K. Lundwall, Inconsistency and Uncertainty in the Charitable Purposes Doctrine, 41 Wayne L. Rev. 1341, 1341–42 (1995).

Ray D. Madoff, Autonomy and End-of-Life Decision Making: Reflections of a Lawyer and a Daughter, 53 Buff. L. Rev. 963 (2005).

Andrew Metz, The Schiavo Autopsy: The Post–Mortem, Newsday, June 16, 2005.

Alan Newman, Incorporating the Partnership Theory of Marriage into Elective–Share Law: The Approximation System of the Uniform Probate Code and the Deferred Community–Property Alternative, 49 Emory L.J. 487 (2000).

Alan Newman, The Intention of the Settlor Under the Uniform Trust Code: Whose Property Is It, Anyway?, 38 Akron L. Rev. 649 (2005).

Burnele V. Powell & Ronald C. Link, The Sense of a Client: Confidentiality Issues in Representing the Elderly, 62 Fordham L. Rev. 1197, 1205 (1994).

Laura Rosenbury, Two Ways to End a Marriage: Divorce or Death, 2005 Utah L. Rev. 1227, 1283.

Leslie Salzman, Rethinking Guardianship (Again): Substituted Decision Making As A Violation of the Integration Mandate of Title II of the Americans with Disabilities Act, 81 U. Colo. L. Rev. 157 (2010).

Ronald J. Scalise, Jr. Honor thy Father and Mother?: How Intestacy Law Goes Too Far in Protecting Parents. 37 Seton Hall L. Rev. 171, 189 (2006).

Frederic S. Schwartz, Models of the Will and Negative Disinheritance, 48 Mercer L. Rev. 1137, 1114–45 (1997).

Robert Mahealani M. Seto and Lynne Marie Kohm, Of Princesses, Charities, Trustees, and Fairytales: A Lesson of the Simple Wishes of Princess Bernice Pauahi Bishop, 21 U. Haw. L. Rev. 393, 411 (1999).

Thomas B. Scheffey, IBM Heiress Case Pushes Legal Boundaries, Connecticut Law Tribune, August 17, 2009.

Thomas Shaffer, The Legal Ethics of Radical Individualism, 65 Tex. L. Rev. 963, 982 (1987). Published originally in 65 Texas Law Review 963 (1987). Copyright 1987 by the Texas Law Review Association.

Jeffrey G. Sherman, Posthumous Meddling: An Instrumentalist Theory of Testamentary Restraints on Conjugal and Religious Choices, 1999 U. Ill. L. Rev. 1273, 1295–97, 1309.

John G. Steinkamp, A Case for Federal Transfer Taxation, 55 Ark. L. Rev. 1, 82 (2002).

Stewart E. Sterk, Asset Protection Trusts: Trust Law's Race to the Bottom? 85 Cornell L. Rev. 1035, 1048–50, 1065–66 (2000).

Stewart E. Sterk, Jurisdictional Competition to Abolish the Rule Against Perpetuities: R.I.P. for the R.A.P., 24 Cardozo L. Rev. 2097, 2104 (2003).

Stewart E. Sterk, Rethinking Trust Law Reform: How Prudent is Modern Prudent Investor Doctrine?, 95 Cornell L. Rev. 851, 902 (2010).

Joshua C. Tate, Conditional Love: Incentive Trusts and the Inflexibility Problem, 41 Real Prop., Prob. & Trust J. 445, 453 (2006).

Jeffrey Toobin, Rich Bitch: The Legal Battle Over Trust Funds for Pets, The New Yorker, September 29, 2008.

Lawrence W. Waggoner, Perpetuities: A Perspective on Wait-and-See, 85 Colum. L. Rev. 1714, 1715–16 (1985). This article originally appeared at 85 Colum. L. Rev. 1714 (1985).

Philip D. Witte, Heir Wars, California Lawyer Magazine, September 2003.

SUMMARY OF CONTENTS

PREFACE iii
ACKNOWLEDGMENTS vii
AUTHOR INDEX xxix
TABLE OF STATUTES xxxiii
TABLE OF CASES xxxvii

CHAPTER ONE. Introduction 1

CHAPTER TWO. Intestate Succession 65

CHAPTER THREE. Protection of the Family 167

CHAPTER FOUR. Wills 227

CHAPTER FIVE. Contesting the Will 413

CHAPTER SIX. The Government's Share: A Brief Introduction to Estate Taxation 508

CHAPTER SEVEN. Trusts 519

CHAPTER EIGHT. Powers of Appointment 737

CHAPTER NINE. Classification and Construction of Future Interests 792

CHAPTER TEN. The Rule Against Perpetuities 869

CHAPTER ELEVEN. Planning for Incapacity 938

CHAPTER TWELVE. Co-ordinating Non-Probate Assets With the Probate Estate 984

CHAPTER THIRTEEN. Estate and Trust Administration 1005

INDEX 1113

TABLE OF CONTENTS

PREFACE iii
ACKNOWLEDGMENTS vii
AUTHOR INDEX xxix
TABLE OF STATUTES xxxiii
TABLE OF CASES xxxvii

CHAPTER ONE. Introduction 1

Sec.
I. The Living and the Dead: Whose Money Is It? 1
Estate of Feinberg 1
Notes and Questions 8
Notes and Questions 14
Ford v. Ford 16
Notes and Questions 22
Notes and Questions 27
Problems 27
II. The Role of the Lawyer, and the Lawyer–Client Relationship 28
Hotz v. Minyard 29
Notes and Questions 32
Problems 33
Barcelo v. Elliott 35
Notes and Questions 42
III. Probate and Non–Probate Transfers 45
A. Probate: What Is It, and Who Needs It? 45
B. Gifts 47
Gruen v. Gruen 47
Notes and Questions 51
C. Joint Interests With Right of Survivorship 52
Franklin v. Anna National Bank 54
Notes and Questions 57
D. The Nonprobate Revolution: Scope and Reasons 60
Notes and Questions 63

CHAPTER TWO. Intestate Succession 65

Sec.
I. Introduction and Representative Statutes 65
II. The Share of the Surviving Spouse 72
Problems 75
Estate of Goick 76
Notes and Questions 80
Despite a Will, Jackson Left a Tangled Estate 82
III. The Share of Lineal Descendants 85
Problems and Questions 87
Problems 90
Note: Conduct–Based Bars to Inheritance 91

Sec.

IV. The Share of Ancestors and Collateral Heirs 93
Problem 94
Estate of Locke 95
Notes and Questions 98
Problems 99
Note on Escheat 99
V. Intestate Succession and Community Property States 100
Estate of Borghi 101
Notes and Questions 106
VI. Defining the Modern Family: Halfbloods, Adoptees, and Non–Marital Children 107
A. Halfbloods 107
Problem 108
B. Adoption 109
Estates of Donnelly 109
Notes and Questions 113
Notes and Questions 114
Estate of Brittin 116
Notes and Questions 120
Bean v. Ford 122
Notes and Questions 127
C. Non–Marital Children and Questions of Paternity 130
Notes and Questions 133
In re Estate of Burden 135
Notes and Questions 139
Problems 140
Problems 142
D. The Impact of Modern Reproductive Technology 142
Questions 145
VII. Simultaneous Death 147
Estate of Villwock 148
Questions 151
Notes and Questions 153
Problems 154
VIII. Disclaimer (Renunciation) 154
Estate of Baird 154
Notes and Questions 158
Problems 163
Note on Assignment of Expectancy Interests 164
Question 164
IX. Advancements 164
Problem 166

CHAPTER THREE. Protection of the Family 167

Sec.

I. An Introduction to the Elective Share 167
II. Traditional Elective Share Statutes 170
Sullivan v. Burkin 170
Notes and Questions 174
Notes and Questions 176

Sec.
III. Modern Elective Share Statutes ---- 178
Notes ---- 191
Problems ---- 193
Notes ---- 195
IV. Waiver of Elective Share Rights ---- 196
Geddings v. Geddings ---- 196
Notes and Questions ---- 198
Notes and Questions ---- 202
V. Other Protections for the Surviving Spouse ---- 203
A. Homestead Allowance, Exempt Property, and Family Allowance ---- 203
Problem ---- 205
B. Protection Against Inadvertent Disinheritance: The Problem of the Pre–Marital Will ---- 206
Prestie v. Prestie ---- 207
Notes and Questions ---- 210
Question ---- 211
Problems ---- 211
VI. The Community Property System ---- 212
VII. Protection of Children: Pretermitted Child Statutes ---- 213
Estate of Glomset ---- 214
Notes and Questions ---- 217
Notes and Questions ---- 219
Problems ---- 220
Heir Wars ---- 220
Notes and Questions ---- 224
Notes and Questions ---- 225

CHAPTER FOUR. Wills ---- 227

Sec.
I. Execution of Wills ---- 227
A. Will Formalities: What are They and Why Have Them? ---- 227
Morris v. West ---- 230
Questions ---- 233
Notes ---- 234
B. The Signature Requirement ---- 235
C. More About the Witness (or Attestation) Requirement ---- 236
Problems ---- 239
D. The Execution Ceremony ---- 241
Note on Safekeeping ---- 242
E. Salvage Doctrines: Substantial Compliance and the UPC's Dispensing Power ---- 243
Estate of Hall ---- 243
Questions ---- 246
Notes ---- 246
Problem ---- 249

Sec.

I. Execution of Wills—Continued
F. Holographic Wills 250
Zhao v. Wong 250
Questions 256
Problem 257
Notes 258
G. Statutory Wills 259
Problems 259
H. Electronic Wills? 260
II. What Constitutes the Will? 260
A. Introduction 260
B. Integration and Incorporation by Reference 262
Estate of Norton 262
Notes and Questions 268
Problem 268
Clark v. Greenhalge 269
Questions 273
Note 274
Notes and Questions 275
Problems 275
C. Facts of Independent Significance 276
Problems 277
In re Tipler's Will 277
Question 281
D. Negative Disinheritance 282
III. Construction Problems Created by the Time Gap Between Will Execution and Death 283
A. Abatement 283
In re Estate of Potter 284
Questions 287
Notes 288
Questions 289
Note on Demonstrative Devises 290
Problems 290
Note on Exoneration of Specific Devises 291
Note on Apportionment of Taxes 291
Problems 293
B. Ademption 293
McGee v. McGee 294
Notes and Questions 299
Question 302
Problems 302
Problems 304
Note on Ademption by Satisfaction 305
C. Lapse 306
Problem 309
Problem 311
Note on Void Devises 311
Problem Areas: When Does the Will Override the Antilapse Statute? 311
Estate of Rehwinkel 311
Notes and Questions 315

Sec.
III. Construction Problems Created by the Time Gap Between Will Execution and Death—Continued
Notes and Questions 319
Morse v. Sharkey 320
Notes and Questions 322
Problems 323
IV. Construction Problems More Generally 324
A. Reading the Will as a Whole 325
Matter of Marine Midland Bank, N.A. 326
Notes and Questions 331
Problem 332
B. Using Extrinsic Evidence 332
1. Is the Will Ambiguous? 333
Estate of Carroll 333
Notes and Questions 337
2. Testator's Circumstances and Behavior 338
Estate of Gibbs 339
Notes and Questions 343
Problems 345
3. Testator's Unattested Statements 346
Problem 346
Britt v. Upchurch 346
Notes and Questions 352
C. Correcting Mistakes 353
Gifford v. Dyer 353
Notes and Questions 354
Knupp v. District of Columbia 355
Notes and Questions 358
Problem 359
V. Revocation of Wills 359
A. Introduction 359
Gushwa v. Hunt 360
B. Revocation by Subsequent Written Instrument 367
Questions 367
Problem 368
Problems 369
C. Revocation by Physical Act 369
Ward–Allen v. Gaskins 370
Questions 374
Notes 375
Problems 377
D. Revocation by Operation of Law 378
Problems 380
Notes 381
E. Revival and Dependent Relative Revocation 382
Problems 383
Note 383
Oliva–Foster v. Oliva 384
Notes and Questions 387
Problems 388

Sec.
VI. Limits on the Power to Revoke: Joint Wills and Will Contracts 389
Garrett v. Read 389
Questions 395
Note on Joint Wills 396
Problems 397
Shimp v. Huff 397
Notes and Questions 403
Problem 404
Note on Contracts to Make Wills 404
VII. Illustrative Will 405

CHAPTER FIVE. Contesting the Will 413

Sec.
I. Testamentary Capacity 413
Barnes v. Marshall 413
Wilson v. Lane 421
Questions 423
Dougherty v. Rubenstein 428
Notes, Questions, and Problems 436
Gonsalves v. Superior Court 438
Notes and Questions 441
Problems 442
II. Undue Influence 442
Haynes v. First National State Bank of New Jersey 443
Notes and Questions 454
Will of Moses 458
Notes and Questions 465
Problem 468
III. Fraud 469
Problem 470
Notes and Questions 471
IV. Tortious Interference with Inheritance 473
Estate of Ellis 473
Questions 478
V. Preparing for the Contest: The Lawyer's Role 482
Questions 483
Question 487
Notes and Questions 488
Problem: Scope of No–Contest Clauses 489
VI. Special Problems Affecting Some Gay, Lesbian and Transgendered Testators 491
Will of Kaufmann 493
Notes and Questions 501
IBM Heiress Case Pushes Legal Boundaries 504
Notes and Questions 507

CHAPTER SIX. The Government's Share: A Brief Introduction to Estate Taxation 508

Problem 515
Problem 517
Note: Gifts Between Spouses 517
Note on the Charitable Deduction 518

CHAPTER SEVEN. Trusts 519

Note on Trusts and Legal Life Estates 520
Note on the Uniform Trust Code 521

Sec.
I. Creation of Trusts 522
  A. Trust Requisites: The Trustee, the Beneficiary, and the Property 522
    1. The Trustee 523
    2. The Need for Identifiable Beneficiaries 526
      Notes and Questions 527
      Rich Bitch; The Legal Battle Over Trust Funds for Pets. 528
      Question 532
    3. Trust Property 532
      Notes 532
  B. Trust Formation: Capacity, Intent, and Formalities 533
    1. Capacity 533
    2. Intent to Create a Trust: The Precatory Language Problem 534
      Spicer v. Wright 534
      Levin v. Fisch 536
      Questions 539
      Problems 539
      Note 540
    3. Trust Formalities 540
      Goodman v. Goodman 540
      Questions 543
      Notes on Formalities 544
II. Using Trusts as an Estate Planning Tool 548
  A. Providing for Minor Children 548
    Problem 549
  B. Building Flexibility Into the Estate Plan: Support Trusts and Discretionary Trusts 550
    Problem 551
    Wells v. Sanford 551
    Questions 555
    Problem 555
    Marsman v. Nasca 555
    Notes and Questions 563
  C. Avoiding Probate 566
    1. Avoiding Probate Without the Use of Trusts 567
      Problem 570

Sec.

II. Using Trusts as an Estate Planning Tool—Continued
2. Avoiding Probate Through the Use of Revocable *Inter Vivos* Trusts ... 570
Questions ... 574
Clymer v. Mayo ... 577
Questions ... 580
Notes ... 580
Heaps v. Heaps ... 582
Questions ... 587
Problem ... 587
Problem ... 592
Committee on Professional Ethics v. Baker ... 593
Questions ... 600
Note ... 600
D. Protecting Beneficiaries from Creditors: Support and Discretionary Trusts, Revocable Trusts, Spendthrift Trusts and Self–Settled Asset Protection Trusts ... 600
1. Support and Discretionary Trusts ... 600
Wilcox v. Gentry ... 602
Questions ... 605
Notes ... 606
2. Spendthrift Trusts ... 607
Scheffel v. Krueger ... 610
Notes and Questions ... 612
Problems ... 613
Notes ... 614
3. Creditors' Rights in Self–Settled Trusts, Including Offshore and Domestic Asset Protection Trusts ... 617
Problems ... 617
Notes ... 618
Federal Trade Commission v. Affordable Media, LLC ... 619
Notes and Questions ... 625
Problems ... 635
Notes and Questions ... 637
E. Planning for Incapacity and/or the Costs of Institutional Care ... 639
1. Planning for Incapacity With Revocable Living Trusts ... 639
Questions ... 640
2. Planning Involving Government Health and Medical Benefits ... 641
a. Support/Discretionary Trusts Created by Someone Other Than the Beneficiary ... 641
Estate of Gist ... 642
Questions ... 646
b. Self–Settled Trusts and Incapacity ... 647
Problem ... 648
Cohen v. Commissioner ... 648
Questions ... 653
Notes ... 654
F. Minimizing Taxation ... 656
1. *Inter Vivos* Trusts ... 656
Estate of Kohlsaat ... 659
Notes and Questions ... 662

Sec.
II. Using Trusts as an Estate Planning Tool—Continued
2. Testamentary Trusts: More on Marital Deduction Planning, and an Introduction to the Generation–Skipping Tax ... 663
a. Maximizing the Assets Available to the Surviving Spouse While Minimizing Taxation ... 664
b. Protecting Assets for Beneficiaries Other Than the Surviving Spouse ... 666
Problems ... 669
c. Generation–Skipping Trusts ... 670
Problem ... 671
III. Trust Modification and Termination ... 671
A. Modification or Termination by Direction of the Trust Settlor ... 672
Connecticut General Life Insurance Co. v. First National Bank of Minneapolis ... 672
Questions ... 674
B. Modification or Termination by Consent ... 675
Adams v. Link ... 676
American National Bank of Cheyenne v. Miller ... 679
Problems ... 683
Notes and Questions ... 685
C. Modification or Termination Without Consent of All Beneficiaries ... 688
1. Mistake ... 689
Walker v. Walker ... 689
Note ... 694
2. Unanticipated Circumstances Affecting Trust Objectives 695
3. Modification or Termination to Provide for Needy Income Beneficiaries: New York's EPTL Section 7–1.6(b) 695
Problem ... 695
IV. Charitable Trusts ... 696
A. Tax Incentives for Charitable Giving ... 697
B. Charitable Purposes ... 698
Shenandoah Valley National Bank of Winchester v. Taylor ... 698
Questions ... 704
Notes ... 704
C. Standing: Who Can Enforce the Charitable Trust's Terms? ... 707
Problem ... 709
D. The Cy Pres Doctrine ... 710
Problem ... 710
Estate of Crawshaw ... 710
Questions ... 720
Notes (and More Questions) ... 720
A Move for Art's Sake Stirs Debate on Bequests ... 724
Questions ... 726
Estate of Wilson ... 726
Notes and Questions ... 733
Tropical Battle of Race, Rights Divides Islanders ... 734
Note ... 735

CHAPTER EIGHT. Powers of Appointment 737

Sec.
I. Terminology and Classification 738
A. Property Law 738
1. The Parties to a Power of Appointment 738
2. Scope of the Power 739
a. General Powers and Special (Non–General) Powers 739
b. Exclusive and Non–Exclusive Powers 740
3. Time of Appointment 740
Problems 741
B. Powers of Appointment and the Internal Revenue Code 742
Problem 742
II. Creation and Exercise 743
Estate of Hamilton 743
Questions 745
Notes 746
Will of Block 747
Notes and Questions 750
Problem 752
Problem 753
III. Scope of the Power 754
Problem 754
A. Exercising a Power by Creating another Trust 755
B. Exercising a Power by Creating Another Power 756
C. Exceeding the Power's Scope 757
1. Limits on the Holder of a Special Power 757
Will of Carroll 757
Questions 760
2. Consequences of Ineffective Appointments 760
Question 763
D. Contracts to Appoint and Releases 763
1. Contracts to Appoint 763
Problem 764
Benjamin v. Morgan Guaranty Trust Co. 764
Question 765
2. Releases 765
Seidel v. Werner 767
Notes, Questions, and Problems 771
IV. Rights of Creditors 772
Problem 772
Problem 775
Note on Powers in Bankruptcy 775
V. Powers of Appointment as a Tax Planning Tool 775
A. Introduction 775
Problem 776
B. When is Property Subject to a Power Included in Donee's Estate? 777
1. The Statute 777

Sec.
V. Powers of Appointment as a Tax Planning Tool—Continued
2. Powers of Invasion Over the Entire Principal of the Trust 779
Problem 779
Best v. United States 780
Questions 785
3. Limited Powers of Invasion: Lapse and the $5,000/5% Power 786
Estate of Kurz v. Commissioner 787
Questions 790

CHAPTER NINE. Classification and Construction of Future Interests 792

Sec.
I. Classification of Future Interests 793
A. Future Interests and Present Interests 793
B. The Categories of Future Interests 794
1. The Basic Classification System 794
2. Future Interests in the Grantor 795
3. Future Interests in Persons Other Than the Grantor 795
a. Traditional Distinctions Among Remainders 795
Webb v. Underhill 797
Notes and Questions 799
Problem 801
b. Executory Interests 801
c. Restatement Simplification 802
II. Construction of Future Interests: Gifts to Individuals 802
A. Should We Imply a Condition of Survival? 803
Uchtorff v. Hanson 803
Questions and Problems 810
Note on the Presumption in Favor of Early Vesting 812
Problem 816
Notes and Questions 821
Problems 821
B. Express Conditions of Survival 822
Matter of Krooss 822
Questions 826
Problems 827
III. Construction of Class Gifts 828
A. Increase in Class Membership 829
In re Evans' Estate 831
Questions 833
Notes 833
Problems 834
B. Decrease in Class Membership: Survivorship Again 835
Problem 835
Usry v. Farr 836
Question 840
Problems 840

Sec.
III. Construction of Class Gifts—Continued
Matter of Marine Midland Bank, N.A. 841
Notes 841
Questions and Problems 843
C. UPC § 2–707: A Reprise 844
Problems and Questions 844
D. Adopted Members of the Class 845
Newman v. Wells Fargo Bank, N.A. 846
Questions 851
Notes 852
E. Class Gifts and Assisted Reproduction 854
F. Gifts to "Heirs" 855
Harris Trust and Savings Bank v. Beach 855
Notes and Questions 861
G. Class Gifts of Income 864
Dewire v. Haveles 864
Notes and Questions 868

CHAPTER TEN. The Rule Against Perpetuities 869

Sec.
I. Making Sense of the Rule: A Bit of Policy, and a Bit of History 870
II. The Rule's Operation 873
A. Which Interests are Subject to the Rule 873
1. Present Interests 874
2. Future Interests in the Grantor 874
3. Future Interests in Transferees 875
B. Applying the Rule: Vesting and Measuring Lives 876
1. When Will an Interest Vest? 876
2. What Does It Mean for an Interest to "Fail" or "Fail to Vest?" 877
3. Interests Can Vest Before They Become Possessory 877
Problem 878
4. "Lives in Being": Choosing Measuring Lives 878
5. Twenty–One Years 883
Problems 884
Note 885
III. Recurring Problems 885
A. When Does the Perpetuities Period Start to Run?: Revocable and Irrevocable Inter Vivos Trusts 885
Cook v. Horn 886
Questions 888
Problems 888
B. Remote Possibilities 889
1. The Fertile Octogenarian 889
Problems 891
Notes 891
2. The Precocious Toddler 892
Notes 893

Sec.
III. Recurring Problems—Continued
3. The Unborn Widow 893
Dickerson v. Union National Bank 893
Notes and Questions 896
4. The Slothful Executor 897
Notes and Questions 897
C. Application to Charitable Gifts and Trusts 898
D. Consequences of Invalidity 899
Problem 901
IV. Class Gifts 901
A. The General Rule 901
Problem 902
B. The Ameliorative Impact of the Class–Closing Rule of Convenience 903
Problem 904
V. Powers of Appointment 905
A. Is the Power Valid? 905
Problem 907
B. Has the Power Been Validly Exercised? 907
1. The Scope of the Relation–Back Doctrine 907
Industrial National Bank of Rhode Island v. Barrett 908
Notes and Questions 911
2. The Second–Look Doctrine 912
Problems 913
C. Validity of Gifts in Default of Appointment 913
Problem 914
Sears v. Coolidge 914
VI. Savings Clauses 917
Estate of Holt 918
Notes and Questions 922
VII. Perpetuities Reform: Legislative and Judicial Salvage Doctrines 924
A. Construction and Reformation 925
B. Wait and See 925
C. USRAP 927
Problems 933
Problem 934
D. Abolition of the Rule 934

CHAPTER ELEVEN. Planning for Incapacity 938

Sec.
I. Introduction 938
II. Managing the Client's Assets 938
A. The Default Regime: Conservatorship 938
Notes and Questions 940
Guardianship: Cases of Financial Exploitation, Neglect, and Abuse of Seniors 942
In re Maher 945
Notes and Questions 950

Sec.
II. Managing the Client's Assets—Continued
B. Planning Around the Default Rules: Powers of Attorney 951
Notes and Questions 956
Estate of Huston 959
Notes and Questions 963
Problem 965
III. Health Care and Death Decisions 965
The Schiavo Autopsy; The Post–Mortem 965
As Man Lay in Coma–Like State, His Brain Was Busy Rebuilding 967
Notes 969
A. The Health Care Default Regime 969
Notes and Questions 971
B. Legal Documents: (Attempting to) Draft Around the Default Regime 972
1. The Durable Health Care Power of Attorney 972
Notes and Questions 974
2. Advance Directives or "Living Wills" 974
Questions and Notes 976
C. Practical Problems: Persuading the Physicians 977
Questions 978
Note 978
D. Physician–Assisted Suicide 979
Questions 981
IV. Long–Term Care at Journey's End 981

CHAPTER TWELVE. Co-ordinating Non–Probate Assets With the Probate Estate 984

Sec.
I. Introduction 984
II. P.O.D. Accounts, Revocable Trusts, and Wills 984
Araiza v. Younkin 984
Notes and Questions 987
III. Retirement Plan Assets 988
Nunnenman v. Estate of Grubbs 989
Notes and Questions 992
Kennedy v. Plan Administrator for DuPont Savings and Investment Plan 994
Notes and Questions 998
Note on Choosing Plan Beneficiaries 999
IV. Life Insurance 999
A. Introduction 999
Lincoln Life and Annuity Company of New York v. Caswell 1001
B. Some Basic Tax–Oriented Estate Planning With Insurance 1002
Problem 1003

CHAPTER THIRTEEN. Estate and Trust Administration 1005

Sec.
I. Estate Administration 1005
A. Do We Need to Administer the Estate? 1006
Problems 1007
B. Where Do We Administer the Estate—Domiciliary and Ancillary Jurisdiction Over Probate 1008
Problem 1008
C. How the Executor Probates the Will 1009
D. Ascertaining and Maximizing the Size of the Estate: Collecting Assets and Disposing of Creditor Claims 1010
1. Collecting Assets 1011
Problems 1011
2. Creditors' Claims 1012
a. Pre–Death Creditors 1012
Tulsa Professional Collection Services, Inc. v. Pope 1014
Notes and Questions 1020
Problems 1021
3. Post–Death Creditors 1021
Vance v. Estate of Myers 1022
Notes and Questions 1025
E. Compensating the Fiduciary (and the Fiduciary's Lawyer) 1027
1. How Should Personal Representatives by Compensated? 1027
Problems 1029
Questions 1029
2. Attorney Fees 1030
Estate of Stevenson 1031
Notes and Questions 1038
Problems 1039
II. The Duty of Loyalty 1041
Questions 1043
Matter of Kinzler 1044
Questions and Notes 1046
Matter of Estate of Rothko 1046
Questions and Notes 1051
III. The Duty of Care 1053
A. The Duty of Care in General 1054
Allard v. Pacific National Bank 1054
Questions 1060
B. Delegation of Fiduciary Obligations 1061
Shriners Hospitals for Crippled Children v. Gardiner 1061
Questions 1064
Note on Delegation 1065
Questions 1066
C. Portfolio Management 1067
In re Estate of Janes 1068
Notes and Questions 1075
Problem 1079
McGinley v. Bank of America, N.A. 1079
Notes and Questions 1085
Questions 1087
D. Safeguarding Property—The Duty Not to Commingle 1087
Questions 1087

Sec.

IV. Duties to Multiple Beneficiaries: Principal and Income 1088
- A. Framing the Problem 1088
- B. Solving the Problem by Drafting: The Unitrust 1089
  - Question 1089
- C. Statutorily Authorized Conversions to Unitrusts 1089
- D. A Statutory Solution: The Uniform Principal and Income Act 1090
  - Questions 1092
  - Problems 1092

V. Accountings and the Duty to Inform Trust Beneficiaries 1092
- *In re Freihofer* 1093
- Questions and Notes 1096
- *Johnson v. Johnson* 1096
- Notes and Questions 1099

VI. Resignation and Removal of Trustees 1101
- A. Resignation 1101
- B. Removal 1102
  - *Kappus v. Kappus* 1102
  - Notes and Questions 1106

VII. Fiduciary Litigation: Who Pays? 1108
- *Rudnick v. Rudnick* 1108
- Notes and Questions 1111

INDEX 1113

AUTHOR INDEX

Aalberts, Robert J. 1079
Abravanel, Evelyn Ginsberg 550–551, 564–556
Alexander, Gregory S. 490, 613, 627, 1041
Alexandre, Michèle 85
Altman, Lawrence K. 1010
Andersen, Roger W. 885
Arash, Dora 663
Ascher, Mark L. 10–12, 100
Atkinson, Rob 723, 1078
Ausness, Richard C. 625, 627

Bailey, Erin C. V. 639
Bailey, James E. 144, 146
Banks, Robert L. 547
Baron, Jane B. 324–25, 533
Barnes, Alison 945
Batts, Deborah A. 225
Beamish, Rita 734–735
Becker, David M. 817, 818, 844, 932
Begleiter, Martin D. 42–43, 44, 45, 489, 645
Beyer, Gerry W. 242, 259, 260, 488, 490, 530, 951
Bird, Gail Boreman 550, 687, 688
Bix, Brian H. 981
Blackstone, William 14
Blattmacher, Jonathan G. 100
Bloom, Ira 191–192, 575, 925, 935,
Boehm, Mike 724–725
Bogert, George G. 673, 1049, 1053, 1059
Bogert, George T. 542, 605, 1053
Bonfield, Lloyd 248
Bott, Alexander J. 154, 180
Boxx, Karen E. 522, 630
Brand, Ronald A. 160
Brashier, Ralph, C. 107, 108, 134, 143, 144, 146, 168–169, 225, 442, 493, 507, 957
Brod, Gail 202
Brody, Evelyn 708
Brown, Richard Lewis 92
Burke, Karen C. 15

Cahn, Naomi 34, 109, 144, 201
Cain, Patricia A. 504, 516
Carnegie, Andrew 12, 508
Champine, Pamela R. 359
Chase, Adam 504
Chester, Ronald 144, 145–146, 220, 225, 226, 425, 685, 709
Clark, Elizabeth G. 942
Clifford, Denis 504
Clowney, Stephen 250
Collett, Teresa Stanton 34, 965
Collins, Dennis W. 397
Cooper, Ilene Sherwyn 134
Cromartie, Martha A. 747
Cunningham, Laura E. 813, 815, 817, 862
Curry, Hayden 504

Dacey, Norman 519
Danforth, Robert T. 521, 607, 626, 638–639
Davies, Robertson 1005
DeFeo, William P. 588
DeFuria, Joseph W. 359
Dessin, Carolyn L. 404, 964
Dickens, Charles 1
Dickinson, Rob G. 488–489
DiRusso, Alyssa A. 65–66, 1091
Dobris, Joel C. 16, 34, 160, 647–648, 870, 935, 936–937, 983, 1068, 1078–1079
Dodge, Joseph M. 667
Domsky, Ronald 178
Douthitt, Amy E. 201–202
Dukeminier, Jesse 45, 813, 817, 880, 885, 926–927, 932, 933, 937

Eason, John K. 639
Eligon, John 457
Emanuel, Anne S. 609
Engel, Barry S. 622, 627
English, David M. 983
Evans, Daniel 292

Featheringill, Carolyn B. 885
Featherston, Thomas 202
Fellows, Mary Louise 66, 88, 165, 491, 492, 540, 936
Fennell, Lee Anne 513
Fetters, Samuel M. 772
Fierstein, Ian G. 46
Fink, Howard 491
Fishman, James 705
Fletcher, Robert L. 911, 923
Fogel, Bradley E.S. 43, 663
Foster, Frances H. 65, 66, 85, 590, 1096, 1100

Foster, Lynn 522, 936
Fratcher, William F. 707, 1111
French, Susan F. 306, 751, 813, 869, 937
Fried, Martin L. 75, 508
Frolik, Lawrence 647
Fuller, Lon 228

Gagliardi, Elaine H. 663
Gallanis, T. P. 84, 492, 1100
Garvey, John L. 315–316, 324, 811
Gary, Susan N. 85, 115, 129, 133, 169, 492, 710, 951
Gerzog, Wendy C. 666–667
Gillett, Mark R. 1091
Gingiss, Randall J. 404, 637
Glendon, Mary Ann 226
Goldenson, Susan M. 983
Goodwin, Iris J. 708
Gorman, Warren F. 425
Graham, Kathy T. 100
Grant, Joseph Karl 260
Gray, John C. 609, 796–797, 869, 872, 887, 906, 910
Grossman, Joanna L. 109
Gulliver, Ashbel G. 52, 228
Guthrie, Chris 109
Guzman, Katheleen R. 145, 164, 1090

Haithman, Diane 724–725
Halbach, Jr., Edward C. 550, 564, 627, 800, 811, 815, 817, 830
Hargrove, Claire G. 260
Hardwick, M. Jeffrey 51
Harper, Robert Matthew 144
Harrison, Jeffrey L. 935
Haskell, Paul G. 609, 805
Hawkins, Francis Vaughan 324
Helmholz, Richard H. 257
Hernandez, Tanya K. 66
Hess, Amy 786, 931
Higdon, Michael J. 128
Hirsch, Adam J. 13–14, 129, 159, 160, 163, 228, 381, 610, 617, 638, 737
Hobbs, Steven H. 34
Hoffman, Jan 980
Hoffman, Sharona 892
Hudson, Kris 236
Huss, Rebecca J. 530

Jenkins, Helen B. 37, 42, 134
Jeffrey, Robert H. 1078
Johanson, Stanley M. 212
Johnson, Jr., Alex M. 723
Johnson, Irene D. 128, 480
Johnson, J. Rodney 931
Johnston, Gerald P. 43, 243
Jones, James T. R. 481

Kaplan, Karen 967–969
Katz, Robert A. 708–709
Kelly-Hill, Linda 92
Kenderdine, Nancy I. 108
Kimbrough, Erich Tucker 844–845
Kindregan, Jr., Charles P. 145
King, Samuel P. 707, 1042
Kinsler, Jeffrey S. 193, 662
Klein, Diane J. 479, 480
Knaplund, Kristine S. 128, 143, 145
Kogan, Terry S. 179
Kohm, Lynne Marie 708
Kolata, Gina 891, 981
Kotlikoff, Laurence J. 15
Kotulak, Ronald 891
Kovach, Richard J. 705
Krasik, Margaret 945
Krier, James E. 937
Kurtz, Sheldon F. 143, 147

Langbein, John H. 12, 45–46, 60–61, 169, 228, 247, 359, 380, 483, 484–486, 490, 519, 523–524, 566, 1043, 1052–1053, 1065–1066, 1067
LaPiana, William P. 160, 163
Laporte, Cloyd 67
Lay, Norvie L. 212
Leach, W. Barton 869, 885, 892–893, 911
Lehman, David 983
Leopold, Aloysius A. 490–491
Leslie, Melanie 224–225, 233, 247–248, 425, 469, 522, 524, 566, 753, 885, 911,1041, 1043, 1046, 1052, 1066, 1076, 1087
Lewis, Browne C. 131, 145
Licata, Kimberly A. 931
Litman, Donna 670
Lindgren, James 229, 236
Link, Ronald C. 33–34, 931, 965
Lischer, Henry J. 637
Lorenzetti, James T. 622
Lorio, Kathryn Venturatos 143–144, 146
Love, Sarajane 1020
Lundwall, Mary K. 705
Lynn, Robert J. 281
Lyons, William H. 606–607

Macey, Jonathan 723

Madoff, Ray D. 465, 469, 491, 501, 976
Maillard, Kevin Noble 424
Makdisi, John 69
Malamud, Deborah C. 12
Mann, Bruce H. 228, 545–546
Margolick, David 12, 482–483
Markey, Maureen E. 885
Massey, Calvin 491
McCaffery, Edward J. 15, 16
McCouch, Grayson M.P. 15, 59
McElwee, L.A. 540
McGovern, Jr., William M. 246, 885
McGrath, Jennifer Tulin 504
McMullen, Judith 647
Meiklejohn, Alexander M. 423
Merric, Mark 522
Metz, Andrew 965–967
Millard, Kevin D. 606
Miller, C. Douglas 248
Miller, John A. 654
Modigliani, Franco 15
Moller, Sid L. 454–455
Monopoli, Paula A. 92, 131–132, 566, 1041
Moran, Gerald P. 610
Morriss, Andrew P. 892

Newman, Alan 169, 179, 210, 521, 522, 575, 606, 607, 647, 686
Nolan, Lawrence C. 146

O'Brien, Raymond C. 85, 145
Orth, John V. 248
Oshins, Steven 522

Padilla, Laura M. 115
Pearce, Russell G. 34, 201
Pearson, Albert M. 491
Pendleton, Megan 133
Pennell, Jeffrey N. 34, 566, 965
Phelan, Mary Elizabeth 42
Poon, Percy S. 1080
Posner, Richard 721
Powell, Burnele V. 33, 965
Powell, Richard R. 168–169
Price, John R. 34

Quinn, Kevin P. 981

Rabin, Edward H. 747, 812
Radford, Mary F. 145, 169, 234, 338
Randall, Gary C. 212
Ratner, James R. 100
Redman, B. 75
Rein, Jan Ellen 127, 853, 965
Repetti, James R. 14
Reppy, William 100
Rhodes, Anne-Marie E. 23, 91, 92
Richardson, Lynda 129
Roberts, Patricia J. 307, 813, 861
Roberts, Patricia G. 854
Rohan, Patrick J. 169
Roosevelt, Theodore 508
Rosenberg, Joseph A. 457, 945
Rosenbury, Laura 168, 180
Roth, Jeffrey 569
Roth, Randall W. 709, 1043
Rothschild, Gideon 623, 627
Rubin, Bonnie Miller 891
Rubin, Daniel S. 627
Rudko, Frances Howell 723

Sablone, Kathleen H. 1091
Saks, Howard J. 983
Salzman, Leslie 944–945
Samuel, Cynthia 213
Scalise, Jr., Ronald 69, 74, 93
Schanzenbach, Max 936
Scheffey, Thomas B. 504–507
Schenkel, Kent D. 228, 988
Schiavo, Frank L. 540
Schiff, Anne R. 145
Schneider, Frederick R. 153, 835, 925, 935
Schoenblum, Jeffrey A. 426, 522, 607
Schuyler, Daniel 592
Schwartz, Charles Patrick 85
Schwartz, Frederic S. 282–283
Schwidetzky, Walter D. 512
Scitovsky, Anne A. 980
Scott, Austin 606, 675, 677, 678, 705, 706, 708,1050
Seto, Robert Mahealani M. 708
Shaffer, Thomas L. 35
Shapo, Helene 144, 145, 178
Sherman, Jeffrey G. 8, 15, 24, 201–202, 467, 503, 507, 664
Sherwin, Emily 248
Siegel, Mark R. 534
Silverman, Rachel Emma 236
Simes, Lewis D. 14, 769, 832
Simon, John G. 723
Sitkoff, Robert 687, 936, 1041, 1052, 1075–1076
Smith, Phyllis C. 630, 639
Smith, Robert B. 1000
Sneddon, Karen J. 1010
Soled, Jay 509
Spaht, Katherine Shaw 213
Spitko, E. Gary 66, 84–85, 469, 492
Spivack, Carla 469
Stake, Jeffrey Evans 627
Stein, Robert A. 46
Steinkamp, John G. 14–15, 509, 663, 786

Sterk, Stewart E. 204, 618–619, 627, 630, 885, 936, 1066–1067, 1076, 1077
Storrow, Richard F. 139
Strohm, Charles Q. 66
Sugarman, F. Skip 169
Sunstein, Cass 980

Tate, Joshua 9, 687, 935
Taylor, Ross 723
Thayer, James B. 324
Thomson, Michael F. 179
Tilly, Jane 983
Tilson, Catherine J. 52, 228
Toobin, Jeffrey 528–529
Tritt, Lee–Ford 144
Turano, Margaret Valentine 175, 179
Turnier, William 657, 935
Turnipseed, Terry 1090
Tuttle, Robert 34, 201

Vallario, Angela M. 43, 178, 345, 937
Vitollo, Timothy J. 613
Volkmer, Ronald R. 42, 100, 169, 179, 191–192, 249, 522

Waggoner, Lawrence W. 75, 81, 88, 143, 147, 169, 195, 359, 380, 381, 811, 815,817, 927, 931–932
Waite, G. Graham 935
Wake, Kenneth L. 488–489
Waldeck, Sarah E. 518
Wang, William K.S. 13, 737
Weiner, Joshua M. 983
Wendel, Peter 115
Wenig, Mary Moers 160, 666
Whitebread, Charles H. 179
Willbanks, Stephanie 179
Wilson, Darryl C. 885
Witte, Philip D. 220–223

Zaritsky, Howard M. 100
Zelenak, Lawrence 667

TABLE OF STATUTES

Table of Current Uniform Probate Code Provisions

Section 1–201	349, 378
Section 2–101	283
Section 2–102	73–75, 93, 151
Section 2–103	73, 93, 151
Section 2–104	152–54
Section 2–105	74
Section 2–106	93, 109
Section 2–107	107
Section 2–109	165
Section 2–113	116
Section 2–114	141
Section 2–118	113
Section 2–119	113–115, 845
Section 2–120	147
Section 2–121	147
Section 2–202	170, 181, 187, 192, 213
Section 2–203	181–82, 189
Section 2–204	181, 183, 189
Section 2–205	181, 183, 189, 190, 193
Section 2–206	181, 185, 189, 192–93
Section 2–207	181, 185, 187, 190–92
Section 2–208	186, 191
Section 2–209	181, 186, 188–89, 191–92
Section 2–212	195
Section 2–213	202–03
Section 2–301	210–11
Section 2–302	218–20, 224
Section 2–402	204
Section 2–403	204
Section 2–404	206
Section 2–405	188, 206
Section 2–501	413
Section 2–502	234–36, 247, 250, 259
Section 2–503	246–49, 250, 376–77, 388
Section 2–504	241
Section 2–507	360, 367–68, 377, 387
Section 2–508	379–80
Section 2–509	388, 383
Section 2–510	274–75
Section 2–511	282, 533, 581
Section 2–512	276
Section 2–513	274–76
Section 2–514	397, 405
Section 2–601	317, 319
Section 2–603	317, 319–20, 322–24
Section 2–604	308
Section 2–605	304
Section 2–606	301–02, 304
Section 2–607	291
Section 2–608	750, 753, 911
Section 2–609	305
Section 2–702	153, 316
Section 2–704	746
Section 2–705	845, 854
Section 2–707	817–18, 821–22, 836, 844–45
Section 2–711	862
Section 2–801	27, 192
Section 2–802	81
Section 2–803	25, 27–28
Section 2–804	319, 378, 380–81, 592, 998
Section 2–901	870, 928
Section 2–902	911, 928, 933
Section 2–903	929
Section 2–904	929
Section 2–905	930, 933
Section 2–906	870
Section 2–907	530
Section 2–1103	161
Section 2–1105	161
Section 2–1106	162, 813
Section 3–301	1009
Section 3–401	1009
Section 3–407	427
Section 3–715	1027
Section 3–721	1028
Section 3–801	1014, 1020
Section 3–803	1014, 1020
Section 3–808	1025–26
Section 3–902	288, 290
Section 3–905	488
Section 3–9A–104(1)	292–93
Section 5–401	939
Section 5–408	939
Section 5–411	941–42
Section 5–413	940
Section 6–101	568
Section 6–203	59
Section 6–204	59
Section 6–301	60, 568
Section 6–302	60, 568
Section 6–305	568
Section 6–306	568
Section 6–307	569

Table of 1969 Uniform Probate Code Provisions

Section 2–508	379

Table of Uniform Trust Code Provisions

Section 105	524
Section 401	546
Section 402	524, 528, 533–34
Section 405	709
Section 406	534
Section 407	545
Section 408	530
Section 409	531

Table of Uniform Trust Code Provisions

Section 411	685–87
Section 412	695
Section 413	720–21
Section 415	694
Section 416	694
Section 501	601–02
Section 502	607
Section 503	614–15
Section 504	602, 606
Section 505	617
Section 601	534
Section 602	675
Section 603	575
Section 604	590
Section 703	1051
Section 705	1102
Section 802	1052
Section 806	1060
Section 810	1087
Section 813	1100
Section 1012	1053
Section 1008	1061, 1086–87

Table of State Statutes

Ariz. Rev. Stat. 14–2901	935
Ark. Stat. 34.77.060	100
Ark. Stat. Ann. 28–9–212	71
Ark. Stat. Ann. 61–134	896
Ark. Stat. Ann. 61–135	896
Cal. Fam. Code, § 297	84
Cal. Gov't Code, §§ 12580–12598	707
California Probate Code, § 66	213
California Probate Code, § 101	213
California Probate Code, § 249.5	144
California Probate Code, § 672(b)	761
California Probate Code, § 681	773
California Probate Code, § 682	773–74
California Probate Code, § 6110	234
California Probate Code, § 6200 et seq.	259
California Probate Code, § 6401	84
California Probate Code, § 6450	123
California Probate Code, § 6454	121, 128
California Probate Code, § 6455	121
California.Probate Code, § 10800	1028
California.Probate Code, § 10801	1028
California.Probate Code, § 10802	1030
California.Probate Code, § 10810	1031, 1039
California.Probate Code, § 10811	1031
California.Probate Code, § 15204	531
California Probate Code, § 15307	616
California Probate Code, § 15404	686
California Probate Code, § 15405	688
California Probate Code, § 15408	695
California Probate Code, § 21311	489
California Probate Code, § 21350	467
California Probate Code, § 21351	467
Colo. Rev. Stat. § 15–11–503	249
Colo. Rev. Stat. § 15–22–101—15–22–112	84, 493
Del. Code Ann., tit. 13, § 920	113
Fla. Stat. § 737.111	545

Table of State Statutes

Fla. Stat. § 742.17	144
Haw. Rev. Stat. 560:2–102	84
Idaho Code § 15–2–201	213
Idaho Code § 16–1509	113
755 Ill. Comp. Stat. 5/2–1	3, 93
755 Ill. Comp. Stat. 5/2–8	3
755 Ill. Comp. Stat. 5/4–10	3
755 Ill. Comp. Stat. 5/15–1	205
755 Ill. Comp. Stat. 35/1 et seq.	975
755 Ill. Comp. Stat. 35/5	976
755 Ill. Comp. Stat. 45/4–1 et seq.	974
755 Ill. Comp. Stat. 45/4–3	974
815 Ill. Comp. Stat. 505/2BB	600
Ind. Code Ann. § 29–1–5–6	377
Iowa Code, § 633.436	289
Kan. Stat. Ann. 59–615	307
La. Rev. Stat. § 9:391.1	144
MCA § 72–2–522	244–45
MCA § 72–2–523	244–246
MCA § 72–2–527	246
MCA § 72–3–310	244
Massachusetts General Laws, Ch. 190B	93
Md. Est. & Trusts Code Ann. § 4–403	307
Miss. Code Ann. § 91–1–5	108
Mo. Rev. Stat. § 474.150	176
Nev. Rev. Stat. Ann. § 147.040	1006
N.H. Rev. Stat. Ann. § 551.10	217
N.H. Rev. Stat. Ann. § 551.12	306, 308
N.J.S.A. 2A:17–19	203
N.J.S.A. 3B:5–3	84
N.J.S.A. 26:7A–4	84
N.J.S.A. 46:2F–9	935
Nev. Rev. Stat. § 133.085	260
N.Y. CPLR § 5206(a)	203
N.Y. EPTL § 1–2.16	90
N.Y. EPTL § 3–2.1	234
N.Y. EPTL § 3–3.2	238
N.Y. EPTL § 3–3.3	306, 308
N.Y. EPTL § 3–3.5	489
N.Y. EPTL § 3–3.6	291
N.Y. EPTL § 3–4.4	301, 308
N.Y. EPTL § 3–4.5	301
N.Y. EPTL § 4–1.1	74
N.Y. EPTL § 4–1.4	92
N.Y. EPTL § 5–1.1A	19
N.Y. EPTL § 5–1.2	92
N.Y. EPTL § 5–3.2	219
N.Y. EPTL § 7–1.1	526
N.Y. EPTL § 7–1.2	526
N.Y. EPTL § 7–1.3	548
N.Y. EPTL § 7–1.5	616
N.Y. EPTL § 7–1.6	696
N.Y. EPTL § 7–1.16	675
N.Y. EPTL § 7–1.17	545
N.Y. EPTL § 7–1.18	546–47
N.Y. EPTL § 7–1.19	686
N.Y. EPTL § 7–3.4	616
N.Y. EPTL § 7–5.2	987, 993
N.Y. EPTL § 7–6.1	530
N.Y. EPTL § 8–1.4	707
N.Y. EPTL § 9–1.2	903
N.Y. EPTL § 9–1.3	892–93, 897–98

Table of State Statutes

N.Y. EPTL § 10–3.3	740
N.Y. EPTL § 10–5.3	763, 771
N.Y. EPTL § 10–6.1	750
N.Y. EPTL § 10–7.2	774
N.Y. EPTL § 10–7.4	774
N.Y. SCPA § 1407	375
N.Y. SCPA § 2307–a	1040
Ohio Rev. Code Ann. § 2105.06	121, 307
Ohio Rev. Code Ann. § 2133.11	975
Ohio Rev. Code Ann. § 5801.04	1100
Pa. Stat. Ann. § 2104	87
Pa. Stat. Ann. § 2203	1000
S.C. Code Ann. § 62–7–401(c)	176
Tenn. Code Ann. § 31–1–105	176
Va. Code Ann. § 20–158	144
Va. Code Ann. § 64.1–64.1	309
Vt. Stat. Ann. 1204(e)	84
Wash. Rev. Code, § 11.04.015	100
Wis. Stat. Ann. § 766.001 et. seq.	100
Wy. Stat. § 2–4–101	72, 87

Table of Internal Revenue Code Provisions

Section 664	503
Section 2010	517
Section 2035	511
Section 2036—2038	657
Section 2041	742, 777–79, 785–86, 790
Section 2042	1003
Section 2044	667
Section 2056	667
Section 2503	657–59
Section 2513	518
Section 2514	742, 766
Section 2518	161
Section 2523(a)	517

TABLE OF CASES

Principal cases are in bold type. Non-principal cases are in roman type. References are to Pages.

A. v. B., 158 N.J. 51, 726 A.2d 924 (N.J. 1999), 34

Adams v. Link, 145 Conn. 634, 145 A.2d 753 (Conn.1958), **676**

Adoption of (see name of party)

Alexander ex rel. Alexander v. Estate of Alexander, 351 Ark. 359, 93 S.W.3d 688 (Ark. 2002), 217

Allard v. Pacific Nat. Bank, 99 Wash.2d 394, 663 P.2d 104 (Wash.1983), **1054**

American Nat. Bank of Cheyenne, Wyo. v. Miller, 899 P.2d 1337 (Wyo.1995), **679**

Ames By and Through Parker v. Reeves, 553 So.2d 570 (Ala.1989), 426

Anderson, Estate of, 65 Cal.Rptr.2d 307 (Cal. App. 2 Dist.1997), 389

Andrews v. Rentz, 266 Ga. 782, 470 S.E.2d 669 (Ga.1996), 455

Angle, In re Estate of, 2000 WL 33223696 (Pa.Com.Pl.2000), 423

Araiza v. Younkin, 116 Cal.Rptr.3d 315 (Cal.App. 2 Dist.2010), **984**

Arkansas Dept. of Human Services Div. of Economic and Medical Services v. Wilson, 323 Ark. 151, 913 S.W.2d 783 (Ark.1996), 653

Arndts v. Bonner, 2004 WL 1532274 (Tenn. Ct.App.2004), 177

Arrowsmith v. Mercantile–Safe Deposit and Trust Co., 313 Md. 334, 545 A.2d 674 (Md.1988), 389, 906

Ashkenazy v. Ashkenazy's Estate, 140 So.2d 331 (Fla.App. 3 Dist.1962), 291

Associated Enterprises, Inc., In re, 234 B.R. 718 (Bkrtcy.W.D.Wis.1999), 533

Auen, Estate of, 35 Cal.Rptr.2d 557 (Cal.App. 1 Dist.1994), 466

Bacardi v. White, 463 So.2d 218 (Fla.1985), 615

Baird, In re, 349 Mont. 501, 204 P.3d 703 (Mont.2009), 1107

Baird, Matter of Estate of, 131 Wash.2d 514, 933 P.2d 1031 (Wash.1997), **154**

Bagley v. Mousel, 271 Neb. 628, 715 N.W.2d 490 (Neb.2006), 345

Baker v. Weedon, 262 So.2d 641 (Miss.1972), 520

Balboni v. LaRocque, 991 So.2d 993 (Fla.App. 4 Dist.2008), 375

Banc of America Inv. Services, Inc. v. Davis, 2009 WL 277050 (Tenn.Ct.App.2009), 993

BancOhio Nat. Bank v. United States, 1988 WL 159144 (S.D.Ohio 1988), 669

Bank One of Milford, N.A. v. Bardes, 25 Ohio St.3d 296, 496 N.E.2d 475 (Ohio 1986), 544

Barcelo v. Elliott, 923 S.W.2d 575 (Tex. 1996), **35**

Barnes v. Marshall, 467 S.W.2d 70 (Mo. 1971), **413**

Barnette v. McNulty, 21 Ariz.App. 127, 516 P.2d 583 (Ariz.App. Div. 2 1973), 674

Barr v. Dawson, 158 P.3d 1073 (Okla.Civ. App. Div. 4 2006), 489

Baxter v. State, 354 Mont. 234, 224 P.3d 1211 (Mont.2009), 981

Beale's Estate, In re, 15 Wis.2d 546, 113 N.W.2d 380 (Wis.1962), 269

Bean v. Ford, 8 Cal.Rptr.3d 541, 82 P.3d 747 (Cal.2004), **122**

Bean v. Wilson, 283 Ga. 511, 661 S.E.2d 518 (Ga.2008), 467

Beatty v. Guggenheim Exploration Co., 225 N.Y. 380, 122 N.E. 378 (N.Y.1919), 471, 547

Beauregard, In re Estate of, 456 Mass. 161, 921 N.E.2d 954 (Mass.2010), 374

Belfield v. Booth, 63 Conn. 299, 27 A. 585 (Conn.1893), 897

Bellows v. Page, 88 N.H. 283, 188 A. 12 (N.H.1936), 526

Benjamin v. Morgan Guar. Trust Co. of New York, 202 A.D.2d 536, 609 N.Y.S.2d 276 (N.Y.A.D. 2 Dept.1994), **764**

Berg, In re Estate of, 783 N.W.2d 831 (S.D. 2010), 424, 428

Berk, In re, 71 A.D.3d 883, 897 N.Y.S.2d 475 (N.Y.A.D. 2 Dept.2010), 950

Best v. United States, 902 F.Supp. 1023 (D.Neb.1995), **780**

Bird v. Plunkett, 139 Conn. 491, 95 A.2d 71 (Conn.1953), 24

Blackstone v. Blackstone, 282 Ga.App. 515, 639 S.E.2d 369 (Ga.App.2006), 91

Blalock v. Riddick, 186 Va. 284, 42 S.E.2d 292 (Va.1947), 376

Blevins v. Moran, 12 S.W.3d 698 (Ky.App. 2000), 315

Block, Matter of Will of, 157 Misc.2d 716, 598 N.Y.S.2d 668 (N.Y.Sur.1993), **747**

Blodgett v. Blodgett, 147 P.3d 702 (Alaska 2006), 23
Blue Ridge Bank and Trust Co. v. McFall, 207 S.W.3d 149 (Mo.App. W.D.2006), 828
Board of Educ. of Montgomery County v. Browning, 333 Md. 281, 635 A.2d 373 (Md.1994), 99, 130
Bob Jones University v. United States, 461 U.S. 574, 103 S.Ct. 2017, 76 L.Ed.2d 157 (1983), 734
Bond & Mortg. Guarantee Co., In re, 303 N.Y. 423, 103 N.E.2d 721 (N.Y.1952), 1052
Bongaards v. Millen, 440 Mass. 10, 793 N.E.2d 335 (Mass.2003), 174
Bonjean's Estate, Matter of, 90 Ill.App.3d 582, 45 Ill.Dec. 872, 413 N.E.2d 205 (Ill. App. 3 Dist.1980), 437
Borghi, In re Estate of, 167 Wash.2d 480, 219 P.3d 932 (Wash.2009), **101**
Bourcet, Matter of Estate of, 175 Misc.2d 144, 668 N.Y.S.2d 329 (N.Y.Sur.1997), 533
Bowles v. Bradley, 319 S.C. 377, 461 S.E.2d 811 (S.C.1995), 845
Brainard v. Commissioner, 91 F.2d 880 (7th Cir.1937), 532
Breeden, Estate of, 208 Cal.App.3d 981, 256 Cal.Rptr. 813 (Cal.App. 4 Dist.1989), 706
Briggs v. Wyoming Nat. Bank of Casper, 836 P.2d 263 (Wyo.1992), 34, 199
Brinker v. Wobaco Trust Ltd., 610 S.W.2d 160 (Tex.Civ.App.-Texarkana 1980), 694
Britt v. Upchurch, 327 N.C. 454, 396 S.E.2d 318 (N.C.1990), **346**
Brittin, In re Estate of, 279 Ill.App.3d 512, 216 Ill.Dec. 50, 664 N.E.2d 687 (Ill.App. 5 Dist.1996), **116**
Broadway Nat. Bank v. Adams, 133 Mass. 170 (Mass.1882), 607
Brookline, Town of v. Barnes, 327 Mass. 201, 97 N.E.2d 651 (Mass.1951), 723, 724
Brooks, In re, 217 B.R. 98 (Bkrtcy.D.Conn. 1998), 625, 637
Brown v. Brown, 2009 WL 1099711 (Ala.Civ. App.2009), 367
Brown v. Independent Baptist Church of Woburn, 325 Mass. 645, 91 N.E.2d 922 (Mass.1950), 899
Brunel, In re Estate of, 135 N.H. 83, 600 A.2d 123 (N.H.1991), 99
Brunner v. Brown, 480 N.W.2d 33 (Iowa 1992), 428
Buckten, Matter of Will of, 178 A.D.2d 981, 578 N.Y.S.2d 754 (N.Y.A.D. 4 Dept.1991), 425
Burchell's Estate, In re, 299 N.Y. 351, 87 N.E.2d 293 (N.Y.1949), 863
Burden, In re Estate of, 53 Cal.Rptr.3d 390 (Cal.App. 2 Dist.2007), **135**
Burke, Matter of, 82 A.D.2d 260, 441 N.Y.S.2d 542 (N.Y.A.D. 2 Dept.1981), 467
Burnett v. First Commercial Trust Co., 327 Ark. 430, 939 S.W.2d 827 (Ark.1997), 358
Burr v. Brooks, 83 Ill.2d 488, 48 Ill.Dec. 200, 416 N.E.2d 231 (Ill.1981), 723

Calligaro, In re Estate of, 19 Misc.3d 895, 855 N.Y.S.2d 873 (N.Y.Sur.2008), 194
Cammack, In re Estate of, 2000 WL 1679492 (Tenn.Ct.App.2000), 396
Campbell v. Campbell, 489 So.2d 774 (Fla. App. 3 Dist.1986), 332
Campbell's Estate, Matter of, 56 Or.App. 222, 641 P.2d 610 (Or.App.1982), 152
Campenello v. Conrow, 127 Misc.2d 91, 485 N.Y.S.2d 469 (N.Y.Co.Ct.1985), 546
Canales, In re Estate of, 837 S.W.2d 662 (Tex.App.-San Antonio 1992), 533
Cantrell v. Cantrell, 2004 WL 3044907 (Tenn. Ct.App.2004), 177
Capaldi v. Richards, 870 A.2d 493 (Del. Supr.2005), 1112
Carmichael v. Heggie, 332 S.C. 624, 506 S.E.2d 308 (S.C.App.1998), 763
Carpenter, Estate of v. Cosby, 2010 WL 1962650 (Miss.App.2010), 377
Carroll, Estate of, 764 S.W.2d 736 (Mo. App. S.D.1989), **333**
Carroll's Will, In re, 274 N.Y. 288, 8 N.E.2d 864 (N.Y.1937), **757**
Carson's Estate, In re, 184 Cal. 437, 194 P. 5 (Cal.1920), 472
Carter v. Bank One Trust Co., 760 N.E.2d 1171 (Ind.App.2002), 747
Cassidy, People v., 884 P.2d 309 (Colo.1994), 600
Certain Scholarship Funds, In re, 133 N.H. 227, 575 A.2d 1325 (N.H.1990), 733
Chappell, In re, 25 Misc.3d 704, 883 N.Y.S.2d 857 (N.Y.Sur.2009), 752
Chase, Matter of, 68 N.J. 392, 346 A.2d 89 (N.J.1975), 452
Chase v. Bowen, 771 So.2d 1181 (Fla.App. 5 Dist.2000), 32
Chatard v. Oveross, 101 Cal.Rptr.3d 883 (Cal. App. 2 Dist.2009), 1111
Chavin v. PNC Bank, 816 A.2d 781 (Del. Supr.2003), 828
Chawla v. Transamerica Occidental Life Ins. Co., 440 F.3d 639 (4th Cir.2006), 1004
Cheatle v. Cheatle, 662 A.2d 1362 (D.C.1995), 23
Chebatoris v. Moyer, 276 Neb. 733, 757 N.W.2d 212 (Neb.2008), 546
Chervitz Trust, In re, 198 S.W.3d 658 (Mo. App. E.D.2006), 756
Chester v. Smith, 285 Ga. 401, 677 S.E.2d 128 (Ga.2009), 234
Chrisp, In re Estate of, 276 Neb. 966, 759 N.W.2d 87 (Neb.2009), 194
Christensen, Estate of v. Christensen, 655 P.2d 646 (Utah 1982), 211
Claflin v. Claflin, 149 Mass. 19, 20 N.E. 454 (Mass.1889), 685
Clark v. Campbell, 82 N.H. 281, 133 A. 166 (N.H.1926), 527

Clark, Estate of, 488 Pa. 1, 410 A.2d 796 (Pa.1980), 159
Clark v. Greenhalge, 411 Mass. 410, 582 N.E.2d 949 (Mass.1991), **269**
Cleveland Bar Assn. v. Sharp Estate Serv., Inc., 107 Ohio St.3d 219, 837 N.E.2d 1183 (Ohio 2005), 600
Clobberie's Case, 1677 WL 114 (KB 1677), 834
Clymer v. Mayo, 393 Mass. 754, 473 N.E.2d 1084 (Mass.1985), 282, **577,** 592
Coates, Estate of, 438 Pa.Super. 195, 652 A.2d 331 (Pa.Super.1994), 923
Cohen, Matter of Estate of, 83 N.Y.2d 148, 608 N.Y.S.2d 398, 629 N.E.2d 1356 (N.Y. 1994), 397
Cohen v. Commissioner of Div. of Medical Assistance, 423 Mass. 399, 668 N.E.2d 769 (Mass.1996), **648**
Collier, Matter of, 381 So.2d 1338 (Miss. 1980), 59
Colombo v. Stevenson, 150 N.C.App. 163, 563 S.E.2d 591 (N.C.App.2002), 315
Committee on Professional Ethics and Conduct of the Iowa State Bar Ass'n v. Baker, 492 N.W.2d 695 (Iowa 1992), **593**
Connall v. Felton, 225 Or.App. 266, 201 P.3d 219 (Or.App.2009), 548
Connecticut General Life Ins. Co. v. First Nat. Bank of Minneapolis, 262 N.W.2d 403 (Minn.1977), **672**
Conservatorship of Morrison, 206 Cal.App.3d 304, 253 Cal.Rptr. 530 (Cal.App. 1 Dist. 1988), 971
Conservatorship of Person of John L., In re, 105 Cal.Rptr.3d 424, 225 P.3d 554 (Cal. 2010), 940
Cook v. Grierson, 380 Md. 502, 845 A.2d 1231 (Md.2004), 28
Cook v. Horn, 214 Ga. 289, 104 S.E.2d 461 (Ga.1958), **886**
Corbett's Estate, In re, 430 Pa. 54, 241 A.2d 524 (Pa.1968), 540
Corwith, Matter of Will of, 163 Misc.2d 831, 622 N.Y.S.2d 424 (N.Y.Sur.1995), 826
Costas, In re, 346 B.R. 198 (9th Cir.2006), 160
Coy v. Ezarski, 731 N.W.2d 19 (Iowa 2007), 300, 303
Cragle v. Gray, 206 P.3d 446 (Alaska 2009), 405
Crane, In re, 164 N.Y. 71, 58 N.E. 47 (N.Y. 1900), 863
Crawshaw, Matter of Estate of, 249 Kan. 388, 819 P.2d 613 (Kan.1991), **710**
Cross v. Cross, 177 Ill.App.3d 588, 126 Ill. Dec. 801, 532 N.E.2d 486 (Ill.App. 1 Dist. 1988), 853
Crummey v. Commissioner, 397 F.2d 82 (9th Cir.1968), 658, 1004
Cruzan by Cruzan v. Director, Missouri Dept. of Health, 497 U.S. 261, 110 S.Ct. 2841, 111 L.Ed.2d 224 (1990), 969
Culver v. Title Guarantee & Trust Co., 296 N.Y. 74, 70 N.E.2d 163 (N.Y.1946), 686

Daley v. Boroughs, 310 Ark. 274, 835 S.W.2d 858 (Ark.1992), 424
Daly, Petition of, 142 Misc.2d 85, 536 N.Y.S.2d 393 (N.Y.Sur.1988), 941
Davis v. Neilson, 871 S.W.2d 35 (Mo.App. W.D.1993), 120, 853
Davis v. Somers, 140 Or.App. 567, 915 P.2d 1047 (Or.App.1996), 44
Deane's Will, In re, 4 N.Y.2d 326, 175 N.Y.S.2d 21, 151 N.E.2d 184 (N.Y.1958), 751
DeBone v. Department of Public Welfare, 929 A.2d 1219 (Pa.Cmwlth.2007), 646
Dellinger, Estate of v. 1st Source Bank, 793 N.E.2d 1041 (Ind.2003), 248
Demaris' Estate, In re, 166 Or. 36, 110 P.2d 571 (Or.1941), 234
Demund v. LaPoint, 169 Misc.2d 1020, 647 N.Y.S.2d 662 (N.Y.Sup.1996), 892
Denison v. Denison, 185 N.Y. 438, 78 N.E. 162 (N.Y.1906), 526
Denner, In re Estate of, 2006 WL 510530 (N.J.Super.Ch.2006), 249
Detzel v. Nieberding, 7 Ohio Misc. 262, 219 N.E.2d 327 (Ohio Prob.1966), 315
DeVoss, Matter of Estate of, 474 N.W.2d 542 (Iowa 1991), 287
Dewire v. Haveles, 404 Mass. 274, 534 N.E.2d 782 (Mass.1989), **864**
Dexia Credit Local v. Rogan, 624 F.Supp.2d 970 (N.D.Ill.2009), 625
Dickerson v. Union Nat. Bank of Little Rock, 268 Ark. 292, 595 S.W.2d 677 (Ark. 1980), **893**
Doctor v. Hughes, 225 N.Y. 305, 122 N.E. 221 (N.Y.1919), 864
Doe v. Kamehameha Schools/Bernice Pauahi Bishop Estate, 470 F.3d 827 (9th Cir. 2006), 736
Doe v. Kamehameha Schools/Bernice Pauahi Bishop Estate, 416 F.3d 1025 (9th Cir. 2005), 736
Doe v. Kamehameha Schools/Bernice Pauahi Bishop Estate, 295 F.Supp.2d 1141 (D.Hawai'i 2003), 735
Donley, In re Guardianship of, 262 Neb. 282, 631 N.W.2d 839 (Neb.2001), 940
Donnelly's Estates, In re, 81 Wash.2d 430, 502 P.2d 1163 (Wash.1972), **109**
Dougherty v. Rubenstein, 172 Md.App. 269, 914 A.2d 184 (Md.App.2007), **428**
Draper, Estate of v. Bank of America, N.A., 288 Kan. 510, 205 P.3d 698 (Kan.2009), 395
Dreher v. Dreher, 370 S.C. 75, 634 S.E.2d 646 (S.C.2006), 176, 591
Drye v. United States, 528 U.S. 49, 120 S.Ct. 474, 145 L.Ed.2d 466 (1999), 159
Duffy, In re, 25 Misc.3d 901, 885 N.Y.S.2d 401 (N.Y.Sur.2009), 1077

Duke, Matter of, 305 N.J.Super. 408, 702 A.2d 1008 (N.J.Super.Ch.1995), 853
Dunklin v. Ramsay, 328 Ark. 263, 944 S.W.2d 76 (Ark.1997), 489
Duran v. Duran, 900 N.E.2d 454 (Ind.App. 2009), 115
Durand's Will, In re, 250 N.Y. 45, 164 N.E. 737 (N.Y.1928), 900
Dyer v. Eckols, 808 S.W.2d 531 (Tex.App.-Hous. (14 Dist.) 1991), 159

Ebitz v. Pioneer Nat. Bank, 372 Mass. 207, 361 N.E.2d 225 (Mass.1977), 733
Eckels v. Davis, 111 S.W.3d 687 (Tex.App.-Fort Worth 2003), 344
Edmundson v. Morton, 332 N.C. 276, 420 S.E.2d 106 (N.C.1992), 305
Egelhoff v. Egelhoff ex rel. Breiner, 532 U.S. 141, 121 S.Ct. 1322, 149 L.Ed.2d 264 (2001), 381, 998
Ellis, In re Estate of, 236 Ill.2d 45, 337 Ill.Dec. 678, 923 N.E.2d 237 (Ill.2009), **473**
Ellis v. West ex rel. West, 971 So.2d 20 (Ala. 2007), 115
Ellison Grandchildren Trust, In re, 261 S.W.3d 111 (Tex.App.-San Antonio 2008), 853
Erickson v. Erickson, 246 Conn. 359, 716 A.2d 92 (Conn.1998), 359
Essen v. Gilmore, 259 Neb. 55, 607 N.W.2d 829 (Neb.2000), 159
Estate of (see name of party)
Estates of Covert, In re, 97 N.Y.2d 68, 735 N.Y.S.2d 879, 761 N.E.2d 571 (N.Y.2001), 24
Estates of Swanson, In re, 344 Mont. 266, 187 P.3d 631 (Mont.2008), 28
Etgen v. Corboy, 230 Va. 413, 337 S.E.2d 286 (Va.1985), 376, 378
Evans v. May, 923 S.W.2d 712 (Tex.App.-Hous. (1 Dist.) 1996), 501
Evans v. McCoy, 291 Md. 562, 436 A.2d 436 (Md.1981), 120, 853
Evans' Estate, In re, 274 Wis. 459, 80 N.W.2d 408 (Wis.1957), **831**

Fabian, In re Estate of, 326 S.C. 349, 483 S.E.2d 474 (S.C.App.1997), 346
Fairbairn, In re Estate of, 46 A.D.3d 973, 846 N.Y.S.2d 779 (N.Y.A.D. 3 Dept.2007), 490
Falise, In re Estate of, 20 Misc.3d 894, 863 N.Y.S.2d 854 (N.Y.Sur.2008), 548
Feinberg, In re Estate of, 235 Ill.2d 256, 335 Ill.Dec. 863, 919 N.E.2d 888 (Ill.2009), **1**
Ferrell–French v. Ferrell, 691 So.2d 500 (Fla. App. 4 Dist.1997), 740
Fidelity Title & Trust Co. v. Clyde, 143 Conn. 247, 121 A.2d 625 (Conn.1956), 705
Finley v. Astrue, 372 Ark. 103, 270 S.W.3d 849 (Ark.2008), 145
Finley v. Finley, 726 S.W.2d 923 (Tenn.Ct. App.1986), 177
First Healthcare Corp. v. Rettinger, 342 N.C. 886, 467 S.E.2d 243 (N.C.1996), 979
First Interstate Bank of Oregon v. Henson–Hammer, 98 Or.App. 189, 779 P.2d 167 (Or.App.1989), 375
First Nat. Bank In Fairmont v. Phillips, 176 W.Va. 395, 344 S.E.2d 201 (W.Va.1985), 130
First Nat. Bank of Dubuque v. Wathen, 338 N.W.2d 361 (Iowa 1983), 853
Flaherty, Matter of Estate of, 446 N.W.2d 760 (N.D.1989), 427, 437
Ford v. Ford, 307 Md. 105, 512 A.2d 389 (Md.1986), **16**
Fordonski, In re Estate of, 678 N.W.2d 413 (Iowa 2004), 248
Ford's Estate, In re, 19 Wis.2d 436, 120 N.W.2d 647 (Wis.1963), 471
Forsee v. United States, 76 F.Supp.2d 1135 (D.Kan.1999), 785
Forsyth v. Rowe, 226 Conn. 818, 629 A.2d 379 (Conn.1993), 655
Foss' Will, In re, 282 A.D. 509, 125 N.Y.S.2d 105 (N.Y.A.D. 1 Dept.1953), 1106
Foster v. Estate of Gomes, 2010 WL 322170 (Fla.App. 5 Dist.2010), 199
Foster v. Oliva, 880 N.E.2d 1223 (Ind.App. 2008), **384**
Fouts, Matter of, 176 Misc.2d 521, 677 N.Y.S.2d 699 (N.Y.Sur.1998), 530
Fowles' Will, In re, 222 N.Y. 222, 118 N.E. 611 (N.Y.1918), 274
Frances Slocum Bank and Trust Co. v. Estate of Martin, 666 N.E.2d 411 (Ind.App.1996), 159
Franklin v. Anna Nat. Bank of Anna, 140 Ill.App.3d 533, 94 Ill.Dec. 870, 488 N.E.2d 1117 (Ill.App. 5 Dist.1986), **54,** 569
Freihofer, Matter of, 172 Misc.2d 260, 658 N.Y.S.2d 811 (N.Y.Sur.1997), **1093**
Fries, In re Estate of, 279 Neb. 887, 782 N.W.2d 596 (Neb.2010), 195
F.T.C. v. Affordable Media, 179 F.3d 1228 (9th Cir.1999), **619**

Gagliardi's Estate, Matter of, 55 N.Y.2d 109, 447 N.Y.S.2d 902, 432 N.E.2d 774 (N.Y. 1982), 526
Gaite's Will Trusts, Re, 1949 WL 10392 (Ch D 1949), 893
Gallaher v. Riddle, 850 A.2d 748 (Pa.Super.2004), 159
Gardiner, In re Estate of, 273 Kan. 191, 42 P.3d 120 (Kan.2002), 85, 501
Garrett v. Read, 278 Kan. 662, 102 P.3d 436 (Kan.2004), **389**
Gaspar, Estate of v. Vogt, Brown & Merry, 670 N.W.2d 918 (S.D.2003), 201
Geddings v. Geddings, 319 S.C. 213, 460 S.E.2d 376 (S.C.1995), **196**
Gerard, Estate of, 911 P.2d 266 (Okla.1995), 455, 465
Gerking v. Wolff, 28 Cal.App.2d 102, 82 P.2d 22 (Cal.App. 4 Dist.1938), 897

Gertner v. Superior Court, 25 Cal.Rptr.2d 47 (Cal.App. 4 Dist.1993), 1021
Gianella v. Gianella, 234 S.W.3d 526 (Mo. App. E.D.2007), 478
Gibbs' Estate, In re, 14 Wis.2d 490, 111 N.W.2d 413 (Wis.1961), **339**
Gifford v. Dyer, 2 R.I. 99 (R.I.1852), **353**
Gillett–Netting v. Barnhart, 371 F.3d 593 (9th Cir.2004), 145
Girard's Estate, In re, 386 Pa. 548, 127 A.2d 287 (Pa.1956), 733
Gist, In re Estate of, 763 N.W.2d 561 (Iowa 2009), **642**
Glomset's Estate, Matter of, 547 P.2d 951 (Okla.1976), **214**
Godwin v. Godwin, 141 Miss. 633, 107 So. 13 (Miss.1926), 569
Goick, In re Estate of, 275 Mont. 13, 909 P.2d 1165 (Mont.1996), **76**
Gonsalves v. Alameda County Superior Court (Picardo), 24 Cal.Rptr.2d 52 (Cal. App. 1 Dist.1993), **438**
Gonzales v. Oregon, 546 U.S. 243, 126 S.Ct. 904, 163 L.Ed.2d 748 (2006), 981
Gonzalez, Matter of, 262 N.J.Super. 456, 621 A.2d 94 (N.J.Super.Ch.1992), 706
Goodman v. Goodman, 128 Wash.2d 366, 907 P.2d 290 (Wash.1995), **540**
Graham's Estate, In re, 216 Kan. 770, 533 P.2d 1318 (Kan.1975), 300
Green v. Green, 559 A.2d 1047 (R.I.1989), 567
Gregg v. Lindsay, 437 Pa.Super. 206, 649 A.2d 935 (Pa.Super.1994), 44
Gregory v. Estate of Gregory, 315 Ark. 187, 866 S.W.2d 379 (Ark.1993), 404
Greiff, Matter of, 92 N.Y.2d 341, 680 N.Y.S.2d 894, 703 N.E.2d 752 (N.Y.1998), 199
Griffith, Estate of v. Griffith, 2010 WL 1077441 (Miss.2010), 234
Grinker, Matter of, 77 N.Y.2d 703, 570 N.Y.S.2d 448, 573 N.E.2d 536 (N.Y.1991), 940
Griswold, Estate of, 108 Cal.Rptr.2d 165, 24 P.3d 1191 (Cal.2001), 142
Gross' Estate, Matter of, 646 P.2d 396 (Colo. App.1981), 343
Gruen v. Gruen, 68 N.Y.2d 48, 505 N.Y.S.2d 849, 496 N.E.2d 869 (N.Y.1986), **47**
Guardianship and Conservatorship of Garcia, In re, 262 Neb. 205, 631 N.W.2d 464 (Neb. 2001), 942
Guardianship of (see name of party)
Gulbankian, State v., 54 Wis.2d 605, 196 N.W.2d 733 (Wis.1972), 243
Gum v. Gum, 1996 WL 112155 (Tex.App.-Beaumont 1996), 426
Gushwa v. Hunt, 145 N.M. 286, 197 P.3d 1 (N.M.2008), **360**

Hall, In re Estate of, 310 Mont. 486, 51 P.3d 1134 (Mont.2002), **243**
Hall's Estate, In re, 60 N.J.Super. 597, 160 A.2d 49 (N.J.Super.A.D.1960), 300
Hamilton, Matter of Estate of, 190 A.D.2d 927, 593 N.Y.S.2d 372 (N.Y.A.D. 3 Dept. 1993), **743**
Hardt v. Vitae Foundation, Inc., 302 S.W.3d 133 (Mo.App. W.D.2009), 709
Hargrove v. Rich, 278 Ga. 561, 604 S.E.2d 475 (Ga.2004), 740
Harrison's Estate, In re, 22 Cal.App.2d 28, 70 P.2d 522 (Cal.App. 4 Dist.1937), 489
Harris Trust and Sav. Bank v. Beach, 118 Ill.2d 1, 112 Ill.Dec. 224, 513 N.E.2d 833 (Ill.1987), **855**
Hartman, Matter of, 347 N.W.2d 480 (Minn. 1984), 841
Harvard College v. Amory, 26 Mass. 446 (Mass.1830), 1067
Haslam v. Alvarez, 70 R.I. 212, 38 A.2d 158 (R.I.1944), 287
Hatch v. Riggs Nat. Bank, 361 F.2d 559, 124 U.S.App.D.C. 105 (D.C.Cir.1966), 688, 864
Hayes v. Hayes' Ex'x, 17 A. 634 (N.J.Ch. 1889), 287
Haynes v. First Nat. State Bank of New Jersey, 87 N.J. 163, 432 A.2d 890 (N.J. 1981), **443**
Heaps v. Heaps, 21 Cal.Rptr.3d 239 (Cal. App. 4 Dist.2004), **582**
Heater, In re Estate of, 266 Ill.App.3d 452, 203 Ill.Dec. 734, 640 N.E.2d 654 (Ill.App. 4 Dist.1994), 163
Hecker v. Stark County Social Service Bd., 527 N.W.2d 226 (N.D.1994), 647
Heggstad, Estate of, 20 Cal.Rptr.2d 433 (Cal. App. 1 Dist.1993), 546
Heller, In re, 6 N.Y.3d 649, 816 N.Y.S.2d 403, 849 N.E.2d 262 (N.Y.2006), 1090
Henderson, Matter of, 80 N.Y.2d 388, 590 N.Y.S.2d 836, 605 N.E.2d 323 (N.Y.1992), 466
Herceg, In re Estate of, 193 Misc.2d 201, 747 N.Y.S.2d 901 (N.Y.Sur.2002), 359
Hill, In re Estate of, 2005 WL 387930 (Tenn. Ct.App.2005), 177
Hillman v. Hillman, 433 Mass. 590, 744 N.E.2d 1078 (Mass.2001), 739
Hilton's Estate, Matter of, 98 N.M. 420, 649 P.2d 488 (N.M.App.1982), 218
Hodel v. Irving, 481 U.S. 704, 107 S.Ct. 2076, 95 L.Ed.2d 668 (1987), 10
Hoesly v. State, Dept. of Social Services, 243 Neb. 304, 498 N.W.2d 571 (Neb.1993), 160
Hoffman, Estate of, 119 Cal.Rptr.2d 248 (Cal. App. 2 Dist.2002), 489
Hoffman's Estate, In re, 175 Ohio St. 363, 195 N.E.2d 106 (Ohio 1963), 567
Holland, Estate of v. Commissioner, T.C. Memo. 1997-302 (U.S.Tax Ct.1997), 662
Holt, Matter of Estate of, 75 Haw. 224, 857 P.2d 1355 (Hawai'i 1993), **918**
Honigman's Will, In re, 8 N.Y.2d 244, 203 N.Y.S.2d 859, 168 N.E.2d 676 (N.Y.1960), 437

Hope, In re Estate of, 223 P.3d 119 (Colo. App.2007), 742

Hotz v. Minyard, 304 S.C. 225, 403 S.E.2d 634 (S.C.1991), **29**

Houston's Estate, In re, 414 Pa. 579, 201 A.2d 592 (Pa.1964), 815, 842

Hughes v. Frank, 1995 WL 632018 (Del.Ch. 1995), 404

Hume, In re Estate of, 984 S.W.2d 602 (Tenn. 1999), 303

Huston, Estate of, 60 Cal.Rptr.2d 217 (Cal. App. 4 Dist.1997), **959**

Hyde, In re, 44 A.D.3d 1195, 845 N.Y.S.2d 833 (N.Y.A.D. 3 Dept.2007), 1078

Industrial Nat. Bank of R. I. v. Barrett, 101 R.I. 89, 220 A.2d 517 (R.I.1966), **908**

In re (see name of party)

Institution for Savings in Roxbury and Its Vicinity v. Roxbury Home for Aged Women, 244 Mass. 583, 139 N.E. 301 (Mass. 1923), 898

Jackson v. Kelly, 345 Ark. 151, 44 S.W.3d 328 (Ark.2001), 478

Jacobs–Zorne v. Superior Court, 54 Cal. Rptr.2d 385 (Cal.App. 2 Dist.1996), 489

Janes, Matter of Estate of, 90 N.Y.2d 41, 659 N.Y.S.2d 165, 681 N.E.2d 332 (N.Y. 1997), **1068**

Janis, In re Estate of, 210 A.D.2d 101, 620 N.Y.S.2d 342 (N.Y.A.D. 1 Dept.1994), 134

Janus v. Tarasewicz, 135 Ill.App.3d 936, 90 Ill.Dec. 599, 482 N.E.2d 418 (Ill.App. 1 Dist.1985), 153

Jee v. Audley, 1787 WL 625 (Ct of Chancery 1787), 889

Jenkins v. Jenkins, 990 So.2d 807 (Miss.App. 2008), 115

Johnson v. Hart, 279 Va. 617, 692 S.E.2d 239 (Va.2010), 42

Johnson v. Johnson, 184 Md.App. 643, 967 A.2d 274 (Md.App.2009), **1096**

Johnson v. La Grange State Bank, 73 Ill.2d 342, 22 Ill.Dec. 709, 383 N.E.2d 185 (Ill. 1978), 178

Jones v. Atchison, 925 F.2d 209 (7th Cir. 1991), 159

Jones v. Hill, 267 Va. 708, 594 S.E.2d 913 (Va.2004), 812

Jones v. Stubbs, 434 So.2d 1362 (Miss.1983), 108

Jotham, In re Estate of, 722 N.W.2d 447 (Minn.2006), 141

JP Morgan Chase Bank, N.A. v. Longmeyer, 275 S.W.3d 697 (Ky.2009), 1101

Julia v. Russo, 984 So.2d 1283 (Fla.App. 4 Dist.2008), 58

Kane v. Superior Court, 44 Cal.Rptr.2d 578 (Cal.App. 2 Dist.1995), 146

Kappus v. Kappus, 284 S.W.3d 831 (Tex. 2009), **1102**

Karsenty v. Schoukroun, 406 Md. 469, 959 A.2d 1147 (Md.2008), 175

Kaufmann's Will, In re, 20 A.D.2d 464, 247 N.Y.S.2d 664 (N.Y.A.D. 1 Dept.1964), **493**

Kearns v. Kearns, 76 A. 1042 (N.J.Ch.1910), 287

Keel v. Estate of Keel, 1998 WL 34032494 (Miss.App.1998), 427

Keenan, Matter of Estate of, 519 N.W.2d 373 (Iowa 1994), 899

Keener v. Keener, 278 Va. 435, 682 S.E.2d 545 (Va.2009), 576

Keisling v. Landrum, 218 S.W.3d 737 (Tex. App.-Fort Worth 2007), 555

Kempton v. Dugan, 224 S.W.3d 83 (Mo.App. W.D.2007), 588

Kennedy v. Plan Adm'r for DuPont Sav. and Inv. Plan, 555 U.S. 285, 129 S.Ct. 865, 172 L.Ed.2d 662 (2009), **994**

Kernkamp v. Bolthouse, 714 So.2d 655 (Fla. App. 5 Dist.1998), 344

Khabbaz, by and through her mother and Next friend, Donna M. Eng v. Commissioner, Social Sec. Admin., 155 N.H. 798, 930 A.2d 1180 (N.H.2007), 145

Kinzler, Matter of, 195 A.D.2d 464, 600 N.Y.S.2d 126 (N.Y.A.D. 2 Dept.1993), **1044,** 1112

Kirk, In re Estate of, 591 N.W.2d 630 (Iowa 1999), 160

Kirkeby, In re, Estate of, 157 Or.App. 309, 970 P.2d 241 (Or.App.1998), 250

Kirkpatrick, In re Estate of, 77 P.3d 404 (Wyo.2003), 114

Kissinger, In re Estate of, 166 Wash.2d 120, 206 P.3d 665 (Wash.2009), 22

Kittson's Estate, In re, 177 Minn. 469, 225 N.W. 439 (Minn.1929), 840

Kleinberg, In re, 38 N.Y.2d 836, 382 N.Y.S.2d 49, 345 N.E.2d 592 (N.Y.1976), 569

Knupp v. District of Columbia, 578 A.2d 702 (D.C.1990), **355**

Knupp v. Schober, 1992 WL 182323 (D.D.C. 1992), 358

Kohlsaat, Estate of v. Commissioner, T.C. Memo. 1997-212 (U.S.Tax Ct.1997), **659**

Kolacy, In re Estate of, 332 N.J.Super. 593, 753 A.2d 1257 (N.J.Super.Ch.2000), 145

Kostin v. Kent, 278 Mich.App. 47, 748 N.W.2d 583 (Mich.App.2008), 987

Kreuzer, Matter of Estate of, 243 A.D.2d 207, 674 N.Y.S.2d 505 (N.Y.A.D. 3 Dept.1998), 903

Krischer v. McIver, 697 So.2d 97 (Fla.1997), 981

Krooss, In re, 302 N.Y. 424, 99 N.E.2d 222 (N.Y.1951), **822**

Kuralt, In re Estate of, 294 Mont. 354, 981 P.2d 771 (Mont.1999), 258

Kuralt, In re Estate of, 315 Mont. 177, 68 P.3d 662 (Mont.2003), 293

Kuralt, In re Estate of, 303 Mont. 335, 15 P.3d 931 (Mont.2000), 258

Kurkowski's Estate, In re, 487 Pa. 295, 409 A.2d 357 (Pa.1979), 1026

Kurz by First Nat. Bank of Chicago, Estate of v. Commissioner, 68 F.3d 1027 (7th Cir.1995), **787**

Lakatosh, Estate of, 441 Pa.Super. 133, 656 A.2d 1378 (Pa.Super.1995), 455, 484

Lalli v. Lalli, 439 U.S. 259, 99 S.Ct. 518, 58 L.Ed.2d 503 (1978), 131

Last Will and Testament of Melson, In re, 711 A.2d 783 (Del.Supr.1998), 458

Latham v. Father Divine, 299 N.Y. 22, 85 N.E.2d 168 (N.Y.1949), 471

Lawrence, In re, 227 B.R. 907 (Bkrtcy. S.D.Fla.1998), 626

Lawrence, In re, 251 B.R. 630 (S.D.Fla.2000), 625

Leavey, In re Estate of, 41 Kan.App.2d 423, 202 P.3d 99 (Kan.App.2009), 235

Lemmons v. Lawson, 266 Ga. 571, 468 S.E.2d 749 (Ga.1996), 827

Levin v. Fisch, 404 S.W.2d 889 (Tex.Civ. App.-Eastland 1966), **536**

Levin v. Smith, 513 A.2d 1292 (Del. Supr.1986), 545

Lewis' Estate, In re, 194 Miss. 480, 13 So.2d 20 (Miss.1943), 569

Lincoln Life and Annuity Co. of New York v. Caswell, 31 A.D.3d 1, 813 N.Y.S.2d 385 (N.Y.A.D. 1 Dept.2006), 993, **1001**

Linthicum v. Rudi, 122 Nev. 1452, 148 P.3d 746 (Nev.2006), 570, 590

Livsey, In re Estate of v. Wood, 183 P.3d 1038 (Okla.Civ.App. Div. 3 2008), 217

Locke, In re Estate of, 148 N.H. 754, 813 A.2d 1172 (N.H.2002), **95**

Lockhead v. Weinstein, 319 Mont. 62, 81 P.3d 1284 (Mont.2003), 81

Lord, In re Estate of, 795 A.2d 700 (Me. 2002), 359

Lucas v. Hamm, 56 Cal.2d 583, 15 Cal.Rptr. 821, 364 P.2d 685 (Cal.1961), 869

Lucero v. Lucero, 118 N.M. 636, 884 P.2d 527 (N.M.App.1994), 424

Ludwig v. AmSouth Bank of Florida, 686 So.2d 1373 (Fla.App. 2 Dist.1997), 923

Lumbard v. Farmers State Bank, 812 N.E.2d 196 (Ind.App.2004), 752

Lung, In re Estate of, 692 A.2d 1349 (D.C. 1997), 291

Lunkes, In re, 406 B.R. 812 (Bkrtcy.N.D.Ill. 2009), 616

Lux v. Lux, 109 R.I. 592, 288 A.2d 701 (R.I. 1972), 835

Lychos, In re Estate of, 323 Pa.Super. 74, 470 A.2d 136 (Pa.Super.1983), 1060

Macaro, In re Estate of, 182 Misc.2d 625, 699 N.Y.S.2d 634 (N.Y.Sur.1999), 27

MacCallum v. Seymour, 165 Vt. 452, 686 A.2d 935 (Vt.1996), 116

MacDonald v. MacDonald, 2005 WL 580530 (Cal.App. 2 Dist.2005), 490

Maenhoudt v. Bank, 34 Kan.App.2d 150, 115 P.3d 157 (Kan.App.2005), 958

Magee v. United States, 93 F.Supp.2d 161 (D.R.I.2000), 654

Maher, Matter of, 207 A.D.2d 133, 621 N.Y.S.2d 617 (N.Y.A.D. 2 Dept.1994), **945**

Maheras, Matter of Estate of, 897 P.2d 268 (Okla.1995), 467

Mahoney v. Grainger, 283 Mass. 189, 186 N.E. 86 (Mass.1933), 333

Malloy, Matter of Estate of, 134 Wash.2d 316, 949 P.2d 804 (Wash.1998), 377

Mampe, In re, 932 A.2d 954 (Pa.Super.2007), 534

Mangels v. Cornell, 40 Kan.App.2d 110, 189 P.3d 573 (Kan.App.2008), 588

Mansur's Will, In re, 98 Vt. 296, 127 A. 297 (Vt.1925), 834

Marks v. Marks, 91 Wash.App. 325, 957 P.2d 235 (Wash.App. Div. 3 1998), 467

Marine Midland Bank, N.A., Matter of, 74 N.Y.2d 448, 548 N.Y.S.2d 625, 547 N.E.2d 1152 (N.Y.1989), **326, 841**

Marsh v. Frost Nat. Bank, 129 S.W.3d 174 (Tex.App.-Corpus Christi 2004), 704

Marshall, In re, 600 F.3d 1037 (9th Cir.2010), 481

Marshall, In re, 253 B.R. 550 (Bkrtcy. C.D.Cal.2000), 481

Marshall v. Marshall, 547 U.S. 293, 126 S.Ct. 1735, 164 L.Ed.2d 480 (2006), 478

Marsman v. Nasca, 30 Mass.App.Ct. 789, 573 N.E.2d 1025 (Mass.App.Ct.1991), **555**

Martignacco, In re Estate of, 689 N.W.2d 262 (Minn.App.2004), 141

Martin v. Palmer, 1 S.W.3d 875 (Tex.App.-Hous. (1 Dist.) 1999), 338

Martino v. Martino, 35 S.W.3d 252 (Tex.App.-Hous. (14 Dist.) 2000), 842

Matlock v. Simpson, 902 S.W.2d 384 (Tenn. 1995), 466

Matter of (see name of party)

Mayberry, Estate of v. Mayberry, 318 Ark. 588, 886 S.W.2d 627 (Ark.1994), 300

McCormick v. Jeffers, 281 Ga. 264, 637 S.E.2d 666 (Ga.2006), 234

McCoy, Matter of Estate of, 844 P.2d 1131 (Alaska 1993), 455, 466

McGee v. McGee, 122 R.I. 837, 413 A.2d 72 (R.I.1980), **294**

McGinley v. Bank of America, N.A., 279 Kan. 426, 109 P.3d 1146 (Kan.2005), **1079**

McQuone v. Brown, 2001 WL 1447232 (Cal. App. 5 Dist.2001), 489

Mears v. Addonizio, 336 N.J.Super. 474, 765 A.2d 260 (N.J.Super.A.D.2001), 1112

Medlock v. Mitchell, 95 Ark. App. 132, 234 S.W.3d 901 (Ark.App.2006), 467

Mergenhagen, In re, 50 A.D.3d 1486, 856 N.Y.S.2d 389 (N.Y.A.D. 4 Dept.2008), 688

Merritt v. Yates, 2000 WL 1483476 (Tenn.Ct. App.2000), 396

Milhoan v. Koenig, 196 W.Va. 163, 469 S.E.2d 99 (W.Va.1996), 423
Miller v. First Nat. Bank & Trust Co., 637 P.2d 75 (Okla.1981), 593
Milton Hershey School, In re, 590 Pa. 35, 911 A.2d 1258 (Pa.2006), 708
Milum v. Marsh ex rel. Lacey, 53 S.W.3d 234 (Mo.App. S.D.2001), 427
M.I. Marshall & Isley Trust Co. v. McCannon, 188 Ariz. 562, 937 P.2d 1368 (Ariz. App. Div. 1 1996), 437
Mitchell, In re, 423 B.R. 758 (Bkrtcy.E.D.Wis. 2009), 607
Molloy v. Bane, 214 A.D.2d 171, 631 N.Y.S.2d 910 (N.Y.A.D. 2 Dept.1995), 160
Moran's Estate, In re, 77 Ill.2d 147, 32 Ill. Dec. 349, 395 N.E.2d 579 (Ill.1979), 152
Morningstar, In re Estate of, 17 A.D.3d 1060, 794 N.Y.S.2d 205 (N.Y.A.D. 4 Dept.2005), 134
Morris v. West's Estate, 643 S.W.2d 204 (Tex.App.-Eastland 1982), **230**
Moseley v. Goodman, 138 Tenn. 1, 195 S.W. 590 (Tenn.1917), 344
Moses' Will, In re, 227 So.2d 829 (Miss. 1969), **458**
Moss v. Axford, 246 Mich. 288, 224 N.W. 425 (Mich.1929), 526
Motes/Henes Trust, Bank of Bentonville v. Motes, 297 Ark. 380, 761 S.W.2d 938 (Ark. 1988), 747
Munn v. Briggs, 110 Cal.Rptr.3d 783 (Cal. App. 4 Dist.2010), 490
Murcury, In re Estate of, 177 Vt. 606, 868 A.2d 680 (Vt.2004), 135, 141
Mushaw v. Mushaw, 183 Md. 511, 39 A.2d 465 (Md.1944), 591

Nelson, In re Estate of, 168 P.3d 235 (Okla. Civ.App. Div. 4 2007), 288
Newbill, Estate of, 781 S.W.2d 727 (Tex.App.-Amarillo 1989), 489
New Jersey Div. of Youth and Family Services v. M.W., 398 N.J.Super. 266, 942 A.2d 1 (N.J.Super.A.D.2007), 91
Newman v. Dore, 275 N.Y. 371, 9 N.E.2d 966 (N.Y.1937), 174, 591
Newman v. Wells Fargo Bank, 59 Cal. Rptr.2d 2, 926 P.2d 969 (Cal.1996), **846**
Nichols v. Eaton, 91 U.S. 716, 23 L.Ed. 254 (1875), 608
Nichols v. Rowan, 422 S.W.2d 21 (Tex.Civ. App.-San Antonio 1967), 234
Noonan's Estate, In re, 361 Pa. 26, 63 A.2d 80 (Pa.1949), 1052
Northern Trust Co. v. Porter, 368 Ill. 256, 13 N.E.2d 487 (Ill.1938), 764
Norton, Matter of Estate of, 330 N.C. 378, 410 S.E.2d 484 (N.C.1991), **262**
Nunnenman v. Estate of Grubbs, 2010 Ark. App. 75 (Ark.App.2010), **989**

O'Neal v. Wilkes, 263 Ga. 850, 439 S.E.2d 490 (Ga.1994), 128
Opatz, Matter of Estate of, 554 N.W.2d 813 (N.D.1996), 159
O'Shaughnessy, United States v., 517 N.W.2d 574 (Minn.1994), 606
Oshkosh Foundation, In re, 61 Wis.2d 432, 213 N.W.2d 54 (Wis.1973), 722
Ottomeier, In re Estate of v. Miller, 85 Wash. App. 1058 (Wash.App. Div. 3 1997), 466

Padilla's Estate, Matter of, 97 N.M. 508, 641 P.2d 539 (N.M.App.1982), 218
Palmer, In re Estate of, 658 N.W.2d 197 (Minn.2003), 141
Pennington, Matter of Estate of, 16 Kan. App.2d 792, 829 P.2d 618 (Kan.App.1992), 1021
People v. ______ (see opposing party)
Peralta v. Peralta, 139 N.M. 231, 131 P.3d 81 (N.M.App.2005), 478
Perkins v. Iglehart, 183 Md. 520, 39 A.2d 672 (Md.1944), 896
Pernod v. American Nat. Bank & Trust Co. of Chicago, 8 Ill.2d 16, 132 N.E.2d 540 (Ill.1956), 695
Petition of (see name of party)
Phelan, In re Estate of, 375 Ill.App.3d 875, 314 Ill.Dec. 275, 874 N.E.2d 185 (Ill.App. 1 Dist.2007), 581
Phillips v. Estate of Holzmann, 740 So.2d 1 (Fla.App. 3 Dist.1998), 529
Phillips v. Najar, 901 S.W.2d 561 (Tex.App.-El Paso 1995), 236
Piel, Matter of, 10 N.Y.3d 163, 855 N.Y.S.2d 41, 884 N.E.2d 1040 (N.Y.2008), 852
Plumley v. Bledsoe, 216 W.Va. 735, 613 S.E.2d 102 (W.Va.2005), 28
Pope, In re Estate of, 2008 WL 2097593 (Miss.App.2008), 465
Pope v. Garrett, 147 Tex. 18, 211 S.W.2d 559 (Tex.1948), 471
Portnoy, In re, 201 B.R. 685 (Bkrtcy.S.D.N.Y. 1996), 625, 626, 637
Potter, In re Estate of, 469 So.2d 957 (Fla.App. 4 Dist.1985), **284**
Potts v. Emerick, 293 Md. 495, 445 A.2d 695 (Md.1982), 547
Powers v. Wilkinson, 399 Mass. 650, 506 N.E.2d 842 (Mass.1987), 854
Pozarny, Estate of, 177 Misc.2d 752, 677 N.Y.S.2d 714 (N.Y.Sur.1998), 582
Prestie v. Prestie, 122 Nev. 807, 138 P.3d 520 (Nev.2006), **207**
Price v. Abate, 2009 WL 559908 (Fla.App. 5 Dist.2009), 234
Probate of Will and Codicil of Macool, In re, 416 N.J.Super. 298 (N.J.Super.A.D.2010), 247
Proprietors of Church in Brattle Square v. Grant, 69 Mass. 142 (Mass.1855), 900
Purce v. Patterson, 275 Va. 190, 654 S.E.2d 885 (Va.2008), 196
Pysell v. Keck, 263 Va. 457, 559 S.E.2d 677 (Va.2002), 201

Ranney, Matter of Will of, 124 N.J. 1, 589 A.2d 1339 (N.J.1991), 248

Morse v. Sharkey, 483 Mich. 48, 764 N.W.2d 1 (Mich.2009), **320**

Rehwinkel, In re Estate of, 71 Wash.App. 827, 862 P.2d 639 (Wash.App. Div. 1 1993), **311**

Reid, In re Estate of, 825 So.2d 1 (Miss.2002), 468

Reisman v. Kaufman, 266 Mich.App. 522, 702 N.W.2d 658 (Mich.App.2005), 755

Richardson Trust, In re, 138 N.H. 1, 634 A.2d 1005 (N.H.1993), 900

Riggs, Estate of, 109 Misc.2d 644, 440 N.Y.S.2d 450 (N.Y.Sur.1981), 129

Rittenhouse's Will, In re, 19 N.J. 376, 117 A.2d 401 (N.J.1955), 449

Robert Paul P., Matter of Adoption of, 63 N.Y.2d 233, 481 N.Y.S.2d 652, 471 N.E.2d 424 (N.Y.1984), 120

Robert T. McLean Irrevocable Trust v. Patrick Davis, P.C., 283 S.W.3d 786 (Mo.App. S.D.2009), 627

Robinson v. Delfino, 710 A.2d 154 (R.I.1998), 58

Roblin's Estate, In re, 210 Or. 371, 311 P.2d 459 (Or.1957), 470

Rogan, United States v., 517 F.3d 449 (7th Cir.2008), 629

Rogan, United States v., 459 F.Supp.2d 692 (N.D.Ill.2006), 629

Rogers, In re Estate of, 81 P.3d 1190 (Hawai'i 2003), 141

Rogiers, In re, 396 N.J.Super. 317, 933 A.2d 971 (N.J.Super.A.D.2007), 91

Rood v. Newberg, 48 Mass.App.Ct. 185, 718 N.E.2d 886 (Mass.App.Ct.1999), 472

Rosenberg's Estate, In re, 196 Or. 219, 248 P.2d 340 (Or.1952), 470

Rosenberg's Estate, In re, 196 Or. 219, 246 P.2d 858 (Or.1952), 470

Rothko's Estate, Matter of, 43 N.Y.2d 305, 401 N.Y.S.2d 449, 372 N.E.2d 291 (N.Y. 1977), **1046**

Rudnick v. Rudnick, 102 Cal.Rptr.3d 493 (Cal.App. 5 Dist.2009), **1108**

Russell v. Chase Investment Services Corp., 212 P.3d 1178 (Okla.2009), 959

Ryan v. Ward, 192 Md. 342, 64 A.2d 258 (Md.1949), 888, 889, 924

Saccu's Appeal From Probate, In re, 97 Conn. App. 710, 905 A.2d 1285 (Conn.App.2006), 1107

Salem United Methodist Church v. Bottorff, 138 S.W.3d 788 (Mo.App. S.D.2004), 675

Sampson v. State, 31 P.3d 88 (Alaska 2001), 981

Sanders, Estate of, 3 Cal.Rptr.2d 536 (Cal. App. 4 Dist.1992), 134

Sarabia, Estate of, 221 Cal.App.3d 599, 270 Cal.Rptr. 560 (Cal.App. 1 Dist.1990), 501

Satterfield v. Bonyhady, 233 Neb. 513, 446 N.W.2d 214 (Neb.1989), 854

Saueressig, In re Estate of, 44 Cal.Rptr.3d 672, 136 P.3d 201 (Cal.2006), 235

Scheffel v. Krueger, 146 N.H. 669, 782 A.2d 410 (N.H.2001), **610**

Schlueter v. Bowers, 994 P.2d 937 (Wyo. 2000), 423

Schmidt, In re, 362 B.R. 318 (Bkrtcy. W.D.Tex.2007), 160

Schmidt's Estate, In re, 261 Cal.App.2d 262, 67 Cal.Rptr. 847 (Cal.App. 1 Dist.1968), 152

Schneider, Estate of v. Finmann, 15 N.Y.3d 306, 907 N.Y.S.2d 119, 933 N.E.2d 718 (N.Y.2010), 42, 43

Scholl v. Murphy, 2002 WL 927381 (Del.Ch. 2002), 423

Schweizer's Estate v. Schweizer's Estate, 7 Kan.App.2d 128, 638 P.2d 378 (Kan.App. 1981), 154

Scott v. Scott, 77 P.3d 906 (Colo.App.2003), 752

Scott v. First Nat. Bank of Baltimore, 224 Md. 462, 168 A.2d 349 (Md.1961), 164

Sears v. Coolidge, 329 Mass. 340, 108 N.E.2d 563 (Mass.1952), **914**

S.E.C. v. Bilzerian, 112 F.Supp.2d 12 (D.D.C. 2000), 625

Security Trust Co. v. Sharp, 32 Del.Ch. 3, 77 A.2d 543 (Del.Ch.1950), 618

Seidel v. Werner, 81 Misc.2d 220, 364 N.Y.S.2d 963 (N.Y.Sup.1975), **767**

Seifert v. Southern Nat. Bank of South Carolina, 305 S.C. 353, 409 S.E.2d 337 (S.C. 1991), 592

Sekanic, Matter of Estate of, 229 A.D.2d 76, 653 N.Y.S.2d 449 (N.Y.A.D. 3 Dept.1997), 134

Seymour v. Biehslich, 371 Ark. 359, 266 S.W.3d 722 (Ark.2007), 490

Shellenbarger, In re Estate of, 86 Cal.Rptr.3d 862 (Cal.App. 2 Dist.2008), 91

Shenandoah Valley Nat. Bank of Winchester v. Taylor, 192 Va. 135, 63 S.E.2d 786 (Va.1951), **698**

Sheridan, In re Estate of, 117 P.3d 39 (Colo. App.2004), 1021

Sherrod v. Cooper, 65 N.C.App. 252, 308 S.E.2d 904 (N.C.App.1983), 834

Shimp v. Huff, 315 Md. 624, 556 A.2d 252 (Md.1989), **397**

Shinn, In re Estate of, 394 N.J.Super. 55, 925 A.2d 88 (N.J.Super.A.D.2007), 203

Shoemaker v. Gindlesberger, 118 Ohio St.3d 226, 887 N.E.2d 1167 (Ohio 2008), 42

Shore, In re, 19 Misc.3d 663, 854 N.Y.S.2d 293 (N.Y.Sur.2008), 1099

Shriners Hospitals for Crippled Children v. Gardiner, 152 Ariz. 527, 733 P.2d 1110 (Ariz.1987), **1061**

Silsby, In re Estate of, 914 A.2d 703 (Me. 2006), 812, 841

Simpson v. Penner, 36 F.3d 450 (5th Cir. 1994), 159

Sinclair v. Sinclair, 284 Ga. 500, 670 S.E.2d 59 (Ga.2008), 490

Singelman v. Singelmann, 273 Ga. 894, 548 S.E.2d 343 (Ga.2001), 427
Sinner, In re Estate of, 2006 WL 2872978 (Iowa App.2006), 812
Smith, In re Estate of, 694 A.2d 1099 (Pa.Super.1997), 52
Smith v. Brannan, 152 Or.App. 505, 954 P.2d 1259 (Or.App.1998), 745
Smith v. O'Donnell, 288 S.W.3d 417 (Tex. 2009), 43
Smith v. Rizzuto, 133 Neb. 655, 276 N.W. 406 (Neb.1937), 1025
Smithers v. St. Luke's–Roosevelt Hosp. Center, 281 A.D.2d 127, 723 N.Y.S.2d 426 (N.Y.A.D. 1 Dept.2001), 710
Snide, Matter of, 52 N.Y.2d 193, 437 N.Y.S.2d 63, 418 N.E.2d 656 (N.Y.1981), 359
Socha, In re, 18 Neb.App. 471, 783 N.W.2d 800 (Neb.App.2010), 1107
Somers v. Firstar Bank, 277 Kan. 761, 89 P.3d 898 (Kan.2004), 685
Soule, In re Estate of, 248 Neb. 878, 540 N.W.2d 118 (Neb.1995), 305
South Carolina Nat. Bank of Charleston (Columbia Branch) v. Copeland, 248 S.C. 203, 149 S.E.2d 615 (S.C.1966), 277
Spacone v. Atwood, 259 B.R. 158 (9th Cir. 2001), 616
Speelman v. Pascal, 10 N.Y.2d 313, 222 N.Y.S.2d 324, 178 N.E.2d 723 (N.Y.1961), 532
Speers, In re Estate of, 179 P.3d 1265 (Okla. 2008), 238
Spelius v. Hollon, 143 Idaho 565, 149 P.3d 840 (Idaho 2006), 235
Spicer v. Wright, 215 Va. 520, 211 S.E.2d 79 (Va.1975), **534**
Spirtos, Estate of, 34 Cal.App.3d 479, 109 Cal.Rptr. 919 (Cal.App. 2 Dist.1973), 1064
Stanton v. Wells Fargo Bank Montana, N.A., 335 Mont. 384, 152 P.3d 115 (Mont.2007), 458
State v. ______ (see opposing party)
Stephan's Estate, In re, 129 Pa.Super. 396, 195 A. 653 (Pa.Super.1937), 706
Stevens v. Casdorph, 203 W.Va. 450, 508 S.E.2d 610 (W.Va.1998), 247
Stevens v. Radey, 117 Ohio St.3d 65, 881 N.E.2d 855 (Ohio 2008), 861
Stevenson, Estate of, 46 Cal.Rptr.3d 573 (Cal.App. 2 Dist.2006), **1031**
Stewart v. Sewell, 215 S.W.3d 815 (Tenn. 2007), 300, 303
St. Joseph's Hospital v. Bennett, 281 N.Y. 115, 22 N.E.2d 305 (N.Y.1939), 705
Stockdale, In re Estate of, 196 N.J. 275, 953 A.2d 454 (N.J.2008), 479
Storr's Agricultural School v. Whitney, 54 Conn. 342, 8 A. 141 (Conn.1887), 899
Strittmater's Estate, In re, 53 A.2d 205 (N.J.Err. & App.1947), 424
Strobel, Matter of, 149 Ariz. 213, 717 P.2d 892 (Ariz.1986), 745, 747
Sullivan v. Burkin, 390 Mass. 864, 460 N.E.2d 572 (Mass.1984), **170,** 591
Sullivan, Estate of, 1998 WL 842263 (Tex. App.-Amarillo 1998), 427
SunTrust Bank v. Merritt, 272 Ga.App. 485, 612 S.E.2d 818 (Ga.App.2005), 338
Symmons v. O'Keeffe, 644 N.E.2d 631 (Mass. 1995), 1107

Taliaferro v. Taliaferro, 260 Kan. 573, 921 P.2d 803 (Kan.1996), 546
Talty, In re Estate of, 376 Ill.App.3d 1082, 315 Ill.Dec. 866, 877 N.E.2d 1195 (Ill.App. 3 Dist.2007), 1046
Taylor v. Hoffman, 209 W.Va. 172, 544 S.E.2d 387 (W.Va.2001), 141
Taylor v. Holt, 134 S.W.3d 830 (Tenn.Ct.App. 2003), 235
Theriault v. Burnham, 2010 WL 3272179 (Me.2010), 478
Thomas v. Arkansas Dept. of Human Services, 319 Ark. 782, 894 S.W.2d 584 (Ark. 1995), 655
Thompson v. Bremer, 34 A.D.2d 801, 311 N.Y.S.2d 980 (N.Y.A.D. 2 Dept.1970), 546
Tipler, In re, 10 S.W.3d 244 (Tenn.Ct.App. 1998), **277**
Tipp, In re Estate of, 281 Mont. 120, 933 P.2d 182 (Mont.1997), 456
Tolman, In re Estate of, 104 Cal.Rptr.3d 924 (Cal.App. 2 Dist.2010), 316
Totten, In re, 179 N.Y. 112, 71 N.E. 748 (N.Y.1904), 567
Town of (see name of town)
Treloar, In re Estate of, 151 N.H. 460, 859 A.2d 1162 (N.H.2004), 217
Trevitte v. Trevitte, 1990 WL 73852 (Tenn. Ct.App.1990), 834
Trimble v. Gordon, 430 U.S. 762, 97 S.Ct. 1459, 52 L.Ed.2d 31 (1977), 131
Troy v. Hart, 116 Md.App. 468, 697 A.2d 113 (Md.App.1997), 160
Truax v. Southwestern College, Oklahoma City, Okl., 214 Kan. 873, 522 P.2d 412 (Kan.1974), 59
Trustees of Amherst College v. Ritch, 151 N.Y. 282, 45 N.E. 876 (N.Y.1897), 544
Trustees of University of Delaware v. Gebelein, 420 A.2d 1191 (Del.Ch.1980), 733
Trust Estate of Jamison, In re, 431 Pa.Super. 486, 636 A.2d 1190 (Pa.Super.1994), 24
Trust Under Agreement of Vander Poel, In re, 396 N.J.Super. 218, 933 A.2d 628 (N.J.Super.A.D.2007), 853

Tulsa Professional Collection Services, Inc. v. Pope, 485 U.S. 478, 108 S.Ct. 1340, 99 L.Ed.2d 565 (1988), **1014**
Tunstall v. Wells, 50 Cal.Rptr.3d 468 (Cal. App. 2 Dist.2006), 487
Turner, In re Estate of, 56 A.D.3d 863, 866 N.Y.S.2d 429 (N.Y.A.D. 3 Dept.2008), 437
Turner v. Adams, 855 S.W.2d 735 (Tex.App.-El Paso 1993), 842

Uchtorff v. Hanson, 693 N.W.2d 790 (Iowa 2005), **803**

United States v. ______ (see opposing party)
United States Trust Co. of Florida Sav. Bank v. Haig, 694 So.2d 769 (Fla.App. 4 Dist. 1997), 1021
University of Southern Indiana Foundation v. Baker, 843 N.E.2d 528 (Ind.2006), 345
Usry v. Farr, 274 Ga. 438, 553 S.E.2d 789 (Ga.2001), **836**
Utley v. Graves, 258 F.Supp. 959 (D.D.C 1966), 609

Vance v. Myers' Estate, 494 P.2d 816 (Alaska 1972), **1022**
Van Der Veen, Matter of Estate of, 262 Kan. 211, 935 P.2d 1042 (Kan.1997), 24
Van Patten, Matter of Estate of, 215 A.D.2d 947, 627 N.Y.S.2d 141 (N.Y.A.D. 3 Dept. 1995), 428
Varney v. Superior Court, 12 Cal.Rptr.2d 865 (Cal.App. 4 Dist.1992), 489
Vaughan, In re Estate of, 2009 WL 3126262 (Tenn.Ct.App.2009), 345
Vaupel v. Barr, 194 W.Va. 296, 460 S.E.2d 431 (W.Va.1995), 467
Vernoff v. Astrue, 568 F.3d 1102 (9th Cir. 2009), 145
Vernum ex rel. Pratt, Estate of v. Estate of Vernum ex rel. Wenmoth, 961 A.2d 181 (Pa.Super.2008), 154
Villwock, Matter of Estate of, 142 Wis.2d 144, 418 N.W.2d 1 (Wis.App.1987), **148**
Vincent, In re Estate of, 98 S.W.3d 146 (Tenn.2003), 291

Wachovia Bank, N.A. v. Levin, 419 B.R. 297 (E.D.N.C.2009), 616
Waldman v. Maini, 195 P.3d 850 (Nev.2008), 153
Walker v. Walker, 433 Mass. 581, 744 N.E.2d 60 (Mass.2001), **689**
Walsh v. St. Joseph's Home For Aged, 303 A.2d 691 (Del.Ch.1973), 277
Ward–Allen v. Gaskins, 989 A.2d 185 (D.C. 2010), **370**
Warren v. Albrecht, 213 Ill.App.3d 55, 157 Ill.Dec. 160, 571 N.E.2d 1179 (Ill.App. 5 Dist.1991), 884, 925
Warren v. Compton, 626 S.W.2d 12 (Tenn.Ct. App.1981), 177
Washburn, In re Estate of, 141 N.H. 658, 690 A.2d 1024 (N.H.1997), 423, 427
Washington v. Glucksberg, 521 U.S. 702, 117 S.Ct. 2258, 138 L.Ed.2d 772 (1997), 978, 980
Webb v. Underhill, 130 Or.App. 352, 882 P.2d 127 (Or.App.1994), **797**
Wege Trust, In re, 2008 WL 2439904 (Mich. App.2008), 1078
Weitzel, Matter of, 778 N.W.2d 219 (Iowa App.2009), 685
Weissinger v. Simpson, 861 So.2d 984 (Miss. 2003), 845
Welch v. Crow, 206 P.3d 599 (Okla.2009), 525
Welch v. Wilson, 205 W.Va. 21, 516 S.E.2d 35 (W.Va.1999), 128
Wells, Estate of v. Sanford, 281 Ark. 242, 663 S.W.2d 174 (Ark.1984), **551**
Wendel's Will, In re, 143 Misc. 480, 257 N.Y.S. 87 (N.Y.Sur.1932), 67
Wendland v. Wendland, 110 Cal.Rptr.2d 412, 28 P.3d 151 (Cal.2001), 970, 975
Westerfeld v. Huckaby, 474 S.W.2d 189 (Tex. 1971), 571, 640
White v. Kansas Health Policy Authority, 40 Kan.App.2d 971, 198 P.3d 172 (Kan.App. 2008), 647
White v. White, 769 A.2d 617 (R.I.2001), 57
Wilber v. Asbury Park Nat. Bank & Trust Co., 59 A.2d 570 (N.J.Ch.1948), 705
Wilcox v. Gentry, 254 Kan. 411, 867 P.2d 281 (Kan.1994), **602**
Wilkerson v. McClary, 647 S.W.2d 79 (Tex. App.-Beaumont 1983), 533
Wilkins, Estate of, 137 Idaho 315, 48 P.3d 644 (Idaho 2002), 275
Williams, In re Estate of, 26 Misc.3d 680, 891 N.Y.S.2d 268 (N.Y.Sur.2009), 134
Williams for and on Behalf of Squier v. Kansas Dept. of Social and Rehabilitation Services, 258 Kan. 161, 899 P.2d 452 (Kan. 1995), 655
Will of (see name of party)
Wilson, Matter of Estate of, 59 N.Y.2d 461, 465 N.Y.S.2d 900, 452 N.E.2d 1228 (N.Y.1983), **726**
Wilson v. Lane, 279 Ga. 492, 614 S.E.2d 88 (Ga.2005), **421**
Wilson v. Wilson, 224 Or.App. 360, 197 P.3d 1141 (Or.App.2008), 195
Wilton, In re, 921 A.2d 509 (Pa.Super.2007), 345
Winans v. Timar, 107 Cal.Rptr.3d 167 (Cal. App. 1 Dist.2010), 468
Wingate v. Estate of Ryan, 149 N.J. 227, 693 A.2d 457 (N.J.1997), 141
Witt v. Rosen, 298 Ark. 187, 765 S.W.2d 956 (Ark.1989), 354
Woodward v. Commissioner of Social Sec., 435 Mass. 536, 760 N.E.2d 257 (Mass. 2002), 144
Wright v. Bloom, 69 Ohio St.3d 596, 635 N.E.2d 31 (Ohio 1994), 58
Wu, In re Estate of, 24 Misc.3d 668, 877 N.Y.S.2d 886 (N.Y.Sur.2009), 239

Young v. Hudgens, 1989 WL 71041 (Tenn.Ct. App.1989), 177
Young v. Ohio Dept. of Human Serv., 76 Ohio St.3d 547, 668 N.E.2d 908 (Ohio 1996), 647

Zahn, Matter of Estate of, 305 N.J.Super. 260, 702 A.2d 482 (N.J.Super.A.D.1997), 291
Zhao v. Wong, 47 Cal.Rptr.2d 707 (Cal.App. 6 Dist.1995), **250**

Zhao v. Wong, 55 Cal.Rptr.2d 909 (Cal.App. 1 Dist.1996), 256
Zsigo, In re Estate of, 2000 WL 33421334 (Mich.App.2000), 427
Zucker v. Mitchell, 62 Wash.2d 819, 384 P.2d 815 (Wash.1963), 545
Zwirn v. Schweizer, 36 Cal.Rptr.3d 527 (Cal. App. 2 Dist.2005), 489

CASES AND MATERIALS

ESTATES AND TRUSTS

FOURTH EDITION

CHAPTER ONE

INTRODUCTION

SECTION I. THE LIVING AND THE DEAD: WHOSE MONEY IS IT?

> *Has a dead man any use for money? Is it possible for a dead man to have any money? What world does a dead man belong to? T'other world. What world does money belong to? This world. How can money be a corpse's? Can a corpse own it, want it, spend it, claim it, miss it?*

Gaffer Hexam, in Charles Dickens, Our Mutual Friend (1865).

Money may be of no value to a corpse, but living people who have accumulated money often have strong opinions about what should happen to "their" money after they die. Trusts and Estates lawyers play an important role in advising and assisting clients who want to arrange for disposition of their assets after death.

Before we consider the lawyer's role in the wealth transmission process, let's consider Gaffer Hexam's questions more seriously. Why should we allow people who have passed to "t'other world" to control wealth in this world? And how much control should we permit people in "t'other world" to exercise? Consider the following case:

Estate of Feinberg

Supreme Court of Illinois, 2009.
235 Ill.2d 256, 335 Ill.Dec. 863, 919 N.E.2d 888.

Max Feinberg's will left his estate to two trusts. These trusts were to benefit his wife, Erla, during her lifetime, and at Erla's death, 50% of the trust assets were to be held in trust for the benefit of the then-living descendants of the couple's two children, Michael and Leila. The trust instrument further provided that any such descendant who married outside the Jewish faith, or whose non-Jewish spouse did not convert to Judaism within one year of marriage would be "deemed deceased for all purposes of this instrument as of the date of such marriage." The share of any such descendant would revert to his or her parent, Michael or Leila.

Max's trust instrument, however, gave Erla a limited power of appointment which enabled her to change the terms of the trust so long as she did not name as remaindermen any persons who did not qualify under the terms of Max's will. Erla exercised that power to direct that at her death, each of her children, and each of her grandchildren who were not deemed deceased under the terms of Max's beneficiary restriction, would receive

$250,000 apiece. If any grandchild were deemed deceased under the beneficiary restriction clause, that child's share would revert to his or her parent.

By the time of Erla's death, all five of the couple's grandchildren had been married for more than one year. Only one of the five had satisfied the beneficiary restriction. One of Michael's daughters, Michele, challenged the validity of the beneficiary restriction. Michael, who was co-executor of his parents' estates, defended the restriction.

The courts below held the beneficiary restrictions invalid as contrary to public policy. Michael appealed.—Eds.

■ GARMAN, J.

ANALYSIS

Michael argues before this court that the beneficiary restriction clause in his father's trust was intended "to encourage and support Judaism and preservation of Jewish culture in his own family," and that it was not binding upon Erla, who exercised her power of appointment consistently with the provision because it expressed her intent as well as Max's. Michael argues, further, that even if Max's beneficiary restriction was not revocable by Erla, the provision does not violate the public policy of this state when it is given effect via his mother's distribution scheme. He asserts that the distribution scheme is a valid partial restraint on marriage of a type that has long been enforced in Illinois and elsewhere. According to Michael, the beneficiary restriction clause has no prospective effect that might subsequently influence a descendant's decisions regarding marriage or divorce because, upon Erla's death, no contingencies remained. He distinguishes the cases relied upon by the appellate court and urges this court to reject the cited Restatement provision as not accurately stating Illinois law.

Michele defends the Restatement provision and argues that this case comes within a line of cases dating back to 1898 in which this court invalidated testamentary provisions that operated to discourage the subsequent lawful marriage by a legatee or to encourage a legatee to obtain a divorce. Specifically, she argues that under *Ransdell v. Boston,* 172 Ill. 439, 50 N.E. 111 (1898), testamentary restrictions on marriage are valid only if they operate to benefit the intended beneficiary. Further, she argues that enforcement of the clause would violate both state and federal constitutions and that it violates public policy by offering a financial inducement to embrace a particular religion.

We note that this case involves more than a grandfather's desire that his descendants continue to follow his religious tradition after he is gone. This case reveals a broader tension between the competing values of freedom of testation on one hand and resistance to "dead hand" control on the other. This tension is clearly demonstrated by the three opinions of the appellate court. The authoring justice rejected the argument that the distribution scheme is enforceable because it operated at the time of Erla's death and could not affect future behavior, stating that its "clear intent

was to influence the marriage decisions of Max's grandchildren based on a religions criterion.'' 383 Ill.App.3d at 997, 322 Ill.Dec. 534, 891 N.E.2d 549. The concurring justice opined that while such restrictions might once have been considered reasonable, they are no longer reasonable. 383 Ill.App.3d at 1000, 322 Ill.Dec. 534, 891 N.E.2d 549 (Quinn, P.J., specially concurring). The dissenting justice noted that under the facts of this case, grandchildren who had complied with the restrictions would "immediately receive their legacy" upon Erla's death (383 Ill.App.3d at 1000, 322 Ill.Dec. 534, 891 N.E.2d 549 (Greiman, J., dissenting)), and that the weight of authority is that a testator has a right to make the distribution of his bounty conditional on the beneficiary's adherence to a particular religious faith (383 Ill.App.3d at 1002, 322 Ill.Dec. 534, 891 N.E.2d 549).

We, therefore, begin our analysis with the public policy surrounding testamentary freedom and then consider public policy pertaining to testamentary or trust provisions concerning marriage.

Public Policy Regarding Freedom of Testation

Neither the Constitution of the United States nor the Constitution of the State of Illinois speaks to the question of testamentary freedom. However, our statutes clearly reveal a public policy in support of testamentary freedom.

The Probate Act places only two limits on the ability of a testator to choose the objects of his bounty. First, the Act permits a spouse to renounce a testator's will, "whether or not the will contains any provision for the benefit of the surviving spouse." 755 ILCS 5/2–8 (West 2008). Thus, absent a valid prenuptial or postnuptial agreement (see, *e.g., Golden v. Golden,* 393 Ill. 536, 66 N.E.2d 662 (1946) (wife can effectively bind herself to accept provisions of husband's will, thereby estopping her from renouncing the will after his death)), the wishes of a surviving spouse can trump a testator's intentions. Second, a child born to a testator after the making of a will is "entitled to receive the portion of the estate to which he would be entitled if the testator died intestate," unless provision is made in the will for the child or the will reveals the testator's intent to disinherit the child. 755 ILCS 5/4–10 (West 2008).

The public policy of the state of Illinois as expressed in the Probate Act is, thus, one of broad testamentary freedom, constrained only by the rights granted to a surviving spouse and the need to expressly disinherit a child born after execution of the will if that is the testator's desire.

Under the Probate Act, Max and Erla had no obligation to make any provision at all for their grandchildren. Indeed, if Max had died intestate, Erla, Michael, and Leila would have shared his estate (755 ILCS 5/2–1(a) (West 2008)), and if Erla had died intestate, only Michael and Leila would have taken (755 ILCS 5/2–1(b) (West 2008)). Surely, the grandchildren have no greater claim on their grandparents' testate estates than they would have had on intestate estates.

The record, via the testimony of Michael and Leila, reveals that Max's intent in restricting the distribution of his estate was to benefit those descendants who opted to honor and further his commitment to Judaism by marrying within the faith. Max had expressed his concern about the potential extinction of the Jewish people, not only by holocaust, but by gradual dilution as a result of intermarriage with non-Jews. While he was willing to share his bounty with a grandchild whose spouse converted to Judaism, this was apparently as far as he was willing to go.

There is no question that a grandparent in Max's situation is entirely free during his lifetime to attempt to influence his grandchildren to marry within his family's religious tradition, even by offering financial incentives to do so. The question is, given our public policy of testamentary freedom, did Max's beneficiary restriction clause as given effect by Erla's appointment violate any other public policy of the state of Illinois, thus rendering it void?

Public Policy Regarding Terms Affecting Marriage or Divorce

The contrary law relied upon by the appellate court to invalidate Max's beneficiary restriction clause is found in three decisions of this court: *Ransdell,* 172 Ill. 439, 50 N.E. 111,*Winterland v. Winterland,* 389 Ill. 384, 59 N.E.2d 661 (1945), and *Estate of Gerbing,* 61 Ill.2d 503, 337 N.E.2d 29 (1975) (which overruled *Winterland* in part). The appellate court concluded that the "language and circumstances" of the testamentary provisions in these cases, "which Illinois courts have found to be against public policy, are strikingly similar to the instant case." 383 Ill.App.3d at 996, 322 Ill.Dec. 534, 891 N.E.2d 549. Specifically, the appellate court invoked the "principle that testamentary provisions are invalid if they discourage marriage or encourage divorce." 383 Ill.App.3d at 995, 322 Ill.Dec. 534, 891 N.E.2d 549.

In *Ransdell,* the testator's will included provisions for his wife, his son, and his daughter. At the time the will was executed, the son and his wife were separated and cross-suits for divorce were pending. The father's bequest to the son provided that the property be held in trust, giving him use and income of the land for life, or "until such time as he * * * shall become sole and unmarried," at which time the trustee was to convey title to the land to him in fee simple. *Ransdell,* 172 Ill. at 440, 50 N.E. 111. If the son died childless while still married to the wife, the land was to go to other devisees. Several years after the father's death, the son, who was still married but living apart from his wife, challenged the provision on public policy grounds.

This court weighed two potentially competing public policies, stating that it was "of the first importance to society that contract and testamentary gifts which are calculated to prevent lawful marriages or to bring about the separation or divorcement of husbands and wives should not be upheld." *Ransdell,* 172 Ill. at 446, 50 N.E. 111. On the other hand, "it is no less important that persons of sound mind and memory, free from restraint and undue influence, should be allowed to dispose of their property by will, with such limitations and conditions as they believe for the best interest of their donees." *Ransdell,* 172 Ill. at 446, 50 N.E. 111. Because the testator had not disinherited his son if he remained married, but made one provision for him in case he remained married (a life estate) and a different provision if he divorced (taking title in fee simple), the condition was not contrary to public policy.

The appellate court cited *Ransdell* for the "general rule that testamentary provisions which act as a restraint upon marriage or which encourage divorce are void as against public policy" and distinguished *Ransdell* from the present case on the basis that the Ransdells' marriage was "already in disrepair" at the time the will was executed. 383 Ill.App.3d at 994, 322 Ill.Dec.534, 891 N.E.2d 549. The appellate court noted that subsequent Illinois cases, however, have "reaffirmed the underlying principle." 383 Ill.App.3d at 995, 322 Ill.Dec. 534, 891 N.E.2d 549.

One such case was *Winterland,* in which the testator created a trust for his wife that, upon her death, was to be distributed equally to their 11 children. However, in a later codicil, the testator directed that the share intended for their son, George, was to be held in trust for him " 'so long as he may live or until his present wife shall have died or been separated from him by absolute divorce.' " *Winterland, 389 Ill. at 385, 59 N.E.2d 661.* George predeceased his wife and she and their son challenged the codicil as promoting divorce, contrary to good morals, and against public policy. *Winterland,* 389 Ill. at 386, 59 N.E.2d 661. This court distinguished *Ransdell* on the basis that the couple's separation was "already an accomplished fact and a divorce suit was then pending" at the time the testator made his will. *Winterland,* 389 Ill. at 387, 59 N.E.2d 661. But where no separation was contemplated, the "natural tendency of the provision" was "to encourage divorce." For that reason, the provision was void. *Winterland,* 389 Ill. at 387–88, 59 N.E.2d 661. This court announced that it is "the public policy of this state to safeguard and protect the marriage relation, and this court will hold as contrary to that policy and void any testamentary provision tending to disturb or destroy an existing marriage." *Winterland,* 389 Ill. at 387, 59 N.E.2d 661.

In *Gerbing,* this court considered the validity of a provision in a testamentary trust that would have terminated the trust and distributed the corpus to the testator's son in the event that his wife predeceased him or the couple divorced and remained divorced for two years. *Gerbing,* 61 Ill.2d at 505, 337 N.E.2d 29. This court restated the general principle that "a devise or bequest, the tendency of which is to encourage divorce or bring about a separation of husband and wife is against public policy." Finding that it was the testator's general intent to benefit her son and that she would have preferred that he take the corpus of the trust, even if he remained married, rather than have him take nothing, this court found the entire provision void, overruling *Winterland* to the extent it held otherwise. *Gerbing,* 61 Ill.2d at 512, 337 N.E.2d 29.

In the present case, the appellate court found the "language and circumstances" of these three cases "strikingly similar" to the present case and saw "no reason to depart from this well-established principle" of these cases. 383 Ill.App.3d at 996, 322 Ill.Dec.534, 891 N.E.2d 549. We disagree with the appellate court's conclusion regarding the similarity of the present case to the cited cases. The beneficiary restriction clause as given effect by Erla's distribution scheme does not implicate the principle that trust provisions that encourage divorce violate public policy. That is, the present case does not involve a testamentary or trust provision that is "capable of exerting * * * a disruptive influence upon an otherwise normally harmonious marriage" by causing the beneficiary to choose between his or her spouse and the distribution. *Gerbing,* 61 Ill.2d at 508, 337 N.E.2d 29. The challenged provision in the present case involves the decision to marry, not an incentive to divorce.

Applicability of Restatement (Third) of Trusts

In reaching its decision, the appellate court also relied on section 29 of the Restatement (Third) of Trusts, and the explanatory notes and comments thereto. 383 Ill.App.3d at 997, 322 Ill.Dec.534, 891 N.E.2d 549.

The appellate court mistakenly compared the present case to an illustration accompanying Comment *j* to section 29 of the Restatement (Third) of Trusts. 383 Ill.App.3d at 997, 322 Ill.Dec.534, 891 N.E.2d 549. The illustration concerns a trust created by an aunt to benefit her nephew, who was to receive discretionary payments until age 18, and all income and discretionary payments until age 30, at which time he would receive an outright distribution of all trust property. However, all of his rights under the trust would end if, before the trust terminated on his thirtieth birthday, he married "a person who is not of R Religion." If he violated this condition, the remainder of the trust would be given to a college. The drafters of the Restatement called this an "invalid restraint on marriage," and stated that the invalid condition and the gift over to the college should not be given effect. Restatement (Third) of Trusts § 29, Explanatory Notes, Comment *j,* Illustration 3, at 62–64 (2003).

Erla's scheme, however, does not operate prospectively to encourage the grandchildren to make certain choices regarding marriage. It operated on the date of her death to determine which, if any, of the grandchildren qualified for distribution on that date. The condition was either met or it was not met. There was nothing any of the grandchildren could have done at that time to make themselves eligible or ineligible for the distribution.

Thus, this is not a case in which a donee, like the nephew in the illustration, will retain benefits under a trust only so long as he continues to comply with the wishes of a deceased donor. As such, there is no "dead hand" control or attempt to control the future conduct of the potential beneficiaries. Whatever the effect of Max's original trust provision might have been, Erla did not impose a condition intended to control future decisions of their grandchildren regarding marriage or the practice of Judaism; rather, she made a bequest to reward, at the time of her death, those grandchildren whose lives most closely embraced the values she and Max cherished.

The trial court and the appellate court erred by finding a violation of public policy in this case. While the beneficiary restriction clause, when given effect via Erla's distribution provision, has resulted in family strife, it is not "so capable of producing harm that its enforcement would be contrary to the public interest." *Kleinwort Benson,* 181 Ill.2d at 226, 229 Ill.Dec. 496, 692 N.E.2d 269.

Other Issues

The several other arguments made by Michele do not alter our conclusion.

Michele argues that the beneficiary restriction clause discourages lawful marriage and interferes with the fundamental right to marry, which is protected by the constitution. She also invokes the constitution in support of her assertion that issues of race, religion, and marriage have special status because of their constitutional dimensions, particularly in light of the constitutional values of personal autonomy and privacy.

Because a testator or the settlor of a trust is not a state actor, there are no constitutional dimensions to his choice of beneficiaries. Equal protection does not require that all children be treated equally; due process does not require notice of conditions precedent to potential beneficiaries; and the free exercise clause does not require a grandparent to treat grandchildren who reject his religious beliefs and customs in the same manner as he treats those who conform to his traditions.

Thus, Michele's reliance on *Shelley v. Kraemer,* 334 U.S. 1, 68 S.Ct. 836, 92 L.Ed. 1161 (1948), is entirely misplaced. In *Shelley,* the Supreme Court held that the use of the state's judicial process to obtain enforcement of a racially restrictive covenant was state action, violating the equal protection clause of the fourteenth amendment. *Shelley,* 334 U.S. at 19, 68 S.Ct. at 845, 92 L.Ed. at 1183. This court, however, has been reluctant to base a finding of state action "on the mere fact that a state court is the forum for the dispute." *In re Adoption of K.L.P.,* 198 Ill.2d 448, 465, 261 Ill.Dec.492, 763 N.E.2d 741 (2002) (citing cases). Indeed, *Shelley* has been widely criticized for a finding of state action that was not " 'supported by any reasoning which would suggest that "state action" is a meaningful requirement rather than a nearly empty or at least extraordinarily malleable formality.' " *Adoption of K.L.P.,* 198 Ill.2d at 465, 261 Ill.Dec. 492, 763 N.E.2d 741, quoting L. Tribe, American Constitutional Law 1698 (2d ed.1988).

Michele argues that the beneficiary restriction clause is capable of exerting an ongoing "disruptive influence" upon marriage and is, therefore, void. She is mistaken. The provision cannot "disrupt" an existing marriage because once the beneficiary determination was made at the time of Erla's death, it created no incentive to divorce.

CONCLUSION

It is impossible to determine whether Erla's distribution plan was the product of her own wisdom, good legal advice, or mere fortuity. In any case, her direction that $250,000 of the assets of Trust B be distributed upon her death to each of the then-living grandchildren of Max who were not "deemed deceased" under the beneficiary restriction clause of Max's trust revoked his plan for prospective application of the clause via a lifetime trust. Because no grandchild had a vested interest in the trust assets and because the distribution plan adopted by Erla has no prospective application, we hold that the beneficiary restriction clause does not violate public policy.

Therefore, we reverse the judgment of the appellate court and remand to the circuit court for further proceedings.

Reversed and remanded.

■ CHIEF JUSTICE FITZGERALD and JUSTICES FREEMAN, THOMAS, KILBRIDE, KARMEIER, and BURKE concurred in the judgment and opinion.

NOTES AND QUESTIONS

1. Consider two accounts of Max and Erla Feinberg's motives when they included the disputed provision in their wills and trust instruments:

> (a) they were trying to control the significant life decisions of their grandchildren by inducing them to marry Jewish spouses.
>
> (b) they were simply expressing their preferences: if Michele (or any other grandchild) were to commit herself to a Jewish spouse, Max and Erla would prefer that Michele share in their estate; if, on the other hand, Michele did not commit herself to a Jewish spouse, Max and Erla would prefer that Michael should take a larger share of their estate.

Do we know which account of Max and Erla's motives is the more accurate one? Would the court care-and should the court care—what motivated Max and Erla when they wrote their wills and trust instruments? See Jeffrey G. Sherman, Posthumous Meddling: An Instrumentalist Theory of Testamentary Restraints on Conjugal and Religious Choices, 1999 U. Ill. L. Rev. 1273, 1309:

> [S]ubjective motive is difficult to divine and easy to manufacture through fanciful posthumous imputation. It is difficult enough to infer what a testator intended to do with her property; to infer why she wanted to do it requires the court to engage in potentially limitless speculation.

2. Why should Michele have any standing to complain? Couldn't her grandparents have cut her out of their wills altogether, leaving their entire estate to Michael? If so, why should Michele be in a position to complain about her grandparents' wills—which at least held out the possibility of inheritance in certain circumstances?

3. What limits, if any, would a court place on enforcement of Max and Erla's stated intentions? Consider the following will provisions:

> (a) "To my granddaughter Michele, so long as she does not convert to another faith within ten (10) years of my death."

> (b) "To my granddaughter Michele, so long as she divorces her Catholic husband, Nick, within ten (10) years of my death."

Would the court have enforced either of those provisions? If not, why not? Suppose Erla, while alive, had promised Michele a substantial sum of money if Michele divorced her husband. Would any "public policy" have prevented Erla from keeping her promise? Why shouldn't Erla be entitled to use in her will the same carrots and sticks as she might have used while she was alive?

4. Professor Joshua Tate suggests that decedents are more frequently using trusts to provide incentives to their designated beneficiaries. He divides those incentives into three categories:

> First are conditions that encourage the beneficiaries to pursue an education. Second are conditions that provide what might be termed moral incentives: incentives that reflect the settlor's moral or religious outlook or promote a particular way of living. Some of these conditions try to encourage the beneficiaries to contribute to charitable causes, while others discourage substance abuse or promote a traditional family lifestyle. Finally, there are conditions designed to encourage the beneficiaries to have a productive career. Within these broad categories are a variety of different incentives that can be tailored to the specific wishes of a particular settlor. Provided that these incentives do not violate public policy, courts generally will enforce them.

Joshua C. Tate, Conditional Love: Incentive Trusts and the Inflexibility Problem, 41 Real Prop., Prob. & Trust J. 445, 453 (2006).

Inheritance Rights More Generally

In England, owners of land—then the principal form of property—had no right to dispose of that property by will until 1540, when Parliament enacted the Statute of Wills, 32 Hen. VIII, c. 1(1540). Instead, real property passed by "descent" to the deceased property owner's "heir"—generally the decedent's oldest son, if decedent had one. If decedent had no sons, his property would pass to his daughters. Decedent had no choice in the matter (unless he made complex arrangements to avoid the rules of descent). With the enactment of the Statute of Wills, decedent for the first time had direct testamentary control over the disposition of real property.

Thus, for Anglo–American courts and legislatures, both the right to receive property and the right to dispose of property, are rooted in positive law, subject to legislative adjustment. And, as we shall see, many states have restricted the right of a decedent to disinherit at least one class of family member—decedent's surviving spouse.

Suppose, however, a state tried to abolish inheritance altogether—to require that all property passes to the state (or, to use the appropriate terminology, to require that all property "escheats" to the state). Would such a statute be constitutional? Although no state has seen fit to abolish inheritance, the United States Supreme Court weighed in on the issue in Hodel v. Irving, 481 U.S. 704, 107 S.Ct. 2076, 95 L.Ed.2d 668 (1987).

Congress had enacted the "Indian Land Consolidation Act", which provided that undivided fractional interests in tracts of land within a reservation would escheat if the interest represented two percent or less of the total acreage in the tract and if the interest earned its owner less than $100 in the year before it was due to escheat. Heirs who, but for the statute, would have succeeded to interests in reservation lands, challenged the statute as an unconstitutional taking. The Supreme Court, in an opinion by Justice O'Connor, agreed, writing:

> ... [T]he regulation here amounts to virtually the abrogation of the right to pass on a certain type of property—the small undivided interest—to one's heirs. In one form or another, the right to pass on property—to one's family in particular—has been part of the Anglo-American legal system since feudal times.... Even the United States concedes that total abrogation of the right to pass property is unprecedented and likely unconstitutional.... Since the escheatable interests are not, as the United States argues, necessarily *de minimis*.... a *total* abrogation of these rights cannot be upheld....
>
> In holding that complete abolition of both the descent and devise of a particular class of property may be a taking, we reaffirm the continuing vitality of the long line of cases recognizing the States', and where appropriate, the United States' broad authority to adjust the rules governing the descent and devise of property without implicating the guarantees of the Just Compensation Clause.... the difference in this case is the fact that both descent and devise are completely abolished....

481 U.S. at 716.

But why should we be so committed to inheritance rights? In a country that embraces equality of opportunity as a goal, inheritance gives a head start to the children of the wealthy and the powerful. Consider the following:

Mark L. Ascher, Curtailing Inherited Wealth, 89 Mich. L. Rev. 69, 69–76 (1990).

One of the most dominant themes in American ideology is equality of opportunity. In our society, ability and willingness to work hard are supposed to make all things possible. But we know there are flaws in our ideology. Differences in native ability unquestionably exist. Similarly, some people seem to have distinctly more than their fair share of good luck. Both types of differences are, however, beyond our control. So we try to convince ourselves that education evens out most differences. Still, we know there are immense differences in the values various parents imbue in their children. And we also know there are vast differences in the educations parents can afford for their children. Here too, however, we feel there is little to be done....

When forced to acknowledge these differences in ability, luck, and educational opportunity, we admit that we do not play on a completely level field. But because each of these differences seems beyond our control, we tend to believe the field is as level as we can make it. It is not. For no particularly good reason, we allow some players, typically those most culturally and educationally advantaged, to inherit huge amounts of wealth, unearned in any sense at all. So long as we continue to tolerate inheritance by healthy, adult children, what we as a nation actually proclaim is, "All men are created equal, except the children of the wealthy."

* * *

About $150 billion pass at death each year. Yet in 1988 the federal wealth transfer taxes raised less than $8 billion [in 2009, the figure was about $14 billion—eds.] Obviously, these taxes could raise much more. If, to take the extreme example, we allowed the government to confiscate all property at death, we could almost eliminate the deficit with one stroke of a Presidential pen. This nation, however, rarely has used taxes on the transfer of wealth to raise significant revenue. Our historical hesitancy in this regard strongly suggests that we as a nation are unwilling to abolish inheritance in order to raise revenue. Nonetheless, thinking about using the federal wealth transfer taxes to abolish inheritance may not be entirely futile....

My proposal views inheritance as something we should tolerate only when necessary—not something we should always protect. My major premise is that all property owned at death, after payment of debts and administration expenses, should be sold and the proceeds paid to the United States government. [Professor Ascher then outlines exceptions to his general rule—generally for protection of spouses, minor children, and disabled descendants.]

My proposal strikes directly at inheritance by healthy, adult children. And for good reason. We cannot control differences in native ability. Even worse, so long as we believe in the family, we can achieve only the most rudimentary successes in evening out many types of opportunities. And we certainly cannot control many types of luck. But we can—and ought to—curb one form of luck. Children lucky enough to have been raised, acculturated, and educated by wealthy parents need not be allowed the additional good fortune of inheriting their parents' property. In this respect, we can do much better than we ever have before at equalizing opportunity....

This proposal sounds radical, perhaps even communistic. Inheritance does seem to occupy a special place in the hearts of many Americans, even those who cannot realistically expect to inherit anything of significance. For example, in 1982, sixty-four percent of the voters in a California initiative voted to repeal that state's inheritance tax. Michael Graetz, who, like me, finds this element of the American psyche puzzling, explains it as a product of "the optimism of the American people. In California, at least, sixty-four percent of the people must believe that they will be in the wealthiest five to ten percent when they die." This fascination with inheritance perhaps explains the minimal public debate about using the federal transfer taxes to raise substantial amounts of revenue. But curtailing inheritance is hardly radical. For years Americans have written seriously and thoughtfully on the subject. My proposal builds on that tradition and reaches the conclusion that substantial limitations on inheritance would contribute meaningfully to the equality of opportunity we offer our children. It also concludes that such limitations are fully consistent with our notions of private property. Neither conclusion is new. What is new is a $200 billion deficit. Now, as at few other times in this nation's history, our government needs new sources of revenue. Accordingly, I suggest changes in the federal wealth transfer taxes that would curtail inheritance and raise revenue. If we cannot, or will not, control the deficit, this generation's primary bequest to its children will be the obligation to pay their parents' debts.

Professor Ascher's article focuses on the inequality generated by inheritance. He notes, and others have emphasized, that the people most likely to inherit significant wealth are also the people whose parents have given them—through education and transmission of cultural values—the most significant head start during their lifetimes. Professor John Langbein has written:

> [I]n striking contrast to the patterns of last century and before, in modern times the business of educating children has become the main occasion for intergenerational wealth transfer. Of old, parents were mainly concerned to transmit the patrimony—prototypically the farm or the firm, but more generally, that "provision in life" that rescued children from the harsh fate of being a mere laborer. In today's economic order, it is education more than property, the new human capital rather than the old physical capital, that similarly advantages a child. . . .

John Langbein, The Twentieth–Century Revolution in Family Wealth Transmission, 86 Mich. L. Rev. 722, 732 (1988).

Inequality, however, may not be the only social harm generated by inheritance. Many—including some people of great wealth—have expressed the fear that excessive inheritance breeds sloth in the children of the wealthy. In Warren Buffett's words, "a very rich person should leave his kids enough to do anything but not enough to do nothing." See also Andrew Carnegie, The Gospel of Wealth, 50 (1933). One can always find anecdotal evidence to support the hypothesis. For a number of examples, all drawn from the heirs to the Johnson & Johnson fortune, see David Margolick, Undue Influence: The Epic Battle for the Johnson & Johnson Fortune (1993), an entertaining account of the challenge to Seward Johnson's will. Wealth gives its bearer the freedom "to be cushioned from market forces." Deborah C. Malamud, Class–Based Affirmative Action: Lessons and Caveats, 74 Tex. L. Rev. 1847, 1872 (1996). That freedom may lead some to take risks that generate great social benefit; it may lead others to a dissolute life.

Why tolerate a social institution that generates both inequality and sloth? One answer is that accumulation of wealth is often a joint effort; members of a wealthy decedent's family—particularly decedent's spouse—may have contributed substantially to decedent's ability to accumulate wealth. Note that even Professor Ascher would permit unlimited inheritance by a surviving spouse. And dependent children may have a right to support during their minority—a right not to be disadvantaged by their parent's premature death.

The more general answer, however, focuses not on the recipients of inheritance, but on the decedent—the person who "earned" the money in the first place. Professors Hirsch and Wang catalogue some of the justifications for inheritance:

Adam J. Hirsch & William K.S. Wang—A Qualitative Theory of the Dead Hand, 68 Ind. L. J. 1, 6–14 (1992).

The traditional rationales for testamentary freedom are as varied as they are controversial. Perhaps oldest is the notion that testators have a natural right to bequeath. Having created wealth by the sweat of her brow, the testator is naturally free to do with it as she pleases—including passing it along to others. Locke and Grotius, among other philosophers, took this view, which after centuries in eclipse has lately drawn flickers of judicial support....

Seemingly as old as the natural rights rationale for freedom of testation are other rationales premised on the sort of utilitarian calculus that Bentham and his disciples methodized. One argument, tracing back to the thirteenth century jurist Henry de Bracton, if not earlier, holds that freedom of testation creates an incentive to industry and saving. Bracton's assumption—shared by modern social scientists—was that persons derive satisfaction out of bequeathing property to others. To the extent that lawmakers deny persons the opportunity to bequeath freely, the subjective value of property will drop, for one of its potential uses will have disappeared. As a result, thwarted testators will choose to accumulate less property, and the total stock of wealth existing at any given time will shrink. Testamentary freedom accordingly fulfills the normative goal of wealth maximization, which is advanced by its proponents as the best available barometer of utility maximization.

* * *

Another argument for freedom of testation, also premised upon the goal of wealth enhancement, is that such freedom supports, as it were, a market for the provision of social services. Social life, like commercial life, is not a one-way street. Though classified by the law as "gratuitous" transfers, bequests within the family may in fact repay the beneficiary for "value" received (though of a sort not recognized as consideration under the common law).... Cast into the icy language of economics, testamentary freedom serves the public interest by promoting the creation of greater stocks of *noncommodity* wealth. The testator's power to bequeath encourages her beneficiaries to provide her with care and comfort—services that add to the total economic "pie."

* * *

A secondary justification for the right of testation is that it would in practice be difficult to curtail. Were lawmakers to rescind the power of the will, testators would find other, less efficient ways to direct the distribution of their wealth. "To attempt therefore to take the disposal out of their hands, at the period of their decease, would be an abortive and pernicious project," William Godwin opined two centuries ago. "If we prevented them from bestowing it in the open and explicit mode of bequest, we could not prevent them from transferring it before the close of their lives, and we should open a door to vexatious and perpetual litigation." ...

* * *

A final justification for freedom of testation, formulated with disarming unaffectedness by Professor Simes, is simply that the power to bequeath comports with political preferences: "the desire to dispose of property by will is very general, and very strong. A compelling argument in favor of it is that it accords with human wishes."

NOTES AND QUESTIONS

1. Blackstone, among others, disputed the Lockean notion that the right to dispose of one's estate emanates from natural law:

> The right of inheritance, or descent to the children and relations of the deceased, seems to have been allowed much earlier than the right of devising by testament. We are apt to conceive at first view that it has nature on its side; yet we often mistake for nature what we find established by long and inveterate custom....
>
> Wills, therefore, and testaments, rights of inheritance and succession, are all of them creatures of the civil or municipal laws, and accordingly are in all respects regulated by them....

2 William Blackstone, Commentaries 11–12 (21st ed. 1844). For a more extensive survey of the attitudes of "worldly philosophers" toward inheritance, see James R. Repetti, Democracy, Taxes and Wealth, 76 N.Y.U. L. Rev. 825, 828–31 (2001). See also John G. Steinkamp, A Case for Federal Transfer Taxation, 55 Ark. L. Rev. 1 (2002), at 82:

> The market economy fostered by our system of government offers the possibility for all to achieve financial success and accumulate wealth. But opportunities are not provided equally and market rewards vary greatly. Hard work alone is not enough. And those who achieve the American Dream cannot justly claim that their financial success was the product only of their individual talent and effort. Financial success in our complex and interdependent economy is always attributable in part to others, be they consumers or other producers, and to the important infrastructure and stable society provided by government.

> Society, consequently, has a legitimate claim on both income and wealth, which it exercises through taxation.

2. Professors Hirsch and Wang discuss the argument that allowing people to dispose of their property after death encourages industry; that in the absence of inheritance, people will work less, because there will be less reason for them to accumulate property.

Suppose the federal government imposed a 100% estate tax next week (perhaps with a modest exemption). How many people do you believe would become less productive as a result? Do people accumulate money to assure an inheritance for their children, or to assure that they will have resources to pay for their own care in old age—care that has become increasingly expensive in recent decades?

Professor Jeffrey Sherman has written:

> It is said that if inheritance and testation were abolished, "everyone would plan to be dead broke on the day of [his] death." Undoubtedly that would be true of some people, but how would they contrive to die broke? A retired individual who, on the basis of what proved to be an underestimate of her remaining life expectancy, decided how much of her wealth to expend each year would find her wealth running out before she did....
>
> In other words, property owners, however benevolently disposed they may be toward their progeny, have grave concerns about their own continued comfort and independence and about the maintenance of their socio-economic stations. The absence of testation rights might affect investment choices but would not be the determining factor.

Jeffrey G. Sherman, Posthumous Meddling: An Instrumentalist Theory of Testamentary Restraints on Conjugal and Religious Choices, 1999 U. Ill. L. Rev. 1273, 1295–97. See also Karen C. Burke and Grayson M. P. McCouch, A Consumption Tax on Gifts and Bequests, 17 Va. Tax Rev. 657, 689–90 (1998) [noting that behavioral foundations of personal consumption, savings, and gratuitous transfers remain largely unexplored].

Professor Sherman's analysis finds support in the work of economists who developed the "Life Cycle Hypothesis," which theorizes that devises are accidental—the result of risk aversity in the face of uncertainty about one's own future needs and date of death. See, e.g., Franco Modigliani, The Role of Intergenerational Transfers and Life Cycle Saving in the Accumulation of Wealth, 2 J. Econ. Persp. 15 (1988). In recent years, some economists and lawyers have questioned the Life Cycle Hypothesis. See Laurence J. Kotlikoff, Intergenerational Transfers and Savings, 2 J. Econ. Persp. 41 (1988); Edward J. McCaffery, The Uneasy Case for Wealth Transfer Taxation, 104 Yale L.J. 283 (1994).

If the Life Cycle Hypothesis is correct, is there any economic justification for inheritance? Who would spend money more wisely—the government or children of rich people? Would a prohibition on inheritance cause people to engage in conspicuous consumption before their deaths?

3. Professor Edward J. McCaffery, skeptical of the Life Cycle Hypothesis, fears that the wealthy might engage in increased consumption if inheritance rights were curtailed. He suggests that increased consumption by the wealthy might be a greater threat to ideals of equality than increased accumulation. Edward J. McCaffery, The Uneasy Case for Wealth Transfer Taxation, 104 Yale L.J. 283, 321 (1994).

Professor Joel Dobris has also questioned the wisdom of the estate tax, except as a symbol of the egalitarian nature of our society. Joel C. Dobris, Federal Transfer Taxes: The Possibility of Repeal and the Post Repeal World, 48 Clev. St. L. Rev. 709, 711 (2000).

4. ***The Politics of Inheritance.*** As the excerpt from Professors Hirsch and Wang indicates, inheritance rights are politically popular. Would you expect those rights to be more or less popular with Congressmen and state legislators than with the public at large? Compared with John Q. Public, is the average Congressman more or less likely to have a personal stake in maintaining the right to inherit?

In every state, the Statute of Wills permits a decedent to write a will disposing of his property at death. As we have noted, we typically call a decedent who writes a will a *testator*. The Feinberg case indicates that courts typically give effect to testator's stated preferences, even when those preferences might be offensive to others. But are there circumstances in which courts will not give effect to testator's intentions, as stated in the will? If so, what reasons justify ignoring decedent's stated preferences?

Consider the following case:

Ford v. Ford

Court of Appeals of Maryland, 1986.
307 Md. 105, 512 A.2d 389.

■ ORTH, J.

I

Pearl Rose Ford murdered her mother, Muriel L. Holland, by stabbing her some 40 times. She wrapped the body in plastic garbage bags and deposited it in the backyard of her home. She now seeks to obtain the property left her under her mother's will. George Benjamin Ford, Jr., her son, asserts that Pearl forfeited her entitlement to the property by the matricide and claims the property as the alternative beneficiary named in the will. The Orphans' Court for Anne Arundel County, in which the will was admitted to probate, ruled that George "be declared the heir" of the estate. The Circuit Court for Anne Arundel County, on appeal by Pearl to it, decided that Pearl was entitled to the property. We ordered that a writ of certiorari be issued to the Court of Special Appeals, to which George appealed, before decision by that court.

II

The Maryland Legislature has not enacted a "slayer's" statute establishing what principles govern when a person kills another and would be tangibly enriched by the death. This Court, however, has addressed the matter in three of its decisions: Price v. Hitaffer, 164 Md. 505, 165 A. 470 (1933); Chase v. Jenifer, 219 Md. 564, 150 A.2d 251 (1959); and Schifanelli v. Wallace, 271 Md. 177, 315 A.2d 513 (1974). Through these cases the Court has created in the common law of this State, the equivalent of a "slayer's" statute, which we shall refer to herein as the "slayer's rule."

Price concerned an appeal from an Orphans' Court order passed in the administration of the estate of an intestate. The order excluded from participation in the distribution of the estate the heirs or personal representatives of the husband of the deceased, who, it was admitted and proved, shot and killed his wife and almost immediately thereafter committed suicide. The question before this Court was:

> Can a murderer, or his heirs and representatives through him, be enriched by taking any portion of the estate of the one murdered?

164 Md. at 506, 165 A. 470. The Court dealt with the question as one of first impression in Maryland and noted the conflicting decisions of other courts of last resort in this country. The decisions at that time represented two views.

> One line of decisions apply the common-law principle of equity that no one shall be permitted to profit by his own fraud, to take advantage of his own wrong, to found any claim upon his own iniquity, or to acquire property by his own crime, and hold that provisions of a will and the statutes of descent and distribution should be interpreted in the light of those universally recognized principles of justice and morality; that such interpretation is justified and compelled by the public policy embraced in those principles or maxims, which must control the interpretation of law, statutes, and contracts. The other and opposite view, as expressed in those decisions which reach a different conclusion, is that, while they recognize the public policy of the common law as declared in the principles and equitable maxims above set forth, such public policy founded upon the common law has been abrogated and denied, and a new and different public policy declared by the Legislature in the enactment of statutes to direct descents and distribution, or governing the execution and effect of testamentary disposition. Some of the courts in the last mentioned group also rely upon constitutional or statutory declarations to the effect that conviction of crime shall not work a corruption of blood or forfeiture of estate.

Id. at 506–507, 165 A. 470. The Court fully discussed the two views and forcefully rejected any view which would "result in sanctioning the enrichment of the perpetrator of the most heinous murder from the estate of his victim." Id. at 516–517, 165 A. 470.

> Suffice it to say that we decline to follow the reasoning supporting any interpretation fraught with consequences so pernicious and so abhorrent to the sense of justice, equity, and morality entertained by what we are pleased to believe is the overwhelming majority of thoughtful and moral people, but prefer to give expression and adherence to the principles and reasoning so forcibly presented by those courts who have in the past adopted the views . . . expressed [in the common law].

Id. at 517, 165 A. 470. We observed in Chase v. Jenifer, 219 Md. at 567, 150 A.2d 251, that the decision in Price, which "was rested upon the maxim that one cannot profit by his own wrong, and on a broad ground of public policy of the common law," was perhaps not then supported by a majority of the courts dealing with the question. "Nevertheless," we declared, "we regard the decision of the Maryland Court [in Price] as settled law." Chase, 219 Md. at 567, 150 A.2d 251. Thus, it is the basic rule of this State that a murderer, or his heirs or representatives through him, ordinarily may not profit by taking any portion of the estate of the one murdered.

The Court in Price indicated that "the equitable maxims of the common law" which it followed in answering the question before it, would apply not only in the case of intestacy but equally to benefits by way of wills and life insurance policies. 164 Md. at 516, 165 A. 470. . . .

* * *

As established by Price, Chase and Schifanelli, the present status of the law of Maryland is:

1) A person who kills another

a) *may not* share in the distribution of the decedent's estate as an heir by way of statutes of descent and distribution, or as a devisee or legatee under the decedent's will, nor may he collect the proceeds as a beneficiary under a policy of insurance on the decedent's life when the homicide is felonious and intentional;

b) *may* share in the distribution of the decedent's estate as an heir by way of statutes of descent and distribution, or as a devisee or legatee under the decedent's will and *may* collect the proceeds as a beneficiary under a policy of insurance on the decedent's life when the homicide is unintentional even though it is the result of such gross negligence as would render the killer criminally guilty of involuntary manslaughter.

2) These principles apply not only to the killer but to those claiming through or under him.

3) The disposition of a criminal case is not conclusive of the character of the homicide or of the criminal agency of the putative killer in a civil proceeding concerning entitlement to assets of the decedent.

a) It is not dispositive that no criminal prosecution was brought against the alleged killer, or that charges against him were dismissed on constitutional, statutory or procedural grounds or otherwise, or that, upon a criminal trial he was found not guilty for whatever reason, or was convicted of murder in the first or second degree or of manslaughter.

b) In the determination of who is entitled to the assets of the decedent, whether the alleged killer was the criminal agent and whether the homicide was intentional and felonious or unintentional is a function within the ambit of the civil proceeding. In short, the lack of or result of a criminal proceeding is not res judicata in a subsequent civil action.

III

It is not disputed that Pearl killed her mother and that under the criminal law she was guilty of first degree murder in that the homicide was "willful, deliberate and premeditated." Md.Code (1957, 1982 Repl.Vol.) Art. 27, 407. Were this the posture of the case, it is clear that under the "slayer's rule" adopted by the Price–Chase–Schifanelli trilogy, Pearl would be precluded from sharing in the estate of her victim; her conduct would be both felonious and intentional. But in addition to the fact that Pearl was the criminal agent of a first-degree murder, it is also undisputed that at the time the crime was committed, she was not criminally responsible by reason of insanity. In short, she stands as guilty of murder in the first degree but insane. See generally Pouncey v. State, 297 Md. 264, 465 A.2d 475 (1983) (Criminal defendant can be found both guilty of the crime and insane at the time of its commission). The question is, therefore, what impact does the fact that Pearl was "insane" at the time she committed the crime have on the "slayer's rule" established by Price–Chase–Schifanelli?

* * *

IV

Pearl Rose Ford went to trial before a jury in the Circuit Court for Anne Arundel County on pleas of not guilty and "not guilty by reason of insanity." While the jury was deliberating its verdicts (four days were consumed before the case went to the jury) she "moved to enter a plea of not guilty by reason of insanity." The court accepted the plea and took the case from the jury. A docket entry reads that Pearl "waived right to jury in open Court" and reflects the verdicts rendered by the judge in these words:

> Finding: That there was sufficient evidence to establish the defendant's guilt if sane. That the defendant is not guilty by reason of insanity.

The court committed her to the Department of Health and Mental Hygiene for examination and evaluation and subsequently ordered that she be treated on an in-patient basis at Crownsville Hospital Center until further order. Although the verdicts as rendered could have been better expressed in light of the existing law, we are satisfied that to all intent and purpose, they were in accord with the required procedure as the equivalent of "Guilty of murder in the first degree" and "Not criminally responsible by reason of insanity under the test for criminal responsibility." In other words, the verdicts were, in effect, albeit not literally, "guilty" and "insane."

* * *

VI

As we have seen, for the slayer's rule to be invoked the killing must have been both felonious and intentional. We have found that it is a function of the trier of fact in a civil proceeding regarding the entitlement of the assets of a decedent alleged to have been killed by a claimant to make an independent determination of the corpus delicti of the crime. The trier of fact must decide on a preponderance of the evidence whether the manner of the decedent's death was homicide, whether the homicide was murder or manslaughter and whether the claimant was the criminal agent. Unlike a criminal prosecution, the civil proceeding does not call for a determination of the degree of murder. Both first and second degree murder are per se felonious and intentional. The civil inquiry, however, must go a step further than is necessary in a criminal prosecution if the finding is that the homicide is manslaughter. See Connor v. State, 225 Md. 543, 558–559, 171 A.2d 699, cert. denied, 368 U.S. 906, 82 S.Ct. 186, 7 L.Ed.2d 100 (1961). Then the trier of fact in the civil proceeding must ascertain whether the manslaughter was voluntary or involuntary. Manslaughter generally, be it voluntary or involuntary, is a felony. Code, Art.27, § 387. But see Code, Art. 27, § 388. Voluntary manslaughter is intentional; involuntary manslaughter is, by definition, unintentional. Rolfes v. State, 10 Md.App.204, 207, 268 A.2d 795 (1970).Schifanelli, 271 Md. 177, 315 A.2d 513, teaches that if the killing is unintentional it is without the ambit of the slayer's rule even though it is felonious. If the civil inquiry were to stop here, a determination that the killing was homicide, that the homicide was murder or voluntary manslaughter and that the claimant was the criminal agent would raise the bar of the slayer's rule.

All the above determinations are to be made on the assumption that the claimant was responsible for his criminal conduct, that he was "sane" at the time of the commission of the killing. The inquiry continues, however, upon the suggestion that the killer was "insane" within the meaning of our criminal responsibility law at the time he committed the offense. The trier of fact must determine whether, at the time the claimant killed the decedent, he lacked substantial capacity to appreciate the criminality of that conduct, or to conform that conduct to the requirements of law, because of a mental disorder or mental retardation. If the claimant were in that category, he would not be criminally responsible for the killing. It is at this point, upon a finding that the claimant was not criminally responsible for his criminal conduct, that the question we noted supra, arises, namely what impact does the fact that the claimant was "insane" at the time of the commission of the crime have on the slayer's rule. The answer is that the slayer's rule is simply not applicable when the killer was not criminally responsible at the time he committed the homicide.

* * *

Our view is not in conflict with the maxims which support the slayer's rule which we have judicially adopted. The rule is based upon principles of equity, justice and morality and on a broad ground of the public policy of the common law. Chase v. Jenifer, 219 Md. at 567, 150 A.2d 251; Price v. Hitaffer, 164 Md. at 511, 516–518, 165 A. 470. Equally a matter of equity, justice and morality and a reflection of public policy is the present enlightened definition of criminal insanity under which punishment for the commission of a crime is prohibited. The terms of that definition simply make the maxims prompting the rule—no one shall be permitted to profit by his own fraud, to take advantage of his own iniquity, or to acquire property by his own crime—inappropriate when a person is criminally insane. A person who suffers a mental disorder or is mentally retarded and falls under the cognitive and volitive components of the criminal responsibility statute does not, by the very terms of those components, act with an unfettered will. His conduct is controlled and his will is dominated by his mental impairment. Fundamentally, a killing is "felonious" when the homicide is a felony. In the frame of reference of the slayer's rule, however, the legislative policy regarding criminal responsibility leads to a qualification of this meaning. We believe that for a homicide to be "felonious" in the context of the slayer's rule, it must be a felony for which the killer is criminally responsible under Maryland's criminal insanity test. Therefore, if a killer is "insane" at the time he killed, the killing is not felonious in the contemplation of the slayer's rule. If the killing is not felonious, even though it may be intentional, the rule does not apply. Our view does not do violence to the broad public policies inherent in both the rule and the criminal insanity statutes. On the contrary, it furthers the principles of equity, justice and morality recognized by both the rule and the statutes.

The result that we reach is in complete accord with the decisions of our sister states which have addressed the problem. Forty-three other states have adopted by legislative enactment a slayer's rule comparable in effect to our rule, and several have embraced such a rule through its case law....

We find that the courts in only 16 of those states, however, have construed the rule, in rendering a decision or by way of *obiter dictum*, in light of the killer's insanity.

... But each and every one of those courts have reached the same result—the slayer's rule does not operate to bar a killer who, at the time of the commission of the homicide, was insane....

... We hold that the slayer's rule does not operate to preclude Pearl Rose Ford from inheriting under the will of her victim, Muriel L. Holland. The judgment of the Circuit Court for Anne Arundel County is affirmed.

■ COLE, J. (dissenting):

... [I]t is clear to me that the fact that the State cannot criminally punish an insane defendant is irrelevant to a determination of whether it is equitable for the killer to inherit from her victim. It is one thing to say that the State should not imprison one who was insane when she committed the murder. It is quite another to say that the insane murderer can profit from her crime. The only relevant focus here must be upon the killer's moral and personal responsibility for the crime.

* * *

I realize that the insane killer committed the crime either because she could not appreciate the criminality of her conduct or because she could not conform her conduct to the requirements of the law. But this reason for the killer's volition has no bearing upon the equitable principle embodied in the slayer's rule. If the insane killer has intentionally killed her victim, if she has acted with the required mens rea for the crime, she is personally and morally responsible for her wrong, and equity demands that she shall not benefit from the deed. It is repugnant to decency to say that an insane murderer can finance her rehabilitation with new found wealth from her victim's estate.

* * *

NOTES AND QUESTIONS

1. If the principle underlying the slayer's rule is that a killer should not profit from her own wrong, why should Pearl Ford inherit her mother's estate?

Is the court concluding that Pearl Ford did not commit a wrong? Would that conclusion be consistent with the Maryland criminal statute, which replaced the defense of "not guilty by reason of insanity" with a plea of "guilty but insane"?

In Estate of Kissinger, 166 Wash.2d 120, 206 P.3d 665 (2009), Joshua Hoge pleaded "not guilty by reason of insanity" to the charge of murdering his mother and stepbrother. In a subsequent proceeding to determine rights to the mother's estate, the Washington Supreme Court nevertheless held that Hoge, who had been diagnosed with schizophrenia and another psychiatric condition, had engaged in the willful and unlawful killing of his mother. As a result, Hoge was not entitled to inherit from his mother. Which approach do you prefer—the approach in Ford or the approach in Kissinger? Why?

2. Should the question in Ford v. Ford turn on whether Pearl Ford had demonstrated sufficiently bad character to disqualify her from inheriting? If so, shouldn't we disqualify murderers from inheriting not merely from their victims, but from anyone? And shouldn't we also disqualify rapists and thieves?

3. Suppose the court had decided that slayers adjudicated insane were disqualified from inheriting from their victims. Would the decision have had any deterrent effect? Would application of the slayer rule cause any insane killers to think twice before killing?

4. According to the court in Ford v. Ford, voluntary manslaughter disqualifies a killer from inheriting; "involuntary" manslaughter does not. Why draw the distinction?

Isn't "involuntary" manslaughter a wrong? Wouldn't the killer profit from his own wrong if permitted to inherit?

Isn't "involuntary" manslaughter deterrable? If not, why do we threaten—in loud and expensive television commercials—to put people in jail for driving while intoxicated?

In Alaska, criminally negligent homicide is a felony, and Alaska's slayer statute disqualifies a person who "feloniously kills the decedent" from inheriting the decedent's property. The Alaska statute also permits the court to set aside the slayer rule in the case of an unintentional killing if the court concludes that application of the rule "would result in a manifest injustice." Suppose a son pleads guilty to criminally negligent homicide of his father, who was dragged to his death after becoming entangled in a dump truck driven by the son. May the son inherit? What factors would be relevant in determining whether the slayer statute should apply? See Blodgett v. Blodgett, 147 P.3d 702 (Alaska 2006) (upholding disqualification).

5. In Colonel Francis Cheatle's last years, his sister Lorene was both the beneficiary of the Colonel's will and the Colonel's principal caretaker. When the Colonel died, their brother Harry alleged that Lorene had hastened the Colonel's death by exercising gross negligence in caring for the Colonel. Harry sought to disqualify Lorene from taking under the Colonel's will. If Harry proved his contentions, should Lorene be disqualified? See Cheatle v. Cheatle, 662 A.2d 1362 (D.C.App.1995) (no disqualification).

6. In Ford v. Ford, does the court ever ask whether Muriel Holland would have wanted Pearl Ford to inherit her estate? Is that question relevant? Should it be? See Anne–Marie Rhodes, Consequences of Heirs' Misconduct: Moving From Rules to Discretion, 33 Ohio N.U. L. Rev. 975, 987 (2007) (arguing that to permit murderer to inherit cannot be tolerated, and "[a] decedent's particular intent is irrelevant.")

If you had to guess, would you guess that Muriel would have wanted Pearl to inherit? Would you guess that Colonel Cheatle would have wanted Lorene to inherit?

7. Suppose testator had a moment of lucidity before death in each of the following cases. Suppose in that moment, testator were asked whether she would want her killer—a 30–year old son—to inherit. What response would you expect if:

1. Testator's son poisons her to assure an inheritance.
2. Testator's son shoots her when she threatens to sabotage the son's marriage.
3. Testator's son shoots her while carelessly cleaning his gun.
4. Testator's son kills her while driving too fast on a slick road.

Do your answers explain why courts, and legislatures, might treat "intentional" or "voluntary" killings differently from "involuntary" ones?

8. Mary writes a will with the following provision:

> "I know my husband, John, gets violent sometimes. If, when he is in one of his violent moods, he happens to kill me, I forgive him, and I still want him to inherit my entire estate."

John, on a tear, kills Mary. Should John inherit Mary's estate? Why or why not? Cf. Matter of Estate of Van Der Veen, 262 Kan. 211, 935 P.2d 1042 (1997), discussing testators' bequests to their son Kent, who murdered both of them:

> The Van DerVeens intended for their daughter to take one-half of their estate. Their knowledge of Kent's troubled nature is reflected in a provision of the Van DerVeens' will that nominates Laura to serve as Kent's guardian and conservator. Nonetheless, they bequeathed one-half of their estate to him. There is nothing in the instrument from which the court could conclude that the Van DerVeens intended for Laura to receive the entire estate in the event of Kent's incapacity or disqualification.

Id. at 222, 935 P.2d at 1049. (The court permitted Kent's son, fathered out-of-wedlock, adopted by another family, and unknown to the Van DerVeens, to take half of their estate).

9. Jim Kevorkian writes a will leaving $100,000 "to my brother Jack." When Jim is diagnosed with an incurable, painful, and protracted disease, Jack (at Jim's request) injects Jim with a solution which kills him. Is Jack entitled to the $100,000? Cf. In re Trust Estate of Jamison, 431 Pa.Super. 486, 636 A.2d 1190 (1994). See generally Jeffrey G. Sherman, Mercy Killing and the Right to Inherit, 61 U. Cin. L. Rev. 803 (1993).

10. Edward and Kathleen, married to each other, write identical wills. Each will leaves decedent's estate to decedent's spouse. Each will also provides that if the spouse does not survive decedent, decedent's estate should be divided equally between the parents of Edward and the parents of Kathleen. Edward shoots Kathleen, and then takes his own life. Are Edward's parents entitled to share in Kathleen's estate? See Matter of Covert, 97 N.Y.2d 68, 761 N.E.2d 571, 735 N.Y.S.2d 879 (2001).

Slayer Statutes and the Uniform Probate Code

The court in Ford v. Ford observes that the Maryland legislature has not adopted a slayer statute. Maryland is in the minority on that point. Most states have enacted statutes to deal with the slayer-heir. A number of the early statutes created as many problems as they solved, because their scope was unclear. For instance, a Connecticut statute expressly prohibited inheritance by heirs or will beneficiaries convicted of murder. Did the statute impliedly sanction inheritance by persons convicted of manslaughter? See Bird v. Plunkett, 139 Conn. 491, 95 A.2d 71 (1953) [holding yes]. If the statute prohibited a slayer from taking by will, did it also apply to a slayer seeking to take under a trust instrument, or seeking to collect on a life insurance policy?

As cases have arisen, many jurisdictions have amended their slayer statutes to account for the situations presented in the cases. Perhaps the most comprehensive slayer statute is the one included in the Uniform Probate Code ("UPC" or "the Code").

First, an introduction to the UPC. Estates law—both substantive and procedural—has always been a local matter in the United States, with considerable differences from state to state. During the 1960s, the National Conference of Commissioners on Uniform State Laws (NCCUSL) began work on the Uniform Probate Code, a statute designed to bring greater uniformity to the law of estates. The Uniform Probate Code was approved by NCCUSL in 1969, and a number of states enacted probate codes based in part or in whole on the UPC.

Meanwhile, NCCUSL, together with the ABA's Real Property, Probate and Trust Law section, established a Joint Editorial Board to consider ways in which the UPC could be strengthened. The Board's efforts resulted in a number of amendments, and, in 1990, in a wholesale revision of Article II of the Code, which deals with "Intestacy, Wills, and Donative Transfers." The Code continues to be amended on a regular basis. Meanwhile, a number of state legislatures have adopted various versions of the Code. In other states, the Code has not been adopted, but has had a discernable impact on state legislation or case law.

Throughout this book, we will examine the UPC's approach to estates law issues. Mastering the UPC, however, is no substitute for mastering your own state's statutory (or common law) approach to estates law issues. We recommend that you compare the UPC provisions to the law applicable in your home state.

How, then, does the UPC deal with the slayer problem? Consider the following:

Uniform Probate Code

Section 2–803. Effect of Homicide on Intestate Succession, Wills, Trusts, Joint Assets, Life Insurance, and Beneficiary Designations.

(a) [Definitions.] In this section:

(1) "Disposition or appointment of property" includes a transfer of an item of property or any other benefit to a beneficiary designated in a governing instrument.

(2) "Governing instrument" means a governing instrument executed by the decedent.

(3) "Revocable," with respect to a disposition, appointment, provision, or nomination, means one under which the decedent, at the time of or immediately before death, was alone empowered, by law or under the governing instrument, to cancel the designation in favor of the killer, whether or not the decedent was then empowered to designate

himself [or herself] in place of his [or her] killer and or the decedent then had capacity to exercise the power.

(b) [Forfeiture of Statutory Benefits.] An individual who feloniously and intentionally kills the decedent forfeits all benefits under this Article with respect to the decedent's estate, including an intestate share, an elective share, an omitted spouse's or child's share, a homestead allowance, exempt property, and a family allowance. If the decedent died intestate, the decedent's intestate estate passes as if the killer disclaimed his [or her] intestate share.

(c) [Revocation of Benefits Under Governing Instrument.] The felonious and intentional killing of the decedent:

(1) revokes any revocable (i) disposition or appointment of property made by the decedent to the killer in a governing instrument, (ii) provision in a governing instrument conferring a general or nongeneral power of appointment on the killer, and (iii) nomination of the killer in a governing instrument, nominating or appointing the killer to serve in any fiduciary or representative capacity, including a personal representative, executor, trustee, or agent; and

(2) severs the interests of the decedent and killer in property held by them at the time of the killing as joint tenants with the right of survivorship [or as community property with the right of survivorship], transforming the interests of the decedent and killer into tenancies in common.

. . .

(e) [Effect of Revocation.] Provisions of a governing instrument are given effect as if the killer disclaimed all provisions revoked by this section or, in the case of a revoked nomination in a fiduciary or representative capacity, as if the killer predeceased the decedent.

(f) [Wrongful Acquisition of Property.] A wrongful acquisition of property or interest by a killer not covered by this section must be treated in accordance with the principle that a killer cannot profit from his [or her] wrong.

(g) [Felonious and Intentional Killing; How Determined.] After all right to appeal has been exhausted, a judgment of conviction establishing criminal accountability for the felonious and intentional killing of the decedent conclusively establishes the convicted individual as the decedent's killer for purposes of this section. In the absence of a conviction, the court, upon the petition of an interested person, must determine whether, under the preponderance of evidence standard, the individual would be found criminally accountable for the felonious and intentional killing of the decedent. If the court determines that, under that standard, the individual would be found criminally accountable for the felonious and intentional killing of the decedent, the determination conclusively establishes that individual as the decedent's killer for purposes of this section.

[subsections h and i are omitted—eds.].

NOTES AND QUESTIONS

1. If UPC § 2–803 had been in effect, how would Ford v. Ford have been decided?

2. Nicole's will provides "I leave all of my property to my husband, O.J." At a criminal trial for Nicole's murder, O.J. is acquitted. If UPC § 2–803 is in effect, is O.J. assured of inheriting Nicole's estate?

Suppose O.J. had been convicted. What effect would the conviction have had on his right to inherit? Why shouldn't conviction and acquittal have the same consequences for inheritance purposes?

3. If O.J. had been convicted, and therefore disqualified from inheriting, how would Nicole's estate have been distributed? Note that UPC § 2–803 (e) provides that the governing instrument should be read "as if the killer disclaimed all revoked provisions...." UPC § 2–801(d)(1), which deals with the effect of disclaimer, provides that disclaimed property generally "devolves as if the disclaimant had predeceased the decedent." If O.J. had died before Nicole, the will would have been ineffective, and Nicole's property would have passed to her heirs—her children—by intestate succession.

We will talk about disclaimer later in the course, but for now, it is enough to know that a disclaimer is the act of turning down a gift, devise, or inheritance.

4. Do you think UPC § 2–803 represents an improvement over the common law approach taken by the Maryland courts? Why or why not? What advantages does UPC § 2–803 create? What disadvantages?

PROBLEMS

1. Melba died intestate—of natural causes—in 1994. Six years earlier, however, Melba's nephew Ray killed two of Melba's siblings—Ray's father and one of Ray's childless aunts. Ray was subsequently convicted of first degree manslaughter for these killings. At Melba's death, Ray asserts a claim as one of Melba's heirs. Ray would not have been entitled to share in Melba's estate if Ray's father had been alive at Melba's death.

> 1. If UPC § 2–803 has been enacted, should Ray be entitled to share in Melba's estate? What arguments would you make for Ray? For Melba's other heirs?
>
> 2. Would your arguments and conclusions be the same in a jurisdiction that has not enacted a slayer's statute? See Estate of Macaro, 182 Misc.2d 625, 699 N.Y.S.2d 634 (1999).

2. Charles inflicted multiple stab wounds on his father, Frederick. Charles then pleaded guilty to murder, and was sentenced to thirty years in prison. Frederick died intestate, survived by his widow (who was not Charles' mother), by Charles, and by Charles' three children. If UPC § 2–803 has been enacted, can Charles' children share in Frederick's estate?

If Charles' children share in Frederick's estate, has Charles profited from his wrong? Should Charles' felonious and intentional killing disqualify both Charles and his descendants? Should Charles' sins be visited on his descendants? See Cook v. Grierson, 380 Md. 502, 514, 845 A.2d 1231, 1238 (2004) ("[I]f we were to adopt the legal fiction that Charles predeceased his father, the children would be placed in a better position than if their grandfather had died of natural causes.").

Should Charles' children be entitled to inherit if the will had named them as beneficiaries? Cf. Plumley v. Bledsoe, 216 W.Va. 735, 613 S.E.2d 102 (2005).

3. Jeannette Swanson shot and killed two of her children, and pled guilty to two counts of deliberate homicide. As part of the pre-sentencing investigation, she went through a series of psychological examinations that led to a diagnosis of mental illness. The doctors concluded that Jeannette believed that she was shooting her children to send them to heaven where they would be safe. As a result, she was sentenced to a state hospital for the term of her natural life. She nevertheless sought to inherit from the children's estates. What result under UPC § 2–803? See Estates of Swanson, 344 Mont. 266, 187 P.3d 631 (2008).

SECTION II. THE ROLE OF THE LAWYER, AND THE LAWYER–CLIENT RELATIONSHIP

In discussing Estate of Feinberg and Ford v. Ford, we have seen two important roles estates lawyers play. First, estates lawyers are sometimes litigators, representing clients with claims to a decedent's estate. (Or, sometimes, litigators must learn some estates law in order to represent claimants to an estate). Second, estates lawyers are sometimes policymakers—devising and evaluating rules for transmission of wealth from one generation to the next. The drafters of the Uniform Probate Code, for instance, participated in a significant law reform effort, and there are often significant opportunities at the state level for estates lawyers to become involved in law reform.

Perhaps the most important role of the estates lawyer, however, is the role of planner. Clients come to lawyers with objectives in mind: they want to assure that their property reaches its intended beneficiaries; they want to minimize taxes; they want to protect beneficiaries from creditor claims.

The lawyer's job, in part, is to help the client achieve her objectives. In part, however, the lawyer's job is to educate the client so the client better understands her objectives and alternatives. The client (and the profession) expect the lawyer to act as a wise counselor. The lawyer's professional training generally enables the lawyer to identify problems and issues which have never occurred to the client. In order to identify those problems, however, the lawyer must accumulate information about the client, the client's family, the client's assets, and the client's wishes. Listening carefully (and asking the right questions) is among the most important skills for an estates lawyer. Only with a complete understanding of the client's situation can the lawyer be an effective planner.

At the same time, however, a lawyer cannot be an effective planner without a thorough understanding of substantive law. Statutes and case law provide a background against which every estates lawyer operates when planning an estate or drafting a will or trust instrument. As you read the cases and statutes presented in this book, ask yourself not simply whether the court reached the "right" result; ask what lessons the materials provide for drafting and planning purposes. Litigation is the estate planner's enemy. In most cases, if a lawyer drafts a document that results in litigation, the lawyer has not done her job—even if the document is ultimately upheld and construed as the lawyer intended it to be construed.

In estates practice, the lawyer does not always have a single, individual client. With great frequency, a married couple may enter a lawyer's office and ask the lawyer to draft wills for each spouse. Sometimes, an elderly testator will bring a child into the office when he consults the lawyer about planning his estate. When more than one person consults with the lawyer, who is the lawyer's client? What responsibilities does the lawyer have to each of the parties? Consider the following case:

Hotz v. Minyard

Supreme Court of South Carolina, 1991.
304 S.C. 225, 403 S.E.2d 634.

■ GREGORY, C.J.:

This appeal is from an order granting respondents summary judgment on several causes of action. We reverse in part and affirm in part.

Respondent Minyard (Tommy) and appellant (Judy) are brother and sister. Their father, Mr. Minyard, owns two automobile dealerships, Judson T. Minyard, Inc. (Greenville Dealership), and Minyard–Waidner, Inc. (Anderson Dealership). Tommy has been the dealer in charge of the Greenville Dealership since 1977. Judy worked for her father at the Anderson Dealership beginning in 1983; she was also a vice-president and minority shareholder. In 1985, Mr. Minyard signed a contract with General Motors designating Judy the successor dealer of the Anderson Dealership.

Respondent Dobson is a South Carolina lawyer practicing in Greenville and a member of respondent Dobson & Dobson, P.A. (Law Firm). Dobson is also a certified public accountant, although he no longer practices as one. In 1985, Dobson sold the tax return preparation practice of Law Firm to respondent Dobson, Lewis & Saad, P.A. (Accounting Firm). Although his name is included in Accounting Firm's name, Dobson is merely a shareholder and director and does not receive remuneration as an employee.

Dobson did legal work for the Minyard family and its various businesses for many years. On October 24, 1984, Mr. Minyard came to Law Firm's office to execute a will with his wife, his secretary, and Tommy in attendance. At this meeting he signed a will, which left Tommy the

Greenville Dealership, gave other family members bequests totaling $250,000.00, and divided the remainder of his estate equally between Tommy and a trust for Judy after his wife's death. All present at the meeting were given copies of this will. Later that afternoon, however, Mr. Minyard returned to Dobson's office and signed a second will containing the same provisions as the first except that it gave the real estate upon which the Greenville dealership was located to Tommy outright. Mr. Minyard instructed Dobson not to disclose the existence of the second will. He specifically directed that Judy not be told about it.

In January 1985, Judy called Dobson requesting a copy of the will her father had signed at the morning meeting on October 24, 1984. At Mr. Minyard's direction, or at least with his express permission, Dobson showed Judy the first will and discussed it with her in detail.

Judy testified she had the impression from her discussion with Dobson that under her father's will she would receive the Anderson Dealership and would share equally with her brother in her father's estate. According to Dobson, however, he merely explained Mr. Minyard's intent to provide for Judy as he had for Tommy when and if she became capable of handling a dealership. Dobson made a notation to this effect on the copy of the will he discussed with Judy. Judy claimed she was led to believe the handwritten notes were part of her father's will.

In any event, Judy claims Dobson told her the will she was shown was in actuality her father's last will and testament. Although Dobson denies ever making this express statement, he admits he never told her the will he discussed with her had been revoked.

In January 1986, Mr. Minyard was admitted to the hospital for various health problems. In April 1986, he suffered a massive stroke. Although the date of the onset of his mental incompetence is disputed, it is uncontested he is now mentally incompetent.

Judy and Tommy agreed that while their father was ill, Judy would attend to his daily care and Tommy would temporarily run the Anderson Dealership until Judy returned. During this time, Tommy began making changes at the Anderson Dealership. Under his direction, the Anderson Dealership bought out another dealership owned by Mr. Minyard, Judson Lincoln–Mercury, Inc., which was operating at a loss. Tommy also formed a holding company which assumed ownership of Mr. Minyard's real estate leased to the Anderson Dealership. Consequently, rent paid by the dealership was greatly increased.

Judy questioned the wisdom of her brother's financial dealings. When she sought to return to the Anderson Dealership as successor dealer, Tommy refused to relinquish control. Eventually, in August 1986, he terminated Judy from the dealership's payroll.

Judy consulted an Anderson law firm concerning her problems with her brother's operation of the Anderson Dealership. As a result, on November 15, 1986, Mr. Minyard executed a codicil removing Judy and her children as beneficiaries under his will. Judy was immediately advised of this development by letter.

In March 1987, Judy met with Tommy, her mother, and Dobson at Law Firm's office. She was told if she discharged her attorneys and dropped her plans for a lawsuit, she would be restored under her father's will and could work at the Greenville Dealership with significant fringe benefits. Judy testified she understood restoration under the will meant she would inherit the Anderson Dealership and receive half her father's estate, including the real estate, as she understood from her 1985 meeting with Dobson. Judy discharged her attorneys and moved to Greenville. Eventually, however, Tommy terminated her position at the Greenville Dealership.

As a result of the above actions by Tommy and Dobson, Judy commenced this suit alleging various causes of action.... We address only the trial judge's ruling on the cause of action against Dobson for breach of fiduciary duty....

ANALYSIS

Judy's complaint alleges Dobson breached his fiduciary duty to her by misrepresenting her father's will in January 1985. As a result, in March 1987 she believed she would regain the Anderson Dealership if she refrained from pursuing her claim against her brother. This delay gave Tommy additional time in control of the Anderson Dealership during which he depleted its assets. Law Firm and Accounting Firm are charged with vicarious liability for Dobson's acts.

The trial judge granted Dobson, Law Firm, and Accounting Firm summary judgment on the ground Dobson owed Judy no fiduciary duty because he was acting as Mr. Minyard's attorney and not as Judy's attorney in connection with her father's will. We disagree.

We find the evidence indicates a factual issue whether Dobson breached a fiduciary duty to Judy when she went to his office seeking legal advice about the effect of her father's will. Law Firm had prepared Judy's tax returns for approximately twenty years until September 1985 and had prepared a will for her she signed only one week earlier. Judy testified she consulted Dobson personally in 1984 or 1985 about a suspected misappropriation of funds at one of the dealerships and as late as 1986 regarding her problems with her brother. She claimed she trusted Dobson because of her dealings with him over the years as her lawyer and accountant.

A fiduciary relationship exists when one has a special confidence in another so that the latter, in equity and good conscience, is bound to act in good faith. Island Car Wash, Inc. v. Norris, 292 S.C. 595, 599, 358 S.E.2d 150, 152 (Ct.App.1987). An attorney/client relationship is by nature a fiduciary one. In re: Green, 291 S.C. 523, 354 S.E.2d 557 (1987). Although Dobson represented Mr. Minyard and not Judy regarding her father's will, Dobson did have an ongoing attorney/client relationship with Judy and there is evidence she had "a special confidence" in him. While Dobson had no duty to disclose the existence of the second will against his client's (Mr.

Minyard's) wishes, he owed Judy the duty to deal with her in good faith and not actively misrepresent the first will. We find there is a factual issue presented whether Dobson breached a fiduciary duty to Judy. We conclude summary judgment was improperly granted Dobson on this cause of action. See Standard Fire Ins. Co. v. Marine Contracting and Towing Co., 301 S.C. 418, 392 S.E.2d 460 (1990) (summary judgment).

Similarly, we find evidence to present a jury issue whether Law Firm should be held vicariously liable for Dobson's conduct since Dobson was acting in his capacity as a lawyer when he met with Judy to discuss the will in January 1985.

* * *

The judgment of the circuit court is reversed in part; [the court affirmed other portions of the trial court's judgment].

NOTES AND QUESTIONS

1. Was Mr. Minyard entitled to keep the contents of his will secret from his daughter Judy? Was he entitled to rewrite his will to cut off all benefit to Judy after Judy consulted a law firm? Was he entitled to offer to restore her interest in the will if Judy dropped her plans for a lawsuit?

If the answers to these questions are yes, how could lawyer Dobson be liable to Judy?

2. Judy had been Dobson's client on tax matters for more than 20 years. When Mr. Minyard asked Dobson to draft a will reducing Judy's share, what should Dobson have done? Was drafting the will a breach of any duty Dobson owed to Judy? A violation of any professional responsibilities? See Chase v. Bowen, 771 So.2d 1181 (Fla. App. 2000) (concluding no breach).

When Judy later consulted Dobson, was she entitled to assume that Dobson was acting in her interest? Did Judy have any reason to know that there was a conflict of interest between herself and her father? Did Dobson have any obligation to provide Judy with information?

3. Suppose Judy had never met Dobson until the day her father executed his wills. Suppose the facts were otherwise the same as in Hotz v. Minyard, that is, Mr. Minyard instructed Dobson to draft a second will and to keep the will secret; Judy asked Dobson about the effect of her father's will. Would Judy's complaint have withstood Dobson's summary judgment motion?

4. What should Dobson have done when

a. Mr. Minyard instructed him not to tell Judy about the second will?

b. Judy asked him to explain the consequences of the will her father had signed at the morning meeting?

c. Mr. Minyard authorized Dobson to instruct Judy that she would be restored to benefits under her father's will if she discharged her other lawyers?

In answering these questions, consider the following excerpts from the ABA's Model Rules of Professional Conduct:

RULE 1.6 CONFIDENTIALITY OF INFORMATION

(a) A lawyer shall not reveal information relating to the representation of a client unless the client gives informed consent, the disclosure is impliedly authorized in order to carry out the representation or the disclosure is permitted by paragraph (b).

> [Paragraph (b) authorizes disclosure to prevent the client from committing a criminal act likely to cause death or serious bodily harm, or in defense of a claim against the lawyer by the client, or arising out of the lawyer's representation of the client—eds.].

RULE 1.7 CONFLICT OF INTEREST: CURRENT CLIENTS

(a) Except as provided in paragraph (b), a lawyer shall not represent a client if the representation involves a concurrent conflict of interest. A concurrent conflict of interest exists if:

(1) the representation of one client will be directly adverse to another client; or

(2) there is a significant risk that the representation of one or more clients will be materially limited by the lawyer's responsibilities to another client, a former client or a third person or by a personal interest of the lawyer.

(b) Notwithstanding the existence of a concurrent conflict of interest under paragraph (a), a lawyer may represent a client if:

(1) the lawyer reasonably believes that the lawyer will be able to provide competent and diligent representation to each affected client;

(2) the representation is not prohibited by law;

(3) the representation does not involve the assertion of a claim by one client against another client represented by the lawyer in the same litigation or other proceeding before a tribunal; and

(4) each affected client gives informed consent, confirmed in writing.

PROBLEMS

1. Burnele V. Powell & Ronald C. Link, The Sense of a Client: Confidentiality Issues in Representing the Elderly, 62 Fordham L. Rev. 1197, 1205 (1994):

> Husband (H) and Wife (W) are an elderly couple. Neither has been previously married. They come to Lawyer (L) for estate planning advice. L has not previously represented either spouse. L advises them of potential conflicts of interest, and H and W consent to joint representation. Contrary to L's best judgment, they agree on mirror wills by which each leaves the bulk of his or her estate to the survivor and the survivor leaves the bulk of the pooled estates to their two children. Both H and W execute their respective wills. A few weeks later, W asks L to prepare a codicil to her will, making a substantial

bequest to W's paramour. W directs L to hold this request in confidence, and indicates that H would probably change his will if he knew about W's request.

What actions should L take?

For discussion of the lawyer's obligation in the marital context, see John R. Price, The Fundamentals of Ethically Representing Multiple Clients in Estate Planning, 62 U. Miami L. Rev. 735 (2008); Naomi Cahn and Robert Tuttle, Dependency and Delegation: The Ethics of Marital Representation, 22 Seattle U. L. Rev. 97 (1998); Teresa Stanton Collett, Love Among the Ruins: The Ethics of Counseling Happily Married Couples, 22 Seattle U. L. Rev. 139 (1998); Steven H. Hobbs, Family Matters: Nonwaivable Conflicts of Interest in Family Law, 22 Seattle U. L. Rev. 57 (1998); Russell G. Pearce, Family Values and Legal Ethics: Competing Approaches to Conflicts in Representing Spouses, 62 Fordham L. Rev. 1253 (1994); Jeffrey N. Pennell, Ethics in Estate Planning and Fiduciary Administration: The Inadequacy of the Model Rules and the Model Code, 45 Rec. Ass'n. B. City N.Y. 715, 740–46 (1990); Joel C. Dobris, Ethical Problems for Lawyers upon Trust Terminations: Conflicts of Interest, 38 U. Miami L. Rev. 1 (1983).

2. Eva and William Briggs have been married for 20 years. Eva approaches a lawyer about drafting a will and trust instrument. The lawyer prepares a trust instrument which requires William's signature, because Eva wants William to waive a valuable right to share in Eva's estate. The lawyer—who previously represented William in connection with an investment problem—advises and encourages William to see his own lawyer in connection with the trust instrument. William tells the lawyer he doesn't want to see another lawyer, and that he will sign whatever Eva wants.

At that point, what should the lawyer do? See Briggs v. Wyoming National Bank of Casper, 836 P.2d 263 (Wyo.1992).

3. A law firm has represented husband and wife in drafting wills in which each spouse left all property to the other. At the time the wills were drafted, neither the wife nor the law firm knew that husband had fathered a child outside the marriage. The firm later learned from the child's mother—who had approached the firm about representing her in a paternity suit—about the nonmarital child. May the law firm disclose the existence of the child to the wife? Must the law firm disclose the existence of the child to the wife? Would your answers be different if the firm learned about the child from the husband rather than from the child's mother? See A. v. B. v. Hill Wallack, 158 N.J. 51, 726 A.2d 924 (1999).

* * *

No one argues that a lawyer should routinely refuse to represent husband and wife when both seek estate planning advice. Many lawyers represent both spouses, but require husbands and wives to sign engagement letters which deal explicitly with the problem of potential conflict. In California, such letters are mandatory. Generally, the interests of husband and wife coincide, and a single lawyer will be able to craft an estate plan for the couple better (and more cheaply) than two separate lawyers, each representing one spouse. What we have been exploring, however, are situations in which conflicts do arise, and in which orthodox learning—embodied in the Model Rules—teaches that the lawyer may no longer represent both spouses. Professor Thomas Shaffer challenges the orthodox learning. He argues that the family unit often is—and should be—the lawyer's client, even when there are conflicts between family members. Suppose, for instance, John and Mary, husband and wife, enter a lawyer's office for estate planning assistance. John instructs the lawyer about the provisions "they" want in their wills, and the lawyer drafts the wills accordingly. Before Mary executes her will, however, the lawyer asks to meet Mary in private, and Mary confesses that some of the provisions are not to her liking, but that she is unwilling to promote family discord by drafting a will inconsistent with her husband's wishes. Should the lawyer advise one of the spouses to see another lawyer in this case—dubbed "The Case of the Unwanted Will?" Consider the following:

Thomas Shaffer, The Legal Ethics of Radical Individualism, 65 Tex. L. Rev. 963, 982 (1987).

> In *The Case of the Unwanted Will,* the most *irresponsible* thing a lawyer could do is to send either of these people to another lawyer, or both of them to two other lawyers. If that is the command of our professional ethics, or even the easiest available "solution" to the case from our regulatory rules, then our ethics and our rules are corrupting. They corrupt the family in general, and *this* family in particular. A lawyer following the rules is irresponsible because in fact, the family is the lawyer's client. The lawyer who sends the family away is not able to respond to his client. He is disabled by a false ethic and, in trying to protect himself, he harms his client.

Do you agree with Professor Shaffer?

* * *

In Hotz v. Minyard, Judy—who actually consulted with Dobson, and who had used Dobson as a lawyer in the past—contended that Dobson owed a duty to her and breached that duty. Does a lawyer ever owe a duty to a person with whom he has never consulted? The issue arises most frequently when a lawyer has carelessly drafted a will or another governing document. Certainly, the lawyer's client—the testator—would have a malpractice claim against the lawyer. But the mistake is not likely to appear—and will certainly not become important—until after testator's death. Do the beneficiaries harmed by the lawyer's negligence have any recourse? Consider the following case:

Barcelo v. Elliott

Supreme Court of Texas, 1996.
923 S.W.2d 575.

■ PHILLIPS, C.J.:

The issue presented is whether an attorney who negligently drafts a will or trust agreement owes a duty of care to persons intended to benefit under the will or trust, even though the attorney never represented the intended beneficiaries. The court of appeals held that the attorney owed no duty to the beneficiaries, affirming the trial court's summary judgment for the defendant-attorney. Because the attorney did not represent the beneficiaries, we likewise conclude that he owed no professional duty to them. We accordingly affirm the judgment of the court of appeals.

I

After Frances Barcelo retained attorney David Elliott to assist her with estate planning, Elliott drafted a will and inter vivos trust agreement for her. The will provided for specific bequests to Barcelo's children, devising the residuary of her estate to the inter vivos trust. Under the trust agreement, trust income was to be distributed to Barcelo during her lifetime. Upon her death, the trust was to terminate, assets were to be distributed in specific amounts to Barcelo's children and siblings, and the remainder was to pass to Barcelo's six grandchildren. The trust agreement contemplated that the trust would be funded by cash and shares of stock during Barcelo's lifetime, although the grandchildren contend that this never occurred. Barcelo signed the will and trust agreement in September 1990.

Barcelo died on January 22, 1991. After two of her children contested the validity of the trust, the probate court, for reasons not disclosed on the record before us, declared the trust to be invalid and unenforceable. Barcelo's grandchildren—the intended remainder beneficiaries under the trust—subsequently agreed to settle for what they contend was a substantially smaller share of the estate than what they would have received pursuant to a valid trust.

Barcelo's grandchildren then filed the present malpractice action against Elliott and his law firm (collectively "Elliott"). Plaintiffs allege that Elliott's negligence caused the trust to be invalid, resulting in foreseeable injury to the plaintiffs.[1] Elliott moved for summary judgment on the sole ground that he owed no professional duty to the grandchildren because he had never represented them. The trial court granted Elliott's motion for summary judgment.

---

1. The plaintiffs alleged that Elliott acted negligently when he:

A. provided in the trust agreement that it would not be effective until signed by the trustee, designated to be First City Bank of Houston, and then failed to obtain the execution of the trust document by the trustee;

B. drafted Mrs. Barcelo's will so as to provide that the residuary of her estate would pass into the trust he sought to create for Mrs. Barcelo, and then provided in the trust agreement that the trust would terminate upon Mrs. Barcelo's death, leaving her residuary to pass by intestacy to her children instead of her six grandchildren, including Plaintiffs, as provided in the trust agreement; and

C. failed to take the necessary steps on behalf of Mrs. Barcelo to fund the trust with the shares of stock....

The court of appeals affirmed, concluding that under Texas law an attorney preparing estate planning documents owes a duty only to his or her client—the testator or trust settlor—not to third parties intended to benefit under the estate plan. 923 S.W.2d 575.

II

The sole issue presented is whether Elliott owes a duty to the grandchildren that could give rise to malpractice liability even though he represented only Frances Barcelo, not the grandchildren, in preparing and implementing the estate plan.

A

At common law, an attorney owes a duty of care only to his or her client, not to third parties who may have been damaged by the attorney's negligent representation of the client. See National Savings Bank v. Ward, 100 U.S. 195, 200, 25 L. Ed. 621 (1879); Annotation, Attorney's Liability, to One Other Than Immediate Client, for Negligence in Connection with Legal Duties, 61 A.L.R. 4th 615, 624 (1988). Without this "privity barrier," the rationale goes, clients would lose control over the attorney-client relationship, and attorneys would be subject to almost unlimited liability. See Helen Jenkins, Privity—A Texas-Size Barrier to Third Parties for Negligent Will Drafting—An Assessment and Proposal, 42 Baylor L. Rev. 687, 689–90 (1990). Texas courts of appeals have uniformly applied the privity barrier in the estate planning context....

Plaintiffs argue, however, that recognizing a limited exception to the privity barrier as to lawyers who negligently draft a will or trust would not thwart the rule's underlying rationales. They contend that the attorney should owe a duty of care to persons who were specific, intended beneficiaries of the estate plan. We disagree.

B

The majority of other states addressing this issue have relaxed the privity barrier in the estate planning context. See Lucas v. Hamm, 56 Cal. 2d 583, 15 Cal. Rptr. 821, 364 P.2d 685, 689 (Cal. 1961), cert. denied, 368 U.S. 987, 82 S. Ct. 603, 7 L. Ed. 2d 525 (1962); Stowe v. Smith, 184 Conn. 194, 441 A.2d 81, 83 (Conn. 1981); Needham v. Hamilton, 459 A.2d 1060, 1062 (D.C.1983); DeMaris v. Asti, 426 So. 2d 1153, 1154 (Fla.Dist.Ct.App. 1983); Ogle v. Fuiten, 102 Ill. 2d 356, 80 Ill. Dec. 772, 774–75, 466 N.E.2d 224, 226–27 (Ill. 1984); Walker v. Lawson, 526 N.E.2d 968, 968 (Ind.1988); Schreiner v. Scoville, 410 N.W.2d 679, 682 (Iowa 1987); Pizel v. Zuspann, 247 Kan. 54, 795 P.2d 42, 51 (Kan. 1990); In re Killingsworth, 292 So. 2d 536, 542 (La.1973); Hale v. Groce, 304 Ore. 281, 744 P.2d 1289, 1292–93 (1987); Guy v. Liederbach, 501 Pa. 47, 459 A.2d 744, 751–53 (Pa. 1983); Auric v. Continental Cas. Co., 111 Wis.2d 507, 331 N.W.2d 325, 327 (Wis. 1983). But see Lilyhorn v. Dier, 214 Neb. 728, 335 N.W.2d 554, 555 (1983); Viscardi v. Lerner, 125 A.D.2d 662, 510 N.Y.S.2d 183, 185 (N.Y.App.Div.

1986); Simon v. Zipperstein, 32 Ohio St.3d 74, 512 N.E.2d 636, 638 (Ohio 1987).

While some of these states have allowed a broad cause of action by those claiming to be intended beneficiaries, see Stowe, 441 A.2d at 84; Ogle, 466 N.E.2d at 227; Hale, 744 P.2d at 1293, others have limited the class of plaintiffs to beneficiaries specifically identified in an invalid will or trust. See Ventura County Humane Society v. Holloway, 40 Cal. App. 3d 897, 115 Cal. Rptr. 464, 468 (Cal. Dist. Ct. App. 1974);DeMaris, 426 So. 2d at 1154; Schreiner, 410 N.W.2d at 683; Kirgan v. Parks, 60 Md. App. 1, 478 A.2d 713, 718–19 (Md. Ct. Spec. App. 1984) (holding that, if cause of action exists, it does not extend to situation where testator's intent as expressed in the will has been carried out); Ginther v. Zimmerman, 195 Mich. App. 647, 491 N.W.2d 282, 286 (Mich.Ct.App.1992) (same); Guy, 459 A.2d at 751–52. The Supreme Court of Iowa, for example, held that a cause of action ordinarily will arise only when as a direct result of the lawyer's professional negligence the testator's intent as expressed in the testamentary instruments is frustrated in whole or in part and the beneficiary's interest in the estate is either lost, diminished, or unrealized. Schreiner v. Scoville, 410 N.W.2d 679, 683 (Iowa 1987).

C

We agree with those courts that have rejected a broad cause of action in favor of beneficiaries. These courts have recognized the inevitable problems with disappointed heirs attempting to prove that the defendant-attorney failed to implement the deceased testator's intentions. Certainly allowing extrinsic evidence would create a host of difficulties. In DeMaris v. Asti, 426 So. 2d 1153, 1154 (Fla.Dist.Ct.App.1983), for example, the court concluded that "[t]here is no authority—the reasons being obvious—for the proposition that a disappointed beneficiary may prove, by evidence totally extrinsic to the will, the testator's testamentary intent was other than as expressed in his solemn and properly executed will." Such a cause of action would subject attorneys to suits by heirs who simply did not receive what they believed to be their due share under the will or trust. This potential tort liability to third parties would create a conflict during the estate planning process, dividing the attorney's loyalty between his or her client and the third-party beneficiaries.

Moreover, we believe that the more limited cause of action recognized by several jurisdictions also undermines the policy rationales supporting the privity rule. These courts have limited the cause of action to beneficiaries specifically identified in an invalid will or trust. Under these circumstances, courts have reasoned, the interests of the client and the beneficiaries are necessarily aligned, negating any conflict, as the attorney owes a duty only to those parties which the testator clearly intended to benefit. See, e.g., Needham, 459 A.2d at 1062.

In most cases where a defect renders a will or trust invalid, however, there are concomitant questions as to the true intentions of the testator. Suppose, for example, that a properly drafted will is simply not executed at the time of the testator's death. The document may express the testator's true intentions, lacking signatures solely because of the attorney's negligent delay. On the other hand, the testator may have postponed execution because of second thoughts regarding the distribution scheme. In the latter situation, the attorney's representation of the testator will likely be affected if he or she knows that the existence of an unexecuted will may create malpractice liability if the testator unexpectedly dies.

The present case is indicative of the conflicts that could arise. Plaintiffs contend in part that Elliott was negligent in failing to fund the trust during Barcelo's lifetime, and in failing to obtain a signature from the trustee. These alleged deficiencies, however, could have existed pursuant to Barcelo's instructions, which may have been based on advice from her attorneys attempting to represent her best interests. An attorney's ability to render such advice would be severely compromised if the advice could be second-guessed by persons named as beneficiaries under the unconsummated trust.

In sum, we are unable to craft a bright-line rule that allows a lawsuit to proceed where alleged malpractice causes a will or trust to fail in a manner that casts no real doubt on the testator's intentions, while prohibiting actions in other situations. We believe the greater good is served by preserving a bright-line privity rule which denies a cause of action to all beneficiaries whom the attorney did not represent. This will ensure that attorneys may in all cases zealously represent their clients without the threat of suit from third parties compromising that representation.

We therefore hold that an attorney retained by a testator or settlor to draft a will or trust owes no professional duty of care to persons named as beneficiaries under the will or trust.

D

Plaintiffs also contend that, even if there is no tort duty extending to beneficiaries of an estate plan, they may recover under a third-party-beneficiary contract theory. While the majority of jurisdictions that have recognized a cause of action in favor of will or trust beneficiaries have done so under negligence principles, some have allowed recovery in contract.

In Texas, however, a legal malpractice action sounds in tort and is governed by negligence principles. See Cosgrove v. Grimes, 774 S.W.2d 662, 664 (Tex.1989); Willis v. Maverick, 760 S.W.2d 642, 644 (Tex.1988). Cf. Heyer v. Flaig, 70 Cal. 2d 223, 449 P.2d 161, 164, 74 Cal. Rptr. 225 (Cal. 1969) (recognizing that third-party-beneficiary contract theory "is conceptually superfluous since the crux of the action must lie in tort in any case; there can be no recovery without negligence"). Even assuming that a client who retains a lawyer to draft an estate plan intends for the lawyer's work to benefit the will or trust beneficiaries, the ultimate question is whether, considering the competing policy implications, the lawyer's professional duty should extend to persons whom the lawyer never represented. For the reasons previously discussed, we conclude that the answer is no.

For the foregoing reasons, we affirm the judgment of the court of appeals.

■ CORNYN, J. (dissenting):

With an obscure reference to "the greater good," the Court unjustifiably insulates an entire class of negligent lawyers from the consequences of their wrongdoing, and unjustly denies legal recourse to the grandchildren for whose benefit Ms. Barcelo hired a lawyer in the first place. I dissent.

By refusing to recognize a lawyer's duty to beneficiaries of a will, the Court embraces a rule recognized in only four states, while simultaneously rejecting the rule in an overwhelming majority of jurisdictions . . .

The threshold question in a negligence action, including a legal malpractice suit, is duty. El Chico Corp. v. Poole, 732 S.W.2d 306, 311 (Tex.1987); see Cosgrove v. Grimes, 774 S.W.2d 662, 664 (Tex.1989) (holding that a legal malpractice action in Texas is grounded in negligence). Whether a defendant owes a duty to the plaintiff depends on several factors, including risk, foreseeability, and likelihood of injury weighed against the social utility of the actor's conduct, the magnitude of the burden of guarding against injury, and the consequences of placing the burden on the defendant. Greater Houston Transp. Co. v. Phillips, 801 S.W.2d 523, 525 (Tex.1990).

The foreseeability of harm in this case is not open to serious question. Because Ms. Barcelo hired Mr. Elliott to accomplish the transfer of her estate to her grandchildren upon her death, the potential harm to the beneficiaries if the testamentary documents were incorrectly drafted was plainly foreseeable. See Lucas, 364 P.2d at 688; see also Heyer v. Flaig, 70 Cal. 2d 223, 449 P.2d 161, 164–65, 74 Cal. Rptr. 225 (Cal. 1969) ("The attorney's actions and omissions will affect the success of the client's testamentary scheme; and thus the possibility of thwarting the testator's wishes immediately becomes foreseeable. Equally foreseeable is the possibility of injury to an intended beneficiary."). Foreseeability of harm weighs heavily in favor of recognizing a duty to intended beneficiaries.

Additionally, the Court's decision means that, as a practical matter, no one has the right to sue for the lawyer's negligent frustration of the testator's intent. A flaw in a will or other testamentary document is not likely be discovered until the client's death. And, generally, the estate suffers no harm from a negligently drafted testamentary document. Heyer, 449 P.2d at 165. Allowing beneficiaries to sue would provide accountability and thus an incentive for lawyers to use greater care in estate planning. Robert L. Rabin, Tort Recovery for Negligently Inflicted Economic Loss, 37 Stan. L. Rev. 1513, 1521 (1985). Instead, the Court decides that an innocent party must bear the burden of the lawyer's error. The Court also gives no consideration to the fair adjustment of the loss between the parties, one of the traditional objectives of tort law.... These grounds for the imposition of a legal duty in tort law generally, which apply to lawyers in every other context, are no less important in estate planning.

Nor do the reasons the Court gives for refusing to impose a duty under these circumstances withstand scrutiny. Contrary to the Court's view, recognizing an action by the intended beneficiaries would not extend a lawyer's duty to the general public, but only to a limited, foreseeable class. Because estate planning attorneys generally do not face any liability in this context, potential liability to the intended beneficiaries would not place them in a worse position than attorneys in any other setting.

The Court also hypothesizes that liability to estate beneficiaries may conflict with the attorney's duty to the client. Before the beneficiaries could prevail in a suit against the attorney, however, they would necessarily have to show that the attorney breached a duty to the decedent. This is because the lawyer's duty to the client is to see that the client's intentions are realized by the very documents the client has hired the lawyer to draft. No conflicting duty to the beneficiaries is imposed.

Searching for other hypothetical problems that might arise if a cause of action for the beneficiaries is recognized, the Court observes that a will not executed at the testator's death could in fact express the testator's true intentions. Granted, such a scenario may be the result of either the testator's indecision or the attorney's negligence. Similarly, a family member might be intentionally omitted from a will at the testator's direction, or negligently omitted because of the drafting lawyer's mistake. In other words, what appears to be attorney negligence may actually reflect the testator's wishes.

But surely these are matters subject to proof, as in all other cases. Nothing distinguishes this class of cases from many others in this respect. The Court fails to consider that the beneficiaries will in each case bear the burden of establishing that the attorney breached a duty to the testator, which resulted in damages to the beneficiaries. Lawyers, wishing to protect themselves from liability, may document the testator's intentions.

* * *

In sum, I would hold that the intended beneficiary of a will or testamentary trust may bring a cause of action against an attorney whose negligence caused the beneficiary to lose a legacy in whole or in part. Accordingly, I would reverse the judgment of the court of appeals and remand this case to the trial court.

■ SPECTOR, J., (dissenting):

The issue in this case is whether the attorney, David Elliott, owed a duty to Frances Barcelo's intended beneficiaries. The majority holds that he did not. The other dissenting justices would recognize a broad cause of action in favor of any person claiming to be an intended beneficiary, regardless of whether the plaintiff is identified in the will or trust instrument. Because I would recognize only a limited cause of action for the intended beneficiaries of wills and trusts, I write separately to dissent.

* * *

I would not go so far as to hold that attorneys who draft wills and trusts have a duty to persons who are not beneficiaries named in the will or trust. Recognizing such a broad cause of action is as likely to frustrate the testator's intent as it is to carry it out. I would, however, allow beneficiaries who are specifically identified on the face of an invalid will or trust to assert a claim.

Recognizing a limited cause of action would subject attorneys who prepare wills and trusts documents to the same standard of care governing attorneys generally. Because I believe that this is sound public policy, I dissent.

NOTES AND QUESTIONS

1. Lawyer David Elliott apparently drafted an invalid trust agreement. Who bears the loss created by the instrument's invalidity? Why?

Presumably, testator paid Elliott for his expertise. What did testator get in return for that payment?

As both the majority and the dissents recognize, the Texas courts are in a distinct minority in holding that a lawyer bears no malpractice liability to will beneficiaries. The malpractice "revolution" of the last several decades has, in the vast majority of states, displaced the privity rule endorsed in Barcelo v. Elliott. Texas, however, is not alone. In a number of states, recent cases have announced continued adherence to the privity rule. See Estate of Schneider v. Finmann, 15 N.Y.3d 306, 907 N.Y.S.2d 119, 933 N.E.2d 718 (2010); Johnson v. Hart, 279 Va. 617, 692 S.E.2d 239 (2010); Shoemaker v. Gindelsberger, 118 Ohio St.3d 226, 887 N.E.2d 1167 (2008). See also Ronald R. Volkmer, Attorney Liability to Nonclients: The Need to Re–Examine Nebraska's Privity Rule, 29 Creighton L. Rev. 295 (1995) [discussing another one of the holdout states]; Mary Elizabeth Phelan, Unleashing the Limits on Lawyers' Liability? Mieras v. DeBona: Michigan Joins the Mainstream and Abrogates the Privity Requirement in Attorney–Malpractice Cases Involving Negligent Will Drafting, 72 U. Det. Mercy L. Rev. 327 (1995) [discussing Michigan's abandonment of the privity rule]. For an excellent discussion, written before Barcelo, of the Texas rule, see Helen B. Jenkins, Privity—A Texas–Size Barrier to Third Parties for Negligent Will Drafting, 42 Baylor L. Rev. 687 (1990).

Is displacement of the privity rule a good thing? Consider the following:

Martin D. Begleiter, Attorney Malpractice in Estate Planning—You've Got to Know When to Hold Up, Know When to Fold Up, 38 Kan. L. Rev. 193, 274–76 (1990).

The first positive effect of the malpractice revolution is that lawyers are held accountable for their mistakes....

Quite simply, an attorney, unlike the proverbial dog, is not entitled to one free bite. If the attorney's negligence in estate planning causes loss to a beneficiary, the attorney should make good that loss. That is not to say that attorneys should make good all "losses" to beneficiaries in wills they drafted.... Many acts or omissions do not constitute negligence, and the attorney is required only to use the degree of care and skill of reasonable lawyers under comparable circumstances.

Closely allied with this fundamental principle is the realization . . . that the imposition of malpractice liability should improve the care with which attorneys perform the tasks involved in estate planning. Some attorneys who do not specialize in estate planning, when sued for malpractice, will cease to practice in this field. More likely, attorneys in the field will improve their procedures for execution, ask more questions of their clients, and pay more attention to the drafting of dispositive instruments.

The concern about malpractice could also result in an increase in specialization. . . . [A]ttorneys who only practice estate planning occasionally may determine that the malpractice exposure is too great to continue to do so or may decide to limit their practices to simple wills and refer all other estate planning matters to attorneys who have a greater knowledge of or more experience in estate planning.

See also Angela M. Vallario, Shape Up or Ship Out: Accountability to Third Parties for Patent Ambiguities in Testamentary Documents, 26 Whittier L Rev 59 (2004); Bradley E.S. Fogel, Attorney v. Client—Privity, Malpractice, and the Lack of Respect for the Primacy of the Attorney–Client Relationship in Estate Planning, 68 Tenn. L. Rev. 261 (2001); Gerald P. Johnston, Avoiding Malpractice Claims That Arise Out of Common Estate Planning Situations, 63 Taxes 780 (1985); Gerald P. Johnston, Legal Malpractice in Estate Planning—Perilous Times Ahead for the Practitioner, 67 Iowa L. Rev. 629, 645–46 (1982).

2. Suppose Frances Barcelo had hired Elliott to draft a contract rather than a trust, and suppose Elliott had drafted an unenforceable contract. Would the privity rule have insulated lawyer Elliott from malpractice liability? Who would have been entitled to recover?

Suppose the invalidity of the contract had not been discovered until after Frances Barcelo's death. Would her executor have been able to recover from lawyer Elliott? Or suppose lawyer Elliott had drafted the will in a way that exposed the estate to unnecessary tax liability. Would the executor have been able to recover for legal malpractice? See Estate of Schneider v. Finmann, 15 N.Y.3d 306, 907 N.Y.S.2d 119, 933 N.E.2d 718 (2010) [New York Court of Appeals reinstates executor's malpractice claim against lawyer whose actions allegedly enhanced the state's tax liability, while reaffirming New York's adherence to privity rule].

In Smith v. O'Donnell, 288 S.W.3d 417, 421 (Tex. 2009), the Texas Supreme Court concluded that "[n]one of the concerns we voiced about third-party malpractice suits apply to malpractice suits brought by an estate's personal representative," reasoning that "when negligent legal advice depletes the decedent's estate in a manner that does not implicate how the decedent intended to apportion his estate, Barcelo's concerns about quarreling beneficiaries and conflicting evidence do not arise." Id. at 422. Why didn't the executor have a claim in the Barcelo case?

3. Consider the majority's objection to malpractice liability to will and trust beneficiaries. Is it difficult to tell, in a case like Barcelo v. Elliott, what testator's intent was? How much uncertainty is there?

4. Justice Spector's dissent and Justice Cornyn's dissent represent two distinct positions on malpractice liability to will beneficiaries—each embraced by a number of states. How are they different? How would each justice resolve the following cases, and why?

a. Lawyer drafts a will devising $5,000 apiece to testator's two brothers, but neglecting to include a residuary clause disposing of the remainder of testator's assets. Rice University has in its possession a letter, sent by testator the day after testator executed her will, indicating (erroneously) that the new will leaves Rice the residue of her estate.

b. Same as (a), except that Rice does not have the letter—Rice only has oral testimony by one of testator's friends that testator had intended most of his estate to go to Rice.

c. Lawyer drafts a will, leaving $5,000 apiece to testator's two brothers, and the remainder to Rice, but has testator execute the will in front of only one witness rather than the two required by statute, causing a court to refuse to probate the will, and leaving Rice with nothing.

In light of your answers, which position do you prefer—Justice Spector's or Justice Cornyn's?

5. Note that none of the opinions in Barcelo v. Elliott decide whether lawyer Elliott's conduct was actually malpractice; the majority merely decides that even if the conduct was malpractice, the grandchildren have no claim against Elliott.

What does constitute malpractice? Suppose, for instance, Lawyer prepares a will which misidentifies one of the charitable beneficiaries. Lawyer brings the will to Testator's hospital room to execute, but discovers the mistake. Lawyer promises to return the next morning with a corrected will. Lawyer does not return until the afternoon. Testator died in the morning without executing the will. Malpractice? See Gregg v. Lindsay, 437 Pa.Super. 206, 649 A.2d 935 (1994) (held, no malpractice).

For a catalogue of the types of errors likely to lead to malpractice liability, see Martin D. Begleiter, Attorney Malpractice in Estate Planning—You've Got to Know When to Hold Up, Know When to Fold Up, 38 Kan. L. Rev. 193, 218–55 (1990). For a discussion of damages, see Martin D. Begleiter, First Let's Sue All the Lawyers—What Will We Get: Damages for Estate Planning Malpractice, 51 Hastings L. J. 325 (2000).

6. A will has no legal effect until the moment of testator's death. Suppose that, after testator's death, the intended beneficiaries discover that testator's lawyer failed to include a residuary clause in the will. The will had been drafted twelve years earlier. The jurisdiction's statute of limitations for negligence claims runs from time of discovery, but the jurisdiction also has a statute of ultimate repose, which bars all negligence claims ten years after the date of the negligent act or omission. Is a malpractice claim against the lawyer time-barred? See Davis v. Somers, 140 Or.App. 567, 915

P.2d 1047 (1996) [holding claim time-barred, and rejecting argument by beneficiaries that lawyer had a continuing duty to ensure that the will accurately reflected testator's intentions].

For a more complete discussion of statute of limitations problem, see Martin D. Begleiter, Attorney Malpractice in Estate Planning—You've Got to Know When to Hold Up, Know When to Fold Up, 38 Kan. L. Rev. 193, 208–18 (1990); Martin D. Begleiter, Article II of the Uniform Probate Code and the Malpractice Revolution, 59 Tenn. L. Rev. 101, 105–07 (1991).

7. *Malpractice Liability as an Impetus for Law Reform.* Estates law has historically been encumbered with a variety of hoary rules which have trapped many an unwary client (and lawyer). Two decades ago, Professor Jesse Dukeminier predicted that the advent of malpractice liability would lead to reform of these rules:

> Malpractice liability, which penalizes lawyers for stumbling over one of the ancient rules, may provide an economic incentive to rationalize the rules and practice, and to eliminate or reform those rules that impose needless costs on the profession, and ultimately on the consumer.

Jesse Dukeminier, Cleansing the Stables of Property: A River Found at Last, 65 Iowa L. Rev. 151, 152 (1979).

Consider the costs Professor Dukeminier has in mind: when a legal rule frustrates testator's intent, some person who was not an object of testator's bounty receives a "windfall." Malpractice liability makes the intended beneficiary whole—but at the expense of the lawyer, and ultimately, the consumer. Malpractice liability does nothing to recover the windfall from the unintended beneficiary.

SECTION III. PROBATE AND NON-PROBATE TRANSFERS

A. PROBATE: WHAT IS IT, AND WHO NEEDS IT?

A course in Trusts and Estates is essentially a study of the wealth transmission process. Few people want to give away their assets during their lives; they want to enjoy those assets until they die, when the assets can no longer do them any good. For that reason, death is the focal point for most gratuitous transfers of wealth.

What happens to Jane Doe's property when she dies? If Jane's property consists only of tangible personal property of little market value—clothes, furniture, and inexpensive jewelry, for instance—Jane's closest relatives may simply divide the property up at Jane's death without using any formal legal processes. So long as no one objects to the division, Jane's relatives have little reason to obtain legal sanction for the division. If Jane wrote a will, the lawyer who drafted it might have an obligation to notify all of the beneficiaries. If the beneficiaries, however, were all content to divide Jane's property informally (presumably in accordance with the will), no formal legal action would be necessary. See John H. Langbein, The

Nonprobate Revolution and the Future of the Law of Succession, 97 Harv. L. Rev. 1108, 1117–18 (1984). One study suggests that the vast majority of "estates" are distributed in this informal way. See Robert A. Stein & Ian G. Fierstein, The Demography of Probate Administration, 15 U. Balt. L. Rev. 54 (1985).

Suppose, however, Jane has a $5,000 savings account, or an automobile, or a house. If Jane's relatives (or the beneficiaries of her will) want to withdraw money from the savings account, how will they convince the bank to release the money? If the relatives want to sell the automobile or the house, how will they convince potential buyers that they have good title? The relatives now need some sort of formal legal document to establish their title to the property. They need to go through the probate process—which varies significantly from state to state. Indeed, within a given state, the process may differ depending upon the size of decedent's estate and the nature of her assets. A number of states offer a simplified process for small estates.

We will study the probate process in more detail later in the course. For now, let us consider a few essentials. If Jane Doe has not left a will, her closest relative, or one of her closest relatives, will generally petition for an appointment as her *personal representative* (traditionally called her *administrator*). When more than one person is interested in becoming administrator, local statutes will generally prescribe priority among the applicants. If Jane Doe has left a will naming an *executor*, the executor will generally petition for "letters testamentary," which entitle the executor to serve as Jane's personal representative. The personal representative then bears responsibility for collecting all of Jane's assets. Because the personal representative has legal authority to act on behalf of Jane's estate, a purchaser can rely on a deed executed by the personal representative, and a bank will be protected if the bank releases funds to the personal representative.

If Jane has left a will, the personal representative will offer the will for probate; she will have to prove that the will was properly executed, and she will provide notice to persons who might have reason to contest the will. If probate is uncontested, or if the personal representative overcomes any challenges to the will's probate, the personal representative will distribute Jane's assets to the persons named in the will—after paying taxes, creditor claims, and expenses of administering the estate. Often, the personal representative will have to submit her accounting to the probate court and/or the devisees for approval.

That, in a nutshell, is the probate process. As we shall see, many testators seek to avoid the probate process because of its reputation—sometimes but not always deserved—for delay and expense. Note that a person can avoid having property pass through the probate process if the owner has divested himself of the property by the time of his death. If the property is not part of Jane's estate, the property does not pass through probate. Often, then, after a testator's death, litigation arises between two classes of people: on one side, the beneficiaries of her estate, who argue that Jane owned the property at her death, and on the other side, people who claimed to have acquired a right to ownership as a result of transactions which took the property outside of Jane's estate. In the next two sections, we consider some of the issues that arise.

B. GIFTS

If, before her death, Jane Doe physically transfers her diamond engagement ring to her daughter Ann, and announces to her entire family that she is giving the ring to Ann, there is little ambiguity about Jane's act: she has made a gift of the ring to Ann, and the ring will not be part of Jane's probate estate. Sometimes, however, a property owner's actions may be more ambiguous. Consider the following case:

Gruen v. Gruen

Court of Appeals of New York, 1986.
68 N.Y.2d 48, 496 N.E.2d 869, 505 N.Y.S.2d 849.

■ SIMONS, J:

Plaintiff commenced this action seeking a declaration that he is the rightful owner of a painting which he alleges his father, now deceased, gave to him. He concedes that he has never had possession of the painting but asserts that his father made a valid gift of the title in 1963 reserving a life estate for himself. His father retained possession of the painting until he died in 1980. Defendant, plaintiff's stepmother, has the painting now and has refused plaintiff's requests that she turn it over to him. She contends that the purported gift was testamentary in nature and invalid insofar as the formalities of a will were not met or, alternatively, that a donor may not make a valid inter vivos gift of a chattel and retain a life estate with a complete right of possession.... [D]efendant appeals ... from the ... judgment entered in Supreme Court awarding plaintiff $2,500,000 in damages representing the value of the painting, plus interest. We now affirm.

The subject of the dispute is a work entitled "SchlossKammer am Attersee II" painted by a noted Austrian modernist, Gustav Klimt. It was purchased by plaintiff's father, Victor Gruen, in 1959 for $8,000. On April 1, 1963 the elder Gruen, a successful architect with offices and residences in both New York City and Los Angeles during most of the time involved in this action, wrote a letter to plaintiff, then an undergraduate student at Harvard, stating that he was giving him the Klimt painting for his birthday but that he wished to retain the possession of it for his lifetime. This letter is not in evidence, apparently because plaintiff destroyed it on instructions from his father. Two other letters were received, however, one dated May 22, 1963 and the other April 1, 1963. Both had been dictated by Victor Gruen and sent together to plaintiff on or about May 22, 1963. The letter dated May 22, 1963 reads as follows:

"Dear Michael:

> "I wrote you at the time of your birthday about the gift of the painting by Klimt.
>
> "Now my lawyer tells me that because of the existing tax laws, it was wrong to mention in that letter that I want to use the painting as long as I live. Though I still want to use it, this should not appear in the letter. I am enclosing, therefore, a new letter and I ask you to send the old one back to me so that it can be destroyed.
>
> "I know this is all very silly, but the lawyer and our accountant insist that they must have in their possession copies of a letter which will serve the purpose of making it possible for you, once I die, to get this picture without having to pay inheritance taxes on it.
>
> "Love,
>
> "s/Victor".

Enclosed with this letter was a substitute gift letter, dated April 1, 1963, which stated:

> "Dear Michael:
>
> "The 21st birthday, being an important event in life, should be celebrated accordingly. I therefore wish to give you as a present the oil painting by Gustav Klimt of SchlossKammer which now hangs in the New York living room. You know that Lazette and I bought it some 5 or 6 years ago, and you always told us how much you liked it.
>
> "Happy birthday again.
>
> "Love,
>
> "s/Victor".

Plaintiff never took possession of the painting nor did he seek to do so. Except for a brief period between 1964 and 1965 when it was on loan to art exhibits and when restoration work was performed on it, the painting remained in his father's possession, moving with him from New York City to Beverly Hills and finally to Vienna, Austria, where Victor Gruen died on February 14, 1980. Following Victor's death plaintiff requested possession of the Klimt painting and when defendant refused, he commenced this action.

The issues framed for appeal are whether a valid inter vivos gift of a chattel may be made where the donor has reserved a life estate in the chattel and the donee never has had physical possession of it before the donor's death and, if it may, which factual findings on the elements of a valid inter vivos gift more nearly comport with the weight of the evidence in this case, those of Special Term or those of the Appellate Division. The latter issue requires application of two general rules. First, to make a valid inter vivos gift there must exist the intent on the part of the donor to make a present transfer; delivery of the gift, either actual or constructive to the donee; and acceptance by the donee (Matter of Szabo, 10 N.Y.2d 94, 98; Matter of Kelly, 285 N.Y. 139, 150 [dissenting in part opn]; Matter of Van Alstyne, 207 N.Y. 298, 306; Beaver v. Beaver, 117 N.Y. 421, 428). Second, the proponent of a gift has the burden of proving each of these elements by clear and convincing evidence (Matter of Kelley, supra, at p. 150; Matter of Abramowitz, 38 A.D.2d 387, 389–390, aff'd on opn 32 N.Y.2d 654).

Donative Intent

There is an important distinction between the intent with which an inter vivos gift is made and the intent to make a gift by will. An inter vivos gift requires that the donor intend to make an irrevocable present transfer of ownership; if the intention is to make a testamentary disposition effective only after death, the gift is invalid unless made by will (see, McCarthy v. Pieret, 281 N.Y. 407, 409; Gannon v. McGuire, 160 N.Y. 476, 481; Martin v. Funk, 75 N.Y. 134, 137–138).

Defendant contends that the trial court was correct in finding that Victor did not intend to transfer any present interest in the painting to plaintiff in 1963 but only expressed an intention that plaintiff was to get the painting upon his death. The evidence is all but conclusive, however, that Victor intended to transfer ownership of the painting to plaintiff in 1963 but to retain a life estate in it and that he did, therefore, effectively transfer a remainder interest in the painting to plaintiff at that time. Although the original letter was not in evidence, testimony of its contents was received along with the substitute gift letter and its covering letter dated May 22, 1963. The three letters should be considered together as a single instrument (see, Matter of Brandreth, 169 N.Y. 437, 440) and when they are they unambiguously establish that Victor Gruen intended to make a present gift of title to the painting at that time. But there was other evidence for after 1963 Victor made several statements orally and in writing indicating that he had previously given plaintiff the painting and that plaintiff owned it. Victor Gruen retained possession of the property, insured it, allowed others to exhibit it and made necessary repairs to it but those acts are not inconsistent with his retention of a life estate. Furthermore, whatever probative value could be attached to his statement that he had bequeathed the painting to his heirs, made 16 years later when he prepared an export license application so that he could take the painting out of Austria, is negated by the overwhelming evidence that he intended a present transfer of title in 1963. Victor's failure to file a gift tax return on the transaction was partially explained by allegedly erroneous legal advice he received, and while that omission sometimes may indicate that the donor had no intention of making a present gift, it does not necessarily do so and it is not dispositive in this case.

Defendant contends that even if a present gift was intended, Victor's reservation of a lifetime interest in the painting defeated it. She relies on a statement from Young v. Young (80 N.Y. 422) that " '[any] gift of chattels which expressly reserves the use of the property to the donor for a certain period, or * * * as long as the donor shall live, is ineffectual' " (id., at p. 436, quoting 2 Schouler, Personal Property, at 118). The statement was dictum, however, and the holding of the court was limited to a determination that an attempted gift of bonds in which the donor reserved the interest for life failed because there had been no delivery of the gift, either actual or constructive (see, id., at p. 434; see also, Speelman v. Pascal, 10 N.Y.2d 313, 319–320)....

Defendant recognizes that a valid inter vivos gift of a remainder interest can be made not only of real property but also of such intangibles as stocks and bonds. Indeed, several of the cases she cites so hold. That being so, it is difficult to perceive any legal basis for the distinction she urges which would permit gifts of remainder interests in those properties but not of remainder interests in chattels such as the Klimt painting here.... As long as the evidence establishes an intent to make a present and irrevocable transfer of title or the right of ownership, there is a present transfer of some interest and the gift is effective immediately (see, Matter of Brady, 228 App. Div. 56, 60, affd. no opn. 254 N.Y. 590; In re Sussman's Estate, 125 N.Y.S.2d 584, 589–591, affd. no opn. 283 App. Div. 1051; Matter of Valentine, 122 Misc. 486, 489; Brown, Personal Property § 48, at 133–136 [2d ed.]; 25 N.Y. Jur., Gifts, § 30, at 173–174; see also, Farmers' Loan & Trust Co. v. Winthrop, 238 N.Y. 477, 485–486). Thus, in Speelman v. Pascal (supra), we held valid a gift of a percentage of the future royalties to the play "My Fair Lady" before the play even existed. There, as in this case, the donee received title or the right of ownership to some property immediately upon the making of the gift but possession or enjoyment of the subject of the gift was postponed to some future time.

Defendant suggests that allowing a donor to make a present gift of a remainder with the reservation of a life estate will lead courts to effectuate otherwise invalid testamentary dispositions of property. The two have entirely different characteristics, however, which make them distinguishable. Once the gift is made it is irrevocable and the donor is limited to the rights of a life tenant not an owner....

Delivery

In order to have a valid inter vivos gift, there must be a delivery of the gift, either by a physical delivery of the subject of the gift or a constructive or symbolic delivery such as by an instrument of gift, sufficient to divest the donor of dominion and control over the property (see, Matter of Szabo, 10 N.Y.2d 94, 98–99, 217 N.Y.S.2d 593, 176 N.E.2d 395, supra; Speelman v. Pascal, 10 N.Y.2d 313, 318–320, supra; Beaver v. Beaver, 117 N.Y. 421, 428–429, supra; Matter of Cohn, 187 App. Div. 392, 395). As the statement of the rule suggests, the requirement of delivery is not rigid or inflexible, but is to be applied in light of its purpose to avoid mistakes by donors and fraudulent claims by donees (see, Matter of Van Alstyne, 207 N.Y. 298, 308; Matter of Cohn, supra, at pp. 395–396; Mechem, Requirement of Delivery in Gifts of Chattels and of Choses in Actions Evidenced by Commercial Instruments, 21 Ill. L. Rev. 341, 348–349). Accordingly, what is sufficient to constitute delivery "must be tailored to suit the circumstances of the case" (Matter of Szabo, supra, at p. 98). The rule requires that " '[the] delivery necessary to consummate a gift must be as perfect as the nature of the property and the circumstances and surroundings of the parties will reasonably permit' " (id.; Vincent v. Rix, 248 N.Y. 76, 83; Matter of Van Alstyne, supra, at p. 309; see, Beaver v. Beaver, supra, at p. 428).

Defendant contends that when a tangible piece of personal property such as a painting is the subject of a gift, physical delivery of the painting itself is the best form of delivery and should be required. Here, of course, we have only delivery of Victor Gruen's letters which serve as instruments of gift. Defendant's statement of the rule as applied may be generally true, but it ignores the fact that what Victor Gruen gave plaintiff was not all rights to the Klimt painting, but only title to it with no right of possession until his death. Under these circumstances, it would be illogical for the law to require the donor to part with possession of the painting when that is exactly what he intends to retain.

Nor is there any reason to require a donor making a gift of a remainder interest in a chattel to physically deliver the chattel into the donee's hands only to have the donee redeliver it to the donor. As the facts of this case demonstrate, such a requirement could impose practical burdens on the parties to the gift while serving the delivery requirement poorly. . . .

Acceptance

Acceptance by the donee is essential to the validity of an inter vivos gift, but when a gift is of value to the donee, as it is here, the law will presume an acceptance on his part (Matter of Kelsey, 26 N.Y.2d 792, affd. on opn. at 29 AD2d 450, 456; Beaver v. Beaver, 117 N.Y. 421, 429, supra). Plaintiff did not rely on this presumption alone but also presented clear and convincing proof of his acceptance of a remainder interest in the Klimt painting by evidence that he had made several contemporaneous statements acknowledging the gift to his friends and associates, even showing some of them his father's gift letter, and that he had retained both letters for over 17 years to verify the gift after his father died. . . .

Accordingly, the judgment appealed from and the order of the Appellate Division brought up for review should be affirmed, with costs.

NOTES AND QUESTIONS

1. Victor Gruen, a Viennese-born architect who escaped to the United States in 1938, when Germany annexed Austria, was best known as the father of the modern shopping mall. Gruen pioneered the multi-level enclosed shopping mall with stores opening into the mall, rather than to an outdoor parking lot. For more on Guren, see M. Jeffrey Hardwick, Mall Maker: Victor Gruen, Architect of an American Dream (2004).

2. In light of the April 1, 1963 letter, why didn't the court conclude that Victor Gruen had given his son not merely a remainder interest in the Klimt painting, but a right to immediate possession?

Suppose, on July 1, 1963, Michael Gruen had demanded possession of the painting, and his father had refused. If Michael then brought an action to recover possession, how do you think the court would have decided the case?

3. Was the effect of Victor Gruen's 1963 letters different from the effect of a will provision leaving the paintings to Michael?

After Victor sent the 1963 letters, would he have been free to sell the painting? Suppose he had written a will disposing of the painting. Would he later have been entitled to sell the painting?

4. Suppose you had been Victor Gruen's lawyer, and Victor had indicated to you that he wanted to be sure his son would not become embroiled in litigation. Would you have recommended that Victor take some action beyond sending the 1963 letters?

5. It is easy to understand why courts would require "donative intent" before finding that a gift has been made. But why require delivery? Suppose Victor Gruen had announced to his entire family "I hereby give my Klimt painting to my son Michael," but had not handed over to Michael either the painting or a letter. Has Victor made a completed gift? If not, why not? On the delivery requirement generally, see Ashbel G. Gulliver & Catherine J. Tilson, Classification of Gratuitous Transfers, 51 Yale L.J. 1 (1941).

6. ***Gifts Causa Mortis.*** Ordinarily, gifts are irrevocable—even if made on one's deathbed. If John gives Mary his car, he cannot take it back. Suppose, however, John believes he is on his deathbed, gives Mary the keys to his car, and says "My car is yours. I have no use for it any more." John has donative intent, and the delivery of the keys undoubtedly qualifies as symbolic (or perhaps "constructive") delivery. If John dies the next week, the car belongs to Mary.

But suppose John unexpectedly recovers. Can he take the car back? Many courts would say yes. They would reason that John's gift was made in contemplation of death, and included an implicit condition that the car would revert to John, if he recovered from the illness. Courts have labeled gifts like this one *gifts causa mortis.* See Estate of Smith, 694 A.2d 1099 (Pa.Super.1997) (checks written just before death by suicide treated as gifts causa mortis; court notes that "donor may retrieve the gifts if the suicide is not completed;" id. at n. 2).

Gifts causa mortis are of no importance as an estate planning device. No lawyer would ever advise a client to make a gift causa mortis. Yet gift causa mortis doctrine is occasionally useful as a litigator's tool. For instance, if decedent recovers from the illness that sparked the gift, but dies a year later from another illness, the estate may argue that a gift made during the first illness was a gift causa mortis, and hence reverted to the donor when he recovered from that illness.

C. Joint Interests With Right of Survivorship

Lifetime gifts are the most obvious sort of non-probate transfer. Because the decedent gives the property away before she dies, there is no property left to pass through decedent's estate. In Gruen v. Gruen, decedent gave away all but his life interest in the painting. Since the life interest expired at decedent's own death, there was nothing left to pass through decedent's probate estate.

Lifetime gifts, however, are not nearly as important in the wealth transmission process as another form of non-probate transfer: transfer by the terms of an instrument creating a joint tenancy with right of survivorship (or its equivalent). To refresh your recollection, if two parties hold property as joint tenants with right of survivorship (or, in the case of married couples, as tenants by the entirety), when the first of the two dies, the decedent's share passes automatically to the survivor—that is the meaning of the words "with right of survivorship." If more than two parties share a joint tenancy with right of survivorship, at the death of the first to die, the decedent's share is divided equally among the surviving joint tenants.

Many people—especially but not exclusively married couples—hold property in joint tenancies, or, in the case of married couples only, in tenancies by the entirety. Sometimes, people acquire joint tenancies by the terms of a relative's will; at other times, people choose to purchase property as joint tenants or tenants by the entirety in order to obtain the survivorship feature associated with those interests. Married couples in particular prefer the survivorship feature because it permits automatic transfer of ownership interests at the death of the first to die.

When a joint tenant or a tenant by the entirety dies, the transfer of property that occurs is a non-probate transfer. The surviving joint tenant takes the property not as decedent's "heir" or by the terms of decedent's will, but by the terms of the instrument that created the joint tenancy. As a result, the property held in joint tenancy never passes through the probate estate of the first to die. Consider the following example:

Example: *By the terms of their mother's will, decedent and her brother acquired a vacation cottage as joint tenants with right of survivorship. Decedent died first, having executed a valid will leaving all of her property to her daughter. At decedent's death, who owns the house?*

Solution: *Because, by the terms of the mother's will, brother and sister each had a right of survivorship, the cottage passed automatically to the brother at decedent's death. The property never passed through decedent's estate, and therefore decedent's daughter has no right to the cottage.*

Joint tenancies and tenancies by the entirety are not restricted to real property; many people hold bank accounts and brokerage accounts as joint tenants with right of survivorship. All joint tenancies—but particularly those in bank accounts—raise questions about the intent of the joint tenants: did they understand the arrangement they were making when they signed documents creating the joint tenancy? In many states, when people buy real property, they are represented by counsel. In other states, even if counsel is not involved, purchasers of real property regard the event as an important one which requires significant care. By contrast, people tend to be more casual when they go to the local bank branch to open an account. To what extent should courts look beyond the papers signed by the account holder in determining whether the account holder has created a joint tenancy with survivorship rights? Consider the following case:

Franklin v. Anna National Bank

Appellate Court of Illinois, 1986.
140 Ill.App.3d 533, 94 Ill.Dec. 870, 488 N.E.2d 1117.

■ WELCH, J.:

Plaintiff, Enola Stevens Franklin, as executor of the estate of Frank A. Whitehead, deceased, commenced this action in the circuit court of Union County against defendant Anna National Bank, alleging that the funds in a joint savings account were the property of the estate. The bank interpleaded Cora Goddard, who asserted her right to the money as the surviving joint owner. After a bench trial, the circuit court entered judgment for Mrs. Goddard. Mrs. Franklin appeals. We reverse.

* * *

Decedent died December 22, 1980. His wife Muriel Whitehead died in 1974. Mrs. Goddard was Muriel's sister. Decedent had eye surgery in May of 1978, and according to Mrs. Goddard was losing his eyesight in 1978. In April of 1978 Mrs. Goddard moved to Union County to help decedent and live with him. On April 17, 1978, Mrs. Goddard and decedent went to the bank, according to Mrs. Goddard to have his money put in both their names so she could get money when they needed it, "and he wanted me to have this money if I outlived him."

A bank employee prepared a signature card for savings account number 3816 and Mrs. Goddard signed it. A copy of this card was in evidence at trial. The signatures of decedent and Mrs. Goddard appear on both sides of the card. It appears that Muriel Whitehead's signature was "whited out" and Mrs. Goddard's signature added. The front of the card states that one signature is required for withdrawals. The back of the card states that all funds deposited are owned by the signatories as joint tenants with right of survivorship.

Mrs. Goddard testified that she did not deposit any of the money in savings account 3816. She made no withdrawals, though she once took decedent to the bank so he could make a withdrawal. According to Mrs. Goddard, on the day she signed the signature card decedent "asked me if I needed my money because they had bought cemetery lots from me, and I told him, not at this time, that I didn't need it. He wanted to know if I needed any more money at that time and I said, no, and I said, just leave it in here and I will get it out whenever I need it." According to Mrs. Goddard, decedent promised to pay her a thousand dollars for the lots; she was never paid. Asked whether she ever had the passbook for savings account 3816 in her possession, Mrs. Goddard answered, "Only while I was at Frank's. It was there."

Later in 1978, Mrs. Franklin began to care for decedent. In January 1979, decedent telephoned the bank, then sent Mrs. Franklin to the bank to deliver a letter to Mrs. Kedron Boyer, a bank employee. The handwritten letter, dated January 13, 1979, and signed by decedent, stated: "I Frank Whitehead wish by Bank accounts be changed to Enola Stevens joint intendency [sic]. Nobody go in my lock box but me." According to Mrs. Franklin, Mrs. Boyer told her to tell decedent he would have to specify what type of account he was referring to. Decedent gave Mrs. Franklin a second letter which Mrs. Franklin delivered to Mrs. Carol Williams at the bank (Mrs. Boyer was absent). This handwritten letter, dated January 13, 1979, stated: "I Frank Whitehead want Enola Stevens and me only go in my lock box. Account type Saving and Checking. In case I can't see she is to take care of my bill or sick." According to Mrs. Franklin, Mrs. Williams said she would take care of it and give the letter to Mrs. Boyer. Mrs. Franklin testified that she signed the savings passbook in the presence of decedent and Mrs. Boyer. Mrs. Franklin took her present last name on May 8, 1979.

Mrs. Boyer, Mrs. Williams, and bank president Delano Mowery all testified at trial. These witnesses explained the usual procedures for account changes. None remembered much of the circumstances surrounding the bank's receipt of the January 13, 1979, letters. According to Mr. Mowery, the bank would not remove a signature from a signature card based on a letter; the most recent signature card the bank had for savings account 3816 was signed by decedent and Mrs. Goddard.

Mrs. Goddard's attorney's assertion at trial that there were no monthly statements on savings account 3816 was uncontradicted.

The trial court found that Mrs. Goddard was the sole owner of the funds in savings account 3816 by right of survivorship as surviving joint tenant, and that no part of the funds became part of decedent's estate.

Mrs. Franklin argues that decedent did not intend to make a gift of savings account 3816 to Mrs. Goddard.

The instrument creating a joint tenancy account presumably speaks the whole truth. In order to go behind the terms of the agreement, the one claiming adversely thereto has the burden of establishing by clear and convincing evidence that a gift was not intended. (Murgic v. Granite City Trust & Savings Bank (1964), 31 Ill. 2d 587, 590, 202 N.E.2d 470, 472.) Each case involving a joint tenancy account must be evaluated on its own facts and circumstances. (In re Estate of Hayes (1971), 131 Ill. App. 2d 563, 568, 268 N.E.2d 501, 505.) The form of the agreement is not conclusive regarding the intention of the depositors between themselves. (In re Estate of Schneider (1955), 6 Ill. 2d 180, 186, 127 N.E.2d 445, 449.) Evidence of lack of donative intent must relate back to the time of creation of the joint tenancy. (In re Estate of Stang (1966), 71 Ill. App. 2d 314, 317, 218 N.E.2d 854, 856.) The decision of the donor, made subsequent to the creation of the joint tenancy, that he did not want the proceeds to pass to the survivor, would not, in itself, be sufficient to sever the tenancy. (In re Estate of Zengerle (1971), 2 Ill. App. 3d 98, 101, 276 N.E.2d 128, 130.) However, it is proper to consider events occurring after creation of the joint account in determining whether the donor actually intended to transfer his interest in the account at his death to the surviving joint tenant. Matter of Estate of Guzak (1979), 69 Ill. App. 3d 552, 555, 388 N.E.2d 431, 433.

We examine the instant facts in light of the above principles: There appears no serious doubt that in January of 1979, just nine months after adding Mrs. Goddard's name to savings account No. 3816, decedent attempted to remove Mrs. Goddard's name and substitute Mrs. Franklin's. The second of decedent's handwritten letters to the bank in January of 1979 indicates decedent's concern that he might lose his sight and be unable to transact his own banking business. These facts show that decedent made Mrs. Goddard (and later Mrs. Franklin) a signatory for his own convenience, in case he could not get his money, and not with intent to effect a present gift. (See Dixon National Bank v. Morris (1965), 33 Ill. 2d 156, 159, 210 N.E.2d 505, 506; Estate of Guzak (1979), 69 Ill. App. 3d 552, 388 N.E.2d 431.) It does not appear that Mrs. Goddard ever exercised any authority or control over the joint account. (See Estate of Guzak (1979), 69 Ill. App. 3d 552, 388 N.E.2d 431.) While decedent's statement that he wanted Mrs. Goddard to have the money in the account if she outlived him suggests decedent's donative intent, taken literally decedent's statement is inconsistent with intent to donate any interest during decedent's lifetime. (See Lipe v. Farmers State Bank of Alto Pass (1970), 131 Ill. App. 2d 1024, 1026, 265 N.E.2d 204, 205.) Mrs. Goddard does not argue that there was a valid testamentary disposition in her favor, nor could we so find on the instant facts.

Of the many cases cited by the parties for comparison with the case at bar, the most persuasive is In re Estate of Schneider (1955), 6 Ill. 2d 180, 127 N.E.2d 445. In Estate of Schneider, the decedent's executor filed a petition alleging the funds in joint bank accounts belonged to the estate and not to Ralston, the surviving joint tenant. Ralston testified that all of the money in the account was deposited by the decedent, that the decedent at no time told Ralston he wanted Ralston to have any of the money, and that when Ralston's name was added to the accounts the decedent said, "I want your name on these bank accounts so that in case I am sick you can go and get the money for me." The trial court concluded that the decedent intended to retain actual ownership of the money. Our supreme court agreed. We reach the same conclusion here. In the case at bar, decedent's attempts to change the account show his consistent view of the account as his own. The surrounding circumstances show decedent's concern for his health and his relatively brief use of Mrs. Goddard (and later Mrs. Franklin) to assure his access to his funds. The money in account No. 3816 should have been found to be the property of the estate.

For the foregoing reasons, the judgment of the circuit court of Union County is reversed, and this cause is remanded for entry of judgment in favor of plaintiff.

Reversed.

NOTES AND QUESTIONS

1. In the Franklin case, the signatures of both Mr. Whitehead and Mrs. Goddard appeared on the signature card associated with the disputed bank account. What rights did the signature card confer on Mrs. Goddard? Did she have the right to withdraw money from the account? If she did have the right to withdraw money, to what use was she entitled to put the money?

If Mrs. Goddard had an unlimited withdrawal right, how could Mr. Whitehead remove her name from the account?

Did Mr. Whitehead intend to give Mrs. Goddard rights beyond that of an "agent" or financial secretary who would act on his behalf because of the difficulties he faced in doing his own banking?

2. Suppose Mr. Whitehead had wanted to give Mrs. Goddard an unlimited right to withdraw from the account, together with a right to take the account balance at his death. How could he have arranged that result when he opened the account?

Do you think the officials at Mr. Whitehead's bank branch had forms that were any more explicit than the one Mr. Whitehead and Mrs. Goddard signed? If not, aren't the forms an invitation to litigation?

3. If you had been Mr. Whitehead's lawyer in the weeks before his death, what actions would you have recommended to reduce the likelihood of subsequent litigation over his accounts?

4. ***Joint Accounts During the Depositor's Lifetime.*** Joint accounts have long been a muddle because of the different purposes for which a depositor might establish a joint account. Consider the three most important reasons:

1. Depositor—especially an elderly or incapacitated depositor—fears that he or she will be physically unable to do his or her own banking, and, for reasons of convenience, wants another person's name on the account.

2. Depositor wants to assure that the account passes to the joint account-holder at depositor's death without the need to go through probate; depositor does not, however, want to confer on the joint account-holder any right to the money during depositor's lifetime.

3. Depositor wants to confer on the joint-account holder all of the rights associated with joint ownership—including the unlimited right to withdraw and use the money on deposit.

Which of these alternatives best describes Mr. Whitehead's reasons?

Most courts have traditionally treated joint accounts as giving each party a right only to the money he or she deposited in the account. See, e.g., White v. White, 769 A.2d 617 (R.I.2001). That is, although each party has power to withdraw all of the money in the account (that is, the bank will not be liable to anyone for paying money to either account-holder), if either party withdraws, without permission, more than the proportion he has deposited, the other party has a claim against him. Failure to advance the claim, however, would constitute ratification of the withdrawal.

The opinion in Franklin v. Anna National Bank clearly reflects this approach. Do you see why? If Mrs. Goddard had an ownership interest beyond her proportion of the deposits (which was zero on the facts of the case), would Mr. Whitehead have been entitled unilaterally to remove Mrs. Goddard's name on the account?

By contrast, some courts conclude that when one person deposits funds into a joint bank account or joint investment account, a presumption arises that the depositor has made a gift of half the property to the other person named on the joint account. See Julia v. Russo, 984 So.2d 1283 (Fla. App. 2008). In the Julia case, the court held that Florida's slayer statute did not preclude decedent's girlfriend from withdrawing funds deposited by decedent in their joint names. The court held that even if the slayer statute were applicable, only the girlfriend's right of survivorship would be extinguished, and the accounts became tenancies in common at the time of decedent's death.

In New York, by statute, a deposit of property in a joint bank account with a right of survivorship creates a presumption that the depositors have created a common law joint tenancy. N.Y. Banking Law § 675 (2011).

5. ***Joint Accounts at Death.*** Courts generally enforce survivorship provisions in joint bank accounts—assuming (1) that the depositor did not revoke the survivorship provision during his lifetime, as Mr. Whitehead did in Franklin v. Anna National Bank; and (2) that decedent's estate does not introduce clear evidence that the now-deceased depositor established the joint account only for convenience.

Because of the uncertainty created when parties seek to introduce evidence about the intent of the deceased depositor, some states, in recent years, have adopted a hard-and-fast rule barring extrinsic evidence to show that the depositor created a joint account for convenience only. See Robinson v. Delfino, 710 A.2d 154 (R.I.1998); Wright v. Bloom, 69 Ohio St.3d 596, 635 N.E.2d 31 (1994).

6. ***P.O.D. Accounts.*** Suppose a depositor does not need to establish a joint account for reasons of convenience, and suppose further that the depositor does not want to confer any withdrawal rights on anyone else during the depositor's lifetime. The depositor does, however, want to assure that the account is paid to a particular person at his death. Can depositor accomplish his objective by creating a "payable on death" or "P.O.D." account?

Historically, the most common judicial answer has been no—that is, courts refused to enforce the provision for payment to a beneficiary upon the depositor's death. Why? Courts reasoned that a P.O.D. account did not transfer any interest to the beneficiary during the depositor's lifetime. As a result, courts treated the designation as equivalent to a will—which becomes effective only at the property owner's death. As we shall see, however, a will is valid only if executed in accordance with testamentary formalities. Since the depositor does not typically comply with those formalities when making a P.O.D. designation, courts often held the designation invalid. See, e.g., Will of Collier, 381 So.2d 1338, 1342 (Miss.1980):

> An analysis of our cases on the subject indicates that the rule is that when an instrument purports to be a deed and is in the words and form of a deed and is acknowledged as such, it should be construed to be testamentary in character and inoperative as a deed of conveyance when, and only when, it affirmatively and clearly appears from the language of the instrument itself, giving due consideration to all its provisions, that it was the intention of the person signing it that the instrument itself would have no effect until his death....
>
> ... Wilma Franklin did not receive any present interest in the certificate when it was issued.... It is patent that the designation "P.O.D. to Wilma Franklin," was an attempt to make a testamentary disposition of the certificate upon the death of Gussie Collier.

See also Truax v. Southwestern College, 214 Kan. 873, 879, 522 P.2d 412, 417 (1974) ("This court has never sanctioned forthright violation of our statute of wills. Neither the passbooks nor the signature cards were executed in accordance with it.")

Does the sharp distinction between a survivorship designation in a joint account and a similar designation in a P.O.D. account serve any purpose? Many legislatures have not thought so, and have enacted statutes making P.O.D. accounts enforceable.

The Uniform Probate Code, Joint Accounts, and P.O.D. Accounts

The Uniform Probate Code provides that depositors may open either single-party or multiple-party accounts, and provides that either type of account may have a P.O.D. designation, an agency designation, or both. In addition, a multiple-party account may be either with or without a right of survivorship. See Uniform Probate Code, § 6–203. Moreover, the drafters of the UPC drafted a form contract of deposit designed to make it easier for a depositor to make a rational choice of the type of account she wants to create. Essentially, the form enables a depositor to check off the options she wants at the time she opens her account, instead of simply signing a "one-size fits all" form presented to her by bank officials. See UPC § 6–204. See generally Grayson M. P. McCouch, Will Substitutes under the Revised Uniform Probate Codes, 58 Brook. L. Rev. 1123, 1136–37 (1993).

Beyond Bank Accounts: T.O.D. Designations in Securities Registration

Today, even people of moderate means often hold some of their assets not in banks, but in mutual funds or brokerage accounts. If it is possible for people to create joint accounts with survivorship rights in bank accounts, is there any reason to prevent people from creating analogous arrangements when they hold their assets in securities or brokerage accounts? Increasingly, the answer is no. For instance, the Uniform Probate Code's treatment of securities and security accounts parallels the code's treatment of bank accounts. UPC § 6–302 authorizes registration of securities "in beneficiary form" whenever a security is owned by one individual or by two or more individuals with right of survivorship. "Beneficiary form" is defined as a registration which indicates "the intention of the owner regarding the person who will become the owner of the security upon the death of the owner." UPC § 6–301.

D. The Nonprobate Revolution: Scope and Reasons

As we have seen, people make gifts and open joint accounts for a variety of reasons—many of which have little to do with an aversion to the probate system. Other forms of transfer—the POD bank account and the TOD brokerage account are two examples—owe their existence almost entirely to a desire to avoid probate. And these accounts represent only a fraction of what Professor John Langbein has dubbed "the nonprobate revolution." For many people, life insurance—which we will discuss in more detail later in the course—will be the most significant form of wealth transmission. And life insurance proceeds, if made payable directly to a named beneficiary, do not pass through the insured's probate estate. Increasingly, estate planners use revocable trusts—which we will also study later—to avoid the probate process. Courts have grudgingly accepted these mechanisms for wealth transmission (sometimes only after legislative action) even though each of them challenges what Professor Langbein has called the "probate monopoly"—"the premise that probate is the sole means by which our legal system permits a transferor to pass his property on death." John H. Langbein, The Nonprobate Revolution and the Future of the Law of Succession, 97 Harv. L. Rev. 1108, 1129 (1984). Consider Professor Langbein's account of current law:

John H. Langbein, The Nonprobate Revolution and the Future of the Law of Succession, 97 Harv. L. Rev. 1108, 1132 (1984).

Modern practice supplies only one theory that can reconcile wills and will substitutes in a workable and honest manner: the rule of transferor's intent. The real state of the law is that the transferor may choose to pass his property on death in either the probate or the nonprobate system or in both. The transferor who takes no steps to form or disclose his intent will be remitted to probate, the state system. The transferor who elects to use any of the devices of the nonprobate system will be protected in his decision, provided that the mode of nonprobate transfer is sufficiently formal to meet the burden of proof on the question of intent to transfer. The alternative formalities of the standard form instruments that serve as mass will substitutes satisfy this requirement so easily that the issue of intent almost never needs to be litigated. The transferor's-intent theory thus replaces the probate monopoly theory. Transferors are free to opt out of probate by selecting any of the well-demarcated nonprobate modes of transfer.

Why have so many forms of non-probate transfer emerged? Again, Professor Langbein offers an answer:

> The probate system has earned lamentable reputation for expense, delay, clumsiness, makework, and worse. In various jurisdictions, especially the dozen-odd that have adopted or imitated the simplified procedures of the Uniform Probate Code of 1969 "UPC", the intensity of hostility to probate may have abated a little. There are, however, intrinsic limits to the potential of probate reform. As Richard Wellman, the principal draftsman of the UPC, forthrightly declared: "The assumption that administration of an estate requires a judicial proceeding is as doubtful as it is costly." Because the Anglo–American procedural tradition is preoccupied with adversarial and litigational values, the decision to organize any function as a judicial proceeding is inconsistent with the interests that ordinary people regard as paramount when they think about the transmission of their property at death: dispatch, simplicity, inexpensiveness, privacy. As long as probate reform still calls for probate, it will not go far enough for the tastes of many transferors, who view probate as little more than a tax imposed for the benefit of court functionaries and lawyers.

Id. at 1116. Professor Langbein contends that probate remains important when real property is involved because of the need to provide marketable title. Id. at 1117. He emphasizes, however, probate has become less necessary as real property has become a less important component of overall wealth:

> The bulk of modern wealth takes the form of contract rights rather than rights in rem—promises rather than things. Promissory instruments—stocks, bonds, mutual funds, bank deposits, and pension and insurance rights—are the dominant component of today's private wealth.

Id. at 1119.

Consider the assets of Wanda, a solidly middle-class individual who is married with two children. Wanda has the following assets: (1) $100,000 in equity in a house she owns with her husband, Harry, as tenants by the entirety; (2) an automobile, furniture, and other personal property worth a total of $30,000; (3) a joint checking account with Harry, in which $5,000 is currently on deposit; (4) an individual retirement account with a value of $150,000; (5) a $300,000 life insurance policy naming Harry as the beneficiary; (6) a mutual fund, in her own name, with a value of $100,000; and (7) a $50,000 vacation cabin she inherited from her parents. If Wanda were to die tomorrow, the following chart illustrates how small a proportion of her assets would pass through her estate:

Wanda's Assets	Estate Assets	Non–Probate Assets
$100,000 house equity		To Harry by right of survivorship created in the deed
$150,000 IRA		Passes to beneficiary designated on IRA account
$300,000 Life Insurance		Passes to beneficiary designated on insurance policy
$100,000 Mutual Fund	Passes Through Estate	
$50,000 Vacation Cabin	Passes Through Estate	

Note that Wanda could arrange to have still fewer of her assets pass through her probate estate if she filed a POD designation with the firm that sold her the mutual funds and put the vacation cabin in joint tenancy. The point is that for many people, only a fraction of their assets are "probate" assets. If Wanda were to write a will, the terms of the will would not govern the disposition of her IRA or her life insurance policy unless she also took steps to make her estate the beneficiary of the IRA and the insurance policy.

What happens when Wanda dies? Who will ensure that her assets reach her beneficiaries and/or her heirs? The details of the process will vary from state to state, and sometimes from county to county, but the following generalizations apply almost everywhere: Whether or not Wanda left a will, someone will bear responsibility for administering her estate. If Wanda left a will, the executor named in the will performs that task. If not, a court-appointed administrator (often a close family member) will oversee the estate. (Both executors and administrators are sometimes referred to as "personal representatives").

Many of the steps the personal representative performs will be the same whether Wanda dies testate (with a will) or intestate (without a will). The following oversimplified chart compares the two processes:

Probate Administration	Intestate Administration
Executor Named in the Will Offers Will for Probate and Petitions Probate Court for Letters Testamentary	Close Family Member Petitions Probate Court for Letters of Administration
Executor provides Notice to Persons With Standing to Challenge the Will	
Executor Collects Estate Assets	Administrator Collects Estate Assets
Executor Pays or Settles Creditor Claims	Administrator Pays or Settles Creditor Claims
Executor Distributes Assets in Accordance With Will	Administrator Distributes Assets in Accordance with Intestate Succession Statute

Note that "letters testamentary" or "letters of administration" are the documents that authorize the executor or administrator to act on the estate's behalf. Without those letters, a brokerage house or bank will not turn over funds to the executor or administrator for payment of claims and ultimate distribution to beneficiaries.

This brief orientation to the probate process serves as an introduction to issues of estate administration. Chapter 13 deals with those issues in greater detail.

NOTES AND QUESTIONS

1. Claire Client consults you about her estate. She informs you that her only significant asset is a $50,000 certificate of deposit at a local bank. Claire wants her nephew, Derek, to receive the certificate at her death. Her only other living relative is a niece, Erin, who lives out of state and never visits. Claire asks you whether she is better off writing a will or designating Derek as the beneficiary pursuant to a "pay on death" option included on a form provided by the bank. Assuming that the state has legislation authorizing P.O.D. accounts, how would you advise Claire?

a. Which alternative is more likely to engender litigation after Claire's death?

b. If Claire changes her mind next year, or three years from now, will it be easier (and cheaper) to change the beneficiary designation or to change her will?

c. Which alternative will be cheaper for Claire right now? Should Claire consider your fee in making her decision?

Is the desire to avoid excessive consultation with lawyers—and not merely an aversion to the probate process—another explanation for the rise in nonprobate transfers? Note that the bank is unlikely to charge for the privilege of executing a beneficiary designation.

2. Much of Professor Langbein's discussion focuses on people who intentionally bypass the probate process. Is every person who signs a bank form, or a brokerage form, designating the account as a joint account with right of survivorship, intentionally bypassing the probate process?

3. ***Tax Consequences of the Nonprobate Revolution.*** One might assume that the drive to avoid probate has been motivated in large measure by a desire to avoid estate taxation. Some people might indeed be motivated by a desire to avoid estate taxation, but for the most part, if they believe that avoiding probate avoids taxes, they are misguided. As we shall see, the federal estate tax statute also applies to *inter vivos* gifts and to a variety of other nonprobate transfers. Although tax considerations remain paramount in the estate plans of many wealthy individuals, tax considerations play little role in the decision to avoid the probate system.

* * *

With this introduction to the differences between probate and nonprobate transfers, it is time—in the next several chapters—to consider what happens to assets that do pass through the probate system. We will later return to nonprobate transfers—particularly to trusts and life insurance.

CHAPTER TWO

INTESTATE SUCCESSION

SECTION I. INTRODUCTION AND REPRESENTATIVE STATUTES

Most Americans die without wills. How should their property be distributed? The doctrinal answer is that the property of a person who dies without a valid will—that is, a person who dies *intestate*—will be distributed in accordance with the intestate succession statutes in effect in the jurisdiction. Suppose, however, you were designing an intestate succession statute. How would you decide what provisions to include?

Many legislators and scholars have concluded that the intestate succession statute should aim to give effect to the probable intent of the decedent. We generally permit people to direct disposition of their assets by writing wills. Some people don't take advantage of their "right" to write wills—perhaps because they are too poor or too uninformed to seek legal advice, perhaps because they find contemplating their own deaths too unpleasant. Should we "punish" these people for their failure to write wills? Or should we try, by statute, to duplicate the dispositions they would have made had they written wills?

Another approach to intestate succession focuses less on decedents' intent and more on social policy. Should we distribute property to those persons most dependent on the decedent's assets, or to the persons who "deserve" the property most? Decedent had an opportunity to write her will; if she didn't do so, why not look to policy as the basis for distributing her assets? In China, for instance, inheritance law penalizes bad behavior and rewards good behavior. See Frances H. Foster, Towards a Behavior-Based Model of Inheritance?: The Chinese Experiment, 32 U. C. Davis L. Rev. 77 (1998).

In the majority of estates, there is little conflict between decedents' intent and social policy. Studies indicate that most people—both those who write wills and those who do not—prefer to have their property pass to close family members, the very people most likely to be dependent on that property, and the very people most likely to have contributed to accumulation of that property. On the other hand, a recent article suggests that intestacy is positively correlated with low socio-economic class and education levels, and that minorities, young people and the unmarried are less likely to have wills than older, white, married people.

With this in mind, some scholars argue that the intestacy laws, premised on the traditional family structure, do a poor job of effectuating the intent of many decedents who have created informal, blended or nontraditional family structures. See, for example, Alyssa A. DiRusso,

Testacy and Intestacy: The Dynamics of Wills and Demographic Status, 23 Quinnipiac Prob. L.J. 36 (2009). Professor Francis Foster has suggested that intestate succession might better be based on a determination of the individual decedent's most likely intent, or even on factors other than the decedent's intent, such as the decedent's actual, as opposed to familial, relationship to prospective beneficiaries. Frances H. Foster, The Family Paradigm of Inheritance Law, 80 N. Car. L. Rev. 200, 268–71 (2001); see also Francis H. Foster, Individualized Justice In Disputes Over Dead Bodies, 61 Vanderbilt L. Rev. 1351 (2008). A more recent article argues that courts could better approximate decedents' intentions by distributing their probate estates to those whom decedents have designated as beneficiaries of their nonprobate property (such as joint tenancies with right of survivorship, joint bank accounts and life insurance policies). See Mary Louise Fellows, E. Gary Spitko & Charles Q. Strohm, An Empirical Assessment of the Potential For Will Substitutes to Improve State Intestacy Statutes, 85 Ind. L.J. 409 (2010).

But even if many decedents would prefer to distribute some of their assets to close friends, intimate partners or even charities, how would courts accurately determine how much a decedent would want to leave to which charities and which friends? Even some scholars who are generally sympathetic to individualized assessment of the intention of decedents concede that "inquiry to ascertain the most likely preferences of the individual decedent may sometimes be a fruitless endeavor of contradictory narratives that fail to yield a definitive understanding of the decedent's preferences." Tanya K. Hernandez, The Property of Death, 60 U. Pitt. L. Rev. 971, 1017 (1999). Moreover, such a system would increase the discretion of probate judges, probate litigation, and the costs of adjudication. Would the high costs that such a system would generate be justified? Perhaps for reasons of administrative convenience, American legislatures have universally preferred a mechanical scheme of intestate succession: we do not focus on the preferences and circumstances of the particular decedent; instead, intestate succession statutes are generally "one size fits all."

The Importance of Intestate Succession

Intestate succession statutes are, of course, important for those people who fail to write a will. But their importance extends beyond those people who die **intestate**. First, as we shall see, some people execute wills that are wholly invalid. Courts may invalidate wills for various reasons—a testator may fail to follow execution formalities or might lack testamentary capacity, to name just two. When a court rejects a will, and the decedent has left no prior, valid will, the intestacy statute directs the distribution of a decedent's estate.

Second, testator may have executed a valid will that fails to completely dispose of all of testator's property. When that occurs, the property that testator's will fails to distribute will be distributed in accordance with the intestacy statute.

Example 1: *Decedent writes a will, which provides "I leave all of my real property to my brother Joe." Decedent dies with $20,000 in stocks and bonds. The will does not dispose of the stocks and bonds, because they are not* real *property. Hence, the stocks and bonds will be distributed by intestate succession.*

Third, a will sometimes refers to the "heirs" of a particular person—either the heirs of the testator himself, or the heirs of some other person. Who are a person's heirs? The people who would succeed to that person's estate by intestate succession. Sometimes wills are even more explicit, devising property to "those people who would succeed to my estate under the intestate succession statute in effect at the time of my death." Again, we can construe the will only if we understand the intestate succession statute.

Example 2: *Decedent writes a will, which provides "I leave $50,000 to my sister Alice, if she survives me. If she does not survive me, I direct that the property be distributed to her heirs (and not to her estate)." Decedent has explicitly provided that if Alice does not survive decedent, the property should pass not to the beneficiaries of Alice's will, but rather to her heirs. Hence if Alice does not survive, the $50,000 will be distributed by intestate succession.*

Fourth, intestate succession is often important for determining who has standing to contest a will. Suppose, for instance, testator's brother believes that testator lacked mental capacity when she wrote her will. Or, suppose testator's cousin believes that a television evangelist exercised undue influence over testator in the drafting of her will. Does the brother, or the cousin, have standing to contest the will? If the contestant would be entitled to take part of the estate by intestate succession, the contestant would have standing to contest. Otherwise, the contestant would have standing only if he had been the beneficiary of a prior will.

In re Wendel's Will, 143 Misc. 480, 257 N.Y.S. 87 (Surr.Ct.1932), furnishes a dramatic example of the importance of intestate succession statutes as a means to limit standing to contest a will. Ella Wendel, an unmarried, childless eccentric whose fortune exceeded $40 million at her death in 1931, left a will. More than 1,600 claimants sought to challenge the will. There were numerous disputes about the relationships between Ella Wendel and the various claimants. The Surrogate Court adopted a procedure which required those contending to be in the nearest degree of kinship to Ella Wendel to prove their claims first, because once the claim of a close relative was established, none of the more distant claimants would have standing to contest. The will contest was eventually settled upon payment of a sum to Ella Wendel's closest relatives. Who represented the Wendel estate? John Marshall Harlan—later of the United States Supreme Court (proving that estates lawyers do sometimes get the recognition they deserve). See Cloyd Laporte, John M. Harlan Saves the Ella Wendel Estate, 59 A.B.A.J. 868 (1973).

Fundamentals of Intestate Succession

Although intestate succession statutes differ significantly from state to state, a number of issues recur. Before examining two intestate succession statutes in detail, let us catalog some of the critical issues to examine in any intestate succession statute.

1. The Share of the Surviving Spouse. The common law developed different rules for intestate succession to real property (often called rules of "descent") and intestate succession to personal property (often called rules of "distribution"). The surviving spouse was not an "heir" of decedent's real property; instead, the spouse had "dower" or "curtesy" rights—lifetime interests—in decedent's real property. By contrast, the surviving spouse was generally entitled to share in distribution of decedent's personal property.

Today, the majority of states apply the same rules to "descent" of real property and "distribution" of personal property. Indeed, in many states, the common law terminology has been abolished. A few states, however, give surviving spouses only life estates in the decedent spouse's real property, but entitle spouses to outright distributions of personal property. See, e.g., Rhode Island 33–1–1 through 33–1–5.

In most states, the statutory trend has been to treat the surviving spouse more generously than at common law. Indeed, as we shall see, in some states, the surviving spouse now takes the entire estate unless the decedent—or the surviving spouse—has children from outside the marriage. What is the rationale for giving the spouse so much of the estate? First, when testators write wills, they typically leave all or most of their estates to their spouses (again, unless there are children from outside the marriage). So, legislators assume decedents who don't write wills would also want their spouses to take the bulk of their estates. Second, a surviving spouse is likely to provide for his or her own children upon the spouse's death. Hence, giving the surviving spouse the lion's share of decedent's estate will not significantly disadvantage the couple's children. Finally, when the couple has minor children, there are significant disadvantages to distributing money to the children; because the children are not capable of dealing with the money on their own, a guardian may have to be appointed—often leading to unnecessary costs and friction.

In many states, domestic partners or partners to a civil union have the same inheritance rights as surviving spouses (more on that later in the chapter).

2. "Descendants" Take to the Exclusion of "Collaterals." Another nearly universal feature of intestate succession statutes is that a decedent's direct lineal descendants take to the exclusion of collateral relatives. Collateral relatives include brothers and sisters, nieces and nephews, cousins and all other relatives who are not direct lineal descendants or ancestors. That is, so long as a decedent has children, grandchildren, or great-grandchildren, virtually all intestate succession statutes preclude a decedent's siblings or any more distant relatives from inheriting. Examine the two statutes reproduced below to see how those statutes reach that result.

Note that many statutes use another word for descendants: "issue." Although a literalist might assume that "issue" is a synonym for "children," the established legal meaning of "issue" includes more remote lineal descendants, including grandchildren and great-grandchildren.

*3. **Distribution Among Collaterals.*** Suppose decedent has no spouse or descendants. How do we decide which relatives are closest to decedent for inheritance purposes? If one or both of decedent's parents are still alive, they generally take to the exclusion of other relatives. Does this reflect the preferences of most decedents? Professor Scalise does not think so:

> Most individuals, if survived by at least one parent and one sibling, prefer their parents and siblings to share in their inheritance, rather than to bestow an exclusive award to their parents. In the Fellows, Simon & Rau study examining public attitudes across five states, the authors discovered that in a situation in which a father, brother, and sister survived a decedent, only 29.2% of the respondents favored awarding all of the estate to a surviving parent. When the hypothetical included both parents and the two siblings, the pattern did not change—only 31.9% favored splitting the estate between the parents and excluding the siblings, while 40.3% wanted to split the estate into fourths, with the father, mother, brother, and sister sharing equally. The study further demonstrated that neither family income nor estate size affect the above preferences.

Ronald J. Scalise, Jr., Honor thy Father and Mother?: How Intestacy Law Goes Too Far in Protecting Parents, 37 Seton Hall L. Rev. 171, 189 (2006); see also John Makdisi, Fixed Shares in Intestate Distribution: A Comparative Analysis of Islamic and American Law, 1984 BYU L. Rev. 267 (1984) (suggesting that parents should share with siblings).

If decedent's parents are dead, which collateral relatives take? Most intestate succession statutes hold that descendants of decedent's parents inherit to the exclusion of relatives who are descended from decedent's grandparents, but not decedent's parents. Thus, decedent's brothers and sisters (or nieces and nephews)—all of whom are descendants of decedent's parents—would inherit to the exclusion of decedent's aunts, uncles, and first cousins—all of whom are descendants of decedent's grandparents. Only if decedent is not survived by any descendants of parents will descendants of grandparents (aunts, uncles, cousins) inherit. The UPC intestacy statute, reproduced below, embodies this approach.

Sometimes, however, intestate succession statutes refer to "degrees of kinship" in order to determine the relative rights of collateral relatives. The Massachusetts statute reprinted later in this chapter is an example. Most statutes that refer to degrees of kinship define kinship according to the "Table of Consanguinity" reproduced below. To determine how many degrees of kinship separate decedent and a particular relative, we must count "up" from the decedent to the common ancestor, and then "down" to the relative in question.

Example 3: *How many degrees of kinship separate decedent and decedent's first cousin? The common ancestor is decedent's grandparent (or more likely, two of decedent's grandparents). We count "up" two degrees from decedent to decedent's grandparent, and then "down" two degrees from the grandparent to the first cousin. The first cousin is, therefore, four degrees of kinship from the decedent.*

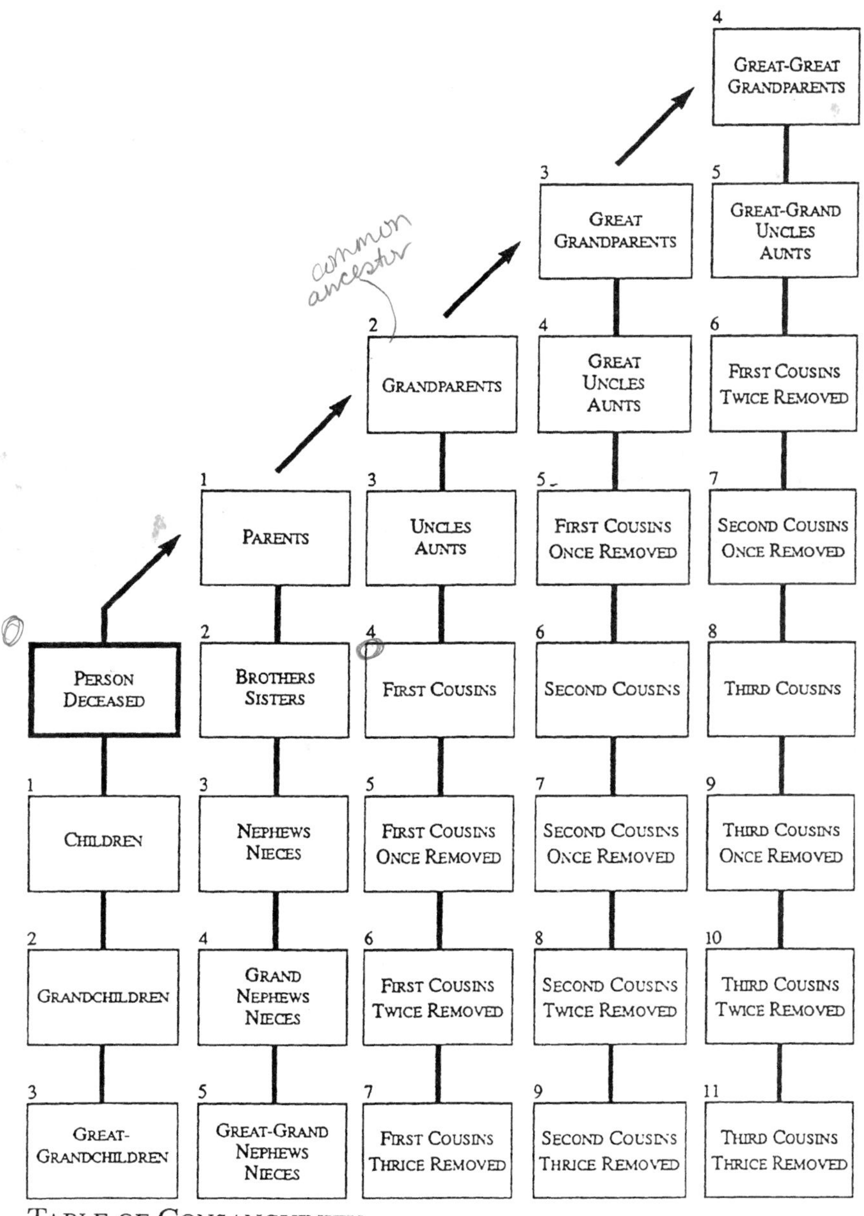

TABLE OF CONSANGUINITY
(Showing Degrees of Relationship)

Not every state follows the Table of Consanguinity in determining the degree of relationship, however. See Ark. Code Ann. § 28–9–212 (directing that the degree of relationship shall be determined by establishing the common ancestor, counting down to the decedent, and then counting down to the relative, and using the greater number, if any, as the degree of relation). As always, it is important to read relevant intestacy statutes and cases closely.

At common law, if decedent had no close relatives, his closest living relatives, no matter how distant, remained entitled to take. Only if decedent had no living relatives would decedent's estate *escheat*, or pass to the state. Many states, however, have enacted what are called "laughing heir" statutes—statutes which preclude inheritance by relatives too remote from decedent. Why are these statutes called "laughing heir" statutes? Because they preclude inheritance by relatives whose glee at their new-found wealth is unmitigated by any grief over the death of decedent.

Examine the Uniform Probate Code. Does it have a laughing heir provision?

4. *Inheritance by Those Not Related By Blood to the Decedent.* Virtually all intestate succession statutes exclude relatives by marriage, other than decedent's own spouse. That is, decedent may well refer to his wife's sister's children as nephews and nieces. Those children are not nieces and nephews for intestate succession purposes, and would not be entitled to inherit unless decedent wrote a will including them. Brothers-in-law and sisters-in-law are also not entitled to take by intestate succession.

In the vast majority of states, step-children are not included in the definition of "descendants" or "issue". A few states, and the UPC, give step-children inheritance rights in extremely limited circumstances.

Adopted children have the same inheritance rights as biological family members to property from their adopted relatives. Other issues presented by adoption are explored later in this chapter.

5. *A Bit More Terminology*. Statutes and judicial opinions occasionally distinguish between a decedent's "heirs at law" and "next of kin." As we have already seen, at common law, the system for "descent" of real property was different from the system for "distribution" of personal property. The persons entitled to take decedent's real property were referred to as his heirs at law. The persons entitled to take his personal property were referred to as his next of kin. Today, the two terms are largely synonymous.

SECTION II. THE SHARE OF THE SURVIVING SPOUSE

WYOMING STATUTES

SECTION 2–4–101 (2010).

(a) Whenever any person having title to any real or personal property having the nature or legal character of real estate or personal estate undisposed of, and not otherwise limited by marriage settlement, dies intestate, the estate shall descend and be distributed . . . to his kindred, male and female, subject to the payment of his debts, in the following course and manner:

(i) If the intestate leaves husband or wife and children, or the descendents of any children surviving, one-half (1/2) of the estate shall descend to the surviving husband or wife, and the residue thereof to the surviving children and descendents of children . . . ;

(ii) If the intestate leaves husband or wife and no child nor descendents of any child, then the real and personal estate of the intestate shall descend and vest in the surviving husband or wife.

UNIFORM PROBATE CODE

SECTION 2–102. SHARE OF SPOUSE.

The intestate share of a decedent's surviving spouse is:

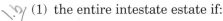

(1) the entire intestate estate if:

(i) no descendant or parent of the decedent survives the decedent; or

(ii) all of the decedent's surviving descendants are also descendants of the surviving spouse and there is no other descendant of the surviving spouse who survives the decedent;

(2) the first [$300,000][1], plus three-fourths of any balance of the intestate estate, if no descendant of the decedent survives the decedent, but a parent of the decedent survives the decedent;

(3) the first [$225,000], plus one-half of any balance of the intestate estate, if all of the decedent's surviving descendants are also descendants of the surviving spouse and the surviving spouse has one or more surviving descendants who are not descendants of the decedent;

(4) the first [$150,000], plus one-half of any balance of the intestate estate, if one or more of the decedent's surviving descendants are not descendants of the surviving spouse.

SECTION 2–103. SHARE OF HEIRS OTHER THAN SURVIVING SPOUSE.

a) Any part of the intestate estate not passing to a decedent's surviving spouse under Section 2–102, or the entire intestate estate if there is no surviving spouse, passes in the following order to the individuals who survive the decedent:

(1) to the decedent's descendants by representation;

(2) if there is no surviving descendant, to the decedent's parents equally if both survive, or to the surviving parent if only one survives;

(3) if there is no surviving descendant or parent, to the descendants of the decedent's parents or either of them by representation;

(4) if there is no surviving descendant, parent, or descendant of a parent, but the decedent is survived on both the paternal and maternal sides by one or more grandparents or descendants of grandparents:

(A) half to the decedent's paternal grandparents equally if both survive, to the surviving paternal grandparent if only one survives, or

1. [UPC 1–109, added to the UPC in 2008, makes all dollar amounts in the UPC subject to annual cost of living adjustments].—eds.

to the descendants of the decedent's paternal grandparents or either of them if both are deceased, the descendants taking by representation; and

(B) half to the decedent's maternal grandparents equally if both survive, to the surviving maternal grandparent if only one survives, or to the descendants of the decedent's maternal grandparents or either of them if both are deceased, the descendants taking by representation;

(5) if there is no surviving descendant, parent, or descendant of a parent, but the decedent is survived by one or more grandparents or descendants of grandparents on the paternal but not the maternal side, or on the maternal but not the paternal side, to the decedent's relatives on the side with one or more surviving members in the manner described in paragraph (4).

(b) If there is no taker under subsection (a), but the decedent has:

(1) one deceased spouse who has one or more descendants who survive the decedent, the estate or part thereof passes to that spouse's descendants by representation; or

(2) more than one deceased spouse who has one or more descendants who survive the decedent, an equal share of the estate or part thereof passes to each set of descendants by representation.

SECTION 2–105. NO TAKER.

If there is no taker under the provisions of this Article, the intestate estate passes to the [state].

As we have seen, the surviving spouse generally takes a significant share of the estate. The Wyoming statute is a fairly traditional one; the surviving spouse shares equally with issue when decedent leaves both spouse and issue. When the decedent is survived by a spouse but no descendants, the Wyoming statute gives the surviving spouse the entire estate. See, also N.Y. EPTL Section 4–1.1(a)(2). The Uniform Probate Code, however, permits parents to share with the spouse (when the estate exceeds $300,000) in those cases. What view of decedent's family situation underlies these provisions? For a critique of statutes permitting parents to share with spouses, see Ronald J. Scalise, Jr., Honor Thy Father and Mother?: How Intestacy Law Goes Too Far in Protecting Parents, 37 Seton Hall L. Rev. 171 (2006).

Note that the Uniform Probate Code takes into account the increasing number of "non-traditional," or "blended," families in which one or both spouses have children born of other marriages, or outside of marriage altogether. The drafters of the Code offer the following rationale for sections 2–102(3) and (4):

> If the decedent leaves surviving descendants and if the surviving spouse (but not the decedent) has other descendants, and thus the decedent's descendants are unlikely to be the *exclusive* beneficia-

> ries of the surviving spouse's estate, the surviving spouse receives the first $225,000 plus one-half of the balance of the intestate estate. The purpose is to assure the decedent's own descendants of a share in the decedent's intestate estate when the estate exceeds $225,000.
>
> If the decedent has other descendants, the surviving spouse receives $150,000 plus one-half of the balance. In this type of case, the decedent's descendants who are not descendants of the surviving spouse are not the natural objects of the bounty of the surviving spouse.

Official Comment, UPC § 2–102. See also Lawrence W. Waggoner, The Multiple–Marriage Society and Spousal Rights Under the Revised Uniform Probate Code, 26 Real Prop. Prob. & Tr. J. 683 (1992); Martin L. Fried, The Uniform Probate Code: Intestate Succession and Related Matters, 55 Albany L. Rev. 927, 929–33 (1992); B. Redman, Entitlement of a Surviving Spouse: A Quandary, 27 Cap. U. L. Rev. 573, 595–97 (1999).

In 2008, the UPC was amended to include 2–103(b), which provides for distribution to decedent's step-children in the event that decedent is not survived by a spouse or any blood or adopted relatives.

As you reread UPC section 2–102, focus on the structure of the statute. If decedent was survived by a spouse, one and only one of the four subsections of section 2–102 is applicable. Your job, in reading the statute, is to determine which of the subsections is applicable to the particular decedent. Thus, if decedent was survived by no issue or parent, or if decedent's only issue are also the surviving spouse's only issue, subsection (1) is applicable; if decedent was survived by a parent and no issue, subsection (2) is applicable; and so on. First figure out which subsection is applicable, and then determine what that subsection provides.

PROBLEMS

1. Charles Childless died survived by his wife, Candace, and his only sibling, a sister, Debbie. If Charles's net probate estate was valued at $400,000, how would his estate be distributed (a) under the Wyoming statute; (b) under the Uniform Probate Code; (c) under the intestate succession statute of your state?

How, if at all, would your answers be different if Charles was also survived by his mother, Bea?

2. Marla Marrier died survived by her husband, Norman, and by their daughter, Olive. Marla died with a $400,000 estate. On the following facts, how much of Marla's estate would Norman be entitled to (a) in Wyoming; (b) under the UPC; and (c) under the intestate succession statute of your state? How would the remainder of Marla's estate be distributed?

1. Neither Marla nor Norman had any children other than Olive.

2. Marla had a son, Peter, by a prior marriage; Norman had no children other than Olive.

3. Norman had a son, Quentin, by a prior marriage; Marla had no children other than Olive.

4. Norman had a son, Quentin, by a prior marriage *and* Marla had a son, Peter, by a prior marriage.

* * *

Intestate succession statutes generally assume that if the parties to a marriage are not divorced, they continue to enjoy an amicable relationship. In reality, however, that is not always the case. What happens when the marital relationship has been dissolved, but the marriage has not been? Consider the following case:

Estate of Goick

Supreme Court of Montana, 1996.
275 Mont. 13, 909 P.2d 1165.

■ ERDMANN, J.:

This is an appeal of an order of the Seventeenth Judicial District Court, Blaine County, granting summary judgment in favor of Barbara Goick, appointing Barbara as a supervised personal representative of decedent Michael Goick's estate, approving the distribution agreement between Barbara and the decedent's children, and denying appellants' motion to compel settlement of the case. We affirm.

We restate the issues as follows:

1. Do the appellants, decedent's mother, brother, and sister, lack standing to appeal?

2. Did the District Court err when it granted summary judgment in Barbara's favor concluding that she was the surviving spouse for purposes of intestate succession?

3. Did the District Court err when it appointed Barbara as personal representative of decedent's estate?

* * *

FACTS

Michael and Barbara Goick were married in 1981 and the marriage produced three children. In December 1990, Michael filed a petition for dissolution. A hearing in the dissolution proceeding was scheduled for April 25, 1991. At that hearing, Michael and Barbara agreed to all issues except the division of household goods, which the parties were to settle within two weeks. The District Court Judge then had the parties present sufficient evidence to support a decree of divorce.

Following the hearing, the judge was apparently asked whether Barbara and Michael were divorced and he responded that they were. The parties were unable to agree on the division of the household goods and, on December 25, 1991, Barbara filed a motion to divide personal property of the marriage. In the motion, she stated her understanding was that the marriage had been dissolved on April 25, 1991, by the District Court. On December 19, 1991, the District Court Judge wrote a memorandum to the attorneys informing them that it was his understanding the parties had refused to sign the settlement agreement negotiated at the April 25 hearing and that he intended to hold the parties to that agreement. On January 7, 1992, Michael's attorney filed an application for withdrawal of attorney to which Michael consented. No further proceedings occurred in the divorce action and no final decree or order was issued. Michael died on November 30, 1992. Two days after his death, Barbara moved to dismiss the divorce proceeding for the reason that Michael had died. On December 3, 1992, an order was issued dismissing the divorce action.

On December 7, 1992, Barbara filed a petition for adjudication of intestacy, determination of heirs, and appointment of personal representative (PR). In the petition, she claimed she was the surviving spouse and was entitled to an appointment as PR. Michael's mother, brother, and sister (the appellants) filed an objection to the petition, claiming Barbara was not the surviving spouse, but rather the ex-wife of Michael. The court appointed a guardian ad litem for the children. Barbara filed a motion for summary judgment asking the court to determine that she was the surviving spouse of Michael. The appellants filed a motion for summary judgment asking the court to find that Barbara was not Michael's surviving spouse.

* * *

On January 27, 1995, a distribution agreement was entered into between Barbara and the children through their guardian ad litem as the only potential heirs of Michael. A notice of distribution agreement was filed, and the appellants filed an objection to the agreement. The District Court approved the agreement on March 21, 1995. The appellants filed a motion asking the court to reconsider the distribution agreement, and the court ordered oral argument. On April 4, 1995, following the hearing, the District Court issued an order granting Barbara's motion for summary judgment on the issue of her status as a surviving spouse, approving the distribution agreement, and appointing Barbara as a supervised personal representative. From that order . . . appellants appeal.

ISSUE 1

Do the appellants, decedent's mother, brother, and sister, lack standing to appeal?

Barbara claims the appellants have no standing to appeal. . . .

The appellants have appealed . . . separate issues to this Court and it is necessary to examine their standing as to each issue. . . .

Appointment of Barbara as PR

Barbara contends that appellants were not heirs to the estate, and so, they could not be injured by Barbara's appointment as PR. The appellants claim they have standing because they are creditors of the estate. In fact, Michael's mother, Wanda Goick, is the only appellant who filed a creditor's claim against the estate. As a creditor, Wanda has priority for appointment as PR if Barbara is determined to be ineligible. See § 72–3–502, MCA. Section 72–3–503, MCA, provides that creditors can object to the appointment of a PR. Wanda objected to Barbara's appointment as PR, and for that reason she has standing to appeal the appointment. Michael's brother and sister are neither creditors nor heirs of the estate, and therefore, they have no standing to appeal her appointment as PR. See Olson v. Dept. of Revenue (1986), 223 Mont. 464, 469–70, 726 P.2d 1162, 1166.

Enforcement of Distribution Agreement

The appellants raise the issue of whether enforcement of the distribution agreement was in error and Barbara argues that they lack standing to challenge the agreement. Under this agreement, Barbara agreed to receive a distribution of one-third of the estate, and the children agreed, through their guardian ad litem, to receive two-thirds of the estate which will be administrated by a corporate trustee.

The distribution agreement provided that Barbara and the children's guardian ad litem agreed

> to enter into a private agreement among successors as to distribution of an estate, pursuant to Section 72–3–915, MCA, in order to settle the litigation in the probate matter pending in Blaine County District Court and to provide for a different distribution than provided under the laws of intestacy.

Section 72–3–915(1), MCA, provides as follows:

> Subject to the rights of creditors and taxing authorities, competent successors may agree among themselves to alter the interests, shares, or amounts to which they are entitled under the will of the decedent or under the laws of intestacy in any way that they provide in a written contract executed by all who are affected by its provisions. The personal representative shall abide by the terms of the agreement subject to his obligation to administer the estate for the benefit of creditors, to pay all taxes and costs of administration, and to carry out the responsibilities of his office for the benefit of any successors of the decedent who are not parties.

The appellants are not successors to the estate and so they are not proper parties to an agreement distributing the estate. They have no legal interest in the distribution of Michael's estate. Furthermore, Wanda's interests as a creditor of Michael's estate are completely provided for by statute.

A party has no standing where there is no personal stake in the outcome of the controversy. Northern Border Pipeline Co. v. State (1989), 237 Mont. 117, 129, 772 P.2d 829, 836.... The appellants have no personal stake in the validity of the agreement. We therefore conclude that the appellants have no standing to claim the distribution agreement was improper. Accordingly, the issue of whether the District Court erred in approving the distribution agreement is not properly before us.

* * *

ISSUE 2

Did the District Court err when it granted summary judgment in Barbara's favor concluding that she was the surviving spouse for purposes of intestate succession?

Wanda, as the sole appellant with standing to litigate this issue, claims that both Barbara and Michael considered themselves divorced and in the April 25, 1991 hearing the District Court Judge informed the parties that they were divorced, even though no final order was ever issued. The District Court held a hearing on this issue in the probate proceeding and concluded that a divorce decree cannot be based on an oral agreement. The court further concluded that Barbara was the surviving spouse for purposes of intestate succession and granted summary judgment in her favor.

* * *

Section 72–2–103(2)(c), MCA (1991), provides that "a person who was a party to a valid proceeding concluded by an order purporting to terminate all marital property rights" is not a surviving spouse of decedent. Wanda claims the April 25, 1991 proceeding conveyed and implied that Barbara and Michael were divorced, thereby "purporting" to terminate all marital property rights. Wanda contends that according to § 72–2–103(2)(c), MCA (1991), Barbara is not a surviving spouse for the purposes of intestacy.

There was no divorce decree or order issued from the April 25, 1991 proceeding, nor was a final settlement even reached as to all marital property rights. Recently, in In re Marriage of Simms (1994), 264 Mont. 317, 871 P.2d 899, we concluded that an oral settlement agreement is not binding on a judge. Whatever settlement was reached in the April 25, 1991 proceeding was merely an oral agreement between the parties and cannot be considered the equivalent of an order where no final order was issued. Accordingly, Barbara's status as a surviving spouse was not terminated pursuant to § 72–2–103(2)(c), MCA (1991).

Wanda further contends principals of equitable estoppel prevent Barbara from claiming that she is the surviving spouse in regard to Michael's estate when she has held herself out as being divorced from Michael for over one and one-half years prior to his death. . . .

In this instance, equitable estoppel would have required that Barbara's representation that they were divorced was made with the intention or expectation that Michael would act upon the representation. It would also require that Michael relied to his detriment upon the representation and that he not be aware that the divorce was not final. Both parties refused to sign the settlement negotiated at the April 25, 1991 hearing. Michael's attorney for the divorce action testified that Michael did not believe the divorce was final and that Michael insisted upon going to trial. This testimony was uncontradicted. It follows that Michael was aware that the divorce was not final and did not act to his detriment even if Barbara was found to have intentionally misrepresented the facts concerning the status of the divorce.

We conclude that Barbara is not estopped from claiming she and Michael were not divorced. The record is clear that no divorce decree or order was ever issued. We therefore conclude that the District Court did not err in holding that Barbara was the surviving spouse for purposes of intestate succession and granting summary judgment in her favor.

ISSUE 3

Did the District Court err when it appointed Barbara as personal representative of decedent's estate?

Wanda's position is that Barbara should not have been appointed PR because she has obvious conflicts of interest over the estate in regard to the children's interests. She argues that Barbara's claim to the estate is directly adverse to that of the children's because the children would receive the entire estate if not for Barbara's self-interest. For that reason, Wanda contends that Barbara cannot act as a fiduciary of the estate for the benefit of the children. The District Court ordered that Barbara be named PR under the court's supervision and that she not take any substantive action without the court's approval.

We review the appointment of a personal representative according to § 72–3–502, MCA, to determine whether a district court has correctly interpreted the law. Estate of Peterson (1994), 265 Mont. 104, 110, 874 P.2d 1230, 1233. If a PR has not been named under a will and there are no devisees, the decedent's surviving spouse has priority for appointment. Section 72–3–502, MCA.

As stated in Issue 2, Barbara is Michael's surviving spouse for purposes of intestate succession. Accordingly, she has priority for appointment over Michael's other heirs, the public administrator, and any creditor. See § 72–3–502, MCA. Her appointment was agreed to by the children through their guardian ad litem. Therefore, the District Court was correct when it determined Barbara had priority for appointment. Furthermore, the children's interests are protected in this situation through the court ordered supervision of the estate's administration. We conclude that the District Court did not err in appointing Barbara as PR of Michael's estate.

NOTES AND QUESTIONS

1. Why should a formal divorce be necessary to disqualify a surviving spouse from taking by intestate succession? Isn't a separation, especially if accompanied by divorce proceedings, enough to establish that decedent wouldn't have wanted the surviving spouse to share in the estate?

Note, however, that a formal divorce is likely to be accompanied by a property settlement, which assures that marital assets are distributed equitably. Had there been such a settlement in Estate of Goick? Although

Michael and Barbara's attorneys had orally agreed to a property settlement, the Goick court determined that an oral settlement agreement is not binding until a judge issues a final order. If the settlement agreement was not binding, and if most of the couple's assets had been held in Michael's name, where would that have left Barbara Goick? Note that in Lockhead v. Weinstein, 319 Mont. 62, 81 P.3d 1284 (2003), the Montana Supreme Court overruled Goick to the extent it held that oral settlement agreements cannot bind parties until the court approves them.

Uniform Probate Code section 2–802 provides that a person whose marriage has been terminated by divorce or annulment does not qualify as a surviving spouse, and that a decree of separation that does not terminate the status of husband and wife is not a divorce for the purposes of 2–802. The section also provides that a surviving spouse does not include "an individual who was a party to a valid proceeding concluded by an order purporting to terminate all marital property rights." § 2–802(b)(3). On the Code's general approach to spousal rights, see Lawrence W. Waggoner, The Multiple–Marriage Society and Spousal Rights Under the Revised Uniform Probate Code, 76 Iowa L. Rev. 223 (1991).

2. ***Standing.*** Why did Michael's mother, Wanda, have standing to challenge Barbara's right to take by intestate succession and hence her right to serve as personal representative? Under the Montana intestate succession statute, even if Barbara had not qualified as a surviving spouse, the entire estate would have been distributed to the couple's children. How, then, would Wanda have benefited from a determination that Barbara was not entitled to take by intestate succession?

Note again the importance of the intestate succession statute in determining standing to challenge a will, or, in this case, an agreement for distribution of the estate. Because neither Michael's siblings nor his mother would have been entitled to take by intestate succession, the court concluded that they lacked standing to challenge the agreement between Barbara and the guardian appointed for the children.

3. ***Compromise Agreements.*** Under the Montana intestate succession statute, derived from the Uniform Probate Code, Barbara Goick, as the surviving spouse would have been entitled to her husband's entire estate. Why did she agree to accept only one-third of the estate?

Note that the Montana statute—reproduced in the Goick opinion—permits not only intestate heirs, but also will beneficiaries, to agree among themselves to distribute decedent's estate in a way that differs from the disposition in decedent's will (or, if there is no will, from the disposition that would result from application of the intestate succession statute). Why would the Montana legislature enact such a statute? Does the Montana statute—and comparable legislation in other states—frustrate the intention of decedents?

4. ***Appointment as Personal Representative.*** In order to distribute decedent's assets after death, someone has to collect those assets. Decedent may have a variety of bank accounts and brokerage accounts, and a variety

of debtors may owe the decedent money. Conversely, decedent may owe money to various creditors, and may have tax bills to pay. Generally, a personal representative is appointed to administer the estate—to collect assets, to pay debts and expenses, and to distribute the estate.

When decedent leaves a will, the will generally appoints an "executor" to perform these functions. When decedent dies intestate, a court will generally appoint a personal representative, often called an "administrator" to perform the same functions. When more than one person seeks appointment as administrator, a statute generally fixes priority among the competing parties. In Montana, for instance, the applicable statute provides that when decedent dies intestate, the surviving spouse has first priority, followed by other heirs, the "public administrator" (a public official appointed to administer estates when no other candidates appear), and finally, creditors of the estate. Thus, if Barbara Goick did not qualify as a surviving spouse, and the other heirs—the couple's children—were not qualified because they had not reached the age of majority, Wanda, who had filed a claim as a creditor, might have been eligible to serve as personal representative.

Why would Wanda (or anyone else) want to serve as personal representative? First, Wanda might not trust Barbara to represent the interests of the estate—either because she suspects Barbara's competence or Barbara's loyalty. Second, in most jurisdictions the personal representative is entitled to compensation out of the estate. In a large estate, the compensation can be quite significant:

Despite a Will, Jackson Left a Tangled Estate

The New York Times
July 7, 2009 Tuesday

> Four days after Michael Jackson died, his family gathered at his brother Jermaine's house in Calabasas, Calif., to hear one of Mr. Jackson's lawyers read a will he drafted in 2002.
>
> After the lawyer, John G. Branca, read the document—which named Mr. Jackson's mother, Katherine, the guardian of his three children and a beneficiary of 40 percent of the estate—the group broke out in applause, according to a person in attendance who insisted on anonymity to speak about a private meeting.
>
> The meeting, which included everyone except Joe Jackson, the father, and Randy, one of the six brothers, was a rare show of unity for the famously fractious family. But in death as in life with the pop superstar, nothing is quite what it seems.
>
> Shortly after the meeting, a lawyer representing Mrs. Jackson began a legal effort to wrest control of her son's estate from Mr. Branca and John McClain, a music executive, both of whom had been named executors.

In a Los Angeles courthouse on Monday, a judge refused Mrs. Jackson's petition and gave temporary authority to Mr. Branca and Mr. McClain. Another hearing to finalize authority is scheduled for Aug. 3.

But the question of Mr. Jackson's business legacy, especially how his music and image will be used to generate income for the family, remains tangled and unresolved.

Over the next few months, a broad cast of players—including the family, the executors, the concert promoter AEG Live, advisers like the Rev. Jesse Jackson and the Rev. Al Sharpton, and a small army of former advisers and hangers-on—will most likely jockey for position in unwinding the singer's estate, estimated at more than $500 million. At the same time they will probably try to avoid an ugly public squabble that could damage the value of the Jackson brand.

* * *

There is more at stake than the singer's assets when he was alive. With explosive sales of music and worldwide hunger for all things Jackson, the estate will need to act quickly to establish a business that can police its property.

There are reports of hundreds of unreleased and potentially lucrative songs; unlicensed T-shirts and memorabilia have already flooded the market.

Since Mr. Jackson's death 10 days ago, Mr. Branca and Mr. McClain have been canvassing former managers and agents to find out whether he had any other wills, investments or cash the two men did not know about.

They are also eager to recover the Neverland Ranch memorabilia from an aborted auction in April. That could put them at odds with Colony Capital, the private equity firm that co-owns Neverland and, according to some people close to the discussions, intends to turn the ranch into a museum along the lines Elvis Presley's Graceland. Mr. Branca and Mr. McClain would prefer to set up a permanent memorial in more tourist-friendly Las Vegas.

AEG, the promoter, filmed Mr. Jackson's final rehearsals for a series of comeback concerts scheduled to begin at London's O2 Arena on July 13. In interviews, Randy Phillips, the chief executive of the company's live division, has said the footage could earn hundreds of millions of dollars that would help AEG recover some of its losses from the canceled shows (any deal would be shared with the estate, thus benefiting the family as well).

* * *

What happens next depends on whether Mr. Branca remains an executor after the Aug. 3 hearing. Mr. Branca, a prominent entertainment lawyer, was associated with Mr. Jackson as early as 1980, and he handled most of Mr. Jackson's big deals, including his 1985 purchase of the Beatles-rich ATV song catalog. In 1987, Mr. Jackson was the best man at Mr. Branca's first wedding. (David Lee Roth, another Branca client, handled the bachelor party.)

After several years apart, Mr. Branca was rehired just a week before Mr. Jackson's death.

"He really knows the ins and outs of the value of Michael's assets, and what can be done with them for the ultimate benefit of the children," Alvin Malnik, a lawyer and onetime financial adviser to Mr. Jackson.

Mrs. Jackson is in a delicate legal position. The trust contains a "no contest" clause, which typically means that if a beneficiary unsuccessfully challenges the will's validity, that person no longer can receive any benefit from the trust.

For that reason, L. Londell McMillan, the lawyer for Mrs. Jackson, did not challenge the will directly, but raised only issues of potential professional conflicts.

"We feel that we can all work together," he said. "But to turn over the keys of the kingdom to people we haven't determined have proper ability to oversee such a large estate, as well as not to be certain there is not a subsequent will, we felt it better to put responsibility in the hands of Mrs. Katherine Jackson."

5. *Same–Sex Relationships.* As of this writing, marriage—with its attendant intestate succession rights—is available to same-sex couples in Massachusetts, New Hampshire, Connecticut, Iowa, Vermont and the District of Columbia. Several other states recognize same-sex marriages performed elsewhere. In a number of other states, same-sex partners can acquire intestate succession rights by registering as domestic partners or entering into a "civil union." See, e.g., N.J. Stat. 3B:5–3 and N.J. Stat. 26:8A–4; Haw. Rev. Stat. 560:2–102; 15 Vt. Stat. Ann. 1204(e); 18–A Me Rev. Stat. § 2–102; 22 Me Rev. Stat. § 2710. Although California recognized same-sex marriages for a brief time, those marriages were banned by Constitutional amendment in 2008. The legitimacy of the Constitutional amendment is being challenged in federal courts, and the case may finally be resolved by the United States Supreme Court. In the meantime, California allows same-sex couples (and any couple if one person is over age 62) to register as domestic partners and to qualify for the same intestate succession rights as spouses. See Cal. Family Code § 297(b)(5); Cal. Prob. Code § 6401. A recent, rather unique Colorado statute authorizes any two individuals to designate each other as the beneficiary of the other for inheritance purposes. Colo. Rev. Stat. §§ 15–22–101–15–22–112.

A number of scholars have suggested that state legislatures should extend intestate succession rights even to partners who have taken no steps to formalize their relationships. See T. P. Gallanis, Inheritance Rights for Domestic Partners, 79 Tul. L. Rev. 55 (2004); E. Gary Spitko, An Accrual/Multi–Factor Approach to Intestate Inheritance Rights for Unmarried Committed Partners, 81 Oregon L. Rev. 255 (2002). For a general discussion of inheritance by domestic partners, see Raymond C. O'Brien, Domestic Partnership: Recognition and Responsibility, 32 San Diego L. Rev. 163 (1995). For arguments that domestic partnership statutes should expressly provide for inheritance by domestic partners, see E. Gary Spitko, The Expressive Function of Succession Law and the Merits of Non–Marital Exclusion, 41 Ariz. L. Rev. 1063, 1068 (1999); Susan N. Gary, Adapting Intestacy Laws to Changing Families, 18 Law & Ineq. J. 1 (2000). See also Frances H. Foster, The Family Paradigm of Inheritance Law, 80 N. Car. L. Rev. 200, 254–57 (2001); Charles Patrick Schwartz, Comment: Thy Will Be Not Done: Why States Should Amend Their Probate Codes to Allow An Intestate Share For Unmarried Homosexual Couples, 7 Conn. Pub. Int. L. J. 289 (2008). And one scholar has argued that spouses in polygamous marriages should be entitled to intestate succession benefits for policy reasons, even though polygamy is not legal in any state. See Michèle Alexandre, Lessons From Islamic Polygamy: A Case For Expanding the American Concept of Surviving Spouse So As To Include De Facto Polygamous Spouses, 64 Wash. & Lee L. Rev. 1461 (2007).

6. *The Problem of the Transgendered Spouse.* Suppose a person elects to have surgery to change gender, and then marries. One might assume that the transgendered spouse would have the same legal rights as any spouse. Yet in Estate of Gardiner, 273 Kan. 191, 42 P.3d 120 (2002), the Kansas Supreme Court held that the marriage between a male and a male-to-female transsexual was void under Kansas law, and that the transsexual was not entitled to inherit from her husband by intestate succession. Were any intestate succession policies served by the court's decision, which permitted decedent's estranged son to inherit his estate?

SECTION III. THE SHARE OF LINEAL DESCENDANTS

When an intestate decedent is not survived by a spouse, decedent's lineal descendants (assuming decedent has lineal descendants) generally succeed to the entire estate. When an intestate decedent is survived by a spouse, the lineal descendants succeed to that portion of the estate which does not pass to the surviving spouse. But in what proportions do those lineal descendants share in the estate? That is the question to which we now turn.

Consider the following family tree:

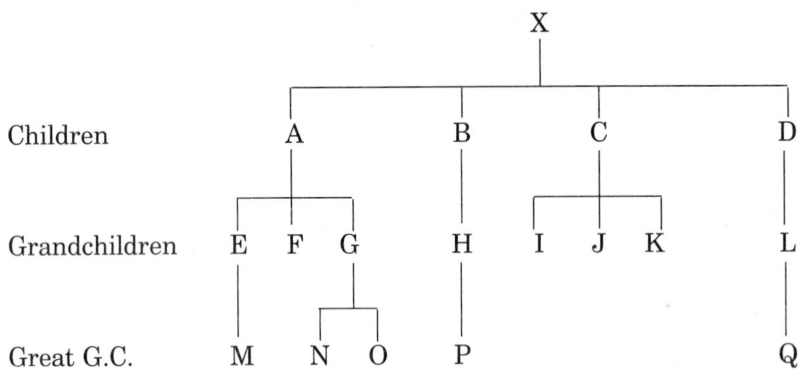

Assume that X is the decedent, who has just died intestate, and without a surviving spouse. Assume that all of the rest of the persons depicted on the diagram are lineal descendants of X—children, grandchildren, and great-grandchildren. Let us consider how X's estate should be distributed.

A first principle of intestate succession is that any living descendant of the decedent cuts off the right of the descendant's own children to inherit. That is, if a decedent is survived by a child, that child's children—decedent's grandchildren—do not take by intestate succession. So, in the family tree depicted above, if A, B, C, and D are alive at X's death, they will share X's estate, to the exclusion of all of X's grandchildren and great-grandchildren. And, of course, A, B, C, and D will share equally in X's estate: one-quarter each.

Suppose, however, one of decedent's children—let's say D—has died before X. How should X's estate now be distributed? Under virtually any intestate succession scheme, D's child, here L, would succeed to D's share. X's other grandchildren—E, F, G, H, I, J, and K—would still take nothing, because their parents are still alive. And L's child Q would, of course, be entitled to nothing because his parent L is alive.

Suppose now that X survived not only D, but all of his children. How should X's estate now be distributed? At this point, statutes differ significantly in their approach. There are two alternatives:

1. ***Strict "Per Stirpes" Distribution.*** The approach taken by the English Statute of Distributions would divide X's estate at the generation of children—the generation closest to the decedent—whether or not any children were actually living at X's death. Then, the descendants of X's children would take their parents share "by stocks," or "per stirpes." Returning to our family tree, if A, B, C, and D all predeceased X, the estate would be divided into four shares, one for each child. E, F, and G would share A's one-quarter interest in the estate; I, J, and K would share C's one-quarter interest. H and L, as their parents' only children, would each take their parent's share—one-quarter of X's estate. X's eight grandchildren would take significantly different shares of X's estate.

What can be said in favor of a strict per stirpes distribution? Its principal advantage is that it gives descendants the same shares they would have received if the order of deaths in the family had been more "normal."

That is, if A, B, C, and D had survived X, the children would have taken equal shares, and B and D, who each had only one child, would most likely have had more of X's estate to pass on to their children at their own deaths. By contrast, at the death of A and C, if they had any portion of X's estate to pass on to their children, they would have had to divide that share among a larger group of children.

Note, however, that the case for a strict per stirpes distribution rests on a number of questionable assumptions: first, that there is a "normal" death order; second, that X's children would not consume their share of X's estate during their own lifetimes, and third, that the children would in fact leave their shares of X's estate to their own children.

2. *"Modern Per Stirpes" Distribution.* The vast majority of American states have abandoned the strict per stirpes distribution in favor of what has sometimes been called a "modern per stirpes" distribution. These states divide decedent's property *at the closest generation to the decedent in which there is at least one descendant living*. Returning to our hypothetical family tree, if A, B, C, and D had all died before X, we would divide X's estate at the generation of grandchildren—the closest generation in which at least one descendant is still alive. Here, assuming all of the grandchildren are alive at X's death, we would divide the estate into eight shares, and give one share to each of the eight grandchildren—E, F, G, H, I, J, K, and L.

Suppose one of the grandchildren—for example, G—had died before X. A modern per stirpes distribution would still divide the estate into eight shares, give seven of those shares to the surviving grandchildren, and divide the eighth share between G's children, N and O. By comparison, consider how the estate would be divided, on the same facts, if the jurisdiction used a strict per stirpes distribution.

* * *

PROBLEMS AND QUESTIONS

1. Read each of the statutory excerpts below and determine whether they describe a strict or modern per stirpes distribution scheme.

WYOMING STATUTES

SECTION 2–4–101 (2010)

* * *

(c) Except in cases above enumerated, the estate of any intestate shall descend and be distributed as follows:

> **(i)** To his children surviving, and the descendents of his children who are dead, the descendents collectively taking the share which their parents would have taken if living;

PENNSYLVANIA STATUTES

SECTION 2104. RULES OF SUCCESSION

The provisions of this chapter shall be applied to both real and personal estate in accordance with the following rules:

(1) TAKING IN DIFFERENT DEGREES.—The shares passing under this chapter to the issue of the decedent, to the issue of his parents or grandparents or to his uncles or aunts or to their children, or grandchildren, shall pass to them as follows: The part of the estate passing to any such persons shall be divided into as many equal shares as there shall be persons in the nearest degree of consanguinity to the decedent living and taking shares therein and persons in that degree who have died before the decedent and have left issue to survive him who take shares therein. One equal share shall pass to each such living person in the nearest degree and one equal share shall pass by representation to the issue of each such deceased person, except that no issue of a child of an uncle or aunt of the decedent shall be entitled to any share of the estate unless there be no relatives as close as a child of an uncle or aunt living and taking a share therein, in which case the grandchildren of uncles and aunts of the decedent shall be entitled to share, but no issue of a grandchild of an uncle or aunt shall be entitled to any share of the estate.

(2) TAKING IN SAME DEGREE.—When the persons entitled to take under this chapter other than as a surviving spouse are all in the same degree of consanguinity to the decedent, they shall take in equal shares.

2. Which distribution scheme—strict per stirpes or modern per stirpes—better reflects the intent of most decedents? Which would you prefer for your own estate? Which do you think your parents would prefer? Surveys suggest that most people prefer the modern per stirpes distribution. See, e.g., Mary Louise Fellows et al., An Empirical Study of the Illinois Statutory Estate Plan, 1976 U. Ill. L. F. 717.

The Uniform Probate Code's "Representation" Provision

Return to our family tree. Suppose now that two of X's children—A and B, survived decedent, but the other two, C and D, did not. Under either the strict per stirpes scheme or the modern per stirpes scheme, A, B, and L would each take one-quarter of X's estate and I, J, and K would share the remaining quarter. That is, four grandchildren of X—I, J, K, and L—would share in the estate, but they would take dramatically different shares: L would take three times as much as her cousins, I, J, and K.

Professor Lawrence Waggoner, who later became the Chief Reporter for the Uniform Probate Code, found this result troubling. See Lawrence W. Waggoner, A Proposed Alternative to the Uniform Probate Code's System for Intestate Distribution Among Descendants, 66 Nw. U. L. Rev. 626 (1971). Why, Waggoner asked, should the shares of I, J, K, and L be equal if their aunts, A and B, had died before X, but unequal if the aunts had survived X? In Waggoner's view, all grandchildren who are entitled to share in X's estate (those whose parents died before X) should take the same share. The 1990 version of the Uniform Probate Code endorsed Waggoner's approach, which is often called distribution *per capita at each generation.* ("Per capita" means "by head;" that is, each person takes a share in her own right, not as a representative of her parents.) This distribution scheme is embodied in section 2–106. Note, however, that this scheme is included in a provision entitled "Representation." Labels can be confusing. The word "representation" under the Uniform Probate Code does not have the same meaning as in the Pennsylvania statute. Make sure you understand the difference. Similarly, statutes often use the term "per stirpes" to refer to either strict or modern per stirpes. The lesson is that one must always carefully read the applicable intestacy statute.

SECTION 2–106. REPRESENTATION.

(a) [Definitions.] In this section:

(1) 'Deceased descendant,' 'deceased parent,' or 'deceased grandparent' means a descendant, parent, or grandparent who either predeceased the decedent or is deemed to have predeceased the decedent under Section 2–104.

(2) 'Surviving descendant' means a descendant who neither predeceased the decedent nor is deemed to have predeceased the decedent under Section 2–104.

(b) [Decedent's Descendants.] If, under Section 2–103(1), a decedent's intestate estate or a part thereof passes 'by representation' to the decedent's descendants, the estate or part thereof is divided into as many equal shares as there are (i) surviving descendants in the generation nearest to the decedent which contains one or more surviving descendants and (ii) deceased descendants in the same generation who left surviving descendants, if any. Each surviving descendant in the nearest generation is allocated one share. The remaining shares, if any, are combined and then divided in the same manner among the surviving descendants of the deceased descendants as if the surviving descendants who were allocated a share and their surviving descendants had predeceased the decedent.

(c) [Descendants of Parents or Grandparents.] If, under Section 2–103(3) or (4), a decedent's intestate estate or a part thereof passes 'by representation' to the descendants of the decedent's deceased parents or either of them or to the descendants of the decedent's deceased paternal or maternal grandparents or either of them, the estate or part thereof is divided into as many equal shares as there are (i) surviving descendants in the generation nearest the deceased parents or either of them, or the deceased grandparents or either of them, that contains one or more surviving descendants and (ii) deceased descendants in the same generation who left surviving descendants, if any. Each surviving descendant in the nearest generation is allocated one share. The remaining shares, if any, are combined and then divided in the same manner among the surviving descendants of the deceased descendants as if the surviving descendants who were allocated a share and their surviving descendants had predeceased the decedent.

* * *

Note that section 2–106(b) applies expressly to the shares of decedent's descendants; section 2–106(c) makes comparable provision for the share of collateral heirs.

Let's examine the statute in operation.

> ***Example 4:*** *Return again to our family tree. Assume this time that A, B, D, G, and H died before X, and that the remainder of X's descendants survived X. If the UPC is in force, how should X's estate be distributed?*
>
> ***Solution:*** *UPC section 2–106(b) tells us to start by dividing X's estate into as many shares as there are (i) surviving descendants in the generation nearest to the decedent which contains one or more surviving descendants and (ii) deceased descendants in the same generation who left surviving descendants. In this case, the closest generation with surviving descendants is the generation of X's children—because one child, C, survived X. So we add the number of descendants in that generation—one—to the number of deceased descendants who left surviving descendants—three—to obtain a total of four shares. The statute tells us to distribute one of the four shares to C.*
>
> *What do we do with the remaining three shares, representing three quarters of X's estate? We recombine them, and then distribute them as if C had predeceased X leaving no descendants. In that event, the nearest generation to X with a living member would have been grandchildren. We take the number of living members of that generation—three (E, F, and L)—and add to that the number of deceased members who left surviving descendants—two (G and H)—for a total of five shares. We then divide the 3/4 of the estate left after distribution to C, and give one share each to E, F, and L: each takes 1/5 of the 3/4 or a total of 3/20 of the estate. We still have two shares left: 6/20, or 3/10 of the estate. What do we do with that portion of the estate? We go through the same process again, dividing equally among N, O, and P, each of whom takes 1/10 of the estate.*

The Uniform Probate Code's representation scheme—although a significant break with tradition—has gained adherents even among states which have not adopted the Code wholesale. See N.Y. E.P.T.L. § 1–2.16.

PROBLEMS

In each of the following situations, how would X's $120,000 estate be distributed (a) under the Wyoming statute; (b) under the Pennsylvania statute; (c) under the Uniform Probate Code, and (d) under the intestate succession statute of your state, assuming that X's descendants are those depicted on the following family tree.

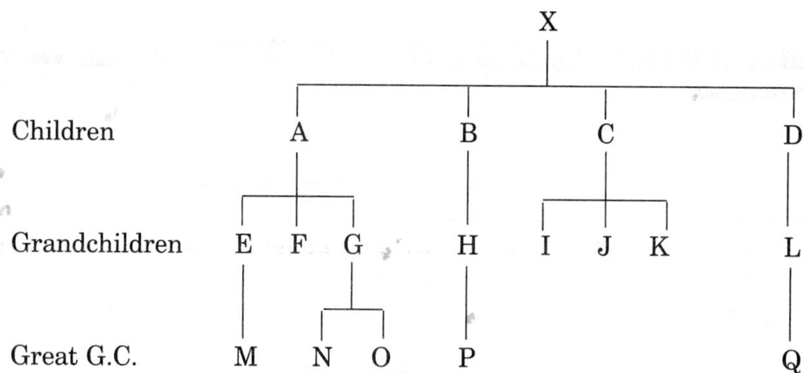

Situation 1: A, B, C, D, G, and L have died before X.

Situation 2: A, E, F, and G have died before X.

Situation 3: A, B, C, G, and H have died before X.

Situation 4: A, B, C, D, F, H, and P have died before X.

In each situation, assume that all descendants of X—other than those explicitly listed—survived X.

NOTE: CONDUCT-BASED BARS TO INHERITANCE

Some U.S. scholars have argued that conduct should—and sometimes does—play an important role in intestacy proceedings. See Ann-Marie Rhodes, On Inheritance and Disinheritance, 43 Real Prop. Tr. & Est. L.J. 433 (2008). You have already been introduced to one such conduct-based rule—the slayer rule, which bars heirs from inheriting from those they have killed. Should an heir who has abandoned or abused the decedent be similarly barred? For example, suppose decedent's father failed to pay child support and severely physically abused decedent during visits. Should decedent's father nonetheless be entitled to a portion of decedent's estate if he is an heir under the state intestacy statute? Absent express statutory authorization, most courts have been reluctant to craft a judicial rule barring inheritance in such circumstances. As one court put it,

> We cannot ... extinguish the right to inherit as an heir from the decedent's estate. To do so would run contrary to the directive from our Supreme Court that [the intestacy statute] "must be limited in strict accordance with the statutory language used therein, and such language can never be extended beyond its plain and ordinary meaning." (citations omitted). Thus, while we are sympathetic we cannot cloak ourselves with the power to make policy decisions that are otherwise reserved for our legislature and regarding which the legislature has remained silent.

Blackstone v. Blackstone, 282 Ga.App. 515, 517–18, 639 S.E.2d 369 (2006); See also, In re Rogiers, 396 N.J.Super. 317, 933 A.2d 971 (2007); In re Estate of Shellenbarger, 169 Cal.App.4th 894, 86 Cal.Rptr.3d 862 (2008).

Occasionally, a court faced with particularly egregious facts may not be so restrained. For example, in New Jersey Division of Youth and Family

Services v. M.W., 398 N.J.Super. 266, 942 A.2d 1 (App. Div. 2008) the court took the unusual step of terminating a mother's intestate right to inherit her son's estate—an estate funded by a million dollar judgment against the state agency charged with protecting children from child abuse. The court stated:

> How cruel, ironic, and inequitable it would be to hold that M.W. retained the right to inherit $1 million from the child she burned, abused, neglected, and abandoned. Equity, morality, and common sense dictate that physically or sexually abusive parents have no right of inheritance by intestacy. The contrary result would bespeak a thoughtless jurisprudence warranting public disrespect. The applicable principle of equity is that "equity will not suffer a wrong without a remedy." (citation omitted).

Id. at 295.

Several state legislatures have enacted statutes expressly authorizing a court to terminate intestacy rights if the heir has abandoned, abused or failed to support a child or spouse. See, e.g., E.P.T.L. 4–1.4 & 5–1.2 (New York); R.C. 2105.10 (Ohio); and KRS 391.033 and 411.137 (Kentucky); See also UPC 2–114 (2008) (directing that "A parent is barred from inheriting from or through a minor child of the parent if there is clear and convincing evidence that immediately before the child's death the parental rights of the parent could have been terminated on the basis of nonsupport, abandonment, abuse, neglect, or other actions or inactions of the parent toward the child"). What is the justification for these statutes? Is the principal aim to effectuate intent, to punish undeserving heirs, or something else? See generally, Anne–Marie E. Rhodes, Abandoning Parents Under Intestacy: Where We Are, Where We Need to Go, 27 Ind. L. Rev. 517 (1994); Paula A. Monopoli, "Deadbeat Dads:" Should Support and Inheritance be Linked?, 49 U. Miami L. Rev. 257 (1994), Richard Lewis Brown, Undeserving Heirs? The Case of the "Terminated Parent," 40 U. Rich. L. Rev. 547 (2006).

Professor Kelly–Hill argues that fault-based statutes are misguided, at least when it comes to spousal rights:

> [I]t may seem unduly harsh to impose the duty of securing divorce or legal separation upon an aggrieved party.... [But r]equiring a legal termination of marriage or separation is the only nonintrusive measure that recognizes that marital privacy is to be protected both during life and at death. No exceptions should be made for the harmed individual who obtains a legal separation that does not terminate property rights, initiates a divorce action but dies before the divorce is finalized, or merely has sufficient grounds for legal separation or divorce. States that have adopted such lesser standards have created "black holes" that can make a surviving spouse ineligible for probate rights because sufficient grounds for divorce exist and, tragically, also ineligible for a property award pursuant to the divorce proceedings because the divorce was not decreed at the time of the decedent's death.

Linda Kelly–Hill, No–Fault Death: Wedding Inheritance Rights to Family Values, 94 Ky. Law J. 319, 354–55 (2005).

SECTION IV. THE SHARE OF ANCESTORS AND COLLATERAL HEIRS

As we have seen, when an intestate decedent has surviving descendants, those descendants almost always take to the exclusion of ancestors and collateral heirs. Many decedents, however, die without surviving descendants. How should their estates be distributed?

Most intestate succession statutes give preference to decedent's parents over collateral relatives. Typically, the parents share equally if both survive. The Uniform Probate Code is illustrative. What these statutes have in mind is the all-too-common situation in which a relatively young person, who has not taken the time to make a will, unexpectedly dies. If that person has not married, and has no children, her parents are likely to be the principal objects of her bounty. In some jurisdictions, however, siblings share equally with parents. See, e.g., 755 Ill. L.C.S. 5/2–1(d). Professor Scalise argues, from empirical evidence, that most decedents would prefer sharing between siblings and parents, a result rejected by the Uniform Probate Code. See Ronald J. Scalise, Jr., Honor Thy Father and Mother?: How Intestacy Law Goes Too Far in Protecting Parents, 37 Seton Hall L. Rev. 171, 189 (2006)

The more difficult problems arise when an intestate decedent is not survived by parents. Generally, as we have seen, descendants of parents (brothers, sisters, and their descendants) take to the exclusion of other collateral relatives. If there are no descendants of parents, descendants of grandparents (uncles, aunts, first cousins, and their descendants) take to the exclusion of descendants of more remote ancestors. The UPC is an example of this type of system, termed a "parentelic" system.

Suppose the living descendants of decedent's parents are people of different generations. For example, suppose decedent is survived by two brothers, and by three nieces—descendants of deceased sisters. How should decedent's estate be distributed? In a parentelic system, the same principles we examined in connection with decedent's lineal descendants are generally applicable with collaterals as well: we would divide the estate into as many shares as decedent has siblings, and give each surviving sibling a share. Descendants of deceased siblings would also share in the estate; precisely how much they would take would depend on whether the state statute mandates a per stirpes distribution (strict or modern) or, instead, a "representation," like the one in UPC § 2–106, that provides for distribution per capita at each generation.

In a system that adopts a "degree of relationship" approach, the estate is distributed to decedent's "next of kin" as defined by the Table of Consanguinity. Consider the following statute:

MASSACHUSETTS GENERAL LAWS, CH. 190B

SECTION 2–103. SHARE OF HEIRS OTHER THAN SURVIVING SPOUSE. [Effective July 1, 2011].

Any part of the intestate estate not passing to the decedent's surviving spouse under section 2–102, or the entire intestate estate if there is no surviving spouse, passes in the following order to the individuals designated below who survive the decedent:

(1) to the decedent's descendants per capita at each generation;

(2) if there is no surviving descendant, to the decedent's parents equally if both survive, or to the surviving parent;

(3) if there is no surviving descendant or parent, to the descendants of the decedent's parents or either of them per capita at each generation;

(4) if there is no surviving descendant, parent, or descendant of a parent, then equally to the decedent's next of kin in equal degree; but if there are 2 or more descendants of deceased ancestors in equal degree claiming through different ancestors, those claiming through the nearest ancestor shall be preferred to those claiming through an ancestor more remote. Degrees of kindred shall be computed according to the rules of civil law.

PROBLEM

Decedent, X, died unmarried, childless, and intestate. X's probate estate has a value of $300,000. His family tree is as follows:

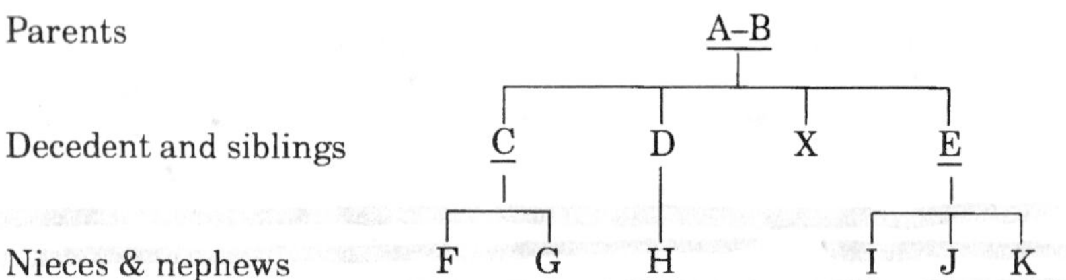

Assume that all underlined individuals died before X. How would X's estate be distributed (a) under the Massachusetts statute? (b) under the Uniform Probate Code? (c) under the intestate succession statute of your state?

* * *

As we have seen, when decedent is survived by descendants, issue of deceased descendants always take, no matter how many generations remote from testator. With collateral descendants, however, many statutes cut off the right to take by stocks at some point. That is, if decedent's closest living relative is a first cousin, and decedent is also survived by descendants of six deceased first cousins, some statutes would give the entire estate to the living first cousin *per capita*—in her own right—and not permit a distribution *per stirpes* to descendants of deceased first cousins. Sometimes, the statutes which cut off the right to take by representation are clear; sometimes they are not, and litigation results. Consider the following case:

Estate of Locke

Supreme Court of New Hampshire, 2002.
148 N.H. 754, 813 A.2d 1172.

■ BRODERICK, J. The appellants, Jean Barber and Marion Hayes, appeal the decision of the Merrimack County Probate Court (O'Neill, J.) determining the heirs of the estate of Geraldine M. Locke under RSA 561:1, II(d) (1997). We affirm.

The relevant facts are not in dispute. Geraldine M. Locke died intestate on September 23, 1999. At her death, Locke had no spouse, children or siblings; her parents and her maternal and paternal grandparents were deceased. Locke's nearest kin, the descendants of her maternal and paternal grandparents, were as follows. On her maternal grandparent side, Locke was survived by Barber and Hayes, both of whom are first cousins of the decedent (fourth degree of kinship to the decedent). On her paternal grandparent side, Locke was survived by the appellees, Ann Stackpole de Pasquale, Carl Stackpole, Frank Stackpole, and Raelene E. Davis Hale, all of whom are first cousins once removed of the decedent (fifth degree of kinship to the decedent). Subsequent to Locke's death, the administratrix of the estate filed a petition for determination of heirs. After a hearing, the probate court ruled that under RSA 561:1, II(d), the appellees were entitled to a distribution of one-half of Locke's estate, that they took equally as to the one-half share of the estate, and that RSA 561:3 (1997) did not preclude them from sharing in the estate as they did not take by representation. This appeal followed.

The appellants argue that RSA 561:1, II(d) and RSA 561:3 provide that first cousins (fourth degree) are entitled to the entire estate to the exclusion of first cousins once removed (fifth degree), because no representation is allowed to collaterals beyond the fourth degree.

* * *

RSA 561:1, II(d) reads:

If there is no surviving issue, parent or issue of a parent but the decedent is survived by one or more grandparents or issue of grandparents, half of the estate passes to the paternal grandparents if both survive, or to the surviving paternal grandparent, or to the issue of the paternal grandparents if both are deceased, the issue taking equally if they are all of the same degree of kinship to the decedent, but if of unequal degree those of more remote degree take by representation; and the other half passes to the maternal relatives in the same manner; but if there be no surviving grandparent or issue of grandparent on either the paternal or the maternal side, the entire estate passes to the relatives on the other side in the same manner as the half.

RSA 561:3 reads:

> No representation shall be allowed among collaterals beyond the fourth degree of relationship to the decedent.

> The statute clearly and unambiguously states that if the decedent has no surviving issue, parent or issue of a parent, but is survived by the issue of grandparents on both the paternal and maternal sides, half of the estate passes to the issue of the paternal grandparents if both paternal grandparents are deceased, while the remaining half of the estate passes to the issue of the maternal grandparents if both maternal grandparents are deceased.

Here, after the estate is properly divided into halves, the statute unambiguously provides for the further independent distribution of each half. Specifically, the issue of the paternal grandparents share equally in one-half of the estate if the issue are all of the same degree of kinship to the decedent. RSA 561:1, II(d). Only if the issue of the paternal grandparents are of unequal degree of kinship do those issue of more remote degree take by representation. Id. In addition, the statute provides for the other half of the estate to pass to the maternal relatives in the same manner, i.e., the issue of the maternal grandparents share equally in one-half of the estate if the issue are all of the same degree of kinship to the decedent.

The appellants contend that a correct reading of the statute, in conjunction with the limitation of representation to the fourth degree of kinship in RSA 561:3, would have us compare the degree of kinship between the issue of the paternal and maternal grandparents and distribute the entire estate to whichever issue have the closer degree of kinship to the decedent. Here, such a reading would favor the issue of the maternal grandparents, as they are first cousins and not first cousins once removed. Such a reading, however, ignores the clear statutory mandate that under such circumstances as exist in this case, the estate is first divided into equal halves. The statute then provides direction for the distribution of each half in turn. We decline to ignore the statutory mandate.

In addition, distribution of the estate based upon a comparison of the degree of kinship between the issue of the paternal and maternal grandparents and the limitation of RSA 561:3 could often result in the entire estate being distributed to either the paternal or maternal side. Only if the degree of kinship on both the paternal and maternal sides is equal would an equal distribution be made. Such a reading, however, would render the final clause of RSA 561:1, II(d) (providing for the entire estate to pass to one side when there are no surviving issue of grandparents on the other side) superfluous in such cases. The legislature is presumed not to have used superfluous words. See Binda v. Royal Ins. Co., 144 N.H. 613, 616, 744 A.2d 634 (2000).

The appellants further contend that by reading RSA 561:1, II(d) and RSA 561:3 together, the term "representation" is defined in a manner which prohibits the first cousins once removed from taking in this case. Specifically, the appellants contend that representation applies to the issue of the paternal and maternal grandparents as a single group, and that representation beyond the fourth degree of kinship to the decedent is prohibited. Consequently, the appellants argue that if the first cousins once removed were to share in the estate, it would be pursuant to representation, but because representation is prohibited beyond the fourth degree of kinship, they cannot share. We disagree.

"Representation" is not defined in either RSA 561:1, II(d) or RSA 561:3. We need not define "representation" here, however, as it is not implicated in this case. While "representation" appears once in RSA 561:1, II(d), it is pertinent only with regard to each half of the estate. If the issue of the paternal grandparents are of unequal degree of kinship, then those issue of more remote degree take a share of the half estate by representation. The same holds true if the issue of the maternal grandparents are of unequal degree of kinship. In the instant case, however, the issue of the maternal grandparents are all of the same degree of kinship (fourth degree) and the issue of the paternal grandparents are all of the same degree of kinship (fifth degree). To say that representation applies to the difference in degree of kinship between the first cousins and the first cousins once removed ignores the clear statutory mandate to split the estate into equal halves and the clear statutory direction for the further independent distribution of each half.

With regard to the distribution of each half of the estate, the claimants are all related to Locke in equal degree. Both appellants are first cousins and they share equally in one-half of the estate. The four appellees are all first cousins once removed and they share equally in one-half of the estate. On each respective side, no individuals of either closer or more remote degree of kinship survive and, therefore, representation is not pertinent. As there are no other living issue with a closer degree of kinship to the maternal or paternal grandparents, respectively, both the first cousins and the first cousins once removed are themselves principals, and they "stand next in degree to [Locke] in their own right, and not by right of representation." Preston v. Cole, 64 N.H. 459, 460, 13 A. 788 (1887). Accordingly, "they take per capita, representation not being necessary to prevent the exclusion of those in a remoter degree." Id. at 459. In sum, the first cousins once removed take in their own right and their degree of kinship is not placed on a scale to be weighed against that of the first cousins.

The appellants also contend there is nothing in RSA 561:3 that restricts its limitation on representation to only one-half of an estate. Their argument fails to acknowledge, however, that RSA 561:1, II(d), and not RSA 561:3, provides a limitation on the applicability of representation, and that the former statute refers to representation only within the context of one-half of an estate.

The appellants rely heavily on legislative history to advance their argument that RSA 561:1, II(d) and RSA 561:3, when read together, define "representation" in a manner which prohibits the first cousins once removed from taking in this case. While legislative history may be helpful in the interpretation of an ambiguous statute, it will not be consulted when the statutory language is plain. Petition of Walker, 138 N.H. 471, 474, 641 A.2d 1021 (1994). "Given the plain language of the statute, we need not delve further in order to glean legislative intent." Appeal of Boucher, 148 N.H. 458, 808 A.2d 537, 539 (2002). The language of RSA 561:1, II(d), as it applies in this case, clearly and unambiguously provides for a division of the estate into two equal halves and for the further independent distribution of each half. If the legislature had intended that either the paternal or maternal side take the entire estate to the exclusion of the other, based upon a comparison of each side's degree of kinship and the limitation of representation in RSA 561:3, it could have declared so in the language of the statute. "It is not for us to put words into the statute . . . where the legislature has chosen not to do so, and it is for the legislature to adjust the statute if it so desires." Id.

Affirmed.

NOTES AND QUESTIONS

1. The New Hampshire intestate succession statute, like many but not all intestate succession statutes, provides that when a decedent is survived only by grandparents or descendants of grandparents, half of the estate passes to issue of paternal grandparents and the other half passes to the issue of maternal grandparents. Note, however, that this preference for equal division does not apply in other instances. Suppose, for instance, decedent's maternal grandparents had multiple marriages, and decedent was the only descendant of both his maternal grandfather and maternal grandmother. Decedent's maternal grandfather had six children other than decedent's mother, while his maternal grandmother had only one child other than decedent's mother. The New Hampshire statute does not provide that descendants of the maternal grandfather share equally with descendants of the maternal grandmother. The situation also arises when decedent's mother and father have had offspring by other spouses; again no intestate succession statute requires equal sharing between the descendants of decedent's mother and the descendants of decedent's father.

In light of the failure to require equal sharing in these instances, does the New Hampshire statute requiring equal division between descendants of maternal grandparents and descendants of paternal grandparents make sense? Note that the Uniform Probate Code includes a comparable provision.

2. Geraldine Locke was survived on her mother's side by two first cousins. Suppose one of those first cousins had died before Geraldine, leaving two children who survived Geraldine. How would the maternal half of Geraldine's estate have been distributed?

Suppose, instead, that Geraldine was survived on her mother's side by her mother's brother and by two daughters of the mother's deceased sister. How would the maternal half of her estate have been distributed? Is the table of consanguinity helpful in explaining why representation is available in one situation and not the other?

What reason is there to provide for representation in some instances, but not in others? Note that in most states, if the intestate succession statute precludes representation, it does so only with respect to more distant collateral relatives.

3. How would the Locke case have been decided under the Massachusetts statute? Under the Uniform Probate Code? Under the intestate succession statute of your state?

PROBLEMS

1. Consider the following family tree. Assume that X is the decedent, D is her mother, E is her father, A and R are her maternal grandparents, and F and Q are her paternal grandparents. Assume that X died unmarried and childless, and assume further that all underlined individuals have predeceased X. How would X's estate be distributed according to the Massachusetts statute? The UPC? The intestate succession statute of your state?

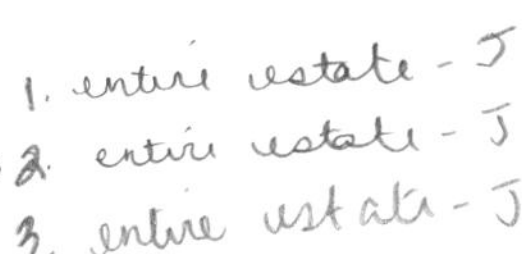

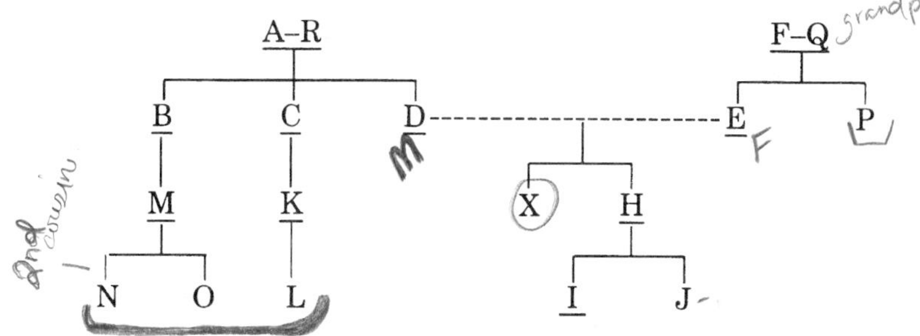

2. Assume the same facts as Problem 1, except that J also died before X. How would X's estate be distributed?

3. Assume the same facts as Problem 1, except that J and P also died before X. How would X's estate be distributed?

4. Assume the same facts as Problem 3, except that K survived X. How would X's estate be distributed?

5. In the family tree above, suppose now that L died intestate, survived only by X (that is, assume all of the other family members listed had died before L). Would X be entitled to take L's estate? Why or why not?

NOTE ON ESCHEAT

When decedent dies intestate and without heirs, the estate typically escheats to the state, or to a governmental entity designated by statute. In Maryland, for instance, estates escheat to the local school district. Cf. Board of Education of Montgomery County v. Browning, 333 Md. 281, 635 A.2d 373 (1994).

Courts often strain to avoid escheat—despite the advent of "laughing heir" statutes. Estate of Brunel, 135 N.H. 83, 600 A.2d 123 (1991) furnishes an example. Decedent died intestate, leaving second cousins as her closest living relatives. New Hampshire had adopted an intestacy statute derived from the Uniform Probate Code, a statute which provided for inheritance only through issue of grandparents. Second cousins, of course, are issue of great-grandparents. Another New Hampshire statute, predating the UPC, but not repealed by the UPC, provided that "[i]f there be no heir, legatee, or devisee of an estate ... the same shall accrue to the state." The court held that because second cousins had been entitled to inherit before introduction of the UPC provision, they still qualified as "heirs!"

SECTION V. INTESTATE SUCCESSION AND COMMUNITY PROPERTY STATES

Eight states (Arizona, California, Idaho, Louisiana, Nevada, New Mexico, Texas and Washington) have community property laws. Alaska has enacted a voluntary, or opt in, community property regime. Ak. Stat. § 34.77.060. For discussion, see Jonathan G. Blattmachr, Howard M. Zaritsky & Mark L. Ascher, Tax Planning with Consensual Community Property: Alaska's New Community Property Law, 33 Real Prop. Prob. & Tr. L. J. 615 (1999). Wisconsin has enacted the Uniform Marital Property Act which contains many basic principles of Community Property. Wis. Stat. Ann. §§ 766.001 et seq. For discussion of the Uniform Marital Property Act, see Kathy T. Graham, The Uniform Marital Property Act: A Solution for Common Law Property Systems? 48 S.D. L. Rev. 455 (2003); William Reppy, The Uniform Marital Property Act: Some Suggested Revisions for a Basically Sound Act, 21 Hous. L. Rev. 679 (1984); Ronald R. Volkmer, Spousal Property Rights at Death: Re-evaluation of the Common Law Premises in Light of the Proposed Uniform Marital Property Act, 17 Creighton L. Rev. 95 (1983/84).

There are considerable variations in detail among the community property states. For instance, Arizona has recently authorized a hybrid form of ownership known as "community property with right of survivorship." See generally James R. Ratner, Community Property, Right of Survivorship, and Separate Property Contributions to Marital Assets: An Interplay, 41 Ariz. L. Rev. 993 (1999).

The community property system, which comes from the civil law, assumes that property acquired during marriage (other than by gift or inheritance) is the product of joint efforts of the husband and wife. Each, therefore, has a half share. Property acquired before marriage or by gift or inheritance is the separate property of the respective spouse.

Each spouse has a power of testamentary disposition only over his or her half of the community property. If the first spouse to die fails to make a will, all of her separate property and her "half" of the community property will be distributed in accordance with the intestacy statute. Consider the following statute:

REVISED CODE OF WASHINGTON

SECTION 11.04.015. DESCENT AND DISTRIBUTION OF REAL AND PERSONAL ESTATE.

The net estate of a person dying intestate, or that portion thereof with respect to which the person shall have died intestate, shall descend subject to the provisions of RCW 11.04.250 and 11.02.070, and shall be distributed as follows:

(1) Share of surviving spouse or state registered domestic partner. The surviving spouse or state registered domestic partner shall receive the following share:

(a) All of the decedent's share of the net community estate; and

(b) One-half of the net separate estate if the intestate is survived by issue; or

(c) Three-quarters of the net separate estate if there is no surviving issue, but the intestate is survived by one or more of his or her parents, or by one or more of the issue of one or more of his or her parents; or

(d) All of the net separate estate, if there is no surviving issue nor parent nor issue of parent.

(2) Shares of others than surviving spouse or state registered domestic partner. The share of the net estate not distributable to the surviving spouse or state registered domestic partner, or the entire net estate if there is no surviving spouse or state registered domestic partner, shall descend and be distributed as follows:

(a) To the issue of the intestate; if they are all in the same degree of kinship to the intestate, they shall take equally, or if of unequal degree, then those of more remote degree shall take by representation.

* * *

Note that the above statute directs different distributions for community property and separate property. As the following case demonstrates, this can give rise to some difficulties.

Estate of Borghi

Supreme Court of Washington, 2009.
167 Wn.2d 480, 219 P.3d 932.

■ STEPHENS, J.:

This case concerns a dispute between the estate of Jeanette L. Borghi (Estate) and her son, Arthur Gilroy, over the characterization of real property acquired by Jeanette Borghi prior to her marriage to Robert Borghi and subsequently titled in both Robert and Jeanette Borghi's names. At the center of this dispute are apparently conflicting presumptions—on the one hand, the well-established presumption that property acquired by a person before marriage is her separate property and, on the other hand, what has been described as a "joint title gift presumption" arising from a change in title to include both spouses' names. *See In re Marriage of Hurd*, 69 Wn. App. 38, 848 P.2d 185 (1993); Laura W. Morgan & Edward S. Snyder, *When Title Matters: Transmutation and the Joint Title Gift Presumption*, 18 J. AM. ACAD. MATRIMONIAL LAW 335 (2003)....

FACTS

Jeanette L. Borghi purchased a parcel of real property in 1966, subject to a real estate contract. The record contains no evidence concerning the terms of or payments under the contract. On March 29, 1975, Jeanette and Robert Borghi married. On July 12 of that year, Cedarview Development Company executed a special warranty deed to "Robert G. & Jeanette L. Borghi, husband and wife." Clerk's Papers at 80. The deed states that it is in fulfillment of the real estate contract.

The Borghis resided on the property from 1975 until 1990. In August 1979, they used the property to secure a mortgage to purchase a mobile home to locate on the property. The 1975 deed was recorded on August 13, 1979.

Jeanette Borghi died intestate on June 25, 2005. Her surviving heirs were Robert Borghi and Arthur Gilroy, her son from a previous marriage. Robert Borghi was appointed personal representative of Jeanette Borghi's estate and filed a petition for declaratory judgment on behalf of the Estate to determine rights in the real property.[2] The superior court commissioner determined that the property was the community property of Robert and Jeanette Borghi, and passed to Robert Borghi under the laws of intestate succession. Arthur Gilroy moved for revision of this decision, which the superior court denied. He then appealed, arguing that the property was Jeanette Borghi's separate property at the time of her death, entitling him to a one-half interest.

The Court of Appeals reversed the superior court and "reluctantly conclude[d] that the property was Mrs. Borghi's separate property." *In re Estate of Borghi*, 141 Wn. App. 294, 304, 169 P.3d 847 (2007). We granted the Estate's petition for review at 163 Wn.2d 1052, 187 P.3d 751 (2008).

ANALYSIS

The question in this case is whether the real property acquired by Jeanette Borghi prior to her marriage to Robert Borghi changed in character from her separate property to community property by the time of her death. More specifically, we must decide whether the inclusion of Robert Borghi's name on the June 12, 1975 deed created a presumption that the property had transmuted from separate to community property or, if not, whether there is sufficient evidence to overcome the underlying separate property presumption and establish an intent to change the character of the property from separate to community property.

We begin with basic principles of Washington community property law. First, presumptions play a significant role in determining the character of property as separate or community property. 19 Kenneth W. Weber, Washington Practice: Family and Community Property Law § 10.1, at 133 (1997) ("Possibly more than in any other area of law, presumptions play an

2. Robert Borghi passed away in October 2006, and Jeanette Borghi's sister now serves as the personal representative of the Estate. *In re Estate of Borghi*, 141 Wn. App. 294, 297, 169 P.3d 847 (2007).

important role in determining ownership of assets and responsibility for debt in community property law."). The presumptions are *true* presumptions, and in the absence of evidence sufficient to rebut an applicable presumption, the court must determine the character of property according to the weight of the presumption. *Id.*

Second, the character of property as separate or community property is determined at the date of acquisition. Harry M. Cross, *The Community Property Law in Washington*, 61 WASH. L. REV. 13, 39 (1986). Under the "inception of title" theory, property acquired subject to a real estate contract or mortgage is acquired when the obligation is undertaken. *Id.*; *see also In re Estate of Binge*, 5 Wn.2d 446, 105 P.2d 689 (1940); *Beam v. Beam*, 18 Wn. App. 444, 453, 569 P.2d 719 (1977). Here, the parties agree that the real property in question was Jeanette Borghi's separate property at the time she married Robert Borghi. Once the separate character of property is established, a presumption arises that it remained separate property in the absence of sufficient evidence to show an intent to transmute the property from separate to community property. 19 WEBER, *supra*, at 134. . . .

The Estate argues that clear and convincing evidence of a transfer of Jeanette Borghi's separate property to community property exists based on the inclusion of Robert Borghi's name on the deed to the property subsequent to the marriage.

* * *

. . . We have consistently refused to recognize any presumption arising from placing legal title in both spouses' names and instead adhered to the principle that the name on a deed or title does not determine the separate or community character of the property, or even provide much evidence. As we stated in *Merritt v. Newkirk*, 155 Wash. 517, 285 P. 442 (1930):

> [T]he fact in itself [(legal title)] is not of controlling moment in determining which of the spouses is the actual owner of the property.
>
> Under our somewhat perplexing statutes relating to the acquisition of property, title to real property taken in the name of one of the spouses may be the separate property of the spouse taking the title, the separate property of the other spouse, or the community property of both of the spouses, owing to the source from which the fund is derived which is used in paying the purchase price of the property.

Id. at 520–21.

The Court of Appeals lamented that this rule is poor policy, suggesting that the contrary rule in *Hurd* "appropriately protects separate property from inadvertent changes in character but allows for gifts by deed." *Borghi*, 141 Wn. App. at 303. This misapprehends the nature of the relevant presumptions. Disregarding title as relevant to the characterization of property does not hinder a party who intends to transmute her separate property into community property from doing so. With respect to real property, a spouse may execute a quitclaim deed transferring the property to the community, join in a valid community property agreement, or otherwise in writing evidence his or her intent. *See Volz*, 113 Wash. at 383; *Verbeek*, 2 Wn. App. at 158; *see generally* Cross, *supra*, at 100–03 (discussing transfers of property between spouses). But in the absence of such evidence, the name in which title is held, including a change in title, tells us nothing or is ambiguous at best. As the Court of Appeals acknowledged in this case, there is no evidence as to why Cedarview included Robert Borghi's name on the deed. *Borghi*, 141 Wn. App. at 302–04. Though it may have done so at Jeanette Borghi's direction, the form of the deed may also have been drafted at the direction of another person, or it may have been a scrivener's error. Nothing in the record answers this question.

More importantly, even when a spouse's name is included on a deed or title at the direction of the separate property owner spouse, this does not evidence an intent to transmute separate property into community property but merely an intent to put both spouses' names on the deed or title. Morgan & Snyder, *supra*, at 354–56. There are many reasons it may make good business sense for spouses to create joint title that have nothing to do with any intent to create community property. *Guye*, 63 Wash. at 353. Allowing a presumption to arise from a change in the form of title inappropriately shifts attention away from the relevant question of whether a gift of separate property to the community is intended and asks instead the irrelevant question of whether there was an intent to make a conveyance into joint title. Morgan & Snyder, *supra*, at 356 (concluding, "Community property law and equitable distribution law should adhere to the stated principle that 'title is irrelevant' and analyze the conveyance in terms of a gift, without any legal presumptions of transmutation").

Further, to apply a presumption based on a change in the name or names in which title is held would create a situation in which a court is asked to resolve an evidentiary question based on nothing more than conflicting presumptions. This case illustrates the conundrum. A court starts with the presumption that the property is Jeanette Borghi's separate property because it was acquired with her own funds before her marriage to Robert Borghi. The parties in this case agree it was initially her separate property. Then, the court must rely on the inclusion of both Robert and Jeanette Borghi's names on the 1975 deed to support a presumption that the property is community property. Applying these presumptions simultaneously, the court reaches an impasse. If we somehow reason that the community property presumption must prevail because it is later in time, then what became of the rule that clear and convincing evidence of actual intent is needed to overcome the original separate property presumption? In sum, applying a gift presumption to counter the separate property presumption in these circumstances would reduce community property principles to a game of King's X. *See* 19 WEBER, *supra*, § 10.7 n.4, at 142. We refuse to do so and instead adhere to the well-settled rule that no presumption arises from the names on a deed or title. To the extent *Hurd* and *Olivares* suggest a gift presumption arising when one spouse places the name of the other spouse on title to separate property, we disapprove these cases.

The remaining question is whether, once the erroneous joint title gift presumption is set aside, the Estate presented clear and convincing evidence that Jeanette Borghi's separate property converted to community property prior to her death. While the Court of Appeals surmised that *someone* must have apprised the vendor on the real estate contract of the desire to have both names included on the fulfillment deed, the Estate concedes this is not evidence of Jeanette Borghi's intent. Moreover, because the property at issue is real property, an acknowledged writing evidencing Jeanette Borghi's intent to transfer her property to the community was required, and no such writing is in evidence. In the absence of clear and convincing evidence to the contrary, the issue must be resolved on the weight of the presumption that the property was Jeanette Borghi's separate property.

CONCLUSION

We hold that the property acquired by Jeanette Borghi prior to her marriage to Robert Borghi was presumptively her separate property. No contrary presumption arose from the fact that a deed was later issued in the names of both spouses, and to the extent *Hurd* and *Olivares* endorse a joint title gift presumption, we disapprove these cases. Because the Estate did not present clear and convincing evidence to overcome the separate property presumption, we hold that the property in question remained Jeanette Borghi's separate property at the time of her death. We affirm the Court of Appeals.

■ ALEXANDER, C.J., and SANDERS and CHAMBERS, JJ., concur.

■ MADSEN, J. (concurring)

* * *

I write separately because the lead opinion says that only a writing may serve as evidence in determining whether Ms. Borghi intended to transform her separate real property into a community asset. Since there is no evidence, written or otherwise, bearing on the question, I do not believe this case requires us to decide what type of evidence is sufficient to overcome the separate property presumption and I would not do so.

■ OWENS, J. (dissenting)

* * *

The lead opinion contends that its rejection of the joint title presumption will not hinder spouses who intend to change separate property to community property, but it absolutely does. Any layperson would reasonably think that retitling his or her separate property in the names of both spouses would cause that property to be jointly owned. It is eminently reasonable for both members of the couple to assume that jointly titled property is thus community property. But under the lead opinion's new rule, families attempting to change the nature of their property by retitling their property will be unable to do so. Instead, families will be forced to use more complex legal forms, likely requiring legal counsel. While the lead opinion's holding may not hinder those affluent families who are able to afford adequate legal assistance, those unable to afford legal counsel will now face unreasonable legal formalities that are counter to common sense. In a day where legal assistance is sadly out of reach for many working families, this new requirement unnecessarily hinders their ability to dispose of their property without engaging in complex legal formalities.

The lead opinion also fails to address how this new rule will apply to unmarried couples in committed, intimate relationships. If one partner in a committed, intimate relationship adds the other partner to the deed of his or her separate property, is the property not considered joint property? What happens to the partner added to the deed, who likely (and reasonably) believed he or she was a joint owner of the property? The idea that this change in title "tells us nothing," ignores the reality of how many families—particularly those without access to legal counsel—organize their property. As a result, the lead opinion refuses to give legal effect to those choices. This decision gives no recourse to those partners who relied on the belief that being added to the deed would provide some protection upon dissolution of a committed, intimate relationship. Instead, the lead opinion would tell those partners they have no legal rights because they did not fill out the correct set of forms. I cannot agree with this reasoning or result....

* * *

Actions have consequences, and listing your spouse on the deed to your property should result in a presumption that you want the property to be community property. The joint titling presumption is based on simple common sense, and Washington families have relied on it for over 20 years. Reversing this policy will unnecessarily complicate the field of family law and lead to unfortunate consequences for the many families unable to afford legal counsel.

I respectfully dissent from the lead opinion.

■ C. JOHNSON, FAIRHURST, and J.M. JOHNSON, JJ., concur with OWENS, J.

NOTES AND QUESTIONS

1. What evidence was there that Jeanette L. Borghi intended to transform the disputed parcel from separate property to community property? Why wasn't this evidence sufficient to establish that she had made a gift to the community?

2. As a result of the court's decision, what steps must a spouse take to transform separate property into community property?

3. Which approach is preferable, the majority's holding or the rule suggested by the dissent? In your opinion, which rule best comports with most property owners' expectations? Which approach best advances the interests of judicial economy?

SECTION VI. DEFINING THE MODERN FAMILY: HALFBLOODS, ADOPTEES, AND NON-MARITAL CHILDREN

For many people in today's America, the family is not a simple entity composed of parents married for life and children born within the marital relationship. Instead, family may be a complex web of relationships affected by divorce, remarriage, adoption, and non-marital relationships. The changing face of the American family has had a significant impact on intestate succession law—and on estates law generally. In this section, we examine how legislatures and courts have responded to the dynamic nature of the family. For a general—and comprehensive—discussion, see Ralph C. Brashier, Children and Inheritance in the Nontraditional Family, 1996 Utah L. Rev. 93 (1996).

A. HALFBLOODS

Suppose two people share only one parent. The two are "halfbloods." Note that halfblood relationships can arise in a variety of different contexts, which might color one's views about the appropriate treatment of halfbloods for intestate succession purposes. Consider the following example:

> ***Example 5:*** *Donald and Ivana, a married couple, had two children, Amy and Barbara. Ten years after Barbara's birth, Donald and Ivana were divorced, and Donald moved to another state, where he and a new wife, Marla, had another child, Carla. Donald died when Carla was 10, and Carla has never met Amy or Barbara. Ivana died when Barbara was 25, and the next year, Barbara, who had not written a will, was killed in a car crash. Should Amy and Carla share Barbara's estate equally?*

Your instinctive answer to that question might be no. In all likelihood, Barbara did not treat Carla as a sister—certainly not in the same way she regarded Amy as a sister. Does that mean that halfbloods should not share equally with wholebloods? Before your answer that question, consider one variation on Example 5: suppose that after Donald left, Ivana had another daughter, Debbie, by a second husband. Debbie lived in the same household with Amy and Barbara until Barbara's death. Should Debbie share equally with Amy? Now, your instinctive answer might be yes.

In drafting an intestate succession statute, which situation should we take as the norm—Carla's or Debbie's? The modern trend is to treat halfbloods equally with wholebloods. Consider the following Uniform Probate Code provision:

SECTION 2–107. KINDRED OF HALF BLOOD.

Relatives of the half blood inherit the same share they would inherit if they were of the whole blood.

* * *

Not all states take the same position. In Florida, and a few other states, if decedent is survived by relatives of the halfblood and relatives of the wholeblood in the same degree, the relatives of the half-blood take half as much as the relatives of the whole blood. See, e.g., Fla. Stat. 732.105.

In Mississippi, wholeblood relatives take to the exclusion of halfblood relatives. The applicable statute provides that "[t]here shall not be, in any case, a distinction between the kindred of the whole and half-blood, except that the kindred of the whole-blood, in equal degree, shall be preferred to the kindred of the half-blood in the same degree." Miss. Code Ann. section 91–1–5. In Jones v. Stubbs, 434 So.2d 1362 (Miss.1983), the court construed the statute to permit decedent's wholeblood nieces and nephews to take to the exclusion of decedent's halfblood sister. How? By concluding that decedent's deceased wholeblood siblings (the parents of the nieces and nephews) would have taken to the exclusion of the halfblood sister, and that the nieces and nephews stepped into their parents' shoes.

Another approach is embodied in Oklahoma law, which provides that halfbloods take equally with wholebloods "unless the inheritance come to the intestate by descent, devise or gift of some one of his ancestors, in which case all those who are not of the blood of such ancestors must be excluded from such inheritance." 84 Okla. Stat. sec. 222. Ancestral property statutes like these are particularly curious, because they apply only to halfbloods. Consider the following example:

> ***Example 6:*** *Decedent died survived by his mother's whole brother and his mother's half-brother, and by no closer relatives. Decedent's only asset—a parcel of real estate—was inherited from his father. Under the Oklahoma statute, who is entitled to the real estate? Presumably, only the mother's whole brother, since, by the terms of the statute, the half-brother would be "excluded" from inheritance of property derived from an ancestor not of his blood. Does this make sense? Note that the mother's whole-brother, who would take the property, shares no blood with decedent's father—the original source of the property!*

For criticism of the Oklahoma statute, and a call for its repeal, see Nancy I. Kenderdine, Oklahoma's Archaic Half–Blood Inheritance Statute—Still Going: A Plea for Repeal, 49 Okla. L. Rev. 81 (1996).

Professor Ralph Brashier has argued that all of the prevailing statutory approaches suffer from the same defect: they rely on bright-line rules that do not capture the wide variety of relationships among half-siblings in modern families. Professor Brashier proposes that states invest probate courts with discretion in determining the intestate share of halfblood claimants. Ralph C. Brashier, Consanguinity, Sibling Relationships, and the Default Rules of Inheritance Law: Reshaping Half-blood Statutes to Reflect the Evolving Family, 58 S.M.U. L. Rev 137 (2005).

PROBLEM

H and W have three children, A, B, and C. After W's death, H marries X and has another child D. A dies with a will that leaves all of her property to B. At B's death, he is survived only by C's child E, and D's two children, F and G. The property B inherited from A is worth $50,000, and B's other property is worth $50,000. How would B's estate be distributed under the Uniform Probate Code? Florida law (which provides for a strict "per stirpes" distribution to issue of parents)? The Mississippi statute? Oklahoma law (which adopts UPC 2–106 "representation" distribution scheme)? Your local statute?

B. ADOPTION

The common law did not recognize adoption. Hence, in this country, adoption is entirely a creature of statute. Mississippi enacted the first American adoption statute in 1846. Massachusetts enacted a more comprehensive statute five years later, and other states followed suit. Guthrie and Grossman, Adoption in the Progressive Era: Preserving, Creating, and Re-Creating Families, 43 Am. J. Leg. Hist. 235, 237 (1999). Professors Guthrie and Grossman observe that adoption statutes served three distinct purposes: family preservation, family creation, and family re-creation. Id. at 236.

Professor Naomi Cahn has explored the contentious debate over inheritance rights of adoptive children, a debate that raged into the 20th century. See Naomi Cahn, Perfect Substitutes or the Real Thing? 52 Duke L. J. 1077, 1126–39 (2003). Even when courts and legislatures conceded that adoptive children could inherit from their adoptive parents, they were often resistant to the idea that those children could inherit from relatives of those adoptive parents when those relatives were not parties to the adoption.

During the middle of the twentieth century, the image of adoption imprinted on the mind of most policymakers was an image of a newborn baby removed from its natural mother's arms and immediately transferred to adoptive parents. Statutes sought to transplant adoptive children—as completely as possible—into their adoptive families, and to cut all ties between the adoptive children and their "natural" families. For intestate succession purposes, as for other purposes, adopted children were to be treated only as children of their adoptive families.

Adoption is now—and always has been—more complicated than the image on which policymakers acted. Adoption by stepparents has always made up a considerable percentage of adoptions. Intestate succession statutes which try to transplant adopted children out of their natural families cause problems when stepparent adoptions are involved. The following case is illustrative:

Estates of Donnelly

Supreme Court of Washington, en banc, 1972.
81 Wash.2d 430, 502 P.2d 1163.

■ NEILL, J.:

May an adopted child inherit from her natural grandparents? Both the trial court and the Court of Appeals (5 Wash. App. 158, 486 P.2d 1158

(1971)), answered "yes." We granted review (79 Wash.2d 1010 (1971)), and disagree. In speaking of heirs and inheritance, we refer to the devolution of property by law in intestacy and not by testamentary or other voluntary disposition.

John J. and Lily Donnelly, husband and wife, had two children, a daughter, Kathleen M., now Kathleen M. Kelly, and a son, John J., Jr. The son had one child, Jean Louise Donnelly, born October 28, 1945. Jean Louise's father, John J. Donnelly, Jr., died on July 9, 1946, less than a year after her birth. Her mother, Faith Louise Donnelly, married Richard Roger Hansen on April 22, 1948. By a decree entered August 11, 1948, Jean Louise was adopted by her stepfather with the written consent of her natural mother. She lived with her mother and adoptive father as their child and kept the name Hansen until her marriage to Donald J. Iverson. Thus she is a party to this action as Jean Louise Iverson.

Lily Donnelly, the grandmother, died October 7, 1964, leaving a will in which she named but left nothing to her two children. All of her property she left to her husband, John J. Donnelly, Sr., Jean Louise Iverson's grandfather.

John J. Donnelly, Sr., the grandfather, died September 15, 1970, leaving a will dated October 16, 1932, in which he left his entire estate to his wife, Lily, who had predeceased him. He, too, named but left nothing to his two children, and made no provision for disposition of his property in event his wife predeceased him. His daughter, Kathleen M. Kelly, as administratrix with wills annexed of the estates of her parents, brought this petition to determine heirship and for a declaration that Jean Louise Iverson, the granddaughter, take nothing and that she, Kathleen M. Kelly, the daughter, be adjudged the sole heir of her mother and father, Lily and John J. Donnelly, Sr., to the exclusion of Jean Louise Iverson, her niece and their granddaughter.

* * *

As the trial court in its memorandum opinion and the Court of Appeals noted, the issue is whether RCW 11.04.085, which says that an adopted child shall not be deemed an heir of his natural parents, cuts off the inheritance from the natural grandparents as well.

... [A] statutory right to inherit one-half of the grandfather's estate is vested in Jean Louise Iverson, the granddaughter, unless that right is divested by operation of RCW 11.04.085, which declares that an adopted child is not to be considered an heir of his natural parents:

> A lawfully adopted child shall not be considered an "heir" of his natural parents for purposes of this title.

When the question of the right of an adopted child to inherit from his natural parents came before us, the intent of the legislature was clear from the literal language of the statute. We held that RCW 11.04.085 prevents an adopted child from taking a share of the natural parent's estate by intestate succession. In re Estate of Wiltermood, 78 Wash.2d 238, 242–43, 472 P.2d 536 (1970). However, reference to the literal language of RCW 11.04.085 does not answer the instant question, i.e., whether, by declaring that an adopted child shall not take from his natural parent, the legislature also intended to remove the adopted child's capacity to represent the natural parent and thereby take from the natural grandparent.

* * *

The legislature has addressed itself to the inheritance rights of adopted children in both the probate and domestic relations titles of RCW. (RCW Titles 11 and 26.) For example, RCW 26.32.140 also directly affects the inheritance rights of an adopted child:

> By a decree of adoption the natural parents shall be divested of all legal rights and obligations in respect to the child, and *the child* shall be free from all legal obligations of obedience and maintenance in respect to them, and *shall be*, to all intents and purposes, and for all legal incidents, *the child, legal heir, and lawful issue of his or her adopter or adopters, entitled to all rights and privileges, including the right of inheritance* and the right to take under testamentary disposition, and subject to all the obligations of a child of the adopter or adopters begotten in lawful wedlock.

(Italics ours.)

* * *

The question at bench should, therefore, be decided in the context of the broad legislative objective of giving the adopted child a "fresh start" by treating him as the natural child of the adoptive parent, and severing all ties with the past. We believe it clearly follows that the legislature intended to remove an adopted child from his natural bloodline for purposes of intestate succession.

* * *

The legislative policy of providing a "clean slate" to the adopted child permeates our scheme of adoption. The natural grandparents are not entitled to notice of any hearing on the matter of adoption. RCW 26.32.080. RCW 26.32.150 provides that, unless otherwise requested by the adopted, all records of the adoption proceeding shall be sealed and not open to inspection.... Thus, the natural grandparents have no assurance that they will know the new name or residence of the adopted child. Indeed, in the usual "out of family" adoption situation the administrator of a deceased natural grandparent's estate will be unable to locate—much less to identify—the post-adoption grandchild.

The consistent theme of the relevant legislation is that the new family of the adopted child is to be treated as his natural family. The only conclusion consistent with the spirit of our overlapping adoption and inheritance statutes is that RCW 11.04.085 was intended to transfer all rights of inheritance out of the natural family upon adoption and place them entirely within the adopted family.

Respondent suggests it is most probable that the legislature never considered the problem of inheritance by adopted persons from their remote natural kin when it passed RCW 11.04.085. Thus, respondent contends that the word "parents" should be strictly construed. We disagree.

On numerous occasions this court has indicated that a statute should be construed as a whole in order to ascertain legislative purpose, and thus avoid unlikely, strained or absurd consequences which could result from a literal reading. That the spirit or the purpose of legislation should prevail over the express but inept language is an ancient adage of the law.

* * *

The broad legislative purpose underlying our statutes relating to adopted children is consistent only with the inference that RCW 11.04.085 was intended to remove respondent, an adopted child, from her natural bloodline for inheritance purposes. If the adopted child cannot take from her natural father, she should not represent him and take from his father.

The chain of inheritance was broken by respondent's adoption. Reversed.

■ HALE, J. (dissenting):

I dissent. This court asks whether an adopted child may inherit from her natural grandparents. Both the trial court and the Court of Appeals, 5 Wash. App. 158, 486 P.2d 1158 (1971), answered yes, and I agree. I would, therefore, adopt the opinion of the Court of Appeals verbatim as declaring the law of the state in this case.

* * *

One can readily agree with the court's proposition that the legislature has designed the adoption and inheritance code so as to make an adopted child the full equal in law with a natural child and, so far as the law can do so, to establish a relationship between adopted parents and adopted children identical to that of natural parents and children. . . .

But nothing in the Court of Appeals opinion militates against the integrity and totality of an adoption. To the contrary, that opinion augments this legislatively declared public policy of upholding and preserving the adoption, where this court's opinion will operate against it. Here, the grandfather's son died; his widowed daughter-in-law eventually remarried, and she consented that her new husband adopt her daughter. The new family relationship created by the marriage and adoption presented none of the circumstances of an adoption designed in law to cut off all familial and legal relationships with the adopted child's natural mother nor her grandparents either. The grandchild continued to live with her natural mother and adoptive father presumably with the full knowledge of her grandfather, whose lineal descendant she remained. None of the factors upon which the legislature legislated to seal the records of adoption against the grandfather existed here. And, although the adoption statute makes this granddaughter no less an adopted daughter of her mother's husband, it ought not to be read to make her less a granddaughter of her natural grandfather either. The statute which the court now says disinherits the granddaughter cannot, as the court now says, serve to give the natural granddaughter a "fresh start" or a "clean slate" in the relationship created by the adoption. One is hard put to find where a statute which operates to cut off the plaintiff grandchild from her grandfather's estate gives her a fresh start or a clean slate. The statute could not, and thus did not sever all ties with the past. While it might have severed whatever legal ties existed between her and her dead father, whose heir she had already been, the adoption could not be reasonably said to do the same with respect to her natural grandfather.

NOTES AND QUESTIONS

1. The majority opinion starts with the following formulation of the question in the case: "May an adopted child inherit from her natural grandparents?" Is that really the question? If this had been a "stranger" adoption, would the dissent have argued that Jean was entitled to inherit from her natural grandparents? In light of the Washington confidentiality statutes, how would Jean have learned that her natural grandparents had died?

2. When Jean's stepfather adopted her, do you think there was any intent to sever Jean's relationship with her natural grandparents?

3. Suppose Jean's father had died, not when she was 9 months old, but when she was 9 years old. Do you think the court's reaction might have been different? Why? How would the human situation have been different 8 years later?

4. Consider the text of the Washington statute. If Jean's mother had died intestate, would a literal reading of the statute have permitted Jean to inherit from her mother? Does your answer suggest that the Washington legislature simply failed to consider stepparent adoptions?

5. A number of state statutes retain the approach of the Washington statute. See, e.g., Del. Code Ann., tit. 13, § 920; Idaho Code § 16–1509. Other states make explicit provision for stepparent adoptions—as does the Uniform Probate Code provision reproduced below.

UNIFORM PROBATE CODE

SECTION 2–118. ADOPTEE AND ADOPTEE'S ADOPTIVE PARENT OR PARENTS.

(a) [Parent–Child Relationship Between Adoptee and Adoptive Parent or Parents.] A parent-child relationship exists between an adoptee and the adoptee's adoptive parent or parents.

SECTION 2–119. ADOPTEE AND ADOPTEE'S GENETIC PARENTS.

(a) [Parent–Child Relationship Between Adoptee and Genetic Parents.] Except as otherwise provided in subsections (b) through (e), a parent-child relationship does not exist between an adoptee and the adoptee's genetic parents.

(b) [Stepchild Adopted by Stepparent.] A parent-child relationship exists between an individual who is adopted by the spouse of either genetic parent and:

(1) the genetic parent whose spouse adopted the individual; and

(2) the other genetic parent, but only for the purpose of the right of the adoptee or a descendant of the adoptee to inherit from or through the other genetic parent.

(c) [Individual Adopted by Relative of Genetic Parent.] A parent-child relationship exists between both genetic parents and an individual who is adopted by a relative of a genetic parent, or by the spouse or surviving spouse of a relative of a genetic parent, but only for the purpose of the right of the adoptee or a descendant of the adoptee to inherit from or through either genetic parent.

(d) [Individual Adopted after Death of Both Genetic Parents.] A parent-child relationship exists between both genetic parents and an individual who is adopted after the death of both genetic parents, but only for the purpose of the right of the adoptee or a descendant of the adoptee to inherit through either genetic parent.

(e) [Child of Assisted Reproduction or Gestational Child Who Is Subsequently Adopted.] If, after a parent-child relationship is established between a child of assisted reproduction and a parent or parents under Section 2–120 or between a gestational child and a parent or parents under Section 2–121, the child is adopted by another or others, the child's parent or parents under Section 2–120 or 2–121 are treated as the child's genetic parent or parents for the purpose of this section.

NOTES AND QUESTIONS

1. How would the Donnelly case have been decided if UPC section 2–119 had been in effect?

2. The Uniform Probate Code permits a child adopted by its stepparent to inherit from or through its other natural parent. Is the statute reciprocal? Suppose, for instance, Ann and Bob Doe have a child, Cindy. Ann and Bob divorce, and Bob marries Danielle, who, with Ann's consent, adopts Cindy. If Ann dies intestate, does Cindy inherit her estate? If Cindy dies intestate (before Ann), does Ann inherit all or part of Cindy's estate? The comments to UPC section 2–119(b) emphasize that "Section 2–119(b)(2) provides that a parent-child relationship also continues to exist between an adopted stepchild and his or her other genetic parent (the noncustodial genetic parent) for purposes of inheritance from and through that genetic parent, but not for purposes of inheritance by the other genetic parent and his or her relatives from or through the adopted stepchild."

When the adoption is not by a stepparent, adoptive relatives typically take to the exclusion of genetic relatives. See, e.g. Estate of Kirkpatrick, 77 P.3d 404 (Wyo. 2003) [adopted person's estate distributed to children of adoptive siblings to the exclusion of children of genetic siblings].

3. Ann and Bill died in a car accident, survived by their three minor children. Soon after, Bill's parents adopted the children. Several years later, Ann's mother died, survived only by her sister and Ann's three children. Did the children's adoption by Bill's parents sever their right to take Ann's mother's estate as her surviving descendants? Assume the relevant intestacy statute provided:

> An adopted person is the child of an adopting parent and *not of the natural parents* except that adoption of a child by the spouse of a natural parent has no effect on the right of the child to inherit from or through either natural parent. . . ."

If you were a judge, how would you rule? See Ellis v. West, 971 So.2d 20 (Ala. 2007) (on similar facts, reversing a lower court determination for the children and applying a strict reading of the statute to deny the children intestate succession rights); Duran v. Duran, 900 N.E.2d 454 (Ind. App. 2009) (woman born out of wedlock and adopted by her maternal grandparents was not an heir entitled to inherit from the estate of her biological father). Would your answer change if the state had enacted UPC section 2–119?

4. ***Inheritance Consequences of Adoptions by Same–Sex Partners and Other Unmarried Partners.*** An increasing number of jurisdictions permit adoption by the unmarried partner of a genetic parent, whether that partner is of the same or the opposite sex. Consider the inheritance consequences of such an adoption under UPC § 2–119. Suppose for instance, that Zack is the genetic child of Yolanda and Xavier. When Yolanda and Xavier divorce, Yolanda forms a relationship with Wayne, but does not marry him. If Wayne adopts Zack, can Zack still inherit from Xavier? From Yolanda? For discussion of the anomalous results generated under the UPC (which does not contemplate such adoptions), see Peter Wendel, Inheritance Rights and the Step–Partner Adoption Paradigm: Shades of the Discrimination Against Illegitimate Children, 34 Hofstra L. Rev. 351, 371–81 (2005); Susan N. Gary, The Parent–Child Relationship Under Intestacy Statutes, 32 U. Mem. L. Rev. 643, 656–62 (2002).

Suppose Ann is Cindy's genetic mother, but Ann's partner Barbara adopts Cindy. If Ann dies, is Cindy entitled to inherit from Ann? See generally Laura M. Padilla, Flesh of My Flesh But Not My Heir: Unintentional Disinheritance, 36 J. Fam. L. 219 (1997).

5. Adoptions greatly expand the possibility that two people might be related to each other in more than one way. Suppose Janice dies, survived by her parents, Willena and Edward, and several siblings. Another sibling, Stephanie, had predeceased her, survived by a child, DeMarcus. After Stephanie's death (but before Janice's death),Willena and Edward adopted DeMarcus. Thus, Janice's nephew became her brother. Under the applicable intestacy statute, Janice's parents and siblings are all heirs entitled to an equal share of her estate. Should DeMarcus be entitled to Stepanie's fractional share as Stephanie's surviving issue, a separate share as a surviving sibling of Janice, or both? See Jenkins v. Jenkins, 990 So.2d 807 (Miss. Ct. App. 2008) (holding that DeMarcus is entitled to take both his own share as sibling and Stephanie's share!). Would the court have come out the same way if Mississippi had adopted UPC 2–113?

SECTION 2–113. INDIVIDUALS RELATED TO DECEDENT THROUGH TWO LINES.

An individual who is related to the decedent through two lines of relationship is entitled to only a single share based on the relationship that would entitle the individual to the larger share.

6. Not all state statutes track the Uniform Probate Code. The Vermont statute precluded an adopted child from inheriting from collateral relatives of the adoptive parent—until the Vermont Supreme Court held that the statute violated the state constitution. MacCallum v. Seymour's Administrator, 165 Vt. 452, 686 A.2d 935 (1996). The court examined the two justifications offered in support of the statute—that the prohibition on adoptee inheritance reflected the presumed intent of collateral relatives, and that the collateral relatives did not consent to the adoption—and dismissed them both, concluding that the statute was "not reasonably related to a valid public purpose, at least with respect to persons who are adopted during their minority." Id. at 941.

Adult Adoptions

In recent years, a number of estates cases have arisen involving a different phenomenon: adult adoptions. In some cases, adults have adopted adults for the express purpose of permitting them to inherit—generally not from the adoptive "parent," but from some relative of the adoptive parent. The situation is especially likely to arise when a long-dead relative has created a future interest in the "children" of a named person. Courts have dealt with those problems as questions of construing the dead relative's grant. See Chapter Nine, *infra.*

Occasionally, the problem arises in the intestate succession context as well. Consider the following case:

Estate of Brittin

Appellate Court of Illinois, Fifth District, 1996.
279 Ill.App.3d 512, 664 N.E.2d 687, 216 Ill.Dec. 50.

■ GOLDENHERSH, J.:

Respondent, Mary Ann Buckman, natural daughter of decedent, Stephen Glenn Brittin, and administrator of his estate, appeals from an order of the circuit court finding petitioners, Deborah J. Roeder, Linda Brittin, Denise Brittin, Stacie Brittin, and Laura Moore, the natural children of decedent's adopted son, William Eugene, to be decedent's legal heirs and reopening decedent's estate.

On appeal, respondent contends the trial court erred in finding petitioners, for purposes of intestate succession, to be the legal heirs of decedent and in reopening decedent's estate. We affirm.

I

The facts are undisputed. The record reveals that when William Eugene was about three years of age, his mother, Estelle Willet, married the decedent, Stephen Glenn Brittin. From age three, Stephen and Estelle raised William as their son. The couple had one natural child, Mary Ann Buckman, respondent herein. Estelle Willet Brittin died on July 28, 1975. Shortly thereafter, on October 20, 1976, Stephen adopted William in an adult adoption proceeding in St. Clair County. William was 46 years old at the time of the adoption and had five children, petitioners herein. The adoption decree specifically provides that William was the child of Stephen Glenn Brittin "and for the purposes of inheritance and all other legal incidents and consequences, shall be the same as if said respondent had been born to Stephen Glenn Brittin and Estelle Willet Brittin (now deceased) in lawful wedlock." William died on May 17, 1979, predeceasing his adoptive father and leaving his five children as his descendants and heirs.

On February 8, 1993, Stephen died intestate leaving Mary, his natural daughter, and petitioners, descendants of his adopted son, William, as his heirs. Decedent's intestate estate was opened on March 10, 1993. The court found respondent to be the sole heir and appointed her administrator of the estate....

On February 9, 1994, petitioners filed a petition to vacate the order of discharge and order finding heirship and to reopen the estate. Petitioners alleged in the petition that they are heirs of the decedent and are entitled to share in decedent's estate as the children of decedent's adopted son. After a hearing, the trial court entered its order finding petitioners legal heirs of decedent and reopening the estate. Respondent filed a motion to reconsider, which was denied on January 30, 1995. Respondent appeals.

II

Respondent contends that petitioners are not descendants of the decedent and may not take, by representation, their deceased father's share of the decedent's estate. Respondent acknowledges that pursuant to section 2–4(a) of the Probate Act (755 ILCS 5/2–4(a) (West 1992)), petitioners' father, as the adopted child of the decedent, is a descendant of his adoptive parent, and had he not predeceased decedent, he would be entitled to half of decedent's estate. However, defendant argues that the legislature, in using the term "adopted child" in section 2–4(a) of the Probate Act, intended to limit intestate succession to the descendants of a child adopted as a minor. Respondent further asserts that the legislature did not intend to include as descendants of an "adopted child" children born to the adopted adult prior to that adult's adoption. According to respondent, because petitioners were already born at the time of decedent's adoption of their father, they are not the descendants of an "adopted child" and therefore cannot take by representation their deceased father's share of decedent's estate. We disagree.

The case before us is one of first impression and requires our consideration of the issue of whether the natural children of an adult adoptee are descendants of the adopting parent for purposes of inheritance. In considering this issue, we must consider whether the legislature, in enacting the statute granting an adopted child the status of a descendant of the adopting parent, intended to limit succession rights of the adoptee's children to the natural children of a child adopted as a minor and to exclude the natural children born to the adult adoptee prior to his adoption by the adopting parent.

* * *

Where the decedent is survived by an adopted child, the adopted child may take a share of the intestate estate as a legal heir of the decedent pursuant to section 2–4(a) of the Probate Act, which provides:

> "§ 2–4. Adopted child and adopting parent. (a) An adopted child is a descendant of the adopting parent for purposes of inheritance from the adopting parent and from the lineal and collateral kindred of the adopting parent. For such purposes, an adopted child also is a descendant of both natural parents when the adopting parent is the spouse of a natural parent." 755 ILCS 5/2–4(a) (West 1992).

* * *

The Adoption Act (750 ILCS 50/1 et seq. (West 1992)) provides for the adoption of an adult as well as the adoption of minor children. Section 3 of the Adoption Act sets forth the conditions under which an adult may be adopted, stating:

> "§ 3. Who may be adopted. A male or female ... adult may be adopted ... provided ... that such adult has resided in the home of the persons intending to adopt him at any time for more than 2 years continuously preceding the commencement of an adoption proceeding, or in the alternative that such persons are related to him within a degree set forth in the definition of a related child in Section 1 of this Act." 750 ILCS 50/3 (West 1992).

* * *

Respondent maintains that section 2–4(a) of the Probate Act does not include adult adoptees because, had the legislature intended to include adopted adult children, it would have changed the word "child" to "person" so as to include all adopted persons. Respondent argues that the legislature has amended section 2–4(a) several times and has not made this change and, therefore, the legislature intended to limit inheritance to minor adopted children. We do not agree with this contention.

* * *

"There are ... two meanings which may be given to the word 'child:' one an offspring or a descendant, when a person is spoken of in relation to his parents; another, a person of immature years.... The word 'child,' when used with reference to the parents, ordinarily has no reference to age, but to the relation. When used without reference to the parents, as indicating a particular individual, it usually bears the meaning of a young person of immature years." Bartholow v. Davies, 276 Ill. at 511, 114 N.E.

at 1019. (NOTE: Bartholow was decided prior to statutory changes allowing the adoption of adults.)

Considering the subject matter and context in which the word "child" is used in section 2–4(a), the plain language of the statute indicates that the legislature intended to use the word "child" in its relational sense; referring to the parent-child relationship between the adoptee and the adopting parent. The word "child," as used here, cannot be interpreted fairly as meaning a minor, in light of section 3 of the Adoption Act which permits adult adoptions. Moreover, there is nothing in section 2–4(a) indicating a distinction between the adoptee's status as an adult or a minor at the time of adoption with regard to the adoptee's classification as a descendant of the adopting parent. The only qualification set forth in the statute is that the adoptee be legally adopted. Nothing more is required. Accordingly, petitioner's deceased father is an adopted child of the decedent and, as such, obtained the right of succession as decedent's legal heir.

III

Respondent next asserts that the children of an adopted adult who were born before the adult's adoption are not the legal heirs of the decedent because they are not the children of an adopted adult. Respondent argues, therefore, that petitioners, as already-born children at the time of their father's adoption, cannot take by representation their predeceased father's share of decedent's estate. This contention is not persuasive.

As discussed above, section 2–4(a) deems all adopted children to be descendants of the adopting parent. This provision places the adopted child and the natural child in equivalent positions with respect to the child's capacity to inherit from an intestate parent. Similarly, the act of adoption itself accords the adoptee the status of a natural child of the adopting parent. In re M.M., 156 Ill. 2d at 62, 619 N.E.2d at 708. As with natural children, the children of the adoptee, by virtue of the adoption, become the grandchildren of the adopting parent, thereby creating a grandparent-grandchild relationship.

Because section 2–4(a) deems an adopted child the descendant of the adopting parent, it logically follows that, for purposes of inheritance, the children of the adopted adult are also descendants and can take as grandchildren of the decedent. Accordingly, if the adopted child predeceases the adopting parent, leaving children, as is the case here, those children, as grandchildren of the adopting parent, are entitled to represent their deceased parent and to receive from the adopting parent's estate the share to which the adopted adult child would have been entitled to receive had he survived the adopting parent. Annotation, Adoption of Adult, 21 A.L.R. 3d 1012, 1034–38, §§ 14, 16 (1968); 2 Am. Jur. 2d Adoption § 205, at 1132 (1994).

* * *

For the foregoing reasons, the judgment of the circuit court of Madison County is affirmed.

NOTES AND QUESTIONS

1. The Illinois adoption statute, quoted by the court in the Brittin case, places limits on adult adoptions; for instance, the "child" must have resided with the "parent" for more than two years preceding the adoption. Not all states impose comparable limitations. Suppose the state statute does not limit consensual adult adoptions. Would you expect a court to reach the same result as in Brittin? See Adoption of Robert Paul P., 63 N.Y.2d 233, 471 N.E.2d 424, 481 N.Y.S.2d 652 (1984) (barring adoption of 50–year old man by his 57–year old gay partner).

Suppose, for instance, a dying father, miffed at his natural children, started adopting a variety of business acquaintances to cut down on the share the natural children would be entitled to inherit from the father's aged mother. Do you think a court would permit the acquaintances to share? Cf. Davis v. Neilson, 871 S.W.2d 35 (Mo.App.1993).

2. In the Brittin case, if Stephen Brittin had not wanted his adopted son's children to inherit, couldn't he have just written a will leaving all of his property to his natural daughter? In light of the trouble he took to adopt William, and to incorporate in the decree a provision declaring that William's inheritance rights would be the same as if he had been Stephen's natural-born son, isn't it clear that the court's result effectuated Stephen's intent?

3. Because a person can generally write a will in favor of the person she chooses to "adopt," the significance of adult adoptions for intestate succession purposes might seem marginal: why bother adopting an adult rather than writing a will in his favor?

There are at least two important differences. First, suppose the adoptive parent knows that her brother's will, (or a trust instrument created by her mother), leaves a significant amount of money to the "parent's" children. If the adoptive parent adopts a "child"—even an adult child—the "child" may become eligible to take under the terms of the will or the trust instrument. Cf. Evans v. McCoy, 291 Md. 562, 436 A.2d 436 (1981). The "parent" cannot achieve a comparable result by writing a will in favor of the "child."

Second, an adult adoption may limit standing to challenge the adoptive parent's will. Suppose, for instance, a gay man in a long-term relationship wants to leave his property to his partner. He expects that his parents, or his siblings, will contest any will he writes. Suppose now that our hypothetical decedent adopts his companion. Will the parents or the siblings have standing to contest the will? Not if the adoption has effectively conferred on the partner the right to take by intestate succession.

Inheritance Without Formal Adoption: Stepparents, Foster Parents, and Equitable Adoption

In cases like Donnelly and Brittin, "parents" took formal legal steps to adopt "children." And, indeed, every state provides a formal legal mechanism for adoptions. Frequently, however, children are raised by adults who are not their natural parents, and who have taken no formal steps to adopt them. These caretakers are as close to parents as the children will ever get. Should the children be entitled to inherit from their substitute parents?

Consider first the case of stepparents. We have seen that if a stepparent adopts her spouse's child, the child is treated as part of the stepparent's natural family for intestate succession purposes. Suppose, however, the stepparent does not adopt the child, but otherwise treats the child as her own. Can the child inherit from the stepparent?

The answer is generally no. In cases like Donnelly, where the child's natural parent has died, no legal doctrine prevents the stepparent from adopting the child. Failure to adopt might, then, constitute some evidence that the stepparent did not want to treat the child as her own. When the child's natural parents are divorced, however, the situation is somewhat different: statutes generally prevent the stepparent from adopting without the consent of the child's natural parents. If the child's natural mother has failed to consent to an adoption, the failure of the child's stepmother to adopt sheds no light on the closeness of the relationship between stepmother and stepchild.

Nevertheless, in the absence of an adoption, most states do not give stepchildren a right to inherit from stepparents. (Ohio permits stepchildren to inherit, but only when the alternative would be escheat to the state. Ohio Rev. Code § 2105.06(J) and (K)).

Consider the California Probate Code, which permits inheritance by stepchildren more broadly.

CALIFORNIA PROBATE CODE

SECTION 6454. FOSTER PARENT OR STEPPARENT.

For the purpose of determining intestate succession by a person or the person's issue from or through a foster parent or stepparent, the relationship of parent and child exists between that person and the person's foster parent or stepparent if both of the following requirements are satisfied:

(a) The relationship began during the person's minority and continued throughout the joint lifetimes of the person and the person's foster parent or stepparent.

(b) It is established by clear and convincing evidence that the foster parent or stepparent would have adopted the person but for a legal barrier.

CALIFORNIA PROBATE CODE

SECTION 6455. EQUITABLE ADOPTION.

Nothing in this chapter affects or limits application of the judicial doctrine of equitable adoption for the benefit of the child or the child's issue.

What is the "judicial doctrine of equitable adoption" discussed in section 6455? Consider the following case:

Bean v. Ford

Supreme Court of California, 2004.
32 Cal.4th 160, 82 P.3d 747, 8 Cal.Rptr.3d 541.

■ WERDEGAR, J.

Terrold Bean claims the right to inherit the intestate estate of Arthur Patrick Ford as Ford's equitably adopted son. The superior court denied the claim, and the Court of Appeal affirmed the denial, for lack of clear and convincing evidence that Ford intended to adopt Bean. After reviewing California case law on equitable adoption, we conclude that no equitable adoption is shown unless the parties' conduct and statements clearly and convincingly demonstrate an intent to adopt. We will therefore affirm the judgment of the Court of Appeal.

Factual and Procedural Background

Born in 1953, Bean was declared a ward of the court and placed in the home of Ford and his wife, Kathleen Ford, as a foster child in 1955. Bean never knew his natural father, whose identity is uncertain, and he was declared free of his mother's control in 1958, at the age of four. Bean lived continuously with Mr. and Mrs. Ford and their natural daughter, Mary Catherine, for about 18 years, until Mrs. Ford's death in 1973, then with Ford and Mary Catherine for another two years, until 1975.

During part of the time Bean lived with the Fords, they cared for other foster children and received a county stipend for doing so. Although the Fords stopped taking in foster children after Mrs. Ford became ill with cancer, they retained custody of Bean. The last two other foster children left the home around the time of Mrs. Ford's death, but Bean, who at 18 years of age could have left, stayed with Ford and Mary Catherine.

Bean knew the Fords were not his natural parents, but as a child he called them "Mommy" and "Daddy," and later "Mom" and "Dad." Joan Malpassi, Mary Catherine's friend since childhood and later administrator of Ford's estate, testified that Bean's relationship with Mary Catherine was "as two siblings" and that the Fords treated Bean "more like Mary rather than a foster son, like a real son was my observation." Mary Catherine later listed Bean as her brother on a life insurance application.

Bean remained involved with Ford and Mary Catherine even after leaving the Ford home and marrying. Ford loaned Bean money to help furnish his new household and later forgave the unpaid part of the debt when Bean's marriage was dissolved. Bean visited Ford and Mary Catherine several times per year both during his marriage and after his divorce. When Ford suffered a disabling stroke in 1989, Mary Catherine conferred with Bean and Malpassi over Ford's care; Ford was placed in a board and care facility, where Bean continued to visit him regularly until his death in 2000.

Mary Catherine died in 1999. Bean and Malpassi arranged her funeral. Bean petitioned for Malpassi to be appointed Ford's conservator, and with Malpassi's agreement Bean obtained a power of attorney to take care of Ford's affairs pending establishment of the conservatorship. Bean also administered Mary Catherine's estate, which was distributed to the Ford conservatorship. When a decision was needed as to whether Ford should receive medical life support, Malpassi consulted with Bean in deciding he should. When Ford died, Bean and Malpassi arranged the funeral.

The Fords never petitioned to adopt Bean. Mrs. Ford told Barbara Carter, a family friend, that "they wanted to adopt Terry," but she was "under the impression that she could not put in for adoption while he was in the home." She worried that if Bean was removed during the adoption process he might be put in "a foster home that wasn't safe."

Ford's nearest relatives at the time of his death were the two children of his predeceased brother, nephew John J. Ford III and niece Veronica Newbeck. Neither had any contact with Ford for about 15 years before his death, and neither attended his funeral. John J. Ford III filed a petition to determine entitlement to distribution (Prob. Code, § 11700), listing both himself and Newbeck as heirs. Bean filed a statement of interest claiming entitlement to Ford's entire estate under Probate Code sections 6454 (foster child heirship) and 6455 (equitable adoption) as well as sections 6402, subdivision (a) and 6450.

After trial, the superior court ruled against Bean. Probate Code section 6454's requirement of a legal barrier to adoption was unmet, since the Fords could have adopted Bean after his mother's parental rights were terminated in 1958. The doctrine of equitable adoption, the trial court found, was inapplicable because "there is no evidence that [Ford] ever told [Bean] or anyone else that he wanted to adopt him nor publicly told anyone that [Bean] was his adopted son." There was thus no clear and convincing evidence of "an intent to adopt."

Bean appealed only on the equitable adoption issue. The Court of Appeal affirmed, agreeing with the trial court that equitable adoption must be proven by clear and convincing evidence. Moreover, the reviewing court held, any error by the trial court in this respect would be harmless because the evidence did not support equitable adoption on any standard of proof "for the same reasons articulated by the trial court."

We granted Bean's petition for review.

Discussion

Chapter 2 of part 2 of division 6 of the Probate Code, sections 6450 to 6455, defines the parent-child relationship for purposes of intestate succession. Section 6450, subdivision (b) provides that such a relationship exists between adopting parents and the adopted child. Section 6453, subdivision (a) provides that the relationship exists between a child and a presumptive parent under the Uniform Parentage Act. Section 6454 delineates the circumstances in which a foster parent or stepparent is deemed a parent for the purpose of succession, requiring both a personal relationship beginning during the child's minority and enduring for the child's and parent's joint lifetimes, and a legal barrier but for which the foster parent or stepparent would have adopted the child. (See generally Estate of Joseph (1998) 17 Cal.4th 203, 208–212 [70 Cal. Rptr. 2d 619, 949 P.2d 472].) Finally, section 6455 provides in full: "Nothing in this chapter affects or limits application of the judicial doctrine of equitable adoption for the benefit of the child or the child's issue." We therefore look to decisional law, rather than statute, for guidance on the equitable adoption doctrine's proper scope and application.

I. Criteria for Equitable Adoption

In its essence, the doctrine of equitable adoption allows a person who was accepted and treated as a natural or adopted child, and as to whom adoption typically was promised or contemplated but never performed, to share in inheritance of the foster parents' property. "The parents of a child turn him over to foster parents who agree to care for him as if he were their own child. Perhaps they also agree to adopt him. They do care for him, support him, educate him, and treat him in all respects as if he were their child, but they never adopt him. Upon their death he seeks to inherit their property on the theory that he should be treated as if he had been adopted. Many courts would honor his claim, at least under some circumstances, characterizing the case as one of equitable adoption, or adoption by estoppel, or virtual adoption, or specific enforcement of a contract to adopt." (Clark, The Law of Domestic Relations in the United States (2d ed. 1988) § 20.9, p. 925.) The doctrine is widely applied to allow inheritance from the adoptive parent: at least 27 jurisdictions have so applied the doctrine, while only 10 have declined to recognize it in that context. (Annot., Modern Status of Law as to Equitable Adoption or Adoption by Estoppel (1980) 97 A.L.R.3d 347, § 3.)

This court decided its only case relating to equitable adoption [in 1957]. (Estate of Radovich, supra, 48 Cal.2d 116.) The question before us was not whether the child could inherit as an equitable adoptee—a final superior court decree established that he could—but the child's status, for purposes of inheritance taxation, as either the decedent's adopted child or a stranger in blood to the decedent. (Id. at pp. 118–119.) The majority took the former view, but its opinion rested on the in rem character of the superior court's probate decree and did not address the contours of the equitable adoption doctrine. (Id. at pp. 119–124.)

Justice Schauer's dissenting opinion, however, addressed the equitable adoption doctrine at some length, concluding the child took solely by virtue of an unperformed contract of adoption and thus as a stranger in blood. (Estate of Radovich, supra, 48 Cal.2d at pp. 129–135 (dis. opn. of Schauer, J.).) Citing sister-state authority, Justice Schauer explained: "When the child takes property in such a case it is as a purchaser by virtue of the contract [citation] and by way of damages or specific performance [citations]. . . . The child shares in the estate of the deceased foster parent as though his own child but not as such. In order to do justice and equity, as far as possible, to one who, though having filled the place of a natural born child, through inadvertence or fault has not been legally adopted, the court enforces a contract under which the child is entitled to property, declaring that as a consideration on the part of the foster parents a portion of their property will pass on their death to the child." (Id. at p. 130.)

* * *

California decisions have explained equitable adoption as the specific enforcement of a contract to adopt. Yet it has long been clear that the doctrine, even in California, rested less on ordinary rules of contract law than on considerations of fairness and intent for, as Justice Schauer put it, the child "should have been" adopted and would have been but for the decedent's "inadvertence or fault." (Estate of Radovich, supra, 48 Cal.2d at pp. 130, 134 (dis. opn. of Schauer, J.), italics omitted.)

Bean urges that equitable adoption be viewed not as specific enforcement of a contract to adopt, but as application of an equitable restitutionary remedy he has identified as quasi-contract or, as his counsel emphasized at oral argument, as an application of equitable estoppel principles. While we have found no decisions articulating a quasi-contract theory, courts in several states have, instead of or in addition to the contract rationale, analyzed equitable adoption as arising from "a broader and vaguer equitable principle of estoppel." (Clark, The Law of Domestic Relations in the United States, supra, at p. 926.) Bean argues Mr. Ford's conduct toward him during their long and close relationship estops Ford's estate or heirs at law from denying his status as an equitably adopted child.

For several reasons, we conclude the California law of equitable adoption, which has rested on contract principles, does not recognize an estoppel arising merely from the existence of a familial relationship between the decedent and the claimant. The law of intestate succession is intended to carry out "the intent a decedent without a will is most likely to have had." (Estate of Griswold (2001) 25 Cal.4th 904, 912 [108 Cal. Rptr. 2d 165, 24 P.3d 1191].) The existence of a mutually affectionate relationship, without any direct expression by the decedent of an intent to adopt the child or to have him or her treated as a legally adopted child, sheds little light on the decedent's likely intent regarding distribution of property. While a person with whom the decedent had a close, caring and enduring relationship may often be seen as more deserving of inheritance than the heir or heirs at law, whose personal relationships with the decedent may have been, as they were here, attenuated, equitable adoption in California is neither a means of compensating the child for services rendered to the parent nor a device to avoid the unjust enrichment of other, more distant relatives who will succeed to the estate under the intestacy statutes. Absent proof of an intent to adopt, we must follow the statutory law of intestate succession.

In addition, a rule looking to the parties' overall relationship in order to do equity in a given case, rather than to particular expressions of intent to adopt, would necessarily be a vague and subjective one, inconsistently applied, in an area of law where "consistent, bright-line rules" (Estate of Furia, supra, 103 Cal.App.4th at p. 6) are greatly needed. Such a broad scope for equitable adoption would leave open to competing claims the estate of any foster parent or stepparent who treats a foster child or stepchild lovingly and on an equal basis with his or her natural or legally adopted children. A broad doctrine of equitable adoption would also render section 6454, in practice, a virtual nullity, since children meeting the familial-relationship criteria of that statute would necessarily be equitable adoptees as well.

While a California equitable adoption claimant need not prove all the elements of an enforceable contract to adopt, therefore, we conclude the claimant must demonstrate the existence of some direct expression, on the decedent's part, of an intent to adopt the claimant. This intent may be shown, of course, by proof of an unperformed express agreement or promise to adopt. But it may also be demonstrated by proof of other acts or statements directly showing that the decedent intended the child to be, or to be treated as, a legally adopted child, such as an invalid or unconsummated attempt to adopt, the decedent's statement of his or her intent to adopt the child, or the decedent's representation to the claimant or to the community at large that the claimant was the decedent's natural or legally adopted child. (See, e.g., Estate of Rivolo, supra, 194 Cal. App. 2d at p. 775 [parents who orally promised child she would "be their little girl" later told her and others they had adopted her]; Estate of Wilson, supra, 111 Cal. App. 3d at p. 248 [petition to adopt filed but dismissed for lack of natural mother's consent]; Estate of Reid (1978) 80 Cal. App. 3d 185, 188 [145 Cal. Rptr. 451] [written agreement with adult child].)

Thus, in California the doctrine of equitable adoption is a relatively narrow one, applying only to those who "though having filled the place of a natural born child, through inadvertence or fault [have] not been legally adopted, [where] the evidence establishes an intent to adopt." (Estate of Furia, supra, 103 Cal.App.4th at p. 5, italics added.) In addition to a statement or act by the decedent unequivocally evincing the decedent's intent to adopt, the claimant must show the decedent acted consistently with that intent by forming with the claimant a close and enduring familial relationship. That is, in addition to a contract or other direct evidence of the intent to adopt, the evidence must show "objective conduct indicating mutual recognition of an adoptive parent and child relationship to such an extent that in equity and good conscience an adoption should be deemed to have taken place." (Estate of Bauer, supra, 111 Cal. App. 3d at p. 560.)

II. Standard of Proof of Equitable Adoption

Bean also contends the lower courts erred in applying a standard of clear and convincing proof to the equitable adoption question. We disagree. Most courts that have considered the question require at least clear and convincing evidence in order to prove an equitable adoption. (See Clark,

The Law of Domestic Relations in the United States, supra, at p. 927; Rein, supra, 37 Vand. L.Rev. at p. 780.) Several good reasons support the rule.

First, the claimant in an equitable adoption case is seeking inheritance outside the ordinary statutory course of intestate succession and without the formalities required by the adoption statutes. As the claim's "strength lies in inherent justice" (Wooley v. Shell Petroleum Corporation, supra, 45 P.2d at p. 932), the need in justice for this "extraordinary equitable intervention" (Rein, supra, 37 Vand. L.Rev. at p. 785) should appear clearly and unequivocally from the facts.

Second, the claim involves a relationship with persons who have died and who can, therefore, no longer testify to their intent. As with an alleged contract to make a will (see Crail v. Blakely (1973) 8 Cal.3d 744, 750, fn. 3 [106 Cal. Rptr. 187, 505 P.2d 1027]), the law, in order to guard against fraudulent claims, should require more than a bare preponderance of evidence. Where "the lips of the alleged adopter have been sealed by death . . . proof of the facts essential to invoke the intervention of equity should be clear, unequivocal and convincing." (Cavanaugh v. Davis (1951) 149 Tex. 573 [235 S.W.2d 972, 978].)

Finally, too relaxed a standard could create the danger that "a person could not help out a needy child without having a de facto adoption foisted upon him after death." (Rein, supra, 37 Vand. L.Rev. at p. 782.) As pointed out in an early Missouri decision, if the evidentiary burden is lowered too far, "then couples, childless or not, will be reluctant to take into their homes orphan children, and for the welfare of such children, as well as for other reasons, the rule should be kept and observed. No one, after he or she has passed on, should be adjudged to have adopted a child unless the evidence is clear, cogent, and convincing . . . ." (Benjamin v. Cronan (1936) 338 Mo. 1177 [93 S.W.2d 975, 981].)

Conclusion

Although the evidence showed the Fords and Bean enjoyed a close and enduring familial relationship, evidence was totally lacking that the Fords ever made an attempt to adopt Bean or promised or stated their intent to do so; they neither held Bean out to the world as their natural or adopted child (Bean, for example, did not take the Ford name) nor represented to Bean that he was their child. Mrs. Ford's single statement to Barbara Carter was not clear and convincing evidence that Mr. Ford intended Bean to be, or be treated as, his adopted son. Substantial evidence thus supported the trial court, which heard the testimony live and could best assess its credibility and strength, in its finding that intent to adopt, and therefore Bean's claim of equitable adoption, was unproven.

NOTES AND QUESTIONS

1. Why weren't Mrs. Ford's statements to Barbara Carter that "they wanted to adopt Terry," but she was "under the impression that she could not put in for adoption while he was in the home" sufficient to bring Bean within the scope of California Probate Code section 6454? Within the scope of equitable adoption doctrine?

2. Suppose Bean had testified that Ford consistently called him "my adopted son." Would the result have been different? If yes, who would have been in a position to rebut such testimony?

3. Could Ford have expressly disinherited Bean? Is that why Bean's equitable estoppel argument was unsuccessful? If functional parents like Arthur Patrick Ford can write wills to provide for (or to disinherit) children like Terry Bean, are the benefits of equitable adoption doctrine worth the litigation costs the doctrine generates?

For a suggestion that the problem might better be approached by making it less intimidating and less expensive for functional parents (who often are the child's natural grandparents) to write wills, see Kristine S. Knaplund, Grandparents Raising Grandchildren and the Implications for Inheritance, 48 Ariz. L. Rev 1, 18–22 (2006).

4. Hattie O'Neal was raised by her mother until her mother's death, when Hattie was eight years old. Hattie then lived with a maternal aunt for four years. The aunt then brought her from New York to Georgia and surrendered custody to a non-relative who wanted a daughter. When the non-relative realized that she was unable to care for Hattie, she brought Hattie to the home of her paternal aunt, Estelle Page (Hattie met her genetic father for the first time when she reached the age of 21). Shortly after Hattie moved in, Page learned that Roswell Cook and his wife wanted a daughter, and Page turned Hattie over to the Cooks. Hattie then lived with Cook until her marriage, and identified herself as Cook's daughter. She also identified Cook as the grandfather of her children. Cook died intestate when Hattie was 42. Hattie sought a share of Cook's estate as an adopted daughter—even though Cook had never taken any formal steps to adopt her.

Would the California Supreme Court have permitted Hattie to inherit from Cook? See O'Neal v. Wilkes, 263 Ga. 850, 439 S.E.2d 490 (1994) (rejecting Hattie's intestate succession claim). But see Welch v. Wilson, 205 W.Va. 21, 516 S.E.2d 35 (1999) (finding equitable adoption based on evidence of decedent's devotion to equitably adopted child, and reciprocation of that devotion). For arguments that courts have construed the equitable adoption doctrine too narrowly to ensure that those whom decedents consider "children" are provided for, see Michael J. Higdon, When Informal Adoption Meets Intestate Succession: The Cultural Myopia of the Equitable Adoption Doctrine,43 Wake Forest L. Rev. 223 (2008); Irene D. Johnson, A Suggested Solution to the Problem of Intestate Succession in Nontraditional Family Arrangements: Taking the "Adoption" (and the Inequity) Out of the Doctrine of "Equitable Adoption", 54 St. Louis U. L.J. 271 (2009) (arguing that "the doctrine is not based on legally defensible theories, makes irrational distinctions among children who are essentially similarly situated, and is not nearly inclusive enough to do justice—especially when so many children today are being raised in nontraditional family arrangements lacking legal sanction").

5. What inferences should we draw from a caretaker's failure to adopt a child over whom the caretaker has long-term actual custody, even if not legal custody? Should we assume that the caretaker made a conscious decision not to adopt? Or is it more likely that the caretaker simply lacked the resources, or the information, necessary to pursue a formal adoption?

By one estimate, nearly one million black children do not live with a genetic parent, and few of them have been formally adopted by their caretakers. Lynda Richardson, Adoptions that Lack Papers, Not Purpose, N.Y. Times, Nov. 25, 1993, at C1.

6. With same-sex couples, the problem may not be resources or access to lawyers, but legal obstacles to adoption. Many states have been unwilling to permit the same-sex partner of a natural parent to adopt the natural parent's child. If the natural parent's partner dies intestate, should the child be able to take by intestate succession?

What arguments would you make for the child? For the collateral heirs of the deceased partner?

7. Even when the court recognizes equitable adoption doctrine, the adoptive "parent" is not entitled to inherit from the adopted "child." Do you understand why? See Estate of Riggs, 109 Misc.2d 644, 440 N.Y.S.2d 450 (1981).

8. On equitable adoption doctrine more generally, see Note, Equitable Adoption: They Took Him into Their Home and Called Him Fred, 58 Va. L. Rev. 727 (1972); see also Jan Ellen Rein, Relatives by Blood, Adoption and Association: Who Should Get What and Why, 37 Vand. L. Rev. 711 (1984); Adam J. Hirsch, Inheritance Law, Legal Contraptions, and the Problem of Doctrinal Change, 79 Or. L. Rev. 527, 547–51 (2000).

Professor Susan Gary, who advocates amending intestacy statutes to provide courts with limited discretion in determining when a child may inherit from his or her functional parent, also acknowledges the dangers in drafting statutes that include functional relationships:

> Expanding intestacy rights to include functional relationships is fraught with risks. Many adults have relationships with children that, although close, are not the sort of relationships that should entitle them to intestacy rights. Grandparents, neighbors, and other relatives of the child all may play important roles in a child's life. Creating an intestacy statute limited to functional parents and not encompassing these other important persons presents a significant challenge. Also, many stepparents have close relationships with their stepchildren and yet may draw a distinction between their biological or adoptive children and their stepchildren.... And the existence of a parent-child relationship does not necessarily equate to dispositive intent.... [T]he practical problems of administering the intestacy laws mean that limitations on who should qualify are important."

Susan N. Gary, The Parent–Child Relationship Under Intestacy Statutes, 32 U. Mem. L. Rev. 643, 673–74 (2002).

9. It is one thing for a child to invoke the equitable adoption doctrine to inherit from the child's own substitute parent. Should a child also be entitled to inherit from the "parent's" family members? In Board of Education of Montgomery County v. Browning, 333 Md. 281, 635 A.2d 373 (1994), the court answered no. Paula Browning was born out of wedlock, but Lawrence, her biological father, adopted her when she was two. Her father married Marian Gibson five months later, and Paula grew up in the couple's household. Marian died in 1986, sixty-five years after Lawrence adopted Paula and sixty-four years after Lawrence and Marian were married. Marian never adopted Paula. Eleanor Hamilton, Marian's sister, died in 1990, intestate and without heirs (other than Paula). Eleanor left an estate of nearly $400,000. Paula invoked the equitable adoption doctrine, and sought to take as Eleanor's heir. The court reaffirmed the equitable adoption doctrine, but held that the doctrine only permits the adopted child to inherit from the adoptive parent, not through the adoptive parent, from the adoptive parent's relatives. As a result, Eleanor's estate escheated to the local school district.

Do you think the result in the Browning case effectuated Eleanor's intent? At least one other case has permitted an equitably adopted child to inherit from a relative of the adoptive parent. In First National Bank in Fairmont v. Phillips, 176 W.Va. 395, 344 S.E.2d 201 (1985), the court permitted an equitably adopted child to inherit from another child of the adoptive parent. The court, however, explicitly reserved judgment on the question at stake in the Browning case: the right of an equitably adopted child to inherit from the adoptive parent's collateral relatives.

C. Non-Marital Children and Questions of Paternity

As we have seen, a decedent's descendants (together with the surviving spouse, if any) have priority under every intestacy statute. In most proceedings, identifying decedent's descendants is a relatively uncomplicated task. Not infrequently, however, the decedent (or one of the decedent's descendants) may have had one or more children out of wedlock. Or occasionally, the biological paternity of a child born to a married couple is in doubt. How does the law address these issues?

At common law, it was presumed that children born to a married woman were the children of her husband (no matter what the reality of the situation). The presumption could be rebutted only by proof of the husband's impotence, sterility, or lack of access to his wife during the period of gestation. In a number of states, the common law presumption has been explicitly codified. In others, the presumption can be overcome by clear and convincing evidence of paternity.

The status of children born to an unmarried woman has evolved dramatically—both in terminology and in legal treatment. Once tarred as "bastards" or, later, "illegitimates", children born outside of marriage now face less (or even non-) judgmental labels; "non-marital children" has become a common one. The legal treatment of non-marital children has also changed. At common law, non-marital children were filius nullius—the children of no one. They were not entitled to inherit from or through either parent. American statutes, even from an early date, ameliorated the common law's harsh treatment: children born outside of marriage were at least accorded the right to inherit from and through their mothers. Until recently, however, most states placed significant restrictions on the right of non-marital children to inherit from and through their fathers.

The United States Supreme Court played a major role in reforming this area of law. Trimble v. Gordon, 430 U.S. 762, 97 S.Ct. 1459, 52 L.Ed.2d 31 (1977), provided the impetus for much of the reform. An Illinois statute provided that a non-marital child could inherit from its father only if the parents had legitimated the child by marrying each other and the father had acknowledged the child during his lifetime. A girl sought to inherit from her intestate father when there had been neither marriage nor acknowledgment. The father had, however, been ordered to support his daughter after a court proceeding in which the court found him to be the girl's father. The Illinois courts, relying on the state's statute, held that she was not entitled to inherit from her father. The United States Supreme Court reversed, holding the statute unconstitutional.

The state had advanced two justifications for the statute: first, the statute encouraged legitimate family relationships; second, the statute facilitated the orderly transmission of decedent's property. The Court easily rejected the argument that, somehow, "persons will shun illicit relations because the offspring may not one day reap the benefits." The state's second argument merited more attention; the Court acknowledged that the problem of proving paternity "might justify a more demanding standard for illegitimate children claiming under their fathers' estates than that required either for illegitimate children claiming under their mothers' estates or for legitimate children generally." 430 U.S. at 770. In Trimble itself, however, the Court concluded that the Illinois statute was infirm because it excluded some categories of non-marital children from inheriting even though their inheritance rights could have been recognized without jeopardizing the orderly settlement of estates.

Subsequently, in Lalli v. Lalli, 439 U.S. 259, 99 S.Ct. 518, 58 L.Ed.2d 503 (1978), the Supreme Court upheld a New York statute which permitted a non-marital child to inherit from its father only when there had been a declaration of paternity before the father's death. The Court held that this procedural requirement bore a substantial relation to the state interest in assuring the orderly settlement of estates.

Nevertheless, the die had been cast: the Court had established that states can justify excluding non-marital children from inheriting only by applying procedural rules designed to assure adequate proof of paternity. For an in-depth discussion of the law's treatment of non-marital children, see Browne Lewis, Children of Men: Balancing the Inheritance Rights of Marital and Non–Marital Children, 39 U. Tol. L. Rev. 1 (2007).

With the advent of DNA testing, courts can efficiently and reliably determine paternity issues. Professor Paula Monopoli questions whether there is any reason for states to retain their complicated parentage rules in light of developing technology. See Paula A. Monopoli, Nonmarital Children and Post–Death Parentage: A Different Path for Inheritance Law?, 48 Santa Clara L. Rev. 857 (2008).

Although legal paternity has a variety of legal consequences, we will focus on its relevance to intestacy proceedings.

UNIFORM PROBATE CODE

SECTION 2–117. NO DISTINCTION BASED ON MARITAL STATUS.

Except as otherwise provided in Sections 2–114, 2–119, 2–120, or 2–121, a parent-child relationship exists between a child and the child's genetic parents, regardless of the parents' marital status.

In determining whether a "parent-child relationship" exists, one must look to the paternity law of the relevant state. Several states have adopted variations of the Uniform Parentage Act (as amended in 2002), a lengthy model statute that sets out procedures and presumptions for determining parental status. Consider the following excerpts:

UNIFORM PARENTAGE ACT

SECTION 201. ESTABLISHMENT OF PARENT-CHILD RELATIONSHIP.

* * *

(b) The father-child relationship is established between a man and a child by:

(1) an unrebutted presumption of the man's paternity of the child under Section 204;

(2) an effective acknowledgment of paternity by the man under [Article] 3, unless the acknowledgment has been rescinded or successfully challenged;

(3) an adjudication of the man's paternity;

(4) adoption of the child by the man; [or]

(5) the man's having consented to assisted reproduction by a woman under [Article] 7 which resulted in the birth of the child [; or

(6) an adjudication confirming the man as a parent of a child born to a gestational mother if the agreement was validated under [Article] 8 or is enforceable under other law].

SECTION 204. PRESUMPTION OF PATERNITY.

(a) A man is presumed to be the father of a child if:

(1) he and the mother of the child are married to each other and the child is born during the marriage;

(2) he and the mother of the child were married to each other and the child is born within 300 days after the marriage is terminated by death, annulment, declaration of invalidity, or divorce [, or after a decree of separation];

(3) before the birth of the child, he and the mother of the child married each other in apparent compliance with law, even if the attempted marriage is or could be declared invalid, and the child is born during the invalid marriage or within 300 days after its termination by death, annulment, declaration of invalidity, or divorce [, or after a decree of separation];

(4) after the birth of the child, he and the mother of the child married each other in apparent compliance with law, whether or not the marriage is or could be declared invalid, and he voluntarily asserted his paternity of the child, and:

(A) the assertion is in a record filed with [state agency maintaining birth records];

(B) he agreed to be and is named as the child's father on the child's birth certificate; or

(C) he promised in a record to support the child as his own; or

(5) for the first two years of the child's life, he resided in the same household with the child and openly held out the child as his own.

(b) A presumption of paternity established under this section may be rebutted only by an adjudication under [Article] 6.

* * *

NOTES AND QUESTIONS

1. In establishing a presumption of paternity when a child is born during a marriage, the Uniform Parentage Act followed well-established common and statutory law. Why might the law establish such a presumption? What type of evidence should be sufficient to overcome the presumption? For an argument that states should adopt the UPA's more functional approach to defining parenthood, see Megan Pendleton, Intestate Inheritance Claims: Determining A Child's Right to Inherit When Biological and Presumptive Paternity Overlap, 29 Cardozo L. Rev. 2823 (2008). For a thorough exploration of the UPA, UPC and various state law approaches to defining parenthood, see Susan N. Gary, We Are Family: The Definition of Parent and Child For Succession Purposes, 34 ACTEC J. 171 (2008).

2. The Uniform Parentage Act prescribes procedures for using DNA evidence to support paternity claims, and many states allow DNA evidence to be admitted for that purpose. Section 608 of the UPA gives courts discretion in granting motions to allow DNA testing to determine parentage. The comments explain:

> This section incorporates the doctrine of paternity by estoppel, which extends equally to a child with a presumed father or an acknowledged father. In appropriate circumstances, the court may deny genetic testing and find the presumed or acknowledged father to be the father of the child. The most common situation in which estoppel should be applied arises when a man knows that a

> child is not, or may not be, his genetic child, but the man has affirmatively accepted his role as child's father and both the mother and the child have relied on that acceptance. Similarly, the man may have relied on the mother's acceptance of him as the child's father and the mother is then estopped to deny the man's presumed parentage.

But see Estate of Sanders, 2 Cal.App.4th 462, 3 Cal.Rptr.2d 536 (1992) (upholding trial court determination barring use of DNA evidence to prove paternity because the California paternity statute failed to expressly establish DNA testing as a method for establishing paternity). In a state that allows DNA evidence, is a child entitled to a court order to exhume the putative father's body for purposes of administering a DNA test? It depends: in some states, paternity must be established during the father's life, so a child seeking to exhume the deceased putative father's body would be out of luck. In those states that do permit proof of paternity after the putative father's death, the answer varies. Some states have statutes authorizing exhumation for testing purposes. See, e.g., O.C.Ga. Ann. § 53–2–27(a) (authorizing a court to "order the removal and testing of deoxyribonucleic acid (DNA) samples from the remains of the decedent and from any party in interest whose kinship to the decedent is in controversy" and authorizing "disinterment of decedent's remains" if reasonably necessary to obtain DNA samples.) In other states the answer is a matter for the common law. See, e.g., Estate of Sekanic, 229 A.D.2d 76, 653 N.Y.S.2d 449 (1997); Estate of Janis, 210 A.D.2d 101, 620 N.Y.S.2d 342 (1994) (holding that the subsection of the NY paternity statute that allows a child to establish paternity with proof that "a blood genetic marker test *had* been administered to the father during life" does not entitle a non-marital child to exhumation); Estate of Morningstar, 17 A.D.3d 1060, 794 N.Y.S.2d 205 (2005) (holding that the statute allows exhumation if the child also claims that the father acknowledged parentage during the child's life); Estate of Williams, 26 Misc.3d 680, 891 N.Y.S.2d 268 (Surr. Ct. 2009) (holding that mother of child born after decedent's death was entitled to DNA testing, even though the deceased never knew the child) See generally Ralph C. Brashier, Children and Inheritance in the Nontraditional Family, 1996 Utah L. Rev. 93, 116–47 (1996); See Ilene Sherwyn Cooper, Posthumous Paternity Testing: A Proposal to Amend EPTL 4–1.2(a)(2)(D), 69 Alb. L. Rev. 947 (2006) (arguing that the New York legislature should revise New York's paternity statute to allow posthumous DNA testing); Cf. Helen Bishop Jenkins, A Study of the Intersection of DNA Technology, Exhumation and Heirship Determination as It Relates to Modern–Day Descendants of Slaves in America, 50 Ala. L. Rev. 39, 49–53 (1998).

Is there a point to cutting off these questions at the death of the "father?" Should the dead "rest in peace?" Professor Helen Bishop Jenkins argues that proof of paternity, principally DNA evidence, should be available to permit persons descended from white masters and their slaves to share in the inheritance of the masters. Helen Bishop Jenkins, DNA and the Slave–Descendant Nexus: A Theoretical Challenge to Traditional Notions of Heirship Jurisprudence, 16 Harv. Blackletter J. 211(2000).

Conversely, suppose the collateral relatives believe that DNA testing will exclude paternity. Should they be entitled to compel the child to submit to DNA testing against her will? See Estate of Murcury, 177 Vt. 606, 868 A.2d 680, 685 (2004) (stating that "compelled genetic testing of a decedent's living relative represents a substantial invasion of privacy").

3. Standing. Who has standing to bring a paternity proceeding? Article 6 of the Uniform Parentage Act addresses this question. Which provisions might become relevant in an intestacy proceeding?

UNIFORM PARENTAGE ACT

SECTION 602. STANDING TO MAINTAIN PROCEEDING.

Subject to [Article] 3 and Sections 607 and 609, a proceeding to adjudicate parentage may be maintained by:

(1) the child;

(2) the mother of the child;

(3) a man whose paternity of the child is to be adjudicated;

(4) the support-enforcement agency [or other governmental agency authorized by other law];

(5) an authorized adoption agency or licensed child-placing agency; [or]

(6) a representative authorized by law to act for an individual who would otherwise be entitled to maintain a proceeding but who is deceased, incapacitated, or a minor [; or

(7) an intended parent under [Article] 8].

Most states that have adopted the Uniform Parentage Act have modified the model statute prior to enactment. Consider the following case:

In re Estate of Burden

California Court of Appeal 2007.
146 Cal. App. 4th 1021, 53 Cal.Rptr.3d 390.

■ PERREN, J.:

Probate Code section 6453, subdivision (b)(2) permits a child born out of wedlock to establish a father-child relationship for intestate succession purposes by providing clear and convincing evidence that the father "has openly held out the child as his own." In this case of first impression, we conclude that evidence of decedent's acknowledgments of respondent as his son during his lifetime are sufficient to meet the burden imposed by section 6453, subdivision (b)(2). We affirm.

STATEMENT OF FACTS AND PROCEDURAL HISTORY

Appellant Tara Burden appeals from an order of the probate court finding that respondent Dale Agnew, her half brother, is entitled to an equal share of the estate of their father, Gregory Allen Burden, under the laws of intestate succession. The court found by clear and convincing evidence that Gregory "openly held out" Dale as his son.

Dale is the son of Gregory Burden and Sally Routt. When Gregory found out that Sally was pregnant, he did not deny fatherhood and proposed marriage. Sally refused Gregory's offer. Sally married Chris Agnew a few months before Dale's birth in October 1971. Dale's birth certificate names Chris as Dale's father, and Chris supported Dale as if Dale were his own child. The parties do not dispute that Gregory is Dale's biological father.

Tara is the daughter of Gregory and Linda Eve Burden. At the time of Tara's birth in December 1981, Gregory and Linda were married and living in California. Gregory and Linda divorced in 1985. Linda received full custody of Tara, and Gregory was given visitation rights. Tara maintained a close relationship with Gregory until his death in August 2004.

Sally did not inform Dale that Gregory was his biological father until September or October 1989, when Dale was 18 years old. During those 18 years, neither Sally nor Dale had any contact with Gregory or any member of his family. After telling Dale that Gregory was his father, Sally took Dale to meet Gregory's mother, Helen; brothers, Kerry and Michael; and sisters, Joyce and Robin.

Shortly after meeting Gregory's family, Dale called Gregory and spoke to him for the first time. Gregory apologized to Dale "for not being there ... for being ... an inactive father." Gregory told Dale that he had a half sister, Tara. However, Gregory did not want Tara to know that Dale was her half brother and refused to allow Dale to come to California and meet her.

Dale next spoke to Gregory in January or February 1990. Dale called Gregory after Gregory returned a photo album containing pictures of Dale that Sally or Helen had sent to him. In that conversation, Gregory mentioned a family resemblance between Dale and himself and between Dale and Tara. Gregory sent a letter to Sally with the photo album. In the letter, Gregory again stated he did not want to become involved in Dale's life.

Dale spoke to Gregory for the last time when Dale called him in 1995 after graduating from college to ask him for help getting into Navy flight school.

After Dale met Gregory's relatives, Dale developed a close relationship with them. Since 1998, he has lived next door to Gregory's mother, Helen, in Ohio, and within 25 miles of Gregory's two brothers and two sisters. Helen and Gregory's brothers babysat Dale's children. Dale testified that everyone in the family knew that Dale was Gregory's son, except Tara. Tara was told of Dale's existence in 1991.

Gregory's brother, sister, and mother all testified that Gregory did not deny being Dale's father. Gregory had minimal contact with his family in Ohio, except that he and his sister, Joyce, had occasional e-mail contact. Joyce and Gregory discussed Dale in three or four e-mails. On February 8,

2004, Gregory sent an e-mail to Joyce replying to one she had sent. After talking at length about Tara, he stated: "Congrats on future grandkids—I say better everyone else than I. Although I am aware that I am told I have two by DA [Dale Agnew] only the future knows if any relationship will ever occur. It is not high on my priority list and may be to another unfair but I have only been a party to conception and by my own choosing. DA has sent pictures and I wish I could say I was the proud grandpa to set them out for display but I have yet to feel the paternal pull in that direction."

Dale sent Gregory greeting cards with pictures of his children, e-mails, father's day cards, birth announcements and a wedding invitation. Gregory did not respond to any of them.

DISCUSSION

* * *

Interpretation of Section 6453, Subdivision (b)(2)

Section 6450 et seq. contains the rules for determining whether there is a parent-child relationship for purposes of inheritance by intestate succession. Section 6450, subdivision (a) states that the "relationship of parent and child exists between a person and the person's natural parents, regardless of the marital status of the natural parents."

Section 6453 contains the rules for determining who is a "natural parent." As relevant here, section 6453 states:

> "(a) A natural parent and child relationship is established where that relationship is presumed and not rebutted pursuant to the Uniform Parentage Act (Part 3 (commencing with Section 7600) of Division 12 of the Family Code).
>
> "(b) A natural parent and child relationship may be established pursuant to any other provisions of the Uniform Parentage Act, except that the relationship may not be established by an action under subdivision (c) of Section 7630 of the Family Code unless any of the following conditions exist: . . .
>
> "(2) Paternity is established by clear and convincing evidence that the father has openly held out the child as his own."

Dale asserts, and the trial court agreed, that he is entitled to one-half of Gregory's estate because he has submitted clear and convincing evidence that Gregory openly held him out as his own child pursuant to section 6453, subdivision (b)(2). Tara asserts that a showing greater than that made by Dale is necessary to meet the requirements of the statute.

* * *

The purpose of the intestate succession provisions of the Probate Code is " 'to carry out . . . the intent a decedent without a will is most likely to have had,' evidently at the time of death, and to do so in a 'more efficient and expeditious' manner." (*Estate of Joseph*, *supra*, 17 Cal.4th at p. 209, quoting from Tent. Recommendation Relating to Wills and Intestate Succession (Nov. 1982) 16 Cal. Law Revision Com. Rep. (1982) pp. 2318, 2319.)

The legislative history of section 6453, subdivision (b)(2) indicates that the clear and convincing evidence standard is "to discourage dubious paternity claims made after a father's death for the sole purpose of inheritance." (*Estate of Sanders* (1992) 2 Cal.App.4th 462, 474 [3 Cal. Rptr. 2d 536].)

Section 6453, subdivision (b)(2)'s predecessor, former section 6408, subdivision (f)(2), required paternity to be established "by clear and convincing evidence that the father has openly and notoriously held out the child as his own." When the statute was renumbered and amended in 1993, the Legislature omitted "and notoriously" and now requires only that the father have "openly held out" the child as his own. (23 Cal. Law Revision Com. Rep. (1993) p. 1011.)

The parties have not cited nor have we found a case construing section 6453, subdivision (b)(2). However, we are not without guidance. We must interpret a statute in context, examining other legislation on the same or similar subjects to ascertain the Legislature's probable intent. We may gain insight into the intended meaning of a phrase or expression by examining use of the same or similar language in other statutes. (*Quarterman v. Kefauver* (1997) 55 Cal.App.4th 1366, 1371 [64 Cal. Rptr. 2d 741].)

One of the presumptions in the Family Code referred to in subdivision (a) of section 6453 contains language identical to that in subdivision (b)(2). Family Code section 7611, subdivision (d) provides that a man is presumed to be the father of a child if he "receives the child into his home and openly holds out the child as his natural child."

Numerous appellate opinions, including one from this court, have interpreted Family Code section 7611, subdivision (d)'s use of the term "acknowledge" as a synonym for "openly holds out." (See, e.g., *Dawn D. v. Superior Court* (1998) 17 Cal.4th 932, 938 [72 Cal. Rptr. 2d 871, 952 P.2d 1139]; *In re Salvador M.* (2003) 111 Cal.App.4th 1353, 1357 [4 Cal. Rptr. 3d 705]; *Brian C. v. Ginger K.* (2000) 77 Cal.App.4th 1198, 1219, 1221 [92 Cal. Rptr. 2d 294]; *In re Julia U.* (1998) 64 Cal.App.4th 532, 541 [74 Cal. Rptr. 2d 920]; *In re Spencer W.* (1996) 48 Cal.App.4th 1647, 1652 [56 Cal. Rptr. 2d 524]; *In re Marriage of Moschetta* (1994) 25 Cal.App.4th 1218, 1226 [30 Cal. Rptr. 2d 893].)

We conclude from this consensus that "openly holds out" is synonymous with "acknowledge." . . .

Here, Gregory did more than privately acknowledge that Dale was his son. As noted by the trial court: "This was proven to the standard of 'clear and convincing evidence' by Greg Burden's written acknowledgement that he was a 'party to conception'; his having asked Dale's mother Sally . . . to marry him; and his admissions to his own mother, brother and sister as well as to Dale and Dale's mother that Dale was his son."

Our interpretation of section 6453, subdivision (b)(2) furthers the statute's legislative purpose. Dale's paternity claim is not "dubious." Although Gregory only grudgingly admitted paternity, he did so on a number of occasions to a number of people, both orally and in writing. This satisfies section 6453, subdivision (b)(2).

Whether or not Gregory would have wanted Dale to inherit is irrelevant. The trial court correctly held that "[t]he law of intestacy ... disregards such evidence of intimacy and lack of intimacy. A decedent who fails to designate inheritance of his assets by a written last testament, is presumed to have known that the laws of intestacy will apply to his estate. [Citation.] For purposes of intestacy, the statutory provisions on inheritance control." (See *Estate of Dye* (2001) 92 Cal.App.4th 966, 980 [112 Cal. Rptr. 2d 362] ["The intestacy laws by their nature will defeat many 'true' intentions. [The d]ecedent could have prevented such 'injustice,' if any, by making a . . . will"].)

Our interpretation of section 6453, subdivision (b)(2) makes it unnecessary to decide whether the trial court erred in admitting evidence of DNA testing. We note, however, that the right to intestate succession in California "does not turn on the judicial determination of paternity, but rather on the factual question whether or not he was acknowledged by [his father] in the prescribed statutory fashion." (*Estate of Ginochio* (1974) 43 Cal. App. 3d 412, 416 [117 Cal. Rptr. 565]; see also *id.* at pp. 416–417 [interpreting former section 255].)

* * *

The order is affirmed. Costs are awarded to respondent.

NOTES AND QUESTIONS

1. The Burden court acknowledges that the intestacy statute has two objectives: to approximate the decedent's intentions and to facilitate the orderly administration of the intestate estate. Yet is seems fairly clear that Gregory did not want to become involved in Dale's life in any way, and that he had no fatherly feelings for him. Does the court's holding approximate Gregory's likely intentions? And why does the court announce, toward the end of the opinion, that "whether or not Gregory would have wanted Dale to inherit is irrelevant?" With what policy objective is this court most concerned?

2. Does it make sense for non-marital children to inherit from genetic fathers they have never known? Why should biology be so important? Consider Dale in particular. Until he was over 18 years old, he believed that Chris Agnew was his father. As far as we know, he treated Agnew as his father, and Agnew supported Dale as his own child. What social policy is advanced by permitting Dale to establish, after he reached the age of majority, that someone else was his genetic father? Should family be defined along strict genetic lines? Isn't that approach inconsistent with the modern approach to adoption, and even to equitable adoption?

Is permitting the child to inherit from a "natural" father with whom the child has never lived a penalty on the father? Reparations for the child? For a general discussion of that issue, see Richard F. Storrow, Parenthood by Pure Intention: Assisted Reproduction and the Functional Approach to Parentage, 53 Hastings L. J. 597 (2002).

Statutes of Limitations

Is there a statute of limitations for determining paternity? Consider the following sections of the Uniform Parentage Act:

SECTION 606. NO LIMITATION: CHILD HAVING NO PRESUMED, ACKNOWLEDGED, OR ADJUDICATED FATHER.

A proceeding to adjudicate the parentage of a child having no presumed, acknowledged, or adjudicated father may be commenced at any time, even after:

(1) the child becomes an adult, but only if the child initiates the proceeding; or

(2) an earlier proceeding to adjudicate paternity has been dismissed based on the application of a statute of limitation then in effect.

SECTION 607. LIMITATION: CHILD HAVING PRESUMED FATHER.

(a) Except as otherwise provided in subsection (b), a proceeding brought by a presumed father, the mother, or another individual to adjudicate the parentage of a child having a presumed father must be commenced not later than two years after the birth of the child.

(b) A proceeding seeking to disprove the father-child relationship between a child and the child's presumed father may be maintained at any time if the court determines that:

(1) the presumed father and the mother of the child neither cohabited nor engaged in sexual intercourse with each other during the probable time of conception; and

(2) the presumed father never openly held out the child as his own.

PROBLEMS

1. In 1986, Hannah Epstein was born to Aviva Epstein, an umarried woman. Financially self-sufficient and content to be a single parent, Aviva did not inform Hannah's biological father, Peter, of Hannah's birth. In 2009, Hannah determined that Peter was probably her father and contacted him. Peter agreed to submit to a DNA test, and the test concluded that Peter was Hannah's father. The two had dinner several times before Peter's untimely death in 2011. If the relevant jurisdiction has adopted the Uniform Parentage Act, may Hannah bring a paternity claim?

As a general matter, why do statutes of limitations exist? What justification is there for disregarding the objectives of limitations statutes in paternity actions?

2. Fewer than 10 states have adopted Uniform Parentage Act section 606. Most states have statute of limitations periods that require paternity actions to be brought by the time a child reaches a particular age, ranging from age 18 to age 23.

Suppose Hannah, in problem 1, above, lives in a state with a limitations period of 23 years. Hannah, age 25, brings a paternity action after Peter's death to establish a right to inherit as his intestate heir. The applicable intestacy statute requires those with an interest in the estate to assert a claim "within a reasonable time, and after reasonable notice ... as prescribed by the court." Hannah argues that the Uniform Parentage Act (as modified by her state) does not preclude her from establishing paternity for intestacy purposes. Should she prevail? See Wingate v. Estate of Ryan, 149 N.J. 227, 693 A.2d 457 (1997); Estate of Rogers, 103 Hawaii 275, 81 P.3d 1190 (2003); Estate of Palmer, 658 N.W.2d 197 (Minn. 2003); Taylor v. Hoffman, 209 W.Va. 172, 544 S.E.2d 387 (2001) (holding that the statute of limitations included in the parentage act does not apply to intestate succession claims). By contrast, the Vermont Supreme Court has construed its statute to impose a limitations period on inheritance claims by non-marital children, and has upheld the statute against constitutional attack. Estate of Murcury, 177 Vt. 606, 868 A.2d 680 (2004).

3. Same as question 1, but suppose that Aviva married Chuck after she discovered she was pregnant, and Chuck raised Hannah as his own child. If Hannah, at age 25, determines that Peter is her biological father, can she file a paternity claim to establish her right to inherit as his intestate heir? Does section 607 give any guidance? In Estate of Martignacco, 689 N.W.2d 262 (Minn.App. 2004), the court—as in Burden—permitted a child to inherit from his genetic father even though the child spent his entire childhood (and much of his adulthood) believing that his mother's husband was his father.

4. Same as problem 3, but suppose Hannah always assumed that Chuck was her biological father. At Chuck's death, Chuck and Aviva's son Ralph contests Chuck's paternity of Hannah in probate court. Under the Uniform Parentage Act, how strong is Ralph's case? See Estate of Jotham, 722 N.W.2d 447 (Minn. 2006) (holding that Uniform Parentage Act statute of limitations bars claim).

Inheritance From a Non–Marital Child

So far, we have dealt with the right of a child to inherit from her genetic father. Does the genetic father have a reciprocal right to inherit from his daughter?

UNIFORM PROBATE CODE

SECTION 2–114. PARENT BARRED FROM INHERITING IN CERTAIN CIRCUMSTANCES.

(a) A parent is barred from inheriting from or through a child of the parent if:

(1) the parent's parental rights were terminated and the parent-child relationship was not judicially reestablished; or

(2) the child died before reaching [18] years of age and there is clear and convincing evidence that immediately before the child's death the parental rights of the parent could have been terminated under law of

this state other than this [code] on the basis of nonsupport, abandonment, abuse, neglect, or other actions or inactions of the parent toward the child.

(b) For the purpose of intestate succession from or through the deceased child, a parent who is barred from inheriting under this section is treated as if the parent predeceased the child.

Another difficult question surrounds the right of the father's relatives to inherit from a non-marital child. The non-marital child may not even know of the existence of these relatives. Should they nevertheless share in the child's estate? Consider the following:

PROBLEMS

1. Joanne was born in 1971, at a time when her mother was married to Willard Wingate, who has always acted as her father. DNA testing will reveal, however, that John Ryan was Joanne's genetic father. If Joanne dies in 2011, survived by her mother, by Willard Wingate, and by Ryan, how would her estate be distributed under the UPC?

2. Denis Griswold was born out-of-wedlock to Betty Morris. John Draves, in response to a court proceeding, confessed that he was the child's father and paid court-ordered support for 18 years. One year after the birth of Denis, Betty Morris married Fred Griswold and began to refer to her son as Denis Griswold. Denis believed Fred Griswold to be his father. Not until he was nearly 40 years old did Denis learn that Draves was his father. At Denis Griswold's death, he was survived by his wife and by two children born to John Draves, who had married and moved out-of-state. Griswold and the Draves children did not know of each other's existence. If, in California, siblings are generally entitled to a share of the estate of a decedent who dies married without issue, should the Draves children share in Denis Griswold's estate? See Estate of Griswold, 25 Cal.4th 904, 24 P.3d 1191, 108 Cal.Rptr.2d 165 (2001).

D. THE IMPACT OF MODERN REPRODUCTIVE TECHNOLOGY

In recent years, medical science has had great success in enabling people to conceive children without sexual intercourse. These medical advances have been a boon to married couples with fertility problems, and they have also increased the parenting opportunities available to same-sex couples:

> These methods currently include intrauterine insemination (previously and sometimes currently called artificial insemination), donation of eggs, donation of embryos, in-vitro fertilization and transfer of embryos, and intracytoplasmic sperm injection.
>
> The woman who becomes pregnant by one of these technologies may do so because she intends to be the child's mother. If she

> intends to be the child's mother, she may be married to a man or a woman (under the law of Connecticut, Iowa, Maine, Massachusetts, New Hampshire, or Vermont), or she may be in a civil union or domestic partnership with another woman (under the law of California, Hawaii, Maryland, New Jersey, Oregon, Washington, or the District of Columbia), or she may be unmarried with or without a partner of the same or opposite sex. Alternatively, the woman who becomes pregnant may be a surrogate who has agreed to bear the child for a married or unmarried couple of the same or opposite sex or for an unpartnered man or woman. To further complicate matters, the sperm that fertilizes the egg may be the sperm of a man who intends to be the child's father or the sperm of a third-party donor who has no such intention and probably was compensated for making the donation. The egg that is fertilized may be the egg of a woman who intends to be the child's mother or the egg of a third-party donor who has no such intention and probably was compensated for making the donation. The possible combinations are legion.

Sheldon F. Kurtz & Lawrence W. Waggoner, The UPC Addresses the Class–Gift and Intestacy Rights of Children of Assisted Reproductive Technologies, 35 ACTEC J. 30 (2009).

But courts and legislatures have struggled to respond to changing times. As Professor Ralph Brashier explains:

> A child can only have two genetic parents. From this genetic origin society decided that the child could only have two legal parents as well. In the traditional family, the genetic and legal parents were the same. The historical emphasis upon ties of blood made it natural that the child should be an expectant heir from and through those genetic, legal parents.
>
> Although today one or both of the child's genetic parents are increasingly not a part of his social family—a family that may include several adults in parent-like roles—we continue to limit the number of legal parents a child may have to two. But who are they? Reluctant legislatures have in many instances failed to remodel existing family laws to reflect fundamental change in family structures; by default, individuals have turned to courts for a legal determination of their familial roles. When legal and genetic parentage are different, inheritance rights today typically follow law, not blood.
>
> Lacking detailed legislative guidance on parentage in nontraditional families, courts have, by and large, engaged in conservative efforts to approximate and preserve a semblance of the traditional family.

Ralph C. Brashier, Children and Inheritance in the Nontraditional Family, 1996 Utah L. Rev. 93, 222–24. For additional discussion, see Kristine S. Knaplund, Legal Issues of Maternity and Inheritance for the Biotech Child of the 21st Century, 43 Real Prop. Prob. & Trust J. 393 (2008); Kathryn Venturatos Lorio, Conceiving the Inconceivable: Legal Recognition of the

Posthumously Conceived Child, 34 ACTEC J. 154 (Winter 2008); Lee–Ford Tritt, Sperms and Estates: An Unadulterated Functionally Based Approach to Parent–Child Property Succession, 62 SMU L. Rev. 367 (2009); Naomi R. Cahn, Parenthood, Genes, and Gametes: The Family Law and Trusts and Estates Perspectives, 32 U. Mem. L. Rev 563 (2002); James E. Bailey, An Analytical Framework For Resolving The Issues Raised By The Interaction Between Reproductive Technology and the Law of Inheritance, 47 DePaul L. Rev. 743, 781–814 (1998); Helene Shapo, Matters of Life and Death: Inheritance Consequences of Reproductive Technologies, 25 Hofstra L. Rev. 1091 (1997); Ralph C. Brashier, Children and Inheritance in the Nontraditional Family, 1996 Utah L. Rev. 93, 177–222; Kathryn Venturatos Lorio, From Cradle to Tomb: Estate Planning Considerations of the New Procreation, 57 La. L. Rev. 27 (1996); Ronald Chester, Freezing the Heir Apparent: A Dialogue on Postmortem Conception, Parental Responsibility, and Inheritance, 33 Hous. L. Rev. 964 (1996).

Although a determination of parentage has many legal ramifications (such as creating support obligations and visitation rights), this text shall focus on intestate succession issues. In recent years, much of the litigation over the identification of intestate heirs has occurred because mothers of posthumously conceived children claim social security survivor benefits for those children. Under federal law, benefits are available to the deceased's minor children if the child would have been an intestate heir under applicable state law.

About a dozen states have statutes that address the posthumously conceived child issue. Of these, eight (Alabama, Delaware, North Dakota, Oklahoma, Texas, Utah, Washington and Wyoming) have enacted the 2002 Uniform Parentage Act, which provides that a father-child relationship is established if a man provides sperm with the intent to become a parent of a child and memorializes this intent in a formal writing that also authorizes posthumous conception. See also, Cal. Prob. Code § 249.5; Fla. Stat. Ann. § 742.17; La. Rev. Stat. Ann. § 9:391.1 (West 2008); Va. Code Ann. § 20–158 (West 2009). For an argument that the New York legislature should adopt a bill that would treat posthumously conceived children as the child of the father for all legal purposes, see Robert Matthew Harper, Dead Hand Problem: Why New York's Estates, Powers and Trusts Law Should Be Amended to Treat Posthumously Conceived Children as Decedents' Issue and Descendants, 21 Quinnipiac Probate L. J. 267 (2008).

In the majority of states the question is left to the courts, which must struggle to interpret intestacy statutes drafted without reproductive technology in mind. In Woodward v. Commissioner of Social Security, 435 Mass. 536, 760 N.E.2d 257 (2002), the Supreme Judicial Court of Massachusetts mirrored the UPA approach, holding that

> In certain limited circumstances, a child resulting from posthumous reproduction may enjoy the inheritance rights of "issue" under the Massachusetts intestacy statute. These limited circumstances exist where, as a threshold matter, the surviving parent or the child's other legal representative demonstrates a genetic rela-

> tionship between the child and the decedent. The survivor or representative must then establish both that the decedent affirmatively consented to posthumous conception and to the support of any resulting child. Even where such circumstances exist, time limitations may preclude commencing a claim for succession rights on behalf of a posthumously conceived child.

See also, Estate of Kolacy, 332 N.J.Super. 593, 753 A.2d 1257 (2000) (concluding that twin girls conceived after their genetic father's death were the intestate heirs of the father); Gillett–Netting v. Barnhart, 371 F.3d 593 (9th Cir. 2004) (awarding social security benefits to posthumously-conceived children).

Not all courts have come to the same conclusion, however. See, e.g.,; Vernoff v. Astrue, 568 F.3d 1102, 1105 (9th Cir. 2009) (holding that posthumously conceived children were not intestate heirs because wife had harvested husband's sperm after death and there was no indication that husband had intended to allow posthumous reproduction); Finley v. Astrue, 372 Ark. 103, 270 S.W.3d 849 (2008) (holding that twins whose test-tube conception had occurred during father's life, but whose mother had not been implanted with the fertilized embryo until after husband's death were not his "children" under the Arkansas intestacy statute). Khabbaz v. Commissioner, Social Security Administration,155 N.H. 798, 930 A.2d 1180 (2007) (finding that posthumously conceived children were not husband's children for intestacy purposes). For interesting reading on this issue, see Raymond C. O'Brien, The Momentum of Posthumous Conception: A Model Act, 25 Contemp. Health L. & Policy 332 (2009); Mary Radford, Postmortem Sperm Retrieval and the Social Security Administration: How Modern Reproductive Technology Makes Strange Bedfellows, 2 Est. Plan. & Community Prop. L.J. 33 (2009); Browne C. Lewis, Dead Men Reproducing: Responding to the Existence of After–Death Children, 16 Geo. Mason L. Rev. 403 (2009); Charles P. Kindregan, Jr., Dead Dads: Thawing an Heir from the Freezer, 35 William Mitchell L. Rev. 433 (2009). Kristine S. Knaplund, Equal Protection, Postmortem Conception, and Intestacy, 53 Kansas L. Rev. 627 (2005); Kristine S. Knaplund, Postmortem Conception and a Father's Last Will, 46 Ariz. L. Rev. 91 (2004); Helene Shapo, Matters of Life and Death: Inheritance Consequences of Reproductive Technologies, 25 Hofstra L. Rev. 1091, 1153–60 (1997); Anne R. Schiff, Arising From the Dead: Challenges of a Posthumous Procreation, 75 N.C. L. Rev. 901 (1997); Katheleen R. Guzman, Property, Progeny, Body Part: Assisted Reproduction and the Transfer of Wealth, 31 U. C. Davis L. Rev. 193 (1997).

QUESTIONS

1. Suppose Harold Husband dies intestate after banking sperm, survived by his wife and a daughter by a prior marriage. In a jurisdiction where courts have recognized inheritance rights in posthumously conceived children, should the court set aside some of the estate assets to provide for any additional children who might be born to him? See Ronald Chester,

Posthumously Conceived Heirs Under a Revised Uniform Probate Code, 38 Real Prop., Prob. & Tr. J. 727 (2004) [advocating draft revision of section 2–108 of the Uniform Probate Code to permit inheritance by children conceived within three years of decedent's death (subject to a number of conditions), and requiring that 50% of the estate be set aside in cases where the prospective postmortem child would, if conceived within three years of decedent's death, be entitled to more than 50% of the estate]. See also Laurence C. Nolan, Critiquing Society's Response to the Needs of Posthumously Conceived Children, 82 Or. L. Rev. 1067 (2003) [advocating legislation to protect the interests of posthumously conceived children]; Compare Ralph C. Brashier, Children and Inheritance in the Nontraditional Family, 1996 Utah L. Rev. 93, 214 [suggesting that such children should be treated as if they have no father].

2. Once Harold Husband dies, who has a right to decide whether his sperm should be implanted or destroyed, and when? See Browne C. Lewis, Dead Men Reproducing: Responding to the Existence of After–Death Children, 16 Geo. Mason L. Rev. 403 (2009) (criticizing courts' reluctance to grant orders allowing surviving spouses to harvest dead husband's sperm). Should Husband be entitled to dispose of his sperm by will? See Kane v. Superior Court, 37 Cal.App.4th 1577, 44 Cal.Rptr.2d 578 (1995); James E. Bailey, An Analytical Framework for Resolving the Issues Raised by The Interaction Between Reproductive Technology and the Law of Inheritance, 47 DePaul L. Rev. 743, 756–81 (1998) (arguing that men and women should be entitled to bequeath gametes, zygotes, preembryos, and embryos); Ronald Chester, Freezing the Heir Apparent: A Dialogue on Postmortem Conception, Parental Responsibility, and Inheritance, 33 Hous. L. Rev. 967, 980–81 (1996) (arguing that men have a constitutional right to dispose of their sperm by will). In the absence of a will, should the sperm be distributed by intestate succession? See generally Kathryn Venturatos Lorio, From Cradle to Tomb: Estate Planning Considerations of the New Procreation, 57 La. L. Rev. 27 (1996).

3. Suppose, over the objections of Harold Husband's child by a prior marriage, Harold's wife uses his sperm to conceive another child. Should the new baby be entitled to take by intestate succession from its half-siblings? Should the half-siblings be entitled to inherit from the child by intestate succession?

The Uniform Probate Code (2008)

In an effort to bring order to chaos, the drafters of the 2008 amendments to the UPC significantly revised the UPC's coverage of parenting determinations, including two new sections specifically geared toward addressing issues created by reproductive technology. The revised UPC is extensive and detailed. Since the issues involving reproductive technologies are only tangentially related to estate planning, we will summarize the highlights as they relate to issues of intestate succession.

The establishment of a parent/child relationship creates intestate succession rights. The UPC takes an "intent" based approach to defining those relationships, focusing on the intentions and actions of participants in assisted reproduction rather than biological or legal relationships. The Code addresses the issue in two sections: section 2–120 concerns assisted reproduction without the use of a surrogate, while section 2–121 deals with reproduction through the use of a surrogate (whom the Code defines as a "gestational carrier").

To assist courts in determining the identity of an intended parent, the UPC creates a variety of presumptions. For example, section 2–120 provides that when the intended mother gives birth to a child using assisted reproductive technology, a sperm donor is presumed to have no parent/child relationship with the resultant child unless the donor is a husband who provides sperm to his wife, or someone who consented to assisted reproduction by the birth mother with the intent to be treated as the other parent of the child. UPC § 2–120(a) & (f). A birth certificate identifying an individual other than the birth mother as the parent of a child of assisted reproduction presumptively establishes a parent/child relationship between the child and the named parent. UPC § 2–120(e). Moreover, any individual who consents to assisted reproduction by the birth mother with an intent to be treated as the other parent to the child can establish a parent/child relationship. Intent can be proved by a written document to that effect or inferred from the individual's acts of functioning as a parent after the child's birth. UPC § 2–120(f). Section 2–120 also limits posthumously conceived child claims by directing that posthumously conceived children are children of the deceased if the child is in utero not later than 36 months after the individual's death, or born not later than 45 months after the individual's death.

Section 2–121 addresses birth through use of a surrogate. A woman who engages in assisted reproduction pursuant to a gestational agreement without the intent to function as the resulting child's parent is—under most circumstances—a "gestational carrier", not the child's parent. UPC § 2–121. Here, the parent-child relationship exists between the "intended parent" and the child. The Code provides several ways to establish the identity of the intended parent.

For more, see Sheldon F. Kurtz & Lawrence W. Waggoner, The UPC Addresses the Class–Gift and Intestacy Rights of Children of Assisted Reproductive Technologies, 35 ACTEC J. 30 (2009).

SECTION VII. SIMULTANEOUS DEATH

In order to take by intestate succession, an heir must survive the decedent. Intestate succession statutes operate on the assumption that decedent would have wanted her closest living relatives to share in her estate, and that, in some sense, decedent's closest living relatives are most deserving of decedent's estate.

What happens, however, if decedent's heir only survives decedent by a short period of time? In that instance, the "deserving" heir does not enjoy decedent's property for long, and decedent's intent may be frustrated—especially if the heir's heirs are not close relatives of the decedent. Consider the following example:

> ***Example 7:*** *Decedent dies intestate survived by her husband and her sister, but no children. The husband dies two weeks after decedent, survived by his brother. How will decedent's estate be distributed?*
>
> ***Solution:*** *Under the Uniform Probate Code (and most other state statutes), decedent's husband will succeed to her entire estate. Then, at the husband's death, the husband's brother will take his entire estate. Decedent's sister will take nothing.*

To avoid this result, decedent would have to write a will. In her will, she could leave some of her estate outright to her sister, or she could give her husband only a life interest in trust. Either way, she could assure that at least some of her estate would ultimately pass to her sister (or perhaps her sister's children). If, however, decedent does not write a will, on the facts of Example 7, decedent's sister will not share in her estate.

Note that on the facts of Example 7, disposition of the couple's estates would have been dramatically different if the husband had died intestate two weeks *before* decedent. In that event, the husband's entire estate would have passed to decedent, and both estates would ultimately have passed to decedent's sister. The husband's brother would have taken nothing.

The problems raised by Example 7 exist whenever a decedent would not want her property to pass to the estate of one of her heirs. Even if the husband in Example 7 had survived decedent by two years instead of two weeks, decedent's intent might have been frustrated if her estate were ultimately distributed to her husband's brother. But in that event, at least her husband—the principal object of her bounty—would have enjoyed the property for a significant period of time. Indeed, there may be less for the husband's brother to receive if the husband had used the property during his own lifetime. As the period for which the heir survives becomes shorter, the problem becomes worse: decedent would receive little solace from knowing that her husband enjoyed her property for two weeks (especially if—as is likely—the distribution process took longer than that!).

When decedent and her heir die at the same time, or in the same disaster, the problem is compounded. A new issue arises: how do we tell who died first? And if we can't tell who died first, what assumptions should we make about who survived? The problem is not limited to intestate succession. The same problem exists when decedent has written a will—if we can't tell who survived, how should we distribute the property? Consider the following case:

Estate of Villwock

Court of Appeals of Wisconsin, 1987.
142 Wis.2d 144, 418 N.W.2d 1.

■ LAROCQUE, J.:

Mary Hintz, Roy Villwock's daughter by a previous marriage, appeals an order that her father's estate be probated in accord with the trial court's finding that Roy preceded his wife, June, in death. The effect of the order is to pass Roy's entire estate to June's estate and in turn to June's heirs as directed by her will. The trial court's determination of the time of Roy's death is a finding of fact and is not clearly erroneous. Section 805.17(2), Stats. Because the trial court found that Roy died before his wife, the provisions of the Uniform Simultaneous Death Act, sec. 851.55(1), Stats., are inapplicable. We affirm.

Roy and June Villwock, critically injured but alive and conscious after a head-on car crash on July 25, 1985, were transported together to a Rhinelander hospital. All five emergency medical technicians on board agreed that Roy suffered cardiopulmonary failure minutes before June similarly failed. Upon arrival at the hospital, each was taken to a separate treatment room where CPR, begun in the ambulance, was continued. A physician eventually pronounced June dead at 8:23 p.m. Another physician, Dr. Bruce Kotila, after giving advanced CPR to Roy, pronounced him dead at 8:34 p.m.

A probate hearing was held to determine the time of Roy's death. Dr. Kotila testified that Roy's heart and lung failure in the ambulance was irreversible despite the efforts to revive him. The trial court accepted Dr. Kotila's testimony and found that Roy died in the ambulance, while his wife was undisputedly still alive and conscious. Roy's will left everything to June and contained no contingency that she need survive him any period of time in order to take under the will. There were no other dispositive provisions in the will. There were no children born to the marriage of Roy and June. June's will left everything to specific members of her family.

Section 146.71, Stats., provides:

> Determination of Death. An individual who has sustained either irreversible cessation of circulatory and respiratory functions or irreversible cessation of all functions of the entire brain, including the brain stem, is dead. A determination of death shall be made in accordance with accepted medical standards.

Prior to the adoption of this statute in 1981, the Wisconsin courts declined to define death. Cranmore v. State, 85 Wis. 2d 722, 774, 271 N.W.2d 402, 428 (Ct.App.1978). The Wisconsin statutory definition of death adopts the uniform Act approved by the National Conference of Commissioners on Uniform State Laws.

Modern advances in life-saving technology have prompted adoption of this uniform law. See Prefatory Note to Uniform Determination of Death Act, 12 U.L.A. 286 (Supp. 1986). The statute allows for two alternative definitions of death. We are only concerned here with the first alternative, which essentially codifies the common law: death is the irreversible failure of the cardiorespiratory system.

Hintz contends that Dr. Kotila's testimony determining Roy's time of death must be disregarded as a matter of law because it is contradictory and speculative. She then concludes that, under the terms of the Uniform Simultaneous Death Act, sec. 851.55, "there is no sufficient evidence that [Roy and June] have died otherwise than simultaneously."[3] We reject her argument.

Dr. Kotila's original death pronouncement of 8:34 p.m. conflicts with his ultimate opinion that death occurred earlier in the ambulance. There also is arguably an inconsistency between his ultimate opinion and his administration of advanced CPR for an hour at the hospital. Dr. Kotila, however, offered explanations for these conflicts. Dr. Kotila explained that his original death pronouncement was not intended to preclude a reevaluation to establish death at an earlier time. Given the demands upon an emergency room physician in a time of crisis, it is not difficult to accept his explanation. Dr. Kotila also explained that CPR was continued for an hour or more to preclude any possibility of an erroneous judgment of death made in haste. This explanation is not incredible as a matter of law. The determination of credibility is the sole province of the trial court. Estate of Sensenbrenner v. Sensenbrenner, 89 Wis. 2d 677, 700, 278 N.W.2d 887, 898 (1979).

Hintz further insists that it is beyond the ability of any medical scientist to fix at a precise moment in time when cardiopulmonary failure was "irreversible." Dr. Kotila testified, however, that the extent of a person's injuries is "a very big factor" in deciding irreversibility. Roy's injuries were undisputedly extensive.

The drafters of the Uniform Determination of Death Act contemplated disputes over irreversibility. The determination of death must be made in accordance with accepted medical standards. "This Act is silent on acceptable diagnostic tests and medical procedures. It sets the general legal standard for determining death, but not the medical criteria for doing so. The medical profession remains free to formulate acceptable medical practices and to utilize new biomedical knowledge, diagnostic tests, and equipment." Prefatory Note to Uniform Determination of Death Act, 12 U.L.A. at 287.

Dr. Kotila is a licensed physician, board certified in internal medicine with nine years' experience in emergency room practices. Although the trial court did not explicitly find that the medical evidence was in accord with accepted standards, it did so implicitly. This court may assume that a missing finding was determined in favor of the order or judgment. Sohns v. Jensen, 11 Wis. 2d 449, 453, 105 N.W.2d 818, 820 (1960). Based upon the qualifications of the expert witness and the fact that his opinion was unchallenged by any other witness or evidence, we will assume that the trial court found that the determination of death was in accord with accepted medical standards.

---

3. Section 851.55(1), Stats., provides:

If the title to property or the devolution thereof depends upon priority of death and there is no sufficient evidence that the persons have died otherwise than simultaneously, the property of each person shall be disposed of as if he or she had survived, except as provided otherwise in this section.

Given the few minutes between Roy's cardiopulmonary failure and that suffered by June, the margin for error, when measured by time, is admittedly narrow. The narrow margin for error is no reason to reject the trial court's fact finding.

> The problem is that the facts are forever gone and no scientific method of inquiry can ever be devised to produce facsimiles that bring the past to life. The judicial process deals with probabilities, not facts, and we must therefore be on guard against making fact skepticism our main preoccupation. However skillfully, however sensitively we arrange a reproduction of the past, the arrangement is still that of the theater. We acknowledge as much when we speak of re-enacting the crime or the accident or perhaps some everyday event; we know better than to speak of reliving it. The most we can hope for is that witnesses will be honest and reasonably accurate in their perception and recollection, [and] that triers of fact will be honest and intelligent in their reasoning,....

R. Traynor, Fact Skepticism and the Judicial Process, 106 U. Pa. L. Rev. 635–36 (1958). The "fact" of the time of Roy's death has been adequately established in this case.

The Simultaneous Death Act is inapplicable. The Villwocks did not die simultaneously. The statute's nontechnical words, if not specifically defined, will be given their ordinary and accepted meaning, which may be ascertained from a recognized dictionary. State v. Wittrock, 119 Wis. 2d 664, 670, 350 N.W.2d 647, 651 (1984). Webster's Third New International Dictionary 2122 (1975) defines "simultaneous" as "occurring at the same time...." Based on the trial court's finding, the deaths here did not occur at the same time.

Order affirmed.

QUESTIONS

1. Suppose Roy and June Villwock had each died intestate, and that the value of Roy's estate totaled $200,000. Suppose further that Roy had been survived by his daughter, Mary Hintz, and June had been survived by various collateral relatives. How would Roy's estate have been distributed if Roy had died before June? If June had died before Roy? [Assume that the Wisconsin intestate succession statute had included provisions identical to UPC §§ 2–102 and 2–103].

2. Suppose now that Roy and June had died simultaneously. If both had died intestate, how would Roy's estate have been distributed?

Why does the Wisconsin simultaneous death act—like most simultaneous death acts—provide that the property of each person should be disposed of as if he or she survived? How does that provision help to effectuate decedent's intent?

3. In Estate of Villwock, the disposition of Roy Villwock's estate turned on whether there was adequate proof that Roy had died a few seconds or a few minutes before June. Does it make sense that death order in a common accident should have such a dramatic impact on distribution of Roy's estate?

4. In which of the following circumstances is the evidence sufficient to establish that death was not simultaneous?:

a. Decedent and her son died as a result of carbon monoxide poisoning while sitting in a parked car left running in a garage. Two pathologists testified that based on the ages of the two (decedent was 79, her son was 41), the son survived decedent. There was no other evidence about death order. See Estate of Moran, 77 Ill.2d 147, 32 Ill.Dec. 349, 395 N.E.2d 579 (1979) (held, insufficient evidence to establish that death was other than simultaneous).

b. Married couple drowned in a lake when their boat capsized. Wife's body was found the next day; husband's body was found three days later. Evidence established that husband had a history of coronary disease. Evidence also established that wife could swim, while evidence about husband's swimming ability was conflicting. Finally, there was evidence that wife had lost her glasses, perhaps during a struggle to survive, while husband's glasses were still in place. See Gerking v. Wolff, 56 Or.App. 222, 641 P.2d 610 (1982) (held, evidence insufficient to establish that either spouse survived the other).

c. Husband and wife were killed in a head-on automobile collision. When ambulance driver reached the scene, he felt no pulse or heartbeat from either spouse. A few minutes earlier, policeman had received no reaction from husband when he turned flashlight beam into husband's eyes; wife was bleeding profusely and making moaning sounds. See Estate of Schmidt, 261 Cal.App.2d 262, 67 Cal.Rptr. 847 (1968) (holding that wife survived husband).

UNIFORM PROBATE CODE

SECTION 2–104. REQUIREMENT OF SURVIVAL BY 120 HOURS; INDIVIDUAL IN GESTATION.

(a) [Requirement of Survival by 120 Hours; Individual in Gestation.] For purposes of intestate succession, homestead allowance, and exempt property, and except as otherwise provided in subsection (b), the following rules apply:

(1) An individual born before a decedent's death who fails to survive the decedent by 120 hours is deemed to have predeceased the decedent. If it is not established by clear and convincing evidence that an individual born before the decedent's death survived the decedent by 120 hours, it is deemed that the individual failed to survive for the required period.

(2) An individual in gestation at a decedent's death is deemed to be living at the decedent's death if the individual lives 120 hours after birth. If it is not established by clear and convincing evidence that an individual in gestation at the decedent's death lived 120 hours after

birth, it is deemed that the individual failed to survive for the required period.

(b) [Section Inapplicable If Estate Would Pass to State.] This section does not apply if its application would cause the estate to pass to the state under Section 2–105.

NOTES AND QUESTIONS

1. Suppose Roy and June Villwock had died intestate. How would Roy Villwock's estate have been distributed if UPC Section 2–104 had been in effect?

2. The Uniform Probate Code includes a parallel provision, Section 2–702, to deal with construction of written instruments. Section 2–702(a) provides that for purposes of the Code itself, a person who is not established to have survived an event by 120 hours is deemed to have predeceased the event. Section 2–702(b) applies the same principle in construing written instruments. Thus, in a case like Estate of Villwock, in construing Roy Villwock's will, Section 2–702(b) would direct a court to treat June Villwock as if she predeceased Roy Villwock. Section 2–702(c) extends this principle to property held in joint tenancies with right of survivorship, directing that if it cannot be proven by clear and convincing evidence that one co-tenant survived the other by 120 hours, each co-tenant's share shall be distributed as though he or she survived the other(s).

Section 2–702(d) provides that survival by 120 hours is not required if "the governing instrument contains language dealing explicitly with simultaneous deaths or deaths in a common disaster and that language is operable under the facts of the case."

Section 2–702 deals not only with wills and trust instruments, but also with life insurance designations. For cases interpreting a prior version of the Uniform Simultaneous Death Act, which did not include a 120–hour survivorship requirement, in the context of a fight over life insurance proceeds, see Janus v. Tarasewicz, 135 Ill.App.3d 936, 90 Ill.Dec. 599, 482 N.E.2d 418 (1985); Waldman v. Maini, 195 P.3d 850 (Nev. 2008).

3. In 1991 the Uniform Simultaneous Death Act was amended to include a 120 hour survivorship requirement, in order to mitigate the types of problems encountered by the court in the Villwock case. In 1997 the Wisconsin legislature adopted the Revised Act. UPC 2–104 and 2–702 were modeled on and are functionally equivalent to the Revised Act. Nearly half the states, however, retain statutes similar to the one construed by the court in the Villwock case. On the experience in individual states, see Alexander J. Bott, North Dakota Probate Code: Prior and Revised Article II, 72 N.D. L. Rev. 1, 34 (1996); Frederick R. Schneider, Recommendations for Improving Kentucky's Inheritance Laws, 22 N. Ky. L. Rev. 317 (1995).

4. Suppose Roy Villwock had hired you to draft his will. Would you have included a provision to deal with simultaneous death? If yes, how would you have drafted the provision?

PROBLEMS

1. Roland and Nancy Schweizer, husband and wife, died in an accident. Roland was killed instantly; Nancy died in the ambulance on the way to the hospital. Each died intestate, and each was survived by four children from a previous marriage. Assume that Roland has an estate of $100,000, and Nancy has an estate of $200,000.

How should each estate be distributed if

(a) UPC Section 2–104 is in effect?

(b) The old Wisconsin statute quoted in Estate of Villwock is in effect?

Cf. Estate of Schweizer, 7 Kan.App.2d 128, 638 P.2d 378 (1981).

2. Phyllis filed for divorce from her husband, Richard. Soon after, Richard made an unannounced visit to Phyllis's home, where he discovered Phyllis and her lover together. Richard shot and killed Phyllis, her lover and then himself. Richard and Phyllis held a significant amount of property as tenants by the entireties. Richard's siblings argued that the simultaneous death statute applied and that they were entitled to Richard's half of the property. Phyllis's heirs argued that the slayer statute governed the outcome, and that one-hundred percent of the couple's property should be distributed to them. Which argument should prevail? See Vernum v. Vernum, 961 A.2d 181 (Pa.Super. 2008) (holding that slayer statute governed the resolution of the dispute and awarding title to Phyllis's heirs).

SECTION VIII. DISCLAIMER (RENUNCIATION)

At common law, an heir was not entitled to "renounce" or "disclaim" property inherited by intestate succession. Title vested in the heir "automatically" at the intestate decedent's death. The heir could, of course, give her interest away as soon as she received it. Why, then, would the heir care about whether she had the right to disclaim her inheritance? Consider the following case:

Estate of Baird

Supreme Court of Washington, en banc, 1997.
131 Wash.2d 514, 933 P.2d 1031.

■ JOHNSON, J.:

The question presented is whether an anticipatory disclaimer of an expectancy interest in an intestate estate is valid and effective under RCW 11.86. We hold the plain language of the statute does not authorize an anticipatory disclaimer of an expectancy interest created by intestacy, and affirm the order of the probate court declaring this disclaimer invalid.

FACTS

Phyllis Baird died intestate on December 29, 1994. She was survived by two children, James Thomas Baird and Julie A. Breckenridge. James Baird has two children, Jayme Baird and Hunter Baird, from his first marriage to Cheryl Kern.

During the later stages of her life, Phyllis Baird suffered from Alzheimer's disease and, as a result, was mentally incapacitated. Susan K. (Saulsbury) Baird was appointed guardian for Phyllis Baird on November 29, 1988, in a guardianship proceeding in Whatcom County. James Baird married Susan (Saulsbury) Baird on November 10, 1992.

On February 9, 1993, James Baird brutally assaulted Susan Baird. As a result of this attack, Susan Baird was permanently disfigured and suffered permanent cognitive defects preventing meaningful employment. Susan Baird filed a personal injury action against James Baird in Whatcom County Superior Court on February 26, 1993, for the injuries suffered in the assault.

James Baird was convicted of first degree assault on March 8, 1994. He received an exceptional sentence of 20 years on June 3, 1994. On March 8, 1994, the same day as his conviction, James Baird executed an instrument purporting to disclaim "any and all interest" he "may have" in his mother's estate. This instrument was filed in his mother's guardianship proceeding that same day.

On October 19, 1994, Susan Baird was awarded a judgment of $2.75 million in her personal injury action against James Baird. One week later, on October 26, 1994, James Baird filed a petition for Chapter 7 bankruptcy. Susan Baird's judgment constitutes approximately 95 percent of the outstanding creditor claims in the bankruptcy proceeding.

As previously stated, Phyllis Baird died intestate on December 29, 1994. Her estate is valued in excess of $500,000. James Baird's share of his mother's estate represents approximately 60 percent of his potential assets available in the bankruptcy proceeding.

On January 26, 1996, Jayme Baird and James Degel, guardian ad litem for Hunter Baird, petitioned the probate court for an order declaring James Baird's disclaimer valid. The bankruptcy trustee opposed the petition. At the same time, Susan Baird filed a motion to intervene in the probate proceeding. On February 14, 1996, the bankruptcy court entered an order abstaining from determining the issue of the validity of the disclaimer pending the resolution of this same issue in the probate proceeding.

On March 25, 1996, the probate court entered orders granting Susan Baird's motion to intervene, and denying the petition to declare the disclaimer valid. Rather, the court declared the instrument invalid without explanation. Jayme and Hunter Baird appealed directly to this court.

We hold anticipatory disclaimers of expectancy interests created by intestacy are not contemplated or authorized by RCW 11.86, and affirm the probate court's order declaring James Baird's disclaimer invalid.

ANALYSIS

Standard of Review

The issue in this case involves statutory construction; issues concerning statutory construction are questions of law reviewed de novo. Rettkowski v. Department of Ecology, 128 Wash. 2d 508, 515, 910 P.2d 462 (1996).

Disclaimers

Disclaimers[4] are defined in RCW 11.86 as "any writing which declines, refuses, renounces, or disclaims any interest that would otherwise be taken by a beneficiary." RCW 11.86.011(4). Statutory disclaimers have their roots in the common law principle that a beneficiary under a will has the right to disclaim or renounce a testamentary gift. Mark Reutlinger & William C. Oltman, Washington Law of Wills and Intestate Succession 163–67 (1985). This rule was based on the theory that no one could be forced to accept a gift. Reutlinger & Oltman, supra, at 163. However, at common law an interest passing via intestacy could not be disclaimed. See S. Alan Medlin, An Examination of Disclaimers Under UPC Section 2–801, 55 Albany L. Rev. 1233, 1235 (1992).

In Washington and other jurisdictions, this particular distinction was abrogated when the law of disclaimer was codified. See, e.g., Laws of 1973, ch. 148. Washington's disclaimer statute, RCW 11.86, was originally enacted in 1973, and almost completely rewritten in 1989. Laws of 1989, ch. 34. The current version of RCW 11.86 substantially conforms with the Uniform Probate Code's section on disclaimers. Compare RCW 11.86 with Unif. Probate Code sec. 2–801 (Supp. 1995).[5] At common law and under our current statute, a properly executed and delivered disclaimer passes the disclaimed interest as if the disclaimant "died immediately prior to the date of the transfer of the interest." RCW 11.86.041(1); see Reutlinger & Oltman, supra, at 164–65. So long as a disclaimer is properly executed and timely delivered, the legal fiction of "relation back" treats the interest as having never passed to the intended beneficiary or heir at law.

In this case, Jayme and Hunter Baird argue that this legal fiction applies and prevents James Baird's interest in his mother's estate from

4. The terms "disclaimer" and "renunciation" are used interchangeably in case law to express what in common law terms is the means to reject a testamentary gift in such a way that it passes to the renouncer's heirs as if he or she had predeceased the testator. See Mark Reutlinger & William C. Oltman, Washington Law of Wills and Intestate Succession 163–64 (1985). Washington statutes uniformly use the term "disclaimer," as will this opinion.

5. We note that while RCW 11.86 codified the law of disclaimers, it also reserves "the right of any person, apart from this chapter, under any existing or future statute or rule of law, to disclaim any interest...." RCW 11.86.080. Thus, the common law rule allowing anticipatory disclaimers based on valuable consideration may continue to authorize that specialized subset of anticipatory disclaimers. See Stewart v. McDade, 256 N.C. 630, 124 S.E.2d 822, 826 (1962) (the disclaimer "of an expectant share to an ancestor, fairly and freely made, in consideration of an advancement or for other valuable consideration, excludes the heir from participation in the ancestor's estate at his death"); see also In re Willets' Estate, 173 Misc. 199, 17 N.Y.S.2d 578 (1939) (court upheld disclaimer of nephew who was aunt's attorney and who borrowed $10,000 from aunt, then disclaimed $10,000 from assets of her estate); McCarthy v. McCarthy, 9 Ill. App. 2d 462, 133 N.E.2d 763 (1956) (upholding attorney's renunciation of an expected right under his client's will because attorney had received fair consideration for the renunciation). That issue, however, is not presently before us.

becoming an asset of his bankruptcy estate.[6] They argue the instrument executed on March 8, 1994 by James Baird met all of RCW 11.86.031(1)'s content requirements and was properly delivered according to RCW 11.86.031(2) by being filed in Phyllis Baird's ongoing guardianship proceeding or, alternatively, in the probate proceeding following Phyllis Baird's death. Thus, Jayme and Hunter Baird assert the disclaimer was valid and effective as of the date their father executed the instrument.

We disagree. The result of adopting the children's argument in this case would be to extend the legal fiction of "relation back" at the potential expense of the bankruptcy estate and Susan Baird. That we will not do. "The doctrine of relation 'is a legal fiction invented to promote the ends of justice.... It is never allowed to defeat the collateral rights of third persons, lawfully acquired.' Johnston v. Jones, 66 U.S. 209, 1 Black 209, 221, 17 L. Ed. 117." In re Estate of Graley, 183 Wash. 268, 274, 48 P.2d 634 (1935) (quoting United States Fidelity & Guar. Co. v. Wooldridge, 268 U.S. 234, 238, 45 S. Ct. 489, 69 L. Ed. 932, 40 A.L.R. 1094 (1925)).

Our disclaimer statute provides: "A beneficiary may disclaim an interest in whole or in part ... in the manner provided in RCW 11.86.031." RCW 11.86.021(1). "Interests" that may be disclaimed include:

> the whole of any property, real or personal, legal or equitable, or any fractional part ... thereof, any vested or contingent interest in any such property.... 'Interest' includes, but is not limited to, an interest created ... by intestate succession.

RCW 11.86.011(2)(a). An intestate interest is created only upon the death of the creator of the interest, i.e., the death of the intestate. See In re Estate of Wiltermood, 78 Wash. 2d 238, 240, 472 P.2d 536 (1970); RCW 11.04.250 and RCW 11.04.290 (vesting of property under descent and distribution chapter). Thus, at the time James Baird executed the instrument at issue, he did not yet have an "interest" in his mother's estate to disclaim.

This definition of "interest" is further supported by the delivery requirements of RCW 11.86. The statute requires that a disclaimer "shall be delivered ... at any time after the creation of the interest, but in all events by nine months after the ... date of the transfer." RCW 11.86.031(2)(b) (emphasis added). As stated above, an intestate interest is not created until the death of the creator/transferor. Thus, James Baird could not have met the statutory delivery requirement on the date the

---

6. Under federal bankruptcy law, a bankruptcy estate includes any interest in property that would have been property of the estate if such interest had been an interest of the debtor on the date of the filing of the petition, and that the debtor acquires or becomes entitled to acquire within 180 days after such date by bequest, devise, or inheritance. 11 U.S.C.A. § 541(a)(5). Applying this definition, James Baird's potential share of his mother's estate would be an asset of the bankruptcy estate. However, if a bankrupt validly executes and delivers a disclaimer prior to the filing of the bankruptcy petition, then the testamentary gift at issue is not part of the bankruptcy estate and descends according to state law. See In re Atchison, 925 F.2d 209 (7th Cir.1991); Stephen E. Parker, Can Debtors Disclaim Inheritances to the Detriment of Their Creditors?, 25 Loy. U. Chi. L.J. 31, 39 (1993).

instrument was executed, or, for that matter, at any time prior to his mother's death, because the "interest" had yet to be created. See In re Will of Heffner, 132 Misc.2d 361, 362, 503 N.Y.S.2d 669 (1986) (anticipatory disclaimer invalid under New York's disclaimer statute for failure to meet notice and filing requirements).

Additionally, James Baird was not a "beneficiary" under RCW 11.86 when he executed the disclaimer. The statute defines a "beneficiary" as "the person entitled, but for the person's disclaimer, to take an interest." RCW 11.86.011(1). James Baird was not entitled to take any interest in his mother's estate prior to her death. See generally Estate of Wiltermood, 78 Wash.2d at 240 (prior to ancestor's death, those who would take according to laws of intestate succession have only the capacity to become heirs, which is at best an expectancy); Rawsthorn v. Rawsthorn, 198 Wash. 471, 481, 88 P.2d 847 (1939) (no one can have an interest at law or in equity, contingent or otherwise, in the property of a living person to which one hopes to succeed as heir at law); In re Marriage of Leland, 69 Wash. App. 57, 71, 847 P.2d 518 (1993) (a contingent future interest in property is greater than a mere expectancy, which is not to be deemed an interest of any kind); see RCW 11.04.250 and RCW 11.04.290 (heirs have legal interests only upon the death of the creator).

We hold that as a matter of law the instrument executed by James Baird on March 8, 1994 is invalid under RCW 11.86 because at that time he did not have an "interest," nor was he a "beneficiary." In sum, RCW 11.86 does not authorize anticipatory disclaimers of expectancy interests.

* * *

CONCLUSION

We hold that the instrument executed by James Baird on March 8, 1994 is invalid as a disclaimer under RCW 11.86.

* * *

The order of the probate court is affirmed and the case is remanded for further proceedings consistent with this opinion.

NOTES AND QUESTIONS

1. As the court notes in Baird, the terms "renunciation" and "disclaimer" are virtual synonyms. Because the Internal Revenue Code uses the term "disclaim," that term has probably become the more prevalent of the two.

2. What did James Baird hope to accomplish by disclaiming his interest in his mother's estate? Who would have benefited if the court had held the disclaimer effective? Who was benefited by the court's decision that the disclaimer was not effective?

3. Suppose James Baird never filed for bankruptcy, and executed his disclaimer on January 1, 1995—three days after his mother's death. Would the disclaimer have been effective? Many courts have used the "relation back" theory—discussed in Baird—to permit disclaiming beneficiaries to avoid creditor claims. Under this theory, if an estate beneficiary executes a disclaimer, the beneficiary's interest is treated as if the beneficiary never received the interest. As a result, the interest is beyond the reach of the beneficiary's creditors. Recent examples include Essen v. Gilmore, 259 Neb. 55, 607 N.W.2d 829 (2000) (beneficiary's renunciation does not constitute fraudulent transfer with respect to judgment creditor); Estate of Opatz, 554 N.W.2d 813 (N.D.1996) (judgment lien does not constitute encumbrance barring right to renounce); Frances Slocum Bank & Trust Co. v. Estate of Martin, 666 N.E.2d 411 (Ind.App.1996) (bank may not enforce lien against property disclaimed by debtor); Dyer v. Eckols, 808 S.W.2d 531 (Tex.App. 1991) (tort creditor may not set aside disclaimer by judgment debtor).

There are a few cases to the contrary, especially from Pennsylvania. In Estate of Clark, 488 Pa. 1, 410 A.2d 796 (1980), the court held that a client with a malpractice judgment against a lawyer was entitled to attach the lawyer's inheritance from his parents, despite the lawyer's disclaimer of his interest in his parents' estates. See also Gallaher v. Riddle, 850 A.2d 748 (Pa. Super. 2004).

Should the relative rights of the creditor and the disclaiming heir depend on the nature of the creditor's claim? Should a claim like Susan Baird's—for injuries suffered as a result of a brutal assault—defeat the claim of creditors even if ordinary contract claims do not? For an affirmative answer, see Adam J. Hirsch, The Problem of the Insolvent Heir, 74 Cornell L. Rev. 587 (1989).

4. ***Federal Tax Liens: The Drye Case.*** Suppose an intestate heir owes the federal government back taxes, for which federal tax liens have been filed. Can the beneficiary disclaim his inheritance so that the property will pass to his daughter free of the federal tax liens? In Drye v. United States, 528 U.S. 49, 120 S.Ct. 474, 145 L.Ed.2d 466 (1999), the Supreme Court held that the disclaimer would not defeat the federal tax lien. Whether the heir's right constituted property within the meaning of the federal tax lien statute was, according to the Court, a matter of federal law. The Court then reasoned that the heir, by deciding whether to disclaim, effectively determines who will receive the property. This power to channel the estate's assets—to determine who receives assets—constitutes property subject to the government's tax lien.

5. ***Disclaimers in Bankruptcy.*** Because the court in Baird concluded that, as a matter of state law, the disclaimer was invalid, neither the state court nor the bankruptcy court had to determine whether a valid disclaimer would be effective against a bankruptcy trustee.

Two federal Courts of Appeals have held that a disclaimer executed before the disclaiming heir petitions for bankruptcy is effective to cut off any rights of the bankruptcy trustee when the disclaimer would be effective under state law. Simpson v. Penner, 36 F.3d 450 (5th Cir. 1994); Jones v. Atchison, 925 F.2d 209 (7th Cir. 1991). Does the Supreme Court's decision in *Drye* cast doubt on the validity of these cases? That is, does *Drye* require application of federal law to determine the validity of a disclaimer in a subsequent bankruptcy proceeding? Although the question is not free from doubt, most courts have held that *Drye* applies only to tax proceedings, not to bankruptcy proceedings. See, e.g., In re Costas, 346 B.R. 198 (9th Cir.BAP 2006).

Whether a disclaimer executed after the heir has petitioned for bankruptcy is effective to cut off the rights of the bankruptcy trustee remains an open question. See e.g., In re Schmidt (Lowe v. Sanflippo), 362 B.R. 318 (Bankr.W.D. Tex. 2007) (holding debtor's post-petition disclaimer of her interest in mother's probate estate invalid and voidable by bankruptcy trustee). For a discussion of the issue, see Adam J. Hirsch, Inheritance and Bankruptcy: The Meaning of the "Fresh Start", 45 Hastings L. J. 175, 183 n.25 (1994).

6. ***Disclaimers and Eligibility for Public Assistance.*** Many public assistance programs impose eligibility limits. If an applicant for public assistance disclaims an interest in an estate, do the disclaimed assets count toward the eligibility threshold? Courts have almost invariably held that the disclaimed assets do count toward the eligibility threshold. See, e.g., Molloy v. Bane, 214 A.D.2d 171, 172, 631 N.Y.S.2d 910, 911 (1995):

> The instant appeal presents a collision of two irreconcilable rules of law. On the one hand, there is a generally recognized right to renounce any and all testamentary or intestate distributions, even when to do so would frustrate one's creditors. On the other hand, public aid is limited and should be spent only on the truly needy. Here, we hold that the policy considerations underlying the latter rule are of paramount importance. Accordingly, while one may renounce a testamentary or intestate disposition, such a renunciation is not without its consequences for purpose of calculating eligibility for Medicaid.

Accord, Hoesly v. State, 243 Neb. 304, 498 N.W.2d 571 (1993). Beyond the eligibility question at issue in Molloy, courts sometimes hold that public agencies may recover from disclaimed assets even when other creditors will not enjoy priority over disclaimed assets. See Troy v. Hart, 116 Md.App. 468, 697 A.2d 113 (1997) (Medicaid fund may recover when applicant disclaimed one-third interest in sister's $300,000 estate); but see Estate of Kirk, 591 N.W.2d 630 (Iowa 1999) (holding that health management company seeking to recover Medicaid benefits extended to wife may not recover assets left to wife by husband when wife's executor disclaimed the assets). See generally Mary Moers Wenig, Disclaimer: Handle With Care, 25 Tax Management Est., Gifts and Tr. Journal 275, 277–78 (2000). On the general problem of asset divestment to plan for the costs of institutional care, see Joel C. Dobris, Medicaid Asset Planning by the Elderly, 24 Real Prop., Prob. & Tr. J. 1, 14–17 (1989).

7. ***The Tax Consequences of Disclaimers.*** Most disclaimers today are tax-driven. This is not the place to detail the tax advantages of disclaimers. For a complete discussion, see Ronald A. Brand & William P. LaPiana: Disclaimers in Estate Planning, A Guide to Their Effective Use (1990). But consider one simple advantage: by disclaiming assets, a beneficiary may be able to funnel assets to his own children without paying estate taxes. At the

same time, if the beneficiary's children are in a lower income tax bracket, the disclaiming beneficiary may also be able to reduce his family's income tax burden.

As an example, consider the following facts: Grandmother Jones dies intestate, leaving an estate of $500,000. Her only child and only heir is Father Jones, now age 65. Father, however, has assets of his own, in excess of $5,000,000. Father will incur a substantial estate tax on his own assets at his death. If Father adds Grandmother's $500,000 to his own estate, a substantial portion of that $500,000—probably 35%—will be lost in federal estate taxation at Father's death. If, however, Father disclaims, what will happen to Grandmother's estate? It will pass as if Father had died before Grandmother. If Father has one daughter, Daughter Jones will take Grandmother's entire $500,000 estate. By disclaiming, Father will have skipped a generation of estate tax; no tax will be due on Grandmother's $500,000 at Father's death.

There are many other situations in which disclaimer generates significant tax advantages. Whether a disclaimer is a "qualified disclaimer," and therefore eligible for the transfer tax benefits available to disclaimers, is governed by Section 2518 of the Internal Revenue Code. To be a "qualified disclaimer", the disclaimant must not have accepted the disclaimed interest or any of its benefits, the disclaimer must be "irrevocable and unqualified," and it must be filed within nine months after the interest is created. If the disclaimant is under 21 at the time of creation, the disclaimant has until nine months after her 21st birthday to disclaim.

The Mechanics of Disclaimer

Suppose an heir (or a will beneficiary) wants to disclaim her interest in an estate. How does the heir go about disclaiming that interest? And what will the effect of the disclaimer be? Consider the following excerpts from the disclaimer provisions of the Uniform Probate Code, which incorporates the Uniform Disclaimer of Property Interests Act (UDPIA):

UNIFORM PROBATE CODE

SECTION 2–1103. SCOPE.

This Part applies to disclaimers of any interest in or power over property, whenever created.

SECTION 2–1105. POWER TO DISCLAIM; GENERAL REQUIREMENTS; WHEN IRREVOCABLE.

(a) A person may disclaim, in whole or part, any interest in or power over property, including a power of appointment. A person may disclaim the interest or power even if its creator imposed a spendthrift provision or similar restriction on transfer or a restriction or limitation on the right to disclaim.

* * *

(b) Except to the extent a fiduciary's right to disclaim is expressly restricted or limited by another statute of this State or by the instrument creating the fiduciary relationship, a fiduciary may disclaim, in whole or part, any interest in or power over property, including a power of appointment, whether acting in a personal or representative capacity...

(c) To be effective, a disclaimer must be in a writing or other record, declare the disclaimer, describe the interest or power disclaimed, be signed by the person making the disclaimer, and be delivered or filed in the manner provided in Section 2–1112. In this subsection:

(1) "record" means information that is inscribed on a tangible medium or that is stored in an electronic or other medium and is retrievable in perceivable form;

(2) "signed" means, with present intent to authenticate or adopt a record, to;

(A) execute or adopt a tangible symbol; or

(B) attach to or logically associate with the record an electronic sound, symbol, or process.

(d) A partial disclaimer may be expressed as a fraction, percentage, monetary amount, term of years, limitation of a power, or any other interest or estate in the property.

(e) A disclaimer becomes irrevocable when it is delivered or filed pursuant to Section 2–1112 or when it becomes effective as provided in Sections 2–1106 through 2–1111, whichever occurs later.

(f) A disclaimer made under this Part is not a transfer, assignment, or release.

SECTION 2–1106. DISCLAIMER OF INTEREST IN PROPERTY.

(a) In this section:

(1) "Future interest" means an interest that takes effect in possession or enjoyment, if at all, later than the time of its creation.

(2) "Time of distribution" means the time when a disclaimed interest would have taken effect in possession or enjoyment.

(b) Except for a disclaimer governed by Section 2–1107 or 2–1108, the following rules apply to a disclaimer of an interest in property:

(1) The disclaimer takes effect as of the time the instrument creating the interest becomes irrevocable, or, if the interest arose under the law of intestate succession, as of the time of the intestate's death.

(2) The disclaimed interest passes according to any provision in the instrument creating the interest providing for the disposition of the interest, should it be disclaimed, or of disclaimed interests in general.

(3) If the instrument does not contain a provision described in paragraph (2), the following rules apply:

(A) If the disclaimant is not an individual, the disclaimed interest passes as if the disclaimant did not exist.

(B) If the disclaimant is an individual, except as otherwise provided in subparagraphs (C) and (D), the disclaimed interest passes as if the disclaimant had died immediately before the time of distribution.

(C) If by law or under the instrument, the descendants of the disclaimant would share in the disclaimed interest by any method of representation had the disclaimant died before the time of distribution, the disclaimed interest passes only to the descendants of the disclaimant who survive the time of distribution.

(D) If the disclaimed interest would pass to the disclaimant's estate had the disclaimant died before the time of distribution, the disclaimed interest instead passes by representation to the descendants of the disclaimant who survive the time of distribution. If no descendant of the disclaimant survives the time of distribution, the disclaimed interest passes to those persons, including the state but excluding the disclaimant, and in such shares as would succeed to the transferor's intestate estate under the intestate succession law of the transferor's domicile had the transferor died at the time of distribution. However, if the transferor's surviving spouse is living but is remarried at the time of distribution, the transferor is deemed to have died unmarried at the time of distribution.

(4) Upon the disclaimer of a preceding interest, a future interest held by a person other than the disclaimant takes effect as if the disclaimant had died or ceased to exist immediately before the time of distribution, but a future interest held by the disclaimant is not accelerated in possession or enjoyment.

For an extensive discussion of the Uniform Act, see William P. LaPiana, Uniform Disclaimer of Property Interests, 14 Probate & Property 57 (2000). For criticism of some of the drafting—particularly with respect to abandonment of the nine-month time limit for filing disclaimers, see Adam J. Hirsch, Revisions in Need of Revising: The Uniform Disclaimer of Property Interests Act, 29 Fla. St. U. L. Rev. 109, 123–30 (2001).

PROBLEMS

1. John Smith dies intestate, survived by his brother, Kurt. At the time of John's death, Kurt is in a nursing home. Kurt dies three months after John. Kurt was in debt to the nursing home at the time of his death. Kurt's wife and executor, Linda, wants to disclaim Kurt's interest in John's estate in order to preserve the assets for their son, Michael. Under the UPC, can Linda disclaim? Does the UPC indicate what effect the disclaimer would have? Cf. Estate of Heater, 266 Ill.App.3d 452, 203 Ill.Dec. 734, 640 N.E.2d 654 (1994) (discussing power of personal representative to disclaim decedent's interest in another estate).

2. Izzy Schultz dies intestate, survived by his son, Herman, and his granddaughter Gertrude, the only child of Izzy's deceased daughter, Frieda.

Herman has four children, Bernie, Morris, Sam, and Zack. Herman asks you how Izzy's estate will be distributed if Herman disclaims his interest. Advise Herman.

NOTE ON ASSIGNMENT OF EXPECTANCY INTERESTS

In Estate of Baird, the court held that James Baird's disclaimer was ineffective because it was executed before Baird's mother's death, at a time when Baird had no interest to disclaim. The court's holding in Baird is consistent with the view that an heir has no property interest in decedent's estate before decedent's death. Indeed, an heir is not an heir until death, but merely an "heir apparent." Why? Because events that might occur during decedent's lifetime could cut off the heir apparent's interest. For instance, if decedent's heir apparent is her brother, decedent could give birth to a child who would prevent the brother from ever becoming an heir.

Perhaps more important, courts were unwilling to recognize property interests in heirs apparent because decedent could always write a will cutting out the heir apparent. Common law courts (and commentators) often say that the heir apparent has "a mere expectancy"—not a property interest—before decedent's death. And they have also held that assignment of an expectancy confers no rights on the assignee. It is that rule that underlies the court's opinion in Baird. Because James Baird had only an expectancy, his disclaimer of his expectancy interest was, in the court's view, ineffective to disclaim his interest.

On the other hand, when an heir apparent (or a will beneficiary) receives consideration for assignment of an expectancy, courts may treat the assignment as a contract to transfer decedent's property when the property passes to the heir, and may enforce the contract in equity. Scott v. First National Bank of Baltimore, 224 Md. 462, 168 A.2d 349 (1961), is illustrative. Pursuant to a separation agreement, husband transferred to his minor child one-half of his expectancy in his father's estate. When the father died, the husband sought to invalidate the assignment. The court enforced the assignment. For a helpful general discussion, see Katheleen R. Guzman, Releasing the Expectancy, 34 Ariz. St. L. J. 775 (2002).

QUESTION

Suppose James Baird had disclaimed his interest in his mother's estate in return for an agreement by his children that they would pay for his legal fees in defending himself against the assault charges. Would the court have held the disclaimer enforceable? What arguments would you make for the children? For Susan Baird?

SECTION IX. ADVANCEMENTS

Suppose that, during decedent's lifetime, decedent gave substantial sums of money to his daughter to enable her to buy a house. Decedent then dies intestate. Decedent's son contends that the sums advanced to the daughter should be counted against the daughter's share of the estate. He argues that intestate succession statutes are designed to treat each of decedent's children equally, and that equal treatment would require that the daughter be credited with sums advanced to her during her lifetime.

What do you think of the son's argument? When a parent gives money to one child during the parent's lifetime, do you think the parent views the gift as a substitute for the child's inheritance? Or do you think the parent views the transfer as a gift over and above any inheritance the child might later receive?

At common law, a substantial gift to a child by a parent raised a presumption that the gift was an advancement of the child's inheritance, and that the gift should be charged against the child's intestate share. The presumption was rebuttable, but the burden of proof was on the child to demonstrate that the parent did not intend an advancement.

Examine the following Uniform Probate Code provision, and consider how the UPC would change the common law treatment of inter vivos transfers:

UNIFORM PROBATE CODE

SECTION 2–109. ADVANCEMENTS.

(a) If an individual dies intestate as to all or a portion of his [or her] estate, property the decedent gave during the decedent's lifetime to an individual who, at the decedent's death, is an heir is treated as an advancement against the heir's intestate share only if (i) the decedent declared in a contemporaneous writing or the heir acknowledged in writing that the gift is an advancement or (ii) the decedent's contemporaneous writing or the heir's written acknowledgment otherwise indicates that the gift is to be taken into account in computing the division and distribution of the decedent's intestate estate.

(b) For purposes of subsection (a), property advanced is valued as of the time the heir came into possession or enjoyment of the property or as of the time of the decedent's death, whichever first occurs.

(c) If the recipient of the property fails to survive the decedent, the property is not taken into account in computing the division and distribution of the decedent's intestate estate, unless the decedent's contemporaneous writing provides otherwise.

* * *

Note that the UPC (and many state statutes) reverse the common law presumption that a lifetime gift should be treated as an advancement. See generally Mary Louise Fellows, Concealing Legislative Reform in the Common–Law Tradition: The Advancements Doctrine and The Uniform Probate Code, 37 Vand. L. Rev. 671 (1984). The UPC requires a writing to establish that a gift is an advancement. How likely is it that a decedent who does not write a will would nevertheless memorialize in writing her intention to treat a gift as an advancement? There may be, however, some cases where decedent does creates such a writing.

Suppose a decedent, or an heir, does acknowledge, in a written memorandum, that an *inter vivos* transfer should be treated as an advancement against the heir's intestate share. How should the estate be distributed? All of the money distributed to heirs as advancements should be added to decedent's net estate, and the total amount (sometimes called the "hotchpot") should then be divided among the heirs in accordance with the provisions of the intestate succession statute. Amounts already received should be charged against the shares of the heirs who received those amounts.

> ***Example 8:*** *Decedent was survived by her three children, A, B, and C. Decedent advanced $30,000 to A during decedent's lifetime, and memorialized the transfer as an advancement against A's intestate share. Three years later, decedent died with an estate of $90,000. How should decedent's estate be distributed?*
>
> ***Solution:*** *The $30,000 received by A should be added to the $90,000 for a total of $120,000. Each of the three children is then entitled to one-third of the total, or $40,000 apiece. Because A has already received $30,000, A is entitled to $10,000 more. B and C each receive $40,000.*

Note that in Example 8, the advancement to A was smaller than the total share of decedent's estate to which A would have been entitled. If A's share had been larger than that total, advancement doctrine does not require A to give back any of the advancement.

> ***Example 9:*** *Same facts as Example 8, except the advancement to A was $50,000. How should decedent's estate be distributed?*
>
> ***Solution:*** *When we add A's $50,000 to the $90,000 in the estate, the total is $140,000. Each child's share would be $46,667. Since A already received more than that, A would not receive anything from the estate, but would not have to give anything back. The $90,000 in the estate would be divided evenly between B and C.*

PROBLEM

During her lifetime, G advanced $50,000 to her daughter A, and $10,000 to her daughter B, each memorialized by a writing declaring her intention that the gifts be treated as advancements. G then died intestate survived by her husband H, and by her three children, A, B, and C, all born of a previous marriage. If G's net estate is valued at $290,000, how should G's estate be distributed if the Uniform Probate Code is in effect?

CHAPTER THREE

PROTECTION OF THE FAMILY

Most people who write wills leave the bulk of their property to close family members, and particularly to spouses. These testators may act out of love, or out of a sense of moral duty to people with whom they have, during their lifetimes, shared fortune and misfortune, but they generally need no legal compulsion to provide for family members. A small percentage of testators, however, would prefer to disinherit close family members, and particularly spouses. To what extent does the law interfere with their preferences?

Within the United States, virtually every state protects a surviving spouse against disinheritance. In most "common law" states, that protection takes the form of a statutory right to a fixed share of the decedent spouse's estate. Community property states provide, as we shall see, even more protection for the surviving spouse.

The protection against disinheritance enjoyed by the surviving spouse does not typically extend to other relatives. Only Louisiana, for instance, provides children—minor or adult—with any significant protection against intentional disinheritance. As we shall see, however, many states protect children against inadvertent disinheritance.

Protecting family members against disinheritance raises important issues of policy, but family protection statutes also raise important issues for the estate planner. In this chapter, we explore both policy and planning.

SECTION I. AN INTRODUCTION TO THE ELECTIVE SHARE

Why should a surviving spouse be entitled to a share of the decedent spouse's estate? The answer lies in the conception of marriage as a partnership. When one spouse foregoes employment, interrupts a career, or makes other sacrifices to assume primary care of children, that spouse may be unable to accumulate assets in her own name. The partnership theory of marriage recognizes that the unemployed spouse's various nonmarket efforts—such as child care and homemaking—though uncompensated, contribute to the family's acquisition of wealth. In England, this partnership idea usually evokes the well-known quotation from Lord Simon of Glaisdale, "The cock bird can feather his nest precisely because he is not required to spend most of his time sitting on it."

Partnership theory also describes sharing behavior between spouses. In this sense the term is not only descriptive but hortatory. A marital regime of sharing principles (which could include equitable division of assets and community property) rather than separate property reflects and encourages marital relations built on trust and loyalty in which spouses divide the various functions within their family, although that division may be economically detrimental to one of the spouses. In this sense, the term also describes the "presumed intent of husbands and wives to pool their fortunes on an equal basis, share and share alike."

Who benefits most from the partnership theory of marriage? Consider the following:

Laura Rosenbury, Two Ways to End a Marriage: Divorce or Death, 2005 Utah L. Rev. 1227, 1283.

. . . [T]he underlying premise of the partnership theory is that intangible contributions to a marriage, such as child care, housework and other care work, should be valued on par with tangible financial contributions, thus leading to an equal or equitable division of tangible assets. This premise most advances the material well-being of those wives who forego market work in order to do care work. Indeed, these women would own no property but for the partnership theory of marriage. But, as feminists have acknowledged in other contexts, historically only certain women—namely white middle-to upper-middle-class women—could afford to forego market work, and, increasingly, many of those women have found that they must work to make ends meet. Thus, today, the partnership theory of marriage most benefits only those women who can afford to stay at home and choose to do so.

Community property states have always embraced the partnership theory of marriage: all property acquired by either spouse during the marriage is assumed to be the product of the joint efforts of the husband and wife. As a result, husband and wife each enjoy a one-half share in the community property. Each spouse, therefore, has a right to dispose by will of one-half of the community property; the other half automatically belongs to the surviving spouse.

Common law states, by contrast, treated property as individually owned, unless husband and wife took title as tenants by the entirety or as joint tenants. As a result, if the husband accumulated great wealth during the marriage, the wealth belonged to him alone, whatever the wife's contributions to the marriage.

Historically, even common law states provided some protections for the surviving spouse, generally in the form of dower and curtesy. Dower gave a widow a life interest in one-third of her deceased husband's lands; curtesy gave the husband a life interest in all of his wife's lands, but the husband acquired a curtesy interest only if children were born to the marriage. See generally Ralph C. Brashier, Disinheritance and the Modern Family, 45

Case W. Res. L. Rev. 83, 89–94 (1994); 2 Richard R. Powell & Patrick J. Rohan, Powell on Real Property 209–10 (1994).

Dower and curtesy performed adequately in a culture where most wealth consisted of real property owned by men, and at a time when marriage was a relatively stable institution. As Americans began to hold more wealth in personal property, dower and curtesy became less effective protections for the surviving spouse.

As a result, most states enacted "elective share" statutes which permitted the surviving spouse to elect to take a statutory percentage (generally one-third) of the decedent spouse's probate estate even if the decedent spouse tried to limit the surviving spouse to a smaller share. The elective share generally applies to both personal property and land. In most states, the elective share has emerged as a substitute for dower and curtesy, and those common law interests have been abolished.

Early elective share statutes were premised on the notion that the surviving spouse—generally the wife—deserved and needed support from her husband, who was generally the family breadwinner, and who generally held title to most of the couple's assets. More recent elective share statutes embrace the partnership theory of marriage. Equality and sharing—not dependence and need—serve as the foundation for many of the more modern elective share statutes—including the Uniform Probate Code. In many respects, these modern elective share statutes operate to approximate (albeit somewhat roughly) the results that would obtain upon death in community property states. For discussion of the theories underlying elective share statutes, see generally Alan Newman, Incorporating the Partnership Theory of Marriage Into Elective–Share Law: The Approximation System of the Uniform Probate Code and the Deferred–Community Property Alternative, 49 Emory L. J. 487 (2000); Mary F. Radford and F. Skip Sugarman, Georgia's New Probate Code, 13 Ga. St. U. L. Rev. 605, 652–54 (1997); Susan N. Gary, Marital Partnership Theory and the Elective Share, 49 U. Miami L. Rev. 567, 577–78 (1995); Ralph C. Brashier, Disinheritance and the Modern Family, 45 Case W. Res. L. Rev. 83 (1994); John H. Langbein & Lawrence W. Waggoner, Redesigning the Spouse's Forced Share, 22 Real Prop. Prob. & Tr. J. 303 (1987); Ronald R. Volkmer, Spousal Property Rights at Death: Re–Evaluation of the Common Law Premises in Light of the Proposed Uniform Marital Property Act, 17 Creighton L. Rev. 95 (1983).

As we examine various types of elective share statutes, ask yourself which theories underlie each statute. As we shall see, elective share statutes differ significantly from state to state, both in form and in substance. Until recently, most guaranteed the surviving spouse a fixed share of the estate—generally one-third—regardless of the duration of the marriage. The most recent version of the Uniform Probate Code takes a different approach, entitling the surviving spouse to far less than one-third of the estate when the parties were recently married, and increasing the share of the surviving spouse with each additional year of marriage, until the share reaches a maximum of 50% of the estate when the spouses have been married for at least 15 years. (Uniform Probate Code § 2–202). In addition, the Code suggests that states guarantee the surviving spouse $75,000 if the elective share percentage would give the surviving spouse a smaller amount.

SECTION II. TRADITIONAL ELECTIVE SHARE STATUTES

Traditionally, elective share statutes allowed a surviving spouse to elect to take a fractional share of the decedent's probate estate—the assets owned by decedent at death. Of course, any crafty testator who wished to disinherit a spouse could find an easy way around the elective share statute: the testator could transfer substantial assets to others before death, either outright or by creating a joint tenancy or a trust with a remainder in someone other than testator's spouse. Courts and legislatures had various responses to this maneuver. Consider the following materials:

Sullivan v. Burkin

Supreme Judicial Court of Massachusetts, 1984.
390 Mass. 864, 460 N.E.2d 572.

■ WILKINS, J.

Mary A. Sullivan, the widow of Ernest G. Sullivan, has exercised her right, under G. L. c. 191, § 15, to take a share of her husband's estate. By this action, she seeks a determination that assets held in an inter vivos trust created by her husband during the marriage should be considered as part of the estate in determining that share. A judge of the Probate Court for the county of Suffolk rejected the widow's claim and entered judgment dismissing the complaint. The widow appealed, and, on July 12, 1983, a panel of the Appeals Court reported the case to this court.

In September, 1973, Ernest G. Sullivan executed a deed of trust under which he transferred real estate to himself as sole trustee. The net income of the trust was payable to him during his life and the trustee was instructed to pay to him all or such part of the principal of the trust estate as he might request in writing from time to time. He retained the right to revoke the trust at any time. On his death, the successor trustee is directed to pay the principal and any undistributed income equally to the defendants, George F. Cronin, Sr., and Harold J. Cronin, if they should survive him, which they did. There were no witnesses to the execution of the deed of trust, but the husband acknowledged his signatures before a notary public, separately, as donor and as trustee.

The husband died on April 27, 1981, while still trustee of the inter vivos trust. He left a will in which he stated that he "intentionally neglected to make any provision for my wife, Mary A. Sullivan and my grandson, Mark Sullivan." He directed that, after the payment of debts, expenses, and all estate taxes levied by reason of his death, the residue of his estate should be paid over to the trustee of the inter vivos trust. The defendants George F. Cronin, Sr., and Harold J. Cronin were named coexecutors of the will. The defendant Burkin is successor trustee of the inter vivos trust. On October 21, 1981, the wife filed a claim, pursuant to G. L. c. 191, § 15, for a portion of the estate.

Although it does not appear in the record, the parties state in their briefs that Ernest G. Sullivan and Mary A. Sullivan had been separated for many years. We do know that in 1962 the wife obtained a court order providing for her temporary support. No final action was taken in that proceeding. The record provides no information about the value of any property owned by the husband at his death or about the value of any assets held in the inter vivos trust. At oral argument, we were advised that the husband owned personal property worth approximately $15,000 at his death and that the only asset in the trust was a house in Boston which was sold after the husband's death for approximately $85,000.

As presented in the complaint, and perhaps as presented to the motion judge, the wife's claim was simply that the inter vivos trust was an invalid testamentary disposition and that the trust assets "constitute assets of the estate" of Ernest G. Sullivan. There is no suggestion that the wife argued initially that, even if the trust were not testamentary, she had a special claim as a widow asserting her rights under G. L. c. 191, § 15. If the wife is correct that the trust was an ineffective testamentary disposition, the trust assets would be part of the husband's probate estate. In that event, we would not have to consider any special consequences of the wife's election under G. L. c. 191, § 15, or, in the words of the Appeals Court, "the present vitality" of Kerwin v. Donaghy, 317 Mass. 559, 572 (1945).

We conclude, however, that the trust was not testamentary in character and that the husband effectively created a valid inter vivos trust. Thus, whether the issue was initially involved in this case, we are now presented with the question (which the executors will have to resolve ultimately, in any event) whether the assets of the inter vivos trust are to be considered in determining the "portion of the estate of the deceased" (G. L. c. 191, § 15) in which Mary A. Sullivan has rights. We conclude that, in this case, we should adhere to the principles expressed in Kerwin v. Donaghy, supra, that deny the surviving spouse any claim against the assets of a valid inter vivos trust created by the deceased spouse, even where the deceased spouse alone retained substantial rights and powers under the trust instrument. For the future, however, as to any inter vivos trust created or amended after the date of this opinion, we announce that the estate of a decedent, for the purposes of G. L. c. 191, § 15, shall include the value of assets held in an inter vivos trust created by the deceased spouse as to which the deceased spouse alone retained the power during his or her life to direct the disposition of those trust assets for his or her benefit, as, for example, by the exercise of a power of appointment or by revocation of the trust.

* * *

We consider first whether the inter vivos trust was invalid because it was testamentary. A trust with remainder interests given to others on the settlor's death is not invalid as a testamentary disposition simply because the settlor retained a broad power to modify or revoke the trust, the right to receive income, and the right to invade principal during his life. Ascher v. Cohen, 333 Mass. 397, 400 (1956). Leahy v. Old Colony Trust Co., 326 Mass. 49, 51 (1950). Kerwin v. Donaghy, 317 Mass. 559, 567 (1945). National Shawmut Bank v. Joy, 315 Mass. 457, 473–475 (1944). Kelley v. Snow, 185 Mass. 288, 298–299 (1904). The fact that the settlor of such a trust is the sole trustee does not make the trust testamentary. In National Shawmut Bank v. Joy, supra at 476–477, we held that a settlor's reservation of the power to control investments did not impair the validity of a trust and noted that "[i]n Greeley v. Flynn, 310 Mass. 23 [1941], the settlor was herself the trustee and had every power of control, including the right to withdraw principal for her own use. Yet the gift over at her death was held valid and not testamentary." We did, however, leave open the question whether such a trust would be testamentary "had the trustees been reduced to passive impotence, or something near it." Id. at 476. We have held an inter vivos trust valid where a settlor, having broad powers to revoke the trust and to demand trust principal, was a cotrustee with a friend (Ascher v. Cohen, supra at 400) or with a bank whose tenure as trustee was at the whim of the settlor (Leahy v. Old Colony Trust Co., supra at 51) . . . . We believe that the law of the Commonwealth is correctly represented by the statement in Restatement (Second) of Trusts § 57 comment h (1959), that a trust is "not testamentary and invalid for failure to comply with the requirements of the Statute of Wills merely because the settlor-trustee reserves a beneficial life interest and power to revoke and modify the trust. The fact that as trustee he controls the administration of the trust does not invalidate it."

We come then to the question whether, even if the trust was not testamentary on general principles, the widow has special interests which should be recognized. Courts in this country have differed considerably in their reasoning and in their conclusions in passing on this question. See 1 A. Scott, Trusts § 57.5 at 509–511 (3d ed. 1967 & 1983 Supp.); Restatement (Second) of Property—Donative Transfers, Supplement to Tent. Draft No. 5, reporter's note to § 13.7 (1982); Annot., 39 A.L.R.3d 14 (1971), Validity of Inter Vivos Trust Established by One Spouse Which Impairs the Other Spouse's Distributive Share or Other Statutory Rights in Property. In considering this issue at the May, 1982, annual meeting of the American Law Institute the members divided almost evenly on whether a settlor's surviving spouse should have rights, apart from specific statutory rights, with respect to the assets of an inter vivos trust over which the settlor retained a general power of appointment. See Proceedings of the American Law Institute, May, 1982, at 59–117; Restatement (Second) of Property—Donative Transfers, Supplement to Tent. Draft No. 5, at 28 (1982).

The rule of Kerwin v. Donaghy, supra at 571, is that "[t]he right of a wife to waive her husband's will, and take, with certain limitations, 'the same portion of the property of the deceased, real and personal, that . . . she would have taken if the deceased had died intestate' (G. L. [Ter. Ed.] c. 191, § 15), does not extend to personal property that has been conveyed by the husband in his lifetime and does not form part of his estate at his death. Fiske v. Fiske, 173 Mass. 413, 419 [1899]. Shelton v. Sears, 187 Mass. 455 [1905]. In this Commonwealth a husband has an absolute right to dispose of any or all of his personal property in his lifetime, without the knowledge or consent of his wife, with the result that it will not form part of his estate for her to share under the statute of distributions (G. L. [Ter. Ed.] c. 190, § 1, 2), under his will, or by virtue of a waiver of his will. That is true even though his sole purpose was to disinherit her." In the Kerwin case, we applied the rule to deny a surviving spouse the right to reach assets the deceased spouse had placed in an inter vivos trust of which the settlor's daughter by a previous marriage was trustee and over whose assets he had a general power of appointment. The rule of Kerwin v. Donaghy has been adhered to in this Commonwealth for almost forty years and was adumbrated even earlier. The bar has been entitled reasonably to rely on that rule in advising clients. In the area of property law, the retroactive invalidation of an established principle is to be undertaken with great caution.... We conclude that, whether or not Ernest G. Sullivan established the inter vivos trust in order to defeat his wife's right to take her statutory share in the assets placed in the trust and even though he had a general power of appointment over the trust assets, Mary A. Sullivan obtained no right to share in the assets of that trust when she made her election under G. L. c. 191, § 15.

We announce for the future that, as to any inter vivos trust created or amended after the date of this opinion, we shall no longer follow the rule announced in Kerwin v. Donaghy. There have been significant changes since 1945 in public policy considerations bearing on the right of one spouse to treat his or her property as he or she wishes during marriage. The interests of one spouse in the property of the other have been substantially increased upon the dissolution of a marriage by divorce. We believe that, when a marriage is terminated by the death of one spouse, the rights of the surviving spouse should not be so restricted as they are by the rule in Kerwin v. Donaghy. It is neither equitable nor logical to extend to a divorced spouse greater rights in the assets of an inter vivos trust created and controlled by the other spouse than are extended to a spouse who remains married until the death of his or her spouse.

The rule we now favor would treat as part of "the estate of the deceased" for the purposes of G. L. c. 191, § 15, assets of an inter vivos trust created during the marriage by the deceased spouse over which he or she alone had a general power of appointment, exercisable by deed or by will. This objective test would involve no consideration of the motive or intention of the spouse in creating the trust. We would not need to engage in a determination of "whether the [spouse] has in good faith divested himself [or herself] of ownership of his [or her] property or has made an illusory transfer" (Newman v. Dore, 275 N.Y. 371, 379 [1927]) or with the factual question whether the spouse "intended to surrender complete dominion over the property" (Staples v. King, 433 A.2d 407, 411 [Me. 1981]). Nor would we have to participate in the rather unsatisfactory process of determining whether the inter vivos trust was, on some standard, "colorable," "fraudulent," or "illusory."

What we have announced as a rule for the future hardly resolves all the problems that may arise. There may be a different rule if some or all of the trust assets were conveyed to such a trust by a third person. Cf. Theodore v. Theodore, 356 Mass. 297 (1969). We have not, of course, dealt with a case in which the power of appointment is held jointly with another person. If the surviving spouse assented to the creation of the inter vivos trust, perhaps the rule we announce would not apply. We have not discussed which assets should be used to satisfy a surviving spouse's claim.... Nor have we dealt with other assets not passing by will, such as a trust created before the marriage or insurance policies over which a deceased spouse had control. Id. at 30, 38.

The question of the rights of a surviving spouse in the estate of a deceased spouse, using the word "estate" in its broad sense, is one that can best be handled by legislation. See Uniform Probate Code §§ 2-201, 2-202, 8 U.L.A. 74-75 (1983). See also Uniform Marital Property Act § 18 (Nat'l Conference of Comm'rs on Uniform State Laws, July, 1983), which adopts the concept of community property as to "marital property." But, until it is, the answers to these problems will "be determined in the usual way through the decisional process." Tucker v. Badoian, 376 Mass. 907, 918-919 (1978) (Kaplan, J., concurring).

We affirm the judgment of the Probate Court dismissing the plaintiff's complaint.

NOTES AND QUESTIONS

1. Suppose, after Sullivan v. Burkin, a Massachusetts testator had consulted you about disinheriting her husband. What advice would you have given her?

2. Suppose a testator's mother has created a trust for the benefit of the testator and testator's children, and has given testator the power to terminate the trust and distribute the trust property to herself. Would Sullivan v. Burkin entitle testator's husband to treat the trust property as part of testator's estate for elective share purposes? See Bongaards v. Millen, 440 Mass. 10, 793 N.E.2d 335 (2003) [holding, in a 4-3 decision, that Sullivan does not extend to trusts created by persons other than testator].

3. As we have seen, elective share statutes sometimes reflect the notion that the parties to a marriage are partners, engaged in a common enterprise, and that neither ought to be able to deprive the other of the fruits of the enterprise. Do the facts in Sullivan v. Burkin fit that pattern? Did the parties engage in any common enterprise for the 19 (or more) years preceding decedent's death?

Consider also Newman v. Dore, 275 N.Y. 371, 9 N.E.2d 966 (1937), a leading case establishing the right of a surviving spouse to elect against *inter vivos* transfers. Decedent was an octogenarian who had married a woman more than 40 years his junior. His wife had, before his death, brought a separation action, alleging that his sexual perversions made him impossible to live with. Decedent had responded by bringing an annulment action of his own, and then by consulting a lawyer about how he might disinherit his wife. As in Sullivan v. Burkin, decedent transferred most of his property into a revocable *inter vivos* trust. The Court of Appeals held the device ineffective to cut off the wife's elective share rights. Do the facts in Newman v. Dore suggest a marriage of equal partners pooling their assets?

Should marital fault be relevant in determining whether a surviving spouse has a right to elect? See Linda Kelly Hill, No–Fault Death: Wedding Inheritance Rights to Family Values, 94 Ky. L. J. 319 (2005).

4. Bear in mind that under most elective share statutes, the surviving spouse must elect between the elective share amount and the amount he or she would receive under the will; the surviving spouse cannot take both. By contrast, at common law, the widow could claim both dower and the provisions made for her in her husband's will. For a more general discussion of problems raised by the right of election, see Margaret Valentine Turano, Love and Death: Marital Problems, Wills and the Right of Election, 49 Brook. L. Rev. 405 (1983).

Like the Massachusetts court in Sullivan v. Burkin, courts in other states have struggled with the fact that certain non-probate transfers, such as revocable trusts and joint bank accounts, allow spouses to maintain full control and ownership of property while evading traditional elective share statutes that limit the surviving spouse's share to a percentage of probate assets. Instead of taking the Sullivan court's approach—crafting specific bright-line rules that expand the reach of elective share statutes—some courts prefer to examine each dispute on a case by case basis, looking for evidence that the deceased spouse's transfer to a nonprobate mechanism was made to defeat the surviving spouse's elective share rights. For example, in Karsenty v. Schoukroun, 406 Md. 469, 959 A.2d 1147 (2008), Maryland's highest court reversed a lower court ruling that assets in a revocable living trust should always be included as part of the elective share estate, stating that

> the question to be determined in any case in which a surviving spouse seeks to invalidate an *inter vivos* transfer is whether the transfer was set up as a mere device or contrivance. If it was, the surviving spouse may have it set aside. This standard places the focus of a court's inquiry on the nature of the underlying transaction, not on the decedent's intent to defraud the surviving spouse. Determining whether an *inter vivos* transfer was a mere device or contrivance is indeed a question of intent; however, the intent that matters is the decedent's intent to structure a transaction by which she or he parts with ownership of the property in form, but not in substance.

Yet the court also emphasized that a revocable living trust, which allows a spouse to retain complete benefit and control over assets, might not necessarily be a "device or contrivance"! Rather, courts should also focus on the motives of the transferee and the transferor, and the extent to which the nonprobate transfers deprive the surviving spouse of her elective share. Clear? What do you think of Maryland's approach?

Some states have gone so far as to enact statutes to address the problem: some statutes focus on the intent of the person making the gift, while others focus on the character of the transfer—was it "illusory" [see, e.g., S.C. Code Ann. § 62–7–401(c) (2005), construed in Dreher v. Dreher, 370 S.C. 75, 634 S.E.2d 646 (2006)]. As you explore the following statutes, consider whether they further the support and partnership theories of the elective share. You might also consider whether the statutes reduce or increase litigation costs.

TENNESSEE CODE ANNOTATED

SECTION 31–1–105. FRAUDULENT CONVEYANCE TO DEFEAT SHARE VOIDABLE

Any conveyance made fraudulently to children or others, with an intent to defeat the surviving spouse of the surviving spouse's distributive or elective share, is, at the election of the surviving spouse, includable in the decedent's net estate under § 31–4–101(b), and voidable to the extent the other assets in the decedent's net estate are insufficient to fund and pay the elective share amount payable to the surviving spouse under § 31–4–101(c).

* * *

MISSOURI REVISED STATUTES

SECTION 474.150. GIFTS IN FRAUD OF MARITAL RIGHTS—PRESUMPTIONS ON CONVEYANCES

1. Any gift made by a person, whether dying testate or intestate, in fraud of the marital rights of his surviving spouse to share in his estate, shall, at the election of the surviving spouse, be treated as a testamentary disposition and may be recovered from the donee and persons taking from him without adequate consideration and applied to the payment of the spouse's share, as in case of his election to take against the will.

2. Any conveyance of real estate made by a married person at any time without the joinder or other written express assent of his spouse, made at any time, duly acknowledged, is deemed to be in fraud of the marital rights of his spouse, if the spouse becomes a surviving spouse, unless the contrary is shown.

NOTES AND QUESTIONS

1. How would Sullivan v. Burkin have been decided if the Tennessee statute had been in effect? The Missouri statute?

2. Under the Tennessee statute, how would you determine whether decedent made a conveyance "with an intent to defeat the surviving spouse of his . . . elective share"? Suppose testator, prior to death, transfers property to her daughter by a prior marriage. Can testator's husband upset the conveyance? Should it matter if, during the wife's final illness, he spent his evenings drinking at bars? See Young v. Hudgens, 1989 WL 71041:

> In determining the transferor spouse's intent, the fact that the surviving spouse may have given the transferor good reason for wanting to give property to someone else supplies a motive for a fraudulent transfer. Moreover, a sincere desire to benefit someone else and an intent to deprive the surviving spouse of his or her elective or distributive share are not mutually exclusive.

By contrast, in Warren v. Compton, 626 S.W.2d 12 (Tenn. App. 1981), testator made significant gifts to his daughter and his long-time lover, who cared for him during his last illness. When his wife sought to upset the transfers, the court rejected her attempt:

> .... We would point out that a strained marriage relationship is a sword which cuts two ways. The surviving spouse could have been so inconsiderate, cold, and self-centered as to justify a transfer of property by the other spouse to those in whom he found solace, comfort, and care. We do not necessarily approve of Mr. Warren's acts, but we are not trying a divorce lawsuit. We are determining whether the transfers were made with the intent to defeat the rights of the surviving spouse. The chancellor heard these people testify and observed their demeanor. He apparently found that the strained marriage relationship, taken in consideration of all other factors, did not establish a fraudulent intent on the part of the husband. We agree.

626 S.W.2d at 18.

In Finley v. Finley, 726 S.W.2d 923 (Tenn. App. 1986), the court identified seven factors it deemed relevant in deciding whether decedent intended to defraud the surviving spouse:

> (1) whether the transfer was made with or without consideration, (2) the size of the transfer in relation to the husband's total estate, (3) the time between the transfer and the husband's death, (4) relations which existed between the husband and the wife at the time of the transfer, (5) the source from which the property came, (6) whether the transfer was illusory, and (7) whether the wife was adequately provided for in the will.

726 S.W.2d at 924. For an overview of the Tennessee elective share statute, see Note, Conveyances Affecting the Surviving Spouse's Elective Share: Tennessee's Past and a Look to the Future, 57 Tenn. L. Rev. 677 (1990). The Tennessee appellate courts continue to wrestle with the "fraudulent conveyance" approach in cases where the decedent spouse makes lifetime transfers to persons other than the surviving spouse. See, e.g., Estate of Hill, 2005 WL 387930 (Tenn. App. 2005); Cantrell v. Cantrell, 2004 WL 3044907 (Tenn. App. 2004); Arndts v. Bonner, 2004 WL 1532274 (Tenn. App. 2004).

The Illinois statute provides that lifetime transfers are not invalid against the spouse unless decedent had an "intent to defraud." 755 Ill. L. C. S. 25/1. The Illinois Supreme Court has held that the statute requires the surviving spouse to prove that decedent lacked intent to make a valid lifetime transfer to a third party. Johnson v. La Grange State Bank, 73 Ill.2d 342, 22 Ill.Dec. 709, 383 N.E.2d 185 (1978). Professor Ronald Domsky has observed that "since the Illinois Supreme Court handed down its decision in Johnson, there is no reported case where a disinherited or disenfranchised spouse has successfully asserted a fraud on the marital right claim." Ronald Domsky, Til Death Do Us Part ... After That, My Dear, You're On Your Own: A Practitioner's Guide to Disinheriting a Spouse in Illinois, 29 S. Ill. U. L. J. 207, 226 (2005).

Why should decedent's intent be relevant at all? How is intent relevant if the purpose of the elective share statutes is to provide support for the surviving spouse? If the purpose is to reflect an equal partnership between the spouses?

3. Is fuzziness in an elective share statute a good thing or a bad thing? In general, fuzzy rules make planning more difficult. For instance, if a Missouri testator asks you how large a wedding gift he can make to his daughter (by a prior marriage) without giving his wife an opportunity to challenge the transfer, what answer would you give him? What questions would you ask before answering?

Do we want to encourage planning by people who seek to disinherit their spouses? Might not fuzzy rules encourage generosity toward spouses in an effort to assure that a court will not upset testator's *inter vivos* transfers?

4. Are elective share statutes that focus on decedent's intent consistent with the partnership theory of marriage—a theory that increasingly governs marital property rights upon divorce? See Angela M. Vallario, Spousal Election: Suggested Equitable Reform for the Division of Property at Death, 52 Cath. U. L. Rev 519 (2003) [arguing that elective share statutes should incorporate principles used for division of property at divorce]; Helene Shapo, The Widow's Mite Gets Smaller: Deficiencies in Illinois Elective Share Law, 24 S. Ill. U. L. J. 95 (1999) (arguing that Illinois courts have embraced the partnership theory in divorce cases, but have ignored partnership theory in elective share cases).

SECTION III. MODERN ELECTIVE SHARE STATUTES

Cases like Sullivan v. Burkin, together with litigation that developed under statutes like those in Tennessee and Missouri, led many scholars and legislators to prefer a more rule-oriented approach to the elective share problem. The New York legislature led the way. In 1966, during a systematic revision of New York's law of estates and trusts, the legislature enacted a statute designed to protect the surviving spouse against specified lifetime transfers, and, at the same time to reduce uncertainty about the validity of other lifetime transfers. The statute required that specified lifetime transfers be added to the value of decedent's probate estate for purposes of computing the surviving spouse's elective share. The 1966 statute, although it has since been modified significantly, served as the foundation for the original Uniform Probate Code treatment of the elective share, which in turn served as the foundation for the most recent version of the Code. Both the original version of the UPC and the current version have been adopted in a number of states, often with local variations. As a result, lawyers must be careful to consult the precise language of the local statute rather than relying on general statements about the UPC's approach to the elective share. See Ronald R. Volkmer, The Complicated World of the Electing Spouse: In Re Estate of Myers and Recent Statutory Developments, 33 Creighton L. Rev. 121, 131–32, 141 (1999). Sometimes, local amendments to the UPC have operated—perhaps unintentionally—to emasculate the effectiveness of the statute as a protection against disinheritance. See Terry S. Kogan & Michael F. Thomson, Piercing the Facade of Utah's "Improved" Elective Share Statute, 1999 Utah L. Rev. 677 [discussing Utah's decision to limit the augmented estate to "marital property"].

The drafters of the 1993 version of the Uniform Probate Code attempted to implement the partnership theory of marriage. In the words of Professor Newman:

> Generally, the objective of the UPC's new elective-share system is to provide the surviving spouse with a right to elect to receive property of sufficient value to result in the surviving spouse's having property with a value equal to approximately half of the couple's marital property, in addition to his or her separate property. The approximation system was designed to accomplish this objective.
>
> The essence of the approximation system is that the length of the marriage conclusively determines for elective-share purposes what portion of each spouse's assets is treated as marital, and thus subject to a surviving spouse's elective-share claim, and what portion is treated as separate, and thus not subject to such a claim. The longer the marriage, the greater the percentage of each spouse's assets that are treated as marital, until after fifteen years of marriage all of each spouse's assets implicitly are so treated. If either spouse has property that he or she brought to the marriage, or received by gift or inheritance during the marriage, over time the UPC's approximation system effectively will convert it, for elective-share purposes, to marital property.

Alan Newman, Incorporating the Partnership Theory of Marriage into Elective–Share Law: The Approximation System of the Uniform Probate Code and the Deferred Community–Property Alternative, 49 Emory L. J. 487 (2000). Some commentators contend that the Code's principal foundation continues to be support of the surviving spouse. See Charles H. Whitebread, The Uniform Probate Code's Nod to the Partnership Theory of Marriage, 11 Prob. L.J. 125 (1992). Others contend that the Code's provisions implement both a support theory and a partnership theory. See Stephanie J. Willbanks, Parting is Such Sweet Sorrow, But Does it Have to Be So Complicated? Transmission of Property at Death in Vermont, 29 Vt. L. Rev. 895, 926 (2005). Still other commentators criticize the Code for abandoning support as its foundation. See Margaret V. Turano, UPC Section 2–201: Equal Treatment of Spouses, 55 Alb. L. Rev. 983 (1992).

In general outline, here is how the UPC works: in any marriage that has lasted for at least 15 years, the Code essentially treats all of the property of both spouses (and most of the property either spouse has transferred without consideration) as a pot of resources owned equally by the two spouses. Therefore, once we figure out what is in the pot at the death of the first spouse to die, if the various *inter vivos* and testamentary transfers have left the surviving spouse with less than half of the pot, the surviving spouse has a right to elect. Thus, if the surviving spouse holds the bulk of the pot as her own assets, she will not generally have a right to elect, even if her spouse left her none of his assets. By contrast, if the surviving spouse held no assets in her own name, she will have a right to elect unless the decedent spouse left her with at least 50% of his own assets.

For shorter marriages, the pot from which the surviving spouse can elect is smaller, and some of the surviving spouse's own assets are excluded from the elective share calculation. The theory behind these provisions is that the marriage has not yet generated a full and equal financial partnership, so each spouse should be able to shield more of his own assets, often earned before the marriage, from claims by the surviving spouse. (Professor Laura Rosenbury notes, however, that the UPC's complicated provisions would not be necessary if the Code "employed definitions of augmented estates that were coextensive with definitions of community property or marital property." Laura Rosenbury, Two Ways to End a Marriage: Divorce or Death, 2005 Utah L. Rev. 1227, 1250). Not all states adopting the UPC have endorsed the UPC's graduated share provisions. See Alexander J. Bott, North Dakota Probate Code: Prior and Revised Article II, 72 N.D. L. Rev. 1 (1996).

The UPC, by limiting surviving spouse protection until the marriage has endured for a significant period, takes account of a common situation: a late-in-life marriage between spouses each of whom have had children before entering into the marriage, and each of whom would like those children to be the principal beneficiaries of their respective estates. Until the marriage has endured for a significant period, the surviving spouse has only a limited right to upset the testamentary scheme of a testator who has chosen to make his children the principal beneficiaries of his estate.

A Statutory "Road Map"

Implementing the Code's partnership theory proved no easy matter. The Code's provisions are complex. Before trying to absorb the statutory detail, consider the statutory scheme. Determining whether a surviving spouse has a right to elect involves four basic steps: (1) compute the value of the decedent spouse's "augmented estate:" the sum of decedent spouse's and surviving spouse's property and non-probate transfers; (2) compute the "marital-property portion" of the augmented estate—the pot of money the spouses have an obligation to share, based on the length of their marriage; (3) compute the surviving spouse's elective share, which is 50% of the marital property portion of the augmented estate; and (4) determine whether the dispositions already made for the surviving spouse, together with a percentage of the spouse's own assets (based on the length of the marriage), are sufficient to satisfy the elective share. If not, decedent's probate and non-probate transfers to others must abate proportionately to satisfy the surviving spouse's elective share amount.

Where and how does the statute tell us to take these steps?

(1) UPC § 2–203(a) tells us what to include in the augmented estate. Essentially, section 2–203(a) tells us to include the following categories of property, each of which is included by virtue of a separate section:

a. Decedent's net probate estate (UPC § 2–204)

b. Decedent's lifetime transfers to people other than the surviving spouse (UPC § 2–205)

c. Decedent's lifetime transfers to the surviving spouse (UPC § 2–206)

d. The surviving spouse's own property, together with property transferred by the surviving spouse (UPC § 2–207).

(2) UPC § 2–203(b) instructs us to determine the "marital-property portion" of the augmented estate by multiplying the augmented estate by a percentage that is keyed to the length of the marriage.

(3) UPC § 2–202(a) tells us that the "elective-share amount" is fifty percent of the marital-property portion of the augmented estate.

(4) UPC § 2–209 then tells us which amounts should be applied in satisfaction of the surviving spouse's elective share. Section 2–209(a)(1) directs us to first apply amounts that will pass to the surviving spouse under the intestacy statute, the will and nonprobate transfers from the deceased spouse. Section 2–209(a)(2) tells us to then apply the "marital-property portion" of the surviving spouse's assets. If the dispositions made for the surviving spouse and the requisite percentage of the spouse's own assets are equal to or greater than the elective share amount, the spouse has no right to additional funds; if the dispositions are less than the elective share amount, section 2–209 sets forth an order of abatement to satisfy the elective share.

With this "road map" as background, let us examine the statute. For a complete understanding of the statutory scheme, it is essential to work out problems that require you to apply the statute. Try your hand at the problems that follow the statute.

UNIFORM PROBATE CODE [2008 REVISION]

SECTION 2–202. ELECTIVE SHARE.

(a) [Elective–Share Amount.] The surviving spouse of a decedent who dies domiciled in this State has a right of election, under the limitations and conditions stated in this Part, to take an elective share amount equal to 50 percent of the value of the marital-property portion of the augmented estate.

(b) [Supplemental Elective–Share Amount.] If the sum of the amounts described in Sections 2–207, 2–209(a)(1), and that part of the elective-share amount payable from the decedent's net probate estate and nonprobate transfers to others under Section 2–209(c) and (d) is less than [$75,000], the surviving spouse is entitled to a supplemental elective-share amount equal to [$75,000], minus the sum of the amounts described in those sections. The supplemental elective-share amount is payable from the decedent's net probate estate and from recipients of the decedent's nonprobate transfers to others in the order of priority set forth in Section 2–209(c) and (d).

(c) [Effect of Election on Statutory Benefits.] If the right of election is exercised by or on behalf of the surviving spouse, the surviving spouse's homestead allowance, exempt property, and family allowance, if any, are not charged against but are in addition to the elective-share and supplemental elective-share amounts.

(d) [Non–Domiciliary.] The right, if any, of the surviving spouse of a decedent who dies domiciled outside this State to take an elective share in property in this State is governed by the law of the decedent's domicile at death.

SECTION 2–203. COMPOSITION OF THE AUGMENTED ESTATE; MARITAL PROPERTY PORTION.

(a) Subject to Section 2–208, the value of the augmented estate, to the extent provided in Sections 2–204, 2–205, 2–206, and 2–207, consists of the sum of the values of all property, whether real or personal, movable or immovable, tangible or intangible, wherever situated, that constitute:

(1) the decedent's net probate estate;

(2) the decedent's nonprobate transfers to others;

(3) the decedent's nonprobate transfers to the surviving spouse; and

(4) the surviving spouse's property and nonprobate transfers to others.

(b) The value of the marital-property portion of the augmented estate consists of the sum of the values of the four components of the augmented estate as determined under subsection (a) multiplied by the following percentage:

If the decedent and the spouse were married to each other:	The percentage is:
Less than 1 year	3%
1 year but less than 2 years	6%
2 years but less than 3 years	12%
3 years but less than 4 years	18%
4 years but less than 5 years	24%
5 years but less than 6 years	30%
6 years but less than 7 years	36%
7 years but less than 8 years	42%
8 years but less than 9 years	48%
9 years but less than 10 years	54%

If the decedent and the spouse were married to each other:	The percentage is:
10 years but less than 11 years	60%
11 years but less than 12 years	68%
12 years but less than 13 years	76%
13 years but less than 14 years	84%
14 years but less than 15 years	92%
15 years or more	100%

SECTION 2–204. DECEDENT'S NET PROBATE ESTATE.

The value of the augmented estate includes the value of the decedent's probate estate, reduced by funeral and administration expenses, homestead allowance, family allowances, exempt property, and enforceable claims.

SECTION 2–205. DECEDENT'S NONPROBATE TRANSFERS TO OTHERS.

The value of the augmented estate includes the value of the decedent's nonprobate transfers to others, not included under Section 2–204, of any of the following types, in the amount provided respectively for each type of transfer:

(1) Property owned or owned in substance by the decedent immediately before death that passed outside probate at the decedent's death. Property included under this category consists of:

(A) Property over which the decedent alone, immediately before death, held a presently exercisable general power of appointment. The amount included is the value of the property subject to the power, to the extent the property passed at the decedent's death, by exercise, release, lapse, in default, or otherwise, to or for the benefit of any person other than the decedent's estate or surviving spouse.

(B) The decedent's fractional interest in property held by the decedent in joint tenancy with the right of survivorship. The amount included is the value of the decedent's fractional interest, to the extent the fractional interest passed by right of survivorship at the decedent's death to a surviving joint tenant other than the decedent's surviving spouse.

(C) The decedent's ownership interest in property or accounts held in POD, TOD, or co-ownership registration with the right of survivorship. The amount included is the value of the decedent's ownership interest, to the extent the decedent's ownership interest passed at the decedent's death to or for the benefit of any person other than the decedent's estate or surviving spouse.

(D) Proceeds of insurance, including accidental death benefits, on the life of the decedent, if the decedent owned the insurance policy immediately before death or if and to the extent the decedent alone and immediately before death held a presently exercisable general power of appointment over the policy or its proceeds. The amount included is the value of the proceeds, to the extent they were payable at the decedent's death to or for the benefit of any person other than the decedent's estate or surviving spouse.

(2) Property transferred in any of the following forms by the decedent during marriage:

(A) Any irrevocable transfer in which the decedent retained the right to the possession or enjoyment of, or to the income from, the property if and to the extent the decedent's right terminated at or continued beyond the decedent's death. The amount included is the value of the fraction of the property to which the decedent's right related, to the extent the fraction of the property passed outside probate to or for the benefit of any person other than the decedent's estate or surviving spouse.

(B) Any transfer in which the decedent created a power over income or property, exercisable by the decedent alone or in conjunction with any other person, or exercisable by a nonadverse party, to or for the benefit of the decedent, creditors of the decedent, the decedent's estate, or creditors of the decedent's estate. The amount included with respect to a power over property is the value of the property subject to the power, and the amount included with respect to a power over income is the value of the property that produces or produced the income, to the extent the power in either case was exercisable at the decedent's death to or for the benefit of any person other than the decedent's surviving spouse or to the extent the property passed at the decedent's death, by exercise, release, lapse, in default, or otherwise, to or for the benefit of any person other than the decedent's estate or surviving spouse. If the power is a power over both income and property and the preceding sentence produces different amounts, the amount included is the greater amount.

(3) Property that passed during marriage and during the two-year period next preceding the decedent's death as a result of a transfer by the decedent if the transfer was of any of the following types:

(A) Any property that passed as a result of the termination of a right or interest in, or power over, property that would have been included in the augmented estate under paragraph (1)(i), (ii), or (iii), or under paragraph (2), if the right, interest, or power had not terminated until the decedent's death. The amount included is the value of the property that would have been included under those paragraphs if the property were valued at the time the right, interest, or power terminated, and is included only to the extent the property passed upon termination to or for the benefit of any person other than the decedent or the decedent's estate, spouse, or surviving spouse. As used in this subparagraph, "termination," with respect to a right or interest in property, occurs when the right or interest terminated by the terms of the governing instrument or the decedent transferred or relinquished the right or interest, and, with respect to a power over property, occurs when the power terminated by exercise, release, lapse, default, or otherwise, but, with respect to a power described in paragraph (1)(i), "termination" occurs when the power terminated by exercise or release, but not otherwise.

(B) Any transfer of or relating to an insurance policy on the life of the decedent if the proceeds would have been included in the augmented estate under paragraph (1)(iv) had the transfer not occurred. The amount included is the value of the insurance proceeds to the extent the proceeds were payable at the decedent's death to or for the benefit of any person other than the decedent's estate or surviving spouse.

(C) Any transfer of property, to the extent not otherwise included in the augmented estate, made to or for the benefit of a person other than the decedent's surviving spouse. The amount included is the value of the transferred property to the extent the aggregate transfers to any one donee in either of the two years exceeded [the amount excludable from taxable gifts under 26 U.S.C. Section 2503(b) on the date next preceding the date of the decedent's death].

SECTION 2–206. DECEDENT'S NONPROBATE TRANSFERS TO THE SURVIVING SPOUSE.

Excluding property passing to the surviving spouse under the federal Social Security system, the value of the augmented estate includes the value of the decedent's nonprobate transfers to the decedent's surviving spouse, which consist of all property that passed outside probate at the decedent's death from the decedent to the surviving spouse by reason of the decedent's death, including:

(1) the decedent's fractional interest in property held as a joint tenant with the right of survivorship, to the extent that the decedent's fractional interest passed to the surviving spouse as surviving joint tenant,

(2) the decedent's ownership interest in property or accounts held in co-ownership registration with the right of survivorship, to the extent the decedent's ownership interest passed to the surviving spouse as surviving co-owner, and

(3) all other property that would have been included in the augmented estate under Section 2–205(1) or (2) had it passed to or for the benefit of a person other than the decedent's spouse, surviving spouse, the decedent, or the decedent's creditors, estate, or estate creditors.

SECTION 2–207. SURVIVING SPOUSE'S PROPERTY AND NONPROBATE TRANSFERS TO OTHERS.

(a) [Included Property.] Except to the extent included in the augmented estate under Section 2–204 or 2–206, the value of the augmented estate includes the value of:

(1) property that was owned by the decedent's surviving spouse at the decedent's death, including:

(i) the surviving spouse's fractional interest in property held in joint tenancy with the right of survivorship,

(ii) the surviving spouse's ownership interest in property or accounts held in co-ownership registration with the right of survivorship, and

(iii) property that passed to the surviving spouse by reason of the decedent's death, but not including the spouse's right to homestead allowance, family allowance, exempt property, or payments under the federal Social Security system; and

(2) property that would have been included in the surviving spouse's nonprobate transfers to others, other than the spouse's fractional and ownership interests included under subsection (a)(1)(i) or (ii), had the spouse been the decedent.

(b) [Time of Valuation.] Property included under this section is valued at the decedent's death, taking the fact that the decedent predeceased the spouse into account, but, for purposes of subsection (a)(1)(i) and (ii), the values of the spouse's fractional and ownership interests are determined immediately before the decedent's death if the decedent was then a joint tenant or a co-owner of the property or accounts. For purposes of subsection (a)(2), proceeds of insurance that would have been included in the spouse's nonprobate transfers to others under Section 2–205(1)(iv) are not valued as if he [or she] were deceased.

(c) [Reduction for Enforceable Claims.] The value of property included under this section is reduced by enforceable claims against the surviving spouse.

SECTION 2–208. EXCLUSIONS, VALUATION, AND OVERLAPPING APPLICATION.

(a) [Exclusions.] The value of any property is excluded from the decedent's nonprobate transfers to others (i) to the extent the decedent received adequate and full consideration in money or money's worth for a transfer of the property or (ii) if the property was transferred with the written joinder of, or if the transfer was consented to in writing before or after the transfer by, the surviving spouse.

(b) [Valuation.] The value of property:

(1) included in the augmented estate under Section 2–205, 2–206, or 2–207 is reduced in each category by enforceable claims against the included property; and

(2) includes the commuted value of any present or future interest and the commuted value of amounts payable under any trust, life insurance settlement option, annuity contract, public or private pension, disability compensation, death benefit or retirement plan, or any similar arrangement, exclusive of the federal Social Security system.

(c) [Overlapping Application; No Double Inclusion.] In case of overlapping application to the same property of the paragraphs or subparagraphs of Section 2–205, 2–206, or 2–207, the property is included in the augmented estate under the provision yielding the greatest value, and under only one overlapping provision if they all yield the same value.

SECTION 2–209. SOURCES FROM WHICH ELECTIVE SHARE PAYABLE.

(a) [Elective-Share Amount Only.] In a proceeding for an elective share, the following are applied first to satisfy the elective-share amount and to reduce or eliminate any contributions due from the decedent's probate estate and recipients of the decedent's nonprobate transfers to others:

(1) amounts included in the augmented estate under Section 2–204 which pass or have passed to the surviving spouse by testate or intestate succession and amounts included in the augmented estate under Section 2–206; and

(2) the marital-property portion of amounts included in the augmented estate under Section 2–207.

(b) [Marital Property Portion.] The marital-property portion under subsection (a)(2) is computed by multiplying the value of the amounts included in the augmented estate under Section 2–207 by the percentage of the augmented estate set forth in the schedule in Section 2–203(b) appropriate to the length of time the spouse and the decedent were married to each other.

(c) [Unsatisfied Balance of Elective–Share Amount; Supplemental Elective–Share Amount.] If, after the application of subsection (a), the elective-share amount is not fully satisfied, or the surviving spouse is entitled to a supplemental elective-share amount, amounts included in the decedent's net probate estate, other than assets passing to the surviving spouse by testate or intestate succession, and in the decedent's nonprobate transfers to others under Section 2–205(1), (2), and (3)(B) are applied first to satisfy the unsatisfied balance of the elective-share amount or the supplemental elective-share amount. The decedent's net probate estate and that portion of the decedent's nonprobate transfers to others are so applied that liability for the unsatisfied balance of the elective-share amount or for the supplemental elective-share amount is apportioned among the recipients of the decedent's net probate estate and of that portion of the decedent's nonprobate transfers to others in proportion to the value of their interests therein.

(d) [Unsatisfied Balance of Elective–Share and Supplemental Elective–Share Amount.] If, after the application of subsections (a) and (c), the elective-share or supplemental elective-share amount is not fully satisfied, the remaining portion of the decedent's nonprobate transfers to others is so applied that liability for the unsatisfied balance of the elective-share or supplemental elective-share amount is apportioned among the recipients of the remaining portion of the decedent's nonprobate transfers to others in proportion to the value of their interests therein.

(e) [Unsatisfied Balance Treated as General Pecuniary Devise.]

The unsatisfied balance of the elective-share or supplemental elective-share amount as determined under subsection (c) or (d) is treated as a general pecuniary devise for purposes of Section 3–904.

Understanding the "Marital–Property Portion."

Notice that UPC § 2–207(a) includes within the augmented estate all of the property of the surviving spouse. But the surviving spouse's right to elect 50% does not apply to the entire augmented estate; instead, UPC § 2–202(a) provides that the right to elect applies only to the "marital-property portion" of the augmented estate. For the marriage that has lasted for 15 years or more, this provision is relatively easy to understand and apply. The marital-property portion includes all (100%) of the surviving spouse's property. This result is entirely consistent with the theory that the spouses have become full partners; each is entitled to half of the joint assets.

For the shorter marriage, however, the UPC assumes, in effect, that some of the assets of each spouse remain separate property, not subject to claims by the survivor. The UPC accomplishes this result not by excluding assets from the augmented estate, but by reducing the percentage of the estate that counts as the marital-property portion. Thus, in a ten-year marriage, 60% of the total augmented estate would count as marital property, and the surviving spouse would be entitled to 50% of that property—which amounts to 30% of the estate (50% of 60%). But if, in a shorter marriage, some of the surviving spouse's own assets are not to be treated as marital assets, they should not be counted as assuring that the survivor obtains an equal share of marital assets. Section 2–209(a)(2) captures this principle by providing that only the marital-property portion of the spouse's assets will be counted towards satisfaction of the elective share. Thus, in a ten-year marriage, 60% of the value of the surviving spouse's assets would be applied toward satisfying her elective share amount; the remainder would be treated as the equivalent of separate assets. Example 1, below, illustrates the UPC's approach.

Satisfaction of the Elective Share

If the total of probate and non-probate transfers to the surviving spouse and the marital-property portion of surviving spouse's assets are insufficient to satisfy the elective share, section 2–209 directs an order of priority for apportioning liability for the balance. First applied are amounts passing to others from decedent's net probate estate and decedent's non-probate transfers to others under section 2–205(1), (2), and (3)(B). If the elective share is still not satisfied, then the recipients of the remaining non-probate transfers are proportionately liable.

Application of the Code: A Few Examples

It is impossible to understand the workings of the UPC's elective share provisions without methodically working through some examples. We will solve two problems, and then leave some problems for you to work out.

Among the most common elective-share problems are those that arise when a couple marries later in life, after one or both partners have experienced a divorce or the death of a first spouse. In many cases, each spouse wants to leave most of the property to his or her children from the previous relationship. Let's examine how the UPC elective share provisions work in that situation.

> ***Example 1: The Second Marriage.*** *Ted Testator and his wife, Ursula, were married for five years before Ted's death. Ted's will left all of his property to, Vanna, his daughter by a prior marriage. Ted's net probate estate was valued at $300,000, and at the time of Ted's death, Ursula had assets of $200,000. Neither Ted nor*

Ursula made any inter vivos transfers. Does Ursula have a right to elect, assuming the UPC is in force? Would the answer be different if Ted and Ursula had been married for 15 years?

Solution: *First, compute the augmented estate. All of the assets of each spouse are included, for a total of $500,000. Next, compute the "marital-property portion" of the augmented estate: Since the parties were married for 5 years, the marital-property portion of the augmented estate is 30% of the augmented estate, or $150,000. Then, calculate the elective share, which is 50% of the marital-property portion of the augmented estate, or $75,000. Finally, what property is charged against Ursula? Note that, by virtue of section 2–209(a)(2), 30% of her own assets are charged against her. As a result, only $60,000 (30% of $200,000) is applied toward her elective share. Ursula is entitled to elect an additional $15,000.*

Note that if Ted and Ursula had been married for 15 years, the marital-property portion of the augmented estate would have been 100%. Ursula's elective share would have been 50% of $500,000 (which equals $250,000)—but all $200,000 of her assets would have been charged against her. As a result, she would have been entitled to elect an additional $50,000.

Now consider how the statute might operate in a more traditional marriage with somewhat more complicated finances.

Example 2: The Long-Term Marriage. *Debbie Decedent dies with a will which leaves "one-half of my property to my husband, Edgar, and the other one-half to be evenly divided between my children Felix and Gertrude." When Debbie died, Debbie and Edgar had been married for 30 years, and had two children, Felix and Gertrude. Debbie, five years before her death, created an irrevocable trust, reserving income to herself for life, and directing that at her death, the principal should be distributed to her alma mater, Georgetown University. The trust principal is, and has been since Debbie created the trust, $50,000. Debbie and Edgar shared a $50,000 joint bank account, with the proceeds payable to the survivor. Debbie had also purchased a $200,000 life insurance policy, and had named her daughter Gertrude as beneficiary. (Note that none of these assets passed through Debbie's probate estate). At Debbie's death, her net probate estate was valued at $300,000, and Edgar's own assets were valued at $200,000. Assuming that the Uniform Probate Code is in effect at Debbie's death, does Edgar have a right to elect? Would Edgar have a right to elect if Edgar had no assets of his own?*

Solution: *First, which assets are included in Debbie's augmented estate under UPC § 2–203?*

$300,000—her net estate—under 2–204.

$50,000—the irrevocable trust—under 2–205(2)(A). Why? Because Debbie retained a right to income until her death.

$25,000—Debbie's share of the joint bank account, under 2–206(2).

$25,000—Edgar's share of the joint bank account, under 2–207(a)(1)(D).

$200,000—the life insurance policy, under 2–205(1)(D).

$200,000—Edgar's own assets, under 2–207.

The total value of the augmented estate is $800,000.

Second, what is the marital-property portion of the augmented estate? Because the couple was married for more than 15 years, 100% of the augmented estate is marital property. Edgar's elective-share amount is 50% of that, or $400,000.

Third, which dispositions will count against Edgar's share? UPC § 2–209(a)(1) tells us to count amounts which pass to Edgar from the net probate estate, and from dispositions included in the augmented estate under section 2–206; section 2–209(a)(1) tells us to count the marital-property portion of Edgar's own assets which in the case of this 30–year marriage, is 100%.

Therefore, we include

$150,000—Edgar's share of Debbie's net probate estate.

$50,000—the joint bank account (half of which was included under 2–206, and the other half of which was included under 2–207).

$200,000—Edgar's own assets, which are included under 2–207.

As a result, $400,000 is applied against Edgar's elective share.

Under the Uniform Probate Code, a surviving spouse always has a formal right to take an elective share. If, however, the decedent spouse has provided adequately for the surviving spouse, the surviving spouse will not benefit by electing, and the decedent spouse's estate plan will remain intact. Debbie's estate illustrates the point. Since Edgar's elective share is $400,000, and, under section 2–209, we apply against Edgar's elective share precisely $400,000 in benefits Edgar has already received or would receive under the will, Edgar has no right to elect anything additional.

How would the solution change if Edgar had no assets of his own? Note that now the augmented estate would include only $600,000, and the marital-property portion of that would be $600,000. Edgar would take only $200,000 of that $600,000 under the terms of the will and testamentary substitutes. Edgar would therefore have a right to elect an additional $100,000. Section 2–209 directs that the beneficiaries of Edgar's estate, the irrevocable trust and the life insurance policy are proportionately liable for that additional $100,000. Since those transfers total $400,000, and Edgar's unsatisfied elective share is $100,000, Edgar would be entitled to 1/4 of the $150,000 passing to the children by will, 1/4 of the $50,000 trust, and 1/4 of the $200,000 life insurance proceeds. (Note that in this instance, under more traditional elective share statutes, Edgar would have no right to elect because Debbie has left him at least one-third of the assets she had under her control.)

NOTES

1. ***Protecting the Spouse with Life Interests in Trust (with an Aside on Disclaimer)*** Suppose a testator chooses to provide for his spouse not by giving her property outright, but instead by providing her with a life interest in a substantial trust. Should the spouse have a right to elect against testator's will? At common law, the answer was no: dower rights, by definition, were life interests; the wife had rights in her husband's property only during her lifetime.

How does the Uniform Probate Code treat life interests in trust? Even a careful reader of the Code will find that the Code's text includes no direct treatment of the issue. Indeed, a plausible reading of the Code suggests that life interests in trust may be used to satisfy the surviving spouse's share. The legislative history of the Code, however, establishes beyond doubt that the surviving spouse has a right to take her elective share absolutely.

First, examine the structure of the Code itself. Section 2–208 provides that the "value" of property "includes the commuted value of any present or future interest and the commuted value of amounts payable under any trust...." Section 2–209 then provides that "amounts ... which pass or have passed to the surviving spouse by testate or intestate succession" should be applied first to satisfy the elective share amount and "to reduce or eliminate any contributions" due from other beneficiaries of the estate. Thus, if testator's will left his entire estate in trust, giving his wife a right to income for her life, one might think that the commuted value of the wife's interests should be applied to satisfy the wife's elective share; if the wife's life expectancy at the husband's death was sufficiently long, the trust, by itself would often satisfy her elective share.

Now turn to the Code's legislative history. An earlier version of the Code explicitly applied against the elective share "amounts included in the augmented estate which would have passed to the spouse but were disclaimed." (See section 2–207(a)(3) of the Code's 1990 version). Under the earlier version, it was clear that the commuted value of a life interest in trust would be applied toward the surviving spouse's elective share. Professor Ira Bloom wrote a trenchant article criticizing that provision. Ira Bloom, The Treatment of Trust and Other Partial Interests of the Surviving Spouse Under the Redesigned Elective Share System: Some Concerns and Suggestions, 55 Alb. L. Rev. 941 (1992). When the drafters of the Code revised the elective share provision in 1993, they eliminated the provision applying against the elective share amounts disclaimed by the spouse. Hence, it is clear that the drafters intended that if decedent provided for the surviving spouse by creating life interests in trust, the surviving spouse could disclaim those interests. As a result, neither the trust principal nor the present value of the surviving spouse's income interest would be applied against the elective share. The surviving spouse would be entitled to take the elective share outright. This result is consistent with the "partnership" theory of marriage on which the Code is based. See generally Ronald R. Volkmer, Spousal Rights at Death: Re-evaluation of the Common

Law Premises in Light of the Proposed Uniform Marital Property Act, 17 Creighton L. Rev. 95, 141–48 (1983).

Nevertheless, the drafting of the current version of the Code is far from ideal. The Code does not indicate that the surviving spouse may disclaim only income interests in trust. But if a surviving spouse can disclaim an absolute interest, and thereby assure that the interest does not count against her elective share, the surviving spouse may upset the testator's testamentary scheme for no good reason. Consider the following example:

> ***Example 3:*** *Testator's will leaves "my house and $50,000 in cash to my wife W, if she survives me, and if she does not, to her son S. I leave the remainder of my estate to my daughter D." Testator and W have been married for 15 years, and at Testator's death, the house is worth $50,000, and Testator has other assets worth $150,000. W has no assets. Does W have a right to elect?*
>
> *If W does not disclaim any interests, she has no right to elect, since the house and the $50,000 (total value, $100,000) will be applied to satisfy her elective share of $100,000 (50% of the marital-property portion of the augmented estate, $200,000). Suppose, however, the wife disclaims her interest in the house (or the house and the cash). Upon disclaimer, the house (or the house and the cash) would pass to S (UPC § 2–801). Does W now have the right to elect, by taking $100,000 from the two beneficiaries, S and D, "in proportion to the value of their interests therein" (UPC § 2–209(b))? That clearly was not the intent of the drafters. But did elimination of the disclaimer provision in the 1990 version throw out the baby with the bathwater?*

2. The Supplemental Amount.

Although the UPC's primary objective is to implement the partnership theory of marriage, it also subscribes to the support theory. Section 2–202(b) provides that the surviving spouse is entitled to have a minimum of $75,000 after the deceased spouse's death. Since this supplemental amount is justified as necessary to ensure support, all of the surviving spouse's assets (not just the marital property portion) and the assets to which the surviving spouse is entitled at the deceased spouse's death (including any additional assets she has a right to elect) are considered in the calculation.

To determine whether a surviving spouse is entitled to a supplemental share, go through the usual calculation to determine the elective share amount. Determine how much the surviving spouse has a right to elect from third party beneficiaries of decedent's probate estate and nonprobate assets. Add this number to 1) the total that the surviving spouse is entitled to receive from the deceased spouse's probate and nonprobate assets (as described in section 2–206), and 2) the total amount of surviving spouse's property and nonprobate transfers to others as described in section 2–207. If the sum is less than $75,000, the surviving spouse has the right to a supplemental amount to bring his or her total property to $75,000.

3. ***The Life Insurance Conundrum.*** Note that UPC §§ 2–205 and 2–206 direct that the value of life insurance policies owned by the deceased spouse and payable to either the surviving spouse or a third person are included in the augmented estate. But state legislatures enacting modern elective share statutes have been reluctant to include life insurance in the list of nonprobate mechanisms included in the estate. See N.Y. EPTL 5–1.1–A(b); Jeffrey S. Kinsler, The Unmerry Widow: Spousal Disinheritance and Life Insurance in North Carolina, 87 N.C. L. Rev. 1461 (2007) (establishing that the North Carolina legislature removed life insurance from the list of nonprobate transfers shortly before enacting the revised elective share statute). Do you have any guesses as to why the scholars who drafted the UPC might have included life insurance while the legislatures who enact statutes are more reluctant?

PROBLEMS

1. Testator, W, dies survived by her husband of 20 years, H, and their son, S. Her will makes the following provisions:

1. $25,000 to H outright.
2. $75,000 in trust, income to be paid to H for life, remainder to S.
3. The balance of my estate to my son, S.

The value of W's net probate estate totaled $150,000.

In addition, at the time of W's death, she and H owned, as tenants by the entirety, with right of survivorship, a house with an equity of $100,000. The house had been purchased in 1992 with money W inherited from her parents. W also had a $100,000 bank account held in trust for S. W had $50,000 in life insurance, with the policy proceeds payable to H. Several years before her death, W had set up an irrevocable trust, with assets worth $100,000, retaining the income for herself for life, with the remainder to go to Cardozo Law School at her death.

If the Uniform Probate Code is in effect, does H have a right to elect against W's will (a) if H had assets of his own (other than his interest in the house) totaling $250,000 at W's death; or (b) if H had no assets of his own at W's death? If H does have a right to elect, how much does H have a right to elect?

Would H have a right to elect if he had been married to W for only 10 years at W's death (assuming again that H had assets of his own totaling $250,000)?

On the same facts, does H have a right to elect under the elective share statute in force in your jurisdiction?

2. Testator, H, dies survived by his wife of 10 years, W, and no children. H's will leaves his entire estate in trust, with income to be distributed to W for life, and the remainder, at W's death, to be paid to Columbia University. Assume that neither H nor W have other assets, and that neither has made any significant transfers during their lifetimes. If, at H's death, the estate is valued at $300,000, and W is healthy and 40 years old, can W disclaim her interest in the trust and elect to take an absolute interest in H's estate? If W does have a right to elect, would you advise her to exercise that right?

3. A 65–year–old client walks into your office, and explains that his assets are currently worth $500,000, and that he has become disenchanted with his wife, who has, in his view, been paying too much attention to other men, and not enough to him. He would like to leave his wife with as little of his estate as possible, and he would prefer to leave the bulk of his money to his children, with a few devises to charitable organizations and some old friends.

How would you advise the client? What steps could he take to disinherit his wife in a jurisdiction that has adopted the Uniform Probate Code? In your state? What disadvantages, if any, would the client suffer if the client took the steps necessary to disinherit his wife?

4. Prior to his second marriage, Chrisp transferred the bulk of his assets to a revocable trust and named his adult sons from his first marriage remainder beneficiaries and successor trustees. He later executed a will leaving his entire probate estate to his second wife. After Chrisp's death, a court rejected his surviving spouse's attempt to include the value of the trust assets in the augmented estate on the ground that the Nebraska elective share statute includes in the estate only transfers made after marriage. See Estate of Chrisp, 276 Neb. 966, 759 N.W.2d 87 (2009). If Nebraska had adopted the UPC elective share statute in its entirety, would the court have come out the same way? Which approach better advances the partnership theory of marriage? The support theory?

5. In compliance with a divorce settlement agreement, Calligaro designated his daughter as a beneficiary of all of his pension and retirement survivor benefits "until her emancipation." Calligaro then married a second time before dying. His second wife exercised her right of election and claimed that the entire value of Calligaro's retirement benefits should be part of the elective share estate, citing New York's elective share statute (which, like the UPC, directs that result). Should her argument prevail? See Estate of Calligaro, 19 Misc.3d 895, 855 N.Y.S.2d 873 (Sur. Ct. 2008) (concluding that the daughter's contractual right under the separation agreement is not subject to the spouse's elective share and so the elective share estate includes only the value of the survivorship benefits payable after the date of the daughter's emancipation).

6. When Fries married Margaret, his second wife, he owned several parcels of real property. Two years after the marriage, Margaret executed quit claim deeds transferring any interest she might have in the parcels to Fries. Fries then transferred the property to his children from a prior marriage. Although Fries' deeds reserved to him no legal rights, he continued to act as the owner of the parcels; he managed the property, collected income and paid the real estate taxes. If, after his death, Margaret claims that the value of the parcels should be included in the augmented estate because Fries retained a life estate, should she prevail? Should the fact that she executed quit claim deeds defeat her claim? See Estate of Fries, 279 Neb. 887, 782 N.W.2d 596 (2010) (reversing lower court's grant of summary judgment in favor of Fries' children and holding that 1) there was a triable issue of fact as to whether Fries retained a life estate, and 2) Margaret did not mean to relinquish her spousal rights when she executed the quit claim deeds in favor of her husband).

NOTES

1. The principal drafter of the UPC's elective share provisions has proposed changing the statute to better account for post-widowhood marriages. Research has revealed significant inaccuracies in the statute's current assumption that, after 15 years, all property is likely to be marital property—especially with respect to post-widowhood marriages. See Lawrence W. Waggoner, The Uniform Probate Code's Elective Share: Time for a Reassessment, 37 U. Mich. J. Law Reform 1 (2003).

2. ***Exercise On Behalf of A Dead or Incapacitated Surviving Spouse.*** Consistent with most state law, the Uniform Probate Code requires that a surviving spouse be living when the petition for an elective share is filed. See UPC § 2–212(a); Wilson v. Wilson, 224 Or.App. 360, 197 P.3d 1141 (2008). Who would want to elect on behalf of a surviving spouse who has died before electing? The beneficiaries under the surviving spouse's will, or the surviving spouse's heirs—who might be different from the beneficiaries under the will of the first spouse to die. The UPC, however, does not permit heirs or estate representatives to elect on the surviving spouse's behalf. (Is this rule consistent with the partnership theory of the elective share? The support theory?)

Suppose, now, that the surviving spouse is not dead, but incapacitated? UPC § 2–212(a) does permit a conservator, guardian, or agent under the authority of a power of attorney to exercise the power on the incapacitated spouse's behalf. However, if the election is exercised on behalf of an incapacitated person, the elective share amounts must be placed in a custodial trust for the benefit of the incapacitated person (UPC § 2–212(b)). If the surviving spouse regains capacity, he may terminate the trust and take the property outright (UPC § 2–212(c)(1)). If the spouse does not regain capacity, the trust property must be distributed through the residuary clause of the decedent spouse's estate, *not* through the surviving spouse's estate. UPC § 2–212(c)(3).

Is UPC § 2–212(c) consistent with the partnership theory of marriage?

3. ***Abandonment and the Elective Share.*** Dorothy and Marril were married in July 1988. The relationship was tumultuous and violent, and Dorothy obtained more than one protective order against Marril. Although Dorothy's health was poor, Marril did little to take care of her, and Dorothy relied on help from her daughter and neighbors. In the year before her death, Dorothy left Marril and moved in with her daughter, who cared for her. Dorothy brought to the marriage several parcels of rental property. Marril was retired, but did not participate in managing the properties.

Should Marril be entitled to an elective share? See Purce v. Patterson, 275 Va. 190, 654 S.E.2d 885 (2008) (affirming lower court determination that Marril had abandoned Dorothy and that statute barred abandoning spouse from exercising a right to elect).

SECTION IV. WAIVER OF ELECTIVE SHARE RIGHTS

Consider two people—each with children of their own, and one or both of whom have significant resources—contemplating marriage. Suppose the partners (or one of them) want to preserve their assets for the benefit of their children. To what extent can each partner assure that her new spouse does not upset her testamentary scheme by asserting elective share rights? Consider the following materials:

Geddings v. Geddings

Supreme Court of South Carolina, 1995.
319 S.C. 213, 460 S.E.2d 376.

■ FINNEY, C.J.:

Respondent (Pinkie Geddings) initiated this action seeking to invoke her right to an elective share of the decedent's probate estate pursuant to S.C. Code Ann. § 62–2–201 (Supp. 1994). Appellants answered alleging Mrs. Geddings had waived her right to an elective share by signing a waiver agreement. After a hearing, the probate judge granted Mrs. Geddings an elective share finding that the purported waiver was void because she did not receive the required statutory fair disclosure. S.C. Code Ann. § 62–2–204 (1987). Appellants appealed the matter to the circuit court which affirmed the probate court's determination. We affirm.

The Geddings were married in 1979. Both had children by their former spouses. In 1988 Mrs. Geddings signed a document presented to her by her husband titled "Waiver of Right to Elect and of Other Rights." In summary the document acknowledged that each had made a will; each desired that the bulk of his/her property go to his/her children by previous marriages; each disclaimed interest in the spouse's estate except as provided in the will admitted to probate at the death of the other spouse; and each had made a full, fair and complete disclosure to each other of all presently-owned assets.

Appellants contend the court erred in concluding the waiver agreement was invalid because Mrs. Geddings did not receive fair disclosure.

As an initial matter, appellants assert the probate court allowed Mrs. Geddings to testify in violation of the Dead Man's Statute S.C. Code Ann. § 19–11–20 (1985). Based on that testimony, appellants claim the court erroneously concluded she had signed the agreement acknowledging fair disclosure when in fact she did not receive fair disclosure. Appellants did not object to Mrs. Geddings' testimony on the ground of violation of the

Dead Man's Statute. Therefore appellants are precluded from raising the question now. Branton v. Martin, 243 S.C. 90, 132 S.E.2d 285 (1963).

The right of election of a surviving spouse may be waived by a written contract signed by the party waiving after fair disclosure. S.C. Code Ann. § 62–2–204 (1987). While South Carolina has not defined what constitutes fair disclosure in this context, other states have in the similar context of antenuptial agreements. Considering the confidential relationship between parties to an antenuptial agreement, the affirmative duty imposed upon each party to disclose his or her financial status transcends what is normally required for a commercial transaction. In re Estate of Lebsock, 44 Colo. App. 220, 618 P.2d 683 (1980). "Fair disclosure contemplates that each spouse should be given information, of a general and approximate nature, concerning the net worth of the other. Each party has a duty to consider and evaluate the information received before signing an agreement." In re Estate of Lopata, 641 P.2d 952 (Colo. 1982); In re Estate of Hill, 214 Neb. 702, 335 N.W.2d 750 (Neb. 1983).

> Fair disclosure means that before signing an antenuptial agreement, each party must disclose to the other the facts that exist at the time of the agreement and which, in the absence of the antenuptial agreement, affect or determine the prospective intestate share of a surviving spouse in the disclosing party's estate or which otherwise affect or determine distribution of property at the disclosing party's death.

In re Estate of Stephenson, 243 Neb. 890, 503 N.W.2d 540 (Neb. 1993).

Both judges found the evidence presented by Mrs. Geddings established she had no real or general knowledge of the total extent of her husband's assets. While Mrs. Geddings had fully disclosed her assets to the decedent, she had no knowledge of the value of husband's estate. The attorney preparing the waiver document testified he did not discuss assets with Mrs. Geddings when it was executed. Mrs. Geddings was excluded from the annual corporate meetings held in her home at Christmas which included only the decedent and his children. There was substantial testimony that decedent was secretive about his financial affairs.

In an action at equity, tried first by the master or special referee and concurred in by the trial judge, the findings of fact will not be disturbed on appeal unless found to be without evidentiary support or against the clear preponderance of the evidence. Townes Assoc., Ltd. v. City of Greenville, 266 S.C. 81, 221 S.E.2d 773 (1976); Dean v. Kilgore, 313 S.C. 257, 437 S.E.2d 154 (Ct. App. 1993) (two-judge rule would apply in appeal from circuit court of an equity case originating in probate court where both courts agreed on material issues).

There was sufficient evidence supporting the factual findings of the probate court concurred in by the circuit court. Accordingly, we AFFIRM.

* * *

NOTES AND QUESTIONS

1. The court in Geddings insists that Mrs. Geddings' waiver of her elective share rights is invalid if her husband failed to disclose his assets at the time of the waiver. Why should a waiver be invalid if the waiving spouse does not know her partner's financial condition?

In Geddings, the waiver was executed after the parties had been married for nine years. Would the court have reached the same result if the waiver had been executed in 1978 instead of 1988? Does the same fiduciary duty exist before the marriage as during the marriage?

"I love you, Sharon, and these documents will advise you of certain rights you have in accordance with federal and state law, as well as variances and privileges you retain in the City of New York."

Tom Cheney © 1993 from The New Yorker Collection. All Rights Reserved.

2. Note that the agreement Mrs. Geddings signed recited that each spouse had made full, fair, and complete disclosure to the other. Is there any reason (other than Mrs. Geddings' self-serving assertions that she didn't know of her husband's assets) to believe that Mrs. Geddings did not receive full disclosure?

Suppose you had been representing Mr. Geddings. What more would you have done to assure that the agreement would be enforced?

Not all states require disclosure to create a valid waiver. See, e.g., Foster v. Gomes, 27 So.3d 145 (Fla. App. 2010) (holding that husband's failure to disclose asset was immaterial to validity of waiver because Florida statute did not require disclosure).

3. Did Mrs. Geddings have her own lawyer when the agreement was signed? Would the court have reached the same result if Mrs. Geddings had signed the agreement after consulting with counsel? Should Mr. Geddings have insisted that Mrs. Geddings hire her own counsel before executing the waiver agreement? Suppose she refused, indicating that she trusted Mr. Geddings and his lawyer implicitly?

In Briggs v. Wyoming National Bank, 836 P.2d 263 (Wyo. 1992), husband of 20 years, in consideration for a 1/17 share in trust assets, executed a document waiving any right to contest his wife's establishment of the trust or transfer of her assets into the trust. The agreement was prepared by wife's lawyer, who had represented husband five or six years earlier in a dispute over an investment. In enforcing the agreement, the court wrote:

> The unrefuted evidence is that, before Mr. Briggs signed the written waiver, Mrs. Briggs and her attorney recommended to him that he review the contents of the trust agreement with another attorney. Mr. Briggs did not equivocate. He affirmatively stated that he did not want to see another attorney, and that he consented to whatever Mrs. Briggs desired to do. Mr. Briggs voluntarily signed the document. He cannot now effectively complain that he did not understand what he was doing because he did not read the agreement or have the advice of an attorney.

836 P.2d at 265. Are you convinced? Consider the dissent's response:

> Since this attorney had represented Mr. Briggs in another matter, it is reasonable that Mr. Briggs might have believed that what he was being told by this attorney, who he could have perceived as representing him, was consistent with this best interest. There would be no reason for Mr. Briggs to suspect that this attorney was acting in something other than his best interests which he perceived as being aligned with his wife's interests at that time.

836 P.2d at 270 [Urbigkit, C.J., dissenting]. If you agree with the dissent, what would you have Mrs. Briggs (and her lawyer) do before Mr. Briggs signs the agreement?

Suppose Mrs. Briggs had procured a lawyer for Mr. Briggs. Would the lawyer's presence have been sufficient to insulate any resulting agreement from subsequent attack? In Matter of Greiff, 92 N.Y.2d 341, 703 N.E.2d 752, 680 N.Y.S.2d 894 (1998), the parties executed a prenuptial agreement waiving their respective elective share rights. When the husband died (three months after the wedding), the wife challenged the agreement. The Surrogate's Court concluded that the husband had exercised bad faith, overreaching, and undue influence—particularly noting that the husband had "selected and paid for" the wife's attorney. The Appellate Division reversed, concluding that the wife had not proven fraud or overreaching. The New York Court of Appeals reversed the Appellate Division's determination, holding that if a party to a prenuptial agreement can show, by a preponderance of the evidence, that the premarital relationship manifested undue and unfair advantage, the burden shifts to the proponents of the agreement to show freedom from fraud, deception, and undue influence. In Greiff itself, the court remanded so that the court below could determine whether the relationship between the couple shifted the burden to proponents of the agreement.

4. The ABA's Model Rules of Professional Conduct include the following provision:

RULE 1.7 CONFLICT OF INTEREST: CURRENT CLIENTS

(a) Except as provided in paragraph (b), a lawyer shall not represent a client if the representation involves a concurrent conflict of interest. A concurrent conflict of interest exists if:

> (1) the representation of one client will be directly adverse to another client; or
>
> (2) there is a significant risk that the representation of one or more clients will be materially limited by the lawyer's responsibilities to another client, a former client or a third person or by a personal interest of the lawyer.

(b) Notwithstanding the existence of a concurrent conflict of interest under paragraph (a), a lawyer may represent a client if:

> (1) the lawyer reasonably believes that the lawyer will be able to provide competent and diligent representation to each affected client;
>
> (2) the representation is not prohibited by law;
>
> (3) the representation does not involve the assertion of a claim by one client against another client represented by the lawyer in the same litigation or other proceeding before a tribunal; and
>
> (4) each affected client gives informed consent, confirmed in writing.

The Comment to Rule 1.7 provides, in part:

> Relevant factors in determining whether there is significant potential for material limitation include the duration and intimacy of the lawyer's relationship with the client or clients involved, the functions being performed by the lawyer, the likelihood that disagreements will arise and the likely prejudice to the client from the conflict. The question is often one of proximity and degree.
>
> For example, conflict questions may arise in estate planning and estate administration. A lawyer may be called upon to prepare wills for several family members, such as husband and wife, and, depending upon the circumstances, a conflict of interest may be present. In estate administration the identity of the client may be unclear under the law of a particular jurisdiction. Under one view, the client is the fiduciary; under another view the client is the estate or trust, including its beneficiaries. In order to comply with conflict of interest rules, the

> lawyer should make clear the lawyer's relationship to the parties involved.
>
> Whether a conflict is consentable depends on the circumstances. For example, a lawyer may not represent multiple parties to a negotiation whose interests are fundamentally antagonistic to each other, but common representation is permissible where the clients are generally aligned in interest even though there is some difference in interest among them. Thus, a lawyer may seek to establish or adjust a relationship between clients on an amicable and mutually advantageous basis; for example, in helping to organize a business in which two or more clients are entrepreneurs, working out the financial reorganization of an enterprise in which two or more clients have an interest or arranging a property distribution in settlement of an estate. The lawyer seeks to resolve potentially adverse interests by developing the parties' mutual interests. Otherwise, each party might have to obtain separate representation, with the possibility of incurring additional cost, complication or even litigation. Given these and other relevant factors, the clients may prefer that the lawyer act for all of them.

Suppose a couple walks into your office and asks you to draft a prenuptial agreement for them. Must you insist that the two parties retain separate lawyers? If not, what obligations do you have to discuss conflicts of interest with the couple? See generally Naomi Cahn & Robert Tuttle, Dependency and Delegation: The Ethics of Marital Representation, 22 Seattle U. L. Rev. 97 (1998).

Suppose you have represented one spouse in business dealings for the past five years. Are your obligations any different?

On the ethical problems of representing more than one family member in a matter where there interests are not perfectly aligned, see Russell G. Pearce, Family Values and Legal Ethics: Competing Approaches to Conflicts in Representing Spouses, 62 Fordham L. Rev. 1253 (1994).

5. A prenuptial agreement provides that "it is the intention of the parties that each of them shall continue to own as his or her separate property ... [that] which they own as of this date" and that "they may hereafter individually acquire additional property ... and it is the intention of the parties hereto that said property shall also be the individual property of the person acquiring the same." Does the agreement waive the parties' elective share rights? See Pysell v. Keck, 263 Va. 457, 559 S.E.2d 677 (2002) (held, no).

6. Husband and wife each inform lawyer that they wish to disinherit the other. Lawyer drafts the wills. Upon wife's death, husband elects against the will. Is the lawyer liable to the wife's estate for malpractice? See Estate of Gaspar v. Vogt, Brown & Merry, 670 N.W.2d 918 (S.D. 2003) (holding lawyer liable for failing to inform wife that without husband's waiver of elective share rights, wife's intent could be frustrated).

On the role of marital contracts more generally, see Jeffrey Sherman, Prenuptial Agreements: A New Reason to Revive an Old Rule, 53 Clev. St.

L. Rev. 359 (2005) (questioning wisdom of enforcing premarital agreements); Thomas Featherston & Amy E. Douthitt, Changing the Rules by Agreement: The New Era in Characterization, Management, and Liability of Marital Property, 49 Baylor L. Rev. 271 (1997) (discussing premarital contracts in community property states); Gail Brod, Premarital Agreements and Gender Justice, 6 Yale J. L. & Feminism 229 (1994).

UNIFORM PROBATE CODE

SECTION 2–213. WAIVER OF RIGHT TO ELECT AND OF OTHER RIGHTS.

(a) The right of election of a surviving spouse and the rights of the surviving spouse to homestead allowance, exempt property, and family allowance, or any of them, may be waived, wholly or partially, before or after marriage, by a written contract, agreement, or waiver signed by the surviving spouse.

(b) A surviving spouse's waiver is not enforceable if the surviving spouse proves that:

(1) he [or she] did not execute the waiver voluntarily; or

(2) the waiver was unconscionable when it was executed and, before execution of the waiver, he [or she]:

(i) was not provided a fair and reasonable disclosure of the property or financial obligations of the decedent;

(ii) did not voluntarily and expressly waive, in writing, any right to disclosure of the property or financial obligations of the decedent beyond the disclosure provided; and

(iii) did not have, or reasonably could not have had, an adequate knowledge of the property or financial obligations of the decedent.

(c) An issue of unconscionability of a waiver is for decision by the court as a matter of law.

(d) Unless it provides to the contrary, a waiver of "all rights," or equivalent language, in the property or estate of a present or prospective spouse or a complete property settlement entered into after or in anticipation of separation or divorce is a waiver of all rights of elective share, homestead allowance, exempt property, and family allowance by each spouse in the property of the other and a renunciation by each of all benefits that would otherwise pass to him [or her] from the other by intestate succession or by virtue of any will executed before the waiver or property settlement.

NOTES AND QUESTIONS

1. How would the Geddings case have been decided if South Carolina had adopted the UPC? Does the UPC require "fair disclosure?" Does the Uniform Probate Code distinguish between prenuptial agreements and agreements executed during the marriage? Which approach do you prefer—the rule established in Geddings, or the UPC provisions?

2. Approximately one month before Stacey and Edward's wedding, Edward presented Stacey with a draft of a prenuptial agreement, which included a waiver of right of election but guaranteed Stacey a $100,000 "death benefit". The agreement was prepared by Edward's attorney, and did not provide that Stacey waived her right to full disclosure. Stacey consulted with her own attorney, who requested that Edward's attorney provide financial information that the agreement referenced but did not include. Edward's attorney sent a document titled "Financial Statement of Edward Shinn" that would serve as Rider A to the agreement. The financial statement listed assets worth $853,750. In fact, there was evidence that Edward's net worth was closer to $6,000,000. Stacey, on the other hand, owned a 1990 Honda Prelude and $121.76 in cash, and had debts totaling $10,000.

Suspecting that the financial information was incomplete, Stacey's attorney requested complete information. Edward responded that Stacey had received all of the information that she was going to get. He informed Stacey's lawyer that she had to accept the agreement "as is" or the marriage was off. Although Stacey left her attorney's office in tears, she later returned to sign the agreement. Three years later Edward died, survived by three children from a prior marriage and his daughter with Stacey. Edward devised his home and the proceeds of a $150,000 life insurance policy to Stacey, and divided the bulk of his estate among his four children. If Stacey argues that the waiver is unenforceable, how would the Geddings court decide the issue? Would your answer be different if UPC section 2–213 were adopted? See, Estate of Shinn, 394 N.J.Super. 55, 925 A.2d 88 (App. Div 2007), cert. denied, 192 N.J. 595, 934 A.2d 637 (2007).

Suppose Edward's financial statement had disclosed assets worth approximately $5,500,000, but the value of his assets at the time was closer to $6,000,000. Should the agreement be enforced?

SECTION V. OTHER PROTECTIONS FOR THE SURVIVING SPOUSE

A. HOMESTEAD ALLOWANCE, EXEMPT PROPERTY, AND FAMILY ALLOWANCE

Suppose that during his lifetime, Oscar Zilch falls on hard times, and racks up debt beyond his current capacity to repay. If Oscar's creditors obtain judgments against him, they are generally free to execute those judgments against Oscar's property. State law, however, typically places some of Oscar's property beyond the reach of creditors. The debtor's clothing is often beyond the reach of creditors (see, e.g., N.J. Stat. Ann., § 2A:17–19). Many states also provide a limited exemption for the family homestead (see, e.g., N.Y. CPLR § 5206(a)). Why? For at least three reasons: (1) to preserve the debtor's basic human dignity; (2) to relieve taxpayers of the obligation to provide for insolvent debtors; and (3) to promote efficiency: items of personal property are likely to be worth more to the debtor than to anyone else and exempting them from creditor execution assures that they stay with the person who values them most. See Stewart E. Sterk, Restraints on Alienation of Human Capital, 79 Va. L. Rev. 383, 413–14 (1993).

Suppose Oscar dies—still in debt. Should his creditors be able to swoop down on his widow and children and satisfy Oscar's debts out of property that was unavailable to them during Oscar's lifetime? In many states the answer is no. The surviving spouse, and often minor children, remain entitled to a homestead exemption, and also remain entitled to keep some personal property away from decedent's creditors. The form of those exemptions differs significantly from state to state.

How does the Uniform Probate Code deal with exemptions? Consider the following:

UNIFORM PROBATE CODE

SECTION 2–402. HOMESTEAD ALLOWANCE.

A decedent's surviving spouse is entitled to a homestead allowance of [$22,500]. If there is no surviving spouse, each minor child and each dependent child of the decedent is entitled to a homestead allowance amounting to [$22,500] divided by the number of minor and dependent children of the decedent. The homestead allowance is exempt from and has priority over all claims against the estate. Homestead allowance is in addition to any share passing to the surviving spouse or minor or dependent child by the will of the decedent, unless otherwise provided, by intestate succession, or by way of elective share.

SECTION 2–403. EXEMPT PROPERTY.

In addition to the homestead allowance, the decedent's surviving spouse is entitled from the estate to a value, not exceeding $15,000 in excess of any security interests therein, in household furniture, automobiles, furnishings, appliances, and personal effects. If there is no surviving spouse, the decedent's children are entitled jointly to the same value. If encumbered chattels are selected and the value in excess of security interests, plus that of other exempt property, is less than $15,000, or if there is not $15,000 worth of exempt property in the estate, the spouse or children are entitled to other assets of the estate, if any, to the extent necessary to make up the $15,000 value. Rights to exempt property and assets needed to make up a deficiency of exempt property have priority over all claims against the estate, but the right to any assets to make up a deficiency of exempt property abates as necessary to permit earlier payment of homestead allowance and family allowance. These rights are in addition to any benefit or share passing to the surviving spouse or children by the decedent's will, unless otherwise provided, by intestate succession, or by way of elective share.

* * *

Note that the Uniform Probate Code's "Homestead Allowance" is significantly different from the homestead allowance in most other state statutes. The UPC allowance applies even if decedent did not own a home; it gives the surviving spouse (or a minor child, if there is no surviving spouse) a flat sum of money, exempt from all creditor claims.

Note also the difference in beneficiaries of the two provisions: the spouse is entitled to the homestead allowance, and if there is no spouse, *minor or dependent* children may take the allowance. The spouse also is entitled to the exempt property, but if there is no spouse, *all* of the decedent's children, jointly, are entitled to the exempt property. Finally, note that the homestead allowance and exempt property are in addition to the amounts the spouse and children take under decedent's will, and in addition to any amounts the spouse would take by elective share.

PROBLEM

At the time for distribution of W's estate, the estate has $150,000 in assets, against which creditors have asserted $80,000 in enforceable claims. W's will provides that her estate should be distributed "$50,000 to my husband H, and the balance to be divided, one-half to H, and one-quarter each to my two children, D and S." At W's death, D is a 25–year–old who is not dependent on W; S is a 17–year–old living with W at her home.

If the Uniform Probate Code is in effect, how should W's estate be distributed

(a) if H, S, and D all survive W?

(b) if only S and D survive W?

How would the estate be distributed if the creditors had asserted $180,000 in enforceable claims?

* * *

Probate is not instantaneous. Estate assets are generally not distributed for months after decedent's death. For that reason, many lawyers counsel that each spouse should have title to some money so that the survivor will have instant access to funds at decedent's death. But suppose decedent spouse held all or most of the couple's assets in his own name. Can the estate administrator or executor make payments to the surviving spouse during the period of estate administration? The answer is generally yes; the surviving spouse and minor children are entitled to support from the estate during the period of administration (see, e.g., 755 Ill. Comp. Stat. Ann. 5/15–1) [spouse entitled to reasonable sum of money to support spouse "in a manner suited to the condition in life of the surviving spouse and to the condition of the estate"; amount not to be less than $10,000]. How does the Uniform Probate Code deal with the problem? By providing for a "Family Allowance":

SECTION 2–404. FAMILY ALLOWANCE.

(a) In addition to the right to homestead allowance and exempt property, the decedent's surviving spouse and minor children whom the decedent was obligated to support and children who were in fact being supported by the decedent are entitled to a reasonable allowance in money out of the estate for their maintenance during the period of administration, which allowance may not continue for longer than one year if the estate is inadequate to discharge allowed claims. The allowance may be paid as a lump sum or in periodic installments. It is payable to the surviving spouse, if living, for the use of the surviving spouse and minor and dependent children; otherwise to the children, or persons having their care and custody. If a minor child or dependent child is not living with the surviving spouse, the allowance may be made partially to the child or his [or her] guardian or other person having the child's care and custody, and partially to the spouse, as their needs may appear. The family allowance is exempt from and has priority over all claims except the homestead allowance.

(b) The family allowance is not chargeable against any benefit or share passing to the surviving spouse or children by the will of the decedent, unless otherwise provided, by intestate succession, or by way of elective share. The death of any person entitled to family allowance terminates the right to allowances not yet paid.

* * *

Section 2–405 of the UPC goes on to limit the Family Allowance to a maximum of $27,000 for the one-year period provided in section 2–404.

B. PROTECTION AGAINST INADVERTENT DISINHERITANCE: THE PROBLEM OF THE PRE–MARITAL WILL

Suppose a married woman dies, leaving a will that was executed three years before her marriage. The will devises her entire estate to her sister. Did she intentionally disinherit her spouse, or did she inadvertently omit him? On one hand, people procrastinate, and rewriting their wills is usually not the first item on a newly-married couple's agenda. It is entirely possible that the testator would have preferred to leave at least a substantial portion of her estate to her husband, but never got around to having a new will drafted. In light of empirical evidence showing that most people want to leave the bulk of their estates to their spouses, it is likely that the testator in this instance would have preferred to benefit her husband—at least to some extent. On the other hand, one might infer that the wife's failure to change the will after three years of marriage is evidence that she intended to keep the old will in effect. After all, she knew she had written a will, knew that her husband would take nothing under the will, and yet made no move to change the will. Which explanation is more persuasive?

Legislation embodies three different approaches to this problem. In a few states, legislatures have assumed that testators who fail to change their pre-marital wills do so inadvertently. Statutes in those states provide that marriage automatically revokes a pre-marital will. As a result, decedent dies intestate, and the surviving spouse takes his intestate share. Should beneficiaries of a pre-marital will be entitled to rebut the presumption that failure to change the will was inadvertent? If so, what evidence should suffice? Consider the following case:

Prestie v. Prestie

Supreme Court of Nevada, 2006.
122 Nev. 807, 138 P.3d 520.

■ HARDESTY, J.:

In this appeal, we consider whether an amendment to an inter vivos trust can rebut the presumption that a pour-over will is revoked as to an unintentionally omitted spouse. We conclude that the plain and unambiguous language of NRS 133.110 does not permit evidence of an amendment to an inter vivos trust to rebut the presumption of a will's revocation as to an unintentionally omitted spouse.... Consequently, we affirm the district court's order revoking the will as to the respondent.

FACTS

In 1987, California residents Maria and W.R. Prestie were married in Las Vegas, Nevada. Maria and W.R. were divorced two years later yet maintained an amiable relationship. W.R. was later diagnosed with macular degeneration and moved to Las Vegas, where he purchased a condominium. Maria also moved to Las Vegas, although she initially resided in a separate residence.

In 1994, W.R. simultaneously executed in California a pour-over will and the W.R. Prestie Living Trust (the inter vivos trust). The pour-over will devised W.R.'s entire estate to the trust. W.R.'s son, appellant Scott Prestie, was named both the trustee and a beneficiary of the inter vivos trust. Neither the will nor the inter vivos trust provided for Maria.

As W.R.'s sight worsened, Maria provided care for W.R. by taking him to his doctor appointments, cooking, and cleaning his condominium. In 2000, Maria moved into W.R.'s condominium to better assist him with his needs. In 2001, W.R. amended the inter vivos trust to grant Maria a life estate in his condominium upon his death. A few weeks later, Maria and W.R. were married for a second time. W.R. passed away approximately nine months later.

Maria eventually petitioned the district court for, among other things, a one-half intestate succession share of W.R.'s estate on the ground that W.R.'s will was revoked as to her under NRS 133.110 (revocation of a will by marriage). Specifically, Maria argued that because she married W.R. without entering into a marriage contract and after he had executed his will, the will was revoked as to her because it did not contain a provision providing for her or a provision expressing an intention to not provide for her.

The probate commissioner found that W.R.'s will was executed before he remarried Maria in 2001 and that the amendment granting Maria a life estate in the condominium was to the inter vivos trust, not to W.R.'s will. The probate commissioner also concluded that, under NRS 133.110, W.R. and Maria did not have a marriage contract and W.R.'s will did not provide for Maria or express an intent to not provide for Maria. Therefore, the probate commissioner recommended that W.R.'s will be revoked as to Maria. The district court subsequently entered an order adopting the probate commissioner's report and recommendations, and Scott Prestie appeals.

DISCUSSION

NRS 133.110—revocation of a will by marriage

NRS 133.110 provides for surviving spouses who are unintentionally omitted from their spouse's will:

> If a person marries after making a will and the spouse survives the maker, the will is revoked as to the spouse, unless provision has been made for the spouse by marriage contract, or unless the spouse is provided for in the will, or in such a way mentioned therein as to show an intention not to make such provision; and no other evidence to rebut the presumption of revocation shall be received.

Scott argues that W.R.'s amendment to the inter vivos trust, which gave Maria a life estate in W.R.'s condominium, means that Maria has been provided for under NRS 133.110. Moreover, Scott contends that W.R.'s amendment to the inter vivos trust rebuts the presumption of revocation under NRS 133.110. We disagree with both of these arguments.

NRS 133.110 is unambiguous, and we have previously explained that it "provides for the presumptive revocation of a will if the testator marries after executing his will and his spouse survives him, unless he has provided for the surviving spouse by marriage contract, by provision in the will, or has mentioned her in such a way as to show an intention not to provide for her." "The sole purpose of [NRS 133.110] is to guard against the unintentional disinheritance of the surviving spouse." Thus, the only evidence admissible to rebut the presumption of revocation for the purposes of NRS 133.110 is a marriage contract, a provision providing for the spouse in the will, or a provision in the will expressing an intent to not provide for the spouse.

Accordingly, we reject the notion that an amendment to a trust, which provides for the spouse, is admissible to rebut the presumption of a will's revocation.[1] The plain language of NRS 133.110 dictates otherwise, and

1. We are cognizant of the fact that modern estate planning regularly utilizes revocable inter vivos trusts with pour-over wills. This approach to estate planning usually results in amendments, if any, being made to the revocable trust and not the pour-over will. Given the clear and unambiguous language of NRS 133.110, we caution that a testator must modify his or her will in order to avoid the consequences resulting from the unintentional omission of a surviving spouse pursuant to NRS 133.110.

"we will not engraft, by judicial legislation, additional requirements upon the clear and unambiguous provisions of NRS 133.110."

W.R. executed his will before remarrying Maria; consequently, Maria could invoke the protections afforded to a spouse under NRS 133.110. Scott concedes that W.R.'s amendment to the inter vivos trust does not constitute a marriage contract and that no other marriage contract providing for Maria exists. Likewise, it is undisputed that W.R.'s will did not contain a provision providing for Maria or a provision expressing an intent to not provide for her. Thus, the district court properly concluded that W.R.'s will is revoked as to Maria, as none of the three limited exceptions contained in NRS 133.110 is present.

NRS Title 13 does not incorporate NRS Title 12 with respect to revocation of wills

Scott argues that NRS Title 13 (trusts) bars Maria's claim as an unintentionally omitted spouse under NRS Title 12 (wills) because NRS 164.005, by reference, contemplates the application of trust amendments in satisfaction of NRS 133.110. We disagree.

NRS 164.005 states:

When not otherwise inconsistent with the provisions of chapters 162 to 167, inclusive, of NRS, all of the provisions of chapters 132, 153 and 155 of NRS regulating the matters of estates:

1. Apply to proceedings relating to trusts, as appropriate; or

2. May be applied to supplement the provisions of chapters 162 to 167, inclusive, of NRS.

We have previously recognized the fundamental rule of statutory construction that "[t]he mention of one thing implies the exclusion of another."

Applying this rule of construction, we conclude that the revocation of a will under NRS 133.110, is unrelated to a trust proceeding. Additionally, NRS 164.005 makes specific mention of NRS Chapters 132, 153, and 155, while making no mention of NRS Chapter 133. By mentioning select chapters, we can imply that the Legislature's exclusion of other chapters was intentional. Nothing in NRS 164.005 or NRS Title 13 contemplates the application of trust amendments in satisfaction of NRS 133.110. Thus, NRS 164.005 has no bearing on the issue of whether W.R.'s will is revoked as to Maria pursuant to NRS 133.110.

CONCLUSION

We conclude that an amendment to an inter vivos trust cannot serve to rebut the presumption that a will is revoked as to an unintentionally omitted spouse. NRS 133.110 unambiguously permits three exceptions to rebut the presumption of revocation, and an amendment to an inter vivos trust is clearly not one of them. We further conclude . . . that NRS 164.005 does not contemplate the application of an inter vivos trust to rebut the unintentional omitted spouse rule of NRS 133.110. . . . Accordingly, we affirm the district court's order.

NOTES AND QUESTIONS

1. Was W. R. Prestie's failure to change his will after his second marriage to Maria inadvertent or intentional? What evidence supports your conclusion? Why might Prestie have modified his revocable trust but not his will? Does it make sense to exclude assets held in a revocable trust from the omitted spouse calculation? See Alan Newman, Revocable Trusts and the Law of Wills: An Imperfect Fit, 43 Real Prop. Tr. & Est. L.J. 523 (2008).

In 2009, the Nevada legislature amended NRS 133.110 to state that an omitted spouse is not entitled to an intestate share if the spouse is provided for by a transfer of property outside of the will and it appears that the maker intended the transfer to be in lieu of a testamentary provision. Would this provision have changed the result in Prestie?

2. If W.R. Prestie had walked into your office after marrying Maria, and had indicated that he wanted to be sure that Maria received a life interest in the condominium, but nothing more, what would you have done? Should W.R.'s estate have a malpractice action against the lawyer who advised him?

3. Other states reject the Nevada statute's presumption that failure to change a pre-marital will is inadvertent. These states leave the elective share provisions as the principal protection for the surviving spouse. Note, however, that the elective share might limit the surviving spouse to one-third of the estate (in most jurisdictions), while in fact, the decedent spouse would have wanted to give the surviving spouse a much greater share of the estate.

The Uniform Probate Code takes a more complex approach to the issue. First, the Code assumes that a pre-marital will does reflect the testator's intent to the extent that it benefits the testator's issue from previous relationships. The Code presumes, however, that the testator's intent to benefit others was negated when she remarried. That presumption is rebuttable. Consider UPC § 2–301:

SECTION 2–301. ENTITLEMENT OF SPOUSE; PREMARITAL WILL.

(a) If a testator's surviving spouse married the testator after the testator executed his [or her] will, the surviving spouse is entitled to receive, as an intestate share, no less than the value of the share of the estate he [or she] would have received if the testator had died intestate as to that portion of the testator's estate, if any, that neither is devised to a child of the testator who was born before the testator married the surviving spouse and who is not a child of the surviving spouse nor is devised to a descendant of such a child or passes under Sections 2–603 or 2–604 to such a child or to a descendant of such a child, unless:

(1) it appears from the will or other evidence that the will was made in contemplation of the testator's marriage to the surviving spouse;

(2) the will expresses the intention that it is to be effective notwithstanding any subsequent marriage; or

(3) the testator provided for the spouse by transfer outside the will and the intent that the transfer be in lieu of a testamentary provision is shown by the testator's statements or is reasonably inferred from the amount of the transfer or other evidence.

(b) In satisfying the share provided by this section, devises made by the will to the testator's surviving spouse, if any, are applied first, and other devises, other than a devise to a child of the testator who was born before the testator married the surviving spouse and who is not a child of the surviving spouse or a devise or substitute gift under sections 2–603 or 2–604 to a descendant of such a child, abate as provided in section 3–902.

QUESTION

How would the Prestie case have been decided if UPC 2–301 had been in effect?

PROBLEMS

1. Testator executed his will in 2003 leaving all of his estate (then valued at approximately $10,000,000) to his granddaughter. By a codicil to this will in 2009, he bequeathed 3,000 shares of Norton Company stock (then worth approximately $200,000) to Virginia, a friend who occupied an adjoining condominium unit, and, in 2010, bequeathed additional shares to Virginia. Testator married Virginia in 2011 when he was 83 and died six weeks later with the will and the two codicils in force. The value of Testator's estate was $9,150,000, including the Norton Company Stock, which was valued at $1,000,000. Granddaughter is Testator's only living descendant.

a. To what would Virginia be entitled . . .

1) under UPC § 2–301?

2) in a jurisdiction that directs that marriage revokes a premarital will as to the spouse (assuming intestate succession provisions identical to the UPC)?

3) in a jurisdiction that gives the surviving spouse an elective share equal to one-third of the estate? See Estate of Christensen v. Christensen, 655 P.2d 646 (Utah 1982).

b. Suppose the will's primary beneficiary was not testator's granddaughter, but his niece. Would the result be different under the UPC?

2. Famous soul singer James Brown died in 2006 with a will, executed in 2000, leaving his estate to his "six living children." In December 2001, Brown entered into a marriage ceremony with Tomi Rae Hynie, who was then married to a Pakistani immigrant. In 2004, Hynie's earlier marriage was annulled as a fraudulent attempt to secure U.S. citizenship for the immigrant. Hynie never entered into another marriage ceremony with Brown. Under the UPC, what rights, if any, would Hynie have against Brown's estate?

How, if at all, would your answer change if the 2000 will had left Brown's entire estate to charity?

SECTION VI. THE COMMUNITY PROPERTY SYSTEM

Recall that eight states (Arizona, California, Idaho, Louisiana, Nevada, New Mexico, Texas and Washington) have community property laws, that Alaska has enacted a voluntary, or opt in, community property regime, and that Wisconsin's Uniform Marital Property Act contains many basic principles of Community Property.

Because the community property system gives each spouse a half share in all property acquired during marriage (other than by gift or inheritance), community property states have no elective share statutes. Property acquired before marriage or by gift or inheritance is the separate property of the respective spouse, and the surviving spouse has no rights in separate property. If the decedent's estate consists entirely of separate property (perhaps because it was earned before the marriage, or because it was inherited either before, or during, the marriage), the surviving spouse is dependent on whatever the decedent wants to give him or her. The theory is that the surviving spouse has a right only to the product of the marriage. If the decedent's wealth is all earned during the marriage, the surviving spouse will get half as his or her share of community property. But, if the money came in before the marriage or by gift or inheritance, the surviving spouse gets nothing—there is no right to separate property.

There are obvious "tracing" problems in determining when the property came in and where it came from. The problem is further complicated by the power of the husband and wife to change property of one kind into property of another kind by agreement or transfer. This process is sometimes called "transmutation." The surviving spouse is usually helped by the strong presumption (and judicial attitude) in favor of classifying property as community property.

Movement of families from community property states into common law states, or from common law states into community property states, creates problems. See Norvie L. Lay, Tax and Estate Planning for Community Property and the Migrant Client (1970); Stanley M. Johanson, The Migrating Client: Estate Planning for the Couple from a Community Property State, 9 Inst. on Est.Pl. & 800 (1975); Gary C. Randall, Of Visigoths, Community Property, Death and Income Tax Basis, 25 Gonz. L. Rev. 237 (1990); Symposium, The Continuing Evolution of American Community Property Law, 1990 Wis. L. Rev. 583. Thus, if a husband earns money while the couple is domiciled in a community property state and invests the money in stock in his name, and the couple moves to a common law state where the husband dies, the wife still has an equitable claim to a half interest in the stock as her community property. And, in many common law states, she will also have an elective share in the deceased husband's half interest! UPC § 2–202 blocks such a double interest. In addition, there is a Uniform Disposition of Community Property Rights at Death Act which solves some of the problems such a move engenders. About a dozen states have adopted the act. Suppose the reverse: the husband earns money in a common law state, retires, and the couple moves to a community property state. Here the money invested in the husband's name would be labeled "separate" because at the time and place acquired, the wife would have no community property right. When the husband now dies domiciled in the community property state, the wife could end up with nothing. She has no community property interest because the property was acquired under a common law system, and she has lost her common law protection because the property is now governed by community property law. This result can be avoided by a statutory provision classifying such property as "quasi community property" and treating it as if it were community property in which each spouse has a one-half interest at the death of the owner (the California approach) or providing the surviving spouse an elective share on the death of the owner (the Idaho approach). Cal. Prob. Code §§ 66, 101; Idaho Code § 15–2–201 et seq. The comparable concept under the Uniform Marital Property Act § 18, is "deferred marital property." Still another approach might be to enact some kind of forced share in all separate property.

SECTION VII. PROTECTION OF CHILDREN: PRETERMITTED CHILD STATUTES

Among the fifty American states, only Louisiana provides children with statutory protection against intentional disinheritance, and Louisiana limits that protection to children under the age of 24 and descendants who are permanently incapable of administering their property. For a discussion of the Louisiana change, see Katherine Shaw Spaht, The Remnant of Forced Heirship: The Interrelationship of Undue Influence, What's Become of Disinherison, and the Unfinished Business of the Stepparent Usufruct, 60 La. L. Rev. 637 (2000); Cynthia Samuel, Letter from Louisiana: An Obituary for Forced Heirship and a Birth Announcement for Covenant Marriage, 12 Tul. Eur. & Civ. L. F. 183, 186 (1997).

Most states, however, protect children against unintentional disinheritance. The statutes—often called pretermitted child statutes—fall into two broad categories: those which protect only children born after execution of testator's will, and those which protect all children who have been unintentionally disinherited. When the statute protects against all unintentional disinheritance, how is decedent's intent to be ascertained? Consider the following case:

Estate of Glomset

Supreme Court of Oklahoma, 1976.
547 P.2d 951.

■ BARNES, JUSTICE.

On the 16th day of October, 1972, the deceased, John Larson Glomset, Sr., and the Appellant, Margie V. Glomset, made and signed joint and reciprocal wills leaving each other all of the other's property in case of death of the other, except in the case of a common disaster, in which instance the whole of the estate was to go to John Larson Glomset, Jr., the son of the deceased.

The deceased's 40–year–old daughter, Carolyn Gay Ghan, was not named in the will. On the 15th day of October, 1973, John Larson Glomset, Sr., died, and on the 17th day of October, 1973, his will was filed for probate. On the 9th day of November the will was admitted to probate, but the question of whether Appellee, Carolyn Gay Ghan, was a pretermitted heir was reserved. On February 7, 1974, a hearing was held, in which Appellee's motion for a declaratory judgment that Appellee was a pretermitted heir, as defined by Title 84 O.S. § 132, and entitled to share in her father's estate, was sustained. The Trial Court found:

> "The Court finds, from a complete reading of the will that the Contestant was omitted therefrom, and that said will provides for her in no manner whatsoever. The Court finds that a complete reading of the will discloses no intent to intentionally not provide for said Contestant. No intention to disinherit Contestant affirmatively appears from the four corners of the will. The Court, therefore, finds that Contestant was unintentionally omitted from deceased's said will, and is, therefore, entitled to have the same share in the estate of the decedent as if decedent had died intestate, all as provided in 84 O.S. § 132."

Appellant questions whether this issue can be determined in a summary judgment proceeding, and, if so, Appellant further disputes the Trial Court's finding that Appellee is a pretermitted heir under the provisions of 84 O.S. § 132.

Title 84 O.S. § 132 provides as follows:

> "When any testator omits to provide in his will for any of his children, or for the issue of any deceased child *unless it appears that such omission was intentional*, such child, or the issue of such child, must have the same share in the estate of the testator, as if he had died intestate, and succeeds thereto as provided for in preceding section." (Emphasis added)

There was no dispute concerning the fact the Appellee was a daughter of the deceased. The only question for our determination is whether or not deceased's omission of Appellee appears to have been intentional.

We must first determine if the intent of the deceased must be determined from the will itself, or if extrinsic evidence is admissible. If extrinsic evidence is not admissible, then there is no question of fact still to be determined, and in that event, since there is only a question of law to be determined, a summary judgment by the Trial Court was proper. In deciding if extrinsic evidence is admissible, we must determine whether or not an intention to disinherit Appellee affirmatively appeared from the four corners of the will. We have previously held that if there are no uncertainties appearing on the face of the will, extrinsic evidence is not admissible. See O'Neill v. Cox, 270 P.2d 663 (Okl. 1954), and Dilks v. Carson, 197 Okl. 128, 168 P.2d 1020 (1946).

There are no uncertainties on the face of the will in this case. The testator admittedly failed to mention his daughter, Appellee Carolyn Gay Ghan, and also failed to indicate any reason for his failure to mention her.

Thus, if we are to follow previous decisions of this court interpreting 84 O.S. § 132, such as In re Daniels' Estate, 401 P.2d 493 (Okl. 1965), then we must find that Appellee is a pretermitted heir and entitled to inherit her proportionate share of her deceased father's estate.

Appellant has failed to set forth a compelling reason why the interpretation of 84 O.S. § 132 should be changed at this time to permit introduction of extrinsic evidence to show intent of the testator where no ambiguity appears on the face of the will.

The writ of certiorari petitioned for is granted, the decision of the Court of Appeals is vacated, and the judgment of the Trial Court is affirmed.

* * *

■ HODGES, VICE CHIEF JUSTICE (dissenting).

The majority opinion holds the will is unambiguous on its face and, therefore, extrinsic evidence is inadmissible to determine the intention of the testator. I believe this perpetuates a misinterpretation of the applicable statute, 84 O.S.1971, § 132.

It is generally recognized that pretermitted heir statutes are not intended to limit a testator's power to dispose of his property by will, or to require him to bestow any part of his estate on any child or descendant. The purpose of the statute is to protect such heirs against omission due to *unintentional* oversight, forgetfulness or mistake. Two broad general classifications of such statutes are recognized: (1) The "Massachusetts-type" statutes, which are usually considered to emphasize the intention of the testator as the material factor in determining whether a child or descendant is disinherited; and (2) "Missouri-type" statutes which omit reference to intention and provide for a total or partial revocation of the will if a child is not named or provided for therein.

Our statute, a "Massachusetts-type" statute, was adopted from the Dakotas. Under comparable statutes providing an omitted child or issue of a deceased child should be entitled to a portion of the testator's estate, "unless it appears that such omission was intentional," the courts of North and South Dakota and the majority of jurisdictions, with the exceptions of

California and Oklahoma, have consistently held since 1868, that extrinsic evidence was admissible to prove that the testator intended to disinherit an omitted child. The pretermitted heir statute raises the presumption that children are not intentionally omitted from a will. However, the presumption is rebuttable by extrinsic evidence and parol testimony.

The purpose and legislative intent of the statute is to protect children unintentionally omitted from the will. It is not to be construed to alter the testamentary intent of the testator by including children he intentionally excluded from his estate.

I would therefore overrule all cases in conflict with the traditional interpretation of the pretermitted heir statute.

Assuming arguendo, the majority view is correct, I further believe the will is ambiguous on its face, and that the testator's intention to disinherit appears from the will itself. The statute which guides our interpretation of intention, 84 O.S.1971, § 152 permits introduction of extrinsic evidence to show the circumstances under which the will was executed.

This court In re Adams' Estate, 203 Okl. 377, 222 P.2d 366 (1950) held that the question of the intention to omit may be drawn from inference of the language as well as the face of the will, and that the drawing of such inference is not only within the power of the court, but is the duty of the court. The court held at page 369:

> "In determining whether the omission of a child is intentional or not, no set form of words, indicating testator's intention to omit such child, is requisite. The will is to be taken as a whole; and if it appears from the entire instrument that testator intended to omit such child, the statute does not apply. * * *
>
> "It is not necessary that testator should name his child, or even refer, in terms, to the fact that it is his child."

Extrinsic evidence should have been admissible because by omitting the daughter from the will she thereby is entitled to her statutory share, while the son who was mentioned in the will receives nothing. Thus on the face of the will an uncertainty is created and extrinsic evidence should be allowed. This extrinsic evidence which was offered, but rejected by the trial court, definitely shows the testator intentionally omitted the daughter. She would not visit her father or even allow her child to visit him. They had not seen each other for some time because of their strained relationship.

I believe a construction which permits a child not mentioned in the will to participate in the distribution of the estate while the other child who is mentioned and designated the contingent beneficiary takes nothing, is a tortured interpretation of the will and the Oklahoma Statutes regarding testamentary intent, and reaches a result totally unintended and uncontemplated by the testator or the statute.

The cause should be remanded to the trial court for determination of the factual question of whether the omission of the daughter was intentional.

I, therefore, respectfully dissent.

NOTES AND QUESTIONS

1. Why did testator's daughter share in his estate while his son did not? Is there any reason to think that result reflected testator's intent?

2. Oklahoma courts continue to adhere to the principles announced in Glomset. For example, in Estate of Livsey, 183 P.3d 1038 (Okla.Civ.Ct. App. 2008), testator's will stated that he had one living child whom he intended to disinherit. Testator left his entire estate to his close friend and the friend's wife. In actuality, testator was survived by six children, all of whom were apparently known to him. Extrinsic evidence indicated that Testator was irreparably estranged from his entire family. Yet the court found that no intent to disinherit the un-mentioned five children could be found on the face of the will, and awarded omitted child shares to each of the five children!

You are an Oklahoma lawyer, and a client has asked you to draft a will leaving all of her property to her husband. What questions would you ask the testator, and how would you draft her will?

3. The dissenting opinion in Glomset characterizes the Oklahoma statute as a "Massachusetts-type" statute. Massachusetts-type statutes permit the excluded child to inherit "unless it appears that such omission was intentional." In most jurisdictions (but not Oklahoma), extrinsic evidence is admissible to prove that the omission was intentional.

By contrast, other jurisdictions have Missouri-type statutes, which permit all children "not named or referred to" in the will to take a share of a deceased parent's estate. See, e.g., N.H.Rev.Stat. Ann. § 551:10. In these jurisdictions, intent is irrelevant; omission of the child (or issue of a deceased child) entitles the omitted descendant to an intestate share. See, e.g., Estate of Treloar, 151 N.H. 460, 859 A.2d 1162 (2004); Alexander v. Alexander, 351 Ark. 359, 93 S.W.3d 688 (2002) (both awarding intestate share to omitted grandchild).

By definition, in states with Missouri-type statutes, extrinsic evidence is not generally available to establish testator's intent.

4. In a jurisdiction that admits extrinsic evidence to establish testator's intent to disinherit a child, what sort of evidence is relevant? Which of the following would have been relevant, and therefore admissible, in Glomset if the court had decided to admit extrinsic evidence:

a. A letter from testator to his daughter explaining that testator trusted his wife to provide for the daughter?

b. Testimony by the lawyer who drafted the will indicating that testator had told the lawyer he wanted to make no provision for his daughter?

c. Testimony by testator's son that testator and the daughter "never got along?"

5. An unmarried client enters your office and asks you to draft a will leaving all of his property to his brother. You ask the client whether he has children, and he tells you he does not. You are worried about a potential (but unlikely) challenge from someone who claims to be a child born outside of marriage. If you were in a jurisdiction with a Missouri-type statute, how would you draft testator's will? Would it be enough to include the following provision:

> "I declare that I have no children whom I have omitted to name or provide for herein."

See Estate of Padilla, 97 N.M. 508, 641 P.2d 539 (App. 1982) [holding that this language was insufficient to establish that the omission was intentional; hence, the omitted child was entitled to share in the estate].

Suppose, instead, you include a provision leaving "$1.00 to any person who seeks to share in my estate as a pretermitted child." Cf. Estate of Hilton, 98 N.M. 420, 649 P.2d 488 (App.1982) [holding that a gift to contestants is sufficient to avoid application of the pretermitted child statute].

6. Why not assume that any testator who wanted to leave property to his children would have done so explicitly? How likely is it that testator forgot that he had children? Should claims by omitted children be limited to children born after the will's execution? Consider the UPC's approach:

SECTION 2–302. OMITTED CHILDREN.

(a) Except as provided in subsection (b), if a testator fails to provide in his [or her] will for any of his [or her] children born or adopted after the execution of the will, the omitted after-born or after-adopted child receives a share in the estate as follows:

(1) If the testator had no child living when he [or she] executed the will, an omitted after-born or after-adopted child receives a share in the estate equal in value to that which the child would have received had the testator died intestate, unless the will devised all or substantially all of the estate to the other parent of the omitted child and that other parent survives the testator and is entitled to take under the will.

(2) If the testator had one or more children living when he [or she] executed the will, and the will devised property or an interest in property to one or more of the then-living children, an omitted after-born or after-adopted child is entitled to share in the testator's estate as follows:

(i) The portion of the testator's estate in which the omitted after-born or after-adopted child is entitled to share is limited to devises made to the testator's then-living children under the will.

(ii) The omitted after-born or after-adopted child is entitled to receive the share of the testator's estate, as limited in subparagraph (i), that the child would have received had the testator included all omitted after-born and after-adopted children with the children to whom devises were made under the will and had given an equal share of the estate to each child.

(iii) To the extent feasible, the interest granted an omitted after-born or after-adopted child under this section must be of the same character, whether equitable or legal, present or future, as that devised to the testator's then-living children under the will.

(iv) In satisfying a share provided by this paragraph, devises to the testator's children who were living when the will was executed abate ratably. In abating the devises of the then-living children, the court shall preserve to the maximum extent possible the character of the testamentary plan adopted by the testator.

(b) Neither subsection (a)(1) nor subsection (a)(2) applies if:

(1) it appears from the will that the omission was intentional; or

(2) the testator provided for the omitted after-born or after-adopted child by transfer outside the will and the intent that the transfer be in lieu of a testamentary provision is shown by the testator's statements or is reasonably inferred from the amount of the transfer or other evidence.

(c) If at the time of execution of the will the testator fails to provide in his [or her] will for a living child solely because he [or she] believes the child to be dead, the child is entitled to share in the estate as if the child were an omitted after-born or after-adopted child.

(d) In satisfying a share provided by subsection (a)(1), devises made by the will abate under section 3–902.

NOTES AND QUESTIONS

1. UPC § 2–302 substantially revises the previous version of the UPC, which did not limit the omitted child to the portion of the estate devised to children living at the time the will was executed. The new version is modeled on the New York statute, N.Y. EPTL § 5–3.2.

2. How would the Glomset case have been decided under UPC § 2–302? Note that the statute, like some other pretermitted child statutes, protect only children born after the execution of the will.

How would the Glomset case have been decided if the daughter had been born after the will's execution?

In light of UPC § 2–302, how would you draft a will to deal with the possibility that a now-childless testator might have children in the future? To deal with the possibility that a testator-parent might have more children in the future?

3. James Brown, the godfather of soul, died in 2006 with a will leaving his estate to his "six living children." The will also provided that Brown did not intend to provide for "any other relatives or persons whether claiming ... to be an heir of mine or not." Ten months later, James Brown, Jr. was born to Tomi Rae Hynie. Brown signed the birth certificate as the father. If UPC § 2–302 were in effect, to what would James Brown, Jr. be entitled?

4. Does UPC § 2–302 confer inheritance rights on a child born after its father's death when the father's frozen sperm are used to artificially inseminate the child's mother? See Ronald Chester, Freezing the Heir Apparent: A Dialogue on Postmortem Conception, Parental Responsibility, and Inheritance, 33 Hous. L. Rev. 964, 984 (1996) [arguing that estate administration concerns should preclude inheritance rights by such children]. New York has recently amended its omitted child statute to preclude inheritance rights by omitted children not yet in gestation at the time of testator's death.

PROBLEMS

1. T dies survived by his wife W, and their daughters A, B, and C. C was born after execution of T's will. The will provides $20,000 for A, $40,000 for B, and the remainder, which turns out to be $240,000, for W. What share of T's estate can C take if UPC 2–302 has been enacted? How would C's share affect the remainder of T's testamentary plan?

2. T dies survived by his wife W, and their daughter C, born after execution of T's will. T's estate has a value of $300,000. The will provides $20,000 for T's sister S, $40,000 for T's alma mater, and distributes the residuary to W. W also has a child D, by a previous marriage. What share of T's estate can C take if the jurisdiction has enacted the Uniform Probate Code?

Heir Wars

By Philip D. Witte.
California Lawyer Magazine, September 2003.

On May 21, 1995, Larry Hillblom, cofounder of DHL Worldwide Express, the giant air express carrier, was flying on business from Pagan in the South Pacific to his home in Saipan. Hillblom was his own man, but he was a lousy pilot.

Well before its destination, the flimsy plane dropped into the sea. Within days, Larry Lee Hillblom, age 52, was declared legally dead.

At the time of his death, Hillblom owned approximately 60 percent of DHL, the domestic corporation, and 22 percent of DHLI, the international company, with a net worth of more than $500 million. In his will, he left almost the entire fortune to a charitable trust benefiting medical research, mainly at the University of California. Drafted in 1982 and never revised, the will contained a single legal flaw rarely seen in the final documents of the rich and well represented: Hillblom did not disinherit any unacknowledged children. Soon after his death, young Asian women—in some cases disturbingly young—flocked to court, each claiming to be the mother of a Hillblom child.

In the bars of Micronesia, the Philippines, and Vietnam, Hillblom was known as the "odd American" who favored young women—virgins, more precisely. He reportedly kept a network of madams on retainer to provide him with a steady supply. "Larry got involved in the kind of culture where that behavior was acceptable, and maybe he convinced himself that it was acceptable," says a close friend.

One woman, Kaelani Kinney, and her half-Caucasian son, whom she called Junior, apparently had a relationship with Hillblom. She sought him out in Saipan's and Palau's public places and loudly demanded child-support payments. Hillblom slipped her money and kept her at bay. But to his friends he denied being Junior's father, insisting that he had had a vasectomy long ago.

Kinney told a different story. She claimed that at the age of 16 she had been introduced to Hillblom at a bar in Palau, her island home and "one of Larry's playgrounds," according to a Hillblom friend. They spent three days together at the Nikko Hotel, and in May 1984 Junior Larry Hillbroom was born—Kinney misspelled the surname on the boy's birth certificate.

[Peter J.] Donnici [a lawyer who had advised Hillblom on business matters] knew about the persistent rumors that Junior was Hillblom's illegitimate son. He advised him to update his will, but Hillblom always shrugged him off. "Twice I said to him point blank, 'Larry, if Junior is your child, let's do something. Let's take care of him and get him out of poverty,'" Donnici recalls. "He told me, 'I don't have any children.'"

Unaccountably, however, [Hillblom's] will failed to include a standard provision disinheriting all pretermitted children. Stranger yet, Hillblom must have been aware of the need to address the issue. While acting as a special CNMI Supreme Court judge in 1992, he and two other justices signed a 13–page opinion holding that pretermitted heirs are entitled to full inheritance rights if they prove by clear and convincing evidence that the deceased was their parent.

It is possible that Hillblom deliberately omitted the clause in his will. The heirs' lawyers have suggested that Hillblom couldn't bring himself to acknowledge his children in his lifetime, but that he intended his estate to pass to those unacknowledged offspring upon his death. Those who knew him best, however, insist that he never would have left anything to his "mistakes," and certainly not to the exclusion of the beneficiary specified in his will.

At the opening hearing of probate in July 1995, Kaelani Kinney and Junior made their claim against the estate.

In all, six women claimed that Hillblom had fathered eight children. Each claim had the ring of authenticity. As their stories filtered out from Saipan, attorneys armed with photos of Hillblom canvassed the seedy bars of Southeast Asia looking for other women who might have had sex with Hillblom and produced an heir.

DNA testing is the usual method for settling paternity cases. But because Hillblom's body was never recovered, the claimants were forced to be creative.

[L]awyers for the claimants turned to indirect genetic evidence. They attempted to secure a court order for DNA samples from Hillblom's mother and two brothers, but citing California's privacy laws they refused to cooperate. The trust later charged that someone from Junior's legal team took a saliva sample from Hillblom's mother while she was in the hospital. The trust and Hillblom family attorneys charged that the act constituted an assault; ultimately, the sample was not used.

Junior's lawyers next sifted through Hillblom's medical records, hoping something might be disclosed that would aid their investigation. That's when they learned about the mole. After the 1993 crash, Hillblom had been airlifted to a clinic in Hawaii and later flown to Davies Medical Center in San Francisco, where he was treated by a University of California physician. Surgeons at Davies had performed a series of facial-reconstruction operations, and in the course of one of them removed a tiny bit of tissue from Hillblom's face. The tissue, thought to be a mole, could prove to be a half billion-dollar blemish.

The hospital asserted the estate owned the tissue sample and refused to release it without its permission. In the legal battle that followed in the California and CNMI courts, Lujan [Junior Hillbroom's lawyer] hired New York lawyers Barry Scheck and Peter Neufeld—recently made famous by their work in the O. J. Simpson case. Lawyers for Davies lost in CNMI superior court and on appeal. After months of legal wrangling, the hospital was ordered to hand over the mole.

At a deposition in the case, however, Davies claimed that there had been an embarrassing mix-up—the mole had come from someone else's face. The hospital claimed it was an honest mistake. During a later deposition, Neufeld asked the chief pathologist if he had any idea what had become of the real Hillblom tissue sample. Surprising a roomful of lawyers, the pathologist reached into the pocket of his lab coat and tossed a block of paraffin wax containing the tissue sample on the conference room table.

In desperation, Neufeld proposed a novel strategy: If Hillblom fathered the children, their blood samples should reveal common genetic material—so-called junk DNA—that would separate them from randomly selected individuals. The approach had never before been used in a paternity case. The lawyers proceeded cautiously because each positive result would diminish the estate, and each negative result would cast doubt on the remaining claims. So they agreed to certain ground rules: The testing would be conducted in secret, and the outcome would not be revealed unless the results supported a claim. Each child agreed to contribute a fixed amount of money from the proceeds of the suit to anyone who tested negative.

Eventually, five of the eight children provided blood samples. Using this indirect method four claimants—Junior Larry Hillbroom, Nguyen Be Lory, Jellian Cuartero, and Mercedita Feliciano—proved, with a high degree of mathematical certainty, to have been fathered by the same man-Larry Hillblom.

As part of subsequent settlement talks, Hillblom's mother agreed to provide a blood sample for $1 million and a portion of the proceeds of the trust's interest from the sale of her son's French chalet. Those tests confirmed that Larry Hillblom had fathered the four children.

But the DHL group did not concede. Even before the test results were disclosed, the group lobbied the CNMI legislature to pass a probate reform law. Lifoifoi, Hillblom's old friend, urged his former colleagues to pass a bill that would retroactively disinherit every illegitimate child in the islands. Called the "Hillblom law" by its detractors, it required the putative father to publicly acknowledge paternity before a child could claim benefits as an heir. [T]he Hillblom law passed in May 1996.

Lujan challenged the law's constitutionality in CNMI superior court and in U.S. district court. The Saipan suit eventually came before CNMI Superior Court Judge Timothy Bellas, who postponed a ruling to give the parties a final chance to settle the case.

By August 1997 negotiations had reached an impasse, with the estate stuck at 40 percent and the children's lawyers holding out for 60 percent. On the eve of the hearing in Judge Bellas's courtroom, the estate met Lujan's terms.

The compromise meant that the four children would receive about $90 million each. But their net was considerably less: Attorneys and experts were paid off the top, and the IRS took more than half of each share. Junior's legal team reportedly cleared about $15 million. Fees for the attorneys and accountants representing the estate exceeded $40 million, but Judge Castro found those expenses excessive and eventually lopped off several million dollars.

The trust benefiting the University of California received about $200 million-much less than it would have received under the terms of Hillblom's will. Still, the children could have been awarded the entire estate had the case gone to trial. "I hope Larry would think that the resolution was a just one," says Donnici.

Donnici also wants to set the record straight about his friend, Larry Hillblom. "There are thousands of girls performing in clubs in the Philippines, Vietnam, Thailand—God knows where else. And there are hundreds of thousands of male patrons who go to those clubs and pay for the pleasures of using those girls. You'll see Chinese executives, Japanese executives, and American executives who are there to have fun. So it's not that Larry was unusual in that regard. Unfortunately, his story was publicized."

Adds Lujan, "Larry was a friend. I don't condone what he did. But we'd be hypocrites—all of us—to condemn him when Larry's the one who made us all rich."

NOTES AND QUESTIONS

1. Suppose UPC § 2–302 had been in effect in the Commonwealth of the Northern Marianas Islands. How much of Larry Hillblom's estates would his non-marital children have taken, assuming they could prove paternity?

2. Suppose Larry Hillblom had retained you to draft his will. What language would you have included to avoid contests by the children?

Protection of Children Against Intentional Disinheritance

As we have seen, most American jurisdictions purport to give testators complete freedom to disinherit their children, so long as they do so explicitly. And, of course, many testators disinherit their children in favor of their surviving spouses—especially when the spouse is also the parent of testator's children. In that situation, courts routinely honor the disinheritance of children.

Consider, however, the situation in which a testator disinherits children in favor of non-relatives. Is "freedom" of testation more imagined than real—especially in light of the near-universal protection of family members against disinheritance in other countries? Consider the following:

Melanie Leslie, The Myth of Testamentary Freedom, 38 Ariz. L. Rev. 235, 270–73 (1996):

Most other Western countries expressly acknowledge a strong public policy of restricting freedom of testation to protect dependents, family members and others who are viewed as having a claim on decedent's assets.... The list of countries with statutory or civil-code protection for testators' children includes Argentina, Austria, Belgium, Brazil, France, Germany, Greece, Italy, Japan, Spain, Sweden and Switzerland.... France's system is illustrative: children can be prevented from receiving a portion of their parent's estate only for cause.

Most common-law countries also restrict testamentary freedom in favor of policies protecting family and other dependents of the testator. For example, at least fifteen common-law jurisdictions, such as New Zealand, England, the states of Australia, and most of the Canadian provinces, have enacted statutes that give courts substantial discretion to deviate from the distributive scheme set forth in the testator's will to provide for the testator's dependents, even where the testator expressly clarified an intention to disinherit. These statutes, generally known as Family Protection Acts or Testator's Dependents Acts, do not exist merely to keep the testator's dependents from becoming wards of the state. Rather, they are imbued with the idea that a testator owes a moral obligation to certain others, regardless of need.

For example, in England, the country that has most influenced United States' wills laws and from which we have inherited our respect for testamentary freedom, the protection afforded runs not only to those related to the testator, but to anyone who can claim entitlement to the testator's assets, such as an ex-spouse or any person who can show they were maintained "in whole or in part" by the decedent. Any qualifying individual is entitled to "reasonable financial provision" from the testator's estate. In determining what financial provision is "reasonable," the court is entitled to consider "all the circumstances," and may make an award "whether or not that provision is required for [the applicant's] maintenance."

Thus, while most of the civilized world recognizes the concept of testamentary freedom to some degree, it forthrightly balances that principle with concern for family members and ideas about morality and justice specific to the particular culture. The United States alone insists on paying lip service to the idea that testamentary freedom is preeminent. Given the practically universal urge to limit testamentary freedom with concerns for family protection and fulfillment of moral duty, it should come as no surprise that the same urges are at play in the common law of the United States. United States courts, however, honor those competing values surreptitiously and to greater and lesser degrees depending on the particular tribunal.

The axiom that wills law is designed only to effectuate testamentary intent is therefore false, and the idea that individuals enjoy complete testamentary freedom is a myth. Generally, individuals have "freedom" to distribute their property along carefully delineated channels in accordance with prevailing norms. Thus, there is the "freedom" to vary the amounts of bequests to children, as long as the primary beneficiaries are the testator's children.

NOTES AND QUESTIONS

1. Professor Leslie argues that courts often protect family members by manipulating testamentary formalities and requirements for establishing undue influence when necessary to assure intestacy when testator's will is not sufficiently generous to family members. Id. Reconsider her argument when we take up will formalities and grounds for will contests.

2. Because of the judicial tendencies Professor Leslie identifies, many lawyers believe that a client should be advised not to disinherit children—unless the client leaves all or most of his estate to his surviving spouse.

3. Some commentators believe that children should receive explicit statutory protection against disinheritance. See Ronald Chester, Disinheritance and the American Child: An Alternative from British Columbia, 1998 Utah L. Rev. 1; Ralph C. Brashier, Protecting the Child from Disinheritance: Must Louisiana Stand Alone?, 57 La. L. Rev. 1 (1996); Deborah A. Batts, I Didn't Ask to Be Born: The American Law of Disinheritance and a Proposal for Change to a System of Protected Inheritance, 41 Hastings L. J. 1197 (1990).

Professor Brashier suggests that a posthumous duty to support minor children—imposed on testator's estate—is one way to provide for those children. Ralph C. Brashier, Disinheritance and the Modern Family, 45 Case W. Res. L. Rev. 83 (1994).

4. Would a system that gives courts discretion to provide for testator's family members be preferable to the UPC's "omitted children" provision? Would the discretionary approach used in England and other common law countries be preferable to American elective share statutes? What advantages of each approach can you identify? Compare Mary Ann Glendon, Fixed Rules and Discretion in Contemporary Family Law and Succession Law, 60 Tul. L. Rev. 1165 (1986) (arguing against American adoption of discretionary approach taken in England and elsewhere) with Ronald Chester, Disinheritance and the American Child: An Alternative from British Columbia, 1998 Utah L. Rev. 1, 32–33 (arguing in favor of a discretionary approach).

CHAPTER FOUR

WILLS

SECTION I. EXECUTION OF WILLS

A. WILL FORMALITIES: WHAT ARE THEY AND WHY HAVE THEM?

Modern contract law has largely dispensed with formalities. Contracts need not be executed under seal. The Statute of Frauds requires a writing before a party may enforce a contract whose performance might not be completed within a year, but the rise of promissory estoppel and like doctrines has made it possible to enforce contracts even without any written document.

Has there been a corresponding decline in formalities in wills law? Consider the following:

TEXAS ESTATES CODE (effective January 1, 2014)

SECTION 251.051. WRITTEN, SIGNED, AND ATTESTED

Except as otherwise provided by law, a last will and testament must be:

(1) in writing;

(2) signed by:

(A) the testator in person; or

(B) another person on behalf of the testator:

(i) in the testator's presence; and

(ii) under the testator's direction; and

(3) attested by two or more credible witnesses who are at least 14 years of age and who subscribe their names to the will in their own handwriting in the testator's presence.

Count the number of formalities the Texas statute requires for a will to be enforceable. The statute requires that the will: (1) must be in writing; (2) must be signed by the testator, or by his proxy, acting under the testator's direction and in his presence; (3) must be attested (witnessed, for the moment); (4) there must be at least two witnesses; (5) the witnesses must be credible; (6) if witnessed, the witnesses must be over 14; (7) the witnesses must sign in their own handwriting; (8) in the presence of the testator.

Why should the legislature be so insistent on formalities when wills are involved? The standard answer focuses on four functions allegedly served by the Statute of Wills: (1) the *protective* function; (2) the *ritual* function; (3) the *evidentiary* function; and (4) the *channeling* function. The first three were identified in a classic article by Ashbel G. Gulliver & Catherine J. Tilson, Classification of Gratuitous Transfers, 51 Yale L.J. 1, 6–7 (1941). The fourth, drawn from Lon Fuller, Consideration and Form, has been emphasized by Professor John Langbein in Substantial Compliance with the Wills Act, 88 Harv. L. Rev. 489, 494 (1975). See also Bruce H. Mann, Formalities and Formalism in the Uniform Probate Code, 142 U. Pa. L. Rev. 1033 (1994).

The formalities of the Statute of Wills are said to protect the testator against fraud, undue influence, mistake, and fraudulent suppression of a valid will after the testator dies. The primary hope is that the presence of witnesses will make scoundrels think twice.

The ritual of will-signing is designed to assure that the will itself is the product of careful reflection by the testator, rather than an offhand statement that reflects a momentary whim. When people dress up, enter an office building, and sign a document in the presence of witnesses, they take the event seriously. See Adam J. Hirsch, Inheritance and Inconsistency, 57 Ohio St. L.J. 1057, 1069 (1996). The cost is that will making may seem daunting and the formality and ritualized nature of the venture may act as a barrier for people who might otherwise make a will.

Requiring a writing generates clear evidentiary advantages: the writing provides a physical record of the testator's wishes. Requiring a formal event surely creates a piece of evidence about which to testify, and requiring witnesses certainly has the effect of providing witnesses to testify about that evidence.

Simply put, channeling provides us with standard expressions of a testator's intent. Channeling encompasses these ideas: (1) formalities provide a known "channel," or canal, for an instrument to travel efficiently through the legal system and into the safe harbor of admission to probate; and (2) the mysteries created by the formalities channel testators to lawyers, who are trained in helping people think about their property, preparing wills, presiding over their execution, storing them, etc. See generally Kent D. Schenkel, Testamentary Fragmentation and the Diminishing Role of the Will: An Argument for Revival, 41 Creighton L. Rev. 155, 177–81 (2008).

Given the importance of making a will, and considering that making a will can be a solitary, or unilateral act (with all the pitfalls that potentially entails), and given the fact that the testator is dead when the will takes effect, it makes some sense to require formalities and witnesses and to hope that testators will look to lawyers for assistance. Clients are likely better off with us than without us.

And, of course, there is always history as an explanation. For instance, in the distant past, when wills were often death-bed events, weak testators, looking at an eternity of hellfire, arguably needed more protection than today's client. Furthermore, prior to the enactment of the English Wills Act of 1837, people were trying to probate all manner of instruments as a decedent's last will and testament. It was, if you will, the 19th century equivalent of probating a cocktail napkin with some scribbles on it and saying, "Your Honor, this napkin proves that the decedent's property belongs to me." Thus, a serious set of formalities serves a filtering function.

Not everyone finds the standard explanations satisfactory. Consider the following:

James Lindgren, The Fall of Formalism, 55 Alb. L. Rev. 1009 (1992).

People are not stupid. Yet for hundreds of years the law of wills has treated them as if they were. Sure, they don't know the law, but they usually know what they want. The fear that they might improvidently give away their property at death has left a legacy of formalism unmatched in American law.

In the law of wills, the story told about people is that their seriously intended statements about their property can't be trusted. They are so weak, old, feeble, and subject to pressure that they need extraordinary protection from themselves. Their spoken words are completely worthless. Their written statements are without meaning unless they're witnessed by two people. Even then, the witnesses must sign in the presence of the giver. And so on.

In the law of contracts, on the other hand, the story is completely different. People are intelligent and competent. They know their own mind. Other people can rely on their seriously made statements. They don't need protection from themselves. Their spoken words are enough to convey millions of dollars. And their written statements have meaning without witnesses.

.... Why do we need wills at all? Why not have an open-ended examination of the dispositive wishes of the decedent, allowing any relevant evidence?

The Uniform Probate Code has streamlined, but not eliminated, the formalities necessary for execution of a will. Compare the formalities in UPC § 2–502 with those in the Texas statute. Note in particular that the most recent version of the UPC allows the testator to dispense with witnesses altogether if the testator arranges to have her signature notarized. States that adopt the UPC after 2008 are likely to follow the UPC's lead. See, e.g. Mass. Gen. L, c. 190B, § 2–502(a)(3).

UNIFORM PROBATE CODE

SECTION 2–502. EXECUTION; WITNESSED WILLS; HOLOGRAPHIC WILLS.

(a) Except as provided in . . . , a will must be:

(1) in writing;

(2) signed by the testator or in the testator's name by some other individual in the testator's conscious presence and by the testator's direction; and

(3) either:

(A) signed by at least two individuals, each of whom signed within a reasonable time after the individual witnessed either the signing of the will as described in paragraph (2) or the testator's acknowledgment of that signature or acknowledgment of the will; or

(B) acknowledged by the testator before a notary public or other individual authorized by law to take acknowledgments.

* * *

To what extent do the wills act formalities serve their purported functions? Consider that question in light of the following case, which focuses on one of the statutory formalities: the requirement that the witnesses witness the will in the presence of the testator:

Morris v. West

Court of Appeals of Texas, Eleventh District, Eastland, 1982.
643 S.W.2d 204.

■ DICKENSON, ASSOCIATE JUSTICE.

This is a probate matter involving a will and codicil which contained proper attestation clauses and self-proving affidavits. Although they appeared to have been properly executed, the jury found that the two attesting witnesses were not in the presence of the testator when the witnesses signed their names to the will and codicil. Judgment on the verdict denied probate and declared that neither document has any testamentary effect. We affirm.

Appellant, Jackson C. Morris, was formerly married to testator's daughter, Lorraine Morris. She contested the probate of her father's will because her one-third share of the residuary estate was given to her ex-husband. The other contestant, Patrick David West, testator's grandson, was omitted from the will. The other beneficiaries and heirs at law took no position on whether or not the will and codicil should be admitted to probate.

This is the second appeal involving this estate. See Morris v. Estate of West, 602 S.W.2d 122 * * *, where this court reviewed a summary judgment denying probate of the will, stating:

The contestants failed to conclusively establish that the subscribing witnesses were not in the presence of the testator when they signed the will. The deposition testimony which we have assumed, but not decided, showed that the witnesses were not in the testator's presence, merely contradicts the attestation clause, and does no more than raise an issue of fact. (Emphasis added)

The jury has now resolved that disputed fact. The jury's verdict may be summarized as follows:

SPECIAL ISSUE NO. 1

Do you find from a preponderance of the evidence at the time Evelyn Cole and Judy Hooker signed their names to the September 14, 1978 document they were in the presence of C. K. West? Answer: No.

SPECIAL ISSUE NO. 2

Do you find from a preponderance of the evidence that Evelyn Cole and Judy Hooker were located in the secretarial office in Mr. Browning's offices at the time they signed their names to the instrument dated September 14, 1978? Answer: Yes.

SPECIAL ISSUE NO. 3

Do you find from a preponderance of the evidence that at the time Evelyn Cole and Judy Hooker signed the instrument dated September 14, 1978 that C. K. West was in the conference room in the offices of Jimmy Browning? Answer: Yes.

SPECIAL ISSUE NO. 4

Do you find from a preponderance of the evidence at the time Evelyn Cole and Judy Hooker signed their names to the February 20, 1979 document they were in the presence of C. K. West? Answer: No.

SPECIAL ISSUE NO. 5

Do you find from a preponderance of the evidence that Evelyn Cole and Judy Hooker were located in the secretarial office in Mr. Browning's offices at the time they signed their names to the instrument dated February 20, 1979? Answer: Yes.

SPECIAL ISSUE NO. 6

Do you find from a preponderance of the evidence that at the time Evelyn Cole and Judy Hooker signed the instrument dated February 20, 1979 that C. K. West was in the conference room in the offices of Jimmy Browning? Answer: Yes.

The record shows that the conference room (in which C. K. West signed the will on September 14, 1978, and in which he signed the codicil on February 20, 1979) is separated from the secretarial office (in which the two witnesses signed the will and codicil) by Mr. Browning's office. The jury believed the deposition testimony that the witnesses left the conference room on each occasion after watching C. K. West sign each instrument, walked down a hallway to the secretarial office where they signed each instrument while C. K. West stayed in the conference room with Mr. Browning, and then returned to the conference room where Mr. Browning signed the self-proving affidavits in his capacity as notary public.

Appellant has briefed nine points of error. All have been considered and overruled.

Point One argues that the trial court erred in overruling appellant's motion for directed verdict and his motion for judgment non obstante veredicto because the witnesses were "in the presence" of C. K. West at the time they signed the will "as a matter of law." Appellant argues that since the entire procedure took place in the same suite of offices, the witnesses were in the "conscious presence" of testator and that his will and codicil should be admitted to probate. We disagree. TEX. PROBATE CODE ANN. section 59 (Vernon 1980) requires the witnesses to sign their names "in the presence of the testator." The jury has found that the witnesses were in the secretarial office when they signed and that C. K. West remained in the conference room. The jury's findings are supported by the evidence. Those rooms are separated by the lawyer's private office. There were two solid walls between the testator and the two witnesses when the witnesses signed their names. The testator could not have seen them sign without arising from his chair, walking some four feet to the hallway and then walking about fourteen feet down the hallway to a point where he could have looked through the doorway and seen the witnesses as they signed their names. * * *

Point Three argues that "there was no evidence or legally insufficient evidence that more than slight physical exertion would have been required for Mr. West to have seen the signing of the will (and codicil, if applicable) from his position." We disagree because, as noted under Point One, he would have had to get up, leave the conference room, and walk down the hallway in order to watch the witnesses sign the will and codicil. Appellant cites Nichols v. Rowan, 422 S.W.2d 21 * * *. In Nichols the court defined "conscious presence" as meaning:

> To be within the testator's presence the attestation must occur where testator, unless blind, is able to see it from his actual position at the time, or at most, from such position as slightly altered, where he has the power readily to make the alteration without assistance.

Clearly, it would have required more than a "slightly altered" position for the testator to have seen the witnesses sign either the will or codicil in this case. In Earl v. Mundy, supra, the witnesses were in the same room with the testator, and he could see all of their movements while they were in the act of signing.

Points Four and Five argue that "there was legally insufficient evidence" that the will and codicil were signed by the witnesses while they were in a different room than testator. Points Six and Seven argue that there was no "clear and unmistakable" evidence that either instrument was signed outside the room in which the testator was sitting and that the evidence did not overcome the sworn acknowledgment by the witnesses in the affidavits which stated they were in the presence of testator when they signed. These points are overruled. The statements of the attestation clause may be rebutted by proper evidence. * * * The "preponderance of the evidence" is the proper burden of proof. * * * Moreover, appellant failed to request issues using his theory of "clear and unmistakable" evidence as the appropriate burden of proof.

Point Eight argues that contestants failed to plead and prove a sufficient interest in the estate to allow them to contest the will. This point is overruled because stipulated facts show that one contestant is decedent's daughter and the other contestant is the son of a child who predeceased testator. They are clearly entitled to contest the will and codicil under TEX. PROBATE CODE ANN. section 10 (Vernon 1980). * * *

The judgment of the trial court is affirmed.

QUESTIONS

1. As a result of the court's decision, how was C.K. West's estate distributed? When a will is held ineffective for failure to comply with testamentary formalities, testator's estate is distributed intestate unless testator had executed a prior will that has never been effectively revoked. In Morris v. West, C.K. West does not appear to have executed a prior will. Who benefitted, then, as a result of the court's decision in Morris v. West? Do you think that played a role in the court's decision? Should it play a role in a court's decision? Can formalities be justified as a mechanism for assuring that testator's property passes to his family unless testator has demonstrated—beyond any reasonable doubt—that he intended to disinherit his heirs? See generally Melanie B. Leslie, The Myth of Testamentary Freedom, 38 Ariz. L. Rev. 235 (1996); Melanie B. Leslie, Enforcing Family Promises: Reliance, Reciprocity, and Relational Contract, 77 N. Car. L. Rev. 551 (1999).

2. Does the presence requirement, as construed by the court in Morris v. West, serve to protect the testator against fraud, undue influence, or forgery? How, if at all, is the potential for chicanery increased because the witnesses witnessed the document while testator was in an adjoining room?

3. Was there any question that C.K. West had given serious consideration to his will? Do testators typically consult lawyers about their wills on a whim? Once testator executes a lawyer-drafted will in the lawyer's office, is there any question that the ceremony involved sufficient ritual to assure testator's seriousness of purpose? Is the testator being punished for choosing an imperfect lawyer?

4. Would the will in Morris v. West have provided a court with any better evidence if the witnesses had signed while in the same room as testator? Did the execution ceremony fulfill the evidentiary function of the Statute of Wills?

5. Would the court have disrupted the channeling function of the Statute of Wills by admitting C.K. West's will to probate? Didn't C.K. West believe he had taken advantage of the legal channels for effectuation of his testamentary intent?

6. After the court's decision in Morris v. West, should Jackson Morris have a claim against lawyer Jimmy Browning for malpractice?

7. How would Morris v. West have been decided if Uniform Probate Code section 2–502 had been in effect at the time of the decision?

NOTES

1. Courts have not applied the traditional "witness presence" requirement consistently. In two recent cases, the Georgia Supreme Court has invalidated wills because the witness was not in the testator's line of vision. See Chester v. Smith, 285 Ga. 401, 677 S.E.2d 128 (2009); McCormick v. Jeffers, 281 Ga. 264, 637 S.E.2d 666 (2006). For discussion of the Georgia cases, see Mary F. Radford, Wills, Trusts, Guardianships, and Fiduciary Administration, 61 Mercer L. Rev. 385 (2009). Some states require not only that the witnesses sign in the presence of the testator, but that they be in each other's presence. See Price v. Abate, 9 So.3d 37 (Fla. App. 2009) (invalidating will for absence of proof that witnesses signed in each other's presence). Yet many courts—including the Texas Court of Civil Appeals—have been less stringent in insisting that testator be able to see the witnesses from a "slightly altered" position in order to satisfy the statute's presence requirement. See Nichols v. Rowan, 422 S.W.2d 21 (1967); In re Demaris' Estate, 166 Or. 36, 110 P.2d 571 (1941) (defining "conscious presence" to include senses other than sight and admitting a will to probate even though a witness signed outside the sight of the testator).

The legislative trend is to eliminate the witness presence requirement, as exemplified by section 2–502 of the Uniform Probate Code and section 6110 of the California Probate Code. See Restatement (Third) Property, § 3.1, cmt. p.

2. ***Must the Witnesses Know They are Witnessing a Will?*** Suppose Jane Smith shows witnesses a document, signs the document in front of them, and asks each of them to read aloud a sentence providing that "the undersigned have witnessed Jane Smith sign this document, and we attest that at the time she signed the document, she was of sound mind and over the age of 18." The witnesses sign the document. If the document is in fact Jane Smith's will, does the will satisfy the formalities of the Texas statute? Does the statute require Jane Smith to inform the witnesses that the document they are signing is a will? Does it require that the witnesses know the document is a will?

A number of statutes explicitly require that testator inform the witnesses that the document is a will. See, e.g., NY EPTL § 3–2.1(a)(3). What purpose is served by a requirement that the testator "publish" the will to the witnesses?

How seriously should courts enforce a publication requirement? In Estate of Griffith, 30 So.3d 1190 (Miss. 2010), the witnesses signed an attestation clause certifying that testator had declared the instrument to be his last will and testament, and signed an affidavit to the same effect. At a hearing before probate court, the witnesses testified that they did not know the document they had witnessed was testator's will. The will left testator's house and a variety of other assets to his brother, and the remainder of his estate to his children. The children contested the will, contending that it did not satisfy the publication requirement. What result?

3. ***What Constitutes a Witness Signature?*** Testator's lawyer prepares a will, and leaves space for two witness signatures. Only one witness signs on the line for witness signatures. The other signature line is blank, but the lawyer who drafted the will (and who was supposed to serve as the second witness) initialed each page of the will. Do the initials constitute a witness signature? See Estate of Leavey, 41 Kan.App.2d 423, 202 P.3d 99 (2009). If not, should anyone have a malpractice claim against the lawyer who supervised the execution ceremony?

4. ***Post Mortem Witness Signature.*** Timothy Saueressig typed a will leaving his property to three friends. Timothy took his will to a friend who owned a Mail Boxes, Etc. franchise, and asked her to notarize his signature on the will. The notary friend and her husband watched as Timothy signed his will, and the notary then notarized Timothy's signature. Timothy apparently believed that this process was sufficient to validate his will. The trial court found that the will was invalid because only one witness, the notary, had signed it. Will proponents argued that the notary's husband, who had witnessed Timothy's signing of the will, ought to be allowed to sign the will as a witness after Timothy's death. Despite clear evidence of intent that Timothy intended the document to be his will, and notwithstanding section 6110's failure to impose a temporal requirement for witness signatures, the California Supreme Court refused to read the statute to allow a witness to sign after testator's death. See Estate of Saueressig, 38 Cal.4th 1045, 44 Cal.Rptr.3d 672, 136 P.3d 201 (2006). The Court justified its decision as necessary to prevent fraud. Do you agree?

The comments to UPC section 2–502 suggest that a witness should be allowed to sign the will after testator's death, as long as the signing occurs within a "reasonable time" of testator's execution. Compare Spelius v. Hollon, 143 Idaho 565, 149 P.3d 840 (2006) [applying 2–502 and permitting probate of will witnessed after testator's death]. Which is the better approach?

B. THE SIGNATURE REQUIREMENT

A testator must sign his will. Almost any imaginable signature will do if it makes a visible impression on the paper and the testator intended the impression to be his signature. A testator can use her first name, initials, nickname or mark. A literate testator can use a mark and the signature or mark can be made with a device other than a writing instrument. A testator's computer generated signature, which testator affixed in the presence of witnesses with the intent to execute his will, was held to satisfy the signature requirement. See Taylor v. Holt, 134 S.W.3d 830 (Tenn. Ct. App. 2003). The purpose of signing is to show the will is final, to show the testator's decision to give the will life.

Most wills acts allow the testator to sign by proxy if the proxy signs at the direction or request of the testator and in the testator's presence. If the signature is a proxy signature, the testator's proxy signs the testator's name. In Phillips v. Najar, 901 S.W.2d 561 (Tex.App.1995), a proxy signed the testator's name to an attested will using a rubber stamp and then the testator marked an "X" on either side of her stamped name. The testator was arthritic and could not write. The case approves both the signature by proxy using a stamp and the use of a mark by a literate testator. Sometimes life imitates law school exams!

Someone may help the testator sign his name, which is not the same as a proxy signature. Obviously, an assisted signature is done in the testator's presence, since it is literally a hands-on event. In this situation, the testator is signing her own name with the aid of an assistant. What problems might an assisted signature cause? Before Melvin Simon died in 2009, the shopping mall magnate with an estate of more than one billion dollars signed a new will increasing the share of his second wife, allegedly by hundreds of millions of dollars, and requested that someone guide his hand to complete his signature so that he would not have to sign with an "X". His daughter by his first marriage has contested the will. See Kris Hudson and Rachel Emma Silverman, Mall Heirs Battle Over will, Wall Street Journal, February 10, 2010. Would Simon have been better off signing with an "X"?

Historically, a testator's signature at any place on the will could satisfy the signature requirement. Beginning in the 19th Century, however, legislatures and courts started requiring testators to sign at the will's end. This requirement, which still exists in some states (New York, for instance) sometimes generates unnecessary litigation. As a result, the Uniform Probate Code eliminates the "at the end" requirement. A signature anywhere in the document will suffice so long as the testator intended the signature to give life to the will.

C. More About the Witness (or Attestation) Requirement

How many witnesses? In the simplest terms, in virtually every state, an ordinary will has to be witnessed. More specifically, it has to be *attested* by the minimum number of *competent* witnesses. Most states require two, but Louisiana and Puerto Rico require as many as five in specific circumstances. "Attest" and "competent" are both terms of art. Attest means to bear witness and competent means qualified to testify in court concerning the material facts of execution. When representing a testator, you would want to have a will witnessed even if the law imposed no legal requirement that wills be attested. But should the law *require* attestation? Professor Lindgren has argued that the law should not. See James Lindgren, Abolishing the Attestation Requirement for Wills, 68 N.C. L. Rev. 541 (1990).

As we have seen, in 2008, the Uniform Probate Code was amended to authorize use of a single attesting witness—if that witness happens to be a notary public. See UPC § 2–502(b)(3)(B). The UPC's drafters recognized the widespread use of notaries to effectuate other important transactions, and noted that often, a client comes to a lawyer's office to execute several documents at the same time, often causing confusion when one of the documents (the will) requires witnesses but no notary, while others require a notary but no other witnesses. The drafters suggest that "[i]t would reduce confusion and the chance for error if all of these documents could be executed with the same formality."

Choosing the Witnesses. Although the Statute of Wills requires witnesses, it does not tell the testator, or the testator's lawyer, whom to choose as witnesses. Does it make a difference? To answer that question, one must understand the function that witnesses serve when the will is probated.

When a will is offered for probate at the testator's death, the proponent must call the witnesses to testify, either in a hearing or via affidavit, that the signatures on the will are indeed theirs. If the will contains no attestation clause or self-proving affidavit (more on those later), or if probate of the will is contested, the witnesses must also provide evidence that the will was executed in compliance with the applicable formalities statute. Consequently, a lawyer should choose witnesses who will be easy to locate and able to testify at the testator's death.

In addition to ensuring that witnesses will be available and competent at testator's death, a lawyer should take care to choose witnesses who will minimize conflict and facilitate probate in the event of a will contest. Suppose, for instance, that your client, a 75–year–old woman, wants to execute a will leaving all of her assets to her 80–year–old husband, thereby disinheriting both of her children by a prior marriage. If, because she has difficulty getting around, you choose to conduct the execution ceremony at her home, should you permit her husband's two children to act as witnesses?

Note the problem. Your client's children may seek to contest the will on some ground—perhaps undue influence, or lack of capacity. If the lawyer representing the estate (maybe you!) has to defend the will, would she want to rely on testimony by the husband's children that the husband had not exercised undue influence, or that testator had capacity at the time she signed the will? Not likely.

So, in choosing witnesses, the lawyer should keep in mind the possibility of a future contest, and should pick witnesses who will be able to offer credible testimony when the will is offered for probate. The more likely a contest, the more careful the lawyer should be in choosing witnesses. If the will is a routine one, in which testator leaves her estate to the natural objects of her bounty, the lawyer need not be as particular in choosing witnesses as when the will disinherits relatives with some expectation of an inheritance.

What happens if testator dies and the witnesses cannot be located or cannot remember the execution ceremony? If testator's lawyer had the witnesses execute a self-proving affidavit, the affidavit serves as evidence that the will was properly witnessed, and the will can be admitted to probate. If the lawyer did not prepare a self-proving affidavit, the situation is more complicated. Most jurisdictions make some provision for probating the will by introducing evidence of the handwriting of the witnesses, or of other facts sufficient to establish that the will was properly executed. See, e.g. NY SCPA § 1405. But when witness testimony is unavailable, probate becomes slower, less routine, and more expensive, even if statute or case law ultimately authorizes probate of the will. And sometimes, courts refuse to probate the will at all because the proponents have not adequately established that the witnesses are unavailable. See, e.g., Estate of Speers, 179 P.3d 1265 (Okla. 2008), where the court held that a will could not be probated, even though signed by two witnesses, because the proponent (decedent's second wife) had failed to produce one of the witnesses, and had also failed to establish that the witness was dead. The court relied on statutory language permitting probate of a will without witness testimony only when the absence or death of the witness is "satisfactorily shown"—while pointing out that evidence that the witness was in fact dead was readily available to the proponent! The moral is clear: a lawyer preparing a will should always have the witnesses execute a self-proving affidavit.

Interested Witnesses. Beyond the common sense of the lawyer, many jurisdictions impose statutory limits on who may serve as a witness. These jurisdictions are concerned that a person who would benefit from the will has incentives to attest to testator's signature and competence even if the execution ceremony was a sham. States take different approaches to the problem. At common law, a will executed by an interested witness failed entirely. Some states purge the entire gift to the interested witness, regardless of whether the witness would have received a gift from a prior will or through intestacy. The Uniform Probate Code includes no disqualification for interested witnesses. The statute below illustrates New York's approach to interested witnesses:

NEW YORK EPTL

SECTION 3-3.2. COMPETENCE OF ATTESTING WITNESS WHO IS BENEFICIARY; APPLICATION TO NUNCUPATIVE WILL.

(a) An attesting witness to a will to whom a beneficial disposition or appointment of property is made is a competent witness and compellable to testify respecting the execution of such will as if no such disposition or appointment had been made, subject to the following:

(1) Any such disposition or appointment made to an attesting witness is void unless there are, at the time of execution and attestation, at least two other attesting witnesses to the will who receive no beneficial disposition or appointment thereunder.

(2) Subject to subparagraph (1), any such disposition or appointment to an attesting witness is effective unless the will cannot be proved without the testimony of such witness, in which case the disposition or appointment is void.

(3) Any attesting witness whose disposition is void hereunder, who would be a distributee if the will were not established, is entitled to receive so much of his intestate share as does not exceed the value of the disposition made to him in the will, such share to be recovered as follows:

(A) In case the void disposition becomes part of the residuary disposition, from the residuary disposition only.

(B) In case the void disposition passes in intestacy, ratably [sic] from the distributees who succeed to such interest. For this purpose, the void disposition shall be distributed under 4–1.1 as though the attesting witness were not a distributee. * * *

Who is an interested witness under this so-called "purging" statute (a statute that purges a witness of his interest in the will)? If a 75–year–old testator leaves all of her property to her 80–year–old husband, the husband would clearly be an interested witness. Would the husband's son be an interested witness? See Restatement (Third) Property § 3.1, cmt. o. (noting that a spouse is an interested witness, but making no comparable statement about other relatives). Does it matter whether the witness knows he is a beneficiary of the will? In Estate of Wu, 24 Misc.3d 668, 877 N.Y.S.2d 886 (Surr. Ct. 2009), the court applied the New York statute and concluded that the statute disqualifies interested witnesses even if they are ignorant of the benefit they would receive under the will. Can that conclusion be justified?

PROBLEMS

1. Matthew, Paul and Luke, decedent's close friends and confidants, witnessed decedent's will. Matthew and Paul were beneficiaries under the will. Matthew received a very modest cash gift, Paul received the residuary estate. Matthew renounced his gift after the will was probated. The decedent's intestate takers, first cousins, claim the will is validly probated but that the residuary passes by intestate succession. Assuming the witnesses are saints, how should the estate be distributed under the New York statute? In a state that purges completely any gift to an interested witness (regardless of whether the witness is an intestate distributee or a legatee under a prior will)? Under the Uniform Probate Code?

What result under the New York statute, if the testator had a prior will with the exact same terms that was witnessed by disinterested witnesses?

2. Testator's will leaves $50,000 to her niece, and divides the rest of her estate between her two children. How should the estate be distributed (a) if the niece and a neighbor, not mentioned in the will, witness the will; or (b) testator's daughter and the neighbor witness the will? Would either answer be different if testator had executed a prior will leaving $30,000 to her niece, $30,000 to a nephew, and the rest of her estate to testator's son?

3. If you were supervising an execution ceremony in a jurisdiction that has enacted the UPC, would you permit will beneficiaries to witness the will? Why or why not?

The Attestation Clause. An attestation clause is a paragraph of boilerplate that states that the will formalities have been satisfied and provides a place for the witnesses' signatures. The content of the clause varies depending on state execution requirements, but a typical clause might read something like this:

> [First witness] and [second witness], as witnesses, state that the Testator declared this instrument to be his Last Will and Testament; that he signed and executed the instrument in our presence, willingly, under no constraint or undue influence; and that he requested that we affix our signatures to this Will.

An attestation clause is not required in any state, but it creates a presumption that the will was validly executed and that the events described in the clause actually occurred. As a result, a will with an attestation clause can be probated even if the witnesses have no memory of the execution ceremony, so long as the witnesses can identify their signatures and the genuineness of the testator's signature is established. The clause can also be used to impeach a hostile witness or to inspire a wavering witness to remember. An attestation clause is understood to be part of the will. Every well-drafted will contains one. See Restatement (Third) of Property, § 3.1, cmt. q.

Self-Proving Affidavits. When a will is offered for probate at the testator's death, the proponent must find the witnesses so that they can lay a foundation for the will by testifying, either in a hearing or via affidavit, that the signatures on the will are indeed theirs. If significant time passes between will execution and testator's death, finding witnesses can be burdensome, even impossible, which can complicate or frustrate the task of probating the will. For this reason, many state statutes now authorize "self-proving affidavits." A self-proving affidavit is attached to the will and signed by the witnesses, the testator and a notary at the time of execution. The affidavit itself is sufficient to get the will admitted to probate, and often eliminates the need to find the witness to establish a foundation for the will at testator's death (unless, of course, there is a will contest).

It can be difficult to understand the difference between an attestation clause and a self-proving affidavit. When a witness signs an attestation clause she is expressing a present intent to act as a witness to the will. She  is attesting. When she signs the self-proving affidavit, she swears that she has already performed the act of witnessing and signing the will. In other words, the self-proving affidavit has the same function as any other type of affidavit—it is a substitute for witness testimony at a hearing or other legal proceeding. Examine the following example of a self-proving affidavit. How is it materially different from an attestation clause?

STATE OF ____________________

ss:

COUNTY OF ____________________

[Testator], [first witness] and [second witness], the testator and witnesses, respectively, whose names are signed to the attached instrument, being first duly sworn, do hereby declare to the undersigned authority that the Testator signed and executed the instrument as his Last Will and Testament, and that he signed willingly and that he executed it as a free and voluntary act for the purposes therein expressed; and that each witness states that she or he signed the Will as witnesses in the presence and hearing of the testator, and that to the best of her knowledge, the Testator was at the time 18 years of age or older, of sound mind, and under no constraint or undue influence.

/s/ ____________________

[Testator]

/s/ ____________________

[Witness]

/s/ ____________________

[Witness]

Subscribed, sworn to, and acknowledged before me, by [Testator], the Testator, and subscribed and sworn to before me by [Witness 1] and [Witness 2], witnesses, this __ day of ______, 2___.

/s/ ____________________

Notary

The Uniform Probate Code (and some other state statutes) allow the drafter to combine the attestation clause and the self-proving affidavit. These statutes provide form language that drafters may use to enable the testator and witnesses to simultaneously execute and self-prove a will. See UPC § 2–504.

D. THE EXECUTION CEREMONY

In thinking about will formalities, the competent estates lawyer must focus on three different, but related questions: first, what formalities should the law (and does the law) require for execution of wills; second, what procedure should a lawyer use in supervising an execution ceremony; third, what should a court do if a will does not fully comply with the required formalities? We have started with a focus on the legally required formalities. Should a lawyer be content to satisfy all statutory formalities? For instance, suppose you draft a will in a jurisdiction that has adopted the Uniform Probate Code. Should you permit the witnesses to witness the will out of the testator's presence?

The answer, of course, is no. Part of your job as testator's lawyer is to minimize future litigation over the will. In conducting an execution ceremony, you should not take short-cuts that might cast suspicion on the validity of the will you have drafted. To some extent, the precautions you take will depend on your common-sense estimate of the risk of future litigation. For example, if a 60–year old testator writes a will leaving all of her property, in equal shares, to her two children, you may have less need to conduct an extended execution ceremony that impresses on the witnesses testator's resolve and competence than if your client is a cranky 80–year old who has chosen to disinherit his children in favor of his new 50–year old flame.

In general, however, all execution ceremonies should include the following steps:

The will should be in final form, with pages numbered and securely fastened. It should contain an attestation clause and, if authorized by state statute, a self-proving affidavit.

There should be at least two witnesses present. Use three if there is a risk of a contest. The drafter often acts as one of the witnesses.

Ordinarily the witnesses are law office personnel. If the witnesses are strangers to the testator, gather everyone in a room, so the witnesses can form an opinion about the testator's capacity. Because it might later be necessary to obtain the witnesses' testimony to probate the will, the witnesses should be easy to find, locally available, and likely to survive the testator. People who take under the will should not be in the room during the ceremony, with the possible exception of the testator's spouse (when the devise to that spouse is traditional and expectable). If devisees are present, there is a risk of a claim of undue influence.

Once the ceremony begins, avoid interruptions and let no one leave the room. Testator, witnesses and attorney should be able to observe and hear each other. The attorney should ask the testator if it is her will and if she wants to sign it. When the attorney is sure the witnesses have heard the answer she should proceed to the signing. She should suggest the testator sign, and point out the place to sign, while getting the attention of the witnesses. The attorney should then ask the testator to declare to the witnesses that the instrument is her will and to request that the witnesses attest and subscribe the will. This is often done with leading questions: "Do you declare this to be your last will and testament and do you request that William Witness and Wilma Witness sign their names as witnesses to this attestation clause that speaks to the due execution of your will?" This also acquaints the witnesses with the attestation clause. The witnesses then sign their names and addresses. As they sign, the signature of the testator should be visible to them. See Restatement (Third) Property, § 3.1 (1999); Gerry W. Beyer, The Will Execution Ceremony–History, Significance and Strategies, 29 S. Tex. L. Rev. 413 (1988).

NOTE ON SAFEKEEPING

Safekeeping of the will is an interesting problem. The testator has an absolute right to her original will, and most clients leave the lawyer's office with the original will in hand. Having said that, most of the problems of revocation that we study are there only because the testator walked out of the lawyer's office holding the original of his will. Simply put, you cannot do something dumb to your will if you do not have it.

Most lawyers see the following as the main options for safekeeping: (1) give the will to the testator with stern injunctions about safekeeping and not making any changes without help from a lawyer; (2) give the will to the nominated executor if a bank is the nominee; (3) deposit the will in the local probate court if the rules of court allow it; or (4) leave the original with the lawyer/drafter.

There are problems with all of these solutions. As indicated, if the testator holds the will there is an increased chance of foolish revocations. If the testator puts the will in a safe deposit box, the box may be sealed at death under local law, thus delaying the probate, and even the discovery, of the will. Giving the will to a bank nominated as executor is a good idea. The problem is that most clients will not be nominating banks as executors. The will deposited in the local courthouse may be forgotten and create more problems than it solves. Leaving the will with the drafting lawyer is a good idea if the lawyer and the firm have a profoundly serious commitment to safekeeping the will and keeping track of their clients. Lawyers with an institutionalized trust and estates practice often make that commitment and their clients are well advised to leave the will with the lawyer and are well served when they do. If safekeeping is provided, there may be an implied moral commitment to represent the executor, even in the face of problems, and the survivors are led to someone the testator considered to be a competent lawyer.

Therein lies the problem. Do you see it? Historically, the juicy part of the trusts and estates practice is representing the executor when the testator dies. If the lawyer holds the original will, she has a good excuse to call the executor after the death and an opportunity to try to make a sale of legal services. This disturbed one court enough to forbid the practice. See State v. Gulbankian, 54 Wis.2d 605, 611, 196 N.W.2d 733, 736 (1972). However, everything that is good for lawyers is not necessarily bad for clients. In the right circumstances, leaving the will with the drafter is the best course of action. See Gerald P. Johnston, An Ethical Analysis of Common Estate Planning Practices—Is Good Business Bad Ethics? 45 Ohio St. L. J. 57, 124–33 (1984).

E. Salvage Doctrines: Substantial Compliance and the UPC's Dispensing Power

We have focused on what formalities legislatures should and do require, and on how lawyers should conduct execution ceremonies. What happens, however, when things don't go quite right—either because of lawyer error, or because the client never involved a lawyer in the process? That is the subject to which we now turn.

Estate of Hall

Supreme Court of Montana, 2002.
310 Mont. 486, 51 P.3d 1134.

■ Regnier, J.

Sandra Kay Ault appeals from the Findings of Fact, Conclusions of Law and Order of the Eighth Judicial District Court, Cascade County. We affirm.

The following issue is dispositive of this appeal:

Did the District Court err in admitting the Joint Will to formal probate?

BACKGROUND

James Mylen Hall ("Jim") died on October 23, 1998. At the time of his death, he was 75 years old and lived in Cascade County, Montana. His wife, Betty Lou Hall ("Betty"), and two daughters from a previous marriage, Sandra Kay Ault ("Sandra") and Charlotte Rae Hall ("Charlotte"), survived him.

Jim first executed a will on April 18, 1984 (the "Original Will"). Approximately thirteen years later, Jim and Betty's attorney, Ross Cannon, transmitted to them a draft of a joint will (the "Joint Will"). On June 4, 1997, Jim and Betty met at Cannon's office to discuss the draft. After making several changes, Jim and Betty apparently agreed on the terms of the Joint Will. Jim and Betty were prepared to execute the Joint Will once Cannon sent them a final version.

At the conclusion of the meeting, however, Jim asked Cannon if the draft could stand as a will until Cannon sent them a final version. Cannon said that it would be valid if Jim and Betty executed the draft and he notarized it. Betty testified that no one else was in the office at the time to serve as an attesting witness. Jim and Betty, therefore, proceeded to sign the Joint Will and Cannon notarized it without anyone else present.

When they returned home from the meeting, Jim apparently told Betty to tear up the Original Will, which Betty did. After Jim's death, Betty applied to informally probate the Joint Will. Sandra objected to the informal probate and requested formal probate of the Original Will.

On August 9, 2001, Judge McKittrick heard the will contest. He issued the Order admitting the Joint Will to probate on August 27, 2001. Sandra appealed.

* * *

DISCUSSION

Did the District Court err in admitting the Joint Will to formal probate?

In contested cases, the proponent of a will must establish that the testator duly executed the will. *See* § 72–3–310, MCA; *Brooks*, 279 Mont. at 519, 927 P.2d at 1026. For a will to be valid, two people typically must witness the testator signing the will and then sign the will themselves. *See* § 72–2–522(1)(c), MCA. If two individuals do not properly witness the document, § 72–2–523, MCA, provides that the document may still be treated as if it had been executed under certain circumstances. One such circumstance is if the proponent of the document establishes by clear and convincing evidence that the decedent intended the document to be the decedent's will. *See* § 72–2–523, MCA; *Brooks*, 279 Mont. at 522, 927 P.2d at 1027.

Sandra urges this Court not to use § 72–2–523, MCA, "to circumvent the statute requiring two witnesses to the execution of a will." Jim and Betty's failure to use witnesses, according to Sandra, was not an innocent omission on their part. She also expresses concern that the improperly witnessed Joint Will materially altered a long-standing agreement to divide the property. She primarily argues, however, that the Joint Will should be invalid as a matter of law because no one properly witnessed it.

Sandra's numerous arguments about why the will was improperly witnessed are irrelevant to this appeal. Neither party disputes that no witnesses were present at the execution of Jim and Betty's Joint Will as required by § 72–2–522, MCA. In the absence of attesting witnesses, § 72–2–523, MCA, affords a means of validating a will for which the Montana Legislature expressly provides. The only question before this Court, therefore, is whether the District Court erred in concluding that Jim intended the Joint Will to be his will under § 72–2–523, MCA. We conclude that the court did not err.

The District Court made several findings of fact that supported its conclusion. In particular, it noted that the Joint Will specifically revoked all previous wills and codicils made by either Jim or Betty. Furthermore, the court found that, after they had executed the Joint Will, Jim directed Betty to destroy the Original Will.

Sandra does not dispute any of the court's factual findings. She argues only that Betty testified that she and Jim had not executed the will even after they had signed it. In making this argument, she points to the following testimony:

Question: Do you know if [Jim] gave [Sandra and Charlotte] a copy of the new will?

Answer: I don't believe he did, no.

Question: Do you know why?

Answer: Well, I guess because we didn't have the completed draft without all the scribbles on it.

Question: So he thought that will was not good yet?

Answer: No, he was sure it was good, but he didn't give it to the girls. And we didn't give it to my son. We didn't give it to anybody.

Question: Why?

Answer: Because it wasn't completely finished the way Ross was going to finish it.

This testimony may suggest that Betty believed that the Joint Will was not in a final form because of "all the scribbles on it." Nevertheless, she immediately goes on to state that she believed the will was good. When asked if it were Jim's and her intent for the Joint Will to stand as a will until they executed another one, she responded, "Yes, it was." The court could reasonably interpret this testimony to mean that Jim and Betty expected the Joint Will to stand as a will until Cannon provided one in a cleaner, more final form. Sandra points to no other evidence that suggests that Jim did not intend for the Joint Will to be his will.

For these reasons, we conclude that the District Court did not err in admitting the Joint Will into final probate. Because Jim directed Betty to destroy the Original Will, we also conclude that the District Court did not err in finding that these acts were acts of revocation of the Original Will under § 72–2–527, MCA.

Affirmed.

QUESTIONS

1. Does the admission to probate of this unwitnessed will frustrate or further the objectives of the formalities statute? What evidence does the Hall court cite in affirming the trial court's finding that there was clear and convincing evidence to establish that Hall intended the joint document to operate as his will? Do you find the evidence compelling? Who probably provided the evidence that the testator ordered his wife to tear up his old will? Who testified about conversations that testator and his wife had in Cannon's office? Should it matter that the boilerplate in the unwitnessed joint will recited that the will revoked all prior wills?

2. If you represented the prevailing parties—the will proponents—in Estate of Hall, could you recover the cost of litigation from lawyer Cannon? What defense could Cannon offer in a malpractice action? Should it be enough for Cannon to argue that he couldn't have committed malpractice because the will was ultimately admitted to probate?

3. Suppose a lawyer challenging the will in the Hall case had argued that to probate the improperly witnessed will would encourage sloppy practice in other cases, and that the Halls' joint will should be denied probate to deter sloppy practice. If you represented proponents of the will, how would you respond to the argument?

NOTES

1. MCA § 72–2–523, on which the Hall court relied in admitting the joint will to probate, is modeled on Uniform Probate Code § 2–503, which provides:

> Although a document * * * was not executed in compliance with § 2–502 [enumerating the wills formalities], the document * * * is treated as if it had been executed in compliance with that section if the proponent of the document * * * establishes by clear and convincing evidence that the decedent intended the document to constitute (i) the decedent's will * * *

See also Restatement (Third) of Property § 3.3 (espousing a rule that excuses "harmless error" in will execution if the will's proponent provides clear and convincing evidence that the testator "adopted" the non-conforming document as her will).

2. In Will of Macool, 416 N.J.Super. 298, 3 A.3d 1258 (2010), Louise Macool's 2007 will left her entire estate to her husband, naming her husband's issue from his prior marriage as contingent beneficiaries in case Louise outlived her husband. A month after her husband's 2008 death, she asked her lawyer to change the will, and gave him a handwritten note with general instructions to treat two of her nieces "the same as the family Macool gets", but with other instructions that the house should be left to the family Macool. Her lawyer typed a version of a will, and labeled it "rough." An hour after leaving her lawyer's office, Louise Macool died without ever reading the will her lawyer had prepared. New Jersey had adopted a statute virtually identical to UPC § 2–503. Should the court have admitted the "rough" will to probate (assuming Louise's nieces offered the will for probate)?

The court refused to admit the will to probate, holding that the statute requires the proponent to "prove, by clear and convincing evidence, that (1) the decedent actually reviewed the document in question; and (2) thereafter gave his or her final assent to it."

3. UPC § 2–503 has been referred to as the "dispensing power," because it creates a judicial power to admit a document to probate even when the document lacks even the basic formalities required by UPC § 2–502. Professor John Langbein has championed the dispensing power as a mechanism for assuring that testator's wishes are given full effect, despite lapses by the lawyer, or by an uncounseled testator. His study of Australian cases convinces him that the dispensing power will eliminate many instances in which courts have frustrated testator intent by adhering rigidly to statutory formalities. John H. Langbein, Substantial Compliance with the Wills Act, 88 Harv. L. Rev. 489 (1975).

Professor Melanie Leslie is not convinced. In an article entitled The Myth of Testamentary Freedom, she argues that courts often invoke formalities selectively, to deny effect to wills when the court believes testator has unfairly deprived his close relatives of an inheritance. The article cites cases like Morris v. West as examples. The article argues that even if a legislature gives courts a dispensing power, they will not be eager to use the power in cases like Morris v. West. Moreover, in cases where the court is convinced that the imperfectly executed document should be probated, existing precedent leaves courts with considerable leeway to admit the document to probate. See generally Melanie B. Leslie, The Myth of Testamentary Freedom, 38 Ariz. L. Rev. 235 (1996). As some support for her position, see Stevens v. Casdorph, 203 W.Va. 450, 508 S.E.2d 610 (1998), where the West Virginia Supreme Court reversed a lower court's admission to probate of a will that disinherited testator's next of kin in favor of his friends. The wheel-chair bound testator executed his will in a bank, and the bank employee witnesses signed the will in their work area, just out of testator's sight. The dissent emphasized that in denying probate of the will the majority declined to follow a 1938 West Virginia case that adopted a "substantial compliance" test for will formalities.

Other scholars, too, have expressed concerns with the trend toward reforming will execution requirements. Professor Emily Sherwin has criticized UPC § 2–503, arguing that the statute might induce testators to be less careful about complying with formalities, and that it will increase litigation. See Emily Sherwin, Clear and Convincing Evidence of Testamentary Intent: The Search for a Compromise Between Formality and Adjudicative Justice, 34 Conn. L. Rev. 453 (2002). See also John V. Orth, Wills Act Formalities: How Much Compliance is Enough? 43 Real Prop. Tr. & Est. L. J. 73 (2008); Lloyd Bonfield, Reforming the Requirements for Due Execution of Wills: Some Guidance from the Past, 70 Tul. L. Rev. 1893 (1996); C. Douglas Miller, Will Formality, Judicial Formalism, and Legislative Reform: An Examination of the New Uniform Probate Code "Harmless Error" Rule and the Movement Toward Amorphism, 43 Florida L. Rev. 167 (1991).

What do you think? Suppose UPC § 2–503 had been enacted when Morris v. West arose. How do you think the court would have decided the case? How would you have argued the case for the proponent? The contestants?

4. **Substantial Compliance.** Although most states have not yet enacted a statute providing for a dispensing power, courts in many states have admitted non-conforming wills to probate by applying the judicially created "substantial compliance" doctrine. Under that doctrine, a court confronting a will that fails to comply strictly with the formalities statute should nonetheless admit the document if the document expresses testator's testamentary intent, and if its form sufficiently conforms to formalities so that the purposes of formalities statutes are served. As one court justified the doctrine:

> Compliance with statutory formalities is important not because of the inherent value that those formalities possess, but because of the purposes they serve. * * * It would be ironic to insist on literal compliance with statutory formalities when that insistence would invalidate a will that is the deliberate and voluntary act of the testator. Such a result would frustrate rather than further the purpose of the formalities. [citations omitted].

See In re Alleged Will of Ranney, 124 N.J. 1, 589 A.2d 1339 (1991) (decided before New Jersey's adoption of UPC section 2–503). In Ranney, the New Jersey Supreme Court held that a will could be admitted to probate even though the witnesses signed the attached self-proving affidavit, but not the will itself. See also, Estate of Fordonski, 678 N.W.2d 413 (Iowa 2004), Estate of Dellinger, 793 N.E.2d 1041 (Ind. 2003) (both admitting wills to probate on facts substantially identical to Ranney).

5. Should a court ever admit to probate a will that lacks the testator's original signature? Prior to the creation of UPC § 2–503, the answer was clearly "no." Although courts in states with a dispensing power or substantial compliance doctrine are still reluctant to admit wills to probate without

a testator's signature, Professor Ronald R. Volkmer illustrates how those doctrines have opened the door for arguments by disgruntled heirs that documents without a signature should be probated. See Ronald R. Volkmer, Formalities of Will Execution Sometimes Eased, 28 Est. Plan. 339 (July 2001).

Professor Volkmer's worst nightmare came to life in Estate of Denner, 2006 WL 510530 (N.J. Super. Ch. 2006). In Denner, testator died with one validly executed will in place. After the valid will was admitted to probate, plaintiff sought to admit three unexecuted documents: the first document was an unexecuted form will with handwritten entries and cross-outs, the second a handwritten list, neither signed nor dated, that the plaintiff alleged was written by testator, and the third an unexecuted will prepared by an attorney. The proponent of the properly executed will filed a motion to dismiss plaintiff's claim on the ground that New Jersey's equivalent of 2–503 did not authorize the court to admit a will that was completely unexecuted. The court rejected the motion, finding that whether any of the three wills were intended by testator to be his will was a question of fact to be determined at trial.

Nipping this type of litigation in the bud, the Colorado legislature enacted 2–503 with an additional requirement that the testator *must* have either signed the document or acknowledged it to be her will. See C.R.S.A. § 15–11–503.

PROBLEM

In 1989, Testator executed a valid will. The will devised Testator's assets to Safe Haven, a local charity. In 1992, Testator drafted a new will. The 1992 will devised Testator's house and the five acres on which it sat to Betsy and Robert Cunningham, Testator's neighbors, in exchange for the Cunninghams' promise to take care of Testator for the remainder of her life. The 1992 will devised the rest of Testator's property to New Hope, a charity that helps runaway children.

After signing the 1992 will, Testator telephoned a notary whom she knew well, and explained that she had just signed "a document" and wanted it notarized. The notary, who recognized Testator's voice, agreed to notarize it, and Testator sent Betsy Cunningham to the notary's place of business with the last page of the will. The notary recognized Testator's signature and notarized the page. Cunningham returned the document to Testator that same day.

Fifteen days later, Testator called Erma Kram, a neighbor and close friend, and asked Kram to witness her will. Kram agreed, and Betsy Cunningham brought the will to Kram's house, where Kram signed the will. Testator was not present. Oscar Smith, another neighbor who knew Testator, was visiting Kram at the time. Smith also signed the will as a witness, although he never spoke to Testator about the will at any time.

Testator has died. Safe Haven has presented the 1989 will for probate. The Cunninghams and New Hope have offered the 1992 will for probate. If the 1992 will is valid, it revokes the 1989 will. If New Jersey law is in effect, what arguments might the proponents of the 1992 will make? How might Safe Haven rebut those arguments? In your opinion, who has the better argument? Would your opinion change if UPC § 2–502 & 2–503 governed? See In re Estate of Kirkeby, 157 Or.App. 309, 970 P.2d 241 (1998).

F. HOLOGRAPHIC WILLS

Very simply put, a holographic will is an unwitnessed will, handwritten and signed by the testator. Holographic wills are recognized in about half the states. We recognize them for a variety of reasons including: a populist distrust of formalism; a historical memory of country life and the frontier, where a dying testator might not be able to find two disinterested witnesses; and a desire to carry out the wishes of the ordinary citizen who has chosen not to hire a lawyer and to leave such a will.

Holographs create as many problems as they solve. The issues they raise can include: whether a testator intended an informal writing to serve as a final expression of testamentary intent; disconnected handwritten pages can be integrated into a single holographic will, or into a valid attested will; claims of forgery; and belated discovery and disclosure of holographic wills after a decedent's affairs have seemingly been settled. Although statutes that allow holographic wills have generated significant amounts of litigation, Professor Stephen Clowney argues that the problems with holographic wills have been exaggerated. Professor Clowney conducted an empirical study of holographic wills in Allegheny County, Pennsylvania, and reached the following conclusions:

> First and foremost, holographs offer testators an inexpensive alternative to state intestacy statutes. Second, holographs grant all willmakers a cost-effective way to make small changes to their larger estate plans. Third, the absence of time-consuming procedural requirements allows anyone caught in a life-or-death situation to author a valid final testament. Finally, holographic wills deserve a second look because, as illustrated by this study, they rarely are contested in courtroom proceedings; in the overwhelming majority of cases, homemade testaments distribute a decedent's property without fuss or objections.

Stephen Clowney, In Their Own Hand: An Analysis of Holographic Wills and Homemade Willmaking, 43 Real Prop. Tr. & Est. L. J. 27, 52–53 (2008).

What suffices to qualify as a valid holographic will? Consider the following case:

Zhao v. Wong

California Court of Appeal, Sixth District, 1995.
40 Cal.App.4th 1198, 47 Cal.Rptr.2d 707.

■ WUNDERLICH, J.

* * *

Tai–Kin Wong (Tai) was a successful 44–year–old businessman who until just before death had a history of good health. He was living with his girlfriend Xi Zhao (Xi), and he enjoyed a close and loving relationship with his large family. On New Year's Eve in 1992, he took ill and died in a hospital emergency room of unexplained causes. Sometime after his death, found in his office was a sealed envelope, decorated with stickers and containing a handwritten note which read "All Tai–Kin Wong's Xi Zhao, my best half TKW 12–31–92." This document—containing no subject, no verb, no description of property, and no indication of its subject matter or purpose—was found by the trial court to be a holographic will, passing Tai's entire estate to Xi.

FACTS AND PROCEDURAL HISTORY

* * * [Tai] had never married and he had no children. For the previous three years, he and Xi had lived together in Saratoga. Tai and Xi had met in 1987 at a scientific conference. They fell in love and began to live together in 1989 after Xi received her doctorate in cell biology. They lived together until the time of Tai's death on New Year's Eve.

* * * Whether their love relationship was flourishing or floundering was disputed at trial. Though supposedly lovers, on the day of Tai's death, New Year's Eve, they had arranged to dine separately—Tai with his close friend, Dr. Jianmin Liu and [Dr. Liu's] girlfriend, and Xi with a man she describes as then a casual social acquaintance, Brien Wilson, a local attorney [Whom she later married.].

The evidence Xi introduced tended to show that she was close to Tai's family, indeed, practically accepted as a member of it. After Mr. Wong [Tai's father] came home from the hospital following a stroke, Tai and Xi took care of him four nights a week, Monday through Thursday. Mr. Wong viewed Xi as his son's companion, and presented her with gifts of money, traditionally given only to family members in Chinese families.

When Tai died on December 31, 1992, it was in the throes of an illness which was similar in its symptoms to sicknesses that had afflicted him two or three times earlier that month.

* * * During the day on New Year's Eve, Tai was working at his office in Fremont. He had business meetings that afternoon until about 4:30, which Xi and others attended. Although not 100 percent healthy, he appeared to be well and to be functioning well. * * * At 7 p.m. Dr. Liu received a call from Tai saying that he was feeling very ill. Dr. Liu's girlfriend advised [Tai] to call "911" which Tai did. His friends agreed to come to the Fremont office from Berkeley. When they reached the office the ambulance had already taken Tai to the hospital. The ambulance attendants found Tai conscious upon their arrival at the office building, but he lost consciousness in the ambulance, never regained it, and died at the hospital before midnight.

By the time Dr. Liu and his girlfriend Jennifer Zhang arrived at the hospital, Tai was in a coma. * * * Meanwhile, Xi was having dinner with

Brien Wilson at a fancy French restaurant in Los Gatos. She had concealed from Tai the fact that she was dining on New Year's Eve with Brien Wilson, a man she moved in with two and one-half months after Tai's death. After dinner, she returned to the Saratoga house, and shortly after her arrival she received a call from Dr. Liu informing her that Tai was in the hospital. (Dr. Liu testified he never did reach Xi on the telephone. Rather, she called him at the hospital after Tai's death.) According to Xi, when she arrived at the hospital, close to midnight, Tai was already dead. While Tai had some symptoms similar to those that characterized his illness 10 days earlier, the cause of death was mysterious and has never been determined.

The questioned document or purported will was discovered in the following way: Xi made no effort to find a will at the residence she shared with Tai. Instead, on January 18, 1993, two weeks after Tai's funeral, Xi, Roy Tottingham (then a business consultant to TTI and now vice-president), Dr. Gin Wu (a TTI employee) and Heston Chau (an old friend of Tai's) searched Tai's office. Xi had asked Danny Wong to help go through Tai's papers, but he refused to do it. These four people, then, including Xi, divided the papers into business documents and personal papers and placed them in separate boxes.

During this search they found a sealed envelope in one of Tai's desk drawers, but Xi could not remember which one nor who saw it first. The upper left hand corner contained Tai's address label, the center of the envelope bore two stickers: a rainbow with the words "You're Special," and a rainbow with the words "Love You." This sealed envelope was placed in the box of Tai's personal papers which itself was sealed. Later the sealed box was placed in Xi's office where it remained unopened.

Dr. Victor Vurpillat, (the co-chief executive officer of TTI when Tai was alive), opened the box in Xi's office sometime later. The only item he removed from the box was the envelope with the stickers. Vurpillat took the envelope and the following day he and Roy Tottingham met with TTI's attorney, together with a probate attorney, John Willoughby, who opened the envelope.

After Tai's death, Xi and Tottingham and Vurpillat incorporated a new company called Transcell Therapeutic Infusion, Incorporated. (TTI, Inc.) Obviously the initials are the same as for Transgenic Technologies, Inc. The new business involves intracellular therapy. * * * Xi claims to have invented the technology used in TTI, Inc. but could not recall when. She was also certain that TTI, Inc.'s processes did not require the use of any TTI or Baekon technology.

Xi filed a petition for probate of the purported will. Xi was first appointed personal representative and Tottingham was appointed special administrator for the purpose of handling Tai's real estate and voting his shares of stock. Mr. Wong, from whom the family had kept word of Tai's death for some six weeks because of Mr. Wong's poor health, filed the will contest on May 14, 1993.

CONTENTIONS OF PARTIES

Appellants contend: the document admitted to probate is not a valid will, because as a matter of law, the words in the document cannot constitute a will and because there is not sufficient evidence of testamentary intent. * * *

DISCUSSION

The document the trial court found to be a will reads as follows: "All Tai Kin Wong's Xi Zhao, my best half." Beneath are the initials "TKW" and the date "12–31–92." The document is completely handwritten. * * *

A holographic will is one entirely in the writing of the testator. The requirements are that it be signed, dated, and that it evidence testamentary intent. [The court is wrong—See Prob. Code 6111.] The trial court resolved the issue of whether the will was in the writing of the testator in favor of proponent Xi. * * * Regarding the third requirement, Witkin says "[I]t must appear that decedent intended to make a testamentary disposition by that particular paper, and if this cannot be shown it is immaterial that his testamentary intentions were [or would have been] in conformity with it." * * *

No particular words are required to create a will. "Thus, a letter or other informal document will be sufficient if it discloses the necessary testamentary intent, i.e., if it appears that the decedent intended to direct the final disposition of his property after his death. The surrounding circumstances may be considered in reaching a conclusion on this issue." * * *

In Estate of Spitzer (1925) 196 Cal. 301, 306 [237 P. 739], the testator was ill. He wrote his brother regarding the property he wanted to go to his wife and daughter. The extrinsic circumstances indicating the letter was meant to be a will were that he told both his brother and his neighbor that he was making a will and sending it to his brother. * * *

In Estate of Button (1930) 209 Cal. 325, 330 [287 P. 964], decedent wrote a long letter to her ex-husband, immediately before she committed suicide. The document was found in the same room in which she was found. In it she said "I'd like to be cremated. You can have the house on 26th ave. and all things of value so you won't be out any money on burying me.' " While the letter went on for many pages and covered many subjects including how ex-husband should care for the parties' son, still the court found these few words at the end of the letter to be a valid holographic will. * * *

Perhaps one of the most extreme examples of a court's finding a document to be a holographic will is Estate of Smilie (1950) 99 Cal. App. 2d 794 [222 P.2d 692]. The decedent, long having quarreled with his wife and stepdaughter, wrote a somewhat illiterate letter to his close friend Max describing a recent altercation and stating he didn't want the stepdaughter to get anything. Smilie wrote: " 'I want you to see that all my bills are paid and that Dot does not get thing. I want you to have all of my after my bill are.' " * * * Observing the principle that one cannot supply words into a will in order to make it have testamentary intent, but that striking certain words as surplusage is permissible, the court found a valid holographic will. The sentence was changed to read " 'I want you to have all.' " * * *

Finally, we discuss a case which in some ways is most on point. In Estate of Blain (1956) 140 Cal. App. 2d 917 [295 P.2d 898], the decedent, Frank Blain, executed a holographic will and put it in his safety deposit box. The will failed to mention his only heir, Sonia Lambert, and nothing in the will indicated that the omission was intentional. Thus, she was presumptively entitled to inherit the entire estate as a pretermitted heir. However, one of the devisees under the holographic will contended that a piece of paper, wrapped around a dinner ring in the safety deposit box, containing the words " 'to Sonia Lambert Frank Blain,' " was an integral part of the will. If so, provision was made for the natural object of Blain's bounty (Sonia), so that the remainder of the holographic will giving all of his property to others would have been valid. * * * The trial court thus grappled with the issue of whether the paper containing the five words including the signature could constitute a document that was testamentary in character, and whether it could be integrated into the seven-page holograph. The trial court found the document was not testamentary in character, it contained no testamentary disposition and exhibited no testamentary intent. * * * Reviewing the sufficiency of the evidence, the appellate court agreed. It pointed out that the document contained no description or specification of any property, and that a holographic will must be complete in itself. * * * In other words, the document must contain some indication that it is intended to convey something upon death, or it is not a will. Testamentary intent may be found when the decedent uses words indicating a transfer of specified property upon the death of the testator. * * * But when the document itself does not express an intention to convey property upon death, it does not exhibit the intent necessary for a will. * * * Evidence before the court indicated Sonia's grandmother had left Sonia the ring and Blain was only holding it for her. Such extrinsic evidence as there was, then, tended to show the ring already belonged to Sonia, and Frank Blain's writing only indicated that it was hers, not that he was giving it to her. (Ibid.) Thus, Frank Blain's attempt to disinherit his only heir was unsuccessful. Because he did not specifically disinherit her in the holographic will, the will was invalid and she took the entire estate. * * *

In most of the cases just discussed, we find descriptions of property and words expressing donative intent. In the cases in which it is a little bit doubtful whether the proffered document is a will, we often have the express statement of the decedent, made shortly before death, that decedent has written his or her will and provided for decedent's loved ones in a certain letter or in a certain document. Clearly such direct extrinsic evidence is extremely probative on the question of whether a document is a will. In the instant case, we have no such helpful extrinsic evidence.

Appellants contend the document admitted to probate cannot, as a matter of law, constitute a will. We agree.

We consider this document which is offered as a holograph to be unique. The document consists of eight handwritten words—five of them constituting two proper names and three of them constituting an appellation, one arrow, a date and initials at the bottom. This series of words contains no recognizable subject, no verb and no object. * * * We conclude that it simply does not contain words sufficient to constitute a valid will.

No particular words are required to create a will. * * * But every will must contain operative words legally sufficient to create a devise of property. * * * In this case, the words are either absent or are so ambiguous in meaning that it is impossible to tell what, if anything, is meant to be given, much less that it is intended to be a transfer of property upon death.

First, no words describe the property allegedly meant to be bequeathed, or even that it is property which is the subject of the note. In attempting to determine the meaning of this first phrase the question is, all of Tai–Kin Wong's what? The trial court found that the absence of a "what" meant all of Tai's property but there is nothing in the document that supports that speculation.

Nor does the document contain any donative words—not "give," "bequeath," "will," or even "want Xi Zhao to have." Instead of a word that indicates a gift or transfer of some sort, Xi contends that the arrow is meant to transfer Tai's entire estate to her upon his death. However, an arrow is not a word at all. It is a symbol with no fixed meaning, either in the general community or as used by the decedent himself. As such, it does not have one meaning which allows it to be used in place of a word, nor can it be used to supply any meaning to the words around it.

Appellants did not find, nor have we, a single case in which a symbol has been used in place of words indicating donative intent in a will. In fact, we have not found a case in which a symbol of no fixed meaning has been used in any material clause of a will. The Probate Code itself assumes that words will be used to create a will. * * * The entire purpose of a will is to express the decedent's wishes for disposition of his or her property after death. If there are insufficient words in the document to do that, or if there are no words at all but ambiguous symbols, the decedent has failed in his or her purpose even if decedent did intend to write a will. The document in this case falls into that category; it simply does not contain operative words legally sufficient to accomplish a transfer of property upon death. Because this first issue is dispositive, we need not address appellants' other assignments of error.

DISPOSITION

Because the questioned document cannot constitute a will as a matter of law, the judgment is reversed and the trial court is directed to enter judgment in appellants' favor. * * *

A petition for a rehearing was denied January 8, 1996, and the opinion was modified to read as printed above. Respondent's petition for review by the Supreme Court was denied February 22, 1996.

APPENDIX

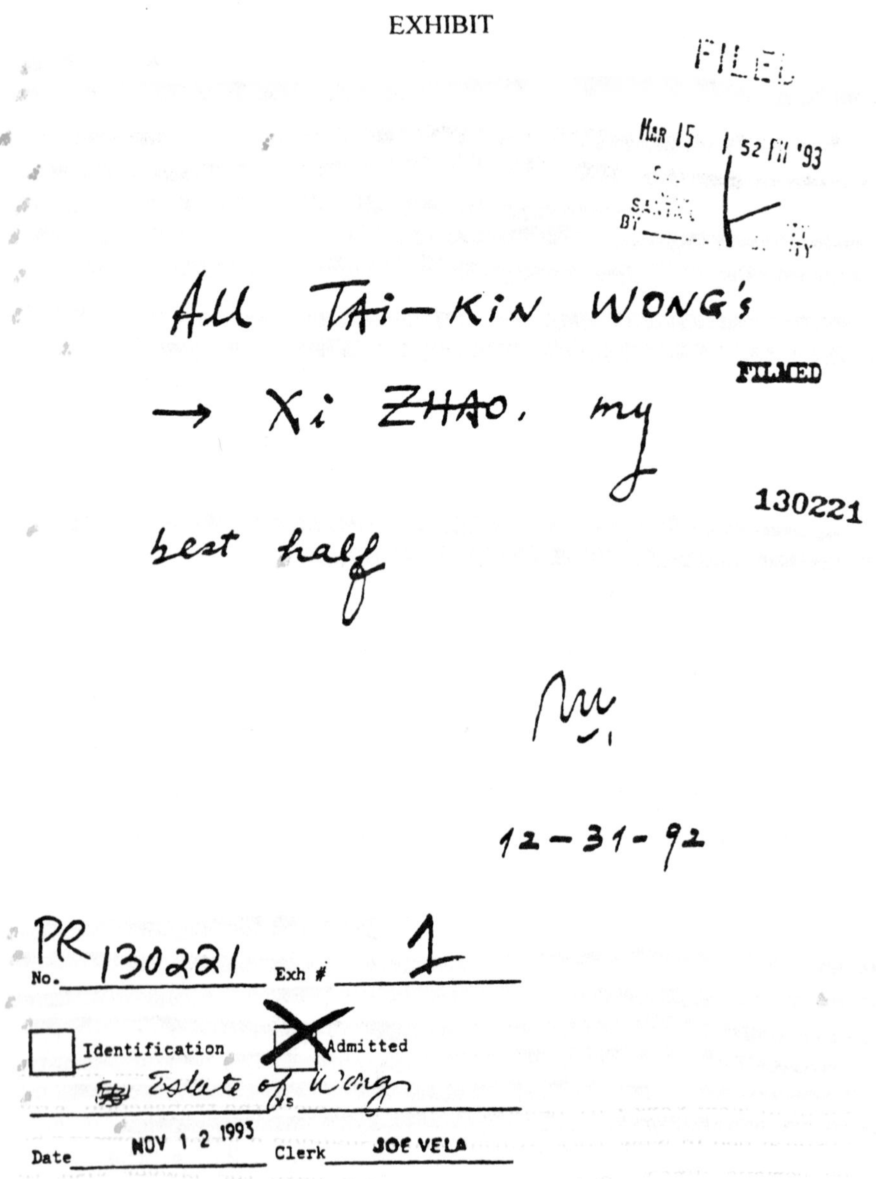

EXHIBIT

FILED

MAR 15 1 52 PM '93

All TAI-KIN WONG's → Xi ZHAO, my best half

FILMED

130221

12-31-92

PR 130221 No. Exh # 1

Identification Admitted

Estate of Wong vs

Date NOV 1 2 1993 Clerk JOE VELA

QUESTIONS

1. In a related case Xi unsuccessfully sued the decedent's brother for slander. See Zhao v. Wong, 48 Cal.App.4th 1114, 55 Cal.Rptr.2d 909 (1996).

In a newspaper interview, decedent's brother claimed that decedent had been murdered through the use of a biological agent, and that Xi had the opportunity, capability and skill to commit the crime. According to decedent's brother, Xi also had a motive; prior to his death, Wong held potentially valuable patents for creating genetically engineered animals.

As a result of the court's decision, how was Tai–Kin Wong's property distributed? Again we ask, do you think this played a role in the outcome of the case? Do you think the court would have come out the way it did if decedent and Xi were married and there were no accusations of misconduct?

2. Did your Property teacher use an arrow to show a transfer of Blackacre from O to A? On the assumption she did, what use of that fact could you make on appeal if you represented Xi? Does the date of the "will" help you in your argument? Do the stickers hurt your argument? Does this "will" have a signature? What obligation did Tai have towards Xi in your mind? What do you make of the fact that Tai and Xi each owned half of the first TTI company, when Tai's half seemingly constituted the bulk of Tai's wealth? What if the "will" had been in Tai's safe deposit box at the bank and found with numerous legal papers? What if, in addition, Tai had told his family he left his estate to Xi? Professor Helmholz, in writing of times long past, tells us that judges "looked at the history of the document and the nature of its contents. If the document had been carefully preserved by the testator, and if its provisions matched his natural and moral obligations towards his family, for instance, then proof . . . was more easily admitted than if circumstances were otherwise." Richard H. Helmholz, The Origin of Holographic Wills in English Law, 15 Legal History 97 (1994). Are things that different today?

3. Does the date of the will suggest to you that holographic wills serve a valid purpose, even in our overlawyered society? Explain.

PROBLEM

Famous television journalist Charles Kuralt maintained a thirty-year relationship with Patricia Shannon—a relationship that he kept secret from his wife and adult children. Twelve years before his death, Kuralt purchased 110 acres of Montana wilderness. Shannon lived on the Montana property, and Kuralt frequently visited her there. In 1997, Kuralt gave Shannon 20 acres of the Montana property. Shannon testified that Kuralt intended to transfer the remaining 90 acres to her later that year, but that he fell ill in New York City before he could complete the transaction. From his hospital bed in New York, Kuralt wrote Shannon a letter informing her of his serious illness, and stating that "I'll have the lawyer visit the hospital to be sure you inherit the rest of the place in MT. if it comes to that." Kuralt died shortly after, without having requested the services of an attorney. Shannon sought to probate the letter as a holographic codicil.

If you were the judge, would you admit the letter to probate? Why or why not? What do you make of the use of the future tense in the language the decedent chose? How is the timing of this "will" different from the timing of Tai's will? Does that suggest that we should have a different attitude towards this "will"?

In the first of four separate opinions dealing with the Kuralt estate, the Montana Supreme Court concluded that summary judgment was inappropriate:

> "[W]e conclude that the extrinsic evidence raises a genuine issue of material fact as to whether Mr. Kuralt intended to gift, rather than sell, the remaining 90 acres of his Madison County property to Shannon. The plain language of the letter of June 18, 1997, indicates, as Shannon points out, that Mr. Kuralt desired that Shannon "inherit" all of his property along the Big Hole River. While other language in the letter—"I'll have the lawyer visit the hospital ... if it comes to that"—might suggest, as the Estate argues and as the District Court concluded, that Mr. Kuralt was contemplating a separate testamentary instrument not yet in existence, it is far from certain that that is the result Mr. Kuralt intended by the letter.
>
> At the very least, when reading the language of Mr. Kuralt's letter in light of the extrinsic evidence showing the couple's future plans to consummate the transfer of the remaining 90 acres vis-a-vis a mock "sale," there arises a question of material fact as to whether Mr. Kuralt intended, given his state of serious illness, that the very letter of June 18, 1997, effect a posthumous disposition of his 90 acres in Madison County.

See Estate of Kuralt, 294 Mont. 354, 981 P.2d 771 (1999). Subsequently, the court upheld a trial court finding that the letter constituted a valid holographic codicil. 303 Mont. 335, 15 P.3d 931 (2000).

Litigation over Kuralt's estate did not end with the Montana Supreme Court's 2000 opinion. The Court's decision that the letter was a valid codicil led to another dispute over whether Shannon or the residuary beneficiaries under Kuralt's original will had to pay the estate taxes generated by the devise of Montana property to Shannon. In 2003, the Montana Supreme Court held that the residuary legatees should pay the taxes.

NOTES

The doctrine of holographic wills gives rise to many doctrinal disputes. One issue is whether a will is valid if the testator affixed her signature somewhere other than at the document's end. Some states require the signature to be at the end of the document, but the majority does not. The UPC allows the testator to sign the will anywhere, which is the better approach.

Another significant issue concerns how much of the purported will is required to be in the testator's handwriting. In some states a holographic will must be entirely in the handwriting of the testator, which gives rise to such issues as whether a will written entirely in the hand of the testator, but written on stationery with a printed letterhead, is entirely in the testator's handwriting. Other states require that a will's "material provisions" be in the testator's handwriting. This rule has spawned litigation over form wills, which contain printed boilerplate and blank spaces that testators fill in by hand. Some, but not all, courts have denied probate to such wills, construing the "material provisions" rule to require that all testamentary language, such as "I bequeath" or "I devise" be in the testator's hand. The modern approach, taken by the UPC, requires only that "material portions" of a holographic will be in testator's handwriting. The comments to section 2–502 suggest that the presence of printed boilerplate is inadequate to invalidate a will, and that a court should consider extrinsic evidence to determine whether the Appellants did not find intent.

Los Angeles Times April 6, 1999

April 6, 1999, Tuesday, Home Edition

SECTION: Calendar; Part F; Page 2; Entertainment Desk

Sharing His Inheritance: *Charles Bronson has settled a dispute with the sister of a Kentucky woman who left him all of her assets in a handwritten will. Audrey Jean Knauer, a fan of Bronson's whom he had never met, left him nearly $292,000 in a 1996 will scribbled atop a grocery list. Knauer, who died in 1997 at age 55, specified the money should go to the Louisville Free Public Library if Bronson didn't want it. Library director Craig Buthod said the dispute was settled out of court, with Bronson agreeing to pay Nancy Koeper, who had protested the will, an undisclosed sum of money. Koeper said in her suit that her sister was mentally ill and obsessed with Bronson. The library will apparently get nothing in the deal, but Bronson's spokeswoman has previously said he would donate whatever he receives to charity.*

G. STATUTORY WILLS

A few states have enacted so-called "statutory wills." Typically, these statutes contain a hopefully well-drafted, simple will that can be used by testators who do not want to hire a lawyer and by lawyers who want to efficiently offer a simple will. See California Probate Code §§ 6200 et seq. The form can be promulgated by the bar association for a modest fee, and commercial publishers can sell the form. See Gerry W. Beyer, Statutory Will Methodologies—Incorporated Forms vs. Fill–In the Forms; Rivalry or Peaceful Coexistence?, 94 Dick.L.Rev. 231 (1990); Restatement (Third) of Property § 3.1, reporter's note 15.

Any number of commercial publishers sell will kits designed to cater to the population of people who want to do a will without the intervention of a lawyer. And, several software publishers sell computer software designed to do the same thing. Of course, lawyers use software, too.

PROBLEMS

1. Frugal Frank, a would be testator, bought a California Statutory Will form from the bar association for $2.00 and went through an execution ceremony that satisfied the local wills act, but that breached, in a highly technical and seemingly unimportant manner, the unique set of formalities established for the statutory will. Frank dies and his Statutory "will" is offered for probate. It is opposed by his heirs. You represent Frank's nominated executor. What arguments will you make? Do you believe the will should be probated? Explain.

2. You clerk for Judge Decent. In a case of first impression, the judge is asked to construe a will drafted with "Lawyer–Free," the most popular will drafting software on the market. The language chosen by the software publisher to do a standard type of trust for minor children is flawed. Taken literally, the language will impose an unfortunate result on the minor children of the testator. The language could be pressed by the Judge into meaning something fairly sensible, although it's a reach when you read the words. How would you advise your judge and why?

H. ELECTRONIC WILLS?

Since 2001, Nevada has authorized electronic wills that contain an electronic signature of the testator and "at least one authentication characteristic of the testator." Nev. Rev.Stat. § 133.085. "Authentication characteristic" is defined to include "a fingerprint, a retinal scan, voice recognition, facial recognition, a digitized signature or other authentication using a unique characteristic of the person." *Id.* § 133.085(6). Why would a lawyer use an electronic will rather than a traditional one? Should other states follow Nevada's lead? See Gerry W. Beyer & Claire G. Hargrove, Digital Wills: Has the Time Come for Wills to Join the Digital Revolution? 33 Ohio N. U. L. Rev. 865 (2007); Joseph Karl Grant, Shattering and Moving Beyond the Gutenberg Paradigm: The Dawn of the Electronic Will, 42 U. Mich. J. L Reform 105 (2008).

SECTION II. WHAT CONSTITUTES THE WILL?

A. INTRODUCTION

Suppose John Smith executes the following document:

* * * * * * * * * * * * * * * * * * *

Will of John Smith

I hereby direct that all of my property be distributed as specified in a memorandum I shall prepare and leave in my bedside table.

I hereby sign this will on January 2, 2007.

John Smith

Witnessed :

Richard Roe

Jane Doe

* * * * * * * * * * * * * * * * * * *

Suppose further that at testator's death, two years later, a typed, unsigned, undated memorandum is found in testator's bedside table, listing various items of property and various recipients. The most valuable assets on the list are designated for Smith's housekeeper. How should testator's estate be distributed?

Note the problems. If we distribute John Smith's estate in accordance with the memorandum in his bedside table, we are permitting Smith to change his will without any testamentary formalities. How do we know the memorandum in his bedside table was actually prepared by Smith? Even if it was prepared by Smith, how do we know that Smith did not prepare a later memorandum that someone else removed from the bedside table? How do we know that the memorandum was not the reflection of an offhand thought rather than his considered wishes? How do we know Smith was of sound mind when he prepared the memorandum?

Because of these problems, most courts would probably distribute Smith's estate by intestate succession, assuming, of course, Smith had no other valid will.

Does this mean that all documents that have an effect on distribution of testator's estate must be accompanied by testamentary formalities? The answer is no. First of all, what counts as a single document? If testator's will consists of four pages, and only the fourth page includes the signature of testator and witnesses, are the first three pages ineffective to pass property because not executed in accordance with the requisite formalities? Of course not. The doctrine of *integration* permits us to treat the four pages as a single "integrated" will.

Second, suppose testator leaves a one-page will in which she leaves her entire estate "to the beneficiaries named in the trust instrument executed by my father on June 1, 1980". So long as the trust instrument is in existence at the time testator executes her will, many of the dangers present in the John Smith will disappear. The doctrine of *incorporation by reference* permits a court to give effect to a will which disposes of property in accordance with an unattested document, so long as the document was in existence at the time the will was executed, and so long as the document is sufficiently identified in the will.

Finally, suppose testator, as in the John Smith will example, makes reference to events which might occur *after* testator executes his will. How can a court escape the argument that to give effect to such events would permit a change in testamentary dispositions without testamentary formalities? Note that a testator's will, read in isolation, often provides an incomplete disposition of testator's estate. Suppose, for instance, testator's will leaves "all of my tangible personal property to my children, in equal shares." After testator executes the will, two significant events occur: (1) she buys a $20,000 oriental rug; and (2) she has another child. Each of these events will change the disposition of testator's estate, even though no new testamentary formalities have taken place. We would nevertheless give effect to testator's will provisions, taking into account the changes that have occurred after execution of the will. Should the result be different if testator's will leaves specified property "to the persons who are, at the time of my death, on the payroll of the ABC Company" (owned by testator)? The doctrine of *facts of independent significance* permits a court to give effect to events which would change the disposition of testator's estate after execution of testator's will—so long as those events have significance apart from a change in testator's dispositive scheme. Thus, the devise to persons on the payroll of ABC Company would qualify (the payroll list has independent significance—significance apart from testator's testamentary scheme), but John Smith's bedside table memorandum would not.

The materials that follow explore these doctrines—together with some significant statutory reforms.

B. Integration and Incorporation by Reference

Very few wills consist of a single page. When one page has been signed and witnessed, how can we be sure that other pages attached to that page constitute part of the same will? If the lawyer assures that all pages are consecutively numbered, initialed by the testator, and securely affixed, courts will generally have little difficulty treating the pages, taken together, as a single, integrated will. Sometimes, however, a lawyer does not supervise the ceremony, or the pages are not prepared at the same time. Problems then arise. Consider the following case:

Estate of Norton

Supreme Court of North Carolina, 1991.
330 N.C. 378, 410 S.E.2d 484.

■ Meyer, J.

This litigation arises out of an effort by propounder Teab Norton to have a paper writing probated in solemn form as the last will and testament of his father, Lawrence Norton, who died on 15 January 1987. The writing sought to be probated is a document consisting of a legal cover sheet and eight sheets of paper. The first page of the document following the legal cover is entitled "Last Will and Testament of Lawrence Norton." Its first paragraph provides:

> I, Lawrence Norton, of Scotland County, North Carolina, do hereby revoke all wills and codicils heretofore made by me, and do hereby make, publish, and declare this my last will and testament in manner and form as follows.

The successive paragraphs, among other things, direct the payment of testator's debts, make certain monetary bequests, and devise specified real properties. The dispositions conclude at the bottom of the sixth page, in mid-sentence of a metes and bounds description of a real property devise. These first six pages are stapled to the flap of the legal cover sheet. The pages do not bear the signatures of any witnesses or a notary public, nor does a date appear, but in the lower right-hand side of each of the six pages is the signature of the testator.

The seventh page of the document is entitled "CODICIL TO LAST WILL AND TESTAMENT OF LAWRENCE NORTON." It states:

> I, Lawrence Norton, of Scotland County, North Carolina, do hereby will, devise, and bequeath to my son, Alton Norton, the following tract of land with the stipulation that it is not to be sold for a period of ten (10) years....

After the metes and bounds description of the property comes the following language:

> IN TESTIMONY WHEREOF, I, the said Lawrence Norton, have signed this typewritten page and the following Certificate of Self–Proven Codicil to my Will which together constitutes this Codicil to my Last Will and Testament and do hereunto set my hand and seal this 17th day of September, 1984.

Beneath this paragraph, Mr. Norton's mark and the signatures of two witnesses appear. Self-proving language, the signatures of a notary and two witnesses, and Mr. Norton's mark are found on the final page. These last two pages are stapled together, and the second page is stapled to the cover sheet, thereby adhering the codicil to the six aforementioned pages. The envelope containing these pages has printed on it "WILL" and then the typewritten words "OF LAWRENCE NORTON AND CODICIL TO WILL OF LAWRENCE NORTON."

Propounder's evidence tended to show the following. On 17 September 1984, decedent had Ms. Blanche Blackwelder, now deceased, type the two-page document entitled "CODICIL TO THE LAST WILL AND TESTAMENT OF LAWRENCE NORTON." That same day, Ms. Blackwelder and a co-worker witnessed the notary public guiding the decedent's hand to make his mark on the document. Decedent had suffered a stroke and needed assistance.

Dorinda Wells, decedent's granddaughter, testified that in September 1984 she had accompanied decedent to Ms. Blackwelder's "to have something typed up requesting that Alton Norton would receive the pond." Decedent later asked Ms. Wells to "staple the ones that he received from

Ms. Blanch[e] [Blackwelder] to the copy of his will" and said that "they had to be attached to the will if they were to be any good." Ms. Wells complied with the request and testified that the document at issue here was the same as the one she stapled together under decedent's direction.

Shirley Stone, former legal secretary for Walter Cashwell, a Laurinburg attorney, testified on deposition that she knew decedent as a regular client of Mr. Cashwell and had seen and notarized decedent's signature on a number of occasions. In particular, she testified that she had typed the aforementioned "LAST WILL AND TESTAMENT OF LAWRENCE NORTON," that the six pages now in existence were the same ones she had typed, and that the signature at the bottom of each of the six pages was that of decedent. Further, Ms. Stone testified that she had prepared a number of different wills for the deceased but that she did not remember when she had prepared the other wills relative to the six-page document at issue here.

C. Whitfield Gibson, the Clerk of Court of Scotland County, testified that soon after decedent's death he inventoried decedent's safe-deposit box at First Union Bank in Gibson, North Carolina. Therein was a brown envelope with no writing on it, inside of which was a white envelope designated "WILL OF LAWRENCE NORTON AND CODICIL TO THE WILL OF LAWRENCE NORTON" that contained the eight-page document propounded as decedent's last will and testament. Clerk Gibson also found another writing within the brown envelope, a two-page document in a white legal cover designated "CODICIL TO WILL OF LAWRENCE NORTON." This document was properly executed 14 February 1975 and begins in midsentence. No reference to a specific will or other paper writing is made in the document.

Ms. Vashti Freeman, formerly with the Gibson Branch of the First Union Bank, testified that decedent had rented a safe-deposit box there and further testified as to the bank's procedures regarding access to safe-deposit boxes. . . .

At the close of propounder's evidence, respondents moved for a directed verdict. This motion was denied. Respondents informed the trial court that they were not offering evidence and renewed their motion for a directed verdict. Propounder also moved for a directed verdict. Both motions were denied. The trial court submitted the following issues to the jury:

> Issue #1: Was the two-page paper writing dated September 17, 1984, executed by Lawrence Norton according to the formalities of law required to make a valid last will and testament or a valid codicil to a last will and testament?
>
> * * *
>
> Issue #2: Were the first six (6) pages of Propounder's Exhibit Number 3 incorporated by reference by Lawrence Norton into the paper writing

dated September 17, 1984 so as to constitute one document propounded by Teab Norton?

* * *

Issue #3: Is the eight-page document identified as Propounder's Exhibit Number 3 and every part thereof the Last Will and Testament of Lawrence Norton?

The jury found in favor of the propounder on each of the issues. After the jury returned its verdict, respondents moved for judgment notwithstanding the verdict as to issues two and three. The trial court granted this motion and entered judgment in favor of respondents.

On appeal, the Court of Appeals unanimously affirmed the trial court. The court did not address the judgment regarding issue number one, as respondents moved for judgment regarding only issues two and three. The court concluded that the first six typewritten pages propounded as decedent's last will and testament, although designated as such, do not constitute a legally valid will because of the lack of witness signatures. Further, while the two-page codicil is valid, as evidenced by the jury's unchallenged determination in issue one, the codicil fails to adequately identify the attached six pages so as to effectuate a valid incorporation by reference. Therefore, propounder's claims on appeal were denied.

The sole question before this Court is whether the Court of Appeals erred in affirming the trial court's decision to award judgment notwithstanding the verdict in favor of respondents because propounder failed to satisfy the legal requirements of testamentary incorporation by reference or otherwise prove that the eight-page document as a whole constituted the final testamentary instrument of Lawrence Norton. We conclude that the Court of Appeals did not err, and we affirm its unanimous decision.

The documents at issue in this case are susceptible of numerous potential interpretations. The six-page document may possibly be conceived as a validly attested will. See N.C.G.S. § 31–3.3 (1984). However, we agree with the Court of Appeals that the stapled pages at issue here cannot constitute a legally valid will. Although decedent's signature on each page suggests that at some time these six pages may have been part of an attested will, the lack of witnesses' signatures vitiates this prospect. The question, therefore, turns on whether the properly executed 1984 codicil gives life to the six pages at issue through incorporation by reference.

* * *

The requirements for an incorporation by reference were articulated by this Court in Watson v. Hinson, 162 N.C. 72, 77 S.E. 1089 (1913):

> It is well recognized in this State that a will, properly executed, may so refer to another unattested will or other written paper or document as to incorporate the defective instrument and make the same a part of the perfect will, *the conditions being that the paper referred to shall be in existence at the time the second will be executed, and the reference to it shall be in terms so clear and distinct that from a perusal of the second will, or with the aid of parol or other proper testimony, full*

> *assurance is given that the identity of the extrinsic paper has been correctly ascertained.*

Id. at 79–80, 77 S.E. at 1092 (emphasis added); see also Siler v. Dorsett, 108 N.C. 300, 302, 12 S.E. 986, 987 (1891) ("[S]uch paper must be described and identified with such particularity as to designate and clearly show, and so that the court can certainly see, what paper is meant to be made part of the will."); Chambers v. McDaniel, 28 N.C. (6 Ired.) 226, 229 (1845) ("[T]he instrument referred to must be so described as to manifest distinctly what the paper is that is meant to be incorporated, and in such a way that the Court can be under no mistake. . . ."). Therefore, the essential inquiry here is whether there is: (1) reliable evidence that the six pages were in existence at the time of the codicil and (2) a "clear and distinct" reference in the codicil itself, or otherwise, such as to provide "full assurance" that the six pages were intended to be incorporated in the testamentary wishes of decedent Lawrence Norton.

Because this issue comes to the Court as a question of whether judgment notwithstanding the verdict was justifiably rendered, we must determine whether the evidence, taken in the light most favorable to propounder, as a matter of law permits an inference in propounder's favor. In re Will of Mucci, 287 N.C. 26, 213 S.E.2d 207 (1975).

* * *

. . . [I]t is apparent that sufficient evidence exists to satisfy the first Watson requirement that the extrinsic document be in existence at the time of the creation of the codicil. Ms. Stone testified that during the period she worked for decedent's attorney, 1970–1977, she had typed the six-page document pursuant to her employer's instructions. Further, she testified that the signature contained on the pages was that of decedent Lawrence Norton. Given that the document was typed before 1977 and that decedent's signature was on the pages at least before 17 September 1984, because as of that date Mr. Norton could no longer inscribe his name, the propounder offered sufficient evidence to satisfy the first prong of the Watson test. Watson, 162 N.C. at 79–80, 77 S.E. at 1092.

However, as to the second Watson requirement (that "the reference . . . be in terms so clear and distinct that . . . full assurance" is provided that the six-page document was intended to be incorporated, id.), we conclude that propounder's claim fails. While decedent had the codicil stapled to the document designated as "his will" and inserted the documents in an envelope that had typed on the outside "WILL OF LAWRENCE NORTON AND CODICIL OF LAWRENCE NORTON," there exists no reference within the codicil itself that is "in terms clear and distinct" designating the six pages as the document to be incorporated. In Watson, we held that a properly executed document, such as the 1984 codicil here, can incorporate another document that is, for whatever reason, defective. Id. However, it is critical that the extrinsic document be adequately identified so as to give "full assurance" that it was the document to be incorporated. We agree with propounder that it is not dispositive that there is no proof that the six pages were physically present at the time of the execution of the 1984 codicil. Nevertheless, without adequate reference derived from the codicil itself or other evidentiary sources, a reviewing court cannot be assured that the decedent intended to incorporate the extrinsic document. The testimony of Ms. Stone established that decedent executed numerous wills prior to his death. This assertion is supported by an examination of the decedent's safe-deposit box, which itself contained a witnessed codicil dated 14 February 1975 that begins in mid-sentence and to which no reference is made in any of the other documents at issue. In the face of this evidence and the fact that the codicil provides no reference to the six pages, we cannot have the "full assurance" that the six pages attached to the codicil were intended by decedent to be incorporated.

* * *

Affirmed.

■ MARTIN, J. (dissenting)

I respectfully dissent....

.... The two-page codicil is a valid testamentary document, the Court of Appeals so held. No one has appealed from that holding. Under N.C.G.S. § 12–3(9), a codicil can be treated as a will. Therefore, documents can be incorporated by reference into a codicil. This is true whether they are attached or not. Further, N.C.G.S. § 31–5.8 provides that a will can be revived through an incorporation by reference. A duly executed codicil may incorporate a paper in the form of a will which was never properly executed as a will. Watson v. Hinson, 162 N.C. at 72, 77 S.E. at 1089. The conditions are that (1) the paper to be incorporated must be in existence at the time of the execution of the incorporating will and (2) the reference to the extraneous document must be in terms so clear and distinct that from a perusal of the second will or with the aid of parol or other proper testimony full assurance is given that the identity of the extrinsic paper has been correctly ascertained.

There is no argument but that the six typewritten pages were in existence at the time that the codicil was executed. No one disputes this point, and the evidence is overwhelming that the six-page document was prepared prior to 1977, and the codicil was executed in 1984.

I now turn my attention to whether the six-page document is sufficiently referred to in the codicil under the facts and circumstances of this case. The codicil refers to itself as a "Codicil to [Norton's] Last Will and Testament." The question is what is the will to which the testator so refers. The propounder argues that the "will" has to mean the will found and attached to the codicil; this seems reasonable to me. Under the facts of this case the six pages were stapled to a lightweight cardboard legal cover together with the two-page codicil. The legal cover had the title: "Will of Lawrence Norton and Codicil to the Will of Lawrence Norton." The stapled papers were inside another legal envelope which bore the same inscription. The evidence further shows that the testator presented the two-page codicil and the six-page document to his granddaughter and asked her to staple them together. He told his granddaughter that the six pages had to be attached to the will "if they were to be any good." This could only mean that he intended the entire eight pages to be his will. At that time he was clearheaded and deliberate in his intention to incorporate the six pages into his will. Thereafter, Norton took the papers to his bank and placed them in his lock box. The lock box was not re-opened until after Norton's death.

.... In looking at the parol evidence and the extrinsic document, it is apparent beyond any misapprehension that the testator intended that the entire eight pages be his last will and testament. The stapling of the six-page document to the duly executed codicil and the testimony as to the facts and circumstances surrounding the stapling of the documents and the placing of them in the safety deposit box of the testator give full assurance as to the identity of the extrinsic paper being incorporated.

.... I conclude that the trial judge erred in entering the judgment notwithstanding the verdict and that the Court of Appeals subsequently erred in affirming this action. My vote is to reverse the Court of Appeals and reinstate the verdict of the jury.

NOTES AND QUESTIONS

1. Suppose, in 2005, Testator prepared a six-page document styled a "last will and testament." The dispositive provisions were all included on the first five pages. The top of the sixth page reads "Dated this ___ day of ___, 2005. I hereby sign my name and declare this document to be my last will and testament." A space for a signature follows, but Testator never dated or signed the document. In 2011, Testator prepared a single page—identical to the sixth page of the "will," stapled the new page to the back of the six-page document, filled in the current date on the new page, signed the new page, and had his signature witnessed. In 2012, Testator dies, and the executor named in the 2005 document submits the entire document for probate. Should the document be admitted to probate?

If so, on what theory? Is this an incorporation by reference case or an integration case? How, if at all, is Estate of Norton different?

2. In Estate of Norton, why doesn't the codicil incorporate the will by reference? What more could Lawrence Norton have done to incorporate the will by reference?

PROBLEM

Beale, a Wisconsin history professor, dictates a 14–page will to his secretary. He takes the will with him as he passes through New York on the way to Moscow. In New York, at a party at the home of a Columbia professor, Beale spreads out the 14 loose pages of the will on a pile on a table, and declares the document to be his will. He then signs the will, and three of the party guests (all professors) sign at the attestation clause. Later, he sends two pages back to his secretary to change the name of the executor. The secretary makes the corrections and sends the pages to Beale in Moscow. After Beale's death, none of the witnesses can identify any of the pages except the page they signed. Should Beale's "will" be admitted to probate? See Estate of Beale, 15 Wis.2d 546, 113 N.W.2d 380 (1962).

Clark v. Greenhalge

Supreme Judicial Court of Massachusetts, 1991.
411 Mass. 410, 582 N.E.2d 949.

■ NOLAN, J.

We consider in this case whether a probate judge correctly concluded that specific, written bequests of personal property contained in a notebook maintained by a testatrix were incorporated by reference into the terms of the testatrix's will.

We set forth the relevant facts as found by the probate judge. The testatrix, Helen Nesmith, duly executed a will in 1977, which named her cousin, Frederic T. Greenhalge, II, as executor of her estate. The will further identified Greenhalge as the principal beneficiary of the estate, entitling him to receive all of Helen Nesmith's tangible personal property upon her death except those items which she "designate[d] by a memorandum left by [her] and known to [Greenhalge], or in accordance with [her] known wishes," to be given to others living at the time of her death. Among Helen Nesmith's possessions was a large oil painting of a farm scene signed by T.H. Muckley and dated 1833. The value of the painting, as assessed for estate tax purposes, was $1,800.00.

In 1972, Greenhalge assisted Helen Nesmith in drafting a document entitled "MEMORANDUM" and identified as "a list of items of personal property prepared with Miss Helen Nesmith upon September 5, 1972, for the guidance of myself in the distribution of personal tangible property." This list consisted of forty-nine specific bequests of Ms. Nesmith's tangible personal property. In 1976, Helen Nesmith modified the 1972 list by interlineations, additions and deletions. Neither edition of the list involved a bequest of the farm scene painting.

Ms. Nesmith kept a plastic-covered notebook in the drawer of a desk in her study. She periodically made entries in this notebook, which bore the title "List to be given Helen Nesmith 1979." One such entry read: "Ginny Clark farm picture hanging over fireplace. Ma's room." Imogene Conway and Joan Dragoumanos, Ms. Nesmith's private home care nurses, knew of the existence of the notebook and had observed Helen Nesmith write in it. On several occasions, Helen Nesmith orally expressed to these nurses her intentions regarding the disposition of particular pieces of her property upon her death, including the farm scene painting. Helen Nesmith told Conway and Dragoumanos that the farm scene painting was to be given to Virginia Clark, upon Helen Nesmith's death.

Virginia Clark and Helen Nesmith first became acquainted in or about 1940. The women lived next door to each other for approximately ten years (1945 through 1955), during which time they enjoyed a close friendship. The Nesmith Clark friendship remained constant through the years. In more recent years, Ms. Clark frequently spent time at Ms. Nesmith's home, often visiting Helen Nesmith while she rested in the room which originally was her mother's bedroom. The farm scene painting hung in this room above the fireplace. Virginia Clark openly admired the picture.

According to Ms. Clark, sometime during either January or February of 1980, Helen Nesmith told Ms. Clark that the farm scene painting would belong to Ms. Clark after Helen Nesmith's death. Helen Nesmith then mentioned to Virginia Clark that she would record this gift in a book she kept for the purpose of memorializing her wishes with respect to the disposition of certain of her belongings.[1] After that conversation, Helen Nesmith often alluded to the fact that Ms. Clark someday would own the farm scene painting.

Ms. Nesmith executed two codicils to her 1977 will: one on May 30, 1980, and a second on October 23, 1980. The codicils amended certain bequests and deleted others, while ratifying the will in all other respects.

Greenhalge received Helen Nesmith's notebook on or shortly after January 28, 1986, the date of Ms. Nesmith's death. Thereafter, Greenhalge, as executor, distributed Ms. Nesmith's property in accordance with the will as amended, the 1972 memorandum as amended in 1976, and certain of the provisions contained in the notebook. Greenhalge refused, however, to deliver the farm scene painting to Virginia Clark because the painting interested him and he wanted to keep it. Mr. Greenhalge claimed that he was not bound to give effect to the expressions of Helen Nesmith's wishes and intentions stated in the notebook, particularly as to the disposition of the farm scene painting. Notwithstanding this opinion, Greenhalge distributed to himself all of the property bequeathed to him in the notebook. Ms. Clark thereafter commenced an action against Mr. Greenhalge seeking to compel him to deliver the farm scene painting to her.

The probate judge found that Helen Nesmith wanted Ms. Clark to have the farm scene painting. The judge concluded that Helen Nesmith's notebook qualified as a "memorandum" of her known wishes with respect to the distribution of her tangible personal property, within the meaning of Article Fifth of Helen Nesmith's will.[2] The judge further found that the notebook was in existence at the time of the execution of the 1980 codicils, which ratified the language of Article Fifth in its entirety. Based on these findings, the judge ruled that the notebook was incorporated by reference

---

1. According to Margaret Young, another nurse employed by Ms. Nesmith, Ms. Nesmith asked Ms. Young to "print[ ] in [the] notebook, beneath [her] own handwriting, 'Ginny Clark painting over fireplace in mother's bedroom.' " Ms. Young complied with this request. Ms. Young stated that Ms. Nesmith's express purpose in having Ms. Young record this statement in the notebook was "to insure that [Greenhalge] would know that she wanted Ginny Clark to have that particular painting."

2. Article Fifth of Helen Nesmith's will reads, in pertinent part, as follows: "that [Greenhalge] distribute such of the tangible property to and among such persons as I *may designate by a memorandum left by me and known to him, or in accordance with my known wishes*, provided that said persons are living at the time of my decease" (emphasis added).

into the terms of the will. Newton v. Seaman's Friend Soc'y, 130 Mass. 91, 93 (1881). The judge awarded the painting to Ms. Clark.

The Appeals Court affirmed the probate judge's decision in an unpublished memorandum and order, 30 Mass. App. Ct. 1109 (1991). We allowed the appellee's petition for further appellate review and now hold that the probate judge correctly awarded the painting to Ms. Clark.

A properly executed will may incorporate by reference into its provisions any "document or paper not so executed and witnessed, whether the paper referred to be in the form of . . . a mere list or memorandum, . . . if it was in existence at the time of the execution of the will, and is identified by clear and satisfactory proof as the paper referred to therein." Newton v. Seaman's Friend Soc'y, supra at 93. The parties agree that the document entitled "memorandum," dated 1972 and amended in 1976, was in existence as of the date of the execution of Helen Nesmith's will. The parties further agree that this document is a memorandum regarding the distribution of certain items of Helen Nesmith's tangible personal property upon her death, as identified in Article Fifth of her will. There is no dispute, therefore, that the 1972 memorandum was incorporated by reference into the terms of the will. Newton, supra.

The parties do not agree, however, as to whether the documentation contained in the notebook, dated 1979, similarly was incorporated into the will through the language of Article Fifth. Greenhalge advances several arguments to support his contention that the purported bequest of the farm scene painting written in the notebook was not incorporated into the will and thus fails as a testamentary devise. The points raised by Greenhalge in this regard are not persuasive. First, Greenhalge contends that the judge wrongly concluded that the notebook could be considered a "memorandum" within the meaning of Article Fifth, because it is not specifically identified as a "memorandum." Such a literal interpretation of the language and meaning of Article Fifth is not appropriate.

"The 'cardinal rule in the interpretation of wills, to which all other rules must bend, is that the intention of the testator shall prevail, provided it is consistent with the rules of law.' " Boston Safe Deposit & Trust Co. v. Park, 307 Mass. 255, 259 (1940), quoting McCurdy v. McCallum, 186 Mass. 464, 469 (1904). The intent of the testator is ascertained through consideration of "the language which [the testatrix] has used to express [her] testamentary designs," Taft v. Stearns, 234 Mass. 273, 277 (1920), as well as the circumstances existing at the time of the execution of the will. Boston Safe Deposit & Trust Co., supra at 259, and cases cited. The circumstances existing at the time of the execution of a codicil to a will are equally relevant, because the codicil serves to ratify the language in the will which has not been altered or affected by the terms of the codicil. See Taft, supra at 275–277.

Applying these principles in the present case, it appears clear that Helen Nesmith intended by the language used in Article Fifth of her will to retain the right to alter and amend the bequests of tangible personal property in her will, without having to amend formally the will. The text of

Article Fifth provides a mechanism by which Helen Nesmith could accomplish the result she desired; i.e., by expressing her wishes "in a memorandum." The statements in the notebook unquestionably reflect Helen Nesmith's exercise of her retained right to restructure the distribution of her tangible personal property upon her death. That the notebook is not entitled "memorandum" is of no consequence, since its apparent purpose is consistent with that of a memorandum under Article Fifth: It is a written instrument which is intended to guide Greenhalge in "distribut[ing] such of [Helen Nesmith's] tangible personal property to and among . . . persons [who] are living at the time of her decease." In this connection, the distinction between the notebook and "a memorandum" is illusory.

The appellant acknowledges that the subject documentation in the notebook establishes that Helen Nesmith wanted Virginia Clark to receive the farm scene painting upon Ms. Nesmith's death. The appellant argues, however, that the notebook cannot take effect as a testamentary instrument under Article Fifth, because the language of Article Fifth limits its application to "a" memorandum, or the 1972 memorandum. We reject this strict construction of Article Fifth. The language of Article Fifth does not preclude the existence of more than one memorandum which serves the intended purpose of that article. As previously suggested, the phrase "a memorandum" in Article Fifth appears as an expression of the manner in which Helen Nesmith could exercise her right to alter her will after its execution, but it does not denote a requirement that she do so within a particular format. To construe narrowly Article Fifth and to exclude the possibility that Helen Nesmith drafted the notebook contents as "a memorandum" under that Article, would undermine our long-standing policy of interpreting wills in a manner which best carries out the known wishes of the testatrix. See Boston Safe Deposit & Trust Co., supra. The evidence supports the conclusion that Helen Nesmith intended that the bequests in her notebook be accorded the same power and effect as those contained in the 1972 memorandum under Article Fifth. We conclude, therefore, that the judge properly accepted the notebook as a memorandum of Helen Nesmith's known wishes as referenced in Article Fifth of her will.

The appellant also contends that the judge erred in finding that Helen Nesmith intended to incorporate the notebook into her will, since the evidence established, at most, that she intended to bequeath the painting to Clark, and not that she intended to incorporate the notebook into her will. Our review of the judge's findings on this point, which is limited to a consideration of whether such findings are "clearly erroneous," proves the appellant's argument to be without merit. First Pa. Mortgage Trust v. Dorchester Sav. Bank, 395 Mass. 614, 621 (1985). The judge found that Helen Nesmith drafted the notebook contents with the expectation that Greenhalge would distribute the property accordingly. The judge further found that the notebook was in existence on the dates Helen Nesmith executed the codicils to her will, which affirmed the language of Article Fifth, and that it thereby was incorporated into the will pursuant to the language and spirit of Article Fifth. It is clear that the judge fairly construed the evidence in reaching the determination that Helen Nesmith intended the notebook to serve as a memorandum of her wishes as contemplated under Article Fifth of her will.

Lastly, the appellant complains that the notebook fails to meet the specific requirements of a memorandum under Article Fifth of the will, because it was not "known to him" until after Helen Nesmith's death. For this reason, Greenhalge states that the judge improperly ruled that the notebook was incorporated into the will. One of Helen Nesmith's nurses testified, however, that Greenhalge was aware of the notebook and its contents, and that he at no time made an effort to determine the validity of the bequest of the farm scene painting to Virginia Clark as stated therein. There is ample support in the record, therefore, to support the judge's conclusion that the notebook met the criteria set forth in Article Fifth regarding memoranda.

We note, as did the Appeals Court, that "one who seeks equity must do equity and that a court will not permit its equitable powers to be employed to accomplish an injustice." Pitts v. Halifax Country Club, Inc., 19 Mass. App. Ct. 525, 533 (1985). To this point, we remark that Greenhalge's conduct in handling this controversy fell short of the standard imposed by common social norms, not to mention the standard of conduct attending his fiduciary responsibility as executor, particularly with respect to his selective distribution of Helen Nesmith's assets. We can discern no reason in the record as to why this matter had to proceed along the protracted and costly route that it did.

Judgment affirmed.

QUESTIONS

1. How many documents did Helen Nesmith's will incorporate by reference? Does the will itself refer to more than a single document? If not, how can the court hold that the will incorporates both the memorandum and the notebook?

2. Suppose Helen Nesmith had never executed the two 1980 codicils to her will. Could the court have held that Helen Nesmith's will had incorporated the notebook by reference? Why not?

3. Suppose the residuary beneficiary of Helen Nesmith's will had been Helen's daughter, rather than executor Greenhalge. If the executor had determined to distribute the painting to the daughter, and Ginny Clark challenged that determination, are you confident that the court would have concluded that the will incorporated the notebook by reference? How are the cases different? Why was the court upset by the conduct of executor Greenhalge in this case?

4. Suppose Helen Nesmith's will had made no reference to a memorandum, but had simply directed Greenhalge to distribute tangible personal property "in accordance with my known wishes." Would Ginny Clark have been entitled to introduce testimony establishing that Helen Nesmith wanted her to have the farm painting? If not, was the testimony of Helen Nesmith's nurses relevant in this case?

NOTE

The incorporation by reference doctrine is explicitly recognized in the vast majority of states. Occasionally, a reference source indicates that the doctrine is not recognized in particular jurisdictions. Those statements are often overstated. For instance, it is often said that New York does not recognize incorporation by reference. Consider, however, Matter of Fowles, 222 N.Y. 222, 118 N.E. 611 (1918). Testator's will created a trust, and provided for distribution of part of the corpus "pursuant to the provisions of such last will and testament as my said wife may leave." The wife's will was in existence at the time the husband and the wife both perished on the Lusitania, but the court was nevertheless confronted with the argument that the husband's trust could not be given effect because the wife's will could not be incorporated by reference. Judge Cardozo rejected the argument:

> It is plain . . . that we are not to press the rule against incorporation to "a drily logical extreme." [citations omitted]. We must look in each case to the substance. We must consider the reason of the rule, and the evils which it aims to remedy. But as soon as we apply that test, the problem solves itself. There is here no opportunity for fraud or mistake. There is no chance of foisting upon this testator a document which fails to declare his purpose.

222 N.Y. at 233, 118 N.E. at 613.

UNIFORM PROBATE CODE

SECTION 2–510. INCORPORATION BY REFERENCE.

A writing in existence when a will is executed may be incorporated by reference if the language of the will manifests this intent and describes the writing sufficiently to permit its identification.

SECTION 2–513. SEPARATE WRITING IDENTIFYING DEVISE OF CERTAIN TYPES OF TANGIBLE PERSONAL PROPERTY.

Whether or not the provisions relating to holographic wills apply, a will may refer to a written statement or list to dispose of items of tangible personal property not otherwise specifically disposed of by the will, other than money. To be admissible under this section as evidence of the intended disposition, the writing must be signed by the testator and must describe the items and the devisees with reasonable certainty. The writing may be referred to as one to be in existence at the time of the testator's death; it may be prepared before or after the execution of the will; it may be altered by the testator after its preparation; and it may be a writing that has no significance apart from its effect on the dispositions made by the will.

NOTES AND QUESTIONS

1. How would Estate of Norton have been decided if the Uniform Probate Code had been in effect? How would Clark v. Greenhalge have been decided?

2. Suppose Helen Nesmith had never written the 1980 codicils to her will. If the Uniform Probate Code had been in effect, would Ginny Clark have been entitled to the farm painting?

What problems would she face under UPC § 2–510? Under UPC § 2–513?

PROBLEMS

1. Ann Acquisitive, a wealthy collector of art, jewelry, and expensive automobiles, enters your office to have a will drafted. She informs you that she constantly acquires new items of considerable value, and that she does not know now how she will want items acquired in the future to be distributed among her four children. Moreover, the number and value of items she acquires in the future might change her views about who should inherit the property she currently owns. Assume that UPC 2–513 is *not* in effect, but that the jurisdiction does recognize the incorporation by reference doctrine. What advice would you give Ms. Acquisitive? How would your advice change if UPC 2–513 or an equivalent statute were in effect?

Do your solutions to this problem suggest why the drafters of the Uniform Probate Code included § 2–513? In light of the problem, why should § 2–513 be limited to tangible personal property? Why not permit reference to a memorandum for intangible personal property (stocks, bonds, and cash) and for real property?

2. In 2005, Tess Testator validly executed a will to which was attached a writing titled "Gift By Memorandum" that was signed by Tess. The Memorandum purported to bequeath several items of valuable tangible personal property to Tess's five adult children. The 2005 will devised the residuary of Tess's estate to Peter Partner, Tess's live-in companion of fifteen years. In 2007, Tess executed a new will. The introductory paragraph revoked "all other and former wills and testamentary powers of any kind heretofore made by me." Paragraph 6 of the 2007 will stated "it is my intention *to make* a separate written instrument leaving items of tangible personal property to various people. All items not listed by me, or *should no list be made* by me, then all items of various personal property not specifically listed to go to specific persons shall pass to Peter Partner." After Tess's death, her children seek to probate the 2005 Memorandum. Should the court admit the Memorandum to probate if the jurisdiction has adopted UPC 2–513? Can your analysis be reconciled with the result in Estate of Wilkins, 137 Idaho 315, 48 P.3d 644 (2002), where the court, on similar facts, admitted the memorandum to probate?

If you agree that the Memorandum should be admitted to probate, how would you counsel a client who wishes to revoke a memorandum made in accordance with 2–513?

C. Facts of Independent Significance

Suppose Testator's will provides "I leave my 100 shares of IBM stock to those people listed on the envelope in which the stocks will be found at my death." At Testator's death, the IBM stock is found in an unsigned envelope, dated after the date of Testator's will, in Testator's desk drawer. Do the persons named on the envelope take the stock?

Generally, the answer is no. To give the IBM stock to the persons listed on the envelope would permit testator to change significant dispositions of wealth without testamentary formalities. We might worry about substitution of envelopes, or we might worry that Testator's envelope scratchings represented only an offhand thought, not a well-planned final disposition of his assets, or that the scratchings were made at a time when Testator was unduly influenced by the person whose name appeared on the envelope as a beneficiary. We could not incorporate the envelope by reference because the envelope was not in existence at the time Testator executed his will. UPC 2–513 doesn't help because the stocks and bonds don't qualify as tangible personal property.

Suppose now that Testator's will provides "I leave my 100 shares of IBM stock to the oldest of my sisters living at the time of my death." After execution of the will, Testator's oldest sister dies. At Testator's death, does his second-oldest sister, his oldest surviving sister, take the stock?

The answer is yes. But how is this case different? If the oldest sister was alive when Testator executed his will but died before the time of Testator's death, the disposition of Testator's estate has changed without any testamentary formalities. The difference is that the event that changed disposition of Testator's estate—the death of his oldest sister—had significance apart from its effect on distribution of Testator's estate. There is no danger that Testator's disposition changed because of Testator's sudden whim; there is no danger that Testator's disposition changed as a result of someone's undue influence. The doctrine of *facts of independent significance* permits a court to give effect to dispositions like the one to Testator's oldest surviving sister. Consider the UPC's approach:

Section 2–512. Events of Independent Significance.

A will may dispose of property by reference to acts and events that have significance apart from their effect upon the dispositions made by the will, whether they occur before or after the execution of the will or before or after the testator's death. The execution or revocation of another individual's will is such an event.

* * *

Note that the doctrine of facts of independent significance is relevant in two kinds of cases: first, when testator's will makes reference to facts or events of independent significance to determine the beneficiaries of the will (as when testator's will makes a devise to his oldest surviving sister); and second, when testator's will makes reference to facts or events of independent significance to determine the property that an ascertained beneficiary will receive (I leave any automobile I may own at my death to my brother, Bob).

PROBLEMS

In each of the following cases, make the arguments for and against giving effect to the disputed provision in testator's will. Consider how the doctrine of facts of independent significance would be relevant, and explain how you would resolve the issue if you were sitting as a probate court judge.

Testator's will leaves

1. "all of the cash and securities in my brokerage account at Merrill Lynch to my daughter Barbara."

2. "all of the cash and securities found in my kitchen drawer to my son Charles."

3. "all of the stocks and bonds found in my safe deposit box to the persons designated on the envelope in which those stocks and bonds are found." Cf. Walsh v. St. Joseph's Home for the Aged, 303 A.2d 691 (Del.Ch.1973).

4. "$1,000 to each of the persons who shall be employed by my company, Testator Inc., at the time of my death."

5. "the residue of my estate to the Houston Foundation, but if at my death my brother shall have died leaving a will creating a trust with charitable beneficiaries, I leave the residue of my estate to the trust created in my brother's last will." Testator's brother died before Testator. The brother's will created a trust with charitable beneficiaries. Cf. South Carolina National Bank of Charleston v. Copeland, 248 S.C. 203, 149 S.E.2d 615 (1966).

After trying your hand at the above problems, see if you understand the holding in the following case:

In re Tipler's Will

Court of Appeals of Tennessee, 1998.
10 S.W.3d 244.

■ LILLARD, J.

This is a will contest. The decedent executed a will, and later executed a holographic codicil to the will. The holograph directed that, if her husband predeceased her, her property should be distributed in accordance with his will. The decedent's husband predeceased her. Enforcement of the holographic codicil was challenged in court by the decedent's heirs. The trial court applied the doctrine of facts of independent significance and ordered the decedent's assets be distributed in accordance with her deceased husband's will. We affirm.

Mrs. Gladys S. Tipler ("Testatrix") executed a formal will on April 2, 1982. This will left the bulk of her estate to her husband, James Tipler ("Husband"), upon the contingency that he survive her. The will did not address the distribution of the estate in the event that Husband predeceased Testatrix. Two days later, Testatrix executed a holographic codicil to the formal will. The codicil reads as follows:

> Should my husband predecesse [sic] me I hereby declair [sic] that his last Will and testament upon his death is our agreement here to four [sic] made between us in Section III of my Will. With the exception Mr. Tipler or myself can elect to make any changes as we desire depending upon which one predeceasest [sic] the other. If no changes are made by either of us this will be our last will and testament.

Thus, the codicil indicated that if Husband predeceased Testatrix, his last will and testament would control the disposition of her estate. At the time the codicil was executed, Husband had not yet executed a will. Husband died in 1990. His will, executed six months prior to his death, created a trust for Testatrix, and directed that upon her death the property be distributed to his relatives. Testatrix died in 1994.

The beneficiaries under Husband's will sought enforcement of Testatrix's codicil in Shelby County Probate Court. This action was challenged by Testatrix' heirs, who would otherwise take under the Tennessee intestacy statute. The Testatrix' heirs asserted that the holographic codicil should not be enforced because it referred to a document not yet in existence, i.e. Husband's will. They argued that Tennessee law requires that for a holographic will to be enforceable, "all its material provisions must be in the handwriting of the testator. ..." *Tenn. Code Ann. § 32–1–105* (1984). Since Testatrix' holograph referred to Husband's will, Testatrix' heirs maintained that material provisions were not in Testatrix' handwriting.

At the trial, the beneficiaries under Husband's will introduced evidence regarding Testatrix' intent. The testimony indicated that Testatrix was not close to her family. One witness stated that Testatrix described her sisters as "greedy," indicating that "if anything happened to her [Testatrix]," her sisters would be like "a bunch of vultures" or "a bunch of barracudas. ..." Evidence indicated that Testatrix "thought of Mr. Tipler's family as her family." Witnesses testified that Testatrix loved her husband dearly and frequently said, "whatever Tippy [Husband] wants is what I want."

After the bench trial, the trial court issued a Memorandum Opinion. The trial court found that the issue of incorporation by reference was not applicable because Husband's will was not in existence at the time Testatrix' codicil was written. The trial court then stated:

> The relevant inquiry is whether the doctrine of facts of independent significance applies in the case at bar. Tennessee recognizes the doctrine of independent significance. *Smith v. Weitzel, 47 Tenn. App. 375, 338 S.W.2d 628, 637 (Tenn. 1960)* ("As to the proposition of

independent significance ... we call attention to Sec. 54.2 of Scott on Trusts"). *Scott on Trusts,* 4th Edition, Section 54.2, page 9, states:

> Section 54.2: Where disposition is determined by facts of independent significance. There is another doctrine of the law of wills that is sometimes confused with the doctrine of incorporation by reference. Even though a disposition cannot be fully ascertained from the terms of the will, it is not invalid if it can be ascertained from the facts that have a significance apart from their effect upon the disposition in the will. Indeed, it is frequently necessary to resort to extrinsic evidence to identify the persons who are to take or the subject matter of the disposition.

Therefore, under the doctrine of independent significance, a court may refer to extrinsic evidence to identify the persons who are to take under the will. In the case at bar, Mrs. Tipler left her residuary estate in Section III to her husband. However, in her holographic codicil, she stated, in her handwriting, that if her husband predeceased her, her residuary estate would pass according to their agreement as indicated in his will.

* * *

A testator may [have] intended for his property to go the same persons who are named in another person's will, and the gift of the testator's property by his will can be upheld on the ground of independent significance. This doctrine of independent significance is an escape mechanism from the strict requirements of incorporation by reference. 2 Bowe–Parker: *Page on Wills,* Section 19.34, page 119.

* * *

In the case at bar, Mrs. Tipler left her residuary estate to Mr. Tipler in her Last Will and Testament, on April 2, 1982. Like the *Klein case,* she modified that provision in her holographic codicil two days later in order to give Mr. Tipler the privilege of naming the persons who would take his part of her estate should he die first. The doctrine of independent significance is satisfied because Mr. Tipler's will had an independent significance of distributing his estate and was not written with the intention of distributing Mrs. Tipler's estate.

After noting that the testator's intent controls in construing a will the trial court then considered the witnesses' testimony to determine Testatrix' intent. The trial court noted that testimony indicating that Testatrix "did not like her family." ... The trial court then ordered that Testatrix' residuary estate be distributed in accordance with Husband's will.

* * *

Testatrix' heirs, who would receive Testatrix' residuary estate if the codicil were invalid, now appeal the decision of the trial court.

On appeal, the Appellants note that *Tennessee Code Annotated § 32–1–105* requires that, for a holographic will to be valid, "the signature and all its material provisions must be in the handwriting of the testator...."

Tenn. Code Ann. § 32–1–105 (1984). The appellants argue that the holograph in this case, which refers ambiguously to an "agreement" between Testatrix and her husband, does not have "all its material provisions" in Testatrix' handwriting since it attempts to incorporate Husband's will. They contend that the holographic codicil would not be valid if it incorporated by reference a document already in existence, and argue that it would be error then to conclude that the holographic codicil could validly incorporate a document not yet in existence when the codicil was executed.

* * *

A number of cases from other jurisdictions involve facts somewhat similar to this case. *See Baxley v. Birmingham Trust Nat'l Bank, 334 So. 2d 848 (Ala.1976); Rogers v. Walton, 141 Me. 91, 39 A.2d 409 (Me. 1943); Leary v. Liberty Trust Co., 272 Mass. 1, 171 N.E. 828 (Mass. 1930); In re Piffard's Estate, 111 N.Y. 410, 18 N.E. 718 (N.Y. 1888). In Piffard's Estate,* a father's will contained an absolute devise and bequest to his daughter. In a later codicil, the testator provided that should the daughter predecease him, the devise and bequest from his estate should be distributed according to the terms of her will. The daughter predeceased the father. The daughter's will was not written at the time of the codicil; therefore, there was no incorporation by reference. The court found that the doctrine of facts of independent significance applied and distributed the assets of the testator's estate according to the terms of the daughter's will. The court of appeals stated that the testator's will refers to the daughter's will, "not as transferring the property by an appointment, but to define and make certain the persons to whom, and the proportions in which, the one-fifth should pass by the father's will in case of the death of the daughter in his lifetime." *In re Piffard's Estate, 111 N.Y. 410, 18 N.E. 718, 719.*

* * *

However, . . . the court did not indicate that the codicils at issue were holographs. Consequently, the facts are distinguishable from this case. In this case, we have a holographic codicil which seeks to incorporate the distribution plan of another will, not in the handwriting of the testator. Tennessee law provides that, to be valid, all the material provisions of a holographic will must be in the handwriting of the testator. *Tenn. Code Ann. § 32–1–105* (1984). Therefore, we must determine whether the holographic codicil in this case contains all material provisions in Testatrix handwriting. Only then will the doctrine of facts of independent significance apply.

The codicil in this case must be considered in light of two important common law principles regarding will construction: the presumption against intestacy and the weight given to the testator's intent. The common law presumption against partial intestacy was codified in *Tennessee Code Annotated § 32–3–101* (1984).[3] This presumption "is applicable when

---

3. *Tennessee Code Annotated § 32–3–101* provides as follows:

A will shall be construed, in reference to the real and personal estate comprised in it, to speak and take effect as if it had been executed immediately before the death of the

the words used, *by any fair interpretation,* will embrace the property not otherwise devised, unless a contrary intention appears from the context." *McDonald v. Ledford, 140 Tenn. 471, 475, 205 S.W. 312, 313 (1917)* (citing *Oldham v. York, 99 Tenn. 68, 41 S.W. 333 (1897)* (emphasis added)). This rule operates to prevent testamentary gifts from lapsing or failing through the incomplete drafting of the will.

... Other than a small bequest to a niece, Testatrix did not provide for her family members in her will. Testimony at trial established that Testatrix was not on good terms with her family members and felt that her husband's family was her family. Under these circumstances, the evidence does not preponderate against the trial court's finding that Testatrix intended that her estate be distributed to her Husband's family through his will and according to his wishes. The evidence of Testatrix's intent was properly considered by the trial court.

In determining whether this codicil contained "all material provisions" in Testatrix' handwriting, we must note that the identity of the beneficiaries is obviously an important item in a will. In this case, the witnesses testimony in this case does not indicate that Testatrix wanted her estate to be distributed to particular members of Husband's family. Rather, it indicates that Testatrix wanted her estate to be distributed to whomever Husband wished. Under these circumstances, a holograph which bequeaths her estate to persons named as beneficiaries under Husband's will would contain all material provisions in Testatrix' handwriting, and therefore would be valid, even though the specific identity of the beneficiaries is contained in another document not in Testatrix' handwriting.

* * *

For the above reasons, we affirm the decision of the trial court. Costs of appeal are assessed against the Appellants, for which execution shall issue, if necessary.

QUESTION

Why was Gladys S. Tipler's codicil, which directed distribution of her assets in accordance with a separate document not yet in existence, valid? To what "act or event" did Tipler's will refer? What significance did the "act or event" have apart from its effect on Tipler's will?

Pour–Over Wills, Facts of Independent Significance and Incorporation by Reference

Historically, one application of the doctrine of facts of independent significance arose when Testator directed that a portion of his estate be distributed to an *inter vivos* trust created by Testator, or by someone else. See generally Robert J. Lynn, Problems with Pour–Over Wills, 47 Ohio St. L.J. 47 (1986). If the trust were not modifiable or revocable, Testator's

testator, and shall convey all the real estate belonging to him, or in which he had any interest at his decease, unless a contrary intention appear by its words in context.

disposition to the trust could be validated by using the incorporation by reference doctrine. Do you see why? If, however, the trust was modified after execution of Testator's will, incorporation by reference was not possible. Again, do you see why?

Nevertheless, if the trust were funded with $1,000,000 in assets, a will provision pouring part of Testator's estate into the trust would be upheld by application of the doctrine of facts of independent significance. Be sure you understand why: note that Testator would not modify or revoke the trust just to change the disposition of his estate; a modification of the trust would immediately affect disposition of the $1,000,000 in the trust. The disposition would have an important present effect, not merely an effect at Testator's death.

As we shall later see, however, testators sometimes have estate planning reasons for creating *unfunded* inter vivos trusts. If Testator's will devised property to an inter vivos trust that held no assets during Testator's life, the doctrine of facts of independent significance might well have failed to validate the will's pour over provision. Do you understand why?

Because pour over wills and inter vivos trusts are useful estate planning tools, every jurisdiction has enacted legislation validating pour over provisions to either funded or unfunded trusts. See, e.g., UPC § 2–511 (titled "Testamentary Additions to Trusts"); Clymer v. Mayo, 393 Mass. 754, 473 N.E.2d 1084 (1985) [holding that Massachusetts's version of the Uniform Testamentary Additions to Trusts Act validated a will that poured over into an unfunded inter vivos trust]. Thus, resort to the doctrines of incorporation by reference or facts of independent significance is no longer necessary to validate a will that pours over to an inter vivos trust. The role that the doctrines played in the development of the revocable inter vivos trust is explored in detail in Chapter 7.

D. NEGATIVE DISINHERITANCE

The preceding two sections demonstrate how documents outside the will can affect the distribution of a decedent's estate. In one instance, however, a number of courts have chosen to ignore language expressly included in decedent's will: when decedent's will purports to disinherit a particular person, the orthodox rule is that the disinheritance provision is ineffective. That is, if T's will provides simply "I hereby disinherit my son S," and the will makes no affirmative provision for any other person, S will take his intestate share. Similarly, if the will provides "I leave my house to my daughter D. I disinherit my son S," the daughter takes the house, but S will take his intestate share of the remainder of T's property, because T's will did not include a valid residuary clause. Only by making affirmative provision for other people would these courts permit T to disinherit an heir. For discussion and criticism of the rule precluding negative disinheritance, see Frederic S. Schwartz, Models of the Will and Negative Disinheritance, 48 Mercer L. Rev. 1137, 1144–45 (1997):

> Certainly it is true that the testator has not specified a recipient for the property that would normally go to the negative beneficiary by hypotheses, there is a partial intestacy. The testator has said only where that property is not to go. But it should be evident that this lacuna in the testator's expressed intent makes the task of giving effect to the testator's intent less problematic, not more so. The only effective expression of the testator's intent with respect to the residue is the disinheritance provision. That provision can be given complete effect by denying the negative beneficiary any share in the residue.
>
> .... A provision disinheriting B2's issue should result in an application of the intestacy statute as if B2 predeceased the testator.

This solution is endorsed in section 2–101(b) of the Uniform Probate Code.

SECTION III. CONSTRUCTION PROBLEMS CREATED BY THE TIME GAP BETWEEN WILL EXECUTION AND DEATH

When most testators execute their wills, they know the extent of their property and the persons to whom they want that property to pass. Often, however, years pass between the execution of the will and testator's death. During those years, the size and nature of testator's property holdings may change significantly. In addition, the beneficiaries named in testator's will may have died. What effect should these changes in property and in beneficiaries have on the distribution of testator's estate?

By case law and by statute, courts and legislatures have developed rules of construction to deal with these changes. *Abatement* rules determine the order of priority among various devisees when the value of the estate is insufficient to satisfy all of the devises in the will. The doctrine of *ademption* applies when testator has devised a particular piece of property—a diamond ring, for instance—which testator disposes of after executing the will. When a devisee named in the will dies before testator's death, the devise generally *lapses* unless the jurisdiction's *antilapse statute* preserves the devise for the devisee's descendants.

One point bears emphasis: all of these rules are rules of construction. They represent the law's best guess about what testator would have wanted when testator did not explicitly consider the situation that actually occurred. Testator (and her lawyer) can avoid the impact of each of these doctrines by appropriate language in the will itself. As you consider the materials in this section, you should consider what sorts of drafting improvements would have avoided the controversy at issue.

A. ABATEMENT

Suppose that at the time testator executes her will, she is quite wealthy, or she expects to be wealthy by the time of her death. As a result, she makes generous devises to a variety of people. When she dies, her property is insufficient to satisfy the devises. How should the estate be distributed? Consider the following case:

In re Estate of Potter

District Court of Appeal of Florida, Fourth District, 1985.
469 So.2d 957.

■ WALDEN, JUDGE.

Mildred D. Potter died testate. Her will provided:

> In the event my husband, EDWIN E. POTTER, shall not survive me, I bequeath and devise my residence known as 14 Sunset Lane, Pompano Beach, Florida, together with all household goods contained therein to my daughter, HELEN POTTER WANKE, if she shall survive me. If my said daughter does not survive me, this bequest shall lapse and such residence shall be sold by my Executor and the proceeds thereof shall become a part of my residuary estate. It is my intention that the properties specifically bequeathed and devised in accordance with the provisions of this Article II of my Will shall pass to the persons named therein free of administrative expenses and free of any liability for estate and inheritance taxes, and I therefore direct my Executor that the said property shall not be considered assets in its hands for any said purposes.

Contemporaneous with the execution of her will, Mrs. Potter executed an amendment to her preexisting *inter vivos* trust, which amendment provided that in the event Mrs. Potter's daughter, Helen, did receive the Pompano Beach residence under the terms of the will, then the trustee "shall thereupon pay over to grantor's son, Edwin E. Potter, Jr., an equivalent amount, out of the trust assets before its division into the two trusts for grantor's son and daughter, free of the trust."

The will also provided that any property specifically bequeathed would pass free of administrative expenses and any liability for estate and inheritance taxes and authorized the executor, if necessary, to request sums to be paid from the trust to the estate to pay debts, administration expenses, taxes, etc. The trust also provided for the trust to pay those expenses of the estate.

Mrs. Potter's husband predeceased her so that upon Mrs. Potter's death, the above-stated terms of the will and the trust became operative. Thus, restating the situation, Mrs. Potter, via her will, wanted her daughter to have the residence, free and clear, and, via her inter vivos trust, wanted her son to have a sum in cash equivalent to the value of the residence received by her daughter.

Unfortunately, there were insufficient assets in the trust to pay Mrs. Potter's son the equivalent sum in cash.

At the personal representative's behest, the trial court entered the appealed order which undertook to interpret the will and trust. It was ruled that Mrs. Potter's intent was to treat the son and daughter equally in the distribution of her estate. Since the assets were insufficient to allow the implementation of the literal provisions of both the will and trust, the trial court ordered the sale of the residence; the payment of taxes and all administration expenses; and, the division of the remainder equally between the son and daughter.

While we disagree with the ultimate conclusion reached by the trial court, we do agree with the finding contained in the appealed order that the trust in question was incorporated by reference into Mrs. Potter's will and that they should be thereby construed together in determining Mrs. Potter's intent. *See* § 732.512(1), Fla.Stat. (1983). Moreover, and as a peripheral consequence, the trust provisions then became testamentary dispositions so as to entitle us to use testamentary terms in describing them.

According to our analysis, the disposition of this appeal is governed by the law concerning devises and abatement.

In our opinion the devise of the residence to Mrs. Potter's daughter constituted a specific devise while the trust proviso requiring payment to Mrs. Potter's son of an equivalent sum of money was tantamount to a general devise.[4]

By way of definition, "A specific legacy is a gift by will of property which is particularly designated and which is to be satisfied only by the receipt of the particular property described." *In re Parker's Estate,* 110 So.2d 498, 500 (Fla. 1st DCA 1959).

On the other hand, "A general legacy is one which may be satisfied out of the general assets of the testator's estate instead of from any specific fund, thing or things. It does not consist of a gift of a particular thing or fund or part of the estate distinguished and set apart from others of its kind and subject to precise identification. A general legacy has a prerequisite of designation by quantity or amount. The gift may be either of money or other personal property." *Park Lake Presbyterian Church v. Henry's Estate*, 106 So.2d 215, 217 (Fla. 2d DCA 1958).

It is our further opinion that general devises abate before specific devises. Redfearn, *Wills and Administration in Florida* § 12.08 (5th Ed.1977), explains such abatement.

> Abatement is the reduction of a legacy or devise on account of the insufficiency of the estate of a testator to pay all his debts, all the costs of administration, and all the legacies in full. The presumption is that the testator intended that all the legacies provided for in his will would be paid in full and that he contemplated that his estate would be sufficient to meet this requirement, but his good intentions are no protection for his legatees and devisees from the just claims of his creditors or from costs of administration. Under the common law and under the probate laws of Florida, the first assets of the estate to be applied to the payment of debts and costs are those charged by the

4. For our purposes the terms, legacy and devise, are synonymous. [Footnote by the Court—eds.]

> testator with this particular indebtedness; next, the assets not devised; then the assets found in the residuary clause of the will are applied. If these assets are insufficient, or if there is no residuary clause or undevised estate, then general legacies must abate pro rata to make up the deficiency; if the general legacies are insufficient to meet these requirements, then specific and demonstrative legacies abate in the manner set forth in section 12.07.

See also 80 Am.Jur.2d *Wills* § 1736 (1975). The above exposition is supported by the provisions of section 733.805, Florida Statutes (1983):

> (1) If a testator makes provision by his will, or designates the funds or property to be used, for the payment of debts, estate and inheritance taxes, family allowance, exempt property, elective share charges, expenses of administration, and devises, they shall be paid out of the funds or from the property or proceeds as provided by the will so far as sufficient. If no provision is made or any fund designated, or if it is insufficient, the property of the estate shall be used for such purposes, except as otherwise provided in § 733.817 with respect to estate, inheritance, and other death taxes, and to raise the shares of a pretermitted spouse and children, in the following order:
>
> (a) Property not disposed of by the will.
>
> (b) Property devised to the residuary devisee or devisees.
>
> (c) Property not specifically or demonstratively devised.
>
> (d) Property specifically or demonstratively devised.
>
> (2) Demonstrative devises shall be classed as general devises upon the failure or insufficiency of funds or property out of which payment should be made, to the extent of the insufficiency. Devises to the decedent's surviving spouse, given in satisfaction of, or instead of, the surviving spouse's statutory rights in the estate, shall not abate until other devises of the same class are exhausted. Devises given for a valuable consideration shall abate with other devises of the same class only to the extent of the excess over the amount of value of the consideration until all others of the same class are exhausted. Except as herein provided, devises shall abate equally and ratably and without preference or priority as between real and personal property. When property that has been specifically devised or charged with a devise is sold or taken by the personal representative, other devisees shall contribute according to their respective interests to the devisee whose devise has been sold or taken, and before distribution the court shall determine the amounts of the respective contributions, and they shall be paid or withheld before distribution is made.

We hold that the trust provision in favor of Mrs. Potter's son constituted a general legacy while the will provision in favor of Mrs. Potter's daughter constituted a specific legacy. Thus, under the circumstances, the general legacy abated prior to the specific legacy with the result here being that Mrs. Potter's daughter should receive the Pompano Beach residence.

By reason of the foregoing and upon authority of *In re Estate of George*, 200 So.2d 256 (Fla. 3d DCA 1967), we reverse the judgment on appeal and remand for further proceedings.

Reversed and Remanded.

■ DOWNEY and HERSEY, JJ., concur.

QUESTIONS

1. Suppose that at the time Mrs. Potter executed her will, her assets included the house on Sunset Lane, valued at $100,000, together with cash and securities valued at $1,000,000. Suppose her will provided:

> "1. I leave the house at 14 Sunset Lane to my daughter Helen.
>
> 2. I leave to my son Edwin, in cash, an amount equivalent to the value of my house at 14 Sunset Lane.
>
> 3. I leave the remainder of my estate to my beloved daughter Gertrude."

How would you classify each devise? Suppose further that Mildred had never created an *inter vivos* trust. If, at the time of Mildred's death, the house was worth $300,000, but Mildred's cash and securities were worth only $200,000, how would the court in Estate of Potter have distributed Mildred's estate?

Why would the court distribute the property that way? Would that distribution effectuate or frustrate Mildred's intention?

2. The court in Estate of Potter holds—in accordance with the general rule—that general devises abate before specific devises. Is there any basis for the general rule? Has it become outdated? Note also that residuary devises generally abate before either general or specific devises.

3. Do you approve of the court's resolution of the Potter case?

4. If the classification of a devise is important in determining abatement order, how would you classify each of the following devises:

> a. "All real estate owned by me or in which I have an interest." (Compare Haslam v. Alvarez, 70 R.I. 212, 38 A.2d 158 (1944) with In re DeVoss, 474 N.W.2d 542 (Iowa 1991)).
>
> b. "The money now due and owing to me from Y." Cf. Hayes v. Hayes, 45 N.J.Eq. 461, 17 A. 634 (1889).
>
> c. "Ten shares of General Motors stock." Cf. Kearns v. Kearns, 77 N.J.Eq. 453, 76 A. 1042 (1910).
>
> d. "My ten shares of General Motors stock."

5. Suppose you had been Mildred Potter's lawyer. How would you have drafted Ms. Potter's will to reflect her apparent intent to treat her two children equally?

NOTES

1. ***Creditor Claims.*** In many cases, the need for abatement arises when creditors assert claims against the estate. Suppose, for instance, decedent dies with $300,000 in securities, but at the time of his death, decedent is liable for $150,000 in business debts and for a $100,000 tort claim. Before death, the creditors had a claim against decedent, and they could have sought to satisfy that claim by executing against decedent's property—here, the securities. The creditor claims do not disappear at decedent's death; they become claims against his estate. Creditor claims generally enjoy priority over claims of estate beneficiaries. As a result, if decedent makes $200,000 in specific and general devises, and his net estate after payment of creditor claims is only $50,000, the devises will abate in the order specified in Potter.

2. ***Ratable Abatement Within Each Class.*** Suppose the value of testator's estate, after payment of creditor claims, and after distribution of all specific devises, is valued at $100,000. Suppose further that testator's will made general devises totaling $250,000. The $100,000 will be distributed ratably among the general devisees. Since the funds available to satisfy general devises equal 40% of the total general devises, each devisee will receive 40% of the devise. Thus, if the will devised $80,000 to one general devisee, that devisee will take $32,000 (40% of $80,000).

What if the only property in the estate consists of specifically devised real property and tangible personal property, and the executor has to sell some of that property to pay debts and costs of administration. How should the executor choose which property to sell, and what rights does the beneficiary of the property sold by the executor have against other specific devisees? See Estate of Nelson, 168 P.3d 235 (Okla. App. 2007) (applying the ratable abatement rule and holding that a specific devisee whose property is sold to pay expenses is entitled to contribution from other specific devisees).

* * *

UNIFORM PROBATE CODE

SECTION 3–902. DISTRIBUTION; ORDER IN WHICH ASSETS APPROPRIATED; ABATEMENT.

(a) Except as provided in subsection (b) and except as provided in connection with the share of the surviving spouse who elects to take an elective share, shares of distributees abate, without any preference or priority as between real and personal property, in the following order: (1) property not disposed of by the will; (2) residuary devises; (3) general devises; (4) specific devises. For purposes of abatement, a general devise charged on any specific property or fund is a specific devise to the extent of the value of the property on which it is charged, and upon the failure or insufficiency of the property on which it is charged, a general devise to the extent of the failure or insufficiency. Abatement within each classification is in proportion to the amounts of property each of the beneficiaries would have received if full distribution of the property had been made in accordance with the terms of the will.

(b) If the will expresses an order of abatement, or if the testamentary plan or the express or implied purpose of the devise would be defeated by the order of abatement stated in subsection (a), the shares of the distributees abate as may be found necessary to give effect to the intention of the testator.

(c) If the subject of a preferred devise is sold or used incident to administration, abatement shall be achieved by appropriate adjustments in, or contribution from, other interests in the remaining assets.

IOWA CODE

SECTION 633.436 GENERAL ORDER FOR ABATEMENT

1. Except as provided in sections 633.211 and 633.212, shares of the distributees shall abate, for the payment of debts and charges, federal estate taxes, legacies, the shares of children born or adopted after the making of a will, or the share of the surviving spouse who elects to take against the will, without any preference or priority as between real and personal property, in the following order:

a. Property not disposed of by the will;

b. Property devised to the residuary devisee, except property devised to a surviving spouse who takes under the will;

c. Property disposed of by the will, but not specifically devised and not devised to the residuary devisee, except property devised to a surviving spouse who takes under the will;

d. Property specifically devised, except property devised to a surviving spouse who takes under the will;

e. Property devised to a surviving spouse who takes under the will.

2. A general devise charged on any specific property or fund shall, for purposes of abatement, be deemed property specifically devised to the extent of the value of the property on which it is charged. Upon the failure or insufficiency of the property on which it is charged, it shall be deemed property not specifically devised to the extent of such failure or insufficiency.

* * *

QUESTIONS

1. How does the Iowa statute differ from the Uniform Probate Code? Which approach is closer to the common law approach? Which do you prefer, and why? In answering that question, consider how each statute would apply to an estate with $200,000 in assets and $50,000 in liabilities if the will made general devises of $20,000 to each of testator's three children, and left the remainder of testator's estate to her husband.

2. How would Estate of Potter have been decided if the Uniform Probate Code had been in effect? Would UPC § 3–902(b) have been relevant in deciding the case?

NOTE ON DEMONSTRATIVE DEVISES

As we have seen, not all devises can be easily categorized as specific or general. One recurring form of problematic devise is the "demonstrative devise"—a devise of a particular amount of money to be drawn from a specified fund. Suppose, for instance, testator devises to his brother "$20,000, and I direct that my stamp collection be sold to satisfy this devise." What happens if testator's estate is insufficient to satisfy all devises, and if the stamp collection itself is only worth $10,000?

The devise to the brother is a demonstrative devise. The demonstrative devise is treated as a specific devise up to the value of the stamp collection, and as a general devise for the balance. Thus, $10,000 of the devise abates with specific devises, while the remaining $10,000 abates with general devises. Do you see how § 3–902 achieves that result?

On the other hand, if the estate is sufficient to satisfy all devises, the brother will take all $20,000, even if the stamp collection itself is worth only $10,000. Do you see how § 3–902 achieves that result?

Sophisticated lawyers rarely draft demonstrative devises.

PROBLEMS

1. Testator's will provides:

> "1. I devise my speedboat, Molasses, to my brother Bob."
>
> "2. I devise $30,000 each to my children, Cindy, Daniel, and Edith."
>
> "3. I devise $30,000 to my daughter, Fran, and I direct that my 2003 Ford Explorer be sold to satisfy this bequest."
>
> "4. I devise the residue of my estate to my alma mater, the University of Pennsylvania."

How would you classify these devises? At Testator's death, her estate consists of Molasses (valued at $10,000), the 2003 Ford Explorer (also valued at $10,000), and $55,000 in cash. If UPC § 3–902 is in effect, how should Testator's estate be distributed?

2. Van Lung's will devised $500,000 to eight enumerated individuals in amounts varying from $25,000 to $100,000. The will directed that these devises be paid out of the stock fund in Lung's investment account. The will then directed that the remainder of Lung's estate be distributed to the Van S. Lung charitable foundation. At Lung's death, his investment account was valued at $700,000, but the stock fund portion of the account was worth only $50,000.

How should Van Lung's estate be distributed?

How would the estate be distributed if he devised "the stock fund in my investment account" to the eight individuals? See Estate of Lung, 692 A.2d 1349 (D.C.App.1997).

Suppose Van Lung had wanted to assure that the eight individuals received their devises regardless of the size of the stock fund, but wanted to give them priority over other devisees with respect to the stock fund. What language would you have recommended that Van Lung use in his will?

NOTE ON EXONERATION OF SPECIFIC DEVISES

Testator's will leaves "my house, located at 10 Main Street, to my sister, Ida." At testator's death, the house has a market value of $100,000, but the house is subject to a $60,000 mortgage. Is Ida entitled to the house free of the mortgage, or does she take the house subject to the mortgage?

The common law rule of *exoneration* held that a specific devisee is entitled to have the mortgage paid at the expense of the residuary estate unless it appeared, from the will itself or surrounding circumstances, that testator intended the devisee to take subject to the mortgage. See, e.g., Ashkenazy v. Ashkenazy's Estate, 140 So.2d 331 (Fla.App.1962).

Increasingly, however, courts and legislatures have adopted the opposite presumption—a presumption of *nonexoneration*. That is, the specific devisee takes subject to a mortgage lien unless testator's contrary intent appears from the will or surrounding circumstances. Section 2–607 of the Uniform Probate Code, entitled "Nonexoneration", provides:

> "A specific devise passes subject to any mortgage interest existing at the date of death, without right of exoneration, regardless of a general directive in the will to pay debts."

See also N.Y. EPTL § 3–3.6(a).

Suppose testator owned a home with his nephew in joint tenancy with right of survivorship. During his life, the testator was solely liable for the underlying mortgage, and testator alone paid the mortgage payments. After testator's death, who is liable on the underlying mortgage, nephew or testator's estate? See Estate of Vincent, 98 S.W.3d 146 (Tenn. 2003); Estate of Zahn, 305 N.J.Super. 260, 702 A.2d 482 (1997) [both concluding, as most courts have, that a will's direction that executor pay testator's "just debts," is insufficient to express an intention that the estate pay off the underlying mortgage on real estate that passed outside of probate].

NOTE ON APPORTIONMENT OF TAXES

Suppose the claims against the estate are not claims by creditors, but claims by the Internal Revenue Service or by state tax authorities. Which beneficiaries bear the burden of those claims? One might think ordinary rules of abatement would apply, and tax claims would come out of the residuary estate. At common law, tax claims were generally treated as claims against the estate, unless the will provided otherwise. (Note that the current Iowa abatement statute—reproduced in the abatement section—applies abatement rules to tax claims).

During the Great Depression, however, application of the common law rule would have significantly distorted the estate plans of many testators. People of wealth generally provided for their principal beneficiaries in the residuary clause of their wills. If investment losses depleted the value of the estate, ordinary abatement rules created a disproportionate impact on residuary devisees. If tax claims, too, were treated as claims against the estate, residuary devisees were doubly disadvantaged. As a result, many states enacted statutes directing apportionment of tax liability among estate beneficiaries. That is, each beneficiary would bear a proportionate share of estate tax liability; the residuary devisee would not bear the entire tax burden. The Uniform Probate Code has adopted this approach. See Section 3–9A–104(1).

Note that when a statute directs apportionment of tax liability, specific devisees will have to satisfy tax claims in order to enjoy the specifically devised property. Many testators do not intend that result. Moreover, many testators do not intend for general devisees to bear any share of tax liability. As a result, wills often include a "direction against apportionment"—an instruction that tax claims should be treated as claims against the estate, reinstating the common law abatement rules for tax claims, and putting tax claims on the same footing as other claims. On the other hand, it is a mistake to view "direction against apportionment" clauses as standard boilerplate that should always be included. If, for example, a testator has significant nonprobate assets that will pass at her death to people other than her will's residuary beneficiary, and if her principal objective is to benefit her residuary beneficiary, a "direction against apportionment" clause can deplete the residuary estate, frustrating testator's intent. See Daniel B. Evans, Tax Clauses to Die For, 20 Probate & Property 38 (2006) (suggesting that including "direction against apportionment" clauses as boilerplate constitutes malpractice). As always, the best approach is to carefully tailor apportionment clauses to your client's particular needs.

Two other points are worth noting. First, the base for the federal estate tax includes not only testator's net probate estate, but also certain lifetime transfers. In that situation, it is important for the drafter of the will (and also the lifetime instruments) to apportion tax liability in a manner that reflects testator's intent. If the drafter does not deal with the problem in the documents, how courts will apportion liability remains uncertain. We will consider this problem in more detail later, in Chapter Eight.

Second, in addition to estate taxes, many states impose inheritance taxes. These taxes are not assessed on the size of the decedent's estate, but on the size of the devise received by each beneficiary. Since inheritance taxes are on the right to receive, there is no apportionment problem: each recipient is primarily liable for the tax on her share. Again, testator's lawyer may draft around the statutory solution.

PROBLEMS

1. Oscar Zilch's will includes the following dispositive provisions:

"1. I devise Rem Brant's painting of mother to Aunt Suzie Zilch.

2. I devise $1,000,000 each to my grandchildren, Zelda, Yolanda, Xavier, and Wanda.

3. I devise the remainder of my estate, in equal shares, to my children, Vernon and Ursula."

At Oscar's death, the painting of mother is valued at $10,000. The remainder of Oscar's estate, after payment of creditor claims and administrative expenses, but before payment of taxes, is valued at $7,000,000. Assume that the federal estate tax due on Oscar's estate is $700,000. If UPC § 3–9A–104(1) is in effect, and the will includes no direction against apportionment, how will the tax liability be apportioned? What effect would a direction against apportionment have on the relative shares of Oscar's devisees?

2. Reporter Charles Kuralt's 1994 properly executed will left the bulk of his estate to his wife, the residuary legatee. Due to the unlimited marital deduction, Kuralt's wife would owe no estate tax at her husband's death. The will also included a direction against apportionment. After Kuralt's death, the will was probated in New York, where Kuralt was domiciled. Soon after, a Montana court determined that a 1997 letter from Kuralt to Patricia Shannon, Kuralt's intimate female companion of over thirty years, was a holographic codicil to the 1994 will. In the short letter, Kuralt expressed an intent to devise to Shannon real property that Kuralt owned in Montana. Shannon claimed that the taxes generated by the gift of the Montana property to her should be paid out of the residue of Kuralt's estate, while Kuralt's wife argued that the taxes should be apportioned. Both New York and Montana law provide that estate taxes should be apportioned among beneficiaries, absent a contrary instruction in testator's will. If you were the judge, how would you rule, and why? See Estate of Kuralt, 315 Mont. 177, 68 P.3d 662 (2003) (holding that taxes should be paid from the residuary estate).

B. ADEMPTION

Where there has been no significant shrinkage in the overall value of testator's estate after execution of testator's will, abatement issues are relatively straightforward. Suppose, however, that testator has specifically devised property, but, before testator's death, testator has disposed of the specifically devised property. Is the specific devisee entitled to the *value* of the specifically devised property, or is the specific devisee entitled to nothing?

The doctrine of ademption provides, in general terms, that the specific devisee is entitled to nothing if the specifically devised property is not in testator's estate at testator's death. We say that the specific devise has been *adeemed* by testator's disposal of the specifically devised property.

The premise on which the ademption doctrine rests is this: by making a specific devise, testator expressed a desire that devisee have particular property—not the value of that property; if testator had wanted the devisee to have the value of the property, testator would have made a general devise, or a demonstrative devise, not a specific one.

In many cases, the doctrine effectuates testator's intent. Suppose, for instance, testator devises a painting to a neighbor who has often admired it (recall the facts in Clark v. Greenhalge, p. ___, *supra*). After execution of testator's will, the painting is destroyed by fire, or testator has sold the painting to pay for her daughter's college education. Testator has not, however, changed her will. Would testator have wanted the neighbor to receive the value of the painting? Probably not. The neighbor was not a principal object of testator's bounty; testator, in all probability, wanted to benefit the neighbor only by giving her the painting—not by giving her money.

This simple case, however, does not capture the variety of circumstances in which lawyers invoke the ademption doctrine. Consider whether application of the doctrine advanced testator's intent in the following case:

McGee v. McGee

Supreme Court of Rhode Island, 1980.
122 R.I. 837, 413 A.2d 72.

■ WEISBERGER, JUSTICE.

This is a complaint for declaratory judgment, in which the plaintiff administrator, Richard J. McGee (Richard), sought directions from the Superior Court in respect to the construction of certain provisions of the will of his mother, Claire E. McGee, and instructions relating to payment of debts and distribution of assets from the testatrix's estate. The sole issue presented by this appeal concerns the question of the ademption of an allegedly specific legacy to the grandchildren of the decedent and the consequent effect of such ademption upon payment of a bequest in the amount of $20,000 to Fedelma Hurd (Hurd), a friend of the testatrix. The provisions of the will pertinent to this appeal read as follows:

"CLAUSE ELEVENTH:

> I give and bequeath to my good and faithful friend FEDELMA HURD, the sum of Twenty Thousand ($20,000.00) Dollars, as an expression to her of my appreciation for her many kindnesses."

"CLAUSE TWELFTH:

> I give and bequeath all of my shares of stock in the Texaco Company, and any and all monies standing in my name on deposit in any banking institution as follows:
>
>> (a) My Executor shall divide the shares of stock, or the proceeds thereof from a sale of same, *with all of my monies, standing on deposit in my name, in any bank*, into three (3) equal parts and shall pay 1/3 over to the living children of my

beloved son, PHILIP; 1/3 to the living children of my beloved son, RICHARD and 1/3 over to the living children of my beloved son, JOSEPH. Each of my grandchildren shall share equally the 1/3 portion given to them." (Emphasis added.)

At the time of the execution of the will and up until a short time before the death of the testatrix, a substantial sum of money was on deposit in her name at the People's Savings Bank in Providence. About five weeks prior to his mother's death, Richard, proceeding pursuant to a written power of attorney as modified by an addendum executed the following month, withdrew approximately $50,000 from these savings accounts. Of this amount, he applied nearly $30,000 towards the purchase of four United States Treasury bonds, commonly denominated as "flower bonds," from the Federal Trust Company in Waterville, Maine (Richard then resided in that state). His objective in executing this transaction was to effect an advantageous method of satisfying potential federal estate tax liability.[5] The bonds, however, did not serve the intended purpose since at the time of Mrs. McGee's death her gross estate was such that apparently no federal estate tax liability was incurred. The remainder of the monies withdrawn from the savings accounts were deposited in Claire McGee's checking account to pay current bills and in a savings account in Richard's name to be transferred to his mother's account as the need might arise for the payment of her debts and future obligations. The sole sum that is now the subject of this appeal is the approximately $30,000 held in the form of United States Treasury bonds.

The complaint for declaratory judgment sought instructions concerning whether the administrator should first satisfy the specific legacy to the grandchildren from the proceeds of the sale of the flower bonds or whether he should first pay the $20,000 bequest to Fedelma Hurd, since the estate lacked assets sufficient to satisfy both bequests.

After hearing evidence and considering legal memoranda filed by the parties, the trial justice found that the bequest to the grandchildren contained in the twelfth clause of the will constituted a specific legacy. He held further, however, that Rhode Island regarded the concept of ademption with disfavor and he sought, therefore, to effectuate the intent of the testatrix. He proceeded to determine that since there is an assumption that one intends to leave his property to those who are the natural objects of his bounty, rather than to strangers, the administrator "should trace the funds used to purchase the Flower Bonds and should satisfy the specific legacy to the grandchildren" under the twelfth clause of the will. Consequently, the trial justice held that the legacy to Fedelma Hurd under the eleventh clause of the will must fail. This appeal ensued.

The McGee grandchildren suggest that the principal design of the testatrix's estate plan, ascertainable from a contemplation of the testamen-

5. Although not otherwise redeemable before maturity, flower bonds may be redeemed at par value, plus accrued interest, upon the owner's death for the purpose of paying the federal taxes on his estate. See *Girard Trust Bank v. United States*, 602 F.2d 938, 940 n. 1 (Ct.Cl.1979). [Note: "Flower bonds" no longer exist—eds.].

tary disposition of her property, was to benefit her family rather than "outsiders." They urge us to consider her intentions—which they assure us were concerned, in part, with protecting the family interests from an anticipated reduction of the estate's value by taxes—in determining whether the transfer of the funds in her accounts did in fact work an ademption. In addition, Richard points out that the decedent did not herself purchase these bonds. On the contrary, Richard acquired them in order to help discharge anticipated tax obligations of the estate and informed his mother of them only subsequently to the purchase. He argues, furthermore, not only that the funds with which he purchased the flower bonds originated in his mother's accounts, but also that since these bonds "are as liquid as cash" they are indeed monies standing in the decedent's name on deposit in a banking institution. He suggests that this description conforms in every respect to the formula drafted into the twelfth clause of her will. Merely the form of the legacy has changed, according to Richard, not its essential character, quality, or substance.

In response, appellant asserts that an ademption occurred by the voluntary act of the testatrix during her lifetime, since her son withdrew the funds as an authorized agent operating under a lawful power of attorney. There is evidence, moreover, that the testatrix subsequently ratified the purchase of the bonds when Richard afterwards told her of his actions and their intended effect upon estate taxes.[6] As a consequence, Hurd asserts that there was no longer any money standing on deposit in the name of the testatrix in any bank with which to discharge the specific legacy to the grandchildren. These transactions resulted in an extinction of the subject matter of the legacy. Hurd argues, in addition, that the intention of the testatrix, even if discernible, is irrelevant to the question of the ademption of the bequest. She therefore contends that her general legacy should be payable from the proceeds of the sale of the flower bonds.

At the outset, we recognize that the instant case concerns specifically the concept of ademption by extinction, a legal consequence that may attend a variety of circumstances occasioned either by operation of law or by the actions of a testator himself or through his guardian, conservator, or agent. *Gardner v. McNeal*, 117 Md. 27, 82 A. 988 (1911); *In re Wright*, 7 N.Y.2d 365, 165 N.E.2d 561, 197 N.Y.S.2d 711 (1960). In particular, a testamentary gift of specific real or personal property may be adeemed—fail completely to pass as prescribed in the testator's will—when the particular article devised or bequeathed no longer exists as part of the testator's estate at the moment of his death because of its prior consumption, loss, destruction, substantial change, sale, or other alienation subsequent to the execution of the will. In consequence, neither the gift, its proceeds, nor similar substitute passes to the beneficiary, and this claim to the legacy is thereby barred. Atkinson, *Handbook of the Law of Wills* § 134 at 741, 743–44 (2d Ed. 1953); 6 Bowe & Parker, *Page on the Law of Wills* § 54.1 at 242,

6. Richard testified his mother "was pleased that [he had] done this because there would be more money available for the children and grandchildren."

§ 54.9 at 256–57 (1962); *Note, Wills: Ademption of Specific Legacies and Devises*, 43 Cal.L.Rev. 151 (1955).

The principle of ademption by extinction has reference only to specific devises and bequests and is thus inapplicable to demonstrative or general testamentary gifts. 6 Page, supra § 54.3 at 245, § 54.5 at 248. In *Haslam v. Alvarez*, 70 R.I. 212, 38 A.2d 158 (1944), we prescribed the criteria for determining the character of a legacy, relying on the earlier case of *Dean v. Rounds*, 18 R.I. 436, 27 A. 515 (1893), wherein we held that "[a] specific legacy, as the term imports, is a gift or bequest of some definite specific thing, something which is capable of being designated and identified." Id. When the testator intends that the legatee shall receive the exact property bequeathed rather than its corresponding quantitative or *ad valorem* equivalent, the gift is a specific one, and when "the main intention is that the legacy be paid by the delivery of the identical thing, and that thing only, and in the event that at the time of the testator's death such thing is no longer in existence, the legacy will not be paid out of his general assets." *Hanley v. Fernell*, 54 R.I. 84, 86, 170 A. 88, 89 (1934). In particular, the designation and identification of the specific legacy in a testator's will describe the gift in a manner that serves to distinguish it from all other articles of the same general nature and prevents its distribution from the general assets of the testator's estate. 6 Page, *supra* § 48.3 at 11–12.

In the case at bar, the trial justice construed the twelfth clause of Mrs. McGee's will as bequeathing a specific legacy to her grandchildren. While it is true that the party who contends the legacy is a specific one must bear the burden of proof on this issue, *DiCristofaro v. Beaudry*, 113 R.I. 313, 320 A.2d 597 (1974), and appellant, in her brief, characterized the twelfth clause as a bequest of a particular residuary gift, the trial justice apparently found that petitioner's contentions met the burden and that the testatrix clearly considered the bequest a specific one.

Without a doubt, the trial justice properly interpreted the McGee grandchildren's bequest, primarily because of the tone of the other provisions, the tenor of the entire instrument, see *Hanley v. Fernell*, 54 R.I. at 86, 170 A. at 89; *Gardner v. Viall*, 36 R.I. 436, 90 A. 760 (1914), and the specificity with which the testatrix described that portion of the twelfth clause relative to the Texaco stock. Additionally, money payable out of a fund—rather than out of the estate generally—described with sufficient accuracy and satisfiable only out of the payment of such fund, *Haslam v. Alvarez*, or a bequest of money deposited in a specific bank, *Hanley v. Fernell*, is, as a rule, a specific legacy. When a will bequeaths "the money owned by one which is on deposit" in a designated bank, although the amount remains unspecified, the gift is nevertheless identifiable and definite, apart from all other funds or property in the testator's estate; and the legacy is specific. *Willis v. Barrow*, 218 Ala. 549, 552, 119 So. 678, 680 (1929); *Prendergast v. Walsh*, 58 N.J.Eq. 149, 42 A. 1049 (Ch.1899). Despite the fact that Mrs. McGee did not name any particular bank in the twelfth clause of her will, she bequeathed all the money in her name "in any bank." In view of the fact that she expected all of her money remaining at her death to go to her grandchildren and, further, the money to be payable from a particular source—that is, accounts in her name in banking institutions—we conclude that the legacy was sufficiently susceptible of identification to render it a specific one.

Accordingly, since the bequest to the grandchildren is specific, we must now determine whether or not it was adeemed by the purchase of the bonds. *Note, Ademption and the Testator's Intent*, 74 Harv.L.Rev. 741 (1961). In connection with the early theory of ademption, the courts looked to the intention of the testator as the basis of their decisions. 6 Page, *supra* § 54.14 at 265. But ever since the landmark case of *Ashburner v. MacGuire*, 2 Bros.C.C. 108, 29 Eng.Rep. 62 (Ch.1786), wherein Lord Thurlow enunciated the "modern theory," courts have utilized the identity doctrine or "in specie" test. This test focuses on two questions only: (1) whether the gift is a specific legacy and, if it is, (2) whether it is found in the estate at the time of the testator's death. Atkinson, *supra* § 134 at 742; Note, 74 Harv.L.Rev. at 742; Comment, *Ademption in Iowa—A Closer Look at the Testator's Intent*, 57 Iowa L.Rev. 1211 (1972). The extinction of the property bequeathed works an ademption regardless of the testator's intent. *In re Tillinghast*, 23 R.I. 121, 123–24, 49 A. 634, 635 (1901); *Humphreys v. Humphreys*, 2 Cox Ch. 184, 30 Eng.Rep. 85 (Ch.1789); 6 Page, *supra* § 54.15 at 266.

The legatees of the twelfth clause argue that the subject matter of the specific bequest, although apparently now unidentifiable in its previous form, actually does exist in the estate of their grandmother but in another form as the result of an exchange or transfer of the original property. But there is a recognized distinction between a bequest of a particular item and a gift of its proceeds, *see generally* Annot., 45 A.L.R.3d 10 (1972); and the testatrix, in the instant case, did recognize the distinction in the twelfth clause of her will by bequeathing the Texaco stock "or the proceeds thereof from a sale of same" but omitting to include similar provisions regarding proceeds in connection with the language immediately following which described the bank-money legacy. It appears that the testatrix's intention, manifest on the face of her will, was that her grandchildren receive only the money in her bank accounts and not the money's proceeds or the investments that represent the conversion of that money into other holdings. Atkinson, *supra* § 134 at 743–44; 6 Page, *supra* § 54.9 at 256–57, § 54.16 at 268–70; see *Gardner v. McNeal*, 117 Md. 27, 82 A. 988 (1911).

In accordance with the generally accepted "form and substance rule," a substantial change in the nature or character of the subject matter of a bequest will operate as an ademption; but a merely nominal or formal change will not. *In re Peirce*, 25 R.I. 34, 54 A. 588 (1903) (no ademption since transfer of stock after consolidation of banks without formal liquidation was exchange and not sale); *Willis v. Barrow*, 218 Ala. 549, 119 So. 678 (1929) (no ademption by transfer of money from named bank to another since place of deposit was merely descriptive); *In re Hall*, 60 N.J.Super. 597, 160 A.2d 49 (1960) (no ademption by transfer of the money from banks designated in will to another one since location was formal description only and did not affect substance of testamentary gift).

Since the money previously on deposit in Mrs. McGee's bank accounts no longer exists at the time of her death, the question arises whether the change was one of form only, rather than substance. We have determined that the change effected by Richard was not merely formal but was substantial. There is no language in the will that can be construed as reflecting an intention of the testatrix to bequeath a gift of bond investments to her grandchildren. The plain and explicit direction of the twelfth clause of the will is that they should receive whatever remained in her bank accounts at the time of her death. Since no sums of money were then on deposit, the specific legacy was adeemed. Clearly, this case is dissimilar to those in which the fund, at all times kept intact, is transferred to a different location, as in *Willis* and *Prendergast*, where the money merely "changed hands," not character. See also In re *Tillinghast,* 23 R.I. 121, 49 A. 634 (1901) (no ademption by mere act of transferring mortgages to own name since they were in specie at the time of testatrix's death). The fact that Mrs. McGee did not herself purchase the bonds is not significant. Disposal or distribution of the subject matter of a bequest by an agent of the testator or with the testator's authorization or ratification similarly operates to adeem the legacy. *Gardner v. McNeal*, 117 Md. 27, 82 A. 988 (1911); *In re Wright*, 7 N.Y.2d 365, 165 N.E.2d 561, 197 N.Y.S.2d 711 (1960); *Glasscock v. Layle*, 21 Ky.Law.Rep. 860, 53 S.W. 270 (Ky.1899).

* * *

Accordingly, we hold that the trial justice erred in allowing the admission of extrinsic evidence regarding Mrs. McGee's intent. We further hold that the specific legacy in the twelfth clause of the testatrix's will is adeemed and the legatees' claim to this bequest is thereby barred. We direct the trial justice to order the petitioner to satisfy the general pecuniary legacy bequeathed in the eleventh clause of the will from the sale of the flower bonds, with the excess to pass under the residuary (fourteenth) clause of the will.

The respondent's appeal is sustained, the judgment below is reversed, and the cause is remanded to the Superior Court for proceedings consistent with this opinion.

NOTES AND QUESTIONS

1. Was the entire devise to the grandchildren in this case specific? Which portion was general? Could you argue that the entire devise was general?

2. Like a majority of courts, the court in the McGee case adopts the "identity" theory of ademption rather than the "intent" theory. As a result, the court did not focus on whether testator would have wanted the devise adeemed. Instead, the identity theory requires the court to focus only on whether the devise was specific (and, of course, on whether the property was a part of testator's estate at testator's death).

Does the identity theory make sense? Note that the theory rests on the premise that we can categorize devises as specific or general. But those categories are significant only for determining how testator's estate should be distributed when unforeseen circumstances have arisen between the time of will execution and the time of testator's death. If the categories themselves are designed to reflect testator's intent, why does it make sense for argument in cases like McGee to focus on whether the devise is "specific" or "general?" Why not instead focus on what testator intended?

3. In McGee itself, what did the grandchildren take? If the amount invested in "flower bonds" exceeded Fedelma Hurd's $20,000 general devise (as it did), who took the balance? Why?

4. Did Claire McGee herself take any action to reduce the value of her devise to her grandchildren? Do you think she understood the consequences of her son's transfer of assets?

In many jurisdictions, if a court-appointed conservator sells or transfers specifically-devised property, the specific devise is not adeemed. See, e.g., Estate of Graham, 216 Kan. 770, 533 P.2d 1318 (1975). Should the court have applied similar analysis in McGee, where the transfer was made by testator's son pursuant to a power of attorney? Compare Coy v. Ezarski, 731 N.W.2d 19 (Iowa 2007) (finding no ademption upon sale of specifically-devised property pursuant to power of attorney) with Stewart v. Sewell, 215 S.W.3d 815 (Tenn. 2007) (finding ademption in similar circumstances, but noting that Tennessee's subsequent adoption of the UPC would alter the result).

5. Suppose Claire McGee had asked you to draft her will. How would you have drafted "Clause Twelfth" to avoid the litigation that resulted in this case?

6. In McGee v. McGee, Clause Twelfth devised all monies standing "in any banking institution." Unfortunately for Claire McGee's grandchildren, Claire's son bought bonds with the money, rather than transferring the money to another banking institution.

Suppose, however, Clause Twelfth had left to the grandchildren "all funds on deposit in my savings account at People's Savings Bank." To what would the grandchildren have been entitled if

a. Claire had transferred her money to the Nickel Savings Bank when People's closed its local branch? See In re Hall, 60 N.J.Super. 597, 160 A.2d 49 (1960) [discussed in McGee v. McGee].

b. Claire had closed her savings account at People's, and bought certificates of deposit at the same institution in order to obtain a higher interest rate? Cf. Estate of Mayberry, 318 Ark. 588, 886 S.W.2d 627 (1994).

c. Nickel Savings Bank had purchased People's, so that Claire's savings account was now held at Nickel?

7. In light of the problems highlighted so far, would you advise a client of modest means to make meaningful specific devises? How often will the devisee care about obtaining the specifically devised property rather than the value of that property?

8. A number of states have enacted statutes to govern ademption issues. Wisconsin, for instance, has, by statute, abolished the common law "identity" theory of ademption, replacing it with a detailed statute informed by the "intent" theory of ademption. Wis. Stat. Ann. 854.08. A number of statutes, including the Wisconsin statute, provide exceptions in cases where a conservator transfers property of an incompetent, and where insurance proceeds remain after adeemed property has been destroyed. See, e.g., N.Y. EPTL 3–4.4; 3–4.5. The Uniform Probate Code formulation is reproduced below:

UNIFORM PROBATE CODE

SECTION 2–606. NONADEMPTION OF SPECIFIC DEVISES; UNPAID PROCEEDS OF SALE, CONDEMNATION, OR INSURANCE; SALE BY CONSERVATOR OR AGENT.

(a) A specific devisee has a right to specifically devised property in the testator's estate at the testator's death and to:

(1) any balance of the purchase price, together with any security agreement, owed by a purchaser at the testator's death by reason of sale of the property;

(2) any amount of a condemnation award for the taking of the property unpaid at death;

(3) any proceeds unpaid at death on fire or casualty insurance on or other recovery for injury to the property;

(4) any property owned by the testator at death and acquired as a result of foreclosure, or obtained in lieu of foreclosure, of the security interest for a specifically devised obligation;

(5) any real property or tangible personal property owned by the testator at death which the testator acquired as a replacement for specifically devised real property or tangible personal property; and

(6) if not covered by paragraphs (1) through (5), a pecuniary devise equal to the value as of its date of disposition of other specifically devised property disposed of during the testator's lifetime but only to the extent it is established that ademption would be inconsistent with the testator's manifested plan of distribution or that at the time the will was made, the date of disposition or otherwise, the testator did not intend ademption of the devise.

(b) If specifically devised property is sold or mortgaged by a conservator or by an agent acting within the authority of a durable power of attorney for an incapacitated principal, or if a condemnation award, insurance proceeds, or recovery for injury to the property is paid to a conservator or to an agent acting within the authority of a durable power of attorney for an incapacitated principal, the specific devisee has the right to a general pecuniary devise equal to the net sale price, the amount of the unpaid loan, the condemnation award, the insurance proceeds, or the recovery.

(c) The right of a specific devisee under subsection (b) is reduced by any right the devisee has under subsection (a).

(d) For the purposes of the references in subsection (b) to a conservator, subsection (b) does not apply if after the sale, mortgage, condemnation, casualty, or recovery, it was adjudicated that the testator's incapacity ceased and the testator survived the adjudication for at least one year.

(e) For the purposes of the reference in subsection (b) to an agent acting within the authority of a durable power of attorney for an incapacitated principal, (i) "incapacitated principal" means a principal who is an incapacitated person, (ii) no adjudication of incapacity before death is necessary, and (iii) the acts of an agent within the authority of a durable power of attorney are presumed to be for an incapacitated principal.

* * *

Note the structure of section 2–606. The statute gives the specific devisee the value of the specifically devised property in several classes of cases where it appears unlikely that the testator would have intended ademption of the devise. Thus, where loss of the specifically devised property was not the result of any voluntary act by the testator—the property was destroyed by fire, or taken by the government in a condemnation proceeding—the specific devisee is entitled to any unpaid condemnation or insurance proceeds. The theory is that testator took no voluntary act, and may not have had time to adjust the will to reflect the change in his property holdings. In those situations, the drafters of the UPC assumed that testator would have preferred the specific devisee to have the proceeds, rather than to take nothing out of the estate. Even if testator has sold specifically devised property, but has not yet collected all monies from the purchaser, the specific devisee is entitled to the balance due on the purchase price. And, the UPC gives the specific devisee the equivalent of a general devise when the specifically devised property has been sold or transferred by a conservator or by "an agent acting within the authority of a durable power of attorney for an incapacitated principal." (Would Claire McGee's son have qualified?)

Perhaps more significant, UPC § 2–606(a)(6) explicitly adopts the intent theory of ademption. The current version of the statute places the burden on the devisee to establish that an ademption has not occurred.

QUESTION

How would McGee v. McGee have been decided if UPC § 2–606 had been in effect in Rhode Island?

PROBLEMS

1. Foster Hume III's will devises a house he owns in Atlanta to his niece, Meredith. Hume devises his residuary estate to a University. A few months before Hume's death, the mortgagee foreclosed on the Atlanta house and sold it at auction. The sale proceeds (after satisfaction of the mortgage) of $55,745.07 were delivered to Hume's executor after his death. There was no evidence that Hume had possessed actual knowledge of the foreclosure proceeding. Under the court's holding in McGee v. McGee, who is entitled to the proceeds from the sale of the Atlanta house? What result under the UPC? See In re Estate of Hume, 984 S.W.2d 602 (Tenn.1999) [decided before Tennessee adopted the UPC; the court reversed two lower courts to hold that the gift was adeemed because pre-UPC ademption doctrine was unconcerned with testator's intent].

Suppose Hume did have actual knowledge of the foreclosure sale. Would that change your answer if McGee is controlling? Under the UPC?

If the UPC were in effect, how would you redraft the will to assure that Meredith does not take any proceeds from a sale of the real property? If you were in Rhode Island, how would you redraft the will to assure that Meredith would be entitled to sale proceeds?

2. Ursula Upscale's will devises "my 2008 Volvo S80" to her brother, Tom. In 2011, Ursula traded in her Volvo (and $40,000 in cash) for a BMW sports car. Ursula then had a head-on collision with a truck. Ursula was killed and the BMW was totaled. Ursula's automobile insurance company is prepared to pay the estate $70,000 for the loss of the BMW. To what, if anything, is Tom entitled (a) under the UPC; (b) under the holding in McGee v. McGee? To what would Tom be entitled under the UPC if the BMW had been uninsured?

3. Upon the death of his wife, Sam Sentimental inherited a diamond ring that had been in his wife's family for three generations. In his will, Sam devised "my wife's diamond ring, which has been in her family for generations, to my wife's sister Rhoda." Sam devised the residue of his estate to his nephew, Quentin. Two years after executing the will, Sam sold the ring for $40,000. At Sam's death, three years later, Sam's estate was valued at $120,000. Under the UPC, is Rhoda entitled to any of Sam's estate?

4. Clara Stewart inherited a house and an undeveloped tract of land near a lake from her second husband. She wrote a will specifically devising the house and the undeveloped tract to her husband's son by a prior marriage, and left all of her remaining property to her own two children by a prior marriage. In her declining years, Clara gave a durable power of attorney to her daughter. Acting pursuant to the power of attorney, the daughter sold the undeveloped tract (which had been appraised for $110,000) to the daughter's own daughter and son-in-law for $80,000, and used the proceeds to pay Clara's nursing home bills. At the time of Clara's death, her estate consisted of the lake house, $50,000 in remaining proceeds from sale of the undeveloped tract, and $100,000 in other property. If the UPC were in effect, how should Clara's assets be distributed? See Stewart v. Sewell, 215 S.W.3d 815 (Tenn. 2007). See also Coy v. Ezarski, 731 N.W.2d 19 (Iowa 2007).

5. At the time Testator executed her will, Testator owned a house, valued at $200,000, and securities worth $100,000. Testator's will left her house to her niece, and the securities to her nephew. In the year before Testator's death, Testator moved into a nursing home, and her sister—acting as a conservator—sold the house to help pay nursing home bills. At testator's death, her estate consisted of $150,000 in cash and securities. How should her estate be distributed if UPC 2–606(b) is in effect?

Changes in Form of Securities

Suppose testator's will devises "my 100 shares of ABC Corp. stock" to her niece. Even if testator never sells the stock, at least two events could occur that give rise to the need for construction of testator's will. First, ABC Corp. could have declared stock splits or stock dividends, multiplying (or reducing) the number of shares held by testator. Second, ABC could have been acquired by another company, leaving testator (and ultimately her estate), with shares of DEF Corp. stock.

A careful drafter will avoid this issue by avoiding devises of "ABC Corporation stock." Suppose, however, the drafter acts on testator's sentimental and foolish wishes to devise particular assets to particular beneficiaries. How should the resulting construction issues be resolved? Consider the UPC's formulation:

UNIFORM PROBATE CODE

SECTION 2–605. INCREASE IN SECURITIES; ACCESSIONS.

(a) If a testator executes a will that devises securities and the testator then owned securities that meet the description in the will, the devise includes additional securities owned by the testator at death to the extent the additional securities were acquired by the testator after the will was executed as a result of the testator's ownership of the described securities and are securities of any of the following types:

(1) securities of the same organization acquired by reason of action initiated by the organization or any successor, related, or acquiring organization, excluding any acquired by exercise of purchase options;

(2) securities of another organization acquired as a result of a merger, consolidation, reorganization, or other distribution by the organization or any successor, related, or acquiring organization; or

(3) securities of the same organization acquired as a result of a plan of reinvestment.

(b) Distributions in cash before death with respect to a described security are not part of the devise.

PROBLEMS

Testator's will devises "100 shares of Hi–Flier Corp. stock" to her sister, Ann. To what is Ann entitled if, two years before Testator's death,

1. Hi–Flier Corp. declared a stock dividend, entitling shareholders to one share for each share they previously held. See Edmundson v. Morton, 332 N.C. 276, 420 S.E.2d 106 (1992).

2. Tip–Top Corp. acquired Hi–Flier, issuing one share of Tip–Top Corp. Stock for each two shares of Hi–Flier stock.

3. Hi–Flier declared a dividend of $5.00 per share, and offered each shareholder the opportunity to take one-tenth of a share of stock in lieu of the $5.00 dividend. Testator took the stock.

NOTE ON ADEMPTION BY SATISFACTION

Suppose testator's will devises property to a particular beneficiary. During testator's lifetime, testator has given property to the same beneficiary. Should the lifetime gift be treated as if it "satisfied" the devise in the will?

If the devise is specific, the case is easy. If testator's will devises her "portrait of mom" to her sister, and testator then gives the portrait to her sister, the devise to the sister is "adeemed by extinction." The sister has received all that the testator intended to give her; she is entitled to nothing more at testator's death.

What if the devise is not specific? Testator's will devises "to each of my three children, one-third of my estate." One year before testator's death, he gives $30,000 to one of his three children. Should that gift be charged against the recipient's share of testator's estate? In general, the answer is no—unless testator has provided, either in the will or in a writing contemporaneous with the gift—that the gift is designed to satisfy the devise in the will. For an application of the principle, see Estate of Soule, 248 Neb. 878, 540 N.W.2d 118 (1995). The Uniform Probate Code is in accord:

SECTION 2–609. ADEMPTION BY SATISFACTION. – maj Rule

(a) Property a testator gave in his [or her] lifetime to a person is treated as a satisfaction of a devise in whole or in part, only if (i) the will provides for deduction of the gift, (ii) the testator declared in a contemporaneous writing that the gift is in satisfaction of the devise or that its value is to be deducted from the value of the devise, or (iii) the devisee acknowledged in writing that the gift is in satisfaction of the devise or that its value is to be deducted from the value of the devise.

(b) For purposes of partial satisfaction, property given during lifetime is valued as of the time the devisee came into possession or enjoyment of the property or at the testator's death, whichever occurs first.

(c) If the devisee fails to survive the testator, the gift is treated as a full or partial satisfaction of the devise, as appropriate, in applying Sections 2–603 and 2–604, unless the testator's contemporaneous writing provides otherwise.

C. LAPSE

We have focused so far on changes in property between the time testator executes her will and the time testator dies. Often, however, difficulties arise not because of changes in property, but because of changes in people—particularly the death of will beneficiaries. We now turn to those difficulties.

Suppose Sal Vationseeker, a wealthy industrialist, makes a $100,000 devise to Reverend Bull Slinger "in recognition of the contribution he has made to the moral fiber of America." Before Sal dies, the reverend is struck dead by lightning. If Sal does not change his will before he dies, what happens to the $100,000 devise? Does it go to Reverend Slinger's estate? To his children?

What do you think Sal would want in this situation? What is the likelihood that Sal knows Reverend Slinger's children or other close relatives? Is there any reason to assume that Sal would prefer his $100,000 to be distributed to Reverend Slinger's children rather than to Sal's own relatives, or to other objects of Sal's bounty?

The common law has generally assumed that when a devisee dies before testator, the testator would not have wanted the devised property to pass to the devisee's descendants or heirs. As a result, a devise "lapses" if the devisee predeceases testator; the devisee's heirs and descendants take nothing. In most American jurisdictions, the common law rule remains intact for devises like the one from Sal to Bull Slinger: the devise lapses if the beneficiary does not survive the testator.

Suppose, now, that Sal makes a $100,000 devise not to the good reverend, but to Sal's daughter, Gladys. He makes another $100,000 devise to his son, Harvey, and still a third $100,000 devise to the children of his deceased son, Irving. Gladys dies after Sal executes his will, but before Sal dies. Gladys is survived by two sons, Jack and Kurt. Should the $100,000 devise to Gladys lapse, or is it more likely that Sal would have wanted his grandsons, Jack and Kurt, to take Gladys' share?

In every American state except Louisiana, the legislature has enacted an "antilapse" statute that would preserve Gladys' $100,000 for her sons (Louisiana protects the sons in other ways). The theory behind antilapse statutes is that when a testator leaves property to a sufficiently close relative, testator would want the issue of that devisee to take the property if the devisee predeceases the testator. Generalization, however, is always dangerous. For an illuminating discussion of lapse issues, and some creative proposals for reform of antilapse statutes, see Susan F. French, Antilapse Statutes are Blunt Instruments: A Blueprint for Reform, 37 Hastings L.J. 335 (1985).

Antilapse statutes vary significantly in operation. In a few states, the antilapse statute applies to all devises, even to those of non-relatives (thus saving devises like the one to Bull Slinger). See, e.g., N.H. Rev. Stat. Ann. § 551.12. In other states, the statute saves only devises to issue, or to issue and siblings. See, e.g., N.Y. EPTL § 3–3.3. In still other states, the statute saves devises to all "relatives," see, e.g., Ohio R.C. § 2107.52, or to a class of relatives defined more broadly than issue and siblings. See, e.g., Kan. Stat. Ann. 59–615 [spouse or relative within sixth degree]. For a comparative study of antilapse statutes, see Patricia J. Roberts, Lapse Statutes: Recurring Construction Problems, 37 Emory L.J. 325 (1988).

Beneficiaries of Antilapse Statutes

Suppose a deceased devisee is within the class of relatives to whom the state's antilapse statute applies. If the statute saves the devise, to whom does the devise pass? Obviously, the devise cannot pass to the dead devisee, but does it pass to the devisee's estate? The general answer is no. Antilapse statutes—except in Maryland—preserve the devise only for the *issue* of the deceased devisee, not for the deceased devisee's will beneficiaries:

> ***Example 1:*** *Testator devises $50,000 to her daughter D, and the residue of her estate to her husband, H. D dies before Testator, leaving a surviving son, S, and a will leaving all of her property to her lover, L. How should Testator's estate be distributed?*
>
> ***Solution:*** *All antilapse statutes save devises to children. As a result, the devise to D does not lapse. However, the devise would not be distributed through D's estate, to L. Instead, the devise would pass to D's issue—here, S.*

Note that in Example 1, if D had died childless, the devise to D would have lapsed—except in Maryland, where L, as the beneficiary of D's will, would have been entitled to take the lapsed devise. Md. Code. Ann. Est. & Trusts § 4–403.

Which approach do you think best reflects the intent of most testators—the Maryland approach or the approach of the vast majority of other states?

Consequences of Lapse

Suppose the applicable antilapse statute does not save a lapsed devise (perhaps because the devisee, like Bull Slinger, is not a relative of testator). What happens to the devised property? The answer to that question depends on the nature of the devise.

Specific and General Devises. If a specific or general devise to an individual beneficiary lapses, the devised property generally passes into the residue of testator's estate. Suppose, for instance, testator devises "$50,000 to Reverend Bull Slinger; $50,000 to my daughter Joan; the remainder of my estate to my wife Laura." If Slinger dies before testator, and the devise lapses, Joan will still take $50,000, and the remainder of the estate will pass to testator's wife Laura.

Residuary Devises. If testator devises the residue of her estate to a single devisee, and if the devise lapses, the residue passes by intestate succession. Suppose, however, testator devises the residue of her estate to more than one devisee. What happens if one of the devisees predeceases the testator, and the antilapse statute does not save the devise?

Until the last several decades, most courts held that the fraction of the residue which would have passed to the deceased devisee would pass instead by intestate succession. In recent decades, many courts have abandoned that view, holding instead that the entire residuary should be distributed to the other residuary devisees; no intestacy should result unless all of the residuary devisees die before testator. Legislation in a number of states—together with the Uniform Probate Code—embodies the modern view that if a devise to one residuary devisee fails, that devisee's share passes to the other residuary devisees.

> ***Example 2:*** *Testator devises the residue of her estate "to be shared by my sister, Patricia, and my good friend Quentin, share and share alike." Quentin dies before Testator [in a jurisdiction whose antilapse statute applies only to devises to "relatives"]. Testator is survived by Patricia, and by a son, Richard [to whom Testator devised $50,000]. How should Testator's estate be distributed?*
>
> ***Solution:*** *At common law, many courts would have held that Patricia and Richard would share Testator's estate because there could be no "residue of a residue." On that view, Richard, as Testator's intestate heir, would take Quentin's share. Today, the Uniform Probate Code, other modern statutes, and many courts, by judicial decision, would hold that Patricia takes the entire residue.*

Among the statutes embodying the modern approach are Uniform Probate Code, § 2–604 and N.Y. EPTL § 3–3.4. Note also that in our example, the residuary devise was to two people as individuals, not to the members of a class, such as "my sisters and brothers" or "my descendants." We will defer the problem of class gifts until after we examine some sample antilapse statutes.

Representative Antilapse Statutes

NEW HAMPSHIRE REVISED STATUTES ANNOTATED

SECTION 551:12. HEIRS OF LEGATEE

The heirs in the descending line of a legatee or devisee, deceased before the testator, shall take the estate bequeathed or devised, in the same manner the legatee or devisee would have taken it if he had survived.

NEW YORK EPTL

SECTION 3–3.3. DISPOSITION TO ISSUE OR BROTHERS OR SISTERS OF TESTATOR NOT TO LAPSE; APPLICATION TO CLASS DISPOSITIONS.

(a) Unless the will whenever executed provides otherwise:

* * *

(2) Instruments executed on or after September first, nineteen hundred ninety-two. Whenever a testamentary disposition is made to the issue or to a brother or sister of the testator, and such beneficiary dies during the lifetime of the testator leaving issue surviving such testator, such disposition does not lapse but vests in such surviving issue, by representation.

(3) The provisions of subparagraph . . . (2) apply to a disposition made to issue, brothers or sisters as a class as if the disposition were made to the beneficiaries by their individual names, except that no benefit shall be conferred hereunder upon the surviving issue of an ancestor who died before the execution of the will in which the disposition to the class was made.

VIRGINIA CODE ANNOTATED

SECTION 64.1–64.1. WHEN CHILDREN OR DESCENDANTS OF DEVISEE, LEGATEE, ETC., TO TAKE ESTATE.

Unless a contrary intention appears in the will, if a devisee or legatee, including a devisee or legatee under a class gift, is (i) a grandparent or a descendant of a grandparent of the testator and (ii) dead at the time of execution of the will or dead at the time of testator's death, the children and descendants of deceased children of the deceased devisee or legatee who survive the testator take in the place of the deceased devisee or legatee. If the takers are all of the same degree of kinship to the deceased devisee or legatee, they take equally. However, if the takers are of unequal degree, then those of more remote degree take by representation.

Note that the Virginia statute reproduced above was based on the 1969 version of the Uniform Probate Code. A number of states have statutes based on the 1969 UPC. As we shall see, the current version of the UPC takes a somewhat different approach.

PROBLEM

Testator's will includes the following dispositive provisions:

"1. $30,000 to my sister, Samantha.

2. $40,000 to my husband's brother, Bernie.

3. $50,000 to my Uncle Jim.

4. $5 to my brother, Carl.

5. The remainder of my estate to my sister's daughter, Nancy, and my husband's daughter, Debbie, in equal shares."

At Testator's death, her estate was valued at $200,005. Testator's husband had predeceased her, and Testator died childless. Samantha and Carl were her only siblings. How should Testator's estate be distributed under the New York statute if Samantha, Bernie, and Jim had predeceased Testator, and

(a) Samantha was survived by her daughter Nancy and her husband Tom; her will left all of her property to Tom; Bernie was survived by his daughter Esther, to whom he left his entire estate; Jim was survived by his son Kurt, to whom he left his entire estate.

(b) Same facts as (a), but Nancy had also predeceased Testator

1. Survived by her husband, to whom she left her entire estate; or

2. Survived by a son, Victor, to whom she left her entire estate.

How would your answers be different if the New Hampshire statute were in effect? The Virginia statute?

Class Gifts

In the materials so far, we have focused on devises to individuals who died before testator. Suppose, however, testator did not make a gift to individuals, but a gift to a class: "to my children" or "to my brothers and sisters" or "to my husband's children." What happens if one or more members of the class predecease the testator?

At common law, if a member of the class predeceased testator, that member's devise lapsed, and the remaining members of the class divided the lapsed devise. Thus, if Testator's will devises $50,000 "to my brother's children," and one of the brother's children predeceases Testator leaving issue, the common law rule would exclude the deceased child's issue, and divide the property among the brother's surviving children.

Most antilapse statutes apply to class gifts as well as gifts to individuals. Examine the New Hampshire, New York, and Virginia statutes. Which of them expressly apply to class gifts? Even when an antilapse statute does not expressly apply to class gifts, courts typically hold that the statute was intended to apply to class gifts as well as to gifts to individuals.

Note, however, that the common law rule remains in effect for those class gifts to which the antilapse statute does not apply:

> ***Example 3:*** *Testator's will leaves "$60,000 to my wife's children by her first marriage." The will leaves the remainder of testator's estate to his own children. The wife had four children by her first marriage; one of the four predeceased Testator leaving issue. How should the $60,000 be distributed under the Virginia statute?*
>
> ***Solution:*** *Note that Virginia's antilapse statute does not apply to devises to a spouse's children. As a result, the devise to the wife's deceased child would lapse, and the other three children would divide the $60,000. By contrast, if Testator's will had left "$60,000 to my children," and Testator had four children, one of whom died before Testator, leaving issue, the issue of the deceased child would take one-fourth of the $60,000, or a total of $15,000.*

If the New Hampshire statute were in effect, would a court reach the same solution in Example 3? Why or why not?

Note that as a drafting matter, gifts to single-generation classes—children, grandchildren, nieces and nephews—invite dispute about the rights of issue of deceased class members. By contrast, if the drafter includes a devise to "issue" or to "issue of my brothers and sisters," the disputes dissolve. Gifts to multi-generational classes automatically include issue of deceased class members. Drafters should use multi-generational language unless the testator wants to exclude issue of deceased class members.

PROBLEM

Testator's will leaves $100,000 "to my nieces," and the remainder of his estate to the American Red Cross. Testator's only sibling had four children: Alice and Bertha, who are still alive; Chelsea, who died before Testator's death, leaving a son, Edgar; and Delilah, who died childless before Testator's death, with a will leaving all of her property to her husband, Frank.

How will Testator's estate be distributed if the Virginia antilapse statute is in effect? The New York statute?

Suppose Testator's will had instead left $25,000 to each of Alice, Bertha, Chelsea, and Delilah. Would distribution of the estate be the same?

NOTE ON VOID DEVISES

At common law, a lapsed devise was a devise to a person who died between the time of will execution and the time of testator's death. By contrast, if the devise was to a person who had died before the time of will execution, the devise was a "void" devise.

For the most part, little turned on whether a devise was deemed "lapsed" or "void." Modern antilapse statutes generally apply to save both lapsed and void devises. In some jurisdictions, however, the distinction remains important when class gifts are involved. For instance, examine the New York antilapse statute. If Testator devises $30,000 "to my brothers," and at the time Testator's will was executed, one of his brothers had already died, do the dead brother's issue share in the $30,000? Would the issue share under the Virginia statute?

PROBLEM AREAS: WHEN DOES THE WILL OVERRIDE THE ANTILAPSE STATUTE?

Remember that antilapse statutes are constructional rules. By using express language in a will, testator (and testator's lawyer) can assure that an antilapse statute will not apply. If, however, the language in the will is not sufficiently precise, litigation may result. Consider the following two cases:

Estate of Rehwinkel

Court of Appeals of Washington, 1993.
71 Wash.App. 827, 862 P.2d 639.

■ PER CURIAM:

Ronald Fossum appeals from an order of summary judgment entered in favor of the estate of Leo August Rehwinkel (hereinafter, Estate). The matter has been referred to the panel for accelerated review pursuant to RAP 18.12. We affirm.

In 1968 Leo Rehwinkel executed his last will and testament. The first section of the will directs that all of Leo's expenses and legal obligations be paid from his estate. The next provision states:

> II.
>
> I give, devise and bequeath the entire residue of my estate, both real and personal property and wherever situated, *to those of the following who are living at the time of my death*, share and share alike:
>
> To my brother, Alex Rehwinkel ... my sister Augusta Stallbaum ... and my following nieces and nephews: Dorothy Schmid ... Velma Best ... George Hagemann ... Helen[e] Anderson ... Hildegard Fingerson ... Richard Stallbaum ... John Ervin Rehwinkel ... Maureen Barrett ... Betty Lou Musto ... the issue by representation (by stirpes and not per capita) of Rudolph Rehwinkel, and the issue by representation (by stirpes and not per capita) of Rosalie Wade.

(Emphasis added by the court.) Section 3 of the will appoints the executor; section 4 revokes all former wills and codicils.

Leo Rehwinkel died in November 1991. His niece, Helene Anderson, one of the named beneficiaries under the will, had died approximately one month earlier.

The will was admitted to probate. Subsequently, Fossum, Helene's son, filed a petition for an order declaring him an heir of Leo Rehwinkel. He argued that under the anti-lapse statute, RCW 11.12.110, he was entitled to the share which his mother would have received had she lived. The Estate filed a motion for summary judgment, contending that Fossum should not be declared an heir of Leo Rehwinkel. On June 1, 1993, the trial court entered an order granting the Estate's motion for summary judgment, dismissing Fossum's petition.

.... This case concerns a question of law regarding interpretation of Leo Rehwinkel's will. See *In re Estate of Lee*, 49 Wash.2d 254, 257, 299 P.2d 1066 (1956). Specifically, we are presented with a single issue regarding application of the anti-lapse statute, RCW 11.12.110, which provides in pertinent part:

> **Death of devisee or legatee before testator.** When any estate shall be devised or bequeathed to any child, grandchild, or other relative of the testator, and such devisee or legatee shall die before the testator, having lineal descendants who survive the testator, such descendants shall take the estate, real and personal, as such devisee or legatee would have done in the case he had survived the testator ... [.]

The anti-lapse statute reflects a legislative determination that, as a matter of public policy, when a testator fails to provide for the possibility that his consanguineous beneficiary will predecease him, the lineal descendants of the beneficiary take his or her share. *In re Estate of Button*, 79 Wash.2d

849, 854, 490 P.2d 731 (1971). "This is said to be a recognition of a natural and instinctive concern for the welfare of those in a testator's bloodline." In re *Estate of Allmond*, 10 Wash. App. 869, 871, 520 P.2d 1388, review denied, 84 Wash.2d 1004 (1974).

> [T]he paramount duty of the court is to give effect to the testator's intent.... Such intention must, if possible, be ascertained from the language of the will itself and the will must be considered in its entirety and effect must be given every part thereof.

In re *Estate of Bergau*, 103 Wash.2d 431, 435, 693 P.2d 703 (1985); accord, *In re Estate of Niehenke*, 58 Wash. App. 149, 152, 791 P.2d 562 (1990), aff'd in part, 117 Wn.2d 631, 818 P.2d 1324 (1991). A presumption arises in favor of the operation of the anti-lapse statute. *In re Estate of Niehenke*, 117 Wash.2d at 640. The burden of showing that the statute should not operate falls upon the party opposing it. All doubts are to be resolved in favor of the operation of the statute, which is to be liberally construed. *In re Estate of Niehenke*, 117 Wash.2d at 640; *In re Estate of Allmond, supra* at 871–72, 520 P.2d 1388. A testator is presumed to be aware of the anti-lapse statute; further, it is presumed that the testator intended the statute to apply unless a contrary intent is shown. *In re Estate of Niehenke*, 117 Wash.2d at 640; 96 C.J.S. Wills § 1217(a), at 1057 (1957). The intent on the part of the testator to preclude operation of the statute must be *clearly* shown. *In re Estate of Niehenke*, 117 Wash.2d at 640. The presumption in favor of the anti-lapse statute does not apply if the testator provides for an alternative disposition. *In re Estate of Button, supra* at 854.

Fossum argues that Leo Rehwinkel's will does not clearly show an intent to preclude operation of the anti-lapse statute. Fossum argues that the trial court decision defeats the intent of the will, which distributes gifts to all "branches" of his family tree. Fossum points out that Leo bequeathed shares of the estate to both Augusta and Alex, the only sister and brother living at the time he executed the will. The will also designated gifts to his nieces and nephews who were living at the time the will was executed; they included the living issue of Augusta, Alex, and his three deceased siblings, Marie, Anna, and John. Finally, the will left gifts to the unnamed issue of his dead niece and nephew, Rosalie and Rudolph. In this way, Fossum contends, Leo left gifts to all "branches" of his family tree. Fossum contends this scheme manifests an intent to benefit all the bloodlines of his family, an intent which is not negated by the limiting language "to those of the following who are living at the time of my death."

The Estate does not dispute the facts of the testamentary scheme. Instead, the Estate argues that the above quoted language in the will manifests the clear intent of the testator to preclude operation of the anti-lapse statute. The Estate argues that this language is a condition precedent to taking under the will: a beneficiary had to be "living at the time of" Leo's death in order to receive a gift.

Our primary duty is to determine the testator's intent from the will in its entirety. *In re Estate of Niehenke*, 117 Wash.2d at 639. Where the testator uses words of survivorship indicating an intention that the devisee shall take the gift only if he survives the testator, the statute does not apply. Annot., *Antilapse Act—Testator's Intention as Defeating Operation of Antilapse Statute*, 63 A.L.R.2d 1172, 1186 (1959).

We agree with the Estate that the language "to those of the following who are living at the time of my death" manifests a clear intent to preclude application of the statute. This phrase clearly provides that only those "who are living at the time of" Rehwinkel's death can take under the will. Fossum does not explain what other meaning this phrase could possibly have, nor do we perceive any.

Research discloses no Washington cases with the same survivorship language. However, our conclusion is supported by the weight of authority from other jurisdictions. In *In re Estate of Leuer*, 84 Misc. 2d 1087, 378 N.Y.S.2d 612 (1976), the language was almost identical to that of the present case. The will directed distribution "among my sisters and brothers living at the time of my death, share and share alike." The court held that where all the testator's siblings predeceased her, the gifts lapsed by virtue of this clause. The court held that this "simple, formal and unambiguous language" evidenced the intent that only the survivors of the class should share in the estate, thereby avoiding application of the anti-lapse statute.

The court in *Shalkhauser v. Beach*, 14 Ohio Misc. 1, 233 N.E.2d 527 (1968) reached the same conclusion. In that case the testator gave "[t]hirty percent (30%) equally among the following who survive me, namely [naming several relatives]." The court in *Shalkhauser* held that this language conditioned the gift on the beneficiary's surviving the testator, and that it was "obvious" the anti-lapse statute had no application in this situation. *Shalkhauser*, at 5.

These cases, then, reject operation of the anti-lapse statute where the will uses survivorship language like that in the instant case. Such language manifests the testator's intent that the named beneficiary take under the will only if he or she survives the testator. *Accord, Slattery v. Kelsch*, 734 S.W.2d 813 (Ky.Ct.App.1987); *Day v. Brooks*, 10 Ohio Misc. 273, 224 N.E.2d 557 (1967); *In re Barrett's Estate*, 159 Fla. 901, 33 So. 2d 159 (1948); *Williams v. Williams*, 152 Fla. 255, 9 So. 2d 798 (1942); *Kunkel v. Kunkel*, 267 Pa. 163, 110 A. 73 (1920).

In arguing that the anti-lapse statute applies, Fossum relies primarily on *Detzel v. Nieberding*, 7 Ohio Misc. 262, 219 N.E.2d 327 (1966). In *Detzel* the will left a gift to the testatrix's sister "provided she be living at the time of" the testatrix's death. The court held that this language did not prevent operation of the anti-lapse statute. The court held that in order to avoid operation of the statute, the will must make an alternative disposition in the event of the death of the beneficiary. *Detzel*, at 274, 219 N.E.2d at 336. In reaching this result, the court in *Detzel* rejected considerable authority to the contrary, including *Kunkel v. Kunkel*, supra.

Two later Ohio cases have declined to follow *Detzel*. In *Day v. Brooks*, supra, the court distinguished *Detzel* on the basis that it related to an individual bequest to one person and on other unspecified grounds. The court in Shalkhauser v. Beach, supra, soundly rejected the *Detzel* court's analysis, calling it "clearly and *completely erroneous.*" *Shalkhauser v. Beach, supra at 6. Accordingly, we do not find* Detzel to be persuasive authority.

We conclude that the weight of authority supports the Estate's position. We hold that the language of distribution to those "who are living at the time of my death" manifests the testator's clear intent that the anti-lapse statute not apply. Accordingly, the gift to Fossum's mother lapsed when she predeceased the testator. The trial court did not err in granting the Estate's motion for summary judgment.

Affirmed.

NOTES AND QUESTIONS

1. If Leo Rehwinkel had known that Helene Anderson would be dead at the time of his death, would he have wanted Helene's son, Ronald Fossum, to take Helene's share? From the language of the will, what argument would you make for Fossum? For the estate?

2. Suppose Rehwinkel had made a single general devise in his will "to Helene Anderson, provided that she be living at the time of my death." If Anderson predeceased Rehwinkel, would her son, Fossum, be entitled to invoke the antilapse statute? Note that this language is similar to the language in Detzel v. Nieberding, 7 Ohio Misc. 262, 219 N.E.2d 327 (1966), discussed and rejected in the Rehwinkel opinion. If the will expressly conditions a devise on survival, how could any court hold that an antilapse statute should apply?

3. Suppose Rehwinkel had made a single general devise in his will "to Helene Anderson," and had included no language regarding survivorship. Suppose further that Rehwinkel's residuary clause had devised "all the rest, residue and remainder of my estate, including legacies or devises that may lapse or fail for any reason, to my sister Augusta Stallbaum." If Anderson predeceased Rehwinkel, would the anti-lapse statute direct that Fossum take her devise? Compare Blevins v. Moran, 12 S.W.3d 698 (Ky. App.2000) [holding that residuary language is boilerplate and insufficient to manifest an intent to preclude application of the anti-lapse statute] with Colombo v. Stevenson, 150 N.C.App. 163, 563 S.E.2d 591 (2002) [holding that similar residuary language does preclude application of the statute]. If Stallbaum predeceased Rehwinkel, leaving a child surviving her, is Stallbaum's child entitled to the residuary devise?

4. Suppose you were drafting Leo Rehwinkel's will, and your goal was to avoid any litigation over the will's meaning. How would you redraft the disputed provision to make it clear that Helene Anderson's devise should lapse unless she survived Rehwinkel? How would you redraft the provision to make it clear that the devise should not lapse? For an excellent discussion of drafting problems, see John L. Garvey, Drafting Wills and

Trusts: Anticipating the Birth and Death of Possible Beneficiaries, 71 Or. L. Rev. 47 (1992).

5. Testator's will provides: "Except as otherwise specifically provided for herein, I have intentionally omitted to provide herein for any of my heirs who are living at the time of my demise." Testator's will leaves property to her daughter, who predeceased testator, leaving issue. Does the will provision preclude daughter's issue from sharing in testator's estate? See Estate of Tolman, 181 Cal.App.4th 1433, 104 Cal.Rptr.3d 924 (2010).

6. ***Note on Simultaneous Death and Antilapse Statutes.*** In Estate of Rehwinkel, Helene Anderson died one month before Leo Rehwinkel. If she had died two months later, she would have been entitled to a share of Rehwinkel's estate, and her son would presumably have become entitled to that share at her death.

Suppose, however, Anderson and Rehwinkel had died in a common disaster. Under the terms of the Uniform Simultaneous Death Act, Anderson would be treated as if she had predeceased Rehwinkel for purposes of distributing Rehwinkel's estate. Therefore, the devise to Anderson would have lapsed.

Now, suppose Anderson had died two days after Rehwinkel. By the terms of the will, she would appear to have qualified to inherit from Rehwinkel. Consider Uniform Probate Code section 2–702(b), entitled "Requirement of Survival by 120 Hours under Governing Instrument":

> Except as provided in subsection (d), for purposes of a provision of a governing instrument that relates to an individual surviving an event, including the death of another individual, an individual who is not established by clear and convincing evidence to have survived the event by 120 hours is deemed to have predeceased the event.

Subsection (d) would not require survival by 120 hours if:

> (1) the governing instrument contains language dealing explicitly with simultaneous deaths or deaths in a common disaster and that language is operable under the facts of the case;
>
> (2) the governing instrument indicates that an individual is not required to survive an event, including the death of another individual, by any specified period or expressly requires the individual to survive the event by a specified period; but survival of the event or the specified period must be established by clear and convincing evidence;. . . .

What effect would a statute comparable to UPC 2–702 have on distribution of Rehwinkel's estate if Anderson had survived Rehwinkel by two days?

The Uniform Probate Code's Antilapse Provision

The Uniform Probate Code's antilapse provision is far more comprehensive—and controversial—than most other antilapse statutes. According to the statute's Official Comment (which goes on for many pages), the statute "resolves a variety of interpretive questions that have arisen under standard antilapse statutes."

In approaching § 2–603, keep in mind that 2–603(b) is the heart of the statute. Section 2–603(b)(1) deals with gifts to individuals, while 2–603(b)(2) deals with class gifts. Perhaps the statute's most controversial provision is 2–603(b)(3), which provides that words of survivorship, by themselves, are not sufficient to remove a devise from application of the antilapse statute.

SECTION 2–601. SCOPE.

In the absence of a finding of a contrary intention, the rules of construction in this Part control the construction of a will.

SECTION 2–603. ANTILAPSE; DECEASED DEVISEE; CLASS GIFTS.

(a) [Definitions.] In this section:

(1) "Alternative devise" means a devise that is expressly created by the will and, under the terms of the will, can take effect instead of another devise on the happening of one or more events, including survival of the testator or failure to survive the testator, whether an event is expressed in condition-precedent, condition-subsequent, or any other form. A residuary clause constitutes an alternative devise with respect to a nonresiduary devise only if the will specifically provides that, upon lapse or failure, the nonresiduary devise, or nonresiduary devises in general, pass under the residuary clause.

(2) "Class member" includes an individual who fails to survive the testator but who would have taken under a devise in the form of a class gift had he [or she] survived the testator.

(3) "Descendant of a grandparent", as used in subsection (b), means an individual who qualifies as a descendant of a grandparent of the testator or of the donor of a power of appointment under the (i) rules of construction applicable to a class gift created in the testator's will if the devise or exercise of the power is in the form of a class gift or (ii) rules for intestate succession if the devise or exercise of the power is not in the form of a class gift.

(4) "Descendants", as used in the phrase "surviving descendants" of a deceased devisee or class member in subsections (b)(1) and (2), mean the descendants of a deceased devisee or class member who would take under a class gift created in the testator's will.

(5) "Devise" includes an alternative devise, a devise in the form of a class gift, and an exercise of a power of appointment.

(6) "Devisee" includes (i) a class member if the devise is in the form of a class gift, (ii) an individual or class member who was deceased at the time the testator executed his [or her] will as well as an individual or class member who was then living but who failed to survive the testator, and (iii) an appointee under a power of appointment exercised by the testator's will.

(7) "Stepchild" means a child of the surviving, deceased, or former spouse of the testator or of the donor of a power of appointment, and not of the testator or donor.

(8) "Surviving", in the phrase "surviving devisees" or "surviving descendants", means devisees or descendants who neither predeceased the testator nor are deemed to have predeceased the testator under Section 2–702.

(9) "Testator" includes the donee of a power of appointment if the power is exercised in the testator's will.

(b) [Substitute Gift.] If a devisee fails to survive the testator and is a grandparent, a descendant of a grandparent, or a stepchild of either the testator or the donor of a power of appointment exercised by the testator's will, the following apply:

(1) Except as provided in paragraph (4), if the devise is not in the form of a class gift and the deceased devisee leaves surviving descendants, a substitute gift is created in the devisee's surviving descendants. They take by representation the property to which the devisee would have been entitled had the devisee survived the testator.

(2) Except as provided in paragraph (4), if the devise is in the form of a class gift, other than a devise to "issue," "descendants," "heirs of the body," "heirs," "next to kin," "relatives," or "family," or a class described by language of similar import, a substitute gift is created in the surviving descendants of any deceased devisee. The property to which the devisees would have been entitled had all of them survived the testator passes to the surviving devisees and the surviving descendants of the deceased devisees. Each surviving devisee takes the share to which he [or she] would have been entitled had the deceased devisees survived the testator. Each deceased devisee's surviving descendants who are substituted for the deceased devisee take by representation the share to which the deceased devisee would have been entitled had the deceased devisee survived the testator. For the purposes of this paragraph, "deceased devisee" means a class member who failed to survive the testator and left one or more surviving descendants.

(3) For the purposes of Section 2–601, words of survivorship, such as in a devise to an individual "if he survives me," or in a devise to "my surviving children," are not, in the absence of additional evidence, a sufficient indication of an intent contrary to the application of this section.

(4) If the will creates an alternative devise with respect to a devise for which a substitute gift is created by paragraph (1) or (2), the substitute gift is superseded by the alternative devise if:

(A) the alternative devise is in the form of a class gift and one or more members of the class is entitled to take under the will; or

(B) the alternative devise is not in the form of a class gift and the expressly designated devisee of the alternative devise is entitled to take under the will.

(5) Unless the language creating a power of appointment expressly excludes the substitution of the descendants of an appointee for the appointee, a surviving descendant of a deceased appointee of a power of appointment can be substituted for the appointee under this section, whether or not the descendant is an object of the power.

(c) [More Than One Substitute Gift; Which One Takes.] If, under subsection (b), substitute gifts are created and not superseded with respect to more than one devise and the devises are alternative devises, one to the other, the determination of which of the substitute gifts takes effect is resolved as follows:

(1) Except as provided in paragraph (2), the devised property passes under the primary substitute gift.

(2) If there is a younger-generation devise, the devised property passes under the younger-generation substitute gift and not under the primary substitute gift.

(3) In this subsection:

(A) "Primary devise" means the devise that would have taken effect had all the deceased devisees of the alternative devises who left surviving descendants survived the testator.

(B) "Primary substitute gift" means the substitute gift created with respect to the primary devise.

(C) "Younger-generation devise" means a devise that (i) is to a descendant of a devisee of the primary devise, (ii) is an alternative devise with respect to the primary devise, (iii) is a devise for which a substitute gift is created, and (iv) would have taken effect had all the deceased devisees who left surviving descendants survived the testator except the deceased devisee or devisees of the primary devise.

(D) "Younger-generation substitute gift" means the substitute gift created with respect to the younger-generation devise.

NOTES AND QUESTIONS

1. UPC § 2–603 operates to save devises to two classes of people: (1) grandparents and their descendants; and (2) stepchildren. Few other antilapse statutes protect devises to stepchildren.

The Official Comment notes that if, after execution of testator's will, testator and the stepchild's parent divorce, the devise to the stepchild itself would be revoked under UPC 2–804. The antilapse statute would not save the revoked devise.

2. Note the interplay between § 2–603(b)(3) and § 2–601. Section 2–603(b)(3) says, in effect, that language of survivorship is an insufficient basis for finding an intention to supersede the UPC's antilapse provisions.

3. If § 2–603 had been in force, how would Estate of Rehwinkel have been decided? Which approach do you prefer—the court's approach or the UPC's?

4. Section 2–603 appears premised on the belief that a comprehensive statute can come closer to approximating testator's intent than the judgment of a common law court. Do you agree? What basis is there for the statutory premise?

Does UPC § 2–603 leave some open questions? Consider the following case:

Morse v. Sharkey

Supreme Court of Michigan, 2009.
483 Mich. 48, 764 N.W.2d 1.

■ PER CURIAM.

In this case, we are called upon to discern the group of individuals who may take under the residuary clause of the testator's will. Petitioner maintains that the residuary clause includes only the surviving siblings of the testator and her late husband, to the exclusion of the surviving heirs of predeceased siblings. In lieu of granting leave to appeal, we would affirm the judgment of the Court of Appeals and hold that the probate court correctly construed the will in petitioner's favor. The class, "brothers and sisters," was unambiguously qualified and limited by the phrase "that survive me." This qualification clearly indicated the testator's intent to exclude her predeceased siblings and their heirs from the class of devisees.

Facts and Procedural History

On January 15, 1979, testator Alice Raymond and her husband Claude Raymond executed mirror-image wills, both leaving their estates to one another upon death. Claude Raymond predeceased the testator in February 2000, and Alice Raymond died at the age of 88 in February 2005. Because the testator's spouse was already deceased, the residuary clause of the will came into effect. It provided that the remainder of the estate would be divided as follows:

> A. Fifty (50%) percent thereof to my brother[s] and sisters that survive me share and share alike or to the survivor or survivors thereof.
>
> B. Fifty (50%) percent thereof to the brothers and sisters of my husband that survive me, share and share alike or to the survivor or survivors thereof.

The testator had eight siblings, but at the time of her death, only two of her siblings were alive. Likewise, the testator's spouse had eight siblings, but only three of her deceased husband's siblings were alive at the time of the testator's death. The petitioner in this case is one of the testator's surviving brothers. The respondents are some of the children and grandchildren of the deceased siblings of Alice and Claude Raymond.

In June 2005, petitioner filed a petition for probate followed by a petition to construe the will. Petitioner argued that only the surviving siblings of the testator and her husband could take under the clear terms of the will. Respondent maintained that the will provided for "the survivor or survivors" of the deceased siblings of Alice and Claude Raymond. Following a hearing, the probate judge agreed with petitioner and denied respondents a share of the estate, reasoning:

> I think in reading the clause one has to look at the first phrase, "Fifty per cent thereof to my brothers and sisters that survive me," then there is a coma [sic]. It would appear to this court that the group Ms. Raymond was dealing with were to [sic] her brothers and sisters. Then she qualified that group by "those who survive me." The remaining clause, in this court's eyes, would be descriptive of the earlier group, the earlier group being "my brothers and sisters that survive me." The remaining phrase, "to share and share alike or to the survivors thereof" would mean to my brothers and sisters, those who predecease me, to those that are left, to share and share alike and to the survivors thereof.

The Court of Appeals affirmed. The majority held that, under the plain language of the will, only the testator's surviving siblings and siblings-in-law could receive a share of the estate, and that the will granted nothing to the descendants of predeceased siblings. Because the testator limited the class of "brothers and sisters" to those who survived the testator, this indicated the testator's intent to exclude any predeceased siblings from the class of devisees.

The Court of Appeals majority further held that the phrase "share and share alike" evinced the intent to bestow a per capita distribution among the surviving siblings. The Court of Appeals majority reasoned that the second clause of the bequest—"or to the survivor or survivors thereof"—modified "my brother[s] and sisters that survive me," confining membership to testator's surviving siblings.

The dissenting judge believed that the plain language of the provision indicated that the estate should be shared by both the surviving siblings *and* the heirs of the deceased siblings. The dissent believed that the majority's interpretation was illogical and redundant, and that the phrase "survivors thereof" must refer to someone *other than* the surviving siblings. Specifically, the dissenting judge believed that the phrase must refer to the descendants of the predeceased siblings.

The respondents appealed in this Court. We heard oral argument on the application for leave to appeal, and now we would affirm the judgment of the Court of Appeals.

Analysis

"The primary goal of the Court in construing a will is to effectuate, to the extent consistent with the law, the intent of the testator." To accomplish this, a court gives effect to the drafter's intent as indicated in the plain language of the will. The will must be read as a whole and harmonized, if possible, with the intent expressed in the document. If there is no ambiguity, the Court is to enforce the will as written. However, if the intent of the testator cannot be gleaned solely by reference to the will because there is an ambiguity, the Court may discern the intent of the testator through extrinsic sources. Additionally, while the probate court's factual findings are subject to review for clear error, a probate court's construction of a will is a question of law subject to de novo review.

The substantive portions of the testamentary provisions are identical, providing for "[f]ifty (50%) per cent thereof to the brothers and sisters that survive me, share and share alike or to the survivor or survivors thereof." We agree with the probate court's ruling in this case that the identified group who may take under the terms of the residuary clause is comprised of the brothers and sisters of Alice and Claude Raymond. However, that group does not include all siblings, but is limited by the phrase "that survive me." Thus, the inclusion of this express limitation necessarily precludes those siblings who predeceased Alice Raymond from taking a portion of the testator's estate under the residuary clause.

We further agree with the probate court that the remaining clause "or to the survivor or survivors thereof" necessarily references the group described earlier in the disjunctive phrase-the surviving brothers and sisters. This is consistent with *In re Holtforth's Estate, 298 Mich 708; 299 NW 776 (1941)*; and *In re Burruss Estate, 152 Mich App 660; 394 NW2d 466 (1986)*. As Justice Cooley noted in *Eberts v Eberts, 42 Mich 404, 407; 4 NW 172 (1880)*, when a will "only makes the gift to persons who survived the testat[or] *there is nothing to go to the issue of others who died before []he did.*" (Emphasis added.)[1]

While the testamentary phrase was imperfectly worded, any other construction, such as that advanced by the Court of Appeals dissent, would permit a gift to the predeceased siblings of the testator, a group that was specifically excluded by the plain language of the will.

We would affirm.

NOTES AND QUESTIONS

1. The Michigan legislature has enacted UPC 2–603 (which is quoted in the footnote to the court's opinion). Did the Michigan Supreme Court hold the statute applicable? Why or why not?

---

1. Although "words of survivorship ... are not, in the absence of additional evidence, a sufficient indication of an intent contrary to the application" of the antilapse statute, *MCL 700.2603(1)(c)*, we agree with the Court of Appeals majority that

> the language of the residuary clause taken as a whole—specially taking into account the use of the three separate statements: "that survive me," "share and share alike," and "the survivor or survivors thereof"—expresses an intent to make a provision for the death of the beneficiaries in a manner contrary to that provided for in the antilapse statute." [*In re Raymond Estate, supra at 35*, citing *In re Burruss Estate, supra at 663, 665*; *In re Holtforth's Estate, supra at 710–711*).]

2. According to the court, what do the words "survivor or survivors" mean in the residuary clause of Alice Raymond's will? What other meaning might "survivor or survivors" have?

3. How would the Morse court have decided the case if each clause had ended after "share and share alike?" Justify your conclusion.

4. Suppose all of Alice Raymond's siblings, and all of her husband's siblings, had predeceased her, leaving issue. How would the court have distributed Alice's estate? Do you think that result would reflect Alice's intent? Does your answer cast doubt on the court's construction of the will (or the statute)?

5. Suppose Alice Raymond had approached you to draft her will. How would you have eliminated the ambiguity that led to this litigation? Suppose your questions revealed that

a. Alice wanted to include only siblings who survived her, and not the issue of siblings who predeceased her?

b. Alice wanted to include siblings who survived and issue of siblings who predeceased her?

PROBLEMS

1. Testator's will leaves a lakefront cottage "to my sister S, if she survives me." The will leaves the rest of his property to his wife, W. At Testator's death, S has died, survived by her two children, A and B. Testator is survived by W and by Testator's own two children, Y and Z. If UPC 2–603 is in effect, how should Testator's estate be distributed?

Would your answer change if

(a) Testator's will also provided "I leave nothing to those ungrateful youngsters, A, B, Y, and Z?"

(b) Testator's will provided "to my sister, S, if she survives me, and not to her descendants if she predeceases me."

(c) Testator's lawyer wrote Testator a letter, before Testator executed the will, indicating that she had included the survivorship language to assure that A and B would not take the cottage?

How would you redraft Testator's will to assure that W takes the cottage if S does not survive Testator? On drafting issues generally, see John L. Garvey, Drafting Wills and Trusts: Anticipating the Birth and Death of Possible Beneficiaries, 71 Oregon L. Rev. 47 (1992).

2. Testator's will leaves all of her property "to my surviving children." Testator is survived by her daughter, D, and the children of a deceased son, A and B. If UPC 2–603 is in effect, how should Testator's estate be distributed? What significance does the UPC attach to the word "surviving" in Testator's will?

How would you redraft Testator's will to assure that D takes all of Testator's property if Testator's son predeceases Testator?

3. Testator's will includes the following provisions:

"1. I devise $10,000 to my daughter D, if she survives me, and if she does not, to my son S.

2. I devise $20,000 to my son S, if he survives me, and if he does not, to my daughter D.

3. I leave the remainder of my estate to my niece, N."

At Testator's death, D has died, survived by a son Y, and S has died, survived by a daughter, Z. How should Testator's $100,000 estate be distributed? [See UPC § 2–603(c); if the statute itself proves too obscure, see the Comment to subsection (c)].

SECTION IV. CONSTRUCTION PROBLEMS MORE GENERALLY

Rules governing abatement, ademption, and lapse have evolved to deal with events the testator (or her lawyer) might not have anticipated at the time testator executed his will. But interpretive issues arise—with frequency—even when there are no "time gap" problems. Courts often define their goal as ascertaining—and effectuating—testator's intentions. But that goal often proves elusive. Consider the following excerpt:

Jane B. Baron, Intention, Interpretation, and Stories, 42 Duke L. J. 630, 638–39 (1992).

[A] testator's thoughts cannot be directly discovered because individual human will is a "formless substance." "The intent of the writer, the ideas existing in his mind, cannot be known to us with certainty: we can only ascertain them to a greater or lesser degree of probability from outward marks or signs." [Francis Vaughan Hawkins, On the Principles of Legal Interpretation, with Reference Especially to the Interpretation of Wills, in James B. Thayer, A Preliminary Treatise on Evidence at the Common Law 577, 580 (1898)]. Chief among these outward marks are the words employed by the writer, but other marks may exist. If the testator's actual thoughts cannot be ascertained directly, then the goal of interpretation must be redefined to some degree. The goal becomes to infer from external marks the internal thoughts they reflect and embody. In pursuit of this goal, words and other external signs are used strategically, as means to an end:

> Every written instrument is the attempted recordation of a series of ideas theretofore had by some definite individual.... Obviously the first task, then, is to squeeze out from each of these segregated paragraphs, sentences, phrases or words, just as near an approximation to the idea sought to be embodied therein, as is obtainable. [Richard R. Powell, Construction of Written Instruments, 14 Ind. L.J. 199, 207 (1939).]

Unfortunately, the strategy is imperfect. The least problematic, most easily accessible set of signs—words—is not a perfect code of signals. Even if words were a perfect code, there would be no guarantee that writers would use the code with perfect accuracy. Complicating matters further is the fact that the words of the will may not have been chosen by the testator, whose ideas are ostensibly at issue, but by the testator's attorney.

* * *

If testator's words are an imperfect guide to testator's intention, what do courts do when confronted with the words? Do they focus on the "plain meaning" of the words, or do they look for evidence beyond the words themselves to illuminate testator's intent? There is no uniform answer to these questions. Interpretive questions have generated controversy in wills law, as they have in constitutional law, in disputes about legislation, and in contract law.

All courts concede, however, that some will provisions are ambiguous. What techniques are acceptable to resolve those ambiguities? First, a careful reading of the will as a whole often sheds light on testator's meaning, even though a particular devise, read in isolation, appears ambiguous. Courts are most receptive to interpretive arguments that do not require them to look beyond the "four corners" of the dispositive document—here, the will. Second, in somewhat more limited circumstances, courts are willing to look at *extrinsic evidence*—evidence found outside the will itself—to resolve ambiguities. Not all extrinsic evidence is equally reliable, and, as we shall see, courts have been reluctant to admit certain types of extrinsic evidence. In addition, many courts have held that extrinsic evidence is admissible only to resolve certain kinds of ambiguity.

We turn now to an exploration of these problems.

A. Reading the Will as a Whole

When a will provision creates an ambiguity obvious on the face of the provision, courts will, as a matter of course, look to the rest of the will to resolve the ambiguity. Suppose, for instance, testator makes a devise of personal property "to my daughters, Jane and Jane, share and share alike." Testator in fact has three daughters, Jane, June, and Mary. Later in the will, testator devises the residue of her estate "to my daughters, Jane and June, share and share alike." The will expressly provides "I intend to leave nothing to my daughter Mary, who has been adequately provided for by her venture capitalist husband."

The devise of personal property is ambiguous on its face; in doctrinal terms, the ambiguity is "patent". Unless testator has two daughters named Jane, the devise as written is incoherent. In a case like that one, almost any court would look to the rest of the will, and conclude that the second reference to "Jane" was meant to be a reference to "June." The rest of the will establishes that testator did not mean the second reference to be "Mary," because testator has intentionally disinherited Mary. The only sensible alternative is to conclude that testator intended Jane and June to share her personal property, just as she intended them to share the residue of her estate.

Suppose, however, the devise at issue is not incoherent on its face. Suppose instead that testator has used a word—children—that has an established legal meaning. Should the court examine the rest of the will when one of the parties contends that testator's use of the word "children" was intended to mean something other than the established legal meaning of the word? Consider the following case:

Matter of Marine Midland Bank, N.A.

Court of Appeals of New York, 1989.
74 N.Y.2d 448, 547 N.E.2d 1152, 548 N.Y.S.2d 625.

■ BELLACOSA, J.:

In concluding that appellants are not entitled to inherit under the relevant gift provision of this disputed will, we reaffirm two basic principles governing the adjudication of decedents' estates by courts: our primary function is to effectuate the testator's intent and the words used to express that intent are to be given their ordinary and natural meaning.

Testator executed his will in 1955 and it was admitted to probate in 1959. At issue is clause (c) of paragraph Fifth, which bequeaths part of the residuary of one of two trusts to the "surviving child or children" of testator's brother Leonard, who predeceased the trust's life tenant, testator's widow, Elsie. A "surviving child" of Leonard, Jacqueline, is respondent before us and claims entitlement to the whole of that residuary portion. Appellants are the widow and children of Leonard's other child, Daniel (Jacqueline's brother), who, like his father, predeceased the life tenant. Daniel's children, as appellants, strive to take under paragraph Fifth's gift provision and urge the courts to construe the word "children" to include grandchildren so that the collateral descendants of the testator, i.e., the grandnephews and grandnieces, can partake of the testamentary plan. Since they are faced with the fundamental proposition that the word "children" will be given its ordinary and natural meaning unless the will as a whole shows an unmistakable intent that different or remoter persons or classes should be included, they argue that the one-time use of the word "issue" in a different, inoperative clause of the will creates ambiguity and warrants forsaking the general rule of construction....

We affirm the order of the Appellate Division because a construction which would substitute for the testator's chosen word a broader, judicially applied definition is unwarranted and would be unsettling to the law of descent and distribution....

Carl V. E. Gustafson was 59 years old, married and childless when he died in 1959. He disposed of virtually his entire estate through two trusts of equal size with an integrated, complementary residuary plan. The trust established in paragraph Sixth provided that testator's brothers, Leonard and Roy, were to be equal income beneficiaries, and upon the death of either of them his one-half interest in the trust (that is, a one-fourth interest in the residuary) would pass to "his child or children". When

Leonard died in 1978, his children, Jacqueline and Daniel, took equally of Leonard's share in this trust. Roy continues his life tenancy in the other portion of this trust. The half of testator's estate reflected in this trust is not involved in this case.

This case and appeal revolve around the trust created in paragraph Fifth of the will, in which Elsie, testator's widow, held a life estate. Upon her death, testator's will directed the corpus of this trust be paid as follows:

> "(a) One-half to my brother, E. Leonard Gustafson.
>
> "(b) One-half to my brother, Roy L. Gustafson.
>
> "(c) If a brother predeceases Elsie Warren Gustafson, then his share of this Trust shall be paid over to his surviving child or children, share and share alike.
>
> "(d) If one of my brothers shall predecease Elsie Warren Gustafson, without issue surviving, then his part of this Trust shall be paid over to his surviving brother."

Roy survived Elsie and took his share pursuant to clause (b). This, too, is not involved in the case.

At issue then is only the portion that would have been Leonard's one-quarter residuary share under clause (a), which, because of Leonard's predeceasing Elsie, must pass through clause (c). Leonard's son, Daniel, having also predeceased Elsie, leaves a widow and children who now seek to take a share of the residuary through this clause, though they are not "surviving child or children".

Courts construing donative instruments are governed by a threshold axiom: a testator's intent, as ascertained "from the words used in the will * * * according to their everyday and ordinary meaning", reigns supreme (Matter of Walker, 64 N.Y.2d 354, 357–358; Matter of Cord, 58 N.Y.2d 539, 544; see also, 4 Page, Wills § 30.7, at 44). In Matter of Villalonga (6 N.Y.2d 477, 484), the natural and ordinary meaning of the word at issue here was held and applied as follows: " '[c]hildren' means immediate offspring, and we reiterate the rule of the [Matter of] Schaufele [252 N.Y. 65, 67] case that it will never be held to include grandchildren 'unless the will as a whole shows that unmistakable intent.' " (Emphasis added.) The will before us cannot clear that high hurdle.

The order of testator's priorities is straightforwardly expressed in paragraph Fifth. First, he provided for his widow as long as she lived. Then, upon her death, his brothers would benefit (para. Fifth [a], [b]). If his brother(s) predeceased his widow, then the focus of testator's beneficial intent shifted to the "surviving child or children" of his brother(s) (para. Fifth [c]), a generation proximate to himself. The final subdivision of this paragraph provides that if a brother dies "without issue surviving", the surviving brother takes all. Thus, if neither issue nor children survived one brother, the other brother (or his children or his issue) would take to prevent a lapse. Accordingly, from the four corners of the will's relevant gift provision, assigning to each word its ordinary meaning, the testamentary scheme is reasonably discernible. Carl Gustafson wanted to benefit: (1)

his widow while she lived; (2) his brothers who survived his widow; and (3) if a brother did not survive his widow, then the brother's child(ren) who did so survive. Those preferences of the testator as to the order and distribution of *his* property are not "incoherent", "inequitable", "inconsistent" or "anomalous", but even if they were, testators are privileged to act in any way they see fit to displace the State's otherwise mandated, homogeneous distribution by intestacy, so long as they are *compos mentis*. Courts, on the other hand, are not privileged to put contrary or even additional words into a testator's actual written expression in order retrospectively to effectuate their own notions of "fair" or "equitable" distribution of estates.

Prowitt v. Rodman (37 N.Y. 42 [1867]) does not support a different result. There, an exception to the plain meaning of "children" was allowed because "the testator intended that the remote descendants should be takers * * * *if there should be a failure of the immediate offspring of [the trust life tenant]*" (id., at 54 [emphasis added]; see also, Matter of Welles, 9 N.Y.2d 277, 280 ["It seems to us that the only possible occasion justifying a more inclusive meaning (of 'children') would be to avoid failure of the estate."]). There is no failure of an estate here, which is the only justification for the exception to the paramount plain meaning rule of construction.

Nor is this case about the testator's intention to disinherit unknown, collateral descendants two generations removed from him. The law of decedents' affairs recognizes no rule requiring a testator to manifest an intent to disinherit in such circumstances. Rather, our rules relate to the testator's intent to bestow a gift and to whom. In that respect, he was plain, precise and orderly, and appellants' claim to a gift in this trust remainder by implication would wrongly extend the plainly expressed and universally understood words. Our ruling, therefore, is natural, not "narrow", and a faithful application of the holding of the governing precedent, not an "extension" of it. Simply put, children means children in the judicial construction of this will.

* * *

As we have consistently held, the plain meaning of the testamentary language itself is the surest path to the judicial discernment of a testator's donative intent. Expanding the application of exceptions to that sound general proposition would soon swallow the rule and render less secure the effectuation of testators' relied upon, expressed intentions. Indeed, to create a new exception out of something called "paramount intent", different from the intent clearly expressed on the face of a will and in its only relevant donative provision, would be seriously unsettling because it would sacrifice predictability, an especially crucial element in the field of decedents' estates where "settled rules are necessary and necessarily relied upon" (Matter of Eckart, 39 N.Y.2d 493, 500).

Accordingly, the order of the Appellate Division should be affirmed, with costs to all parties filing briefs payable out of the residuary trust at issue.

■ CHIEF JUDGE WACHTLER and JUDGES ALEXANDER and TITONE concur.

■ HANCOCK, JR., J. (dissenting in part in an opinion in which JUDGES SIMONS and KAYE concur):

I would modify the order of the Appellate Division and hold that the term "children" in paragraph FIFTH (c) of the will includes grandchildren and, therefore, that Leonard's share must be divided equally between his son Daniel's surviving children, collectively, and his daughter, Jacqueline.

In my view, construing "children" narrowly here and, thereby, disinheriting the lineal descendants of one of the testator's brothers is unwarranted and represents a distinct—and unfortunate—*extension* of the "unmistakable intent" rule. In Matter of Villalonga (6 N.Y.2d 477), where we applied that rule and declined to read "children" broadly, we emphasized that: (1) the will there was "a simple one * * * and not afflicted with the weakness of ambiguity" (id., at 481), (2) "[t]here [was] no interchangeable use made of the terms 'children' and 'issue' " (id., at 481), and (3) "[n]or [did] the general distributive scheme disclose a testamentary purpose to benefit children of predeceased immediate offspring together with surviving immediate offspring" (id.). Those very factors—the *absence* of which led our court to construe "children" narrowly in Villalonga—are *present* in this case.

The will here is ambiguous. The ambiguity arises, in part, from the interchangeable use of the terms "children" and "issue" in paragraph FIFTH. Also, the use of *"issue"* in paragraph FIFTH (d) manifests a clear intention to benefit a predeceasing brother's surviving lineal descendants—not just the brother's immediate offspring as a narrow reading of "children" in paragraph FIFTH (c) suggests. Moreover, the intent of the testator as indicated by the language and structure of the entire will seems straightforward: to make gifts to his brothers or their respective family lines, treating them equally. Indeed, there is nothing in the testamentary scheme to suggest that the testator wanted to disinherit the family of his brother's son (Daniel's family), in favor of that brother's other child (Jacqueline), on the seemingly unrelated and meaningless contingency of his brother's son predeceasing his widow.

Significantly, the Villalonga court itself reaffirmed the well-established exception to the rule it applied, viz., that where uncertainty exists, "children" should be given a broad construction to avoid an inequitable result (id., at 482–483). Quoting Matter of Paton (111 N.Y. 480, 486), our court reiterated that, "[o]f course, if the language employed 'is equally susceptible of one or another interpretation, we should, on every principle of right, and within the spirit of the authorities, give it that which is *most equitable and consonant with the dictates of justice*' " (6 N.Y.2d, at 484 [emphasis added]; see also, id., at 486 [Desmond, J., dissenting]; Matter of Blodgett, 286 N.Y. 602, aff'g. 250 App. Div. 324 and 261 App. Div. 878; Matter of Brown, 93 N.Y. 295, 295–299; Prowitt v. Rodman, 37 N.Y. 42, 54, 58; Guernsey v. Guernsey, 36 N.Y. 267, 271; Mowatt v. Carow, 7 Paige 328; 4 Kent's Com 419, n). Accordingly, we should construe "children" in paragraph FIFTH (c) as "issue" and, thereby, avoid an incoherent interpretation of paragraph FIFTH (c) and (d) and, at the same time, avoid the patent inequity which otherwise results.

The majority's attempt to reconcile paragraph FIFTH (c) and (d) avoids neither problem. Nor does it withstand scrutiny. Paragraph FIFTH (d) cannot fairly be read—as the majority contends—as providing that, "if neither issue nor children survived one brother, the other brother *(or his children or his issue)* would take to prevent a lapse." (Majority opn, at 453 [emphasis added].) Plainly, the language of paragraph FIFTH (d) does not so provide. It does no more than give the share of the estate in question to the "surviving brother" if the other dies "without issue surviving". There is no language in paragraph FIFTH (d) itself that directs or permits "issue" (or "children") to take. Only paragraph FIFTH (c) can be read as providing for that, and then, only if "children", as used by the testator, is construed to mean "issue".

Indeed, the majority's contention, that paragraph FIFTH (d) permits a devise to a brother's "issue" under certain circumstances, plainly undercuts their position and supports the view taken here. Their contention necessarily recognizes the basic point that "issue" (i.e., children of deceased children) were intended to be beneficiaries in some situations. But because, as noted, such a disposition cannot be effected under paragraph FIFTH (d), it follows that it can only be made under paragraph FIFTH (c)—i.e., by construing "children" in paragraph FIFTH (c) broadly as permitting "issue" to take.

Similarly, other provisions in the will either make little sense or run counter to the testator's over-all design if "children" is narrowly construed. For example, the distribution under paragraph sixth, providing for the direct gifts to the testator's two brothers,[7] would have failed if one of them had died with grandchildren or other issue, but with no surviving immediate offspring. And the very same would be true for paragraph EIGHTH—which was explicitly intended to cover any bequest elsewhere in the will that might fail.[8] Under that paragraph, as under paragraphs FIFTH and SIXTH, if "children" is read narrowly, there would be no provision for the very real contingency of a brother dying with no surviving sons or daughters, but with grandchildren or other lineal descendants still alive. Thus, paragraph EIGHTH, intended to avoid intestacy, would actually have permitted intestacy if read strictly.

I would resolve the ambiguities, and avoid the otherwise resulting inconsistencies and anomalies in the will, by broadly construing "children" to mean "issue". Such a construction would, in my view, yield the most reasonable and fair result—i.e., permitting Leonard's son's family (Daniel's family) as well as Leonard's daughter (Jacqueline) to share in the estate—and, thereby, avoid the certainly unintended inequity of depriving Daniel's

7. Paragraph SIXTH (e) provides: "If a brother predeceases me, then his share of the Trust provided hereby shall be paid over to his child or children, share and share alike."

8. Paragraph EIGHTH provides: "If any Trust or Legacy hereunder shall be voided; or, if any intestacy develops * * * then such legacy or intestacy shall be * * * paid over to my brothers * * * or to the child or children of a deceased brother, share and share alike."

children on the mere happenstance that their father died before their great uncle's widow. Finally, construing "children" broadly would, thus, give effect to the testator's paramount intent.

NOTES AND QUESTIONS

1. In the first paragraph of the court's opinion, Judge Bellacosa identifies two basic principles: (a) courts strive to effectuate the testator's intent; and (b) words used to express that intent are to be given their ordinary and natural meaning.

Are the two principles consistent? If we want to effectuate testator's intent, shouldn't we focus on the meaning *testator* attached to those words, not on the "ordinary and natural" meaning of the words?

2. On the majority's construction of Carl Gustafson's will, how would Gustafson's estate have been distributed if both Jacqueline and Daniel (the two children of Carl's brother, Leonard) had died before Elsie, leaving surviving children (grandchildren of Leonard)? If Leonard's grandchildren would not take Leonard's share, who would? By its terms, would section (d) be applicable?

Do your answers to these questions suggest that the majority's construction of the word "children" makes Carl's testamentary scheme incoherent? Shouldn't that counsel rejection of the majority's construction?

3. The majority in Marine Midland champions a "plain meaning" approach on the ground that any alternative approach would "sacrifice predictability" in an area where rules are relied upon.

If the dissenters in Marine Midland had prevailed, do you think any lawyers would have relied, in drafting wills, on the court's decision to construe "children" to mean "issue?"

If you were drafting Carl Gustafson's will, and you wanted to be sure that only living children of Leonard would take, how would you redraft the will? If you wanted to be sure that all issue of Leonard would take, how would you redraft the will? Would the result in Marine Midland have any appreciable effect on your drafting choices?

4. Suppose, in Article II of testator's will, testator devises a parcel of real property to "my three nephews." The residuary clause of testator's will devises the residue "to my three nephews, Able, Baker, and Charlie." Able and Baker are the sons of testator's sister; Charlie is the son of testator's wife's brother. Testator's half-brother also had a son, David. How would the Marine Midland majority distribute the real property devised in Article II? Is the hypothetical distinguishable from Marine Midland itself?

Would the hypothetical be distinguishable if testator's half-brother had two sons, David and Edward?

5. Does the Marine Midland dissent look beyond the "four corners" of the will to ascertain Carl Gustafson's intent? If not, does the dissent's approach open up the will construction process to unreliable self-serving evidence?

Does the dissent's approach increase the cost of litigation by permitting parties to introduce live witnesses—or affidavits—to establish testator's "true" intent? What harm, if any, would result from examining testator's entire document in order to determine testator's intent?

PROBLEM

Testator's will devises "to my brother Richard and my nephew Harold, in equal proportions, all of my real estate together with an undivided one-third interest in my partnership holdings. I further give and bequeath unto Robert Guthrie and Charles Campbell an undivided one-sixth interest apiece in my partnership holdings in said concern."

To how much of Testator's partnership holdings is Richard entitled? How would you use the devise to Guthrie and Campbell to shed light on the question? Cf. Campbell v. Campbell, 489 So.2d 774 (Fla.App.1986).

B. Using Extrinsic Evidence

Often, one of the parties to a will construction proceeding believes that evidence from outside the will itself will shed useful light on the meaning of the words testator used in her will. Why not permit all such evidence to be admitted in the hope that some of the evidence may increase the court's understanding of the language in the will? One answer is that admitting all potentially useful evidence would be inefficient—the gain in understanding will be outweighed by the cost—to the parties and the court—of protracted proceedings to determine the meaning of testator's words. Another answer is that many kinds of extrinsic evidence are easily fabricated, especially after testator's death.

Consider, for instance, a will that provides "I leave all of my property to my children." Testator's stepson wants to testify that testator had told him "I consider you my son, and my will leaves my property to all of my children, which of course includes you." The testimony might be probative on the meaning of the word "children" in testator's will, but the testimony is also unreliable. The stepson has every reason to lie. Moreover, the testator is dead, and therefore is in no position to rebut the stepson's assertions.

Sometimes, the problem with extrinsic evidence is not fabrication, but relevance. Suppose, for instance, one of testator's children—not the step-son—offers to testify that testator told her (three years after executing his will) that testator intended for the stepson to share in his estate. Even if true, is the testimony relevant? The question is testator's intention when testator executed his will; not his intention at the time he spoke to his daughter. Testator might have changed his mind about his stepson after execution of the will, but that change in mind will not affect disposition of his estate unless testator has executed a will memorializing the change.

Does this mean that courts should never admit extrinsic evidence? Such a rule would be ridiculous. In a sense, extrinsic evidence is necessary to interpret every will. Suppose Testator leaves "my engraved Montblanc pen to my husband." We cannot tell from the will itself that the particular piece of black plastic with a gold nib is a "Montblanc pen," nor can we tell that the balding man who calls himself "Mr. Testator" is the "husband" to whom Testator's will refers. Only by examining facts outside the will can we draw the connections necessary to distribute Testator's property in accordance with her will.

The difficult questions then, are deciding what sorts of extrinsic evidence should be admissible, and in what situations. We now turn to those questions.

1. IS THE WILL AMBIGUOUS?

Courts often say that extrinsic evidence is admissible to shed light on testator's intent only when the will itself is ambiguous. Mahoney v. Grainger, 283 Mass. 189, 186 N.E. 86 (1933), is a leading case. Testator, a 64–year–old woman, consulted a lawyer about preparation of her will. She told the lawyer that her 25 first cousins were her closest relatives, and that she wanted them to share equally. She neglected to tell the lawyer that she also had an elderly aunt. The lawyer drafted the will to leave testator's residuary estate to "my heirs at law living at the time of my decease, absolutely; to be divided among them equally, share and share alike . . ." At testator's death, her cousins sought to introduce extrinsic evidence to establish that testator intended them—and not the aunt—to take under the will. The court rejected their effort and permitted the aunt to take:

> It is only where testamentary language is not clear in its application to facts that evidence may be introduced as to the circumstances under which the testator used that language in order to throw light upon its meaning. Where no doubt exists as to the property bequeathed or the identity of the beneficiary there is no room for extrinsic evidence; the will must stand as written.

If the test, however, focuses on whether the language of the will is clear, we must ask "clear" to whom? To the judge reading the will? To the ordinary lawyer? To the man on the street? To the testator? Consider the following case:

Estate of Carroll

Court of Appeals of Missouri, 1989.
764 S.W.2d 736.

■ GREENE, J.:

Plaintiffs, who are the children of the brothers and sisters of Dortha Carroll, deceased, appeal from a trial court judgment which construed the will of Archie L. Carroll, who was the surviving husband of Dortha, in a manner that excluded plaintiffs from being considered as beneficiaries of Archie's estate.

The relevant facts are not in dispute. Archie and Dortha had been married for over 57 years, and had no children. Dortha had eight nieces and nephews who were the children of her brothers and sisters. Archie had twelve nieces and nephews who were the children of his brothers and sisters. On May 9, 1978, the parties executed separate wills. In his will, Archie's residuary estate was bequeathed to Dortha. It also provided that in the event Dortha predeceased Archie, on Archie's death his residuary estate be liquidated and the proceeds be equally divided between "my nieces and nephews that are living as of the date of my death." Dortha's will contained similar provisions, and provided that if Archie predeceased her the residuary estate was to go to "my nieces and nephews that are living as of the date of my death." The wills were drafted by an attorney who was one of the witnesses to the wills. Dortha died July 5, 1980. Archie died September 19, 1986, leaving as his last will and testament the will dated May 9, 1978.

Plaintiffs then filed a petition to construe the will, seeking a declaration that Archie's bequest to "my nieces and nephews that are living as of the date of my death" included them, as well as children of Archie's brothers and sisters. At trial, plaintiffs offered the testimony of eleven witnesses, plus several exhibits. This evidence consisted of testimony regarding statements Archie had made to some of the witnesses stating an intention to benefit the children of the brothers and sisters of Dortha, and that he regarded them as his nieces and nephews as well as the nieces and nephews from his side of the family. There was also testimony that Dortha and Archie did not distinguish between nieces and nephews by consanguinity and those by affinity when referring to nieces and nephews, and that there was a warm family relationship between Archie and Dortha's blood kin.

* * *

The trial court stated that it would receive all of the offered evidence with the reservation that it would only be considered if it found the phrase "my nieces and nephews" in Archie's will to be ambiguous.

The trial court then made findings, and entered judgment which reads as follows:

> 1. That Article 'TWO' of the Last Will and Testament of Archie L. Carroll directs that 'my estate shall be sold, liquidated and turned into cash and my residuary estate shall then be divided equally between my nieces and nephews that are living as of the date of my death.'
>
> 2. Plaintiffs, who are the nieces and nephews of Dortha Carroll, the deceased wife of Archie L. Carroll, and who preceded him in death, maintain that the language of Article 'TWO' was meant and intended by the testator to include the nieces and nephews of Dortha Carroll as well as the nieces and nephews of Archie L. Carroll.
>
> 3. Under the law applicable to wills, the Court must give effect to words clear in meaning and capable of ready definition. Only when the

terms of the will as written are not plain or when the will cannot be given effect as written because of some latent ambiguity may the Court consider outside evidence for the purpose of ascertaining intention.

4. The phrase 'my nieces and nephews' is clear and unambiguous and means the children of brothers and sisters.

THEREFORE, IT [IS] ADJUGED [sic], ORDERED AND DECREED that:

Only the children of the brothers and sisters of Archie L. Carroll are legatees under the terms of the Last Will and Testament of Archie L. Carroll and the personal representative is ordered to distribute the estate of Archie L. Carroll in accordance with the will so construed.

* * *

In their first point relied on, plaintiffs contend the trial court erred in declaring that the phrase " 'my nieces and nephews' " meant only the children of the brothers and sisters of the testator, not including the children of the brothers and sisters of the deceased spouse. This amounts to an argument that the trial court relied on an improper declaration of law in deciding this issue.

Since the will was professionally prepared, the words "my nieces and nephews" have legal effect and meaning. Crist v. Nesbit, 352 S.W.2d 53, 56 (Mo.App.1961). "[W]ords with a well-known technical meaning should be construed according to their technical meaning unless a contrary meaning clearly appears from the context of the will," after considering the will as a whole. Norris v. Norris, 731 S.W.2d 844, 845 (Mo. banc 1987). There is nothing in Archie's will that expresses an intent on his part to have the term "my nieces and nephews" considered in any manner other than in its legal and technical sense.

In their brief, plaintiffs have not cited a single case from any state supporting their theory that the term "my nieces and nephews" includes the children of the sisters and brothers of one's spouse, and seemingly rely on dictionary definitions that the terms "niece" and "nephew" include the sons and daughters of a brother-in-law or a sister-in-law, citing Webster's Third New International Dictionary of the English Language, Unabridged (1969) and Black's Law Dictionary (5th ed. 1979). However, Black's Law Dictionary (rev. 4th ed. 1968), defines "nephew" in the following way: "In legal usage only children of brothers and sisters are called 'nephews' and 'nieces,' children of husband's or wife's brothers and sisters being so called only by courtesy." There is ample textbook and appellate opinion authority in support for such statement.

In 94 A.L.R. 30 (1935), it is stated the "testator is always presumed to use the words in which he expresses himself according to their strict and primary acceptance.... [I]t is an inflexible rule of construction that the words of the will shall be interpreted in their strict and primary sense, and in no other, although they may be capable of some popular or secondary interpretation...." In 80 Am.Jur.2d Wills § 1198 (1975), it is stated:

> The general rule is that the testator must be presumed to have used words in his will in their ordinary or primary sense and meaning.... 'Niece' and 'nephew' in their primary and ordinary sense mean the immediate descendants of the brothers and sisters of the person named.

In 95 C.J.S. Wills § 667 (1957), it is stated:

> Usually, the terms 'nephews' and 'nieces' do not include nephews and nieces of the testator's spouse, unless such intention appears or is expressed by the will as a whole, or where the testator referred to his nephews and nieces, but in fact had none of his own blood. In the absence of controlling language to the contrary, bequests to 'nephews and nieces' are held to mean only nephews and nieces by consanguinity, not affinity; and it is only by courtesy that the children of a husband's or wife's brothers and sisters are called nephews and nieces.

An observation to the same effect is also contained in the definitions of "Nephew" and "Niece" at the beginning of 66 C.J.S. (1950). While there is no Missouri case in point on the issue, case law from other jurisdictions is unanimous in support of the textbook observations just referred to. In Terney v. Belton, 239 Or. 101, 396 P.2d 557 (en banc 1964), the question was whether the word "nephew" appearing in an inheritance tax statute included the son of a brother-in-law of the deceased. After observing that the legal meaning of the word "nephew" applied only to the son of a brother or sister, the Supreme Court of Oregon stated the presumption was that the Oregon legislature, when using the word "nephew" in the statute, was using it in accordance with its legal meaning. Id. at 558.

* * *

If Archie, or his lawyer who drafted his will, had intended to include the children of the brothers and sisters of Dortha as beneficiaries under his will, it would have been easy for them to have done so, simply by referring to "our nieces and nephews" instead of "my nieces and nephews," or better still, by stating, "the children of (the named brothers or sisters of each spouse)." However, this was not done. "My" is the possessive form of the pronoun "I," while "our" is a possessive form of the pronoun "we." American Heritage Dictionary of the English Language (1970).

The clear and unambiguous legal meaning of the words "my nieces and nephews" means the children of the brothers or sisters of the declarant. The trial court's ruling to that effect was a proper declaration of law.

In their remaining point relied on, plaintiffs claim the trial court erred in not considering extrinsic evidence to the effect that the testator regarded the siblings of his deceased spouse as his nieces and nephews, and intended to provide for them in his will.

The trial court, in explaining why it did not consider such evidence in deciding the issue, declared:

> Under the law applicable to wills, the Court must give effect to words clear in meaning and capable of ready definition. Only when the terms of the will as written are not plain or when the will cannot be given

> effect as written because of some latent ambiguity may the Court consider outside evidence for the purpose of ascertaining intention.

The court went on to declare the phrase " 'my nieces and nephews' " to be clear and unambiguous and to mean the children of the brothers and sisters of Archie.

A testator's intention must be determined by the will itself, and not by attempting to guess at what the testator may have meant. Estate of Ihl v. Oetting, 682 S.W.2d 865, 867 (Mo.App.1984). Since the technical or legal meaning of the words "my nieces and nephews" as used in the will means the children of the brothers and sisters of the testator, and no contrary intent is expressed anywhere in the will, no ambiguity exists regarding the meaning of such words. Therefore, extrinsic evidence regarding the testator's intent was inadmissible. Matter of Morrissey, 684 S.W.2d 876, 878 (Mo.App.1984). The trial court was correct in refusing to consider such evidence. The point has no merit.

Judgment affirmed.

NOTES AND QUESTIONS

1. Suppose the children of Dortha Carroll's siblings had hired you to represent them on an appeal to the Missouri Supreme Court. How would you have argued the case? What error would you contend the Court of Appeals has made?

2. The court in Estate of Carroll acknowledges that Webster's Third International Dictionary defines nephews and nieces to include children of sisters-in-law and brothers-in-law, but appears to believe that the definition in legal encyclopedias, not ordinary dictionaries, should be determinative. Do you agree? If the Carrolls had read the wills their lawyer had prepared for them, and had seen the words "nephews and nieces" used, would they have had any reason to correct the lawyer, given their own understanding of the words?

3. Suppose that on the date Dortha and Archie executed their wills, all of the children of Archie's siblings had already died. Suppose further that some of them had left children—Archie's grandnephews and grandnieces. At Archie's death, who would have been entitled to take? Would extrinsic evidence have been admissible to establish Archie's intent?

4. Other courts have been more willing to admit extrinsic evidence to establish that the meaning testator attached to the words he used was different from the apparently "clear" meaning of those words. For example, on facts essentially identical to those in Estate of Carroll, the Court of Appeals of Texas reversed a trial court's grant of summary judgment in favor of testator's nieces and nephews by blood. As in Carroll, testator and his wife had executed wills with mirror provisions. Testator's will devised his entire estate to his wife, or, if his wife predeceased him, to "my nieces and nephews." The husband died second, and his nieces and nephews argued that testator's wife's nieces and nephews should be excluded from the distribution of testator's estate. In finding that the wife's nieces and nephews had established a triable issue of fact regarding the testator's intent, the court found that doubt existed as to what the testator meant by the term "nieces and nephews," and that the argument that "nieces and nephews" included only testator's blood relatives "lack[ed] merit in current English usage." See Martin v. Palmer, 1 S.W.3d 875 (Tex.App.1999).

The Restatement (Third) of Property: Wills & Other Donative Transfers (2003) endorses this more "liberal" approach. Restatement section 11.1 defines ambiguity:

> An ambiguity in a donative document is an uncertainty in meaning that is revealed by the text or by extrinsic evidence other than direct evidence of intention contradicting the plain meaning of the text.

Section 11.2(a) goes on to provide that ambiguities should be "resolved by construing the text of the donative document in accordance with the donor's intention, to the extent that the donor's intention is established by a preponderance of the evidence." Finally, § 10.2 provides:

> In seeking to determine the donor's intention, all relevant evidence, whether direct or circumstantial, may be considered. Thus, the text of the document and relevant extrinsic evidence may both be considered.

How would the drafters of the Restatement have decided Estate of Carroll? Matter of Marine Midland Bank?

5. In construing Archie Carroll's will, would the language of Dortha Carroll's will be helpful? Does the fact that Archie and Dortha used identical language to dispose of their residuary estates suggest that they intended identical beneficiaries to take? Is the content of Dortha's will "extrinsic evidence" in the construction of Archie's will?

6. Suppose a trust document gives trustee the absolute discretion to determine how to invest trust assets. Should a trustee be entitled to introduce a letter from settlor to trustee as evidence that the settlor directed trustee to make certain lower yielding investments? See SunTrust Bank v. Merritt, 272 Ga.App. 485, 612 S.E.2d 818 (2005) (allowing trustee to introduce extrinsic evidence of settlor's investment preferences as a defense to beneficiary's claim that the trustee made poor investment decisions). See Mary Radford, Wills, Trusts and Guardianships, and Fiduciary Administration, 57 Mercer L. Rev. 403 (2005) (criticizing the SunTrust Bank court for stretching to find a latent ambiguity where none existed).

2. TESTATOR'S CIRCUMSTANCES AND BEHAVIOR

Suppose testator, in a will written two years before her death, leaves property "to my daughter." Testator, in fact, has two daughters, Tammy and Vanna. A reading of the will itself does not indicate which of the two daughters was to inherit the property. Tammy wants to introduce evidence that (a) testator had lived with her for the last 20 years of her life; (b) that testator did not speak with Vanna after Vanna married outside the faith, 25 years before testator's death; and (c) that since Vanna's marriage, testator has, every year, made donations to the local church "in Vanna's memory." Should the evidence be admitted?

Generally, the answer is yes. Although the will appears clear on its face—the word "daughter" is not inherently ambiguous—ambiguity arises when we try to match the words in the will with the facts in the world. Lawyers often say that the will includes a "latent" ambiguity. When the will includes a latent ambiguity, extrinsic evidence of the sort Tammy wants to introduce is generally admissible.

Why? Because the evidence is both probative and reliable. The fact that testator spoke to only one daughter—Tammy—during the last 20 years of her life is relevant in determining what testator meant when she used the word "daughter". Similarly, evidence that she treated Vanna as if she were dead—her frequent contributions in Vanna's "memory"—helps explain why she saw no need to identify Tammy with greater particularity in her will.

Moreover, the evidence is reliable in the sense that it is not easily fabricated. If testator has lived with Tammy for 20 years, or has made contributions in Vanna's memory, many disinterested people will be available to verify those facts. In addition, there is no danger that admitting the evidence would subvert the Statute of Wills: testator would not move in with Tammy, or make contributions in Vanna's memory, merely to avoid writing a new will. (By contrast, if we admitted the oral testimony by testator's clergyman—presumably a reliable person—that testator had told him that she intended Tammy to take her estate, we might worry that admitting such evidence would permit testator to change her will without testamentary formalities).

In cases of latent ambiguity, then, courts routinely admit evidence of testator's circumstances or behavior to enable the court to correlate the language of the will with the facts in the world. How far should this principle extend? Consider the following case:

Estate of Gibbs

Supreme Court of Wisconsin, 1961.
14 Wis.2d 490, 111 N.W.2d 413.

Petitions by respondent Robert W. Krause for the construction of a portion of the wills of George Gibbs and his wife Lena Adele Gibbs.

Mrs. Gibbs died April 11, 1960, and Mr. Gibbs died May 27, 1960. Mrs. Gibbs' will was executed October 21, 1958, and Mr. Gibbs executed his will May 5, 1960.

* * *

Subparagraph 2(g) of Article Third of Mrs. Gibbs' will is identical with subparagraph 2(i) of Article Second of Mr. Gibbs' will. Each reads as follows:

> To Robert J. Krause, now of 4708 North 46th Street, Milwaukee, Wisconsin, if he survives me, one per cent (1%).

Respondent Robert W. Krause of Milwaukee, who has never resided at 4708 North 46th Street, alleged that he had been an employee of Mr. Gibbs for thirty years and was a friend of the family of both Mr. and Mrs. Gibbs for many years. He alleged that Robert J. Krause who lives at 4708 North 46th Street was unknown to the Gibbs and that each of them intended to name respondent as legatee.

At the hearing, respondent offered evidence in support of his allegations. It was received over objection of Robert J. Krause. It appeared that Robert J. Krause was not acquainted with Mr. or Mrs. Gibbs except that he recalled a conversation in 1955 with a lady who might have been Mrs. Gibbs. The court found that the address given in the wills had been inadvertently stated and that both decedents intended to refer to respondent Robert W. Krause as legatee. Orders were accordingly entered in each estate on February 23, 1961. Robert J. Krause appealed.

■ FAIRCHILD, J.:

* * *

Respondent testified that he met Mr. Gibbs about 1928. From 1930 to 1949 he was employed as superintendent of a steel warehouse where Mr. Gibbs was his superior. They worked in close contact ..... Mrs. Gibbs had made a few visits at the plant before 1949 and respondent had seen her there. Mr. Gibbs did not visit respondent's home, although on a few occasions had telephoned him at home. Mr. Gibbs always called respondent "Bob."

Miss Krueger, who had been the Gibbs housekeeper for 24 years up to 1958 and was a legatee under both wills, corroborated much of respondent's testimony. She also testified that Mr. Gibbs had told her he made a will remembering various people including "the boys at the shop," referring to them as "Mike, Ed, and Bob."

* * *

Of the individuals named in the wills as legatees, all except two were shown to be relatives of Mr. or Mrs. Gibbs, former employees, neighbors, friends, or children of friends. The two exceptions were named near the end of the will and proof as to them may have been inadvertently omitted. "Mike," named in the will, was a warehouse employee under the supervision of respondent.

* * *

Prior to 1950 respondent had lived at several different locations. From 1950 until April, 1960, he lived at 2325 North Sherman Boulevard. We take judicial notice that this address and 4708 North 46th Street are in the same general section of the city of Milwaukee, and that both are a number of miles distant from the Gibbs home. We also take judicial notice that the telephone directory for Milwaukee and vicinity listed 14 subscribers by the name of Robert Krause with varying initials in October, 1958, and 15 in October of 1959. The listing for appellant gives his middle initial J. as well as his street address.

The only evidence which suggests even a possibility that Mr. or Mrs. Gibbs may have known of appellant may be summarized as follows:

For a time, appellant had a second job as a part-time taxi driver, and he recalled an elderly lady who was his passenger on a lengthy taxi trip in June, 1955. He did not recall where he picked her up. He had driven her across the city, waiting for her while she visited in a hospital, and then driven her back across the city. The place where he let her out, however, was not her home. He did not recall that she had given him her name, but she had inquired as to his. They had conversed about the illness of appellant's wife and his working at an extra job in order to make ends meet. She had expressed sympathy and approval of his efforts. Presumably when he was notified that his name appeared in the Gibbs wills as legatee, he endeavored to find an explanation of his good fortune and concluded that the lady in question must have been Mrs. Gibbs. The 1955 taxi ride, however, could not explain the gift to Robert Krause in the 1953 wills, and it is clear that the same legatee was intended in the Krause bequests in all the wills. Moreover, appellant's description of his taxi passenger differed in several particulars from the description of Mrs. Gibbs given by other witnesses.

2. *Propriety of considering extrinsic evidence.* As stated above, the county court could reach no other conclusion upon consideration of the extrinsic evidence than that Mr. and Mrs. Gibbs intended to designate respondent as their legatee. The difficult question is whether the court could properly consider such evidence in determining testamentary intent.

Under rules as to construction of a will, unless there is ambiguity in the text of the will read in the light of surrounding circumstances, extrinsic evidence is inadmissible for the purpose of determining intent.

A latent ambiguity exists where the language of the will, though clear on its face, is susceptible of more than one meaning, when applied to the extrinsic facts to which it refers.

There are two classes of latent ambiguity. One, where there are two or more persons or things exactly measuring up to the description in the will; the other where no person or thing exactly answers the declarations and descriptions of the will, but two or more persons or things answer the description imperfectly. Extrinsic evidence must be resorted to under these circumstances to identify which of the parties, unspecified with particularity in the will, was intended by the testator.

Had the probated wills used the language of the 1953 wills "To Robert Krause of Milwaukee," such terms would have described both appellant and respondent, as well as a number of other people. Upon such ambiguity of the first type above mentioned becoming apparent, extrinsic evidence would be admissible in order to determine which Robert Krause Mr. and Mrs. Gibbs had in mind as their legatee.

Had the will said "To my former employee, Robert J. Krause of 4708 North 46th Street," neither appellant nor respondent would have exactly fulfilled the terms. Latent ambiguity of the second type would thus have appeared, and again extrinsic evidence would be admissible to determine what individual testators had in mind.

The wills containing, as they do, similar bequests to a long list of individuals, each bearing some relationship of blood, friendship, or former employment to Mr. or Mrs. Gibbs, come close to implying that every legatee named has some such relationship. Nevertheless the wills do not refer to Krause as standing in any particular relationship.

The terms of the bequest exactly fit appellant and no one else. There is no ambiguity.

> "An ambiguity is not that which may be made doubtful by extrinsic proof tending to show an intention different from that manifested in the will, but it must grow out of the difficulty of identifying the person whose name and description correspond with the terms of the will." [citation omitted]

Under the circumstances before us, can a court properly consider evidence showing that some of the words were used by mistake and should be stricken or disregarded? It is traditional doctrine that wills must not be reformed even in the case of demonstrable mistake. This doctrine doubtless rests upon policy reasons. The courts deem it wise to avoid entertaining claims of disappointed persons who may be able to make very plausible claims of mistake after the testator is no longer able to refute them.

Although the courts subscribe to an inflexible rule against reformation of a will, it seems that they have often strained a point in matters of identification of property or beneficiaries in order to reach a desired result by way of construction. In Will of Stack, where the will devised "Block 64," the court included part of block 175 in the provision to conform to the unexpressed intent of the testator. In Will of Boeck, where the will devised the "northeast quarter of the northwest quarter" of a section, which was not owned by the testator, the court held such provision passed the southeast quarter of the northwest quarter, to conform to the misexpressed intent of the testator. In Moseley v. Goodman, where testator bequeathed property to "Mrs. Moseley," the court denied the claim of Mrs. Lenoir Moseley to the gift and held that Mrs. Trimble had been intended by the testator. Mrs. Trimble was known to the testator by the nickname "Mrs. Moseley."

In Miller's Estate, testator left property to "William Wilson's children." Relying on evidence that testator frequently confused William Wilson with his brother Seth, the court held the gift should go to the children of Seth Wilson, who had been intended by the testator. In Groves v. Culph, testator devised a remainder interest in part of lot 15 to his daughter. The court, to conform to testator's true intent, included part of lot 16 in this devise. In Castell v. Togg and Geer v. Winds the testator omitted a child from his will by mistake. The court inserted in the will the gift which had been intended for the child by the parent. In Beaumont v. Feld a bequest to "Catharine Earnley" was proven to have been intended for Gertrude Yardley, and was given to the latter, and in Masters v. Masters, a gift to "Mrs. Sawyer" was given to Mrs. Swopper, because testator knew no one by the former name. In the two cases last mentioned, no one with the name given in the will claimed the gift.

We are also aware of the rule which allows a court in probating a will to deny probate to a provision in the document which was included by mistake. British courts will deny probate to a single word, or part of a sentence, thereby completely altering the provided dispositions.

We conclude that details of identification, particularly such matters as middle initials, street addresses, and the like, which are highly susceptible to mistake, particularly in metropolitan areas, should not be accorded such sanctity as to frustrate an otherwise clearly demonstrable intent. Where such details of identification are involved, courts should receive evidence tending to show that a mistake has been made and should disregard the details when the proof establishes to the highest degree of certainty that a mistake was, in fact, made.

We therefore consider that the county court properly disregarded the middle initial and street address, and determined that respondent was the Robert Krause whom testators had in mind.

Orders affirmed.

NOTES AND QUESTIONS

1. Suppose Mr. and Mrs. Gibbs had wanted to leave property to Robert J. Krause. How would you have drafted their wills to assure that their intended beneficiary received the property without the need for litigation? Should a lawyer have to go to such lengths to avoid claims by testator's greedy employee?

2. Ben Franklin's will devises $100,000 "to the Trustees of Pennsylvania State University." The Trustees of the University of Pennsylvania—who contend that they were the intended beneficiary of the devise—seek to introduce evidence that Ben was an alumnus of the U. of P., and that Ben had given generously to the University in the past.

Would the court in Gibbs have admitted the evidence? If the evidence had been admitted, would it establish that the University of Pennsylvania should receive the devise? Cf. In re Estate of Gross, 646 P.2d 396 (Colo. App.1981).

3. Testator devises property "to my daughter, Vanna Black." Testator's other daughter, Tammy—who wants to convince the court that the will's apparent reference to Vanna was in fact a reference to Tammy—seeks to introduce evidence that testator lived with Tammy for the last 20 years of her life, and that testator had made a number of gifts "in memory of my daughter Vanna." Should the evidence be admitted? Is Gibbs distinguishable, and if so, how?

Consider Moseley v. Goodman, 138 Tenn. 1, 195 S.W. 590 (1917) [discussed in Estate of Gibbs]. Testator's will left $20,000 to "Mrs. Moseley" and $20,000 to "Mrs. Moseley's housekeeper." Testator was in the business of selling cigars. He bought cigars made by R.L. Moseley. At testator's death, R.L. Moseley's wife sought to exclude the following evidence: testator referred to one Trimble, the salesman from whom he purchased Moseley cigars, as "Moseley," and referred to Trimble's wife as "Mrs. Moseley." When testator became ill, he rented a room at an apartment house owned by Trimble, and was attended there by Mrs. Trimble and by Mrs. Anna Lang, a housekeeper employed by Mrs. Trimble. Held, the evidence was admissible, and Mrs. Trimble and Mrs. Lang were entitled to the $20,000 devises.

4. Courts can differ on whether a will contains a latent ambiguity. Consider the following case: A valid codicil to testator's will directed testator's executor to pay all estate expenses "from my Smith Barney Shearson account," and to pay the balance of that account to testator's niece. At testator's death, Smith Barney held the following assets in testator's name: money funds totaling $33,000, stocks valued at $1,100, and bonds worth $234,675. Testator's executor (her son) argues that the niece is entitled only to the remaining money funds, but *not* the stocks and bonds. Should the court admit extrinsic evidence to clarify testator's intent, or is the will clear on its face? See Kernkamp v. Bolthouse, 714 So.2d 655 (Fla.App.1998) [reversing trial court's determination that will was clear and that niece should receive all assets held by Smith Barney, and remanding with instructions to consider extrinsic evidence of testator's intent to clear up latent ambiguity].

5. Courts also admit extrinsic evidence to resolve ambiguities in inter vivos trust documents. In Eckels v. Davis, 111 S.W.3d 687 (Tex. App. 2003), the settlor's inter vivos trust document identified two investment accounts by number. After the trust was executed, the account numbers were changed for investment reasons. The court admitted extrinsic evidence to identify the accounts, and held that the gift of the account proceeds did not adeem.

6. ***The Patent/Latent Distinction.*** Courts and commentators have sometimes distinguished between latent and patent ambiguities. The ambiguity in Estate of Gibbs was latent because it did not appear on the face of the document; the ambiguity became apparent only with reference to extrinsic evidence. A patent ambiguity, by contrast, is one that is apparent on the face of the will. For instance, if the will leaves testator's house to John in one provision of the will, and leaves the same house to Jane in another provision, the ambiguity is patent. Similarly, if the will omits language that would be necessary to read the will as a coherent whole—as, for instance, if the only dispositive provision of the will provided: "I devise to John Smith" without including any description of the property devised—the ambiguity is patent.

Although courts have traditionally been ready to admit extrinsic evidence to resolve latent ambiguities, some courts have been more hesitant to admit extrinsic evidence to resolve patent ambiguities. Patent ambiguities are, in cause and effect, quite similar to mistakes, and as we shall see, courts have historically been unwilling to admit extrinsic evidence to reform mistakes in wills.

Many commentators would abolish all distinctions between latent and patent ambiguities. The Restatement (Third) of Property: Wills and Other Donative Transfers section 11.1, comment a (2003) provides that "although it is customary to distinguish between latent and patent ambiguities, no legal consequences attach to the distinction." The Indiana Supreme Court recently declared that "the distinction between patent and latent ambiguities is not useful, and it is proper to admit extrinsic evidence to resolve any ambiguity." See University of Southern Indiana Foundation v. Baker, 843 N.E.2d 528 (Ind.2006). But see, contra, Bagley v. Mousel, 271 Neb. 628, 715 N.W.2d 490 (2006) [holding that parol evidence is inadmissible to resolve patent ambiguities].

For an argument that attorneys should incur malpractice liability for creating patent ambiguities, see Angela M. Vallario, Shape Up Or Ship Out: Accountability to Third Parties for Patent Ambiguities in Testamentary Documents, 26 Whittier L. Rev. 59 (2004).

PROBLEMS

1. Henry Wilton's will devised "my saddle and bridle, my double and single harness and tack, all my horse-drawn vehicles, and any Rose Tree Hunt memorabilia to my good friend, John Brislin." Brislin asserts a right to all items owned by testator that have actual reference to foxes, fox hunting, and horses, and any item used by testator in connection with horses. Those items have a total value of $80,000, while items with a Rose Tree Hunt Club insignia have a total value of $1,700. Is Wilton's will ambiguous? If so, is the ambiguity latent or patent? If you represented Brislin, what sort of evidence would you want to introduce to support your client's claim? See Estate of Wilton, 921 A.2d 509 (Pa. Super. 2007).

2. Neil Vaughan's will left "the farm I own in Robinette Valley" to his second cousin, and the remainder of his estate to his children. At his death, he owned two farms in Robinette Valley, one of which was contiguous to the cousin's farm. Does the cousin inherit one farm or two? See Estate of Vaughan, 2009 WL 3126262 (2009).

3. In 1942, twenty-one year old Lucy Ann Smith gave birth to a son, John. Lucy Ann, who was not married, lived with her parents, D.J. and Martha, and Lucy Ann's six siblings. Shortly after the birth, D.J and Martha held a family conference with the oldest children, and the family swore that they would tell everyone that John's parents were D.J. and Martha, and that

Lucy Ann was John's sister. From that day forward, the siblings behaved as though John were their brother, and John believed that he was.

In 1971, D.J. was killed in a car accident. The obituary listed John as D.J.'s son, and John received an intestate share of his "father's" estate. In 1989, when John was 47 years old, he discovered that Lucy Ann was his mother. In 1994, Julia (D.J. and Martha's oldest child) died. Her will, which was executed in 1976, left her $200,000 estate "to my brothers and sisters living at my death." Julia's executor refused to give John a portion of Julia's estate.

Should John be entitled to a share of Julia's estate? See In re Estate of Fabian, 326 S.C. 349, 483 S.E.2d 474 (1997).

3. TESTATOR'S UNATTESTED STATEMENTS

PROBLEM

Testator's will leaves "my farm property" to her niece, Irene, and the residue of her estate to her daughter Jane. At Testator's death, she owns a 100–acre tract of land. Her home is located on the east end of the 100–acre parcel, and a retail store selling produce and nursery stock is located on the west end of the parcel. No fences separate out the various uses.

At Testator's death, Irene and Jane disagree about the scope of the devise. Irene seeks to introduce testimony by Irene's mother Linda (Testator's sister) that, on the day she executed the will, she "made sure that Irene would get the farm, including the house and the retail store." Jane seeks to introduce testimony by a neighbor, Karl, that Testator had, at several times before her death, offered to sell to Karl "the farm property" but had made it clear to Karl that the offer didn't include the residence or the retail store.

Should Karl's testimony be admitted? Should Linda's? In assessing the issues, consider the following case:

Britt v. Upchurch

Supreme Court of North Carolina, 1990.
327 N.C. 454, 396 S.E.2d 318.

■ FRYE, J.:

The issues presented in this appeal are whether the Court of Appeals erred (1) in holding that the affidavit of the attorney who drafted the testator's will was admissible at trial to show the testator's intent; and (2) in reversing the trial court's grant of summary judgment for plaintiff. We conclude that the trial court was correct in refusing to consider the affidavit and in granting summary judgment for plaintiff. We therefore reverse the decision of the Court of Appeals.

Walter Hartman, the father of plaintiff, executed his will on 12 March 1979. At that time Mr. Hartman was married to Ada Cassie Hartman, his second wife, who was the mother of the defendant in this action. Mr. Hartman's will provided in Article IV: "I give and bequeath unto my said wife my residence at 2615 Cooleeme (sic) Street, Raleigh, North Carolina, for the term of her natural life. I give and devise the remainder interest in said property to my daughter, BLANCHE LOUISE HARTMAN BRITT." Article VIII, the residuary clause of the will, provided: "All of the remainder and residue of my property, I give, devise, and bequeath to my wife, ADA CASSIE HARTMAN in fee simple. If my wife shall predecease me, I give, devise and bequeath said residue to my daughter *Blanche Hartman Britt*."

At the time of his death, Mr. Hartman was living in the same home he had lived in since he purchased it in 1948. The house itself is located on lot 36 which is shown on the county tax records as 2615 Cooleemee Street. At the same time Mr. Hartman purchased lot 36, his mother purchased the adjoining lot 37, a vacant lot which is shown on the tax records as 2613 Cooleemee Street. Mr. Hartman's mother conveyed lot 37 to him by deed in 1956. Thus, at the time of execution of the will and at the time of his death, Mr. Hartman owned lots 36 and 37.

Mr. Hartman died on 24 February 1983, and Ada Cassie Hartman, his widow, died on 5 April 1988. Ms. Hartman's will provided in Article III: "I give and bequeath to my daughter, Yvonne G. Upchurch, all my personal and real property." Yvonne G. Upchurch, the defendant, attempted to sell lot 37, claiming title to lot 37 under her mother's will, contending that it passed to her mother under the residuary clause of Mr. Hartman's will.

On 6 October 1988, plaintiff brought this action in the Superior Court of Wake County to quiet title to lot 37. Plaintiff claimed title to lot 37 under Article IV of her father's will. On 1 November 1988, plaintiff filed a motion in limine to exclude any evidence, oral or written, of Thomas F. Adams, Jr., regarding Mr. Hartman's testamentary intent. Thomas F. Adams, Jr., was the attorney who drafted Mr. Hartman's will. On 13 January 1989, the trial judge granted the motion. On that same day, defendant moved for summary judgment. In support of this motion, defendant filed copies of the deeds to lots 36 and 37 as well as affidavits from employees of the tax offices of both the City of Raleigh and Wake County showing that lots 36 and 37 were listed separately in the tax records in both offices, lot 36 as a vacant lot identified as 2613 Cooleemee Street and lot 37 as a house and lot identified as 2615 Cooleemee Street. Plaintiff filed her own affidavit in opposition to defendant's motion for summary judgment, and on 8 February 1989 the trial judge granted plaintiff's motion for summary judgment, declaring her to be the owner of lots 36 and 37.

Defendant appealed to the Court of Appeals, both from the order granting summary judgment in favor of plaintiff and from the order excluding evidence from Mr. Adams concerning Mr. Hartman's testamentary intent. The Court of Appeals held that the description of the property in the will, "my residence at 2615 Cooleemee Street," created a latent ambiguity and that extrinsic evidence, including an affidavit signed by Mr. Adams, was admissible to show Mr. Hartman's intent when he executed the will. Britt v. Upchurch, 96 N.C. App. 257, 260, 385 S.E.2d 366, 368 (1989). The Court of Appeals further held that since the evidence in Mr. Adams' affidavit was admissible, and since plaintiff's affidavit presented evidence of contrary intent, material issues of fact were presented, and summary judgment was inappropriate. Id.

We agree with the Court of Appeals that the description of the property in the will creates a latent ambiguity and that extrinsic evidence is admissible in order to ascertain the testator's intent. We do not agree that Mr. Adams' affidavit should be admitted as evidence of Mr. Hartman's intent.

The general rule in North Carolina is that a latent ambiguity presents a question of identity and that extrinsic evidence may be admitted to help identify the person or the thing to which the will refers. Redd v. Taylor, 270 N.C. 14, 22, 153 S.E.2d 761, 766 (1967). This extrinsic evidence is admissible "to identify a person or thing mentioned therein." Id. This evidence is not admissible "to alter or affect the construction" of the will. Id. at 23, 153 S.E.2d at 767 (quoting McLeod v. Jones, 159 N.C. 74, 76, 74 S.E. 733, 734 (1912)). "Surrounding circumstances as well as the declarations of the testator are relevant to the inquiry." Id. "Surrounding circumstances" do not refer to the intent of the testator, rather these circumstances mean the "*facts* of which the testator *had knowledge* when she made her will." Wachovia Bank and Trust Co. v. Wolfe, 245 N.C. 535, 540, 96 S.E.2d 690, 694 (1957) (emphases in the original). "Declarations of *intent* by a testator . . . are not admissible to control the construction of his will or to vary, contradict, or add to its terms." Redd v. Taylor, 270 N.C. at 23, 153 S.E.2d at 767 (emphasis added). See also Holmes v. York, 203 N.C. 709, 166 S.E. 889 (1932) (objection properly sustained to proffered testimony of witness that testatrix "told him she did not intend the land to go to O.C. York under her will," id. at 711, 166 S.E. at 890); and Reynolds v. Trust Co., 201 N.C. 267, 159 S.E. 416 (1931) (objection properly sustained to deposition testimony of attorney that "[w]ill as drafted by me was drawn strictly in accordance with [testator's] instructions, and I recall very clearly that we discussed the difference between the two paragraphs mentioned," id. at 277, 159 S.E. at 420).

The reasoning behind these rules is succinctly stated in Thomas v. Houston, 181 N.C. 91, 106 S.E. 466 (1921), "[w]ills are made by testators, not by witnesses." Id. at 94, 106 S.E. at 468. By allowing testimony from someone else of what testator intended to say in his will, the will could be altered, revoked or annulled by verbal testimony, and this would conflict with the requirement that wills be in writing. In re Will of Cobb, 271 N.C. 307, 311, 156 S.E.2d 285, 289 (1967). Allowing extrinsic evidence of what the testator said he intended to do "would open a door for frauds and perjuries of the most alarming character." Id. (quoting Harrison v. Morton & Brown, 32 Tenn. (2 Swan) 461, 469 (1852)).

In his affidavit, Mr. Adams stated:

> It is my best recollection that Mr. Hartman mentioned to me on the day he came to execute his Will that he owned a vacant lot adjacent to the lot on which the residence was located.
>
> It is also my best recollection that I suggested that the Will be redrawn to clarify that this lot was or was not deemed to be part of the lot on which his residence was located. My best recollection of his response was to the effect that he had had one or more heart attacks and was very ill; that he wanted to sign his Will without waiting for it to be rewritten; that he wanted his Wife to have the vacant lot and the residuary clause was sufficient to devise it to her; that everyone knew that it was not a part of his residence lot and had never been cleared and made a part of the yard (he said that it was covered by trees and undergrowth); and that the residence lot and the vacant lot were purchased at separate times.

This affidavit is not a factual account of what Mr. Hartman said or did which might shed light on how he used the term "my residence at 2615 Cooleemee Street." Rather, it is a statement of the attorney's "best recollections" of his suggestions to the testator and "the effect" of the testator's response. The affidavit does purport to set forth some facts of which the testator had knowledge, such as, the lot was covered by trees and undergrowth. When viewed in its entirety, however, the affidavit is, in essence, only the attorney's conclusions or impressions of what the testator meant or intended to say in his will. Such evidence is not admissible.

Defendant argues that the attorney's affidavit should be admitted in evidence because case law provides that declarations of the testator are allowed where a latent ambiguity is present. For this proposition, defendant cites Thomas v. Summers, 189 N.C. 74, 126 S.E. 105 (1925); Redd v. Taylor, 270 N.C. 14, 153 S.E.2d 761; and Fulwood v. Fulwood, 161 N.C. 601, 77 S.E. 763 (1913). While defendant is correct that these cases hold that "declarations" of the testator are admissible, the "declarations" in these cases do not appear to be declarations of testamentary intent; rather they are testator's declarations which cast light upon the testator's usage of particular terms in the will.

In Thomas, the testatrix left a will devising "my home place on McIver Street." Thomas, 189 N.C. at 74, 126 S.E. at 106. Evidence was introduced which showed that at the time of her death, the testatrix owned two adjacent lots on McIver Street which were purchased at separate times. Lot 4 where testatrix' house was located was purchased in October 1915, and lot 5, which was a vacant lot adjoining lot 4, was purchased in November 1915. Id. at 74–75, 126 S.E. at 106. Further evidence showed that testatrix planted flowers on lot 5, although it had no building located on it, and she put a fence between lot 5 and lot 6, which she once owned but later sold. She also planted fruit trees and grapevines on lot 5.

When plaintiffs and defendants in Thomas both claimed lot 5, the court allowed testimony from a witness that testatrix, before her death, had asked the witness to build an iron fence around lots 4 and 5. The witness was allowed to testify further that testatrix had asked the witness three or four more times if he had put up the fence, to which he replied that he had not been able to get the proper materials to proceed with the construction. Id. at 75, 126 S.E. at 106. Further evidence was admitted that testatrix, claiming that it was her home place, refused to sell lot 5. This Court concluded that the language used in the will presented a latent ambiguity and that all of the evidence discussed above was admissible to show what the testatrix meant by the term "my home place on McIver Street." Id. at 76, 126 S.E. at 107. While in Thomas the Court clearly stated, "the declarations of the testator at the time of making the will and at other times ... were competent evidence," id. at 77, 126 S.E. at 107 (emphasis added), the "declarations" were not direct declarations of testamentary intent; rather, they were declarations of the testatrix which showed what she considered to be her home place.

In Redd, the testatrix left a will which provided in part: "If Warren & Jane Redd take care of my beloved husband F. M. Redd and me ... They are to have the part of the Farm on the Albemarle Road that they want in fee Simple. The rest of the farm to go with the rest of my estate." Redd, 270 N.C. at 17, 153 S.E.2d at 763. This Court held that the devise of "the part of the Farm on Albemarle Road that they want in fee Simple" created a latent ambiguity. Id. at 22, 153 S.E.2d at 766.

When the Redds claimed the entire farm, the trial court admitted other claimants' evidence which showed that the Redds had sought to purchase from the testatrix the part of the farm which they leased from her for a nursery. Id. at 19, 153 S.E.2d at 765. The trial court also admitted evidence from witnesses that the testatrix told them that she did not want to sell the land to the Redds but that they would get it in her will. Id. at 20, 153 S.E.2d at 765. In its opinion, the Court did not say whether the testimony regarding the testatrix' intention to leave the property to the Redds was properly admitted. The Court held, "Parole evidence of testatrix declarations that the Redds had sought to buy the land they had leased from her since 1951 was sufficient and competent to identify it as the land they wanted when she wrote the codicil." Id. at 24, 153 S.E.2d at 768. In view of the Court's earlier statement of the general rule, "[d]eclarations of intent by a testator ... are not admissible to control the construction of his will," id. at 23, 153 S.E. at 767, Redd does not stand for the proposition that direct declarations of testamentary intent are admissible to explain a latent ambiguity.

Fulwood involved a will which devised "the homestead tract of land." Fulwood, 161 N.C. at 602, 77 S.E. at 764. This Court again found that the language of the will presented a latent ambiguity. Id. However, the Court did not specify which declarations of the testator were allowed to help fit the description found in the will to the land owned by the testator. Id. Thus, Fulwood only provides the statement of the general rule that declarations of the testator at the time of making the will are admissible without explaining the nature of these declarations or whether they were declarations of testamentary intent.

None of the cases cited by defendant for the proposition that declarations of the testator at the time of making the will are admissible to remove a latent ambiguity stand for the extension of that rule to include the testator's direct declarations of intent as to which particular beneficiary will receive each parcel of land. To allow such declarations of intent would allow a will to be made by a witness rather than by the testator.

Since the affidavit contains the impressions of the attorney as to Mr. Hartman's intent concerning who was to get lot 37, it is inadmissible as extrinsic evidence to explain the latent ambiguity in the will. Therefore, the trial judge was correct in not allowing this affidavit to be considered on the issue of what was meant by the phrase "my residence at 2615 Cooleemee Street."

We now address whether the trial judge was correct in granting summary judgment in favor of plaintiff. The Court of Appeals held that material issues of fact exist in this case, and therefore summary judgment is inappropriate. Britt v. Upchurch, 96 N.C. App. at 260, 385 S.E.2d at 368. However, this holding was dependent upon the Court of Appeals' holding that Mr. Adams' affidavit was admissible to show Mr. Hartman's intent, thus creating a material conflict with the extrinsic evidence offered by plaintiff.

.... Since we have held that the attorney's affidavit was properly excluded by the trial judge when ruling on defendant's summary judgment motion, we must look at the evidence which was properly before the judge when ruling on the motion. The evidence before the trial judge on the summary judgment motion included: (1) the copies of the deeds for lots 36 and 37 as well as affidavits attesting to the genuineness of these documents; (2) affidavits concerning the tax records for lots 36 and 37 in the Wake County Tax Office and the City of Raleigh Tax Office; and (3) plaintiff's affidavit explaining how the two lots were acquired and used by the Hartman family.

In her affidavit, plaintiff asserted that at the same time her parents purchased the house on lot 36 her grandmother purchased the adjoining lot 37 on behalf of her father. She further stated that, when the family moved into the house located on lot 36, lot 37 was overgrown with honeysuckle, poison ivy, and other weeds. According to plaintiff, the Hartman family cleared lot 37 and landscaped it by planting various trees, bushes, and other plants. As noted earlier, the affidavit contained the information that Mr. Hartman built a garage on lot 37 and partially paved a driveway from the door of the garage across lot 36 to the street. Mr. Hartman also built a tool shed on lot 37 and used it to park the family's second car. Plaintiff stated that her father built a concrete sidewalk from the house on lot 36 to the garage on lot 37 and built several slate walkways across the property. The family dog was housed in a doghouse and dog pen constructed on lot 37. Plaintiff provided other facts in the affidavit which tended to show that the Hartman family used both lots 36 and 37 as their "residence."

To support her theory that "my residence at 2615 Cooleemee Street" refers only to lot 36, defendant offered evidence that the two lots (1) were purchased at different times; (2) were listed separately on the tax records; and (3) had different street addresses. Nothing else appearing, the fact that the lots were purchased at different times would explain why they were listed separately on the tax records. We also attach little significance to the different street addresses since there is no evidence that the testator used a different street address for lot 37 or was even aware that it carried an address other than 2615 Cooleemee Street. We conclude that defendant's forecast of evidence is not sufficient to raise a genuine issue of material fact as to whether Mr. Hartman considered "my residence at 2615 Cooleemee Street" to include both lots 36 and 37.

The question is really what Mr. Hartman considered to be his residence, and details of how Mr. Hartman and his family used the two lots are helpful in answering that question. Defendant has offered no admissible evidence to counter the evidence presented by plaintiff in her affidavit as to the facts showing that the family used both lots 36 and 37 as their residence. When viewed as a whole, the forecast of evidence points without contradiction to both lots 36 and 37 being used as a single residence by the Hartman family and that "my residence at 2615 Cooleemee Street" refers to both lots 36 and 37 rather than just to lot 36. There being no genuine issue of material fact, the trial judge was correct in granting plaintiff's motion for summary judgment.

The decision of the Court of Appeals is reversed, and the judgment of the trial court is reinstated.

NOTES AND QUESTIONS

1. How were the statements in Britt v. Upchurch different from the statements in Thomas v. Summers or Redd v. Taylor, discussed by the Britt v. Upchurch court in the course of its opinion?

2. Recall Estate of Carroll. If the court had concluded that "nephews and nieces" were ambiguous, would it have admitted testimony that testator had, during his lifetime, referred to his wife's siblings' children as "nephews and nieces?"

3. Why distinguish between testator's direct statements of testamentary intent and testator's informal statements which might shed light on testator's intent? Are direct statements of intent more susceptible to fabrication? Or is the problem that direct statements of intention—but not testator's informal statements—would undermine the language of the will itself as the definitive expression of testator's intent?

4. Direct statements of testator's intention are routinely admitted in cases of equivocation: when testator's description of a person or property could fit one of two people or things equally well. Suppose, for instance, testator leaves $10,000 to "my cousin Sam." Testator has two cousins—one named Samuel and the other named Samantha. Testator's statement to his wife (or his lawyer) that he had just executed a will leaving $10,000 to Samantha would be admissible to resolve the ambiguity.

5. The Restatement (Third) of Property: Wills and Other Donative Transfers abandons altogether the prohibition on admission of direct statements of intent. See § 10.2, cmt. f.

C. CORRECTING MISTAKES

In the preceding sections, we have been dealing with ambiguous wills—wills susceptible of more than one meaning. Suppose, however, the language of the will is susceptible of only one meaning—but that meaning does not reflect testator's intent. That is, suppose the will, as written and executed, contains a mistake that neither testator nor testator's lawyer caught.

Consider the following hypothetical: After leaving $10,000 to her sister, Zelda, Ann Airhead's will provides "I leave the remainder of my entire estate to Jonah Hill, whose good looks and sex appeal have served as an inspiration to me for years." Ann's lawyer, Bob Brainless, is prepared to testify that he got his notes mixed up after his interview with Ann, and substituted Jonah Hill for Brad Pitt. Ann's sister is willing to testify that Ann has purchased videocassettes of every Brad Pitt movie ever made, and that she had read many letters Ann had sent to Pitt promising Pitt her estate. At Ann's death, Zelda offers Ann's will for probate.

What should the court do? Should it probate the will and permit Hill to take? Should the court simply decide that the will is invalid (in whole or in part) and that Ann's estate should pass by intestate succession? Or should the court reform the will and substitute Pitt for Hill as the beneficiary?

Could the problem be characterized as one of ambiguity rather than mistake? How would the court in Estate of Gibbs, p. 339, *supra*, have treated the problem?

Consider these questions in the light of the following case:

Gifford v. Dyer

Supreme Court of Rhode Island, 1852.
2 R.I. 99, 57 Am.Dec. 708.

This was an appeal from a decree of the Court of Probate of Little Compton, proving and approving the last will and testament of Abigail Irish. The will was dated December 4, 1850, and the testatrix died December 6, 1850. After several bequests of small sums to the children of Robin Gifford and to others, she gives and bequeaths the rest and residue of her property, one half to John Dyer, who was her brother-in-law, and the other half to her two nephews, Jesse and Alexander Dyer. Robin Gifford, the only child of the testatrix, was not mentioned in the will. It appeared in evidence, that at the date of the will, Robin Gifford had been absent from home, leaving a family, for a period of ten years, unheard from; that all the neighbors considered him dead, and that his estate had been administered upon as of a person deceased. The scrivener who drew the will, testified as follows: "After I had read the will to her, she asked if it would make any difference if she did not mention her son. I asked if she considered him living. She said she supposed he had been dead for years; she said, if it would make any difference, she would put his name in, for they will break the will if they can. I think that was the expression she used. I think she said what she had given to her grand-children was in lieu of what he would have, but am not positive. I think her son left in 1841, and was not heard of to my knowledge. She was speaking of a home at Mr. Dyer's and said, what she had given him would pay him well. She said her grand-children had not been to see her while she was sick." It appeared that the testatrix had resided with John Dyer for some time previous to her death.

* * *

■ GREENE, C. J., delivered the opinion of the court. It is very apparent in the present case, that the testatrix would have made the same will, had she known her son was living. She did not intend to give him anything, if living.

But if this were not apparent and she had made the will under a mistake as to the supposed death of her son, this could not be shown *dehors* the will. The mistake must appear on the face of the will, and it must also appear what would have been the will of the testatrix but for the mistake. Thus, where the testator revokes a legacy, upon the mistaken supposition that the legatee is dead, and this appears on the face of the instrument of revocation, such revocation was held void. Campbell v. French, 3 Vesey 321.

NOTES AND QUESTIONS

1. Brooks executed a will leaving $20,000 to Margolis and $15,000 to Witt. Later, he executed a codicil revoking the devises to Margolis and Witt "since I have in the interim made *inter vivos* gifts to" Margolis and Witt. Margolis and Witt offer to prove that Brooks never made any *inter vivos* gifts. On the standard articulated in Gifford v. Dyer, are Margolis and Witt entitled to their devises if they prove that Brooks never made any gifts? See Witt v. Rosen, 298 Ark. 187, 765 S.W.2d 956 (1989) [Held, Margolis and Witt do not inherit].

Incidentally, the winning lawyer in Witt v. Rosen was one Vincent Foster, of the Rose Law Firm in Little Rock. Foster later became an advisor to President Clinton, and his mysterious and untimely suicide became a focal point in the investigation of the Whitewater land scandal.

2. Gifford v. Dyer and Witt v. Rosen are cases in which testator has allegedly formed a mistaken impression about the world around her (or him). In Gifford, testator mistakenly believed her son was dead; in Witt, testator mistakenly (or so the beneficiaries asserted) believed he had made gifts to the beneficiaries. Cases like these are often referred to as cases involving "mistake in the inducement". The allegation made by the excluded beneficiaries is, in effect, "if testator only knew the true facts, testator would have left us money."

Courts are understandably reluctant to honor mistake in the inducement claims because every testator is under some misimpressions at the time the testator executes his or her will. Testator may be misinformed about the wealth of her children, the fidelity of her husband, the value of her property, or the size of the estate tax that will be levied on her estate. If we were to hold that "mistakes" of this sort were sufficient to upset a duly executed will provision, many wills would be denied probate or subject to reformation.

* * *

Should courts respond differently when, as in the Hill/Pitt hypothetical, the mistake is a scrivener's error—testator knew what she wanted, but the lawyer did not adequately express her wishes in the will as executed?

In practice, courts are far more inclined to reform a will by using the eraser end of the pencil than by using the pencil's point. Is the risk of judicial error higher when a court is asked to correct the error by inserting the name of an intended beneficiary? Consider the following case:

Knupp v. District of Columbia

District of Columbia Court of Appeals, 1990.
578 A.2d 702.

■ NEWMAN, J.

This is an appeal from a judgment of the Superior Court construing a will. The problem at issue is that the will's sixth paragraph states that the residual estate is to pass to the person specified in the eighth paragraph of the will, but the eighth paragraph does not name a residual legatee. Appellant explains that the inconsistency is a result of an error on the part of the attorney who drafted the will: that although the testator allegedly instructed the attorney to name appellant as the beneficiary of the residual estate, the attorney forgot to insert such a clause in the will. Appellant argued in the construction proceeding in Superior Court that, based upon extrinsic evidence showing that the testator intended the appellant to be the beneficiary of the residual estate, the court should interpret the will to give Appellant the residual estate. The trial court held that it was without power to reform the will by inserting the name of a legatee alleged to have been omitted by mistake. As a consequence, the residue would go to the District of Columbia by escheat. See D.C. Code § 19–701 (1981). We agree with the Superior Court's ruling and, thus, we affirm.

I

The facts of this case show that the testator, a District of Columbia resident, executed a will from his hospital bed in March 1986 and died approximately one month thereafter. Paragraph Six of the will states:

> I direct my Executor to sell or otherwise convert into cash such of the rest and remainder of my estate as, in his judgment, is or may be necessary to pay my just debts, expenses of administration, funeral

> expenses, expenses of last illness, estate and inheritance (and other) taxes, and the cash legacies specified in subparagraphs A through G, inclusive, of paragraph SEVENTH hereof. I request that the remaining assets of my estate that are not required to be sold in order to pay debts, expenses, taxes, and cash legacies as provided in the preceding sentence be retained in kind by said Executor and distributed in kind to the residual legatee as stipulated in paragraph EIGHTH hereof.

Paragraph eighth of the will states, in pertinent part:

> I hereby nominate and appoint RICHARD L. KNUPP, . . ., as Executor of this my last will and testament, and I direct that no bond or security be required of him. I ask that he retain MILTON W. SCHOBER, . . ., as attorney for my estate.

Nowhere does paragraph eighth name a residual beneficiary.

The will was drafted by Milton W. Schober, the attorney referred to in the eighth paragraph of the will and the drafter of the testator's two prior wills. In his two prior wills, the testator left significant bequests to his personal friend, Richard L. Knupp ("Knupp"). Appellant alleges that in this will testator also intended Knupp to benefit. Allegedly, approximately one month prior to his death, the testator told Schober to draft a new will which would leave specific dollar amounts to several named beneficiaries and which would leave the bulk of the estate to Knupp, as residual beneficiary. Schober drafted the new will and the testator signed it. The will, however, did not name the residual legatee. Schober submitted an affidavit to the trial court admitting that he mistakenly failed to designate a residual beneficiary in the will even though the testator had instructed him to name Knupp. Schober also provided the trial court with notes he took of his conversations with the testator to prove that the testator intended Knupp to be the residual legatee.

In an order dated November 16, Judge Barnes found that the will was ambiguous on its face and that the court should consider extrinsic evidence to determine the testator's intent. In a supplemental order, though, Judge Barnes ruled that as a matter of law, specific extrinsic evidence concerning the names of omitted legatees must be excluded.

II

The general rule in construing a will in the District of Columbia is that the testator's intent is the guiding principle. Wyman v. Roesner, 439 A.2d 516, 520 (D.C.1981); see also In re Estate of Kerr, 139 U.S. App. D.C. 321, 433 F.2d 479 (1970). If the intent is clear from the language of the will, the inquiry ends there. Wyman, supra at 520; see also Brinker v. Humphries, 90 U.S. App. D.C. 180, 181, 194 F.2d 350, 352 (1952); Association of Survivors of the 7th G.A. Regiment v. Larner, 55 App. D.C. 156, 158, 3 F.2d 201, 203 (1925). However, "if the language 'upon its face and without explanation, is doubtful or meaningless' . . . a court may examine extrinsic evidence in order to understand the will." Wyman, supra, at 520 (quoting Baker v. National Savings & Trust, 86 U.S. App. D.C. 161, 162, 181 F.2d

273, 274 (1950)); accord Starkey v. District of Columbia, 377 A.2d 382, 383 (D.C.1977).

While the intent of the testator is the "polestar in construction of a will," In re Estate of Kerr, supra, 139 U.S. App. D.C. at 331, 433 F.2d at 489, extrinsic facts are not always permitted into evidence in order to prove the testator's intent. Certain conditions must be present to warrant the introduction of extrinsic evidence. First, there must be some ambiguity in order for a court to consider extrinsic evidence. See, e.g., Wyman, supra, 439 A.2d at 520. In addition, in all cases in which such evidence is received, it can be "utilized only for the purpose of interpreting something actually written in the will and never to add provisions to the will." 7th G.A. Regiment, supra, 55 App. D.C. at 158, 3 F.2d at 203. As one treatise states:

> evidence of surrounding circumstances is admissible to enable the court to understand the meaning of the words which the testator has used in his will, it is not admissible to add to the will provisions which cannot fairly be inferred from the language which is used therein, or to take from the will provisions which are clearly expressed therein.

4 BOWE–PARKER: PAGE ON WILLS, § 32.2 at 237 (citing Brown v. Wells, 45 App. D.C. 428 (1916), Atkins v. Best, 27 App. D.C. 148 (1906)).

When an ambiguity exists regarding the testator's intent, often a court will allow extrinsic facts into evidence to clear up the ambiguity. As the Supreme Court noted over a century ago:

> It is settled doctrine that, as a latent ambiguity is only disclosed by extrinsic evidence, it may be removed by extrinsic evidence. Such an ambiguity may arise upon a will, either when it names a person as the object of a gift, or a thing as the subject of it, and there are two persons or things that answer such name or description; or, secondly, it may arise when the will contains a misdescription of the object or subject: as where there is no such person or thing in existence, or, if in existence, the person is not the one intended, Or the thing does not belong to the testator.

Patch v. White, 117 U.S. 210, 217, 6 S. Ct. 617, 29 L. Ed. 860 (1886). See also 7th G.A. Regiment, supra, 55 App. D.C. at 158, 3 F.2d at 203 ("[A]mbiguity may arise when a will names a person as the object of a gift, or a thing as the subject of it, and there are two persons or things that equally well answer such name or description. In such a case, it is apparent that extrinsic evidence is not only useful, but indispensable to a proper interpretation of the will."); Mitchell v. Merriam, 88 U.S. App. D.C. 213, 188 F.2d 42 (1951) (where testatrix devised property to "my nephew Edward A. Mitchell" and testatrix had both a nephew and a grand nephew named Edward A. Mitchell, the court allowed in extrinsic evidence to show which of the two individuals the testatrix was referring to in her will); In re Miller's Estate, 127 F. Supp. 23 (D.D.C.1955) (where testatrix's will stated "I give and bequeath to my cousin, Sue McCook ... any monies that are left after my just debts are paid," extrinsic evidence was allowed in order to determine whether testatrix intended the word "monies" to be restricted to cash and money on deposit in bank accounts or whether the word should be understood in the colloquial sense as meaning all personal property).

Any ambiguity in the will under consideration in this case is not of the sort that can be corrected by the consideration of extrinsic evidence. There is no language in the will that could lead a court to infer that the testator intended Knupp to be the recipient of the residual estate; thus, it was proper for the court not to admit the extrinsic evidence.

* * *

For the aforementioned reasons, the decision is hereby Affirmed.

NOTES AND QUESTIONS

1. What reason was there for the court in Knupp to refuse to reform testator's will? Was it clear from the face of the will that the scrivener had made an error? Is this case significantly different from a case in which the lawyer includes a residuary clause, but leaves the residue of the estate to "##XX00"? If the lawyer had left the residue to "##XX00," could the court have treated the case as one of ambiguity rather than mistake? Note that any ambiguity would have been "patent," and that some courts have refused to admit extrinsic evidence to resolve patent ambiguities.

2. Other courts, too, have declined to allow extrinsic evidence to re-write a will when the scrivener neglects to provide for a residuary legatee, even when there is clear evidence of testator's intent. See e.g., Burnett v. First Commercial Trust Co., 327 Ark. 430, 939 S.W.2d 827 (1997). Whatever label we attach to the problem, what reason is there to permit testator's estate in a case like Knupp to escheat to the District of Columbia? Is the judicial policy of refusing to correct scrivener's errors consistent with the general trend in wills law toward relaxing rules when necessary to effectuate testamentary intent?

After this case, Knupp sued attorney Schober for malpractice. The court granted Knupp's motion for summary judgment, finding that there was no issue of fact regarding whether Schober's conduct was reasonable or defensible. See Knupp v. Schober, 1992 WL 182323 (1992). Will the draconian results in such cases create an incentive for lawyers to be more careful in future cases—especially if wills like the one in this case give rise to malpractice claims by disappointed beneficiaries?

Or is this a case where additional incentives are unnecessary because the prospect of litigation to reform the document will itself induce even minimally competent lawyers to take adequate care? In other words, how likely do you think it is that results like the one in Knupp will have an effect on lawyer behavior?

3. The Restatement (Third) of Property: Wills and Other Donative Transfers (2003) disapproves the result in the Knupp case, and would permit use of extrinsic evidence to reform a mistaken omission in a will. See § 11.2, comment p and illustration 16. A number of scholars, too, have argued that courts should be more willing to reform wills for mistake, even if reformation requires inserting new language into the will. See John H. Langbein & Lawrence W. Waggoner, Reformation of Wills on the Ground of Mistake: Change of Direction in American Law? 130 U. Pa. L. Rev. 521 (1982); Joseph W. DeFuria, Mistakes in Wills Resulting from Scriveners' Errors: The Argument for Reformation, 40 Cath. U. L. Rev. 1 (1990).

Those arguments have not fallen on deaf ears. A few appellate courts have held that extrinsic evidence was properly admitted to prove testators' intent in light of scriveners' errors, see, e.g., Estate of Lord, 795 A.2d 700 (Me. 2002); Erickson v. Erickson, 246 Conn. 359, 716 A.2d 92 (1998). Courts have admitted extrinsic evidence even when the drafter accidentally omitted the name of the residuary legatee. See Estate of Herceg, 193 Misc.2d 201, 747 N.Y.S.2d 901 (Surr. Ct. 2002).

Professor Pamela R. Champine, however, argues that the Restatement (Third) of Property goes too far, and recommends an approach to mistake correction that she sees as a reasonable compromise between the traditional rule and the Restatement Third's approach. See Pamela R. Champine, *My* Will Be Done: Accommodating the Erring and the Atypical Testator, 80 Neb. L. Rev. 387 (2001).

PROBLEM

Testator's lawyer prepares wills for Harvey and Rose Snide, husband and wife. Harvey's will leaves all of his property to Rose; Rose's will leaves all of her property to Harvey. By mistake, Harvey executes Rose's will, and Rose executes Harvey's. Harvey dies, and a guardian for one of the couple's minor children refuses to consent to probate of either will. What would the Knupp court do? What should the court do? See Matter of Snide, 52 N.Y.2d 193, 418 N.E.2d 656, 437 N.Y.S.2d 63 (1981).

SECTION V. REVOCATION OF WILLS

A. INTRODUCTION

The objects of a testator's bounty are rarely the same when testator is 80 as when testator was 40. Over time, parents die, spouses may divorce, and children and grandchildren may be born. Some relatives will treat testators better over time; relations with others may become strained. Moreover, the financial situation of testator—and of potential will beneficiaries—will change over time. As a result, a thirty-year old will may not reflect testator's intention at the time of testator's death. Legal doctrine recognizes this situation, and permits a testator to revoke her will. Indeed, in some situations—in particular, divorce—legal doctrine introduces a presumption of revocation to carry out the testator's imagined intent.

There are three ways to revoke a will. They are: (1) revocation by a subsequent written instrument—either by an express clause of revocation or by inconsistent subsequent provisions; (2) revocation by a physical act to the original will—either to the paper the will is written on or to the writing on the paper; and (3) revocation by operation of law due to a change in the circumstances of the testator.

UNIFORM PROBATE CODE

SECTION 2–507. REVOCATION BY WRITING OR BY ACT.

(a) A will or any part thereof is revoked:

(1) by executing a subsequent will that revokes the previous will or part expressly or by inconsistency; or

(2) by performing a revocatory act on the will, if the testator performed the act with the intent and for the purpose of revoking the will or part or if another individual performed the act in the testator's conscious presence and by the testator's direction. For purposes of this paragraph, 'revocatory act on the will' includes burning, tearing, canceling, obliterating, or destroying the will or any part of it. A burning, tearing, or canceling is a 'revocatory act on the will', whether or not the burn, tear, or cancellation touched any of the words on the will.

(b) If a subsequent will does not expressly revoke a previous will, the execution of the subsequent will wholly revokes the previous will by inconsistency if the testator intended the subsequent will to replace rather than supplement the previous will.

(c) The testator is presumed to have intended a subsequent will to replace rather than supplement a previous will if the subsequent will makes a complete disposition of the testator's estate. If this presumption arises and is not rebutted by clear and convincing evidence, the previous will is revoked; only the subsequent will is operative on the testator's death.

(d) The testator is presumed to have intended a subsequent will to supplement rather than replace a previous will if the subsequent will does not make a complete disposition of the testator's estate. If this presumption arises and is not rebutted by clear and convincing evidence, the subsequent will revokes the previous will only to the extent the subsequent will is inconsistent with the previous will; each will is fully operative on the testator's death to the extent they are not inconsistent.

Sometimes, a testator takes a "belt and suspenders" approach to revocation, attempting to revoke both by an express writing and by crossing out portions of the will. In the following case, decided in a state that has adopted the UPC provision on revocation, even this double-barreled approach proved unsuccessful. In reading the case, consider what the lawyer who supervised the revocation did wrong.

Gushwa v. Hunt

Supreme Court of New Mexico, 2008.
145 N.M. 286, 197 P.3d 1.

■ BOSSON, JUSTICE.

The New Mexico Probate Code specifies the means by which a testator may revoke a prior will. *See NMSA 1978, § 45–2–507(A)* (1993) stating that a will may be revoked by either executing a subsequent will or by performing a revocatory act on the will). The district court, concluding that the purported revocation in this case was legally ineffective, granted summary judgment, and the Court of Appeals affirmed in a well-reasoned opinion. On certiorari, we affirm most of that opinion, reversing only a small part and remanding for the district court to adjudicate a remaining allegation of fraud and to consider the propriety of a constructive trust in this case.

BACKGROUND

In June 2000, Decedent George Gushwa executed his Last Will and Testament (the Will) while his wife, Zane Gushwa, the Petitioner in this appeal, was in the hospital. Decedent was assisted in preparing the Will by his niece, Betty Dale, and her husband, Ted Dale (Ted). The Will provided that Decedent's separate property be held in trust for the support of Wife, during her life, and upon her death it was to be distributed to Decedent's nieces and nephews. Wife received no permanent distribution under the Will. Decedent named Ted as the trustee, and gave the original Will to him for safekeeping. The Dales were not beneficiaries under the Will.

Shortly thereafter, it appears that Decedent decided he wanted to revoke the Will. According to Wife, Decedent called Ted to regain possession of the original Will, but Ted refused to send it. Ted denies receiving such a request from Decedent. Instead, Ted submitted an affidavit stating that Wife called him and requested that he send *her* the original Will. Ted then notified Decedent's attorney and asked whether he should send Wife the original Will, because Ted knew that Decedent did not want her to see it. Decedent's attorney told Ted to contact Decedent, which Ted did. According to Ted, Decedent asked him to discuss the Will only in general terms with Wife, and told Ted which pages of the Will to send to Decedent. Ted then sent photocopies of those pages to Decedent.

In January 2001, Decedent contacted another lawyer to help him revoke the Will. In February 2001, his new lawyer assisted him in drafting a document entitled "Revocation of Missing Will(s)," in which Decedent repeatedly stated that he wanted to revoke his previous Will. At the same time, on the advice of counsel Decedent wrote "Revoked" on the copy of three pages of the Will, presumably the same three pages that he received from Ted, and attached those pages to the Revocation of Missing Will(s) document. That document was signed by Decedent and two witnesses and was notarized. In April 2001, Decedent received a photocopy of the entire Will from his previous attorney and wrote "Revoked" on each page of that copy of the Will.

Decedent died in 2005. After his death, Wife filed an application for informal appointment of a personal representative. Wife asserted that her husband died intestate and that she was not aware of any unrevoked testamentary instruments. In her application, Wife listed the names of several interested parties, including Wanda Hunt (Wanda), Decedent's niece, the Respondent in this appeal. Wanda objected to Wife's application, arguing that the June 2000 Will had not been revoked and was still in force, because Decedent had failed to follow the statutory formalities for revocation set forth in the Probate Code.

In response to Wanda's objections, Wife argued that the June 2000 Will had been revoked by the Revocation of Missing Will(s) document, and also by Decedent's act of writing "Revoked" on the photocopied pages of the Will. She further contended that Ted's behavior prevented Decedent from obtaining possession of the original Will so that he could write "Revoked" on the original instead of just a copy. Wife asked the district court to impose a constructive trust upon Decedent's estate if the court found that the Will had not been successfully revoked under the statute. In July 2006, the district court agreed with Wanda that Decedent's will had not been revoked in a manner consistent with the requirements of the Probate Code and granted summary judgment in her favor and against Wife.

The Court of Appeals affirmed the district court.

DISCUSSION

This appeal raises two questions under the Probate Code and one question of equity. First, we consider whether Decedent's execution of the Revocation of Missing Will(s) document satisfies the requirements of *Section 45-2-507(A)(1)*, dealing with revocation by writing. Second, we determine whether Decedent's act of writing "Revoked" on a photocopy is a revocatory act within the meaning of *Section 45-2-507(A)(2)*. Finally, we examine whether the allegations of fraud against Ted create a genuine issue of material fact that, if proven, might justify relief and preclude summary judgment.

Revocation by Writing

At the outset, we note that our Probate Code, unlike that of other states, does not allow for revocation of a will by any "other writing." *Compare § 45-2-507(A)(1)* ("A will or any part thereof is revoked ... by executing a subsequent will that revokes the previous will or part expressly or by inconsistency....") *with Fla. Stat. § 732.505(2)* (2002) ("A will or codicil, or any part of either, is revoked ... [b]y a subsequent will, codicil, or *other writing* executed with the same formalities required for the execution of wills declaring the revocation." (Emphasis added.)).

Wife argues that the Revocation of Missing Will(s) document should be given the effect of a subsequent will because of its language expressly revoking Decedent's prior will. Wife relies on the definition of "will" contained in the definitions section of the Probate Code. *See NMSA 1978, § 45-1-201(A)(53)* (1995) (defining a will as "any testamentary instrument that ... revokes or revises another will").

Wife's position, however, is at odds with the Code's specific language describing the only legally effective methods of revocation. If a will could be revoked by any writing that simply revoked another will, without the necessary testamentary language—or that it be in fact a "subsequent will"—then a will could be revoked by "any other writing," contrary to the Code's specific language and the legislative intent to limit the available means of revocation. Because our Probate Code requires revocation by a subsequent will, we are guided by this more specific statement rather than a generic definition. Accordingly, we reject Wife's argument that the Revocation of Missing Will(s) document satisfies the requirements of *Section 45–2–507(A)(1).* It clearly does not, regardless of Decedent's intent. Our Probate Code requires an exacting attention to form as well as intent to validate a revocation. *See Martinez, 1999 NMCA 93, P 11, 127 N.M. 650, 985 P.2d 1230.*

Similarly, Wife's argument that other language in the Revocation of Missing Will(s) document gives it the effect of a subsequent will does not persuade us. Instead, the language chosen by Decedent clearly shows that he knew he was not drafting a subsequent will.

First, in the Revocation of Missing Will(s) document, Decedent explained in writing his correct understanding of the two methods by which a testator can revoke a will—drafting a subsequent will or performing a revocatory act on the will. Decedent then listed acceptable revocatory acts, including burning or canceling. After establishing that he knew how to revoke a will, and what acts constitute a revocatory act on a will, Decedent then "attest[ed] that [he] canceled the first three (3) pages of the will executed ... on or about June 6, 2000, with the express intent to revoke the same." Thus, it is clear from the Revocation of Missing Will(s) document that if Decedent intended to revoke the Will, it was not by drafting a subsequent will, but by performing a revocatory act on the photocopy of the Will.

Additionally, Decedent used conditional language in the Revocation of Missing Will(s) document which strongly suggests that he did not intend the Revocation document to act as a subsequent will. Decedent wrote that he retained the option of drafting a subsequent will. Decedent stated that he knew that his property would pass through intestate succession "*if* [he did] not make a subsequent will." (Emphasis added.) In other words, the Revocation of Missing Will(s) document, though an expression of intent, was not a subsequent will in Decedent's mind. In addition, while Decedent excluded Ted and Betty from inheriting any of his property, he explained that they were not to inherit "whether by will or by intestate succession," leaving open the possibility of a subsequent will.

Our review of the statutory requirements for revocation by a subsequent will, along with our analysis of the language Decedent selected for use in the Revocation of Missing Will(s) document, persuades us that the Revocation of Missing Will(s) document was never intended to be a subsequent will and should not be given the effect of a subsequent will by this Court. Therefore, as a matter of law consistent with the clear language of the Probate Code, this document did not revoke Decedent's prior will.

The Effect of a Revocatory Act on a Photocopy of the Will

In addition to revoking a will by executing a subsequent will, the Probate Code provides that a will may be revoked by performing a revocatory act on the will. *Section 45–2–507(A)(2).* ("A will . . . is revoked . . . by performing a revocatory act on the will if the testator performed the act with the intent and for the purpose of revoking the will. . . .").

Wife argues that a majority of modern courts hold that a testator's revocation of a copy of will is a legally effective revocation of the original will. In support of her argument, Wife relies on an annotation that contains only six cases, all decided prior to 1952. *See 79 Am. Jur. 2d Wills § 516* (2002). These cases do not support Wife's position because the courts were considering the legal efficacy of fully executed duplicate copies, not photocopies of an original will.

Wife acknowledges that these cases address duplicate originals, but she contends that under our rules of evidence the distinction between a duplicate original and a photocopy "is a distinction without a difference." Relying on Rule 11–1003 NMRA, "Admissibility of Duplicates," Wife argues that a photocopy of a will should have the same evidentiary value as a duplicate original will.

In making her argument that a photocopy of a will and an executed original will should be given the same evidentiary weight, Wife fails to appreciate that under our rules of evidence a duplicate is only admissible to the same extent as the original: to prove the contents of the original. Instead, Wife is attempting to give the photocopy the same legal significance as an executed original, which our Probate Code does not permit.

Instead, our Probate Code mandates that a revocatory act be performed "on the will." *Section 45–2–507(A)(2).* While the Code does not explicitly require that the act be performed on the original or on an executed original, such a requirement is implicit in the statutory term "will." The Probate Code sets forth specific testamentary requirements for executing a will. *See NMSA 1978, § 45–2–502* (1995) ("[A] will must be: A. in writing; B. signed by the testator or in the testator's name by some other individual in the testator's conscious presence and by the testator's direction; and C. signed by at least two individuals. . . ."). Requiring that the revocatory act be performed on an original, or on a fully executed copy, simply comports with the statutory requirements for executing a will. *See In re Estate of Tolin, 622 So. 2d 988, 990 (Fla. 1993)* ("[The probate code] prescribes the manner used to properly execute a will or codicil. The use of the terms 'will or codicil,' which have specific statutory definitions, shows a legislative intent that in order to effectively revoke a will or codicil by a physical act, the document destroyed must be the original document.").

There is a real and valuable distinction between a photocopy admitted only to prove the contents of a will and a photocopy admitted as a legally effective original.

Further, we agree with our Court of Appeals that treating photocopies differently from originals is important as a matter of policy. As that Court explained, the requirement of an original can protect against fraudulent reproduction of unauthorized wills. *See Gushwa, 2007 NMCA 121, P 21, 142 N.M. 575, 168 P.3d 147.* Photocopies can be readily produced and the existence of multiple copies of a will can engender confusion, especially when the issue is whether the will has been validly revoked. *Id.*

We are also informed by case law from other jurisdictions where courts have held that a revocatory act performed on a mere photocopy is legally ineffective. *See Tolin, 622 So. 2d at 990* (holding that the decedent's attempted revocation was ineffective, even though the decedent "destroyed a document which 'was an exact copy of the fully executed original . . . and was in all respects identical to the original except for the original signatures' "); *In re Krieger, 191 A.D.2d 994, 595 N.Y.S.2d 272, 272 (App. Div. 1993)* (holding "that a will cannot be revoked by the physical destruction of an unexecuted conformed copy"). Accordingly, we hold that Decedent's revocatory acts performed on a mere photocopy of his original Will do not comport with the statutory requirements of *Section 45-2-507(A)(2).*

Imposition of a Constructive Trust

Because we conclude that Decedent's attempt to revoke the Will was legally ineffective, we decline to remand for a trial on that issue. We are, however, mindful of the inequity that this holding may work under the circumstances of this particular case if, as alleged, Decedent was fraudulently prevented from regaining possession of his original Will.

Our courts have correctly held that "statutes providing for revocation of wills are mandatory and that generally a will may be revoked only in the manner prescribed by statute." *Martinez, 1999 NMCA 93, P 9, 127 N.M. 650, 985 P.2d 1230* (citing *Albuquerque Nat'l Bank v. Johnson, 74 N.M. 69, 71, 390 P.2d 657, 658 (1964)).* To ameliorate the occasional inequities that such a formal approach may unintentionally produce, courts have resorted to equitable remedies such as the imposition of a constructive trust. *See Tolin, 622 So. 2d at 990–91.*

A court will impose a constructive trust "to prevent the unjust enrichment that would result if the person having the property were permitted to retain it." *In re Estate of Duran, 2003 NMSC 8, P 34, 133 N.M. 553, 66 P.3d 326.* Courts have held that certain conduct, "such as fraud, constructive fraud, duress, undue influence, breach of a fiduciary duty, or similar wrongful conduct[,]" may warrant the imposition of a constructive trust. *Id.* (quoted authority omitted). "If a court imposes a constructive trust, the person holding legal title is subjected to an equitable duty to convey the property to a person to whom the court has determined that duty is owed." *Id.*

Wife maintains that Ted wrongfully prevented Decedent from regaining possession of his original Will. Decedent's niece, Wanda, disputes these allegations with an affidavit from Ted. In response to Wife's allegation that he refused to send Decedent the original Will, Ted denies ever receiving a call from Decedent requesting the original Will. Instead, he explains that it was Wife, not Decedent, who called him asking for the original Will. Ted also states that Decedent instructed him not to send Wife the original and to send Decedent a copy of only certain pages of the Will.

Viewing this evidence in the light most favorable to Wife, as the party opposing summary judgment, and drawing all inferences in favor of a trial on the merits, we conclude that summary judgment was not appropriate with respect to this issue. *See Handmaker, 1999 NMSC 43, P 18, 128 N.M. 328, 992 P.2d 879*. A disputed issue of material fact remains unresolved, namely whether Ted wrongfully prevented Decedent from obtaining the original Will, thereby making it virtually impossible for Decedent to comply with the statutory requirements for revocation. Thus, we remand to the district court to adjudicate that issue and decide whether, as a consequence, a constructive trust should be imposed under the facts of this case.

CONCLUSION

We affirm in part and reverse in part and remand to the district court for further proceedings consistent with this Opinion.

■ CHAVEZ, CHIEF JUSTICE (dissenting).

I recognize that the Revocation of Missing Will(s) document is not an ideal will, and indeed that Decedent apparently believed that it did not constitute a will under New Mexico law. Decedent used language suggesting that he did not consider the document a will and that he intended to revoke his prior will by the ineffective means of performing a revocatory act on a partial photocopy of his prior will. Because of this confusion, the majority concludes as a matter of law that Decedent's document was not a will, and as such failed to satisfy New Mexico's statutory requirements for the revocation of a prior will. I respectfully disagree. The document met all of the formalities necessary to create a will, and the district court's responsibility was simply to determine the testator's intent.

Had Decedent executed, in accordance with the statutory formalities, a document purporting to be a will requesting that his property be disposed of through the intestacy laws, but specifying that nothing from his estate would be given to certain relatives, I see no reason why our courts should refuse to give effect to his desires. In other words, such a document would be a valid will. Furthermore, if Decedent executed such a subsequent will, it seems clear that the New Mexico Probate Code would obligate us to conclude that the previous will had been revoked, *even if* the new will did not explicitly recite language revoking the previous will. *Section 45-2-507(C)* ("The testator is presumed to have intended a subsequent will to replace rather than supplement a previous will if the subsequent will makes a complete disposition of the testator's estate."). Unfortunately, our decision is not so simple, since the disputed Revocation of Missing Will(s) document contains additional language suggesting that Decedent did not perceive it to be a will.

I would reverse the district court because it should not have decided the issue of the will's testamentary nature as a matter of law. The document appears to satisfy the statutory requirements for a will. The real issue is Decedent's intent, which the evidence strongly suggests was to dispose of his property and revoke the prior will. Due to the ambiguity of the Revocation of Missing Will(s) document, there still exists a genuine issue of material fact on this subject.

For the foregoing reasons, I respectfully dissent.

B. REVOCATION BY SUBSEQUENT WRITTEN INSTRUMENT

A client (call him George Gushwa) walks into your office and explains that he wants to revoke a will he has previously executed. Would you ask him how he wants to have his estate distributed? If so, wouldn't you generally advise the client to execute a new will to give effect to his current wishes? When a lawyer is involved, wills are almost inevitably revoked by execution of a new will. Most well-drafted wills contain an express revocation clause like this: "I hereby revoke all wills and codicils I have previously made." When a new, validly exercised will contains such language, the new will revokes all prior wills.

Gushwa is unusual because the lawyer supervised revocation of a will without helping testator prepare a new will. But the opinion in *Gushwa* raises questions that might arise more frequently when revocation is not supervised by a lawyer. Consider the following:

QUESTIONS

1. Testator types a document entitled "Revocation of Will." The document consists of a single declarative sentence: "I hereby revoke all wills I have previously made." Testator then signs and dates the document. If UPC § 2–507 were in effect, would the document revoke testator's prior wills? Why not?

2. Suppose testator typed and executed the same document, but did so in front of two disinterested witnesses, and asked the two witnesses to witness revocation of his will, and to attest to the revocation. The witnesses then sign the document below testator's signature. According to the court in *Gushwa*, would the document be effective to revoke testator's will? Would it be effective under the Florida statute discussed by the court?

3. Suppose now that testator executes the purported revocation in the manner described in question 2, but adds a sentence saying "I understand that my estate will now be distributed to my heirs at law." Would the *Gushwa* court have found the document effective to revoke testator's prior wills? Would the language about distribution to my heirs at law qualify to make the revocation document a "will" within the meaning of UPC § 2–507? In Brown v. Brown, 21 So.3d 1 (Ala. App. 2009), testator executed a revocation document providing that I "do hereby revoke all last wills and testaments heretofore made by me; it being my intention and desire to die without a will." The court, quoting heavily from *Gushwa*, concluded that the document was ineffective to revoke the will. Is *Brown* distinguishable from *Gushwa?* In light of *Gushwa* and *Brown*, would you support enactment of UPC 2–507 without making changes to the statutory language?

As we have seen, the safest way to revoke a prior will is to execute a new one that expressly revokes all prior wills. But suppose testator—uncounseled by a lawyer, or counseled by a poor lawyer—executes a new will without expressly revoking all prior wills. Does the new will revoke all prior wills? According to UPC § 2–507(b), the answer depends on testator's intent: did testator intend the new will to supplement the prior will, or to serve as a complete substitute for the prior will? In light of the UPC's language, consider the following:

PROBLEM

Testator executed a 2005 will leaving "all of my property" to her sister. In 2010, she executed a document which she declared to be "my last will and testament." The document provides "I leave all of my real property to my brother." If testator dies in 2012, owning a small cabin and $50,000 in cash, how should testator's estate be distributed?

Revocation by Codicil

We tend to think of the decedent's last will and testament as a single instrument. Though that is often the case, the decedent's last will and testament may also be the combination of two or more instruments. The combination often consists of a will plus one or more codicils. Thus, I might execute a will in January of 2003 and change a gift in that original will in a codicil dated February 2, 2006 and also change my executor in a second codicil dated March 3, 2011.

An example of a codicil follows.

CODICIL

I, JANE ROE, of the City, County and State of New York, having made my Will dated June 1, 2007, do make, publish, and declare this to be a Codicil to said Will.

FIRST: I hereby revoke Article THIRD (a) of my said Will and substitute the following in its place:

> "THIRD: (a) I give and bequeath the sum of One Thousand Dollars ($1,000) to my sister ANN ROE if she survives me."

SECOND: I hereby ratify and confirm my said Will except as any part of it is revoked or modified by this Codicil.

IN WITNESS WHEREOF, I JANE ROE, have to this, a Codicil to my Will, dated June 1, 2007, subscribed my name this 2d day of July, in the year Two Thousand and Eleven.

____

Jane Roe

Subscribed by the Testator in the presence of us and of each of us, and at the same time published, declared, and acknowledged by her to us to be a Codicil to her Last Will and Testament dated June 1, 2007, and thereupon we, at the request of the said Testator, in her presence and in the presence of each other, have hereunto subscribed our names as witnesses this 2nd day of July, 2011.

____________________________ residing at ____________

____________________________ residing at ____________

As you can see, this well-drafted codicil expressly revokes part of the decedent's original will. If the testator dies with the will and the codicil in effect, what would you probate as the last will and testament of the testator? Do you see why thoughtful lawyers try to avoid codicils unless time is very short or there is some question about the testator's capacity?

PROBLEMS

1. Testator devises Blackacre to Able in his will. In a later codicil that gives no further guidance, Testator devises Blackacre to Baker. Who gets Blackacre?

2. Testator devises $1,000 to Charlie in her will. In a later codicil that gives no further guidance, Testator devises $2,000 to Charlie. Both instruments are probated. No further information is available. How much does Charlie get? How would you redraft Testator's codicil to eliminate any ambiguity?

C. REVOCATION BY PHYSICAL ACT

Oscar Owner, long-time owner of a major league baseball team, conducts a ceremony at home plate before an important game. In front of a packed stadium, he announces that he has decided to revoke his only will because he would prefer to die intestate. He then takes a match to his will, and burns it up. If the Uniform Probate Code is in effect, has Oscar revoked his will? Of course he has. Under virtually any statute, such a public destruction of the will would provide ample evidence of testator's intent. In light of the formalities that attend execution of wills, few testators are likely to burn, tear or obliterate their wills unless they intend to revoke.

It is also true, however, that few testators burn their wills in front of 50,000 people. What happens if, at testator's death, her will is found with some or all of the dispositive provisions crossed out? Or, what happens if her will is not found at all [but her lawyer has a copy of the executed will]? Consider these questions in light of *Gushwa* and the following case:

Ward–Allen v. Gaskins

District of Columbia Court of Appeals, 2010.
989 A.2d 185.

■ FISHER, J.:

Sustaining objections to a codicil executed by Anna Creech in 1995, the Superior Court admitted her 1992 will to probate. We reverse and remand for further proceedings consistent with this opinion.

I. Facts

On August 13, 1992, Anna Creech executed a will ("1992 will") which contained eighteen items. Several of those items bequeathed various possessions to specific persons. For example, in Item VI, Ms. Creech left her china closet to her nephew, Cleveland Mitchell. In Item XIII, Ms. Creech bequeathed "the entire residue of my estate, whether real, personal or mixed, of every kind, nature and description whatsoever ... to all of my nieces and nephews who survive me." In addition, in Item XIV, Ms. Creech nominated Mr. Mitchell as her personal representative, and named one of her nieces, appellee Lettie Gaskins, as his alternate.

On August 11, 1995, Ms. Creech executed a codicil ("1995 codicil") to the 1992 will, explicitly revoking Items VI, XIII, and XIV. She now bequeathed her china closet to Special T. Allen instead of Mr. Mitchell; she devised her real property (her home at 131 U Street, N.E.), to Bettye Ward Garner and Bobbie Jean Ward–Allen as tenants in common; and, although she again nominated Mr. Mitchell as her personal representative, she named Ms. Ward–Allen as the alternate instead of Ms. Gaskins.[1] Ms. Creech ratified, confirmed, and republished her 1992 will "in all respects except as altered or modified by this First Codicil thereto."

Anna Creech died on December 15, 2001, at the age of 94. Nearly five years later, on November 7, 2006, Ms. Ward–Allen filed a petition for standard probate in which she sought appointment as Ms. Creech's personal representative. Ms. Ward–Allen attached the 1992 will and a copy of the 1995 codicil to her petition. In June 2008, two of Ms. Creech's nieces, Lettie Gaskins and Jessie Marie Davis, filed objections to admission of the 1995 codicil and to Ms. Ward–Allen's petition for standard probate. They based their objections on the fact that Ms. Ward–Allen filed a copy of the 1995 codicil, instead of the original, with the register of wills.

After a hearing in August 2008, the trial judge sustained appellees' objections to probating a copy of the 1995 codicil because there was too "much uncertainty about what became of the original" and Ms. Ward–Allen did not meet her burden to "prove what happened to it." He then denied Ms. Ward–Allen's petition for standard probate and admitted the 1992 will to probate. The court also appointed Ms. Gaskins as personal representative, Mr. Mitchell having previously renounced the appointment.

---

1. Ms. Garner is Ms. Creech's niece, Ms. Ward–Allen is Ms. Creech's grandniece, and Special Allen is Ms. Creech's great grandniece. All of them lived with Ms. Creech at her home and cared for her for twenty or twenty-five years.

Ms. Ward–Allen filed a notice of appeal; Ms. Gaskins is the only appellee to have filed a brief in this court.

II. Analysis

A. Revocation and Revival

In the District of Columbia, a testator may revoke a will or codicil in two ways. He may expressly revoke the instrument (or a part thereof) by executing "a later will, codicil, or other writing declaring the revocation." *D.C. Code § 18–109 (a)(1)* (2001). Alternatively, revocation may be accomplished by "burning, tearing, cancelling, or obliterating the will or codicil, or the part thereof, with the intention of revoking it, by the testator himself, or by a person in his presence and by his express direction and consent." *D.C. Code § 18–109 (a)(2).* Both of these forms of revocation are at issue in this case.

There is no dispute that in her 1995 codicil, Ms. Creech explicitly "revoke[d]" critical items from the 1992 will. "[I]n place of said Item[s]," she, among other changes, appointed a new alternate personal representative and disposed of her home differently. These revocations became effective upon execution of the 1995 codicil. *D.C. Code § 18–109(a)* (a will may be revoked in part); *In re Burleson, 738 A.2d 1199, 1205 (D.C. 1999)* ("[W]e now hold that under *D.C. Code § 18–109,* a prior will may be revoked upon the *execution* of a subsequent will....") (emphasis in original).

Even if it were true, as the trial court seems to have concluded, that Ms. Creech revoked the 1995 codicil by destroying it (more on that later), the court erred by admitting the 1992 will to probate in its entirety. *D.C. Code § 18–109(b)* provides that: "A will or codicil, or a part thereof, after it is revoked, may not be revived otherwise than by its re-execution, or by a codicil executed as provided in the case of wills, and then only to the extent to which an intention to revive is shown." As we explained in *Burleson,* "under *D.C. Code § 18–109,* a prior will [once revoked] ... may not be revived unless [it] has been re-executed or a codicil [is] executed in accordance with other statutory provisions." *In re Burleson, 738 A.2d at 1205.* In other words, revocation of the codicil would not reinstate Items VI, XIII, and XIV of the earlier will. *Id. at 1205–06* ("[E]ven if we were to assume, from the fact that the original 1994 will was not found at the time of his death, that Burleson intended to revoke his 1994 will, ... this would not change the fact that the 1993 will was rendered void upon execution of the 1994 will containing a revocation clause."); *In re Smith, 77 F. Supp. 217, 219 (D.D.C. 1948)* ("The revocation of the second will does not reinstate the earlier will.").

Here, as in *Burleson,* it is undisputed that the codicil had been properly executed, and no evidence was "presented suggesting that the deceased had revived the [earlier] will by re-executing [it] or executing a [new] codicil." *In re Burleson, 738 A.2d at 1206.* Thus, Items VI, XIII, and XIV of Ms. Creech's 1992 will have not been revived and may not be admitted to probate.

B. The Missing Codicil

As we have mentioned, *D.C. Code § 18–109(a)(2)* allows a will or codicil to be revoked by "burning, tearing, cancelling, or obliterating ... with the intention of revoking it." The District of Columbia therefore recognizes an evidentiary presumption that applies if the original of a will or codicil cannot be found at the time of its maker's death:

> "If a will or codicil, known to have been in existence during testator's lifetime, and in his custody, or where he had ready access to it, can not be found at his death, a presumption arises that such will was destroyed by testator in his lifetime with the intention of revoking it; and in the absence of rebutting evidence this presumption is sufficient to justify a finding that the will was revoked."

Webb v. Lohnes, 69 App. D.C. 318, 321, 101 F.2d 242, 245 (1938) (quoting 1 PAGE ON WILLS, § 773 (2d ed. 1926)). The presumption is not rebutted merely by producing a copy of the executed original. *In re McKeever, 361 A.2d 166, 171 (D.C. 1976)* ("We hold that the decedent's revocation of the original will in her possession also revoked the carbon copy of the same will in her safe deposit box."). On the other hand, it is "generally agreed that the presumption [of revocation] is rebuttable[,]" *Gilbert v. Gaybrick, 195 Md. 297, 306, 73 A.2d 482, 485 (1950)*; it is not absolutely necessary that the original be produced or that its absence be satisfactorily explained.

Once the presumption of revocation is triggered, the party seeking to probate a copy of the will or codicil must show, by a preponderance of evidence, that the testator did not destroy the lost will or codicil with the intent of revoking it. *Webb, 69 App. D.C. at 321, 101 F.2d at 245.* A variety of evidence may be offered in an attempt to meet this burden. *See In re Barfield, 736 A.2d 991, 998 (D.C. 1999)* (to prevail, proponent of will that could not be found at decedent's death must "offer[ ] facts to rebut the presumption of revocation"); *Clark v. Turner, 87 U.S. App. D.C. 54, 55, 183 F.2d 141, 142 (1950)* ("A [Proponent of lost will] must show either that the will was in existence at the time of decedent's death or ... he must be able to show that the testatrix intended that the will remain in force, thus rebutting the presumption of revocation."); *Webb, 69 App. D.C. at 322, 101 F.2d at 245* (considering that decedent had "access to the will and daily opportunity to destroy it," whether any "witness claim[ed] to have seen the will or heard any statement from [decedent] that it was still in existence," and whether "evidence [demonstrated] continuing interest and friendly relationship between the [decedent and beneficiary]."); *New York State Library School Ass'n v. Atwater, 227 Md. 155, 158, 175 A.2d 592, 594 (1961)* (considering testator's statements, within two years of her death, referring to the existence of the missing will, but "intimating that she might revoke or change [it]"); *Plummer v. Waskey, 34 Md. App. 470, 481–84, 368 A.2d 478, 485–86 (1977)* (citing 95 C.J.S. WILLS § 385, at 285–87) (listing types of evidence that can overcome the presumption) (considering the state of relations between the testator and beneficiary, as well as evidence that testator had been contemplating making a new will shortly before her death).

In this case, appellant Ward–Allen testified that she sent the original copy of the codicil to Mr. Mitchell, in North Carolina, because she knew that Ms. Creech had nominated him to be her personal representative and that he would need the document. When Ms. Ward–Allen ultimately filed a petition for standard probate, she had not recovered the original, and she filed a copy of the codicil.

Appellant contends she "testified that she had possession of the original of that codicil after Anna Creech died. . . ." This may well have been what she intended to say, but the record is less than clear. The questions and answers did not always follow a logical progression, and Ms. Ward–Allen made confusing statements about whether she mailed the original before or after Ms. Creech died.[2] To add to the uncertainty, Ms. Ward–Allen's two witnesses, Ms. Garner and Special Allen, remembered "seeing the original codicil right before she sent [it to Mr. Mitchell]," but thought that occurred in 1995. Unfortunately, we do not know if, or when, Mr. Mitchell received the original codicil because he did not appear at the hearing, nor did Ms. Ward–Allen's attorney depose him. Moreover, although the court said, "I believe Ms. Ward–Allen's testimony about her sending it to Mr. Mitchell," it did not make any findings regarding when that occurred.

It is crucial that this uncertainty be resolved. If Ms. Ward–Allen had the original codicil *after* Ms. Creech's death, then Ms. Creech obviously had not destroyed it. *See Tilghman v. Bounds, 214 Md. 533, 538, 136 A.2d 226, 228 (1957)* (There was "evidence tending to show that the will was in existence at and after the time of the death of the testatrix . . . [and none demonstrating] that she executed any later will, or that the [will, when last seen by witness,] had been altered or mutilated in any way."; allowing copy of will to be probated). If Ms. Ward–Allen sent the original to Mr. Mitchell *before* Ms. Creech's death, then Ms. Creech would have lost the opportunity to revoke the codicil by destroying the original. *D.C. Code § 18–109 (a)(2)* (revocation of a will or codicil by destroying it may only be accomplished "by the testator himself, or by a person in his presence and by his express direction."). The presumption of revocation would not apply unless she somehow regained access to it. These factual questions should be resolved on remand.

---

2. For example, Ms. Ward–Allen responded to Judge Wertheim's question, "[w]hen did you have possession of it, before or after she passed?" by saying, "A[w]ell, see. I knew where she kept it. I had it before she passed." After that comment, Ms. Ward–Allen explained that, as one of Ms. Creech's caretakers, she had access to all of Ms. Creech's important papers. Because of Ms. Creech's advanced age, "I had to take her almost every place she went[,] . . . [and] I was also her right hand." Later in the discussion, Ms. Ward–Allen said, "when the late Anna Creech deceased, . . . [a]t the time, I realized that Cleveland Mitchell, Jr. was the personal representative for the late Anna Creech. So, I, I realized that he had to have all the original documents in his hand. Therefore, . . . I sent the [codicil] by mail. . . ." There is no clear answer as to whether Ms. Ward–Allen mailed the original codicil before or after Ms. Creech passed away.

As we have said, only portions of the 1992 will may be admitted to probate. If the court concludes on remand that Ms. Creech revoked the codicil, she will have made no valid provision disposing of the residue of her estate (including her real property and the china closet) and those items will pass under the laws governing intestacy. In remanding, we reiterate that "[t]he primary function of a court in construing the terms of a will is to determine the intent of the testator and to give that intention full effect unless it is contrary to law." *O'Connell v. Riggs Nat'l Bank, 475 A.2d 405, 407 (D.C. 1984)*; *see also Washington Loan & Trust Co. v. Convention of Protestant Episcopal Church, 54 App. D.C. 14, 19–20, 293 F. 833, 838–39 (1923)* ("If [the testator's] intention does not conflict with any rule of law or public policy, . . . it is the court's duty to be diligent in seeing that it is obeyed. Nice distinctions by which the clearly stated will of a testator would be defeated should not be resorted to or encouraged.").

III. Conclusion

For the reasons we have explained, the 1992 will cannot be probated in its entirety. Further proceedings are necessary to determine whether Anna Creech revoked her 1995 codicil. If so, then much of her property will be treated as if she died intestate. If not, the codicil should be admitted to probate. We reverse and remand for further proceedings consistent with this opinion.

So ordered.

QUESTIONS

1. Why didn't the court admit the 1995 codicil to probate instead of remanding? What questions of fact remained for resolution by the trial court? What would Ward–Allen have had to prove to be entitled to probate the 1995 codicil?

2. The Supreme Judicial Court of Massachusetts recently made the following observation about lost wills:

> When a will is traced to the testator's possession or to where he had ready access to it and the original cannot be located after his death, there are three plausible explanations for the will's absence: (1) the testator destroyed it with the intent to revoke it; (2) the will was accidentally destroyed or lost; or (3) the will was wrongfully destroyed or suppressed by someone who was dissatisfied with its terms.

Estate of Beauregard, 456 Mass. 161, 921 N.E.2d 954 (2010). What reason is there for courts to presume that explanation (1) represents the truth?

3. In light of the explanations for lost wills outlined in question 2, what result should courts reach in the following cases:

a. Testator's lawyer testifies that he gave the original will to testator. The will leaves testator's daughter, his sole heir, income for life, with remainder to be distributed to her children upon her death. At death, the will was not found. Testator's daughter had keys to testator's house and safe deposit box. See First Interstate Bank of Oregon v. Henson–Hammer, 98 Or.App. 189, 779 P.2d 167 (1989).

b. Same facts, but testator's daughter had no keys to the house or safe deposit box.

c. Testator executed a will dividing the bulk of his property between his two surviving children, and leaving grandchildren born to a deceased child a much smaller amount. Testator kept the will at home. Although none of the children or grandchildren had access to the house, a variety of nurses and caretakers did. At death, the will was not found. See Balboni v. LaRocque, 991 So.2d 993 (Fla.App. 2008).

4. In light of the *Gushwa* and *Ward–Allen* cases, what advice would you give a client about custody of the original will?

5. Suppose a client of yours had physical custody of her will. She calls you and indicates that she wants to revoke the will immediately, and doesn't have time to execute a new will. If she wants to revoke the will by physical act, what act or acts would you recommend? Why?

NOTES

1. ***Proof of Lost Wills.*** If the presumption is rebutted the proponent of the will (in all likelihood the nominated executor) still has to prove the contents of the missing, but not revoked, will. There are various ways to prove the contents, with a photocopy of the lost original being the easiest to imagine. Courts in many states will listen to lesser forms of proof, such as the drafter's testimony. Some states do not wish to taint their judicial process with weak proof of the content of lost wills or do not want to waste judicial resources on such inquiries. Those states may require specific forms of proof of the will's contents or establish special procedures for proving the will. Statutes establishing these special procedures are called "lost and destroyed will statutes." They create a second hurdle, after the wills act, that the will must get over.

Here is an example of a lost and destroyed wills act:

NEW YORK SCPA

SECTION 1407. PROOF OF LOST AND DESTROYED WILL.

A lost or destroyed will may be admitted to probate only if

1. It is established that the will has not been revoked, and

2. Execution of the will is proved in the manner required for the probate of an existing will, and

3. All of the provisions of the will are clearly and distinctly proved by each of at least two credible witnesses or by a copy or draft of the will proved to be true and complete.

What good is there to be said about lost and destroyed wills acts? What bad is there to be said?

2. ***Revocation by Marks Made on the Will.*** Recall that in *Gushwa,* testator, at his lawyer's direction, had written "Revoked" on each page of a copy of his previously executed will. If George Gushwa had written the words "revoked" across the front of each page of the original of his will, that marking would have revoked the will. Why should the result be different because he wrote the same words across a copy? Suppose testator had taken a photocopy of his will, crossed out every provision, torn off the signature and told his lawyer he had revoked the will. Applying the analysis articulated in *Gushwa,* would the will still be valid? Do you approve of this result? Does this rule still make sense? The drafters of the Restatement (Third) of Property think not. Comments to the Restatement suggest that if the testator mistakes a copy for the original, and her intent to revoke the will can be proved by clear and convincing evidence, the failure to revoke the original will can be excused as harmless error, and the revocation can be valid. See Restatement (Third) Property, § 4.1, cmt. f. Would the result be the same under UPC § 2–503?

3. ***Loss or Destruction of Duplicate Originals.*** Sophisticated lawyers have the client sign only one original will. If, for some reason, a testator signs two original wills with the same exact terms, the two wills are "duplicate originals." Generally, only one duplicate original need be offered for probate. What happens, however, if one of the duplicate originals cannot be found after testator's death?

If the "lost" duplicate original was the only one in the testator's custody, courts generally indulge in the presumption that testator destroyed the duplicate original, and thereby revoked the will. See, e.g., Blalock v. Riddick, 186 Va. 284, 42 S.E.2d 292 (1947). What happens, however, if *both* duplicate originals had been in testator's custody, and one was lost or otherwise defaced? Cf. Etgen v. Corboy, 230 Va. 413, 337 S.E.2d 286 (1985).

4. ***Proxy Revocation by Physical Act.*** Virtually all states recognize proxy revocation by physical act. The testator must intend a revocation and the act must be done by the proxy in the testator's presence and by her direction.

Assume a testator sends a dated, handwritten, signed note to her lawyer that says, "Tear up my will as soon as you get this note." Assume that note is not a holographic instrument of revocation. Is the will revoked if the lawyer immediately tears the will in half and puts the two halves in the testator's client file? If your answer is "no," can the two halves be probated? Are your answers the same if the lawyer *shreds* the original, which is the only version of the will in existence, and no one can remember the terms of the shredded will?

Partial Revocation by Physical Act

Suppose Ebeneezer Stooge's duly executed will makes three provisions:

1. I devise $20,000 to my son Moe.
2. I devise $10,000 to my friend Larry.

3. I devise the remainder of my estate to my son Curly.

Suppose further that testator crosses out the devise to Larry, and initials or signs the cross-out. Or, suppose testator physically cuts the devise to Larry out of the will. How should testator's estate be distributed at testator's death?

Most states allow partial revocation of a will by physical act, on the basis that the local statute expressly or impliedly sanctions such revocations. What language in 1990 UPC § 2–507 allows such partial revocations?

If testator crosses out "my friend Larry," and writes in "my cousin Vinny," neither Larry nor Vinny is entitled to inherit. Do you see why? See, e.g. Carpenter v. Cosby, 34 So.3d 1230, 1234 (Miss. App. 2010) (holding that scratched out paragraphs were revoked, but additions are invalid "because she didn't have two witnesses sign on those amendments.")

If the partial revocation changes the construction of the remainder of a clause or increases a provision made for someone other than the residuary devisee, some courts will not validate the revocation on the theory that the change constitutes a testamentary transfer that requires formalities. The court in Estate of Malloy, 134 Wash.2d 316, 949 P.2d 804 (1998) took an extreme view and held invalid testator's partial revocation because the revocation would decrease the amount available to certain general devisees and increase the gift to the residuary legatee. The Restatement (Third) Property disapproves of cases like Malloy as inconsistent with statutes that allow partial revocation. See Restatement (Third) Property, § 4.1, cmt. i. Nonetheless, most jurisdictions do not allow a testator to directly change or modify (as opposed to revoke) a provision for a devisee by physical act. Do you understand why? Does the distinction make sense?

A few states flatly refuse to permit partial revocation by physical act. See Ind. Code 29–1–5–6. The standard explanations for the no partial revocation by physical act rule are formalistic and literalistic readings of particular state statutes and a concern about the scope of the testator's intent to revoke when it is clear that something less than a complete revocation is intended.

PROBLEMS

1. Reconsider Ebeneezer Stooge's will. Suppose, with present intent to revoke, Stooge writes these words across Article Two: "This gift is void." Does Larry get his money under 1990 UPC § 2–507? In a state that refuses to recognize partial revocations by physical act? In a state that refuses to recognize partial revocations by physical act, but follows the substantial compliance approach to will formalities? A state that does not recognize partial revocation by physical act, but in which the legislature has adopted 1990 UPC § 2–503's dispensing power?

2. With present intent to revoke, Stooge cuts out Article Two and destroys it. No one remembers what Article Two said. How should Stooge's estate be distributed in a state that refuses to recognize partial revocations by physical act?

3. Testator properly executed duplicate originals of an ordinary attested will. He made general bequests of $50,000 to each of his three daughters, and then, in the fourth paragraph, he left his residuary estate to his lover. He explicitly left his only son with nothing. Testator kept one duplicate original of the will in his home, and the other in a safe deposit box. Testator's lover then left him, and testator committed suicide. After his death, the duplicate original left in his house was found with the fourth paragraph crossed out in pencil. The other duplicate original remained intact in the safe deposit box. How should testator's estate be distributed under the UPC? In a state that does not permit partial revocation by physical act? Cf. Etgen v. Corboy, 230 Va. 413, 337 S.E.2d 286 (1985).

D. REVOCATION BY OPERATION OF LAW

Testator writes a will leaving all of her property to her husband. Three years later, testator and her husband divorce. Testator never changes her will. Should her ex-husband inherit her property? If we focus on testator's intent, most of us will intuitively respond, no. How would a court reach that result? Consider the following statutes:

UNIFORM PROBATE CODE

SECTION 1-201. GENERAL DEFINITIONS.

* * * (18) "Governing instrument" means a deed, will, trust, insurance or annuity policy, account with POD designation, security registered in beneficiary form (TOD), transfer on death (TOD) deed, pension, profit-sharing, retirement, or similar benefit plan, instrument creating or exercising a power of appointment or a power of attorney, or a donative, appointive, or nominative instrument of any similar type.

SECTION 2-804. REVOCATION OF PROBATE AND NONPROBATE TRANSFERS BY DIVORCE; NO REVOCATION BY OTHER CHANGES OF CIRCUMSTANCES.

(a) [Definitions.] In this section:

(1) 'Disposition or appointment of property' includes a transfer of an item of property or any other benefit to a beneficiary designated in a governing instrument.

(2) 'Divorce or annulment' means any divorce or annulment, * * * A decree of separation that does not terminate the status of husband and wife is not a divorce for purposes of this section.

(3) 'Divorced individual' includes an individual whose marriage has been annulled.

(4) 'Governing instrument' means a governing instrument executed by the divorced individual before the divorce or annulment of his [or her] marriage to his [or her] former spouse.

(5) 'Relative of the divorced individual's former spouse' means an individual who is related to the divorced individual's former spouse by blood, adoption, or affinity and who, after the divorce or annulment, is not related to the divorced individual by blood, adoption, or affinity.

* * *

(b) [Revocation Upon Divorce.] Except as provided by the express terms of a governing instrument, a court order, or a contract relating to the division of the marital estate made between the divorced individuals before or after the marriage, divorce, or annulment, the divorce or annulment of a marriage:

(1) revokes any revocable (i) disposition * * * of property made by a divorced individual to his [or her] former spouse in a governing instrument and any * * * disposition * * * in a governing instrument to a relative of the divorced individual's former spouse,* * * (iii) nomination in a governing instrument, nominating a divorced individual's former spouse or a relative of the divorced individual's former spouse to serve in any fiduciary or representative capacity, including a personal representative, executor, trustee, conservator, agent, or guardian; * * *

(d) [Effect of Revocation.] Provisions of a governing instrument are given effect as if the former spouse and relatives of the former spouse disclaimed all provisions revoked by this section or, in the case of a revoked nomination in a fiduciary or representative capacity, as if the former spouse and relatives of the former spouse died immediately before the divorce or annulment.

(e) [Revival if Divorce Nullified.] Provisions revoked solely by this section are revived by the divorced individual's remarriage to the former spouse or by a nullification of the divorce or annulment.

(f) [No Revocation for Other Change of Circumstances.] No change of circumstances other than as described in this section and in Section 2–803 effects a revocation.

Section 2–508 of the pre–1990 Uniform Probate Code (in effect in many jurisdictions) provides, in relevant part, as follows:

> If after executing a will the testator is divorced or his marriage annulled, the divorce or annulment revokes any disposition or appointment of property made by the will to the former spouse, any provision conferring a general or special power of appointment on the former spouse, and any nomination of the former spouse as executor, trustee, conservator, or guardian, unless the will expressly provides otherwise. Property prevented from passing to a former spouse because of revocation by divorce or annulment passes as if the former spouse failed to survive the decedent, and other provi-

sions conferring some power or office on the former spouse are interpreted as if the spouse failed to survive the decedent. If provisions are revoked solely by this section, they are revived by testator's remarriage to the former spouse. For purposes of this section, divorce or annulment means any divorce or annulment which would exclude the spouse as a surviving spouse within the meaning of Section 2–802(b). A decree of separation which does not terminate the status of husband and wife is not a divorce for purposes of this section. No change of circumstances other than as described in this section revokes a will.

PROBLEMS

1. Charlie and Francine were married in middle age. It was a second marriage for both. The only children they had were from prior marriages. While married, each executed a will leaving all probate property to the other, if living, and if not living, half to one's children and half to the other's children. Each nominated the other as executor. Thereafter, they divorced. Charlie died without making a new will, survived by Francine, her children, and his children.

Who gets Charlie's probate property under pre–1990 § 2–508 of the UPC? Who is his executor? Assuming no other relevant law or contract provisions, who gets his life insurance if the beneficiary designation purports to give it to Francine and if pre–1990 § 2–508 is in effect? If you were a creative judge, faced with your answer to the preceding question, what would you do about it?

Who gets Charlie's probate property under 1990 UPC § 2–804? Who gets the insurance? Does Charlie's estate get the "right" executor if he and Francine were partners in an unusual and complex business, and remained partners after the divorce? Do we care enough to do anything about it, if Charlie didn't?

2. Linda and Joel were married in college. It was a first marriage for both. They had one child. While married, Joel executed a will leaving all his probate property to Linda, if living, and if not living, all to a trust for their child, Eliot, until he reaches age 25. He appoints Linda as his executor and he inadvertently appoints Linda as the trustee of the trust. Do you see why we say inadvertently? Thereafter, they divorced. Later, Joel died, survived by Linda and Eliot, aged four. Linda, a loving parent, is raising Eliot. Who is the executor of Joel's probate estate (which is going entirely to the trust for Eliot) and who is Eliot's trustee under 1990 UPC § 2–804? Are you happy with this result? How would a creative judge solve the problem?

This section is discussed in Lawrence W. Waggoner, Spousal Rights in Our Multiple Marriage Society: The Revised Uniform Probate Code, 26 Real Prop., Prob. & Tr. J. 683, 689–701 (1992). See also John H. Langbein, The Nonprobate Revolution and the Future of the Law of Succession, 97 Harv. L. Rev. 1108 (1984).

For an argument that section 2–804 is too narrow, and that implied revocation is appropriate in a broader range of circumstances, see Adam J. Hirsch, Text and Time: A Theory of Testamentary Obsolescence, 86 Wash. U. L. Rev. 609 (2009).

NOTES

1. ***Non-probate assets governed by ERISA.*** While David and Donna were married, David designated Donna as the beneficiary under David's life insurance policy and a pension plan. Both the policy and the pension plan were provided by David's employer and were governed by federal law, specifically, the Employee Retirement Income Security Act of 1974 (ERISA). Later, David and Donna divorced, and David died intestate two months later without having changed the beneficiary designations. David's children by a prior marriage sued for the proceeds, citing a state statute that provided for automatic revocation of beneficiary designations of non-probate assets in favor of the former spouse upon divorce. The United States Supreme Court held that the federal statute, which directed that the proceeds of the non-probate assets should be paid to the individual designated as beneficiary in the contract, pre-empted state law. Donna received the proceeds. See Egelhoff v. Egelhoff, 532 U.S. 141, 121 S.Ct. 1322, 149 L.Ed.2d 264 (2001).

2. ***Pre-marital wills.*** It is easy to imagine a single person with a will leaving everything to her parents, getting married, never getting around to making a new will, and thereafter dying. Suppose Sally executed a will leaving everything to her favorite charity. Thereafter, she met Fred, fell in love, and married him. Somehow, she never got around to executing a new will. What if Sally dies under her premarital will? Who gets her property?

There are three basic solutions. In some states the marriage revokes the entire will. Then Fred would get his intestate share and the balance of Sally's estate would also pass by intestacy. In a second set of states, marriage does not revoke the will, but Fred would be entitled to take an elective share [see Chapter 3, section IV, supra]. In a third set of states, Fred would be a "pretermitted" or "omitted" spouse. Then the will would not be revoked. Rather, Fred would get his omitted spouse's share and the balance of Sally's probate estate would pass under her will. Sometimes, the surviving spouse's share turns out to be the same as an intestate share, but technically the survivor claims as an omitted spouse, not as an intestate taker. The UPC solution is elegant and somewhat complicated. Section 2–301 takes into account gifts under the will to the testator's issue by prior unions and to the surviving spouse. It is designed to help the decedent who truly forgot to do a new will, so it can be avoided. How would you draft a will for a client who was about to get married? The section is discussed in Lawrence W. Waggoner, Spousal Rights in Our Multiple Marriage Society: The Revised Uniform Probate Code, 26 Real Prop., Prob. & Tr. J. 683, 748–51 (1992).

E. REVIVAL AND DEPENDENT RELATIVE REVOCATION

Suppose testator wrote a will in 2003, and then wrote a second will in 2009, explicitly revoking the 2003 will. In 2011, testator burned the 2009 will, but did not execute a new will. If testator died in 2012, would a court probate his 2003 will, or would testator have died intestate?

In general, the answer is that testator would have died intestate. Revocation of testator's last will does not reinstate a prior will. Why not? Because reinstatement of the prior will would require testamentary formalities, and the act of burning, tearing, or mutilating the 2009 will was not accompanied by those formalities. Thus, if, in 2012, testator were to sign the 2003 will again, in front of witnesses, testator would have effectively reinstated that will. Similarly, if testator were to execute a codicil to the previously revoked 2003 will, testator would have "republished" the original will by codicil, and the 2003 will would be reinstated.

Consider the cases, however, in which testator burns the 2009 will without conducting any additional ceremony. Does the rule that revocation does not reinstate prior wills make sense? Consider the following two examples:

> ***Example 4:*** *Testator, estranged from her children, writes a 2003 will leaving all of her property to the United Way. In 2009, testator writes a new will, leaving all of her property to the Salvation Army. In 2011, testator, fed up with news stories of mismanagement of charities and reconciled with her children, burns the 2009 will.*
>
> ***Example 5:*** *Testator, in 2003, writes a will leaving half of her property to the United Way, and dividing the other half equally between her two daughters. In 2009, testator, estranged from one of her daughters, writes a new will, dividing the property equally between the United Way and the other daughter. In 2011, testator, reconciled with her formerly estranged daughter, burns her 2009 will in front of the entire family, announcing that "Now I have my will back the way I want it."*

In Example 4, should revocation of the 2009 will revive the 2003 will? Not if our goal is to effectuate testator's intent. But what about in Example 5? Here, to permit testator to die intestate would frustrate testator's consistent intent to leave half of her property to the United Way. Is there a way to revive the 2003 will in Example 5, but not Example 4? The Uniform Probate Code's answer is "yes". Consider the UPC's formulation:

SECTION 2–509. REVIVAL OF REVOKED WILL.

(a) If a subsequent will that wholly revoked a previous will is thereafter revoked by a revocatory act under Section 2–507(a)(2), the previous will remains revoked unless it is revived. The previous will is revived if it is evident from the circumstances of the revocation of the subsequent will or from the testator's contemporary or subsequent declarations that the testator intended the previous will to take effect as executed.

(b) If a subsequent will that partly revoked a previous will is thereafter revoked by a revocatory act under Section 2–507(a)(2), a revoked part of the previous will is revived unless it is evident from the circumstances of the revocation of the subsequent will or from the testator's contemporary or subsequent declarations that the testator did not intend the revoked part to take effect as executed.

(c) If a subsequent will that revoked a previous will in whole or in part is thereafter revoked by another, later, will, the previous will remains revoked in whole or in part, unless it or its revoked part is revived. The previous will or its revoked part is revived to the extent it appears from the terms of the later will that the testator intended the previous will to take effect.

PROBLEMS

1. Testator validly executed will number 1, which left Blackacre to Nephew and testator's residuary estate to Yale University. Consider two variations:

a. Testator executed will number 2, which left Blackacre to Niece and testator's residuary estate to Yale. Testator later burned will number 2.

b. Testator executed a codicil to will number 1. The codicil provided: "I leave Blackacre to Niece." Testator later burned the codicil.

If Testator made no other statements, and no other evidence of Testator's intent is available, how would Testator's estate be distributed in variations (a) and (b), assuming UPC § 2–509 is in effect? What justification is there for the difference in treatment?

2. Testator validly executed will number 1, which provided "I leave my tangible personal property to my daughter D, and the rest of my estate to Columbia University." Testator later executed will number 2, which provided "I leave all of my property to my daughter, D." Finally, Testator executed will number 3, which provided "I revoke [will number 2] and leave all of my tangible personal property to my grandson G." If UPC § 2–509 is in effect, how should Testator's estate be distributed?

NOTE

Suppose testator executes a will, and then a codicil. If testator subsequently revokes the codicil, has testator also revoked the will? The standard answer is "no". Revocation of the codicil leaves the will, without the revoked codicil, intact.

Is that the answer given by the court in the *Ward–Allen* case? Note that the court based its conclusion on the District of Columbia statute, which incorporated an earlier version of the Uniform Probate Code.

Does the current version of the UPC adopt the approach reflected in *Ward–Allen?* See UPC § 2–509(b).

Dependent Relative Revocation

Consider this simple story. Testator's valid first will leaves everything to her friend Ellen, who is not a relative of Testator's. Testator then "revokes" that valid first will, intending to execute a new will in favor of Ellen, with a different trust company as executor. The "revocation" is facially successful, but the second will fails for some reason. Which would the testator rather have—the first will or no will? If the testator would rather have the first will, how can a court give effect to that will? Consider the following case:

Oliva–Foster v. Oliva

Indiana Court of Appeals, 2008.
880 N.E.2d 1223.

■ BARNES, JUDGE

Debra Oliva–Foster and Patrick Oliva, Jr., ("the children") appeal the trial court's denial of their motion for summary judgment and grant of Judith Oliva's motion for summary judgment. We affirm.

Issue

The children present several issues, which we consolidate and restate as whether the trial court in granting summary judgment properly applied the doctrine of dependent relative revocation to revive their father's 1995 will.

Facts

Patrick Oliva executed a will in 1995 in the office of his attorney, Mario Zappia. The 1995 will named Judith Oliva, his spouse, as the primary beneficiary. Judith is not the children's mother. He named his daughter Debra, Patrick Jr.'s two children, and Judith's daughter Cheryl as contingent beneficiaries. Patrick left his son, Patrick, Jr., out of the 1995 will.

Patrick executed a new will on March 13, 2002, again in the office of Attorney Zappia. The 2002 will again named Judith as the primary beneficiary. This will, however, included Patrick, Jr., as a contingent beneficiary along with Debra and Cheryl. When he returned home from the attorney's office, Patrick instructed Judith to tear up his 1995 will. She tore it up in Patrick's presence. Patrick explained that this way "Pat, Jr. will not know that he was ever taken out of the will." App. p. 144. Under the 2002 will, the children would inherit from their father only if Judith did not survive him.

Patrick passed away on March 16, 2003. The 2002 will was admitted to probate on April 29, 2003. The children filed a will contest on July 23, 2003. They contended the 2002 will was improperly executed and invalid. Specifically, the children alleged that the witnesses did not sign the will in the presence of each other and of the decedent.

During the course of litigation, Attorney Zappia recovered an electronic copy of the 1995 will. Following this discovery, Judith and the children entered cross motions for summary judgment. The children argued that the 2002 will was invalid, the 1995 will was revoked and could not be revived, and the estate should pass by intestate succession. Indiana's intestacy laws would divide the estate between Judith and the children. Judith argued that even if the 2002 will were invalid, the 1995 will would be revived by the doctrine of dependent relative revocation, and the estate would still pass to her.

The trial court granted Judith's motion for summary judgment and denied the children's. This appeal followed.

Analysis

The children contend that the trial court misapplied Indiana law in granting summary judgment in favor of Judith.

Judith contends, and the trial court agreed, that in the event the 2002 will is invalid, the 1995 will would be revived by the doctrine of dependent relative revocation. Our supreme court recognized this doctrine in *Roberts v. Fisher, 230 Ind. 667, 676, 105 N.E.2d 595, 598 (1952)*, and explained:

> [I]f a testator mutilates or destroys a will with a present intention of making a new one immediately and as a substitute, the new will is not made, or, if made, fails of effect for any reason, it will be presumed that the testator preferred the old will to intestacy, and the old one will be admitted to probate in the absence of evidence overcoming the presumption.

In that case, on November 30, 1942, Amy Roberts's attorney drafted her will. Amy kept one copy and the attorney kept the original plus one copy. After an "estrangement" between Amy and certain beneficiaries of her will, she struck out items on the copy as well as her signature and the witnesses signatures. *Roberts, 230 Ind. at 672, 105 N.E.2d at 597.* On November 21, 1944, Amy called her attorney and discussed making a new will. During that conversation, her attorney advised that she should not only merely cross out parts of the old will, but that she should destroy it. That day he sent her a letter with the original will enclosed, instructing her to destroy it. *Id. at 673, 105 N.E.2d at 598.* Two days later the original was destroyed in the presence of her attorney.

Only forty days elapsed between the time Amy destroyed her will and her death. She did not make a new will during that time. At the time of her death, the copy of her will with stricken signature and paragraphs was found in her home. The trial court found this will could be revived by the doctrine of dependent relative revocation, but our supreme court disagreed. *Id. at 677–78, 105 N.E.2d at 599.*

Although it recognized the doctrine of dependent relative revocation, the supreme court concluded it did not apply to Amy's will because the mutilation of the copy was not done with a "present intention to make a new will immediately." *Id., 105 N.E.2d at 600.* Without such intention, the court concluded the destruction amounted to an absolute revocation. *Id. at 678, 105 N.E.2d at 600*. Although our supreme court concluded that Indiana's probate statutes did not foreclose the doctrine, it warned that the doctrine should "be cautiously applied." *Id. at 676, 105 N.E.2d at 599.*

The facts here reveal that Patrick only ordered the tearing up of his 1995 will after the creation and signing of his 2002 will. In fact, these events occurred immediately after returning home from his attorney's office. Patrick's act of instructing the 1995 will to be torn apart was clearly conditional on the creation and legitimacy of the new 2002 will. These facts indicate that Patrick destroyed the 1995 will because he intended the 2002 will to take its place. As such, we conclude that the doctrine of dependant relative revocation can be applied to revive the 1995 will. This result also avoids intestacy. "[T]he law does not favor and will avoid intestacy whenever possible." *Steele v. Chase, 151 Ind. App. 600, 607, 281 N.E.2d 137, 140 (1972)*. It is especially relevant here where intestate succession would be contrary to Patrick's intentions as evident in both of his wills.

The children contend that the 2002 will was created before the 1995 will was torn apart, and thus the chain of events cannot qualify for an application of the dependent relative revocation doctrine. They point out that the testator did not destroy the 1995 will with a present intention to make a new one—rather the new will was already drafted and signed. On this point, Judith argued to the trial court that other states had utilized dependent relative revocation without a perfect timeline. The trial court succinctly summarized the party's positions and stated: "simply by destroying the will on the way home from the lawyer as opposed to destroying it before you go to the lawyer's, those two cases should be treated differently?" Tr. p. 10. We think not. Patrick was free to destroy his prior 1995 will because a new will was in place and he depended on that will to be probated. The children also contend that Patrick's destruction of the 1995 will amounted to an absolute revocation and it cannot be revived. We disagree. Considering that Patrick only ordered that will to be torn up after completing his new will, it is clear this destruction was conditioned on the ability to probate his estate under the new will.

Finally, it is important to note that probate of the 1995 will will result in the same outcome as the 2002 will—Judith is the sole beneficiary of Patrick's estate. It is on this narrow set of facts that we conclude the dependent relative revocation doctrine is applicable here.

Conclusion

The trial court did not err by granting summary judgment in favor of Judith. By correctly applying the doctrine of dependent relative revocation, the trial court concluded that even if the 2002 will would be found invalid, the 1995 will would be revived and create the same result. As such, there were no issues of material fact left for trial and summary judgment was properly granted. We affirm.

NOTES AND QUESTIONS

1. Suppose Patrick Sr.'s 2002 will had left his two children $10,000 each, and the balance of his estate, which amounted to $200,000, to his wife. Suppose further that the 2002 will had not been signed in front of witnesses. After signing the 2002 will, Patrick Sr. tears up the 1995 will (which had left nothing to the two children), indicating that "now the children will never know that I cut them out of the earlier will." At Patrick Sr.'s death, could the court apply the doctrine of dependent relative revocation? If so, how much would the children take? Does your answer explain why the comment to UPC § 2–507 calls DRR "the law of second best?"

2. Suppose now that the 2002 will had given the children, collectively, all of Patrick Sr.'s estate. After signing the will (with no witnesses), Patrick tears up the 1995 will (which had left his entire estate to his wife) in front of three old friends, telling them "now that adulterer won't get a dime from me." Would a court apply DRR? How would Patrick Sr.'s estate be distributed?

3. The premise underlying DRR is that testator's revocation of his will was based on a mistake—often a mistake about the effect of the revocation. Since testator was laboring under the burden of a mistake when he "revoked" his will, courts ignore the "revocation," and treat the revoked will as if it were still in effect. Section 4.3 of the Restatement (Third) of Property renames DRR the doctrine of "ineffective revocation."

A slightly different way of making the same point is that testator's revocation was conditioned on a set of facts that did not actually occur. In Oliva–Foster, for instance, Patrick's revocation was conditioned on his belief that his new disposition would be given effect. Since that disposition would not be given effect, the condition did not occur, and the revocation was therefore ineffective. In other words, Patrick **D**idn't **R**eally **R**evoke!

Generally, however, when a court is deciding whether to apply DRR, the court is trying to decide if testator would rather have died with the "revoked" will or without it. Testator's intent is the key.

Consider § 4.3 of the Restatement (Third) of Property:

Section 4.3 Ineffective Revocation (Dependent Relative Revocation)

> (a) A partial or complete revocation of a will is presumptively ineffective if the testator made the revocation:
>
> > (1) in connection with an attempt to achieve a dispositive objective that fails under applicable law, or
> >
> > (2) because of a false assumption of law, or because of a false belief about an objective fact, that is either recited in the revoking instrument or established by clear and convincing evidence.

(b) The presumption established in subsection (a) is rebutted if allowing the revocation to remain in effect would be more consistent with testator's probable intention.

PROBLEMS

1. In 2000, Testator validly executed a will leaving all of his property to his daughter. In 2005, he validly executed a second will, leaving three-fourths of his property to his daughter, and one-fourth to his son. In 2010, he took both wills to his lawyer's office and, in the presence of the lawyer, tore up the 2005 will, saying that he wanted to reaffirm the first will.

If the Uniform Probate Code's revival provision (§ 2–509) were in effect, how should Testator's estate be distributed if Testator died in 2012?

Now, suppose you are in a jurisdiction where the only way to revive a revoked will is by reexecution or republication by codicil. How should Testator's estate be distributed? If you were representing the daughter, would DRR be useful to you? If the court applied DRR, how much would the daughter receive? Does this problem illustrate why DRR is a doctrine of the "second best"? Do you see why DRR will have a diminished role as a salvage doctrine if revival rules become more intent-effectuating?

2. Testator's valid will contained a gift of $10,000 to Frank. Testator crossed out $10,000 and wrote in $15,000 in her own handwriting. How much money, if any, does Frank get? To answer this problem take things step-by-step. First, how do you characterize the cross out? Next, how do you characterize the writing in of the $15,000? Next, ask yourself what did testator really want? Finally, how, if at all, can you use DRR to get Testator as close as possible to what she wanted? How could you give Testator what she wanted under UPC § 2–503 (the dispensing power)? Can you explain why DRR is the law of second best in terms of this problem?

3. Testator's valid will contained a gift of $10,000 to Franklyn. Testator crossed out $10,000 and wrote in $1 in her own handwriting. How much money, if any, does Franklyn get? Can you explain?

4. Testator's husband had given her a testamentary power of appointment over property he had owned. That is, the husband did not give Testator the property, but instead gave her the power to dispose of the property in her will. If Testator did not exercise the power, the property would pass to "takers-in-default" designated by the husband. (We will discuss powers of appointment in greater detail in Chapter Eight). In 1982, Testator executed a will that exercised the power of appointment. Then, in 1993, Testator, who wanted to avoid probate of most of her assets, conveyed the bulk of her own property into a newly-created lifetime trust to benefit the same people as would have taken under her 1982 will. Testator then executed a new will expressly revoking the 1982 will and pouring her assets into the lifetime trust. Due to an omission by Testator's lawyer, the will did not exercise her husband's power of appointment.

If you represent the beneficiaries under Testator's 1982 will (and 1993 trust), how would you use DRR to assist your clients? See Anderson v. Irwin, 56 Cal.App.4th 235, 65 Cal.Rptr.2d 307 (1997). But see Arrowsmith v. Mercantile–Safe Deposit & Trust Co., 313 Md. 334, 545 A.2d 674 (1988).

SECTION VI. LIMITS ON THE POWER TO REVOKE: JOINT WILLS AND WILL CONTRACTS

In general, a testator is free to revoke her will at any time before her death. What if testator and her spouse agree, while both are alive, on a disposition of their collective assets? Suppose further that they execute wills reflecting their agreement, or they execute a single joint will. After the first spouse dies, is the survivor entitled to renege on the agreement and revoke the will? Consider the following case:

Garrett v. Read

Kansas Supreme Court, 2004.
278 Kan. 662, 102 P.3d 436.

■ BEIER, J.:

This dispute over the wills of the parents in a blended family requires us to decide whether the district court erred in (1) admitting a scrivener attorney's testimony about a contemporaneous oral agreement between the parents; (2) holding that the wills were contractual, rendering a later will executed by the surviving parent ineffective; and (3) imposing a constructive trust on the estate property or proceeds.

Plaintiffs Elizabeth Garrett, Calvin Humble, Dale Humble, and Patricia Humble are the children of John Humble. In 1967, their father married Sarah Puffinbarger, who had two daughters, defendants Deloris Read and Dorothy Brookhauser, and one son, Gary Lee Puffinbarger, from her previous marriage. Gary eventually predeceased his mother, leaving Sarah and three of her grandchildren, third-party plaintiffs Christie Cambers, Gregory Puffinbarger, and Melanie Crumby.

In 1984, lawyer Timothy Fielder prepared nearly identical wills for Sarah and John. Each will first directed that any funeral expenses and debts be paid from the estate. Each will also provided that one of Sarah's daughters would receive a grandfather clock. The remaining estate was bequeathed to the surviving spouse "absolutely." If one spouse predeceased the other, or if the spouses died at the same time, each will provided that the rest of the estate was to be divided into sevenths. One-seventh would be distributed to each of the six surviving children of the two spouses. The remaining one-seventh would be split evenly among Gary's children.

John died in October 1984, and his entire estate passed to Sarah.

In 1993, Sarah met with Fielder and executed a new will, revoking her 1984 will. The 1993 will retained the grandfather clock provision, but it changed the disposition of the rest of Sarah's estate, directing that it be divided into only two equal shares, one for each of her daughters. John's four children and Gary's three children were disinherited.

Sarah died in October 2001.

John's children filed this lawsuit, seeking a constructive trust on four-sevenths of the estate property. They alleged the 1993 will was invalid because the 1984 wills had been contractual. Gary's children intervened as third-party plaintiffs, also arguing that the 1984 wills were contractual and that Sarah could not violate her agreement with John by denying them their one-seventh share.

Plaintiffs and third-party plaintiffs both relied on the 1984 wills' reciprocal provisions as evidence of the contract between Sarah and John. Plaintiffs also relied on Fielder's deposition testimony.

Fielder testified that an agreement existed between Sarah and John at the time they executed their 1984 wills. He had explained joint and mutual wills to them and suggested including contractual language in the documents. Although they agreed they wanted contractual wills, they wanted the surviving spouse to be able to liquidate estate assets and spend all of the proceeds, if necessary. They also believed that an equal distribution among their seven children or their offspring would best reflect the assets each had brought into the marriage; they wanted the surviving parent to be prevented from changing the shares designated for the deceased parent's children; yet they wanted the surviving parent to be able to alter the shares of that parent's own children. Fielder said this was the intention behind the use of the word "absolutely" in the wills.

Fielder also testified that, before Sarah executed her 1993 will, he informed her that she and John had entered into an agreement. Sarah told him she had taken care of John's children outside of the will by means of joint property and investments. Fielder prepared the 1993 will in reliance on this statement.

Defendants and third-party plaintiffs filed motions in limine. Defendants contended Fielder's testimony should be barred as parol evidence contradicting the wills. Third-party plaintiffs argued Fielder's testimony was admissible only to prove the agreement to leave the estate to the children and grandchildren in sevenths; they asserted any further testimony from Fielder was inadmissible parol evidence. The district court denied the motions in limine, relying on *In re Estate of Chronister*, 203 Kan. 366, 454 P.2d 438 (1969), and *In re Estate of Tompkins*, 195 Kan. 467, 407 P.2d 545 (1965). Thus all of Fielder's testimony was admitted into evidence.

All parties filed motions for summary judgment. The district court found the evidence of an agreement between Sarah and John was uncontroverted. As a result, Sarah's 1993 will could not alter the 1984 wills' designation of shares for John's children but could alter the shares designated for her own children. Thus the district court granted plaintiffs' motion for summary judgment, denied defendants' motion for summary judgment, and denied third-party plaintiffs' motion for summary judgment.

The district court imposed a constructive trust in favor of plaintiffs in an amount equal to four-sevenths of the worth of Sarah's estate that had passed to the defendants.

Defendants and third-party plaintiffs appealed to the Court of Appeals, and this court transferred the case pursuant to K.S.A. 20–3018(c).

Standard of Review

* * *

All three groups of parties filed dispositive motions in the district court. There were no genuine issues of material fact, which made this case amenable to consideration for summary judgment. We therefore turn to discussion of the controlling legal issues.

Admission of Attorney Scrivener's Testimony

Generally, "all relevant evidence is admissible. K.S.A. 60–407(f). Relevant evidence is defined as 'evidence having any tendency in reason to prove any material fact.' K.S.A. 60–401(b)." *State v. Dreiling,* 274 Kan. 518, 549, 54 P.3d 475 (2002). There can be no serious question in this case regarding the relevance of the scrivener's testimony....

Defendants argued that the 1984 wills were unambiguous and that Fielder's testimony therefore was barred by the parol evidence rule. In fact, our previous cases do not establish ambiguity as the analytical touchstone defendants want to make it.

This court has held:

"Extrinsic evidence is admissible in connection with the instruments themselves to show that separate wills, which are mutual and reciprocal in their bequests and devises, were executed in pursuance of an agreement between the testators, notwithstanding the absence of recitals in the wills designating or referring to such agreement. Such evidence may consist of writings, acts and declarations of the parties, testimony of other persons, and evidence of all the surrounding facts and circumstances." *Eikmeier v. Eikmeier*, 174 Kan. 71, Syl. P 1, 254 P.2d 236 (1953).

This court has also stated that "the rule that parol evidence is never admissible to change or vary the terms and provisions of an unambiguous will does not render inadmissible extrinsic evidence that a will was executed pursuant to an agreement." *In re Estate of Tompkins*, 195 Kan. 467 at 474 (citing *Eikmeier*, 174 Kan. 71, 254 P.2d 236, Syl. P 2). "The admission of such evidence may result in proving the will to have been non-contractual as well as contractual. [Citations omitted.]" *Tompkins*, 195 Kan. at 474....

Many other Kansas cases also support the approach taken by the district court here. See, *e.g., In re Estate of Stratmann*, 248 Kan. 197, 207, 806 P.2d 459 (1991) (where wills contain no contractual language, court must "search extrinsic evidence for guidance"); *In re Estate of Wade*, 202 Kan. 380, 387, 449 P.2d 488 (1969) (proof of existence of agreement between testators may be developed through extrinsic evidence); *In re Estate of Zahradnik*, 6 Kan. App. 2d 84, 91–93, 626 P.2d 1211 (1981) (error for district court not to allow extrinsic evidence to establish existence of contract, even though will contained no contractual language, where distributions of property identical and wills use plural pronouns).

It was not an abuse of discretion for the district court to allow Fielder's testimony. The language of the wills supported the existence of a mutual understanding between Sarah and John to leave the bulk of their estate to the surviving parent for full use during that person's lifetime, then to the six children and one set of grandchildren evenly. Testimony regarding such an agreement was not barred by the parol evidence rule. See *Eikmeier*, 174 Kan. 71, 254 P.2d 236, Syl. P 1; *Tompkins*, 195 Kan. at 474. Plaintiffs were not required to demonstrate first that the language of the wills was ambiguous in order to admit testimony regarding the oral agreement.

Third-party plaintiffs nevertheless continue to argue that Fielder's testimony was admissible only to the extent that it proved the existence of an agreement regarding distribution of seven equal shares. They claim Fielder's testimony about the further agreement that the surviving parent would have a right to alter the shares of his or her own children should have been inadmissible.

We disagree. Fielder's further testimony about this topic explained more than the choice of the word "absolutely." The testimony did not alter or amend the language of the wills; it further demonstrated the existence of the basic agreement to divide the bulk of the estate into sevenths; and it demonstrated the existence of a sensible limitation on that agreement, reserving to the surviving parent the right to alter the distributions to his or her own children. It was not an abuse of discretion to allow Fielder's testimony regarding this additional facet of the oral agreement between John and Sarah.

Contractual Wills

> "Whether a will is contractual in character involves a question of fact, the determination of which must be established by competent evidence." *In re Estate of Chronister*, 203 Kan. 366, 454 P.2d 438, Syl. P 1.
>
> "The firmly established rule ... for the construction of wills, to which all other rules are subordinate, is that the intention of the testator as garnered from all parts of the will is to be given effect, and that doubtful or inaccurate expressions in the will shall not override the obvious intention of the testator. In construing a will the court must put itself as nearly as possible in the situation of the testator when he made the will and from a consideration of the situation and from the language used in every part of the will, determine as best it can the purpose of the testator and the intentions he endeavored to convey by the language used. [Citation omitted.]" *In re Estate of Tompkins*, 195 Kan. at 471.

The district court accurately described the evidence regarding whether the 1984 wills were contractual as uncontroverted. The only evidence consisted of the language of the wills and Fielder's testimony.

Defendants contend that the 1984 wills were not contractual because no plural pronouns, contractual terms, or mention of consideration appear in their language. This court has stated that use of plural pronouns and contractual terms supports the presumption that wills are contractual, but this is not the end of the inquiry. This court has also held that separate wills without mention of an agreement between the testators, may be contractual wills if that interpretation is supported by the evidence. See *Chronister*, 203 Kan. at 371–72.

In *Chronister*, 203 Kan. at 367, Herbert and Mabel Chronister executed a joint will leaving their estate to the surviving spouse "for his or her own personal use and benefit forever" and then to the nieces and nephews of Herbert. After Herbert died, Mabel changed her will to leave a large portion of the estate to her sister and her sister's children, with the remainder to Herbert's nieces and nephews.

This court reviewed previous cases, finding that in some cases wills had contractual language contained therein, but in other cases "wills have been construed as contractual on the basis of specific provisions or terms, one of the common denominators usually being a provision for the disposition of property after the death of the survivor." 203 Kan. at 369. We decided the joint and mutual will of Herbert and Mabel was contractual in spite of the language stating the estate passed to the survivor forever and said: "Provisions of like nature [in wills] have commonly been said to evidence, in the case of joint wills, an understanding between the joint testators by which they intended to bind themselves." 203 Kan. at 373. We held that identical disposition of property, the use of plural pronouns, the mutual exclusion of heirs, and a "full and explicit provision ... for disposition of the testators' remaining property after the death of the survivor" in the joint will were indicative of the agreement between them. 203 Kan. at 373.

* * *

In an opinion affirmed and adopted by this court, the Court of Appeals set out factors that could be considered to determine whether a will is contractual. See *Bell v. Brittain*, 19 Kan. App. 2d 1073, 880 P.2d 289 (1994), *aff'd* 257 Kan. 407, 893 P.2d 251 (1995). The Court of Appeals stated:

"The fact that a will does not contain a reference to a contract is not conclusive in determining whether a will is contractual. The intent of the testators to be bound by a joint and mutual will need not be expressly recited, but may be determined circumstantially by language and other expressions used in the will. Language indicating a contractual will includes: (1) a provision in the will for the distribution of property on the death of the survivor; (2) a carefully drawn provision for the disposition of any share in case of a lapsed residuary bequest; (3) the use of plural pronouns; (4) joinder and consent language; (5) the identical distribution of property upon the death of the survivor; (6) joint revocation of former wills; and (7) consideration, such as mutual promises." 19 Kan. App. 2d 1073, 880 P.2d 289, Syl. P 5.

The *Bell* panel found that a mutual will meeting some of the stated provisions was contractual. 19 Kan. App. 2d at 1077–80. Under the *Bell* facts, the will provided for a distribution at the death of the survivor, used plural pronouns, used language that "appeared to qualify as joinder and consent language[,]" had identical distributions, and evidenced consideration. The will did not provide for a lapsed bequest; nor did it revoke all former wills. 19 Kan. App. 2d at 1078–79. The panel also noted that the family of a predeceased son had been expressly disinherited. 19 Kan. App. 2d at 1079. Based on these factors, the panel held that the will, on its face, evidenced an agreement between the testators "that the parties intended the will to be joint, mutual, and contractual." 19 Kan. App. 2d at 1079–80. As a result, the panel upheld the district court's grant of summary judgment. 19 Kan. App. 2d at 1079–80.

The uncontroverted facts here lead to the same conclusion. The 1984 wills were nearly identical, leaving the entire estate to the surviving parent and then to the children and one set of grandchildren, evenly divided. Both of the 1984 wills left a grandfather clock to one of Sarah's daughters, and the wills provided for the family of Sarah's predeceased son, evidencing a "full and explicit provision for the disposition" of the estate at the death of the surviving spouse. See *In re Estate of Chronister*, 203 Kan. 366, 373, 454 P.2d 438 (1969). Further, Fielder testified that Sarah and John communicated their wishes to be bound by their agreement with each other to leave a portion of the estate's assets to one another's children. They also wanted the freedom to change the distributions to their own children. Under the circumstances, it is apparent that John and Sarah wanted the surviving spouse to ensure that the children of the deceased parent were included if the estate was not consumed during the surviving parent's lifetime.

The uncontroverted evidence establishes that the 1984 wills were contractual and that Sarah retained the right to disinherit any of her children and grandchildren. Summary judgment in favor of plaintiffs was appropriate. Denial of summary judgment in favor of defendants and third-party plaintiffs also was appropriate.

Constructive Trust as Remedy

This court has stated:

"A single instrument may be both a will contractual in nature, and a contract testamentary in nature; as a will it is revocable but as a contract it is enforceable; and although a contractual will revoked by execution of a second will, cannot be probated, it may nonetheless be enforced as a contract against the estate of the testator breaching it." *Reznik v. McKee, Trustee*, 216 Kan. 659, Syl. P 2, 534 P.2d 243 (1975).

Sarah's revoked 1984 will was no longer in effect at the time of Sarah's death in 2001. However, because it was contractual, her estate remained subject to its terms. Because the 1984 will could not be probated, plaintiffs were correct to seek imposition of a constructive trust as their remedy.

"A constructive trust arises wherever the circumstances under which property was acquired make it inequitable that it should be retained by the person who holds the legal title." *Logan v. Logan*, 23 Kan. App. 2d 920, Syl. P 6, 937 P.2d 967, *rev. denied* 262 Kan. 961 (1997). To prove a constructive trust, there must be a showing of one of the two types of fraud: actual or constructive. 23 Kan. App. 2d 920, 937 P.2d 967, Syl. P 7.

Actual fraud is not at issue in this case. "Constructive fraud is a breach of a legal or equitable duty which, irrespective of moral guilt, the law declares fraudulent because of its tendency to deceive others or violate a confidence, and neither actual dishonesty or purpose or intent to deceive is necessary." 23 Kan. App. 2d 920, 937 P.2d 967, Syl. P 7. Two additional elements also must be proved: "There must be a confidential relationship[, and] the confidence reposed must be betrayed or a duty imposed by the relationship must be breached." 23 Kan. App. 2d 920, 937 P.2d 967, Syl. P 8.

* * *

In this case, the district court found that there was an agreement between John and Sarah regarding distribution of their property after the death of the survivor. The relationship between spouses qualifies as a confidential relationship. In addition, this confidential relationship was based on John's trust in Sarah to distribute four-sevenths of the estate to his children. See *Heck*, 23 Kan. App. 2d at 67. The agreement imposed a duty upon Sarah, and she breached this duty by executing the 1993 will and disinheriting plaintiffs. The district court properly imposed a constructive trust.

Affirmed.

3d party plaintiffs could have been disinherited

QUESTIONS

1. Did Sarah expressly promise, either in her will or in any other writing, not to revoke her will? What evidence establishes a contract not to revoke between Sarah and John? Should testimony by the drafting attorney suffice to establish the terms of a contract?

2. Most married couples have wills that are substantially identical. Does the Garrett case suggest that all such reciprocal wills are non-revocable? How would you draft to ensure that a surviving spouse had the ability to revoke a reciprocal will?

3. Would Sarah have breached the contract not to revoke her will if, after John's death:

(a) she had won the lottery and devised her lottery winnings to New York University?

(b) she had adopted a child and devised 25% of the collective estate to her adopted child?

(c) she had made lifetime gifts of $50,000 to each of two favored nieces? See Estate of Draper v. Bank of America, N.A., 288 Kan. 510, 205 P.3d 698 (2009).

(d) she executed a codicil to her will that increased a general bequest to her niece from $5,000 to $10,000?

(e) she remarried, she and her new husband generated significant wealth, and she executed a new will giving the bulk of her assets to her new husband?

In light of your answers, would you recommend that a couple in a marriage or civil union execute a contract not to revoke their reciprocal wills?

4. Examine attorney Fielder's conduct in the Garrett case. Fielder testified that Sarah and John each wanted to leave a fixed portion of their assets to the other's children, but wanted the freedom to change the distributions to their own children. Does the fact that John's children prevailed indicate that Fielder was right to draft the wills the way that he did? How would you have planned the couples' estate to avoid litigation?

5. The court in Garrett concludes that Sarah's 1993 will constitutes a breach of her contract with her husband. Does the court refuse to probate the revised will? If not, how does the court give effect to her 1984 will?

Note that if Sarah had contracted with the First Baptist Church to pay the church $50,000 in return for services provided by the church, and Sarah had not paid by the time of her death, the church would be a creditor of Sarah's estate, and would be entitled to payment before money was distributed to Sarah's will beneficiaries. Does the court in this case conclude that the beneficiaries under the 1984 will are creditors of Sarah's estate? If so, how much does Sarah's estate owe the creditors?

6. Suppose that shortly after John's death, Sarah made a gift of $20,000 to her best friend, Mabel. At Sarah's death, would the beneficiaries of the reciprocal will have a claim to the $20,000? Would it be different if Sarah transferred $30,000 into a joint bank account with right of survivorship in Mabel? Compare Merritt v. Yates, 2000 WL 1483476 (Tenn.App.2000) [holding that surviving spouse's transfer of assets to joint account and revocable trust of which her son was beneficiary was not a "reasonable" use of the couple's joint funds, and impressing the assets with a constructive trust for the final beneficiaries] with Estate of Cammack, 2000 WL 1679492 (Tenn.App.2000) [finding surviving spouse's gifts of marital property to her own children valid because "the contract required [the surviving spouse] to refrain from changing her will after the testator's death [and] the record contains no evidence that she breached that promise"].

NOTE ON JOINT WILLS

Occasionally, married couples execute a single, joint will instead of two separate wills. When parties execute joint wills, courts often find contract obligations even when the language imposing binding obligations is less than crystal clear.

Consider the Uniform Probate Code's formulation—dealing not only with reciprocal wills, but also with joint wills and any other will contracts:

Reciprocal and Joint Wills and the Uniform Probate Code

SECTION 2–514. CONTRACTS CONCERNING SUCCESSION.

A contract to make a will or devise, or not to revoke a will or devise, or to die intestate, if executed after the effective date of this Article, may be established only by (i) provisions of a will stating material provisions of the contract, (ii) an express reference in a will to a contract and extrinsic evidence proving the terms of the contract, or (iii) a writing signed by the decedent evidencing the contract. The execution of a joint will or mutual wills does not create a presumption of a contract not to revoke the will or wills.

How would Garrett v. Read have been decided if the Uniform Probate Code had been in effect? For criticism of the UPC's formulation, see Dennis W. Collins, Oral Contracts to Make a Will and the Uniform Probate Code: Boon or Boondoggle, 20 Creighton L. Rev. 413 (1987).

PROBLEMS

1. Harry and Rae, a childless couple, executed mutual wills making devises to named relatives of each spouse, and leaving the residue to the surviving spouse. The parties also entered into a contract making each will irrevocable except upon the consent of the other spouse. Harry died first, and at his death, his will was not found. Rae enters your office. She wants to know whether she can take all of Harry's estate outright by intestate succession, and whether she will be bound to distribute the estate, at her death, in accordance with the agreement she made with Harry. Advise Rae. See Estate of Cohen, 83 N.Y.2d 148, 629 N.E.2d 1356, 608 N.Y.S.2d 398 (1994).

2. Fred, age 65, and Helen, age 55, enter your office. They are in agreement that they want their estates to pass to the survivor at the death of the first to die, and that they want the survivor to have complete freedom to use estate assets during the survivor's lifetime. At the survivor's death, they want $20,000 to pass to each of three nieces, and the balance to be paid to the First Baptist Church.

What questions would you ask of Fred and Helen, and what course of action would you recommend?

* * *

Perhaps the most significant change that might occur after a will becomes irrevocable is the remarriage of the surviving spouse. If the surviving spouse has been the party to a will contract, what rights should a subsequent spouse have against the estate of the party to the will contract? The following case addresses that issue.

Shimp v. Huff

Court of Appeals of Maryland, 1989.
315 Md. 624, 556 A.2d 252.

■ MURPHY, C.J.

In his treatise, The Law of Wills, § 34 at 69 (3rd ed. 1947), George W. Thompson warns that "[a]s a general rule, joint wills are not regarded with much favor by the courts, and are . . . apt to invite litigation." The joint will of Lester and Clara Shimp has fulfilled Thompson's prediction by causing this Court for a second time to resolve conflicts arising from that will. In Shimp v. Shimp, 287 Md. 372, 412 A.2d 1228 (1980) (Shimp I), we addressed the issue of whether Lester and Clara's joint will could operate as a binding contract and thereby limit the survivor's right to dispose of property by a testamentary plan which differed from that contained in the joint will. In the present case, the issue is whether Lester Shimp's second wife, upon his death, is entitled to receive an elective share and a family allowance under Maryland Code (1974, 1988 Cum.Supp.) § 3–203 and § 3–201 of the Estates and Trusts Article when Lester had previously contracted, by virtue of a joint will with his first wife, to will his entire estate to others.

* * *

I.

Lester Shimp married his first wife, Clara, in 1941. At the time of their marriage, neither Lester nor Clara possessed any property of consequence. Subsequently, in 1954, they acquired a farm which they sold in 1973; thereafter they bought a home. Lester and Clara took title to both the farm and the home as tenants by the entireties.

On May 8, 1974, in Washington County, the couple executed an instrument titled "Last Will and Testament of Clara V. Shimp and Lester Shimp." It stated in relevant part:

> WE, CLARA V. SHIMP AND LESTER SHIMP, of Washington County, Maryland, being of sound and disposing mind, memory and understanding, and capable of making a valid deed and contract, do make, publish and declare this to be our Last Will and Testament, hereby revoking all other Wills and Codicils by each of us made.
>
> After the payment of all just debts and funeral expenses, we dispose of our estate and property as follows:
>
> ITEM I. A. MUTUAL BEQUEST—We mutually give to whichever of us shall be the survivor the entire estate of which we may respectfully own at our death.
>
> B. SURVIVOR'S BEQUEST—The survivor of us gives the entire estate of his or her property which he or she may own at death as follows:
>
> 1) Unto James Shimp, if he is living at the death of the survivor of us, the sum of One Thousand ($1,000.00) Dollars.
>
> 2) Unto Emma Plotner, if living at the death of the survivor of us, the sum of One Thousand ($1,000.00) Dollars.
>
> 3) Unto Mary Virginia Huff and Betty Jane Moats all household goods and machinery to do with as they desire. This bequest is made unto them due to the care that they have given us.

4) All of the rest and residue of the estate of the survivor is hereby devised unto Mary Virginia Huff, Betty Jane Moats, Paul R. Mijanovich and Ruth C. Thomas to be divided equally among them. In the event of the death of any of said persons, their children shall inherit the share to which the parent would have been entitled, if living.

* * *

ITEM III. We, the Testators, do hereby declare that it is our purpose to dispose of our property in accordance with a common plan. The reciprocal and other gifts made herein are in fulfillment of this purpose and in consideration of each of us waiving the right, during our joint lives, to alter, amend or revoke this Will in whole or in part, by Codicil or otherwise, without notice to the other, or under any circumstances after the death of the first of us to die. Unless mutually agreed upon, this Last Will and Testament is an irrevocable act and may not be changed.

Clara died in 1975 in Washington County. At the time of her death she did not own property solely in her name and possessed no probate estate. Lester did not offer the will for probate following his wife's death. He did, however, file a petition in the Circuit Court for Washington County seeking declaratory relief and requesting the right to execute a new last will and testament. The court found that the will was revocable, but that the contract under which the will was executed might be specifically enforced in equity or damages recovered upon it at law. Lester appealed to the Court of Special Appeals, see Shimp v. Shimp, 43 Md.App. 67, 402 A.2d 1324 (1979), and ultimately, by writ of certiorari, the case came before us.

In Shimp I, we found that the Shimps had executed their joint will pursuant to and in accordance with a valid, binding contract. 287 Md. at 387, 412 A.2d 1228. We held that Lester was "entitled to a declaratory decree stating that he may revoke his will but that an enforceable contract was entered into between him and his wife.... [and that] [a]t his death it may be specifically enforced in equity or damages may be recovered upon it at law." Id. at 388, 412 A.2d 1228. Thereafter, Lester did not execute another will or otherwise disturb the testamentary plan set forth in the joint will.

On April 4, 1985, in Washington County, Lester married Lisa Mae; they remained married until his death on January 11, 1986. Lester was not survived by any children.

Following Lester's death, Clara and Lester's joint will was admitted to probate in Washington County. Mary Virginia Huff and Wallace R. Huff were appointed Personal Representatives of the Estate on January 30, 1986. Lisa Mae and Lester had not entered into any marital agreement waiving Lisa Mae's marital rights, and she sought payment of a family allowance and filed an election for her statutory share of Lester's estate. On June 4, 1986, the Personal Representatives declined to pay Lisa Mae either her family allowance or her elective share. On July 10, 1986, Lisa Mae filed suit for a declaratory judgment in the Circuit Court for Washington County, requesting that the court pass an order that she was entitled to both a family allowance and an elective share of Lester's estate.

* * *

III.

While we have not previously addressed the issue of a surviving spouse's right to take an elective share in conflict with claims under a contract to convey by will, courts in other jurisdictions have examined the issue under varying factual situations....

In a number of these cases one spouse, after entering into a divorce or separation agreement which requires that spouse to leave part or all of the estate to the first spouse, remarries and then dies ..... In other cases, the decedent has contracted to make a will leaving property to children or other relatives.... Still other cases have arisen where the decedent had remarried after entering into an agreement to will property in exchange for services, ... or for forbearance from legal action, ... or to facilitate an adoption.... In some cases, the decedent has executed a will conforming to the contract, while in others he has breached the contract by executing a nonconforming will or by dying intestate

A.

The majority of these cases arise from the decedent having breached a contract to devise property by executing a nonconforming will or by dying intestate. In these cases, the claimants under the contract generally proceed on a theory of specific performance. While the rights of beneficiaries of a contract vest after the contract is made, nevertheless, where suit is brought for specific performance of the contract, "the after-acquired rights of third parties are equitable considerations to be regarded in adjudicating the questions." Owens v. McNally, 113 Cal.444, 45 P. 710 at 713 (1896). In determining whether to award specific performance to contract beneficiaries, courts have considered several different factors, including whether the surviving spouse had notice of the contract prior to the marriage, see, e.g., Patecky v. Friend, 220 Or. 612, 350 P.2d 170 at 175 (1960), the length of the marriage and the natural affection shared between the decedent and the surviving spouse, see, e.g., In re Arland's Estate, 131 Wash. 297, 230 P. at 157 at 158 (1924), whether the surviving spouse would be deprived of the entire estate by enforcement of the contract, see, e.g., Wides v. Wides' Executor, 299 Ky. 103, 184 S.W.2d 579 at 584 (1944), and the public policy concerning the marriage relationship and the rights of surviving spouses, see, e.g., Wides, supra, 184 S.W.2d at 584; Budde v. Pierce, 135 Vt. 152, 375 A.2d 984 at 986–87 (1977). In a great many cases consideration of these factors has led the court to determine that the superior equities were with the surviving spouse ..., while in other cases it has not....

B.

In those cases where the decedent has executed a will conforming to the contract, the claimants cannot seek specific performance, and courts, therefore, do not use equitable powers in resolving these cases. Instead, courts have analyzed the conflicting claims by characterizing the competing claimants as either creditors or legatees and evaluating their claims under the applicable priority rules. In a number of cases involving divorce settlements, the courts have found that where the decedent executes a will, which conforms to the terms of a contract, the beneficiaries take as legatees under the will and not as contract creditors. See, e.g., Donner, supra, 364 So.2d at 755; Dunham, supra, 320 N.Y.S.2d at 954; Tanenbaum, supra, 16 N.Y.S.2d at 510; Lewis, supra, 123 N.Y.S.2d at 862–63; Hoyt, supra, 21 N.Y.S.2d at 111. Consequently, because the applicable statutes give a higher priority to a surviving spouse's elective share than to testamentary bequests, the courts upheld the surviving spouse's claim over the claims of the contract beneficiaries....

* * *

[T]his analysis leads to the anomalous result that the contract beneficiaries are in a better position where the decedent breaches the contract than where the decedent fully and properly performs in accordance with it. See In Re Erstein's Estate, supra, 129 N.Y.S.2d at 321 ("[i]t would be anomalous if the rights of the promisees would be substantially greater in the case of intestacy than they would be had the testator left a will which carried out his promise").

C.

* * *

Other courts have relied upon the public policy surrounding the marriage relationship as the basis for upholding the surviving spouse's claim to an elective share over the claims of contract beneficiaries. These courts cite the general principle that "contracts in restraint of marriage are void as against public policy, while anything which tends to prevent marriage, or to disturb the marriage state, is viewed by the law with suspicion and disfavor." Owens, supra, 45 P. at 713. See also Bedal, supra, 218 P. at 648 (indicating that a contract to devise property to a third party could be characterized as a contract in restraint of marriage; and that "inasmuch as the contract for sole heirship would deprive any children subsequently born of their natural rights of inheritance, and would likewise deprive the parents of their right to dispose of property by gift or devise to subsequently born or adopted children, or to a spouse of either on a subsequent marriage, such a type of contract offends against the common instincts of natural loyalty, affection, and duty, and is therefore contrary to the public good and welfare"). They characterize contracts which require a decedent to devise his entire estate to a third party as being contracts which might restrain or discourage marriage. Therefore, to prevent having these contracts declared void as against public policy, courts have construed the contract to imply that when entering into the agreement the parties contemplated that the testator might remarry....

IV.

This case does not present a claim for specific performance because Lester performed his obligation under the contract and died leaving a will which conformed to the contract. Thus, we need not consider whether the superior equities lie with the Personal Representatives or with Lisa Mae.

Because Lester died leaving a will which conformed to the contract, we might consider drawing an analogy between the present case and the divorce cases, wherein courts found that where the decedent died leaving a conforming will, the contract beneficiaries were more properly characterized as legatees rather than contract creditors. Under this approach, we would find the respondents to be legatees under Lester's will whose interest in the estate, like the interest of any other legatee under any will, is subject to the abatement procedure outlined in § 3–208 of the Estates and Trusts Article. Under this procedure Lisa Mae's elective share would have priority over the respondents' claims and their share of the estate would be abated. Nevertheless, we acknowledge, as the court did in Erstein's Estate, supra, that this method of resolving the issue of priority leads to the anomalous result that the contract beneficiaries' rights would be greater where the contract is breached than where the testator performs in accordance with its terms. Consequently, we decline to adopt this theory as the controlling law in this case.

Instead, we find the question of priorities between a surviving spouse and beneficiaries under a contract to make a will should be resolved based upon the public policy which surrounds the marriage relationship and which underlies the elective share statute. As we noted previously, "the right of a person to transfer property upon his death to others . . . is not a natural right but a privilege granted by the State." Safe Dep. & Tr. Co., supra, 181 Md. at 355, 29 A.2d 906. Furthermore, "[t]he right to make a will is a purely statutory right," which the State may limit by statute. Johns v. Hodges, 62 Md. 525, 539 (1884). The Legislature on several occasions has limited this right by enacting restrictions such as those contained in § 3–203, which grants a surviving spouse the right to receive an elective share of a decedent's estate, regardless of the provisions contained in the decedent's will. In addition, § 3–204 suggests that the right to receive the elective share is a personal right, which cannot be waived by the unilateral acts of others, including the actions of the deceased spouse. These statutes and principles of law suggest that there is a strong public policy in favor of protecting the surviving spouse's right to receive an elective share. This Court on other occasions has recognized the strong public policy interest in protecting the surviving spouse's elective share from the unilateral acts of a deceased spouse. For example, in a number of cases this Court has declared transfers in fraud of marital rights to be void. See, e.g., Mushaw v. Mushaw, 183 Md. 511, 39 A.2d 465 (1944). See also Sykes, Inter Vivos Transfers in Violation of the Rights of Surviving Spouses, 10 Md.L.Rev. 1 (1949). We have indicated that this doctrine also applies to transfers made prior to the marriage. Collins v. Collins, 98 Md. 473, 484, 57 A. 597 (1904).

In addition to the public policy underlying these statutes, the public policy surrounding the marriage relationship also suggests that the surviving spouse's claim to an elective share should be afforded priority over the claims of beneficiaries of a contract to make a will. Like the majority of other courts, we have recognized the well settled principle that contracts which discourage or restrain the right to marry are void as against public policy. Bostick v. Blades, 59 Md. 231, 232–33 (1883). In executing a will, a testator is presumed to know that a spouse might renounce the will, thus extinguishing or reducing legacies contained in the will, and if the testator does not provide for this contingency then the beneficiaries under the will might lose the property left them. Webster v. Scott, 182 Md. 118, 121, 32 A.2d 475 (1943); see also Mercantile Trust Co. v. Schloss, 165 Md. 18, 27–28, 166 A. 599 (1933). Thus, we find that the respondents' rights under the contract were limited by the possibility that the survivor might remarry and that the subsequent spouse might elect against the will. Consequently, we conclude that their claims under the contract are subordinate to Lisa Mae's superior right to receive her elective share.

* * *

NOTES AND QUESTIONS

1. In Shimp v. Huff, Lisa Mae Shimp sought to take an "elective share" of Lester's estate. As we have already seen, most states protect a surviving spouse against intentional disinheritance. That is, even if a decedent leaves the spouse nothing in decedent's will, the surviving spouse may "elect" to take a share of the estate.

Note the careful strategy pursued by Lester's lawyer in Shimp v. Huff. After Clara's death, Lester brought a declaratory judgment action to determine whether the joint will created a binding contract. If the court had held that no contract was created, Lester could have executed a new will in favor of any beneficiaries he chose. When the court held that the joint will did create a binding contract, Lester chose not to execute a new will. Instead, after his marriage, he left Lisa Mae to rely on her elective share rights. As a result, the beneficiaries under the joint will could not bring a claim for breach of contract, because Lester never breached.

Suppose Lester had written a new will after Clara's death. Suppose further that the beneficiaries of the joint will asserted contract claims against Lester's estate. What relief would the court have given the beneficiaries of the joint will? Consider two situations:

(a) Lester's new will devises 10% of his estate to Lisa Mae, and the rest to the beneficiaries of the joint will.

(b) Lester's new will devises 90% of his estate to Lisa Mae, and the rest to the beneficiaries of the joint will.

If Lester's subsequent will had devised only 10% of his estate to Lisa Mae, would she have had a right to take more than that?

2. Until Lester's remarriage to Lisa Mae, the beneficiaries of the joint will had a contract claim that Lester could not defeat by writing a new will. Upon Lester's remarriage, that contract claim becomes subject to Lisa Mae's rights. Why? Does the court give a satisfactory explanation?

Suppose there had been no joint will. Before marrying Lisa Mae, however, Lester had accumulated significant debt to a physician. The physician would have a contract claim against Lester (and his estate). If Lester then married Lisa Mae, would the physician's contract claim be subject to Lisa Mae's right of election? Why should the physician's contract claim be treated differently from the contract claim advanced by beneficiaries of the joint will?

3. In Shimp v. Huff, Lester and Lisa Mae were married for less than one year before Lester's death. Are the equities in favor of Lisa Mae so clear? What if Lester's property had largely been inherited from Clara's family. Should Lisa Mae be entitled to a significant share of those assets?

4. As the court in Shimp v. Huff indicates, a number of courts have held that beneficiaries of will contracts are creditors who take priority over subsequent spouses asserting elective share rights. See, e.g., Gregory v. Estate of Gregory, 315 Ark. 187, 866 S.W.2d 379 (1993). In the Gregory case, the beneficiaries of the joint will were the children of the parties to the joint will. In Shimp v. Huff, Clara and Lester were childless. Should that make a difference?

On the general problem raised in Shimp v. Huff, see Randall J. Gingiss, Second Marriage Considerations for the Elderly, 45 S.D. L. Rev. 469, 477–82 (2000); Carolyn L. Dessin, The Troubled Relationship of Will Contracts and Spousal Protection: Time for an Amicable Separation, 45 Cath. U. L. Rev. 435 (1996).

PROBLEM

Abner and Beulah enter your office seeking advice about their estates. They have agreed that all of their property should pass to the survivor, and that at the death of the survivor, the remaining property should pass to the couple's two children. Beulah is concerned, however, that Abner might remarry after her death, and that Abner's future spouse might make a claim to the property. Abner, confident that he will not remarry, is happy to accommodate Beulah's wishes. In light of Shimp v. Huff, what recommendations would you make to Abner and Beulah?

NOTE ON CONTRACTS TO MAKE WILLS

On occasion, a person finds it useful to contract to make a will in favor of someone else. Perhaps the situation is most common when an elderly person seeks lifetime care, and promises the caretaker all or a share of testator's estate in return for that care. Hughes v. Frank, 1995 WL 632018 (1995), illustrates the problem—and the typical solution:

Alden, a difficult woman afflicted with Parkinson's disease, became dependent on Hughes, a caretaker. Alden never paid Hughes a salary, but, according to Alden's bookkeeper, she promised that Hughes would receive everything upon Alden's death. Alden's will, however, left Hughes only $125,000, while Alden's estate was worth $2.1 million. The court concluded that Alden and Hughes had entered into a binding oral contract, and that Hughes was entitled to specific performance.

Recall UPC § 2–514. Would the UPC permit enforcement of the oral contract in Hughes v. Frank? See Cragle v. Gray, 206 P.3d 446 (Alaska 2009) (holding that the UPC makes oral succession contracts unenforceable; testator's granddaughter, who had orally agreed to provide care in return for inheriting testator's house, was not entitled to the house).

Will contract problems also arise when, upon divorce, one spouse promises to devise property to the other, or to the children of the marriage.

SECTION VII. ILLUSTRATIVE WILL

Now that you have become familiar with a variety of wills law principles, let us examine an actual will (edited to eliminate clauses with little instructional value). Do not treat the Jacqueline Onassis will as a model; wills should be tailored to the needs of individual testators.

As you read the will, focus on why each phrase in the will was included. Is the language simply boilerplate, or does it serve an important function? Ask yourself how the disposition of testator's property would have been different if the language had not been included. Also ask yourself how you might improve the drafting of the will.

LAST WILL AND TESTAMENT OF JACQUELINE K. ONASSIS

I, JACQUELINE K. ONASSIS, of the City, County and State of New York, do make, publish and declare this to be my Last Will and Testament, hereby revoking all wills and codicils at any time heretofore made by me.

FIRST: A. I give and bequeath to my friend RACHEL (BUNNY) L. MELLON, if she survives me, in appreciation of her designing the Rose Garden in the White House my Indian miniature "Lovers watching rain clouds," Kangra, about 1780, if owned by me at the time of my death, and my large Indian miniature with giltwood frame "Gardens of the Palace of the Rajh," a panoramic view of a pink walled garden blooming with orange flowers, with the Rajh being entertained in a pavilion by musicians and dancers, if owned by me at the time of my death.

B. I give and bequeath to my friend MAURICE TEMPELSMAN, if he survives me, my Greek alabaster head of a woman if owned by me at the time of my death.

C. I give and bequeath to my friend ALEXANDER D. FORGER, if he survives me, my copy of John F. Kennedy's Inaugural Address signed by Robert Frost if owned by me at the time of my death.

D. Except as hereinabove otherwise effectively bequeathed, I give and bequeath all my tangible personal property, including, without limitation, my collection of letters, papers and documents, my personal effects, my furniture, furnishings, rugs, pictures, books, silver, plate, linen, china, glassware, objects of art, wearing apparel, jewelry, automobiles and their accessories, and all other household goods owned by me at the time of my death to my children who survive me, to be divided between them by my Executors, in the exercise of sole and absolute discretion, in as nearly equal portions as may be practicable, having due regard for the personal preferences of my children.

SECOND: A. I have made no provision in this my Will for my sister, Lee B. Radziwill, for whom I have great affection because I have already done so during my lifetime. I do wish, however, to remember her children and, thus, I direct my Executors to set aside the amount of Five Hundred Thousand Dollars ($500,000) for each child surviving me of my sister, Lee B. Radziwill.

B. I give and bequeath the amount of Two Hundred and Fifty Thousand Dollars ($250,000) to each child of mine who survives me.

C. I give and bequeath to NANCY L. TUCKERMAN, if she survives me, the amount of Two Hundred and Fifty Thousand Dollars ($250,000).

D. I give and bequeath to MARTA SQUBIN, if she survives me, the amount of One Hundred and Twenty–Five Thousand Dollars ($125,000).

E. I give and bequeath to my niece ALEXANDRA RUTHERFURD, if she survives me, the amount of One Hundred Thousand Dollars ($100,000).

F. I give and bequeath to PROVIDENCIA PAREDES, if she survives me, the amount of Fifty Thousand Dollars ($50,000).

G. I give and bequeath to LEE NASSO, if she survives me, the amount of Twenty–Five Thousand Dollars ($25,000).

H. I give and bequeath to MARIE AMARAL, if she survives me, the amount of Twenty–Five Thousand Dollars ($25,000).

I. I give and bequeath to EFIGENIO PINHEIRO, if he survives me, the amount of Twenty–Five Thousand Dollars ($25,000).

THIRD: A. I give and devise any and all interest owned by me at the time of my death in the real property located in the City of Newport, State of Rhode Island, which I inherited from my mother, Janet Lee Auchinclosss, and which is known as "Hammersmith Farm," including all buildings thereon and all rights and easements appurtenant thereto and all policies of insurance relating thereto, to HUGH D. AUCHINCLOSS, JR., if he survives me, or, if he does not survive me, to his children who survive me, in equal shares as tenants-in-common.

B. Except as hereinbefore otherwise effectively devised, I give and devise all real property owned by me at the time of my death, including all buildings thereon and all rights and easements appurtenant thereto and all policies of insurance relating thereto, to my children who survive me, in equal shares as tenants-in-common, or, if only one of my children survive me, to such survivor, or, if none of my children survive me, I authorize, but do not direct, my Executors to sell any such real property and I direct that the net proceeds of sale together with any such property not so sold be added to my residuary estate and thereafter held, administered, and disposed of as a part thereof.

C. I give, devise and bequeath all stock owned by me at the time of my death in any corporation which is the owner of any building in which I have a cooperative apartment, together with any lease to such apartment and all right, title and interest owned by me at the time of my death in and to any agreements relating to said building and the real property on which it is located, to my children who survive me, in equal shares as tenants in common, or, if only one of my children survive me, to such survivor, or, if none of my children survive me, I authorize, but do not direct, my Executors to sell any such stock and I direct that the net proceeds of sale together with any such stock not so sold be added to my residuary estate and thereafter held, administered and disposed of as a part thereof.

FOURTH: Under the Will of my late husband, John Fitzgerald Kennedy, a marital deduction trust was created for my benefit over which I was accorded a general power of appointment. I hereby exercise such power of appointment and direct that, upon my death, all property subject to such power be transferred, conveyed and paid over to my descendants who survive me, per stripes.

FIFTH: All the rest, residue and remainder of my property and estate, both real and personal, of whatsoever kind and wheresoever situated, of which I shall die seized or possessed or of which I shall be entitled to dispose at the time of my death (my "residuary estate"), after the payment therefrom of the taxes directed in Article NINTH hereof to be paid from my residuary estate (my "net residuary estate"), I give, devise and bequeath to the Trustees hereinafter named, IN TRUST, NEVERTHELESS, to hold as THE C & J FOUNDATION (sometimes hereinafter referred to as the "Foundation") and to manage, invest and reinvest the same, to collect the income thereof and to dispose of the net income and principal thereof for the following uses and purposes subject to the following terms and conditions:

A. Payment of Annuity Amount. The Trustees shall hold and manage the Foundation property for a primary term which shall commence with the date of my death and shall end on the 24th anniversary thereof.

B. Upon the expiration of the Foundation's primary term, the assets of the Foundation (other than any amount due to the qualified charitable beneficiaries) shall be disposed of in the following manner:

1. If no descendant of any child of mine is then living, the assets of the Foundation shall be transferred, conveyed and paid over as follows: (a) one-half (1/2) thereof (or the entire amount thereof if neither my sister, Lee B. Radziwill, nor any descendant of hers is then living) to the then living descendants of my cousin Michel Bouvier, per stirpes; and (b) the other one-half (1/2) thereof (or the entire amount thereof if no descendant of my cousin Michel Bouvier is then living) to the then living descendants of my sister, Lee B. Radziwlll, per stirpes, or, if no such descendant of hers is then living, to my said sister, if she shall then be living.

2. If one or more descendants of any child of mine is then living, the assets of the Foundation shall be transferred, conveyed and paid over as follows: (a) one-half (1/2) thereof (or the entire amount if no descendant of my son, John F. Kennedy, Jr., is then living) to the then living descendants of my daughter, Caroline B. Kennedy, per stirpes; and (b) one-half (1/2) thereof (or the entire amount if no descendant of my daughter, Caroline B. Kennedy, is then living) to the then living descendants of my son, John F. Kennedy, Jr., per stirpes.

. . .

EIGHTH: In the event that any beneficiary or beneficiaries hereunder upon whose survivorship any gift, legacy or devise is conditioned and the person or persons, including myself, upon whose prior death such gift, legacy or devise takes effect shall die simultaneously or under such circumstances as to render it impossible or difficult to determine who survived the other, I hereby declare it to be my will that such beneficiary or beneficiaries shall be deemed not to have survived but to have predeceased such person or persons, and that this my Will and any and all of its provisions shall be construed on such assumption and basis.

NINTH: A. All estate, inheritance, legacy, succession or transfer or other death taxes (including any interest and penalties thereon) imposed by any domestic or foreign taxing authority with respect to all property owned by me at the time of my death and passing under this my Will (other than any generation-skipping transfer tax imposed by Chapter 13 of the Code, or any successor section or statute of like import, and any comparable tax imposed by any other taxing authority) shall be paid without apportionment out of my residuary estate and without apportionment within my residuary estate and with no right of reimbursement from any recipient of any such property. By directing payment of the aforesaid taxes from my residuary estate only in so far as those taxes are generated by property passing under this my Will, it is my express intention that the property over which I possess a general power of appointment and to which I refer in Article FOURTH of this my Will shall bear its own share of such taxes.

B. Should my Estate, after payment of all of my debts and funeral expenses, the expenses of estate administration and the taxes referred to in this Article NINTH, be insufficient to satisfy in full all of the preresiduary bequests and devises which I make under Articles FIRST through THIRD hereof, I direct that the bequests and devises in (1) Paragraphs A, B and C of Article FIRST, (2) Article SECOND and (3) Paragraph A of Article THIRD shall abate last after the abatement of the bequests and devises in Paragraph D of Article FIRST and Paragraphs B and C of Article THIRD.

. . .

ELEVENTH: In addition to, and not by way of limitation of, the powers conferred by law upon fiduciaries, subject, however, to the directions and prohibitions in Article FIFTH hereof, I hereby expressly grant to my Executor with respect to my estate and the Trustees with respect to each of the trust estates herein created, including any accumulated income thereof, the powers hereinafter enumerated, all of such powers so conferred or granted to be exercised by them as they may deem advisable in the exercise of sole and absolute discretion:

(1) To purchase or otherwise acquire, and to retain, whether originally a part of my estate or subsequently acquired, any and all stocks, bonds, notes or other securities, or any variety of real or personal property, including securities of any corporate fiduciary . . .; and to make or retain any such investment without regard to degree of diversification.

(2) To sell (including to any descendant of mine), lease, pledge, mortgage, transfer, exchange, convert or otherwise dispose of, or grant options with respect to, any and all property at any time forming a part of my estate or any trust estate, in any manner, at any time or times, for any purpose, for any price and upon any terms, credits and conditions; and to enter into leases which extend beyond the period fixed by statute for leases made by fiduciaries and beyond the duration of any trust.

(3) To borrow money from any lender, including any corporate fiduciary, for any purpose connected with the protection, preservation or improvement of my estate or any trust estate, and as security to mortgage or pledge upon any terms and conditions any real or personal property of which I may die seized or possessed or forming a part of any trust estate.

(4) To vote in person or by general or limited proxy with respect to any shares of stock or other security; directly or through a committee or other agent, to oppose or consent to the reorganization, consolidation, merger, dissolution or liquidation of any corporation, or to the sale, lease, pledge or mortgage of any property by or to any such corporation; and to make any payments and take any steps proper to obtain the benefits of any such transaction.

(5) To the extent permitted by law, to register any security in the name of a nominee with or without the addition of words indicating that such security is held in a fiduciary capacity; and to hold any security in bearer form.

(6) To complete, extend, modify or renew any loans, notes, bonds, mortgages, contracts or any other obligations which I may owe or to which I may be a party or which may be liens or charges against any of my property, or against my estate, although I may not be liable thereon; to pay, compromise, compound, adjust, submit to arbitration, sell or release any claims or demands of my estate or any trust against others or of others against my

estate or any trust upon any terms and conditions, including the acceptance of deeds to real property in satisfaction of bonds and mortgages; and to make any payments in connection therewith.

(7) To make distributions in kind (including in satisfaction of pecuniary bequests) and to cause any distribution to be composed of cash, property or undivided fractional shares in property different in kind from any other distribution without regard to the income tax basis of the property distributed to any beneficiary or any trust.

TWELFTH: A. I appoint ALEXANDER D. FORGER and MAURICE TEMPELSMAN Executors of this my Last Will and Testament. If either of them should fail to qualify or cease to act as Executor hereunder, I authorize, but do not direct, the other, in the exercise of sole and absolute discretion, to appoint as a co-Executor such individual or such bank or trust company as he, in the exercise of sole and absolute discretion, shall select. Any such appointment shall be made by an instrument in writing filed with the clerk of the appropriate court.

B. Should it be necessary for a representative of my estate to qualify in any jurisdiction wherein any Executor named herein cannot or may not desire to qualify as such, any other Executor acting hereunder shall, without giving any security, act as Executor in such jurisdiction and shall have therein all the rights, powers, privileges, discretions and duties conferred or imposed upon my Executor by the provisions of this my Will, or, if no Executor can or wishes to qualify as Executor in such other jurisdiction, or, if at any time and for any reason there shall be no Executor in office in such other jurisdiction, I appoint as Executor therein such person or corporation as may be designated by the Executors acting hereunder. Such substituted Executor shall, without giving any security, have in such other jurisdiction all the rights, powers, privileges, discretions and duties conferred or imposed upon my Executors by the provisions of this my Will.....

...

D. I appoint my daughter, CAROLINE B. KENNEDY, my son, JOHN F. KENNEDY, JR., ALEXANDER D. FORGER and MAURICE TEMPELSMAN Trustees of the trust created under Paragraph A of Article FIFTH of this my Will and therein designated THE C & J FOUNDATION.

...

G. Any Executor or Trustee may resign from office without leave of court at any time and for any reason by filing a written instrument of resignation with the clerk of the appropriate court.

...

K. Except as provided by law, I direct that my Executors shall not be required to file any inventory or render any account of my Estate and that no Executor, Trustee, or donee of a power in trust shall be required to give any bond. If, notwithstanding the foregoing direction, any bond is required by any law, statute or rule of court, no sureties shall be required thereon.

L. I authorize and empower the Trustees or Trustee of each trust created hereunder to transfer the trust assets to, and to hold and administer them in, any jurisdiction in the United States and to account for the same in any court having jurisdiction over said assets.

M. I direct that any and all powers and discretion conferred by law and by this my Will upon my Trustees including, but not by way of limitation, the right to appoint successor and co-Trustees, may be exercised by the Trustees from time to time qualified and acting hereunder.

N. Whenever the terms "Executors" or "Executor" and "Trustees" or "Trustee" are used in this my Will, they shall be deemed to refer to the Executors or Executor or the Trustees or Trustee acting hereunder from time to time.

THIRTEENTH: A. Disposition in this Will to the descendants of a person per stirpes shall be deemed to require a division into a sufficient number of equal shares to make one share for each child of such person living at the time such disposition becomes effective and one share for each then deceased child of such person having one or more descendants then living, regardless of whether any child of such person is then living, with the same principle to be applied in any required further division of a share at a more remote generation.

B. As used in this Will, the terms "child," "children," "descendant" and "descendants" are intended to include adopted persons and the descendants of adopted persons, whether of the blood or by adoption.

IN WITNESS WHEREOF, I, JACQUELINE K. ONASSIS, have to this my Last Will and Testament subscribed my name and set my seal this 22 day of March, in the year One Thousand Nine Hundred and Ninety–Four.

____

Jacqueline K. Onassis Subscribed and sealed by the Testatrix in the presence of us and of each of us, and at the same time published, declared and acknowledged by her to us to be her Last Will and Testament, and thereupon we, at the request of the said Testatrix, in her presence and in the presence of each other, have hereunto subscribed our names as witnesses this 22nd day of March 1994.

____

____

STATE OF NEW YORK

COUNTY OF NEW YORK

Each of the undersigned, individually and severally being duly sworn, deposes and says:

The within Will was subscribed in our presence and sight at the end thereof by JACQUELINE K. ONASSIS, the within-named Testatrix, on the 22nd day of March, 1994, at 1040 Fifth Avenue in the State of New York.

Said Testatrix at the time of making such subscription declared the instrument so subscribed to be her Last Will and Testament.

Each of the undersigned thereupon signed his or her name as a witness at the end of said Will at the request of said Testatrix and in her presence and sight and in the presence and sight of each other.

Said Testatrix was, at the time of so executing said Will, over the age of 18 years and, in the respective opinions of the undersigned, of sound mind, memory and understanding and not under any restraint or in any respect incompetent to make a will.

The Testatrix, in the respective opinions of the undersigned, could read, write and converse in the English language and was suffering from no defect of sight, hearing or speech or from any other physical or mental impairment which would affect her capacity to make a valid will. The Will was executed as a single, original instrument and was not executed in counterparts. Each of the undersigned was acquainted with said Testatrix at said time and makes this affidavit at her request. The within Will was shown to the undersigned at the time affidavit was made, and was examined by each of them as to the signature of said Testatrix and of the undersigned. The foregoing instrument was executed by the Testatrix and witnessed by each of the undersigned affiants under the supervision of Georgiana J. Slade, an attorney-at-law.

Severally sworn to before this 22nd day of March, 1994

____
(witness)

____
(witness)

____
Notary

CHAPTER FIVE

CONTESTING THE WILL

As we have seen, before a will is admitted to probate, the proponents of the will—generally the executor or the will beneficiaries—must establish that the will has been executed in accordance with the requisite testamentary formalities. Suppose the proponents have succeeded in demonstrating that testator complied with the applicable Statute of Wills. Are they home free? No, they are not. Even if the will complies with statutory formalities, contestants—those seeking to establish that the will is invalid—may argue that the will, or a part of the will, should not be admitted to probate because the testator lacked testamentary capacity, or because the will's dispositive provisions were unduly influenced by one of the will beneficiaries. In this section, we explore those grounds for contest. We also explore the special problems of gay and lesbian testators, who frequently fear contests when they execute wills in favor of their partners.

SECTION I. TESTAMENTARY CAPACITY

It is hornbook law that testator can only execute a valid will if testator has "testamentary capacity." The Uniform Probate Code provides that "[a]n individual 18 or more years of age who is of sound mind may make a will." Uniform Probate Code § 2–501. As we shall see, determining whether testator is of "sound mind" is not always an easy matter. But start by considering a more basic question. Why should capacity matter at all? So long as the testator has the ability to formulate a statement of his preferences, why shouldn't we give effect to those stated preferences, without regard to how bizarre testator's behavior might be, and without regard to any medical diagnoses of testator's condition? After all, testator managed to accumulate, or to hold on to, the property during life; why shouldn't testator be free to dispose of the property at death? Consider the following cases:

Barnes v. Marshall

Supreme Court of Missouri, 1971.
467 S.W.2d 70.

■ HOLMAN, J.:

This action was filed to contest a will and two codicils executed by Dr. A. H. Marshall a short time before his death which occurred on July 29, 1968. The plaintiff is a daughter of the testator. The defendants are the beneficiaries of the alleged will. A number are relatives of testator, but many are religious, charitable, and fraternal organizations. A trial resulted in a verdict that the paper writings were not the last will and codicils of Dr. Marshall. A number of the defendants have appealed. We will hereinafter refer to the appellants as defendants. We have appellate jurisdiction because the will devises real estate and also because of the amount in dispute.

One of the "Points Relied On" by defendants is that the verdict is against the greater weight of the credible evidence. Since this court will not weigh the evidence in a case of this nature this point, strictly speaking, would not present anything for review. However, in considering the argument under that point we have concluded that defendants actually intended to present the contention that plaintiff did not make a submissible case and that the trial court erred in not directing a verdict for defendants, and we will so consider the point. The petition charged that testator was not of sound mind and did not have the mental capacity to make a will. The transcript contains more than 1,100 pages and there are a large number of exhibits. We will state the facts as briefly as possible and we think they will clearly support our conclusion that the submission is amply supported by the evidence.

The will, executed April 30, 1968, made specific bequests of testator's home and office furniture and equipment. The remainder of the net estate was devised to trustees, with annual payments to be made from the income to various individuals, churches, charities, and fraternal organizations. Plaintiff, her husband and two children were to receive $5.00 each per year. The estate was appraised in the inventory at $525,400.

The Marshalls had three children: plaintiff who lived in St. Louis, Mary Taylor Myers who lived in Dexter, Missouri, and died in May 1965, and Anetta Ester Vogel who lived near Chicago and who died about a month after her father's death.

In stating the evidence offered by plaintiff we will deal specifically with five witnesses: three lay witnesses because of contentions concerning their testimony, hereinafter discussed, and the two medical witnesses because of the importance we attribute to their testimony. There were many other witnesses whose testimony we will endeavor to summarize in a general way.

Ward Barnes, husband of plaintiff, testified that he visited in the Marshall home frequently from the time of his marriage in 1930 until Dr. Marshall's death; that Mrs. Marshall was a very cultured, refined, patient, and accommodating woman; that he spent a great deal of time with testator and soon learned that testator would dominate the conversation in accordance with a certain pattern; that testator told him that he discontinued his medical practice at the command of the Lord so that he might use his time in saving the nation and the world; that testator had told him

> "that the Lord had revealed to him the secrets of heaven; that he was the only man on earth to whom the Lord had revealed these secrets; that he had told him that heaven was a glorious place and that when

> he went to heaven he would have a beautiful crown and a wonderful throne sitting next to Thee Lord. He said that there were three powers in heaven, the Lord, Thee Lord, and God, and he said that this throne that he would have would be on the right hand side of Thee Lord in heaven. He said that heaven was a wonderful place, Thee Lord had revealed to him that whatever pleasures man had on earth he would have in heaven. If it was whiskey, if it was gambling, if it was women, that these would be provided him."

He stated that testator had also told him that the Lord had given him a special power of calling upon the Lord to right the wrongs which people had done to him; that many times he related instances of various people whom he had "turned over to the Lord" and the Lord had meted out justice at his instance by taking away the person's wealth, and usually that the person lost his health, had a long period of suffering, and eventually died; that when testator related stories about the men he had turned over to the Lord he would become highly emotional, would pound on the table with his fists, would call these men dirty profane names, his face would become flushed, and the veins in his neck would stand out; that testator had told him that he (testator) had run for Congress on two occasions and had run for President of the United States (although apparently never nominated by any party) on two or three occasions; that he had told him that

> "if he were made President of the United States he would cancel all public debt, that he would call in all government bonds and discontinue the interest on all of these obligations, and that he would then print money and control the currency, and that he would kill the damn bankers and the crooks and the thieves that were robbing the people in political office and that the world would then be able to settle down and live in peace."

He stated that on one occasion testator took him to his office and showed him a number of young women who were mailing out material in the interest of his candidacy; that he had said it was costing him "thousands of dollars to mail this material out, but the Lord had told him to do it and he had no right to go counter to what the Lord had told him to do." He further stated that in one of his campaigns for President testator had purchased a new car and had many biblical quotations and sayings of his own printed all over the automobile; that he had observed him, campaigning from this car, at the corner of Grand and Lindell Boulevard in St. Louis.

Witness Barnes further testified that testator had told him that Mrs. Marshall had inherited a piece of land and that when it was sold he took part of the money and gave her a note for $3,500; that later Mrs. Marshall had pressed him for payment and had conferred with Moore Haw, an attorney, and that because of that testator had locked her out of the house; that Mrs. Marshall then filed a suit and caused him to pay her the $3,500; that eventually the Marshalls were reconciled and resumed their life together; that at the time Mrs. Marshall died he and plaintiff went immediately to Charleston and at testator's request plaintiff made the funeral arrangements; that testator went to his wife's bedroom and searched the room looking for money and called him and plaintiff in to help him; that he found only a few dollars and then became enraged, "his fists clenched * * * his hands were shaking, his body was trembling; his face was red and he was—you could see he was in a terrible emotional state as he stood there shaking his fists and shouting. He said, 'I know she had more money than that. * * * Your mother made me pay and that scoundrel Moore Haw, the dirty, low down * * * made me pay that thirty-five hundred dollars,' and he said, 'I want my money back. I want you to give it to me.' " Witness further testified that of the $3,500 testator had paid his wife in 1941 Mrs. Marshall had given plaintiff $1,500; that from the time of his wife's death until his own death testator had frequently demanded that plaintiff send him $3,500 and stated that if she didn't he would cut her out of his will; that it was his opinion that from the time he first became acquainted with him until his death Dr. Marshall was not of sound mind.

Frank Eaves testified that he had known testator for about eight years before his death; that he was Plant Supervisor for Crenshaw Packing Company and that testator would come to the plant about once a week; that he had heard testator talk about having the Lord come down on people, making them suffer, and having them killed; that he said his furnace didn't work and he had the Lord put a curse on it and it had worked good ever since; that he said he "talked directly to God and God told him things"; that when he would discuss subjects of that kind "his face would get real red, his eyes would bug out, the vessels would stand out on his neck, he would slobber and shout, and pound on anything available"; that he would sometimes come in dressed in nothing but his nightgown and his house shoes; that on one occasion he came to the plant with nothing on but a housecoat; that he was talking about a rash on his body and opened his housecoat and exposed his private parts to the female secretary and others present. Mr. Eaves was of the opinion that testator was of unsound mind over the period he had known him.

William West testified that he was a drug clerk in the Myers Drug Store in Dexter; that he had known testator from 1951 until his death; that testator came in the drug store about once a month during that period; that he had heard testator say that he talked directly to the Lord and the Lord told him the things he was to do; that one of these was that he should save the world and should be prime minister of the United States; that he also talked about turning people over to the Lord for punishment and when he did so the Lord would mete out the punishment and the men would die, or lose their wealth or something of that nature; that when he would talk about such things he used loud abusive language, his face would be flushed, and he would pound the table; that at the funeral of testator's daughter, Mrs. Myers, he (the witness) started to assist Mrs. Marshall, who was then about 80 years old, out of her chair and Dr. Marshall "slapped me on the arm and told me to keep my hands off of her"; that he was present when Mrs. Marshall was trying to get out of the car and in so doing exposed a portion of her leg and testator "bawled her out for it." Witness was of the opinion that testator, during the time he had known him, was of unsound mind.

Dr. Charles Rolwing testified that he first saw testator professionally in 1940; that at that time testator complained of heart trouble but he was unable to find any evidence of such; that he was of the opinion that he was then suffering from manic-depressive psychosis for which there is no cure and that it would gradually get worse; that he also attended testator from the first part of May 1968 until his death in July; that at that time he was suffering from a serious heart ailment; that he was at that time still suffering from manic-depressive psychosis; that he was of the opinion that on April 30, May 17, and May 24, 1968, testator was of unsound mind.

Plaintiff also presented the testimony of Dr. Paul Hartman, a specialist in psychiatry and neurology, who testified in response to a hypothetical question. This question hypothesized much of the evidence related by the other witnesses for plaintiff and utilizes ten pages of the transcript. In response thereto Dr. Hartman expressed the opinion that Dr. Marshall was of unsound mind on the dates he executed his will and codicils; that he would classify Dr. Marshall's mental disease as manic-depressive psychosis with paranoid tendencies; that it was his opinion that Dr. Marshall was incapable of generalized logical thinking.

In addition to the foregoing evidence plaintiff testified herself and offered more than a dozen other witnesses, all of whom related unusual conduct and statements of testator. Plaintiff also offered a large number of exhibits in the nature of letters from testator and various publications containing advertisements and statements written by testator. There was evidence that plaintiff had been a dutiful daughter, had been solicitous of testator and her mother, had visited them frequently and often would take prepared food which she knew they liked. A number of these witnesses testified that testator had told them of various men who had wronged him and that he had turned them over to the Lord who meted out punishment in the form of financial loss, illness, death, or all three; that when he would tell of these things he would speak loud, get excited, his face would become red, his eyes bulge out, and he would gesture violently; that testator was unreasonably jealous of his wife and often said that all women who wore short skirts, or smoked, were immoral.

There was testimony that on the Christmas before the death of his daughter, Mary Myers, the Myers and Barnes families ate Christmas dinner with the Marshalls, and after the dinner testator "jumped on" Mary about her skirt being short and continued doing so until Mary became so upset that she and her husband had to leave.

A number of witnesses testified concerning the fact that testator would go to various public establishments dressed in his nightgown and bathrobe. An article written by testator and published in a local newspaper under date of June 4, 1942, under the heading of "DR. MARSHALL SAYS," contained the following:

> "Providence they say always raises up a great leader in every crisis * * *. I am that great leader. I am that prophet that Moses and all the other prophets have spoken about. I am the Messiah that the people of this world have been talking and praying about and believing and hoping that he would soon show up. I am the inspired prophet."

In contending that plaintiff did not make a submissible case defendants point to the testimony of their witnesses to the effect that testator was of sound mind and was calm, quiet, and collected on the day the will was executed. The difficulty with that argument is that in determining this question "we must disregard the evidence offered by defendants unless it aids plaintiffs' case, accept plaintiffs' evidence as true, and give them the benefit of every inference which may legitimately be drawn from it." Sturm v. Routh, Mo. Sup., 373 S.W.2d 922, 923.

It is also contended that most of plaintiff's evidence dealt with testator's "sickness, peculiarities, eccentricities, miserliness, neglect of person or clothing, forgetfulness, anger, high temper, unusual or peculiar political and religious views, jealousy, mistreatment of family, unusual moral views, and repeating of stories, which are not evidence of testamentary incapacity or of unsound mind."

As we have indicated, we do not agree with defendants' contentions. We have stated a portion of the evidence and it need not be repeated here. It is sufficient to say that we think testator's stated views on government, religion, morals, and finances go beyond the classification of peculiarities and eccentricities and are sufficient evidence from which a jury could reasonably find he was of unsound mind. When we add the strong medical testimony to that of the lay witnesses there would seem to be no doubt that a submissible case was made.

Defendants also point out that there is evidence that a person suffering from manic-depressive psychosis has periods of normalcy between the abnormal periods of elation or depression and that testator was in a normal period at the time the will was executed. The mental condition of testator at the precise time the will was executed was a question for the jury to decide. The jury was obviously persuaded that he was not of sound mind and since there was evidence to support that verdict it is conclusive.

Plaintiff's evidence relating to the mental condition of testator encompassed the period from 1940 until his death in 1968. The next point briefed by defendants is that the court erred in admitting evidence of occurrences years prior to the execution of the will because it was too remote to have any probative value. It is true, as defendants contend, that "[evidence], not too remote, of mental unsoundness either before or after the will's execution is admissible, provided it indicates that such unsoundness existed at the time the will was made." Rothwell v. Love, Mo. Sup., 241 S.W.2d 893, 895. There can be no question, however, but that evidence concerning testator's mental condition long prior to the execution of the will is admissible if it tends to show his condition at the time of said execution. Holton v. Cochran, 208 Mo. 314, 106 S.W. 1035, l.c. 1069; Buford v. Gruber, 223 Mo. 231, 122 S.W. 717 [4]; Clingenpeel v. Citizens' Trust Co., Mo. Sup.,

240 S.W. 177. Dr. Rolwing testified that he treated testator in 1940 and that he was of unsound mind at that time; that he was suffering from manic-depressive psychosis, an incurable mental disease which would gradually get worse. That testimony was certainly admissible as it would have a direct bearing on testator's mental condition at the time the will was executed. And in view of that testimony it was appropriate to admit other evidence concerning testator's statements and conduct tending to support the submission of mental incapacity occurring during the intervening period. This point is accordingly ruled adversely to defendants' contention.

The next point briefed by defendants is that the court erred in permitting lay witnesses Ward Barnes, Frank Eaves, and William L. West to express an opinion that testator was of unsound mind. This for the reason that the facts related by those witnesses were not inconsistent with sanity and hence the necessary foundation was not established. The rule regarding the competency of lay witnesses to express an opinion on the issue as to whether a person is or is not of sound mind is that "a lay witness is not competent to testify that, in the opinion of such witness, a person is of unsound mind or insane, without first relating the facts upon which such opinion is based; and, when the facts have been stated by such lay witness, unless such facts are inconsistent with such person's sanity, the opinion of such lay witness that the person under consideration was insane or of unsound mind, is not admissible in evidence and may not be received. * * * In this connection it has repeatedly been determined that evidence of sickness, old age, peculiarities, eccentricities in dress or oddities of habit, forgetfulness, inability to recognize friends, feebleness resulting from illness, and other facts or circumstances not inconsistent with the ability to understand the ordinary affairs of life, comprehend the nature and extent of one's property and the natural objects of his bounty, and which are not inconsistent with sanity, cannot be used as a basis for the opinion testimony of a lay witness that a person is of unsound mind or insane. * * * 'The rule is well settled that, ordinarily, before a lay witness will be permitted to give his opinion that a person is of unsound mind, he must first detail the facts upon which he bases such opinion, but if he expresses an opinion that such person is of sound mind, he is not required to detail the facts upon which he founds his opinion. The reason for the rule is obvious. An opinion that a person is of unsound mind is based upon abnormal or unnatural acts and conduct of such person, while an opinion of soundness of mind is founded upon the absence of such acts and conduct.' " Lee v. Ullery, 346 Mo. 236, 140 S.W.2d 5, 9, 10.

Because of this point we have heretofore detailed the testimony of these three witnesses in the factual statement and such need not be repeated here. We think it is obvious that each witness detailed sufficient facts upon which to base the opinion stated. Those facts went far beyond a mere showing of peculiarities and eccentricities. They were clearly inconsistent with the conclusion that testator was of sound mind. The facts detailed by these witnesses are quite different from those stated by the witnesses in Lewis v. McCullough, Mo. Sup., 413 S.W.2d 499, the case upon which defendants rely.

The defendants also contend that the court erred in refusing to permit their witness, Harris D. Rodgers, to express an opinion that testator was of sound mind. This witness operated an abstract business in Benton, Missouri, which is about 20 miles from Charleston. However, he had known testator for about 35 years and had seen and visited with him on an average of from two to four times a year. We have concluded that we need not determine whether or not the court erred in excluding this testimony. This for the reason that it is "well settled that, if in a specific instance the evidence should not have been excluded, the error is harmless if the same evidence is found in the testimony of the same or other witnesses, given before or after the objection was sustained." Steffen v. Southwestern Bell Telephone Co., 331 Mo. 574, 56 S.W.2d 47, 48. In this instance defendants offered ten lay witnesses who were permitted to testify that in their opinion testator was of sound mind. With such an abundance of testimony on that issue it seems apparent to us that the exclusion of the opinion of one additional witness could not have been prejudicial. No reversible error appearing this point is ruled adversely to defendants.

Defendants' final contention is that the court erred in refusing to give their proffered Instruction No. P–1. They say that the instructions given were not sufficient to properly instruct the jury and that P–1 was necessary to clarify the issues. The instructions given submitted the issue as to whether testator was of sound and disposing mind and memory at the time he signed the documents. Also given was Instruction No. 8 which is MAI 15.01 and which defines the phrase "sound and disposing mind and memory."

Instruction P–1 reads as follows:

> "The Court instructs the jury that, in determining the issue of whether Dr. A. H. Marshall was of sound and disposing mind and memory, you may take into consideration the instrument itself and all its provisions, in connection with all other facts and circumstances in evidence. But, under the law of the State of Missouri, Dr. A. H. Marshall was not obligated to leave any part of his estate to the plaintiff, Julia Amma Barnes, and he was not obliged to mention plaintiff in his will. A man who is of sound and disposing mind and memory as defined by Instruction No. ___ has the right to dispose of his property by will as he may choose, even to the entire exclusion of those who, but for the will, would be the heirs of his estate; and if after considering all the evidence in the case, including the instrument itself and all its provisions, you believe that Dr. A. H. Marshall was of sound and disposing mind and memory, you will not further consider whether said disposition was appropriate or unappropriate. The jury should not substitute its judgment for the testator's judgment, nor should they determine the case upon the wisdom or the justice of the disposition made by the testator of his property; whether such disposition is just or right is a question for the testator, and for none other than the testator."

It will be noted that P–1 is clearly a cautionary instruction. And the rule is well established that "[the] giving of cautionary instructions is largely within the discretion of the trial court and unless such discretion is abused it will not be interfered with on appeal." Bucks v. Hamill, 358 Mo. 617, 216 S.W.2d 423, 425. We also have the view that the instruction is somewhat argumentative in its nature.... Moreover, it appears that the manner in which P–1 is prepared is out of harmony with the direction that "instructions shall be simple, brief, impartial, free from argument * * *." S. Ct. Rule 70.01(e). The ultimate issues were properly submitted to the jury and we do not consider it necessary or desirable that P–1 should have been given. The trial court did not abuse its discretion in refusing to give it and hence no reversible error occurred.

The judgment is affirmed. All concur.

Wilson v. Lane

Supreme Court of Georgia, 2005.
279 Ga. 492, 614 S.E.2d 88.

■ FLETCHER, C. J.

After Executrix Katherine Lane offered Jewel Jones Greer's 1997 last will and testament for probate, Floyd Wilson filed a caveat, challenging Greer's testamentary capacity. A Jasper County Superior Court jury found that Greer lacked testamentary capacity at the time she executed her will, but the trial court granted Lane's motion for judgment notwithstanding the verdict. Wilson appeals. Because we agree that there was no evidence to show that Greer lacked testamentary capacity, we affirm.

A person is mentally capable to make a will if she "has sufficient intellect to enable [her] to have a decided and rational desire as to the disposition of [her] property. ..." In this case, the propounders introduced evidence that the will in question distributed Greer's property equally to 17 beneficiaries, 16 of whom are blood-relatives to Greer. The only non-relative beneficiary is Katherine Lane, who spent much of her time caring for Greer before her death in 2000. The drafting attorney testified that in his opinion, at the time the 1997 will was signed, Greer was mentally competent, and that she emphatically selected every beneficiary named in the will. Numerous other friends and acquaintances also testified that Greer had a clear mind at the time the will was signed.

Thus, the propounders established a presumption that Greer possessed testamentary capacity. The caveators, however, never presented any evidence whatsoever showing that Greer was incapable of forming a decided and rational desire as to the disposition of her property, even when the evidence is examined in the light most favorable to their case.

The caveators challenged Greer's capacity by showing that she was eccentric, aged, and peculiar in the last years of her life. They presented testimony that she had an irrational fear of flooding in her house, that she had trouble dressing and bathing herself, and that she unnecessarily called the fire department to report a non-existent fire. But "[t]he law does not withhold from the aged, the feeble, the weak-minded, the capricious, the notionate, the right to make a will, provided such person has a decided and rational desire as to the disposition of his property." Although perhaps persuasive to a jury, "eccentric habits and absurd beliefs do not establish testamentary incapacity." All that is required to sustain the will is proof that Greer was capable of forming a certain rational desire with respect to the disposition of her assets.

In addition to Greer's eccentric habits, the caveators also introduced evidence of a guardianship petition filed for Greer a few months after the will was executed, the testimony of an expert witness, and a letter written by Greer's physician. None of that evidence, however, was sufficient to deprive Greer of her right to make a valid will, as none of it showed that she was incapable of forming a rational desire as to the disposition of her property.

The expert admitted that he had never examined Greer, and that his testimony was based solely on a cursory review of some of Greer's medical files. Further, he was equivocal in his testimony, stating only that "*it appears* that she was in some form of the early to middle stages of a dementia of the Alzheimer's type." Regardless of the stigma associated with the term "Alzheimer's," however, that testimony does not show how Greer would have been unable to form a rational desire regarding the disposition of her assets. Indeed, the expert offered no explanation of how her supposed condition would affect her competency to make a valid will.

The testimony of Greer's physician also failed to show how she lacked testamentary capacity. In 1996, the physician wrote a letter stating that Greer "was legally blind and suffered from senile dementia ...." But the doctor testified that he was "not sure whether she had senile dementia at the time or not, even though I wrote that." He stated further that he only wrote the letter to try and assist Greer in obtaining help with her telephone bill because she had been having trouble with her eyes. In any event, a vague reference to "senile dementia" cannot eliminate testamentary capacity. If it could, it would undermine societal confidence in the validity and sanctity of our testamentary system.

Finally, ... Lane filed a guardianship petition in 1998, after the will was executed, proclaiming that Greer was no longer capable of managing her own affairs alone. According to the testimony, however, the petition was filed solely in order to satisfy the Department of Family and Children Services' concerns regarding Greer's ability to continue living on her own, and thus to allow Greer to remain in her home. Even if Greer's inability to live alone existed at the time the will was executed, which was not proven by any evidence, that fact bears no relation to her ability to form a rational desire regarding the disposition of her assets.

* * *

... [I]n this case, no testimony, expert or otherwise, was offered to establish that at the time the will was executed, Greer suffered from a form of dementia sufficient in form or extent to render her unable to form a decided and rational desire regarding the disposition of her assets .... At most, there was evidence that Greer was an eccentric woman whose mental health declined toward the end of her life. Accordingly, the evidence demanded a verdict upholding the validity of the will, and the trial court was correct to reverse the jury's contrary verdict.

Judgment affirmed.

QUESTIONS

1. Dr. Marshall appears to have been a volatile, abusive man with peculiar (although, at times, personally comforting) views about religion, politics, and morality. These beliefs may have made him an annoyance (and a laughingstock) during his lifetime, but despite his peculiarities, Dr. Marshall managed to function well enough to amass an estate of $525,400, and to give explicit directions about how that estate should be distributed. Why should his peculiarities deprive him of the right to dispose of his estate as he wished?

2. Would the Wilson v. Lane court have upheld the jury verdict that Dr. Marshall lacked capacity? What standard did that court articulate for determining whether Jewel Greer lacked capacity?

Testamentary capacity is a legal concept, not a medical one. Typically, the articulated standard for capacity is relatively low. The Supreme Court of Appeals of West Virginia, quoting a 90–year old formulation, recently put it this way:

> It is not necessary that a testator possess high quality or strength of mind, to make a valid will, nor that he then have as strong mind as he formerly had. The mind may be debilitated, the memory enfeebled, the understanding weak, the character may be peculiar and eccentric, and he may even want capacity to transact many of the business affairs of life; still it is sufficient if he understands the nature of the business in which he is engaged and when making a will, has a recollection of the property he means to dispose of, the object or objects of his bounty, and how he wishes to dispose of his property.

Milhoan v. Koenig, 196 W.Va. 163, 166, 469 S.E.2d 99, 102 (1996). See generally Alexander M. Meiklejohn, Contractual and Donative Capacity, 39 Case W. Res. L. Rev. 307 (1988–89).

3. The Wilson court found that there was no support for the jury's determination that Jewel Greer lacked capacity even though she suffered from Alzheimer's disease and, within one year of Greer's execution of her will, her caretaker filed a guardianship petition alleging that Greer was incapable of managing her own affairs. Several courts have held that a testator with senile dementia or Alzheimer's disease may still have capacity to execute a will. Is this approach justifiable? See, for example, Schlueter v. Bowers, 994 P.2d 937 (Wyo.2000); Estate of Angle, 2000 WL 33223696 (Pa.Com.Pl.2000); Scholl v. Murphy, 2002 WL 927381 (Del.Ch.2002). But see, Estate of Washburn, 141 N.H. 658, 690 A.2d 1024 (1997) (invalidating will in favor of caretaker on evidence that at time will was executed testator was suffering from Alzheimer's disease and no longer recognized close relatives).

In other cases, courts have upheld testator's capacity to make a will even *after* a guardian or conservator has been appointed to manage testator's affairs. See, e.g., Estate of Berg, 783 N.W.2d 831 (S.D. 2010); Lucero v. Lucero, 118 N.M. 636, 884 P.2d 527 (N.M.App.1994). Why would a court permit a testator to execute a will after a determination that testator was not capable of managing her own affairs?

4. Should testator's will itself be relevant in determining testator's capacity? Suppose Dr. Marshall's will had left $20,000 to charitable organizations, and divided the remainder of his estate equally among his daughters. If the daughters had contested, in order to invalidate the charitable devise, would the jury have concluded that Dr. Marshall lacked capacity? If the jury had found no capacity, would the court have upheld the jury verdict?

Did the Wilson court view the dispositive provisions of Jewel Greer's will as relevant to the capacity determination? Should it have?

5. Testator, a woman who appeared "entirely reasonable and normal" in her dealings with the outside world—including her lawyer and her bank—wrote numerous memos and comments in the margins of books indicating a hatred of men. The memos indicated that "she looked forward to the day when women would bear children without the aid of men, and all males would be put to death at birth." For several years, she worked as a volunteer for the National Women's Party, and her will left her entire estate to the party—cutting out her closest relatives, cousins with whom she had very little contact. Should the will be invalidated for lack of capacity? See In re Strittmater's Estate, 140 N.J.Eq. 94, 53 A.2d 205 (1947) (invalidating will).

Would your answer be different if testator had been survived by a sister and a brother, and had left her entire estate to her sister? If she had left all of her money to the Republican party? Would the Strittmater case have been decided the same way had it arisen in 2011 instead of 1947?

Incapacity litigation was sometimes used in the antebellum south to invalidate wills of decedents who left property to their slave mistresses. See Kevin Noble Maillard, The Color of Testamentary Freedom, 62 S.M.U. L. Rev. 1783 (2009).

6. ***Lucid Intervals.*** In many capacity cases, the proponent of the will tries to rebut evidence of incapacity by showing that even if testator often lacked capacity, testator executed the will during a "lucid interval"—a period during which testator did have sufficient understanding to make a will.

Daley v. Boroughs, 310 Ark. 274, 835 S.W.2d 858 (1992), is illustrative. The trial court had upheld testator's will against a capacity challenge. The Arkansas Supreme Court summarized the medical evidence:

> It is true that the medical records for the previous three days refer to the testator's confusion and disorientation and his need to be restrained. It is further true that the charge nurse, Margaret Townsend, questioned the testator's competency during this period, but she was not on duty on August 21. Dr. Lisa Bishop testified that the testator had trouble following commands and was confused, though she also was not tending the testator the night he executed the will and admitted that she did not know if he was competent at that time. The testimony of Dr. Geisle Urrutibeheity and Dr. Robert Searcy may also cast doubt on the testator's competency, but their testimony is not conclusive on this point. Dr. Urrutibeheity observed the testator two hours after he signed the new will and would offer no opinion at trial as to his competency when he made the will. Dr. Searcy never actually saw the testator and, though he posited a theory of incompetency based on the incomplete medical records, he admitted the possibility of a lucid interval, and that eyewitness accounts would have validity.

Id. at 285, 835 S.W.2d at 864. In spite of the medical evidence, the court upheld the will, relying on testimony of lay witnesses, combined with the possibility of a lucid interval. See also Will of Buckten, 178 A.D.2d 981, 578 N.Y.S.2d 754 (1991).

Justifications for the Capacity Requirement

One justification for invalidating the will of a person who lacks capacity is that the will does not reflect testator's "true" desires—the desires testator would have had were it not for testator's "illness". Is that justification coherent? In Dr. Marshall's case, wasn't Dr. Marshall defined by his peculiarities? Would it be possible to fathom what Dr. Marshall would have been like—and what he would have wanted—without his mental illness?

Does the notion that we should give effect only to testator's "true" desires make more sense when testator's behavior changed significantly in the period before testator executed the will, due to Alzheimer's disease or rapidly progressing senile dementia? See generally Warren F. Gorman, Testamentary Capacity in Alzheimer's Disease, 4 Elder L.J. 225 (1996).

Another justification for requiring capacity rests on the notion that family members may be entitled to an inheritance—either because they have relied on the prospect of inheritance, or because they have developed expectations about inheritance which ought not to be disappointed unless testator has a rational basis for disinheriting them. Is this justification more persuasive? If accepted explicitly, would it undermine testamentary freedom altogether? See Ronald Chester, Less Law, But More Justice?: Jury Trials and Mediation as Means of Resolving Will Contests, 37 Duq. L. Rev. 173 (1999) (arguing that "despite the common law focus on the mind of the testator, the proper inquiry in will contests goes to the fairness of the resulting distribution, particularly as it effects children"); Melanie B. Leslie, Enforcing Family Promises: Reliance, Reciprocity and Relational Contract, 77 N. C. L. Rev. 551 (1999) (arguing that courts adjudicating will contests look closely at the quality of the relationship between testator and the disinherited family member to determine whether the relationship gave rise to implicit duties and understandings contractual in nature).

Standing to Contest

In Barnes v. Marshall, testator's daughter—an heir—contested his will. Typically, testator's heirs, and any beneficiaries who would take larger amounts under prior wills, have standing to contest. That is, people with a financial interest in invalidating the last will have standing to contest the will. Suppose, however, a beneficiary has a contingent interest in a prior will, and a more certain, but smaller, interest in the challenged will. Does the beneficiary have standing to contest? Cf. Ames v. Reeves, 553 So.2d 570 (Ala.1989).

Jurisdictions divide about the right of an administrator or executor under a prior will to contest a subsequently executed will. Trustees under prior wills generally can contest because they have a financial interest as title holders. Creditors generally have no standing to contest, because the contest will not affect the size of the estate. Courts divide, however, about whether the creditors of an heir, or of the beneficiary of a prior will, have standing to contest. See Note, 50 Notre Dame Law. 309 (1974).

Proving Incapacity

The Role of the Jury. As Barnes v. Marshall indicates, courts treat testamentary capacity as a question of fact. In most states, juries decide capacity questions. Juries are notoriously sympathetic to disinherited relatives. For an empirical study, see Jeffrey A. Schoenblum, Will Contests—An Empirical Study, 22 Real Prop., Prob. & Tr. J. 607 (1987) (concluding that contestants prevail far more often before juries than before judges).

It is easy to understand why juries favor contestants. Close family members appear before them, putting their best foot forward. The testator, by contrast, is dead, and not available to explain why she has chosen to disinherit close family members.

When a jury finds that testator lacks capacity, what recourse is available to the proponents of the will? In theory, anyway, they cannot simply argue that the jury reached the wrong conclusion on the evidence. Instead, they will have to argue that there was no evidence to support the jury verdict, or in other words, that "reasonable jurors could not have differed" as to testator's capacity.

As Barnes v. Marshall illustrates, this argument may sometimes be a hard argument to make. On the other hand, the Wilson v. Lane court was persuaded. The dissenting opinion, omitted here, argued that the majority failed to apply this standard correctly. Do you agree?

In some states, proponents may be able to argue that the jury's verdict was "against the great weight and preponderance" of the evidence. See, e.g., Gum v. Gum, 1996 WL 112155 (Tex.App.1996). Alternatively, they can take two other avenues pursued by the lawyers in Barnes v. Marshall: they can argue that the trial court improperly admitted certain testimony, or they can argue that the trial court issued improper instructions to the jury. Note that these approaches may only entitle proponents to a new trial, not to a judgment admitting the will to probate—although appellate courts often find a way to direct a verdict for proponents.

Note also that some states—California is a notable example—ban juries from will contest cases.

Burden of Proof. Courts differ about who bears the burden of proof on the capacity issue. Some states hold that the proponents of the will bear the burden of proving capacity. See, e.g., Keel v. Keel, 1998 WL 34032494 (Miss.App.1998); Estate of Washburn, 141 N.H. 658, 690 A.2d 1024 (1997). Others hold that the contestants bear the burden of proving incapacity. See, e.g., Singelman v. Singelmann, 273 Ga. 894, 548 S.E.2d 343 (2001); Estate of Flaherty, 446 N.W.2d 760 (N.D.1989). Uniform Probate Code § 3–407 provides that contestants have both the initial burden of proof and the ultimate burden of persuasion on issues of incapacity.

Suppose a testator executes a valid self-proving affidavit along with her will. Does the affidavit create a presumption of capacity? See Milum v. Marsh, 53 S.W.3d 234 (Mo.App.2001) (holding that a self-proving affidavit creates a presumption of testamentary capacity); Estate of Sullivan, 1998 WL 842263 (Tex.App.1998) (stating that even when will proponent produces self-proving affidavit, "the burden of persuasion on the issue of testamentary capacity never shifts from the proponent").

Lay Witnesses. Incapacity cases frequently turn on testimony of witnesses who have no legal or medical expertise. Many testators will not have been examined by physicians or psychologists in the time period surrounding will execution, so that lay testimony about testator's behavior may be the most persuasive evidence about testator's capacity. Such evidence is routinely admitted. In fact, in one recent case the court upheld a trial court's determination that the testator had testamentary capacity even though all expert witnesses testified that capacity was lacking, and the only witnesses to testify that testator had capacity were lay witnesses. See Estate of Zsigo, 2000 WL 33421334 (Mich.App.2000). The testimony of lay witnesses is subject to the limitation discussed in Barnes: the witness may not state a conclusion about testator's capacity without relating the facts on which the conclusion is based.

Medical Testimony. As Barnes v. Marshall and Wilson v. Lane illustrate, medical testimony is often critical in litigation over testamentary capacity. In broad terms, medical testimony is of two types: testimony by physicians who examined decedent, and testimony by physicians who didn't.

In the Marshall case, Dr. Charles Rolwing had examined testator in 1940 and again in the months before testator's death in 1968. If the question at hand was Dr. Marshall's capacity at the time he executed his will and codicils in 1968, why was Dr. Rolwing's testimony about Dr. Marshall's condition in 1940 relevant? What basis does the court offer for sustaining admission of testimony so remote in time from execution of the will? When a physician has examined testator close to the time of will execution, the physician's testimony is always relevant and admissible.

In Wilson v. Lane, Jewel's physician had written a letter one year before Jewel executed her will, which stated that Jewel was suffering from dementia. The jury must have found this evidence persuasive. Why wasn't the letter sufficient to convince the court to uphold the jury's verdict that Jewel lacked capacity?

Suppose the physician has not examined the testator during the testator's lifetime. What role should the physician's testimony play? In both Barnes and Wilson, the trial courts admitted the testimony of physicians who formed opinions based solely on testator's records and/or the evidence related by the other witnesses at trial. Suppose one of these expert witnesses had reached his conclusions not based on the testimony of witnesses at trial but based on interviews with some of testator's acquaintances who did not testify at trial. Would the expert's conclusions have been admissible? Would the expert have been entitled to testify about the facts on which he based his conclusions? See Brunner v. Brown, 480 N.W.2d 33 (Iowa 1992) (holding that expert who did not examine testator was entitled to state opinions based on interviews, but not to testify about the contents of the interviews, because statements made by the parties interviewed were inadmissible hearsay); Estate of Berg, 783 N.W.2d 831 (S.D. 2010) (holding that trial court properly considered, but gave little credence to, medical testimony by physicians who had never examined testator during his lifetime).

What if the only evidence of incapacity is medical testimony by a physician who never examined testator? Should that testimony be sufficient to overcome a motion for summary judgment, or for directed verdict? That issue arose in Estate of Van Patten, 215 A.D.2d 947, 627 N.Y.S.2d 141 (1995), where the court held that this evidence was insufficient to create a triable issue of fact regarding whether testator had capacity. How difficult do you think it would be for a lawyer to find a physician willing to testify, based on hypothetical facts, that a dead testator lacked testamentary capacity? Does your answer suggest why the court reached its conclusion in the Van Patten case?

* * *

In Barnes v. Marshall and Wilson v. Lane, contestants sought to prove that testators lacked all capacity to write a will. In other cases, contestants seek to prove that even if testator generally had capacity to conduct everyday affairs, testator was plagued by an "insane delusion" which renders the will invalid. Consider the following case:

Dougherty v. Rubenstein

Court of Special Appeals of Maryland, 2007.
172 Md.App. 269, 914 A.2d 184.

■ EYLER, J.

The "insane delusion rule" of testamentary capacity came into being almost 200 years ago, as the invention of British jurists in *Dew v. Clark*,

162 Eng. Rep. 410 (Prerog. 1826). The rule was devised to cover a gap in the existing law, which held that "idiots and persons of non-sane memory" could not make wills, *see* 34 & 35 Hen. 7, ch. 5 (1534), but accepted as valid the will of a testator "who knew the natural objects of his or her bounty, the nature and extent of his or her property, and could make a 'rational' plan for disposition, but who nonetheless was as crazy as a March hare[.]" Eunice L. Ross & Thomas J. Reed, *Will Contests* § 6:11 (2d. (1999)).

In the *Dew* case, a father insisted that his grown daughter, who by all accounts was a well-behaved, sweet, and docile person, was the devil incarnate. The father's wife had died in childbirth, ...

By the time his daughter was 8 or 9 years old, the father spoke of her only as wicked, having vices not possible of a girl that young, depraved in spirit, vile, of unequaled depravity, deceitful, and violent in temper. He told others that she was a child of the devil and a "special property of Satan." *Id.* at 426. When the child came to live with him, he treated her as a servant and physically tortured her.

In 1818, the father made a will that disinherited his daughter. Three years later, he was the subject of a writ "*de lunatico inquirendo*" and was declared by a court of chancery to be of unsound mind. He died later that year.

In a caveat proceeding by the daughter, the evidence showed that the daughter was known by all for her good disposition and that the father had boasted to others that he lavished his daughter with love and material items, when the exact opposite was true. The probate court found that, although in 1818, when the will was made, the father's behavior was usual in all respects, except toward his daughter, his warped thinking about her was a delusion that "did and could only proceed from, and be founded in, insanity." *Dew, supra,* 162 Eng. Rep. at 430. The court further found that the father's "partial insanity" or "monomania"—insanity about a particular subject—about the evil nature of his daughter had caused him to disinherit her. On that basis, the court held that the father had been without testamentary capacity when he made his will, and set the will aside.

* * *

In the case before us, James J. Dougherty, IV ("Jay"), the appellant, invoked the insane delusion rule before the Circuit Court for Harford County, sitting as the Orphans' Court, in an effort to set aside the June 9, 1998 Will of his father, James J. Dougherty, III ("James"), the decedent, which disinherited him. Jay is James's only child. According to Jay, James's Will was the product of an insane delusion that Jay had stolen his money. The Will named James's sister, Janet C. Rubenstein, the appellee, personal representative ("PR") of James's estate and bequeathed virtually all of James's assets to Rubenstein and his two other sisters, Elizabeth J. Hippchen and Dorothy D. Schisler. The estate was comprised mainly of

James's house, valued at about $200,000. James died on October 29, 2004, at age 59, of congestive heart failure. On December 10, 2004, Jay filed a petition for judicial probate in the Circuit Court for Harford County, sitting as the Orphans' Court, asking that he be named PR of the Estate, in place of Rubenstein, and that the Will not be admitted into probate. He filed a list of interested persons that included his three paternal aunts. On December 14, 2004, Rubenstein delivered a copy of James's Will to the Register of Wills.

* * *

The evidence, viewed in a light most favorable to the verdict, showed the following.

* * *

On October 26, 1990, James executed a Last Will and Testament that appointed Rubenstein as PR and left his estate to Jay.

Throughout the 1990's, James's health deteriorated due, in large part, to alcohol abuse.[1] On several occasions, he experienced breathing difficulties that necessitated a trip to the emergency room. Eventually, he developed a dependency on certain prescription narcotics. At one time, he was admitted to an in-patient substance abuse program, but left before completing it.

* * *

The chain of events most immediately relevant to the issue on appeal began on December 9, 1997, when James suffered a minor stroke and was admitted to Fallston General Hospital. He was diagnosed with congestive heart failure and dilated cardiomyopathy (an enlarged heart caused by alcohol abuse). During the hospitalization, James often was disoriented and confused and had trouble expressing himself and understanding what was being said to him. He was rarely oriented to where he was or what day or time it was.

On December 18, 1997, the doctors at Fallston General transferred James to Harford Memorial Hospital's psychiatric unit for evaluation. James's confused state of mind and inability to communicate persisted during his stay at Harford Memorial. His speech was garbled. He was observed to be prone to confabulation and paranoia.

Linda Freilich, M.D., an internist, was in charge of James's medical care during his Harford Memorial admission. She diagnosed him with dementia. Dr. Freilich and a second doctor, Lakshmi P. Baddela, M.D., executed "Physician's Certificate of Disability" affidavits, attesting that James was suffering from dementia, that the condition was "lifelong" or "permanent," and that:

> [D]ue to the present condition of dementia, he is without sufficient capacity to consent to the appointment of a guardian of his person and

1. There was testimony that James was in the habit of drinking one to two bottles of gin a day.

property and affairs or to consent to the care and confinement of his person or the management of his property and affairs[.]

Dr. Freilich recommended that James be placed in a nursing home. Jay and his wife Christy decided instead to place him in the Cantler's Personal Care Home ("Cantler Home"), which the doctors referred to as a boarding home. James adamantly objected, insisting that he be returned to his own house to live.

On January 5, 1998, James was discharged from Harford Memorial and was transported to the Cantler Home. There, he was assigned a small private bedroom with access to a common area and to a bathroom that he shared with three other residents. The other residents of the Cantler Home were considerably older than James, who was 52.

By all accounts, James was miserable at the Cantler Home. He complained incessantly to his sisters, his mother, his friends, and Jay and Christy about being there. He told his sisters that he did not have access to the telephone because it was located in a locked area of the home. When Richard Hodges, an old friend, visited James at the Cantler Home, the first thing James said was that he wanted help to "get out." James told him that the owners of the home kept the residents locked downstairs, even for meals. James said he had asked Jay and Christy to "get me out of here," but they would not, because they wanted "to keep me here."

James's sisters and his mother visited him at the Cantler Home and were disturbed by the conditions they saw. James was in a small area sitting on a hard chair. The first thing he said when they walked in was, "Get me out of here before I go crazy like the rest of them." One of the sisters sat on a chair not realizing it was covered with urine from another boarder.

Every other day, Jay tried to visit James at the Cantler Home. James "wanted nothing to do with [him]," however, because James was angry that Jay had placed him in the home instead of letting him move back to his own house. About a week after James moved into the Cantler Home, Jay and Christy left for an annual five-day ski trip with Christy's family. While they were away, Rubenstein removed James from the Cantler Home and returned him to his house.

When Jay and Christy returned from their trip, they learned that James was back at home. They went to see him. Jay had started handling his father's financial affairs when James was admitted to the hospital, and therefore was in possession of all of James's financial records. Jay and Christy brought the financial records with them because James "needed to take [them] back over." James lashed out at Jay, accusing him of stealing his money and saying that, to James, Jay "didn't exist." Jay tried to show James the financial records, to prove that nothing had been stolen, but James would not look at the records or listen to what Jay had to say.

Over the next few weeks, Jay tried to reason with James, but James ignored him. He insisted that Jay had stolen money from him. James told

Jay, "As far as I'm concerned, you are dead." That was the last time the two saw each other.

On January 23, 1998, James executed a new Power of Attorney appointing Rubenstein as his attorney-in-fact. A week later, James came under the care of Richard DeSantis, M.D., for whom Rubenstein was working as a secretary. Dr. DeSantis is an internist and endocrinologist. For the next two years, Dr. DeSantis treated James's heart condition. According to Dr. DeSantis, James did not exhibit any symptoms of dementia aside from some minor speech difficulties, which could have been caused by his stroke.

In late spring of 1998, James met with Ed Seibert, a lawyer and longtime friend, and asked him to draft a new will for him. There was no evidence that anyone encouraged or urged James to see a lawyer or assisted him in doing so. James went to Seibert's office by himself.

Seibert testified that, when he and James met, James's demeanor was "just as lucid as you and I." He described his conversation with James as follows:

> It seemed to be perfectly normal up to a point. The point I am talking about has to do with the antipathy he generated or seemed to be suffering toward his son.
>
> I told him, Look—he didn't want any part of his son in the Will. At that time I said, [']Look, [James], you should consider this twice. Don't leave him out. Leave him something. Put his name in it. Do something. You can't, because he is your only heir, really.[']
>
> So I did admonish him about that, but he was bound and determined to leave [Jay] out altogether. . . . I wanted to know why, and all he told me was that his son had cleaned out his bank account.
>
> I know nothing about how that was done. I am just saying what he told me. [Jay] also had placed him somewhere where he was virtually in a prison and he couldn't get out, and it was a terrible thing for him, and it affected him badly. So he didn't want [Jay] remotely mentioned, or even indirectly referred to in that Will. So I did what he asked me to do.

On June 9, 1998, James returned to Seibert's office to execute his new Will. Seibert's daughter, Heather, and his daughter-in-law, Susanne Reising, signed as witnesses. Both described James's demeanor that day as normal. According to Seibert, from what he saw, there was no reason to think that James was not competent to make his Will or that anyone had exerted undue influence over him to get him to change his Will.

From 1998 until his death in 2004, James lived alone. There was much conflicting testimony about his mental state during those years. The sisters, a nephew, and several family friends testified that James's mental state improved dramatically once he left the Cantler Home and that, from then on, he essentially cared for himself. Two family friends and Jay's stepfather testified that James was not the same person he had been before the late 1997 hospitalizations, and that he required considerable outside assistance in his daily activities. The evidence showed that, during this time period, James drove a car, wrote his own checks, and dressed and groomed himself. Several witnesses testified that James devoted time to his favorite hobby of flying model airplanes.

James complained to almost all of his friends and family members that Jay had stolen his money. Fred Visnaw, the son of a close friend of James, witnessed many conversations between his own father and James about James's belief that Jay had stolen money from him. On three occasions, Visnaw's father tried to reason with James about these thoughts, but James's mind was made up. On one occasion, Visnaw himself tried to intervene with James on Jay's behalf, to no avail.

Another of James's friends, Hodges, testified that James told him he was going to "cut [Jay] out" because Jay had stolen from him. Two of James's sisters, Rubenstein and Schisler, also testified that they were aware that James thought that Jay had stolen money from him. The parties stipulated, however, that there was absolutely no evidence that Jay had ever actually stolen any money from James.

James also continued to complain to many of his friends and family members that Jay had put him in the Cantler Home against his wishes. He described the Cantler Home as a prison. He believed that Jay had sent him there to live permanently.

James died on October 29, 2004, never having reconciled with his son. Jay was not notified of his father's death. There was no obituary published. Jay learned of his father's death through a friend, in early December of 2004.

Drs. Freilich and DeSantis each testified at trial and opined about James's mental state in the months before and after June 1998, when the Will was executed. Dr. Freilich opined that James was suffering from dementia; Dr. DeSantis opined that he was not.

* * *

The judge ruled from the bench. He found that when James was a patient at Harford Memorial in late 1997–early 1998, he clearly "had no capacity to execute a Will." The judge rejected Dr. Freilich's opinion, however, that James had dementia and that it was permanent and progressive. He found that, after James was released from the hospital, in early January 1998, he improved substantially, and was able to care for himself. He concluded that James's recovery and ability to take care of himself for six years before he died were inconsistent with a diagnosis of permanent and progressive dementia; and that Dr. Freilich probably had mistaken the acute effects of the stroke and alcohol withdrawal for dementia.

The judge further found that, when James executed the Will, on June 9, 1998, he "was lucid, he was coherent, he understood the extent of his assets and the object of his bounty, except for the [possible] issue of [an] insane delusion[.]" He then explained his understanding of that issue:

> Was this Will the product of an insane delusion? Even if [James] was competent by being coherent and lucid, if the Will was the product of an insane delusion, then the Will is invalid. Here [James] had the belief that Jay stole from him, and if that was an insane, untrue delusion, that would, I think, invalidate the June 1998 Will that disinherited his son, Jay.
>
> *Under the law that's been quoted to me and I have consulted, the delusion, or the wrong impression, ... the incorrect fact must be the product of a mental disease.*

(Emphasis added.)

The judge reiterated that he could not accept Dr. Freilich's opinion about dementia and therefore "can't go on and then say [James's] irrational belief about his son's theft was the product of a mental disease."....

DISCUSSION

The sole issue for decision in this appeal is whether the trial judge erred in concluding that the Will was not the product of an insane delusion on the part of the testator.

* * *

A testator's "insane delusion," also called "monomania," is in the law a type of unsoundness of mind that will invalidate his will, for lack of capacity, if the delusion produced the disposition made in the will. The testator's delusion must have been *insane* and his will must have been a consequence of the insane delusion, however. *Benjamin v. Woodring*, 268 Md. 593, 601, 303 A.2d 779 (1973). *See also Sellers v. Qualls,* 206 Md. 58, 66, 110 A.2d 73 (1954) (holding that testatrix's delusion that her sister tried to poison her, even if insane, did not control the making of her will and therefore will would not be set aside on that basis); *Brown v. Fidelity Trust Co.*, 126 Md. 175, 182–83, 94 A. 523 (1915) (holding that even if grantor of trust was operating under an insane delusion when she disposed of certain property, the trust would not be set aside because there was no evidence that the trust resulted from the delusion).

The Court of Appeals has said that an "insane delusion" is "a belief in things impossible, or a belief in things possible, but so improbable under the surrounding circumstances, that no man of sound mind could give them credence." *Johnson, supra*, 105 Md. at 85–86. It also has defined the term to mean "a false belief for which there is no reasonable foundation ... concerning which [the testator's] mind is not open to permanent correction through argument or evidence." *Doyle v. Rody*, 180 Md. 471, 479, 25 A.2d 457 (1942). Eccentricity, peculiar beliefs (such as in spiritualism or healing powers), and hostility or aversion to one relative or another are not, standing alone, insane delusions. *See Brown v. Ward*, 53 Md. 376 (1880) (testatrix who spoke to spirits, believed they could heal diseases, did not believe in the Bible, and despised some of her relatives was not suffering from an insane delusion when she made her will).

"Insane delusion" or "monomania" insanity is not a general defect of the mind. It is an insanity directed to something specific, that is, a particular person or thing. A testator can be laboring under the influence of an insane delusion while otherwise acting and appearing competent. . . .

* * *

Jay . . . argues that the application of the insane delusion rule to the evidence adduced at trial compelled a finding that James disinherited him due to an insane delusion that Jay had stolen his money. Jay points out that there was no evidence that he had stolen James's money (or that any of James's money had been stolen), as the parties stipulated, and therefore James's belief plainly was false; that no amount of reasoning could get James to change his mind about his false belief, and James's mind was not open to being changed, even by records that would have shown conclusively that no money was missing; that the false belief arose soon after a hospitalization during which James was unable to understand what was being said to him or to communicate and was disoriented; that while James's functional abilities improved over time, after he was discharged from the Cantler Home, he could not overcome the false belief that Jay had stolen his money; and all of the evidence, and especially that of Mr. Siebert, a disinterested person, showed that James left nothing to Jay in his Will because he was convinced that Jay already had all of his money.

Beginning with the last point, we note that the orphans' court indeed found that James's false belief that Jay had stolen from him had caused James to disinherit Jay. The court observed that James also was angry with Jay for moving him into the Cantler Home but that "that was not a false belief"; and that, if the false belief (about stealing money) was an insane delusion "then it's going to invalidate the Will. If it is not, then the Will stands, given the other findings I made." So, the court in fact found, as Jay argues it was compelled to find, that the delusion about his having stolen money prompted James to disinherit him.

We disagree, however, that the law of insane delusions compelled a finding by the orphans' court that James's delusion that Jay stole his money was an *insane* delusion. To be sure, James's delusion shared many of the characteristics of the insane delusions in the *Johnson*, *Doyle*, and *Benjamin* cases. James and Jay were close relatives, and Jay would be expected to have been the object of James's bounty. James came suddenly to believe that Jay had harmed him by stealing his money, when there was no evidence to support that belief, and he refused to hear the evidence that would refute it. James's false belief did not subside, but became central to his thinking about Jay, causing hostility and aversion.

This case is factually distinguishable [from precedent]. In those cases, there simply was no explanation, whether or not rational, for the testator's sudden false belief, and therefore the delusion only could have come from within the testator's own mind. In this case, the delusion entered James's mind when he was a resident, not by choice, of the Cantler Home, which for him was a terrible experience that he blamed completely upon Jay. As James saw it, he was confined to a home similar to a nursing home, without privacy or access to a telephone, in the company of residents who were enfeebled by old age, and with no hope of being let out. The witnesses who testified about having visited James in the Cantler Home confirmed that the accommodations were insufficient for him and that he felt like he had been imprisoned—and that he was of the view that Jay had failed him by forcing him in and by not coming to his aid to get out.

From the time he arrived at the Cantler Home forward, James was convinced that Jay had betrayed him by not letting him go home instead. James's delusion that Jay also had betrayed him by stealing his money was a generalization, albeit not a logical one, drawn from his true belief that Jay had been the decision-maker who had kept him in the Cantler Home until his sisters rescued him. In essence, this is what the trial judge found from the evidence: that James's delusion was an outgrowth of a stubborn conviction that Jay had "done something wrong" by "imprisoning" him at the Cantler Home. Although it was false, and it prompted James to disinherit Jay, it was not an inexplicable delusion that only could have come into being as the product of an insane mind.

The facts as found by the orphans' court did not compel a finding that James was suffering from an insane delusion, under the law of testamentary capacity. The court's finding that James was suffering from a delusion that Jay had stolen his money, but that the delusion was not an insane delusion, was a reasonable interpretation of the evidence. Accordingly, we shall not disturb it on appeal.

NOTES, QUESTIONS, AND PROBLEMS

1. Did the parties argue over whether Jay had stolen his father's money? If Jay did not steal the money, why wasn't James Dougherty suffering from an insane delusion?

2. As we have seen, courts are reluctant to reform wills based on alleged mistakes of fact—largely because all of us are laboring under mistakes of fact every day. If courts invalidated wills whenever a contestant could prove that testator had a mistaken belief at the time the will was executed, few wills would survive.

How is an insane delusion different from a mistake of fact? Shouldn't courts be equally hesitant to entertain insane delusion cases?

3. Quentin Quarterback had a sexual relationship with Priscilla Pornstar. Pornstar later gave birth to a daughter, Angel. Quarterback insists that Angel is not his daughter, and leaves Angel nothing in his will, instead dividing his estate between his wife and various charities. Can Angel set aside the will on the theory that Quarterback executed the will while plagued by an insane delusion? How should Quarterback's estate be distributed in each of the following circumstances:

(a) Angel proves, by DNA testing completed after Quarterback's death, that Quarterback was in fact her father.

(b) Angel confronts Quarterback, during his lifetime, with DNA evidence establishing that Quarterback was her father; Quarterback insists that the evidence was fabricated or wrong, and leaves Angel nothing in his will.

(c) In his will, Quarterback acknowledges the existence of the DNA tests, expresses the view that such tests are inaccurate, and writes "even if Angel Pornstar were my daughter, I would not want her to share in my estate because of the headaches she caused me during my lifetime."

(d) In his will, Quarterback acknowledges that Angel is his daughter, but expressly disinherits her.

The belief by testators that their children were sired by someone else is a staple of insane delusion cases. See, e.g., Estate of Flaherty, 446 N.W.2d 760 (N.D.1989) (upholding jury verdict of insane delusion).

4. Another frequent "insane delusion" is the belief that testator's spouse has been unfaithful. Does the existence of a "fact" which supports testator's belief preclude an insane delusion claim? How significant must the fact be?

Suppose, for instance, testator had repeatedly told her friends that her husband had been unfaithful, based largely on a birthday card sent to her husband by a woman friend. Testator also became suspicious because her husband insisted on answering the telephone whenever it rang. If testator's will cuts out her husband, should her husband be entitled to set aside the will as the product of an insane delusion? Cf. In re Honigman's Will, 8 N.Y.2d 244, 168 N.E.2d 676, 203 N.Y.S.2d 859 (1960) (upholding jury's finding of insane delusion).

Should it matter that the husband would be entitled to assert elective share rights? Should the effect on the will beneficiaries matter? Consider two situations:

(a) testator's will leaves all of her property to her children by a prior marriage; and

(b) testator's will leaves all of her property to her brothers; testator died childless.

Which is a more likely case for a finding of insane delusion, and why?

5. Other insane delusion claims have arisen when testator believed that some of her relatives were trying to kill her, see M.I. Marshall & Ilsley Trust Co. v. McCannon, 188 Ariz. 562, 937 P.2d 1368 (App.1996), when testator believed that some of her relatives were trying to commit her to a nursing home, see Estate of Bonjean, 90 Ill.App.3d 582, 45 Ill.Dec. 872, 413 N.E.2d 205 (1980), or when testator believed that one of her children was stealing from her, see Estate of Turner, 56 A.D.3d 863, 866 N.Y.S.2d 429 (2008).

* * *

When an elderly or infirm potential client walks into a lawyer's office and asks the lawyer to prepare a will, does the lawyer have an obligation to ascertain whether the potential client has capacity to execute a will? Consider the following case:

Gonsalves v. Superior Court

Court of Appeal of California, First District, 1993.
19 Cal.App.4th 1366, 24 Cal.Rptr.2d 52.

■ Perley, J.:

In this writ proceeding, we consider the duty of an attorney to determine the testamentary capacity of a client seeking to make a will.

FACTS—PROCEDURAL HISTORY

On June 1, 1992, Dolores F. Picardo, real party herein, filed a complaint arising from the fact that she had been disinherited as beneficiary of the estate of her aunt, Dorothy Dvorak. The estate was left to Colleen Ganaye through a trust and will drafted by Attorney Linda M. Gonsalves and executed by Dvorak on June 7, 1991. In the . . . cause of action for professional negligence . . ., real party alleged that with a reasonable amount of diligence, petitioners [attorney Gonsalves, her partner, Paul Kozachenko, and the law firm of Gonsalves & Kozachenko—eds.] would have known of the lack of testamentary capacity of the deceased and should have refused to permit the execution of the documents. Gonsalves either deliberately conspired with Ganaye or negligently acted to defeat real party's right of inheritance.

On May 7, 1993, petitioners filed a motion for summary judgment. They argued (1) that Gonsalves had no reason to doubt Dvorak's testamentary capacity, (2) that they owed no duty to plaintiff and thus could not be liable for professional negligence.... In support of the motion, petitioners filed the declaration of Dr. Smith, the surgeon who had operated on Dvorak for the colon cancer from which Dvorak died in July of 1991. Dr. Smith stated that he treated, Dvorak, a 78–year–old woman, from May 1991 and last saw her in the office on July 8, 1991. "[D]uring this entire time, she was mentally alert and fully mentally competent. She required some pain medication and antinausea medication, but these did not interfere with her mental abilities whatsoever." In a later declaration, Dr. Smith stated he saw Dvorak twice a day between May 22, 1991, and June 7, 1991. Immediately after surgery she suffered from confusion, disorientation and may have experienced hallucinations as a result of pain medication which commonly has that effect. He examined her on June 7, 1991, the day she was discharged and she was "alert, articulate, coherent, capable of understanding and following instructions, and was in full possession of her mental faculties."

Notations in hospital records as to Dvorak's condition read: "June 3, 1991 10:50 a.m.: [discharge planning note:] 'I spoke with patient this am—she was independent and lived alone prior to admission. She stated she would be going to a friend's home and the friend would assist her. We discussed the ostomy.... 'June 4, 1991 4:00 p.m.: [social services note: Routine visit by oncology social worker.] Patient is in excellent spirits and expresses pleasant surprise at' easy 'procedures for colostomy management. She feels well trained and capable despite earlier apprehension. She says she is coping well emotionally, relying on her strong religious faith and pleasant memories to dismiss sadness. She looks forward to working with her younger friend, who has become like a daughter or granddaughter to her.' 'June 7, 1991: [Condition Upon Discharge:] Awake, alert, ... ostomy instructions given ... denies pain.' "

In a declaration, petitioner Gonsalves stated that on June 4, 1991, she received a telephone call from Colleen Ganaye, a stranger to her. Ms. Ganaye told her that her friend, Dorothy Dvorak, was hospitalized with terminal cancer and had requested Ms. Ganaye to assist her in setting up an appointment with an attorney to discuss estate planning matters. Ms. Gonsalves telephoned Dvorak in the hospital and set up an appointment for June 5. She met alone with her for about 45 minutes. She was sitting up in her hospital bed and appeared healthy, well-rested and alert. She was coherent and articulate throughout the meeting. She stated that she wanted Ganaye to handle her affairs upon her incapacity and she wanted her to inherit her estate. She told her that her closest living relatives were her niece, Dolores Picardo, and a nephew. She stated that she did not want to leave anything to Ms. Picardo. She wanted to include disinheritance language in her estate planning documents because she felt that Ms. Picardo might try to contest the will. Gonsalves asked Dvorak if she wished to state her intentions on videotape and Dvorak thought that would be helpful. In accordance with the instructions, Gonsalves prepared a durable power of attorney, a living trust and a pour-over will. The documents were executed on June 7, 1991. The event took place at Ganaye's home while Ganaye was at work. The only persons present were Kristine Rosales, Mary Caldwell, Dvorak and Gonsalves.

Caldwell confirmed in deposition that Dvorak appeared "bright, cheerful, talkative, alert, and responsive." She also mentioned that Colleen Ganaye had befriended Dvorak many years before and that she had visited Ganaye's house on numerous occasions when Dvorak was present.

Rosales also confirmed that Dvorak was in good spirits. Because of the videotaping, "Dorothy kind of joked about does my hair look okay, am I going to look okay when somebody looks at this. I want to look nice."

The video tape shows Gonzales asking Dvorak if she intends to leave her property to Ganaye and not to Picardo and if she understands the terms of her will. Dvorak replies affirmatively with an alert, responsive and calm demeanor.

Declarations by real party, real party's daughter, and Carol Dvorak, stepdaughter-in-law of the deceased, emphasized the close relationship of Dvorak and real party, Dvorak's frailties and confusion. Dr. David Berke, personal physician for Dvorak since the mid–1970's, filed a declaration stating that "Dorothy Dvorak has for many years been subject to hallucinations, and during the last year of her life was increasingly depressed." He saw her at an unspecified date at the hospital and observed that she was totally confused and would not be in a position to execute a last will and testament. Based upon his knowledge of Dvorak "for many years, and knowing her condition at and about the time involved, she was subject and could be subjected to undue influence without recognizing the consequences of her act."

Respondent court denied the motion for summary judgment and petitioners filed the instant petition. We issued an alternative writ on September 9, 1993. On September 30, 1993, respondent court granted the motion for summary judgment and entered judgment in favor of petitioners. Although the instant petition is moot, at the request of real party in interest, we will resolve the issues presented on the merits since real party's attorney states that it is his intention to seek appellate review of the order granting summary judgment.

DISCUSSION

DOES AN ATTORNEY WHO FAILS TO INVESTIGATE A CLIENT'S TESTAMENTARY CAPACITY INCUR LIABILITY TO A PERSON DISINHERITED BY THE WILL DRAWN BY THE ATTORNEY?

Since the case of Lucas v. Hamm, it has been settled in California that intended beneficiaries of a will who lose their testamentary rights because of failure of the attorney who drew the will to properly fulfill that attorney's obligations under his or her contract with the testator may recover damages as third party beneficiaries and also on a tort liability theory for breach of duty owed directly to the beneficiaries. (Lucas v. Hamm (1961) 56 Cal.2d 583, 588 [15 Cal.Rptr. 821, 364 P.2d 685]; Heyer v. Flaig (1969) 70 Cal.2d 223, 226 [74 Cal.Rptr. 225, 449 P.2d 161] disapproved on another point in Laird v. Blacker (1992) 2 Cal.4th 606, 617 [7 Cal.Rptr.2d 550, 828 P.2d 691]; Bucquet v. Livingston (1976) 57 Cal.App.3d 914, 921 [129 Cal.Rptr. 514].)

In determining whether to extend liability to such third party beneficiaries, the Supreme Court considered whether the imposition of such liability "would impose an undue burden on the profession" and announced: "We are of the view that the extension of his liability to beneficiaries injured by a negligently drawn will does not place an undue burden on the profession, particularly when we take into consideration that a contrary conclusion would cause the innocent beneficiary to bear the loss." (Lucas v. Hamm, supra, 56 Cal.2d at p. 589.)

The same considerations lead to the conclusion that attorney liability should not be extended in favor of those who are disinherited by the will of a testator without testamentary capacity. First, the disinherited beneficiary in this situation, unlike the beneficiary in the Lucas v. Hamm situation, has a remedy since he or she may contest the probate on the ground of lack of testamentary capacity. Second, such an extension of Lucas v. Hamm would be an intolerable burden to place upon attorneys. It would put an attorney in the position of potential liability to either the beneficiary disinherited if he or she draws the will or the potential beneficiary if he or she refuses to draw the will. Third, the potential for such liability would unjustifiably deny many persons the opportunity to make their wills. Many factors which might suggest a lack of testamentary capacity to some attorneys as well as to those unfamiliar with the law in this area do not denote lack of such capacity. As the court said in Estate of Selb (1948) 84 Cal.App.2d 46, 49 [190 P.2d 277]: "It has been held over and over in this state that old age, feebleness, forgetfulness, filthy personal habits, personal eccentricities, failure to recognize old friends or relatives, physical disability, absent-mindedness and mental confusion do not furnish grounds for holding that a testator lacked testamentary capacity." Even delusions or hallucinations do not show incompetency if not related to the testamentary act. (Estate of Perkins (1925) 195 Cal. 699, 704 [235 P. 45]; see also Estate of Fritschi (1963) 60 Cal.2d 367, 372 [33 Cal.Rptr. 264, 384 P.2d 656], decedent in hospital with fatal cancer; physically weak, disturbed and under heavy dosage of drugs determined to have testamentary capacity.)

The facts of the instant case illustrate the potential problem for the dying testator and his attorney. The declarations filed in this case suggest that had Gonsalves consulted both Dr. Smith and Dr. Berke for an opinion on testamentary capacity, she might have received diametrically opposed opinions. Faced with potential liability to Picardo who she knew would be disinherited, Gonsalves might have declined to draw the will despite her own view that Dvorak had the requisite competence.

The primary duty of the attorney is to the client and is fulfilled if the attorney, convinced of testamentary capacity by his or her own observations and experience with the client, draws the will as requested. We conclude that an attorney who fails to investigate the testamentary capacity of his or her client is not liable in tort to a former beneficiary disinherited by the will drawn by the attorney. The attorney obviously is not liable in contract since the disinherited person is not a third party beneficiary of the contract between attorney and testatrix.

* * *

We agree with petitioners that, as a matter of law, they were entitled to summary judgment. Since respondent court has now granted summary judgment to petitioners, we discharge the alternative writ and deny the petition as moot.

NOTES AND QUESTIONS

1. Does the court in the Gonsalves case suggest that the lawyer bears no responsibility for determining whether the client has capacity to execute the will? If the lawyer is not liable in tort or in contract, should the lawyer simply draft the will, no matter how confused the client might seem?

2. Even if the lawyer would not be liable to the disinherited heir, might the lawyer nevertheless be subject to disciplinary proceedings if the lawyer drafted a will for a clearly incompetent client? How likely is it that a disciplinary committee would take action against a lawyer who drafted a will for an apparently incompetent client?

3. Suppose lawyer Gonsalves believed that testator lacked capacity at the time testator executed the will. Dolores Picardo, testator's niece, contests the will. During the trial, Picardo's lawyer calls Gonsalves to testify, and asks whether, in Gonsalves' judgment, testator had capacity. What should Gonsalves say? Should the possibility of contest act as a constraint on the lawyer when the lawyer is convinced the client does not have capacity?

PROBLEMS

1. Testator's son comes to you and asks you to draft a will for testator. He informs you, accurately, that he is testator's only heir, but that he would prefer if, for tax reasons, testator left her entire estate to his two children. Testator is in a nursing home. When you consult her about her wishes, testator says "I don't understand these legal terms. You decide what is best for me." Testator appears confused, and, during your visit, forgets your name and why you are there. She also appears disoriented in the nursing home. Should you draft the will?

Would this problem—the desire to generate tax advantages for a beneficiary when the testator lacks capacity—be better addressed by authorizing a person to execute a will on behalf of an incapacitated testator? Some jurisdictions now authorize conservators to execute wills on behalf of an incapacitated testator. See Ralph C. Brashier, Policy, Perspective, and the Proxy Will, 61 S.C.L. Rev. 63 (2009).

2. Testator's son tells you that testator, who is currently in a nursing home, wants to draft a new will. When you visit testator to ascertain his wishes, he informs you that he wants to cut out his "no-good daughter", whose name he often forgets. He also tells you that he wants to divide his estate equally between his wife and his son. When you remind him that his wife has been dead for five years, he says "then give it all to my son." Discussion with the nurses at the home reveals that testator asks where he is at least five times a day. Should you draft the will? How, if at all, is this case different from Problem 1?

SECTION II. UNDUE INFLUENCE

When contestants challenge a will based on "undue influence" they argue that the written will does not reflect the testator's "true" intent. The contestants generally argue that the written will reflects the successful effort of a will beneficiary to substitute his own wishes for those of a testator susceptible to the beneficiary's influence. Contestants need not argue that testator lacked capacity to make a will (although contestants often advance undue influence and lack of testamentary capacity as grounds for invalidating the same will).

But what sort of influence is undue? Testators often respond to pressures exerted by potential beneficiaries. Suppose, for instance, testator's son says to her, on numerous occasions, "I'm short of money. I've lost my job and I'm having trouble making ends meet. Please help me out in your will." If testator—a successful businesswoman—responds by leaving her son more money than she leaves her other children, has the son exercised "undue influence?" Of course not. The son may have influenced the mother's testamentary dispositions, but the son's influence has not been "undue"; the mother simply deems her son's financial condition a relevant factor in disposing of her estate, and acts accordingly.

Suppose now that the son's plea is combined with a "threat" of sorts: "if you don't leave me the bulk of your estate, I won't be able to take care of you during your period of illness." If the mother leaves the son the bulk of her estate, will an "undue influence" attack on the mother's will succeed? Remember that the mother and the son could enter into an explicit contract, whereby the son agrees to provide lifetime care in return for the mother's promise to leave him all or part of her estate. If such a contract would be enforceable, is there any reason to invalidate a mother's will when she responds to the son's implicit offer to care for the mother on condition that the mother remember him in her will?

If even a threat does not amount to undue influence, what does? Consider the following case:

Haynes v. First National State Bank of New Jersey

Supreme Court of New Jersey, 1981.
87 N.J. 163, 432 A.2d 890.

■ HANDLER, J.

This is a will contest in which the plaintiffs, two of the decedent's six grandchildren, seek to set aside the probate of their grandmother's will and two related trust agreements. The major issue presented is whether the will is invalid on the grounds of "undue influence" attributable to the fact that the attorney, who advised the testatrix and prepared the testamentary instruments, was also the attorney for the principal beneficiary, the testatrix's daughter, in whom the testatrix had reposed trust, confidence and dependency....

In an unreported opinion upholding the probate of the will and related trusts, the trial court held that the circumstances created a presumption of undue influence but that this presumption had been rebutted by defendants....

* * * [The Appellate Division sustained the Trial Court on this issue] * * *

I

The issues raised by this appeal, particularly whether the contested will was invalid as a result of "undue influence," require a full exposition of the facts.

Mrs. Isabel Dutrow, the testatrix, was the widow of Charles E. Dutrow, an employee of Ralston Purina Co. who had acquired substantial stock in that corporation. Upon his death the stock, aggregating almost eight million dollars, was distributed to his widow and their two daughters, both outright and in trust.

Betty Haynes, one of the daughters of Charles and Isabel Dutrow, came with her two sons to live with her parents in the Dutrow family home in York, Pennsylvania in 1941 while Betty's husband was in military service during World War II. Following Charles Dutrow's death in 1945 and her own divorce, Betty and her sons continued to live with Mrs. Dutrow in York. The relationships between mother and daughter were extremely close, Mrs. Dutrow having deep affection for Betty, as well as her grandsons whom she practically raised. The two boys, however, left the York home sometime around 1968 to the considerable aggravation and disappointment of their grandmother. But Betty remained with her mother until Betty's death in June 1973.

At the time of Betty's death, she had been living with her mother for more than 30 years. Mrs. Dutrow was then 84 years old and suffered from a number of ailments including glaucoma, cataracts and diverticulitis, and had recently broken her hip. Mrs. Dutrow, distraught over the death of her closest daughter and somewhat alienated from the Haynes children, decided to move in with her younger daughter, Dorcas Cotsworth, and Dorcas' husband, John, who had homes in Short Hills and Bay Head, New Jersey. This decision was a reasonable one, freely made by Mrs. Dutrow, who despite her age, physical condition and feelings of despair was and remained an alert, intelligent and commanding personality until the time of her death.

During her lifetime, Mrs. Dutrow executed a great many wills and trust agreements. All of these instruments, as well as those her husband had executed prior to his death, were prepared by the longstanding family attorney, Richard Stevens, of Philadelphia. By June 1967 Stevens had prepared five wills and several codicils for Mrs. Dutrow.

As of the time she moved in with the Cotsworths, Mrs. Dutrow's estate plan reflected a basic disposition to treat the Haynes and the Cotsworth family branches equally. During the last four years of her life, however, while living with daughter Dorcas, Mrs. Dutrow's will went through a series of changes which drastically favored Dorcas and her children while diminishing and excluding the interests of the Haynes brothers. These changes, and their surrounding circumstances, bear most weightily upon the issue of undue influence.

Shortly after moving in with Dorcas, following a conference between her daughter and Stevens, the first of many will and trust changes was made by Mrs. Dutrow on July 25, 1973. Under the new provisions of the will, Mrs. Dutrow's residuary estate was to be divided into two equal trusts, one for Dorcas, the principal of which Dorcas could invade up to certain limits and the other a trust with income to each of the Haynes boys without a power of invasion. A new will and an inter vivos trust with almost identical provisions, including approximately 60,000 shares of Ralston Purina stock, were later executed on November 24, 1973 and December 4, 1973, respectively. Mrs. Dutrow also gave Dorcas 5,000 shares of stock outright to compensate her for the expense of having Mrs. Dutrow live with her.

During the time these instruments were being drawn, Dorcas and her husband, John Cotsworth, began actively to express their views about Mrs. Dutrow's estate plans to Stevens. In a meeting between Stevens, Mrs. Dutrow, and the Cotsworths on November 13, 1973 at the Cotsworth home in Short Hills, John Cotsworth gave Stevens two charts of Mrs. Dutrow's estate which Cotsworth had prepared. According to Stevens' testimony at trial, the import of the charts was to make "substantial outright gifts to the members of the Cotsworth family and smaller gifts to [plaintiffs, the Haynes children]." Stevens further testified that Mrs. Dutrow had told him at this meeting that the pressure upon her by the Cotsworths to change her will was enormous. On November 19, 1973, John Cotsworth wrote Stevens a long letter in which he summarized what he, Cotsworth, saw as Mrs. Dutrow's "objectives" with regard to her estate plans and then detailing in over five pages the calculations as to how these "objectives" could be achieved. An important aspect of his proposal was to deplete substantially the estate to simplify Mrs. Dutrow's "money worries." Cotsworth further noted at the beginning of this letter to Stevens that "[o]ur joint obligation—you and the family—is to accomplish these objectives with minimum tax effects upon the total estate. Obviously you are in a far better position to work out the details than I am, but you appear reluctant to go as fast or as far as I have suggested for reasons that are not clear to us."

Then, on November 26, 1973, Cotsworth proceeded to consult Grant Buttermore, his own lawyer, regarding Mrs. Dutrow's estate plans. Buttermore had been the attorney for the Cotsworth family and the Cotsworth family business, the Berry Steel Corporation, for six to seven years and had provided substantial legal advice concerning the corporation. He had also prepared wills for both Mr. and Mrs. Cotsworth and some of their children. For all intents and purposes, Buttermore can be viewed as having been the family attorney for the Cotsworths.

On November 29, 1973, following the initial contact by her husband, Dorcas Cotsworth went to Buttermore concerning the trust agreement of November 24 that Stevens had prepared for her mother. As a result, Buttermore called Stevens while Dorcas was in his office and discussed the matter of Mrs. Dutrow's domicile. This subject, in addition to a proposal concerning "gifting" by Mrs. Dutrow, had earlier been broached to Buttermore by John Cotsworth. Both lawyers agreed that Mrs. Dutrow's domicile should be changed to New Jersey for tax purposes and Buttermore made the change on the instrument by hand. Later that day Buttermore wrote to Stevens to confirm the results of the call, as well as the fact that the Cotsworths were personally involved in Mrs. Dutrow's estate planning, *viz:*

> We are in the process of reviewing Mrs. Dutrow's estate with her and Mr. and Mrs. Cotsworth along the lines suggested by Mr. Cotsworth in his outline heretofore submitted to you.

Buttermore concluded this letter by relaying Mrs. Dutrow's request to Stevens to provide "a complete list of all [her] assets * * * in order that we may make a proper analysis."

Stevens immediately responded, writing separate letters to Buttermore and Mrs. Dutrow on November 30. He gave Buttermore a skeletal list of Mrs. Dutrow's assets with no detail. At the same time he also undertook to make some technical corrections of Mrs. Dutrow's will, which was executed, as noted, on December 4. In the letter accompanying the will, he mentioned his conversation with Buttermore and his "assumption" that Mrs. Dutrow wanted him to give Buttermore the information he was requesting.

The response to this communication was a letter written to Stevens on December 3, 1973 in Dorcas Cotsworth's handwriting on her personal stationary, and signed by Dorcas and Mrs. Dutrow, which contained the following:

> These are my mother's observations as she sits here besides me—and she insists she is *not* being pressured. . . .
>
> Mother and I have discussed this so often—now she says get it over and let me forget it—as it worries her with everything undone.
>
> * * *
>
> Her desire and intent is to have Dorcas rewarded while alive—to have an Irrevocable Trust set up to let Dorcas have income and right to sprinkle money to Grandchildren when necessary. * * *
>
> When Dorcas dies then the per stirpes takes over. * * *
>
> Mother approves of Mr. Grant Buttermore knowing all details and keeping in this estate.

A meeting of Buttermore and John Cotsworth with Stevens was scheduled for December 13, 1973. Prior to this meeting Buttermore met with Mrs. Dutrow alone, as he testified was his customary practice, "so that I could get the intent directly from * * * the testatrix." During this two hour conference, according to Buttermore, he explained various legal and tax aspects of estate planning to Mrs. Dutrow. He also told her "that intent was much more important and controlled over the other two items, meaning taxation and liquidity." Buttermore also reviewed at length Mrs. Dutrow's assets and her present will and trusts. Among other things, Mrs. Dutrow, according to Buttermore's testimony, said that "her first priority was to make sure she had enough to last during her lifetime," for which purpose Mrs. Dutrow said she would need $26,000 per year. Buttermore also explained to Mrs. Dutrow that the practical effect of the per stirpes disposition of the November 24 trust agreement would be to enable the two plaintiffs, the Haynes brothers, ultimately to "receive twice as much as each of the other grandchildren," to which Mrs. Dutrow responded, according to Buttermore, "I didn't realize that."

Buttermore testified that he told Stevens at the December 13 meeting that Mrs. Dutrow "wanted to go to the per capita basis equally among the grandchildren." Stevens, according to Buttermore, was very skeptical that Mrs. Dutrow wanted to do this and asked Buttermore to doublecheck it with her. Buttermore replied that "[i]n my mind she'd already made that decision after our talk on December the eleventh."

On December 17 and 18, a concerned Stevens wrote Buttermore letters confirming the discussion of December 13, and on December 18, specifically adverted to the possibility of "undue influence." There is no indication in the record that Buttermore responded to Stevens on this matter.

Buttermore, in response to a call from Dorcas Cotsworth, again met alone with Mrs. Dutrow in Short Hills on January 11 to discuss a problem concerning some back dividends. While he was with her, Buttermore, at his own initiative, told her what had happened during his December 13 meeting with Stevens and John Cotsworth and reviewed with her Stevens' letter of December 17 concerning her estate plans. Following that exchange, Buttermore related, Mrs. Dutrow instructed *him* to "draw the papers." Although Stevens had previously asked Buttermore to write him in Vermont, where he was vacationing, if there were any further developments concerning Mrs. Dutrow's estate planning, Buttermore did not do so, apparently believing that Mrs. Dutrow, who complained of Stevens' absence, did not desire or need Stevens to be further involved. Thus, Buttermore, still the Cotsworths' attorney, also stepped in, exclusively, as Mrs. Dutrow's attorney for purposes of planning her estate.

Significantly, at this juncture, drastic changes in Mrs. Dutrow's estate planning materialized. According to Buttermore, he and Mrs. Dutrow then proceeded to discuss in detail her wishes for a new will and trust agreements. Mrs. Dutrow assertedly indicated that she wanted "to leave [her estate] equally * * * between the grandchildren," and did not care about the adverse tax consequence which Buttermore claimed he had explained to her. Buttermore also seemed to minimize the effect of the proposed change allegedly requested by Mrs. Dutrow by pointing out to her that altering the particular trust in question would not accomplish her goals; although all six grandchildren would inherit equally under the particular trust in question, the consequence of other trusts already in existence would be that the two Haynes grandchildren would "still be getting greater in the end" than Mrs. Cotsworth's children. During that meeting, Buttermore also apparently showed Stevens' letter of December 18 concerning undue influence to Mrs. Dutrow.

These discussions resulted in the near total severance of the Haynes children from their grandmother's estate. Assertedly, at Mrs. Dutrow's request, Buttermore promptly prepared two new trust agreements, which provided for the payment of income with full right of invasion of principal to Dorcas Cotsworth during her lifetime and that, upon Dorcas' death, "the then remaining balance in said trust shall be divided equally among settlor's grandchildren." In addition, Mrs. Dutrow's new will provided for the bequest of all her tangible personal property to Dorcas Cotsworth, "or if she does not survive me to my grandchildren who survive me, equally." These instruments were executed by Mrs. Dutrow on January 16, 1974.

On January 19 Buttermore sent Stevens copies of the new instruments along with a letter in which he explained that after going over everything "meticulously with Mrs. Dutrow," the new instruments had been prepared "along the lines we have discussed" and that, in Stevens' absence, Mrs. Dutrow had become "quite upset with the Fidelity Bank and decided that she wanted to immediately revoke" the existing trust agreements and will. Stevens testified to astonishment at the proposed distribution. He also expressed surprise about the provision in both trust agreements, which permitted Dorcas Cotsworth to withdraw the principal each year so that, if exercised, there might be nothing left when she died.

In early May 1974 Buttermore again met with Mrs. Dutrow to make some changes in the trust agreements. The most important change allowed the corporate trustee First National State Bank of New Jersey to distribute principal, "in its sole discretion," to Dorcas Cotsworth and any of Mrs. Dutrow's grandchildren (i.e., plaintiffs as well as Dorcas' children). This was in contrast to the original terms of this trust agreement, as executed by Mrs. Dutrow in January 1974, which allowed for such discretionary distribution by the bank only to Mrs. Cotsworth and her children, not to plaintiffs. According to Buttermore's testimony, this change was clearly Mrs. Dutrow's idea.

On April 24, 1975, Mrs. Dutrow amended the revocable trust agreement and added a codicil to her will in order to add *in terrorem* clauses to each instrument. Both the amendment and the codicil were prepared by Buttermore. At trial, Buttermore said that Mrs. Dutrow had decided to add the clause after reading that J. Paul Getty had included such a clause in his will to prevent litigation.

Buttermore next met with Mrs. Dutrow to discuss her estate on December 11, 1975. At this meeting, according to Buttermore's testimony, Mrs. Dutrow told him that she had decided to give her estate, other than special bequests or amounts, to Dorcas Cotsworth, to enable Dorcas to enjoy it during Dorcas' lifetime. Buttermore testified that he was "taken by surprise" by this proposal and tried to explain to Mrs. Dutrow that this change would result in additional taxes of between $700,000 and $800,000 when Dorcas died. But, according to Buttermore, Mrs. Dutrow insisted on making the change. The necessary amendments to the revocable trust agreement were prepared by Buttermore and executed by Mrs. Dutrow on January 9, 1976, providing for distribution of the principal to Dorcas upon Mrs. Dutrow's death, or, if Dorcas was not then living, equally among Mrs. Dutrow's grandchildren. A new will executed the same day provided, as had previous wills, that Dorcas would inherit all of Mrs. Dutrow's tangible personal property. The final change made by Mrs. Dutrow in her estate plans before she died in September 1977, was to amend the revocable trust to give $10,000 to each of her grandchildren at her death, apparently realizing that otherwise the Haynes children would likely not inherit anything.

The last testamentary document executed by the testatrix was a will dated April 8, 1976. It contained no further major changes in her dispositions. Mrs. Dutrow died on September 27, 1977 and her final will was admitted to probate by the Surrogate of Ocean County on October 12, 1977, with the First National State Bank of New Jersey as executor.

II

In any attack upon the validity of a will, it is generally presumed that "the testator was of sound mind and competent when he executed the will." Gellert v. Livingston, 5 N.J. 65, 71, 73 A.2d 916 (1950). If a will is tainted by "undue influence," it may be overturned. "Undue influence" has been defined as "mental, moral or physical" exertion which has destroyed the "free agency of a testator" by preventing the testator "from following the dictates of his own mind and will and accepting instead the domination and influence of another." In re Neuman, 133 N.J.Eq. 532, 534, 32 A.2d 826 (E. & A. 1943). When such a contention is made

> the burden of proving undue influence lies upon the contestant unless the will benefits one who stood in a confidential relationship to the testatrix and there are additional circumstances of a suspicious character present which require explanation. In such case the law raises a presumption of undue influence and the burden of proof is shifted to the proponent. [In re Rittenhouse's Will, 19 N.J. 376, 378–379, 117 A.2d 401 (1955)]

Accord, * * * [citations omitted] * * * In re Hopper, 9 N.J. 280, 282, 88 A.2d 193 (1952), 5 N.J. Practice (Clapp, Wills and Administration) § 62 (3rd ed. 1962).

The first element necessary to raise a presumption of undue influence, a "confidential relationship" between the testator and a beneficiary, arises

> where trust is reposed by reason of the testator's weakness or dependence or where the parties occupied relations in which reliance is naturally inspired or in fact exists. * * * [In re Hopper, supra, 9 N.J. at 282, 88 A.2d 193]

Here, the aged Mrs. Dutrow, afflicted by the debilitations of advanced years, was dependent upon her sole surviving child with whom she lived and upon whom she relied for companionship, care and support. This was a relationship sustained by confidence and trust. The determination of the trial court, in this case, that there was a confidential relationship between the testatrix and the chief beneficiary of her will is unassailable.

The second element necessary to create the presumption of undue influence is the presence of suspicious circumstances, which, in combination with such a confidential relationship, will shift the burden of proof to the proponent. Such circumstances need be no more than "slight." In re Blake's Will, supra, 21 N.J. at 55–56, 120 A.2d 745; In re Rittenhouse's Will, supra, 19 N.J. at 379, 117 A.2d 401; Gellert v. Livingston, supra, 5 N.J. at 71, 73 A.2d 916; In re Week's Estate, 29 N.J.Super. 533, 540, 103 A.2d 43 (App.Div.1954).

In this case there were suspicious circumstances attendant upon the execution of the will. There was a confidential relationship between the testatrix and her attorney, who was also the attorney for the daughter and the daughter's immediate family. Furthermore, following the establishment of the confidential relationship of the daughter's attorney with the testatrix, there was a drastic change in the testamentary dispositions of the testatrix, which favored the daughter. These factors collectively triggered the presumption that there was undue influence in the execution of the will.

On this record, the trial court correctly posited a presumption of undue influence that shifted the burden of proof on this issue to the proponents of the will. The court concluded ultimately on this issue, however, that the proponents, the defendants, had overcome the presumption of undue influence. The trial judge determined that Mrs. Dutrow was of firm mind and resolve, that the final testamentary disposition, though markedly different from previous plans, was not unnatural or instinctively unsound and it represented her actual intent. Further, the court found the explanation for Mrs. Dutrow's final testamentary disposition to be candid and satisfactory.

* * *

In this jurisdiction, once a presumption of undue influence has been established the burden of proof shifts to the proponent of the will, who must, under normal circumstances, overcome that presumption by a preponderance of the evidence. In re Week's Estate, supra, 29 N.J.Super. at 538–539, 103 A.2d 43. * * * [citations omitted] * * * See generally 5 N.J. Practice, supra, § 62. As stated by Judge Clapp in In re Week's Estate, supra:

> In the case of a presumption of undue influence, apparently because the presumption is fortified by policy, the proponent must, according to the language of the cases, prove, to the satisfaction of the trier of fact, that there was no undue influence. In connection with this presumption, unlike other presumptions, the courts do not speak as to the burden of going forward with the evidence. However, we conclude, the moment this presumption is erected, both the burden of proof * * * and the burden of going forward with proof, shift to the proponent and are identical and coincident. To meet each of these assignments, the proponent must establish by the same quantum of proof—that is, by a preponderance of the proof—that there is no undue influence. [29 N.J.Super. at 538–539, 103 A.2d 43 (citations omitted)]

In re Week's Estate, supra, recognized, however, that there were situations calling for a stronger presumption of undue influence and a commensurately heavier burden of proof to rebut the presumption. While in that case the presumption of undue influence was deemed to be rebuttable by a preponderance of evidence, the court acknowledged other cases where the presumption of undue influence is so heavily weighted with policy that the courts have demanded a sterner measure of proof than that usually obtaining upon civil issues. That is the situation, for instance, where an attorney benefits by the will of his client and especially where he draws it himself. [29 N.J.Super. at 539, 103 A.2d 43.]

It has been often recognized that a conflict on the part of an attorney in a testimonial situation is fraught with a high potential for undue influence, generating a strong presumption that there was such improper influence and warranting a greater quantum of proof to dispel the presumption. Thus, where the attorney who drew the will was the sole beneficiary, the Court required "substantial and trustworthy evidence of explanatory facts" and "candid and full disclosure" to dispel the presumption of undue influence. In re Blake's Will, 21 N.J. 50, 58–59, 120 A.2d 745 (1956). And, where an attorney-beneficiary, who had a preexisting attorney-client relationship with the testatrix, introduced the testatrix to the lawyer who actually drafted the challenged will, this Court has required evidence that was "convincing or impeccable," In re Rittenhouse's Will, supra, 19 N.J. at 382, 117 A.2d 401, "convincing," In re Hopper, supra, 9 N.J. at 285, 88 A.2d 193, and, "clear and convincing," In re Davis, supra, 14 N.J. at 170, 101 A.2d 521. Accord, In re Baker's Will, supra; see In re Estate of Lehner, 142 N.J.Super. 56, 360 A.2d 400 (App.Div.1975), rev'd on other grounds, 70 N.J. 434, 360 A.2d 383 (1976); cf. In re Estate of Churik, supra, 165 N.J.Super. at 5, 397 A.2d 677 (applying lower burden of proof where testator advised by independent attorney); In re Week's Estate, supra (same).

* * *

It is not difficult to appreciate the policy reasons for creating an especially strong presumption of undue influence in cases of attorney misconduct. Such professional delinquency is encompassed by our official rules governing the professional ethics of attorneys. Our disciplinary rules cover all gradations of professional departures from ethical norms, and, the existence of an ethical conflict exemplified in this case is squarely posited under DR 5–105.[2] This ethical rule prohibits an attorney from engaging in professional relationships that may impair his independent and untram-

---

2. DR 5–105 Refusing to Accept or Continue Employment if the Interests of Another Client May Impair the Independent Professional Judgment of the Lawyer.

(A) A lawyer shall decline proffered employment if the exercise of his independent professional judgment in behalf of a client will be or is likely to be adversely affected by the acceptance of the proffered employment, except to the extent permitted under DR 5–105(C).

(B) A lawyer shall not continue multiple employment if the exercise of his independent professional judgment in behalf of a client will be or is likely to be adversely affected by his representation of another client, except to the extent permitted under DR 5–105(C).

(C) In situations covered by DR 5–105(A) and (B) except as prohibited by rule, opinion, directive or statute, a lawyer may represent multiple clients if he believes that he can adequately represent the interests of each and if each consents to the representation after full disclosure of the facts and of the possible effect of such representation on the exercise of his independent professional judgment on behalf of each.

(D) If a lawyer is required to decline employment or to withdraw from employment under DR 5–105, no partner or associate of his or his firm may accept or continue such employment.

meled judgment with respect to his client. This disciplinary stricture should be practically self-demonstrative to any conscientious attorney. There is nothing novel about the ethical dilemma dealt with by DR 5–105. A lawyer cannot serve two masters in the same subject matter if their interests are or may become actually or potentially in conflict. [In re Chase, 68 N.J. 392, 396, 346 A.2d 89 (1975)].

So pervasive and fundamental is the ethical reach of DR 5–105 that ethical violations of this disciplinary rule based upon conflicts of interest have been found in a myriad of situations and in almost every walk of professional life. Such conflicts often arise where there is dual representation. E.g., In re Krakauer, 81 N.J. 32, 404 A.2d 1137 (1979); In re Dolan, 76 N.J. 1, 384 A.2d 1076 (1978). See "Developments of the Law—Conflicts of Interest in the Legal Profession," 94 Harv.L.Rev. 1244, 1292–1315 (1961). A conflict of interest, moreover, need not be obvious or actual to create an ethical impropriety. The mere possibility of such a conflict at the outset of the relationship is sufficient to establish an ethical breach on the part of the attorney. In re Kushinsky, 53 N.J. 1, 5, 247 A.2d 665 (1968); In re Braun, 49 N.J. 16, 18, 227 A.2d 506 (1967); In re Blatt, 42 N.J. 522, 524, 201 A.2d 715 (1964); In re Kamp, 40 N.J. 588, 595, 194 A.2d 236 (1963). Even where the representation of two clients has become a routine practice on the part of the bar generally, when the latent conflict becomes real, the attorney must fully disclose all material information and, if need be, extricate himself from the conflict by terminating his relationship with at least one party. Cf. Lieberman v. Employers Ins. of Wausau, 84 N.J. 325, 338–340, 419 A.2d 417 (1980) (conflict of interest on part of insurance defense counsel who normally represented both the insured and the insurer).

Accordingly, it is our determination that there must be imposed a significant burden of proof upon the advocates of a will where a presumption of undue influence has arisen because the testator's attorney has placed himself in a conflict of interest and professional loyalty between the testator and the beneficiary.[3] In view of the gravity of the presumption in such cases, the appropriate burden of proof must be heavier than that which normally obtains in civil litigation. The cited decisions which have

3. In re Estate of Lehner, 70 N.J. 434, 360 A.2d 383 (1976), was the case primarily relied upon by the trial judge as requiring only a preponderance of the evidence. In *Lehner,* where the attorney who had drawn the testator's will was under a later will named as sole beneficiary, the Appellate Division articulated a standard of proof that we understand to mean and equate with the level of clear and convincing evidence, *viz:*

> The presumption is "overborne by *substantial and trustworthy* evidence of explanatory facts to the contrary." In re Blake's Will, supra, 21 N.J. at 58 [120 A.2d 745] * * * [T]he proponent's testimony "did not have the *convincing* or *impeccable* quality required by our decisions to remove the aura of suspicion." In re Rittenhouse's Will, supra, 19 N.J. at 382 [117 A.2d 401]. [142 N.J.Super. 56, 66–67, 360 A.2d 400 (1975).]

In reversing the Appellate Division, this Court disagreed with its conclusion that the presumption of undue influence had not been overcome. Nevertheless, the Court did not directly or by implication reject the authorities relied upon by the Appellate Division which indicated that the proper burden of overcoming the presumption of undue influence in such circumstances was greater than a preponderance of the evidence.

dealt with the quantum of evidence needed to dispel the presumption of influence in this context have essayed various descriptions of this greater burden, *viz:* "convincing," "impeccable," "substantial," "trustworthy," "candid," and "full." Our present rules of evidence, however, do not employ such terminology. The need for clarity impels us to be more definitive in the designation of the appropriate burden of proof and to select one which most suitably measures the issue to be determined. See, e.g., In re Weeks' Estate, supra. Only three burdens of proof are provided by the evidence rules, namely, a preponderance, clear and convincing, and beyond a reasonable doubt. *Evid.R.* 1(4). The standard in our evidence rules that conforms most comfortably with the level of proofs required by our decisions in this context is the burden of proof by clear and convincing evidence. In re Davis, supra, 14 N.J. at 170, 101 A.2d 521; cf. Sarte v. Pidoto, 129 N.J.Super. 405, 411, 324 A.2d 48 (App.Div.1974) (*de facto* use of a standard stricter than preponderance of the evidence entails proof by clear and convincing evidence under rules of evidence). Hence, the presumption of undue influence created by a professional conflict of interest on the part of an attorney, coupled with confidential relationships between a testator and the beneficiary as well as the attorney, must be rebutted by clear and convincing evidence.

Applying these principles to this case, it is clear that attorney Buttermore was in a position of irreconcilable conflict within the common sense and literal meaning of DR 5–105. In this case, Buttermore was required, at a minimum, to provide full disclosure and complete advice to Mrs. Dutrow, as well as the Cotsworths, as to the existence and nature of the conflict and to secure knowing and intelligent waivers from each in order to continue his professional relationship with Mrs. Dutrow. DR 5–105(C). Even these prophylactic measures, however, might not have overcome the conflict, nor have been sufficient to enable the attorney to render unimpaired "independent professional judgment" on behalf of his client, DR 5–105(B); see Lieberman v. Employers Ins. of Wausau, supra, 84 N.J. at 338–340, 419 A.2d 417. Any conflict, of course, could have been avoided by Buttermore simply refusing to represent Mrs. Dutrow. DR 5–105(A), (B); see In re Davis, supra, at 171, 101 A.2d 521. But, Buttermore was apparently insensitive or impervious to the presence or extent of the professional conflict presented by these circumstances. He undertook none of these measures to eliminate the dual representation or overcome the conflict.[4]

4. In this case, we recognize that Buttermore believed in good faith that he was taking proper precautions to overcome or avoid the consequences of the improper conflict and did not believe or perceive that his position involved an impermissible conflict of interest in light of these measures. He also expressed the view that frequently estate planning involves members of an entire family and therefore no conflict exists for an attorney who has professional relationships with members of the family, in addition to the testator. This position is, of course, inconsistent with our explicit holding that such conduct, as exemplified by the facts of this case, violates DR 5–105. Since this application of DR 5–105 to such situations has not been generally acknowledged, we do not think it fair that ethical sanctions be pursued retroactively in this case for such conduct, since there are no additional aggravating circumstances. See In re Smock, 86 N.J. 426, 432 A.2d 34 (1981).

Consequently, a strong taint of undue influence was permitted, presumptively, to be injected into the testamentary disposition of Mrs. Dutrow.

Accordingly, the attorney's conduct here, together with all of the other factors contributing to the likelihood of wrongful influence exerted upon the testatrix, has engendered a heavy presumption of undue influence which the proponents of the will must overcome by clear and convincing evidence.

This determination that clear and convincing evidence must be marshalled to overcome the presumption of undue influence appropriately requires that the matter be remanded to the trial court for new findings of fact and legal conclusions based upon application of this burden of proof. We remand, recognizing that there is considerable evidence in the record as to Mrs. Dutrow's intelligence, independence and persistence, of her alienation, to some extent, from the Haynes children, and as to her natural intent primarily to benefit her children, rather than her grandchildren.

* * *

Accordingly, the judgment below is reversed and the matter remanded, Jurisdiction is not retained.

■ CLIFFORD, J. dissenting in part. [Justice Clifford's dissent concerned the no-contest clause and is omitted]

For reversal—JUSTICES SULLIVAN, PASHMAN, CLIFFORD, SCHREIBER and HANDLER—5.

NOTES AND QUESTIONS

1. How did Mrs. Dutrow's estate plan change between the time of Betty Haynes' death in 1973 and the time of Mrs. Dutrow's own death four years later? Who was disadvantaged as a result of the changes?

2. If anyone unduly influenced Mrs. Dutrow in this case, who unduly influenced her?

3. ***The Significance of a "Confidential Relationship".*** When Dorcas Cotsworth and her lawyer, Grant Buttermore, gave Mrs. Dutrow advice, do you think Mrs. Dutrow assumed that they were acting in their own interests, or in Mrs. Dutrow's interest?

Suppose Mrs. Dutrow's niece, on an annual visit, had suggested that Mrs. Dutrow ought to devise $50,000 to the niece. Would Mrs. Dutrow have believed that the niece was acting in her own interest, or in Mrs. Dutrow's interest? Why might Mrs. Dutrow attribute a different motivation to Dorcas or to lawyer Buttermore?

As the court indicates, a "confidential relationship" between testator and beneficiary is necessary to raise a presumption of undue influence. (On presumptions in undue influence law, see Sid L. Moller, Undue Influence and the Norm of Reciprocity, 26 Idaho L. Rev. 275 (1990)). The court, quoting In re Hopper, goes on to say that a confidential relationship is one

> where trust is reposed by reason of the testator's weakness or dependence or where the parties occupied relations in which reliance is naturally inspired or in fact exists.

Suppose, for instance, that Mrs. Dutrow routinely relied upon Dorcas to act on her behalf—to find the right doctors, to make the right investments, to deal with insurance reimbursements. Wouldn't Mrs. Dutrow also assume that Dorcas was acting on her behalf when Dorcas advised her about her will? That is, if Dorcas had gained Mrs. Dutrow's confidence, should we permit Dorcas to act in her own self-interest when advising Mrs. Dutrow about her will? The general answer is no: if a will beneficiary enjoys a confidential relationship with testator, and there is reason to believe that the beneficiary used the testator's confidence and trust to benefit herself, the beneficiary has unduly influenced the testator.

4. ***Suspicious Circumstances.*** It is generally quite natural for a testator to leave all or much of his estate to people with whom testator enjoys a relationship of trust and confidence—especially testator's closest family members. The mere fact that a person who enjoys a confidential relationship with testator is also a will beneficiary does not, therefore, create a presumption of undue influence. Instead, as the court in the Haynes case indicates, suspicious circumstances must be present.

If, for instance, the will beneficiary had no discussions with testator about disposition of testator's estate, no presumption of undue influence arises. See, e.g., Andrews v. Rentz, 266 Ga. 782, 470 S.E.2d 669 (1996) (directed verdict for proponent of will, a caretaker and friend not related to testator, in the absence of evidence that beneficiary had ever spoken with testator about will).

When are circumstances sufficiently suspicious to create a presumption of undue influence? Courts often treat dispositions as suspicious when made to persons who do not appear to be the natural objects of testator's bounty. See, e.g., Estate of McCoy, 844 P.2d 1131 (Alaska 1993) (devise to lawyer rather than testator's sister). Circumstances may be suspicious even if the parties accused of undue influence benefit only by collecting fees as fiduciaries rather than beneficial interests in testator's estate. See Matter of Gerard, 911 P.2d 266 (Okla.1995) (person unrelated to decedent benefits from control of trust in which substantial fees are involved).

Even when the persons accused of undue influence are natural objects of testator's bounty—usually close relatives—courts may find suspicious circumstances when, as in the Haynes case, testator's will has changed dramatically over time to benefit the supposed influencer.

5. ***Testator's "Weakened Mental State."*** A robust, independent testator is generally less susceptible to undue influence than a dependent, weakened testator. Courts often require evidence of "weakened intellect" or "weakened mental state" before they will sustain a finding of undue influence. See, e.g., Estate of Lakatosh, 441 Pa.Super. 133, 143–44, 656 A.2d 1378, 1384 (1995). At the very least, courts treat the physical and mental condition of testator "as it affects his or her ability to withstand the

influence" as a relevant factor in undue influence cases. Estate of Tipp, 281 Mont. 120, 933 P.2d 182 (1997).

The Haynes Case and the Lawyer's Role

1. The court in the Haynes case concludes that lawyer Buttermore had a conflict of interest. Why? What reason was there to believe that Buttermore could not, or would not, effectively represent Mrs. Dutrow's interests when advising her about her estate plan? Was Buttermore a beneficiary of Mrs. Dutrow's will?

Rule 1.7 of the ABA's Model Rules of Professional Conduct provides:

> (a) Except as provided in paragraph (b), a lawyer shall not represent a client if the representation involves a concurrent conflict of interest. A concurrent conflict of interest exists if:
>
> (1) the representation of one client will be directly adverse to another client; or
>
> (2) there is a significant risk that the representation of one or more clients will be materially limited by the lawyer's responsibilities to another client, a former client or a third person or by a personal interest of the lawyer.
>
> (b) Notwithstanding the existence of a concurrent conflict of interest under paragraph (a), a lawyer may represent a client if:
>
> (1) the lawyer reasonably believes that the lawyer will be able to provide competent and diligent representation to each affected client;
>
> (2) the representation is not prohibited by law;
>
> (3) the representation does not involve the assertion of a claim by one client against another client represented by the lawyer in the same litigation or other proceeding before a tribunal; and
>
> (4) each affected client gives informed consent, confirmed in writing.

If the Model Rules had been in effect in New Jersey at the time Buttermore drafted Mrs. Dutrow's will, would Buttermore have been in violation of the Rules?

Suppose Buttermore had disclosed potential conflicts to Mrs. Dutrow. If she had then executed a document acknowledging Buttermore's disclosure and requesting that he act as her lawyer, would Buttermore have complied with his ethical obligations?

2. When John Cotsworth approached Buttermore about Mrs. Dutrow's estate plan, what should Buttermore have done? How should he have responded to Cotsworth—his long-time client?

Leaving aside ethical questions, was Buttermore's plan to disinherit the grandsons wise? How sympathetic would you expect a court to be to Mrs. Dutrow's will?

3. One of the more sensational estates trials in recent years took place not in probate court, but in a criminal prosecution. Brooke Astor's son, Anthony Marshall, and a lawyer who worked on Mrs. Astor's estate plan were convicted of defrauding and stealing from Mrs. Astor. See John Eligon, Brooke Astor's Son Guilty in Scheme to Defraud Her, New York Times, October 9, 2009. Consider the following account of the behavior of two lawyers who were *not* charged in the criminal case:

> In the Astor trial, prosecutors were highly critical of the way two prominent lawyers handled changes to Mrs. Astor's will. Although those lawyers—Henry Christensen III and G. Warren Whitaker—were not charged with crimes, prosecutors said they contributed to the fraud against Mrs. Astor by having her sign documents that did not reflect her wishes and that she was not competent enough to understand.
>
> Mr. Whitaker ... testified that even people with severe mental defects could legally execute a will if they understood what they were doing when they signed it.
>
> Mr. Whitaker drafted an amendment to Mrs. Astor's will that gave Mr. Marshall control of a $60 million portion of her estate, and testified that she understood what she was doing when she signed it in January 2004, even though she was 101 and had Alzheimer's disease. Prosecutors said that Mr. Marshall and Mr. Morrissey tricked her into signing it, and they charged them with conspiracy.

John Eligon, In Astor Trial, a Lesson for Estate Lawyers, New York Times, October 25, 2009.

Suppose Anthony Marshall, acting under the power of attorney his mother had given to him, hired Whitaker to draft the amendment, and paid Whitaker from his mother's funds. Was Whitaker in a position to represent Mrs. Astor's interests or Marshall's? What should Whitaker have done? Was it enough to ascertain whether Mrs. Astor understood what she was doing when she signed the will? How would Whitaker deal with potential undue influence issues? If you had been Whitaker, what advice would you have given to Marshall? The criminal and civil litigation over the $180 million Astor estate cost millions, and left Marshall with a prison sentence. Should Whitaker be liable to anyone for his role in Mrs. Astor's estate planning? If so, to whom? For more general discussion of the Astor case, see Joseph A. Rosenberg, Regrettably Unfair: Brooke Astor and the Other Elderly in New York, 30 Pace L. Rev. 1004 (2010).

4. Suppose—after your admission to the bar—a family member asks you to draft a will in which you are named as a beneficiary, or in which your spouse is named as a beneficiary. Should you draft the will?

Rule 1.8(c) of the ABA's Model Rules provides:

> A lawyer shall not solicit any substantial gift from a client, including a testamentary gift, or prepare on behalf of a client an instrument giving the lawyer or a person related to the lawyer any substantial gift unless the lawyer or other recipient of the gift is related to the client. For purposes of this paragraph, related persons include a spouse, child, grandchild, parent, grandparent or

other relative or individual with whom the lawyer or the client maintains a close, familial relationship.

If Rule 1.8(c) is in effect, can you prepare a will for your mother naming your spouse as a beneficiary? Even if there would be no ethical violation, would preparing such a will be good practice? Why or why not?

In re Melson's Estate, 711 A.2d 783 (Del.Supr.1998) is instructive. In that case, testator had a will leaving her estate equally to her two sons, John and Joseph. Shortly before her death, John drafted a new will for her. The new will gave 3/4 of testator's estate to John and his children, and only 1/4 of testator's estate to Joseph. Testator executed the will from her hospital bed while Joseph was out of town for the weekend. When Joseph challenged the will on grounds of undue influence, the court held that John had the burden to prove the absence of undue influence because 1) the testator had weakened intellect, 2) John and testator had a confidential relationship, and 3) John received a substantial benefit under the will.

By contrast, in Stanton v. Wells Fargo Bank Montana, 335 Mont. 384, 152 P.3d 115 (2007), testator's former son-in-law (the ex-husband of testator's deceased daughter) drafted testator's will, which left the bulk of testator's estate to the drafter. The Montana Supreme Court conceded that the actions of the son-in-law—a lawyer—"could constitute a violation of Rule 1.8(c)", but held that a violation of professional conduct rules should not "create any presumption that a legal duty has been breached." The court then upheld the bequest to the lawyer-drafter over the objections of a charitable beneficiary of testator's prior will and trust agreement. Does the result make sense? Is there any explanation (other than the desire to exercise undue influence) for the son-in-law's failure to inform testator that she would be better off having her will drafted by the lawyer who had drafted her previous wills?

* * *

In the Haynes case, the relationship of trust and confidence between Mrs. Dutrow on the one hand, and her daughter and lawyer Buttermore on the other hand, was fairly evident. In other cases, however, the relationship may not be so clear—yet much will turn on whether a confidential relationship exists. When will a court find a confidential relationship, and what should testator (or her lawyer) do when testator wants to write a will benefitting her confidante? Consider the following case:

Will of Moses

Supreme Court of Mississippi, 1969.
227 So.2d 829.

■ SMITH, J.:

[Mrs. Fannie Traylor Moses died on February 6, 1967. Clarence Holland, an attorney, sought to probate a will executed in 1964, which made him the principal beneficiary of her estate. (An earlier will had made Mrs.

Moses' sister the principal beneficiary). The Chancellor found that the will had been the product of undue influence, and Holland appealed.—eds.]

... [A]ppellant's chief argument is addressed to the proposition that even if Holland, as Mrs. Moses' attorney, occupied a continuing fiduciary relationship with respect to her on May 26, 1964, the date of the execution of the document under which he claimed her estate, the presumption of undue influence was overcome because, in making the will, Mrs. Moses had the independent advice and counsel of one entirely devoted to her interests. It is argued that, for this reason, a decree should be entered here reversing the chancellor and admitting the 1964 will to probate....

A brief summary of facts found by the chancellor and upon which he based his conclusion that the presumption was not overcome, follows:

Mrs. Moses died at the age of 57 years, leaving an estate valued at $125,000. She had lost three husbands in less than 20 years. Throughout the latter years of her life her health became seriously impaired. She suffered from serious heart trouble and cancer had required the surgical removal of one of her breasts. For 6 or 7 years preceding her death she was an alcoholic.

* * *

The exact date on which Holland entered Mrs. Moses' life is unclear. There is a suggestion that she had met him as early as 1951. Their personal relationship became what the chancellor, somewhat inaccurately, characterized, as one of "dubious" morality. The record, however, leaves no doubt as to its nature. Soon after the death of Mrs. Moses' last husband, Holland, although 15 years her junior, began seeing Mrs. Moses with marked regularity, there having been testimony to the effect that he attended her almost daily. Holland was an attorney and in that capacity represented Mrs. Moses. She declared that he was not only her attorney but her "boyfriend" as well....

After Mrs. Moses died, the 1964 will was brought forward by another attorney, also an associate of Holland, who said that it had been entrusted to him by Mrs. Moses, together with other papers, for safekeeping. He distinguished his relation with Holland from that of a partner, saying that he and Holland only occupied offices together and shared facilities and expenses in the practice of law. He also stated that he saw Mrs. Moses on an "average" of once a week, most often in the company of Holland.

Throughout this period, Mrs. Moses was a frequent visitor at Holland's office, and there is ample evidence to support the chancellor's finding that there existed a continuing fiduciary relationship between Mrs. Moses and Holland, as her attorney.

* * *

The evidence supports the chancellor's finding that the confidential or fiduciary relationship which existed between Mrs. Moses and Holland, her attorney, was a subsisting and continuing relationship, having begun before the making by Mrs. Moses of the will of August 22, 1961, under the terms of which her jewelry had been bequeathed to Holland, and having ended only with Mrs. Moses' death. Moreover, its effect was enhanced by the fact that throughout this period, Holland was in almost daily attendance upon Mrs. Moses on terms of the utmost intimacy. There was strong evidence that this aging woman, seriously ill, disfigured by surgery, and hopelessly addicted to alcoholic excesses, was completely bemused by the constant and amorous attentions of Holland, a man 15 years her junior. There was testimony too indicating that she entertained the pathetic hope that he might marry her. Although the evidence was not without conflict and was, in some of its aspects, circumstantial, it was sufficient to support the finding that the relationship existed on May 26, 1964, the date of the will tendered for probate by Holland.

The chancellor's factual finding of the existence of this relationship on that date is supported by evidence and is not manifestly wrong. Moreover, he was correct in his conclusion of law that such relationship gave rise to a presumption of undue influence which could be overcome only by evidence that, in making the 1964 will, Mrs. Moses had acted upon the independent advice and counsel of one entirely devoted to her interest.

Appellant takes the position that there was undisputed evidence that Mrs. Moses, in making the 1964 will, did, in fact, have such advice and counsel. He relies upon the testimony of the attorney in whose office that document was prepared to support his assertion.

This attorney was and is a reputable and respected member of the bar, who had no prior connection with Holland and no knowledge of Mrs. Moses' relationship with him. He had never seen nor represented Mrs. Moses previously and never represented her afterward. He was acquainted with Holland and was aware that Holland was a lawyer.

* * *

The attorney's testimony supports the chancellor's finding that nowhere in the conversations with Mrs. Moses was there touched upon in any way the proposed testamentary disposition whereby preference was to be given a nonrelative to the exclusion of her blood relatives. There was no discussion of her relationship with Holland, nor as to who her legal heirs might be, nor as to their relationship to her, after it was discovered that she had neither a husband nor children.

It is clear from his own testimony that, in writing the will, the attorney-draftsman, did no more than write down, according to the forms of law, what Mrs. Moses told him. There was no meaningful independent advice or counsel touching upon the area in question and it is manifest that the role of the attorney in writing the will, as it relates to the present issue, was little more than that of scrivener. The chancellor was justified in holding that this did not meet the burden nor overcome the presumption.

* * *

Holland, of course, did not personally participate in the actual preparation or execution of the will. If he had, under the circumstances in evidence, unquestionably the will could not stand. It may be assumed that Holland, as a lawyer, knew this.

* * *

The chancellor's finding that the will was the product of Holland's undue influence is not inconsistent with his conclusion that "Her (Mrs. Moses) mind was capable of understanding the essential matters necessary to the execution of her will on May 26, 1964, at the time of such execution." A weak or infirm mind may, of course, be more easily over persuaded. In the case under review, Mrs. Moses was in ill health, she was an alcoholic, and was an aging woman infatuated with a young lover, 15 years her junior, who was also her lawyer. If this combination of circumstances cannot be said to support the view that Mrs. Moses suffered from a "weakness or infirmity" of mind, vis-a-vis Holland, it was hardly calculated to enhance her power of will where he was concerned. Circumstances in evidence, both antecedent and subsequent to the making of the will, tend to accord with that conclusion.

The sexual morality of the personal relationship is not an issue. However, the intimate nature of this relationship is relevant to the present inquiry to the extent that its existence, under the circumstances, warranted an inference of undue influence, extending and augmenting that which flowed from the attorney-client relationship. Particularly is this true when viewed in the light of evidence indicating its employment for the personal aggrandizement of Holland. For that purpose, it was properly taken into consideration by the chancellor.

* * *

The chancellor was justified in finding that the physical absence of Holland during Mrs. Moses' brief visit to the office of the attorney who wrote the will did not suffice to abate or destroy the presumption of undue influence.

* * *

■ ROBERTSON, J. (dissenting):

I am unable to agree with the majority of the Court that Mrs. Moses should not be allowed to dispose of her property as she so clearly intended.

* * *

There is no proof in this voluminous record that Holland ever did or said anything to Mrs. Moses about devising her property to anybody, much less him. It is conceded that in the absence of the presumption of undue influence that there is no basis to support a finding that Holland exercised undue influence over Mrs. Moses. This being true, the first question to be decided is whether the presumption of undue influence arises under the circumstances of this case.

It is my opinion that the presumption did not arise. The fact, alone, that a confidential relationship existed between Holland and Mrs. Moses is not sufficient to give rise to the presumption of undue influence in a will case....

It was not contended in this case that Holland was in any way actively concerned with the preparation or execution of the will. Appellees rely solely upon the finding of the chancellor that there were suspicious circumstances. However, the suspicious circumstances listed by the chancellor in his opinion had nothing whatsoever to do with the preparation or execution of the will. These were remote antecedent circumstances having to do with the meretricious relationship of the parties, and the fact that at times Mrs. Moses drank to excess and could be termed an alcoholic, but there is no proof in this long record that her use of alcohol affected her will power or her ability to look after her extensive real estate holdings. It is common knowledge that many persons who could be termed alcoholics, own, operate and manage large business enterprises with success. The fact that she chose to leave most of her property to the man she loved in preference to her sisters and brother is not such an unnatural disposition of her property as to render it invalid.

In this case, there were no suspicious circumstances surrounding the preparation or execution of the will, and in my opinion the chancellor was wrong in so holding. However, even if it be conceded that the presumption of undue influence did arise, this presumption was overcome by clear and convincing evidence of good faith, full knowledge and independent consent and advice.

* * *

When she got ready to make her will she called Honorable Dan H. Shell for an appointment. Shell did not know her, although he remembered that he had handled a land transaction for her third husband, Walter Moses, some years before. Shell had been in the active practice of law in Jackson since 1945; he was an experienced attorney with a large and varied practice.

* * *

She came alone to his office on March 31, 1964, and advised him that she wanted him to prepare a will for her. Mr. Shell testified that she was alert, intelligent and rational, and knew exactly what she was doing.

Mr. Shell was asked the question: "To what extent did you try to influence Mrs. Fannie Moses in drafting her will?" He answered:

> "I didn't try to influence her at all. I asked her about the property and I asked her marital background, because I needed to know whether or not there would be a spouse who might have renunciation rights, I needed to know if she had children and as to whether or not she wanted to pretermit them if there were children. I wanted to know the general value of the properties so that I could advise her as to whether or not she might have an estate tax problem, and I ascertained that she probably did have and so advised her, but she said that it didn't matter to her, that *this was the way she wanted to leave the property, so I drew the will in accordance with her specific directions.*" (emphasis added)

He advised her that he needed specific legal descriptions of her various properties. She got this information and brought it to his office. He prepared the first draft of the will and mailed it to her on May 1, 1964. Shell testified:

> "Then she called me in just a few days and pointed out that the will was not correct, that the property which I had described as being devised to Robert Miller was not the right tract of land and it should have been another piece of property that I had incorrectly devised to Clarence Holland and it should have been devised to Robert Miller, and the tract I had devised to Robert Miller should have been devised to Clarence Holland."

> "Well, of course, I wanted it *as she wanted it*, so I immediately began to go about the revision. She sent in—I don't believe she came personally, or if she did she left with the receptionist some tax receipts which she thought would help me identify that property that I had misdescribed, and I did rewrite the will, and on May 21st I wrote her a short letter and sent her an original and two copies of the will as I had revised it. I did not see her when she came in later on May 26th or 27th—I don't remember what day it was—I was not in the office, I was in Court trying a case in Circuit Court, and I did not see her when she came in and actually signed the will, but I wrote the will on two separate occasions." (emphasis added)

His testimony imports verity, and it stands uncontradicted.

The majority was indeed hard put to find fault with his actions on behalf of his client. It is easy for us who are removed from the active practice of law to criticize our brethren who are "on the firing line." The question is, did he do all that was reasonably required of him to represent his client in the preparation of her will. He was not required to be perfect, nor was he required to meet a standard of exact precision. He ascertained that Mrs. Moses was competent to make a will; he satisfied himself that she was acting of her own free will and accord, and that she was disposing of her property exactly as she wished and intended. No more is required.

On May 26, 1964, Mrs. Moses came alone to Mr. Shell's office. She told Mrs. Mary L. Ward, one of Shell's secretaries, that she had her will, that Mr. Shell had fixed it exactly as she wanted it, and that she was ready to sign it. She signed it in the presence of Mrs. Ward and Antoinette Neely, another secretary in Shell's law firm, and they each signed as an attesting witness. Mrs. Ward testified that Mrs. Moses was alert, friendly and her usual self on this occasion.

Shell was asked the direct question:

> "Q. Now in connection with the drawing of this will, what did Clarence Holland have to do with that?"

He answered:

> "A. Not one thing on earth."

Shell was asked:

"Q. From that time up until the time of her death, did you ever discuss the matter with him?

A. About his being a devisee under the will, or even writing a will?

Q. Yes."

He answered:

"A. No. That was none of his business, as far as I was concerned. It was confidential between Mrs. Moses and myself."

* * *

.... Mrs. Moses was 54 years old ... when she executed her will. She went alone to the law office of an independent, capable and experienced attorney. She herself told him how she wanted to devise her property. This was on March 31, 1964. After she had pointed out an error in the first draft to Mr. Shell he corrected and rewrote the will and mailed it to her on May 21, 1964. She went alone to his office on May 26, 1964, and signed her last will in the presence of two disinterested witnesses. Almost two months had elapsed between her first conference with Shell and the actual execution of the will.

There is not one iota of testimony in this voluminous record that Clarence Holland even knew of this will, much less that he participated in the preparation or execution of it. The evidence is all to the contrary. The evidence is undisputed that she executed her last will after the fullest deliberation, with full knowledge of what she was doing, and with the independent consent and advice of an experienced and competent attorney whose sole purpose was to advise with her and prepare her will exactly as she wanted it.

In January 1967, about one month before her death and some two years and eight months after she had made her will, she called W. R. Patterson, an experienced, reliable and honorable attorney who was a friend of hers, and asked him to come by her home for a few minutes. Patterson testified:

"She said, 'Well, the reason I called you out here is that I've got an envelope here with all of my important papers in it, and that *includes my last will and testament,*' and says, 'I would like to leave them with you if you've got a place to lock them up in your desk somewhere there in your office.' "

"* * * And she said, *'Now, Dan Shell drew my will for me two or three years ago,' and she says, 'It's exactly like I want it,' and says, 'I had to go to his office two or three times to get it the way I wanted it, but this is the way I want it,* and if anything happens to me I want you to take all these papers and give them to Dan,' and she says, 'He'll know what to do with them.' " (emphasis added)

What else could she have done? She met all the tests that this Court and other courts have carefully outlined and delineated. The majority opinion says that this still was not enough, that there were "suspicious circumstances" and "antecedent agencies", but even these were not connected in any shape, form or fashion with the preparation or execution of her will. They had to do with her love life and her drinking habits and propensities.

* * *

If full knowledge, deliberate and voluntary action, and independent consent and advice have not been proved in this case, then they just cannot be proved. We should be bound by the uncontradicted testimony in the record; we should not go completely outside the record and guess, speculate and surmise as to what happened.

I think that the judgment of the lower court should be reversed and the last will and testament of Fannie T. Moses executed on May 26, 1964, admitted to probate in solemn form.

NOTES AND QUESTIONS

1. If Fannie Taylor Moses had married Clarence Holland, would the result in this case have been the same? Although the relationship between husband and wife is often a relationship of trust and confidence, courts rarely find that the marital relationship, combined with a substantial devise to the spouse, gives rise to a presumption of undue influence. Estate of Pope, 5 So.3d 427 (Miss. App. 2008) is a recent exception. Two years after his wife of 50 years died, testator married a woman who had become his primary caregiver and immediately changed his will to leave everything to his new wife. The court upheld a jury verdict in favor of testator's children, holding that the confidential relationship between husband and wife created a presumption of undue influence. See generally Ray D. Madoff, Unmasking Undue Influence, 81 Minnesota L. Rev. 571, 585–86 (1997).

Will of Moses may be a historical relic, but elderly people with money remain easy prey for younger partners who flatter them with attention. Thus, in Estate of Gerard, 911 P.2d 266 (Okla.1995), the Oklahoma Supreme Court sustained a finding of undue influence when the Crabtrees, a married couple, supervised preparation of new wills and trust instruments cutting out the septuagenarian testator's wife, and giving the couple effective control of the trust by making Mr. Crabtree executor of the estate. The court noted:

> "The Crabtrees assumed an increasing role in Dr. Gerard's affairs during the final months of his life. Joyce Crabtree was responsible for much of his medical care. There was testimony that Joyce Crabtree was seen climbing into bed with Dr. Gerard. She hugged him and told him she loved him."

Id. at 271. How easy is it for a court to separate out a loving, committed, relationship outside of marriage from a relationship—perhaps sexual—designed only to generate financial benefits?

2. Suppose the genders of Moses and Holland had been reversed. Do you think the court would have reached the same result? Or does the court's opinion reflect its own biases about what sorts of May–December romances are "normal"?

3. Suppose Clarence Holland had not been a lawyer. Would the court have reached the same result?

4. ***Other confidential relationships involving non-relatives.***

a. ***Lawyer Client.*** Courts inevitably become suspicious whenever a testator executes a will naming his lawyer as a beneficiary. Most predatory lawyers are clever enough to avoid drafting wills in which they are named as beneficiaries, but all too often, the lawyer is unable to resist having a hand in the drafting process. See, e.g., Matlock v. Simpson, 902 S.W.2d 384 (Tenn.1995) (court upsets jury determination permitting attorney-draftsman to take under the will; clear and convincing evidence necessary to overcome presumption of undue influence); Estate of Ottomeier, 85 Wash. App. 1058 (1997) (lawyer-beneficiary drafts testator's will, but drives testator to another lawyer's office to review the will; court upholds trial court order invalidating will when testator conceded to reviewing lawyer that "she was too blind to read the will; and that [drafting lawyer] should receive some money but she was not certain how much").

Because of the fiduciary relationship between lawyer and client, courts look upon wills in which the lawyer is named as beneficiary with great disfavor, and the lawyer is generally unable to overcome the presumption of undue influence—even if the lawyer did not draft the will herself. Thus, in Matter of Henderson, 80 N.Y.2d 388, 605 N.E.2d 323, 590 N.Y.S.2d 836 (1992), the New York Court of Appeals held that Irvin Husin, the lawyer-beneficiary of testator's will, was not entitled to summary judgment even when the will was drafted by another lawyer, Martin Weinstein, located by testator through the auspices of the local bar association. The court wrote:

> According to Weinstein's deposition, he met briefly with Henderson before actually drafting the will, but never seriously inquired into the reasons for her decision to leave such a large portion of her assets to Husin and to virtually disinherit her sister.... Rather than conducting an independent review of her personal situation, Weinstein prepared Henderson's will primarily on the basis of Husin's four-page memo outlining Henderson's assets and testamentary wishes, which named Husin and his family members. Consequently, it could be inferred that Henderson did not receive the benefit of counselling by an independent attorney and that her will was essentially the indirect product of her discussions and relationship with Husin.

Id. at 393–94, 605 N.E.2d at 326. See, e.g., Estate of Auen, 30 Cal.App.4th 300, 35 Cal.Rptr.2d 557 (1994) (noting that although lawyer "did not personally draft the 1990 will there is evidence that she participated in its drafting" and that she "added her own comments to [testator's] handwritten notes, notes which were used by [lawyer-drafter] to draft the 1990 will"); Estate of McCoy, 844 P.2d 1131 (Alaska 1993) (lawyer-beneficiary did not draft testator's will, but asked a colleague to draft the will; colleague prepared the will without consulting testator).

Occasionally, the lawyer gets to keep the devise. Thus, in Vaupel v. Barr, 194 W.Va. 296, 460 S.E.2d 431 (1995), where testator made her lawyer, a long-time friend, the residuary beneficiary of her estate, the court went so far as to grant summary judgment to the lawyer-beneficiary, noting that when the testator informed the lawyer, who had drafted her previous wills, that she wanted to make him a beneficiary, the lawyer immediately informed testator that another lawyer would have to draft the will.

Courts generally view relationships between testators and other types of fiduciaries, such as agents under a power of attorney, as confidential. See, e.g., Medlock v. Mitchell, 95 Ark.App. 132, 234 S.W.3d 901 (2006).

b. ***Spiritual Advisors.*** Testators often enjoy confidential relationships with their clergymen, and unscrupulous clergymen may have a particular hold on aged testators—the promise of eternal salvation. Indeed, in days past, the mortmain statutes routinely invalidated excessive gifts to religious organizations. See generally Jeffrey G. Sherman, Can Religious Influence Ever be Undue Influence? 73 Brook. L. Rev. 579 (2008).

Although mortmain statutes are on the wane, courts continue to scrutinize gifts to religious organizations for signs of undue influence. The spiritual advisor need not benefit personally for the gift to be suspect. See Estate of Maheras, 897 P.2d 268 (Okla.1995); see also, Marks v. Marks, 91 Wash.App. 325, 957 P.2d 235 (1998) (affirming trial court determination that testator's bequest to religious group was invalid, even though there was no evidence of undue influence, because church leader helped testator draft her will and thus engaged in the unauthorized practice of law!). Professor Sherman concludes that "[t]he best solution to this problem of clerical overreaching is to treat all relationships between a testator and her spiritual advisor as per se confidential for purposes of the law of undue influence." Sherman, supra, at 638.

c. ***Nursing Home Operators and Other Caregivers.*** In an era in which many elderly and infirm people live in nursing homes, the owners and operators of those nursing homes have significant opportunity to influence testamentary dispositions. A disposition in favor of a nursing home operator is inherently suspicious. See, e.g., Matter of Burke, 82 A.D.2d 260, 441 N.Y.S.2d 542 (1981). Bequests to nurses and caregivers also provoke suspicion. See, e.g. Bean v. Wilson, 283 Ga. 511, 661 S.E.2d 518 (2008).

5. ***The California Statutory Approach.*** In California, a statute declares invalid any donative transfer to the drafter of an instrument making the transfer, or to a care custodian of the transferor, subject to narrow statutory exceptions. California Probate Code § 21350. A testator who wants to make a transfer to a drafter or a care custodian must submit the instrument to an independent attorney for review. That attorney must then counsel the client, must attempt to assure that the transfer was not the product of undue influence, fraud, duress, or menace, and must prepare a certificate for delivery to the transferor and the drafter. California Probate Code § 21351.

The certificate itself, however, does not conclusively rebut the presumption of undue influence. In Winans v. Timar, 183 Cal.App.4th 102, 107 Cal.Rptr.3d 167 (2010), the Court of Appeal reversed a trial court's award of summary judgment to a caretaker who had obtained a certificate of independent review, holding that questions of fact remained about whether the independent attorney had provided adequate counseling to testator.

6. One undue influence case involves a law student who made the most of his legal education. In Estate of Reid, 825 So.2d 1 (Miss.2002), twenty-four year old Michael Cupit knocked on the door of Mary Lea Reid, a seventy-eight year old widow, expressing an educational interest in her historic antebellum home. The two began a relationship which, to the embarrassment of Reid's friends, included a great deal of "physical affection." Shortly thereafter, Cupit entered law school. Three years later, Cupit (perhaps having completed courses in property law, trusts and estates and family law) put his legal knowledge to work; Cupit first arranged to have Reid execute a deed conveying all of her real property to him; then, Cupit helped Reid draft a will leaving all of her property to him, and, for good measure, he obtained Reid's power of attorney. Finally, in a dramatic application of the "belts and suspenders" approach to lawyering, Cupit helped Reid adopt him as her son (thus rendering him Reid's only heir at law). When Reid's next-of-kin challenged the legal procedures, the Mississippi Supreme Court upheld the lower courts' nullification of the deed, will and power of attorney on grounds of "undue influence, overreaching, breach of fiduciary relationship, breach of an attorney-client relationship" and "breach of a position of trust." Sadly for Cupit, the court also upheld the nullification of the adoption as a fraud on the court.

7. ***The Role of Independent Advice or Counsel.*** Even apart from the California statute discussed in note 5, supra, courts generally acknowledge that a presumption of undue influence can be rebutted by proof that testator acted after obtaining the counsel of persons independent of the alleged influencer. But when has testator obtained independent counsel? Consider the following problem:

PROBLEM

Fannie Moses walks into your office and informs you of her intent to leave the bulk of her estate to her lover and lawyer, Clarence Holland. You explain to her that courts often presume undue influence when a testator leaves money to a lawyer who is not related to testator by blood or marriage. She reaffirms her intent to make Holland a beneficiary of her will, and asks you to take whatever steps would be necessary. What would you do? How would you improve on the course of action pursued by Dan Shell?

Increasingly, scholars have come to ask whether undue influence doctrine is designed, as often suggested, to protect the testator, or whether the doctrine is designed instead to enforce the norm that testators should provide for close family members. After studying 160 undue influence cases decided over a five-year period, Professor Melanie Leslie concluded:

> [C]ourts often evaluate potential beneficiaries from their own perspective, as opposed to that of the testator, thus appearing less concerned with effectuating testamentary intent than in forcing the testator to distribute his or her estate in accordance with prevailing notions of morality.

Melanie B. Leslie, The Myth of Testamentary Freedom, 38 Ariz. L. Rev. 235, 246 (1996); see also Ray D. Madoff, Unmasking Undue Influence, 81 Minn. L. Rev. 571, 575–77 (1997).

Professor Carla Spivack argues for abolition of the Undue Influence doctrine, emphasizing that the doctrine wastes judicial time on frivolous suits, and gives discontented heirs leverage to force a settlement with will beneficiaries, distorting decedent's intent and depleting the value of the estate. Carla Spivack, Why the Testamentary Doctrine of Undue Influence Should be Abolished, 58 Kan. L. Rev. 245, 286–87 (2010).

Recognizing that some courts (perhaps unwittingly) use capacity and undue influence doctrine to enforce social norms, Professor E. Gary Spitko suggests allowing the nonconforming testator to direct in her will that any contest concerning the will shall be adjudicated by an arbitrator appointed by the testator. This would enable the testator to appoint a decision-maker who will honor testator's concerns and values. See E. Gary Spitko, Gone But Not Conforming: Protecting the Abhorrent Testator from Majoritarian Cultural Norms Through Minority–Culture Arbitration, 49 Case W. Res. 275 (1999).

SECTION III. FRAUD

For a testator to be unduly influenced, the testator must be susceptible to influence. As we have seen, a confidential relationship between testator and beneficiary may lead the testator to believe that the beneficiary has testator's own interests at heart, and therefore makes testator susceptible to the beneficiary's influence. And testator's susceptibility is even greater if testator has become dependent on the beneficiary, or if testator's mind has weakened.

Suppose, however, testator remains intellectually alert, and manages his own affairs. His daughter baldly lies to him in order to induce him to disinherit her brother. Does the brother have any remedy? Consider the following statement:

> "Fraud which causes testator to execute a will consists of statements which are false, which are known to be false by the party who makes them, which are material, which are made with the intention of

> deceiving testator, which deceive testator, and which cause testator to act in reliance upon such statements."

In re Estate of Rosenberg, 196 Or. 219, 246 P.2d 858, 248 P.2d 340 (1952).

PROBLEM

John and June had two children, Charlie and Ruth. Charlie became an unemployed wanderer, and a great disappointment to his father. After several decades of marriage, John and June separated, and John moved to a hotel. One cause of the separation was John's anger over Ruth's financial support of Charlie. Soon after, John suffered a stroke and moved to a nursing home. Ruth visited John regularly, but John refused to see Charlie.

June died leaving a will that devised her diamond ring (worth $1,000) to Ruth, and the rest of her property, valued at $1,500, equally to both children. Charlie also received $12,301.06 worth of non-probate assets. After the expenses of administration and taxes were paid by that estate, Ruth received $61.90 and the diamond ring. Charles received from his mother in total, $12,367.96.

Soon after June's death, Ruth visited her father in the nursing home and angrily told him that her mother had "left everything to Charlie." In response, John asked Ruth to hire a lawyer, and she suggested her husband's cousin, whom John knew because they were members of the same lodge. John directed the lawyer to prepare a will leaving Charlie one dollar and the rest of his property to Ruth.

After John's death, Charlie contested the will, alleging that Ruth's statement that she took nothing from her mother's estate was fraudulent and made to induce John to leave everything to Ruth.

1. Did Ruth intend to deceive her father? If your answer is yes, why should Ruth's intent matter if her statements did, in fact, induce her father to cut Charlie out of his will? See In re Roblin's Estate, 210 Or. 371, 311 P.2d 459 (1957).

If Ruth had no intent to deceive, how would the problem be different from a case in which a beneficiary claims that testator's will was the product of testator's mistaken belief? How do courts typically treat allegations of mistaken belief?

2. Suppose Ruth had intended to deceive her father. Would Charlie have prevailed in this case? Why or why not?

How can a court tell whether a beneficiary's statement to testator induced a particular will disposition? Suppose testator had written a will cutting out Charlie after Ruth uttered the following statements—all with intent to deceive testator into cutting Charlie out of his will:

(a) "Charlie's wife is a gold-digger."

(b) "Charlie is trying to commit you to an institution."

(c) "It was Charlie who robbed your house last year. He needed money to buy drugs."

In which cases would Charlie be likely to succeed on a fraud claim? Would the fraud claim succeed if Ruth's statements were true? Cf. In re Ford's Estate, 19 Wis.2d 436, 120 N.W.2d 647 (1963) (holding that statements were not fraudulent when they may have been true).

NOTES AND QUESTIONS

1. In the problem above, suppose instead that John had been prepared to execute a will leaving all of his property to Charlie, perhaps on the belief that Ruth could care for herself, while Charlie was destitute. If Ruth then made statements designed to induce testator into cutting Charlie out, and if those statements did lead testator to cut Charlie out, would Charlie be entitled to reformation of the will to conform with testator's apparent intention? The conventional answer is no. That does not mean Charlie would be without remedy: Charlie could seek imposition of a constructive trust on any proceeds inherited by Ruth. The constructive trust, as we have already seen is a remedial device designed to prevent a person from unjustly retaining title to property. In Judge Cardozo's famous words:

> A constructive trust is the formula through which the conscience of equity finds expression. When property has been acquired in such circumstances that the holder of the legal title may not in good conscience retain the beneficial interest, equity converts him into a trustee.

Beatty v. Guggenheim Exploration Co., 225 N.Y. 380, 386, 122 N.E. 378, 380 (1919).

The constructive trust has also been invoked to aid beneficiaries of an unexecuted will who contend that beneficiaries of an earlier will fraudulently prevented testator from revoking the old will and executing the new one. See, e.g., Pope v. Garrett, 147 Tex. 18, 211 S.W.2d 559 (1948).

Latham v. Father Divine, 299 N.Y. 22, 85 N.E.2d 168 (1949), presents the most graphic illustration of the use of the constructive trust to prevent fraud. Testator had written a will benefitting Father Divine, the leader of a religious cult, and his followers. Shortly before testator's death, she had lawyers prepare a new will leaving property to her first cousins. The cousins alleged that Father Divine and his followers

> conspired to kill, and did kill, the deceased by means of a surgical operation performed by a doctor engaged by the defendants [Father Divine and his followers] without the consent or knowledge of any of the relatives of the deceased.

85 N.E.2d at 169. The cousins sought imposition of a constructive trust on estate proceeds payable to Father Divine on the ground that he and his followers had fraudulently prevented execution of the new will. The Court of Appeals held that the complaint was sufficient to withstand a motion to dismiss.

Note that in the Latham case, the cousins did not seek to invalidate testator's earlier will—the one in favor of Father Divine. Why not? Because the cousins were not testator's heirs, and hence would not have benefited from invalidation of the earlier will. Why didn't the heirs seek to invalidate the earlier will? They did—but dropped their contest after reaching a compromise with Father Divine!

2. J. Gamble Carson, already married to another woman, entered into a marriage ceremony with Alpha O. Carson, who did not know of the prior marriage (or of other marriages J. Gamble had also, apparently, solemnized). Alpha wrote a will leaving her property "to my husband J. Gamble Carson." Alpha died after living happily with J. Gamble for one year. If Alpha's relatives contest her will on the ground of fraud, should the court, on these undisputed facts:

a. direct a verdict for J. Gamble;

b. direct a verdict for Alpha's heirs; or

c. send the case to a jury?

What arguments would you make for each party? If the court sends the case to a jury, what questions of fact must the jury decide? Would your answers be different if Alpha and J. Gamble had lived together for six days? Six years? See Estate of Carson, 184 Cal. 437, 194 P. 5 (1920).

3. ***Fraud and non-disclosure.*** Martha Moon had two adult children: a son, Todd, and a daughter, June. Over a fifteen-year period beginning in 1972, Martha often instructed Todd that if she ever became seriously ill he should remove her jewelry from her safe deposit box and place it in his safe so that the items would not become part of her taxable estate at her death. In 1991, an ailing Martha removed her jewelry from the safe deposit box and placed it in her dresser drawer. Shortly thereafter, she became ill and was hospitalized. When Todd went to her safe deposit box to get the jewelry, he discovered it missing and informed his mother of that fact. An addled Martha, forgetting both her past instructions to Todd and that she had removed her jewelry from the box, panicked and accused Todd of accessing her safety deposit box without her consent and stealing the jewelry. Todd consulted June, who assured him that she knew the jewelry was in Martha's drawer, and that she would explain everything to Martha. Instead, June said nothing and stood by while her mother changed her will, disinheriting Todd and leaving everything to June. If the evidence clearly establishes that Martha changed her will because she falsely believed that her son stole her jewelry, did the sister commit fraud by failing to correct her mother's mistaken impression? Should a court invalidate the will, thus insuring that the son receives half of his mother's estate?

In Rood v. Newberg, 48 Mass.App.Ct. 185, 718 N.E.2d 886 (1999) the court confronted this issue. The court noted that fraud doctrine generally requires a false representation, and that non-disclosure does not usually amount to fraud. However, the court found that non-disclosure could amount to fraud *if* the non-disclosing party owed a duty to the testator. Here, there was a confidential relationship between the will beneficiary and testator, which gave rise to a duty to disclose to testator that she was mistaken in her beliefs. The court upheld the probate court's invalidation of certain testamentary bequests to the beneficiary.

SECTION IV. TORTIOUS INTERFERENCE WITH INHERITANCE

In 2007, eighty-year old Thelma Testator executed a valid will leaving the bulk of her entire estate to her close (younger) friend and next-door neighbor, Louise, who has taken care of Thelma since she was diagnosed with terminal cancer. Sometime after the execution, Thelma's nephew, Roger, an attorney and Thelma's only relative, had Thelma execute a deed to Thelma's home (her principal asset) to herself and Roger as joint tenants with right of survivorship. Roger did not explain to Thelma that the paper he asked her to sign was a deed. Instead, he told her that her signature would facilitate probate of the house. Thelma has died, and the probate court has distributed the rest of Thelma's estate, valued at $200, to Louise. Roger claims title to the house. Does Louise have any recourse? Consider the following case:

Estate of Ellis

Supreme Court of Illinois, 2009.
236 Ill.2d 45, 337 Ill.Dec. 678, 923 N.E.2d 237.

■ BURKE, J.

Grace Ellis executed a will in 1964 naming Shriners Hospitals for Children (Shriners) as beneficiary of her estate if she died without direct descendants. In 1999, she executed a new will naming James G. Bauman as sole beneficiary. Bauman was the pastor of the church of which Ellis was a member. When Ellis died in 2003, the 1999 will was admitted to probate. It was not until 2006 that Shriners became aware of its interest in the 1964 will. Shriners filed the instant action to contest the 1999 will based on theories of undue influence and fraud and included a tort count for intentional interference with an expectancy of inheritance. The circuit court of Cook County dismissed all counts as untimely pursuant to section 8–1 of the Probate Act of 1975 (755 ILCS 5/8–1 (West 2006)). On appeal, Shriners challenged only the dismissal of the tort claim. The appellate court affirmed the trial court's judgment. 381 Ill. App. 3d 427, 887 N.E.2d 467, 320 Ill. Dec. 323.

We allowed Shriners' petition for leave to appeal (210 Ill. 2d R. 315(a)) and now hold that Shriners' tort claim for intentional interference with an expectancy of inheritance is not limited by the six-month limitation period in section 8–1. Accordingly, we reverse the appellate court's judgment and remand to the trial court for further proceedings.

BACKGROUND

On December 3, 1964, Ellis executed a will designating her elderly parents as the primary beneficiaries of her estate, and designating her descendants and petitioner Shriners as contingent beneficiaries. On August 9, 1999, Ellis executed a new will designating Bauman as sole primary beneficiary and Ellis' surviving heirs at law as contingent beneficiaries of her estate.

Ellis died on October 8, 2003, at the age of 86, leaving no direct descendants. Her estate was worth more than $2 million dollars. The 1999 will was filed with the clerk of the circuit court of Cook County on October 9, 2003, and admitted to probate on October 29, 2003. Bauman was named independent executor of the estate.

Shriners first became aware of its interest in the 1964 will when Bauman filed the will with the circuit court in 2006 as part of a separate will contest brought by several of Ellis' heirs at law. Shriners filed its "Petition to Contest Will and For Other Relief" on August 8, 2006. Shriners alleged that Ellis met Bauman in 1994 and became a member of St. John's Lutheran Church in Glenview, Illinois, where Bauman was a pastor. Ellis subsequently gave Bauman powers of attorney over her health care and property, changed title to more than $1 million of her assets to Bauman, and purchased gifts and an automobile for Bauman. Counts I and II of the petition contested the validity of the 1999 will based on theories of undue influence and mental incapacity. Both counts requested the vacation of the order admitting the 1999 will to probate, and the admission to probate of the 1964 will.

Count III, the count that is at issue in this appeal, set forth a tort claim for intentional interference with an expectancy of inheritance. It alleged that: (1) but for the 1999 will obtained by Bauman, Shriners would have received Ellis' entire estate; (2) with knowledge of the 1964 will, Bauman set forth on an intentional scheme to interfere with Shriners' expectancy for his personal benefit; (3) Bauman interfered with Shriners' expectancy by abusing his position of trust, unduly influencing Ellis to execute a new will and to buy him gifts, violating his fiduciary duty to Ellis, taking advantage of her age and diminished capacity, and failing to notify beneficiaries and interested parties after her death; and (4) but for Bauman's actions, the bequest to Shriners would have been received. Shriners asked that the circuit court enter judgment against Bauman. In its prayer for relief, it requested compensatory damages in excess of $2 million dollars, an accounting of all *inter vivos* transfers and gifts, and punitive damages.

Bauman filed a motion to dismiss the petition, asserting that it was filed more than six months after admission to probate of the 1999 will, in violation of section 8–1 of the Probate Act of 1975 (755 ILCS 5/8–1 (West 2006)).

Section 8–1 provides, in relevant part:

> "Within 6 months after the admission to probate of a domestic will * * *, any interested person may file a petition in the proceeding for the administration of the testator's estate or, if no proceeding is

pending, in the court in which the will was admitted to probate, to contest the validity of the will." 755 ILCS 5/8–1 (West 2006).

The circuit court granted Bauman's motion, dismissed the entire petition with prejudice, and denied Shriners leave to amend.

On appeal, Shriners challenged only the dismissal of the tort claim in count III. The appellate court affirmed.

ANALYSIS

The sole issue in this appeal is the timeliness of Shriners' tort claim. As noted, the appellate court applied the six-month limitation period for filing a will contest set forth in section 8–1 of the Probate Act of 1975. This six-month limitation period is jurisdictional and not subject to tolling by fraudulent concealment or any other fact not expressly provided for by the Probate Act. Whether the six-month limitation is applicable to a tort claim is a question of statutory construction subject to *de novo* review. People v. Lewis, 223 Ill. 2d 393, 402, 860 N.E.2d 299, 307 Ill. Dec. 645 (2006).

Shriners contends that the appellate court's application of section 8–1 of the Probate Act of 1975 to a tort claim for intentional interference with expectancy of inheritance contradicts the clear and unambiguous language of the statute and confuses the tort with a will contest. We agree. Under the plain language of section 8–1, the six-month statutory limitation period applies to a "petition * * * to contest the validity of the will." 755 ILCS 5/8–1 (West 2006). A tort action for intentional interference with inheritance is distinct from a petition to contest the validity of a will, in several important respects. The single issue in a will contest is whether the writing produced is the will of the testator. Mount v. Dusing, 414 Ill. 361, 365, 111 N.E.2d 502 (1953); Hall v. Eaton, 259 Ill. App. 3d 319, 321, 631 N.E.2d 805, 197 Ill. Dec. 583 (1994). Any ground which, if proved, would invalidate the will, including undue influence, incapacity, fraud, or revocation, may state a cause of action. *Hall*, 259 Ill. App. 3d at 321. The object of a will contest proceeding is not to secure a personal judgment against an individual defendant but is a *quasi in rem* proceeding to set aside a will.

By contrast, in a tort claim for intentional interference with inheritance, "[o]ne who by fraud, duress or other tortious means intentionally prevents another from receiving from a third person an inheritance or gift that he would otherwise have received is subject to liability to the other for loss of the inheritance or gift." Restatement (Second) of Torts § 774B (1979). The "widely recognized tort" does not contest the validity of the will; it is a personal action directed at an individual tortfeasor. See Marshall v. Marshall, 547 U.S. 293, 312, 164 L. Ed. 2d 480, 498, 126 S. Ct. 1735, 1748 (2006) (the tort claim "seeks an *in personam* judgment against [the defendant], not the probate or annulment of a will"). Although some of the evidence may overlap with a will contest proceeding, a plaintiff filing a tort claim must establish the following distinct elements: (1) the existence of an expectancy; (2) defendant's intentional interference with the expectancy; (3) conduct that is tortious in itself, such as fraud, duress, or undue influence; (4) a reasonable certainty that the expectancy would have been realized but for the interference; and (5) damages. See In re Estate of Roeseler, 287 Ill. App. 3d 1003, 1021, 679 N.E.2d 393, 223 Ill. Dec. 208 (1997); In re Estate of Knowlson, 204 Ill. App. 3d 454, 457, 562 N.E.2d 277, 149 Ill. Dec. 813 (1990); Nemeth v. Banhalmi, 99 Ill. App. 3d 493, 499, 425 N.E.2d 1187, 55 Ill. Dec. 14 (1981); Restatement (Second) of Torts § 774– (1979). The remedy for a tortious interference action is not the setting aside of the will, but a judgment against the individual defendant, and, where the defendant has himself received the benefit of the legacy, a constructive trust, an equitable lien, or "a simple monetary judgment to the extent of the benefits thus tortiously acquired." Restatement (Second) of Torts § 774B(e) (1979). Thus, a tort claim for intentional interference with an expectancy is not a "petition * * * to contest the validity of the will" under the plain statutory language of section 8–1.

Although section 8–1 does not expressly limit a tort action, Illinois courts nevertheless have restricted the tort in certain circumstances where a plaintiff forgoes an opportunity to file a tort claim within the six-month period for a will contest. In *Robinson*, after the will and codicil were admitted to probate, plaintiffs entered into a settlement agreement with the estate, agreeing not to file a will contest in exchange for $125,000. More than six months later, plaintiffs filed a complaint for tortious interference with expectancy of inheritance. This court held that the tort action should have been dismissed where plaintiffs chose not to avail themselves of a will contest remedy.

This court noted in *Robinson* that the public policy underlying the enactment of section 8–1 is "an attempt to make the administration of an estate as orderly as possible because of the gravity of the interests at stake." *Robinson*, 97 Ill. 2d at 186. See also Pedersen v. Dempsey, 341 Ill. App. 141, 143, 93 N.E.2d 85 (1950) (reasons for restricting a will contest include "the pressing importance of securing an orderly settlement of estates, to prevent embarrassment to creditors and others, and to avoid as much confusion as possible in the vast amount of property rights and titles that pass through probate"). We said that to allow the plaintiffs to maintain a tort action "which in its practical effect would invalidate a will that has become valid under the Probate Act of 1975 * * * would permit the issue of undue influence, which would have been grounds for a will contest, to be litigated years after the will was admitted to probate and immune from contest on this issue." *Robinson*, 97 Ill. 2d at 186.

The concern articulated in *Robinson* about the "practical effect" of allowing the plaintiffs to maintain the tort action must be read in the context of the facts of that case. Unlike Shriners, the plaintiffs in *Robinson* could have obtained complete relief had they filed a timely will contest. Instead, they settled with the estate and agreed not to file any further claims arising from the will and codicil. In the instant case, we cannot say that a will contest was "available" to Shriners, nor that a successful will contest would have furnished the relief sought by Shriners in its tort action. The parties agree that Shriners was unaware of its bequest in the 1964 will until more than two years after the 1999 will had been admitted to probate. Our holding in *Robinson* was limited to not recognizing the tort action where plaintiffs have an opportunity to contest a probated will but choose not to do so, and subsequently enter into an agreement to take no further court action. Unlike the plaintiffs in *Robinson*, Shriners did not choose to forgo an opportunity to contest the probated will. It never had that opportunity. Once the 1999 will was admitted to probate, and the six-month jurisdictional period had passed with no will contest having been filed, the validity of the will was established for all purposes. *Robinson*, 97 Ill. 2d at 182–83.

Furthermore, a will contest would not have provided sufficient relief to Shriners because it would not have extended to the alleged *inter vivos* transfers of property. Shriners alleged that Bauman depleted Ellis' estate by inducing her to transfer assets worth more than $1 million to him prior to her death. In a successful will contest, Shriners could have recovered only assets that were part of the estate upon Ellis' death but could not have reached the assets transferred during her lifetime.

The court in In re Estate of Jeziorski, 162 Ill. App. 3d 1057, 1059, 516 N.E.2d 422, 114 Ill. Dec. 267 (1987), recognized under similar circumstances that a will contest alone could not fully compensate the plaintiffs. There, the plaintiffs filed an action to contest the decedent's will and also a claim for tortious interference with an expectancy. The plaintiffs alleged that the defendants had fraudulently procured *inter vivos* transfers from the decedent and that substantially all of the probate assets were outside of the estate. The trial court granted the defendants' motion to strike the tort claim, holding that heirs or legatees may not maintain an action for tortious interference where a will has been admitted to probate. *Jeziorski*, 162 Ill. App. 3d at 1059. The appellate court reversed and allowed the entire complaint to proceed in the probate division. The court rejected the defendants' contention that the will contest proceeding was sufficient to protect the parties' expectancies because, even if the plaintiffs had prevailed in a will contest proceeding, it would not have provided them the relief which they were seeking. *Jeziorski*, 162 Ill. App. 3d at 1063. Similarly, in the case at bar, had Shriners filed a timely will contest, it would not have provided a remedy for the alleged *inter vivos* transfers.

Accordingly, we find that section 8–1 does not apply to the tort action filed by Shriners against Bauman. We emphasize that our holding applies to the particular parties under the circumstances of this case and does not extend to a plaintiff who fails to bring a tort claim within the period for filing a will contest, where the will contest remedy was available.

CONCLUSION

For the foregoing reasons, we reverse the judgments of the appellate court and the circuit court and remand the cause to the circuit court for further proceedings consistent with this opinion.

Reversed and remanded.

QUESTIONS

1. Why didn't Shriners contest the 1999 will within the statutory six month period? If the problem was notice, why didn't Shriners receive notice? The applicable Illinois statutes require the petitioner in a probate proceeding to list, in the petition, all heirs and legatees of the testator (755 ILCS 5/6–4), and to "mail a copy of the petition to . . . each of the testator's heirs and legatees whose names and post office addresses are stated in the petition." 755 ILCS 5/6–10. Did Bauman ignore the statutory requirement?

The Illinois statute also made provision for notice by publication if the name or address of an heir or legatee is not stated in the petition. Would notice by publication have been helpful to Shriners? Why or why not?

2. If Shriners had known of the 1964 will and the probate proceeding, would that knowledge have barred Shriners from proceeding with a tortious interference claim? What relief did Shriners seek in the tortious interference action? How, if at all, could Shriners have obtained that relief within the context of a probate proceeding?

3. Suppose testator had made no *inter vivos* transfers to Bauman. Would the court have dismissed the tortious interference claim? Why or why not? Does your answer depend on whether Shriners had known of the 1964 will?

4. Many state courts strictly limit the tort to plaintiffs who cannot be made whole through a successful will contest. See, e.g., Jackson v. Kelly, 345 Ark. 151, 44 S.W.3d 328 (2001) (holding that, where testator's will devised her entire estate to her son and disinherited her daughter, testator's daughter could not sustain an action in tort against her brother after she failed to establish undue influence in probate court proceeding); see also Gianella v. Gianella, 234 S.W.3d 526 (Mo. App. 2007).

5. Suppose Shriners had never been named in testator's will. The beneficiaries of testator's last will learn that testator wants to write a will naming Shriners as the principal beneficiary. They plot to prevent testator from seeing a lawyer to draft a new will. Does Shriners have a tortious interference claim? Note that these facts resemble the claim that reached the Supreme Court in the Anna Nicole Smith case, Marshall v. Marshall, 547 U.S. 293, 126 S.Ct. 1735, 164 L.Ed.2d 480 (2006), discussed below.

How is this situation different from Latham v. Father Divine cited in Note 1 on page 471? Could the cousins in that case have prevailed on a tortious interference claim?

6. ***Burden of Proof.*** A number of states require a will contestant to establish undue influence by "clear and convincing" evidence. These same states may require that plaintiff establish tortious interference by a "preponderance of the evidence." See, e.g. Theriault v. Burnham, 2 A.3d 324 (Me.2010); Peralta v. Peralta, 139 N.M. 231, 131 P.3d 81 (2005). Is there any justification for the difference?

Consider the following facts: Bauman induces testator to leave his entire estate to Bauman, induces no lifetime transfers, and notifies Shriners immediately when offering the 1999 will for probate. What advice would you give to Shriners? How, if at all, would your advice change if

Bauman had also induced testator to make a $500,000 transfer during testator's lifetime?

7. *Statute of Limitations.* Suppose Bauman had induced testator to make an *inter* vivos transfer in 1995. After testator's death, could Shriners have prevailed on a tortious interference claim based on that transfer? At what point does the statute of limitations begin to run against Shriners? Would Shriners have had a claim against Bauman at any time before testator's death? Why or why not? Should it matter that Shriners had no claim against Bauman if *testator* had a claim?

8. *Punitive Damages?* If Shriners prevails at trial, to what remedies will Shriners be entitled? Who will pay the judgment?

As Professor Diane Klein explains, because the tort claim is an action at law,

> Compensatory and punitive damages are recoverable by a person tortiously injured by a third party's interference with his or her expected inheritance. As a legal claim in personam against the interfering tortfeasor, the costs of prosecuting and defending the action are borne by the parties, not the estate.

Diane J. Klein, Revenge of the Disappointed Heir: Tortious Interference with Expectation of Inheritance—A Survey With Analysis of State Approaches in the Fourth Circuit, 104 W. Va. L. Rev. 259 (2002).

By contrast, punitive damages are not typically available in undue influence cases. Even when an undue influence challenge succeeds, the prevailing parties do not obtain "compensation" from the undue influencer; instead, the estate is distributed in accordance with testator's instructions. In the words of the New Jersey Supreme Court,

> "because ... there has been no loss suffered by the estate, the only remedy sought is the admission of a particular will to probate. In that context, nothing in the way of compensatory damages is sought... and, by extension, there can be no basis for a claim for punitive damages."

Estate of Stockdale, 196 N.J. 275, 953 A.2d 454 (2008).

Nevertheless, in the Stockdale case, the court held that, in a limited set of undue influence cases, punitive damages should be available. In particular, where a stranger to the estate manages to obtain access to testator's assets by exercising undue influence, and those assets cannot be restored to the estate through usual probate mechanisms, the estate would have a compensatory claim against the stranger, and that compensatory claim could give rise to a punitive damages claim. Id. at 313–314, 953 A.2d at 476. In Stockdale, for instance, a neighbor who had obtained the confidence of a woman in her late 80s or early 90s, arranged for the woman to convey the house to him, and then used the woman's assets to pay for utilities on the house, while also "spiriting away" the woman's furniture. The court noted that these assets could not be restored to the woman's estate through usual probate mechanisms, and therefore could support claims for compensatory and punitive damages.

Should punitive damages be available more generally in undue influence cases? Under current law, what disincentives are there to prevent exercise of undue influence—particularly by non-family members who would otherwise not benefit from a testator's estate?

9. For a thorough exploration of courts' differing approaches to the tort, see Diane J. Klein, The Disappointed Heir's Revenge, Southern Style: Tortious Interference with Expectation of Inheritance—A Survey with Analysis of State Approaches in the Fifth and Eleventh Circuits, 55 Baylor L. Rev. 79 (2003); Diane J. Klein, A Disappointed Yankee In Connecticut (or Nearby) Probate Court: Tortious Interference With Expectation of Inheritance—: A Survey With Analysis Of State Approaches in the First, Second and Third Circuits, 66 U. Pitt. L. Rev. 235 (2004). For an extensive analysis of the tort, see Irene D. Johnson, Tortious Interference with Expectancy of Inheritance or Gift—Suggestions for Resort to the Tort, 39 U.Tol. L.Rev. 769 (2010).

* * *

Perhaps the most famous case involving tortious interference involves the model/actress Anna Nicole Smith, whose legal name was Vickie Lynn Marshall. Anna met her second husband, oil billionaire J. Howard Marshall, when he dropped in at Gigi's in Houston, where Anna was working the day shift as an exotic dancer. Anna was 26; Marshall was 89. Legend has it that Marshall was smitten after Anna performed a lap dance for him, and he began to pursue her aggressively. Shortly thereafter, Smith saw an ad in the newspaper to audition for Playboy Magazine. As the bankruptcy court tells it, the rest is history:

> She appeared on the cover photo of Playboy Magazine in March, 1992, as the centerfold Playmate of the month in the May, 1992 issue, and as the Playmate of the Year for 1992. She is also known for her television appearances as a model for Guess Jeans. J. Howard promoted and encouraged this career before and during their marriage and paid for acting lessons for her.
>
> After a courtship that lasted some two and a half years, Vickie agreed to marry J. Howard in June, 1994, and they were married immediately. At that time J. Howard was 89 years old, and Vickie was 26. This was the third marriage for J. Howard, and the second for Vickie. J. Howard had two sons from his first marriage, J. Howard Marshall III and Pierce. Vickie had a son from her prior marriage. While a prenuptial agreement was drafted, it was never signed by the parties.
>
> * * *
>
> As an inducement to marry him, J. Howard promised Vickie that he would leave her half of what he had. J. Howard made this promise repeatedly, both before and after the marriage.
>
> In December, 1992 J. Howard instructed Harvey Sorensen, an attorney who represented him from time to time, to arrange a [significant] gift to Vickie, "his future wife...." A few days earlier J. Howard

> also instructed Jeff Townsend, another attorney who did work for J. Howard, to arrange for Edwin Hunter to prepare a "catch-all trust" for Vickie's benefit. Neither of these projects was completed because Pierce fired Sorensen and conspired with Hunter to prevent the drafting and execution of the documents that would have accomplished the gift that J. Howard had directed.

In re Marshall, 253 B.R. 550 (Bankr. C.D.Cal.2000).

Pierce, terrified that his father would give money to Anna (Vickie), vowed to engage in "World War III" if Anna attempted to obtain any of Marshall's assets after his death, and by all accounts, he did. Anna made a claim for Marshall's assets in a Texas probate court, but lost when a jury ruled in favor of Pierce on all counts. Meanwhile, Anna filed for bankruptcy in California. Pierce filed a creditor's claim in the bankruptcy, alleging that Anna had defamed him. In response, Anna filed a counterclaim alleging tortious interference with a gift. After a trial, the bankruptcy court found Pierce liable, and awarded Anna punitive damages, citing Pierce's bad behavior during discovery which included destroying documents, failing to produce documents, falsely invoking attorney-client privilege, and ignoring court-imposed monetary sanctions. In total, Anna's judgment came to almost one half billion dollars.

The Ninth Circuit ultimately reversed the bankruptcy court determination, holding that the probate exception to the bankruptcy code deprived the bankruptcy court of jurisdiction. The Supreme Court of the United States reversed the Ninth Circuit, with the Bush administration weighing in on the side of Anna Nicole. Pierce died one month later.

The Supreme Court remanded the case to the Ninth Circuit for a determination of other issues. On September 7, 2006, Anna gave birth to a baby girl, Dannielynn. Anna's only son Daniel, age 20, died unexpectedly and mysteriously while visiting his mother and new sister in the hospital. Then, in February of 2007, Anna Nicole died from an accidental prescription drug overdose, prompting litigation over where she should be buried and over which of four men was Dannielynn's father.

In 2010, after the death of all of the original parties, the Ninth Circuit, on remand, concluded that the Texas probate court's factual findings precluded Anna Nicole from establishing the elements of her counterclaim. As a result, Pierce's estate was entitled to judgment. In re Marshall, 600 F.3d 1037 (9th Cir. 2010).

Yet another bizarre aspect of the Anna Nicole Smith saga was a dispute over Anna's burial place. See James T. R. Jones, Anna Nicole Smith and the Right to Control Disposition of the Dead, Louisville Bar Briefs, Vol 7., No. 5 (May 2007).

SECTION V. PREPARING FOR THE CONTEST: THE LAWYER'S ROLE

Often, even when a lawyer believes testator has capacity to make a will, and is not subject to undue influence, the lawyer also believes a will contest is likely. In that event, a major part of the lawyer's job is to plan for the contest that seems likely—or even inevitable. The planning function is important in estates of every size, but one of the most celebrated will contests of recent decades provides a useful focus for considering the options available to the lawyer. The estate of Seward Johnson—heir to the Johnson & Johnson pharmaceuticals fortune—became the subject of a nasty contest between Johnson's children and his wife. The contest featured major New York law firms on each side of the controversy, and generated a popular book by a former legal affairs columnist for the New York Times. The book, David Margolick's *Undue Influence* (1993), is a fascinating and gossipy account of the Johnson family, the preparation of Johnson's will, and the resulting trial. For now, though, let's consider what Johnson's lawyers might have done to avoid the debacle that ultimately resulted: a will contest in which Johnson's wife, the principal beneficiary of his will, agreed to pay $40 million out of the estate to settle the contest brought by Johnson's children, and in which the estate was depleted by another *$25 million* to pay both sides' legal fees. Professor John Langbein's review of Margolick's book provides useful background:

John H. Langbein, Book Review, 103 Yale L.J. 2039, 2039–40 (1994).

Basia Piasecka, a thirty-year-old Polish emigre, landed in New York in 1968 seeking work. Through Polish connections, she found her way to kitchen employment in the New Jersey home of Seward Johnson and his second wife, Essie. Within months, Basia became Seward's mistress. Seward, then seventy-three, was an heir to the Johnson & Johnson pharmaceuticals fortune. Although Johnson & Johnson treated Seward as a nominal officer, he played no role in the company. He spent his decades philandering and dabbling in oceanography through a foundation that he established. In 1971 Seward divorced Essie, settling $20 million on her to dissolve their thirty-two-year marriage. Weeks later Seward married Basia, who was more than forty years his junior. Their marriage endured a dozen years, until Seward died from cancer in May 1983.

Seward's estate was valued at his death in excess of $400 million. Seward was survived by his six adult children, four of whom were older than Basia. Seward had shown little interest in the children when they were young, and his relationship with them as adults was largely perfunctory, although Basia cultivated amicable relations with the children throughout her marriage to Seward. As adults, the children were embarrassing wastrels, constantly in debt to their trust funds. They fared as badly in their marriages and family lives as in their careers and business affairs. The extravagant marital and extramarital adventures of one of Seward's daughters, Mary Lea, would strain credulity in a work of cheap fiction. Beginning in the 1940's, Seward had used inter vivos trusts to settle Johnson & Johnson stock worth tens of millions on each child. In the many wills that he executed across the next four decades, he excluded his children from benefitting further in his estate. After marrying Basia, Seward revised his estate plan several times, making ever larger provision for her. His last will, executed in April 1983 when his struggle with cancer was near the end, devised a little of his estate to his foundation and the rest to Basia. The will excluded the children, as well as their spouses and descendants.

At about the time that he married Basia, Seward hired the prominent New York law firm of Shearman & Sterling to take charge of his estate planning. The firm placed Seward's affairs in the hands of a young associate, Nina Zagat.

* * *

QUESTIONS

Suppose you had been Nina Zagat. Would you have anticipated a will contest? If so, what would you have told Seward about the anticipated contest? Would you have told him that there was a possibility that, no matter what steps he took, the contest might succeed? If you said that to Seward, might he have decided to take his legal business elsewhere?

What steps would you have recommended to Seward, and how would you have couched your recommendations? Consider the following:

1. Would it have been useful to have a psychiatrist examine Seward at the time he wrote his will? Are there any reasons for *not* suggesting a psychiatric examination? If so, what are they?

2. Would it have been useful to videotape Seward's execution ceremony? Note that in the Gonsalves case, testator's lawyer arranged a videotaping of the execution ceremony. What risks, if any, accompany videotaping of the execution ceremony? See Estate of Lakatosh, 441 Pa.Super. 133, 145, 656 A.2d 1378, 1384–85 (1995), where the court had this to say about an audiotape prepared by testator's lawyer:

> ... Attorney Jacobs testified at trial that, because Roger was to receive the bulk of Rose's estate and was not her blood relative, he thought it wise to make the tape as evidence of the will's validity, should it be challenged. Instead of reinforcing the integrity of the will, the audio tape supports the proposition that Rose suffered from a weakened intellect.
>
> The audio tape revealed that Rose was easily distracted and clearly had difficulty remaining focused on the issue of the will. Also, as pointed out by the trial court, even though Attorney Jacobs repeatedly attempted to re-direct Rose's attention to the issue of the will, she could not remain focused or coherent.

3. Whom would you have selected to witness Seward Johnson's will? Why?

4. Would you have suggested to Seward that he modify his intended disposition to avoid a will contest? What modifications might have been helpful to Seward, and why? Is it the lawyer's role to suggest will dispositions to the client, or should the lawyer simply ascertain testator's intent and draft an instrument that gives testator's property to testator's intended beneficiaries?

* * *

Consider Professor Langbein's take on the lawyering done on Seward Johnson's behalf:

> When a legal system is as ill-equipped as ours is to dispose effectively of marginal capacity suits, the system places a considerable premium on taking preventive measures to forestall attack. Seward Johnson's estate cried out for such contest planning. The indicia of potential contest were visibly present when the will was drafted. The will disinherited the children totally, from a $400 million estate. The children were known to have had no particular affection for Seward and Basia, hence no incentive to avoid besmirching the couple's names with the ugly evidence of eccentricity, vulnerability, and overbearing that is the currency of undue influence suits.

Basia, who had to defend the will, was an intrinsically unsympathetic figure—half the testator's age, imperious and temperamental, an arriviste flaunting a life of unimaginable luxury near her former haunts as cook and chambermaid.

Had Seward's lawyers responded to these flashing warning lights, three broad strategies were open to them to protect the estate against the threat of contest.

A. Obtaining Evidence of Capacity

Because the "worst evidence" principle of American probate law requires the testator to be dead before the court decides whether he was capable when he was alive, good planners take steps to generate and preserve favorable evidence of the testator's capacity and independence. Counsel should have arranged for Seward to explain why he chose to exclude the children, and why he chose to favor Basia. Sometimes counsel advises the testator to write this explanation in a letter, or counsel works with the testator to prepare an affidavit. Sometimes it is arranged for the testator to be video taped reading from a script or speaking from notes. Another variant is for the lawyer to interview the testator for a stenographic transcript or video record, asking the testator to explain the will, and giving him the opportunity to show his deliberation and volition.

Seward Johnson remained vigorous despite his long decline until his last few days, yet no steps were taken at the times he executed his series of wills to create and preserve this kind of powerfully persuasive evidence of his testamentary capacity, independence, and freedom from imposition.

B. Involving Potential Witnesses

Another common precaution is to arrange for persons who are likely to survive the testator to inform themselves about his condition at the time of the making of the will, so that they can testify about the subject in the event of contest. Such persons might include both medical experts new to the testator, and persons who have been long familiar with him and are thus able to form a comparative view of his capacity at the time of the making of the will. These persons interview the testator about his condition, the contents of his will, and his reasons for disinheriting his "natural objects." Under this drill, the witnesses execute fairly contemporaneous affidavits, reciting their contact with the testator and their reasons for concluding that the testator was of sound mind and acting freely. Occasionally, the planner arranges for these persons to serve as supernumerary attesting witnesses, who attend and attest the execution of the will; other planners prefer to confine the involvement of these potential witnesses outside the will.

Seward Johnson's lawyers made only an isolated and ineffectual use of this technique. On the day Seward executed his last will, Nina Zagat had an attending physician sign a canned certificate reciting that Seward was "of sound mind and memory and aware of his acts."

C. The No–Contest Clause

A third avenue of defense is to include a no-contest clause in the will. In Seward Johnson's case, he would have needed to alter his testamentary plan somewhat, and provide modest but conditional devises for each child. The condition would have been that all the children's devises would be canceled if any child contested the will. Very shortly before Seward's death, lawyers at Shearman & Sterling gave passing thought to drafting a no-contest clause to include in Seward's will but ultimately did nothing about it.

* * *

Why were the common defensive measures not taken in planning the Johnson estate?.... [I]n the course of the penultimate round of will drafting two months before Seward's death, Seward inquired of Shearman & Sterling's Nina Zagat whether the children might be able to contest the will. She assured him that there were no grounds for contest.

One is left to wonder whether the enormous executor compensation that Shearman & Sterling wrote into Seward's will played some role in the firm's seemingly wishful failure to attend to proper contest planning. The best defense against the allegation that Basia and Nina conspired to impose Basia's scheme upon Seward's will would have been a videotape or affidavit, in which Seward explained not only why he favored Basia and disinherited his children, but also why he chose to lavish millions on avoidable executor fees for Nina.

103 Yale L.J. at 2045–47.

* * *

No–Contest Clauses

Professor Langbein asks why Seward Johnson's lawyers chose not to include a no-contest clause in Johnson's will. What is a no-contest clause (also called an *in terrorem* clause because of its objective—striking terror in the heart of potential contestants)? In the Haynes case, lawyer Buttermore inserted no-contest clauses in Mrs. Dutrow's will and in the trust instruments he drafted for Mrs. Dutrow. The clause included in one of the trust instruments, which was nearly identical to the clause in Mrs. Dutrow's will, was as follows:

> If any beneficiary under this trust shall contest the validity of, or object to this instrument, or attempt to vacate the same, or to alter or change any of the provisions hereof, such person shall be thereby deprived of all beneficial interest thereunder and of any share in this Trust and the share of such person shall become part of the residue of the trust, and such person shall be excluded from taking any part of such residue and the same shall be divided among the other persons entitled to take such residue.

Consider the effect of such a clause. Suppose Mrs. Dutrow's will had left $10,000 to each of the Haynes grandchildren, and the remainder of her estate to Dorcas Cotsworth. Suppose further that the New Jersey courts routinely enforced no-contest clauses. If the Haynes grandchildren had approached you about contesting Mrs. Dutrow's will, what advice would you have given to them?

Consider the following questions:

1. What would a grandchild have received from Mrs. Dutrow's will if the grandchild chose not to contest the will?

2. What would a grandchild have received if the grandchild contested the will, and the contest proved unsuccessful?

3. What would a grandchild have received if the grandchild contested the will, and the contest proved successful?

4. Was this the typical grandparent/grandchild relationship? Does that inform the decision?

5. Suppose one grandchild contested the will. Would the other grandchild be entitled to retain his $10,000 bequest?

Note, in particular, Question 3: if a grandchild had successfully contested the will, the no-contest clause would have been invalidated along with the rest of the will, and the grandchild would have been able to take the share he would have received under Mrs. Dutrow's last validly executed will.

Suppose a testator included a provision expressly excluding all grandchildren if any of them were to contest the will. Would such a provision be enforceable? See Tunstall v. Wells, 144 Cal.App.4th 554, 50 Cal.Rptr.3d 468 (2006)[holding that such a provision would not be contrary to public policy].

No-contest clauses, then, require the contestant to make an evaluation of the likelihood that the contest will prove successful. If the likelihood is small, the contestant might choose not to contest, in order to preserve whatever provisions testator made for the contestant.

QUESTION

The Seward Johnson estate was valued at $400 million. Would a no-contest clause have been effective to prevent the children from contesting the will if the will itself

(a) left the children nothing?

(b) left the children $500,000 each?

(c) left the children $20,000,000 each?

Explain your answers. Do your answers suggest why Seward Johnson's lawyers may have chosen not to include a no-contest clause? Would you have wanted to be the lawyer who informed Seward Johnson that he could best avoid a will contest by leaving each of his ungrateful children $20 million?

No–Contest Clauses and Probable Cause

In the Haynes case, as noted, Mrs. Dutrow's will included a no-contest clause. Does that mean that the Haynes grandchildren would have been entitled to nothing if their contest ultimately proved unsuccessful? No, it doesn't, because the court held the no-contest clause unenforceable on the facts of the Haynes case, where the contest was made in good faith and based on probable cause.

The New Jersey courts had long held no-contest clauses enforceable, subject to exceptions not relevant in the Haynes case. In 1977, however, after Mrs. Dutrow's death, the New Jersey legislature enacted a statute patterned on § 3–905 of the Uniform Probate Code, reproduced below. While the New Jersey Supreme Court held that the statute was not, by its terms, applicable to Mrs. Dutrow's will, the court also held, in a portion of the opinion not reproduced above, that "the legislative handling of the subject is, and should be, strongly influential in the judicial quest for the important social values which are constituent elements of the common law . . ."

What was "the legislative handling of the subject"?

UNIFORM PROBATE CODE

SECTION 3–905. PENALTY CLAUSE FOR CONTEST.

A provision in a will purporting to penalize any interested person for contesting the will or instituting other proceedings relating to the estate is unenforceable if probable cause exists for instituting proceedings.

* * *

NOTES AND QUESTIONS

1. When does a contestant have "probable cause" to institute proceedings? Did the children have probable cause to contest Seward Johnson's will?

If a court concludes that the proponents are not entitled to summary judgment, does that mean that the contestants had probable cause? If the contestants can establish the existence of a confidential relationship between the principal beneficiary and the testator, what more need the contestants prove to establish probable cause?

2. Why would the drafters of the UPC have included a provision like § 3–905? The provision is certainly a good one for estates litigators, but is it a good one for anyone else? UPC § 3–905 reduces the risk associated with contesting a will. Is that a good thing?

Would you expect a provision like UPC § 3–905 to increase the likelihood of settlement of will contests or to decrease the likelihood? Why? See generally Martin D. Begleiter, Anti–Contest Clauses: When You Care Enough to Send the Final Threat, 26 Ariz. St. L. Rev. 629 (1994) (criticizing the UPC approach); Gerry W. Beyer, Rob G. Dickinson & Kenneth L. Wake, The Fine Art of Intimidating Disgruntled Beneficiaries with In

Terrorem Clauses, 51 S.M.U. L. Rev. 225 (1998) (recommending that the Texas legislature adopt a statute which would enforce no-contest clauses even when the contestant has a good faith basis for bringing the contest).

3. The UPC's approach to no-contest clauses has not yet won general acceptance. See, e.g., Dunklin v. Ramsay, 328 Ark. 263, 944 S.W.2d 76 (1997) (enforcing no-contest clause). California has recently amended its statutes to bar enforcement of no contest clauses against beneficiaries who have "probable cause." Cal. Prob. Code § 21311.

In New York, no-contest clauses are enforceable even against contestants who have probable cause. N.Y. EPTL § 3–3.5(b). New York, however, makes an exception for contests based on allegations that the will was the product of forgery or that the will was revoked. N.Y. EPTL § 3–3.5(b)(1).

Why are forgery and revocation different? Is it because contests on those grounds expose less of testator's "dirty laundry," and therefore would be less objectionable to testator?

PROBLEM: SCOPE OF NO-CONTEST CLAUSES

Gary Greedy's wife left a will devising $1,000,000 to Gary. The will also included a no-contest clause identical to the one used in Mrs. Dutrow's will. Gary enters your office seeking a larger share of his wife's $4,000,000 estate. He wants to know whether he risks losing his devise if

(a) he asserts a right to take an elective share of his wife's estate. See Barr v. Dawson, 158 P.3d 1073 (Okla.Civ.App. 2006).

(b) he challenges a trust created for the wife's descendants on the ground that the trust violates the Rule Against Perpetuities. See In re Harrison's Estate, 22 Cal.App.2d 28, 70 P.2d 522 (1937).

(c) he seeks construction to determine whether a devise of "my country home" includes the furniture in the house. See N.Y. EPTL § 3–3.5(b)(3)(E); McQuone v. Brown, 2001 WL 1447232 (2001).

(d) he challenges the qualifications of his wife's sister, who was named in the will to serve as executor. See Estate of Newbill, 781 S.W.2d 727 (Tex.App.1989); Estate of Hoffman, 97 Cal.App.4th 1436, 119 Cal.Rptr.2d 248 (2002).

(e) he seeks a determination that certain property did not pass through his wife's estate because he and his wife owned the property as joint tenants with right of survivorship. See Jacobs–Zorne v. Superior Court, 46 Cal.App.4th 1064, 54 Cal.Rptr.2d 385 (1996).

(f) he asserts a creditor's claim against the estate alleging that his wife breached an oral promise to devise to him $2,000,000? Compare Varney v. Superior Ct., 10 Cal.App.4th 1092, 12 Cal.Rptr.2d 865 (1992), with Zwirn v. Schweizer, 134 Cal.App.4th 1153, 36 Cal.Rptr.3d 527 (2005).

(g) he brings an action against his wife's sister for tortious interference with inheritance. See Munn v. Briggs, 185 Cal.App.4th 578, 110 Cal.Rptr.3d 783 (2010).

(h) he brings an action to determine whether he is the beneficiary of his wife's individual retirement account under ERISA? See MacDonald v. MacDonald, 2005 WL 580530 (Cal. App. 2005).

(i) he (unsuccessfully) seeks to probate a subsequent will leaving him more than $1,000,000. See Seymour v. Biehslich, 371 Ark. 359, 266 S.W.3d 722 (2007).

(j) he cooperates with lawyers contesting the will on behalf of a child who received a smaller share of the estate than the wife's other children. See Estate of Fairbairn, 46 A.D.3d 973, 846 N.Y.S.2d 779 (2007).

Advise Gary.

Could Gary's wife's lawyer have drafted a no-contest clause which would be triggered by any or all of Gary's potential claims?

Some jurisdictions enable litigants to obtain a declaratory judgment that a particular motion or action would not trigger the no-contest provisions in a will. See, e.g., Sinclair v. Sinclair, 284 Ga. 500, 670 S.E.2d 59 (2008).

Ante–Mortem Probate and Other Tools for Reducing Will Contests

In none of the will contests discussed in this chapter have the courts had the benefit of testimony from the one person whose state of mind is most relevant—the testator. Why? Because the contest occurs after testator's death. Does this system make sense, or should we permit testator to test a will's validity before her death?

During the 1970s, there was a significant movement toward a system of ante-mortem probate. A number of scholars suggested that a procedure permitting evaluation of testator's will before testator's death would reduce the incidence of will contests by disappointed heirs seeking compromise settlements. Each scholar suggested a somewhat different model for ante-mortem probate. See Howard Fink, Ante–Mortem Probate Revisited: Can an Idea Have Life After Death?, 37 Ohio St. L. J. 264 (1976); John H. Langbein, Living Probate: The Conservatorship Model, 77 Mich. L. Rev. 63 (1978); Gregory S. Alexander, The Conservatorship Model: A Modification, 77 Mich. L. Rev. 86 (1978); Gregory S. Alexander & Albert M. Pearson, Alternative Models of Ante–Mortem Probate and Procedural Due Process, 78 Mich. L. Rev. 89 (1979).

Three states—Arkansas, North Dakota, and Ohio—enacted ante-mortem probate statutes in the late 1970s, and Alaska has authorized ante-mortem probate more recently. What effect have the statutes had? See Aloysius A. Leopold & Gerry W. Beyer, Ante–Mortem Probate: A Viable Alternative, 43 Ark. L. Rev. 131, 172–74 (1990):

> Compared to those of North Dakota and Arkansas, the Ohio ante-mortem statutes have generated the greatest use, perhaps owing to the larger population of Ohio resulting in the increased interest in ante-mortem probate....
>
> * * *
>
> Despite the greater awareness of the ante-mortem probate alternative in Ohio, it nonetheless appears that the statute is infrequently used. In the first eight years of its availability, approximately eight ante-mortem probate cases were filed in Franklin County, one of Ohio's largest counties. It is believed that even fewer cases were filed in other counties. The statute appears to be used most frequently when an attorney has prepared a will for a person who is under guardianship or who is elderly.

The National Conference of Commissioners on Uniform State Laws considered a draft statute on ante-mortem probate, but later dropped the project for lack of support. Why did ante-mortem probate not garner more significant support? Consider the following:

> A ... failing of living probate is the high price it exacts from testators in return for an ephemeral assurance that their wills are secure from challenge. That price includes physical and mental examination, participation in the court proceeding, the cost of an attorney and of a guardian ad litem (depending upon the proposal adopted), and the risk of family disharmony. These costs will inevitably deter many testators from using the proceeding regardless of the benefits obtained.

Mary Louise Fellows, The Case Against Living Probate, 78 Mich. L. Rev. 1066, 1094 (1980). Do you agree with Professor Fellows?

Ray Madoff explores whether and to what extent mediation can be used to minimize will disputes. See Mediating Probate Disputes: A Study of Court–Sponsored Programs, 38 Real Prop. Prob. & T. J. 697 (2004). In another article, she argues that families involved in will disputes are less inclined than those involved in divorces to settle or engage in mediation, probably because wills doctrine inadvertently encourages parties to seek a judicial determination. See Ray D. Madoff, Lurking in the Shadow: The Unseen Hand of Doctrine in Dispute Resolution, 76 S. Cal. L. Rev. 161 (2003).

Finally, Professor Calvin Massey suggests that states enact statutes to allow people to designate heirs-at-law. This would nip will contests in the bud by denying standing to closest family members. See Calvin Massey, Designation of Heirs: A Modest Proposal to Diminish Will Contests, 37 Real Prop. Prob. & Tr. J. 577 (2003).

SECTION VI. SPECIAL PROBLEMS AFFECTING SOME GAY, LESBIAN AND TRANSGENDERED TESTATORS

Disappointed heirs often react as much to the personal rejection associated with a will leaving them out as to the financial loss. If heirs also have difficulty accepting the testator's way of life, the likelihood of contest is even greater. As a result, gay men and lesbians can face significant hurdles when they try to channel their assets to their partners. And, because a majority of states withhold marital privileges from same-sex partners, individuals in those partnerships cannot be assured of an intestate share of his or her companion's property. See Susan N. Gary, Adapting Intestacy Laws to Changing Families, 18 Law & Ineq. 1 (2000) (exploring ways that the law could be reformed to provide for intestate distributions in non-traditional families); E. Gary Spitko, The Expressive Function of Succession Law and the Merits of Non–Marital Inclusion, 41 Ariz. L. Rev. 1063 (1999) (showing how intestacy laws negatively impact gay and lesbian families, and criticizing the drafters of the Uniform Probate Code for failing to rectify this result); T.P. Gallanis, Default Rules, Mandatory Rules, and the Movement for Same–Sex Equality, 60 Ohio St. L. J. 1513 (1999) (also showing how the intestacy rules fail to account for gay and lesbian families); Mary Louise Fellows, Committed Partners and Inheritance: An Empirical Study, 16 Law & Ineq. J. 1 (1998) (recommending that the Uniform Probate Code be amended to provide an intestacy share to decedent's "committed partner.")

As a result of the law, a non-traditional family's need for estate planning may be even greater than in more traditional families. This need came to a head during the AIDS crisis of the 1980s and 1990s, which disproportionately affected gay men and made estate planning essential even for relatively young people. When a young person dies, the risk of conflict between the person's partner and family of origin may be even stronger than it ordinarily would be; biological families may have had insufficient time to understand and accept testator's homosexuality, and therefore may bear greater anger and hurt both at the testator and at the prospect (and reality) of premature death.

As of this writing in early 2011, five states (New Hampshire, Massachusetts, Connecticut, Iowa, and Vermont) and the District of Columbia recognize same sex marriage. Several other states recognize same-sex marriages performed elsewhere. A constitutional challenge to California's prohibition on gay marriage appears likely to reach the United States Supreme Court. Moreover, a number of other states, while not recognizing same sex marriage, grant to same-sex couples all of the privileges, benefits and obligations of marriage. As a result, in more and more states, committed same-sex couples have elective share and intestacy rights, as well as all other rights that a spouse may have under the applicable state probate code.

When a state treats a partner as an intestate heir with rights equivalent to the spouse, the state reduces the number of relatives who might have standing to contest the will; because the testator dies with a "spouse," the testator's will may be contested only if testator has a child or parent who wishes to contest it. Collateral relatives will not have standing. More importantly, when a will challenge is successful, the results will be less devastating to the remaining partner, because the partner is legally entitled to at least a large fraction of testator's estate. It is important to note, however, that because the federal government does not legally recognize same-sex partnerships, neither a same-sex marriage, civil union, reciprocal beneficiary designation or a domestic partnership can grant important federal rights, such as the marital deduction, Social Security benefits, immigration protections and veterans' benefits.

A recent Colorado statute takes a different approach, authorizing any two individuals to designate each other as the beneficiary of the other for estate planning and other purposes. Colo. Rev. Stat. §§ 15–22–101–15–22–112. Even if the parties to a designated beneficiary agreement do not execute wills or other estate planning documents, a designated beneficiary is entitled to inherit by intestate succession.

Of course, the move towards recognition of same-sex relationships has not been universal. In fact, the majority of states have passed so called "Defense of Marriage Acts"; statutes designed to bar same sex marriages in those states and to prevent their state courts from recognizing same-sex marriages entered into in other states.

For an in-depth look at how current law fails to take account of the needs of a wide variety of non-traditional families, see Ralph C. Brashier, Inheritance Law and the Evolving Family (Temple Univ. Press 2004).

When a gay or lesbian testator writes a will giving his or her estate to a partner, contests sometimes result. Few of those cases reach the appellate courts. The following case is a notable exception:

Will of Kaufmann

Supreme Court of New York, Appellate Division, 1964.
20 A.D.2d 464, 247 N.Y.S.2d 664, Aff'd 15 N.Y.2d 825, 205 N.E.2d 864, 257 N.Y.S.2d 941 (1965).

■ McNALLY, J.:

This will contest is limited to the issue of undue influence. The contestants are the distributees of, and the proponent is unrelated to, the decedent. Two juries have found undue influence. On the prior appeal, by a divided court, the decree denying probate was reversed and a new trial directed because of error (14 A. D. 2d 411). Appellant argues the proof in its totality fails to establish a jury question on the issue of undue influence. . . .

The instrument offered for probate is dated June 19, 1958. The decedent, Robert D. Kaufmann, was then 44, unmarried, a millionaire with a substantial income. Robert's sole distributees were two brothers, Joel and Aron. Joel is married and his sons are Richard and Lee, infants over 14 years of age. Aron is unmarried and an invalid.

Robert had inherited all his wealth from his parents. He had no liking or aptitude for business. His inherited wealth consisted principally of minority interests in various family enterprises in which he did not actually participate.

In and prior to 1947 Robert was intimately and warmly associated and identified with his relatives; he lived with his brother Joel in Washington and was particularly attached to and fond of his nephews, Richard and Lee. In 1947 Robert took up painting, an interest which he pursued and developed with increasing involvement with the passage of time and with a great measure of artistic success. During the latter part of 1947 or early 1948, Robert came to New York City and set up his own establishment. He was then about 34.

* * *

It would appear that Robert and the proponent, Walter A. Weiss, met in 1948. Weiss was the senior of Robert by five years. Weiss did not testify at either of the two trials. In his pretrial examination Weiss stated he was an attorney who did not practice. His pedigree, resources and means of income in 1948 do not appear.

* * *

In 1949 Weiss moved into Robert's apartment at 965 Fifth Avenue. Weiss lived with Robert until the latter's death on April 18, 1959.

* * *

Robert and Weiss traveled to Paris in 1950 for a few months; to Europe, West Indies, the Virgin Islands, Haiti, Greece and other countries during 1952 and 1953 and around the world in 1956. Robert paid all expenses. Weiss claims to have paid his share of living and travel expenses but we have no evidence other than his declaration on that score.

* * *

In 1949 Robert opened a checking account with Bankers Trust Company. Weiss was given power to draw against this account. Soon thereafter a similar arrangement was made as to an account with Chemical Bank New York Trust Co. Thereafter, until Robert's death, Weiss had the power to draw against all Robert's bank accounts. In 1951 Weiss acquired a general power of attorney from Robert. Weiss had unrestricted access to Robert's safe-deposit box.

The record establishes that since 1950 those selected by Weiss rendered medical and legal services to Robert. In 1951 Robert changed his attorneys. On June 13, 1951 he executed a new will. This enlarged Weiss' share of Robert's estate. In addition to personal effects and paintings, the will devises to Weiss the 74th Street residence and one half of the residue, and he is made the trustee of several trusts and one of three executors, the others being Robert's brother, Joel, and Robert's psychiatrist, Dr. Janet M. Rioch. Weiss' expectancy under the provisions of this will was over $500,000.

Contemporaneously with the will of June 13, 1951 Robert signed a letter of the same date purporting to explain his will. The letter affirms the will contains unusual provisions in that "a sizeable portion" of Robert's estate is devised to a man "not a member of my family". The letter to Robert's brothers proceeds to state the reasons for the provisions. It recites that Robert first met Weiss in 1946; that Robert's outlook was then "approaching the nadir"; he was a "frustrated time-wasting little boy"; he was "terribly unhappy, highly emotional and filled to the brim with a grandly variegated group of fears, guilt and assorted complexes". It states that Robert fortunately met Walter who encouraged him to submit to psychoanalysis. In addition, the letter goes on to state:

> "Walter gave me the courage to start something which slowly but eventually permitted me to supply for myself everything my life had heretofore lacked: an outlet for my long-latent but strong creative ability in painting * * * a balanced, healthy sex life which before had been spotty, furtive and destructive; an ability to reorientate myself to actual life and to face it calmly and realistically. All of this adds up to Peace of Mind—and what a delight, what a relief after so many wasted, dark, groping, fumbling immature years to be reborn and become adult!"
>
> "I am eternally grateful to my dearest friend—best pal, Walter A. Weiss. What could be more wonderful than a fruitful, contented life and who more deserving of gratitude now, in the form of an inheritance, than the person who helped most in securing that life? I cannot believe my family could be anything else but glad and happy for my own comfortable self-determination and contentment and equally grateful to the friend who made it possible."
>
> "Love to you all,"
>
> "Bob."

The letter is accompanied by an envelope addressed to Robert's brothers and the Kaufmann family. The envelope is unsealed. The letter and envelope thereafter accompanied the three succeeding wills prepared by attorneys other than the one who drew the will of 1951. Prior to 1954, the 1951 letter was in the possession of the attorney who had drawn the 1951 and the 1953 wills. In or about May, 1954, the letter of June 13, 1951 and the letter of October 23, 1952, hereafter described, came into the possession of Weiss who caused them to be delivered with the 1953 will to the attorneys who thereafter prepared the last two wills.

* * *

The 1951 letter is not based on reality. Robert had become aware of his desire to paint, had received instruction and had started painting prior to his meeting with Weiss. The will of 1950 provides for a bequest of $2,500 to Leo Steppat "my art teacher". Weiss had nothing to do with Robert's creative ability in painting. In attributing to Weiss the "start [of] something which slowly but eventually permitted me to supply for myself everything my life had heretofore lacked: an outlet for my long-latent but strong creative ability in painting", the letter is not in accord with the record. Weiss in his pretrial statement acknowledged he did not know why Robert attributed to him his painting career.

The letter refers to the "courage" acquired from Weiss "to supply for myself * * * a balanced, healthy sex life which before had been spotty, furtive and destructive". The implication is that Weiss in some fashion was identified with Robert's sex life. Weiss' pretrial statement emphatically denied it.

* * *

The will of April 8, 1953 designates Weiss sole executor. Shortly thereafter, on May 28, 1953, Weiss' confidential memorandum to Robert states: "6. WILLS—Your will should be gone over, since there is at least one point needs changing."

* * *

The emotional base reflected in the letter of June 13, 1951 is gratitude utterly unreal, highly exaggerated and pitched to a state of fervor and ecstasy. The jury could have found, in addition, that Weiss conveyed to Robert false accusations as to Joel's integrity and mismanagement of the family enterprises. If the accusations were intended to and did cause Robert to disinherit members of his family in whole or in part, Weiss exercised undue influence. (Matter of Anna, 248 N. Y. 421, 427; Matter of Budlong, 126 N. Y. 423, 432.)

On May 5, 1954 Weiss forwarded to attorney Lloyd Garrison the will of April 8, 1953 together with the letters of June 13, 1951 and October 23, 1952, and a covering letter stating that Robert "wants to make a new will as soon as possible". Mr. Garrison, by letter dated May 10, 1954, acknowledged the documents and stated he had discussed the matter with his partner, Mr. Rochlin. A draft of the proposed will was transmitted to Robert with Rochlin's letter dated May 21, 1954. The draft provided for the appointment of Weiss and Garrison as executors and trustees. The draft followed a conference between Robert and Rochlin on May 6, 1954. On May 25, 1954 Robert signed a letter to Rochlin returning the draft and requesting changes including a provision for the appointment of Weiss as sole executor instead of the provision in the draft appointing Weiss and Garrison jointly.

The May 6 conference was solely between Robert and Rochlin. Among the matters discussed was Robert's investment in the Multi–Deck Corporation ..... Robert said he wanted the stock in the company to go to Weiss with provision in his will that it was to bear its share of the estate tax. Robert directed that one half of the residuary go to his two nephews, Richard and Lee. They also discussed the executors to be named and Rochlin was told to designate Weiss and Garrison executors and trustees. The 1953 will contained an interrorem clause providing that the devise to one contesting the will shall lapse. Rochlin informed Robert his firm's policy was to recommend to a client not to put such a clause in his will.

Significantly, Robert at the time spoke of the letter of June 13, 1951. Rochlin read the letter. Robert inquired whether it was advisable to leave the letter with his will. Rochlin said he would talk with Garrison about it. Rochlin's office memorandum of June 10, 1954 states that on the previous day, when the 1954 will was executed, Robert again read the letter and on Rochlin's recommendation it was placed with the will together with the burial instructions of October 23, 1952. It does not appear what, if any, discussion was had between Robert and Rochlin; Robert did not discuss the letter with Garrison.

* * *

On October 21, 1955 a new will was executed substantially like the 1954 will with the additional provision for the devise of the Quogue property to Weiss.

* * *

On May 22, 1958 Garrison caused to be delivered to Robert a five-page memorandum directing his attention to the fact that his then will provided for Aron, his father's former secretary, his former art teacher and other provisions. Other questions were raised. The final paragraph reads: "My suggestion is that you consider these questions with Walter [Weiss] and that then we should get together for a brief discussion, because I know from experience that in the course of discussion other questions will arise, and that we cannot work this all out by correspondence."

* * *

No draft of the will was submitted to Robert; he did not meet with Garrison as suggested by the latter and they had no discussion or talk regarding the radical departure from the testamentary plan of the 1955 will. The execution of the will on June 19, 1958 offered for probate took 15 to 20 minutes and involved only the formalities.

* * *

Weiss and Robert lived together from 1949 to the date of Robert's death. The evidence enabled the jury to find that Robert became increasingly dependent on Weiss socially and businesswise. Moreover, it supports the view that this dependence was encouraged and that Weiss took affirmative steps to insulate Robert from his family and persons he sought to cultivate.

Robert gave Weiss his unbounded confidence and trust. Weiss exploited Robert, induced him to transfer to him the stewardship formerly exercised by Joel, increased Robert's need for dependency, prevented and curtailed associations which threatened his absolute control of Robert and alienated him from his family.

Weiss, in his memorandum of April 4, 1951, attributes to Joel the following description of his role which the jury could have found to be the fact: "I believe Joel finds it most acceptable to his pride to consider that I have instigated an independent will in you for my own purposes; that you serve my selfish desire to mix into his all-important, fascinating business machinations—all out of some kind of misguided weakness of will!"

Weiss was responsible for the displacement of the attorneys who prepared the 1950 will; he introduced Robert to Garrison who prepared the instrument offered for probate. Weiss recommended the doctors who treated Robert; he employed all help who came in contact with Robert. Mail and telephone communications were routed through Weiss. Family mail at times was destroyed and did not reach Robert. Correspondence purporting to be from Robert was dictated by Weiss.

* * *

Anne McDonnell, the housekeeper and cook, testified Weiss was master of the household and brooked no interference from Robert. She also testified there were occasions when Weiss insisted that Robert sign papers without opportunity to read them and that Robert complied.

Watkins, a banker friend of Robert's father, testified he talked at length with Robert about the Fairfax matter. On one occasion Weiss was present and did all the talking while Robert was mute. On another occasion Watkins was alone with Robert and his only response was: "That's the way Walter [Weiss] wants it."

Robert perceptibly lost weight during the latter years, in part due to a low cholesterol diet. He became disinterested in his attire and appearance. After 1950 he received extensive psychiatric treatment, the nature of which does not appear.

In 1955 Robert complained of inability to sleep. His inability to sleep continued until his death. He took large quantities of pills for the condition which included doriden, miltown, seconal and nembutal—medication to reduce tension and induce sleep. He was unable to sleep without medication. On April 18, 1959, asleep at his home in Key West, Robert died in a fire which destroyed the house.

The record is replete with financial matters pertaining to Robert's interest in family investments. The suggestion is that Robert became estranged from his family because of financial matters. The jury could have found that Robert did not wish to be concerned with matters of business; that the differences based thereon were introduced by Weiss for the purpose of causing a breach between Robert and his family.

* * *

The record becomes clear if it is viewed in the light of a skillfully executed plan by Weiss to gain the confidence of Robert, displace Joel as manager of his financial affairs, assume control of Robert's bank accounts, safe-deposit box, household and property as if it were his. The only impediment against completely relieving Robert of his worldly goods was the circumstance that his investments in the main were closely tied in with those of Joel and his brother Aron. To overtly seize Robert's property would risk a challenge by his family. So long as Robert was under his control and influence, Weiss was assured of a life of ease and luxury. He, therefore, need only direct Robert toward making him his principal beneficiary in the event of his death. This he could do without the knowledge of the family. The result was to be substantiated by written declarations of Robert assigning reasons for the unnatural disposition.

* * *

Following the death of Robert, Weiss disclaimed knowledge of the letter of June 13, 1951; disclaimed knowledge of the details of the change of beneficiaries as to the insurance policies and averred initial knowledge after Robert's death of the instrument offered for probate. In all of these respects the jury could have found Weiss lied deliberately.

Contestants' medical expert testified the record evidence delineated a personality with pathological dependency; one unable to deal with reality, insecure, unstable and who tends to submit unreasonably to the will of another. There was no expert medical testimony to the contrary.

One may make testamentary disposition of his worldly goods as he pleases. The motives and vagaries or morality of the testator are not determinative provided the will is the free and voluntary disposition of the testator and is not the product of deceit. There are two principal categories of undue influence in the law of wills, the forms of which are circumscribed only by the ingenuity and resourcefulness of man. One class is the gross, obvious and palpable type of undue influence which does not destroy the intent or will of the testator but prevents it from being exercised by force and threats of harm to the testator or those close to him. The other class is the insidious, subtle and impalpable kind which subverts the intent or will of the testator, internalizes within the mind of the testator the desire to do that which is not his intent but the intent and end of another. (Marx v. McGlynn, 88 N. Y. 357; Rollwagen v. Rollwagen, 63 N. Y. 504, 519.)

If it appeared to the satisfaction of the jury that Weiss willfully alienated Robert from his family by falsely accusing Joel of fraud and mismanagement in the conduct of the family business enterprises for the purpose of causing Robert to disinherit members of his family, then the jury properly could have found undue influence. (Matter of Anna, 248 N. Y. 421, supra; Tyler v. Gardiner, 35 N. Y. 559, 595.)

The fact that the relation between Robert and Weiss may have afforded Robert some satisfaction did not enable Weiss deceitfully, improperly and insidiously to turn Robert against his family. (Matter of Budlong, 126 N. Y. 423, 432, supra; Rollwagen v. Rollwagen, supra, p. 520.)

* * *

Weiss' deliberately false pretrial testimony is that he first learned he was a testamentary beneficiary of Robert after his death. The record shows indisputably Weiss' involvement with each of the wills since 1950; copies were in the vault to which he had the right of access he frequently exercised. In May, 1954 Weiss caused the prior will and the letters of June, 1951 and October, 1952 to be delivered to Garrison. Here, again, Weiss disassociates himself from circumstances cogently pointing to his involvement in and responsibility for the testamentary disposition made by Robert.

The record enabled the jury to find that the instrument of June 19, 1958 was the end result of an unnatural, insidious influence operating on a weak-willed, trusting, inexperienced Robert whose natural warm family attachment had been attenuated by false accusations against Joel, subtle flattery suggesting an independence he had not realized and which, in fact, Weiss had stultified, and planting in Robert's mind the conviction that Joel and other members of the family were resentful of and obstructing his drive for independence.

The fact that the instrument offered for probate was prepared by reputable, competent attorneys is a relevant circumstance but does not preclude a finding that the undue influence here involved was active, potent and unaffected by the interposition of independent counsel. (Matter of Anna, 248 N. Y. 421, 425, supra.) Far more extensive interposition by independent counsel has been held not to be conclusive on the existence of undue influence. (Smith v. Keller, 205 N. Y. 39, 43.)

* * *

The issue of undue influence was submitted to the jury without the benefit to the contestants of any presumption. The charge placed the unrelieved burden of establishing undue influence upon the contestants. The issue was given to the jury in the aspect most favorable to the appellant; appellant made no exception to the charge. The record overwhelmingly sustains the verdict on undue influence on the basis of the charge made.

The decree denying probate of the instrument dated June 19, 1958 should be affirmed, with costs to respondents payable out of the estate.

* * *

■ Witmer, J. (dissenting):

* * *

The verdict in this case rests upon surmise, suspicion, conjecture and moral indignation and resentment, not upon the legally required proof of undue influence; and it cannot stand.

The record shows that the testator was intelligent and generally healthy. The evidence that he lost weight was explained by his doctor who said that he had placed him upon a no-fat diet. True, the testator was not wholly like other people. He had little zest for business, which fact set him apart from his family. He had artistic ability, and particularly loved to paint. So did Weiss. They had common interests. Testator felt and said that he had uncommon ability as a painter and that some day he would be known for his artistic work. In this, he was not wholly wrong, for it appears that eighty museums have accepted his work for permanent display.

The record is replete with evidence of the friendly relation, indeed love and affection, that existed between testator and Weiss for a decade. There is no substantial evidence that their relationship was not one of mutual esteem and self-respect. The isolated incidents of testator bowing to Weiss' wishes on certain occasions over this period fall far short of conclusively pointing to a subserviency, when viewed in the light of all the evidence. True, testator relied upon Weiss in business and administrative matters, but that is not to say that testator was not essentially in command. There is evidence that at times testator made his own business decisions. The fact that Weiss advised testator in his business dealings with his brothers is not inconsistent with his position as testator's financial advisor. . . .

The issue in this case is not what were the morals of these men, nor whether testator led a normal life, nor whether Weiss has been proved a liar. The issue is, does the propounded instrument represent the intrinsic wishes and will of the testator, or was it the product of the command of Weiss which the testator did not really want to follow, but was unable to resist? The veracity of Weiss, it is true, may not be ignored in considering this issue.

* * *

There was, thus, no question of fact for the jury; and proponents' motion for a directed verdict should have been granted. The decree appealed from should therefore be reversed, with costs to all parties appearing separately and filing briefs, payable out of the estate, and the matter remitted to the Surrogate's Court with directions to admit the will to probate.

NOTES AND QUESTIONS

1. Suppose Robert Kaufmann had been Roberta Kaufmann, the stereotypical 1960s wife in a "Leave it to Beaver" family. On the facts presented, do you think any jury would have invalidated Roberta's will because of undue influence by her husband Walter? For a recent discussion of the Kaufmann case, see Ray D. Madoff, Unmasking Undue Influence, 81 Minn. L. Rev. 571, 592–600 (1997).

2. Suppose the jury in the Kaufmann case had held that Walter Weiss did not unduly influence Robert Kaufmann. Would the Appellate Division have upheld the jury verdict? Is the problem here the judicial definition of undue influence or the likelihood that juries will bring their own prejudices to bear on the facts presented to them?

3. Do you think the 1951 letter written by Robert Kaufmann, in which he extols Walter Weiss for enriching his life, was helpful in rebutting claims of undue influence? If not, why not?

4. Two more recent cases have been less willing to infer undue influence from the existence of a homosexual relationship. See Evans v. May, 923 S.W.2d 712 (Tex.App.1996) (upholding will benefitting of 30–year life mate of testator); Estate of Sarabia, 221 Cal.App.3d 599, 270 Cal.Rptr. 560 (1990) (jury, after deliberating for 19 minutes, rejects claim of undue influence by gay lover).

5. ***Estate planning and the transgendered.*** A recent case dramatically illustrates the need for estate planning when one party to a marriage is transgendered; in such a case, even a marriage license may not be enough to ensure that a surviving spouse takes a share of her husband's intestate estate. In Estate of Gardiner, 273 Kan. 191, 42 P.3d 120 (2002), J'Noel Gardiner, a post-operative male to female transsexual, was denied an intestate share of her husband's estate. Decedent Marshall G. Gardiner, a wealthy businessman, had married J'Noel four years after the successful completion of her sex-change treatment, and he knew that she had been born with male sex organs. Marshall's estranged son Joseph argued that the marriage was void, relying on a Kansas law limiting marriage to "two parties of the opposite sex." The district court granted summary judgment to Joseph, answering the question "[c]an a physician change the gender of a person with a scalpel, drugs and counseling, or is a person's gender immutably fixed by our Creator at birth?" with a definitive "once a man, always a man." Although the Court of Appeals reversed, the Kansas Supreme Court reinstated the district court's determination, reasoning that the Kansas legislature, in limiting marriage to two people of the opposite sex, could not have meant to define J'Noel as female:

> The words "sex," "male," and "female" are words in common usage and understood by the general population. Black's Law Dictionary, 1375 (6th ed. 1999) defines "sex" as "the sum of the peculiarities of structure and function that distinguish a male from a female organism; the character of being male or female." Webster's New Twentieth Century Dictionary (2nd ed. 1970) states the initial definition of sex as "either of the two divisions of organisms distinguished as male or female; males or females (especially men or women) collectively." "Male" is defined as "designating or of the sex that fertilizes the ovum and begets offspring: opposed to *female*." "Female" is defined as "designating or of the sex that produces ova and bears offspring: opposed to *male*." [Emphasis added.] According to Black's Law Dictionary, 972 (6th ed. 1999) a marriage "is the legal status, condition, or relation of one man and one woman united in law for life, or until divorced, for the discharge to each other and the community of the duties legally incumbent on those whose association is founded on the distinction of sex."
>
> The words "sex," "male," and "female" in everyday understanding do not encompass transsexuals. The plain, ordinary meaning of "persons of the opposite sex" contemplates a biological man and a biological woman and not persons who are experiencing gender dysphoria. A male-to-female post-operative transsexual does not fit the definition of a female. The male organs have been removed, but the ability to "produce ova and bear offspring" does not and never did exist. There is no womb, cervix, or ovaries, nor is there any change in his chromosomes. As the *Littleton* court noted, the transsexual still "inhabits ... a male body in all aspects other than what the physicians have supplied." 9 S.W.3d at 231. J'Noel does not fit the common meaning of female.

Planning Strategies for Gay, Lesbian or Transgendered Testators

If the Gardiner case emphasizes the need for estate planning in non-traditional unions, and the Kaufmann case illustrates the uphill battle same-sex couples face even if they do take the trouble to plan their estates, what strategies are available to those testators who live in states barring same-sex marriage or civil unions? Consider some alternatives.

1. ***No-Contest Clauses.*** Note that in Will of Kaufmann, Robert Kaufmann's lawyer advised against use of a no-contest clause. Are there

particular reasons why no-contest clauses might be ill-suited to gay and lesbian testators? See generally Jeffrey G. Sherman, Undue Influence and the Homosexual Testator, 42 U. Pitt. L. Rev. 225, 248–53 (1981).

Suppose testator's assets total $200,000. If testator is survived by three sisters and two brothers, and testator wants to leave all or most of his assets to his life-partner, how would you draft a no-contest clause to accomplish testator's goal?

Is it possible that, even if an appropriate no-contest clause could be drawn, "the condition against contest may only fuel the anger of the contestants." Comment, In the Shadow of Death: A Guide to Estate Planning for the Client with AIDS, 3 J. Pharmacy & Law 109, 117 (1994).

2. *Lifetime Agreements with Testator's Family of Origin.* If testator believes that members of his family of origin would be receptive, testator can enter into contracts with them by which they release their right to contest testator's will. These contracts can provide testator with some reassurance against contest—but only if family members are sufficiently open-minded to make such agreements—the very situation in which contest is least likely.

Suppose testator contracts with her three siblings, each of whom agrees not to challenge testator's will, which leaves the bulk of testator's estate to her life-partner. Testator's sister dies, leaving two sons. Are the sons bound by the agreement?

3. *Charitable Remainder Trusts.* The Internal Revenue Code permits a testator to take a charitable deduction for the remainder interest in a charitable remainder annuity trust or a charitable remainder uni-trust. 26 U.S.C. secs. 664(d)(1) and (d)(2). By creating a charitable remainder trust, the gay testator may kill two birds with one stone: first, the testator may obtain a charitable deduction for part of his estate and, second, the testator may obtain an important ally in any will contest—the holder of the charitable remainder, who will want to defend the trust against contest by testator's legal heirs. Indeed, the state Attorney General, as enforcer of charitable trusts, may also come to the aid of the testator's named executor.

Of course, the charitable remainder trust device does not permit the surviving member of the couple to retain an absolute interest in the trust property; the device works only for a testator willing to limit his partner to a life interest.

4. *Non-Probate Alternatives.* Suppose a same-sex couple maintains all (or a significant percentage) of their assets in joint names—either in joint bank accounts or brokerage accounts, or in joint tenancy. Upon the death of one member of the couple, will the property pass through the probate process? If not, how much would a will contest accomplish for the contestants?

If testator and a partner choose to hold assets in their joint names, many lawyers recommend that testator's will expressly indicate that the joint ownership arrangement was intended to convey ownership rights on the surviving partner, and was not intended merely as a matter of convenience. For tax reasons that are beyond the scope of this casebook, many lawyers who advise estate-taxable same-sex partners suggest they not hold title as joint tenants with right of survivorship.

Because non-probate transfers tend to be less susceptible to after-death contests, many lawyers advise gay clients to make liberal use of testamentary substitutes, which take assets out of the probate process. See Hayden Curry & Denis Clifford, A Legal Guide for Lesbian and Gay Couples, 9:24–9:25 (6th ed. 1991); Adam Chase, Tax Planning for Same–Sex Couples, 72 Denv. U. L. Rev. 359 (1995). However, joint tenancies are not appropriate for all couples, since they can generate negative tax consequences (which are beyond the scope of this book). See Patricia A. Cain, A Review Essay: Tax and Financial Planning for Same–Sex Couples: Recommended Reading, 8 Law & Sex. 613 (1998). Funded revocable trusts can be especially helpful.

* * *

Of course, not all families contest and modern courts may be increasingly sympathetic to homosexual devisees, especially in areas where there are large numbers of homosexual voters. For an in-depth analysis of ethical issues faced by estate planners who represent non-traditional couples, see Jennifer Tulin McGrath, The Ethical Responsibilities of Estate Planning Attorneys in the Representation of Non–Traditional Couples, 27 Seattle U. L. Rev. 75 (2003).

Adoption of Same–Sex Partners

IBM Heiress Case Pushes Legal Boundaries

By Thomas B. Scheffey.
Connecticut Law Tribune, August 17, 2009.

Two decades ago, no states had civil unions, let alone marriage for same-sex couples.

But blue-chip lawyers in New York and Connecticut nevertheless suggested a recipe for romantic and economic happiness for an IBM heiress and her longtime female lover: They should get an adult adoption.

But what started as an outside-the box way to formalize a relationship has turned into a long-running court battle over the potential inheritance of $10 million or more.

The legal battle stretches from the islands of Maine to the Gold Coast of Connecticut. It has involved probate courts in both states and, most recently, the Supreme Court of Maine.

The story starts with Olive Watson, now 61, who is the granddaughter of IBM founder Thomas Watson and the daughter of Thomas Watson Jr., of Greenwich, who ran the legendary business for decades and amassed a large fortune before his death in 1993.

Her longtime lover is a woman named Patricia Spado.

"They went to all the family gatherings together. They were a couple. But there was no marriage permitted," said Bridgeport lawyer Michael Koskoff, of Koskoff, Koskoff & Bieder, who currently represents Spado. "They wanted to see what they could do to set up a binding financial relationship. So they went to consult with several attorneys."

The women wanted to formalize their relationship and to ensure financial stability for Spado, who had quit her interior design job to be with Watson full time. They consulted top New York trust lawyer William Zabel, who proposed adult adoption. New York didn't allow adult same-sex adoptions, but Maine seemed more accommodating. It is one of just three states where an adult adoption would have worked, Olive Watson was told.

Fortunately, the Watson clan has a $20 million, 300–acre vacation compound on the Maine island of North Haven with its own private air strip. Maine's adoption statute at the time only required that the adoptee be "living" in Maine. Even though Olive Watson was a few months younger, she would become the "mother" and Spado would become the adoptive "daughter." And so the formal proceedings took place in 1991, after the two women spent several weeks at the North Haven compound.

In 1992, the couple broke up. At the time, Olive Watson paid Patricia Spado a $500,000 settlement for clear title to some jointly held real estate, but reassured Spado in a letter that she would never contest the legality of the adoption.

That became a key point at the end of 1993, when the IBM chief died. By being adopted by Olive Watson, Spado was arguably a grandchild of Thomas Watson Jr. And he left trusts to his grandchildren, including those who were adopted, that were worth more than $10 million each, according to lawyers familiar with the matter.

The trustees of the Watson trusts opposed the idea of Spado inheriting money. They said it was never Thomas Watson Jr.'s intent to treat an adult same-sex partner as a grandchild.

Supreme Reversal

In an opinion issued last month, a unanimous Maine Supreme Court ruled that the adoption of Patricia Spado, under the statute in force at the time, was perfectly legal. "Adoption jurisdiction is conferred on the Probate Court of a county when an adoptee 'lives' in the county," the Maine court wrote. So the whole legal issue hung from a thread—whether Patricia Spado was truthful when she told the probate judge back in 1991 that she "lived" in Maine even though she had been there only a few weeks.

Deciding the term "lives" was ambiguous, the court delved into the legislative history of the statute. Over the past 80 years, through multiple amendments, the legislature never defined the word "lives" in the adoption statute. Construing the term liberally is generally in the best interest of the child, and adoption is to be encouraged, the court reasoned. There was no fraud on the court by Patricia Spado, the Maine Supreme Court decided, and her adoption by Olive Watson is legally valid, it concluded.

The ruling delighted Koskoff. "I'm sure that it is the first decision ever to grant legal status to the adoption of a same-sex partner as a matter of law—certainly by any Supreme Court of any state," he said.

"The case has gotten much stronger as a result of this Maine decision. It was very specific, saying they were not going to start looking at the reasons behind an adoption. That's going to help us in Connecticut."

The Connecticut portion of the case has been based in Greenwich Probate Court.

[Spado's] lawyers made a claim in Greenwich Probate Court to clarify her rights under the Watson trusts. They argued on Spado's behalf that Connecticut statutes and its public policy treated adopted children like biological children, and that the trusts' terms did, too.

But in 2006, Greenwich probate court judge David W. Hopper ruled against Spado's status as a grandchild under the Watson trusts.

Hopper focused on interpreting the intent of Thomas Watson Jr. He placed significant weight on the fact that Watson referred specifically to his 15 grandchildren in the trust, and his lack of knowledge that Olive Watson had adopted Patricia Spado.

"The fact that Spado and Olive [Watson] deliberately did not inform [Thomas] Watson of the adoption leads to the clear conclusion that they may well have been concerned with what Watson might do had he been informed," Hopper wrote.

He concluded by stating that Spado acknowledged that one motivation for the adoption was to enable her claim to be a beneficiary under the trusts. "It is a reasonable conclusion that Watson did not intend to benefit someone who is adopted for no reason other than to obtain his money," Hopper wrote.

But Koskoff said there is well-established language that can be placed in a trust if a grantor wishes to include minor adopted children but exclude adopted adults. That language did not appear in the documents establishing the Watson trusts, he said.

"No Ambiguity"

Spado has appealed Hooper's ruling. In October, they'll get a brand new hearing before a Stamford Superior Court judge. Attorney Koskoff said the Maine Supreme Court decision gives him an edge.

"The only basis for the claim in Connecticut, that [Spado] is not the grandchild, is that there is some ambiguity in the term 'adopted,'" said Koskoff. "And the Maine Supreme Court has said there is no ambiguity. An adopted child is an adopted child is an adopted child."

At least one legal expert backs Koskoff's interpretation. New York Law School Professor Arthur Leonard has been writing about the legal significance of adult adoptions for decades, and has a legal blog on current development in the law of same-sex couples.

In an e-mail exchange, he commented: "Since Spado was legally adopted by Watson in Maine, she is a legal child of Watson. As courts generally interpret the Full Faith and Credit Clause of the U.S. Constitution, an adoption decree by a state court is entitled to full faith and credit by courts of other jurisdictions."

The Maine decision isn't likely to be susceptible to attack on the grounds that it might be decided differently in Connecticut, Leonard said. "Generally speaking, there is no 'public policy' exception to this obligation. This means that in the Connecticut litigation, the court must extend to Spado the same status as would be extended to any other adoptive child of a child of Thomas and Olive Watson."

The Watson trusts are represented by Cummings & Lockwood's Robert P. Dolian and B. Cort Delany, who were unavailable and did not return calls for comment. Greenwich trust lawyer Henry Pascarella is the guardian ad litem for any unborn, unknown or unascertained beneficiaries under the three Watson trusts, and Woodbridge trusts and estates lawyer David W. Schneider represents him.

"We're disappointed by the Maine Supreme Court decision," Schneider said. In the Connecticut probate court, Pascarella and Schneider had opposed recognizing Spado as a grandchild, saying to do so would be "a travesty."

They will be part of the upcoming Superior Court proceeding. "I expect this to be litigated," said Schneider, "and then there are, of course, two levels of appeal beyond that."

NOTES AND QUESTIONS

1. Suppose, after the breakup, Olive Watson had wanted to prevent Patricia Spado from inheriting any portion of her father's estate. Could she have taken steps to "divorce" her daughter? Should that serve as a deterrent to adult adoption?

2. Few same-sex couples view themselves as parent and child, and few are likely to take such a cynical view towards the legal system that they would willingly use legal forms to achieve a result that does not reflect the nature of their relationship. See Ralph C. Brashier, Children and Inheritance in the Nontraditional Family, 1996 Utah L. Rev. 93, 169–172. Professor Brashier writes:

> These second-best attempts are also disturbing when viewed as parent-child relationships. Adoption by one homosexual of his or her partner, like a heterosexual's adoption of his or her spouse, simply does not fit with society's expectations of a true parent-child relationship. In fact, gay and lesbian adoptions of their partners may be on the wane; many homosexuals appear to have concluded that they will not accept adoption as a second-best substitute for legally recognized marriage.

Id. at 171–72. See generally Jeffrey G. Sherman, Undue Influence and the Homosexual Testator, 42 U. Pitt. L. Rev. 225, 253–62 (1981).

CHAPTER SIX

THE GOVERNMENT'S SHARE: A BRIEF INTRODUCTION TO ESTATE TAXATION

Why should a decedent be able to leave any wealth to family members? Andrew Carnegie—not known for socialist tendencies—wrote (reflecting the sexism of his era):

> [T]he parent who leaves his son enormous wealth generally deadens the talents and energies of the son, and tempts him to lead a less useful and less worthy life than he otherwise would.

Andrew Carnegie, The Gospel of Wealth 50 (1933). Carnegie's notion that inheritance creates a disincentive for children to productive activity led many in the early 20th century to advocate a federal tax on estates. Others, President Theodore Roosevelt among them, also emphasized the inequality of opportunity generated by large inheritance. In arguing for an estate tax, Roosevelt (also no slouch on the sexism front) wrote:

> No advantage comes either to the country as a whole or to the individuals inheriting the money by permitting the transmission in their entirety of the enormous fortunes which would be affected by such a tax; and as an incident to its function of revenue raising, *such a tax would help to preserve a measurable equality of opportunity for the people of the generations growing to manhood.*

17 Works of Theodore Roosevelt 504–05 (Memorial ed. 1925) (emphasis added).

Neither Carnegie nor Roosevelt suggested an absolute prohibition on inheritance. First, whatever incentive to sloth inheritance might provide for rich children, the prospect of passing wealth to children may create at least some incentive for parents to continue to engage in productive activity after they have accumulated enough wealth to provide for their own needs. Second, a prohibition on inheritance would not have a prayer of enactment.

Since 1916, however, a federal estate tax has been in effect in the United States (with a one year hiatus in 2010). (The federal government had earlier imposed estate or inheritance taxes to raise revenue during wartime. See Martin Fried, Wartime Necessities, Trusts and Estates, January 2004, at 20). When compared with the size of the federal budget, the estate tax is not a major source of revenue, but the tax has served historically as an expression of national commitment to egalitarian ideals. Warren Buffet, one of the world's wealthiest men, has defended the estate tax as a tool that prevents the development of a "plutocracy," and he has publicly stated that repealing it would be like "choosing the 2020 Olympic team by picking the eldest sons of the gold-medal winners in the 2000 Olympics."

The estate tax targets the wealthy; a decade ago, two percent of Americans paid estate and gift taxes. See John G. Steinkamp, A Case for Federal Transfer Taxation, 55 Ark. L. Rev. 1 (2002). In light of recent amendments, the current percentage is far smaller. All of the middle class escapes federal estate taxation altogether. Under current law, individuals with less than $5,000,000 in assets and married couples owning less than $10,000,000 in assets are exempt from federal transfer tax entirely, while individuals who die with estates greater than that amount face a marginal tax rate of 35%.

In addition to the federal estate tax, most states have death, inheritance, or gift taxes of one sort or another. For all but the wealthiest decedents, these state transfer taxes may now be more significant than the federal estate taxes. Although state tax rates are universally lower than the federal 35% rate, state death and inheritance taxes often affect estates far smaller than $5,000,000. Nevertheless, because state death, inheritance, and estate taxes vary significantly from state to state, we provide only limited treatment of them here.

A Bit of History, A Bit of Politics

If faced with a significant tax on one's estate, a sensible wealthy person would choose to give away assets before death, diminishing the size of the estate, and therefore, the amount of tax. When the federal estate tax was first enacted, wealthy people did just that. See Jay A. Soled, Reassigning and Assessing the Role of the Gift Tax, 83 B.U. L. Rev. 401 (2003). As a result, Congress enacted a gift tax to reduce opportunities for tax avoidance.

Until 1976, however, the wealthy could still reduce their tax liability substantially by giving assets away during life. This was the result of two structural defects. First, the gift tax rate was significantly lower than the federal estate tax rate. Second, the law entitled each person to a separate exemption from gift taxes and estate taxes, so that those who used up their lifetime exemption still had a full exemption available at death. In addition to the opportunity for tax savings through lifetime gifts, those families wealthy enough to pass assets over a generation, i.e., to leave significant assets to grandchildren rather than children, were able to avoid one entire generation of estate and gift taxation. These incentives to tax avoidance were especially important in light of the high marginal tax rates; before 1976, many people of moderate means were subject to the estate tax, and the marginal tax rate on an estate over $10,000,000 was 77%!

In 1976 Congress substantially reformed the federal transfer tax system in several major respects. First, it "unified" the estate and the gift taxes by creating a shared rate table for the two taxes, at rates ranging from 18 to 70 percent, and by substituting a "unified credit" for the two separate exemptions of prior law. The effect of the unified credit is to exempt a certain level of wealth transfers from tax, whether those transfers take place during life (gift tax) or at death (estate tax). In 1976 Congress set that exempt level of wealth transfers (which we'll refer to from now on as the "exemption amount") at $175,625. That meant that individuals who transferred wealth of less than $175,625 during their life and at death were wholly free of any obligation to pay gift or estate taxes, and that more wealthy individuals only paid tax to the extent that their wealth transfers exceeded that amount. In 1976, therefore, individuals of moderate means could be subject to the transfer taxes.

In the intervening years, Congress has steadily and dramatically increased the exemption amount (the current level is $5,000,000) so that only the wealthier segment of the population is subject to the transfer taxes. Another major change Congress made in 1976 was to enact a new federal transfer tax to backstop the estate and gift taxes: the tax on generation-skipping transfers. That tax was intended to prevent wealthy individuals from avoiding estate and gift taxes by essentially "skipping over" one generation. While the 1976 version of the tax was severely flawed and ultimately repealed, it laid the groundwork for a more effective and workable generation-skipping tax that is still in effect today. A detailed description of the generation-skipping transfer tax is beyond the scope of this book.

In most cases, a married couple functions as a single economic unit; the couple pools most of its resources rather than carefully segregating husband's resources from wife's resources. What estate tax consequences should follow when the first spouse dies? For a long time, the estate tax statute permitted a limited marital deduction; if the decedent spouse devised property to the surviving spouse, part—but not all—of that devise would qualify for the marital deduction and pass free of tax. That regime ended in 1981, with enactment of the unlimited marital deduction. Now, any property transferred by one spouse to the other passes free of gift and estate tax.

Legislation enacted in 2001 provided for a gradual phaseout of the estate tax, culminating with complete elimination in 2010. For complicated budgetary reasons, however, the 2001 legislation provided for reinstatement of the tax—with an exemption of only $1,000,000—starting in 2011. The general expectation had been that Congress would act before 2010 to remedy this anomaly, but Congress didn't act until the final days of 2010. By its terms, the 2010 legislation is effective only through 2012, although many predict it will be extended beyond that date. (Congress, of course, often proves prognosticators wrong). The new legislation increases the exemption to $5,000,000 per person, and decreases the rate to 35%. The statute also indexes the exemption for inflation. Another critical feature of the new legislation is the introduction of "portability," which permits a married couple to exempt $10 million from the estate tax even without engaging in careful estate planning. We will discuss portability shortly.

The Mechanics of the Federal Estate Tax

The federal transfer taxes (gift, estate, and generation-skipping) are designed to impose a once-a-generation tax on the transfer of wealth. The estate and gift taxes are largely unified, which means that lifetime transfers and transfers at death are aggregated in measuring the amount of wealth subject to the tax. As noted above, because of the unified credit, aggregate wealth transfers up to the exemption amount are free of tax, and for wealthy individuals who transfer more than the exemption amount, estate and gift taxes apply at a 35% rate.

The statutory scheme imposing the estate and gift taxes dates back to 1976, when there were multiple rate brackets to apply and the exemption amount was quite low. Congress has patched it sloppily to accommodate the changes in the law made since. Much of the complexity is no longer necessary because under current law the estate tax basically imposes a 35% flat-rate tax on transfers in excess of the exemption amount. Thus, to compute the estate tax liability of an estate when the decedent has made no taxable gifts, one can proceed as follows:

1. Determine the taxable estate. The taxable estate is not merely decedent's probate estate. Under section 2033 of the Code, all property owned by decedent at death is included in the decedent's gross estate, but sections 2035 through 2044 include a variety of other property interests that may not pass through decedent's probate estate, including life insurance proceeds (subject to qualifications), employee death benefits, and the decedent's interest in joint tenancies. Once we have computed the gross estate, sections 2053 through 2056 provide deductions against the gross estate, most significantly the marital deduction and the charitable deduction. For now, we will not focus on these various inclusions and deductions, but we will return to them at various points during the course.

2. Subtract the exemption amount—$5,000,000 in 2011—from the taxable estate.

3. Multiply the balance by .35.

Example 1: *Decedent dies in 2011 with a taxable estate of $8,000,000, and has made no gifts during his lifetime. What is the estate tax due on that estate?*

Solution: *To compute the estate tax due, we subtract $5,000,000 from $8,000,000, and then multiply by 35%. Thus, the tax due is .35 × $3,000,000, or a total of $1,050,000.*

Terminology: The Unified Credit

Until recently, the estate tax included a progressive rate structure; the larger the estate, the higher the rate. The simple computational process outlined above was inconsistent with a progressive rate structure. As a result, the statute operated—and still operates—to allow each decedent a "unified credit" against the estate tax. (As we shall see, the credit is a "unified" credit because it applies against both the estate tax and the gift tax). The unified credit is equal to the tax on the exemption amount applicable in the year of the decedent's death. (The unified credit, however, is not equal to 35% of the exemption amount because the credit structure builds on tax tables that include graduated rates. We will not deal with that complication in this chapter). Because the marginal rate on all amounts in excess of the exemption amount is 35%, we can compute the estate tax due without explicit reference to the unified credit.

Nevertheless, as a result of the statutory scheme, lawyers frequently refer to the unified credit.

The Annual Gift Exclusion

So far, we have not considered what constitutes a taxable gift. Should the $50 scarf you bought for Aunt Blanche at Christmas be a taxable gift? What about the $10,000 motorcycle your (wealthy and generous) parents bought you as a college graduation present? And what about the $20,000 your (even more wealthy and generous) parents paid last year toward your law school tuition?

26 U.S.C. 2503 deals with these problems. Section 2503(e) explicitly excludes payments made as tuition to educational institutions, and payments made to providers of medical care. Note that to qualify for the exclusion, the payments must be made directly to providers; if your mother pays you $20,000 to reimburse you for amounts you paid to your law school, your mother has made a gift that does not qualify for the tuition exclusion.

Section 2503(b) deals with the scarf, the motorcycle, and other "gifts" as follows:

> In the case of gifts (other than gifts of future interests in property) made to any person by the donor during the calendar year, the first $10,000 of such gifts to such person shall not ... be included in the total amount of gifts made during such year.

The Taxpayer Relief Act of 1997 amended section 2503(b) to include an inflation adjustment: the exclusion will be $10,000 multiplied by a cost-of-living adjustment using 1997 as the base year. The amendment also provides, however, that if the adjusted amount is not a multiple of $1,000, the "amount shall be rounded to the next lowest multiple of $1,000." As a result, in 2011, the exclusion stood at $13,000. For purposes of problems in this book, we will treat the annual exclusion as if it remains at $13,000.

The import of section 2503(b) is this: if a donor gives $13,000 gifts to five different people—children, siblings, friends—none of the gifts have any estate tax consequences. If the donor makes a single gift of $50,000 to one person, the first $13,000 of the gift is not treated as a taxable gift; the remaining $37,000 is treated as a taxable gift.

The $13,000 annual exclusion—originally enacted to avoid taxation of occasional gifts—has become an effective estate planning device. See generally Walter D. Schwidetzky, Estate Planning: Hyperlexis and the Annual Exclusion Rule, 32 Suffolk U. L. Rev. 211, 214 (1998). Consider the following example:

Example 2: *Jones has three children, five grandchildren, and assets worth $8,000,000. How much estate tax would be saved if Jones gave $13,000 to each of his children and grandchildren in each of the three years before his 2011 death?*

Solution: *Jones will have made $312,000 in gifts subject to the annual exclusion. He will save 35% of that, or $109,200, in estate tax.*

To elaborate, if Jones made no gifts, and died with an estate worth $8,000,000, the estate tax would be $1,050,000 (See Example 1, supra). If Jones gave away $104,000 during each of the three years before his death, for a total of $312,000, his estate would be reduced to $7,688,000. The estate tax would be $940,800 (35% of $2,688,-000).

For those most concerned about the bite of the estate tax, that is, the most wealthy, the $13,000 annual exclusion provides a significant opportunity to reduce taxes at death by making gifts during life. Indeed, for some scholars, the major puzzle is why, in light of the tax advantages of lifetime giving, the level of lifetime giving is as low as it is. See Lee Anne Fennell, Death, Taxes, and Cognition, 81 N.C. L. Rev 567 (2003).

Integrating the Gift Tax and the Estate Tax

Suppose a donor makes a $50,000 gift to his daughter. Does the donor have to pay tax on the gift? Does the donor have to file a tax return? Must the daughter pay tax on the gift received? The donor does have to file a return, but no tax will be due if the gift is the first large gift the donor has made. The daughter, as donee, pays no tax on the gift received.

In basic outline, the rules are simple: a donor does not have to file a gift tax return for any gift that qualifies for the $13,000 annual exclusion, or for the tuition and medical care exclusion. For other gifts, the donor must file a return, reporting the taxable gift. The donor will not, however, be obligated to pay any gift tax until the donor has used up the $5,000,000 lifetime exemption from estate and gift taxes.

Although the estate and gift taxes are largely integrated, two advantages to lifetime gifts remain. First, by making a lifetime gift, the donor of the gift avoids tax on any appreciation in the value of the property between the time of the gift and the time of the donor's death. The value of property given away is essentially "frozen" for federal transfer tax purposes. Suppose, for instance, donor had made a gift of securities worth $100,000 in 2011. Assuming donor has not used up her $5,000,000 exemption, no tax will be due on the gift during her lifetime. If she subsequently uses up her exemption, tax will become due, but only on the date-of-gift value of $100,000. By contrast, if she retained the securities until her death, and the securities have increased in value to $200,000, the securities would be valued at $200,000 for estate tax purposes. As a result, an owner who expects the value of property to appreciate often finds it advantageous to give the property away before the appreciation occurs. (Of course, in recent years, depreciation of securities has been as common as appreciation, reducing the value of this "advantage" of making lifetime gifts.)

Second, the amount of gift tax actually paid on lifetime gifts is excluded from the estate tax base. Put in tax jargon, the gift tax is "tax exclusive" while the estate tax is "tax inclusive."

To take a simple example, suppose Brown has used up his unified credit. Brown is deciding whether to make a lifetime gift. Suppose Brown has $135,000 available to give.

> *Case 1: Brown makes a lifetime gift of $100,000 to his daughter. Brown pays tax of $35,000—35% of the value of the gift—and the daughter receives $100,000.*
>
> *Case 2: Brown does not make a lifetime gift. Instead he retains the $135,000 in his estate. His estate will be liable for $47,250 (35%) in additional estate tax, and the daughter, if she is the estate beneficiary, receives only $87,750.*

Note further that if Brown does not have $135,000 in cash, but instead has an asset worth $135,000 that Brown expects will appreciate, the estate tax savings will be even greater. If the asset appreciates by $100,000 between the time of the gift and the time of Brown's death, Brown will have saved an additional $35,000 in estate tax.

Does this example mean that it is always advantageous to make lifetime gifts? Not always. First, some people want or need their assets during their own lives; lifetime gifts diminish the security they may want during their old age (although a concern about security may be diminished with a $5,000,000 exemption). Second, the "tax exclusive" advantage of lifetime gifts does not apply to gifts made within three years of death. Section 2035(b) of the Code mandates that gift taxes paid on gifts made within three years of death be added back into decedent's estate for purposes of computing the estate tax. Third, there is a significant income tax advantage to passing property through one's estate rather than by *inter vivos* gift: the "stepped-up basis." The donor's cost basis travels with the gift when the donor makes an *inter vivos* gift; by contrast, when a testator passes an asset through the estate, the estate beneficiary's basis is the value of the asset at the time of transfer.

Consider this difference in concrete terms. Capital gains on the sale of property are subject to federal income tax. That is, if Smith purchases one share of ABC Corporation stock at $50, and sells that share five years later at $500, Smith has realized a gain of $450, which is subject to income tax (albeit at favorable capital gains rates). The $50 purchase price is Smith's "basis" in the stock. If Smith gives the stock to Jones, Jones retains the same $50 basis in the stock; if Jones later sells the stock for $500, Jones must pay income tax based on the $450 gain. Suppose, however, the stock passes through Smith's estate at Smith's death. If Jones acquires the stock through Smith's estate, Jones takes the stock with a "stepped-up basis:" the market value of the stock at Smith's death. So, for instance, if the value of the stock is $500 at Smith's death, and Jones sells the stock for $500 as soon as he receives it, Jones is not liable for any income tax on the sale. The stepped-up basis is a significant tax advantage, and often makes it preferable to pass assets through one's estate rather than by *inter vivos* gift. Often, a potential donor must balance the income tax advantages of the stepped-up basis against the estate tax advantage of locking in the value of a gift before the gift appreciates significantly in value.

PROBLEM

Donor has the following assets:

a. 1000 shares of HiFlier Corp., bought five years ago for a total price of $1,000,000, and now worth $5,000,000.

b. 1000 shares of Slow'n'Steady Corp., bought eight years ago for a total price of $4,000,000, and still worth $4,000,000.

Donor would like to take advantage of the "tax exclusive" nature of the gift tax by making a lifetime gift of $2,000,000. Donor's estate will be large enough that she expects to use up her unified credit.

1. What would you recommend if you expect that neither asset will appreciate significantly between now and the date of Donor's death?

2. Assuming no further appreciation, how much estate and gift tax will donor have saved if she takes your recommendation rather than allowing all of her assets to pass through her estate?

3. What income tax consequences would your recommendation have?

4. What recommendation would you make if the capital gains tax rate were 25% and you expected the HiFlier stock to increase in value by another $4,000,000 by the time of Donor's death?

The Marital Deduction

So far, we have discussed the estate tax as if each decedent were an unmarried individual. How does the estate tax situation differ when a married couple is involved? Assets held by the married couple are sometimes held jointly (often with a right of survivorship), but they are often held in the name of one spouse or the other. If, for instance, most of the couple's assets are held in the husband's name, and the husband dies first, should the wife have to deplete the resources otherwise available to her in order to pay estate tax? Since 1981, the statutory answer has been no. The estate tax is treated as a tax on transmission of wealth between generations; Congress does not require taxation of the husband's estate at his death, only to have the property taxed again at the wife's death. One tax each generation suffices. Section 2056(a) of the code provides:

> Allowance of Marital Deduction. For purposes of the tax imposed by section 2001, the value of the taxable estate shall, except as limited by subsection (b), be determined by deducting from the value of the gross estate an amount equal to the value of any interest in property which passes or has passed from the decedent to his surviving spouse, but

> only to the extent that such interest is included in determining the value of the gross estate.

Suppose, for instance, decedent's gross estate is $10,000,000. If decedent leaves $3,000,000 of that amount to a spouse, that $3,000,000 is "deducted" from the gross estate to leave a taxable estate of $7,000,000. The marital deduction permits the married couple to avoid taxation on transfers to each other, whether during their lifetimes or at death, and also to defer taxation until the death of the surviving spouse. Should the same benefits be available to same-sex couples? See Patricia A. Cain, Death Taxes: A Critique From the Margin, 48 Clev. St. U. L. Rev. 677 (2000). Note that the federal Defense of Marriage Act precludes same-sex couples from claiming the benefit of the marital deduction even if the couple has formalized their relationship through a marriage or civil union in a state that recognizes same sex unions.

Many couples have so-called "simple wills" that leave all of the decedent's property to the surviving spouse. Such wills are adequate for couples of moderate means. But until the 2010 introduction of portability into the estate tax, couples with taxable estates needed more complicated wills to minimize their collective tax burden. Consider the following example:

> ***Example 3 (traditional law):*** H and W are a married couple with total assets of $9,000,000—$7,000,000 held by the wife, W, and $2,000,000 held by the husband, H. Suppose H died first in 2011, leaving all of his property to W, and W died a year later, leaving all of her property to the couple's children. Under traditional estate tax law (before the 2010 amendments), how much tax is due at H's death, and how much tax is due at W's death?
>
> ***Solution:*** Because H left all of his property to W, his entire estate would qualify for the marital deduction, leaving H with no taxable estate. Moreover, even if H had left his estate to someone other than his wife, his taxable estate would be smaller than the $5,000,000 exemption, so no tax would be due. Now consider the situation at W's death. If H left all $2,000,000 to W, W would have had a taxable estate of $9,000,000—generating an estate tax, at 2011 rates, of $1,400,000.

H and W could have avoided all federal estate tax on their estates by complicated planning. That planning would include a transfer by W of funds to H so that W's own estate would not exceed W's exemption amount ($5,000,000 in 2011). That transfer alone would not have solved the problem if H's will left the amount transferred right back to W. If H did that, W's estate would be back up to $9,000,000, generating $1,400,000 in tax. So, to avoid tax, H (and W) could draft instruments devising significant amounts to persons other than each other (typically, the couple's children), to assure that neither spouse died with a taxable estate larger than $5,000,000.

The 2010 legislation was designed to eliminate the need for this careful planning by making the exemption amount "portable." Section 2010(c)(2) provides that a decedent's exemption shall include the sum of decedent's own exemption and any unused exemption of a deceased spouse.

Consider how portability works by re-examining the facts in example 4:

> ***Example 3 (current statute):*** H and W are a married couple with total assets of $9,000,000—$7,000,000 held by the wife, W, and $2,000,000 held by the husband, H. Suppose H died first in 2011, leaving all of his property to W, and W died a year later, leaving all of her property to the couple's children. Under the current statute, how much tax is due at H's death, and how much tax is due at W's death?
>
> ***Solution:*** As under traditional law, H's estate qualifies for the marital deduction, leaving H with no taxable estate. Because H's estate all qualifies for the marital deduction, H uses up none of his exemption. At W's death, then, W can use both W's own exemption and H's exemption for a total of $10,000,000. Because W's estate is only $9,000,000, W's estate generates no tax.

Although portability reduces the need for lifetime estate planning, H's executor (or the executor's lawyer) must take care to file a federal estate tax return at H's death—even though no tax is due at that time. (Generally, an executor need not file an estate tax return when the decedent's estate is smaller than the exemption amount). Section 2010(c)(5) makes it clear that the surviving spouse may only make use of a deceased spouse's unused exemption when the deceased spouse's executor "files an estate tax return ... and makes an election on such return" authorizing use of any unused exemption at the surviving spouse's death.

PROBLEM

Ann Attorney, a sixty-five year old partner in a two-person law firm, recently died with an estate valued at $2,000,000 (including the value of her share of the law practice). Her will left all of her property to her husband, Ben Builder, age 66. Ben, who has been named executor of Ann's estate, has assets of his own worth $1,000,000. Ben approaches you and asks whether he should hire an accountant to prepare a federal estate tax return for Ann's estate. How would you advise Ben? Would your answer be different if Ben's own assets were worth $10,000,000? If they were worth $100,000?

NOTE: GIFTS BETWEEN SPOUSES

Just as a disposition to a spouse by will qualifies for the marital deduction, a gift by one spouse to the other generates no tax consequences. Section 2523(a) allows a deduction for the full value of gifts made between spouses. Hence, if one spouse transfers assets to the other, the transfer has no gift tax consequences.

Moreover, since each spouse can make use of the $13,000 exclusion, a married couple may give $26,000 a year to each of their children, grandchildren, or other donees without incurring any tax consequences. And, if one spouse makes a gift of $26,000, the gift will be treated as two $13,000 gifts, one by each spouse, so long as the other spouse consents. 26 U.S.C. 2513(a). Hence, if one spouse owns the bulk of the couple's assets, that spouse's $26,000 gifts fully qualify for the annual exclusion (so long as the other spouse agrees and does not make any gifts to the same donee).

NOTE ON THE CHARITABLE DEDUCTION

Built into the estate tax is another deduction of considerable importance: an unlimited deduction for contributions to qualified charitable organizations. The deduction means, in effect, that when a wealthy decedent leaves part of her estate to charity, the government foots 35% of the bill. Abolition of the estate tax would eliminate this tax subsidy for charitable giving, provoking concerns about a potential reduction in charitable giving. For analysis, and a suggested reform, see Sarah E. Waldeck, An Appeal to Charity: Using Philanthropy to Revitalize the Estate Tax, 24 Va. Tax Rev. 667 (2005).

Estate Tax Planning: What's Left?

The combination of portability with a $5,000,000 exemption significantly reduces the importance of estate tax planning even for relatively wealthy taxpayers. Sophisticated planning strategies remain valuable for estates larger than $5,000,000, but those strategies are beyond the scope of this course. For estates between $1,000,000 and $5,000,000—the bread and butter of many estates practitioners—two other tax concerns will often take center stage.

First, state estate tax statutes do not always track the federal statute. Many have exemptions far lower than the federal statute, and lawyers would be well-advised to insure that the estate planning documents they draft take account of state-specific provisions.

Second, many moderately wealthy clients hold a large proportion of their assets in IRAs or other forms that have not yet been subject to income taxation. An estates lawyer needs to familiarize herself with strategies that enable the client to minimize the income tax burden.

These concerns, however, are beyond the scope of this course.

CHAPTER SEVEN

TRUSTS

You have already been introduced to the trust in your study of the elective share and in your study of wills. What is a trust, and why would anyone use one?

The trust is a product of history—of the division of jurisdiction between law courts and courts of equity. But the trust has endured through the centuries because it has proven extraordinarily useful in a wide variety of legal contexts. See generally John H. Langbein, The Secret Life of the Trust: The Trust as an Instrument of Commerce, 107 Yale L.J. 165 (1997). Our focus here is on the trust as a device for transmission of wealth.

A trust is an entity in which ownership is divided between the trustee (who is sometimes said to hold "legal" title to the trust property) and the beneficiaries (said to hold "beneficial" title). The trustee—not the beneficiary—has the right to manage the trust property, but also has the obligation to manage the property in the beneficiary's interest—not the trustee's own interest. In other words, if you wanted to buy some property held in trust, you would go to the trustee; if you were looking for a rich friend, you would look to the trust beneficiary.

Estate planners find trusts useful in a variety of ways. The creator of a trust (generally called the "settlor" or sometimes "trustor") may want to leave property to people—whether adults or children—with limited capacity to manage money. By creating a trust, the settlor can repose management responsibilities in a trustee who is (the settlor hopes) up to the task. Indeed, as we shall see, if the objects of the settlor's bounty are better at spending money than managing it, the settlor, through use of appropriate language in the trust instrument, may even be able to insulate profligate beneficiaries from claims by their creditors.

Perhaps even more important, the settlor can use a trust to increase flexibility in an estate plan. For instance, a settlor concerned that her children might have differing needs after her death might not want to leave each child outright bequests, but might prefer instead to confer on a trustee discretion to distribute money among the children according to their needs, or according to the settlor's more explicit directions.

Many trusts (called "testamentary trusts") are created by will. In recent decades, however, many settlors have created trusts (called "*inter vivos* trusts" or "living trusts") while they are alive. A primary motivation for some of these trusts has been avoidance of probate. In *How to Avoid Probate*, a 1966 book that topped the best-seller list (Masters and Johnson's *Human Sexual Response* was second on the list), estate planner Norman Dacey almost single-handedly popularized the living trust.

Although changes in the tax laws have made it somewhat more difficult (and somewhat less lucrative) than it once was to use trusts as a means for avoidance of federal estate and income taxation, opportunities still exist to reduce tax liability through the use of trusts.

Because the trust is so flexible, lawyers are constantly finding new uses for trusts. Among the most popular in recent years are a variety of trusts designed to protect the assets of elderly and institutionalized clients against claims by the government or other medical care providers; asset protection trusts structured to avoid the settlor's creditors; and dynasty trusts created to take advantage of the repeal of the Rule Against Perpetuities in some jurisdictions.

NOTE ON TRUSTS AND LEGAL LIFE ESTATES

Settlors often create trusts to maintain control over property (and, indirectly, over people) past their own deaths. Thus, a wealthy settlor may want to provide generously for her husband, but at the same time may want to assure that the husband (or, perhaps, a subsequent wife) does not dissipate settlor's assets, leaving too little for settlor's children. An outright bequest to the husband provides no protection to the children, while an outright bequest to the children may leave the husband without the resources settlor wants him to enjoy. By using a trust, the settlor can accomplish both objectives; the settlor can direct the trustee to pay income to the husband for life, and to distribute the principal to the children at the husband's death. As we will see later, the settlor can also direct the trustee to pay the husband some of the principal in accordance with limitations imposed by the settlor. Indeed, as we shall see, the settlor can refine the trust language to account for a variety of potential future events.

If the goal is to shift beneficiaries upon the death of the husband (or upon the death of a child, or anyone else), why not simply convey the property to the husband for life, with a remainder to the children? That is, why not create a legal life estate rather than a trust? A number of factors counsel against creating legal life estates. Rarely would it be advisable for a lawyer to recommend creating a legal life estate rather than a trust.

First, when a life tenant and remaindermen share ownership of property, no one person has power to sell a fee simple interest in the property. If, for instance, the property is no longer producing substantial income, the life tenant is powerless to sell the property and use the proceeds to purchase property that does generate income—absent consent of the remaindermen, or, perhaps, a court order (Cf. Baker v. Weedon, 262 So.2d 641 (Miss. 1972), illustrating how difficult it may be for even an impoverished legal life tenant to obtain a court-ordered sale of the property). By contrast, if a trustee owns the property under a properly drafted instrument that includes a power of sale, the trustee could exchange the unproductive property for other property that better meets the needs of the intended beneficiary or beneficiaries.

Second, a legal life tenant has no power to lease the property for a period beyond the expiration of the life estate. Anyone taking a lease from a life tenant, then, assumes the risk that the life tenant might die before the expiration of the lease term. This would generally operate to depress the price the lessee would be willing to pay, hurting the life tenant without producing commensurate gain for the remaindermen. Again, by conveying the property in trust, and conferring on the trustee a power to lease the property, the settlor avoids this difficulty.

Third, when ownership is divided between a legal life tenant and remaindermen, the life tenant's management responsibilities are often murky. Does the life tenant have to make repairs if the cost of the repairs exceeds the return the life tenant would realize on repair expenditures? What power does the life tenant have to remove minerals? These questions fall within the domain of the law of waste—not noted for crisp rules designed to provide ready guidance to the life tenant.

By contrast, when the owner of property creates a trust, the owner vests decision-making power in the trustee. The trustee decides what repairs are necessary and whether sale or lease of the property would be advisable. With respect to potential buyers and tenants, the trustee has the powers of a fee owner.

Although the problems associated with legal life estates are serious when land is involved, the disadvantages of the legal life estate are compounded when the assets at issue are publicly held securities, or worse, ownership interests in small businesses. As a result, legal life estates are seldom encountered except with land. For the property owner seeking to divide ownership over time, the trust is virtually always the preferred mechanism.

NOTE ON THE UNIFORM TRUST CODE

In 2000, the National Conference of Commissioners on Uniform State Laws promulgated The Uniform Trust Code (hereafter referred to as the "UTC"), and amended it in 2001, 2003, 2004 and 2005. Though the UTC purports largely to restate and clarify the common law of trusts, many of its provisions have generated controversy. For example, commentators and practitioners have argued over the Code's notification provisions, the scope of creditor protections, and whether the UTC dilutes important fiduciary protections enjoyed by beneficiaries under the common law.

For an article exploring the debate over the notification provisions, see Alan Newman, The Intention of the Settlor Under the Uniform Trust Code: Whose Property Is It, Anyway?, 38 Akron L. Rev. 649, 675–78 (2005). For articles considering whether the UTC diminishes or bolsters creditors' rights, see Robert T. Danforth, Symposium: Trust Law in the 21st Century: Article Five of the UTC and the Future of Creditors' Rights in Trusts, 27 Cardozo L. Rev. 2551 (2006); Jeffrey A. Schoenblum, Symposium: Trust Law in the 21st Century: In Search of a Unifying Principle for Article V of the Uniform Trust Code: A Response to Professor Danforth, 27 Cardozo L.

Rev. 2609 (2006); Alan Newman, The Rights of Creditors of Beneficiaries Under the Uniform Trust Code: An Examination of the Compromise, 69 Tenn. L. Rev. 771 (2002); Mark Merric and Steven J. Oshins, How Will Asset Protection of Spendthrift Trusts Be Affected by the UTC?, 31 Est. Plan. 478 (Oct. 2004).

For articles debating whether the UTC weakens fiduciary protections, see Melanie B. Leslie, Fiduciary Duties and the Limits of Default Rules, 94 Geo. L.J. 67 (2005); Melanie B. Leslie, In Defense of the No Further Inquiry Rule: A Response to Professor Langbein, 47 Wm. & Mary L. Rev. 541 (2005); Melanie B. Leslie, Common Law and Common Sense, 27 Cardozo L. Rev. 2713 (2006); Karen E. Boxx, Symposium: Trust Law in the 21st Century: Distinguishing Trustees and Protecting Beneficiaries: A Response To Professor Leslie, 27 Cardozo L. Rev. 2753 (2006).

Thanks to aggressive lobbying by trust institutions, the UTC has quickly been adopted by more than two dozen states and the District of Columbia.

For interesting and thoughtful discussions of the UTC see, Alan Newman, The Intention of the Settlor Under the Uniform Trust Code: Whose Property Is It, Anyway?, 38 Akron L. Rev. 649, 675–78 (2005); Lynn Foster, The Arkansas Trust Code: Good Law for Arkansas, 27 U. Ark. Little Rock L. Rev. 191 (2005); Ronald R. Volkmer, The Nebraska Uniform Trust Code: Nebraska Trust Law in Transition, 37 Creighton L. Rev. 61 (2003).

SECTION I. CREATION OF TRUSTS

A. TRUST REQUISITES: THE TRUSTEE, THE BENEFICIARY, AND THE PROPERTY

Suppose Ann Smith, a woman of means whose principal assets are invested in publicly traded securities, wants to provide for her somewhat impulsive daughter, Barbara, during Barbara's lifetime, and to assure that at Barbara's death, Ann's assets pass to Barbara's children. Ann wants her niece, Carol, to manage the portfolio during Barbara's lifetime. Ann's intended beneficiaries are clear, she knows precisely what property she wants to use to provide for those beneficiaries, and she has identified a potential "trustee" for the property. If Ann, after consulting her lawyer, decides to create a trust—either during her lifetime or by will—her lawyer will draft a trust instrument in which she describes with care the trust beneficiaries, the trust property, and the trustee (or trustees). No one is likely to challenge the trust instrument for want of adequate property, beneficiaries, or trustee.

Ann Smith may be a typical client, but an estates lawyer must also be prepared for the less typical client whose potential beneficiaries are less traditional, or whose assets are somewhat more ephemeral. It is established law that every trust must have at least one beneficiary. See Restatement

(Third) of Trusts § 44 (2003) (stating that a trust is valid only if it names a beneficiary who is ascertainable at the time of creation or who will become ascertainable during the period measured by the Rule Against Perpetuities). Trusts must also have trust property (see *id.*, § 2, comment i). In this section, we explore the implications of these requirements for the estates lawyer.

1. THE TRUSTEE

As we have seen, the trustee is the person or entity who holds "legal" title to the trust property. To the outside world, the trustee appears as the "owner" of the trust property. The primary obligations of the trustee are to manage and distribute trust property exercising due care. The trustee cannot act out of self-interest as it carries out these duties. Rather, it must subordinate its best interests to the best interests of the trust beneficiaries. In other words, the trustee is a *fiduciary* who owes *duties of care and loyalty* to the trust beneficiaries.

For instance, suppose, as in the Ann Smith hypothetical, the trust property consists of publicly traded securities. At a basic level, it is the trustee's responsibility to pay the income generated by those securities to the designated trust beneficiaries. In addition, if some of the investments in the trust's portfolio no longer seem prudent, it is the trustee's responsibility to sell them and acquire prudent investments. We explore the details of the trustee's fiduciary duties in detail later in the book.

Statutes and case law provide a set of rules spelling out fiduciary obligations, but the settlor of the trust can vary many, if not most, of those obligations in the terms of the trust instrument. Indeed, contract has come to play an increasingly important role in defining the trustee's duties:

John H. Langbein, The Contractarian Basis of the Law of Trusts, 105 Yale L. J. 625, 629, 650–51 (1995)

... My theme is that despite decades of pulpit-thumping rhetoric about the sanctity of fiduciary obligations, fiduciary duties in trust law are unambiguously contractarian. The rules of trust fiduciary law mean to capture the likely understanding of the parties to the trust deal, which is why both the duty of loyalty and the duty of prudence yield to the more particularized intentions that the parties may choose to express or imply in their trust deal....

... The rules of trust law apply only when the trust instrument does not supply contrary terms. Because the parties can oust the trust default regime, we say that they choose it by deciding not to oust it. The default character of trust law has become more insistent in modern times, as the trust has lost its connection to the relatively inflexible patterns of conveyancing, and as trust assets and trust purposes have become more variable....

As in contract, so in trust, the autonomy of the parties is not wholly unrestrained. There are the obvious public policy prohibitions against trusts for illegal purposes. There are the traditional definitional minima—there must be trust property and beneficiaries capable of enforcing the trust.... There are also limits on self-serving exculpation clauses in trust that echo the unconscionability protections in contract. Thus, in trust as in contract, the courts will intervene against market failure. But these limits hardly pinch in ordinary circumstances....

Notwithstanding Professor Langbein's view, most states delineate a mandatory core of duties that cannot be eliminated or modified in the trust agreement. For instance, in all states the trustee has a non-waivable duty to act in good faith, in the best interests of the trust beneficiaries and in accordance with the settlor's objectives. In addition, most state courts would decline to enforce a trust provision purporting to shield a trustee from liability for grossly negligent or reckless actions. And many states impose non-negotiable requirements that the trustee notify trust beneficiaries of the existence of the trust, the identity of the trustee, the nature of the beneficiaries' interests, and their right to receive information about trust management. Several go further and impose a non-waivable duty to provide regular accountings to the beneficiaries. See generally, Uniform Trust Code § 105.

Is the characterization of fiduciary duties as mere default rules advisable from a policy perspective? See, Melanie B. Leslie, Fiduciary Duties and the Limits of Default Rules, 94 Geo. L.J. 67 (2005).

A trust will not fail for want of a trustee. A vacancy in the office of trustee might arise for a number of reasons. First, the trust instrument might fail to name a trustee. Second, at the trust's inception the trustee may fail to qualify—the trustee may be dead or may decline to serve, or a court might refuse to confirm the appointment (because of incompetence or lack of legal capacity to act as trustee). Third, after the trust has been created the appointed trustee might die, be removed, or resign.

When the trust instrument does not account for these contingencies, a court will appoint a trustee to fill the vacancy and assure continuation of the trust. Obviously, a well-drafted trust instrument provides for these contingencies; if it doesn't, the client didn't get what he or she paid for.

Relationship Between Trustees and Beneficiaries: The Merger Doctrine

A trust settlor may name the sole trustee one of the beneficiaries of the trust, and may name the sole beneficiary one of the trustees of the trust. Moreover, the settlor may name the same two or three parties as trustees and as beneficiaries of the trust. The same person may not, however, serve as sole trustee and sole beneficiary. See UTC § 402(a)(5); Restatement (Third) of Trusts § 69 (2003).

There is, of course, little reason for a settlor to appoint the same person as sole beneficiary and sole trustee, but circumstances might arise in which the same person becomes sole trustee and sole beneficiary. Suppose, for instance, settlor creates a trust, naming her husband as sole trustee and life beneficiary, and providing that the principal is to be distributed to settlor's daughter at the husband's death. If the daughter dies before the husband, leaving her father, settlor's husband, as her only heir, the husband has become the sole trustee and sole beneficiary. In that circumstance, the husband's legal title and equitable title "merge," and the trust terminates. The husband holds the property free of any trust. Restatement (Third) of Trusts § 69, cmt. d (2003). But generally, as long as there is at least one trustee who is not a beneficiary, or one beneficiary—however contingent her interest—who is not the trustee, the trust will be valid. See Welch v. Crow, 206 P.3d 599 (Okla.2009) (holding that merger doctrine did not apply where sole trustee was sole income beneficiary but settlor named contingent remaindermen).

Active and Passive Trusts: A Little History, A Little Hornbook Law

The modern trust is a direct descendant of the use, a popular land ownership device in England from the 13th century until enactment of the Statute of Uses in 1535. English lawyers developed the use to achieve objectives that continue to face estate planners today—avoiding taxes, protecting assets from creditors—and to avoid the common law prohibition on wills of land. S, the owner of land would convey the land to T (the equivalent of the modern trustee) for the use of B (the equivalent of the modern trust beneficiary). Originally, T had no enforceable obligation to B; S and B had to rely on T's trustworthiness to assure that the arrangement had its intended effect. Ultimately, however, as some Ts proved untrustworthy, use beneficiaries were able to convince the Chancellor, but not the law courts, to enforce the use obligation. Hence, the origins of the beneficiary's interest as an "equitable" interest, in contrast to the trustee's "legal" interest.

Although uses became extraordinarily popular with conveyancers—by some accounts, nearly all English land was subject to uses by 1500—their success as a tax avoidance device made them unpopular with the king. The result, in 1535, was enactment of the Statute of Uses. The Statute decreed that henceforth, the equitable interests of use beneficiaries would be treated as legal interests, thus undermining the tax avoidance advantages of the use. Thus, B became the outright owner of Blackacre, instead of T.

The Statute of Uses, however, did not apply to personal property. Moreover, English courts held that the Statute did not apply to active uses—those which involved not merely a dummy titleholder, but a titleholder with "active" managerial responsibilities. These exceptions to the Statute of Uses led to the development of modern trust law, and simultaneously created one doctrinal rule of modest importance: if a trust imposes no active duties on the trustee, the trust is invalid as a "passive" trust, and the beneficiary acquires legal as well as equitable title. Although the English Statute of Uses only invalidated passive trusts of land, not personalty, American statutes and cases typically hold passive trusts invalid whether the subject matter is land or personalty. See, e.g., N.Y. EPTL §§ 7–1.1, 7–1.2; Bellows v. Page, 88 N.H. 283, 188 A. 12 (1936).

Why would anyone care whether a trust is passive? A beneficiary might want to challenge a trust as passive simply to avoid paying commissions to the named trustee. Perhaps most often, the beneficiary's challenge rests on a desire to own the property outright—in particular, to have control over the trust property, rather than merely beneficial ownership. See, e.g. Estate of Gagliardi, 55 N.Y.2d 109, 432 N.E.2d 774, 447 N.Y.S.2d 902 (1982) (invalidating a trust as "passive" where settlor took property in his own name, in trust for named beneficiaries, without any indication about trust duration); Denison v. Denison, 185 N.Y. 438, 78 N.E. 162 (1906) (construing a trust as passive and avoiding invalidity under the Rule Against Perpetuities).

2. THE NEED FOR IDENTIFIABLE BENEFICIARIES

No trust fails for want of a trustee, but no trust exists in the absence of a beneficiary. The requirement that trusts have identifiable beneficiaries is designed, in part, to assure that someone has power to enforce the trust. A well-drafted will or trust instrument clearly designates the trust beneficiaries. On occasion, however, settlors create litigation issues by describing beneficiaries in vague terms, or by failing entirely to name a beneficiary. When this occurs, should courts respond by trying to ascertain testator's intent, or by invalidating the trust?

Consider Caroline Girard's will, which made the following provisions:

> I give, devise and bequeath all the rest, residue and remainder of my property to Henry W. Axford with the instructions to pay the same to the person who has given me the best care in my declining years and who in his opinion is the most worthy of my said property. I make him the sole judge and request that his signature with the signature of the person receiving said property shall be a sufficient release for my said executor.

Mary Piers took care of Caroline from the time the will was executed until her death, and Axford designated Mary as the person entitled to the residue of Caroline's estate. Caroline's sisters (her intestate heirs) argued that Caroline intended to create a trust, with Henry as trustee, but her attempt failed for failure to name an ascertainable beneficiary.

In Moss v. Axford, 246 Mich. 288, 224 N.W. 425 (1929), the court upheld the trust on the following grounds:

> It is enough if the testator uses language which is sufficiently clear to enable the court by extrinsic evidence to identify the beneficiary. If by such evidence the court can make the identification necessary to give effect to the intention of the testator, the devise will be sustained.

Do you think the court would have upheld Axford's designation if he had named someone other than Mary Piers as the beneficiary?

NOTES AND QUESTIONS

1. Testator's will bequeaths $500,000 to her trustee with the direction that she "pay the interest annually to my nieces and nephews for their lives." Testator leaves the residue of her estate to a local charity. Testator is survived by five siblings ranging in age from 30 to 40 years old. Suppose the charity argues that the trust must fail because the beneficiaries are not definitely ascertainable—testator's siblings can have additional children who would be entitled to distributions. Should the trust be upheld? See Restatement (Third) of Trusts § 46(1).

2. Suppose Testator created a trust to benefit "my friends." Because no particular person, or even any identifiable group of people, has a right to enforce trust obligations against the named trustee, courts traditionally have held that such a trust is invalid for failure to name definite beneficiaries. See, e.g., Clark v. Campbell, 82 N.H. 281, 286, 133 A. 166, 170 (1926) (concluding that a trust for friends fails for indefiniteness because "[t]he word 'friends' unlike 'relations' has no accepted statutory or other controlling limitations, and in fact has no precise sense at all").

But when a settlor's attempt to create a trust to benefit individuals other than settlor's heirs fails for lack of identifiable beneficiaries, the resulting distribution of settlor's assets to those heirs clearly frustrates settlor's intent. As a result, both the Restatement (Third) and the UTC attempt to give courts tools for effectuating testator's intent in those cases. Consider the following:

> **Restatement (Third) of Trusts § 46**
>
> **Members of an Indefinite Class as Beneficiaries**
>
> (1) Except as stated in (2), where the owner of property transfers it upon intended trust for the members of an indefinite class of persons, no trust is created.
>
> (2) If the transferee is directed to distribute the property to such members of the indefinite class as the transferee shall select, the transferee holds the property in trust with power but no duty to distribute the property to such class members as the transferee may select; to whatever extent the power (presumptively personal) is not exercised, the transferee will then hold for reversionary beneficiaries implied by law.
>
> **Comment on Subsection (1):** Although a disposition is expressed simply as a trust for the members of an indefinite class, a literal interpretation would seem doubtful as a matter of transferor intention and (unless the transferor is alive to take by resulting trust) would wholly defeat whatever specific objective the transferor had in mind. An interpretation is therefore preferred that would give the disposition some effect reasonably consistent with the transferor's general objective. Thus, the disposition may be interpreted as intended to create a trust for members of the described class as determined or selected by the designated trustee, in which case the situation falls within Subsection (2). See Comment *d*. Or, if the disposition is interpreted as one

intended to benefit those members of an otherwise indefinite class that are or may become identifiable [by the court after evaluation of extrinsic evidence], a valid trust is created.

See also UTC § 402(c) (stating that "a power in a trustee to select a beneficiary from an indefinite class is valid. If the power is not exercised within a reasonable time, the power fails and the property subject to the power passes to the persons who would have taken the property had the power not been conferred").

Rich Bitch;
The Legal Battle Over Trust Funds for Pets.

September 29, 2008
Jeffrey Toobin

The life of Leona Helmsley presents an object lesson in the truism that money does not buy happiness. Born in 1920, she overcame a hardscrabble youth in Brooklyn to become a successful condominium broker in Manhattan, eventually alighting, in the nineteen-sixties, at a firm owned by Harry B. Helmsley, one of the city's biggest real-estate developers. The two married in 1972, and Leona became the public face of their empire, the self-styled "queen" of the Helmsley chain of hotels. In a series of ads that ran in the *Times Magazine* and elsewhere, Helmsley's visage became a symbol of the celebration of wealth in the nineteen-eighties. She wouldn't settle for skimpy towels, the ads proclaimed—"Why should you?"

In private, as it turned out, the grinning monarch wasn't just demanding but despotic. Throughout her life, Leona left a trail of ruin-embittered relatives, fired employees, and, fatefully, unpaid taxes. Knowing that the Helmsleys had used company funds to renovate their sprawling mansion, Dunnellen Hall, in Greenwich, Connecticut, disgruntled associates leaked the records to the *Post*. Among the charges billed to the company were a million-dollar dance floor installed above a swimming pool; a forty-five-thousand-dollar silver clock; and a two-hundred-and-ten-thousand-dollar mahogany card table. In 1988, the U.S. Attorney's office charged the couple with income-tax evasion, among other crimes. (Harry Helmsley avoided trial because of ill health; he died in 1997, at the age of eighty-seven.) At the trial, a housekeeper famously testified that Leona had told her, "We don't pay taxes. Only the little people pay taxes," and the public warmed itself on a tabloid bonfire built under the Queen of Mean. Leona was convicted of multiple counts and served eighteen months in federal prison.

In time, following her release, she became largely a recluse, and she died at Dunnellen Hall on August 20, 2007.

After her husband died, Leona Helmsley got a dog named Trouble, a Maltese bitch. In her will, which she signed two years before her death, Helmsley put aside twelve million dollars in a trust to care for Trouble. * * *

"Leona had never had a dog before she got Trouble," Elaine Silverstein, a co-founder of the Miami agency that created the "queen" advertisements for the Helmsley hotels, told me. "She treated her like a person, and took her everywhere. She would take that dog to bed with her every night." After Helmsley's release from prison, she returned for a time to her hotels' ads, but for one campaign she insisted that Silverstein feature Trouble instead. The ad showed the tiny white dog perched on a red velvet chair, and text that said, " 'Trouble,' the Helmsley's favorite four-legged guest," recommends that you call for reservations. "It didn't make much sense for a dog to endorse a hotel, but that's what Leona wanted," Silverstein said. * * *

The twelve-million-dollar trust for Trouble also created problems. The will stated that custody of Trouble should go to Rosenthal, Leona's brother, or to her grandson David, and the trust agreement directed them to "provide for the care, welfare and comfort of Trouble at the highest standard." But neither man wanted the dog. After the will was made public, Trouble received death threats, which may have had something to do with their refusal. (Both men declined to comment.) So the trustees had to find the dog a home. Moreover, the bequest to Trouble was so self-evidently excessive for a single, aging dog that the trustees decided to take steps to reduce it.

Trusts for Pets. How could Leona Helmsley create an enforceable trust to benefit Trouble, an animal with no legal capacity to sue the trustee? Traditionally, such trusts were unenforceable. Eventually some sympathetic courts developed the "honorary trust" doctrine. An honorary trust operates like a power or a conditional gift. That is, a trust for an animal would not fail outright, but the trustee would be entitled to take the trust funds so long as the trustee used them for the animal's benefit. If the trustee failed to use the funds for the animal's benefit, or if the animal died, the honorary trust would fail, and the property would pass back into the residue of the Settlor's estate, or, if the honorary trust were the residuary bequest, by intestate succession. See Restatement (Third) of Trusts § 47 (2003); Phillips v. Holzmann, 740 So.2d 1 (Fla. Ct. App.1998). It was hoped that the settlor's heirs would have an incentive to ensure that the trustee used the money appropriately.

BIZARRO By DAN PIRARO

BIZARRO © 1991 by Dan Piraro. Reprinted with permission of Universal Press Syndicate. All Rights Reserved.

In 1996, the New York legislature took the unusual step of enacting a statute authorizing trusts for pets. The idea took hold, and a majority of states have enacted similar legislation. See UPC 2–907; UTC § 408. The statutes authorize a settlor to designate an individual with power to enforce trust obligations. If the settlor fails to designate such an individual, the statute authorizes a court to appoint someone to enforce the trust's terms, thus moving a step beyond the honorary trust device. See also, In re Fouts, 176 Misc.2d 521, 677 N.Y.S.2d 699 (Sur.Ct.1998) (applying N.Y. EPTL § 7–6.1 and appointing individuals to enforce a trust to benefit five chimpanzees proficient in sign language).

For a review of state law governing trusts for pets, see Gerry W. Beyer, Pet Animals: What Happens When Their Humans Die?, 40 Santa Clara L. Rev. 617 (2000). For more on planning for pets, see Rebecca J. Huss, Separation, Custody and Estate Planning Issues Relating to Companion Animals, 74 U. Colo. L. Rev. 181 (2003).

Non-Charitable "Purpose" Trusts. Occasionally, a settlor creating a trust does not seek to benefit particular people but to accomplish a particular objective. Consider another provision of Leona Helmsley's will, which bequeathed $3 million dollars to the "Leona Helmsley Perpetual Care Trust" to provide for the care of the cemetery plots of her husband, her son, her parents, her sister and herself:

> My Trustees shall distribute any part of the trust income and principal, at any time or times, as my Trustees shall determine in their sole discretion is advisable (i) for the care, cleaning, maintenance, repair and preservation of the interior and exterior of the Final Resting Places, and (ii) for the care, planting and cultivation of the lawn, trees, shrubs, flowers, plants or hedges located on the cemetery plots on which the Final Resting Places are located. I direct that my trustees arrange for the Mausoleums to be acid washed or steam cleaned at least once a year. Any undistributed net income shall be added to principal... I direct my Trustees maintain the Final Resting Places in excellent condition, and to arrange for inspection of the Final Resting Places as often as may be necessary (but not less than quarterly) to ensure their proper care and maintenance.

Like trusts for pets, non-charitable "purpose trusts" lack an identifiable beneficiary and were thus unenforceable at common law. A few states have enacted statutes authorizing trusts for specific purposes, such as the New York statute that allows trusts for the maintenance of graves and burial plots (Leona Helmsley was a New York resident). The reporters for the Restatement (Third) of Trusts and the UTC have again created tools to allow courts to authorize non-charitable purpose trusts, although they take different approaches to the problem. Consider the Restatement:

> **§ 47 Trusts for Noncharitable Purposes**
>
> (1) If the owner of the property transfers it in trust for indefinite or general purposes, not limited to charitable purposes, the transferee holds the property as trustee with the power but not the duty to distribute or apply the property for such purposes ...
>
> (2) If the owner of property transfers it in trust for a specific noncharitable purpose and no definite or ascertainable beneficiary is designated, unless the purpose is capricious, the transferee holds the property as trustee with the power exercisable for a reasonable period of time, normally not to exceed 21 years, to apply the property to the designated purpose; if and to whatever extent the power is personal and not exercised, or the property exceeds what reasonably be needed for the purpose, the trustee holds the property and or the excess for the reversionary beneficiaries implied by law.

The UTC takes a different approach to the problem. UTC § 409 authorizes twenty-one year trusts for non-charitable purposes enforceable by a person designated by the settlor or the court. And California law provides that "[a] trust created for an indefinite or general purpose is not invalid for that reason if it can be determined with reasonable certainty that a particular use of the trust property comes within that purpose." Cal. Prob. Code, sec. 15204.

QUESTION

What is the difference between the Restatement (Third)'s approach to purpose trusts and the approach taken by the UTC and the California statute? Which approach is preferable?

3. TRUST PROPERTY

No one would litigate over a trust unless something of value were at stake. But it is sometimes unclear whether the subject of the trust constitutes "property," and, more particularly, whether it constituted "property" at the time the trust was created. If a court concludes that the subject of the trust constitutes a "mere expectancy" rather than "property," then the court will conclude that the trust was invalid. The comments to the Restatement (Third) give the classic example of an expectancy; the expectation of receiving property at another's death. See Restatement Third § 41, cmt. a. For example, if Sarah Settlor declares that she holds in trust "all the property that I will receive under my mother's will" and Sarah's mother is still alive, Sarah has not created a valid trust. Sarah has no current property interest in her mother's estate—she merely expects to receive that property. But other than that obvious example, determining whether an expectation is a property interest or a "mere expectancy" is not always so simple. Consider the following two cases:

In Brainard v. Commissioner, 91 F.2d 880 (7th Cir. 1937), the court held that a trust failed for lack of property when settlor attempted to place in trust for relatives any profits he might receive as a result of stock trading during the following year. The settlor had attempted to create the trust in order to assure that those profits would be taxed at the (lower) tax rate applicable to his beneficiaries—his wife, mother, and infant children. In invalidating the trust, the court concluded that "the taxpayer based his declaration of trust upon an interest which at that time had not come into existence and in which no one had a present interest."

By contrast, in Speelman v. Pascal, 10 N.Y.2d 313, 178 N.E.2d 723, 222 N.Y.S.2d 324 (1961), the New York Court of Appeals upheld an assignment of a percentage of the profits to be derived from the musical stage version of George Bernard Shaw's *Pygmalion*—even though that version had not yet been written. A theatrical producer held the rights to make a musical version of the play, and assigned them to his secretary (who was also his lover). The court held that the secretary acquired an enforceable right to the future profits from what became *My Fair Lady*.

How is Speelman distinguishable from Brainard? Would the result in Speelman have been different if the producer had not yet, at the time of the assignment to his secretary, acquired the rights to produce a musical version of *Pygmalion*? In light of these holdings, can you tell the difference between a property interest and a "mere expectancy?"

NOTES

1. ***Identification of Trust Property.*** In Brainard, the court held that no trust had been created because settlor had no property interest at the time

he attempted to create the trust. In other cases, the requirement of trust property has been used to invalidate trusts when the property subject to the trust has been insufficiently identified. See, e.g., Wilkerson v. McClary, 647 S.W.2d 79 (Tex.App.1983) (holding trust invalid for failure to identify trust property where settlor had four bank accounts and settlor declared that he held "a checking/savings account" in trust); In re Associated Enter., Inc., 234 B.R. 718 (Bankr. W.D. Wis. 1999) (finding that assets were not held in trust when trust document recited only that the trustee held "Stocks/Bonds/Funds and Real Property" in trust). See Restatement (Third) of Trusts § 40, cmt. e (2003) (declaring that "the subject matter of a trust must be definite and ascertainable. There is no trust property if . . . [the property description] is so indefinite that it cannot be ascertained").

Does inability to identify precisely the subject matter of the trust justify leaving the named beneficiary with nothing? In Wilkerson, couldn't the court have concluded that the smallest of the four accounts was subject to the trust? For criticism of Wilkerson and mechanical application of the rule that a trust fails when trust property is inadequately identified, see Jane B. Baron, The Trust Res and Donative Intent, 61 Tul. L. Rev. 45 (1986).

2. *Standby Trusts.* Testator's lawyer might, as part of an estate plan, draft a trust instrument designed to receive testator's assets at death, and then to distribute those assets to designated beneficiaries. These trusts, sometimes called "standby trusts" or "pour-over trusts," may not actually be funded with any assets during testator's lifetime. Most states have adopted some version of the Uniform Testamentary Additions to Trusts Act, which expressly validates pour-over gifts to standby trusts, even if the standby trust is unfunded prior to the settlor's death. See also, UPC § 2–511. Therefore, when unfunded standby trusts are challenged, courts usually uphold the trusts. See, e.g., Estate of Canales, 837 S.W.2d 662 (Tex.App.1992); In re Bourcet's Estate, 175 Misc.2d 144, 668 N.Y.S.2d 329 (Sur.Ct. 1997). Note, however, that the trustees of a standby trust have no significant trust duties until the trust becomes funded at the testator's death. Standby trusts are studied in greater detail later in this chapter.

B. TRUST FORMATION: CAPACITY, INTENT, AND FORMALITIES

1. CAPACITY

Just as a testator must have capacity to create a valid will, a settlor must have capacity to create a valid trust. See UTC § 402(a)(1). The capacity standard varies depending on the type of trust the settlor seeks to create and the circumstances surrounding creation. If the trust is testamentary, the capacity standard is satisfied if the testator had capacity to make the will creating the trust. See UTC § 402, cmt.; Restatement (Third) of Trusts § 11(1) (2003). The requirement of testamentary capacity is explored in Chapter 5, *supra*.

What is the capacity standard when a settlor attempts to create an *inter vivos* trust? The capacity standard for revocable trusts is the same as that for wills. See UTC § 601; Restatement (Third) of Trusts § 11(2) (2003). If the trust is irrevocable, the capacity standard varies depending upon the reason for the trust's creation. If the settlor uses the irrevocable trust as a gift substitute, she must meet the capacity standard that is required for outright gifts. UTC § 402, cmt.; Restatement (Third) of Trusts § 11(3) (2003); Restatement (Third) of Property: Wills and Other Donative Transfers § 8.1 (2003). The gift standard adds an additional requirement to the testamentary capacity test; in addition to the factors that a testator must be capable of understanding, the settlor of an irrevocable trust must also understand "the effect that the disposition may have on the future financial security of the settlor/donor and of those who may be dependent on him or her." See Restatement (Third) of Trusts § 11(3), cmt. c (2003). If the settlor creates the irrevocable trust as part of a negotiated or adversarial transaction, then the settlor must possess the capacity to contract. See Restatement (Third) of Trusts, § 11(3), cmt. c (2003); Restatement (Second) of Contracts § 12.

Like wills, trusts may be challenged on grounds of fraud, duress or undue influence. See UTC § 406; Restatement (Third) of Trusts § 12 (2003), § 62 (2003); In re Mampe, 932 A.2d 954, 2007 Pa. Super. 269 (2007) (affirming judgment of trial court that revocable trust was product of undue influence). For a thorough analysis, see Mark R. Siegel, Unduly Influenced Trust Revocations, 40 Duq. L. Rev. 241 (2002). See Chapter 4, *supra,* for a study of these doctrines.

2. INTENT TO CREATE A TRUST: THE PRECATORY LANGUAGE PROBLEM

To create a private express trust, a settlor must express an intent to impose an enforceable duty on the trustee. See UTC § 402(a)(2); *See* Restatement (Third) of Trusts § 13 (2003). In most cases, the intent requirement poses no serious problem; competent lawyers typically use care to designate a trustee or trustees, and to indicate in the trust instrument that the transfer is "in trust."

On occasion, however, testators annex "precatory words"—words of request or entreaty—to devises or bequests, and thus create doubt whether an absolute gift or trust is intended. Is such language a polite testator's manner of imposing fiduciary duties on a trustee, or does it express merely a hope or wish, which in no sense is intended to be binding?

In considering the two cases that follow, be sure to ask yourself how the drafter of the instrument could have avoided the ambiguity that led to litigation.

Spicer v. Wright

Supreme Court of Virginia, 1975.
215 Va. 520, 211 S.E.2d 79.

■ POFF, J.

Leila Wilson Spicer died March 22, 1968, survived by her husband, Meade T. Spicer, Jr., her sole heir at law. In her holographic will dated

May 20, 1966, admitted to probate, she named her sister, Anne Beecher Wilson as "executor" without bond. Miss Wilson died on June 8, 1970. Russell Alton Wright qualified as Mrs. Spicer's administrator d.b.n.c.t.a. and as such filed a bill seeking aid and guidance in the construction of the will. He named as defendants Meade T. Spicer, Jr.; Archer L. Yeatts, III, Administrator of the Estate of Anne Beecher Wilson, deceased; the heirs at law and distributees of Miss Wilson; and certain parties unknown. John W. Edmonds, III, was appointed Guardian *ad litem* for Meade T. Spicer, Jr.

The third paragraph of the will provided:

> My estate of every kind and description, personal, real estate, etc., I give to my sister, Anne Beecher Wilson to be disposed of as already agreed between us.

By final decree entered February 7, 1974, incorporating a letter opinion dated December 19, 1973, the chancellor held "that Anne Beecher Wilson acquired a fee simple title to the estate of Leila Wilson Spicer ... free of and from all trusts". We granted Meade T. Spicer, Jr., by his Guardian *ad litem,* an appeal. By order entered in this Court on November 26, 1974, it appearing that Meade T. Spicer, Jr., died on October 18, 1974, Katharine S. Edmonds, Executrix of the Estate of Meade T. Spicer, Jr., deceased, was substituted as party appellant * * *.

Appellant contends that the language of the will, "to be disposed of as already agreed between us", is imperative and connotes an intent to create an express trust; that such testamentary intent is corroborated by the extrinsic evidence; and that since the terms of the agreement are unknown and the express trust cannot be enforced, "[t]he property must be held as a resulting trust for Mrs. Spicer's heir and next of kin—her husband."

In Burton v. Irwin, 212 Va. 104, 181 S.E.2d 624 (1971), the testatrix devised her estate by holographic will to her brother whom she named "executor and trustee". The last sentence of the will provided: "My Brother knows my wishes and will carry them out, to the best of his ability." The chancellor held that an express trust was intended, that the trust failed for indefiniteness, and that a "naked trust was created or implied in favor of the heirs at law and distributees" of the testatrix. We said that "[t]he question is whether the testatrix intended to create a trust for undesignated beneficiaries and unspecified purposes which must fail for indefiniteness or whether she intended to leave her entire estate in fee simple to her brother. If she created a void trust then her net estate will be held by Burton as trustee under a resulting trust for the benefit of her heirs at law and distributees." 212 Va. at 105–106, 181 S.E.2d at 626. Reversing the chancellor's decree, we held that "the language found in Mrs. Mallory's will falls short of establishing an intent to create a trust and that it constitutes a devise and bequest of her property in fee simple and absolute estate to her brother William L. Burton." 212 Va. at 110, 181 S.E.2d at 629.

Here, we are faced with essentially the same question. We must decide whether the language of Mrs. Spicer's will, read in context with the extrinsic evidence, is sufficient to establish an intent to create an express trust; if so, that trust fails for indefiniteness and a resulting trust arises in favor of Meade T. Spicer, now deceased; if not, Miss Wilson takes the entire estate in fee simple.

As we said in *Burton* "[p]recatory words are *prima facie* construed to create a trust when they are directed to an executor * * * [but] no trust is created by precatory language directed to a legatee unless there is testamentary intent to impose a legal obligation upon him to make a particular disposition of property." 212 Va. at 109, 181 S.E.2d at 628.

* * *

The extrinsic evidence showing the close relationship between Mrs. Spicer and Miss Wilson reinforces the import of the language of the will that, at the time the will was written, the two sisters had "already agreed" how the property of the testatrix was "to be disposed of". But such evidence fails to establish a "testamentary intent to impose a legal obligation * * * to make a particular disposition of property" or to show that the agreement was one designed "to impose duties which are enforceable in the courts." Restatement of Trusts § 25, Comment a at 69 (2d ed. 1959). If the extrinsic evidence had sufficiently identified the beneficiary agreed upon and the terms of the benefits agreed upon, that evidence and the precatory language considered together would be sufficient to establish a testamentary intent to impose a legally enforceable duty, and to create a trust. Since the evidence did not, the precatory language standing alone imposes nothing more than an undefined moral obligation. * * *

We hold that the language Mrs. Spicer employed is precatory, that the extrinsic evidence is insufficient to render that language imperative or to establish a testamentary intent to impose a legal obligation to make a particular disposition of property, that no express trust was intended or created, and that the language constitutes an absolute testamentary grant to Miss Wilson. Our holding in no way impairs those rights which the parties have agreed vested in the surviving spouse under Code § 64–16 on the date of Mrs. Spicer's death.

Finding no error below, we affirm the chancellor's decree.

Affirmed.

Levin v. Fisch

Texas Court of Civil Appeals, 1966.
404 S.W.2d 889.

■ Collings, J.

Laura Fisch brought suit against Suzanne Cohen Levin and Jay Howard Cohen, individually and as independent executors of the estate of Bertha Cohen, deceased. Plaintiff, a sister of the deceased, claimed that she had an interest in said estate under the provisions of the last will and testament of Bertha Cohen. Defendants are the children of Bertha Cohen, deceased. It was stipulated that Bertha Cohen died on November 28, 1959, in Houston, Harris County, Texas, that the last will and testament of Bertha Cohen, dated April 11, 1958, was admitted to probate on January 27, 1960 by the Probate Court of Harris County, Texas, and that the defendants are the duly appointed and acting independent executors of the estate of Bertha Cohen, deceased....

* * *

The will provided for specific bequests to appellants. In addition to the provision for specific bequests, paragraph V of the will, the interpretation of which is here in controversy, is as follows:

> All of my other property of whatsoever nature, real, personal, or mixed, I give, devise and bequeath to my two children, Suzanne Cohen Levin and Jay Howard Cohen, to be divided equally between them so that each shall receive an equal share with the other in said property. It is my desire that each year out of the annual rent proceeds, rents and revenues from such property during such year so received by my said daughter and son they pay to my sister Mrs. Laura Fisch the sum of $2,400.00, provided such net proceeds, rents and revenues, received by them from such property for such year is sufficient to meet such payment. In the event the net revenues from such property for any given year should be insufficient to meet such payment for such year, then the amount of the payment to my said sister for such year should be reduced in the amount of such deficiency. It is my desire that my children continue such payments during the remainder of my said sister's life time provided that should my sister LAURA FISCH get married, then my said children should not, after the date of such marriage continue such payment. In the event my said sister should marry, then the payment to her during the year of such marriage, should be prorated as of the date of such marriage....

* * *

Appellants point out that the testatrix Bertha Cohen unequivocally devised and bequeathed to appellants all of her property not theretofore devised. Appellants contend that the phrase "It is my desire" considered in connection with the language used "within the four corners of the instrument", is not ambiguous, and should be given its ordinary and natural meaning, and should not be interpreted as a bequest or a mandatory instruction to appellants to pay to her sister, Mrs. Fisch, the $2,400.00 annual payment indicated in the will. Appellants contend that if Bertha Cohen had intended to bestow upon her sister, Laura Fisch, any right to the annual net rents and revenues from the properties which she had previously and unequivocally devised to appellants, she would have directed appellants in their capacity as executors to make such distribution. The word "desire" in its ordinary and primary meaning is precatory, but is often construed when used in a will as directive or mandatory when it clearly appears that such was the intention of the testator from a consideration of the instrument as a whole and the surrounding circumstances.

In support of the judgment appellee relies upon Colton v. Colton, 127 U.S. 300 (1888). In that case the testator devised and bequeathed to his wife all of his estate, both real and personal, and then continued as follows: "I recommend to her the care and protection of my mother and sister and request her to make such gift and provision for them as in her judgment will be best." In discussing the question of whether the above provision was precatory or mandatory the court stated:

> According to its context and manifest use, an expression of desire or wish will often be equivalent to a positive direction, where that is the evident purpose and meaning of the testator—And in such a case as the present, it would be but natural for the testator to suppose that a request, which, in its terms, implied no alternative, addressed to his widow and principal legatee, would be understood and obeyed as strictly as though it were couched in the language of direction and command—. . . .

* * *

The record in this case which is not disputed shows the following facts and circumstances surrounding the testator when the will was executed. The deceased, Bertha Cohen and the appellee Laura Fisch were sisters. Appellants are the children of Bertha Cohen. On April 11, 1958, when Bertha Cohen executed the will she and Laura Fisch were both widows, approximately fifty years of age. Bertha Cohen owned property of the value of approximately one million dollars, and the value of property owned by Laura Fisch was approximately Twenty-five Thousand Dollars. The appellant Cohen was twenty years of age and appellant Levin was twenty-five years old. Appellants had one year previously inherited from their father property of the approximate value of one million dollars. For two years prior to her death Bertha Cohen paid appellee the sum of $200.00 per month. She also made other gifts to appellee and her daughter of clothing and money. The record shows that appellee was in poor health and unable to work full time, and that her income was approximately $300.00 per month.

Appellants rely principally on Byars v. Byars et al., 182 S.W.2d 363, (Sup.Ct. 1944), in which it was held that the word "request" in its ordinary or natural meaning when used in a will is precatory and not mandatory. Our Supreme Court in that case noted the statement of the rule set out in the Colton case, supra, and then distinguished the facts in the Byars case as follows:

> No facts are presented in this case, as in Colton v. Colton, 127 U.S. 300, showing the situation of the testator when the will was drawn and the circumstances of the surviving wife and the other persons named, from which the inference might be drawn that the precatory paragraph of the will was intended to be mandatory. There is the single circumstance that the request is by the husband to the surviving wife. . . .

In 95 C.J.S. Section 602b the rule which in our opinion is applicable in Texas is stated as follows:

> Whether Precatory or Mandatory. In determining whether particular words are to be construed as precatory or mandatory, the court will look to the expressed intent of the testator, as found from the context of the will and surrounding circumstances; and words which, in their ordinary meaning, are precatory will be construed as mandatory only when it is evident that such was the testator's intent....

* * *

The trial court correctly found that there was no genuine issue of fact in the case. Based upon the rule announced in the above cited cases and authorities it is our opinion that it was the intention of the testatrix that the words of "desire" as used in the will were a positive directive and imposed an obligation on appellants to comply therewith. The provision of the will for the payment to appellee of $2,400.00 annually was set out specifically as well as the desire or direction of the testatrix that such payments should be discontinued in certain specified contingencies. The language in question considered in context and in connection with the language of the will as a whole, and the surrounding facts and circumstances is in our opinion more clearly mandatory than that of the Colton case. The court properly entered summary judgment in favor of appellee, Laura Fisch.

QUESTIONS

1. Why did the will in Levin v. Fisch create a trust, while the will in Spicer v. Wright did not?

2. Why did the husband's guardian in Spicer argue that his wife's will created a trust? Would the husband have been a beneficiary of the trust?

3. How would you have drafted the instrument in Spicer to create a trust? To make it clear that no trust was intended? Similarly, redraft the instrument in Levin to eliminate the ambiguity that spawned the litigation.

4. As a result of the court's decision in Levin v. Fisch, what duties were imposed on the trustees? Recall that testator instructed her children to pay to her sister $2,400/month "out of the annual rent proceeds, rents and revenues" from her property. Suppose the trustees sold the real property that generated "rent proceeds, rents and revenues." Would their obligation to Laura end? Suppose that the trustees not only sold the real property that they inherited from their mother, but spent the sale proceeds and the rest of their inheritance. Would Laura have legal standing to complain?

PROBLEMS

1. "I bequeath $10,000 to my accountant, John Smith, who is instructed as to my charitable wishes." Outright gift to the accountant?

2. "I bequeath $10,000 to my beloved brother, John Smith, who is instructed as to my charitable wishes." Outright gift? See Estate of Corbett, 430 Pa. 54, 241 A.2d 524 (1968).

3. "I bequeath $10,000 to my beloved brother, John Smith, but I ask him to use part of the money to care for our ailing cousin, Adam." Outright gift?

4. "I bequeath $10,000 to my beloved brother, John Smith, but I ask him to pay $50 per month to care for our ailing cousin, Adam." Outright gift?

NOTE

In construing precatory language, how closely should we search to determine testator's actual meaning? Should we ask what this testator meant when she drafted her will, or should we focus on what a competent estate planner would have meant by the words used? See generally Mary Louise Fellows, In Search of Donative Intent, 73 Iowa L. Rev. 611 (1988). For an examination of how different states have dealt with the precatory language problem, see Frank L. Schiavo, Does the Use of "Request," "Wish," or "Desire" Create a Precatory Trust or Not?, 40 Real Prop. Prob. & Tr. J. 647 (2006).

For an excellent discussion of the problems associated with precatory language, including drafting suggestions, see L.A. McElwee, Precatory Language in Wills: Mere Utterances of the Sibyl? 11 Prob. L.J. 145 (1992).

3. TRUST FORMALITIES

Goodman v. Goodman

Supreme Court of Washington, 1995.
128 Wash.2d 366, 907 P.2d 290.

■ Johnson, J.

This case involves a family dispute between Clive Goodman's mother, Gladys Goodman, and his children over property he transferred to Gladys before his death in 1983. A jury found Gladys held Clive's property in trust for his children and wrongfully withheld the property. The trial judge granted judgment notwithstanding the verdict, having found the children commenced the action after the limitations period had run.... We reverse.

Clive Goodman died in November 1983 after a three-year struggle with a liver disease. His illness required frequent hospitalizations and complicated medical procedures. About five years before his death, Clive gave Gladys general power of attorney. About one year before his death, he transferred his major asset, Ozzie's East Tavern, to Gladys. Gladys sold the tavern on an installment contract in 1982 for $70,000; she deposited the proceeds of the sale in her bank account.

Clive was survived by four children: Scott, Craig, Michelle, and his stepdaughter Tamara. When Clive died in 1983, Scott was seventeen, Craig was sixteen, Michelle was thirteen, and Tamara was twenty-one. He was also survived by Shirley Golden, his first wife and mother of all the children. Shirley and Clive had divorced in 1972, but remained close friends until his death.

Some eight years after Clive's death, when Scott was 25 years old, he asked Gladys for the first time for money from the sale of Ozzie's East and Clive's other assets. When Scott asked Gladys for the money, she reportedly told him she had taken care of Clive and felt she deserved it.

Scott then hired an attorney and was appointed personal representative of Clive's estate. He sued Gladys in that capacity in 1991, alleging that Clive intended Gladys to hold Clive's property for the benefit of his children until they were the age of majority or were able to receive and manage the property on their own. Gladys pleaded laches as an affirmative defense and counterclaimed for offset of money she had loaned to Clive or had paid on his behalf.

At trial, Shirley testified Clive had a will, had transferred all of his property to Gladys, and intended his children to have his property when they were old enough to responsibly manage it. She testified that shortly after the funeral, Gladys told her there was no will but she would give the children Clive's money when they were old enough to be responsible. Shirley relayed this information to the children. The children did not have a problem with Gladys holding Clive's property in trust. Shirley thought about hiring an attorney at this time but could not afford one. She stated:

> I wasn't concerned at all about the moneys. I felt very confident that there wouldn't be a problem with it. She [Gladys] told me the same things Dee [Clive] had told me.

Shirley first became concerned when Scott asked Gladys about the property in 1991.

Clive's stepdaughter Tamara testified she had seen Clive's will in 1977 and briefly discussed it with him. Based on that conversation, she believed Clive's property would be divided among the children. About one year after Clive's death, Tamara heard from relatives that all of Clive's property was in Gladys' name, and the children were not entitled to anything. She believed she discussed this with her siblings and Shirley around Christmas 1983. Shirley does not recall discussing this with Tamara.

Gladys testified she never had a conversation with Shirley regarding Clive's property or a will. She also testified Clive gave her the money to repay numerous loans and out of love and appreciation.

At the close of Scott's case, Gladys moved for a directed verdict on the grounds the limitations period had run. The trial court reserved ruling on this motion.

At the close of testimony, the trial court instructed the jury to decide whether Clive transferred his property to Gladys as a gift or to hold in trust for the benefit of the children. It defined a trust as:

> A trust can be defined as a right of property, real or personal, held by one party for the benefit of another. It is a confidence placed in one person, who is termed a trustee, for the benefit of another, respecting property which is held by the trustee for the benefit of another. A trust need not be in writing. A trust can arise or be implied from circumstances as a result of the presumed intention of the parties as gathered from the nature of the transaction between them.

Clerk's Papers at 28.

Gladys did not offer a jury instruction on the statute of limitations defense, nor did she except to the trial court's failure to give one.

The jury found Gladys held the property in trust for the benefit of Clive's children, and the children incurred damages of $60,000 as a result of Gladys' wrongful retention of the trust property. They also found Gladys was entitled to an offset of $11,000.

Following the verdict, the trial court granted Gladys' motion for a JNOV, finding that the children should have discovered the cause of action more than three years before Scott commenced the action. The Court of Appeals agreed. It found the statute of limitations issue presented a factual question, but affirmed the trial court because the facts were susceptible of only one reasonable interpretation: the children were put on notice of facts, which with the exercise of due diligence would have led to discovery of the wrongdoing as each of them turned eighteen and received nothing. Because the youngest child turned eighteen more than three years before the commencement of the action, the suit was time barred....

Viewing the evidence in the light most favorable to the nonmoving party, we hold the statute of limitations defense presented a question of fact that could not be decided as a matter of law.

The parties and the courts below have referred to the trust as a constructive trust. A constructive trust is an equitable remedy imposed by courts when someone should not in fairness be allowed to retain property. *Farrell v. Mentzer*, 102 Wash. 629, 174 P. 482 (1918); see *generally* George T. Bogert, Trusts § 77 (6th ed. 1987). An express trust, on the other hand, arises because of expressed intent and involves a fiduciary relationship in which the trustee holds property for the benefit of a third party. *In re Lutz*, 74 Wash. App. 356, 365, 873 P.2d 566 (1994).

Scott's theory in this case, consistent with the jury instructions, was that Clive intended Gladys to hold his personal property in trust until the children reached majority or were mature enough to handle it. In support of this theory, Shirley testified:

> A. The only thing[] that was said, was the day of the funeral.... [Gladys] said that she was not giving them [the children] any money until they got older. Because she didn't want them blowing it.
>
> Q. Did you relay that to the children?
>
> A. Yes.
>
> Q. Did she indicate how much older they would have to get?

A. Until they were responsible. See, we have had a few problems with Scott. And—just took him a little longer than it does other people to grow up.

Q. Well, did you ever explain to them what you perceived to be Mrs. Goodman's role in holding onto the property?

A. Well, they just knew that their grandmother was going to—give them the money after they reached a certain age. I didn't know what the certain age was. One child could be—responsible at this age. Another one won't. So I didn't know what she was waiting for. Or—I never questioned it because Dee had told me that they were going to be taken care of, they weren't going to get their money until they were—older.

Consistent with this and other testimony, the jury found Clive intended Gladys to hold his property in trust for the children. This being the case, the trust at issue is properly characterized as an express trust.

An action based on an express (or constructive trust) is subject to the three-year statute of limitations contained in RCW 4.16.080.... The statute of limitations on an express trust action begins to run when the beneficiary of the trust discovers or should have discovered the trust has been terminated or repudiated by the trustee.

.... The jury found Gladys held Clive's property in trust for the children. Although no findings were made concerning the terms of the trust, the trial testimony supports Scott's view that Clive intended Gladys to hold the property until the children reached majority or were mature enough to handle it. Had the evidence only been that Clive intended Gladys to hold his property until the children reached majority, the repudiation would have occurred when each child turned eighteen and received nothing as the trial court found. But given the jury's verdict and the evidence that Clive intended the children to have his property when they were mature enough to handle it, it can hardly be said as a matter of law that the repudiation occurred when each child turned eighteen. A reasonable interpretation of the evidence is the repudiation occurred in 1991 when Gladys told Scott for the first time she deserved Clive's money and would not give him anything. Under these circumstances, when Gladys repudiated the trust is susceptible to more than one reasonable interpretation, and the trial court erred....

QUESTIONS

1. As we have seen, legislatures and courts worry a lot about formalities when a decedent seeks to make a transfer by will. Yet, in many states, courts are willing to enforce a trust agreement without any written evidence of the terms of the trust, without any signature, and without any witnesses. What justifies such a dramatic difference between the treatment of wills and trusts? See generally Bruce H. Mann, Formalities and Formalism in the Uniform Probate Code, 142 U. Pa. L. Rev. 1033, 1060 (1994) (noting that rise in testamentary substitutes led to increased criticism of strict formalities in wills law).

2. Suppose Clive Goodman had never transferred title to Ozzie's East Tavern during his lifetime, but had instead executed a will leaving all of his property to his mother, Gladys. After probate of the will, Clive's ex-wife testifies that Gladys had told her Clive had given her the property as trustee for Clive's children. In an action by Clive's son Scott to enforce the trust, what result? See Trustees of Amherst College v. Ritch, 151 N.Y. 282, 45 N.E. 876 (1897) (holding that equity compels will beneficiary to comply with "secret" trust).

3. Suppose Clive's ex-wife testifies that Clive had declared to her, at a funeral, that he was holding Ozzie's East Tavern in trust for the children. Clive continued to operate the tavern. Three years after the supposed declaration, Scott brings an action against Clive to recover income derived from operation of the Tavern. What result?

4. Suppose that, instead of transferring title to his mother, Clive had transferred title to his sons Scott and Craig. At Clive's funeral, Scott informs his mom that he and Craig will turn over a share to sister Michelle when she is old enough to be responsible. At age twenty-five, Michelle seeks a share, and her brothers refuse. What result?

5. After Goodman v. Goodman, a Washington client informs you of his desire to make an outright gift to his mother of an apartment building worth $100,000. He is concerned that his ex-wife or his greedy children might, after his death, make claim to the apartment house. What advice would you give the client?

6. Suppose Gladys Goodman had never sold Ozzie's East. Suppose instead she had mortgaged the tavern, and then defaulted on the mortgage. What rights would the children have against the mortgagee? Suppose there was no mortgage, but Gladys' judgment creditors sought to foreclose on the tavern? What rights would the children have against the creditors? See Bank One of Milford, N.A. v. Bardes, 25 Ohio St.3d 296, 496 N.E.2d 475 (1986).

NOTES ON FORMALITIES

1. *Statute of Frauds.* In all but a few American states, no writing is necessary to establish a trust of personal property. (That does not, of course, mean that no writing is desirable. A lawyer who advises a client to establish an oral trust is asking for trouble.). The original English Statute of Frauds did, however, apply to trusts of land, and most American jurisdictions purport to require writings for trusts of land. The court in Goodman v. Goodman does not mention the rule—despite the fact that the original trust property, the tavern, appears to have been real property, and despite the fact that the Washington Supreme Court has, in its own words, "repeatedly and consistently held that parol evidence is not admissible to establish an express trust in land." Zucker v. Mitchell, 62 Wash.2d 819, 823, 384 P.2d 815, 818 (1963).

A few jurisdictions explicitly permit oral trusts of land. See, e.g., Levin v. Smith, 513 A.2d 1292 (Del.1986).

The Uniform Trust Code sanctions oral trusts (unless otherwise prohibited by state statute), but would require that the trust's terms be proved by clear and convincing evidence, a higher standard than that employed by most states. See UTC § 407.

2. *A Writing and Other Formalities Required in Some States.* In recent years, both the Florida and New York legislatures have enacted statutes requiring trusts, including trusts of personal property, to be in writing and executed with formalities. See Fla. Stat. 737.111; N.Y. EPTL section 7–1.17. The Florida statute provides:

FLORIDA STATUTES

SECTION 737.111 EXECUTION REQUIREMENTS FOR EXPRESS TRUSTS.

(1) The testamentary aspects of a trust defined in section 731.201(34), are invalid unless the trust instrument is executed by the grantor with the formalities required for the execution of a will.

(2) The testamentary aspects of a trust created by a nonresident of Florida, either before or after this law takes effect, are not invalid because the trust does not meet the requirements of this section, if the trust is valid under the laws of the state or country where the settlor was at the time of execution.

(3) The testamentary aspects of an amendment to a trust are invalid unless the amendment is executed by the settlor with the same formalities as a will.

(4) For the purposes of this section, the term "testamentary aspects" means those provisions of the trust that dispose of the trust property on or after the death of the settlor other than to the settlor's estate.

* * *

The New York statute requires the signatures of the settlor and at least one trustee (unless the settlor is the sole trustee) and either 1) acknowledgment by a notary, or 2) the signatures of two witnesses. See N.Y. EPTL section 7–1.17.

How would the Goodman case have been decided under the Florida statute? What do you think motivated the statute? Is the statute a good idea?

3. *Declarations of Trust vs. Transfers in Trust.* A trust settlor may create an *inter vivos* trust by declaring that she holds the trust property, as trustee, in trust for named beneficiaries, or by transferring the trust property to someone else as trustee for the benefit of the named beneficiaries. A trust document that creates a trust and names someone other than the settlor as trustee is often called a deed of trust.

4. *Delivery.* When a settlor transfers the property in trust to someone else as trustee, the settlor must *deliver* the trust property to the named trustee. See, e.g., Thompson v. Bremer, 34 A.D.2d 801, 311 N.Y.S.2d 980 (1970), aff'd 28 N.Y.2d 566, 268 N.E.2d 324, 319 N.Y.S.2d 611 (1971); Restatement (Third) of Trusts § 16 (2003). The delivery requirement for transfers in trust, like the delivery requirement for *inter vivos* gifts, is designed to assure that the settlor truly intended to make a transfer; if I announce to you that I have given you my gold watch, but continue to wear the watch on my arm, can we be sure that my words were intended to speak more loudly than my actions? If, however, along with my statement, I give you the watch, I have eliminated any ambiguity.

What constitutes delivery, however, may vary from state to state. Suppose a settlor executes a deed of trust that recites "Settlor hereby transfers and delivers to Trustee all property listed on attached Schedule A." Schedule A lists Blackacre (settlor's vacation home) and 1,000 shares of AT & T common stock as trust assets. If Settlor delivers the trust document to the trustee, but does not execute a deed transferring title to Blackacre to Trustee and does not re-register the stock in Trustee's name, has Settlor satisfied the delivery requirement? Compare N.Y. E.P.T.L. § 7–1.18 (directing that no trust is created unless and until Settlor transfers title to real property to trustee and re-registers the stock in trustee's name) with Restatement (Third) of Trusts § 16 cmt. b (2003) (suggesting that delivery of the trust document would satisfy the delivery requirement), and Chebatoris v. Moyer, 276 Neb. 733, 757 N.W.2d 212 (2008) (finding that execution of trust document and acceptance by trustees was sufficient to transfer title to real property into trust). Notwithstanding the Restatement's position, would a prudent lawyer fail to transfer title to titled assets?

Courts sometimes use the delivery requirement to invalidate trusts when there is no question about settlor's intent. The court may mistrust settlor's capacity, or be concerned about settlor's other relatives, and the delivery requirement may provide a convenient foundation for invalidating the trust. (Cf. Thompson v. Bremer, *supra*).

When a settlor declares herself trustee, most courts hold that actual delivery is unnecessary so long as the trust declaration clearly identifies the trust assets, reasoning that the settlor cannot deliver property to herself. Cf. Taliaferro v. Taliaferro, 260 Kan. 573, 921 P.2d 803 (1996) (upholding a declaration of trust even though settlor had never formally transferred title to the trust property). See also, UTC § 401(2), cmt.; Restatement (Third) of Trusts § 10, cmt. e (2003). Moreover, courts generally uphold declarations of trusts of real property even if the settlor has not recorded the declaration or any instrument of transfer. See Estate of Heggstad, 16 Cal.App.4th 943, 20 Cal.Rptr.2d 433 (1993). However, courts tend to scrutinize carefully the supposed settlor's treatment of the property after the declaration to determine whether settlor had intended to create a trust. See, e.g., Campenello v. Conrow, 127 Misc.2d 91, 485 N.Y.S.2d 469 (1985) (finding no trust where settlor had recorded deed in which he declared that he held property in trust for his children, because settlor had mortgaged the property and treated it as his own).

In a few states, however, the settlor/trustee must satisfy the delivery requirement by transferring title or changing the registration of the trust property from the settlor as an individual to the settlor "as trustee." In such states, failure to transfer title will invalidate the trust as to those assets. See e.g., N.Y. EPTL § 7–1.18.

5. *Constructive and Resulting Trusts.* The private express trust—the focus of attention in this chapter—shares the "trust" label with two other, significantly different, devices: the constructive trust and the resulting trust.

The constructive trust is not really a trust at all, but a remedial device used by courts to achieve results which do not easily fit within other doctrinal frameworks. No one "intends" to create a constructive trust. Instead, the constructive trust—discussed in Goodman v. Goodman—is a flexible remedial device often used to prevent unjust enrichment. In Judge Cardozo's words:

> A constructive trust is the formula through which the conscience of equity finds expression. When property has been acquired in such circumstances that the holder of the legal title may not in good conscience retain the beneficial interest, equity converts him into a trustee.

Beatty v. Guggenheim Exploration Co., 225 N.Y. 380, 386, 122 N.E. 378, 380 (1919). For instance, when A devises property to B, without mention of any trust, but relying on B's oral promise to hold the property in trust for C, courts have held that B holds as a constructive trustee for C. See Potts v. Emerick, 293 Md. 495, 445 A.2d 695 (1982); Restatement (Third) of Trusts § 7, cmt. d (2003). In effect, the court wishes A had made B trustee of an express trust, and construed events as if A had created an express trust. See generally Robert L. Banks, Jr., A Survey of the Constructive Trust in Tennessee, 12 Memphis St. L. Rev. 71 (1981).

A resulting trust generally arises when a settlor intends to create a trust, but the trust fails for some reason. For instance, when a settlor transfers property to a trustee in trust for beneficiaries too indefinite to permit enforcement, does the trustee obtain beneficial as well as legal title? Of course not. Instead, courts say that the trustee holds the property on a "resulting trust" for the benefit of the settlor or settlor's successors-in-interest. Practically, all that means is that once the court concludes that the express trust fails, the "trustee" must transfer the property back to settlor. Similarly, if the trust has more property than necessary to accomplish its purposes, the trustee is said to hold the remainder on a resulting trust for the benefit of settlor or settlor's successors-in-interest. In a sense, the resulting trust is an implied equitable reversion in the settlor. See Restatement (Third) of Trusts § 7 (2003).

The other important category of resulting trust is the "purchase money resulting trust." At common law, if Jones paid for land, but arranged for the seller to transfer title to Smith, the presumption was that Jones had not made a gift to Smith, but that Jones retained beneficial title to the property—that is, Smith held title in trust for Jones. See Restatement (Third) of Trusts § 7, cmt. c (2003). The underlying premise was that Jones would never pay money for property to be transferred to Smith. Surely, if Jones paid the money, Jones intended creation of a trust. In many jurisdictions, the purchase money resulting trust has been abolished by statute. See, e.g., N.Y. EPTL Section 7–1.3.

The resulting trust and the constructive trust are not estate planning tools. They are important principally as devices litigators might use to rescue estates when the testator's plans have gone awry. Thus, in Goodman v. Goodman, Scott Goodman's lawyer—undoubtedly concerned that the court would not enforce an express trust because the trust had not been reduced to writing—argued that Scott's grandmother held the property as constructive trustee. Similarly, in Estate of Falise, 20 Misc.3d 894, 863 N.Y.S.2d 854 (Sur. Ct. 2008), the Surrogate Court determined that decedent's nephew—the named beneficiary on several bank and IRA accounts worth more than $400,000—held those assets in a constructive trust for decedent's children. There was evidence that decedent had left a letter instructing his nephew as to how the money should be distributed and that the nephew had destroyed the letter after distributing small fractions of the money to decedent's children. Decedent's children testified that their father had told them that he had put the accounts in the nephew's name to avoid probate, and that nephew would distribute almost all of the money to them after decedent's death. Despite the fact that New York law requires an executed writing to establish a trust, the Surrogate Court held in favor of decedent's children on the theory that nephew held the funds in a "constructive trust." But see Connall v. Felton, 225 Or.App. 266, 201 P.3d 219 (2009) (reversing a lower court decision that decedent's stepson held decedent's home in a "resulting trust" for her children, where decedent had executed a deed transferring her home to her stepson but reserving a life estate in herself).

SECTION II. USING TRUSTS AS AN ESTATE PLANNING TOOL

As you studied the trust's basic elements, you saw that trusts enable property owners to provide for enjoyment of property over successive generations. Trusts enable property owners to accomplish a variety of other important estate planning objectives as well. Specifically, property owners use trusts (and related mechanisms) to provide for minor children when their parents die before the age of maturity, to give trustees flexibility in meeting beneficiaries' needs, to protect beneficiaries from creditors, to avoid probate, to plan for incapacity and the costs of institutional care and to achieve flexibility in the estate plan while obtaining maximum estate tax advantages. The following sections explore in turn each of these important estate planning objectives.

A. PROVIDING FOR MINOR CHILDREN

A chief estate planning concern of parents of minor children is to provide for the children's long-term care in the event that the parents die before the children reach adulthood. In a two-parent family, each parent's will should provide for two contingencies; the death of the testator prior to the partner, and the death of the testator after (or concurrently with) the partner (for a discussion of drafting with respect to "simultaneous death," see Chapter Two, Section VI, *supra*). For single parents, a well drafted plan providing for minor children is especially important. Divorced parents may wish to devise assets to minor children without involving former spouses in the management or distribution of those assets. Trusts can facilitate planning for all of these families.

Increasingly, settlors are using revocable *inter vivos* trusts as the main component of their estate plans. Section II C.2. of this chapter addresses the creation and use of revocable *inter vivos* trusts. For many parents, however, the disadvantages of a revocable trust would outweigh the benefits. For those parents, testamentary trusts are sufficient to carry out their objectives.

A well drafted will that provides for minor children should contain two key provisions; first, the testator should nominate a custodial guardian to assume primary care of minor children in the event the children are left parentless. Second, the will should create a testamentary trust for the children's benefit. Nominating the children's guardian as testamentary trustee has the advantage of convenience. Some clients, however, may prefer to appoint a different person or financial institution to act as trustee. The will provisions should offer guidelines concerning how the trustee is to distribute the income and principal to the minor beneficiaries (the specifics regarding trustee discretion are discussed in subsection C., *infra*).

A parent also may wish to transfer non-probate assets, such as a retirement account or the proceeds of a life insurance policy, to minor children. The testator can consolidate the administration of those assets by naming a trustee as beneficiary of those assets. This enables all of the testator's assets to be administered as part of the same trust.

PROBLEM

Myrna Smith, age 32, has asked you to draft her will. Myrna has a husband, John, and a son, Paul, age 2. John has quit his job, and is taking care of Paul full time. Myrna is the sole breadwinner. Myrna and John each have $50,000 in assets. In addition, Myrna has a pension plan that allows her to name alternative beneficiaries in the event of her death. John is named as alternative beneficiary. The intestacy statute in the relevant state directs an intestate distribution of ½ to the spouse and ½ to the children of the deceased.

Myrna is confident that John would take care of Paul should Myrna die before Paul reaches majority, and she wants to name John the sole beneficiary of her estate. What other dispositive provisions should Myrna's will include? Should she make any changes to her pension plan's beneficiary designation? What other document(s) should be part of the family's estate plan?

B. Building Flexibility Into the Estate Plan: Support Trusts and Discretionary Trusts

Suppose a person wants more than one person to benefit from her estate. She can simply divide her estate assets among the intended beneficiaries, but that approach does not enable the testator to provide for each beneficiary when that beneficiary needs resources the most. To divide benefits over time, the testator can create a trust, reserving income to one (or more) beneficiaries, and providing for payment of the principal to other beneficiaries at the death of the income beneficiary or beneficiaries. Even that approach, however, does not permit the testator to take account of future events that might make it appropriate to devote more (or less) of the estate to one particular beneficiary, or to some group of beneficiaries. *Support Trusts* and *Discretionary Trusts* enable the testator to account for events not known at the time the testator dies or at the time a settlor creates an *inter vivos* trust. They also enable a testator to provide for the unknown needs of incapacitated beneficiaries. See Gail Boreman Bird, Diagnosis: Mental Incapacity, Rx: Protective Trust, 116 Tr. and Est. 676 (1977).

When settlor creates a discretionary trust, the settlor imposes no mandatory obligation on the trustee. Instead, the settlor gives the trustee discretion to pay income (and/or to invade principal) for the benefit of one or more described beneficiaries. The settlor says, in effect, "I trust you, trustee, to do what is best for the described beneficiaries, and to make the payments I would believe appropriate." See generally Edward C. Halbach, Jr., Problems of Discretion in Discretionary Trusts, 61 Colum. L. Rev. 1425 (1961).

By contrast, a settlor creates a support trust by giving the trustee power to pay income for the support of a named beneficiary. The settlor need not simply use the word "support"; the trust instrument might authorize payment of income for the "support and education," or for the "maintenance" of the beneficiary's lifestyle. The trustee is then obligated to pay the beneficiary the amounts necessary for support. A pure support trust, then, imposes a mandatory duty on the trustee; the trustee's responsibility is to ascertain what the beneficiary needs for support, and then to pay that amount to the beneficiary. Alternatively, settlor might create a trust that has both mandatory and discretionary characteristics. In one common form, a settlor requires the trustee to pay income to the beneficiary and to invade the principal if necessary to provide for the income beneficiary's support. Consider another hybrid:

Evelyn Ginsberg Abravanel, Discretionary Support Trusts, 68 Iowa L. Rev. 273, 278–79 (1983).

Although a support trust is deemed to contain an ascertainable standard by which the trustees' distributive decisions can be measured, the trustee is vested with considerable dispositive discretion. The "discretionary" aspect of even a pure support trust arises by reason of the imprecise nature of the support standard.

* * *

Frequently, the discretionary element of a support trust is made explicit, as when discretionary language is combined with language that, if taken alone, would be deemed to create a pure support trust. For example, a property owner transfers certain assets "to T, in trust, to pay to W or apply so much of the income or principal of the trust, from time to time, as T shall, *in his uncontrolled discretion, deem necessary for the support and maintenance* of W," with remainder over to some third person upon the termination of the life tenant's interest. This language creates a species of trust termed a discretionary support trust.

PROBLEM

The primary estate planning concern for Phil T. Rich, a 75–year old with considerable means, is to assure adequate provision for his 68–year old wife of 18 years. At the same time, however, Phil would like assets not needed by his wife to pass, at his death, to his two daughters by a prior marriage, now aged 38 and 35, rather than to his wife's son by a prior marriage, now aged 45. Phil has heard that a "support trust" or a "discretionary trust" might be well-suited to meet his goals.

In light of the materials that follow, advise Phil about the advantages and disadvantages of creating, by will, a discretionary trust or a support trust, and draft a provision appropriate to Phil's needs. In the course of the exercise, consider the following:

(1) Whom should Phil select as trustee: his wife, one or both of his children, his 70–year–old sister (whose judgment he trusts and who has great affection for both his wife and his children), or a corporate trustee?

(2) What powers should Phil confer upon the trustee with respect to trust income? Trust principal?

Wells v. Sanford

Supreme Court of Arkansas, 1984.
281 Ark. 242, 663 S.W.2d 174.

■ HOLLINGSWORTH, J.

The central issue raised in this appeal is whether the assets of a testamentary trust should be used to support a woman who has been declared incompetent before her own assets, as controlled by her guardian, are used.

Nora Wells was declared physically incompetent in 1974 and Elvan G. Sanford, one of the appellees, was appointed her guardian. In 1977, Hiram Wells, Nora Wells' son, executed his Last Will and Testament. The Will contained the following provisions:

II

> If my mother, Nora Wells, is living at the time of my death, then I give, devise, and bequeath my entire estate to Elvan G. Sanford, as Trustee to be held in trust for the use and benefit of my mother as long as she lives. I authorize the Trustee to expend for the support and maintenance of the said Nora Wells, such sums as may be necessary as long as she lives.

III

> If my mother, Nora Wells, is not living at the time of my death, then I give, devise, and bequeath my estate to Elvan G. Sanford and/or Koleta J. Sanford, his wife, to have and to hold as their absolute property. If my mother, Nora Wells, survives me, any of my estate left at her death I hereby direct said Elvan G. Sanford and/or Koleta J. Sanford to receive any and all of balance of estate left as their absolute property.

Hiram Wells died in 1979 leaving only real property as the corpus of the testamentary trust. Nora Wells, now 91, resides in a nursing home and owes an unpaid bill there of $23,749.74. Her property consists solely of: (1) 109 acres of realty owned by her in fee and subject to the guardianship of Elvan Sanford; and (2) her life interest in the 80 acres of realty constituting the testamentary trust of Hiram Wells. Sanford, as guardian, petitioned the Baxter County Probate Court for permission to sell the guardianship assets of Nora Wells and apply the proceeds to her support. Subsequently, J. C. Wells and Irene Bain, appellants here and Nora Wells' children, petitioned the Baxter County Chancery Court to direct the trustee to sell the trust assets and apply those proceeds for Nora Wells' support. The cases were consolidated for trial. The court delayed ruling on the petition to sell the guardianship assets until a new guardian was appointed and joined in the petition. The court dismissed the appellants' petition to sell the trust assets finding that Hiram Wells intended that his testamentary trust be used to support Nora Wells only in the event her own property was insufficient to maintain her. We reverse.

In his decree, the chancellor found that if Nora Wells had predeceased Hiram Wells, all of his estate would have gone to the Sanfords. Since Hiram predeceased Nora, his property went into trust for the "use and benefit" of Nora during her life, with the balance of the trust estate going to the Sanfords. The chancellor stated:

> 5. That Nora Wells has ample assets which may be used for her.
>
> 6. The central issue of the case is whether or not Hiram intended that the phrase "sums necessary for the support and maintenance" of Nora Wells means that his estate was to be appropriated to maintain Nora even when she had sufficient means or whether he intended to have his estate held available for her support in the event those means were exhausted.
>
> 7. In the literal sense, no funds would be "necessary" for Nora's support until her own ran out. In addition, if Hiram's funds are used

to support Nora before her funds run out, the effect is to increase Nora's estate and possibly benefit Hiram's brother and sister whom Hiram intended to pass in favor of the Sanfords. On the other hand, if Nora's funds were used first, she will still be taken care of, a result consistent with Hiram's purpose, but any funds remaining will ultimately benefit the Sanfords, who were the next objects of his bounty.

We have said before that unless something appears in the will indicating a different purpose, it is ordinarily presumed that the testator intended the beneficiary to be supported and maintained from estate income or from sale of part of the corpus. *Cross v. Pharr*, 215 Ark. 463, 221 S.W.2d 24 (1949).

The intention of the testator is derived from the four corners of the will, considering the language used and giving meaning to all of its provisions. *Armstrong v. Butler*, 262 Ark. 31, 553 S.W.2d 453 (1977). We construe the words and sentences used in a will in their ordinary sense in order to arrive at the testator's true intention. *Fowler v. Hogue, Trustee*, 276 Ark. 416, 635 S.W.2d 274 (1982). We have held that when there is nothing in the will to indicate that the testator did not understand the meaning of the words he used, we must presume that he did. *Lewis v. Bowlin*, 237 Ark. 947, 377 S.W.2d 608 (1964). Furthermore, in *Lewis* we quoted our holding in *Moody v. Walker*, 3 Ark. 147 (1840) where we stated:

> When technical phrases or terms of art are used, it is fair to presume that the testator understood their meaning, and that they expressed the intention of his will, according to their import and signification. When certain terms or words have by repeated adjudication received a precise, definite and legal construction, if the testator in making his will uses such terms or similar expressions, they shall be construed according to their legal effect.

Under *Cross,* supra, and its progeny we have given the term "necessary for support" a legal construction. We have held that a trust written in those terms is to be used to support the beneficiary regardless of the beneficiary's own assets. We must presume that Hiram Wells intended that the words he used would be given their legal effect. To find, as the chancellor did, that Hiram intended that his mother use her own assets first, thereby decreasing her estate, expressly so that Hiram's brother and sister would not inherit their mother's estate, would be allowing the testator to control the disposition of someone else's property. It is axiomatic that a testator can only convey by will such property as he owns and that he cannot, through his will, control the estate of another. *Refeld et al. Executors v. Bellette et al.*, 14 Ark. 148 (1853); 94 C.J.S. Wills § 76 (1956).

The appellants rely on *Cross v. Pharr*, *supra,* which involves a devise of property by the testator to F. E. Pharr in the nature of a trust for the lifetime of the testator's wife. During her life, the trustee was to pay Mrs. Pharr the income from the estate "when and as the same may be needed by my said wife." In *Cross*, the parties claimed that the widow's private means were sufficient for her support. We held:

> It is true that the will directs payment of the net income "when and as the same may be needed"; and should we construe J. W. Pharr's plan as one reserving the income to actual necessities arising after Mrs. Pharr had exhausted her own funds, appellants would be correct. *This, however, is not sufficiently shown to have been the testator's desire.* It is pointed out that the income, when apportioned to the entire period affected, amounted to but $525 a year. *Unless something appears in the will indicating a different purpose*, it is ordinarily presumed that the *trustor intended the beneficiary* to be supported and maintained from estate income, or as is sometimes the case, from sale of a part of the corpus.

That case mandates a similar result here. Our decision in *Cross* was based on what was sufficiently shown to have been the testator's desire based on what appeared in the will. Similarly, in *Martin v. Simmons First Nat'l Bank, Trustee*, 250 Ark. 774, 467 S.W.2d 165 (1971), we held that the appellant was not required to exhaust all of her resources before her medical expenses could be paid for out of the corpus of a trust left by her sister. In both cases, as here, we found that the appellant was the primary object of the testator's bounty, with others given consideration incidentally.

Here the clause in Hiram Wells' will created a presumption that he intended that Nora Wells be supported by the trust assets during her lifetime. Under *Cross* that is sufficient. Absent language by the testator manifesting an intention that the trust assets be withheld until the guardianship assets were exhausted, the presumption is that the trust assets are available for use immediately. Our different conclusions do not result so much from a disagreement with the chancellor on the law involved as from its application to the facts in this case.

The function of a court in dealing with a will is purely judicial; and its sole duty and its only power in the premises is to construe and enforce the will, not to make for the testator another will which might appear to the court more equitable or more in accordance with what the court might believe to have been the testator's unexpressed intentions. *Park v. Holloman*, 210 Ark. 288, 195 S.W.2d 546 (1946).

* * *

The appellants' final point on appeal is not properly before this court. The appellants argue that judicial supervision of the trust is not inappropriate because of the conflict of interest inherent in Sanford's position as trustee of the trust, remainderman of the trust, and guardian of the trust's beneficiary. A new guardian has been appointed for Nora Wells. The appellees counter by quoting our decision in *Thompson, Trustee v. Dunlap*, 244 Ark. 178, 424 S.W.2d 360 (1968), where we held that a court may not, on its own motion, supervise the administration of the trust, absent a direction by the creator of the trust that it be so supervised. Judicial supervision is not an issue here. Our decision today directs that the trust assets be used to support Nora Wells, irrespective of her own assets, and authorizes the sale of those assets, if necessary, to comply with our decision. We leave undisturbed the trustee's discretion as to the invasion of the trust assets. Absent an abuse of that discretion, we do not interfere. Restatement (Second) of Trusts § 187 (1959).

QUESTIONS

1. The court in its opinion says "[i]t is axiomatic that a testator can only convey by will such property as he owns and that he cannot, through his will, control the estate of another." Is the court's statement true? Redraft Hiram Wells' will to assure that less of his mother's property passes to Hiram's siblings.

2. Suppose Hiram had given his trustee discretion to use income and to invade principal for his mother's benefit, without making any reference to his mother's support. Would the trustee have been entitled to refuse payment to the mother?

PROBLEM

Testator left several million dollars in trust, naming his second wife income beneficiary. The trust document provided:

> The trust's primary purpose shall be to provide for the support, maintenance, and health of my wife in the standard of living to which she is accustomed at my death. If my wife's own income and other financial resources from sources other than from this trust are not sufficient to so maintain her in such standard of living, the Trustee shall distribute, from time to time, as much of the current trust net income, or accumulated trust net income, as shall be necessary to so maintain her. If my wife's own income and other financial resources, together with distributions of current and accumulated trust net income from this trust, are not sufficient to maintain her in such standard of living, then the Trustee shall distribute as much of the trust corpus as shall be necessary to so maintain her.

After testator's death, testator's wife's separate income of $1,200/month is grossly insufficient to maintain the standard of living she enjoyed with her husband. Because the wife owns separate property valued at $300,000, trustee refuses to make distributions to the wife until she has essentially exhausted her own resources (specifically, until all she has left is "one home and one vehicle"). If the wife sues the trustee, should the court direct the trustee to make payments to the wife? See Keisling v. Landrum, 218 S.W.3d 737 (Tex.App.2007).

Marsman v. Nasca

Appeals Court of Massachusetts, 1991.
30 Mass.App.Ct. 789, 573 N.E.2d 1025, Appeal Denied, 411 Mass. 1102, 579 N.E.2d 1361.

■ DREBEN, J.

This appeal raises the following questions: Does a trustee, holding a discretionary power to pay principal for the "comfortable support and maintenance" of a beneficiary, have a duty to inquire into the financial resources of that beneficiary so as to recognize his needs? If so, what is the remedy for such failure? A Probate Court judge held that the will involved in this case imposed a duty of inquiry upon the trustee. We agree with this conclusion but disagree with the remedy imposed and accordingly vacate the judgment and remand for further proceedings.

1. *Facts*.... Sara Wirt Marsman died in September, 1971, survived by her second husband, T. Frederik Marsman (Cappy), and her daughter by her first marriage, Sally Marsman Marlette. Mr. James F. Farr, her lawyer for many years, drew her will and was the trustee thereunder.

Article IIA of Sara's will provided in relevant part:

> "It is my desire that my husband, T. Fred Marsman, be provided with *reasonable maintenance, comfort and support* after my death. Accordingly, if my said husband is living at the time of my death, I give to my trustees, who shall set the same aside as a separate trust fund, one-third (1/3) of the rest, residue and remainder of my estate ...; they shall pay the net income therefrom to my said husband at least quarterly during his life; and *after having considered the various available sources of support for him*, my trustees shall, if they deem it necessary or desirable from time to time, in their sole and uncontrolled discretion, pay over to him, or use, apply and/or expend for his direct or indirect benefit such amount or amounts of the principal thereof as they shall deem advisable for his *comfortable support and maintenance*."

(Emphasis supplied).

Article IIB provided:

> "Whatever remains of said separate trust fund, including any accumulated income thereon on the death of my husband, shall be added to the trust fund established under Article II—...."

Article IIC established a trust for the benefit of Sally and her family. Sally was given the right to withdraw principal and, on her death, the trust was to continue for the benefit of her issue and surviving husband.

The will also contained the following exculpatory clause:

> "No trustee hereunder shall ever be liable except for his own willful neglect or default."

During their marriage, Sara and Cappy lived well and entertained frequently. Cappy's main interest in life centered around horses. An expert horseman, he was riding director and instructor at the Dana Hall School in Wellesley until he was retired due to age in 1972. Sally, who was also a skilled rider, viewed Cappy as her mentor, and each had great affection for the other. Sara, wealthy from her prior marriage, managed the couple's financial affairs. She treated Cappy as "Lord of the Manor" and gave him money for his personal expenses, including an extensive wardrobe from one of the finest men's stores in Wellesley.

In 1956, Sara and Cappy purchased, as tenants by the entirety, the property in Wellesley which is the subject of this litigation. Although title to the property passed to Cappy by operation of law on Sara's death, Sara's will also indicated an intent to convey her interest in the property to Cappy. In the will, Cappy was also given a life estate in the household furnishings with remainder to Sally.

After Sara's death in 1971, Farr met with Cappy and Sally and held what he termed his "usual family conference" going over the provisions of the will. At the time of Sara's death, the Wellesley property was appraised at $29,000, and the principal of Cappy's trust was about $65,600.

Cappy continued to live in the Wellesley house but was forced by Sara's death and his loss of employment in 1972 to reduce his standard of living substantially. He married Margaret in March, 1972, and, shortly before their marriage, asked her to read Sara's will, but they never discussed it. In 1972, Cappy took out a mortgage for $4,000, the proceeds of which were used to pay bills. Farr was aware of the transaction, as he replied to an inquiry of the mortgagee bank concerning the appraised value of the Wellesley property and the income Cappy expected to receive from Sara's trust.

In 1973, Cappy retained Farr in connection with a new will. The latter drew what he described as a simple will which left most of Cappy's property, including the house, to Margaret. The will was executed on November 7, 1973.

In February, 1974, Cappy informed the trustee that business was at a standstill and that he really needed some funds, if possible. Farr replied in a letter in which he set forth the relevant portion of the will and wrote that he thought the language was "broad enough to permit a distribution of principal." Farr enclosed a check of $300. He asked Cappy to explain in writing the need for some support and why the need had arisen. The judge found that Farr, by his actions, discouraged Cappy from making any requests for principal.

Indeed, Cappy did not reduce his request to writing and never again requested principal. Farr made no investigation whatsoever of Cappy's needs or his "available sources of support" from the date of Sara's death until Cappy's admission to a nursing home in 1983 and, other than the $300 payment, made no additional distributions of principal until Cappy entered the nursing home.

By the fall of 1974, Cappy's difficulty in meeting expenses intensified.[1] Several of his checks were returned for insufficient funds, and in October,

---

1. After Sara's death, Cappy's income was limited, particularly considering the station he had enjoyed while married to Sara. In 1973, including the income from Sara's trust of $2,116, his income was $3,441; in 1974 it was $3,549, including trust income of $2,254; in 1975, $6,624, including trust income of $2,490 and social security income of $2,576. Margaret's income was also minimal; $499 in 1974, $4,084 in 1975, including social security income of $1,686. Cappy's income in 1976 was $8,464; in 1977, $8,955; in 1978, $9,681; in 1979, $10,851; in 1980, $11,261; in 1981, $12,651; in 1982, $13,870; in 1983, $12,711; in 1984, $12,500; in

1974, in order that he might remain in the house, Sally and he agreed that she would take over the mortgage payments, the real estate taxes, insurance, and major repairs. In return, she would get the house upon Cappy's death.

Cappy and Sally went to Farr to draw up a deed. Farr was the only lawyer involved, and he billed Sally for the work. He wrote to Sally, stating his understanding of the proposed transaction, and asking, among other things, whether Margaret would have a right to live in the house if Cappy should predecease her. The answer was no. No copy of the letter to Sally was sent to Cappy. A deed was executed by Cappy on November 7, 1974, transferring the property to Sally and her husband Richard T. Marlette (Marlette) as tenants by the entirety, reserving a life estate to Cappy. No writing set forth Sally's obligations to Cappy.

The judge found that there was no indication that Cappy did not understand the transaction, although, in response to a request for certain papers by Farr, Cappy sent a collection of irrelevant documents. The judge also found that Cappy clearly understood that he was preserving no rights for Margaret, and that neither Sally nor Richard nor Farr ever made any representation to Margaret that she would be able to stay in the house after Cappy's death.

Although Farr had read Sara's will to Cappy and had written to him that the will was "broad enough to permit a distribution of principal," the judge found that Farr failed to advise Cappy that the principal of his trust could be used for the expenses of the Wellesley home. The parsimonious distribution of $300 and Farr's knowledge that the purpose of the conveyance to Sally was to enable Cappy to remain in the house, provide support for this finding. After executing the deed, Cappy expressed to Farr that he was pleased and most appreciative. Margaret testified that Cappy thought Farr was "great" and that he considered him his lawyer.

Sally and Marlette complied with their obligations under the agreement. Sally died in 1983, and Marlette became the sole owner of the property subject to Cappy's life estate. Although Margaret knew before Cappy's death that she did not have any interest in the Wellesley property, she believed that Sally would have allowed her to live in the house because of their friendship. After Cappy's death in 1987, Marlette inquired as to Margaret's plans, and, subsequently, through Farr, sent Margaret a notice to vacate the premises. Margaret brought this action in the Probate Court.

After a two-day trial, the judge held that the trustee was in breach of his duty to Cappy when he neglected to inquire as to the latter's finances. She concluded that, had Farr fulfilled his fiduciary duties, Cappy would not have conveyed the residence owned by him to Sally and Marlette. The judge ordered Marlette to convey the house to Margaret and also ordered Farr to reimburse Marlette from the remaining portion of Cappy's trust for the expenses paid by him and Sally for the upkeep of the property. If Cappy's

---

1985, $12,567; in 1986, $12,558. The largest portion from 1975 on came from social security benefits.

trust proved insufficient to make such payments, Farr was to be personally liable for such expenses. Both Farr and Marlette appealed from the judgment, from the denial of their motions to amend the findings, and from their motions for a new trial. Margaret appealed from the denial of her motion for attorney's fees. As indicated earlier, we agree with the judge that Sara's will imposed a duty of inquiry on the trustee, but we disagree with the remedy and, therefore, remand for further proceedings.

2. *Breach of trust by the trustee.* Contrary to Farr's contention that it was not incumbent upon him to become familiar with Cappy's finances, Article IIA of Sara's will clearly placed such a duty upon him. In his brief, Farr claims that the will gave Cappy the right to request principal "in extraordinary circumstances" and that the trustee, "was charged by Sara to be wary should Cappy request money beyond that which he quarterly received." Nothing in the will or the record supports this narrow construction. To the contrary, the direction to the trustees was to pay Cappy such amounts "as they shall deem advisable for his comfortable support and maintenance." This language has been interpreted to set an ascertainable standard, namely to maintain the life beneficiary "in accordance with the standard of living which was normal for him before he became a beneficiary of the trust." *Woodberry v. Bunker*, 359 Mass 239, 243 (1971). *Dana v. Gring*, 374 Mass. 109, 117 (1977). See *Blodget v. Delaney*, 201 F.2d 589, 593 (1st Cir.1953).

Even where the only direction to the trustee is that he shall "in his discretion" pay such portion of the principal as he shall "deem advisable," the discretion is not absolute. "Prudence and reasonableness, not caprice or careless good nature, much less a desire on the part of the trustee to be relieved from trouble ... furnish the standard of conduct." *Boyden v. Stevens*, 285 Mass. 176, 179 (1934), quoting from *Corkery v. Dorsey*, 223 Mass. 97, 101 (1916). *Holyoke Natl. Bank v. Wilson*, 350 Mass. 223, 227 (1966).

That there is a duty of inquiry into the needs of the beneficiary follows from the requirement that the trustee's power "must be exercised with that soundness of judgment which follows from a due appreciation of trust responsibility." *Boyden v. Stevens*, 285 Mass. at 179. *Woodberry v. Bunker*, 359 Mass. at 241.

Farr, in our view, did not meet his responsibilities either of inquiry or of distribution under the trust. The conclusion of the trial judge that, had he exercised "sound judgment," he would have made such payments to Cappy "as to allow him to continue to live in the home he had occupied for many years with the settlor" was warranted.

3. *Remedy against Marlette.* The judge, concluding that, had Farr not been in breach of trust, "[C]appy would have died owning the house and thus able to devise it to his widow, the plaintiff," ordered Marlette to convey the house to Margaret. This was an inappropriate remedy in view of the judge's findings. She found that, although the relationship between Cappy and Sally was "close and loving," there was "no fiduciary relation between them" and that Sally and Marlette "were not unjustly enriched by

the conveyance." She also found that "Sally and Richard Marlette expended significant monies over a long period of time in maintaining their agreement with [C]appy."

Because the conveyance was supported by sufficient consideration (the agreement to pay the house expenses) and because Sally and Marlette had no notice of a breach of trust and were not themselves guilty of a breach of fiduciary duty, they cannot be charged as constructive trustees of the property. *Jones v. Jones*, 297 Mass. 198, 207 (1937). That portion of the judgment which orders Marlette to convey the property is vacated.

4. *Remainder of Cappy's trust.* The amounts that should have been expended for Cappy's benefit are, however, in a different category. More than $80,000 remained in the trust for Cappy at the time of his death. As we have indicated, the trial judge properly concluded that payments of principal should have been made to Cappy from that fund in sufficient amount to enable him to keep the Wellesley property. There is no reason for the beneficiaries of the trust under Article IIC to obtain funds which they would not have received had Farr followed the testatrix's direction. The remedy in such circumstances is to impress a constructive trust on the amounts which should have been distributed to Cappy but were not because of the error of the trustee....

* * *

The amounts to be paid to Cappy's estate have not been determined. On remand, the Probate Court judge is to hold such hearings as are necessary to determine the amounts which should have been paid to Cappy to enable him to retain possession of the house.

5. *Personal liability of the trustee.* Farr raises a number of defenses against the imposition of personal liability, including the statute of limitations, the exculpatory clause in the will, and the fact that Cappy assented to the accounts of the trustee. The judge found that Farr's breach of his fiduciary duty to inquire as to Cappy's needs and his other actions in response to Cappy's request for principal, including the involvement of Sally in distributions of principal despite Sara's provision that Cappy's trust be administered separately, led Cappy to be unaware of his right to receive principal for house expenses. The breach may also be viewed as a continuing one. In these circumstances we do not consider Cappy's assent, see *Swift v. Hiscock*, 344 Mass. at 693, or the statute of limitations to be a bar. See *Greenfield Sav. Bank v. Abercrombie*, 211 Mass. 252, 259 (1912); *Allen v. Stewart*, 214 Mass. at 113; *Akin v. Warner*, 318 Mass. at 675–676. The judge also found that Margaret learned of Cappy's right to principal for house expenses only when she sought other counsel after his death.

The more difficult question is the effect of the exculpatory clause. As indicated in part 3 of this opinion, we consider the order to Marlette to reconvey the property an inappropriate remedy. In view of the judge's finding that, but for the trustee's breach, Cappy would have retained ownership of the house, the liability of the trustee could be considerable.

Although exculpatory clauses are not looked upon with favor and are strictly construed, such "provisions inserted in the trust instrument without any overreaching or abuse by the trustee of any fiduciary or confidential relationship to the settlor are generally held effective except as to breaches of trust 'committed in bad faith or intentionally or with reckless indifference to the interest of the beneficiary.' " *New England Trust Co. v. Paine*, 317 Mass. 542, 550 (1945), S.C., 320 Mass. 482, 485 (1946). See *Dill v. Boston Safe Deposit & Trust Co.*, 343 Mass. 97, 100–102 (1961); *Boston Safe Deposit & Trust Co. v. Boone*, 21 Mass. App. Ct. 637, 644 (1986). The actions of Farr were not of this ilk and also do not fall within the meaning of the term used in the will, "willful neglect or default."

Farr testified that he discussed the exculpatory clause with Sara and that she wanted it included. Nevertheless, the judge, without finding that there was an overreaching or abuse of Farr's fiduciary relation with Sara, held the clause ineffective. Relying on the fact that Farr was Sara's attorney, she stated: "One cannot know at this point in time whether or not Farr specifically called this provision to Sara's attention. Given the total failure of Farr to use his judgment as to Cappy's needs, it would be unjust and unreasonable to hold him harmless by reason of the exculpatory provisions he himself drafted and inserted in this instrument."

Assuming that the judge disbelieved Farr's testimony that he and Sara discussed the clause, although such disbelief on her part is by no means clear, the conclusion that it "would be unjust and unreasonable to hold [Farr] harmless" is not sufficient to find the overreaching or abuse of a fiduciary relation which is required to hold the provision ineffective. See Restatement (Second) of Trusts § 222, comment d (1959). We note that the judge found that Sara managed all the finances of the couple, and from all that appears, was competent in financial matters.

There was no evidence about the preparation and execution of Sara's will except for the questions concerning the exculpatory clause addressed to Farr by his own counsel. No claim was made that the clause was the result of an abuse of confidence. See *Boston Safe Deposit & Trust Co. v. Boone*, 21 Mass. App. Ct. at 644.

The fact that the trustee drew the instrument and suggested the insertion of the exculpatory clause does not necessarily make the provision ineffective. Restatement (Second) of Trusts § 222, comment d. No rule of law requires that an exculpatory clause drawn by a prospective trustee be held ineffective unless the client is advised independently. Cf. *Barnum v. Fay*, 320 Mass. 177, 181 (1946).

The judge used an incorrect legal standard in invalidating the clause. While recognizing the sensitivity of such clauses, we hold that, since there was no evidence that the insertion of the clause was an abuse of Farr's fiduciary relationship with Sara at the time of the drawing of her will, the clause is effective.

The judgment is vacated, and the matter is remanded to the Probate Court for further proceedings to determine the amounts which, if paid, would have enabled Cappy to retain ownership of the residence. Such amounts shall be paid to Cappy's estate from the trust for his benefit prior to distributing the balance thereof to the trust under Article IIC of Sara's will.

* * *

Dunkley v. Peoples Bank & Trust Co., 728 F.Supp. 547 (W.D.Ark.1989). Settlor provided:

> Trustee shall distribute to my spouse from time to time as much of the net income and principal of the Family Trust, even to the extent of exhausting principal, as the trustee believes desirable from time to time for the health, support in reasonable comfort, education, best interests, and welfare of my spouse, considering all circumstances and factors deemed pertinent by the trustee.

She provided further:

> My primary concern during the life of my spouse is for the health and support in reasonable comfort of my spouse, and the trustee need not consider the interest of any other beneficiary in making distributions to my spouse for those purposes under this paragraph.

After settlor's death, her husband, Rushke, sought large distributions of principal, and sought change of the corporate trustee as each trustee frustrated his wishes. Finally, husband found a trustee, Cooper, willing to authorize distribution of most trust principal for purchase of a $140,000 home in Chicago, of all places, for "medical reasons!" (The husband lived in Arkansas at the time, but had more family in the Chicago area). The trustee knew at the time that husband owned another home with a value of $90,000 to $110,000, and that trust proceeds of $122,000 (from another trust) had recently been distributed to him.

The court held the trustee bank had breached its fiduciary duties to the remaindermen, condemning the practices of the bank's trust department:

> [T]he court finds it incredible that this organization would have allowed decisions such as the one made in this case to be made only by one individual without any control or supervision by any other person or committee in the bank.
>
> The court is convinced that persons who hire banks to act as trustees of estates such as this one do not intend that one individual have the power that Mr. Cooper had. Instead, they believe, and have a right to believe, that the "entire bank" is working for them in providing the business judgment necessary to properly care for their life savings.
>
> Mr. Ruschke, after "running off" at least one other trustee because the trust officer would not agree with his interpretation of the trust, approached Rick Cooper and told him that he needed $140,000 "for medical reasons" so he could buy a house in the

> Chicago area. Cooper told him that was possible, because as he testified in his deposition, he believed at the time that he had no duty to any other beneficiary because of the terms of the trust instrument. After making the determination that the trust instrument authorized such a distribution, it is even more incredible that he required almost no showing of either the need for the distribution or the real purpose for it. All that he required was a letter from a doctor saying that it would be a good idea for Mr. Ruschke to be allowed to move close to his family, and an offer and acceptance showing that Mr. Ruschke intended to buy a house in Wisconsin for $123,000. For Mr. Cooper, it was sufficient for Mr. Ruschke to explain the $17,000 excess by saying that it was needed for house repairs and moving costs. No proof whatsoever of those needs was required.
>
> With that little showing, Cooper then delivered a $140,000 cashier's check to Ruschke and he apparently used it to purchase a home which he has now deeded to three of his sons. Cooper apparently did not consider at all the fact that Mr. Ruschke had substantial funds largely of a liquid nature that could be used for this purpose. Instead, he allowed Mrs. Ruschke's estate, in spite of her attempt to control it for the benefit of her son, to be almost entirely depleted . . .

The court directed the bank to make the trust whole by returning to the trust the amount wrongfully paid to the Mr. Rushke, and indicated that the bank could recover from Mr. Rushke any amounts wrongfully paid to him.

NOTES AND QUESTIONS

1. In both Marsman and Dunkley, the trust instrument provided the trustee with discretion, but also provided guidance to the trustee about the way in which the trustee should exercise that discretion; in Marsman, the trustee was to make payments for "comfortable support and maintenance," while in Dunkley, settlor indicated that her concern was for her spouse's "health, support in reasonable comfort, education, best interests, and welfare."

Suppose, instead, settlor in each case had given the trustee discretion, or "absolute discretion" to invade principal, but had provided no standards against which that discretion was to be measured. Would the court in each case then have upheld the trustee's action?

Restatement (Third) of Trusts § 50 (1)(2003) provides:

> A discretionary power conferred upon the trustee to determine the benefits of a trust beneficiary is subject to judicial control only to prevent misinterpretation or abuse of the discretion by the trustee.

Comment c elaborates:

> Although the discretionary character of a power of distribution does not ordinarily authorize the trustee to act beyond the bounds of

> reasonable judgment, a settlor may manifest an intention to grant the trustee greater than ordinary latitude in exercising discretionary judgment. How does such an intention affect the duty of the trustee and the role of the court?
>
> It is contrary to sound policy, and a contradiction in terms, to permit the settlor to relieve a "trustee" of all accountability. Once it is determined that the authority over trust distributions is held in the role of trustee (contrast non fiduciary powers mentioned in Comment *a*) words such as "absolute" or "unlimited" or "sole and uncontrolled" are not interpreted literally. Even under the broadest grant of fiduciary discretion, a trustee must act honestly and in a state of mind contemplated by the settlor. Thus, a court will not permit the trustee to act in bad faith or for some purpose or motive other than to accomplish the purposes of the discretionary power. Except as the power is for the trustee's personal benefit, the court will also prevent the trustee from *failing* to act, either arbitrarily or from a misunderstanding of the trustee' duty or authority.
>
> Within these limits, it is a matter of interpretation to ascertain the *degree* to which the settlor's use of language of extended (e.g., "absolute") discretion manifests an intention to relieve the trustee of normal judicial supervision and control in the exercise of a discretionary power over trust distributions.

In light of the Restatement formulation, what value is there in conferring absolute discretion on a trustee? Why would a settlor *want* to give absolute discretion to a trustee, rather than requiring the trustee to act reasonably?

2. Note that in the Marsman case, the trust instrument provided that the trustee should invade principal for Cappy's benefit "after having considered the various available sources of support for him." Suppose the trust instrument had not included such language. Would the trustee have been *required* to consider other sources of support? Would the trustee have been *entitled* to consider outside sources?

If the trust had been a pure discretionary trust, without any ascertainable standards, the trustee would have been entitled, but not required, to consider outside income. When the trust instrument provides standards, as the instrument did in Marsman, the issue is more complicated. Professor Abravanel writes:

> When a settlor superimposes discretionary language on a support standard, the trustee is not violating a rule of law if he chooses to consider other sources of the beneficiary's income in determining whether to make a distribution to that beneficiary. If the grant of express trustee discretion in the context of a hybrid trust is to be afforded any scope, the trustee should be at liberty to consider or not to consider outside sources of the beneficiary's income.

Evelyn Ginsberg Abravanel, Discretionary Support Trusts, 68 Iowa L. Rev. 273, 294–95 (1983). See also Edward C. Halbach, Jr., Problems of Discretion in Discretionary Trusts, 61 Colum. L. Rev. 1425 (1961). Professor Abravanel concedes, however, that courts do not always agree. In fact, the

Restatement (Third) of Trusts § 50, cmt. e, creates a presumption that the trustee is to consider other resources available to the beneficiary unless it is clear that the settlor intended otherwise.

As a drafter, how would you proceed if:

(a) settlor wanted trustee to withhold payment if beneficiary had adequate sources of outside income;

(b) settlor wanted trustee to exercise discretion as if beneficiary had no outside income; and

(c) settlor wanted to leave to the trustee all decisions about the effect of outside income?

3. In deciding whether to invade principal, should the trustee consider the needs of the remaindermen? That is, should the trustee's actions have been sustained if the remainderman in Marsman had been quite poor, and the remaindermen in Dunkley quite wealthy?

How would you draft a discretionary trust instrument if you wanted the trustee to pay attention to the remainderman's concerns? If you didn't want the trustee to do so?

4. ***Spray Trusts.*** In Marsman and Dunkley, the trustee had discretion to invade the principal of the trust for the benefit of the life beneficiary. In other trusts, the trustee has discretion to pay the income to one or more named beneficiaries. Thus, a settlor could create a trust giving the trustee discretion to pay income to any of settlor's children, as their needs might appear. Because trustee has discretion to "spray" the income among the various beneficiaries, this form of discretionary trust is sometimes called a "spray" trust or a "sprinkle" trust.

5. ***Professional Responsibility Issues.*** In the Marsman case, lawyer Farr's conduct raises a variety of questions about ethical practice. The ABA's Model Rules of Professional Conduct include the following Conflict of Interest Provision:

RULE 1.7 CONFLICT OF INTEREST: CURRENT CLIENTS

(a) Except as provided in paragraph (b), a lawyer shall not represent a client if the representation involves a concurrent conflict of interest. A concurrent conflict of interest exists if:

(1) the representation of one client will be directly adverse to another client; or

(2) there is a significant risk that the representation of one or more clients will be materially limited by the lawyer's responsibilities to another client, a former client or a third person or by a personal interest of the lawyer.

(b) Notwithstanding the existence of a concurrent conflict of interest under paragraph (a), a lawyer may represent a client if:

(1) the lawyer reasonably believes that the lawyer will be able to provide competent and diligent representation to each affected client;

(2) the representation is not prohibited by law;

(3) the representation does not involve the assertion of a claim by one client against another client represented by the lawyer in the same litigation or other proceeding before a tribunal; and

(4) each affected client gives informed consent, confirmed in writing.

In light of that provision, consider the following:

a. When drafting a will or trust instrument for a client, should a lawyer offer to serve as a trustee? What if the client initiates the discussion by asking the lawyer if she would serve? The attorney has a financial incentive to serve as trustee, since trustees are typically paid commissions (based on the size of the estate) for their service. Can a lawyer give disinterested advice about the wisdom of appointing herself as trustee?

b. If it is appropriate for a lawyer to draft a trust instrument under the terms of which the lawyer agrees to serve as trustee, may the lawyer include a clause exculpating herself from liability for breach of fiduciary duty? What does the court in Marsman say? Is the court's discussion satisfactory?

c. When Cappy and Sally entered Farr's office to discuss executing a deed to the house, were either or both of them Farr's clients? What should Farr have done when they told him what they wanted and asked him to draw up a deed? Should Farr have recommended a lawyer to Cappy?

Suppose Sally had been a steady client of Farr's, providing Farr with business which generated $10,000 a year in fees. Would it be unreasonable to expect Farr to inform Cappy that conveyance of the house might be unnecessary to meet Cappy's financial needs? Does that mean Farr should not represent Cappy, even if Cappy does consent?

See generally Paula A. Monopoli, Drafting Attorneys as Fiduciaries: Fashioning an Optimal Ethical Rule for Conflicts of Interest, 66 U. Pitt. L. Rev. 411 (2005); Jeffrey N. Pennell, Ethics in Estate Planning and Fiduciary Administration: The Inadequacy of the Model Rules and the Model Code, 45 Rec. Ass'n. B. City N.Y. 715 (1990).

6. ***Exculpating Trustees for Breach of Duty.*** Suppose that an attorney other than Farr had drafted Sally's trust document, but that Farr was named trustee. Should that attorney have included the clause exculpating Farr from liability for negligent acts? What are the pros and cons of such a clause? Would you recommend one for your client? See Melanie B. Leslie, Fiduciary Duties and the Limits of Default Rules, 94 Geo. L.J. 67 (2005) (arguing that most settlors are unaware of the meaning and potential impact of exculpatory clauses, and might not agree to them if they had full information). But see, John H. Langbein, Mandatory Rules in the Law Of Trusts, 98 Nw. L. Rev. 1105 (2004) (stating that fiduciary duties are, and should be, default rules that are freely modifiable by the parties).

C. AVOIDING PROBATE

Americans have developed—not without reason—a near obsession with avoiding probate. Although the average person's fears about the probate process may be exaggerated, probate often entails costs and delays. The principal costs are (1) commissions paid to the executor or administrator selected to administer the estate; and (2) legal fees paid to the lawyer who steers the estate through the probate process. These costs vary significantly from state to state.

There are a number of ways to hold property so that it passes outside of probate on an individual's death. Some mechanisms, such as Totten trusts, joint accounts, joint tenancies, and accounts with payable on death provisions, are not technically trusts, although they may resemble trusts in various ways. Because those vehicles enable a property owner to transfer assets at death without going through probate, the following paragraphs explore those probate avoidance vehicles. We will then explore the revocable living trust.

1. AVOIDING PROBATE WITHOUT THE USE OF TRUSTS

"Totten trusts"

A Totten trust is the somewhat misleading name given to bank accounts held "in trust" for designated beneficiaries. The name derives from In re Totten, 179 N.Y. 112, 71 N.E. 748 (1904), in which the New York Court of Appeals first sustained a bank account trust against the claim that it constituted an invalid testamentary transfer. Totten trust accounts are not really trusts—the depositor retains full control over the account during her life. She can withdraw funds or close the account at will, and she owes no duty to the designated beneficiaries. Totten trusts, which have been around for more than one hundred years, arose as a cheap and easy way to avoid probate. To create a Totten trust, the depositor need only fill out the appropriate bank form.

From time to time, Totten trusts have been challenged by those entitled to a testator's probate estate by will or intestacy, or by disinherited spouses seeking to exercise a right of election. As in the Totten case, claimants usually argue that because the trust account is tantamount to absolute ownership in the funds, the beneficiary designation is an invalid testamentary disposition because it was not made in compliance with the will execution statute, and therefore the funds in the account should be considered part of testator's probate estate. Courts in most states now generally reject that argument so long as the depositor's intent to create a trust account is clear. See, e.g., Green v. Green, 559 A.2d 1047 (R.I. 1989); but see Hoffman's Estate, 175 Ohio St. 363, 195 N.E.2d 106 (1963).

Professor Jeffrey Roth has suggested that the settlor of a Totten trust be enabled to provide, by appropriate instruments, for conversion of a Totten trust into a real trust, with a successor trustee, at the settlor's death. Jeffrey Roth, Successor Trustees of Tentative Trusts: Trust Law Phantoms, 38 St. Louis U. L. J. 407 (1993).

P.O.D. Bank Accounts and Contracts with P.O.D. Provisions

Suppose Jane Smith opens an account in her own name, but provides that the funds will be "payable on death to John Smith." P.O.D. accounts are functionally identical to Totten trust accounts. John has no right to the funds during Jane's lifetime, but if Jane dies without closing the account or revoking the designation, John will receive the account funds at Jane's death.

As with Totten trusts, courts have occasionally held that John is not entitled to the funds because the P.O.D. provision constitutes a testamentary transfer without testamentary formalities. The trend is toward enforcement, and the Uniform Probate Code moves substantially in that direction. The 1989 revision of article VI of the Uniform Probate Code "consolidates treatment of POD accounts and trust accounts so that the same rules apply to both, since both types of account operate identically and serve the same function of passing property to a beneficiary at the death of the account owner." Uniform Probate Code, Article VI, Prefatory Note (1989 Revision). Section 6–101 validates P.O.D. accounts. Section 6–204 provides a form contract of deposit which would enable depositors to choose between a "single-party account" and a "multiple-party account." On a single-party account, the depositor would then choose whether to include a P.O.D. designation, or, alternatively to have assets pass to the depositor's estate at death. On a multiple-party account, the depositors could choose whether to create a right of survivorship, and whether to include a P.O.D. designation at the death of the surviving depositor. The UPC includes no separate form for Totten trusts, because a single-party account with a P.O.D. designation is the functional equivalent of a Totten trust.

In addition to P.O.D. bank accounts, a variety of other contractual arrangements allow one party to the contract to designate a beneficiary to receive contract proceeds in the event of the party's death. Examples include pension plans, individual retirement plans, insurance policies or employee benefit plans. Here again, the trend is toward enforcing these contractual provisions, notwithstanding the lack of compliance with testamentary formalities. Uniform Probate Code section 6–101 provides explicitly that a wide variety of nonprobate transfers on death are nontestamentary.

Today, even people of moderate means often hold some of their assets in mutual funds or brokerage accounts. The Uniform Probate Code's treatment of securities and security accounts parallels the Code's treatment of bank accounts. UPC Section 6–302 authorizes registration of securities "in beneficiary form" whenever a security is owned by one individual or by two or more individuals with right of survivorship. "Beneficiary form" is defined as a registration which indicates "the intention of the owner regarding the person who will become the owner of the security upon the death of the owner." UPC section 6–301.

How does one accomplish registration in beneficiary form, and what consequences does such registration generate? Consider the following Uniform Probate Code sections:

SECTION 6–305. FORM OF REGISTRATION IN BENEFICIARY FORM.

Registration in beneficiary form may be shown by the words "transfer on death" or the abbreviation "TOD," or by the words "pay on death" or the abbreviation "POD," after the name of the registered owner and before the name of a beneficiary.

SECTION 6–306. EFFECT OF REGISTRATION IN BENEFICIARY FORM.

The designation of a TOD beneficiary on a registration in beneficiary form has no effect on ownership until the owner's death. A registration of a security in beneficiary form may be canceled or changed at any time by the sole owner or all then surviving owners without the consent of the beneficiary.

Section 6–307 goes on to provide that at the death of the owner, securities in beneficiary form pass to the beneficiary or beneficiaries who survive the owner.

Joint Accounts

Jane Smith and her husband John have a joint bank account. During the lifetime of Jane and John, either has power to withdraw all of the funds, but, in most states, each generally has a claim against the other for withdrawals in excess of the amount deposited by the withdrawing account holder! That is, Jane and John do not jointly "own" the money in the account; John has a claim only to his contribution to the present balance. But see, In re Kleinberg, 38 N.Y.2d 836, 382 N.Y.S.2d 49, 345 N.E.2d 592 (1976) (stating that, under New York law, a deposit to a joint account by one co-tenant is an irrevocable gift to the other tenant of one-half the deposit amount).

What happens to the funds on deposit if Jane dies? Typically, the documents creating a joint account include a survivorship feature, and statutes in many states expressly authorize banks to pay over all of the funds in such an account to either holder of the account. Thus, if one of the account holders were to die, the other could withdraw the funds without worrying about probate. Occasionally, however, a court will hold that such a statute protects the bank against wrongful payment, but does not entitle the surviving account holder to funds contributed by the decedent. Instead, such a court might hold that the joint account was established only for the convenience of the decedent, and that decedent's estate has a claim against the surviving account holder. See Godwin v. Godwin, 141 Miss. 633, 107 So. 13 (1926) (later overruled in In re Lewis' Estate, 194 Miss. 480, 13 So.2d 20 (1943)); cf. Franklin v. Anna Nat'l Bank, 140 Ill.App.3d 533, 94 Ill.Dec. 870, 488 N.E.2d 1117 (1986) (Chapter 1, supra).

Joint Tenancies with Right of Survivorship

Suppose Jane and John own their home as joint tenants with right of survivorship. During their joint lives, both Jane and John have a right to occupy the entire home. Either of them may sever the right of survivorship by transferring his or her fractional share to a third party (turning the owners into tenants in common). What happens if Jane dies? If she has not severed the right of survivorship during her life, her interest in the home does not pass through probate, but instead passes automatically to John.

This is true even if Jane's will purports to bequeath her interest in the home to someone other than John.

Some states allow married couples to hold real property as tenants by the entireties. This estate is similar to a joint tenancy, except that one spouse may not unilaterally sever the right of survivorship.

PROBLEM

Louise Larson is an unmarried woman with one adult son, Martin. Louise has a checking account with an average monthly balance of $15,000, and securities currently worth $200,000. She also owns her home, free and clear of any mortgage. Currently, Louise has in place a simple will that devises all of her real and personal property to Martin.

1. If Louise were to die tomorrow, which of her assets would pass through probate?

2. How could she restructure her holdings to avoid probate? Assume that avoiding probate is her only estate planning goal.

2. AVOIDING PROBATE THROUGH THE USE OF REVOCABLE *INTER VIVOS* TRUSTS

If a person divests himself of all assets during his lifetime, there is no estate to probate at death. Most people, however, are justifiably leery of giving away their assets to friends or family members who might be none too eager to care for the donor in her time of need. Enter the revocable *inter vivos* trust (often referred to as a "living trust"), a remarkably flexible mechanism that allows the settlor to retain almost total control over her property while avoiding probate. How is this accomplished? Typically, the settlor will make herself the trustee and the life beneficiary, give herself broad management powers, including the power to revoke the trust and invade the principal, and will designate—subject to revocation, of course—those people entitled to take the remaining property at settlor's death. During settlor's life, the remainder beneficiaries have no incentive, or standing, to challenge the settlor/trustee's actions. See In Linthicum v. Rudi, 122 Nev. 1452, 148 P.3d 746 (2006). At the settlor's death, the successor trustee simply distributes the trust principal to the remainder beneficiaries. There is no need to involve a court at all.

Of course, it is unlikely that the settlor will transfer every last asset to the revocable trust; the settlor may die owning items of personal property and miscellaneous sums of money outright. For that reason, most estate plans that employ revocable living trusts also include a "pour over" will. The will serves a "mopping up" function—it directs the probate court to distribute testator's probate assets to the successor trustee of the living trust, to be managed and distributed in accordance with the trust's terms. Although the pour over will must be probated, if the ownership of settlor's assets is properly structured only a small fraction of testator's assets will pass through probate.

Although an irrevocable trust also accomplishes the goal of avoiding probate, it is a poor mechanism for that purpose because it forever prevents the settlor from changing her mind about the trust's terms. For that reason, a settlor will ordinarily create an irrevocable trust when her goal is to make a gift, and a revocable trust when her goal is to avoid probate.

The Evolution of the Revocable Living Trust: From Invalid to Ubiquitous

Because a revocable trust retains for the settlor complete control and enjoyment of the trust assets, and allows the settlor to revoke the trust entirely at her discretion, it is virtually indistinguishable from a will from a functional perspective. Yet most settlors do not execute living trust documents in compliance with will formalities (because most states do not require those formalities for trust creation). For that reason, the first courts to consider challenges to revocable trusts often invalidated those trusts as "invalid testamentary dispositions," on the theory that the settlor/trustee owed fiduciary duties to no one. Over time, however, courts realized that revocable *inter vivos* trusts served an important purpose, and they increasingly rejected challenges to their validity. As one court put it,

> A document which can stand as a trust is not rendered invalid because it avoids the need for a will. Good reasons often exist for a presently operative trust in preference to a will, which cannot be operative until death and which can accomplish nothing during lifetime. "If an owner of property can find a means of disposing of it *inter vivos* that will render a will unnecessary for the accomplishment of his practical purposes, he has a right to employ it. The fact that the motive of a transfer is to obtain the practical advantages of a will without making one is immaterial." National Shawmut Bank of Boston v. Joy, 315 Mass. 457, 471, 53 N.E.2d 113, 122 (1944). A settlor's business or property may be of such character that it cannot endure even a short period of suspension of operations between death and probate. See Notes, Use of *Inter Vivos* Trusts in Agricultural Estate Planning, 55 Iowa L. Rev. 1328 (1970). A settlor may wish to avoid the expense of administration, attorney fees or executor's fees. A settlor may ... desire some fiduciary to take over the management of the trust corpus in the likely event of incompetency by reason of sickness or age. The reasons one might have for making a transition during lifetime are varied. Living trusts often afford better management, greater protection, more privacy and considerable economy.

Westerfeld v. Huckaby, 474 S.W.2d 189 (Tex. 1971). Revocable living trusts are now valid in all states.

Sample Revocable Trust

Following is an excerpt from a revocable trust document. The excerpt is not designed to give the reader a comprehensive form for a revocable living trust, but rather to highlight key provisions:

Declaration of Trust

2007 Imelda Saint James Revocable Living Trust

Article One: Establishment of Trust

Imelda Saint James (hereinafter called the "Settlor" or the "Trustee," depending on the context) hereby declares that she has set aside and holds in trust the property in Schedule A attached hereto. Property now or hereafter subject to this trust shall be referred to as the "Trust Property" and shall be held, administered and distributed in accordance with the terms of this instrument. The trust created shall be known as the "2007 Imelda Saint James Revocable Living Trust." The Settlor is the trust's primary beneficiary.

Article Two: Operation of the Trust During Settlor's Lifetime

A. Distribution of Income and Principal.

1. During the lifetime of the Settlor, the entire net income from the trust estate shall be added to and become principal, forming a common fund. The Trustee shall distribute from such common fund to or for the benefit of the Settlor, at her request made from time to time, such sums, at such times, and for such periods as the Settlor shall direct.

2. If the Settlor, in the opinion of the Trustee, is for any reason unable to request payments, then the Trustee may pay to or apply for the benefit of the Settlor so much of the trust estate as the Trustee may deem proper or necessary to provide the Settlor with health, support, comfort, enjoyment and happiness.

B. Liberal Invasion of Principal for Settlor. The Trustee shall exercise in a liberal manner the power to invade principal for the Settlor's benefit, and the rights of the remaindermen of the trusts shall be considered of secondary importance.

C. Incapacity of the Settlor. If at any time, either in the Trustee's discretion or as certified in writing by the licensed physician having responsibility for Settlor's care and treatment, the Settlor has become physically or mentally incapacitated, whether or not a court of competent jurisdiction has declared her incompetent, mentally ill or in need of a conservator, the Trustee shall pay for the account of or apply for the benefit of the Settlor the amounts of income and principal necessary in the Trustee's discretion for the proper health, support, comfort, enjoyment, welfare and happiness of the Settlor until the incapacitated Settlor, either in the Trustee's discretion or as certified by a licensed physician, is again able to manage her own affairs, or until the Settlor's death.

D. Distribution to Parties Other Than Settlor. The Settlor may at any time direct the Trustee in writing to pay single sums or periodic payments out of the trust estate to any other person or organization.

Article Three: Distribution on Settlor's Death

Upon the death of the settlor, after payment or provision for payment of amounts described in Article VIII, the Trustee shall divide the trust estate into as many equal shares as there are children of the Settlor then living and deceased children of the Settlor leaving issue then living. Each share shall be distributed as follows:

A. Each share allocated to a living child of the Settlor shall be distributed to such child outright and free of trust.

B. Each share allocated to a deceased child of the Settlor shall be distributed to that deceased child's issue, *per stirpes*.

Article Four: Administrative Provisions of Trust

A. Successor Trustee. If the Settlor should die, resign, become mentally incapacitated (as defined by Article Two C, herein), or otherwise become unwilling or unable to act as Trustee, then Settlor's son, Melvin James, shall act as successor Trustee. If Melvin James should for any reason fail to qualify or cease to act as Trustee, then Settlor's daughter, Sally James, shall act as successor trustee. Each person designated or acting as Trustee hereunder shall have the power to designate one or more successor trustees to act when he or she becomes unable or unwilling to act as Trustee. If both Melvin James and Sally James shall fail to qualify or cease to act as Trustee, then the person(s) so designated shall act as successor Trustee, with the preference given first to successors designated by Melvin James, then those designated by Sally James, and finally, then those designated by any such designee while acting as Trustee.

B. Compensation and Bond of Trustee. Any Trustee named herein or designated hereunder shall be entitled to reasonable compensation from the trust estate for services rendered as Trustee. No Trustee or successor Trustee shall be required to give bond, unless otherwise provided for in such designation.

C. Powers of the Trustee [omitted]

[Eds. note: This section gives the Trustee broad powers to hold and manage the Trust Property, including but not limited to the power to sale, lease, borrow, insure, litigate and invest trust assets].

Article Five: Rights Reserved by Settlor

A. Revocation During Settlor's Lifetime. The Settlor may at any time revoke this instrument in whole or in part by an instrument in writing signed by the Settlor and delivered to the Trustee. If the Settlor revokes this instrument, the Trustee shall deliver to the Settlor, or her designee, all of the designated portion of the Trust Property. If the Settlor revokes this trust instrument entirely or with respect to a major portion of the Trust Property, the Trustee shall be entitled to retain sufficient assets reasonably necessary to secure payment of liabilities lawfully incurred by the Trustee in the administration of the trust, including Trustee's fees that have been earned, unless the Settlor shall indemnify the Trustee against loss or expense. Upon Settlor's death, this trust shall immediately become irrevocable.

B. Amendment During Settlor's Lifetime. The Settlor may at any time during her life amend any of the terms of this instrument by an instrument in writing, signed by her and delivered to the Trustee. No amendment shall substantially increase the duties or liabilities of the Trustee without the Trustee's consent, nor shall the Trustee be obligated to act under such amendment unless the Trustee accepts it.

C. Powers Personal to the Settlor. Settlor's powers to revoke or amend this instrument are personal to her and shall not be exercisable on her behalf by any guardian, conservator, or other person, except that revocation or amendment may be authorized, after notice to the Trustee, by the court that appointed the guardian or conservator.

D. Investment Powers. The Settlor may, at any time, direct the Trustee in writing to invest the trust estate in specific securities, properties or investments; to retain as part of the Trust Property any securities, properties or investments at any time held hereunder, for such length of time as such directions may provide; or to sell, encumber, lease, manage, control, or dispose of any Trust Property. The Trustee shall not be liable for any loss sustained or incurred by reason of compliance with any such written directions of the Settlor.

Executed at ______, this ___ day of ______, ______.

Trustee: Settlor:

______________________________ ______________________________

State of __________)
) ss.
County of __________)

On this the ___ day of __________________, ___, before me __________________, the undersigned Notary Public personally appeared Imelda Saint James, personally known to me (or proved to me on the basis of satisfactory evidence) to be the person whose name is subscribed to the within instrument and acknowledged that she executed it.

Witness my hand and official seal.

____
Notary's Signature

QUESTIONS

1. What rights does the Settlor have to income generated by the investment of trust assets? To trust principal?

2. Suppose paragraph 5A were omitted. What result?

3. What steps must Settlor take to revoke or modify the trust instrument during her life? Could you improve upon the drafting of the revocation and modification provisions?

4. Suppose Settlor is diagnosed with Alzheimer's disease. If Settlor loses the ability to manage her affairs, what will happen to the trust? Suppose Settlor resists the idea that she has lost capacity, and insists on (badly) managing the trust assets. Can those closest to her protect her from herself?

5. If control of the trust is transferred to a successor trustee, how much of the trust income or principal may that trustee distribute to Settlor?

6. In addition to listing trust property on schedule A, should the drafting attorney take any additional steps to identify the property held in this trust?

7. Suppose Settlor resigns the trusteeship, and her son Melvin becomes trustee. Sally believes that Melvin is pursuing a reckless and dangerous investment strategy, which may include self-dealing. Does Sally, as a remainder beneficiary, have standing to demand an accounting and, if the facts warrant it, standing to sue Melvin for breach of fiduciary duty? Would it matter if Settlor's reason for resigning as trustee was that she had become incompetent? See UTC § 603(a) (directing that beneficiaries of revocable living trusts have no rights to enforce the trust during the settlor's lifetime). See also, Alan Newman, Revocable Trusts and the Law of Wills: An Imperfect Fit, 43 Real Prop. Tr. & Est. L.J. 523 (2008) (explaining that the original draft of the UTC provided that remainder beneficiaries could enforce the trust if the settlor lacked capacity, but that provision was removed after objections from estate planning attorneys). How might you draft the trust to address this issue?

8. Because revocable living trusts are will substitutes, courts have begun to apply will construction doctrines, such as abatement, apportionment, and anti-lapse statutes, to the interpretation of revocable trusts. See Alan Newman, Revocable Trusts and the Law of Wills: An Imperfect Fit, 43 Real Prop. Tr. & Est. L.J. 523 (2008) (exploring the trend toward treating revocable trusts as wills); Ira Mark Bloom, Unifying the Rules For Wills and Revocable Trusts in the Federal Estate Tax Apportionment Arena: Suggestions For Reform, 43 Real Prop. Tr. & Est. L.J. 447 (2008).

9. No–contest clauses. Increasingly, settlors are inserting no-contest clauses in revocable trust instruments. In the absence of careful drafting, these clauses can cause confusion about whether raising issues in probate court can trigger the trust's no-contest provision. Consider the following recent example:

Settlor executed a pour-over will and a revocable trust leaving his estate to his children in equal shares. The trust contained a no-contest clause, which provided that "any person that objects to or contests any provision of this Trust, in whole or in part, shall forfeit his or her entire distribution otherwise payable under this Trust and receive only $1.00 under this Trust and will receive no other distribution from my Trust nor from my estate." Settlor's will did not contain a no-contest clause. At Settlor's death, one of Settlor's sons—the successor trustee of the revocable trust—allegedly informed his siblings that "there is no will." Settlor's daughter then applied to be the personal administrator of Settlor's probate estate, claiming that he died intestate. Settlor's other children then produced Settlor's will for probate, and the trustee refused to give the daughter her share of the trust assets, claiming that her act of initiating an intestacy proceeding and applying to be personal administrator violated the trust's no-contest clause. Should the trustee prevail? See Keener v. Keener, 278 Va. 435, 682 S.E.2d 545 (2009) (reversing the lower court to hold that daughter's acts did not trigger the no contest clause).

Pour Over Wills

A settlor who wishes to devise her assets in further trust may use an *inter vivos* trust and a pour over will to consolidate the management and distribution of her probate and non-probate assets after her death. For example, settlor can execute an *inter vivos* trust document and then a "pour over" will provision that distributes her residuary estate to the trustee of the *inter vivos* trust. She may also designate the successor trustee of her living trust as the beneficiary of her retirement account and other non-probate assets. Of course, settlor could consolidate management of her assets without an *inter vivos* trust by creating a testamentary trust and naming the testamentary trustee as the beneficiary of her non-probate assets. However, this option is more costly than using an *inter vivos* trust. First, surrogate or probate courts usually have continuing jurisdiction over testamentary trusts, and the testamentary trustee may have to file periodic accountings with the court, adding a level of administrative complexity. Second, transferring non-probate assets into a testamentary trust renders those assets probate assets, which delays their distribution and adds to the cost of probate. Most settlors, then, use *inter vivos* trusts as the receptacle for probate and non probate assets.

If the settlor's primary concern is to consolidate the management of her assets after her death (as opposed to avoiding probate), she may decide not to fund her revocable trust during her life. Because an unfunded revocable trust's sole function is to receive the settlor's assets upon the settlor's death, it is sometimes referred to as a "standby trust."

Historically, pour over will provisions were vulnerable to attack by disgruntled heirs. Heirs argued that the pour over provisions in the wills were invalid because they directed that probate assets be distributed in accordance with an invalid testamentary document (the revocable trust). In the case of an unfunded standby trust, heirs also argued that the receptacle trust was invalid because it lacked *property*, one of the trust requisites. In response, trustees resorted to two wills doctrines: incorporation by reference and facts of independent significance. First, the trustee might argue that the will validly incorporated the *inter vivos* trust by reference. This argument had a drawback, however. Because incorporation by reference doctrine requires the incorporated document to be in existence at the will's execution, revocable trusts that had been amended or modified could not be incorporated by reference. This undermined one of the primary attractions of revocable trusts; flexibility in dealing with assets during settlor's life. Successful application of incorporation by reference also had the disadvantage of turning the trust into a testamentary trust, which generally meant that the probate court retained jurisdiction over the trust.

The second argument available to trustees was the doctrine of facts of independent significance. A trustee might argue that the living trust had an independent lifetime purpose (in addition to its testamentary function), and thus the pour over will provision was valid. This argument often succeeded, but only if the settlor had transferred property to the trust during her life. If, however, the settlor's will poured over into an *unfunded* standby trust, the trust's sole function was to distribute the settlor's assets upon the settlor's death, and the doctrine of facts of independent significance could not be used to validate the pour over provision. Consider the arguments made in the following case:

Clymer v. Mayo

Supreme Judicial Court of Massachusetts, Essex, 1985.
393 Mass. 754, 473 N.E.2d 1084.

■ HENNESSEY, CHIEF JUSTICE.

* * * [Professor Clara A. Mayo (the decedent), of Boston University, was married to James P. Mayo, Jr. from 1958 to 1978. The Mayos had no children. Professor Mayo was an only child and her heirs at law are her parents, Mr. and Mrs. Weiss.

On 2 February 1973, the Mayos executed wills and trust indentures wherein each spouse was made the other's principal beneficiary. In Professor Mayo's will, Mr. Mayo was to receive her personal property. The residue of her estate was to pour over into her revocable and amendable *inter vivos* trust. The trust was to continue after Professor Mayo's death, with the income (and limited amounts of principal) payable to Mr. Mayo. Upon Mr. Mayo's death, a portion of the trust assets would continue to be held in trust for the benefit of Professor Mayo's nieces and nephews until the last of them reached age 30, at which time the principal would be distributed to various educational institutions. Professor Mayo and John P. Hill were trustees. On the date the trust was established, Professor Mayo changed the beneficiary of her Boston University Group life insurance from Mr. Mayo to the trustees of her trust. A month later she changed her retirement annuity contracts to designate the trustees as beneficiaries. At the time of its creation, the trust was not funded. Its future assets were to consist of the proceeds of the policies and the property to be poured over from the will.

In 1975, the Mayos separated. In June, 1977, Professor Mayo changed the beneficiary of her Boston University Life Insurance policy from the trustees to Ms. LaFrance, a friend. The trustees as beneficiaries under her

retirement contracts were not changed. On 3 January 1978, the Mayos were divorced. Under the property settlement, Mr. Mayo waived any right, title or interest in Professor Mayo's "securities, savings accounts, savings certificates and retirement fund" and her "furniture, furnishings and art." Mr. Mayo remarried and executed a new will in favor of his new wife. Professor Mayo died on 21 November 1981 with her will in force and without having revoked or amended her trust. The life insurance was paid to Ms. LaFrance. Three cases are consolidated for the appeal. In the portion of the opinion presented here, the court deals with the contention of the Weisses, Professor Mayo's parents, that there was no valid pour-over will because there was no valid trust (the trial court had held the trust valid).]
* * *

Validity of "Pour-over" Trust.

The Weisses claim that the judge erred in ruling that the decedent's trust was validly created despite the fact that it was not funded until her death. They rely on the common law rule that a trust can be created only when a trust res exists. New England Trust Co. v. Sanger, 337 Mass. 342, 348, 149 N.E.2d 598 (1958). Arguing that the trust never came into existence, the Weisses claim they are entitled to the decedent's entire estate as her sole heirs at law.

In upholding the validity of the decedent's pour-over trust, the judge cited the relevant provisions of G.L. c. 203, § 3B, inserted by St.1963, c. 418, § 1, the Commonwealth's version of the Uniform Testamentary Additions to Trusts Act. "A devise or bequest, the validity of which is determinable by the laws of the commonwealth, may be made to the trustee or trustees of a trust established or to be established by the testator * * * including a funded or unfunded life insurance trust, although the trustor has reserved any or all rights of ownership of the insurance contracts, if the trust is identified in the will and the terms of the trust are set forth in a written instrument executed before or concurrently with the execution of the testator's will * * * *regardless of the existence, size or character of the corpus of the trust*" (emphasis added). The decedent's trust instrument, which was executed in Massachusetts and states that it is to be governed by the laws of the Commonwealth, satisfies these statutory conditions. The trust is identified in the residuary clause of her will and the terms of the trust are set out in a written instrument executed contemporaneously with the will. However, the Weisses claim that G.L. c. 203, § 3B, was not intended to change the common law with respect to the necessity for a trust corpus despite the clear language validating pour-over trusts, "regardless of the existence, size or character of the corpus." The Weisses make no showing of legislative intent that would contradict the plain meaning of these words. It is well established that "the statutory language is the principal source of insight into legislative purpose." Bronstein v. Prudential Ins. Co. of America, 390 Mass. 701, 704, 459 N.E.2d 772 (1984). Moreover, the development of the common law of this Commonwealth with regard to pour-over trusts demonstrates that G.L. c. 203, § 3B, takes on practical meaning only if the Legislature meant exactly what the statute says concerning the need for a trust corpus.

This court was one of the first courts to validate pour-over devises to a living trust. In Second Bank–State St. Trust Co. v. Pinion, 341 Mass. 366, 371, 170 N.E.2d 350 (1960), decided prior to the adoption of G.L. c. 203, § 3B, we upheld a testamentary gift to a revocable and amendable *inter vivos* trust established by the testator before the execution of his will and which he amended after the will's execution. Recognizing the importance of the pour-over devise in modern estate planning, we explained that such transfers do not violate the Statute of Wills despite the testator's ability to amend the trust and thereby change the disposition of property at his death without complying with the statute's formalities. "We agree with modern legal thought that a subsequent amendment is effective because of the applicability of the established equitable doctrine that subsequent acts of independent significance do not require attestation under the statute of wills." Id. at 369, 170 N.E.2d 350.

At that time we noted that "[t]he long established recognition in Massachusetts of the doctrine of independent significance makes unnecessary statutory affirmance of its application to pour-over trusts." Id. at 371, 170 N.E.2d 350. It is evident from *Pinion* that there was no need for the Legislature to enact G.L. c. 203, § 3B, simply to validate pour-over devises from wills to funded revocable trusts.

However, in *Pinion,* we were not presented with an unfunded pour-over trust. Nor, prior to G.L. c. 203, § 3B, did other authority exist in this Commonwealth for recognizing testamentary transfers to unfunded trusts. The doctrine of independent significance, upon which we relied in *Pinion,* assumes that "property was included in the purported *inter vivos* trust, prior to the testator's death." Restatement (Second) of Trusts § 54, comment f (1959). That is why commentators have recognized that G.L. c. 203, § 3B, "[m]akes some * * * modification of the *Pinion* doctrine. The act does not require that the trust res be more than nominal or even existent." E. Slizewski, Legislation: Uniform Testamentary Additions to Trusts Act, 10 Ann.Surv. of Mass.Law § 2.7, 39 (1963). See Osgood, Pour Over Will: Appraisal of Uniform Testamentary Additions to Trusts Act, 104 Trusts 768, 769 (1965) ("The Act * * * eliminates the necessity that there be a trust corpus").

By denying that the statute effected such a change in the existing law, the Weisses render its enactment meaningless. "An intention to enact a barren and ineffective provision is not lightly to be imputed to the Legislature." Insurance Rating Bd. v. Commissioner of Ins., 356 Mass. 184, 189, 248 N.E.2d 500 (1969). By analogy, in Trosch v. Maryland Nat'l Bank, 32 Md.App. 249, 252, 359 A.2d 564 (1976), the court construed Maryland's Testamentary Additions to Trusts Act as "conditionally abrogating the common law rule * * * that a trust must have a corpus to be in existence." Despite minor differences in the relevant language of Maryland's Estates and Trusts Act, § 4–411,[2] and our G.L. c. 203, § 3B, we agree with the court's conclusion that "the statute is not conditioned upon the existence of a trust but upon the existence of a trust *instrument*" (emphasis in original). Id. at 253, 359 N.E.2d 564. The Weisses urge us to follow Hageman v. Cleveland Trust Co., 41 Ohio App.2d 160, 324 N.E.2d 594 (1974), rev'd on other grounds, 45 Ohio St.2d 178, 182, 343 N.E.2d 121 (1976), where the court held that an *inter vivos* trust had to be funded during the settlor's life to receive pour-over assets from a will. However, in reaching this conclusion the court relied on a statute differing from G.L. c. 203, § 3B, in its omission of the critical phrase: "regardless of the existence, size or character of the corpus of the trust." See Ohio Rev.Code Ann. § 2107.63 (Baldwin 1978).

For the foregoing reasons we conclude, in accordance with G.L. c. 203, § 3B, that the decedent established a valid *inter vivos* trust in 1973 and that its trustee may properly receive the residue of her estate. We affirm the judge's ruling on this issue.

[The court went on to hold that the provisions of the trust in favor of Mr. Mayo were revoked by operation of law—eds.]

* * *

QUESTIONS

1. Why did Clara Mayo's estate plan include a revocable trust when she might have opted for a simple will?

2. Would Clara Mayo's pour-over will provision have been effective if the Massachusetts legislature had not enacted the Uniform Testamentary Additions to Trusts Act? The Pinion case, cited by the court, was decided prior to the statute's enactment. Could the Clymer court have validated Mayo's pour-over will simply by following Pinion? If not, could the trustee have resorted to incorporation by reference doctrine to validate the revocable trust?

NOTES

1. Clara Mayo led an impressive life. As a child, she and her parents fled Austria to escape the Nazis, and they eventually settled in New York. Clara attended Cornell University, where she majored in philosophy and studied psychology under Urie Bronfenbrenner. After working as a research social psychologist, she eventually became a professor of psychology at Boston University. Prof. Mayo devoted much of her life to studying problems of

---

2. Maryland Estates and Trusts Code Ann. § 4–411 (1974), reads: "A legacy may be made in form or in substance to the trustee in accordance with the terms of a written *inter vivos* trust, including an unfunded life insurance trust although the settlor has reserved all rights of ownership in the insurance contracts, if the trust instrument has been executed and is in existence prior to or contemporaneously with the execution of the will and is identified in the will, without regard to the size or character of the corpus of the trust or whether the settlor is the testator or a third person."

racism and sexism. She was one of the first to study school busing as a way to end segregation in schools. She eventually became an expert in the treatment of African Americans in U.S. courts, and was the director of the graduate program in African American Studies at Boston University.

2. Since *Clymer v. Mayo,* the Uniform Testamentary Additions to Trusts Act has been amended, and the current version is incorporated into the Uniform Probate Code. The majority of states have enacted either a version of the Uniform Act, or an equivalent statute validating will provisions which "pour" assets into *inter vivos* trusts. Consider the Uniform Probate Code's current formulation:

SECTION 2–511. TESTAMENTARY ADDITIONS TO TRUSTS.

> (a) A will may validly devise property to the trustee of a trust established or to be established (i) during the testator's lifetime by the testator, by the testator and some other person, or by some other person, including a funded or unfunded life insurance trust, although the settlor has reserved any or all rights of ownership of the insurance contracts, or (ii) at the testator's death by the testator's devise to the trustee, if the trust is identified in the testator's will and its terms are set forth in a written instrument, other than a will, executed before, concurrently with, or after the execution of the testator's will or in another individual's will if that other individual has predeceased the testator, regardless of the existence, size or character of the corpus of the trust. The devise is not invalid because the trust is amendable or revocable, or because the trust was amended after the execution of the will or the testator's death.
>
> [Subsections (b) and (c) of the statute are omitted].

In the few states where pour over will provisions are not authorized by statute, courts continue to struggle to validate those provisions by stretching the doctrines of incorporation by reference or facts of independent significance. See, e.g., In re Estate of Phelan, 375 Ill.App.3d 875, 314 Ill.Dec. 275, 874 N.E.2d 185, app. Denied, 226 Ill.2d 615, 317 Ill.Dec. 503, 882 N.E.2d 77 (2008) (finding that pour-over will incorporated settlor's revocable trust by reference, even though settlor executed revocable trust document after she executed will, on the grounds that the trust was "in existence" at the time of will execution because the document had been drafted).

3. In Clymer v. Mayo, Clara Mayo created a revocable living trust to receive the proceeds of her life insurance policies after her death. The use of a trust to receive life insurance proceeds has significant advantages when estate liquidity is an issue. Suppose, for instance, the insured's principal asset is a closely held business. Upon the insured's death, the main burden of taxes, debts, and administration expenses falls on the probate estate, creating heavy demands for cash. To avoid a "fire sale" of the business, the estate might find it helpful to have available proceeds from life insurance policies. The insured can accomplish that result by making the policies payable to the estate, but that would give the executor a claim for fees on the insurance proceeds, and would make the proceeds available for creditor claims. It might also increase state death tax liability. Alternatively, the insured can create an insurance trust with a provision authorizing the trustee to purchase assets from the insured's estate at prevailing prices, and to make loans to the estate. To create the trust, a person must first execute a revocable trust document, and then name the trustee of the revocable trust as the beneficiary of a life insurance policy.

Revocable trusts that exist to receive life insurance proceeds should not be confused with irrevocable life insurance trusts. Estate planners use the latter to minimize estate taxes.

The Dark Side of Revocable Trusts

Revocable living trusts are now valid in every state, and their popularity has exploded, due in part to aggressive marketing efforts of financial consultants and estate planners (not all of whom are lawyers). The law's trend is to treat revocable living trusts like wills. To that end, the Restatement (Third) of Trusts provides that revocable living trusts are subject to the same policy constraints and rules of construction applicable to wills. As you may recall from your study of wills law, formalities are thought to provide several useful functions: (1) the *protective* function; (2) the *ritual* function; (3) the *evidentiary* function; and (4) the *channeling* function.

Settlors who use forms to create revocable trusts may stumble without competent legal guidance. See, e.g., In re Pozarny, 177 Misc.2d 752, 677 N.Y.S.2d 714 (Sur. Ct. 1998) (struggling to interpret settlor's trust document, purchased as a "kit," which consisted of unintegrated papers in a loose-leaf notebook).

If a settlor creates a revocable living trust without complying with formalities, can the court be sure that she was free from undue influence at the time of creation? Can the court be confident that the settlor seriously intended the trust to govern the final disposition of her assets? Does this suggest that legislatures should abolish will formalities for testamentary documents as well? Or, has the law's willingness to recognize revocable living trusts undermined important protections provided by formalities statutes?

A second problem with revocable living trusts is that settlors may have difficulty living with them. Most clients understand what a will is and how it operates. They may have more difficulty grasping the concept of the revocable living trust, however. Conceptual confusion can lead to big problems down the road. Consider the following case:

Heaps v. Heaps

Court of Appeal of California, 2004.
124 Cal.App.4th 286, 21 Cal.Rptr.3d 239.

■ SILLS, J.

I. INTRODUCTION

This case illustrates the sort of unexpected complications that can arise from the so-called living trusts, which are hawked so aggressively these days. The bottom line here is that the casual use of a living trust as a quickie estate planning device meant that a husband was worth a lot less than his second wife thought he was worth when she married him. Unbeknownst to her, the husband's erstwhile assets had already been tied up for the first wife's children because of an overly broad clause involving how the trust would hold title.... We will therefore affirm a judgment which requires the second wife to pay over assets that she thought were the husband's, and later thought were hers, to the first wife's children.

II. BACKGROUND

In 1985, during the course of a long marriage, George and Barbara Heaps—the husband's first wife—executed a revocable living trust with both spouses acting as their own trustees. The trust would, however, become irrevocable with the death of one of the original trustors. Upon that death, the trust was to be split into two trusts: a "family" trust consisting of the maximum amount of assets that would pass to the "estate of the Trustor" free of estate tax and a "marital" trust for the remainder. George and Barbara's son William Heaps and son-in-law Frank Ciotti would join the survivor as co-trustees of the family trust, but the surviving spouse would remain sole trustee of the marital trust. The trust also provided that the surviving spouse would have the right to an annual principal invasion of the assets of the *family* trust, up to the greater of 5 percent of the assets or $5,000. However, to make that invasion, the trust (section 3.06 to be specific) required the surviving spouse to first "make such request on or before December 1 of each year only."

This case concerns the only important asset put into that trust, a residence on Circle Haven owned by George and Barbara at the time the trust agreement was made. Title to the Circle Haven property was transferred to the trust via quitclaim deed in 1985. The quitclaim deed transferring the property to the trust was, however, never recorded. It was just given to George and Barbara's attorney.

Barbara would live another nine years, and die in 1994. But four years before her death in 1990, George and Barbara sold the Circle Haven property for $320,000. In return for the Circle Haven property, George and Barbara got back a note and an all-inclusive deed of trust in the amount of $236,000, *title to which was taken as joint tenants.*

Of course, taking title as joint tenants was, in retrospect, to be expected: Since the quitclaim deed to the trust was never recorded, the buyers of the Circle Haven property would have no reason to expect to receive title *from* the trust. As far as the buyers were concerned, title was directly in the names of George and Barbara as joint tenants.

There is no question that on Barbara's death the trust became irrevocable. The question on which this case turns is, rather, whether the proceeds from the sale of the Circle Haven property were still *in* the trust as of Barbara's death in 1994.

If those proceeds were property of George and Barbara individually, then the actions of George and his second wife Mary Ann, whom he married a few months after Barbara's death in February, were perfectly legitimate. Those actions were these: In 1996, George and his second wife Mary Ann created their own family trust, and executed a quitclaim deed to transfer any interest in the Circle Haven property and in the all-inclusive trust deed received in return for that property to that new trust. What's more, after George died in 2002—in fact, during the pendency of this very case—Mary Ann transferred all the assets from the 1996 trust to her own revocable trust.

However, if the proceeds were still in the 1985 trust, the 1996 and 2002 transfers were, in effect, conversions of property not belonging to George or Mary Ann. For what it is worth, there is no evidence in the record that George himself ever treated the 1985 trust as having any force or validity after Barbara's death.

III. TERMS OF THE TRUST

Two clauses in particular bear on the question of whether, by taking title as joint tenants, George and Barbara took the proceeds of the Circle Haven property out of the trust. We now quote them verbatim.

First is the portion of the trust agreement involving amendment [emphasis added by court]:

"Section 1.06 Amendment and Revocation

"At any time during the joint lives of the Trustors, jointly as to Community Property and individually as to his or her own separate property, Trustors may, *by a duly executed instrument*,

"a) Amend this trust agreement (including its technical provisions) in any manner and/or

"b) Revoke this trust agreement in part or in whole, in which latter event any and all trust properties shall forthwith revert to such Trustor free of trust. Such instrument of amendment or revocation shall be effective immediately upon its proper execution by Trustor(s), but *until a copy has been received by a trustee*, that Trustee shall not incur any liability or responsibility either (i) for failing to act in accordance with such instrument or (ii) for acting in accordance with the provisions of this trust agreement without regard to such instrument." (Italics added.)

Second is the portion of the trust agreement concerning holding title:

"Section 5.06 Manner of Holding Title

"The Trustee may hold securities or other property held by Trustee in trust pursuant to this Declaration in Trustee's name as Trustee under this Declaration, in *Trustee's own name without a designation showing it to be Trustee under this Declaration*, in the name of Trustee's nominee, or the Trustee may hold such securities unregistered in such condition that ownership will pay by delivery." (Italics added.)

IV. DISCUSSION

A. *The Terms of the Trust Agreement Require Something More to Take Property Out of the Trust Than a Mere Change in Title*

The basic rule governing the interpretation of these clauses is exceedingly simple: "The whole of a contract is to be taken together, so as to *give effect to every part*, if reasonably practicable, each clause *helping to interpret the other*." (Civ. Code, § 1641, italics added.)

At oral argument, counsel for Mary Ann eloquently argued that pulling assets out of living trusts should not be difficult for people who are both the trustees and beneficiaries of such a trust. And that idea certainly makes sense in the abstract, and dovetails nicely with her central legal theory, which is that merely by taking *title* to the proceeds as joint tenants, George and first wife Barbara were exercising the power they necessarily had to pull assets out of the trust.

But the theory fails because the only way we can "give effect to every part" is to interpret the trust agreement to require, when assets are being withdrawn from the trust, something—anything in fact—*in addition* to merely taking title in a form that would be in some name other than the trust's.

The first clause, section 1.06, is fairly prosaic. A "duly executed instrument" was needed to amend the trust. Since George and Barbara were their own trustees, presumably a signed memo to themselves purporting to amend the trust would have been sufficient.[3]

But the second clause, section 5.06, is a landmine, ostensibly buried in the trust agreement to make it easy and convenient for the trust to hold property—but in the end, too easy and convenient. By saying that title to trust property could be held *in any way*, it necessarily meant that selling an asset and taking title in a name other than that of the trust's would not, by itself, take the property out of the trust. The whole point of section 5.06 is that title could be taken in the name of the trustors as distinct from the trust itself and the property would still be *in* the trust.

By the same token, the fact that after Barbara's death George simply ignored the 1985 trust he had entered into with Barbara could not take the Circle Haven proceeds out of the trust. After all, section 5.06 was obviously

3. The provision for delivery to the trustee was probably a result of taking a more conventional trust and not editing it so as to adapt it for cases where the trustors are their own trustees—editing, as journalists say, "with a shovel." The provision, of course, has its comic aspect: George and Barbara could have made a modification of their trust by signing a memo to themselves, which would have been effective at the moment of signing, but George and Barbara would suffer no liability to themselves as trustees if they didn't deliver it to themselves! Delivery, for what it is worth, is not an issue in this case. The dispositive thing here is that there was nothing at all, delivered or undelivered, to indicate that by selling Circle Haven the proceeds were to be taken out of the trust.

put in the trust so that it would be easy to ignore the existence of the trust and still maintain assets in it. But there is a price to be paid for such convenience. In computerese, section 5.06 made "remain in trust" the default setting. Some affirmative action *beyond merely a change in form of title* on the part of the trustors was required to click off that default.

Having determined that the placement of assets within the trust became irrevocable with Barbara's death in 1994, it follows that George and Mary Ann's attempt to place those assets in another trust in 1996, and Mary Ann's subsequent attempt to further place those assets in yet a third trust in 2002, constituted conversion of the assets of the original trust. Conversion exists if there is substantial interference or "an exertion of wrongful dominion over the personal property of another in denial of or inconsistent with his rights therein." (*George v. Bekins Van & Storage Co.* (1949) 33 Cal.2d 834, 837 [205 P.2d 1037].)

* * *

C. *No Laches*

On the merits, Mary Ann's laches theory is that Frank and William should have begun this action after their mother died eight years earlier, even though their father was still living. But that idea doesn't fly, because Frank and William weren't informed of the fact that they had actually become trustees of the family trust on Barbara's death. Accordingly, they could justifiably assume that George, as surviving trustee, would deal fairly with the trust assets during the remainder of his life, so there would be no need to exercise their rights as regards the trust assets until his death. And, in fact, Frank and William began litigating within two months of George's death, which was hardly an unreasonable passage of time.

D. *Damages*

1. VALUE OF THE TRUST

Mary Ann first contends that the trial court had no substantial evidence with which to determine the value of the 1985 trust at the time of Barbara's death. The argument is based on the idea that a schedule of assets created by Frank was inadmissible because it is partially based on nonadmitted evidence. However, since the schedule was a general compilation of documents that could not be examined individually by the court without great loss of time, it was admissible. (See Evid. Code, § 1523, subd. (d) ["oral testimony of the content of a writing is not made inadmissible . . . if the writing consists of numerous accounts or other writings that cannot be examined in court without great loss of time, and the evidence sought from them is only the general result of the whole"].)

2. DISTRIBUTIONS

We have already discussed the anomaly that, under the literal terms of the trust, George and Mary Ann had to write a memo to themselves (or its substantive equivalent) to amend the trust. Mary Ann also argues that she should be credited with moneys that George *would* have been entitled to if he had "forced" the trustees to give it to him. She notes that this would include all the income from both trusts. Moreover, she says that George could have revoked his one-half interest in the trust, and could also (though this would be more speculative) have exercised his annual right to invade 5 percent or $5,000 of principal.

This whole line of argument fails because George, for some reason—perhaps because he thought that by ignoring it it would go away—never acknowledged the existence of the 1985 trust to anyone, even himself. Mary Ann's argument thus has an if-pigs-had-wings quality. It is essentially circular: If George had exercised his rights he would have had the right to the money, ergo he should have the right to the money. The argument fails because there is no authority within the four corners of the trust by which a court should be compelled to *impute* the exercise of rights within the framework of the trust to someone who was intent on ignoring the trust altogether.

Of course, if you step back and look at the record in broader terms, George's inertness makes a certain kind of sense: One can reasonably infer that George did not want to acknowledge to Mary Ann that assets she thought *were his* were really tied up in an earlier trust made for the benefit of the children of first wife. For George to have formally revoked his one-half interest in the trust, or formally requested the 5 percent principal distributions or general income distributions, would have been to acknowledge that those assets weren't really his.

Lastly, Mary Ann argues that the trial court failed to recognize her own contributions to the trust (i.e., the 1996 trust) in its award. But Mary Ann certainly would not have contributed to the 1985 trust prior to Barbara's death in 1994, when the trust became irrevocable. Since the award is based on the trust's value at that time, Mary Ann's contributions to the 1996 trust are irrelevant.

V. DISPOSITION

The judgment is affirmed. Respondents shall recover their costs on appeal.

QUESTIONS

1. Why did George and Barbara Heaps fail to follow the procedure described in their own trust document for modifying the trust by removing assets?

2. At the time of trust creation, what objectives might George and Barbara have had when they placed their assets in a revocable living trust? Given those probable objectives, what drafting errors did their attorney make?

PROBLEM

When William and Jane married, William had three children from a previous marriage, and Jane had four. William and Jane each executed a revocable living trust. Both trust instruments provided that the trusts were revocable during the lifetime of the settlor, that the settlor's spouse would receive the income after the settlor's death, and at the death of the spouse the principal would be distributed in seven equal shares to their children. Jane died, and the trustee distributed the income of her trust to William. William remarried, revoked his trust (unbeknownst to Jane's children) and executed a new revocable trust that left the trust property only to his own children. At William's death, the trustee distributed the principal of Jane's trust to all seven children, and the principal of William's trust to William's three children.

Jane's children believe they are entitled to a portion of William's trust. If you represent Jane's children, what arguments might you advance? See Kempton v. Dugan, 224 S.W.3d 83 (Mo. App. 2007).

Would Jane's children's claim be stronger if William and Jane had settled one, instead of two, revocable trusts? See Mangels v. Cornell, 40 Kan.App.2d 110, 189 P.3d 573 (2008).

What drafting lessons might you learn from this problem?

Is the Revocable Trust Right for Every Client?

Marketers of revocable trusts emphasize the advantage of avoiding probate with its attendant costs, delays, and loss of privacy. However, George Heaps gained none of these advantages through his attempted use of an *inter vivos* trust. Clearly, an attorney had recommended to the Heaps that they create a revocable living trust. Was that recommendation wise? Would you recommend a revocable living trust to every client?

Consider the view of one probate court judge:

> Write a will? Prepare a living trust? Purchase an annuity? Deliver cash gifts? These are the decisions that make up the critical pieces of a well constructed estate plan—a plan that deserves to be built upon a foundation of accurate, reliable information. Avoiding probate is not a plan, it is a commercially manufactured scheme designed to lure an uninformed public away from the good counsel of a licensed legal professional. The lofty promises to eliminate estate costs and realize huge tax savings are summarily dismissed by reasonable people. Good estate planning is not accomplished by performing a legal 'sleight of hand.' As any good plan, it is the result of clear thought and deliberate action.

William P. DeFeo, Avoiding Probate Court: A Judge's Perspective, 19 Quinnipiac Prob. L.J. 53 (2005).

In fact, revocable trusts are not the best option for every client. The following paragraphs explore some basic factors that should be considered in determining whether a revocable living trust is right for your client:

1. THE PROS AND CONS OF AVOIDING PROBATE

Marketers of revocable living trusts often argue that such trusts are preferable to wills because they save the costs (both in time and money) associated with probate. But whether a revocable trust generates savings is a more complex issue than might first appear. First, the costs of drafting a revocable trust and accompanying pour-over will, and then transferring assets to the trust, might exceed the cost of drafting and executing a simple will. Transferring assets to the trust may engender recording fees and brokerage commissions, and there may be costs associated with re-registering securities and other assets in the trustee's name. In addition, if the settlor names a professional fiduciary trustee or co-trustee, the co-trustee will be entitled to trustee commissions during the settlor's life and after her death.

The use of a revocable trust will not entirely eliminate expenditures at the settlor's death. The settlor's executor or administrator must file an estate tax return, analyze the settlor's assets and liabilities and pay creditors. And to the extent that some of settlor's assets were not held in trust, probate proceedings will still be necessary.

On the other hand, avoiding probate through the use of a funded revocable trust has advantages. Even if probate is necessary, costs of probate will be substantially less if most assets are held in a revocable trust (because probate costs are generally tied to the size of the probate estate). Of course, the savings might be offset by the trustee's commissions during settlor's life. In addition to engendering fewer costs at decedent's death, the trustee can immediately distribute assets to decedent's dependents. By contrast, the family of the testator with a simple will must wait until the court appoints an executor. Although most states have family homestead and maintenance statutes that authorize a court to dispense funds to family members pending completion of the probate process, family members must apply for those funds and wait for the court's approval before they will receive those assets. Finally, an individual who owns real property in states other than the state of his domicile can avoid the costs of ancillary probate by transferring title to all of his real property to a revocable *inter vivos* trust.

2. THE NEED TO PLAN FOR INCAPACITY

Revocable living trusts can make the transition to old age or incapacity less awkward. The settlor can provide for a successor trustee to assume management of trust assets in the event of settlor's incapacity. This avoids the need for a costly, time consuming and possibly painful guardianship or conservatorship proceeding. For further discussion of using a revocable trust to plan for incapacity, see Section II E, infra.

3. PRIVACY CONCERNS

A will must be filed with the court during the probate process, and thus becomes a public document. A trust, however, is private and the trustee need not divulge the contents of the trust document to any third party. For this reason, settlors with strong concerns for privacy may prefer a revocable living trust to a will.

There are, however, limits to the privacy afforded the settlor of the revocable living trust. In any litigation over the trust, the trustee will probably be required to produce the trust document during discovery. Moreover, the trustee may have to provide copies of the trust document to financial institutions that invest trust assets. In most cases, however, a revocable trust is more private than a will. For an argument that trust privacy is undermining both attempts to create a uniform trust law and the move to unify the doctrines applying to wills and will substitutes, see Frances H. Foster, Privacy and the Elusive Quest for Uniformity in the Law of Trusts, 38 Ariz. St. L.J. 713 (2006).

4. MINIMIZING THE CHANCES OF A SUCCESSFUL WILL CONTEST

After settlor's death, disgruntled heirs may challenge settlor's revocable trusts by claiming that the settlor lacked capacity or was the victim of fraud or undue influence. But challenging a revocable trust on those grounds may be more difficult than contesting a will. First, remainder beneficiaries of revocable trusts do not have standing to challenge the trust provisions during the settlor's life. See Linthicum v. Rudi, 122 Nev. 1452, 148 P.3d 746 (2006) (holding that contingent remaindermen, who claimed that settlor lacked capacity, could proceed only by filing a guardianship petition against settlor). Second, even challenges that are filed after settlor's death can be difficult to win. If the settlor funded the trust during her life and lived in accordance with the trust's terms prior to her death, those facts provide solid evidence of settlor's intent to have the trust instrument dictate the distribution of her assets at death. In many states, however, the statute of limitations for contesting a will is considerably shorter than the statute of limitations for contesting a revocable trust. For example, UTC section 604 provides that a contestant must file a contest within 120 days of receipt of an optional warning notice or three years following settlor's death, whichever is first. In practice, however, few settlors are likely to provide the optional warning—because they will not want to deal with the animosity the warning is likely to trigger. As a result, the longer three-year statute will apply. This long limitations period can undercut the effectiveness of the revocable trust in providing a smooth transition at settlor's death.

5. ASSET MANAGEMENT NEEDS

Individuals with substantial assets may wish to devote time to work, travel or leisure pursuits instead of to asset management. Others may be unable to perform investment tasks competently. Those individuals could simply execute a power of attorney in favor of a trusted friend or family member. The better course is to hold assets in trust and name a professional trustee. Or, a settlor can retain control over management decisions but free herself from the burden of record keeping and other administrative details by appointing a professional to serve as co-trustee with the settlor. Alternatively, the settlor can enter into a management arrangement with a bank trust department or other investment adviser.

In sum, revocable living trusts are most advantageous for older people with substantial assets. On the other hand, young adults with insubstantial assets will probably find that the expense (in time and money) of holding assets in a revocable trust outweighs the benefits. A determination of whether clients in between those extremes can benefit from a living trust will depend on careful consideration of each client's individual needs and circumstances.

Protecting the Spouse Against Revocable Trusts

Although challenges to revocable *inter vivos* trust as testamentary do not succeed today, when settlor's *spouse* challenges a revocable *inter vivos* trust as illusory because the settlor retained full control over the trust's assets until the moment of death, the spouse often prevails.

Suppose a settlor transfers all of his assets into a revocable trust, reserving to himself broad powers of revocation and management. The trust instrument provides that at settlor's death, trust assets should be paid to someone other than the surviving spouse. At death, settlor's estate will have no assets. What relief is available to the surviving spouse?

Under many modern elective share statutes (including the UPC), the revocable trust will be included in the "augmented estate" or will otherwise be available to satisfy the surviving spouse's claims. See also, Restatement (Third) of Trusts § 25, cmt. a (2003) (stating that surviving spouses should be able to include revocable *inter vivos* trusts in the elective share calculation). At common law, dower and curtesy would have protected the surviving spouse against unilateral transfers from the decedent spouse to the trust. But, in those jurisdictions that abolished dower and curtesy, and substituted elective share provisions applicable only against the net probate estate, the surviving spouse faced a serious problem: by use of a revocable *inter vivos* trust, the decedent spouse could attempt to cut the surviving spouse off with nothing.

In that context, a number of courts, led by the New York Court of Appeals in Newman v. Dore, 275 N.Y. 371, 9 N.E.2d 966 (1937), concluded that the revocable trust was "illusory," and hence invalid to perpetrate what was sometimes called a "fraud on the widow's share." (New York's elective share statute now includes revocable trusts as testamentary substitutes in computing the estate against which the surviving spouse may elect.) See also Dreher v. Dreher, 370 S.C. 75, 634 S.E.2d 646 (2006). In evaluating the validity of revocable trusts as a device to cut off the surviving spouse, some courts focus on settlor's intent (see, e.g., Mushaw v. Mushaw, 183 Md. 511, 39 A.2d 465 (1944)), while others, including Newman v. Dore, *supra*, focus on the degree of control reserved by settlor.

In Sullivan v. Burkin, 390 Mass. 864, 460 N.E.2d 572 (1984) (*supra*, Chapter 3), the Massachusetts Supreme Judicial Court announced that it would subsequently adopt another rule protecting the surviving spouse against disinheritance by use of revocable trusts:

> The rule we now favor would treat as part of the estate of the deceased for the purposes of G.L. c. 191, § 15 [the forced heirship statute—eds.]

> assets of an *inter vivos* trust created during the marriage by the deceased spouse over which he or she alone had a general power of appointment, exercisable by deed or will. This objective test would involve no consideration of the motive or intention of the spouse in creating the trust. We would not need to engage in a determination of "whether the [spouse] has in good faith divested himself [or herself] of ownership of his [or her] property or has made an illusory transfer" (*Newman v. Dore*, 275 N.Y. 371, 379, 9 N.E.2d 966 [1937]) or with the factual question whether the spouse "intended to surrender complete dominion over the property" (*Staples v. King*, 433 A.2d 407, 411 [Me. 1981]). Nor would we have to participate in the rather unsatisfactory process of determining whether the *inter vivos* trust was on some standard, "colorable," "fraudulent", or "illusory".

Because many jurisdictions do not have statutes expressly including revocable trusts in an augmented estate for elective share purposes, the illusory trust doctrine remains important. See, e.g. Seifert v. Southern Nat'l Bank of South Carolina, 305 S.C. 353, 409 S.E.2d 337 (1991) (holding that proceeds of revocable trust should be included in husband's estate for purposes of calculating elective share; South Carolina had adopted version of UPC, but had refused to adopt augmented estate provisions). See generally Daniel Schuyler, Revocable Trusts—Spouses, Creditors and Other Predators, Ch. 74–13, 8th Annual Institute on Estate Planning (Univ. Of Miami 1974).

Often, lawyers seeking to invalidate a revocable trust cite cases in which a court has invalidated a trust to protect a surviving spouse. Generally, this tactic proves unsuccessful. Whether a trust is illusory for the purpose of protecting a surviving spouse has little to do with whether the trust should be held invalid for failure to comply with testamentary formalities.

Changed Marital Circumstances and Revocable Trusts

PROBLEM

To avoid probate, Sarah Settlor creates a revocable living trust. Sarah conveys all of her assets to herself as trustee of the trust. At the time she creates the trust, Sarah is married to Sam, and the trust instrument provides that at Sarah's death, Sam should act as successor trustee, and should distribute the trust principal to himself. Two years later, Sarah becomes enamored of another man, and obtains a divorce. Sam, grief stricken, dies the next month, intestate, survived by his brother, Bob. How should Sarah's assets be distributed if she then dies intestate, survived by her new husband?

Would the answer be the same if instead of drafting a trust instrument, Sarah had deposited all of her assets in a bank account trust?

Would the answer be the same if Sarah had created an *irrevocable* trust?

See UPC § 2–804 (divorce revokes revocable dispositions). See also Clymer v. Mayo, 393 Mass. 754, 473 N.E.2d 1084 (1985) (court applies to revocable trust a statute providing that divorce revokes will executed before the divorce; court, however, restricts holding "to the particular facts of this case—specifically the existence of a revocable pour-over trust funded entirely at the time of the decedent's death"); Miller v. First National Bank & Trust Co., 637 P.2d 75 (Okla.1981) (holding that divorce operates to revoke revocable *inter vivos* trust).

How should Sarah Settlor's lawyer draft the trust instrument to anticipate the possibility of marital difficulties? Will people in Sarah's position heed the lawyer's advice? Will they appreciate the lawyer who raises questions about potential marital difficulties?

Marketing Revocable Trusts: Professional Responsibility Issues

Committee on Professional Ethics v. Baker

Supreme Court of Iowa, 1992.
492 N.W.2d 695.

■ LAVORATO, J.

Before us is a report of the Grievance Commission recommending that attorney William D. Baker be reprimanded.

* * *

Baker is a sole practitioner and has practiced law in Des Moines since 1967. He focuses primarily on real estate, probate, estate planning, and trusts.

Rex Voegtlin is a certified financial planner and sole shareholder of Diversified Resource Management, Inc., located in West Des Moines. During 1989 and 1990 Voegtlin was presenting seminars in which he touted living trusts as an estate planning device. (Living or loving trusts have been promoted as a way of avoiding probate.) One of Voegtlin's advertisements concerning these seminars is in evidence. The ad urges people to attend and learn "how to avoid probate and minimize estate taxes with an estate plan that includes a living trust." In a newsletter—also in evidence—Voegtlin condemns probate as too expensive and time consuming.

In 1989 James Miller, a lawyer, was a trust officer for Hawkeye Bank and Trust of Des Moines, a former client of Baker's. In the summer of that year Miller attended one of Voegtlin's seminars and met him for the first time. Sometime after that meeting the two agreed to work jointly in putting on Voegtlin's seminars. Miller's reason for doing so was to attract new business for his bank....

Shortly before Miller agreed to these joint seminars, he and Voegtlin met with Baker in August 1989.

* * *

.... Baker told the two he would accept referrals from them for the preparation of living trusts and related documents, and he began doing so in the fall of 1989.

* * *

Over time the seminars and referrals developed this way. Voegtlin would advertise a free seminar in which the benefits of a living trust would be explained. Voegtlin and Miller would divide up the time during which each would speak. Voegtlin would close the seminar by offering free individual consultations. . . .

Before the consultations, these "clients"—as Voegtlin described them—would complete a general information planning form in which they would list their names, addresses, family members, and assets. At the consultations, which were held in Voegtlin's office, the clients would present the form at which point Voegtlin and Miller would review it as well as the clients' goals. The primary goal was, of course, to avoid probate.

Voegtlin and Miller would then talk about the various estate planning options the clients had. They would discuss the living trust in a general way—what it can do and what it cannot do. Voegtlin would diagram on a blackboard how a living trust works. The use of marital trusts, family trusts, and generation-skipping trusts was explained—how they worked and how they fit into an estate plan. The diagram would be individualized to include the clients' beneficiaries by name and the names of the trustees.

Voegtlin would also diagram how a will works so the clients could understand the difference between a living trust and a will. Voegtlin would then take a Polaroid picture of the diagrams and give it to the clients. Miller would talk about the duties of a bank trustee and what a bank does on a day-to-day basis when acting as a trustee.

Eventually during the consultations, Voegtlin, Miller, and the clients would reach a consensus as to which estate plan was best for the clients. By this time Voegtlin and Miller had made a determination as to which documents would be necessary to carry out the estate plan.

At this point Voegtlin and Miller would tell the clients that the clients needed to employ a licensed attorney to prepare the documents. If the clients had an attorney, the two would suggest that the clients' attorney be employed. If the clients had no attorney, the two would give the clients a list of attorneys to consider. Baker was among those attorneys listed. The two told the clients that most clients chose Baker because he was a competent attorney, his fees were reasonable, and he was prompt. The evidence shows that from October 1989 through October 1991, Baker accepted about 100 of these referrals. Fewer than ten were received by other attorneys.

Frequently Voegtlin would telephone Baker during the consultations. Voegtlin would tell him that the clients who were there wanted to proceed with the living trust and wanted him to do the legal work. Voegtlin would use a speaker phone so that the clients could also talk to Baker. Voegtlin would remain and listen to the conversation.

Sometimes Voegtlin would not follow this procedure. Instead Voegtlin or Miller would bring the materials discussed at the consultations to Baker and ask if he would accept the referral. A few times clients themselves would go to Baker's office with the materials. The materials would include

(1) a copy of the financial form, (2) a general outline of the terms to be included in the clients' living trust, and (3) a description of other necessary documents.

Baker would then call the clients to go over their materials and discuss any questions that either he or they might have. Baker would ask if they were still interested. Some were; others were not. If the clients expressed an interest in proceeding, Baker would tell them that he would prepare a draft of what they wanted and send the draft to them for their review. If the clients did not proceed, Baker would not charge them for any work he might have done for them.

If the clients wanted to proceed, Baker would tell them to bring the trust documents to a meeting at Voegtlin's office. At the meeting Baker would go through the documents and explain them to the clients. Voegtlin was often, but not always, at these meetings. The clients executed the documents at these meetings unless corrections were necessary. If corrections were necessary, the corrections were made and the documents were either executed then or later.

* * *

Not surprisingly, the documents frequently named Voegtlin or Diversified as the person to fund the trust. Voegtlin's wife—also a certified financial planner—usually performed this task. Funding the trust simply means having the clients sign whatever forms or documents that are necessary to transfer personal property from the clients' names to the living trust. Voegtlin's fee for funding the trust and financial advice related to this task was $1000. The advice, for example, might include recommending exchanging a low-interest producing asset for a higher-interest producing one.

In May 1990 Voegtlin asked Baker to furnish him with a sample living trust and accompanying documents that Baker was using for the clients Voegtlin and Miller were referring to him. Voegtlin told Baker he wanted sample documents to show clients who were interested in seeing what Baker's trust looked like. Voegtlin apparently used these documents in his seminars.

* * *

In July 1990 the Committee on professional Ethics and Conduct of the Iowa State Bar Association published interpreting opinions 90–1 and 90–2. Formal opinion 90–32 was published in November 1990. The subject of each opinion was the marketing of living trusts. Opinion 90–32 stated that it was improper for Iowa lawyers to participate in living trust programs like those conducted by Diversified. After publication of opinions 90–1 and 90–2, Baker was the only attorney who continued accepting referrals from Voegtlin.

In February 1991 two members of the UPC met with Baker concerning its investigation of Voegtlin and Diversified. At Baker's disciplinary hearing, one of the two investigating UPC members testified this way:

Q. Would it be fair to say, based on the information that Mr. Baker gave you, that Mr. Voegtlin would tell Mr. Baker specific documents that would be needed in a given situation? A. That was my understanding, that they had sort of a standard package of documents that Mr. Baker indicated were developed early on that he got from Hawkeye Bank when Hawkeye Bank was involved in doing these trusts, that he had modified them in some respects but the basic package of documents Mr. Baker had and then at Mr. Voegtlin's direction would decide we need will A or will B or trust A or trust B or whatever type was needed.

* * *

Q. ... When does it say Voegtlin's doing this? A. My understanding was that Mr. Voegtlin, when he called Mr. Baker, would tell him that "We need pour-over will A," or, "We need pour-over will B," or, "We need just A or B," and described the client's specific situation and that Voegtlin was giving the legal advice and directing him as to what documents to prepare.

* * *

Q. When you talked with Mr. Baker about what he might recommend to clients, did he tell you that he merely explained the pros and cons of living trusts to the clients and let them make up their own mind, or did he say that he recommended living trusts to his clients? ... A. My understanding is by the time that the people got to Mr. Baker that it was a done deal, in that the decisions had already been discussed with Mr. Voegtlin about what they needed, that they needed the living trust, and that he basically then prepared the documents for their signature.

* * *

Q. Was there any discussion with Mr. Baker as to whether when he got a referral from Mr. Voegtlin he ever recommended anything to them other than the living trust? A. That was one thing I was curious about, is whether as an attorney he was exercising some independent judgment on these clients, and I asked him about that, and he had indicated that he had about 50 to 60 referrals from Mr. Voegtlin over what I understood to be some time period from about 1989, and he indicated he had never suggested to the client that the living trust was not appropriate for their situation.

* * *

In April 1991 two members of the UPC met with Voegtlin and his attorney about procedures Voegtlin used in recommending living trusts and referring legal matters. The UPC did not make a determination that Voegtlin was involved in the unauthorized practice of law. Apparently, the UPC is delaying its determination because of this disciplinary proceeding against Baker. The UPC has, however, referred the matter to the attorney general's office for investigation of consumer fraud.

The Committee on Professional Ethics and Conduct filed a complaint against Baker in October 1991. The complaint alleges that Baker's involvement with Voegtlin in the living trust marketing scheme violated several disciplinary rules and ethical considerations of the Iowa Code of Professional Responsibility for Lawyers and formal opinion 90–32.

* * *

After finding that the allegations of the complaint were true, the commission recommended that Baker be publicly reprimanded for (1) aiding in the unauthorized practice of law; (2) permitting others to influence his professional judgment in providing legal services to clients referred to him, resulting in a conflict of interest; and (3) accepting improper referrals.

* * *

I. *Aiding in the Unauthorized Practice of Law.*

We first turn our attention to the commission's finding that Baker aided Voegtlin in the unauthorized practice of law. Whether we agree with this finding requires a two step analysis. First, did Voegtlin's actions constitute the unauthorized practice of law? If so, did Baker aid those actions?

A. *Voegtlin's actions.* This court has refrained from attempting an all-inclusive definition of the practice of law. Rather it decides each case in this area largely on its own particular facts. *Bump v. Barnett*, 235 Iowa 308, 315, 16 N.W.2d 579, 583 (1944). EC 3–5 of the Iowa Code of Professional Responsibility for Lawyers takes the same tack: "It is neither necessary nor desirable to attempt the formulation of a single, specific definition of what constitutes the practice of law." EC 3–5.

However, EC 3–5 goes on to tell us what the practice of law includes:

> *However, the practice of law includes*, but is not limited to, representing another before the courts; giving of legal advice and counsel to others relating to their rights and obligations under the law; and preparation or *approval of the use of legal instruments by which legal rights of others are either obtained, secured or transferred* even if such matters never become the subject of a court proceeding. Functionally, the practice of law relates to the rendition of services for others that call for the professional judgment of a lawyer. The essence of the professional judgment of the lawyer is his educated ability to relate the general body and philosophy of law to a specific legal problem of a client; and thus, the public interest will be better served if only lawyers are permitted to act in matters involving professional judgment. Where this professional judgment is not involved, nonlawyers, such as court clerks, police officers, abstracters, and many governmental employees, may engage in occupations that require a special knowledge of law in certain areas. But the services of a lawyer are essential in the public interest whenever the exercise of professional legal judgment is required.

* * *

From the evidence in this case, it is clear that Voegtlin's actions met one of the practicing law tests articulated in EC 3–5: "approval of the use of legal instruments by which legal rights of others are either obtained, secured or transferred." Voegtlin met with the clients. He advised them about what they needed in the way of estate planning. He advised them in particular about what documents they would need and how those documents would need to be tailored to meet their particular situation. In the words of one UPC investigator, by the time the clients got to Baker "it was a done deal." Baker was merely a scrivener. Voegtlin had already made the major decisions; he, rather than Baker, was exercising professional judgment. The "smoking gun" on this point is found in the supplemental financial planning letter. This document acknowledges that the financial planning letter and related instruments were recommended by Voegtlin.

* * *

For all of these reasons, we agree with the commission that Voegtlin was engaged in the unauthorized practice of law.

B. *Baker's actions*. DR 3–101(A) prohibits a lawyer from aiding a nonlawyer in the unauthorized practice of law. EC 3–1 exhorts the legal profession to actively discourage the unauthorized practice of law. EC 3–3 reminds lawyers that the disciplinary rules prohibit a lawyer from submitting to the control of others in the exercise of the lawyer's judgment. EC 3–4 also reminds lawyers that "[p]roper protection of members of the public demands that no person be permitted to act in the confidential and demanding capacity of a lawyer unless he is subject to the regulations of the legal profession."

We agree with the commission that in one way or another Baker violated DR 3–101(A), EC 3–1, EC 3–3, and EC 3–4. From our review of the record, we see Voegtlin's seminars, his newsletters, and his referrals to Baker as nothing more than a scheme on Voegtlin's part to reap substantial fees. Indeed, he targeted clients having estates in excess of $600,000. The scheme worked because Voegtlin preached through his seminars and newsletters that clients should use a living trust because our probate system "takes too long and is too expensive." Voegtlin controlled the whole process from the initial interview to the final meeting when the clients executed the documents in his office. He did so by recommending the living trust, the necessary tailored documents to effectuate it, and a lawyer who he believed would not counsel against his advice. In fact, when Voegtlin sold clients on a living trust, Baker never once counseled against using it.

Instead of discouraging Voegtlin from these actions, Baker actually encouraged them in a number of ways. First, Baker allowed Voegtlin to exercise the professional judgment Baker should have exercised. Second, Baker allowed Voegtlin to act in a confidential capacity with the clients who were referred to Baker. Third, Baker furnished Voegtlin with forms to be used at his seminar. Fourth, Baker accepted approximately 100 referrals from Voegtlin. Last, Baker gave Voegtlin advice on his newsletters.

Our experience with "living trusts" teaches us that they may be a very poor substitute for probate. Unlike probate fees, the fees charged by nonlawyers like Voegtlin who tout living trusts are not subject to court scrutiny. Lack of court scrutiny can easily lead to unnecessary and excessive fees. The point is whether a living trust is appropriate in a given case calls for the exercise of independent professional judgment by a lawyer.

II. *Engaging in Conflicts of Interest.*

The commission found that Baker permitted Voegtlin to influence his professional judgment in providing legal services to clients referred to Baker, resulting in a conflict of interest.

This finding is predicated on alleged violations of DR 5–107(B) and EC 5–1.

DR 5–107(B) provides:

> *A lawyer shall not permit a person who recommends*, employs, or pays *him to render legal services for another to direct or regulate his professional judgment in rendering such legal services.*

(Emphasis added.)

EC 5–1 provides:

> The professional judgment of a lawyer should be exercised, within the bounds of the law, solely for the benefit of his client and free of compromising influences and loyalties. Neither his personal interests, the interests of other clients, *nor the desires of third persons should be permitted to dilute his loyalty to his client.*

(Emphasis added.)

The commission found sufficient evidence to establish a violation of DR 5–107(B) and EC 5–1. We agree.

We have already found that Voegtlin, not Baker, exercised professional judgment as to the appropriateness of a living trust and the particular documents necessary to effectuate it. We have also referred to the reasons why Voegtlin promoted living trusts. All of this is another way of saying that Baker permitted Voegtlin to "direct or regulate his professional judgment" in rendering legal services to the referred clients. DR 5–107(B).

All of this is also another way of saying that Baker permitted Voegtlin's desires to "dilute [Baker's] loyalty to his client[s]." EC 5–1. Like the commission; we find that the prospect of receiving additional referrals constituted the "compromising influences" mentioned in EC 5–1. The number of referrals was many—approximately 100 in all. And the fees generated by them were substantial—approximately $40,000 in total. It is significant to us that Baker came to eventually realize that he was the only lawyer receiving these referrals, and that fact bothered him.

* * *

IV. *Discipline.*

[The court concluded that discipline in excess of reprimand would not be appropriate].

.... [A]dditional facts enter our decision on discipline here. First, Baker has for many years enjoyed an excellent reputation as an active practicing lawyer. Second, Baker fully cooperated with all investigations related to the complaint. Third, no client referred by Voegtlin (1) complained about any living trust or other documents Baker prepared or (2) suffered any financial loss based upon these documents....

We do not condone Baker's behavior in this matter. He was ill-advised to continue accepting referrals from Voegtlin when it became apparent that such conduct might be improper. What he should have done is to follow the old ethics adage, "if you have doubt, don't do it." Baker did the opposite. We view his past professional judgment as misguided, and we expect him to guard against even the appearance of impropriety in his future professional relationships.

We reprimand Baker for aiding Voegtlin in the unauthorized practice of law and for allowing Voegtlin to direct or regulate Baker's professional judgment in rendering legal services to Baker's clients.

QUESTIONS

Over the course of six months, five clients have consulted you indicating that their investment advisor (a college classmate of yours) has recommended that they ask you to prepare revocable *inter vivos* trusts for them. In each case, you explored with the client the mechanics of the trust, and indicated that creation of a revocable trust was consistent with the client's objective. When a sixth client enters your office with the same story, what should you do, given the court's opinion in Baker?

Does it matter whether you and your classmate have a social relationship? Whether you refer clients to your classmate for investment advice?

NOTE

The practices at issue in Baker have become widespread, and have resulted in discipline of lawyers in a number of states. See, e.g., People v. Cassidy, 884 P.2d 309 (Colo. 1994) (six month suspension from practice). In a 2005 case, the Supreme Court of Ohio imposed a fine of $1,027,260 against a group of non-lawyer financial advisers who sold revocable living trusts with the (nominal) help of "review attorneys." See Cleveland Bar Assoc. v. Sharp Estate Serv., Inc., 107 Ohio St.3d 219, 837 N.E.2d 1183 (2005). Other states have enacted statutes regulating the drafting of living trusts. 815 Ill. Comp. Stat. Ann. sec. 505/2–B.

D. Protecting Beneficiaries from Creditors: Support and Discretionary Trusts, Revocable Trusts, Spendthrift Trusts and Self-Settled Asset Protection Trusts

1. SUPPORT AND DISCRETIONARY TRUSTS

Many a trust settlor creates a trust to assure that the trust beneficiary or beneficiaries receive a dependable source of income. Suppose for instance, a settlor, concerned about her son's financial acumen, creates a trust, naming a bank as trustee, and providing that the bank is to pay income to the son until the son reaches age 40, and then to terminate the trust and distribute the principal to the son. The settlor, by postponing distribution of the principal until the son reaches age 40, may be trying to assure that the son does not dissipate his inheritance before he becomes more mature.

Suppose, however, that after the trust is created, the son, at age 25, wants to buy a yacht. Having no money of his own, the son executes the following instrument, and delivers it to a yacht seller:

> I hereby assign to Barbara Boatseller all of my right, title, and interest in the income and principal of the trust created by my mother on September 1, 1997.

Boatseller, knowing the size of the trust, is happy to postpone immediate payment in return for this assurance that ultimately, the trust principal will be hers. And, in almost every state, the son's assignment is enforceable. Once Boatseller provides the trustee with notice of the assignment, trustee is obligated to pay income, as it accrues, to Boatseller. Once the son reaches age 40, the trustee will be obligated to pay Boatseller the principal (unless a court terminates the trust and pays Boatseller early because the trust no longer serves any discernible purpose). The result is that settlor's intention has been frustrated: she has not assured a steady income for her son.

Now suppose the son made no voluntary assignment to Boatseller, but instead gave Boatseller a note for $200,000 in exchange for the yacht. If the son defaulted on the note, and Boatseller obtained a judgment against the son, Boatseller, as a judgment creditor, would be entitled to garnish the trust income in the hands of the trustee, forcing the trustee to pay the trust income to Boatseller rather than the son, subject to reasonable limits imposed by the court. See UTC § 501; Restatement (Third) of Trusts § 56. Again, the settlor's intention would have been frustrated.

Suppose, however, the settlor had created a support trust for her son's benefit, using the following language:

> I direct my trustee to pay to my son as much of the income as shall be necessary to provide for his support, education, and maintenance.

If the son assigned his rights to the trust to Boatseller, would the trustee be obligated to pay Boatseller the trust income? Note that the trust instrument does not require—or permit—the trustee to pay out all trust income; the trustee is limited to paying sums necessary to provide for support. If the yacht is not necessary for the son's support, trustee is not obligated (or permitted) to pay Boatseller trust income or principal. At the same time, despite the assignment, trustee may pay trust income directly to the son to use for his support, or to suppliers of goods and services necessary for the son's support, education, or maintenance.

What if the son made no assignment to Boatseller, but instead gave Boatseller a note for $200,000 in exchange for the yacht? Would Boatseller have any rights against the trustee? Again, the answer is no; because settlor has authorized the trustee to use the trust's funds only for the support of the beneficiary, a creditor who is not providing support is not entitled to garnish the beneficiary's interest in the trust.

Finally, suppose that the son enrolls in college. Because the trust is a support trust that expressly defines "support" as including education, the trustee would have the duty to pay for the son's college tuition. If, for some reason, the trustee did not pay and the university obtained a judgment for outstanding tuition payments, what rights would the creditor have to the assets held in trust? At common law, and today in a majority of states, the university would have exactly the same rights as the son; if the son sued the trustee for breach of fiduciary duty for failing to pay college tuition, he would prevail. Similarly, the university has the right to attach the trust assets in satisfaction of the debt.

The drafters of the UTC, however, changed the law in this respect. In a state that has adopted the UTC, the university can attach the son's interest in the trust, but if the trustee fails to pay the debt, the university is prevented from compelling a distribution or arguing that the trustee's failure to pay the debt constitutes a breach of fiduciary duty. Only the son would have standing to make that argument. See UTC § 504. The only creditors with power to compel a distribution are those whose claims are based on alimony and child support. To reiterate, although section 501 authorizes a court to allow a creditor to attach the beneficiary's interest in a trust, section 504 bars almost all creditors from complaining if the trustee fails to make a distribution for goods or services that the trustee is obligated to provide to the beneficiary! What does it mean to say that the university has a "right" to attach the beneficiary's interest if it is up to the trustee to determine whether to honor that "right"? Does the UTC approach make sense? Because the UTC has been adopted in almost half of the states, make sure you understand the difference between the common law approach (reiterated in the Restatement (Third)) and the UTC on this point.

Under the law of any state, then, a support trust provides a beneficiary with substantial protection against creditor claims. In common law states, only providers of necessaries can attach trust assets. In UTC states, even providers of necessaries have no legal right to argue that the trustee who doesn't want to pay them must pay. At the same time, however, the support trust limits the trustee's power to use the money for any purposes other than support of the beneficiary. What if the settlor wants to confer on the trustee power to pay money for purposes other than support? Can the settlor give the trustee discretion, and still insulate the beneficiary's interest from creditor claims? Consider the following case:

Wilcox v. Gentry

Supreme Court of Kansas, 1994.
254 Kan. 411, 867 P.2d 281.

■ McFarland, J.

Ron and Nancy Wilcox appeal from the district court's judgment holding that any payments made by the trustee of the Frank Gentry Trust

(Trust) which are made for the benefit of Isabell Gentry and not paid directly to Isabell, are not subject to garnishment. The Court of Appeals affirmed the judgment appealed from, but reversed, *sua sponte*, a continuing garnishment order entered by the district court relative to payments made by the trustee directly to Isabell Gentry.... The matter is before us on petition for review.

In 1985, Frank Gentry created a revocable Trust. During his lifetime, Frank was the beneficiary of the Trust. Upon Frank's death certain trust property was to be distributed to named individuals. The residue of the Trust's assets was to be divided into five equal shares. Four of these shares were to be distributed to the four individuals designated as their recipients. This action concerns the fifth share. The applicable Trust provision in Article III, Section D.5, is as follows:

> (e) One share shall remain in trust until the death of Isabell Gentry. The trustee, in his sole discretion, may make such distributions of income and principal to her or on her behalf as the trustee deems advisable after giving due consideration to all sources of funds available to her. Upon the death of Isabell Gentry, the trust shall terminate and the balance of the trust and accumulated income shall be distributed to the then surviving beneficiaries in proportion to the beneficial interests they would have been entitled to, under D. 5.(a), (b), (c) and (d) above, had Grantor died on the actual date of Isabell Gentry's death. In the event Isabell Gentry should predecease the Grantor, this share shall be equally divided between Mary Margaret Gentry and Eric Gentry, or pass fully to the survivor.

The district court and the Court of Appeals characterized the Trust provisions applicable to Isabell Gentry in (e) as being discretionary in nature. This determination is unchallenged herein and we agree we are dealing with a discretionary trust. The Trust contains no spendthrift provision.

Ron and Nancy Wilcox obtained a judgment against Isabell Gentry for fraud in the sale of a residential property. Their judgment was for $40,000 actual damages and $11,667.35 punitive damages. They garnished the Trust to seek satisfaction of their judgment. Frank Gentry, grantor and sole beneficiary during his lifetime, had died previously, thereby activating section 5(e) relative to Isabell.

* * *

The district court held that any trustee payments directly to Isabell were subject to garnishment but that trustee payments for Isabell's benefit were not. The propriety of the district court's determination relative to payments made for Isabell's benefit is the only aspect of the judgment from which an appeal was taken.

In the case before us, the issue is not whether the trustee can be compelled to pay income or principal. The issue before us is, if the trustee exercises its discretion and makes a payment on behalf of the beneficiary, whether such payment is subject to the creditors' garnishment.

This makes Restatement (Second) of Trusts § 155(2) the applicable statement, as it provides:

> (2) Unless a valid restraint on alienation has been imposed in accordance with the rules stated in §§ 152 and 153, if the trustee pays to or applies for the beneficiary any part of the income or principal with knowledge of the transfer or after he has been served with process in a proceeding by a creditor to reach it, he is liable to such transferee or creditor.

As previously stated, there is no valid restraint on alienation (spendthrift provision) involved herein. This section makes no distinction between payments directly to the beneficiary or on the beneficiary's behalf.

Pertinent comments to subsection (2) are found therein as follows:

> h. *Effect of payment by trustee to beneficiary after assignment.* Although in the case of a discretionary trust a transferee or creditor of the beneficiary cannot compel the trustee to pay over any part of the trust property to him, yet if the trustee does pay over any part of the trust property to the beneficiary with knowledge that he has transferred his interest or after the trustee has been served with process in a proceeding by a creditor of the beneficiary to reach his interest, the trustee is personally liable to the transferee or creditor for the amount so paid, except so far as a valid provision for forfeiture for alienation or restraint on alienation has been imposed as stated in §§ 150, 152 and 153.
>
> * * *
>
> i. *Effect of applying property by trustee for beneficiaries after assignment.* If the trustee applies for the benefit of the beneficiary income or principal, he is liable to an assignee of the beneficiary's interest or to a creditor of the beneficiary, if he makes such application after he has knowledge of the assignment or after he has been served with process in a proceeding brought by a creditor of the beneficiary to reach the beneficiary's interest.

In IIA Scott on Trusts § 155.1, p. 160–61 (4th Ed. 1987), the following pertinent discussion appears:

> Although the trustee need not pay any part of the trust fund to the beneficiary or to his creditors, but may withhold it entirely, but if he does determine to pay part of it to him, he should pay it to the creditors who now stand in his shoes. The English courts, however, have here made a distinction. They have held that the trustee can properly *apply* the trust fund for the use of the beneficiary even though he is bankrupt or his creditors have brought a proceeding to reach his interest. The distinction thus drawn between payment to the beneficiary and applying trust funds for his benefit seems to be arbitrary and without any sound basis in public policy. The result is that the beneficiary is enabled to enjoy the benefit of the trust in spite

of his insolvency, as long as the trustee is willing to apply the trust estate for his benefit.

In Bogert, Trusts and Trustees § 228, pp. 524–32 (Rev.2d Ed.1992), distinctions between discretionary and spendthrift trusts are discussed, and the following is stated relative to a creditor's ability to reach trust funds:

> If the trust is a true "discretionary" trust, the nature of the interest of the beneficiary, rather than any expressed restraint on his power to alienate or the rights of his creditors, determines questions of voluntary or involuntary alienation. The beneficiary cannot secure the aid of a court in compelling the trustee to pay or apply trust income or principal to him since the terms of the trust permit the trustee to withhold payments at his will. Until the trustee elects to make a payment the beneficiary has a mere expectancy. Nor can a creditor compel the trustee to exercise his discretion to make payments. If the beneficiary attempts to transfer his interest, or his creditors seek to take it, before the trustee has made an election to pay or apply, the transferee or creditor has no remedies against the trustee because he stands in the shoes of the beneficiary.
>
> * * *
>
> If, however, the trustee exercises his discretion by making a decision to pay to or apply for the beneficiary, then the beneficiary can force the trustee to confer such a benefit on him, and he can transfer his right and his creditors can take advantage of it, if the trust does not have a spendthrift clause. If the trustee receives notice of an attempted voluntary transfer, or is served with process by a creditor of the beneficiary, before the making of his decision to allocate trust property to the beneficiary, he will be liable to the assignee or creditor if he thereafter uses his discretion and elects to pay to the beneficiary. In such a case his duty is to pay to the assignee or creditor if he decides to pay or apply, unless the discretionary trust instrument contains a spendthrift clause, or a statute gives rights to the creditor as in the case where the surplus of income over that needed for support is made liable to creditors.

The above-cited treatises are persuasive. We see no valid reason for treating payments to a beneficiary differently from payments made on behalf of the beneficiary as far as creditors are concerned. If the creditor has the right to reach payments made to the beneficiary excluding payments made on behalf of the beneficiary serves only to encourage circumvention of that right. We adopt Restatement (Second) of Trusts § 155(2) and find it determinative of this issue. The district court and the Court of Appeals erred in holding that only funds paid directly to a discretionary trust beneficiary are subject to garnishment by a creditor.

QUESTIONS

1. Ron and Nancy Wilcox prevailed on their appeal. Can they compel the trustee to pay them any money? If not, how, if at all, was the court's decision helpful to them? If you were the lawyer for the Wilcoxes, how would you advise them to proceed in light of the court's decision?

2. Suppose you were the trustee in this case. After the court's decision, would you make any distributions of income or principal (a) to Isabell or (b) to the Wilcoxes? Why or why not?

3. In light of Wilcox, would you recommend a discretionary trust to a settlor who wants to provide for her son, while keeping trust assets away from the son's creditors?

4. In 1951, Lawrence O'Shaughnessy's grandparents created trusts directing the trustees, in their discretion, to pay to Lawrence "all or such part of the principal or the annual net income of the trust estate as they shall see fit during his lifetime." In 1986, the Internal Revenue Service sought to collect a $412,000 income tax deficiency assessed against Lawrence. Can the IRS compel the trustees to pay trust income or principal? Can the trustees pay Lawrence income or principal? See United States v. O'Shaughnessy, 517 N.W.2d 574 (Minn.1994).

5. Would the Wilcox case have been decided differently if UTC § 504 had been adopted by the Kansas legislature?

NOTES

1. The Restatement (Third) of Trusts reaffirms the Restatement (Second)'s language imposing personal liability on the trustee if the trustee distributes trust funds to or for the benefit of the trust beneficiary after being served with process by a creditor who seeks to attach the beneficiary's interest in the trust. See Restatement (Third) of Trusts § 60, cmt. c (2003).

2. Recall that UTC § 504 departs from common law to provide that creditors (except ex-spouses and dependent children) have no right to argue that a trustee has abused its discretion in failing to make a trust distribution. Suppose that the UTC had been adopted in Kansas, and that the trustee in Wilcox made a payment to Ron and Nancy *after* their creditor had attached their interest in the trust. Could the trustee be held personally liable for that maneuver? The comments to the UTC are silent on that issue. On one hand, in depriving the creditor of the right to argue that a clearly breaching trustee has abused its discretion, the drafters seem to imply that a trustee cannot be personally liable for making a payment to someone other than the creditor. On the other hand, section 106 provides that the "common law of trusts and principles of equity" supplement the UTC where it is silent. See Alan Newman, The Rights of Creditors of Beneficiaries Under the Uniform Trust Code: An Examination of the Compromise, 69 Tenn. L. Rev. 771 (2002) (concluding that UTC would not resolve controversy over this issue).

For articles discussing the UTC's approach to creditor's rights, See, Kevin D. Millard, Rights of a Trust Beneficiary's Creditors Under the Uniform Trust Code, 34 ACTEC J. 58 (2008); William H. Lyons, Discretionary Trusts, Support Trusts, Discretionary Support Trusts, Spendthrift Trusts, and Special Needs Trusts Under the Nebraska Uniform Trust Code, 86 Neb. L. Rev. 231 (2007); Alan Newman, Spendthrift and Discretionary Trusts: Alive and Well Under the Uniform Trust Code, 40 Real Prop. Prob. & Trust J. 567 (2005); Robert T. Danforth, Symposium: Trust Law in the 21st Century: Article Five of the UTC and the Future of Creditors' Rights in Trusts, 27 Cardozo L. Rev. 2551 (2006); Jeffrey A. Schoenblum, Symposium: Trust Law in the 21st Century: In Search of a Unifying Principle for Article V of the Uniform Trust Code: A Response To Professor Danforth, 27 Cardozo L. Rev. 2609 (2006).

2. SPENDTHRIFT TRUSTS

The most common mechanism for keeping trust assets away from a beneficiary's creditors is inclusion of a "spendthrift" provision in the trust instrument. For instance, the trust instrument might provide:

> "The interests of my trust beneficiary, whether in trust income or trust principal, shall not be capable of assignment, anticipation, or seizure by legal process."

Lawyers typically refer to trusts which include such provisions as "spendthrift trusts." Spendthrift provisions are valid only if they prevent both voluntary assignments and involuntary garnishment by the beneficiary's creditors. See UTC § 502(a); Restatement (Third) of Trusts § 58 (2003). Do you see which words prevent voluntary assignment? Garnishment?

UTC section 502(b) directs that a spendthrift clause like the one above is sufficient to restrain both voluntary and involuntary transfer of the beneficiary's interests. Courts, however, often inspect the trust document carefully to determine whether, the spendthrift clause notwithstanding, the document actually enables the beneficiary to alienate his or her interest. For example, in In re Mitchell, 423 B.R. 758 (Bankr. E.D. Wis. 2009), the bankruptcy court held that a spendthrift provision was invalid where the trust document stated:

> [the beneficiary] may withdraw the balance from the principal of his or her share any time or times. The Trustee shall make payment without question upon the child's written request. The right of withdrawal shall be a privilege which may be exercised only voluntarily and shall not include an involuntary exercise.

The Mitchell court cited the Restatement (Second) of Trusts for the proposition that "if a beneficiary is entitled to have the principal paid or conveyed to him immediately or at any time he may call for it, a restraint on alienation of his interest is invalid." See also, Restatement (Third) of Trusts § 58 cmt. a. Do you see why careful drafting is important?

Since their introduction, spendthrift trusts have been controversial. Those who support them emphasize the ideal of free testation, and argue that there is no public policy justification for declaring spendthrift trusts invalid. Consider the following excerpt:

Broadway National Bank v. Adams, 133 Mass. 170 (1882):

> [T]he reasons of the rule [prohibiting restrictions on alienation] do not apply in the case of a transfer of property in trust. By the creation of a trust like the one before us, the trust property passes to the trustee with all its incidents and attributes unimpaired. He takes the whole legal title to the property, with the power of alienation; the *cestui que trust* takes the whole legal title to the accrued income at the moment it is paid over to him. Neither the principal nor the income is at any time inalienable. . . .
>
> . . . The founder of this trust was the absolute owner of his property. He had the entire right to dispose of it, either by an absolute gift to his brother, or by a gift with such restrictions or limitations, not repugnant to law, as he saw fit to impose. His clear intention, as shown in his will, was not to give his brother an absolute right to the income which might hereafter accrue upon the trust fund, with the power of alienating it in advance, but only the right to receive semiannually the income of the fund, which upon its payment to him, and not before, was to become his absolute property. His intentions ought to be carried out, unless they are against public policy.
>
> . . . . The only ground upon which it can be held to be against public policy, is that it defrauds the creditors of the beneficiary.
>
> It is argued that investing a man with apparent wealth tends to mislead creditors, and to induce them to give him credit. The answer is, that creditors have no right to rely upon property thus held, and to give him credit upon the basis of an estate which, by the instrument creating it, is declared to be inalienable by him, and not liable for his debts. By the exercise of proper diligence they can ascertain the nature and extent of his estate, especially in this Commonwealth, where all wills and most deeds are spread upon the public records. There is the same danger of their being misled by false appearances, and induced to give credit to the equitable life tenant when the will or deed of trust provides for a cesser or limitation over, in case of an attempted alienation, or of bankruptcy or attachment, and the argument would lead to the conclusion that the English rule is equally in violation of public policy. We do not see why the founder of a trust may not directly provide that his property shall go to his beneficiary with the restriction that it shall not be alienable by anticipation, and that his creditors shall not have the right to attach it in advance, instead of indirectly reaching the same result by a provision for a cesser or a limitation over, or by giving his trustees a discretion as to paying it.

* * *

See also, Nichols v. Eaton, 91 U.S. 716, 726, 23 L.Ed. 254 (1875), wherein the Court states that spendthrift trusts are not unfair to creditors, because creditors can ascertain the restrictions on the beneficiary's income and choose whether to extend credit. This is especially true in the computer age.

Opponents of spendthrift trusts argue that such trusts are not morally justifiable because they insulate spendthrifts from responsibility for their actions, and are unsound as a policy matter because they harm creditors who cannot take adequate precautionary measures. John Chipman Gray, perhaps best known for his formulation (and exhausting discussion) of the Rule Against Perpetuities, fiercely opposed spendthrift trusts as suitable only for certain classes of people—infants, lunatics, and married women—but certainly not for grown men! Gray wrote:

> The general introduction of spendthrift trusts would be to form a privileged class, who could indulge in every speculation, could practice every fraud, and, provided that they kept on the safe side of the criminal law, could yet roll in wealth. They would be an aristocracy, though certainly the most contemptible aristocracy with which a country was ever cursed.

John C. Gray, Restraints on the Alienation of Property 174 (1883). See also Paul G. Haskell, Teaching Moral Analysis in Law School, 66 Notre Dame L. Rev. 1025, 1047 (1991) ["... Testator's use of the spendthrift provision, and the law which upholds it, are not morally defensible."].

Professor Anne S. Emanuel views spendthrift trusts as unfair to creditors and takes issue with the argument that creditors may protect themselves from spendthrifts by gathering financial information prior to extending credit:

> This argument fails on two grounds. First, while testamentary trusts are public records, *inter vivos* trusts are not; the point simply does not apply to a significant number of trusts. Second, the creditor did not necessarily "recklessly" extend credit. The creditor might hold a tort judgment, or a claim for child support or unpaid taxes.
>
> With reference to contract creditors, ... [the argument is] that the creditor should identify security before extending credit. The creditor who relies on apparent affluence without determining its source does so at his own risk. This position, despite its appeal, has two flaws. First, it increases initial transaction costs in all extensions of credit in order to control relatively few situations. Second, by making the determination of whether a claim is entitled to satisfaction turn on whether it is a contract claim, transaction costs are increased by adding a layer of complexity. Claimants forced into litigation will classify claims as something other than contract claims, *e.g.*, as the tort of negligent breach of contract.

Anne S. Emanuel, Spendthrift Trusts: It's Time to Codify the Compromise, 72 Neb. L. Rev. 179, 192–93 (1993). See also Utley v. Graves, 258 F.Supp. 959 (D.D.C.1966), *rev'd*, 382 F.2d 451 (D.C.Cir.1967):

> That a person should be able to live according to the standards to which he claims to be accustomed and at the same time repudiate any obligation to pay for anything that he purchases on credit, is manifestly inequitable and repugnant to the ideas of right and wrong. That persons who are sufficiently sophisticated and incredulous may decline to extend credit to him, and refuse to sell him anything or render him

> any service except for current payment in cash, is not an adequate answer. There are numerous small business concerns that are unable to maintain a complete credit department and ascertain the fact that a person, although seemingly affluent, is living on the income of a spendthrift trust.

For a modern rejoinder, see Adam J. Hirsch, Spendthrift Trusts and Public Policy: Economic and Cognitive Perspectives, 73 Wash. U. L.Q. 1, 91–92 (1995) [arguing that allowing spendthrift trusts, even self-settled ones, is consistent with other asset protection mechanisms, including incorporation, holding property in tenancies by the entirety and contributing to an ERISA-qualified pension plan]. See also Gerald P. Moran, A Radical Theory of Jurisprudence: The "Decisionmaker" as the Source of Law—The Ohio Supreme Court's Adoption of the Spendthrift Trust Doctrine as a Model, 30 Akron L. Rev. 393 (1997) (discussing Ohio's departure from its earlier refusal to recognize spendthrift trusts).

Are spendthrift trusts fair to creditors? Consider the following case:

Scheffel v. Krueger

Supreme Court of New Hampshire, 2001.
146 N.H. 669, 782 A.2d 410.

■ DUGGAN, J.

The plaintiff, Lorie Scheffel, individually and as mother and next friend of Cory C., appeals a Superior Court (Hollman, J.) order dismissing her trustee process action against Citizens Bank NH, the trustee defendant. See *RSA 512:9Bb* (1997). We affirm.

In 1998, the plaintiff filed suit in superior court asserting tort claims against the defendant, Kyle Krueger. In her suit, the plaintiff alleged that the defendant sexually assaulted her minor child, videotaped the act and later broadcasted the videotape over the Internet. The same conduct that the plaintiff alleged in the tort claims also formed the basis for criminal charges against the defendant. See *State v. Krueger, 776 A.2d 720, 146 N.H., 2001 N.H. LEXIS 108 (2001).* The court entered a default judgment against the defendant and ordered him to pay $551,286.25 in damages. To satisfy the judgment against the defendant, the plaintiff sought an attachment of the defendant's beneficial interest in the Kyle Krueger Irrevocable Trust (trust).

The defendant's grandmother established the trust in 1985 for the defendant's benefit. Its terms direct the trustee to pay all of the net income from the trust to the beneficiary, at least quarterly, or more frequently if the beneficiary in writing so requests. The trustee is further authorized to pay any of the principal to the beneficiary if in the trustee's sole discretion the funds are necessary for the maintenance, support and education of the beneficiary. The beneficiary may not invade the principal until he reaches the age of fifty, which will not occur until April 6, 2016.

The beneficiary is prohibited from making any voluntary or involuntary transfers of his interest in the trust. Article VII of the trust instrument specifically provides:

> No principal or income payable or to become payable under any of the trusts created by this instrument shall be subject to anticipation or assignment by any beneficiary thereof, or to the interference or control of any creditors of such beneficiary or to be taken or reached by any legal or equitable process in satisfaction of any debt or liability of such beneficiary prior to its receipt by the beneficiary.

Asserting that this so-called spendthrift provision barred the plaintiff's claim against the trust, the trustee defendant moved to release the attachment and dismiss the trustee defendant. The trial court ruled that under *RSA 564:23* (1997), this spendthrift provision is enforceable against the plaintiff's claim and dismissed the trustee process action.

* * *

We first address the plaintiff's argument that the legislature did not intend *RSA 564:23* to shield the trust assets from tort creditors, especially when the beneficiary's conduct constituted a criminal act. . . .

We begin by examining the language found in the statute. *RSA 564:23*, I, provides:

> In the event the governing instrument so provides, a beneficiary of a trust shall not be able to transfer his or her right to future payments of income and principal, and a creditor of a beneficiary shall not be able to subject the beneficiary's interest to the payment of its claim.

The statute provides two exceptions to the enforceability of spendthrift provisions. The provisions "shall not apply to a beneficiary's interest in a trust to the extent that the beneficiary is the settlor and the trust is not a special needs trust established for a person with disabilities," *RSA 564:23*, II, and "shall not be construed to prevent the application of RSA 545–A or a similar law of another state [regarding fraudulent transfers]," *RSA 564:23*, III. Thus, under the plain language of the statute, a spendthrift provision is enforceable unless the beneficiary is also the settlor or the assets were fraudulently transferred to the trust. The plaintiff does not argue that either exception applies.

Faced with this language, the plaintiff argues that the legislature did not intend for the statute to shield the trust assets from tort creditors. The statute, however, plainly states that "a creditor of a beneficiary shall not be able to subject the beneficiary's interest to the payment of its claim." *RSA 564:23*, I. Nothing in this language suggests that the legislature intended that a tort creditor should be exempted from a spendthrift provision. Two exemptions are enumerated in sections II and III. Where the legislature has made specific exemptions, we must presume no others were intended. See *Brahmey v. Rollins, 87 N.H. 290, 299, 179 A. 186 (1935).* "If this is an omission, the courts cannot supply it. That is for the Legislature to do." Id. (quotation omitted).

The plaintiff argues public policy requires us to create a tort creditor exception to the statute. The cases the plaintiff relies upon, however, both involve judicially created spendthrift law. See *Sligh v. First Nat. Bank of Holmes County, 704 So. 2d 1020, 1024 (Miss.1997); Elec. Workers v. IBEW–NECA Holiday Trust, 583 S.W.2d 154, 162 (Mo.1979).* In this State, the legislature has enacted a statute repudiating the public policy exception sought by the plaintiff. Compare *RSA 564:23*, I, with *Athorne v. Athorne, 100 N.H. 413, 416, 128 A.2d 910 (1957).* This statutory enactment cannot be overruled, because "it is axiomatic that courts do not question the wisdom or expediency of a statute." *Brahmey, 87 N.H. at 298.* Therefore, "no rule of public policy is available to overcome [this] statutory rule." Id.

The plaintiff next argues that the trust does not qualify as a spendthrift trust under *RSA 564:23* because the trust document allows the beneficiary to determine the frequency of payments, to demand principal and interest after his fiftieth birthday, and to dispose of the trust assets by will. These rights, the plaintiff asserts, allow the beneficiary too much control over the trust to be recognized as a trust under *RSA 564:23*. Beyond the exclusion of trusts settled by the beneficiary, see *RSA 564:23*, II, the statute does not place any limitation on the rights a beneficiary is granted under the trust instrument. Rather, by its plain language the statute applies where a trust's "governing instrument ... provides, a beneficiary ... shall not be able to transfer his or her right to future payments of income and principal, and a creditor of a beneficiary shall not be able to subject the beneficiary's interest to the payment of its claim." *RSA 564:23*, I. In this case, the trust instrument contains such a provision. Because the settlor of this trust is not the beneficiary, the spendthrift provision is enforceable. The legislature did not see fit to pronounce further limitations and we will not presume others were intended. See *Brahmey, 87 N.H. at 299.*

Finally, the plaintiff asserts that the trial court erred in denying her request that the trust be terminated because the purpose of the trust can no longer be satisfied. The plaintiff argues that the trust's purpose to provide for the defendant's support, maintenance and education can no longer be fulfilled because the defendant will likely remain incarcerated for a period of years. The trial court, however, found that the trust's purpose "may still be fulfilled while the defendant is incarcerated and after he is released." See, e.g., *RSA 622:55* (Supp. 2000). The record before us supports this finding.

Affirmed.

■ Barry and Fauver, JJ., Superior Court Justices, specially assigned under *RSA 490:3*, concurred; Gray and Manias, JJ., Retired Superior Court Justices, specially assigned under *RSA 490:3*, concurred.

NOTES AND QUESTIONS

1. Suppose Kyle Krueger had not been a spendthrift trust beneficiary, but had worked for a living. How would Corey C.'s mother have satisfied her judgment? Why does the law allow successful plaintiffs to attach defendants' wages? Does it make sense to make a wage earner pay for the consequences of his actions, yet shield the trust beneficiary from responsibility for his? For an argument that involuntary tort creditors should be entitled to attach assets held in spendthrift trusts, see Timothy J. Vitollo, Applying Hamilton Orders to Spendthrift Interests, 43 Real Prop. Tr. & Est. L.J. 169 (2008).

2. In Broadway Nat'l Bank, excerpted in the text preceding Scheffel v. Krueger, the court justified enforcement of the spendthrift trust as a reflection of the settlor's intent. The court recognized, however, that in other areas of law, common law courts have refused to give effect to a grantor's intent. In particular, the court cites the common law's refusal to enforce restraints on alienation. Thus, if, in a will, testator devises real property to her son, with the proviso "neither my son nor his heirs shall have power to sell the property, nor shall the property be subject to the claims of my son's creditors," the proviso would simply be unenforceable, and the property would be subject to the claims of the son's creditors.

What distinguishes spendthrift trusts? If the son's legal interest in the house is subject to creditor claims, why shouldn't the son's interest in a spendthrift trust equally be subject to those claims?

3. The merger doctrine applies to spendthrift trusts. Thus, if the sole income beneficiary becomes the sole trustee, or visa versa, the trust terminates, and the beneficiary takes the trust principal outright. This could create a problem for a beneficiary facing creditor claims. To avoid having the trust assets attached by creditors, the beneficiary may refuse to act as trustee (in which case the court will appoint a trustee). Or, if merger occurred because other equitable interests were extinguished, causing the entire equitable interest to vest in the remaining beneficiary, the beneficiary may promptly disclaim the additional equitable interest to which she has become entitled. See Restatement (Third) of Trusts § 69, cmt. d (2003).

4. If your grandmother were about to create a trust for your benefit, would you want the trust to be spendthrift? Note that while spendthrift trusts restrict the ability of creditors to reach the beneficiary's interest in the trust property, they also restrict the beneficiary's ability to assign his interest voluntarily. Is this a restriction on autonomy a beneficiary would welcome? Is it a restriction the law should permit the settlor to impose? See Gregory S. Alexander, The Dead Hand and the Law of Trusts in the Nineteenth Century, 37 Stan. L. Rev. 1189, 1193 (1985) ("[W]ithin the individualistic regime of consolidated property there is no objective basis for choosing between the autonomy of the donor and that of the donee ...; any resolution of that problem is a 'naked preference.' ").

PROBLEMS

Ben is the income beneficiary of a $100,000 trust, which generates $10,000 of income annually. Creditor has a money judgment against Ben for $8,000. The judgment was for Ben's breach of a contract to supply widgets. Consider Creditor's rights in (a) a jurisdiction that adheres to the common law (Restatement) approach; and (b) a jurisdiction that has adopted the UTC.

1. What are Creditor's rights against the trustee if the trust instrument provides:

a. "The trustee shall pay to Ben the entire net income of the trust, at least annually."

b. "The trustee shall pay to Ben so much of the income of the trust as the trustee deems necessary for Ben's education, support and maintenance."

c. "The trustee shall pay to Ben so much of the income of the trust as the trustee deems appropriate in the trustee's absolute discretion."

2. How would Creditor's rights be different if Creditor were Ben's landlord?

3. In each of these circumstances, how would the creditor's rights change if the trust instrument provided, in addition,

> "The interests of my trust beneficiary, whether in trust income or trust principal, shall not be capable of assignment, anticipation, or seizure by legal process."

4. What are Creditor's rights once Ben has the trust income in his hands?

Public Policy Exceptions to Spendthrift Trusts

Notwithstanding cases such as Scheffel v. Krueger, supra, courts have carved out a few exceptions to the protections afforded spendthrift trust beneficiaries. Consider the Uniform Trust Code:

SECTION 503. EXCEPTIONS TO SPENDTHRIFT PROVISION.

(a) In this section, "child" includes any person for whom an order or judgment for child support has been entered in this or another State.

(b) Even if a trust contains a spendthrift provision, a beneficiary's child, spouse, or former spouse who has a judgment or court order against the beneficiary for support or maintenance, or a judgment creditor who has provided services for the protection of a beneficiary's interest in the trust, may obtain from a court an order attaching present or future distributions to or for the benefit of the beneficiary.

(c) A spendthrift provision is unenforceable against a claim of this State or the United States to the extent a statute of this State or federal law so provides.

NOTES

1. ***Claims for Alimony and Support.*** UTC § 503 is consistent with the approach of the vast majority of states. See also Restatement (Third) of

Trusts § 59 (2003). What is the rationale for making an exception for claims based on alimony and child support? Consider this excerpt from Bacardi v. White, 463 So.2d 218 (Fla. 1985):

> Respondents urge that we approve the district court's decision and hold that the settlor's intent prevails over any public policy arguments which would allow the alienation of disbursements from the trust. They contend that an ex-wife's debt is no different than any ordinary debt even though it represents unpaid alimony and related attorney's fees and that, therefore, her claim should be treated the same as the claim of any other creditor. They assert that it is clear from reading the spendthrift provision that the settlor did not intend Adriana Bacardi to participate as a beneficiary and that this intent precludes garnishment.
>
> This case involves competing public policies. On the one hand, there is the long held policy of this state that recognizes the validity of spendthrift trusts. On the other hand, there is the even longer held policy of this state that requires a former spouse or a parent to pay alimony or child support in accordance with court orders.
>
> * * *
>
> We have weighed the competing public policies and, although we reaffirm the validity of spendthrift trusts, we conclude that in these types of cases the restraint of spendthrift trusts should not be an absolute bar to the enforcement of alimony orders or judgments. Florida's interest in the enforcement of these awards under certain limited circumstances is paramount to the declared intention of the settlor and the restraint of a spendthrift trust.

2. Suppose a client approaches you about creating a spendthrift trust for the benefit of his son. The client knows of the son's marital difficulties, and wants to assure that the son's wife cannot reach any interest in the trust. Is there any way to effectuate your client's goal while assuring that the son continues to benefit from the trust? Is there a way to keep the money away from the wife, while assuring that the son collects income until the wife makes a claim for support or alimony? If yes, try to draft an instrument accomplishing that objective.

3. ***Claims for Attorneys Fees.*** Note that under the UTC, and the law of most states, if a trust beneficiary hires a lawyer to protect his interest in a spendthrift trust, the lawyer has a claim against the trust proceeds. (Did you expect anything different?).

4. ***Claims for Necessaries.*** Suppose a trustee of a spendthrift trust receives a demand for payment not from the beneficiary's spouse, but from the beneficiary's landlord, or from the beneficiary's physician, seeking recompense for services rendered. Is the trustee obligated to pay under UTC section 503?

In some states, a provider of necessary services may enforce her claim against the beneficiary's interest in a spendthrift trust. What might the justification be for this exception?

5. ***Other Limits on Power to Shelter Income from Creditors.*** Can a wealthy benefactor provide a beneficiary with unlimited income, all of which is unavailable to creditors (other than, perhaps, suppliers of necessaries)? A number of states have enacted statutes purporting to give creditors the right to reach a debtor's interest in a spendthrift trust to the extent that the debtor's interest exceeds the debtor's needs for education and support. See, e.g., Cal. Prob. Code, sec. 15307; N.Y. EPTL Section 7–3.4. These statutes, however, provide creditors with limited recourse because courts—particularly in New York—have construed them to insulate from creditor claims all income necessary to maintain the debtor-beneficiary's "station in life." That is, if a beneficiary is used to living in the lap of luxury, creditors cannot reach assets necessary to keep the beneficiary in that lap.

6. ***Spendthrift Protection of Remainder Interests.*** Suppose Settlor's trust directs the trustee to distribute the income to Sam, her spouse, for life, and "at the death of my spouse, the trustee shall terminate the trust and distribute the principal to my daughter Belinda." The trust also includes a spendthrift provision. During Sam's life, one of Belinda's creditors seeks to attach Belinda's remainder interest (knowing that the creditor will not receive any money until Sam's death). Does the spendthrift clause bar the creditor's attempt to attach Belinda's interest? Compare Wachovia Bank v. Levin, 419 Bankr. 297 (E.D.N.C. 2009) (determining that Pennsylvania law construes spendthrift clauses broadly to include protection of remainder interests) with In re Lunkes, 406 B.R. 812 (Bankr.N.D. Ill. 2009) (citing the Restatement (Second) of Trusts to hold the spendthrift clause invalid as to the remainderman).

7. ***Spendthrift Trusts in New York.*** In most jurisdictions, a trust settlor must include a spendthrift provision to insulate trust interests from creditor claims. In New York, however, all income interests in trusts have spendthrift protection unless the trust instrument expressly confers on the income beneficiary a power to transfer rights under the trust. N.Y. EPTL Section 7–1.5. Remainder interests, however, do not receive automatic protection.

8. ***Spendthrift Trusts in Bankruptcy.*** As we have seen, spendthrift trusts are frequently justified as a mechanism for protecting beneficiaries against their own improvidence. It would be peculiar, then, to deny protection to the most improvident of beneficiaries—those who find themselves in bankruptcy proceedings. And, indeed, the bankruptcy act insulates spendthrift trusts from claims by the trustee in bankruptcy. 11 U.S.C. section 541(c)(2) provides:

A restriction on the transfer of a beneficial interest of the debtor in a trust that is enforceable under applicable nonbankruptcy law is enforceable in a case under this title. See Spacone v. Atwood, 259 B.R. 158 (9th Cir.BAP 2001) (holding that debtor's retirement trust, which was established for debtor by debtor's employer, qualified as a valid spendthrift trust under California law, and thus was not property of the bankruptcy estate). For a discussion of the interplay between spendthrift trusts and the Bankruptcy Code, see Adam J. Hirsch, Inheritance and Bankruptcy: The Meaning of the "Fresh Start," 45 Hastings L.J. 175, 241–43, esp. n. 222 (1994).

3. CREDITORS' RIGHTS IN SELF-SETTLED TRUSTS, INCLUDING OFFSHORE AND DOMESTIC ASSET PROTECTION TRUSTS

UNIFORM TRUST CODE

SECTION 505. CREDITOR'S CLAIM AGAINST SETTLOR.

(a) Whether or not the terms of a trust contain a spendthrift provision, the following rules apply:

(1) During the lifetime of the settlor, the property of a revocable trust is subject to claims of the settlor's creditors.

(2) With respect to an irrevocable trust, a creditor or assignee of the settlor may reach the maximum amount that can be distributed to or for the settlor's benefit. If a trust has more than one settlor, the amount the creditor or assignee of a particular settlor may reach may not exceed the settlor's interest in the portion of the trust attributable to that settlor's contribution.

(3) After the death of a settlor, and subject to the settlor's right to direct the source from which liabilities will be paid, the property of a trust that was revocable at the settlor's death is subject to claims of the settlor's creditors, costs of administration of the settlor's estate, the expenses of the settlor's funeral and disposal of remains, and [statutory allowances] to a surviving spouse and children to the extent the settlor's probate estate is inadequate to satisfy those claims, costs, expenses, and [allowances].

PROBLEMS

Settlor creates an irrevocable trust, and transfers $2,000,000 to the First National Bank as trustee. Two of Settlor's creditors seek to attach the trust assets to satisfy their judgments. Creditor A's judgment is for medical costs that Settlor incurred from an emergency appendectomy. Creditor B's judgment is based on a breach of contract claim for the sale of widgets. Under UTC section 505 what rights does either creditor have to attach the trust assets if the trust instrument provides as follows:

1. Trustee shall distribute all income to Settlor during Settlor's life, and shall distribute the principal to Settlor's children after Settlor's death.

2. Trustee shall distribute to Settlor income and/or principal as necessary to provide for Settlor's health, education, maintenance and support. At Settlor's death, Trustee is directed to distribute any remaining principal to Settlor's children.

3. Trustee shall pay to Settlor such amounts of income and/or principal as Trustee, from time to time and in Trustee's sole and uncontrolled discretion, deems appropriate. At Settlor's death, any remaining trust assets shall be distributed to Settlor's children.

4. Would any of your answers to problems 1–3 change if Settlor's trust also included a spendthrift clause?

5. Would any of your answers to problems 1–3 change if the trust instrument provided that Settlor could revoke the trust at any time during his life?

6. Suppose that Settlor dies before Creditors A and B can attach the trust assets. Do the creditors have any recourse?

NOTES

1. When is a trust self-settled? Suppose, for instance, John gives Mary $100,000 to create a spendthrift trust for John's benefit. Although Mary may nominally be the settlor of the trust, John's creditors will be entitled to reach his interest because he furnished the consideration for the trust. Similarly, if two people create reciprocal spendthrift trusts for each other's benefit, both trusts will be treated as self-settled, and the spendthrift provisions will be ineffective. See, e.g., Security Trust Co. v. Sharp, 32 Del.Ch. 3, 77 A.2d 543 (1950).

2. The disdain American courts and legislatures historically have expressed towards self-settled spendthrift trusts has created opportunities for offshore jurisdictions seeking to attract trust business:

> ***Stewart E. Sterk: Asset Protection Trusts: Trust Law's Race to the Bottom? 85 Cornell L. Rev. 1035, 1048–50 (2000):***
>
> Consider the Cook Islands' International Trusts Act of 1984. By its terms, the statute applies only to international trusts, not to trusts established for the benefit of residents of the Cook Islands—a sure sign that the purpose of the statute was to attract foreign capital. To that end, the statute includes numerous measures that make the Cook Islands a favorite trust situs for settlors seeking to avoid creditor claims. First, the statute makes self-settled spendthrift trusts fully enforceable. Second, the statute provides that creditors may not reach the settlor's interest in an international trust even if the settlor retains a right to revoke the trust. As a result, once a settlor's assets enter a Cook Islands international trust, the settlor's creditors may not attach the settlor-beneficiary's interest.
>
> Third, ... [u]nder the statute, even if a creditor proves that the settlor intended to defraud by transferring assets into a trust, the creditor may not reach the trust assets unless the settlor was insolvent at the time the creditor's claim arose.... Finally, the statute expressly provides that no Cook Islands court shall enforce or recognize a foreign judgment against a Cook Islands trust, or a settlor, trustee, or beneficiary of the trust, if the judgment is based upon application of a law inconsistent with the statute.

> Many offshore jurisdictions embrace to varying degrees these three features of the Cook Islands statute—authorization of self-settled trusts, evisceration of fraudulent transfer protection, and refusal to enforce foreign judgments.... [T]hese new asset protection provisions are undoubtedly responsible, at least in part, for the one trillion dollars or more currently held in offshore trusts.

* * * * * * * * * * *

Do American courts have any weapons against settlors who use offshore trusts to keep their creditors away from their assets? Consider the following case:

Federal Trade Commission v. Affordable Media, LLC

United States Court of Appeals, Ninth Circuit, 1999.
179 F.3d 1228.

■ WIGGINS, J.

A husband and wife, Denyse and Michael Anderson, were involved in a telemarketing venture that offered investors the chance to participate in a project that sold such modern marvels as talking pet tags and water-filled barbells by means of late-night television. Although the promoters promised that an investment in the project would return 50 per cent in a mere 60 to 90 days, the venture in fact was a Ponzi scheme, which eventually unraveled and left thousands of investors with tremendous losses. When the Federal Trade Commission brought a complaint against the telemarketing duo, they claimed that they were simply innocent dupes rather than a modern day telephonic Bonnie and Clyde.

While the investors' money was lost in the fraudulent scheme, the Andersons' profits from their commissions remained safely tucked away across the sea in a Cook Islands trust. When the Commission brought a civil action to recover as much money as possible for the defrauded investors, the Andersons advanced two incredible propositions. First, they claimed that they should retain the 45 percent commissions they received for their role in the fraud, even though they acknowledged that the investors were defrauded. They claimed this entitlement because they merely sold the toxic investments that fueled the scheme and propped up the duplicitous house of cards. Second, the Andersons claimed that they were unable to repatriate the assets in the Cook Islands trust because they had willingly relinquished all control over the millions of dollars of commissions in order to place this money overseas in the benevolent hands of unaccountable overseers, just on the off chance that a law suit might result from their business activities. The learned district court was skeptical of both arguments and choose to grant the Commission its requested preliminary relief.

An old adage warns that a fool and his money are easily parted. This case shows that the same is not true of a district court judge and his common sense. After the Andersons refused to comply with the preliminary injunction by refusing to return their illicit proceeds, the district court found the Andersons in civil contempt of court. The Andersons appealed. We have jurisdiction under *28 U.S.C. § 1292*(a)(1) and we affirm.

On April 23, 1998, the Federal Trade Commission (the "Commission") filed a complaint in the United States District Court for the District of Nevada, charging the Andersons, Financial, and others with violations of the Federal Trade Commission Act (the "Act") and the Telemarketing Sales Rule for their participation in a scheme to telemarket fraudulent investments to consumers. Upon motion by the Commission, the district court issued an ex parte temporary restraining order against the defendants. After hearings on April 30 and May 8, 1998, the district court entered a preliminary injunction against the defendants, which incorporated the provisions of the temporary restraining order. Both the temporary restraining order and the preliminary injunction required the Andersons to repatriate any assets held for their benefit outside of the United States.

In July, 1995, the Andersons had created an irrevocable trust under the law of the Cook Islands. The Andersons were named as co-trustees of the trust, together with AsiaCiti Trust Limited ("AsiaCiti"), a company licensed to conduct trustee services under Cook Islands law. Apparently, the Andersons created the trust in an effort to protect their assets from business risks and liabilities by placing the assets beyond the jurisdiction of the United States courts. As discussed more fully below, the provisions of the trust were intended to frustrate the operation of domestic courts, by removing the Andersons as trustees and preventing AsiaCiti from repatriating any of the trust assets to the United States if a so-called "event of duress" occurred.

In response to the preliminary injunction, the Andersons faxed a letter to AsiaCiti on May 12, 1998, instructing AsiaCiti to provide an accounting of the assets held in the trust and to repatriate the assets to the United States to be held under the control of the district court. AsiaCiti thereupon notified the Andersons that the temporary restraining order was an event of duress under the trust, removed the Andersons as co-trustees under the trust because of the event of duress, and refused to provide an accounting or repatriation of the assets. The trust assets were therefore not repatriated to the United States and the Andersons have provided only limited information to the district court and the Commission regarding the trust assets.

On May 7, 1998, the Commission moved the district court to find the Andersons in civil contempt for their failure to comply with the temporary restraining order's requirements that they submit an accounting of their foreign assets to the Commission and to repatriate all assets located abroad. At a hearing on June 4, 1998, the district court found the Andersons in civil contempt of court for failing to repatriate the trust assets to the United States and failing to provide an accounting of the trust's assets. The district court, however, continued the hearing until June 9, then until June 11, and finally until June 17, in an effort to allow the Andersons to purge themselves of their contempt. In attempting to purge themselves of their contempt, the Andersons attempted to appoint their children as trustees of the trust, but AsiaCiti removed them from acting as trustees because the event of duress was continuing. At the June 17 hearing, the district court indicated that it believed that the Andersons remained in control of the trust and rejected their assertion that compliance with the repatriation provisions of the trust was impossible. At the close of the June 17 hearing, the district judge ordered the Andersons taken into custody because they had not purged themselves of their contempt. The Andersons timely appealed the district court's issuance of the preliminary injunction and finding them in contempt. We affirm the district court.

The ... issue on appeal is the district court's finding the Andersons in contempt for refusing to repatriate the assets in their Cook Islands trust.

The standard for finding a party in civil contempt is well settled:

> The moving party has the burden of showing by clear and convincing evidence that the contemnors violated a specific and definite order of the court. The burden then shifts to the contemnors to demonstrate why they were unable to comply.

Stone v. City and County of San Francisco, 968 F.2d 850, 856 n. 9 (9th Cir.1992) (citations omitted).

The temporary restraining order required the Andersons, in relevant part, to "transfer to the territory of the United States all funds, documents and assets in foreign countries held either: (1) by them; (2) for their benefit; or (3) under their direct or indirect control, jointly or singly." These provisions were continued in the preliminary injunction. It is undisputed that the Andersons are beneficiaries of an irrevocable trust established under the laws of the Cook Islands. The Andersons do not dispute that the trust assets have not been repatriated to the United States. Instead, the Andersons claim that compliance with the temporary restraining order is impossible because the trustee, in accordance with the terms of the trust, will not repatriate the trust assets to the United States.

A party's inability to comply with a judicial order constitutes a defense to a charge of civil contempt. The Andersons claim that the refusal of the foreign trustee to repatriate the trust assets to the United States, which apparently was the goal of the trust, makes their compliance with the preliminary injunction impossible.

Although the Andersons assert that their "inability to comply with a judicial decree is a complete defense to a charge of civil contempt, regardless of whether the inability to comply is self-induced," we are not certain that the Andersons' inability to comply in this case would be a defense to a finding of contempt. It is readily apparent that the Andersons' inability to comply with the district court's repatriation order is the intended result of their own conduct. Their inability to comply and the foreign trustee's refusal to comply appears to be the precise goal of the Andersons' trust.[4]

---

4. The Andersons' trust created the circumstances in which a foreign trustee would refuse to repatriate assets to the United States by means of so-called duress provisions. Under

The Andersons claim that they created their trust as part of an "asset protection plan." These "so-called asset protection trusts are designed to shield wealth by moving it to a foreign jurisdiction that does not recognize U.S. judgments or other legal processes, such as asset freezes." Debra Baker, Island Castaway, ABA Journal, October 1998, at 55. The "asset protection" aspect of these foreign trusts arises from the ability of people, such as the Andersons, to frustrate and impede the United States courts by moving their assets beyond those courts' jurisdictions:

> Perhaps most importantly, situs courts typically ignore United States courts' demands to repatriate trust assets to the United States. A situs court will not enforce a United States order from a state court compelling the turnover of trust assets to a creditor that was defrauded under United States law, or assets that were placed into a self-settled spendthrift trust.

James T. Lorenzetti, The Offshore Trust: A Contemporary Asset Protection Scheme, *102 Com. L. J. 138, 143–144 (1997).*

Because these asset protection trusts move the trust assets beyond the jurisdiction of domestic courts, often times all that remains within the jurisdiction is the physical person of the defendant. Because the physical person of the defendant remains subject to domestic courts' jurisdictions, courts could normally utilize their contempt powers to force a defendant to return the assets to their jurisdictions. Recognizing this risk, asset protection trusts typically are designed so that a defendant can assert that compliance with a court's order to repatriate the trust assets is impossible:

> Another common issue is whether the client may someday be in the awkward position of either having to repatriate assets or else be held in contempt of court. A well-drafted [asset protection trust] would, under such a circumstance, make it impossible for the client to repatriate assets held by the trust. Impossibility of performance is a complete defense to a civil contempt charge.

Barry S. Engel, Using Foreign Situs Trusts For Asset Protection Planning, *20 Est. Plan. 212, 218 (1993).*

Given that these offshore trusts operate by means of frustrating domestic courts' jurisdiction, we are unsure that we would find that the Andersons' inability to comply with the district court's order is a defense to a civil contempt charge. We leave for another day the resolution of this more difficult question because we find that the Andersons have not

---

the trust agreement, an event of duress includes "the issuance of any order, decree or judgment of any court or tribunal in any part of the world which in the opinion of the protector will or may directly or indirectly, expropriate, sequester, levy, lien or in any way control, restrict or prevent the free disposal by a trustee of any monies, investments or property which may from time to time be included in or form part of this trust and any distributions therefrom." Upon the happening of an event of duress, the trust agreement provides that the Andersons would be terminated as co-trustees, so that control over the trust assets would appear to be exclusively in the hands of a foreign trustee, beyond the jurisdiction of a United States court.

satisfied their burden of proving that compliance with the district court's repatriation order was impossible.

In the asset protection trust context, moreover, the burden on the party asserting an impossibility defense will be particularly high because of the likelihood that any attempted compliance with the court's orders will be merely a charade rather than a good faith effort to comply.... With foreign laws designed to frustrate the operation of domestic courts and foreign trustees acting in concert with domestic persons to thwart the United States courts, the domestic courts will have to be especially chary of accepting a defendant's assertions that repatriation or other compliance with a court's order concerning a foreign trust is impossible. Consequently, the burden on the defendant of proving impossibility as a defense to a contempt charge will be especially high.

Given these considerations, we cannot find that the district court clearly erred in finding that the Andersons' compliance with the repatriation order was not impossible because the Andersons remain in control of their Cook Islands trust.

The Andersons claim that they have "demonstrated to the district court 'categorically and in detail' that they can not comply with the repatriation section of the preliminary injunction." The district court was not convinced and neither are we. While it is possible that a rational person would send millions of dollars overseas and retain absolutely no control over the assets, we share the district court's skepticism.

The Andersons had previously been able to obtain in excess of $1 million from the trust in order to pay their taxes. Given their ability to obtain, with ease, such large sums from the trust, we share the district court's skepticism regarding the Andersons' claim that they cannot make the trust assets subject to the court's jurisdiction.

Moreover, beyond this general skepticism concerning the Andersons' lack of control over their trust, the specifics of the Andersons' trust indicate that they retained control over the trust assets. These offshore trusts allow settlors, such as the Andersons, significant control over the trust assets by allowing the settlor to act as a cotrustee or "protector" of the trust.

The district court's finding that the Andersons were in control of their trust is well supported by the record given that the Andersons were the protectors of their trust. A protector has significant powers to control an offshore trust. See Gideon Rothschild, "Establishing and Drafting Offshore Asset Protection Trusts," *23 Est. Plan. 65, 70 (1996)* ("The use of a trust protector or advisor is common among foreign trusts. This person ... has the power to replace trustees and veto certain actions by the trustees."). A protector can be compelled to exercise control over a trust to repatriate assets if the protector's powers are not drafted solely as the negative powers to veto trustee decisions or if the protector's powers are not subject to the anti-duress provisions of the trust. See id. ("The protector's powers should generally be drafted as negative powers and subject to the anti-duress provisions to protect against an order compelling the protector to exercise control over the trust."). The Andersons' trust gives them affirmative powers to appoint new trustees and makes the anti-duress provisions subject to the protectors' powers,[5] therefore, they can force the foreign trustee to repatriate the trust assets to the United States.

Perhaps the most telling evidence of the Andersons' control over the trust was their conduct after the district court issued its temporary restraining order ordering the repatriation of the trust funds. The Andersons sent a notice to the foreign trustee, ordering it to repatriate the trust assets because the district court had issued a temporary restraining order. The foreign trustee removed the Andersons from their positions as co-trustees and refused to comply with the repatriation order. After the Andersons claimed that compliance with the repatriation provisions of the temporary restraining order was impossible, the Commission revealed to the court that the Andersons were the protectors of the trust. The Andersons immediately attempted to resign as protectors of the trust. This attempted resignation indicates that the Andersons knew that, as the protectors of the trust, they remained in control of the trust and could force the foreign trustee to repatriate the assets.

The Andersons contend that even though they are the protectors of the trust, it is impossible for them to repatriate the trust assets. The Andersons' argument, that "there is a misstep in the FTC's logic," ignores the fact that they bear the burden of proving impossibility, not the Commission. Their pointing to a few provisions of the trust, alone, is insufficient to carry their burden or to establish that the district court's finding that they remain in control of their trust was clearly erroneous.[6]

Because we see no clear error in the district court's finding that the Andersons remain in control of their trust and could repatriate the trust assets, the district court did not abuse its discretion in holding them in contempt. We, therefore, affirm the district court's finding the Andersons

5. For example, the trust provides the protectors with discretion to conclusively determine that an event of duress has not occurred: "For the purpose of determining whether an Event of Duress has occurred pursuant to paragraph (c) and paragraph (d) of this clause (1)(a)(vi) of this Deed, the written certificate of the Protector to that effect shall be conclusive."

6. The provisions of the trust also make clear that the Andersons' position as protectors gives them control over the trust. In provisions of the trust agreement that the Andersons conveniently fail to reference, the trust agreement makes clear that the Andersons, as protectors, have the power to determine whether or not an event of duress has occurred: "For the purpose of determining whether an Event of Duress has occurred pursuant to paragraph (c) and paragraph (d) of this clause (1)(a)(vi) of this Deed, the written certificate of the Protector to that effect shall be conclusive." Moreover, the very definition of an event of duress that the Andersons assert has occurred makes clear that whether or not an event of duress has occurred depends upon the opinion of the protector: "The issuance of any order, decree or judgement of any court or tribunal in any part of the world which in the opinion of the Protector will or may directly or indirectly, expropriate. . . ." Therefore, notwithstanding the provisions of the trust agreement that the Andersons point to, it is clear that the Andersons could have ordered the trust assets repatriated simply by certifying to the foreign trustee that in their opinion, as protectors, no event of duress had occurred.

in contempt. Given the nature of the Andersons' so-called "asset protection" trust, which was designed to frustrate the power of United States' courts to enforce judgments, there may be little else that a district court judge can do besides exercise its contempt powers to coerce people like the Andersons into removing the obstacles they placed in the way of a court. Given that the Andersons' trust is operating precisely as they intended, we are not overly sympathetic to their claims and would be hesitant to overly-restrict the district court's discretion, and thus legitimize what the Andersons have done.

AFFIRMED.

NOTES AND QUESTIONS

1. Suppose the Andersons had, in 1995, established an irrevocable domestic trust reserving income to themselves for life, and directing that the trust principal be paid to their children at the death of the survivor. Suppose further that the trust instrument named Chauncey Upright as trustee, and included a spendthrift provision. Could the Federal Trade Commission have reached the trust income or principal?

How did the creation of the Cook Islands trust improve the Andersons' position?

2. Why would the California courts—or the courts of any other state—hold that a trust created by a California resident, and funded with property accumulated in California, should be governed by Cook Islands law, when Cook Islands law would permit the California resident to avoid obligations to California creditors? For cases refusing to apply the law of a foreign country to trusts created by domestic settlors, see, e.g., Dexia Credit Local v. Rogan, 624 F.Supp.2d 970, aff'd 602 F.3d 879(7th Cir. 2010); In re Portnoy, 201 B.R. 685 (Bankr. S.D.N.Y.1996); In re Brooks, 217 B.R. 98 (Bankr. D. Conn. 1998). For an argument that U.S. courts should honor offshore trusts if certain conditions are met, see Richard C. Ausness, The Offshore Asset Protection Trust: A Prudent Financial Planning Device or the Last Refuge of a Scoundrel?, 45 Duq. L. Rev. 147 (2007).

Suppose a California court were to hold that any trust created by a California resident is, with respect to creditor claims, governed by the law of California. What effect would the court's holding have? Would California courts have power to enforce it? Does the difficulty of obtaining jurisdiction over property in a Cook Islands trust explain why the FTC sought, and the Affordable Media court imposed, contempt sanctions against the Andersons? Other courts have followed Affordable Media in imposing contempt sanctions. See S.E.C. v. Bilzerian, 112 F.Supp.2d 12 (D.D.C. 2000); In re Lawrence, 251 B.R. 630 (S.D.Fla. 2000).

3. What kinds of assets are best suited for offshore trusts? Would the settlor be better off transferring to the trust $1,000,000 in shares of a Fortune 500 company, or the deed to an apartment building worth $1,000,000? Why?

4. Suppose, after the Affordable Media decision, three months pass and the trustee still refuses to repatriate the trust assets. Can the district court continue to hold the Andersons in contempt? If not, how effective will contempt sanctions be as a weapon against settlors who create offshore trusts?

5. The Andersons were telemarketers who set up the trust before engaging in the Ponzi scheme discussed by the court. Suppose instead that Mrs. Anderson had been a physician who had established an offshore trust to avoid potential malpractice liability. Would the court's reaction have been the same?

Offshore trusts have been heavily marketed to physicians and other professionals as a protection against large potential jury awards.

6. In imposing contempt sanctions, the Anderson court used an indirect method to induce repatriation of offshore trust assets. Another indirect method involves withholding a discharge in bankruptcy from the trust settlor. Ordinarily, a debtor who seeks protection of the Bankruptcy Code obtains discharge of his debts. (11 U.S.C. § 727(a)). Several courts have denied discharge to settlors of offshore trusts, concluding that the settlor falls within one of the statute's exceptions. See, e.g. In re Lawrence, 227 B.R. 907 (Bankr. S.D.Fla. 1998); In re Portnoy, 201 B.R. 685 (Bankr. S.D.N.Y. 1996).

7. Trust Protectors. The Andersons' trust documents named the Andersons themselves as trust "protectors." More commonly, someone other than the settlor is named as a trust protector. What is a protector? Professor Danforth explains:

> [M]any offshore jurisdictions recognize the role of a "trust protector," a person granted special . . . to control the administration of the trust, with respect to such matters as removal and replacement of trustees, control over discretionary actions of the trustees, etc. By use of the trust protector mechanism, a settlor is able to vest in some trusted person substantial control over trust administration, while at the same time being able to resist the claim that the settlor himself or herself (whose actions will be subject to the authority of a United States court) retains such control. If the trust protector is a United States person (and thus subject to the authority of a United States court), the trust instrument will typically give the protector no affirmative powers, but only veto powers, with the consequence that a United States court will be unable to compel the protector to force administration of the trust in a certain manner.

Robert T. Danforth, Rethinking the Law of Creditors' Rights in Trusts, 53 Hastings L J 287, 309 (2002). See also Edward C. Halbach, Jr., Significant Trends in the Trust Law of the United States, 32 Vand. J. Transnat'l L 531 (1999).

In light of Professor Danforth's explanation, do you see why the Andersons erred in naming themselves as trust protectors?

Although trust protectors were originally created to facilitate off-shore asset protection, lawyers are increasingly naming trust protectors to police typical private express trusts. Ordinarily, the trust settlor will name a close friend, relative, accountant, or attorney as the protector. Trust protectors can be given a range of powers, including the power to veto or change trust distributions, correct trust errors, or move the trust's location. Protectors are often given the power to amend the trust in light of changed circumstances, such as changes in tax laws or the circumstances of particular beneficiaries.

The trust protector mechanism is not without risk. Because the concept is new, there is no background law to guide courts in dealing with conflicts that may arise between protectors and trustees, or protectors and beneficiaries. Moreover, it is unclear whether courts will find that trust protectors are fiduciaries, or just holders of discretionary powers. The first court to consider a breach of fiduciary duty claim by a beneficiary against a trust protector has held that trust protectors may assume fiduciary duties. See Robert T. McLean Irrevocable Trust v. Davis, 283 S.W.3d 786 (Mo. Ct. App. 2009) (reversing lower court's dismissal of beneficiary's claim against trust protector on grounds that trust beneficiary stated a claim by alleging that the settlor intended protector to function as a fiduciary, and that the protector failed to monitor trustees who squandered $500,000 of trust assets). Careful drafting is therefore a must.

For an analysis of potential problems, and how courts might resolve them, see Richard C. Ausness, The Role of Trust Protectors in American Trust Law, 45 Real Prop. Tr. & Est. L.J. 319 (2010); Stewart E. Sterk, Symposium: Trust Law in the 21st Century: Trust Protectors, Agency Costs, and Fiduciary Duty, 27 Cardozo L. Rev. 2761 (2006), Gregory S. Alexander, Symposium: Trust Law in the 21st Century: Trust Protectors: Who Will Watch the Watchmen? 27 Cardozo L. Rev. 2807 (2006); Jeffrey Evans Stake, Symposium: Trust Law in the 21st Century: A Brief Comment on Trust Protectors, 27 Cardozo L. Rev. 2813 (2006).

8. Some estate planners have argued that even if American creditors ultimately have the right to pierce offshore trusts, the trusts have considerable value to settlors because the practical difficulty of reaching trust assets will dissuade many creditors, or induce them to settle on terms favorable to the settlor/debtor. See, e.g. Gideon Rothschild and Daniel S. Rubin, Offshore Trusts—Onshore Litigation, 13 Prob. & Prop. 28 (1999); Barry Engel, Roundtable Discussion, 32 Vand J. Transnat'l L. 779, 785 (1999). If they are right, would you recommend offshore trusts to clients fearful of future liability? Consider the following:

U. S. Department of Justice

United States Attorney
Northern District of Illinois

Patrick J. Fitzgerald
United States Attorney

Federal Building
219 South Dearborn Street, Fifth Floor Chicago, Illinois 60604

FOR IMMEDIATE RELEASE
THURSDAY MAY 29, 2008
www.usdoj.gov/usao/iln

U.S. Charges Former Edgewater Hospital Owner Peter Rogan with Lying to Obstruct Government Efforts to Collect $64.2 Million Civil Health-Care Fraud Judgment; Defendant Detained in Canada

CHICAGO—The former owner and chief executive of the bankrupt Edgewater Hospital and Medical Center is facing federal perjury and obstruction of justice charges here relating to Government efforts to collect a $64.2 million civil health-care fraud judgment against him. The defendant, Peter G. Rogan, was charged in a two-count criminal complaint that was filed in U.S. District Court on May 23 and unsealed yesterday, Patrick J. Fitzgerald, United States Attorney for the Northern District of Illinois, and Robert D. Grant, Special Agent-in-Charge of the Chicago Office of the Federal Bureau of Investigation, announced today.

Rogan, 62, formerly of Valparaiso, Ind., who has been living in Vancouver, British Columbia, since 2006, was detained on Monday by the Canada Border Services Agency upon returning to Vancouver from a trip to China. Rogan was denied admission to Canada based on Canadian immigration law, and he is now facing Canadian immigration proceedings to determine whether or not he may be admitted into Canada.

Rogan at one time owned Edgewater Hospital and later sold it, but continued to control the hospital and medical center through various management companies he owned. The hospital, located at 5700 North Ashland, closed in December 2001 and entered bankruptcy in 2002, when four doctors, a vice president and the management company pleaded guilty to federal criminal health-care fraud charges involving the payment of kickbacks for patient referrals and medically unnecessary hospital admissions, tests, and services.

Rogan was not charged criminally at that time, but in 2002, the United States filed a civil lawsuit against him alleging that was responsible for

Edgewater's submission of millions of dollars of false claims for reimbursement under the Medicare and Medicaid programs, *United States v. Peter Rogan, et al.*, 02 C 3310 (N.D. Il.). In September 2006, following a bench trial, U.S. District Judge John Darrah entered a judgment against Rogan for $64,259,032.50, and found that Rogan had testified falsely, destroyed documents and obstructed justice, *United States v. Rogan*, 459 F. Supp.2d 692 (N.D. Il. 2006). The judgment was upheld on appeal earlier this year, *United States v. Rogan*, 517 F.3d 449 (7th Cir. 2008).

After the September 2006 judgment, the Government began efforts to collect from Rogan, using post-judgment procedures including depositions, citations and subpoenas to discover the nature, extent and location of any assets he owned or controlled. To date, Rogan has made no payments toward the debt, according to the new charges against him.

In late 2006, the Government filed a motion in the civil proceedings asserting that Rogan had access to many millions of dollars that were being held in offshore accounts. Specifically, court documents alleged that Rogan was the discretionary beneficiary of the Peter G. Rogan Irrevocable Trust, which was established in 1996 in the Bahamas. The Government alleged that there was between $30 and $35 million in this and other trusts in the names of his children, and that the trust in Rogan's name alone generated dividend and/or interest income of approximately $760,000 a year.

On Dec. 21, 2006, Rogan responded to the Government's motion by filing an affidavit with the Court in which he denied that he exercised any control over the trust and its income or assets, that he had no control over distributions from the trust, and that he did not have ready access to the assets of the trust. The new criminal charges allege that those statements were false, and that, in fact, Rogan controlled the trust and its income and assets, and that he had ready access to its funds.

According to the criminal complaint, in 2007 and 2008, Oceanic Bank and Trust Ltd., (Bahamas), which served as trustee of Rogan's trust until 2006, produced trust records to the Government in response to a subpoena. According to the records, the complaint alleges, between 1996 and 2004, Rogan directly or indirectly directed the trustee to make distributions totaling approximately $8.15 million to himself or to others he specified. Those distributions are detailed in the complaint affidavit—ranging in amounts from $50,000 to $3.4 million—and included funds that Rogan directed to be paid to his wife for personal expenses; for service and maintenance on his 48–foot boat named "Fringe Benefit;" for legal fees; and $2.9 million that he testified he used to pay restitution owed by Bainbridge Management L.P., resulting from its guilty plea in the Edgewater criminal fraud case.

Between July 2004 and November 2006, the new charges allege that Rogan's wife or agent—instead of Rogan himself—communicated directly with Oceanic to cause the distribution of at least $6.5 million in additional trust funds to accounts in his wife's name, which she then used to make payments to her husband and his creditors.

The United States is being represented by Assistant U.S. Attorneys Daniel Gillogly and Andrew Boutros.

If convicted, perjury carries a maximum penalty of five years in prison and obstruction of justice carries a maximum of 10 years, and both counts carry a maximum fine of $250,000. . . .

Domestic Asset Protection Trusts

Once it became clear that protection against creditors was so important to some wealthy people that they would go to the trouble and expense of creating trusts in the Cook Islands, or Jersey in the Channel Islands, or a variety of other offshore jurisdictions, legislators in some American states began to consider whether they might attract trust business by offering comparable protection closer to home. No American state has gone as far as the Cook Islands, but several states have authorized trusts in which the settlor can maintain a beneficial interest free from creditor claims. Alaska and Delaware were the pioneering states, but Nevada and Rhode Island were not far behind. Currently, about a dozen states have statutes authorizing self-settled asset protection trusts. So far, enthusiasm for asset protection trusts has been limited to lightly populated states—where most of the trust business is likely to come from out-of-state, and where most of the creditors left out in the cold will also be out-of-staters. See Stewart E. Sterk, Asset Protection Trusts: Trust Law's Race to the Bottom, 85 Cornell L. Rev. 1035, 1069 (2000). For an analysis of the early statutes, see Phyllis C. Smith, The Estate and Gift Tax Implications of Self–Settled Domestic Asset Protection Trusts: Can You Really Have Your Cake and Eat It Too?, 44 New Eng. L. Rev. 25 (2009); Karen E. Boxx, Gray's Ghost—A Conversation About the Onshore Trust, 85 Iowa L. Rev. 1195, 1204–08 (2000).

Because states' principal objective in enacting asset protection statutes was to attract trust business to state banking institutions, state statutory requirements for the creation of an asset protection trust are similar. Specifically, the trustee must either be an individual resident of the particular state, or a qualified trust or banking institution doing business in the state. The statutes require that the trustee have some administrative duties, such as keeping records or filing tax returns, and the settlor must physically locate some of the trust assets within the state. Although the key feature of the asset protection trust is the settlor's ostensible surrender of control over the trust assets, in reality a settlor may retain a significant degree of control.

Examine the relevant provisions of the Delaware Asset Protection Statute:

12 Del. C. § 3570. Definitions

As used in this subchapter:

* * *

(4) "Disposition" means a transfer, conveyance or assignment of property ... or the exercise of a power so as to cause a transfer of property, to a trustee or trustees, ...

* * *

(6) "Qualified disposition" means a disposition by or from a transferor to a qualified trustee or qualified trustees, with or without consideration, by means of a trust instrument.

* * *

(9) "Qualified trustee" means a person who:

a. In the case of a natural person, is a resident of this State other than the transferor or, in all other cases, is authorized by the law of this State to act as a trustee and whose activities are subject to supervision by the Bank Commissioner of the State, the Federal Deposit Insurance Corporation, the Comptroller of the Currency, or the Office of Thrift Supervision or any successor thereto; and

b. Maintains or arranges for custody in this State of some or all of the property that is the subject of the qualified disposition, maintains records for the trust on an exclusive or nonexclusive basis, prepares or arranges for the preparation of fiduciary income tax returns for the trust, or otherwise materially participates in the administration of the trust.

c. For purposes of this subchapter, neither the transferor nor any other natural person who is a nonresident of this State nor an entity that is not authorized by the law of this State to act as a trustee or whose activities are not subject to supervision as provided in paragraph a. of this subsection shall be considered a qualified trustee; however, nothing in this subchapter shall preclude a transferor from appointing one or more advisers, including but not limited to:

1. Advisers who have authority under the terms of the trust instrument to remove and appoint qualified trustees or trust advisers;

2. Advisers who have authority under the terms of the trust instrument to direct, consent to or disapprove distributions from the trust; and

3. Advisers described in § 3313 of this title, whether or not such advisers would meet the requirements imposed by paragraphs a. and b. of this subsection.

For purposes of this subsection, the term "adviser" includes a trust "protector" or any other person who, in addition to a qualified trustee, holds 1 or more trust powers.

d. A person may serve as an investment adviser described in § 3313 of this title, notwithstanding that such person is the transferor of the qualified disposition, but such a person may not otherwise serve as adviser of a trust that is a qualified disposition except with respect to the retention of the veto right permitted by subsection (10)b. of this section.

* * *

f. In the case of a disposition to more than 1 trustee, a disposition that is otherwise a qualified disposition shall not be treated as other than a qualified disposition solely because not all of the trustees are qualified trustees.

(10) "Trust instrument" means an instrument appointing a qualified trustee or qualified trustees for the property that is the subject of a disposition, which instrument:

a. Expressly incorporates the law of this State to govern the validity, construction and administration of the trust;

b. Is irrevocable, but a trust instrument shall not be deemed revocable on account of its inclusion of 1 or more of the following:

1. A transferor's power to veto a distribution from the trust;

2. A power of appointment (other than a power to appoint to the transferor, the transferor's creditors, the transferor's estate or the creditors of the transferor's estate) exercisable by will or other written instrument of the transferor effective only upon the transferor's death;

3. The transferor's potential or actual receipt of income, including rights to such income retained in the trust instrument;

* * *

5. The transferor's receipt each year of a percentage (not to exceed 5) specified in the trust instrument of the initial value of the trust assets or their value determined from time to time pursuant to the trust instrument or of a fixed amount that on an annual basis does not exceed 5% of the initial value of the trust assets;

6. The transferor's potential or actual receipt or use of principal if such potential or actual receipt or use of principal would be the result of a qualified trustee's or qualified trustees' acting:

A. In such qualified trustee's or qualified trustees' discretion;

B. Pursuant to a standard that governs the distribution of principal and does not confer upon the transferor a substantially unfettered right to the receipt or use of the principal; or

C. At the direction of an adviser described in paragraph (9)c. of this section who is acting:

I. In such adviser's discretion; or

II. Pursuant to a standard that governs the distribution of principal and does not confer upon the transferor a substantially unfettered right to the receipt of or use of principal. For purposes of this paragraph, a qualified trustee is presumed to have discretion with respect to the distribution of principal unless such discretion is expressly denied to such trustee by the terms of the trust instrument.

7. The transferor's right to remove a trustee or adviser and to appoint a new trustee or adviser (other than a person who is a related or subordinate party with respect to the transferor within the meaning of § 672(c) of the Internal Revenue Code of 1986 [26 U.S.C. § 672(c)] and any successor provision thereto);

8. The transferor's potential or actual use of real property held under a qualified personal residence trust within the meaning of such term as described in § 2702(c) of the Internal Revenue Code of 1986

[26 U.S.C. § 2702(c)] and any successor provision thereto or the transferor's possession and enjoyment of a qualified annuity interest within the meaning of such term as described in Treasury Regulation § 25.2702–5(c)(8) [26 C.F.R. 25.2702–5(c)(8)] and any successor provision thereto;

* * *

c. Provides that the interest of the transferor or other beneficiary in the trust property or the income therefrom may not be transferred, assigned, pledged or mortgaged, whether voluntarily or involuntarily, before the qualified trustee or qualified trustees actually distribute the property or income therefrom to the beneficiary, and such provision of the trust instrument shall be deemed to be a restriction on the transfer of the transferor's beneficial interest in the trust that is enforceable under applicable nonbankruptcy law within the meaning of § 541(c)(2) of the Bankruptcy Code (11 U.S.C. § 541(c)(2)) or any successor provision thereto.

* * *

12 Del. C. § 3572. Avoidance of qualified dispositions

(a) Notwithstanding any other provision of this Code, no action of any kind, including, without limitation, an action to enforce a judgment entered by a court or other body having adjudicative authority, shall be brought at law or in equity for an attachment or other provisional remedy against property that is the subject of a qualified disposition or for avoidance of a qualified disposition unless such action shall be brought pursuant to the provisions of § 1304 or § 1305 of Title 6. The Court of Chancery shall have exclusive jurisdiction over any action brought with respect to a qualified disposition.

(b) A creditor's claim under subsection (a) of this section shall be extinguished unless:

(1) The creditor's claim arose before the qualified disposition was made, and the action is brought within the limitations of § 1309 of Title 6 in effect on the later of the date of the qualified disposition or August 1, 2000; or

(2) Notwithstanding the provisions of § 1309 of Title 6, the creditor's claim arose concurrent with or subsequent to the qualified disposition and the action is brought within 4 years after the qualified disposition is made.

In any action described in subsection (a) of this section, the burden to prove the matter by clear and convincing evidence shall be upon the creditor.

* * *

(d) Notwithstanding any law to the contrary, a creditor, including a creditor whose claim arose before or after a qualified disposition, or any other person shall have only such rights with respect to a qualified disposition as are provided in this section and §§ 3573 and 3574 of this title, and no such creditor nor any other person shall have any claim or cause of action against the trustee, or advisor described in § 3570(9)c of this title, of a trust that is the subject of a qualified disposition, or against any person involved in the counseling, drafting, preparation, execution or funding of a trust that is the subject of a qualified disposition.

* * *

(g) If, in any action brought against a trustee of a trust that is the result of a qualified disposition, a court takes any action whereby such court declines to apply the law of this State in determining the validity, construction or administration of such trust, or the effect of a spendthrift provision thereof, such trustee shall immediately upon such court's action and without the further order of any court, cease in all respects to be trustee of such trust and a successor trustee shall thereupon succeed as trustee in accordance with the terms of the trust instrument or, if the trust instrument does not provide for a successor trustee and the trust would otherwise be without a trustee, the Court of Chancery, upon the application of any beneficiary of such trust, shall appoint a successor trustee upon such terms and conditions as it determines to be consistent with the purposes of such trust and this statute. Upon such trustee's ceasing to be trustee, such trustee shall have no power or authority other than to convey the trust property to the successor trustee named in the trust instrument or appointed by the Court of Chancery in accordance with this section.

* * *

12 Del. C. § 3573. Limitations on qualified dispositions

With respect to the limitations imposed by § 3572 of this title, those limitations on actions by creditors to avoid a qualified disposition shall not apply:

(1) To any person to whom the transferor is indebted on account of an agreement or order of court for the payment of support or alimony in favor of such transferor's spouse, former spouse or children, or for a division or distribution of property in favor of such transferor's spouse or former spouse, but only to the extent of such debt; or

(2) To any person who suffers death, personal injury or property damage on or before the date of a qualified disposition by a transferor, which death, personal injury or property damage is at any time determined to have been caused in whole or in part by the tortious act or omission of either such transferor or by another person for whom such transferor is or was vicariously liable but only to the extent of such claim against such transferor or other person for whom such transferor is or was vicariously liable.

12 Del. C. § 3574. Effect of avoidance of qualified dispositions

(a) A qualified disposition shall be avoided only to the extent necessary to satisfy the transferor's debt to the creditor at whose instance the disposition had been avoided, together with such costs, including attorneys' fees, as the court may allow.

* * *

(d) For purposes of this subchapter, attachment, garnishment, sequestration, or other legal or equitable process shall be permitted only in those circumstances permitted by the express terms of this subchapter.

* * *

PROBLEMS

Your client, Dr. Amanda Ames, an oncologist, is a resident of New York. She is divorced and has one child, age 4. Dr. Ames has consulted you because she recently read an article that recommended that doctors place their assets in asset protection trusts to guard against potential malpractice liability and other types of creditor claims. Because New York law does not recognize or enforce self-settled spendthrift trusts, Dr. Ames inquires whether she can shield her assets by taking advantage of the Delaware asset protection statute.

1. Suppose that Dr. Ames wants to create a Delaware asset protection trust (aka a "self-settled spendthrift trust"). She desires to have as much access to and control over the trust property as possible during her life, and wants the trust property to be distributed to her daughter at her death. Assume you decide that creation of a Delaware asset protection trust is in Dr. Ames's best interests, and you agree to create one for her (in accordance with ethical standards).

a. What key provisions should the trust document contain to ensure that it qualifies as a Delaware asset protection trust?

b. Dr. Ames wishes to retain as much control as possible over the trust property. Will inclusion of any of the following provisions deny Dr. Ames the protection afforded by the Delaware statute?

(1) The trust instrument names Dr. Ames as sole trustee.

(2) The trust instrument requires the trustee to distribute all trust income to Dr. Ames on a quarterly basis.

(3) The trust instrument directs the trustee to distribute such amounts of the trust principal to Dr. Ames as she, from time to time, requests in writing.

c. What additional provisions might the trust contain to ensure that Dr. Ames has access to trust principal when she needs it?

d. What provisions should the trust contain to maximize Dr. Ames' ability to control the investment of trust assets?

e. May Dr. Ames transfer title to her New York home to the trustee of her trust? If so, will Dr. Ames' New York home be protected from most creditors if she continues to live in it?

2. Suppose that on December 1, 2007, Dr. Ames creates a trust that complies with the terms of the Delaware statute, and that she transfers all but $50,000 of her assets to the trust. Soon thereafter, First National Bank files suit in a Delaware court, seeking to attach Dr. Ames's trust assets to satisfy a New York judgment that the bank obtained in November of 2006. The basis for the judgment was Dr. Ames' default on $100,000 of credit card debt.

a. Can the Bank attach the trust assets as necessary to satisfy its judgment? To answer this question, you will also need to consider the following Delaware statute:

6 Del. C. § 1304. Transfers fraudulent as to present and future creditors

(a) A transfer made or obligation incurred by a debtor is fraudulent as to a creditor, whether the creditor's claim arose before or after the transfer was made or the obligation was incurred, if the debtor made the transfer or incurred the obligation:

(1) With actual intent to hinder, delay or defraud any creditor of the debtor; or

(2) Without receiving a reasonably equivalent value in exchange for the transfer or obligation, and the debtor:

a. Was engaged or was about to engage in a business or a transaction for which the remaining assets of the debtor were unreasonably small in relation to the business or transaction; or

b. Intended to incur, or believed or reasonably should have believed that the debtor would incur, debts beyond the debtor's ability to pay as they became due.

(b) In determining actual intent under subsection (a)(1), consideration may be given, among other factors, to whether:

(1) The transfer or obligation was to an insider;

(2) The debtor retained possession or control of the property transferred after the transfer;

(3) The transfer or obligation was disclosed or concealed;

(4) Before the transfer was made or obligation was incurred, the debtor had been sued or threatened with suit;

(5) The transfer was of substantially all the debtor's assets;

(6) The debtor absconded;

(7) The debtor removed or concealed assets;

(8) The value of the consideration received by the debtor was reasonably equivalent to the value of the asset transferred or the amount of the obligation incurred;

(9) The debtor was insolvent or became insolvent shortly after the transfer was made or the obligation was incurred;

(10) The transfer occurred shortly before or shortly after a substantial debt was incurred; and

(11) The debtor transferred the essential assets of the business to a lienor who transferred the assets to an insider of the debtor.

* * *

b. It is unethical for an attorney to assist a client in violating the law. In light of your answer to problem 2a, what questions would you ask a client who wants to create an asset protection trust? See Henry J. Lischer, Jr., Professional Responsibility Issues Associated With Asset Protection Trusts, 39 Real Prop., Prob. & Tr. J. 561 (2004).

c. Suppose Dr. Ames' ex-husband obtains a judgment against Dr. Ames for two year's worth of unpaid alimony. Can he attach the trust assets?

d. Suppose Martha Stewart, a (former) close friend of Dr. Ames, successfully sues the doctor for personal injuries she sustained in Dr. Ames' home in January of 2008. If Martha seeks to enforce her judgment against the trust in a Delaware court, will she succeed?

NOTES AND QUESTIONS

1. Suppose the Bank described in Problem 2 sought to enforce its judgment against the trust in a New York court. Suppose further that the bank could not establish that Dr. Ames' transfer of her property to the trust was fraudulent. Would a New York court apply Delaware law and enforce the spendthrift provision? The issue remains unresolved. The courts of states that do not recognize asset protection trusts, and the federal bankruptcy courts, may as a choice-of-law matter apply the law of the trust settlor's domicile to invalidate asset protection provisions in out-of-state trusts. See Randall J. Gingiss, Putting a Stop to Asset Protection Trusts, 51 Baylor L. Rev. 987, 1013–18 (1999). A number of courts have already taken this approach with respect to offshore trusts. See, e.g., In re Portnoy, 201 B.R. 685 (Bankr.S.D.N.Y.1996); In re Brooks, 217 B.R. 98 (Bankr.D.Conn.1998). If courts take the same approach with domestic asset protection trusts, the full faith and credit clause of the federal constitution would require Delaware (or any other state in which settlor has created an asset protection trust) to recognize a judgment in favor of the settlor's creditors. Such a conclusion would, of course, undermine the value of a domestic asset protection trust.

On the other hand, if states offering domestic asset protection trusts begin to capture much of the country's trust business, larger states may begin to compete by abolishing their long-standing prohibition on self-settled spendthrift trusts.

2. Is there anything wrong with self-settled spendthrift trusts? Professor Adam Hirsch writes:

> It bears noticing that in a variety of contexts lawmakers already allow persons unilaterally to enhance their financial security by insulating a portion of their assets from creditors' claims. If an individual engages in commercial activity, of course, she can protect nonbusiness assets from business creditors by incorporating, or by forming a limited partnership or a limited liability company. Within limits set by the law of fraudulent conveyances, individuals can also protect assets from nonbusiness creditors by converting them into exempt property, by conveying separate property into a tenancy by the entirety, or by making voluntary contributions to an ERISA-qualified pension plan. In the wake of these venerable contrivances, the prohibition against self-settled spendthrift trusts appears all the more unthematic.

Adam J. Hirsch, Spendthrift Trusts and Public Policy: Economic and Cognitive Perspectives, 73 Wash. U. L.Q. 1, 91–92 (1995). See also, Adam J. Hirsch, Symposium: Trust Law in the 21st Century: Fear Not the Asset Protection Trust, 27 Cardozo L. Rev. 2685 (2006). Are you persuaded?

The changing landscape has stimulated some to consider whether the traditional approach to self-settled trusts has been too generous toward creditors. Professor Robert Danforth has argued that when the settlor's interest in the trust is discretionary, the settlor's creditors ought not to be entitled to reach that interest, at least when the trustee enjoys independence from the settlor. He argues that the when the settlor has created an irrevocable discretionary trust, the settlor's creditors should generally have no more right to compel payment than the settlor would have. And, he argues, the trustee's fiduciary duties limit the settlor's right to demand payment. See Robert T. Danforth, Rethinking the Law of Creditors' Rights in Trusts, 53 Hastings L. J. 287, 348–60 (2002). Professor Danforth, concedes, however, that limits on asset protection trusts (APTs) remain important:

> APTs should be respected only in those circumstances in which there are legitimate limitations on the settlor's access to trust assets. To curtail excessive distributions to the settlor, one option would be to place a ceiling on distributions, by reference to a standard—such as one for the settlor's health, support, and education. Another option would be to require that the trust have multiple beneficiaries (both during the settlor's lifetime and after the settlor's death), so that the trustee is accountable to persons other than the settlor, whose interests would be financially adverse to the settlor's interest. To take this concept one step further, APT legislation could require that distributions to the settlor be made by an independent trustee and also require the consent of a person with a substantial adverse beneficial interest.

Id. at 365–66.

3. Do asset protection trusts put trustees at risk? As Erin Bailey explains:

> The orthodox rule is that trusts are not legal entities that can be sued in their own right. This reality traditionally forced claimants to sue the trustee in its *personal* capacity, compelling the trustee to then seek reimbursement (indemnification) from trust assets for any resulting *personal liability*. Asset protection trusts purpose to protect a settlor's assets from creditors—good news for the settlor but potentially bad news if the unwary trustee is sued in its personal capacity and the asset protection trust shields the trustee from its entitled reimbursement. It is not known whether courts will respect the asset protection objective or if they do, leave trustees holding the proverbial bag. * * *

See Erin C. V. Bailey, *Asset Protection Trusts Protect the Assets But What About the Trustees?*, Prob. & Prop. 58 (Jan./Feb. 2007).

4. Neither the UTC nor the Restatement (Third) of Trusts authorize self-settled spendthrift trusts.

Professor John Eason has written important articles on in-depth issues raised by asset protection trusts. See John K. Eason, Symposium: Trust Law in the 21st Century: Policy, Logic and Persuasion in the Evolving Realm of Trust Asset Protection, 27 Cardozo L. Rev. 2621 (2006); John K. Eason, Retirement Security Through Asset Protection: The Evolution of Wealth, Privilege, and Policy, 61 Wash & Lee L. Rev. 159 (2004); John K. Eason, Developing the Asset Protection Dynamic: A Legacy of Federal Concern, 31 Hofstra L. Rev. 23 (2002); John K. Eason, Home From the Islands: Domestic Asset Protection Trust Alternatives Impact Traditional Estate and Gift Tax Planning Considerations, 52 Fla. L. Rev. 41, 73–100 (2000).

5. The IRS recently issued a private letter ruling that asset protection trusts that are valid under applicable state law are not includable in the settlor's gross estate. See Ltr. Rul. 200944002. For an argument that these trusts should be includable in the settlor's taxable estate because the settlor retains control over the assets, see Phyllis C. Smith, The Estate and Gift Tax Implications of Self-Settled Domestic Asset Protection Trusts: Can You Really Have Your Cake and Eat It Too?, 44 New Eng. L. Rev. 25 (2009).

E. PLANNING FOR INCAPACITY AND/OR THE COSTS OF INSTITUTIONAL CARE

1. PLANNING FOR INCAPACITY WITH REVOCABLE LIVING TRUSTS

A revocable trust can facilitate planning for old age. An elderly settlor can name a professional fiduciary trustee and delegate management of the assets to the trustee for as long as the trust endures. If the settlor prefers to retain control over her assets for as long as possible, she may name herself trustee, and provide for a successor trustee to assume control if and when the settlor becomes incompetent. Needless to say, a well drafted instrument should provide a standard for determining when incompetency occurs so as to avoid the prospect of litigation down the line. Revocable trusts eliminate the need for a durable power of attorney, although well drafted estate plans usually have both. Durable powers of attorney are discussed in Chapter 11, *infra.*

QUESTIONS

1. In Westerfeld v. Huckaby, 474 S.W.2d 189 (Tex. 1971), the settlor attempted to provide for incapacity through the following language:

> In the event of my death or legal incapacity, I hereby nominate and appoint as SUCCESSOR TRUSTEE: Arthur L. Huckaby—1717 Dowling Street Houston Harris County, Texas to be Successor Trustee.

Is this language sufficient to ensure a smooth transition in the event the settlor becomes incapacitated? How would you improve upon it?

2. Re-examine some excerpts from the sample revocable living trust, *supra:*

> [From Article 2C]:
>
> Incapacity of the Settlor. If at any time, either in the Trustee's discretion or as certified in writing by the licensed physician having responsibility for Settlor's care and treatment, the Settlor has become physically or mentally incapacitated, whether or not a court of competent jurisdiction has declared her incompetent, mentally ill or in need of a conservator, the Trustee shall pay for the account of or for the benefit of the Settlor the amounts of income and principal necessary in the Trustee's discretion for the proper health, support, comfort, enjoyment and welfare of the Settlor until the incapacitated Settlor, either in the Trustee's discretion or as certified by a licensed physician, is again able to manage her own affairs, or until the Settlor's death.
>
> [From Article 4A]:
>
> Successor Trustee. If the Settlor should die, resign, become mentally incapacitated (as defined by Article Two C, herein), or otherwise become unwilling or unable to act as Trustee, then Settlor's son, Melvin James, shall act as successor Trustee. If Melvin James should for any reason fail to qualify or cease to act as Trustee, then Settlor's daughter, Sally James, shall act as successor trustee. Each person designated or acting as Trustee hereunder shall have the power to designate one or more successor trustee to act when he or she becomes unable or unwilling to act as Trustee. If both Melvin James and Sally James shall fail to qualify or cease to act as Trustee, then the person(s) so designated shall act as successor Trustee, with the preference given first to successors designated by

Melvin James, then those designated by Sally James, and finally, then those designated by any such designee while acting as Trustee.

Does the language provide for a smooth transition in the event of the settlor's incapacity? How is it different than the language in Westerfeld v. Huckaby?

2. PLANNING INVOLVING GOVERNMENT HEALTH AND MEDICAL BENEFITS

Often, the costs of caring for an incapacitated person far exceed a family's resources. Even those families fortunate enough to have accumulated significant assets can deplete those funds to care for an incapacitated family member. For that reason, incapacitated people often apply for and receive financial assistance through a variety of government programs, chief among them Medicaid, a federal program that pays medical costs for indigent people. Although Medicaid is a federal program, it is administered through the states, and states impose their own qualifying thresholds and rules governing eligibility. To qualify for Medicaid or other state benefits, an applicant must show that his or her income and assets are below the state maximum threshold. Thus, families must often "spend down" their assets to qualify. But "spending down" can, by definition, leave healthy family members impoverished. In addition, the incapacitated person may end up receiving the lowest quality care.

The law in this area is quite complicated, and a thorough understanding of Medicaid and state welfare benefits must be saved for an elder law course. Our goal is to highlight ways in which families can (and cannot) use the trust mechanism to qualify for government benefits while preserving some assets to supplement care for the disabled family member or to avoid impoverishing the entire family.

a. Support/Discretionary Trusts Created by Someone Other Than the Beneficiary

Bethany, a thirty-year old woman, is the beneficiary of a discretionary support trust established by her grandmother many years ago. Bethany becomes incapacitated as a result of an accident, and she requires permanent institutional care. Her parents, as her guardians, apply for state medical aid on her behalf. Because Bethany has not been able to work for the six months since her accident, she has no income and minimal assets. The trust principal has a current value of $500,000. Will the state consider the trust principal an "available asset" in determining whether Bethany qualifies for government benefits? Consider the following materials:

Estate of Gist

Supreme Court of Iowa 2009.
763 N.W.2d 561.

■ WIGGINS, J.

We must decide whether the district court correctly allowed the State to enforce its Title XIX lien against a trust containing a spendthrift clause. Because we find the trust is a discretionary trust with standards, we conclude our common law allows the State to recover its lien for necessities supplied to the beneficiary from the trust, in spite of the spendthrift provision. We also conclude the lack of symmetry between Medicaid's eligibility requirements and Medicaid's ability to recover from an estate does not preclude recovery. Therefore, we affirm the decision of the district court.

In 1974, Alice and Glenn Pirie signed a joint will leaving all assets to the surviving spouse. If at the time of death there was not a surviving spouse, the property was to go to their daughter Elenore Gist, in trust for her lifetime. After Elenore's death, the assets would go to Glenn and Alice Pirie's granddaughters, Susan Eral and Colleen Conrad f/k/a Susan and Colleen Gist. In May 1982, after the death of Glenn Pirie, Alice Pirie signed a codicil to the will appointing Elenore's daughters, Conrad and Eral as trustees for the testamentary trust.

Conrad and Eral assumed their role as trustees on August 15, 1983, after the death of Alice Pirie. Elenore Gist was forty-seven years old at the time. Elenore began receiving Title XIX benefits under the Iowa medical assistance program in 1995. She continued receiving those benefits until her death on July 19, 2006.

By January 31, 2007, Conrad and Eral completed the final report and accounting for the Elenore Gist Trust. The court set the date for the hearing on that final report for March 12, 2007. On March 6, the Iowa Department of Human Services filed a claim in probate court against the trust for the amounts it paid under Title XIX. The department also filed an objection to the final report of the trust claiming the final report failed to provide the department reimbursement for the monies it paid to Elenore under Title XIX. The department claimed Gist owed $396,570.20 to the State for services she received under Title XIX. By March 9, Eral and Conrad had filed an amended denial of the claim.

The district court ruled on the claim and objection and found the trust was a discretionary support trust set up for Elenore Gist and as such, it should be used to repay her Title XIX debt. Eral and Conrad appeal.

In this appeal, we must decide whether the district court erred in finding the testamentary trust created for Elenore Gist was subject to Gist's Title XIX medical assistance debt. If we determine that the trust is subject to the debt, we must then determine whether the trust's identification as a spendthrift trust defeats the State's claim for reimbursement. Finally, we must decide whether the lack of symmetry between Medicaid's eligibility requirements and Medicaid's ability to recover from an estate precludes the State from recovery.

* * *

The relevant provisions of the Piries' will creating the trust for Elenore are as follows:

> The trustee shall pay to Elenore for so long as she shall live at quarterly intervals, or more often the income from the trust assets or so much thereof as may be necessary to provide her with a reasonable standard of living, considering any other means of support or resources which she may have. If the income shall be insufficient to provide her with a reasonable standard of living the trustee may invade the principal or corpus of the trust assets. While provision is hereinafter made for the disposition of any trust assets which may remain at Elenore's death it shall not be an objective of this trust to preserve the trust estate intact for the remaindermen beneficiaries nor to deny Elenore a reasonable standard of living for the purpose of enhancing the value of the trust estate or even preserving it for the benefit of the beneficiaries. The discretion of the trustees shall therefore extend to disbursing the whole of the trust estate for Elenore's benefit during her lifetime but, if possible, the trustee shall make provision for her burial expenses.
>
> * * *
>
> All assets of the trust and the income therefrom shall be free from the claims of any and all creditors of the beneficiaries thereof and shall not be used for the payment of their debts or obligations except as may be necessary to carry out the purposes of the trust. No beneficiary shall have any power or right to assign, sell, pledge, hypothecate or in any other manner deal with the trust property. All restrictions herein contained shall apply equally to include every person having a claim against, or making a demand against the beneficiaries whether such claim or demand is imposed by law or otherwise, except that lawful taxes may be collected from the trust assets to the extent permitted by law.

The last paragraph of the quoted language is a spendthrift provision.

The State claims Iowa Code section 249A.5 allows it to recover from the estate the monies it paid on Elenore's behalf under Title XIX. Section 249A.5 provides:

> The provision of medical assistance to an individual who is fifty-five years of age or older, or who is a resident of a nursing facility, intermediate care facility for persons with mental retardation, or mental health institute, who cannot reasonably be expected to be discharged and return to the individual's home, creates a debt due the department from the individual's estate for all medical assistance provided on the individual's behalf, upon the individual's death.

Iowa Code § 249A.5(2) (2005). The Code defines "estate" under chapter 249A as property in which a recipient has "any legal title or interest at the time of the recipient's ... death, to the extent of such interests, including but not limited to interests in jointly held property, retained life estates, and interests in trusts." *Id.* § 249A.5(2)(*c*). Iowa adopted this recovery statute in 1994. 1994 Iowa Acts ch. 1120, § 10 (codified at Iowa Code § 249A.5(2) (1995)). The assets included within the expansive definition of "estate" are subject to probate. Iowa Code § 249A.5(2)(*d*); *see also In re Estate of Serovy,* 711 N.W.2d 290, 293–94 (Iowa 2006) (holding the estate included assets held in joint tenancy and allowing for recovery of those assets).

* * *

The trust agreement created by the joint will of the Piries gave the trustee the discretion to distribute the income of the trust to Elenore "as may be necessary to provide her with a reasonable standard of living, considering any other means of support or resources which she may have." The trust gave the trustee the discretion to invade the principal or corpus to provide her with a reasonable standard of living. The trust did not limit the principal and corpus payments to the mere support of Elenore, but allowed those payments to provide her with a reasonable standard of living. This language created a discretionary trust with standards.

We have stated that for purposes of section 249A.5(2)(*c*) a beneficiary has an "interest" in a trust to the extent the assets are available to the trust beneficiary. *Id.* at 55. In a discretionary trust with standards, the beneficiary has the right to require the trustee to pay him the amount, which in the exercise of reasonable discretion is needed to support him. *Id.* at 54. Additionally, the beneficiary may transfer his interest and a creditor may reach it. *Id.* Accordingly, a beneficiary's interest in the discretionary trust with standards is the kind of interest encompassed by section 249A.5(2)(*c*). Therefore, Elenore's interest in the trust is the kind of interest encompassed by section 249A.5(2)(*c*), unless the spendthrift clause of the trust precludes the State from reaching that interest.

* * *

Having determined the Gist Trust is the type of trust from which the State is entitled to reimbursement for its Title XIX claim, we must determine whether the spendthrift clause protects the assets of the trust. The trustees argue that the Iowa Trust Code's provisions on spendthrift trusts prevent the State from seeking reimbursement from the trust on its Title XIX lien ..... The trustees cite Iowa Trust Code sections 633A.2301 and 633A.2302, which provide in relevant part:

633A.2301. Spendthrift protection recognized

Except as otherwise provided in section 633A.2302, all of the following provisions shall apply:

1. A term of a trust providing that the interest of a beneficiary is held subject to a "spendthrift trust", or words of similar import, is sufficient to restrain both voluntary and involuntary transfers of the beneficiary's interest.

...

4. A creditor or assignee of a beneficiary of a spendthrift trust may not compel a distribution that is subject to the trustee's discretion despite the fact that:

   a. The distribution is expressed in the form of a standard of distribution.

   b. The trustee has abused its discretion.

Iowa Code § 633A.2301.

633A.2302. Exception to spendthrift protection

A term of a trust prohibiting an involuntary transfer of a beneficiary's interest shall be invalid as against claims by any creditor of the beneficiary if the beneficiary is the settlor.

Id. § 633A.2302.

On its face, these sections of the Iowa Trust Code appear to end the analysis because the Code does not contain an exception to the spendthrift protection in the trust for services or supplies provided for necessities. *See* Restatement (Third) of Trusts § 59(b) (2003) (providing an exception to a spendthrift provision in a trust for "services or supplies provided for necessities"). However, our analysis must continue based on section 633A.1104 of the Iowa Trust Code, which provides, "[e]xcept to the extent that this chapter modifies the common law governing trusts, the common law of trusts shall supplement this trust code." Iowa Code § 633A.1104.

Our common law does have an exception to a spendthrift provision for services or supplies provided for necessities. *In re Estate of Dodge,* 281 N.W.2d 447, 451–52 (Iowa 1979). There we held a creditor's claim may be enforced against the trustee of a support trust subject to a spendthrift clause if (1) the claim is for necessary goods or services, not officiously rendered, which the settlor intended to provide the beneficiary through trust funds; and (2) the withholding of payment for the goods and services is not properly within the discretion granted the trustee by the trust instrument. *Id.* at 451.

The Iowa Trust Code is silent as to a necessity exception. Sections 633A.2301 and 633A.2302 do not provide that its exceptions are exclusive. As section 633A.1104 clearly establishes, the common law of trusts shall supplement the trust code. Our common law has recognized a necessity exception since 1979. Accordingly, the common law necessity exception in *Dodge* still applies notwithstanding enactment of the Iowa Trust Code. *See* Martin D. Begleiter, *In the Code We Trust–Some Trust Law for Iowa at Last,* 49 Drake L.Rev. 165, 210–11 (2001) (opining that section 633A.1104 retains the necessity exception).

Applying the exception as set forth in *Dodge,* the State provided Elenore with necessary goods or services. The settlor of the trust intended for the trust to provide a reasonable standard of living for Elenore, which includes the goods and services provided by the State. Additionally, because this was a discretionary trust with standards, the withholding of payment for the goods and services was not properly within the discretion granted the trustee by the instrument. *Barkema,* 690 N.W.2d at 54. Therefore, the spendthrift provision of the trust does not prevent the State from collecting its Title XIX lien.

The final argument made by the trustees to prevent the State from enforcing its Title XIX lien is that there should be symmetry between the determination of whether an asset is available during the lifetime of the beneficiary for Medicaid eligibility purposes and the determination made for estate recovery purposes of whether an asset is included in the decedent's estate under Iowa Code section 249A.5. In other words, if an asset does not make a person ineligible for Medicaid, that asset should not be used to reimburse the State for its Medicaid payments.

The trustees claim it is unfair not to have symmetry. Whether there should be symmetry between the eligibility for Medicaid and the recovery allowed by the State under section 249A.5 is not a decision for this court. That is a policy decision to be made by the legislature, the branch of government responsible for enacting the laws governing Medicaid. Moreover, there are valid reasons for this policy decision.

By not requiring a person to spend all of his or her assets in order to be eligible for Medicaid, the legislature has allowed the recipient to use his or her funds for items not covered by Medicaid. Although the legislature could have just as easily required a recipient to spend all assets before being eligible for Medicaid, that requirement would create a significant hardship on Iowa families because Medicaid does not cover one hundred percent of a person's expenses. The legislature took a more humanitarian approach by allowing recipients to keep certain assets to pay for items not covered by Medicaid. To the extent such assets are not exhausted at the time of the recipient's death, however, the legislature allows the State to recoup its payments from those assets. As a court, we defer to the legislature on these matters. Consequently, the lack of symmetry is not a reason for us to hold the State is not entitled to reimbursement of its Title XIX lien.

* * *

AFFIRMED.

QUESTIONS

1. Did the trustee of Elenore's trust have a duty to pay for Elenore's medical expenses? If so, why weren't the trust assets an available resource for Medicaid qualification purposes?

2. Did Iowa Code section 249A.5 explicitly give the state the power to seek reimbursement from the assets held in a spendthrift trust? If not, does the Iowa Trust Code allow support creditors to attach assets held in a spendthrift trust? How does the court justify its decision?

3. Not all states consider discretionary support trusts (with or without spendthrift clauses) "unavailable" for Medicaid eligibility purposes. Many states consider such assets "available," while others hold that the question whether trust assets are available turns on the trust settlor's intent. See, DeBone v. Department of Public Welfare, 929 A.2d 1219 (Pa. Cmwlth. Ct. 2007) (finding that testator "intended" the assets of a discretionary support spendthrift trust to be available because applicant was the only income beneficiary and the trust was created largely for tax reasons).

Supplemental Needs Trusts

A supplemental needs trust provides the beneficiary with comforts and additional medical support that he or she would not be entitled to have if she depended entirely on government assistance. If the trust is properly drafted, the trust principal will not be counted as an "available" resource for Medicaid, social security and other government benefits.

To qualify as a valid supplemental needs trust, the trust instrument must be funded with assets of someone other than the beneficiary herself. The trust document should prevent the trustee from paying for the beneficiary's basic support needs, and must expressly state that the trust's purpose is to provide care that supplements specific government benefits to which the beneficiary is entitled. The trust instrument should give the trustee complete discretion to make distributions, and it should direct that the trust should be administered to ensure that the beneficiary does not lose his or her eligibility for benefits. The state has no right to reimbursement from a supplemental needs trust at the beneficiary's death; the assets will be distributed as provided in the trust instrument. See, White v. Kansas Health Policy Authority, 40 Kan.App.2d 971, 198 P.3d 172 (2008); Young v. Ohio Dep't of Human Servs., 76 Ohio St.3d 547, 668 N.E.2d 908 (1996); Hecker v. Stark County Social Serv. Bd., 527 N.W.2d 226 (N.D. 1994). See also Alan Newman, The Rights of Creditors of Beneficiaries Under the Uniform Trust Code: An Examination of the Compromise, 69 Tenn. L. Rev. 771 (2002). On the general problem of creating trusts to benefit a disabled child, see Judith McMullen, Family Support of the Disabled: A Legislative Proposal to Create Incentives to Support Disabled Family Members, 23 U. Mich. J.L. Reform 439 (1990); Lawrence Frolik, Discretionary Trusts for a Disabled Beneficiary, 46 U. Pitt. L. Rev. 335 (1985).

b. *Self-Settled Trusts and Incapacity*

Joel C. Dobris, Medicaid Asset Planning by the Elderly: A Policy View of Expectations, Entitlement and Inheritance, 24 Real Prop., Prob. & Trust J. 1, 5–8 (1989).

.... Elderly individuals want to live in the family house as long as possible and they want to pass it on to the next generation, especially if there is even a hope of it being used by a family member. In addition, the elderly want to pass a decent inheritance to their children and grandchildren. Finally, they also want to keep their good names. They do not want to cheat and they do not want to go on "welfare". They simply want access to a nursing home if they need it.

* * *

Most children do not want to put their parents in a nursing home.... But children also want "their inheritances." Simply put, the engine that drives the divestment of assets to qualify for Medicaid is the children. They feel entitled to an inheritance that, if denied, they regard as a breach of the social compact, as they read it.

PROBLEM

Oscar Zilch, age 70, and his wife, Olive, age 65, have approached you for advice. The couple own, as tenants by the entirety, a house valued at $100,000, and Oscar owns $200,000 in securities. They each draw monthly Social Security checks, and Oscar receives a small pension from one of his employers. Both Oscar and Olive are in excellent health, but they want to assure (1) that if one of them has to enter a nursing home, the other will have the resources to maintain the couple's current standard of living; and (2) that, at death, they can pass as much money as possible to their only child, Zelda, now age 41 and living in another state.

After reading the following materials, advise Oscar and Olive about their alternatives.

Cohen v. Commissioner

Supreme Judicial Court of Massachusetts, 1996.
423 Mass. 399, 668 N.E.2d 769.

[Eds. Note: This opinion consolidates four cases wherein settlors attempted to qualify for Medicaid by placing assets in various types of discretionary trusts. A summary of the terms of three of those trusts follows:

1) *Cohen.* In June, 1983, Mary Ann Cohen placed her own assets in a trust with the following terms:

> The Trustees may, from time to time and at any time, distribute to or expend for the benefit of the beneficiary (Cohen), so much of the principal and current or accumulated net income as the Trustees may in their sole discretion, determine.... The Trustees, however, shall have no authority whatsoever to make any payments to or for the benefit of any Beneficiary hereunder when the making of such payments shall result in the Beneficiary losing her eligibility for any public assistance or entitlement program of any kind whatever. It is the specific intent of the Grantor hereof that this Trust be used to supplement all such public assistance or entitlement programs and not defeat or destroy their availability to any beneficiary hereunder.

2) *Comins.* On January 1, 1985, Lilyan and Sydney Comins placed their home in a trust, retaining the income interest for life as long as they are not institutionalized. If both are institutionalized, the trustee is permitted only to:

> apply for the benefit of each of the primary beneficiaries only so much of the net income as is necessary and appropriate to provide each with those health, medical, social, and personal benefits and services, and only those benefits and services which are not otherwise available to each primary Beneficiary from other sources as or when needed for his or her welfare.

With respect to the principal, the instrument provided:

> *Principal with respect to Donor.* [The Trustee shall pay to an institutionalized beneficiary] so much of the principal of the Trust as is necessary and appropriate to provide him/her with those benefits and services, and only those benefits and services, which are not otherwise available to him/her from other sources as or when needed for his/her welfare.
>
> Withdrawal of Principal. The Trustee shall also pay over or apply for the benefit of each primary Beneficiary an amount of principal as either primary Beneficiary shall direct in writing, not exceeding the lesser of $5,000 or 5% of the principal ... provided, however, that the Trustee shall make no distributions of principal under this paragraph to a primary Beneficiary during or with respect to any time during which such primary Beneficiary is institutionalized....

3) *Kokoska.* Kokoska was a severely disabled, middle-aged woman, whose disabilities were a result of brain damage sustained during surgery. She received a substantial amount of money in 1968 as a result of the settlement of an ensuing malpractice action. In 1983, her conservator arranged to have the remaining proceeds placed in a trust, and at that time she applied for Medicaid. The relevant portions of the trust state:

> ARTICLE ONE. PURPOSE OF THE TRUST. "The purpose of this Trust is to provide for the supplemental care, comfort, health, maintenance, support, education, habilitation and welfare of the Primary Beneficiary ... taking into account the benefits of ... assistance the Primary Beneficiary otherwise receives as a result of his or her disability ... from any state or federal government or governmental agency ... (hereinafter 'The Benefits').... [T]he trust estate shall be used to the maximum extent possible to supplement such Benefits as are received by the Primary Beneficiary....
>
> ARTICLE TWO. DISPOSITION OF INCOME. "[T]he trustee shall pay to or for the benefit of the Primary Beneficiary such portion of the net income of the Trust as in the Trustee's discretion is advisable for the Primary Beneficiary's care, comfort, health, maintenance, support, education, habilitation, and welfare. The Trustee may make payments of income on account of the Primary Beneficiary for the purchase of such property, goods, or services as from time to time are excluded from the Primary Beneficiary's eligibility for or receipt of Benefits. Without intending to be an exclusive or controlling list, such property, goods, and services may include those specified by federal and state Medicaid eligibility guidelines....
>
> ARTICLE THREE. DISPOSITION OF PRINCIPAL. ¿¿[T]he Trustee ... may make payment from time to time of so much of the principal of the Trust as is advisable in the discretion of the Trustee to meet the needs of the Primary Beneficiary as set forth in article two."

In each case, the Division of Medical Assistance denied the plaintiffs eligibility for Medicaid because it determined that the trust assets were "available" resources for determining eligibility. An excerpt from the opinion follows]:

■ FRIED, J.

I

The Medicaid program was established in 1965 as Title XIX of the Social Security Act, 42 U.S.C. § 1396 et seq., to provide health care to needy persons. The program, which makes funds available to individuals and those who furnish services to them, is administered by the States, but the State programs must comply with Federal statutes and regulations in order to qualify for the Federal funds which pay for a significant part of the program. See *Harris v. McRae*, 448 U.S. 297, 301, 65 L. Ed. 2d. 784, 100 S. Ct. 2671 (1980); *Haley v. Commissioner of Pub. Welfare*, 394 Mass. 466, 467–468, 476 N.E.2d 572 (1985). The issue presented in these cases arises from the wish of persons with some means, perhaps even considerable means, to preserve their assets in the face of the large medical expenses faced particularly by elderly persons. While the Medicare program, 42 U.S.C. § 1395 et seq. (1994), is designed to provide medical insurance for elderly and disabled persons generally, the coverage of that program is not complete. Supplemental private insurance is expensive and rarely comprehensive, and certain expenses—particularly long-term institutional care—confront especially elderly individuals and their families with expenses that are likely to deplete their resources entirely. See generally Gordon, How to Protect Your Life Savings from Catastrophic Illness and Nursing Homes (1990). Many of those same expenses, though perhaps on a less generous scale, are covered for the indigent by Medicaid. See *Harris*, supra at 301–302.

In response, attorneys and financial advisers hit upon the device of having a person place his or her assets in trust so that those assets would provide for that person's comfort and well being, maybe even leaving something over to pass on his or her death, while creating eligibility for public assistance. See H.R. Rep. No. 265, 99th Cong., 1st Sess., pt. 1, at 71–72 (1985) (Committee on Energy and Commerce). The theory behind this maneuver was that, because the assets are in trust, they do not count as the grantor's assets and thus do not raise the grantor above the level of indigency-needed to qualify for public assistance. Courts in this State and elsewhere had ruled in various contexts that, if an individual settled assets in an irrevocable trust and the disposition of those assets was at the discretion of a trustee, no beneficiary of the trust would have a right to call for them, and so the assets could not be considered available to the beneficiary. See *Randolph v. Roberts*, 346 Mass. 578, 579–580, 195 N.E.2d 72 (1964) (creditor denied access to assets of testamentary spendthrift trust to reimburse itself for beneficiary's welfare disability charges).... The parties have not cited any case in any jurisdiction that has applied this reasoning to a trust in which the grantor or settlor is also the beneficiary, a so-called self-settled trust, nor have we decided such a case. Indeed, as we show below ..., the law as to self-settled trusts is to the contrary.

Nevertheless, individuals faced with health care costs that threatened to deplete their assets seized upon this jurisprudence as sanctioning their seeming impoverishment through self-settled trusts. Thus, a grantor: was able to qualify for public assistance without depleting his assets; could once more enjoy those assets if he no longer needed public assistance; and, if such a happy time did not come, could let them pass intact pursuant to the terms of the trust to his heirs. The grantor was able to have his cake and eat it too.

There was considerable dissatisfaction with the ensuing state of affairs. The bill containing the provisions now before this court was referred in 1985 to the House Committee on Energy and Commerce. In its report recommending passage, the committee wrote:

> The Committee feels compelled to state the obvious. Medicaid is, and always has been, a program to provide basic health coverage to people who do not have sufficient income or resources to provide for themselves. When affluent individuals use Medicaid qualifying trusts and similar "techniques" to qualify for the program, they are diverting scarce Federal and State resources from low-income elderly and disabled individuals, and poor women and children. This is unacceptable to the Committee.

H.R. Rep. No. 265, 99th Cong., 1st Sess., pt. 1, at 72 (1985).

The provisions, as finally enacted in 1986 and referred to here as the MQT statute, are the same in all relevant respects to those reported by the committee.... Building on the predicate that a person's eligibility for Medicaid assistance depends on whether the resources available to that person exceed a specified maximum, the MQT statute first provides that:

> In the case of a medicaid qualifying trust [described in paragraph (2)], the amounts from the trust deemed available to a grantor, for purposes of subsection (a)(17), is the maximum amount of payments that may be permitted under the terms of the trust to be distributed to the grantor, assuming the full exercise of discretion by the trustee or trustees for the distribution of the maximum amount to the grantor. For purposes of the previous sentence, the term "grantor" means the individual referred to in paragraph (2).

42 U.S.C. § 1396a(k)(1). Subsection (2) then goes on to define the term "medicaid qualifying trust":

> (2) For purposes of this subsection, a "medicaid qualifying trust" is a trust, or similar legal device, established (other than by will) by an individual (or an individual's spouse) under which the individual may be the beneficiary of all or part of the payments from the trust and the distribution of such payments is determined by one or more trustees who are permitted to exercise any discretion with respect to the distribution to the individual.[7]
>
> * * *

---

7. Subsection (3) provides that "this subsection shall apply without regard to—(A) whether or not the medicaid qualifying trust is irrevocable or is established for purposes other

In 1993, Congress amended the provision relating to irrevocable MQTs to provide:

> (i) if there are any circumstances under which payment from the trust could be made to or for the benefit of the individual, the portion of the corpus from which, or the income on the corpus from which, payment to the individual could be made shall be considered resources available to the individual, and payments from that portion of the corpus or income—(I) to or from the benefit of the individual, shall be considered income of the individual, and (II) for any other purpose, shall be considered a transfer of assets by the individual subject to subsection (c); and (ii) any portion of the trust from which, or any income on the corpus from which, no payment could under any circumstances be made to the individual shall be considered, as of the date of establishment of the trust (or, if later, the date on which payment to the individual was foreclosed) to be assets disposed by the individual for purposes of subsection (c), and the value of the trust shall be determined for purposes of such subsection by including the amount of any payments made from such portion of the trust after such date.

42 U.S.C. § 1396p(d)(3)(B).[8]

This amendment, which, unlike the MQT statute, explicitly applies only to trusts established after the effective date of the statute, see Pub. L. 103–66, § 13611(e)(2)(C), 107 Stat. 627 (1993), resolves in favor of the Commonwealth beyond any possibility of argument the issue presented in these cases: if, in any circumstances any amount of money might be paid to a beneficiary, the maximum of such amount is deemed to be available to the beneficiary.

* * *

Drawing these strands together, we interpret the statute to define what is an MQT. See 42 U.S.C. § 1396a(k)(2). And that is any trust established by a person (or that person's spouse) under which that person may receive any payments. This general definition is qualified only by the requirement that the trustees must be permitted to exercise some discretion—that is, the conditions for distribution may not be completely fixed for all circumstances. If there is an MQT, then subsection (1) of the MQT statute, with which we have been occupied, tells us how much money is to be deemed to be available. That amount is the greatest amount that the trustees in any set of circumstances might have discretion to pay out to the beneficiary. Thus, if there is a peppercorn of discretion, then whatever is the most the beneficiary might under any state of affairs receive in the full

---

than to enable a grantor to qualify for medical assistance under this title; or (B) whether or not the discretion described in paragraph (2) is actually exercised." 42 U.S.C. § 1396a(k)(3).

8. The amendment provides that subsection (d) "shall apply without regard to—(i) the purposes for which a trust is established, (ii) Whether the trustees have or exercise any discretion under the trust, (iii) any restrictions on when or whether distributions may be made from the trust, or (iv) any restrictions on the use of distributions from the trust." 42 U.S.C. § 1396p(d)(2)(C).

exercise of that discretion is the amount that is counted as available for Medicaid eligibility.[9]

* * *

The judgments of the Superior Court are affirmed.

QUESTIONS

1. Why didn't the settlors in Cohen and its companion cases create spendthrift trusts to insulate their assets from the claims of the state as creditor?

2. The court in Cohen decided that the settlor-beneficiaries of the various trusts were not eligible for Medicaid reimbursement. Did the court also decide that the trustees were obligated to invade trust principal to pay for institutional care?

Examine the trust instruments drafted for Cohen, Comins, and Kokoska. After the court's decision, what responsibility did the trustee have, in each case, for maintaining the settlor-beneficiary?

Suppose, in each case, the nursing home had admitted the beneficiary with an expectation of payment either from the trust or from Medicaid. After the court's decision, would the nursing home be able to compel the trustee to use trust assets to pay nursing home bills? If the answer is no, would you expect nursing homes to admit patients who are beneficiaries of trusts like these?

3. In the Cohen opinion, Justice Fried notes that if the trust instruments had conferred on the trustee no discretion to invade principal for the benefit of the settlor-beneficiary, the trust principal would not be treated as an asset of the beneficiary for purposes of determining Medicaid eligibility. See also Arkansas Dept. of Human Services v. Wilson, 323 Ark. 151, 913 S.W.2d 783 (1996). Does this exception permit wholesale evasion of Medicaid eligibility limits? Are there reasons a trust settlor might not want to create an irrevocable trust, reserving to herself all income but relinquishing all right to invade principal?

4. Suppose a mother and daughter walk into your office and tell you that they have heard that the mother will not be able to qualify for Medicaid because she has assets totaling $200,000. Mother and daughter both tell you that the mother is willing to convey her assets to her daughter if that will qualify the mother for Medicaid should the need arise in the future, and the daughter agrees that she will treat the assets as if they belonged to her mother; that is, any proposed transfer would be, as far as they are

---

9. It is the requirement of that peppercorn of discretion that the 1993 amendment removes, providing that eligibility is to be measured by the maximum amount available under the trust under any circumstances, whether or not the trustee enjoys any discretion.

Section (2) of the MQT statute also requires some trustee discretion for a trust to count as an MQT at all. This condition is also absent from the 1993 amendment. See Matter of Kindt, 542 N.W.2d 391, 396 n. 2 (Minn.Ct.App.1996) (listing differences between MQT statute and 1993 amendment).

concerned, transfers in name only, designed only to qualify mother for Medicaid.

If you arrange the transfers the parties have suggested, are you violating any professional obligation? How would you respond to mother and daughter? Consider Model Rules of Professional Conduct, Rule 1.2(d):

> A lawyer shall not counsel a client to engage, or assist a client, in conduct that the lawyer knows is criminal or fraudulent, but a lawyer may discuss the legal consequences of any proposed course of conduct with a client and may counsel or assist a client to make a good faith effort to determine the validity, scope, meaning or application of the law.

What other dangers would such an arrangement generate? Suppose the daughter subsequently refused to turn the money over to the mother? See John A. Miller, Voluntary Impoverishment to Obtain Government Benefits, 13 Cornell J. L. & Pub. Pol'y. 81 (2003).

5. The Health Insurance Portability and Accountability Act of 1996 imposes criminal penalties on anyone who:

> for a fee knowingly and willfully counsels or assists an individual to dispose of assets (including by any transfer in trust) in order for the individual to become eligible for medical assistance under a State plan under title XIX, if disposing of the assets results in the imposition of a period of ineligibility for such assistance under section 1917(c).

42 U.S.C. § 1320a–7B(a)(6). In light of the statute, what risks does a lawyer take in the situation discussed in Question 4? Lawyers attacked the constitutionality of the statute. Attorney General Janet Reno informed Congress that the Justice Department would not enforce the statute because "the counseling prohibition in that provision is plainly unconstitutional under the First Amendment and because assistance prohibition is not severable from the counseling prohibition." As a result of the Justice Department's position, a federal district court concluded that a lawyer challenge to the statute was not justiciable because it presented no case or controversy. Magee v. United States, 93 F.Supp.2d 161, 165 (D.R.I. 2000).

NOTES

1. ***The Problem of the "Community Spouse."*** Medicaid regulations invariably require consideration of the assets of both partners to a marriage in determining whether either spouse is eligible for Medicaid benefits. See 42 U.S.C. § 1396r–5(c)(1)(A) ("There shall be computed (as of the beginning of the first continuous period of institutionalization ... of the institutionalized spouse)—(i) the total value of the resources to the extent either the institutionalized spouse or the community spouse has an ownership interest ...").

When one spouse needs institutional care, this creates a dilemma for the spouse who will continue to live in the community—often called the "community spouse." Only by "spending down" the couple's assets will the institutionalized spouse qualify for Medicaid, but spending down the assets to Medicaid eligibility limits will significantly reduce the community spouse's standard of living.

The Medicaid statute does provide limited protection to the community spouse. Although the resources of both spouses are considered in determining eligibility for Medicaid, after one spouse is institutionalized, the statute provides the community spouse some protection against claims by the state. The statute precludes imposition of a lien on the couple's home (42 U.S.C. § 1396p(a)(2)(A)), and provides that during periods of institutionalization, the community spouse's income shall not be deemed available to the institutionalized spouse. 42 U.S.C. § 1396r–5(b)(1). In particular, if trust income is paid solely to the community spouse, the income is not treated as available to the institutionalized spouse. 42 U.S.C. § 1396r–5(b)(2)(B)(ii)(I).

As the Cohen case indicates, the Medicaid statute changes frequently, so the practitioner is well-advised not to rely on cases or secondary materials written before the statute's latest incarnation.

2. ***Self-Settled Supplemental Needs Trusts.*** In Cohen and its companion cases, settlor-beneficiaries were apparently trying to preserve their assets to pass on to estate beneficiaries. In a number of cases, as in the case of Kokoska, when disabled persons have received tort recoveries or settlements, persons acting on their behalf have attempted to create trusts to supplement public assistance, while preserving the principal for estate beneficiaries. Courts have consistently thwarted such efforts, treating the trusts as if they had been created by the beneficiary. See Williams for and on Behalf of Squier v. Kansas Dept. of Social and Rehab. Servs., 258 Kan. 161, 899 P.2d 452 (1995); Thomas v. Arkansas Dep't of Human Servs., 319 Ark. 782, 894 S.W.2d 584 (1995); Forsyth v. Rowe, 226 Conn. 818, 629 A.2d 379 (1993).

But federal law does authorize specific types of self-settled supplemental needs trusts. Consider the following:

Comment: Third–Party Special Needs Trust: Dead or Alive In A Uniform Trust Code World, 16 Tex. Wesleyan L. Rev. 249 (2010):

> In 1993, Congress passed federal law that allows a person with disabilities to retain their resources in a special needs trust under exceptions to the amendments of the Omnibus Budget and Reconciliation Act (OBRA–93). These trusts are considered self-funded trusts because the assets used to fund the trust belong to the disabled beneficiary. This type of trust shelters the assets that were already "in the pocket" of the disabled person, such as a homestead or other real or personal property, from the assets that are considered when determining eligibility for governmental assistance. The funds placed in the trust are put into a "non-countable" category and allow the individual to preserve eligibility for governmental assistance. To become a beneficiary of a special needs trust, the individual must be considered "disabled" as defined by 42 U.S.C. § 1382c(a)(3)(A), (C). The individu-

al "must be unable to engage in any substantial gainful activity by reason of any medically determinable physical or mental impairment which can be expected to result in death or which has lasted or can be expected to last for a continuous period of not less than twelve months (or, in the case of a child under the age of eighteen, if he suffers from any medically determinable physical or mental impairment of comparable severity)."

[Congress] created two types of self-funded trusts. First, the "Payback" or "(d)(4)(A)" trust that is permitted through 42 U.S.C. § 1396p(d)(4)(A). This type of trust is created for the sole benefit of a disabled person under the age of sixty-five. The trust is created by a parent, grandparent, legal guardian, or court with the assets of the disabled person. After the disabled individual's death, the funds remaining in the trust must be repaid to the state Medicaid agency up to an amount that was provided by the agency to the disabled person. There is no obligation however to conserve funds for the state.

The second type of federally permitted trust is the "Pooled" or "(d)(4)(C)" trust which is permitted through 42 U.S.C. § 1396p(d)(4)(C). This type of trust is created and managed by a non-profit agency. Assets are pooled from other beneficiaries for investment and management purposes, and each beneficiary maintains a separate sub-account. The account is created for the sole benefit of a disabled person by the individual's parents, grandparents, legal guardian, court, or the disabled individual themselves. On the individual's death, the remaining amount left in the sub-account is distributed to the other disabled individuals known by the agency. A Pooled trust would most likely be created when the family cannot identify a suitable trustee, the bank trust fees are costly, or the family prefers that the amount remaining in the trust after the beneficiary's death be passed to disabled individuals rather than be given back to the state. The main difference between the two federally created trusts is that (d)(4)(C) pooled trust can be created by the disabled individual and the (d)(4)(A) trust cannot.

F. MINIMIZING TAXATION

1. *INTER VIVOS* TRUSTS

Many laypersons are under the misperception that they can realize significant transfer tax and income tax savings by transferring property into trust during their lifetimes. In fact, in most estate plans, *inter vivos* trusts create few tax advantages, and the primary motivations for creating them are usually non-tax concerns about management of trust property and protection of beneficiaries.

To a large extent revocable *intervivos* trusts act as will substitutes, and while they play an important role in probate avoidance, they offer no significant tax savings when compared to a traditional will. During the settlor's lifetime, the trust is essentially ignored for income tax purposes; all of the income of the trust is taxed to the settlor. On the settlor's death, the assets are included in his estate for estate tax purposes as though he owned the trust property outright (I.R.C. § 2038).

Irrevocable trusts are essentially substitutes for outright gifts. So long as the settlor of an *irrevocable* trust parts with all interest and control over the transferred property, creation of the trust will be taxed just like an outright gift of the property, with one exception discussed below. On the settlor's death, the assets in the trust will not be included in the settlor's estate (so long as the settler retains no powers with respect to the trust, §§ 2036–2038). As a result, by creating an irrevocable trust (or by making a lifetime gift), the settlor can avoid estate taxation on the appreciation in value of the trust property between the time the trust is created and the time of testator's death.

There is one significant difference between making gifts in trust as compared to outright gifts, and that has to do with the annual exclusion. Only "present interests" in property qualify for the annual exclusion from gift tax, so as a general proposition transfers in trust will not qualify for the annual exclusion. Section 2503(c) allows a limited exception to this rule in the case of certain trusts created for the beneficiary of a minor. "Minors trusts," however, are unappealing to many clients because in order to qualify for the exception the trust assets must be distributed to the minor when she reaches age 21.

Because of the limitations of the present interest requirement, planners have sought ways to avoid it. A judicial rule has developed which generously allows the annual exclusion for transfers to a "*Crummey Trust*," discussed below.

Very sophisticated estate plans do use irrevocable trusts for estate taxation minimization (and avoidance). Given the current size of the exemption amount, these tools will be appropriate for only the wealthiest clients, and some of them involve very aggressive planning. Some examples of the types of trusts employed include irrevocable insurance trusts, "Grantor Retained Annuity Trusts" or "GRATs", and Intentionally Defective Grantor Trusts "IDGTs". A detailed discussion of these planning techniques is beyond the scope of this book.

Irrevocable trusts do not provide the opportunity for significant income tax savings. If the beneficiary is in a lower tax bracket than the settlor, some amount of income tax can be saved if income is distributed to the beneficiary, but if the beneficiary is a child under the age of 18, the beneficiary's income will be taxed at her parents' rate, resulting in no tax savings. Moreover, to the extent that transfers to irrevocable trusts might generate significant income tax savings, those same savings could be achieved by making outright gifts. See generally William Turnier, The Role of Gift Giving in Estate Planning, 59 N.C. L. Rev. 377 (1981).

For most estate planning clients, tax avoidance, then, rarely provides the sole justification for creation of *inter vivos* trusts. But where non-tax concerns lead the settlor to make transfers in trust, the estate planner's job is to ensure that settlor makes maximum use of available tax benefits (such as the annual exclusion), and that settlor encounters no tax detriments (such as inadvertent inclusion in the settlor's estate at death).

Crummey Trusts

Recall that 26 U.S.C. § 2503(b) creates an annual gift exclusion ($13,000 in 2011, indexed for inflation). Suppose a property owner wants to take full advantage of the gift tax annual exclusion, but does not want to make outright gifts to her intended beneficiaries. Some of the beneficiaries may be minors; others may not be "ready," in the property owner's mind, to manage gifts of, say, $13,000 per year. Can the property owner simply create $13,000 irrevocable trusts for each of the beneficiaries, postponing the beneficiaries' right to trust principal until some time in the future? The answer is no—unless the settlor takes care in creating the trusts.

Under the "present interest" rule discussed above, if a property owner makes a gift of a future interest, the gift will be taxed even if its value is below the amount of the annual exclusion. (Of course, no tax may be due immediately; the donor may not yet have used up her $5,000,000 lifetime exemption from estate and gift taxation. But to the extent the donor uses her exemption during her lifetime, it will be unavailable at death).

A clever estate planner devised the following scheme to qualify for the annual exclusion while limiting the beneficiary to a future interest in a trust: why not create a trust which gives the ultimate beneficiary the right to withdraw the property owner's annual contribution to the trust for a limited period—say, 30 days—upon which the right to withdraw lapses? The gift is arguably not a gift of a future interest, because the beneficiary has an absolute right to withdraw the money during the year in which the "gift" is made. But the limited time for withdrawal, together with the limited savvy of the beneficiary, makes it extremely unlikely that the money will actually be withdrawn. Moreover, the property owner has a stick to make sure the beneficiary doesn't withdraw the money: if the beneficiary withdraws this year's share, there won't be a share next year.

The Commissioner of Internal Revenue challenged this clever scheme in Crummey v. Commissioner, 397 F.2d 82 (9th Cir. 1968). The taxpayer won. Following the decision in Crummey, the Internal Revenue Service issued Revenue Ruling 73–405, which approved the use of the Crummey device to obtain the benefit of the annual exclusion while limiting the beneficiary's practical access to the proceeds of the gift. The Ruling provides:

> [I]t is not the actual use, possession, or enjoyment by the donee which marks the dividing line between a present interest and a future interest, but rather the right conferred upon the donee by the trust instrument to such use, possession, or enjoyment. A gift in trust to a minor is not a "future interest" if the donee has a present right to the use, possession or enjoyment, although such use, possession, or enjoyment may require the appointment of a legal guardian....

> [I]t is now concluded that a gift in trust for the benefit of a minor should not be classified as a future interest merely because no guardian was in fact appointed. Accordingly, if there is no impediment under the trust or local law to the appointment of a guardian and the minor donee has a right to demand distribution, the transfer is a gift of a present interest that qualifies for the annual exclusion allowable under section 2503(b) of the Code.

As a result of the Crummey litigation and Revenue Ruling 73–405, many owners of property have found it attractive to create what have come to be called "Crummey trusts." Indeed, estate planners have sought to expand use of the Crummey trust device. How far can a taxpayer go to take advantage of the annual exclusion? Consider the following case:

Estate of Kohlsaat

United States Tax Court, 1997.
T.C. Memo. 1997–212.

■ SWIFT, J.

Respondent determined a deficiency of $337,474 in the Federal estate tax of the Estate of decedent Lieselotte Kohlsaat.

* * *

After settlement of some issues, the issue for decision is whether, in the computation of petitioner's Federal estate tax, decedent's inter vivos transfer of property to an irrevocable trust is eligible under section 2503(b) for the annual gift tax exclusion with respect to each of 16 contingent beneficiaries of the trust.

FINDINGS OF FACT

Some of the facts have been stipulated and are so found. Petitioner is the Estate of Lieselotte Kohlsaat, deceased, Peter Kohlsaat, coexecutor. Decedent died a resident of New Jersey. When the petition was filed, Peter Kohlsaat resided in Cresskill, New Jersey.

On March 27, 1990, decedent formed the Lieselotte Kohlsaat Family Trust as an irrevocable trust (the trust) and transferred to the trust a commercial building owned by decedent and managed for many years by various Kohlsaat family members. At the time of decedent's transfer of the building to the trust, the building was valued at $155,000. Thereafter, no other transfers were made to the trust.

Under provisions of the trust, Beatrice Reinecke (Beatrice) and Peter Kohlsaat (Peter), decedent's two adult children, were designated as cotrustees and primary beneficiaries of the trust. Beatrice and Peter each received an interest in one-half of the corpus and income of the trust, and each received a special power to appoint the corpus of his or her one-half share of the trust to his or her children or grandchildren.

Under the trust provisions, 16 contingent remainder beneficiaries were designated. Beatrice's three children and eight grandchildren were designated as contingent remainder beneficiaries in Beatrice's one-half share of the trust, and Peter's spouse and four sons were designated as contingent remainder beneficiaries in Peter's one-half share of the trust.

Beatrice and Peter, as well as the 16 contingent beneficiaries, were each given the right—following each transfer of property to the trust—to demand from the trust an immediate distribution to them of property in an amount not to exceed the $10,000 annual gift tax exclusion under section 2503(b) that was considered to be available to each beneficiary. Each beneficiary's right to demand a distribution lapsed 30 days after a transfer of property to the trust. The guardian of any minor beneficiary was authorized to exercise the minor beneficiary's right to demand a distribution of property from the trust.

On April 2, 1990, within 6 days of decedent's transfer of the commercial building to the trust, the beneficiaries of the trust were timely notified of their rights to demand distributions of trust property of up to $10,000 each. None of the beneficiaries exercised his or her right to demand a distribution from the trust, and none of the beneficiaries requested notification of future transfers of property to the trust.

No understandings existed between decedent, the trustees, and the contingent beneficiaries to the effect that the beneficiaries would not exercise their rights to demand distributions from the trust.

On petitioner's Federal estate tax return, petitioner treated the interests of the 16 contingent beneficiaries as qualifying for 16 annual gift tax exclusions under section 2503(b) with regard to decedent's 1990 transfer of the commercial building to the trust.

On audit of petitioner's Federal estate tax return, respondent denied the above 16 annual gift tax exclusions claimed by petitioner on the grounds that the contingent beneficiaries did not hold present interests in the trust.

OPINION

* * *

The annual exclusion provides that gifts made to beneficiaries during a calendar year shall be excluded from taxable gifts to the extent they do not exceed $10,000 per beneficiary per year. Sec. 2503(b); sec. 25.2503–2(a), Gift Tax Regs. Gifts qualifying for the annual exclusion are not counted in the computation of an estate's Federal estate tax liability. Sec. 2001(b).

Only gifts of present interests in property qualify for the annual gift tax exclusion. Gifts of future interests in property (i.e., interests in property that are limited to commence in use, possession, or enjoyment at some future date) do not qualify for the annual exclusion. Sec. 2503(b); sec. 25.2503–3(a), Gift Tax Regs.

Generally, interests in property qualify as present interests in property where they represent the unrestricted right to immediate use, possession, or enjoyment of property or income from property. Sec. 25.2503–3(b), Gift Tax Regs.

Where trust beneficiaries, including minor and contingent beneficiaries, are given unrestricted rights to demand immediate distributions of trust property, the beneficiaries generally are treated, under section 2503(b), as possessing present interests in property. Estate of Cristofani v. Commissioner, 97 T.C. 74, 84–85 (1991); see also Crummey v. Commissioner, 397 F.2d 82, 88 (9th Cir.1968), affg. in part and revg. in part T.C. Memo. 1966–144; Perkins v. Commissioner, 27 T.C. 601, 605–606 (1956).

In Estate of Cristofani v. Commissioner, supra, contingent beneficiaries of a trust were given the unrestricted right to legally demand immediate distribution to them of trust property following a transfer of property to the trust. The contingent beneficiaries were treated as holding present interests in the trust, and the settlor's transfers of property to the trust were treated as qualifying for the annual gift tax exclusion.

* * *

Respondent argues that understandings existed between decedent and the 16 contingent beneficiaries of decedent's trust to the effect that the beneficiaries would not exercise their rights to demand distributions of trust property, that these understandings negate decedent's donative intent, and that the substance-over-form doctrine should apply to deny the annual gift tax exclusions with regard to the interests held by the 16 contingent beneficiaries.

We disagree.

Pursuant to the provisions of the trust, for a 30–day period following a transfer of property to the trust, the contingent beneficiaries were given unrestricted rights to legally demand immediate distribution to them of trust property. The evidence does not establish that any understandings existed between decedent and the beneficiaries that the contingent beneficiaries would not exercise those rights following a transfer of property to the trust. At trial, several credible reasons were offered by the trust beneficiaries as to why they did not exercise their rights to demand a distribution of trust property. The fact that none of the beneficiaries exercised their rights or that none of the beneficiaries requested notification of future transfers of property to the trust does not imply to us that the beneficiaries had agreed with decedent not to do so, and we refuse to infer any understanding.

The evidence does not support respondent's contention that the contingent beneficiaries believed they would be penalized for exercising their rights to demand distributions of trust property or that the trustees purposefully withheld information from the beneficiaries.

Further, the contingent beneficiaries received actual notice from the trustees with regard to their rights. Decedent intended to benefit the contingent beneficiaries by giving them interests in the trust. The contingent beneficiaries were decedent's relatives.

For the reasons stated above, the contingent beneficiaries' unrestricted rights to demand immediate distributions of trust property are to be treated as present interests in property. Decedent's transfer of the commercial building to the trust qualifies for 16 annual gift tax exclusions under section 2503(b) with regard to the present interests of the 16 contingent beneficiaries therein.

NOTES AND QUESTIONS

1. Why didn't the beneficiaries of the trust exercise their right to withdraw $10,000 from the trust? To the extent that the remainder interests of Peter's spouse and the various children and grandchildren were contingent, wouldn't it have been in their interests to withdraw $10,000?

2. Suppose the various beneficiaries had agreed, in writing, not to exercise any withdrawal rights conferred on them by settlor. Would the withdrawal rights qualify for the annual gift tax exclusion? See Estate of Holland, T.C. Memo. 1997–302 (1997), indicating that an express agreement would disqualify the withdrawal rights, but finding, on the facts of that case, that there had been no express agreement. Why should the existence of an express agreement be critical?

3. Suppose Lieselotte Kohlsaat had wanted to make her son Peter the only beneficiary of the trust, and had wanted the trust property distributed to Peter at her death. Could Lieselotte have created a Crummey trust giving withdrawal rights to the same sixteen people? What risk would Ms. Kohlsaat have run? Under what circumstances would you recommend giving withdrawal rights to persons who do not have remainder interests in the trust?

4. Suppose one of Lieselotte Kohlsaat's grandchildren had exercised a right to withdraw $10,000. What obligations would the grandchild's demand impose on the trustees? Note that the trust property in Kohlsaat was a building. Would the trustee's have been obligated to sell the building? To deal with this problem, many lawyers recommend that a Crummey trust be funded, at least in significant part, with liquid assets.

5. The device used in the Kohlsaat case is a controversial one. Although the IRS has lost several cases in which taxpayer made arrangements similar to that in Kohlsaat, the Service has continued to litigate these cases. The lawyer who creates a trust like the one in Kohlsaat should understand that she puts her client at some risk. For criticism of the IRS's continued litigation of these cases, despite consistent case law upholding use of these withdrawal powers, see Jeffrey S. Kinsler, Has the Internal Revenue Service's Challenge of Semi–Naked Lapsing Powers Become Frivolous?, 15 Widener L. J. 299 (2006).

6. Notice is critical in the Crummey trust scheme; the holder of the right to withdraw must receive adequate notice of the withdrawal right, and must enjoy a reasonable time to exercise that right once notice has been received. The beneficiary should always receive notice in writing, and, for evidentiary purposes, the beneficiary should be required to acknowledge receipt of the notice. The IRS has issued a number of private letter rulings indicating that a 30–day withdrawal period—after receipt of the notice—suffices to qualify trust contributions for the annual gift tax exclusion. Professor Bradley Fogel notes, however, that the notices are often designed to discourage exercise:

> Crummey notices are generally drafted in language that is sufficiently stilted as to make it apparent that the notice was written by the attorney. Thus, Crummey notices not only notify the power-holder of the existence of the power, they also effectively, albeit silently, communicate that the power is not meant to be exercised. Even if the power-holder were inclined to exercise the power, he would be unlikely to risk angering the donor by choosing to exercise the withdrawal power. Indeed, Crummey powers are very rarely exercised.

Bradley E.S. Fogel, Back to the Future Interest: The Origin and Questionable Legal Basis of the Use of Crummey Withdrawal Powers to Obtain the Federal Gift Tax Annual Exclusion, 6 Fla. Tax Rev. 189, 211–213 (2003). See generally Dora Arash, Crummey Trusts: An Exploitation of the Annual Exclusion, 21 Pepp. L. Rev. 83, 93–95 (1994).

7. For a thorough critique of Crummey trusts, including an extensive analysis of the Kohlsaat case, see Bradley E.S. Fogel, The Emperor Does Not Need Clothes—The Expanding Use of "Naked" Crummey Withdrawal Powers to Obtain Federal Gift Tax Annual Exclusions, 73 Tul. L. Rev. 555 (1998). By contrast, Professor Elaine Gagliardi endorses Crummey's focus on objective legal rights rather than the grantor's subjective intent:

> Focus on the taxpayer's tax avoidance motive or intent imbues planning techniques with unnecessary uncertainty. In contrast, the objective economic substance test rejects the more subjective analysis asserted by the Service, and provides more certainty to the estate planning process.

Elaine Hightower Gagliardi, Economic Substance in the Context of Federal Estate and Gift Tax: The Internal Revenue Service Has It Wrong, 64 Mont. L. Rev. 389, 419 (2003). For a more general discussion of Crummey trusts, see, John G. Steinkamp, Common Sense and the Gift Tax Annual Exclusion, 72 Neb. L. Rev. 106 (1993). For a general discussion of the Code's definition of future interest, and a proposal for reform, see Jeffrey G. Sherman, 'Tis a Gift to Be Simple: The Need for a New Definition of "Future Interest" for Gift Tax Purposes, 55 U. Cin. L. Rev. 585 (1987).

2. TESTAMENTARY TRUSTS: MORE ON MARITAL DEDUCTION PLANNING, AND AN INTRODUCTION TO THE GENERATION-SKIPPING TAX

When married couples seek tax advice, two situations typically arise:

(1) Each spouse wants to give the other spouse all of the couple's property, and to trust the surviving spouse to dispose of whatever is left at the survivor's death. This situation is common in the so-called "traditional" family, where both spouses share the same children. In this situation, the lawyer's goal is to give the surviving spouse as much control over the property as possible, without generating adverse tax consequences.

(2) The decedent wants to provide for the surviving spouse, but to control the ultimate distribution of the property after the surviving spouse's death. This situation is common in a multiple-marriage family, where decedent's spouse is not necessarily the parent of decedent's children, and where the spouse may have children who are not also the decedent's children.

Until the introduction of portability into the estate tax law (recall the discussion of portability in Chapter 6), testamentary trusts offered significant tax advantages to clients in both situations. The new legislation significantly reduces the need for testamentary trusts in the "traditional" family situations, but trusts remain very useful for "multiple-marriage" families.

a. Maximizing the Assets Available to the Surviving Spouse While Minimizing Taxation

Suppose each spouse in a married couple wants to leave all assets to the other, trusting the surviving spouse to distribute those assets among the couple's issue (or to other persons) by the terms of the surviving spouse's will. The couple's lawyer could draft wills for each spouse leaving all property to the other spouse, and providing an alternative disposition if the other spouse were to die first. Consider the tax consequences associated with those wills.

Both before and after the 2010 revision of the estate tax law, no estate tax would be due at the death of the first spouse to die. The marital deduction would leave the decedent spouse with no taxable estate, so the survivor would take the decedent's assets free of any estate tax.

Under the law that applied through 2009, however, this hypothetical estate tax plan generated a significant tax disadvantage for the couple: at the surviving spouse's death, the survivor could use only the survivor's own exemption; the couple essentially wasted the credit of the first spouse to die. Recall that the credit is equal to the estate tax on the exemption amount applicable in the year of decedent's death. Consider the following example (using today's $5,000,000 exemption amount):

> ***Example 1:*** *Harry dies with an estate of $4,000,000, leaving all $4,000,000 to his wife, Wanda. Wanda dies two years later, with an estate of $9,000,000 ($5,000,000 of her own money, plus the $4,000,000 she inherited from Harry). At Harry's death, no tax was due because his entire estate qualified for the marital deduction. At Wanda's death, however, under pre–2010 law, her taxable state would have been $9,000,000. She would be able to use her*

$5,000,000 exemption, and then be taxed at 35% of the $4,000,000 balance. (The portability provisions of the 2010 law solve this problem, by allowing Wanda's estate to make use of Harry's unused exemption.)

Before 2010, to minimize the couple's total estate tax bill, the couple's lawyer had to structure their estate plan so that the predeceased spouse's estate would make use of that spouse's exemption amount. To do so, some portion of the estate needed to be left in such a way that it would not qualify for the marital deduction. The goal was for the first decedent to die to leave a taxable estate equal to the exemption amount. Of course, the lawyer could have accomplished that result by having each spouse make a large devise to the children in order to make use of the exemption, but that solution would not have achieved the couple's non-tax goals, because the surviving spouse would not have the use of those assets during his or her lifetime. So instead the estate plan was constructed to leave the estate of the first spouse to die in a manner that would provide the surviving spouse the use of all the property, but would avoid including a portion of that property in the survivor's estate.

Lawyers typically accomplished this result for their clients by drafting "credit shelter trusts," also called "bypass trusts" because the trust property bypassed the estate of the surviving spouse. Consider the following example:

Example 2: *Harry has an estate of $6,000,000; Wanda, his wife, has an estate of $4,000,000. Harry's will leaves to Wanda as trustee, an amount equal to the exemption amount (this was often described by a formula, with reference to the largest amount that can pass free of the federal estate tax by reason of the unified credit.) He directs Wanda to pay income to herself for life, and provides that at Wanda's death, the property should be divided among the couple's three children. The will leaves the balance of his estate to Wanda. If Harry dies first, followed by Wanda, what estate tax is due and when?*

Solution: *At Harry's death, the trust principal is included in his taxable estate, because it does not qualify for the marital deduction. How much is the trust principal? If he died in 2011, the trust principal would equal the exemption amount of $5,000,000, which is the largest amount that could pass free of the federal estate tax by reason of the unified credit applicable in 2011. The remaining $1,000,000 passes directly to Wanda, and qualifies for the marital deduction. Hence, no tax is due at Harry's death. At Wanda's death, the $5,000,000 in the credit shelter trust is* ***not*** *included in her estate, because Harry has directed in his will that the property pass directly to the children at Wanda's death; Wanda doesn't have a power to dispose of the property as she sees fit. At Wanda's death, her taxable estate would consist of her $4,000,000 in assets plus the $1,000,000 she received from Harry, or $5,000,000. Because that does not exceed the exemption amount, her estate would owe no tax.*

The same strategy—use of a credit-shelter trust—would minimize the couple's tax liability under law as revised in 2011, but the introduction of portability makes the strategy largely unnecessary for most couples. Today, if Harry left all $6,000,000 to Wanda, leaving himself with no taxable estate, Wanda would be entitled, at her death, to the benefit of her own unified credit, augmented by any of Harry's unified credit that was not used at his death. Because Harry did not use any of his credit, Wanda would be entitled to use all of it. As a result, no tax would be due at Wanda's death, even though she died with a $10,000,000 estate.

Although they may be rarely necessary from a federal estate tax perspective, credit-shelter trusts will remain a part of the legal landscape for some time to come, for at least two reasons. First, many clients whose wills were drafted before 2010 will not have changed their wills in light of the new statute (especially because the new statute does not generate any particular tax benefits for those who change their wills after enactment). Second, state estate tax law may not change as quickly as federal law, and in some states, lawyers may continue to draft credit shelter trusts to minimize state estate taxation. Finally, because the provisions of the 2010 law are set to expire in 2012, there is no guarantee that portability and the $5,000,000 exemption will be permanent. Planners may wish to build flexibility into estate plans to deal with the possibility that the law may change once again.

b. Protecting Assets for Beneficiaries Other Than the Surviving Spouse

In the preceding section, we considered the decedent who wants to leave essentially all assets to the surviving spouse, but who wants simultaneously to minimize tax burdens. Now let us turn to the decedent who also wants to minimize taxation and to provide for the surviving spouse during her lifetime, but wants to ensure that his assets pass to designated beneficiaries (e.g., his children) following the death of the surviving spouse. He may also want some assets to be available to those other beneficiaries if needed while the surviving spouse is alive. For this decedent, the tax problem is not using up his unified credit, but, instead, assuring that his dispositions, beyond the unified credit, qualify for the marital deduction.

Suppose Harry and Wanda in our example 2 each have children by prior marriages. Harry wants to give Wanda a life interest in his property, but wants to ensure that after Wanda's death his property will pass to his children—not Wanda's. At the same time, Harry wants to take advantage of the marital deduction to defer all estate taxation until Wanda's death. Should Harry be entitled to accomplish these objectives simultaneously? Some critics, recognizing that men would seek to achieve these objectives far more often than women, object to legislation that permits decedents to have their cake and eat it too. See Wendy C. Gerzog, The Illogical and Sexist QTIP Provisions: I Just Can't Say It Ain't So, 76 N.C. L. Rev. 1597 (1998); Mary Moers Wenig, Taxing Women: Thoughts on a Gendered Ecoomy, 6 S. Cal. Rev. L. & Women's Stud. 561 (1997); Wendy C. Gerzog,

The Marital Deduction QTIP Provisions: Illogical and Degrading to Women, 5 UCLA Women's L. J. 301, 304 (1995); but see Lawrence Zelenak, Taking Critical Tax Theory Seriously, 76 N.C. L. Rev. 1521 (1998); Joseph M. Dodge, A Feminist Perspective on the QTIP Trust and the Unlimited Marital Deduction, 76 N.C. L. Rev. 1729 (1998).

Harry can simultaneously accomplish these two objectives—obtaining the marital deduction while controlling ultimate disposition of the property through use of a device known as a *qualified terminable interest property trust*, known almost universally as a *QTIP Trust.*

Section 2056, the marital deduction statute, generally permits a decedent's estate to take the marital deduction only for absolute dispositions to the surviving spouse or their rough equivalents; if the spouse receives only a life estate, or a life interest in trust, the marital deduction is not generally available (See I.R.C. § 2056(b)(1), reproduced below). Congress became persuaded that this general rule, which had long been in effect, was unfair to decedents who had, because of death or divorce, married more than once; a decedent could not take full advantage of the marital deduction while still assuring that the bulk of her estate passed, at her spouse's death, to her own children.

In 1981, to remedy this problem, Congress created the qualified terminable interest property provision embodied in section 2056(b)(7). The statute permits a decedent to create a trust which gives her surviving spouse only a life interest, and to have the trust qualify for the marital deduction. So long as the trust mandates annual (or more frequent) payment of income to the surviving spouse, and assures that no one else will acquire any power to invade the trust principal during the spouse's lifetime, decedent's executor may elect to have the trust qualify for the marital deduction. Section 2044 assures that QTIP property will be taxed at least once, by providing that if property qualifies for the marital deduction under section 2056(b)(7), the value of that property is included in the estate of the surviving spouse.

Examine the statute to see how the drafters articulated that result:

Section 2056. Bequests, etc., to surviving spouse.

(a) Allowance of marital deduction. For purposes of the tax imposed by section 2001, the value of the taxable estate shall, except as limited by subsection (b), be determined by deducting from the value of the gross estate an amount equal to the value of any interest in property which passes or has passed from the decedent to his surviving spouse, but only to the extent that such interest is included in determining the value of the gross estate.

(b) Limitation in the case of life estate or other terminable interest.

(1) General rule. Where, on the lapse of time, on the occurrence of an event or contingency, or on the failure of an event or contingency to occur, an interest passing to the surviving spouse will terminate or fail, no deduction shall be allowed under this section with respect to such interest—

(A) if an interest in such property passes or has passed (for less than an adequate and full consideration in money or money's worth) from the decedent to any person other than such surviving spouse (or the estate of such spouse); and

(B) if by reason of such passing such person (or his heirs or assigns) may possess or enjoy any part of such property after such termination or failure of the interest so passing to the surviving spouse; and no deduction shall be allowed with respect to such interest (even if such deduction is not disallowed under subparagraphs (A) and (B))—

(C) if such interest is to be acquired for the surviving spouse, pursuant to directions of the decedent, by his executor or by the trustee of a trust.

For purposes of this paragraph, an interest shall not be considered as an interest which will terminate or fail merely because it is the ownership of a bond, note, or similar contractual obligation, the discharge of which would not have the effect of an annuity for life or for a term. * * *

(7) Election with respect to life estate for surviving spouse.

(A) In general. In the case of qualified terminable interest property—

(i) for purposes of subsection (a), such property shall be treated as passing to the surviving spouse, and

(ii) for purposes of paragraph (1)(A), no part of such property shall be treated as passing to any person other than the surviving spouse.

(B) Qualified terminable interest property defined. For purposes of this paragraph—

(i) In general. The term "qualified terminable interest property" means property—

(I) which passes from the decedent,

(II) in which the surviving spouse has a qualifying income interest for life, and

(III) to which an election under this paragraph applies.

(ii) Qualifying income interest for life. The surviving spouse has a qualifying income interest for life if—

(I) the surviving spouse is entitled to all the income from the property, payable annually or at more frequent intervals, or has a usufruct interest for life in the property, and

(II) no person has a power to appoint any part of the property to any person other than the surviving spouse.

Subclause (II) shall not apply to a power exercisable only at or after the death of the surviving spouse. To the extent provided in regulations, an annuity shall be treated in a manner similar to an income interest in property (regardless of whether the property from which the annuity is payable can be separately identified).

(iii) Property includes interest therein. The term "property" includes an interest in property.

(iv) Specific portion treated as separate property. A specific portion of property shall be treated as separate property.

(v) Election. An election under this paragraph with respect to any property shall be made by the executor on the return of tax imposed by section 2001. Such an election, once made, shall be irrevocable.

* * *

In example 2, above, if Harry is concerned about preserving assets for his children following Wanda's death, and perhaps making some assets available for his children during Wanda's life, Harry could structure his estate plan as follows: first, the $1,000,000 that he left Wanda outright in the first example would instead go into a Q-tip trust. That trust would be for Wanda's exclusive benefit during her life, and on her death would pass to her children. Second, the exemption amount would fund the "credit shelter" or "bypass trust", which could allow for distributions of income or principal to Harry's children as well as Wanda during Wanda's life. On Wanda's death the trust would go to Harry's children.

Under this plan, if Harry predeceases Wanda, his estate will pay no tax. This is because the Q-tip trust qualifies for the marital deduction (assuming his executor properly elects), and the $5,000,000 in the credit shelter trust is within Harry's exemption. On Wanda's death, the Q-tip trust will be taxed as part of her estate, but the credit shelter trust will not; it will "bypass" her estate entirely. Her estate will owe no tax unless her own assets, when combined with the assets in the Q-tip trust, exceed $5,000,000.

PROBLEMS

1. Decedent, in her will, creates a trust, directing that income be paid to her husband during his life, with the principal to be distributed to decedent's children at the husband's death. Another clause in decedent's will provides:

> "No interest of any beneficiary in a trust created by this will shall be capable of anticipation or assignment."

May decedent's executor elect to treat the trust as QTIP property and claim the marital deduction? Cf. BancOhio Nat'l Bank v. United States, 1988 WL 159144 (S.D. Ohio 1988).

2. Decedent is survived by his second wife, Maria, their daughter, Anna (age 21), and Laura (age 40), decedent's child from a first marriage. Decedent's will bequeaths to Laura outright "the largest amount that can pass free of the federal estate tax by virtue of the unified credit." Decedent's residuary clause creates a QTIP trust, directing the trustee to pay all of the trust income to Maria, and to distribute the remainder to their daughter Anna. At decedent's death in 2011, his estate has a value of $14,000,000. Maria's assets total $1,000,000. If Maria and decedent were married for 10 years, can Maria take an elective share under the elective share statute in your state? Under the Uniform Probate Code? If so, would any of decedent's estate planning objectives be frustrated?

If you had been decedent's attorney, how would you have planned his estate to minimize or eliminate any elective share problems?

For a thorough analysis of issues arising from the intersection of the elective share and the federal estate tax, see Donna Litman, The Interrelationship Between the Elective Share and the Marital Deduction, 40 Real Prop. Prob. & Trust J. 539 (2005).

c. *Generation–Skipping Trusts*

Consider the extraordinarily wealthy family, with assets far larger than any one generation could consume. If each member of the family made full use of the marital deduction and the unified credit, all assets would still be subject to estate tax at each generation. Suppose, however, a wealthy decedent chose not to leave assets to her children, but instead gave those assets directly to her grandchildren, or better, created a trust giving the children an income interest for life, with a remainder to the grandchildren. Would those assets be taxable in the estates of decedent's children? Until 1986, the answer was, generally, no.

Generation-skipping trusts created the potential for enormous tax savings. Suppose, for instance, a decedent had $10,000,000 in assets, and, for simplicity, one child. Compare the following two dispositions (absent the generation-skipping tax, to which we will return in a moment):

> ***Example 3:*** *When decedent dies in 2011, her will leaves her entire estate to her child. Five years later, in 2016, the child dies, leaving his entire estate (which we assume, for simplicity, is his mother's estate, neither diminished nor augmented over the course of time) to his children. What estate tax is due and when? (Assume, for this question, that the estate tax in 2016 is identical to the tax in 2011).*
>
> ***Solution:*** *At decedent's death, the $10,000,000 estate generates an estate tax of $1,750,000 ($5,000,000 × .35). Decedent's child's estate equals the balance, or $8,250,000. The tax on that amount, at the child's death in 2016, is $1,397,500 ($3,250,000 × .35) [assuming the 2016 exemption amount remains $5,000,000]. Decedent's grandchildren receive a total of $6,852,500.*
>
> ***Example 4:*** *Decedent's will leaves her entire estate to a trustee, with income payable to the child for life, and directions to distribute the principal, at the child's death, to decedent's grandchildren. What estate tax is due and when?*

> ***Solution:*** *As in Example 3, at decedent's death, the tax is $1,750,000, leaving $8,250,000 for distribution to the trust. But at decedent's child's death, the child has no taxable estate. Hence, no tax is due, and the grandchildren receive all $8,250,000.*

Examples 3 and 4 illustrate the enormous tax savings that were long available (largely to the very rich) by using generation-skipping trusts. In the Tax Reform Act of 1986, however, Congress enacted the Generation–Skipping Transfer Tax, significantly curtailing the tax benefits of generation-skipping trusts.

The thrust of the tax is this: in cases like Example 4, even though no assets pass through decedent's child's estate, we must treat the distribution of trust principal *as if* the principal were distributed through the child's estate. That is, the generation-skipping tax is designed to assure that wealth is taxed once each generation. The tax also applies to "direct skips", i.e. transfers directly to the transferor's grandchildren. So it can apply even if a transfer isn't in trust.

The tax itself is complicated, and no one should prepare an estate plan for a multi-million dollar estate without significantly more tax background than we can cover in a basic Trusts and Estates course. Hence, we will not examine the statutory details here. One important point is relevant: each individual transferor enjoys a $5,000,000 exemption from the Generation–Skipping Transfer Tax. The exemption is tied to the annual exemption from the estate tax. In practice, this means that in 2011, an individual can create a $5,000,000 trust, providing for income to children for life and ultimate distribution to grandchildren, without incurring generation-skipping tax liability. Since each spouse in a married couple can use the exemption, a married couple who dies in 2011 can shield $10,000,000 from tax in the estates of their children.

PROBLEM

Sarah Settlor, 88 years old, has an estate valued at $4,000,000. Sarah has two children, Zelda age 65. and Xavier, age 62. Zelda currently has $8,000,000 in assets, and Xavier has $6,500,000. Neither Zelda nor Xavier expects to need Sarah's assets, and indeed, both are making gifts of $13,000 per year to their own children to take advantage of the annual gift tax exclusion. Sarah approaches you about drafting a will, and asks whether tax concerns are relevant with her $4,000,000 estate. How would you advise her?

SECTION III. TRUST MODIFICATION AND TERMINATION

Once a trust has been created, who has power to modify its terms, and under what circumstances? When and how does the trust terminate altogether? This section explores those questions.

A. MODIFICATION OR TERMINATION BY DIRECTION OF THE TRUST SETTLOR

The trust settlor—who created the trust in the first place—has considerable power over trust termination and modification. First, the settlor can, by appropriate language in the instrument creating the trust, reserve to herself the power to revoke or modify the trust. Second, the trust instrument will almost invariably specify a time for trust termination, and will include directions for distribution of trust assets upon termination.

When the settlor reserves a power to revoke, issues often arise about whether settlor has followed her own directions for trust modification or revocation. Consider the following case:

Connecticut General Life Insurance Co. v. First National Bank of Minneapolis

Supreme Court of Minnesota, 1977.
262 N.W.2d 403.

■ YETKA, J.

Appeal from judgment and order denying appellant's motion for amended findings of fact, conclusions of law, and order for judgment. The plaintiff, Connecticut General Life Insurance Co., filed a complaint in interpleader on September 9, 1974. After answers and counterclaims were filed, plaintiff deposited disputed life insurance proceeds with the court and was dismissed from the proceedings. After a trial without a jury, the District Court in Hennepin County determined that the disputed insurance proceeds were to be paid to the First National Bank of Minneapolis, as trustee of the John W. Aughenbaugh Trust. Mrs. Marilyn Aughenbaugh appeals from that determination. We affirm.

On February 2, 1965, Connecticut General Life Insurance Co. (Connecticut General) issued John W. Aughenbaugh a life insurance policy. At that time there was in existence a Last Will and Testament of John W. Aughenbaugh, executed on or about March 16, 1964, which left his estate to Elizabeth Ann Aughenbaugh. On May 4, 1967, John W. Aughenbaugh executed a new will. On the same date he executed an instrument creating the John W. Aughenbaugh Revocable Insurance Trust (the trust). First National Bank of Minneapolis (respondent) was named as trustee. Part of the funding for the trust was to be provided by the Connecticut General policy. The trust was not funded in any respect except by the insurance policies listed. The respondent, First National Bank of Minneapolis, was made beneficiary of the Connecticut General Insurance policy; the trust beneficiaries were Elizabeth Ann Aughenbaugh and three Aughenbaugh children. There were other trusts created in the instrument but they are not in issue in the present case.

In February 1972 the last premium was paid. At that time John W. Aughenbaugh and Elizabeth Ann Aughenbaugh were married and living in

Minneapolis. On November 10, 1972, they were divorced, and on February 14, 1973, John W. Aughenbaugh and Marilyn L. Melaas (appellant) were married in Nevada.

In April 1973 Aughenbaugh and his second spouse moved to Arizona. On or about October 16, 1973, John W. Aughenbaugh executed a document entitled "Will." The will purported to "supercede and cancel any previous wills or trusts established by me." It was entrusted by John Aughenbaugh to his wife Marilyn after it was executed. He died on October 21, 1973. The will was probated in Arizona. After several exchanges of documents between Connecticut General and appellant, the present action was instituted raising the issue as to whether the will executed by John W. Aughenbaugh on October 16, 1973, operated to revoke the John W. Aughenbaugh Revocable Insurance Trust, created May 4, 1967. The trial court held in the negative.

Appellant appears to raise five points in her brief, but three of those issues depend primarily upon whether the trust is *inter vivos* or testamentary in nature. The remaining two issues involve interpretation of the trust agreement itself.

(1) Is a revocable life insurance trust *inter vivos* or testamentary?

* * *

[In the omitted portion the Court upheld the trust as nontestamentary.]

* * *

(2) Revocation of the trust by will.

It is the general rule that where a settlor reserves the power to revoke a trust by a transaction *inter vivos*, as for example by notice to the trustee, he cannot revoke the trust by his will. Restatement, Trusts (2d) § 330, comment *j*; Bogert, Trusts and Trustees, § 1001 (2 ed.); IV Scott on Trusts, § 330.8 (3 ed.). The trust involved in the present case includes the following clause:

> "3.1) *Reservations Affecting the Trust.* Donor reserves the right to amend this agreement from time to time in any and all respects; to revoke the trust hereby created, in whole or in part; and to change the identity or number (or both) of the trustee or trustees hereunder, *by written instrument executed by Donor and delivered to any trustee* (or to Donor's wife if no trustee is acting at a particular time) *during Donor's lifetime*; provided, however, that the duties and responsibilities of the Trustee shall not be substantially increased by any such amendment without its written consent." (Italics supplied.)

The trial court interpreted this clause to mean that the trust could only be *revoked* by written instrument as set forth above. We agree.

Although the clause is not a model of good drafting, appellant concedes that the obvious intent of the section and the requirement of written notice is to protect the trustee. But once this purpose is conceded, any claimed ambiguity in this section of the trust disappears. Maximum protection for the trustee is provided by requiring all major changes to be made by notice to the trustee.

This position, taken by the trial court, appears reasonable because the trustee would wish to know of any major change in its duties; revocation or amendment of the trust would constitute as major a change as an increase or decrease in the number of trustees. The sense of the clause, taken as a whole, is that changes which do not substantially increase the duties and responsibilities of the trustee may be made unilaterally by giving written notice, but that the trustee must concur in substantial increases in its duties.

Affirmed.

QUESTIONS

1. Once a trust settlor has decided to reserve a power to revoke, why would he limit his flexibility in deciding how to revoke?

2. Examine carefully Clause 3.1 in John Aughenbaugh's trust instrument. If you had been arguing on behalf of Aughenbaugh's second wife, how would you have dealt with the language italicized by the court? As a matter of construction, which argument is better?

3. Was there any question about John Aughenbaugh's intent in this case? If not, why should the court frustrate his intent by holding the revocation invalid?

4. In light of the Connecticut General case, how would you draft a provision reserving to the settlor a power to revoke? Consider the following:

> "I hereby reserve unto myself the power and right at any time during my lifetime, before actual distribution to the beneficiary hereunder, to revoke in whole or in part or to amend the Trust hereby created without the necessity of obtaining the consent of the beneficiary and without giving notice to the beneficiary. Any-one of the following acts shall be conclusive evidence of such revocation of this Trust:
>
> (a) the delivery to the issuer or transfer agent of the shares by me of written notice that this Trust is revoked in whole or in part;
>
> (b) the transfer by me of my right, title and interest in and to said Shares;
>
> (c) the delivery by me to the issuer or transfer agent of the Shares of written notice of the death of the beneficiary hereunder. * * * "

In Barnette v. McNulty, 21 Ariz.App. 127, 516 P.2d 583 (1973), the court held that this provision did not limit settlor's ability to revoke by oral statements. The trust document had been taken from Norman Dacey's controversial "How to Avoid Probate." Can you improve on Dacey's language?

5. Suppose John Aughenbaugh had not expressly reserved a power to revoke the trust. Would a court give effect to a later instrument purporting to revoke it? Historically (and in most states today), trusts were presumed to be irrevocable unless the settlor expressly reserved a right to revoke. The new trend is to recognize revocable living trusts as will substitutes, and to reconcile trusts law with wills law by presuming that living trusts are revocable unless the instrument states otherwise. Compare N.Y. E.P.T.L. § 7–1.16 (directing that all trusts are presumed irrevocable unless settlor expressly reserves the right to revoke), with Restatement (Third) of Trusts § 63, cmt. c (2003) (creating a presumption that a trust is revocable if settlor has retained a beneficial interest in the trust); UTC § 602 (providing that "unless the terms of a trust expressly provide that the trust is irrevocable, the settlor may revoke or amend the trust").

6. Suppose John Aughenbaugh *had* reserved a power to revoke, but had specified no method of revocation. Would a court give effect to a will provision purporting to revoke the trust instrument? Remember that a will is treated as an instrument that becomes effective at the testator's death, not during the testator's lifetime. See generally 81 A.L.R.3d 959 (1977) (collecting cases, and concluding that courts are generally reluctant to construe will provisions as effective revocations of *inter vivos* trusts); but see Restatement (Third) of Trusts § 63, cmt. h (2003) (providing that when settlor fails to specify how a revocable trust should be revoked, the trust may be revoked "in any way that provides clear and convincing evidence of settlor's intent to do so", including "by a will . . . that is executed after the creation of the trust and remains unrevoked at settlor's death, and that refers expressly to the trust or the power . . ."); see also UTC § 602(C)(2)(a) (same as Restatement).

7. Suppose that an elderly trust settlor directed that his trust instrument be delivered to him at the nursing home where he was living. Settlor then tore the distributive provisions out of the trust instrument. Did Settlor revoke the trust? There is no common law precedent that suggests that settlors can revoke trusts by physical act. But the comments to UTC § 602 state that "[w]hile revocation of a trust will ordinarily continue to be accomplished by signing and delivering a written document to the trustee, other methods, such as a physical act or an oral statement coupled with a withdrawal of the property, might also demonstrate the necessary intent." Consequently, the court in Salem United Methodist Church v. Bottorff, 138 S.W.3d 788 (Mo.App. 2004) noted that because Missouri had adopted the UTC, a trust might now be revocable by physical act. Is it wise to extend the wills doctrine of revocation by physical act to trusts?

B. MODIFICATION OR TERMINATION BY CONSENT

Suppose the settlor has reserved no power to revoke the trust. What reasons are there to require continuation of the trust if the settlor and all of the beneficiaries want to terminate it? Moreover, after the settlor's death, should the trust continue if all of the beneficiaries agree to terminate the trust?

Adams v. Link

Supreme Court of Errors of Connecticut, 1958.
145 Conn. 634, 145 A.2d 753.

■ KING, ASSOCIATE JUSTICE.

The defendants Link and the United States Trust Company of New York are the executors and trustees under the will and codicil of Mildred A. Kingsmill, late of Darien. Mrs. Kingsmill left, as her sole heirs at law, two brothers, Orson Adams, Jr., and Alvin P. Adams, and a sister, Ethel A. Martin. This action grows out of, although it is distinct from, an appeal by Orson Adams, Jr., and Alvin P. Adams, two of the three heirs at law, from the admission of the will and codicil to probate.

In the view which we take of the case, only the right to terminate the trust created in paragraph sixth of the will need be considered. This paragraph disposed of the residue by a trust. It provided for the payment of the net income for life, in monthly or quarterly instalments at their written election, to Joan K. Pringle and Mayes M. Foeppel, neither of whom was an heir at law. At the death of the survivor, the trust was to terminate and distribution of the corpus was to be made to the New York Association for the Blind. In fact, Joan K. Pringle predeceased the testatrix, leaving Mayes M. Foeppel as the sole income beneficiary and entitled, under the terms of the trust, to the entire net income for life.

During the pendency of the appeal from probate, a so-called compromise agreement was entered into between Mayes M. Foeppel, party of the first part, the New York Association for the Blind, party of the second part, and the three heirs at law of the testatrix, parties of the third part. The agreement in effect provided that (1) the appeal from the admission of the will and codicil to probate would be withdrawn; (2) 15 per cent of the residuary estate, i.e. the trust corpus, would be paid outright to the three heirs at law in equal shares; (3) 37 per cent would be paid outright to the New York Association for the Blind; and (4) 48 per cent would be paid outright to Mayes M. Foeppel less a deduction of $15,000 which would be used to establish a new trust, the precise terms of which are not material. Basically, it was for the education of a son of Alvin P. Adams, and upon completion of his education the trust would terminate and any unused corpus and interest would be returned to Mayes M. Foeppel. The compromise agreement was by its express terms made subject to the approval of the Superior Court. The defendant executors and trustees refused to participate in the agreement or to carry it out. The present action, the plaintiffs in which include all parties to the agreement except the New York Association for the Blind, which was made a party defendant, seeks in effect (a) the approval of the agreement by the Superior Court, and (b) a decree compelling the defendant executors and trustees to carry it out. Since the provision for the New York Association for the Blind was a charitable gift, the attorney general was made a defendant to represent the public interest, under the provisions of § 212 of the General Statutes. The court refused to approve the agreement, and from this action the plaintiffs took this appeal.

While the parties have extensively argued and briefed a number of questions, one basic proposition is dispositive of, and fatal to, the position taken by the plaintiffs. No corrections of the finding which could benefit them in this view of the case can be made.

The fundamental effect of the compromise agreement, if approved by the court, would be to abolish the trust. Our rule as to the right of the beneficiaries of a testamentary trust to have it terminated has been set forth in a number of cases, including Ackerman v. Union & New Haven Trust Co., 90 Conn. 63, 71, 96 A. 149; De Ladson v. Crawford, 93 Conn. 402, 411, 106 A. 326, and Hills v. Travelers Bank & Trust Co., 125 Conn. 640, 648, 7 A.2d 652, 123 A.L.R. 1419. The rule has also in effect been applied to the right of the beneficiaries to terminate an *inter vivos* trust. Gaess v. Gaess, 132 Conn. 96, 101, 42 A.2d 796, 160 A.L.R. 432. Here a testatrix, in her will, established a trust in admittedly clear and unambiguous language; she has now died; and the trust beneficiaries and the heirs at law have joined in a plan to set aside the trust and substitute a distribution of the testatrix' estate more to their liking. Such a testamentary trust may be terminated only by a decree of a court of equity, regardless of any stipulation by all parties in interest. Peiter v. Degenring, 136 Conn. 331, 336, 71 A.2d 87. Our rule as set forth in Hills v. Travelers Bank & Trust Co., supra, is: Conditions precedent which should concur in order to warrant termination of a testamentary trust by judicial decree are (1) that all the parties in interest unite in seeking the termination, (2) that every reasonable ultimate purpose of the trust's creation and existence has been accomplished, and (3) that no fair and lawful restriction imposed by the testator will be nullified or disturbed by such a result. "The function of the court [of equity] with reference to trusts is not to remake the trust instrument, reduce or increase the size of the gifts made therein or accord the beneficiary more advantage than the donor directed that he should enjoy, but rather to ascertain what the donor directed that the donee should receive and to secure to him the enjoyment of that interest only." Hills v. Travelers Bank & Trust Co., supra [125 Conn. 640, 7 A.2d 655]; Peiter v. Degenring, supra. The underlying rationale of our rule is the protection, if reasonably possible, of any reasonable, properly expressed, testamentary desire of a decedent. 3 Scott, Trusts (2d Ed.) § 337.

It appears that all the interested beneficiaries have joined in the agreement under consideration. For the purposes of this case only, we will assume, without in any way deciding, that the plaintiffs are correct in their claim that the defendant executors and trustees have no standing to attack the compromise. This assumption is permissible because the compromise was in terms made contingent upon court approval, and this approval could not be compelled by any agreement of the trust beneficiaries among themselves. Peiter v. Degenring, supra. Thus we may assume, without deciding, that the first condition precedent under our rule is satisfied. But see Loring, A Trustee's Handbook (5th Ed.) § 122, p. 316, § 123, p. 318. The second and third conditions precedent have not, however, been satisfied. The obvious objectives of the testatrix were to provide (a) an assured income for life for Mayes M. Foeppel, and (b) at her death an intact corpus for the New York Association for the Blind. In carrying out these objectives, the testatrix took two important steps. In the first place, the management of the trust corpus was committed to trustees selected by her and in whose financial judgment she is presumed to have had confidence. Secondly, expenditure of any principal by the life beneficiary was precluded. Taken together, these two steps would tend to achieve, and in all reasonable probability would achieve, the testatrix' two basic objectives. To abolish the trust and turn over a fraction of the corpus outright to the life beneficiary would be to enable her in a moment to lose the protection of the practically assured life income provided by the testatrix. The two basic objectives of the trust's creation and existence were reasonable and commendable and cannot be fully accomplished prior to the death of the life beneficiary. Peiter v. Degenring, supra, 136 Conn. 337, 71 A.2d 90; 3 Scott, op. cit., § 337.1, p. 2454. Obviously, had the testatrix intended to entrust the life beneficiary with the handling of any part of the corpus, she would have so provided by a simple, outright gift.

The plaintiffs attempt to avoid the impact of our rule by two main claims. The first is that since the protection accorded the life beneficiary could be lost by her voluntary alienation of the income or by its involuntary alienation through attachment or seizure under an order in equity, the testatrix could not have intended to protect the beneficiary. This amounts in effect to a claim that only a spendthrift trust is protected from termination by agreement of all interested beneficiaries. The case against termination under our rule is of course even stronger where a spendthrift trust is involved, as in Mason v. Rhode Island Hospital Trust Co., 78 Conn. 81, 84, 61 A. 57. 3 Scott, op. cit., § 337.2. But the operation of our rule is not restricted to such trusts. The mere fact that the testatrix failed to provide the maximum possible protection for the life beneficiary by creating a spendthrift trust under the terms of what is now § 3195d of the 1955 Cumulative Supplement does not warrant a conclusion that she intended no protection at all, so that we can consider that the trust no longer has any purpose. Id., p. 2454.

* * *

The plaintiffs also claim that whatever the rule may be in cases involving no will contest, a more liberal rule applies where, as here, the termination of the trust is a part of the settlement of such a contest. Some support for this position may be found in cases cited in 3 Scott, Trusts (2d Ed.) § 337.6. The rationale of our rule as to the power to set aside or terminate a trust is not, however, such that its applicability would be affected by the mere fact that the motivation of a trust termination agreement is the compromise of a will contest. It is true that such contests are not infrequently compromised by agreements involving the transfer of legacies or devises, in whole or in part, by beneficiaries under the will. Where such gifts are alienable this is permissible, since no violence is done to the provisions of the will. But that is not this case. Here the provisions of the will itself are being drastically changed so as to abolish a trust contrary to our rule. This cannot be done. It follows that the court below was not in error in denying approval of the agreement. Indeed, it was the only decision which could properly have been made. This conclusion makes unnecessary the consideration of the other grounds of appeal.

There is no error.

* * *

How would the court in Adams v. Link have decided the following case?

American National Bank of Cheyenne v. Miller

Supreme Court of Wyoming, 1995.
899 P.2d 1337.

■ KAUTZ, DISTRICT JUDGE

This appeal considers whether the beneficiaries of a trust can compel its early termination on the grounds it lacks any remaining material purpose. As collateral matters, this case addresses whether a trustee (who is not also a beneficiary) has standing to challenge the early termination of a trust, and whether the cost of a supersedeas bond was properly allocated to the trustee individually.

The district court found all the beneficiaries of the Evelyn S. Plummer Trust consented to its early termination, and continuation of the trust served no remaining material purpose of the Grantor. An order terminating the trust was issued over the objection of the Trustee, who appealed....

We affirm the district court's summary judgment terminating the trust....

ISSUES

Appellant Trustee states the following issue:

In Wyoming, an irrevocable trust should not be revoked in a manner which is contrary to its express provisions because of the suggested expediency of the beneficiaries.

In their brief, Appellees rephrase the issues as:

I. Whether the trial court properly entered summary judgment terminating the Evelyn S. Plummer Trust?

A. Whether this Court should adopt the rule of RESTATEMENT (SECOND) OF TRUSTS § 337 (1957), which allows termination of trusts with no remaining material purpose by consent of all beneficiaries?

B. Whether all of the beneficiaries of the Evelyn S. Plummer Trust have consented to its termination?

C. Whether there is any material purpose for continuing the Plummer Trust?

II. Whether this appeal should be dismissed because Appellant lacks standing to appeal from the trial court's order of summary judgment?

A. Whether any aggrieved party is before this Court?

B. Whether the Bank can appear on behalf of the unborn heirs of the Trust beneficiaries?

C. Whether the Bank is itself an "aggrieved party," in either its personal or fiduciary capacity?

III. Whether the trial court acted within its discretion in ordering Appellant to post a supersedeas bond from its own assets rather than from the assets of the Trust?

FACTS

Appellant is the Trustee of the Evelyn S. Plummer Trust, established by Mrs. Plummer in 1967. Mrs. Plummer had one child, Vivian Miller. Vivian Miller married Appellee Grant E. Miller. The Millers had three children, Appellees Davin, Hickey and Miller, Jr.

In summary, the trust instructed the Trustee to utilize the trust estate:

1. To support Mrs. Plummer during her lifetime, and pay her debts and expenses upon her death.

2. After Mrs. Plummer's death, to pay $200.00 per month to Vivian and Grant E. Miller, or the survivor of them, and to assist with educational expenses of their children (Davin, Hickey and Miller, Jr.).

3. After the death of both Vivian and Grant E. Miller, to divide the trust estate into "as many equal shares as there are then living children" of Vivian and Grant E. Miller. Those shares are to be distributed:

a. 20% to each child at age 23 or college graduation, whichever is earlier; b. 20% to each child at age 28; c. 20% to each child at age 35.

4. When the last of the 20% payments to the grandchildren has been made, to distribute all the balance of the trust estate to the Chiles P. Plummer and Evelyn S. Plummer scholarship fund at the University of Wyoming.

Mrs. Plummer died in 1976 and Vivian Miller passed away in 1992. Grant E. Miller relinquished and assigned his interests in the $200.00 per month payments to Davin, Hickey and Miller, Jr. Those individuals are all over 35 years of age.

Grant E. Miller, Davin, Hickey, Miller, Jr., and the University of Wyoming all consented to termination and distribution of the trust now, even though Grant E. Miller is still living. The Trustee, however, did not consent and refused to terminate the trust.

Appellees brought an action for declaratory relief, requesting that the district court declare the trust be terminated. In response to a Motion for Summary Judgment, the district court issued detailed Findings of Fact and Conclusions of Law in support of an Order directing the trust be terminated.

The Trustee appealed that ruling, and requested the district court's order be stayed during the appeal. Appellees objected to the stay, arguing the trust would incur taxes on income, which if distributed, the University of Wyoming would not have to pay. Appellees argued they would lose the use and benefit of the trust estate during the appeal. The district court then required the Trustee to post a supersedeas bond at its own expense, and not at the expense of the trust.

DISCUSSION

A. Standing

Appellees have raised the issue of the Trustee's standing to bring this appeal. Appellees assert only an "aggrieved party" has standing to appeal. They then argue that only beneficiaries can be aggrieved parties to an order terminating the trust. As a consequence, Appellees believe a trustee has no standing unless it is acting on behalf of an aggrieved beneficiary.

It is true that standing is jurisdictional. In the *Matter of Various Water Rights in Lake DeSmet*, 623 P.2d 764, 767 (Wyo.1981). "For a party to have standing to sue means that he has sufficient stake, in an otherwise justiciable controversy, to obtain a judicial resolution *Spratt v. Security Bank of Buffalo*, 654 P.2d 130, 134 (Wyo.1982).

A trustee, however, acts on behalf of both the beneficiaries and the grantor of the trust. A fundamental duty of a trustee is to carry out the terms of the trust. 76 Am. Jur. 2d Trusts §§ 374, 375 (1992). "The clearly expressed intention of the settlor should be zealously guarded...." *First Nat'l Bank & Trust Co. v. Brimmer*, 504 P.2d 1367, 1371 (Wyo.1973).

A trustee has an obligation to defend the trust in order to carry out the material purposes of the trust. Wyo. Stat. § 4–8–103(c)(xxv) (Supp. 1995) recognizes that a trustee has the power (and standing) to

> "prosecute or defend actions, claims or proceedings for the protection of trust assets and of the trustee in the performance of his duties;...." (emphasis added)

One of the duties specified for the Trustee in the Plummer Trust was to hold and manage the trust estate, subject to certain conditions, until the death of Grant E. Miller. Although there is a dispute as to whether such a duty constitutes a material purpose of the trust, the Trustee in this case had the power, and standing, to defend its performance of that duty. This Trustee would not know, until after the resolution of this case, that in Wyoming beneficiaries can direct the termination of a trust where there are no remaining material purposes of the trust.

We hold that in this case the Trustee had standing.

B. Termination of the Trust

The trial court granted summary judgment directing the trust be terminated. In doing so, the district court held "where all the beneficiaries of a trust consent to termination, and there is no material purpose in continuing the trust, the beneficiaries can compel termination of the trust. Restatement (Second) of Trusts '337."

"Summary judgment is appropriate when no genuine issue of material fact exists and when the prevailing party is entitled to have a judgment as a matter of law." *Sandstrom v. Sandstrom*, 884 P.2d 968, 971 (Wyo.1994). In testing the propriety of the summary judgment here, we will first review the law applied by the trial court, and then determine whether there were issues of fact material to a resolution of the case under the appropriate legal principles.

Whether the beneficiaries of a trust can terminate that trust prior to the time specified for termination in the trust document is an issue that has not previously been decided in Wyoming. The Restatement (Second) of Trusts § 337 (1959) summarizes a general rule as to when beneficiaries can compel the early termination of a trust:

> (1) Except as stated in Subsection (2), if all of the beneficiaries of a trust consent and none of them is under an incapacity, they can compel the termination of the trust.
>
> (2) If the continuance of the trust is necessary to carry out a material purpose of the trust, the beneficiaries cannot compel its termination.

We find the principles of § 337 to be sound, and adopt them as the law of Wyoming. This rule balances between protecting and enforcing a grantor's instructions regarding a trust, and providing for distribution to beneficiaries at the earliest time after all the grantor's material purposes have been fulfilled. The law should guard and enforce a grantor's wishes and purposes, so long as they remain unfulfilled. When those purposes have been fulfilled, however, the law should provide for the most expeditious termination and distribution of the trust estate. The rule we adopt here accomplishes both purposes.

The record in this case does not reflect any issue of material fact, based on the rule adopted above. Grant E. Miller, Davin, Hickey, Miller, Jr., and the University of Wyoming all consented to termination of the trust. There are no other beneficiaries of the trust. There is no remaining material purpose for continuation of the trust.

The Trustee mistakenly believes there are unborn contingent beneficiaries of the trust who did not consent to its termination. The trust terms, however, make it clear there are no unborn, contingent beneficiaries. The trust provides that if Grant E. Miller dies before Davin, Hickey, and Miller, Jr., those individuals each receive a share of the trust estate, with the balance being distributed to the University of Wyoming. Because Davin, Hickey, and Miller, Jr. are each over 35 years of age, vesting would occur immediately. If Davin, Hickey or Miller, Jr. die before Grant E. Miller, neither they nor their heirs would receive any part of the trust estate. This is so because the trust provides for per capita distribution to Grant E. Miller's children when it directs:

> "Upon the death of the last survivor of Vivian Miller and Grant E. Miller, the entire Trust Estate ... shall be divided into as many equal

> shares as *there are then living children of said Vivian Miller and Grant E. Miller*". (emphasis added)

No heirs of Davin, Hickey or Miller, Jr., could possibly be involved.

There is no remaining material purpose of the trust. A grantor's intent is to be found, if possible, within the trust instrument itself. *First Nat'l Bank & Trust Co.*, 504 P.2d at 1369; *Kerper v. Kerper*, 780 P.2d 923, 939 (Wyo.1989). The trust instrument here identifies several purposes. Two of those purposes are for support of beneficiaries—monthly income for Grant E. Miller and educational assistance for Davin, Hickey and Miller, Jr. All of these beneficiaries have waived their support for continuation of the trust.

If Grant E. Miller were deceased, the other beneficiaries would receive their interest in the trust without regard for educational support because those beneficiaries are over the age of 35. Educational support was a material purpose of the trust only until those beneficiaries reached age 35.

The trust has no spendthrift provisions. Grant E. Miller could, and did, renounce and assign his monthly support interest to his children. Consequently, his monthly support is no longer a material purpose of the trust.

The Trustee argues Grant E. Miller's life as a measuring life for distribution to his children constitutes a material purpose of the trust. In other words, the Trustee urges the grantor's purpose was to delay her grandchildren's receipt of their interests until Grant E. Miller's death.

The trust does indicate an intent to delay the grandchildren's enjoyment of their interests. However, Grant E. Miller's life is not the measurement the grantor chose to use. The trust clearly establishes Davin, Hickey and Miller, Jr., reaching age 35 as the measurement or condition for the delay of distribution to them. Reference to Grant E. Miller's life time in the trust does not quantify a delay in distribution to Davin, Hickey and Miller, Jr., but relates only to his own support.

Because Grant E. Miller has waived and transferred his right to monthly support, and because Davin, Hickey and Miller, Jr., have reached the age of 35, there is no remaining material purpose for the trust.

* * *

PROBLEMS

Testator, who died unmarried and childless, left all of her property in trust, and directed the trustee to divide the trust income among ten beneficiaries, as follows: $5,000 per year to each of six cousins, $50,000 per year to three nephews, and the balance of the income to a favorite niece. Testator directed trustee to make payments to each beneficiary until that beneficiary's death, and to terminate the trust at the death of the surviving beneficiary. At termination, testator directed that the principal, plus any accumulated income, should be paid to an art museum.

Testator's niece and nephews have died, as have four of the six cousins; two cousins survive. The trust principal now totals $5,000,000, and the art museum wants to purchase a number of works in the expectation that prices will soon rise.

1. Suppose the art museum offers to pay the two cousins (each now 70 years old) $100,000 apiece in return for their consent to trust termination. The cousins agree. If the trustee refuses to consent to the beneficiaries' agreement, what arguments might the beneficiaries advance in support of their position? How might the trustee respond to those arguments?

2. Suppose the museum instead agrees to modify the trust to leave $1,000,000 in the trust, and to increase payments to the surviving cousins to $20,000 per year each, with the remainder of the trust principal to be paid to the museum. If the cousins agree, should a court permit modification?

3. Consider section 65 of The Restatement (Third) of Trusts (2003), which provides:

§ 65. Termination or Modification by Consent of Beneficiaries

> (1) Except as stated in Subsection (2), if all of the beneficiaries of an irrevocable trust consent, they can compel the termination or modification of the trust.
>
> (2) If termination or modification of the trust under Subsection (1) would be inconsistent with a material purpose of the trust, the beneficiaries cannot compel its termination or modification except with the consent of the settlor or, after the settlor's death, with authorization of the court if it determines that the reason for termination outweighs the material purpose.

Comment d elaborates:

> Material purposes are not readily to be inferred. A finding of such a purpose generally requires some showing of a particular concern or objective on the part of the settlor, such as concern with regard to a beneficiary's management skills, judgment, or level of maturity....
>
> The mere fact that a settlor has created a trust for successive beneficiaries does not prevent the beneficiaries from terminating or modifying the trust to reallocate the beneficial interests among themselves if they wish to do so. A trust plan to provide successive enjoyment is not itself sufficient to indicate, for example, that the settlor had a material purpose of depriving the beneficiaries of the property management or otherwise protecting them from the risks of their own judgment. In the absence of additional circumstances indicating a further purpose, the inference is that the trust was intended merely to allow one or more persons to enjoy the benefits of the trust property during the period of the trust and to allow the other beneficiary or beneficiaries to receive the property thereafter.

What impact would the Restatement (Third) have on your analysis of Problem 1?

4. Suppose a client asks you to draft a testamentary trust that provides his only child Martha with income for her life, and distributes the remainder to Martha's children at her death. The client informs you that he wishes to name his long-time investment advisor, Wilma Wise, as trustee of the trust, because he thinks that Wilma would do a much better job of managing the assets than would Martha. Given the language and comments of Restatement (Third), how would you draft the trust to ensure that Martha could not terminate it after your client's death? Would your answer be different if the client asked you to draft an *inter vivos* trust with the same terms?

NOTES AND QUESTIONS

1. The rule that the beneficiaries of the trust cannot agree to terminate the trust when termination would frustrate the wishes of the settlor is commonly referred to as the "Claflin doctrine," after Claflin v. Claflin, 149 Mass. 19, 20 N.E. 454 (1889). The Restatement (Third), quoted above, would abandon the Claflin doctrine and substitute a test that would have courts balance the reasons for termination against the settlor's material purpose. UTC § 411(b) rejects the position taken by the Restatement (Third), and instead endorses the Claflin doctrine. Section 411(b) provides that trust beneficiaries may terminate or modify the trust "if the court concludes that continuance of the trust is not necessary to achieve any material purpose of the trust," or that "modification is not inconsistent with a material purpose of the trust."

Which approach is more sensible? Professor Chester argues that the Claflin doctrine should be rejected: "The living, providing they are legally interested parties and can all agree, should be able to bring to an end an individual's estate plan when it no longer suits them, unless there remains some need for "guardianship-like' protection." See Ronald Chester, Inheritance, Wealth and Society 128 (1982). Professor Sitkoff notes that the Claflin doctrine can be inefficient because it "entrenches the trustee and locks in a certain minimal level of beneficiary-trustee agency costs." On the other hand, he notes, the Claflin doctrine might be valuable to beneficiaries as a whole because "it increases the willingness of grantors to create a trust in the first place." See Robert H. Sitkoff, An Agency Costs Theory of Trust Law, 89 Cornell L. Rev. 621, 659–60 (2004).

2. In both Adams v. Link and American Nat'l Bank of Cheyenne v. Miller, the trustees opposed termination of the trust even though all beneficiaries supported termination. Why would the trustees oppose termination? Is any justification apparent, other than a desire to preserve their own right to commissions and their reputation among the wealthy for sticking up for their settlor-customers?

3. There is some controversy about the effect that a spendthrift clause should have on the beneficiaries' ability to terminate an irrevocable trust. Many courts have taken the position that the beneficiaries may not compel termination of a spendthrift trust, because termination would interfere with a material purpose of the settlor. See Matter of Weitzel, 778 N.W.2d 219 (Iowa App. 2009); Somers v. Firstar Bank, 277 Kan. 761, 89 P.3d 898

(2004). Some statutes expressly direct that result. For example, California Probate Code, § 15404(b) provides:

> (a) Except as provided in subdivision (b), if all beneficiaries of an irrevocable trust consent, they may compel modification or termination of the trust upon petition to the court.
>
> (b) If the continuance of the trust is necessary to carry out a material purpose of the trust, the trust cannot be modified or terminated unless the court, in its discretion, determines that the reason for doing so under the circumstances outweighs the interest in accomplishing a material purpose of the trust. Under this section the court does not have discretion to permit termination of a trust that is subject to a valid restraint on transfer of the beneficiary's interest. . . .

In New York, where all trusts are spendthrift unless the settlor provides otherwise, the beneficiaries ordinarily may not consent to trust termination once the settlor has died—unless the settlor has explicitly made the trust non-spendthrift. See Culver v. Title Guarantee & Trust Co., 296 N.Y. 74, 70 N.E.2d 163 (1946). However, if the beneficiaries can show that "continuation of the trust is economically impracticable, that the express terms of the disposing instrument do not prohibit its early termination, and that such termination would not defeat the specified purpose of the trust and would be in the best interests of the beneficiaries," a court may terminate a spendthrift trust. See E.P.T.L. 7–1.19.

On the other hand, the drafters of the Restatement (Third) of Trusts advise that a spendthrift clause is only "some indication" that the settlor had a material purpose inconsistent with termination because the settlor may have inserted the clause as a matter of routine, or simply to facilitate the beneficiaries' successive enjoyment of the trust property. See Restatement (Third) of Trusts § 65, cmt. e (2003).

UTC section 411(c) gives states a choice. As Professor Newman explains:

> The UTC, as originally promulgated, did not address the material-purpose subject generally, but provided in section 411(c) that the inclusion of a spendthrift provision in the instrument "is not presumed to constitute a material purpose of the trust." The 2004 amendments to the UTC, however, bracket section 411(c) because several states that have enacted the Code have not agreed with the provision and have either deleted it or have revised it to state that a spendthrift provision is presumed to constitute a material purpose of the trust. In UTC-adopting jurisdictions in which spendthrift provisions are treated as constituting material purposes under pre-UTC law, the deletion of section 411(c) would likely continue that result.

See Alan Newman, The Intention of the Settlor Under the Uniform Trust Code: Whose Property Is It, Anyway?, 38 Akron L. Rev. 649 (2005).

Finally, if a trust is a pure discretionary trust and not protected by a spendthrift provision, should the beneficiaries be entitled to terminate the trust if they all consent? See Restatement (Third) of Trusts § 65, cmt. e (2003) (stating that "discretionary provisions, ... may represent nothing more than a settlor's plan for allocating the benefits of his or her property flexibly among various beneficiaries rather than revealing some significant concerns or protective purposes that would prevent the beneficiaries from joining together to terminate a trust and divide or distribute the property as they wish ...").

With increasing frequency, settlors are creating so-called "incentive trusts", designed not only to provide for future generations but to ensure that trust beneficiaries live healthy and productive lives. For example, a settlor might require a beneficiary to earn a minimum salary to qualify for trust distributions. Professor Joshua Tate considers whether rules that make trust termination too easy might unwisely undermine such trusts. See Joshua Tate, Conditional Love: Incentive Trusts and the Inflexibility Problem, 41 Real Prop. Prob. & Tr. J. 445 (2006). On the material purpose doctrine generally, see Gail Boreman Bird, Trust Termination: Unborn, Living and Dead Hands—Too Many Fingers in the Trust Pie, 36 Hastings L. J. 563, 577–93 (1985).

4. ***Termination While the Settlor Is Still Alive.*** Suppose the trust in Adams v. Link had been an *inter vivos* trust, and that settlor, during her lifetime, had consented to termination. Would the court have terminated the trust? Suppose, in American Nat'l Bank v. Miller, the beneficiaries had consented to termination before the settlor's death, and the settlor had objected. Would the court have terminated the trust?

If all of the beneficiaries of a trust consent to termination, the only reason for keeping the trust in effect is deference to the wishes of the settlor. If, however, the settlor consents to the termination, the only reason for maintaining the trust disappears. Thus, both the Restatement (Third) of Trusts § 65 (2003) and Uniform Trust Code § 411(a) allow a settlor to terminate or modify a trust if all beneficiaries consent, even if termination or modification is inconsistent with the material purpose of the trust.

5. ***Who Are the Trust's Beneficiaries?*** In American Nat'l Bank of Cheyenne v. Miller, the trust instrument provided for division of the trust principal, at the death of the survivor of Grant and Vivian Miller, "into as many equal shares as there are then living children" of the Millers. Once Vivian Miller died, no additional children of Grant and Vivian could be born. As a result, at the time the trust beneficiaries sought termination, it was clear that all possible beneficiaries had consented. Suppose, however, that the instrument had provided for distribution, at the death of Grant and Vivian Miller, to the "issue then living" of Grant and Vivian. Would termination by consent have been possible?

Consider the problem: if Davin Miller (a child of Grant and Vivian) were to die before his father, neither Davin nor his estate would be entitled to any share of trust principal. Instead, if Davin had children of his own, those children would be entitled to the trust principal. If, however, the consent of all potential issue of Grant and Vivian is necessary to permit termination of the trust, termination by consent would be impossible; some potential issue are unborn, while others might still be minors, without capacity to bind themselves. Cf. In re Mergenhagen, 50 A.D.3d 1486, 856 N.Y.S.2d 389 (App. Div. 2008) (holding that amendment to trust was invalid because the minor contingent beneficiaries had not consented to the amendment in writing).

UTC § 401(e) provides that if not all of the beneficiaries consent to a proposed modification or termination of the trust, the court may order modification or termination if the court is satisfied that, (1) if all of the beneficiaries had consented, the trust could have been modified or terminated under this section; and (2) the interests of a beneficiary who does not consent will be adequately protected.

In some jurisdictions, courts may appoint a guardian ad litem to represent the interests of unborn beneficiaries, and then require consent of the guardian before permitting trust termination. See Cal. Prob. Code, § 15405; Hatch v. Riggs National Bank, 361 F.2d 559 (D.C.Cir. 1966).

If a guardian is appointed to represent the interests of unborn beneficiaries, what responsibility does the guardian have? Suppose settlor creates an irrevocable *inter vivos* trust, reserving income to herself, and providing that at her death, principal is to be divided among her next of kin. Twenty years later, settlor discovers that the trust income is insufficient to provide for her support, and seeks modification to permit limited invasion of principal. Her two children consent, and a guardian is appointed to represent the interests of unborn persons who might become settlor's next of kin. Should the guardian consent? On what terms?

The California statute provides that "[i]n determining whether to give consent, the guardian ad litem may rely on general family benefit accruing to living members of the beneficiary's family as a basis for approving a modification or termination of the trust." Cal. Prob. Code § 15405. Would the California statute alter your answers? See generally Gail Boreman Bird, Trust Termination: Unborn, Living and Dead Hands, Too Many Fingers in the Trust Pie, 36 Hastings L.J. 563, 600–05 (1985).

C. Modification or Termination Without Consent of All Beneficiaries

Courts typically enforce trusts according to their terms because trust instruments typically reflect the intentions of trust settlors. What happens, however, when a court becomes convinced that enforcing the trust according to its terms would frustrate settlor's intentions?

The problem can arise because the instrument was poorly drafted, and never reflected settlor's intent. But even a well-drafted instrument may not anticipate the circumstances that might arise over the lifetime of a trust—which might extend over two generations. As time passes, the language of the trust instrument may become less reliable as a guide to settlor's intentions because it is not clear how testator would have responded to the changed circumstances. Courts (and legislatures) have developed a number of doctrines designed to permit escape from the language of the trust instrument.

1. MISTAKE

Suppose settlor creates a trust with a clear tax objective in mind. The trust's language fails to achieve that objective. Can a court reform the trust instrument to accomplish testator's objective? Consider the following excerpt:

Walker v. Walker

Supreme Judicial Court of Massachusetts, 2001.
433 Mass. 581, 744 N.E.2d 60.

■ MARSHALL, C.J.

The plaintiffs commenced this action in the Supreme Judicial Court for Suffolk County pursuant to *G. L. c. 215, § 6*, seeking to reform the Donald D. Walker Revocable Trust. They alleged that, due to a mistake, the trust as presently written fails to accomplish the settlor's goals. Because of the Federal tax implications discussed below, and because it is uncertain whether the Internal Revenue Service would abide by a decision on a matter of State law, such as this, other than a decision from the State's highest court, see *Loeser v. Talbot, 412 Mass. 361, 362, 589 N.E.2d 301 (1992)*, a single justice reported the case to the full court.

The plaintiffs are the trustees of the trust. The defendants are the presently identifiable beneficiaries of the trust and the Commissioner of Internal Revenue (commissioner). As commonly happens when the commissioner is named as a defendant and served with process in a case such as this, he has chosen not to participate. *Berman v. Sandler, 379 Mass. 506, 509 n. 5, 399 N.E.2d 17 (1980)*. All of the other parties have stipulated to the relevant facts, and each of the defendants other than the commissioner has assented to the relief sought. A guardian ad litem has been appointed to represent the interests of any unborn or unascertained individuals; the guardian ad litem also has joined in the stipulation of facts and assented to the relief sought.

* * *

1. Facts. Donald D. Walker (Donald), settlor of the Donald D. Walker Revocable Trust, dated April 27, 1988, died on January 31, 1989. He was survived by his spouse, E. Virginia Walker (Virginia), and two children, Marcia B. Walker and Penelope B. Walker. The trust instrument identifies Donald and Virginia as the initial cotrustees, and they served in that capacity until Donald's death, at which time Virginia became the sole trustee. In accordance with the terms of the trust, Virginia subsequently appointed Rockland Trust Company to serve as cotrustee.[10] The trust was revocable during Donald's lifetime and became irrevocable on his death.

The trust instrument called for distribution of the trust property, on Donald's death, to one or more of three trusts: a general marital trust, a

---

10. Virginia and Rockland Trust Company continue to serve as cotrustees. Virginia has named her children, Marcia and Penelope, to serve as successor cotrustees (along with Rockland Trust Company) in the event that she ceases to serve as trustee for any reason.

special marital trust, and a nonmarital deduction trust. Article III, paragraph A, which creates the general marital trust, Article III, paragraph B, which creates the special marital trust, and Article IV, which sets forth various administrative provisions for the two marital trusts, expressly indicate that those trusts were intended and designed to provide Donald's estate with the maximum marital deductions permitted by law for purposes of Massachusetts and Federal estate taxes,[11] and that they should be interpreted and administered accordingly. Under the terms of both marital trusts, Virginia is to receive net income generated from any property in those trusts during her lifetime. Under Article III, paragraph C, entitled "Payments of Principal from Marital Trusts," the trustees are also authorized to distribute to Virginia, during her lifetime, all or any portion of the principal of those trusts as they deem in their discretion to be advisable, and Virginia, as beneficiary, also has the power to demand all or any portion of the principal of the general marital trust during her lifetime.

In Article III, paragraph A, Virginia is granted the power to appoint, in her own will, the principal of the general marital trust, as well as any income that has accrued but remains undistributed at the time of her death. Her power of appointment expressly includes the power to appoint general marital trust principal to her own estate. In Article III, paragraph B, she is granted the power to appoint, in her will, special marital trust principal to one or more of Donald's issue and their spouses.

Under the express terms of Article III, paragraphs A and B, the general marital trust and the special marital trust were to be funded only to the extent necessary to eliminate (or minimize as far as possible) the Federal and Massachusetts estate taxes on Donald's estate.... Because of the size of Donald's estate, however, no estate taxes would have been due when he died, so no property from the Donald D. Walker Revocable Trust was distributed to either of the marital trusts. Those trusts went unfunded. Only the nonmarital deduction trust was funded. It received all of the trust property....

Under Article III, paragraph D, which creates the nonmarital deduction trust, Virginia is to receive, during her lifetime, the net income

---

At the time the parties filed their statement of agreed facts, Virginia was eighty-one years old, Marcia was forty-eight years old, and Penelope was forty-two years old. Marcia and Penelope are Donald's only issue; neither one of them is married or has any children.

11. Article III, paragraph A provides in relevant part: "if any part of the Grantor's estate is subject to the Massachusetts estate tax, then there shall be set aside in a separate trust, to be known as the General Marital Trust, an amount (the 'general marital amount') equal to the maximum marital deduction allowable in determining the Grantor's Massachusetts estate tax ... provided, however, that the general marital amount shall not exceed the minimum amount which ... would eliminate the Massachusetts estate tax otherwise payable by reason of the Grantor's death after taking into account all credits, exemptions, and other deductions."

Article III, paragraph B provides in relevant part: "there shall be set aside as a separate trust, to be known as the Special Marital Trust, the smallest amount (the 'special marital amount') which if given outright to [Virginia] at the Grantor's death would eliminate or minimize insofar as possible the total federal and state estate taxes otherwise payable by reason of the Grantor's death after taking into account all credits, exemptions, and deductions."

generated from the principal of that trust. On her death, the principal is to be paid to Donald's then living issue. Unlike the language in the marital trusts, the language creating the nonmarital deduction trust gives Virginia no right, as beneficiary, to appoint principal through her will. However, Article III, paragraph F, entitled "Discretionary Power to Pay Principal," which applies to the nonmarital deduction trust, gives Virginia, in her capacity as trustee, unbridled discretion to pay principal from the nonmarital deduction trust to herself as beneficiary. As explained below, it is this language that the parties contend was mistakenly included in the trust document. Specifically, Article III, paragraph F states:

> "In addition to the payments of income hereinabove provided, the Trustee is (or Trustees are) authorized at any time or from time to time to make or apply distributions or payments of principal of the trust property to or for the benefit of the Grantor's said spouse, E. Virginia Walker, in such portions or amounts, including the entire trust property, as the Trustee or Trustees may deem advisable. In making the discretionary payments or distributions of principal under this paragraph F, it is the Grantor's desire that the Trustee or Trustees exercise the power to make such payments or distributions in a liberal manner, and so may, but need not, take into account other resources available to said beneficiary."

The inclusion of this provision giving Virginia, as trustee, the authority to make discretionary payments of principal to herself, as beneficiary, constitutes a general power of appointment within the meaning of I.R.C. § 2041(b)(1) (1986). As a result, the property subject to the power, in other words all property in the nonmarital deduction trust, will be includible in Virginia's gross estate at the time of her death, regardless of whether she exercises the power. I.R.C. § 2041(a)(2) (1986). The parties claim that this result is contrary to Donald's intent to have the nonmarital deduction trust property pass free of estate taxes in both his estate and Virginia's estate. To support their claim that Donald so intended, they rely on the structure and language of the trust instrument and on an affidavit from the attorney who drafted the instrument. That attorney, now retired, states in his affidavit as follows:

> "5. I do not recall specific discussions with Mr. Walker as to whether he intended the assets in the Non-marital Deduction Trust to pass free of estate taxes following Mrs. Walker's death. However, my practice was to draft Non-marital Deduction Trusts so that the assets of these trusts would pass free of estate taxes upon the deaths of both the donor and the donor's spouse.
>
> "6. My memory as to Mr. Walker's intentions has been aided by a review of the Walker Trust and correspondence from me to Mrs. Virginia Walker following Mr. Walker's death.
>
> "7. With the aid of these documents, it is my memory that Mr. Walker intended the assets in the Non-marital Deduction Trust to pass free of estate taxes upon Mrs. Walker's death.
>
> "8. I believe that the relief which the plaintiffs request in the Complaint, including limiting Mrs. Walker's discretion as Trustee over

the principal of the Non-marital Deduction Trust by an ascertainable standard, will conform the Walker Trust to Mr. Walker's intent, by removing the assets of the Non-marital Deduction Trust from Mrs. Walker's gross estate."

The parties ask that we permit the trust to be reformed in three respects: (1) by inserting a so-called ascertainable standard in Article III, paragraph F, which would limit the scope of Virginia's power as trustee under that paragraph in a way that would cause her not to have a general power of appointment; (2) by inserting in Article V, which governs the succession of trustees, a provision requiring that there be a corporate cotrustee serving at all times; and (3) by inserting a new paragraph in Article V reciting Donald's intention (a) that no principal or income of any trust be included in the estate of any trustee, (b) that no trustee have the power to act in any fashion that would subject his or her estate to estate taxes, and (c) that in the event a trustee's estate would be so affected, his or her power to act may be exercised only by a cotrustee who will not be so affected. The parties maintain that these changes will ensure, as Donald intended, that the property in the nonmarital deduction trust not be included in Virginia's gross estate for estate tax purposes.[12]

2. Discussion. It is well settled that, as a matter of Massachusetts law, a trust instrument may be reformed to conform to the settlor's intent. DiCarlo v. Mazzarella, 430 Mass. 248, 250, 717 N.E.2d 257 (1999). *Putnam v. Putnam, 425 Mass. 770, 772, 682 N.E.2d 1351 (1997). Simches v. Simches, 423 Mass. 683, 686–687, 671 N.E.2d 1226 (1996).* Thus "we may require the trust to be reformed on clear and decisive proof that the instrument fails to embody the settlor's intent because of scrivener's error." *DiCarlo v. Mazzarella, supra.* See *Shawmut Bank, N.A. v. Buckley, 422 Mass. 706, 714, 665 N.E.2d 29 (1996).* "We have allowed the reformation of trust instruments which produced tax results that were clearly inconsistent with the settlor's tax objectives." *BankBoston v. Marlow, 428 Mass. 283, 285, 701 N.E.2d 304 (1998).* See *Putnam v. Putnam, supra,* and authorities cited.

"To ascertain the settlor's intent, we look to the trust instrument as a whole and the circumstances known to the settlor on execution." *DiCarlo v. Mazzarella, supra at 250,* quoting *Pond v. Pond, 424 Mass. 894, 897, 678 N.E.2d 1321 (1997).* In addition, we have indicated our willingness to accept extrinsic evidence, such as an attorney's affidavit, that demonstrates that there has been a mistake. "Indeed, the crucial evidence of intent and mistake may well be available from the lawyer who drafted (or misdrafted) the instrument rather than from the settlor." *Putnam v. Putnam, supra at 772.* See *Loeser v. Talbot, 412 Mass. 361, 366 n. 7, 589 N.E.2d 301 (1992); Berman v. Sandler, 379 Mass. 506, 511, 399 N.E.2d 17 (1980).*

---

12. The parties indicate that the value of the nonmarital deduction trust assets shortly before they filed their stipulation of facts was $798,931. To illustrate the effect that the requested reformation might have on her estate, they have supplied us with calculations demonstrating that, had she died in 1998 (when the stipulation was filed), Virginia's estate would have recognized a savings of $365,476 in total Federal and Massachusetts estate taxes as a result of reformation.

The evidence in this case more than adequately demonstrates that Donald, as settlor of the Donald D. Walker Revocable Trust, intended to eliminate, or to minimize to the fullest extent possible, any adverse estate tax consequences not only to his own estate, but also to Virginia's estate. He did this by availing himself of the maximum marital deductions permitted by Massachusetts and Federal law in the general and special marital trusts, by funding those trusts only to the extent needed to take advantage of those deductions, and by giving Virginia no power as beneficiary of the nonmarital deduction trust to appoint principal of that trust. The absence of a power (as beneficiary) to appoint nonmarital deduction trust property plainly was intended to keep the property from being included in her gross estate.[13] Moreover, we have in this record the drafting attorney's affidavit confirming both the settlor's and his intentions to construct the nonmarital deduction trust such that the trust property would not be included in Virginia's estate.

To remedy the unintended result, the parties seek to reform Article III, paragraph F by inserting a so-called ascertainable standard governing trustee distributions of principal to Virginia, and by deleting the problematic language concerning liberal discretionary distributions. Inclusion of an ascertainable standard will effectively negate a general power of appointment, I.R.C. '2041(b)(1)(A), remove the nonmarital deduction trust property from Virginia's estate, and thereby conform the instrument to Donald's intent. The standard sought to be imposed tracks the language of I.R.C. '2041(b)(1)(A).[14] For the reasons stated herein, we shall allow this proposed reformation.

The plaintiffs represent that this reformation of Article III, paragraph F will ensure that, "regardless of the identity of the trustee, or of application of fiduciary standards to the trustee's conduct in office, Mrs. Walker will not possess a general power of appointment and the assets of the Nonmarital Deduction Trust would not be included in her gross taxable estate." Nevertheless, they also ask that we reform the trust instrument by inserting two other provisions that they claim will "further" Donald's intent.[15] They make no argument that these additional provisions are necessary to effectuate Donald's intent. We therefore decline to address these provisions.

---

13. The inclusion of powers of appointment in the General marital trust and special marital trust apparently was intended to comply with the requirements for a marital deduction applicable at that time.

14. The parties propose to reform Article III, paragraph F to read as follows: "Power to Pay Principal. In addition to the payments of income hereinabove provided, the Trustee is (or Trustees are) authorized at any time or from time to time to make or apply distributions or payments of principal of the trust property to or for the health, education, support or maintenance of the Grantor's said spouse, E. Virginia Walker, in such portions or amounts, including the entire trust property, as the Trustee or Trustees may deem advisable."

15. First, they propose inserting, in Article V, a requirement that "there shall be at all times one corporate Trustee serving hereunder provided that such corporate Trustee must be a trust company or bank qualified to act as such in Massachusetts, possessing trust powers, and having a combined capital and surplus of not less that $10,000,000[]," and "that upon the

3. Conclusion. We remand this case to the county court for entry of a judgment reforming Article III, paragraph F of the Donald D. Walker Revocable Trust in conformance with this opinion.

So ordered.

NOTE

The tax planning that led to the "mistake" in the Walker case has become unnecessary in light of the "portability" rules in the 2010 estate tax revision, but the court's approach to reformation remains illustrative. Reformation for mistake is not limited to the tax context, and courts are willing to admit extrinsic evidence to establish mistake. Uniform Trust Code § 415 goes so far as to provide that,

> a court may reform the terms of a trust, even if unambiguous, to conform the terms to the settlor's intention if it is proved by clear and convincing evidence that both the settlor's intent and the terms of the trust were affected by a mistake of fact or law, whether in expression or inducement.

Application of the mistake doctrine is particularly appropriate in the tax context because the settlor's tax objectives are often clear, and the language used in the instrument could have been designed for no purpose other than achieving those objectives. See Uniform Trust Code § 416 (allowing court to grant a request to modify a trust to achieve settlor's tax objectives).

As we have seen, courts are extraordinarily reluctant to reform wills for mistake. Why should these same courts be willing to permit reformation of trust instruments? For some of the silly consequences of the doctrinal distinction, see Brinker v. Wobaco Trust Limited, 610 S.W.2d 160 (Tex.Civ. App.1980) (acknowledging that a testamentary disposition is not subject to reformation, and then struggling to conclude that a pour-over provision in a will did not make the trust testamentary with respect to the assets poured into the trust).

Can a trust settlor obtain reformation of a trust instrument on the ground that she did not understand the trust instrument? Consider the following:

> It is further argued that it is unlikely an elderly lady in poor health would be capable of understanding a trust agreement

---

removal of the corporate Trustee serving hereunder, there shall be a replacement corporate Trustee to serve in its place."

They also propose inserting the following language in Article V: "It is the Grantor's intention that no part of the principal or income of any of the trusts hereunder shall ever be included for estate tax purposes in the estate of any Trustee hereunder by reason of any right, power or authority conferred, or any duty imposed, upon said Trustee, and the Grantor directs that any Trustee whose estate may be thus affected for estate tax purposes shall not[] possess under this Trust any such right, power or authority, or be subject to any such duty, and such rights, powers, authorities and duties shall be exercised only by a Trustee who will not be so affected."

> several pages long, couched in precise and formal legal phraseology; and that "Few laymen, younger, more vigorous and experienced in business would understand it." The argument proves too much. If such a contention had merit very few modern legal instruments could withstand attacks of the kind made in this case. The general rule is that if the words are written as the parties intended they should be written or supposed they were written when the instrument was signed, then no matter how much they may be mistaken as to the meaning of those words no relief can be granted, either at law or in equity.

Pernod v. American National Bank & Trust Co. of Chicago, 8 Ill.2d 16, 132 N.E.2d 540 (1956). Is the excerpt consistent with reforming trust instruments for failure to achieve their intended tax consequences?

2. UNANTICIPATED CIRCUMSTANCES AFFECTING TRUST OBJECTIVES

Suppose a settlor has created a spendthrift trust, and has given the trustee limited discretion to invade principal for the income beneficiary's benefit. Over time, distributions of trust principal have reduced the value of trust property to the point that administration costs—principally trustee fees—approach the annual income on the trust property. Suppose further that state law prohibits the termination of an irrevocable spendthrift trust absent the settlor's consent. May the trustee and the beneficiaries nevertheless terminate the trust? Consider the following provision from the Restatement (Third) of Trusts:

Section 66. Power of Court to Modify: Unanticipated Circumstances

> (1) The court may modify an administrative or distributive provision of the trust, or direct or permit the trustee to deviate from an administrative or distributive provision, if because of circumstances not anticipated by the settlor the modification or deviation will further the purposes of the trust.

See also UTC § 412(a). Would the Restatement provision permit termination of a trust whose assets had declined precipitously? In California, a statute gives the trustee authority to terminate a trust—without even obtaining court consent—if the trust principal falls below $20,000. Cal. Prob. Code, section 15408. UTC § 412(b) allows a court to modify trust terms "if continuation of the trust on its existing terms would be impracticable or wasteful or impair the trust's administration."

3. MODIFICATION OR TERMINATION TO PROVIDE FOR NEEDY INCOME BENEFICIARIES: NEW YORK'S EPTL SECTION 7–1.6(b)

PROBLEM

Settlor creates a trust, providing that all trust income should be paid to settlor's son during his lifetime, and, at the son's death, the principal should be distributed to son's issue. Settlor is now dead, the son is 70 years old and in need of costly medical attention. Settlor's son has two children, age 38 and 33, and four grandchildren.

1. Is termination by consent, and distribution of some of the principal to son, feasible? Examine all potential difficulties.

2. If one of son's children refuses to consent, or if a guardian appointed for grandchildren—born or unborn—refuses to consent, can son compel trustee to make a payment to defray the cost of medical treatment? Is your answer different if the following statute has been enacted?

NEW YORK EPTL

SECTION 7–1.6(b)

> Notwithstanding any contrary provision of law, the court having jurisdiction of an express trust, hereafter created or declared, to receive income from property and apply it to the use of or pay it to any person, unless otherwise provided in the disposing instrument, may in its discretion make an allowance from principal to any income beneficiary whose support or education is not sufficiently provided for, whether or not such person is entitled to the principal of the trust or any part thereof; provided that the court, after a hearing on notice to all those beneficially interested in the trust in such manner as the court may direct, is satisfied that the original purpose of the creator of the trust cannot be carried out and that such allowance effectuates the intention of the creator.

3. Do you see why many lawyers believe that most trusts should contain a power to invade principal for the income beneficiary?

SECTION IV. CHARITABLE TRUSTS

Although most gratuitous transfers of wealth are made to family members, many people also choose to give money to charities—both during their lifetimes and by will. Ordinary charitable gifts—$100 to the local church, $10,000 to one's alma mater—generally present no significant trust law issues (unless, as we shall see, the church or the alma mater are no longer in existence at the time the transfer is to become effective, or the testator misnames the charity in her will). But suppose a philanthropist wants to impose a continuing obligation to use her money for a particular philanthropic purpose: scholarships for law students, or maintenance of a soup kitchen. How can the philanthropist assure that her instructions will continue to be followed?

The private express trust—the focus of most of this chapter—will not help our philanthropist, for two reasons. First, as we have seen, a private express trust must have identifiable beneficiaries—people who have a right to enforce duties imposed on the trustee. Although many people may benefit from scholarships or soup kitchens, so long as the philanthropist does not confer a right to a scholarship, or to soup, on particular people, no one will be entitled to enforce trust duties on the "trustee." As a result, the trust would not qualify as a private express trust. Second, as we shall see when we discuss the Rule Against Perpetuities, in many jurisdictions private express trusts may not endure forever. If the philanthropist wants to assure that scholarship funds are permanently available, a private express trust will not accomplish his objective.

Charitable trust doctrine developed to deal with these problems. If the settlor's objectives do sufficient social good to be deemed "charitable," a trust for those charitable purposes will be enforced even without identifiable beneficiaries. Who will enforce the trust obligations? The state, through its Attorney General. That is, if the settlor's purposes are deemed sufficiently worthy, the state will expend its resources to assure that the charitable trustee adheres to the settlor's intent. For the same reasons, neither legislatures nor courts have imposed any limits on the duration of charitable trusts.

A. Tax Incentives for Charitable Giving

Why does anyone make substantial contributions to charitable enterprises? Altruism and a desire for immortality each provide significant reasons, but the Internal Revenue Code provides extra reasons to consider charitable giving.

The federal estate and gift tax laws permit a 100% deduction for gifts to qualifying charities. Consider the effect of this deduction on a wealthy testator whose estate tax rate is 35%. Suppose this testator, having made substantial bequests to her family and friends, is deciding what to do with an additional $1,000,000. Testator can give all $1,000,000 to a charity without incurring any federal estate tax liability. By contrast, if testator chooses to give the money to family members, only $650,000 will reach those family members; the rest will be paid in federal estate taxes (ignoring, for now, the effect of any state taxes).

If testator has any desire to benefit particular charities, then, the tax system provides a significant incentive for charitable giving. What's more, if testator's will or *inter vivos* trust benefits one or more charities, representatives of those charities will lavish attention on testator during her lifetime, and may be willing to memorialize testator after her death—unlike the government, and perhaps unlike members of testator's family.

Moreover, if testator wants to postpone the effective date of the charitable gift until after the lifetime of a spouse, the Internal Revenue Code will oblige. By placing property in trust for the life of a spouse, followed by a charitable remainder and using an "annuity trust" or "unitrust", the transfer can be made free of federal estate tax. There is a 100% marital deduction for the life interest in the spouse and a 100% charitable deduction for the remainder. Similarly, testator could create a QTIP trust with a charitable remainder. The details of these trusts are beyond our scope, but they are attractive options for wealthy testators.

In addition, if testator makes lifetime charitable gifts, the Internal Revenue Code provides an income tax deduction for those gifts—making them still more attractive for some wealthy individuals.

B. Charitable Purposes

When does a trust qualify for treatment as a charitable trust? Consider the following case:

Shenandoah Valley National Bank of Winchester v. Taylor

Supreme Court of Appeals of Virginia, 1951.
192 Va. 135, 63 S.E.2d 786.

■ Miller, J.

Charles B. Henry, a resident of Winchester, Virginia, died testate on the 23rd day of April, 1949. His will dated April 21, 1949, was duly admitted to probate and the Shenandoah Valley National Bank of Winchester, the designated executor and trustee, qualified thereunder.

Subject to two inconsequential provisions not material to this litigation, the testator's entire estate valued at $86,000, was left as follows:

> "SECOND: All the rest, residue and remainder of my estate, real, personal, intangible and mixed, of whatsoever kind and wherever situate, * * *, I give, bequeath and devise to the Shenandoah Valley National Bank of Winchester, Virginia, in trust, to be known as the 'Charles B. Henry and Fannie Belle Henry Fund', for the following uses and purposes:
>
> "(a) My Trustee shall invest and reinvest my trust estate, shall collect the income therefrom and shall pay the net income as follows:
>
>> "(1) On the last school day of each calendar year before Easter my Trustee shall divide the net income into as many equal parts as there are children in the first, second and third grades of the John Kerr School of the City of Winchester, and shall pay one of such equal parts to each child in such grades, to be used by such child in the furtherance of his or her obtainment of an education.
>>
>> "(2) On the last school day of each calendar year before Christmas my trustee shall divide the net income into as many equal parts as there are children in the first, second and third grades of the John Kerr School of the City of Winchester, and shall pay one of such equal parts to each child in such grades, to be used by such child in the furtherance of his or her obtainment of an education."

By paragraphs (3) and (4) it is provided that the names of the children in the three grades shall be determined each year from the school records, and payment of the income to them "shall be as nearly equal in amounts as it is practicable" to arrange.

Paragraph (5) provides that if the John Kerr School is ever discontinued for any reason the payments shall be made to the children of the same grades of the school or schools that take its place, and the School Board of Winchester is to determine what school or schools are substituted for it.

Under clause "THIRD" the trustee is given authority, power and discretion to retain or from time to time sell and invest and reinvest the estate, or any part thereof, as it shall deem to be to the best interest of the trust.

The John Kerr School is a public school used by the local school board for primary grades and had an enrollment of 458 boys and girls so there will be that number of pupils or thereabouts who would share in the distribution of the income.

The testator left no children or near relatives. Those who would be his heirs and distributees in case of intestacy were first cousins and others more remotely related. One of these next of kin filed a suit against the executor and trustee, and others challenging the validity of the provisions of the will which undertook to create a charitable trust.

Paragraph No. 10 of the bill alleges:

> "That the aforesaid trust does not constitute a charitable trust and hence is invalid in that it violates the rule against the creation of perpetuities."

Other heirs and distributees appeared and joined in the cause and asked that the trust be declared void and the estate distributed among testator's next of kin.

The cause was heard upon the bill and a demurrer filed by the executor and trustee. The demurrer was overruled and the contention of the heirs and distributees sustained. From decrees that adjudicated the principles of the cause and held that the trust was not charitable but a private trust and thus violative of the rule against perpetuities and void, this appeal was awarded.

The sole question presented is: does the will create a valid charitable trust?

Construction of the challenged provisions is required and in this undertaking the testator's intent as disclosed by the words used in the will must be ascertained. If his dominant intent as expressed was charitable, the trust should be afforded efficacy and sustained.

But on the other hand, if the testator's intent as expressed is merely benevolent, though the disposition of his property be meritorious and evince traits of generosity, the trust must nevertheless be declared invalid because it violates the rule against perpetuities.

"A charitable trust is created only if the settlor properly manifests an intention to create a charitable trust." Restatement of the Law of Trusts, sec. 351, p. 1099.

Authoritative definitions of charitable trusts may be found in 4 Pomeroy's Equity Jurisprudence, 5th Ed., sec. 1020, and Restatement of the Law of Trusts, sec. 368, p. 1140. The latter gives a comprehensive classification definition. It is:

"Charitable purposes include:

"(a) the relief of poverty;

"(b) the advancement of education;

"(c) the advancement of religion;

"(d) the promotion of health;

"(e) governmental or municipal purposes; and

"(f) other purposes the accomplishment of which is beneficial to the community."

In the recent decision of Allaun v. First, etc., National Bank, 190 Va. 104, 56 S.E.2d 83, the definition that appears in 3 M.J., Charitable Trust, sec. 2, p. 872, was approved and adopted. It reads:

> 'A charity,' in a legal sense, may be described as a gift to be applied, consistently with existing laws, for the benefit of an indefinite number of persons, either by bringing their hearts under the influence of education or religion, by relieving their bodies from disease, suffering or constraint, by assisting them to establish themselves for life, or by erecting or maintaining public building or works, or otherwise lessening the burdens of government. It is immaterial whether the purpose is called charitable in the gift itself, if it is so described as to show that it is charitable. Generally speaking, any gift not inconsistent with existing laws which is promotive of science or tends to the education, enlightening, benefit or amelioration of the condition of mankind or the diffusion of useful knowledge, or is for the public convenience is a charity. It is essential that a charity be for the benefit of an indefinite number of persons; for if all the beneficiaries are personally designated, the trust lacks the essential element of indefiniteness, which is one characteristic of a legal charity. (190 Va. p. 108.)

See also, Collins v. Lyon, 181 Va. 230, 24 S.E.2d 572; Protestant Episcopal Education Soc. v. Churchman, 80 Va. 718.

In the law of trusts there is a real and fundamental distinction between a charitable trust and one that is devoted to mere benevolence. The former is public in nature and valid; the latter is private and if it offends the rule against perpetuities, it is void.

* * *

Appellant contends that the gift qualifies as a charitable trust under the definition in Allaun v. First, etc., Nat. Bank, supra. It is also said that it not only meets the requirements of a charitable trust as defined in Restatement of the Law of Trusts, supra, but specifically fits two of those classifications, viz.:

"(b) trusts for the advancement of education;

"(f) other purposes the accomplishment of which is beneficial to the community."

We now turn to the language of the will for from its context the testator's intent is to be derived. Sheridan v. Krause, 161 Va. 873, 172 S.E. 508, 91 A.L.R. 1067. Its interpretation must be free from and uninfluenced by the unyielding rule against perpetuities. Yet, when the testator's intent is ascertained, if it is found to be in contravention of the rule, the will, in that particular, must be declared invalid.

* * *

In clause "SECOND" of the will the trust is set up, and by clause "THIRD" full power is bestowed upon the trustee to invest and reinvest the estate and collect the income for the purposes and uses of the trust. In paragraphs (1) and (2), respectively, of clause "SECOND" in clear and definite language the discretion, power and authority of the trustee in its disposition and application of the income are specified and limited. Yearly on the last school day before Easter and Christmas each youthful beneficiary of the testator's generosity is to be paid an equal share of the income. In mandatory language the duty and the duty alone to make cash payments to each individual child just before Easter and Christmas is enjoined upon the trustee by the certain and explicit words that it "shall divide the net income * * * and shall pay one of such equal shares to each child in such grades."

Without more, that language and the occasions specified for payment of the funds to the children being when their minds and interests would be far removed from studies or other school activities definitely indicate that no educational purpose was in the testator's mind. It is manifest that there was no intent or belief that the funds would be put to any use other than such as youthful impulse and desire might dictate. But in each instance immediately following the above-quoted language the sentence concludes with the words or phrase "to be used by such child in the furtherance of his or her obtainment of an education." It is significant that by this latter phrase the trustee is given no power, control or discretion over the funds so received by the child. Full and complete execution of the mandate and trust imposed upon the trustee accomplishes no educational purpose. Nothing toward the advancement of education is attained by the ultimate performance by the trustee of its full duty. It merely places the income irretrievably and forever beyond the range of the trust.

Appellant says that the latter phrase, "to be used by such child in furtherance of his or her obtainment of an education", evinces the testator's dominant purpose and intent. Yet it is not denied that the preceding provision "shall divide the net income into as many equal parts * * * and shall pay one of each equal parts to such child" is at odds with the phrase it relies upon. The appended qualification, it says, however, discloses a controlling intent that the 450 or more shares are to be used in the furtherance of education, and it was not really intended that a share be paid to each child so that he or she could during the Christmas or Easter holidays, or at any other time, use it "without let or hindrance, encumbrance or care." With that construction we cannot agree. In our opinion, the words of the will import an intent to have the trustee pay to each child his allotted share. If that be true,—and it is directed to be done in no uncertain language—we know that the admonition to the children would be wholly impotent and of no avail.

In construing wills, we may not forget or disregard the experiences of life and the realities of the occasion. Nor may we assume or indulge in the belief that the testator by his injunction to the donees intended or thought that he could change childhood nature and set at naught childhood impulses and desires.

Appellant asserts that literal performance of the duty imposed upon it—pay to each child his share—would be impracticable and should not be done. Its position in that respect is stated thus: "We do not understand that under the law of Virginia a court would pay money for education into the hands of children who are incapable of handling it." It then says that the funds could be administered by a guardian or under sec. 8–751, Code, 1950, (where the amounts are under $500), a court could direct payment to be made to the recipient's parents.

With these statements, we agree. But because the funds could be administered under applicable statutes has no bearing upon nor may that device be resorted to as an aid to prove or establish the testator's intent. We are of opinion that the testator's dominant intent appears from and is expressed in his unequivocal direction to the trustee to divide the income into as many equal parts as there are children beneficiaries and pay one share to each. This expressed purpose and intent is inconsistent with the appended direction to each child as to the use of his respective share and the latter phrase is thus ineffectual to create an educational trust. The testator's purpose and intent were, we think, to bestow upon the children gifts that would bring them happiness on the two holidays, but that falls short of an educational trust.

If it be determined that the will fails to create a charitable trust for *educational purposes* (and our conclusion is that it is inoperative to create such a trust), it is earnestly insisted that the trust provided for is nevertheless charitable and valid. In this respect it is claimed that the two yearly payments to be made to the children just before Christmas and Easter produce "a desirable social effect" and are "promotive of public convenience and needs, and happiness and contentment" and thus the fund set up in the will constitutes a charitable trust. 2 Bogert on Trusts, sec. 361, p. 1090, and 3 Scott on Trusts, sec. 368, p. 1972.

The definition of the word "charity" as it appears in Collins v. Lyon, supra, is relied upon to sustain this position. In that decision the meaning of the word "charity" as given in Wilson v. First Nat. Bank, 164 Iowa 402, 145 N.W. 948, was quoted with approval as follows:

> The word 'charity', as used in law, has a broader meaning and includes substantially any scheme or effort to better the condition of society or any considerable portion thereof. It has been well said that any gift not

inconsistent with existing laws, which is promotive of science or tends to the education, enlightenment, benefit, or amelioration of the condition of mankind or the diffusion of useful knowledge, or is for the public convenience, is a charity.

Numerous cases that deal with and construe specific provisions of wills or other instruments are cited by appellant to uphold the contention that the provisions of this will, without reference to and deleting the phrase "to be used by such child in the furtherance of his or her obtainment of an education" meet the requirements of a charitable trust. Many of those cases are listed below. * * * [Citations omitted.] * * *

Upon examination of these decisions, it will be found that where a gift results in mere financial enrichment, a trust was sustained only when the court found and concluded from the entire context of the will that the ultimate intended recipients were poor or in necessitous circumstances.

A trust from which the income is to be paid at stated intervals to each member of a designated segment of the public, without regard to whether or not the recipients are poor or in need, is not for the relief of poverty, nor is it a social benefit to the community. It is a mere benevolence—a private trust—and may not be upheld as a charitable trust. Restatement of the Law of Trusts, sec. 374, p. 1156:

* * *

Nor do we find any language in this will that permits the trustee to limit the recipients of the donations to the school children in the designated grades who are in necessitous circumstances, and thus bring the trust under the influence of the case styled Appeal of Eliot, 74 Conn. 586, 51 A. 558.

The conclusion there reached was that where a trust is set up and a class is designated as beneficiary which generally contains needy persons, the testator will be presumed to have intended as recipients those members of the class who are in necessitous circumstances.

Payment to the children of their cash bequests on the two occasions specified would bring to them pleasure and happiness and no doubt cause them to remember or think of their benefactor with gratitude and thanksgiving. That was, we think, Charles B. Henry's intent. Laudable, generous and praiseworthy though it may be, it is not for the relief of the poor or needy, nor does it otherwise so benefit or advance the social interest of the community as to justify its continuance in perpetuity as a charitable trust. * * *

[Omitted is that portion of the opinion in which the court held the cy pres statutes inapplicable because the trust was not for a "charitable, benevolent, or eleemosynary purpose". See Va.Code, 1950, §§ 55–31, 55–32.] * * *

No error is found in the decrees appealed from and they are affirmed.

Affirmed.

QUESTIONS

1. Who stands to benefit from the court's holding in the Shenandoah case?

2. Suppose Charles Henry's will had provided:

> "I devise the residue of my estate to Mrs. Jane Doe, currently a teacher at the John Kerr school. I request, but do not require, that, on the last calendar day before Christmas, she distribute the net income into as many equal parts as there are children in the first, second, and third grades at the school, to be used by each such child in the furtherance of his or her education."

How would the residue have been distributed? If Charles Henry trusted Jane Doe, would this hypothetical provision have avoided the difficulties created by his actual will?

Might a court have treated the language in this clause as mandatory rather than precatory? If so, what would have happened to the trust principal at Jane Doe's death?

3. Suppose Charles Henry's will had created a trust, but provided that, at the specified times, the trustee

> "Shall divide the net income into as many equal parts as there are children in the first, second and third grades of the John Kerr School whose families have incomes in the bottom third of all families who send students to the school."

Would the trust have been upheld? Why? What if the trust had provided for distribution of all income, in equal parts, to all undergraduates at William and Mary College?

4. Testator's will bequeathed $1,000,000 to The United States President, Vice President, and Speaker of the House as Trustees. The will directs the trustees to invest the money until there are sufficient funds to create a trust of $1,000,000 for every U.S. citizen (man, woman and child) over the age of 18, a process that the testator estimated would take 346 years. Testator's will emphasized that no person should be denied his or her share based on race, religion, marital status, sexual preference, or amount of wealth. Did testator create a valid charitable trust? See Marsh v. Frost National Bank, 129 S.W.3d 174 (Tex. App. 2004) (holding that trust had no charitable purpose because testator's desire to "financially enrich the American public", while "generous and benevolent," does not "necessarily benefi[t] ... the community"). Does the holding make sense? What policy goals are served by declining to give this trust charitable status?

NOTES

1. If the attempt to create a charitable trust in the Shenandoah case seems fanciful, consider the following:

Mary K. Lundwall, Inconsistency and Uncertainty in the Charitable Purposes Doctrine, 41 Wayne L. Rev. 1341, 1341–42 (1995).

Today charitable trusts may be created for a wide variety of purposes. Testators have attempted to create charitable trusts to build hospitals, churches, and libraries. They have set aside property to establish volunteer firefighting brigades, "to provide for the payment of pensions to retired professors," and to maintain a home for "indigent widows and maiden ladies." Testators have also attempted to do the following: establish scholarships for those who receive the lowest scores in a golf tournament, create a Christmas fund for employees, establish an annual horse race named in honor of a testator's deceased daughter, and provide shoes for indigent actors. Trusts have also been created to distribute Bibles and to espouse vegetarianism. One testator even attempted to establish a charitable trust to hire musicians to play dirges and march to the cemetery on his birthday and other holidays.

Citations to the various attempts appear in Professor Lundwall's article.

2. ***Charitable Corporations.*** A philanthropist seeking to make a charitable bequest need not use the trust form. The philanthropist can instead create a charitable corporation or foundation, or make a gift to an existing charitable corporation. See generally James Fishman, The Development of Nonprofit Corporation Law and an Agenda For Reform, 34 Emory L.J. 617, 650–57 (1985) [contrasting and comparing charitable trusts with charitable corporations]. As with a charitable trust, the philanthropist can impose restrictions on the corporation's use of the funds. St. Joseph's Hospital v. Bennett, 281 N.Y. 115, 22 N.E.2d 305 (1939), is the leading case establishing that restricted gifts to charitable corporations should be treated, for perpetuities purposes, like charitable trusts.

3. ***Trusts for Education.*** Trusts for the advancement of education include trusts to endow professorships, scholarships, loan funds, primary schools, secondary schools, colleges, universities, art museums, public libraries, and the like. In addition, trusts to promote research, to provide for the publication of scholarly treatises, for the delivery of lectures, and to give training for citizenship, character, and leadership are treated as charitable.

Suppose, however, settlor creates a trust, with the income to be used for the education of her descendants. Is the trust charitable? See 4A Austin W. Scott, Trusts, sec. 375.3 (Fratcher ed. 1989) [No]. Should it be? Professor Richard J. Kovach has argued for the creation of "family development trusts" that would permit tax-free transfer of wealth to family members for worthy purposes. See Richard J. Kovach, Family Development Deductions—An Alternative to Repealing the Estate Tax, 35 U. Rich. L. Rev. 27 (2001). Do you agree?

Suppose the settlor creates a trust for the purpose of disseminating his own ideas. Is the trust charitable? See Wilber v. Asbury Park National Bank & Trust Co. 142 N.J.Eq. 99, 59 A.2d 570 (1948), *aff'd* 2 N.J. 167, 65 A.2d 843 (1949) (court holds no, after finding settlor's "Random Scientific Notes" irrational); Fidelity Title & Trust Co. v. Clyde, 143 Conn. 247, 121 A.2d 625 (1956) (court holds no, after characterizing work as pornographic). Would the result have been different if trust settlor had been Albert Einstein or Jeremy Bentham? Suppose settlor created a trust for the promotion of another person's "irrational" or "pornographic" ideas? Should treatment of the trust depend on the court's assessment of the merits of the ideas, or do cases like Wilber and Fidelity Title simply suggest greater scrutiny when settlor's purpose—perpetuation of his own ideas—seems selfish rather than charitable?

Do you see why lawyers might advise a clients with novel "ideas" to (1) during the client's lifetime, establish a charitable corporations designed to further those ideas, and (2) devise property to the corporation?

4. ***Relief of Poverty.*** Trusts for the relief of poverty are charitable. Suppose, however, settlor attempts to create a trust to assist named charitable individuals. Is the trust charitable? Ordinarily, the problem is of little practical relevance because even if not charitable, the trust would be enforceable as a private express trust. What happens, however, if the named beneficiaries have died? See In re Gonzalez, 262 N.J.Super. 456, 621 A.2d 94 (1992) [money given by donors for medical treatment of named individual returned to donors when individual died before treatment; court held trust non-charitable, and therefore, held *cy pres* inapplicable].

5. ***Trusts for Religious Purposes.*** Although religion is clearly one of the categories of charity, courts sometimes find pretexts to invalidate trusts for unorthodox beliefs. See Stephan's Estate, 129 Pa.Super. 396, 195 A. 653 (1937) (invalidating trust for upkeep of spiritualist camp).

6. ***Non-traditional Charitable Purposes.*** Suppose settlor creates a trust for distribution "to persons, entities, and causes advancing the principles of socialism and those causes related to socialism." Is the trust charitable? See In re Estate of Breeden, 208 Cal.App.3d 981, 256 Cal.Rptr. 813 (1989) (yes). Would the result be the same if the trust were for advancing the principles of fascism? Communism? The Republican Party? In the Breeden case, the court wrote:

> Although a trust to promote the success of a specific political party is not charitable (see IVA Scott, Law of Trusts (4th ed. 1989) sec. 374.6, p. 221; 41 A.L.R.3d 833, 836–837), the promotion of a particular cause or doctrine remains charitable regardless whether it is embraced as well by a political party (Rest.2d, Trusts, sec. 374, com.k., pp. 260–261). In fact, in Buell v. Gardner (1914) 83 Misc. 513, 144 N.Y.S. 945, the court upheld as charitable a gift in trust establishing a temperance fund to be used to defray the expenses of the Prohibition Party because the purpose of the devise was charitable—to advance the cause of temperance and not the fortunes of any political party.

Id. at 816. Are you persuaded by the court's distinction between trusts to benefit a political party and trusts to benefit the ideas promulgated by the party?

C. STANDING: WHO CAN ENFORCE THE CHARITABLE TRUST'S TERMS?

1. The Attorneys General as Monitors. The Attorney General in each state has standing to enforce charitable trusts. How can the Attorney General keep track of charitable trusts? Some states have enacted statutes requiring charitable organizations to file reports with the Attorney General (see, e.g., N.Y. EPTL Section 8–1.4; Cal. Gov't Code, sections 12580–12598 [based on Uniform Supervision of Trustees for Charitable Purposes Act, 7B U.L.A. 730 (1985)]). The sheer number of charitable trusts, combined with underfunding problems, makes it unlikely that the Attorney General's office will carefully monitor any particular trust, absent prompting by interested parties or egregious misconduct.

When settlor initially creates a charitable trust, other estate beneficiaries have incentive and standing to challenge potential uses of charitable trust funds. Suppose, however, settlor gives money to a local church, and directs that the income be used to provide flowers each Sunday. Who is likely to notify the Attorney General if, ten years later, the church buys artificial flowers and starts using the money to provide Sunday breakfast for needy parishioners? Settlor could create a reverter clause in the instrument, giving his heirs an incentive to monitor the church, but if settlor considers that course unattractive, the church may face no effective constraint beyond the moral force of settlor's wishes.

Litigation involving the Bishop trust illustrates the challenges involved in monitoring charitable trustees. The Bishop Trust, which may be the largest charitable trust in the United States, was established in 1884 through the will of Princess Bernice Pauahi Bishop, the last direct descendant of the King who unified the Hawaiian Islands. Princess Bishop, who married a New York banker and turned down the chance to be queen, left the bulk of her estate in charitable trust for the construction and maintenance of two schools designed to educate children of Hawaiian descent. At the time the trust was created, its principal asset was 375,000 acres of Hawaiian land. In the 1960s, land reform in Hawaii resulted in the forced sale of some of the Bishop land, generating an estimated two billion dollars. By the late 1990s, the Bishop trust had diversified into health care, banking, oil and natural gas, among other investments, and had assets estimated at $6 billion. At the same time, the schools were enrolling just under seven percent of the children in the state of Hawaiian ancestry—the same percentage as 30 years earlier. Allegations of trustee mismanagement and conflict of interest prompted the governor to seek an investigation by the Attorney General, which ultimately resulted in removal or resignation of the trustees. See generally Samuel P. King & Randall W. Roth, Broken Trust 110 (2006); Evelyn Brody, A Taxing Time for the Bishop Estate: What is the I.R.S. Role in Charity Governance? 21 U. Haw. L. Rev. 537, 550–56 (1999).

2. Beneficiaries and Former Beneficiaries As Monitors. The Bishop Trust and other cases have led some to argue that standing ought to be given to other interested parties. For example, Professors Seto and Kohm argue that,

> [T]he theoretical basis for the exclusive standing rule—that the attorney general is in fact more capable of watching over trustees than interested alumni, donors, or students—is repudiated by a manifest inability on the part of the attorney general's offices to secure enough manpower, money, and statutory authority to support a vigilant supervisory program.

Robert Mahealani M. Seto and Lynne Marie Kohm, Of Princesses, Charities, Trustees, and Fairytales: A Lesson of the Simple Wishes of Princess Bernice Pauahi Bishop, 21 U. Haw. L. Rev. 393, 411 (1999). Should charitable trust beneficiaries be given standing to enforce trust terms? What might the pros and cons of such a rule be? If courts or legislatures were to confer standing on charitable beneficiaries, who would qualify as beneficiaries? In In re Milton Hershey School, 590 Pa. 35, 911 A.2d 1258 (2006), the Pennsylvania Supreme Court denied standing to an alumni association, which had argued that the Milton Hershey School trustees were not properly applying trust funds to help orphaned children, because the association was not named as a beneficiary in the trust document, and because the trust instrument explicitly provided that alumni were to be excluded as beneficiaries upon graduation from the school.

3. **Donors As Monitors.** A current, although very controversial, trend is toward allowing donors to have standing to enforce the terms of charitable gifts, whether made in trust or to foundations or nonprofit corporations. Professor Iris Goodwin explores the problem:

> In considering donor standing, there is one additional, quite significant consideration. Public charity occupies a large part of what is termed "civil society." Recent studies argue that, while America was once the *exemple par excellence* of a vital civil society (thought to be the secret of our healthy democracy), participation in all areas of American life now exhibits a marked decline. Thus, it can be argued, given the fragile state of civil society, a liberalization of the standing rules is an important incentive to continued participation by donors—and a boon to the vitality of civil society. However, other commentators go further than merely noting a decline in participation in American society to point out that, as civil society has atrophied, institutions once at its center have become privatized. Viewed in this light, the advent of donor standing—if the result is to strengthen the hand of a private party vis-a-vis the charity—has a less salubrious import.... [Yet] [i]f a mission is to be truly public, it must at some point transcend the person whose private vision was its source. By the same token, the donor in pursuit of a legacy must come to appreciate that if her charitable vision is to survive in any guise, it must over time engage or enlist the vision of other contributors, thereby potentially becoming something larger than itself.

See Iris J. Goodwin, Donor Standing to Enforce Charitable Gifts: Civil Society vs. Donor Empowerment, 58 Vand. L. Rev. 1093 (2005). See also, Robert A. Katz, Can Principal–Agent Models Help Explain Charitable Gifts and Organizations?, 2000 Wis. L. Rev. 1 (explaining that whether the settlor should have power to enforce may depend on whether we regard the charity as existing to advance the donor's interests or to advance the interests of the beneficiaries).

With little fanfare and no explanation, the UTC reverses well-settled common law to provide that the settlor of a charitable trust may enforce its terms. UTC § 405(c). See Ronald Chester, Grantor Standing to Enforce Charitable Transfers Under 405(c) of the Uniform Trust Code and Related Law: How Important Is It and How Extensive Should It Be?, 37 Real Prop. Prob. & Tr. J. 611 (2003). Should the policies embodied in UTC section 405 be extended to donors of restricted gifts not in trust? At least one court has rejected donor standing when the gift was not made in trust. See, Hardt v. Vitae Foundation, Inc., 302 S.W.3d 133 (Mo. App. 2009).

Is the settlor of a charitable trust ideally suited to enforce its terms? If so, what should the scope of standing be? Consider the following problem:

PROBLEM

In 1996, Winston Dithers, a recovered alcoholic devoted to the treatment and understanding of the disease of alcoholism, donated $10,000,000 in trust to Mercy Hospital, as trustee, to establish an alcohol treatment center. The trust instrument provided that all trust assets must be used for the benefit of the Dithers Center. The trust instrument specified that the Dithers Center treatment program would involve five days of detoxification in the hospital, followed by rehabilitation in a "free-standing, controlled, uplifting and non-hospital environment," removed from the hospital setting. The Hospital purchased a building to house the rehabilitation program, and in 1999, the Dithers Alcoholism Treatment and Training Center opened. Dithers remained actively involved in the Center's program, which was a source of tension with the Hospital staff, who sometimes disagreed with Dithers about appropriate methods of treatment.

In 2000, Dithers died. Dithers' wife, Thelma, took it upon herself to see that the terms of Dithers' trust were honored. In 2004, the Hospital announced that it was closing the Dithers Center and selling the building, and that it would move the alcohol abuse treatment program to the main hospital. When Thelma challenged the Hospital's decision, the Hospital President informed her that the trust did not have enough money to sustain the Dithers Center as an entity separate from the hospital. Thelma notified the Attorney General, who investigated and discovered that the Hospital had "loaned" restricted assets from the Dithers Charitable Trust to its general fund. After the Attorney General demanded that the Hospital return the funds, it returned to the trust $4 million of the nearly $5 million it had "borrowed", but paid no interest. The Attorney General then closed the case.

Thelma seeks to sue the Hospital to enforce the terms of the gift. Specifically, she seeks injunctive relief to require the Hospital to 1) return all of the funds borrowed from the Trust, 2) pay interest to the trust on all funds borrowed, 3) cease efforts to sell the Center's building, and 4) run the rehabilitation program in a manner consistent with practices that her husband believed were most effective. The hospital and the Attorney General argue that Thelma lacks standing to maintain her claims. Should the court grant Thelma standing to pursue some or all of her claims? Cf. Smithers v. St. Luke's–Roosevelt Hospital Center, 281 A.D.2d 127, 723 N.Y.S.2d 426 (N.Y. App. Div. 2001).

For more on the law regarding enforcement of charitable trusts, see Susan N. Gary, Regulating the Management of Charities: Trust Law, Corporate Law, and Tax Law, 21 U. Haw. L. Rev. 593 (1999).

D. The Cy Pres Doctrine

PROBLEM

Oscar Zilch, a prominent lawyer who is also an alumnus of Long Island University, devises $200,000 to the trustees of Long Island University for the purposes of establishing the Oscar Zilch Law School at the University. The devise is clearly insufficient to establish a law school.

1. You represent the trustees of Long Island University. At Oscar's death, what advice do you give the trustees about the bequest? Can the university use the money for any other purpose?

2. You represent the residuary beneficiaries of Oscar's estate, who want to know whether they can obtain the $200,000. What advice would you give them?

3. You represent Hofstra University, which would like to get its hands on the money for use in its law school. Hofstra is also located on Long Island, and Oscar graduated from Hofstra's law school. What advice would you give Hofstra?

4. You represent the state Attorney General. What position do you take in this controversy?

Estate of Crawshaw

Supreme Court of Kansas, 1991.
249 Kan. 388, 819 P.2d 613.

■ Six, J.

This case involves the application of the cy pres doctrine to a testamentary trust. We are presented with a first impression review of K.S.A. 1990 Supp. 59–22a01, which codified the cy pres doctrine judicially recognized by this court.

The residuary legatee contending charities are the Marymount Memorial Educational Trust Fund (MMETF) and the Salvation Army.

The Salvation Army appeals, contending the district court erred in applying the cy pres doctrine. The Salvation Army reasons that the testamentary trust language evidenced a specific charitable intent to benefit students at Marymount College.

The Court of Appeals disagreed and affirmed the district court's application of cy pres. *In re Estate of Crawshaw*, 15 Kan. App. 2d 273, 806 P.2d 1014 (1991). We granted the Salvation Army's petition for review.

* * *

We affirm the application of the cy pres doctrine and the selection of MMETF; however, we modify the trial court's ruling concerning the administration of the Crawshaw trust by MMETF and its trustee.

Facts

Chester D. Crawshaw bequeathed the bulk of his estate to two residuary beneficiaries: the Salvation Army with its Kansas Office at Wichita, Kansas (15% of residue outright) and Marymount College located at Salina, Kansas (85% of residue in trust).

Crawshaw died testate on May 4, 1989. Paul S. Gregory was appointed administrator with will annexed. Crawshaw's will designated Marymount as trustee of a testamentary trust with a purpose to provide loans to nursing and other students at Marymount. Because Marymount ceased operation on June 30, 1989, it filed a petition for an order directing administration of the trust. Alleging that Crawshaw manifested a general charitable intent, Marymount requested the district court to apply the cy pres doctrine as set forth in K.S.A. 1990 Supp. 59–22a01. Marymount also requested the transfer of Crawshaw's testamentary trust funds to MMETF.

The Salvation Army: (1) denied general charitable intent; (2) objected to MMETF as a proper successor trustee; (3) alleged Crawshaw did not manifest charitable intent to benefit students attending colleges other than Marymount; and (4) asked the court to determine that the bequest should be distributed to the Salvation Army as the remaining beneficiary of Crawshaw's residuary estate.

Gregory alleged that Crawshaw had general charitable intent and that the bequest to Marymount is impossible to distribute. Gregory sought a determination from the district court as to the proper entity to receive the bequest.

Fort Hays State University Endowment Association (FHSUEA) filed a petition for order directing administration of the trust. FHSUEA also requested transfer of the funds of Crawshaw's testamentary trust to FHSUEA under K.S.A. 1990 Supp. 59–22a01 to be administered for the benefit of Fort Hays State University students. The trial court denied the petition of FHSUEA.

FHSUEA is not a party to this appeal.

Stipulation

The parties agreed to the following stipulated facts:

"1. Chester D. Crawshaw, a resident of Osborne, Kansas, died testate on May 4, 1989. On May 12, 1989 his Last Will and Testament ... was admitted to probate in Osborne County District Court, Probate Division. (Petition to Probate Will). Paul S. Gregory was appointed as administrator with Will annexed. (Letters Testamentary).

"2. The Last Will and Testament of Chester D. Crawshaw provides for the distribution of the personal effects of the deceased, and further provides for certain legacies to four individuals, said legacies totaling $350.00. (Last Will and Testament). The residuary estate is valued in excess of $140,000.00. (Inventory and Appraisement).

"3. Upon distribution of these bequests and legacies, the Will directs that the personal property and real property remainder of the estate be sold and converted to cash and that the proceeds be distributed as follows:

> "A. I direct that said Executor first pay all of my just debts, including my funeral expenses and expenses of my last sickness, and the costs of administering my estate, and all legacies provided for by this, my Last Will and Testament.
>
> "B. I give, devise and bequeath fifteen percent (15%) of the rest, residue and remainder of the funds, proceeds and property of my estate to the Salvation Army, with Kansas office at Wichita, Kansas, to be used by it as it shall deem fit, without any restrictions whatever.
>
> "C. I give, devise and bequeath the remaining eighty-five percent (85%) of the rest, residue and remainder of the funds, proceeds and property of my estate to Marymount College, located at Salina, Kansas, in trust, or in the event that said college does not have the legal capacity to accept and administer the herein created trust, then, in trust, to the official Board or Association of said college having the legal capacity to accept and administer the herein created trust, in any event hereinafter referred to as Trustee, and that said trust is created for the purposes, and subject to the conditions, hereinafter stated:
>
> > "1. That such trust fund, with its accretions, shall perpetually be called and known as the 'Mary Anna and Chester D. Crawshaw Trust Fund'.
> >
> > "2. That said trust fund shall be paid to said legatee and devisee by my Executor at the time of the final settlement of my estate.
> >
> > "3. The funds herein provided for may be loaned to students in the nursing department of said college. If there are no eligible candidates in said nursing department for this fund in any academic year, then the administrators may grant a loan to any other student or students attending said college.
> >
> > "4. The administration of the fund shall be left entirely to the Trustee.

* * *

"4. Chester D. Crawshaw was not Catholic but his deceased wife was Catholic and they were married in the Catholic Church. Chester D. Crawshaw received a Methodist burial service. Chester D. Crawshaw was not a Marymount College alumni, director, employee, former employee, teacher, or former teacher, nor is it known that he had any other type of special personal relationship with Marymount College.

* * *

"8. The Marymount Memorial Educational Trust Fund (hereinafter referred to as 'MMETF') was established on September 13, 1989 by and between Marymount College of Kansas and George K. Fitzsimons, Bishop of the Roman Catholic Diocese of Salina in Kansas. (Petition of Marymount College, Par. 7; and MMETF Trust Agreement (Exhibit 'C')).

* * *

"11. FHSU Endowment Association is a not-for-profit corporation and the objects and purposes to be transacted and carried on by said Endowment Association are as follows:" To raise funds for the purposes for which this corporation is created; to support educational undertakings at Fort Hays State University and to receive and hold in trust any property, real and personal, given, devised, bequeathed, given in trust, or in any other way transferred to this corporation for the use and/or benefit of Fort Hays State University, or of any student or employee therein as such, or of any school, division, department or branch thereof or for the carrying on at said institution of any line or work, teaching or investigation which the donor, grantor or testator may designate." (Petition of FHSU Endowment Association, Par. 8).

"12. Fort Hays State University has an established School of Nursing that offers both a bachelors and a masters degree in nursing. (Petition of FHSU Endowment Association, Par. 9)."

The Trial Court's Ruling

The district court found that Crawshaw had general charitable intent to benefit nursing and other students. The trial judge reasoned:

> "[T]his will does not give the money to any college, but does create its own separate trust fund and puts a name on it, indicating that these funds are to be provided under the name of the Crawshaws and given out in that manner. The Court also finds that the method of giving the money is charitable in nature. Even though it's intended to draw some interest, it's still only to guarantee that the fund continues and is able to provide for its existence in the future. The Court finds that the Crawshaws did not have any particular—neither one of them were graduates of Marymount College. It truly was his intent to benefit nursing students and other students. The Court finds general charitable intent by the nature of his will."

The district court then found that MMETF was the appropriate entity to administer the trust.

* * *

The Kansas Rule

The testamentary trust in question contained no alternate disposition in the event the bequest lapsed or became void. In Kansas, a lapsed or void bequest falls into the residuum and will be disposed of by the residuary clause, if one has been provided. *Trustees of Endowment Fund of Hoffman Memorial Hosp. Ass'n. v. Kring*, 225 Kan. 499, 506, 592 P.2d 438 (1979). Crawshaw's will contained a residuary clause with two provisions: the first was a bequest of 15% of the residue outright to the Salvation Army; the second was a bequest of 85% of the residue creating the trust that is the subject of this action. If the trust fails, all proceeds would be distributed to the remaining residuary legatee, the Salvation Army.

Contentions of the Parties

The Salvation Army asserts that the will unambiguously indicates Crawshaw's specific charitable intent to benefit only students at Marymount. Therefore, it contends, the district court and the Court of Appeals erred in applying rules of judicial construction and in looking beyond the provision of the will establishing the testamentary trust.

The Salvation Army relies on the testamentary trust language in the will. Clauses C.3. and C.5. of Crawshaw's will (set out in the stipulation) refer to "said college." The Salvation Army argues that the C.3., C.5. provisions unambiguously indicate Crawshaw's intent to benefit nursing and other students only at Marymount College. The Salvation Army suggests it is inappropriate to look beyond this language. If we disregard these limitations, the Salvation Army reasons, we would not be construing Crawshaw's will but constructing a new one, which we should not do.

Marymount and Gregory argue that both the district court and the Court of Appeals appropriately found that Crawshaw had general charitable intent and applied the cy pres doctrine, as codified by K.S.A. 1990 Supp. 59–22a01. They contend that it is appropriate to look beyond the specific will provision creating the testamentary trust to determine Crawshaw's intent. They also contend that an examination of the will and extrinsic evidence of Crawshaw's relationship with Marymount indicate that Crawshaw had general charitable intent to facilitate higher education. Marymount was merely an agent to effect Crawshaw's gift.

Marymount and Gregory assert that Crawshaw's intent may not be determined from a single provision. We are encouraged to look at the entire will. They emphasize other provisions in the will which they assert demonstrate Crawshaw's general charitable intent.

Our attention is invited first to the opening paragraph of the testamentary trust:

> [T]o Marymount College, located at Salina, Kansas, in trust, or, in the event that said college does not have the legal capacity to accept and administer the herein created trust, then, in trust, to the official Board or Association of said college, having the legal capacity to accept and administer such trust.

This provision indicates, according to Marymount and Gregory, that Crawshaw did not want the trust to fail because of a problem with the named trustee. They advance the theory that Crawshaw named Marymount as an agent to carry out his purpose of furthering higher education. Marymount asserts that Clause C.3. demonstrates that Crawshaw anticipated the problem of a lack of eligible nursing students. He wished to benefit other students, indicating his general charitable intent to benefit higher education. In addition, the clause utilizes "may," which is precatory.

Clause C.4. leaves the administration of the fund entirely to the trustee. Marymount reasons that the C.4. language is evidence of Crawshaw's intent to give the trustee maximum flexibility to change the way the fund is administered. C.4. also permits the trustee to carry out the objectives of the trust in spite of changing circumstances.

Clause C.1. states: "That such trust fund, with its accretions, shall perpetually be called and known as the 'Mary Anna and Chester D. Crawshaw Trust Fund.' " Gregory asserts that Crawshaw would not have wanted this perpetual fund to cease to exist merely because Marymount terminated its educational programs.

Gregory also points out the disparity of the bequests to the Salvation Army (15%) and to the trust fund (85%). Gregory contends that Crawshaw's interest in higher education was superior to his interest in the charitable nature of the Salvation Army.

Finally, Marymount asserts that few charitable trusts are devoid of any designation as to where the funds should be spent. It argues that if the Salvation Army's view, specific charitable intent by virtue of the mention of the specific college where the scholarship fund is to be spent, is accepted, the cy pres doctrine will be effectively abolished.

The Cy Pres Doctrine

Cy pres is a common-law doctrine that has been recognized by Kansas courts, but never applied because this court and the Court of Appeals have always found specific charitable intent. *Trustees of Endowment Fund of Hoffman Memorial Hosp. Ass'n. v. Kring*, 225 Kan. 499; *Shannep v. Strong*, 160 Kan. 206, 160 P.2d 683 (1945); and *In re Estate of Coleman*, 2 Kan. App. 2d 567, 584 P.2d 1255, rev. denied 225 Kan. 844 (1978).

The Court of Appeals, in Coleman, succinctly described the cy pres doctrine.

> The doctrine of cy-pres permits a court to implement a testator's intent and save a gift to charity by substituting beneficiaries when the named charitable beneficiary is unable to take the gift. In order for the doctrine to apply, several conditions must be met. First, the gift must be to a charitable organization for a charitable purpose. Second, it must be impossible, impractical or illegal to carry out the donor's stated charitable purpose. Finally, it must appear that the donor had a general charitable intent. The fundamental concept of the doctrine is that a donor may have a general charitable intent, and that the particular charitable institution he has designated as recipient of the

> gift is only an agent for effectuating that gift. Therefore, when it becomes impossible for the gift to take effect exactly as the donor specified, the court must look for another agent, as nearly like the designated one as possible, that will receive the gift and effectuate the general charitable intent expressed in the will or gift instrument.

2 Kan.App.2d at 574.

The cy pres doctrine should not be applied if the testator has: (1) manifested a specific charitable intent; (2) has anticipated possible failure of the trust; or (3) has made an alternate disposition of the property if the charitable gift should fail. Kring, 225 Kan. at 504.

In 1988, the Kansas legislature enacted K.S.A. 1990 Supp. 59–22a01, which provides in part:

> (a) If a trust for charity is or becomes ... impossible or impracticable of fulfillment or if a devise or bequest for charity, at the time it was intended to become effective is ... impossible or impracticable of fulfillment, and if the settlor or testator, manifested a general intention to devote the property to charity, any judge, on application of any ... interested party ... may order an administration of the trust, devise or bequest as nearly as possible to fulfill the manifested general charitable intention of the settlor or testator. In every such proceeding, the attorney general, as representative of the public interest, shall be notified and given an opportunity to be heard. The provisions of this act shall not be applicable if the settlor or testator has provided, either directly or indirectly, for an alternative plan in the event the charitable trust, devise or bequest is or becomes illegal or impossible or impracticable of fulfillment.

K.S.A. 1990 Supp. 59–22a01(c)(1) states: " 'Charity' and 'charitable' includes, but is not limited to, any eleemosynary, religious, benevolent, educational, scientific, artistic or literary purpose."

K.S.A. 1990 Supp. 59–22a01 codifies the common-law doctrine of cy pres. Marymount asserts that the legislature intended to broaden the application of the doctrine.

* * *

In the absence of Crawshaw providing a specific guidance provision, our task of determining whether he had a general charitable intent could be advanced if we were able to answer two questions: First, if Crawshaw had known that Marymount College would not be in existence at the time his will was admitted to probate, would he have wanted the trust funds to go for loans to nursing and other students generally; or second, would he have wanted the funds of his entire residuary estate to go to the Salvation Army? These two inquiries arise from a counter-factual proposition. It is difficult to determine what Crawshaw would have wanted by assuming that certain events that did not occur had occurred.

A court will seldom have sufficient information about the preferences of a testator to determine how the testator's thought process in a counter-factual situation should guide the court; consequently, we must look for guidance to our past cy pres decisions.

In *Shannep v. Strong*, 160 Kan. 206, the testator devised two quarter sections of land to a trustee to manage and pay the income to " 'the United Brethren in Christ Church Association at Burns, Marion Couney [county], Kansas,' " a local church. 160 Kan. at 207. After the church ceased to exist, the testator's widow, as the residuary legatee, filed an action to have the trust declared as lapsed and to have the land pass to her under the residuary clause. The board of trustees of the parent church intervened and claimed to be entitled to the income from the trust as the successor of the local church. We stated that the primary consideration in construction of a will is the testator's intention which must be ascertained from all provisions within the four corners of the will and not from any single or isolated provision. 160 Kan. at 211. The question in Shannep was whether the testator intended to create a trust for religion generally or a trust for the benefit of a particular church in a particular community. We found that the testator intended to benefit the particular local church, not religion generally, and declined to apply the cy pres doctrine.

Three decades after Shannep, the Court of Appeals considered the cy pres doctrine in *Coleman*, 2 Kan. App. 2d 567. *Coleman* construed a residuary clause in the will of the testator leaving the residue: (1) two-fifths to the American Cancer Society, (2) two-fifths "to the College of Emporia, a Presbyterian educational institution located at Emporia, Kansas," and (3) one-fifth to the Presbyterian Manor, a Presbyterian home for the aged. 2 Kan. App. 2d at 569.

The College of Emporia closed its doors on December 31, 1973. The testator died on August 3, 1975. The will was executed in 1965. Sterling College, a Presbyterian College similar to the College of Emporia, urged the trial court to apply the cy pres doctrine and substitute Sterling College as beneficiary. The Court of Appeals stated the question was whether the testator had a general charitable intention to benefit Presbyterian higher education or a narrow, special intention to benefit the College of Emporia, and no other Presbyterian college. 2 Kan. App. 2d at 575. Sterling College asserted that the modern tendency is to presume a general charitable intent in any charitable gift that may be negated by either the gift instrument or extrinsic evidence. The Court of Appeals declined to create such a presumption, reasoning that the presumption favoring charitable gifts, the presumption against intestacy, and the duty of the court to uphold the intent of the testator adequately protect charitable gifts. Coleman held that the entity seeking the application of the cy pres doctrine has the burden to demonstrate, either by extrinsic evidence or by evidence within the will itself, that the donor had the requisite general charitable intent. 2 Kan. App. 2d at 577.

The *Coleman* court found one "crucial" fact supporting the trial court's finding that there was no general charitable intent. 2 Kan. App. 2d at 577. The testator executed his will shortly after being made aware of the College of Emporia's financial plight which bolstered the theory that he named the College of Emporia as a residuary legatee with the specific thought of aiding that particular Presbyterian college. Although there was no evidence of a special personal relationship between the testator and the college (he was not an alumnus or a trustee), there was a special personal relationship between the testator and other named beneficiaries. The Court of Appeals found these facts supported the theory that the testator wished to benefit the College of Emporia rather than Presbyterian higher education.

Syllabus para. 5 in *Coleman*, 2 Kan. App. 2d 567, is instructive:

> In determining whether the testator had a general charitable intent, courts may consider all available, admissible evidence, both intrinsic and extrinsic, which is indicative of the testator's intent. Among the factors which may be considered are the existence of a reversionary or gift-over provision, the existence of a limitation or reservation on the use of the gift, whether the bulk of the estate was bequeathed to charity, and whether specific devises and bequests were made to individuals who would have taken the estate by intestacy.

* * *

In the case at bar, the Court of Appeals found the facts "remarkably similar" to those in *Coleman* with the exception of the personal relationship. 15 Kan. App. 2d at 282. The court focused on the *Coleman* testator's knowledge of the College of Emporia's financial trouble. This knowledge was crucial in finding specific charitable intent in *Coleman*. This crucial finding is missing in Crawshaw's relationship with Marymount.

We view *Coleman* as a well-written comprehensive opinion setting forth the factors to be considered in determining general charitable intent. Those factors are supported by case law from other jurisdictions. See *Howard Savings Inst. v. Peep*, 34 N.J. 494, 170 A.2d 39 (1961); *Board of Trustees of UNCBCH v. Heirs of Prince*, 311 N.C. 644, 319 S.E.2d 239 (1984) (applying the statute which K.S.A. 1990 Supp. 59–22a01 apparently was modeled after); and Bogert, Trusts and Trustees § 437, 137–43 (1991).

We agree with the analysis of the Court of Appeals in the case at bar. First, charitable trusts are favorites in the law and should receive a liberal construction. *In re Estate of Freshour*, 185 Kan. 434, 441, 345 P.2d 689 (1959); *In re Estate of Porter*, 164 Kan. 92, 100, 187 P.2d 520 (1947). Second, we should consider the entire will and extrinsic evidence regarding Crawshaw's relationship with Marymount rather than considering only the individual clauses as urged by the Salvation Army. *Shannep*, 160 Kan. at 211; *Coleman*, 2 Kan. App. 2d at 577.

We reason that Crawshaw had general charitable intent. We base our conclusion on the following facts:

1. The will contained no gift over provision;

2. The will contained provisions indicating Crawshaw did not wish the will to fail;

3. The trust was to be perpetual and was named after Crawshaw and his wife;

4. Crawshaw made small specific bequests to his heirs and did not include them in the residuary clause;

5. The bulk of his estate was given to charity;

6. The bulk of the residuum, 85%, was given to Marymount as a perpetual trust named after Crawshaw versus 15% outright to the Salvation Army. This indicates Crawshaw placed importance on his name living on with the scholarship loan fund;

7. Crawshaw had no known personal relationship with Marymount, supporting the theory that Marymount was an agent to effect his general charitable intent of furthering higher education.

The Marymount Memorial Education Trust Fund

At the hearing before the district court, Marymount argued that it would fulfill Crawshaw's intention and administer the fund as set out in his will, the exception being that the students benefiting would not be those attending Marymount College.

* * *

The district court's order requires that the bequest be transferred to the trustee of the MMETF and administered under terms of that fund.

The trustee of MMETF is George K. Fitzsimons, Bishop of the Roman Catholic Diocese of Salina in Kansas.

The MMETF trust agreement provides, in part:

> ARTICLE I
>
> This trust shall be known as the 'Marymount Memorial Educational Trust Fund'. A primary objective and purpose of this charitable trust is to perpetuate the name of Marymount College as an institution of higher learning dedicated to the excellence of academic education and professional training in the field of nursing. For this reason the trustee is requested to administer the trust estate exclusively for educational purposes and in a manner that will further those educational objectives associated with Marymount College during the years of its existence. The trustee is further requested to carry out to the maximum extent practicable the expressed intent of any original settlor or testator of existing scholarship funds which may be added to and become a part of the trust estate. *These requests, however, are precatory only and shall not impose any legal obligation on the trustee or limit the trustee from exercising any discretionary right or power otherwise conferred by the provisions of this trust agreement.* (Emphasis added.)

Other provisions in the agreement allow the trustee to make distributions of income or principal to any charitable organization or for any charitable purpose. The Crawshaw testamentary trust could be used for charitable purposes unrelated to Crawshaw's general charitable intent to benefit students, particularly nursing students. Counsel for the MMETF acknowledged this fact during oral argument.

K.S.A. 1990 Supp. 59–22a01(a) provides that any judge "may order an administration of the trust, devise or bequest as *nearly as possible to fulfill the manifested general charitable intention of the settlor or testator.*" (Emphasis added.)

We restrict the administration of the Crawshaw testamentary trust within the MMETF trust to comply with Crawshaw's intent as expressed in his will.

The MMETF trustee, in administering Crawshaw funds, shall be controlled by the terms of the Crawshaw testamentary trust. Our affirmance of Bishop Fitzsimons, or his successor in trust, as the cy pres trustee of the "Mary Anna and Chester D. Crawshaw Trust Fund" is contingent upon his written acceptance of the limitation upon his use of Crawshaw trust funds established in this opinion. The trustee's written acceptance shall be filed with the district court not later than 20 days after the date of the mandate in this case. In the event such trustee does not file the written acceptance, the district court shall name another trustee to administer the Crawshaw trust in accordance with the terms of that trust and this opinion.

If during administration, the stated conditions of the Crawshaw trust prove to be impracticable, the trustee may petition the district court for instructions to, as nearly as possible, effect the intention of the testator.

The judgments of the district court and Court of Appeals are affirmed as modified.

QUESTIONS

1. Suppose Chester Crawshaw had made a general devise of $50,000 to Marymount College instead of devising Marymount 85% of his residuary estate. Would the result in the case have been different? Would the identities of the residuary legatees matter?

2. Suppose Crawshaw (or his wife) had been a graduate of Marymount. Would the result in the case have been different?

3. Suppose you had been retained to draft Crawshaw's will. What would you have done to avoid the litigation in this case?

NOTES (AND MORE QUESTIONS)

1. Uniform Trust Code section 413(a) provides:

> (a) Except as otherwise provided in subsection (b), if a particular charitable purpose becomes unlawful, impracticable, or impossible to achieve, or wasteful:
>
> (1) the trust does not fail, in whole or in part

(2) the trust property does not revert to the settlor or the settlor's successor's in interest; and

(3) The court may apply cy pres to modify or terminate the trust by directing that the trust property be applied or distributed, in whole or in part, in a manner consistent with the settlor's charitable purposes.

(b) A provision in the terms of a charitable trust that would result in distribution of the trust property to a noncharitable beneficiary prevails over the power of the court under subsection (a) to apply cy pres to modify or terminate the trust only if, when the provision takes effect:

(1) the trust property is to revert to the settlor and the settlor is still living; or

(2) fewer than 21 years have elapsed since the date of the trust's creation.

Would the Crawshaw court's task have been easier or more difficult if section 413(a) had been in effect? *See also,* Restatement (Third) of Trusts § 67 (2003) (employing substantially similar language). For an argument that the UTC approach is misguided, see Alberto B. Lopez, A Revaluation of Cy Pres Redux, 78 U. Cin. L. Rev. 1307 (2010).

2. *The Economics of Cy Pres.* Is the *cy pres* doctrine efficient? Consider the following justification offered by Judge Posner:

> . . . [T]he dilemma of whether to enforce the testator's intent or to modify the terms of the will in accordance with changed conditions since his death is often a false one. A policy of rigid adherence to the letter of the donative instrument is likely to frustrate both the donor's purposes and the efficient use of resources. . . . [S]uppose that Senator Bacon had given the city a tuberculosis sanatorium. . . . As the incidence of tuberculosis declined and advances in medical science rendered the sanatorium method of treating tuberculosis obsolete, the value of the donated facilities in their intended use would have diminished. Eventually, it would have become clear that the facilities would be more valuable in another use. . . . [E]nforcement would in all likelihood be contrary to the purposes of the donor, who intended by his gift to contribute to the cure of disease, not to perpetuate useless facilities.
>
> The foregoing discussion may seem tantamount to denying the competence of a donor to balance the value of a perpetual gift against the cost in efficiency that such gifts frequently impose. But since no one can foresee the future, a rational donor knows that his intentions might eventually be thwarted by unpredictable circumstances and may therefore be presumed to accept implicitly a rule permitting modification of the terms of the bequest in the event that an unforeseen change frustrates his original intention.

Richard Posner, Economic Analysis of Law 556 (5th ed. 1998).

3. ***How Impossible Must Strict Compliance with Settlor's Instructions Be?: The Buck Trust.*** In the Crawshaw case, Marymount College had closed, so strict compliance with testator's instructions was not feasible. Suppose, however, strict compliance is possible, but seems arguably not to advance settlor's broader purposes. That problem faced a California trial court in Estate of Buck, a 1986 case not officially reported, but reprinted in 21 U.S.F.L.Rev. 691 (1987).

When Beryl Buck died, widowed and childless, in 1975, her estate's principal asset was $9 million of stock in a privately held oil company. She left the residue of her estate to the San Francisco Foundation, a community trust, and directed that the funds be used

> for exclusively non-profit charitable, religious or educational purposes in providing care for the needy in Marin County, California, and for other non-profit charitable, religious, or educational purposes in that county.

Id. at 693. Marin County is one of the wealthiest counties in the nation. Moreover, in 1979, after a bidding war, Shell Oil bought the stock in the Buck trust for $260 million.

In 1984, the San Francisco Foundation, as trustee, sought judicial application, pursuant to the *cy pres* doctrine, to use Buck funds outside of Marin County. The foundation argued that if Mrs. Buck had known that the trust assets would increase so substantially, she would have permitted expenditure of the money in a broader geographical area. The court refused to apply *cy pres*, and rejected the argument that compliance with the literal terms of Mrs. Buck's will was inappropriate because her philanthropy would be ineffective if limited only to Marin County:

> The cy pres doctrine should not be so distorted by the adoption of subjective, relative, and nebulous standards such as "inefficiency" or "ineffective philanthropy" to the extent that it becomes a facile vehicle for charitable trustees to vary the terms of a trust simply because they believe that they can spend the trust income better or more wisely elsewhere.... There is no basis in law for the application of standards such as "efficiency" or "effectiveness" to modify a trust, nor is there any authority that would elevate these standards to the level of impracticability.

21 U.S.F.L.Rev. 691 at 752. See also In re Oshkosh Foundation, 61 Wis.2d 432, 213 N.W.2d 54, 57 (1973) (rejecting effort to expand trust disbursements beyond city limits):

> No argument is here made that the purpose of the trust has become either impossible or illegal. Rather it is claimed that compliance with the trust has become "impracticable" because it has become "unfair".... But cy pres does not warrant a court substituting a different plan for that set forth in the trust solely because trustee or court, or both, believe the substituted plan to be a better plan.

Estate of Buck generated a wealth of commentary—much of it unfavorable. See Simon, American Philanthropy and the Buck Trust, 21 U.S.F.L.Rev. 641 (1987); Note, Relaxing the Dead Hand's Grip: Charitable Efficiency and the Doctrine of Cy Pres, 74 Va. L. Rev. 635 (1988); Note, Phantom Selves: The Search for a General Charitable Intent in the Application of the Cy Pres Doctrine, 40 Stan. L. Rev. 973 (1988).

Cases like Buck explain why the UTC and The Restatement (Third) of Trusts (2003) expand the scope of *cy pres* to allow courts to reform trusts when their operation becomes wasteful.

In general, academic commentators favor broad application of *cy pres*. See, e.g., Alex M. Johnson, Jr., Limiting Dead Hand Control of Charitable Trusts: Expanding Use of the Cy Pres Doctrine, 21 U. Haw. L. Rev. 353 (1999); Frances Howell Rudko, The Cy Pres Doctrine in the United States: From Extreme Reluctance to Affirmative Action, 46 Clev. St. L. Rev. 471 (1998); Alex M. Johnson, Jr. & Ross Taylor, Revolutionizing Judicial Interpretation of Charitable Trusts: Applying Relational Contracts and Dynamic Interpretation to Cy Pres and America's Cup Litigation, 74 Iowa L. Rev. 545 (1989). Professor Atkinson would go a step further, and permit charities to ignore the settlor's charitable instructions, even without judicial sanction. Rob Atkinson, Reforming Cy Pres Reform, 44 Hastings L.J. 1112 (1993). But see Jonathan Macey, Private Trusts for the Provision of Private Goods, 37 Emory L.J. 295 (1988).

4. ***Participants in Cy Pres Litigation.*** Once it becomes clear that settlor's instructions cannot feasibly be followed, each *cy pres* dispute raises two distinct but related questions: first, should the doctrine be applied at all (that is, did settlor have a general charitable intent); second, how should the doctrine be applied—who should take the settlor's funds, and on what terms?

The parties interested in those two issues will often be different. In Crawshaw, for instance, the Salvation Army, as residuary beneficiary, was quite interested in whether *cy pres* should be applied, but once the court decided that the doctrine was applicable, the Salvation Army was not terribly concerned with the terms on which the Marymount Trust Fund would hold Mr. Crawshaw's money.

Many *cy pres* cases involve disputes among charitable entities, each with their own proposals for using charitable trust monies after it has been determined that the testator's instructions are impossible to effectuate. See, e.g., Town of Brookline v. Barnes, 327 Mass. 201, 97 N.E.2d 651 (1951) [settlor creates trust for town for purpose of establishing a public hospital; when it becomes clear that funds are insufficient, court chooses town's scheme for a health center over neighboring hospital's plan to expand its operations]; Burr v. Brooks, 83 Ill.2d 488, 48 Ill.Dec. 200, 416 N.E.2d 231 (1981) (dispute among city, not-for-profit corporation, and school district, each seeking to capture trust funds).

When disputes like these arise, the Attorney General sometimes takes a position among various charitable purposes, but courts are not bound by the Attorney General's position. See Town of Brookline v. Barnes, 327 Mass. 201, 97 N.E.2d 651 (1951). Instead, courts use their own judgment in choosing the substitute taker most likely to approximate settlor's wishes.

A Move for Art's Sake Stirs Debate on Bequests

By Mike Boehm and Diane Haithman.
Los Angeles Times, December 14, 2004.

In a case watched for its possible effect on philanthropy, a Pennsylvania judge Monday ruled that art intended to stay put—the treasured, highly idiosyncratic but deficit-ridden Barnes Foundation collection—can be uprooted despite the terms of the donor's bequest.

The decision opens the way for the cloistered collection amassed by pharmaceutical tycoon Albert C. Barnes to be moved from suburban Merion, Pa., and housed in a more conventional, $100-million showplace in downtown Philadelphia. There, attendance and revenue are expected to soar.

Students who take courses at the Barnes Foundation had tried to stop the move, saying it would dishonor Barnes' wish to create an intimate educational institution—not a conventional museum—built around his whopping collection of Renoirs, Cezannes, Matisses, Picassos, Rousseaus and Modiglianis, among others. The Barnes trove, considered by many art experts to be the best private collection in the country, is said to be worth from $6.5 billion to more than $30 billion.

The ruling poses questions for those with large sums to bequeath: If Barnes' trust can be substantially changed, can their wishes, too, prove to have a life span of less than "in perpetuity"?

"I think that any time there is a decision to break the original donor's intentions, it has a negative effect on philanthropy," said Gene Tempel, executive director of the Center on Philanthropy at Indiana University.

But the Barnes situation seems unique, said Southwestern University law professor Robert Lind, author of "Art and Museum Law": "I don't see it as a harbinger of similar situations arising down the road."

Barry Munitz, president of the J. Paul Getty Trust in Los Angeles, said that although the case gained enormous attention, especially from people in a position to make big bequests of cash and art, he doubted that it would have a damping effect. In 2000, the Getty gave the Barnes Foundation $500,000 to help it plan a solution to its fiscal jam.

For art aesthetes, the worry is that moving the Barnes collection for the sake of making it more accessible—and revenue-enhancing—will destroy the visual and intellectual effect its creator, who died in 1951, had in mind. He specified that the paintings, sculptures and furnishings should remain exactly where he placed them, in unorthodox configurations that, for some expert beholders, reveal an ingenious and visionary understanding of the relationships among works of art.

"The Barnes was an anti-museum, because he hated museums," said Christine Steiner, a former Getty Trust general counsel who specializes in art law. "There are no museums quite as quirky and strange. The era of quirky collectors is over."

"It's very sad," said Bruce J. Altshuler, director of New York University's museum studies program. "Museums, as a whole, are becoming less and less 'different.' " And museum leaders, Altshuler added, are becoming more insistent that gifts not come with lots of donor restrictions on how art can be displayed.

The Barnes Foundation's trustees had argued in a September hearing that they were going broke in an affluent suburban residential district, where municipal rules aimed at preserving neighborhood tranquility limited gallery operations. Without transplantation, they said, the Barnes Foundation—which has a $1.2–million annual deficit, according to testimony—would eventually collapse.

Lawyers for the students, who had won friend-of-the-court status, countered that Barnes had less drastic ways of curing its financial woes: It could amass more than $40 million by selling real estate holdings elsewhere, as well as thousands of lesser artworks and a highly valued Courbet painting that's not part of Barnes' carefully choreographed gallery displays. That, and boosting admission prices, would erase the deficit and bring financial stability, argued the students' attorneys, Terrance A. Kline and Paul M. Quinones.

. . .

In his 31–page opinion, Montgomery County Orphans' Court Judge Stanley Ott ruled that selling off Barnes Foundation art and property would net $20 million—not enough to keep the operation solvent. Transplanting the collection to an established museum district in downtown Philadelphia would be "the least drastic modification" to Barnes' initial wishes that would ensure that his foundation could survive and serve the educational purpose that was Barnes' overall aim, Ott decided.

Three Philadelphia-based philanthropies, the Pew Charitable Trusts, the Annenberg Foundation and the Lenfest Foundation, have promised to help the Barnes Foundation raise $100 million to build a new home near the Philadelphia Museum of Art and the Rodin Museum, and an additional $50 million for an endowment to safeguard the foundation's long-term solvency.

At the core of the design, said Kimberly Camp, the Barnes Foundation's executive director, will be an exact replica of the existing layout, so that all of the art can be hung exactly as it is in Merion. Additional classroom and exhibition space will be built around that core. Barnes attorney Ralph Wellington said that no more than about 100 people would be allowed to enter per hour, about the same as peak hourly attendance at the current location.

QUESTIONS

1. Was it impossible for the Foundation to continue to operate Albert Barnes' museum in a manner consistent with his vision? Impracticable? Wasteful?

2. Note that the Foundation's directors obtained pledges to assist them in raising more than $150,000,000 to move the museum and render it solvent. Couldn't the Foundation's directors have launched the same fundraising campaign to keep the museum in its original location?

3. What is more important: honoring Barnes' vision, or ensuring that the Barnes' collection is a vital part of Philadelphia life?

Estate of Wilson

New York Court of Appeals, 1983.
59 N.Y.2d 461, 452 N.E.2d 1228, 465 N.Y.S.2d 900.

■ COOKE, CH. J.

These appeals present the question whether the equal protection clause of the Fourteenth Amendment is violated when a court permits the administration of private charitable trusts according to the testators' intent to finance the education of male students and not female students. When a court applies trust law that neither encourages, nor affirmatively promotes, nor compels private discrimination but allows parties to engage in private selection in the devise or bequest of their property, that choice will not be attributable to the State and subjected to the Fourteenth Amendment's strictures.

The factual patterns in each of these matters are different, but the underlying legal issues are the same. In each there is imposed a decedent's intention to create a testamentary trust under which the class of beneficiaries are members of one sex.

In Matter of Wilson, article eleventh of Clark W. Wilson's will provided that the residuary of his estate be held in trust (Wilson Trust) and that the income "be applied to defraying the education and other expenses of the first year at college of five (5) young men who shall have graduated from the Canastota High School, three (3) of whom shall have attained the highest grades in the study of science and two (2) of whom shall have attained the highest grades in the study of chemistry, as may be certified to by the then Superintendent of Schools for the Canastota Central School District." Wilson died in June, 1969 and for the next 11 years the Wilson Trust was administered according to its terms.

In early 1981, the Civil Rights Office of the United States Department of Education received a complaint alleging that the superintendent's acts in connection with the Wilson Trust violated title IX of the Education Amendments of 1972 (U.S. Code, tit. 20, § 1681 et seq.), which prohibits gender discrimination in Federally financed education programs. The Department of Education informed the Canastota Central School District that the complaint would be investigated. Before the investigation was completed, the school district agreed to refrain from again providing names of students to the trustee. The trustee, Key Bank of Central New York, initiated this proceeding for a determination of the effect and validity of the trust provision of the will.

The Surrogate's Court held that the school superintendent's co-operation with the trustee violated no Federal statute or regulation prohibiting sexual discrimination, nor did it implicate the equal protection clause of the Fourteenth Amendment. The court ordered the trustee to continue administering the trust.

A unanimous Appellate Division, Third Department, modified the Surrogate's decree. The court affirmed the Surrogate's finding that the testator intended the trust to benefit male students only and, noting that the school was under no legal obligation to provide the names of qualified male candidates, found "administration of the trust according to its literal terms is impossible." (87 A.D.2d, p. 101.) The court then exercised its cy pres power to reform the trust by striking the clause in the will providing for the school superintendent's certification of the names of qualified candidates for the scholarships. The candidates were permitted to apply directly to the trustee.

Matter of Johnson also involves a call for judicial construction of a testamentary trust created for the exclusive benefit of male students. By a will dated December 13, 1975, Edwin Irving Johnson left his residuary estate in trust (Johnson Trust). Article sixth of the will provided that the income of the trust was to "be used and applied, each year to the extent available, for scholarships or grants for bright and deserving young men who have graduated from the High School of [the Croton–Harmon Union Free] School District, and whose parents are financially unable to send them to college, and who shall be selected by the Board of Education of such School District with the assistance of the Principal of such High School."

Johnson died in 1978. In accordance with the terms of the trust, the board of education, acting as trustee, announced that applications from male students would be accepted on or before May 1, 1979. Before any scholarships were awarded, however, the National Organization for Women, filed a complaint with the Civil Rights Office of the United States Department of Education. This complaint alleged that the school district's involvement in the Johnson Trust constituted illegal gender-based discrimination.

During the pendency of the Department of Education's investigation, a stipulation was entered into between the executrix of the will, the president of the board of education, and the Attorney–General. The parties sought "to avoid administering the educational bequest set forth in Article Sixth in a manner which is in conflict with the law and public policy prohibiting discrimination based on sex". The stipulation provided that "all interested parties agree to the deletion of the word 'men' in Article Sixth of the Will and the insertion of the word 'persons' in its place." The Attorney–General then brought this proceeding by petition to the Surrogate's Court to construe article sixth of the will.

The Surrogate found that the trustee's unwillingness to administer the trust according to its terms rendered administration of the trust impossible. The court, however, declined to reform the trust by giving effect to the stipulation. Rather, it reasoned that the testator's primary intent to benefit "deserving young men" would be most closely effected by replacing the school district with a private trustee.

A divided Appellate Division, Second Department, reversed, holding that under the equal protection clause of the Fourteenth Amendment, a court cannot reform a trust that, by its own terms, would deny equal protection of law. The court reasoned that inasmuch as an agent of the State had been appointed trustee, the trust, if administered, would violate the equal protection clause. Judicial reformation of the trust by substituting trustees would, in that court's view, itself constitute State action in violation of the Fourteenth Amendment. The court determined that administration of the trust was impossible and, in an exercise of its cy pres power, reformed the trust by eliminating the gender restriction.

II

* * *

When a court determines that changed circumstances have rendered the administration of a charitable trust according to its literal terms either "impracticable or impossible", the court may exercise its cy pres power to reform the trust in a matter that "will most effectively accomplish its general purposes" (EPTL 8–1.1, subd. [c]). In reforming trusts pursuant to this power, care must be taken to evaluate the precise purpose or direction of the testator, so that when the court directs the trust towards another charitable end, it will "give effect insofar as practicable to the full design of the testator as manifested by his will and codicil" (*Matter of Scott*, 8 N.Y.2d 419, 427; see Bogert, Trusts and Trustees [rev. 2d ed.], § 442).

The court, of course, cannot invoke its cy pres power without first determining that the testator's specific charitable purpose is no longer capable of being performed by the trust (see, e.g., *Matter of Scott*, supra; *Matter of Swan*, 237 App. Div. 454, affd sub nom. *Matter of St. Johns Church of Mt. Morris*, 263 N.Y. 638; *Matter of Fairchild*, 15 Misc. 2d 272). In establishing these trusts, the testators expressly and unequivocally intended that they provide for the educational expenses of male students. It cannot be said that the accomplishment of the testators' specific expression of charitable intent is "impossible or impracticable." So long as the subject high schools graduate boys with the requisite qualifications, the testators' specific charitable intent can be fulfilled.

Nor are the trusts' particular limitation of beneficiaries by gender invalid and incapable of being accomplished as violative of public policy. It is true that the eradication in this State of gender-based discrimination is an important public policy. Indeed, the Legislature has barred gender-based discrimination in education (see Education Law, § 3201–a), employment (see Labor Law, §§ 194, 197, 220–e; General Business Law, § 187), housing, credit, and many other areas (see Executive Law, § 296). As a result, women, once viewed as able to assume only restricted roles in our society (see *Bradwell v. State*, 16 Wall [83 U.S.] 130, 141), now project significant numbers "in business, in the professions, in government and, indeed, in all walks of life where education is a desirable, if not always a necessary, antecedent" (*Stanton v. Stanton*, 421 U.S. 7, 15). The restrictions in these trusts run contrary to this policy favoring equal opportunity and treatment of men and women. A provision in a charitable trust, however, that is central to the testator's or settlor's charitable purpose, and is not illegal, should not be invalidated on public policy grounds unless that provision, if given effect, would substantially mitigate the general charitable effect of the gift (see 4 Scott, Trusts [3d ed.], § 399.4).

Proscribing the enforcement of gender restrictions in private charitable trusts would operate with equal force towards trusts whose benefits are bestowed exclusively on women. "Reduction of the disparity in economic condition between men and women caused by the long history of discrimination against women has been recognized as * * * an important governmental objective" (*Califano v. Webster*, 430 U.S. 313, 317). There can be little doubt that important efforts in effecting this type of social change can be and are performed through private philanthropy (see, generally, Commission on Private Philanthropy and Public Needs, Giving in America: Toward a Stronger Voluntary Section [1975]). And, the private funding of programs for the advancement of women is substantial and growing (see Bernstein, Funding for Women's Higher Education: Looking Backward and Ahead, Grant Magazine, vol. 4, No. 4, pp. 225–229; Ford Foundation, Financial Support of Women's Programs in the 1970's [1979]; Yarrow, Feminist Philanthropy Comes Into Its Own, N.Y. Times, May 21, 1983, p. 7, col. 2). Indeed, one compilation of financial assistance offered primarily or exclusively to women lists 854 sources of funding (see Schlacter, Directory of Financial Aids for Women [2d ed., 1981]; see, also, Note, Sex Restricted Scholarships and the Charitable Trust, 59 Iowa L. Rev. 1000, 1000–1001, & nn. 10, 11). Current thinking in private philanthropic institutions advocates that funding offered by such institutions and the opportunities within the institutions themselves be directly responsive to the needs of particular groups (see Ford Foundation, op cit., at pp. 41–44; Fleming, Foundations and Affirmative Action, 4 Foundation News No. 4, at pp. 14–17; Griffen, Funding for Women's Programs, 6 Grantsmanship Center News, No. 2, at pp. 34–45). It is evident, therefore, that the focusing of private philanthropy on certain classes within society may be consistent with public policy. Consequently, that the restrictions in the trusts before this court may run contrary to public efforts promoting equality of opportunity for women does not justify imposing a per se rule that gender restrictions in private charitable trusts violate public policy.

* * *

Although not inherently so, these trusts are currently incapable of being administered as originally intended because of the school districts' unwillingness to co-operate. These impediments, however, may be remedied by an exercise of a court's general equitable power over all trusts to permit a deviation from the administrative terms of a trust and to appoint a successor trustee.

A testamentary trust will not fail for want of a trustee (see EPTL 8–1.1; see, also, *Matter of Thomas*, 254 N.Y. 292) and, in the event a trustee is unwilling or unable to act, a court may replace the trustee with another (see EPTL 7–2.6; SCPA 1502; see, also, *Matter of Andrews*, 233 App. Div. 547; 2 Scott, Trusts [3d ed.], § 108.1). Accordingly, the proper means of continuing the Johnson Trust would be to replace the school district with someone able and willing to administer the trust according to its terms.

When an impasse is reached in the administration of a trust due to an incidental requirement of its terms, a court may effect, or permit the trustee to effect, a deviation from the trust's literal terms (see 9A Rohan, N.Y. Civ. Prac., pars. 7–2.4[3]—7–2.4[4]). This power differs from a court's cy pres power in that "[through] exercise of its deviation power the court alters or amends administrative provisions in the trust instrument but does not alter the purpose of the charitable trust or change its dispositive provisions" (Bogert, Trusts and Trustees [rev. 2d ed.], § 394, p. 249; see, e.g., *Trustees of Sailors' Snug Harbor v. Carmody*, 211 N.Y. 286; *Matter of Bruen*, 83 N.Y.S.2d 197; *Matter of Godfrey*, 36 N.Y.S.2d 414, aff'd no opn. 264 App. Div. 885). The Wilson Trust provision that the school district certify a list of students is an incidental part of the trust's administrative requirements, which no longer can be satisfied in light of the district's refusal to co-operate. The same result intended by the testator may be accomplished by permitting the students to apply directly to the trustee. Therefore, a deviation from the Wilson Trust's administrative terms by eliminating the certification requirement would be the appropriate method of continuing that trust's administration.

III

It is argued before this court that the judicial facilitation of the continued administration of gender-restrictive charitable trusts violates the equal protection clause of the Fourteenth Amendment (see U.S. Const., 14th Amdt, § 1). The strictures of the equal protection clause are invoked when the State engages in invidious discrimination (see *Moose Lodge No. 107 v. Irvis*, 407 U.S. 163, 173, 176–77; *Burton v. Wilmington Parking Auth.*, 365 U.S. 715, 721; *Civil Rights Cases*, 109 U.S. 3). Indeed, the State itself cannot, consistent with the Fourteenth Amendment, award scholarships that are gender restrictive (see *Mississippi Univ. for Women v. Hogan*, 458 U.S. 718; *Kirchberg v. Feenstra*, 450 U.S. 455; *Stanton v. Stanton*, 421 U.S. 7, supra).

The Fourteenth Amendment, however, "erects no shield against merely private conduct, however discriminatory or wrongful." (*Shelley v. Kraemer*, 334 U.S. 1, 13; see *Blum v. Yaretsky*, 457 U.S. 991, 1002; *Jackson* *v. Metropolitan Edison Co.*, 419 U.S. 345, 349; *Moose Lodge No. 107 v. Irvis*, 407 U.S. 163, 171–179, *supra; Evans v. Abney*, 396 U.S. 435, 445). Private discrimination may violate equal protection of the law when accompanied by State participation in, facilitation of, and, in some cases, acquiescence in the discrimination (see, e.g., *Burton v. Wilmington Parking Auth.*, 365 U.S. 715, *supra; Reitman v. Mulkey*, 387 U.S. 369; *Shelley v. Kraemer*, 334 U.S. 1, *supra*). Although there is no conclusive test to determine when State involvement in private discrimination will violate the Fourteenth Amendment (see *Reitman v. Mulkey, supra*, at p. 378), the general standard that has evolved is whether "the conduct allegedly causing the deprivation of a federal right [is] fairly attributable to the state" (*Lugar v. Edmondson Oil Co.,* 457 U.S. 922, 937). Therefore, it is a question of "state responsibility" and "[only] by sifting facts and weighing circumstances can the * * * involvement of the State in private conduct be attributed its true significance" *(Burton v. Wilmington Parking Auth.*, 365 U.S. 715, 722, *supra*).

* * *

The State generally may not be held responsible for private discrimination solely on the basis that it permits the discrimination to occur (see *Flagg Bros. v. Brooks*, 436 U.S. 149, 164; *Jackson v. Metropolitan Edison Co.*, 419 U.S. 345, 357, *supra; Moose Lodge No. 107 v. Irvis*, 407 U.S. 163, 176, *supra; Evans v. Abney*, 396 U.S. 435, *supra*). Nor is the State under an affirmative obligation to prevent purely private discrimination (see *Reitman v. Mulkey*, 387 U.S. 369, 376, 377, *supra*). Therefore, when the State regulates private dealings it may be responsible for private discrimination occurring in the regulated field only when enforcement of its regulation has the effect of compelling the private discrimination (*see Flagg Bros. v. Brooks, supra*; *Moose Lodge No. 107 v. Irvis, supra; Shelley v. Kraemer,* 334 U.S. 1, *supra;* cf. *Adickes v. Kress & Co.*, 398 U.S. 144, 170).

* * *

A court's application of its equitable power to permit the continued administration of the trusts involved in these appeals falls outside the ambit of the Fourteenth Amendment. Although the field of trusts is regulated by the State, the Legislature's failure to forbid private discriminatory trusts does not cause such trusts, when they arise, to be attributable to the State (see *Flagg Bros. v. Brooks*, 436 U.S. 149, 165, *supra;* see, also, *Evans v. Abney*, 396 U.S. 435, 458 [Brennan, J., dissenting], *supra*). It naturally follows that, when a court applies this trust law and determines that it permits the continued existence of private discriminatory trusts, the Fourteenth Amendment is not implicated.

In the present appeals, the coercive power of the State has never been enlisted to enforce private discrimination. Upon finding that requisite formalities of creating a trust had been met, the courts below determined the testator's intent, and applied the relevant law permitting those intentions to be privately carried out. The court's power compelled no discrimination. That discrimination had been sealed in the private execution of the wills. Recourse to the courts was had here only for the purpose of facilitating the administration of the trusts, not for enforcement of their discriminatory dispositive provisions.

This is not to say that a court's exercise of its power over trusts can never invoke the scrutiny of the Fourteenth Amendment. This court holds only that a trust's discriminatory terms are not fairly attributable to the State when a court applies trust principles that permit private discrimination but do not encourage, affirmatively promote, or compel it.

The testators' intention to involve the State in the administration of these trusts does not alter this result, notwithstanding that the effect of the courts' action respecting the trusts was to eliminate this involvement. The courts' power to replace a trustee who is unwilling to act as in Johnson or to permit a deviation from an incidental administrative term in the trust as in Wilson is a part of the law permitting this private conduct and extends to all trusts regardless of their purposes. It compels no discrimination. Moreover, the minimal State participation in the trusts' administration prior to the time that they reached the courts for the constructions under review did not cause the trusts to take on an indelible public character (see *Evans v. Newton*, 382 U.S. 296, 301; *Commonwealth of Pennsylvania v. Brown*, 392 F2d 120).

In sum, the Fourteenth Amendment does not require the State to exercise the full extent of its power to eradicate private discrimination. It is only when the State itself discriminates, compels another to discriminate, or allows another to assume one of its functions and discriminate that such discrimination will implicate the amendment.

Accordingly, in Matter of Wilson, the order of the Appellate Division should be affirmed, with costs payable out of the estate to all parties appearing separately and filing separate briefs.

In Matter of Johnson, the order of the Appellate Division should be reversed, with costs payable out of the estate to all parties appearing separately and filing separate briefs and the decree of the Surrogate's Court, Westchester County, reinstated.

■ MEYER, J., [concurring in Matter of Wilson and dissenting in Matter of Johnson].

I would affirm in both cases. Although the Constitution does not proscribe private bias, it does proscribe affirmative State action in furtherance of bias.

In Matter of Wilson the trust is private and the only involvement of a public official (the superintendent of schools) is his certification of a student's class standing, information which is, in any event, available to any student applying to the trustee for a scholarship. There is, therefore, no State action.

In Matter of Johnson, however, the trustee is the board of education, a public body. The establishment of a public trust for a discriminatory purpose is constitutionally improper, as Presiding Justice Mollen has fully spelled out in his opinion. For the State to legitimize that impropriety by replacement of the trustee is unconstitutional State action. The only permissible corrective court action is, as the Appellate Division held, excision of the discriminatory limitation.

NOTES AND QUESTIONS

1. Did the court in the Wilson case apply the *cy pres* doctrine? If not, how did the court avoid invalidating the trust?

Note that in other cases, courts have applied *cy pres* to save charitable trusts when the designated trustee is a public official who could not, consistent with the constitution, obey the settlor's discriminatory directions. See In re Certain Scholarship Funds, 133 N.H. 227, 575 A.2d 1325 (1990) (permitting scholarship recipient to be a "student" rather than a "boy"). In Ebitz v. Pioneer National Bank, 372 Mass. 207, 361 N.E.2d 225 (1977), the court construed the term "young men" to include women, reasoning that settlor had not intended to draw gender distinctions when settlor created a scholarship fund to benefit "young men to acquire a legal education."

2. Would the court have reached the same result if the trust in Wilson had been designed to benefit "five (5) young *white* persons who shall have graduated from Canastota High School...."? Suppose the trust had been for the benefit of "five (5) young Christian persons?"

Could the public trustees have administered the trust if the trust had been to benefit five *girls*? See Trustees of University of Delaware v. Gebelein, 420 A.2d 1191 (Del.Ch.1980) (holding that public trustee could enforce gender discrimination in favor of women because purpose was to correct for past discrimination).

3. What limits, if any, should courts impose on the right of settlors to discriminate in designating beneficiaries of charitable trusts? If courts prohibited discrimination on the basis of religion, for instance, would that prohibition have any effect on the volume of charitable giving? See In re Girard's Estate, 386 Pa. 548, 613, 127 A.2d 287, 318 (1956), rev'd sub nom Pennsylvania v. Board of Dir. of City Trusts, 353 U.S. 230, 77 S.Ct. 806, 1 L.Ed.2d 792 (1957) [Bell, J., concurring]:

> If the present contention of the City is correct its effect will be catastrophic on testamentary church and charitable bequests, as well as on the law of Wills in Pennsylvania. The constitutional prohibition against discrimination—the Fourteenth Amendment—is not confined to color; it *prohibits the States* from making any discrimination because of race, creed or color. It follows logically and necessarily that if an individual cannot constitutionally leave his money to an orphanage or to a private home and college for poor white male orphans, he cannot constitutionally leave his money to a Catholic, or Episcopal, or Baptist, or Methodist, or Lutheran or Presbyterian Church; or to a Synagogue for Orthodox Jews; or to a named Catholic Church or to a named Catholic priest for Masses for the repose of his soul, or for other religious or charitable purposes. That would shock the people of

Pennsylvania and the people of the United States more than a terrible earthquake or a large atomic bomb.

Charitable trusts receive favorable treatment not available to other trusts—exemption from the Rule Against Perpetuities, and from the requirement that beneficiaries be identified. Should courts extend these benefits to trusts that discriminate on the basis of race or gender? If your answer is yes, explain why?

Note that even if a discriminatory trust is treated as charitable for state law purposes, the discriminatory trust may not be entitled to federal tax exemptions extended to qualified charities under the Internal Revenue Code. See Bob Jones University v. United States, 461 U.S. 574, 103 S.Ct. 2017, 76 L.Ed.2d 157 (1983).

Tropical Battle of Race, Rights Divides Islanders

By Rita Beamish.
Washington Post, September 14, 2003.

A river of crimson T-shirts stretched more than a mile down Waikiki's main thoroughfare. With Hawaiian chants and the blowing of conch shells, the throng of demonstrators moved slowly past befuddled tourists along the oceanfront.

"Ku i ka pono. Ku 'e i ka hewa!" they chanted, in a display of solidarity that included the governor and lieutenant governor, education officials, students, families and elders. Their chant translated: "Stand up for justice. Resist injustice!"

The sight of several thousand marchers drew attention last Sunday in the tourist mecca of Waikiki, but the impetus for the demonstration came from a federal courthouse three miles away. There, three anti-discrimination lawsuits may undo a catalogue of services available only to those of aboriginal Hawaiian ancestry—health care, housing and even a prestigious private school.

Two separate civil rights suits take on one of the state's most revered institutions, Kamehameha Schools, which was founded by the will of a Hawaiian princess to educate her people....

[T]he two cases against Kamehameha Schools seek admission for non-Hawaiians. One of them roused especially high passions this fall, after a court ordered the admission of a non-Hawaiian boy to the sprawling Honolulu hilltop campus while his lawsuit is pending. U.S. District Judge David Ezra said his order does not prejudge the merits of the case, which alleges a violation of the 1866 Civil Rights Act.

Lingle said Kamehameha Schools "is perhaps the single most important institution for preserving Hawaiian culture for next generations." It is known for its strong academics and cultural pride. Its choir gained fame in the recent Disney animated film "Lilo and Stitch."

In the late 1960s, when elsewhere "it wasn't considered good to be Hawaiian," said teacher Joanne Quindica, Kamehameha opened a new world to her. At school, she said, "I could feel the heart of the Hawaiians." Kealohilani Ohuna, a 1993 graduate, said, "Kamehameha Schools is one of the last things Hawaiians have, and we have to hold on to that."

Kamehameha openly states that it will not admit non-Hawaiians while it has qualified applicants—children take an entrance exam—with a drop of Hawaiian blood. With a trust of $5.4 billion and three campuses, its stated mission is "to improve the capability and well-being of people of Hawaiian ancestry." The trust voluntarily gave up federal funding but retains its nonprofit tax standing.

The 1883 will of Princess Bernice Pauahi Bishop, last of the direct royal line, directed construction of Kamehameha Schools and said spaces should be reserved for indigents and orphans, with "preference to Hawaiians of pure or part aboriginal blood." Historically, the trustees have extended the preference to the entire student body.

"She believed at least through education she might be able to better prepare her people to survive in this new world, so that they could compete in the Western world and under the new rules, but also be able to know who they were, where they came from, the roots of their culture," said Constance Lau, chairman of the schools' board of trustees. The Hawaiian population had been decimated by Western-imported diseases. Over time, expressions of Hawaiian language and culture were forbidden or discouraged.

Trust officials also cite state and federal data showing that Hawaiians today lag in school readiness and in public school performance, are disproportionately represented in prisons and homeless shelters, and have a poverty rate twice that of non-Hawaiians. Rather than any "invidious discriminatory purpose," the schools' admissions policy "is in furtherance of the Congressionally recognized compelling public interest in remedying the effects of past discrimination against native Hawaiians," Kamehameha's court briefs say.

However, John Goemans, the attorney who brought the Rice case and now represents both plaintiffs suing Kamehameha Schools, sees no nuance in the civil rights law. "All you've got to do is show there's a racial admission policy. It doesn't matter what the intent was," he said. He also contended that data on the Hawaiians' plight are skewed because the statistics include multiethnic people with only a little Hawaiian blood.

. . .

NOTE

In Doe v. Kamehameha Schools, 295 F.Supp.2d 1141 (D. Hawai'i 2003), the plaintiff, a non-Native Hawaiian minor, asserted that he was denied admission to the school because of his race, and the school's admission policy granting a preference to children of Native Hawaiian ancestry violated

§ 1981. After the district court held that the school's affirmative action plan served a legitimate remedial purpose, and that the plan reasonably related to that purpose, a three-judge panel of the Ninth Circuit reversed, finding that "the school's absolute bar to admission on the basis of race is invalid." 416 F.3d 1025 (9th Cir. 2005). The Ninth Circuit granted rehearing *en banc*, and the court, in an 8–7 decision, affirmed the district court. See Doe v. Kamehameha Schools/Bernice Pauahi Bishop Estate, 470 F.3d 827 (9th Cir. 2006).

CHAPTER EIGHT

POWERS OF APPOINTMENT

We have already discussed powers of appointment at a number of points in the course. Powers of appointment are an indispensable feature of estate planning because first, they introduce flexibility into the estate plan, and second, when structured properly, they can generate significant tax advantages. See generally Adam Hirsch & William K.S. Wang, A Qualitative Theory of the Dead Hand, 68 Ind. L.J. 1, 38–49 (1992).

Consider a brief illustration:

Mother, 70 years old and ill, has significant assets, and wants to assure Father, age 65 and healthy, full use of those assets during his lifetime. Mother also wants to assure that the assets are available for the couple's children, Sister, age 35, and Brother, age 32, at Father's death. That is, Mother wants to assure that Father does not use the assets to benefit a future wife or some other family member. What are Mother's options?

Mother could create a trust, with income to be paid to Father during his lifetime, and principal to be divided equally between Sister and Brother at Father's death. Suppose, however, Mother does not know what Sister and Brother's relative needs will be at Father's death. If Mother trusts Father to evaluate their needs, Mother need not provide for equal division; she can instead give Father a power to appoint the property between Sister and Brother, essentially postponing any decision about how her property should be divided until Father's death, when Sister and Brother's needs may be clearer. (In addition, by giving Father a power of appointment, Mother gives Sister and Brother an incentive to be nicer to Father).

Alternatively, consider a case in which estate tax consequences motivate Mother to create a power of appointment. Mother wants to give Father all of her assets, but also wants to take full advantage of her own unified credit. Mother can create a "credit shelter trust" or "bypass trust" which gives Father broad powers to use trust income, limited power to invade trust principal, and a special power to appoint between Sister and Brother. In this way, she assures that the trust property does not qualify for the marital deduction, and hence passes through her own estate, using up her unified credit. At the same time, despite the broad powers Mother has given Father, the trust property will not be treated as part of Father's taxable estate.

There are two sources of legal rules governing powers of appointment—state property law and the Internal Revenue Code (the "Code"). Because property law's treatment of powers differs from the Code's in a few critical respects, we first review the legal property law rules. We then address the critical differences in the Code.

Section I. Terminology and Classification

A. Property Law

What, precisely, is a power of appointment? According to the Restatement (Third) of Property: Wills and Other Donative Transfers, § 17.1 (Tentative Draft No. 5, 2006),

> *A power of appointment is a power that enables the donee of the power, acting in a non-fiduciary capacity, to designate recipients of beneficial ownership interests in the appointive property.*

Under state law, then, because the holder of the power is not a fiduciary, her failure to exercise the power would not expose her to legal liability.

The issues that surround powers of appointment will be a lot easier to understand if you start by mastering the terminology. In each of three areas—the "parties" to a power, the scope of the power, and the time of exercise—definitions are important.

1. THE PARTIES TO A POWER OF APPOINTMENT

The person who creates the power of appointment—the person whose money or property will be distributed when the power is exercised—is called the ***donor*** of the power.

The person who exercises the power—the person who actually decides how the donor's property should be distributed—is called the ***donee*** of the power.

The people to whom the donee appoints the property are the ***appointees.*** As we shall see, the donor often restricts the people to whom the donee may appoint. The class of people eligible to receive the appointive property are called the ***objects of the power*** or the ***class of permissible appointees.***

Finally, who takes if the donee never exercises the power of appointment? The people who would take in the absence of exercise—whether or not they are explicitly named in the instrument creating the power—are called the ***takers in default.***

> ***Example 1:*** *Mother creates a trust, providing that "trust income should be paid to Father for life, and at Father's death, Father may appoint the trust principal among our children. If Father does not appoint, the trust property shall pass to our children in equal shares."*
>
> *Mother, who created the power, is the donor of the power. Father, who has the authority to exercise the power, is the donee of the power. The children form the class of permissible appointees, and any children to whom Father eventually appoints are appointees. The children are also the takers in default, because the trust*

property would be distributed to them if Father fails to exercise the power.

2. SCOPE OF THE POWER

a. *General Powers and Special (Non–General) Powers*

Suppose the donor of a power of appointment wants to give the donee complete freedom to choose the beneficiaries of the appointive property. The donor can give the donee a **general power**, which entitles the donee to appoint to anyone—including herself or her estate.

Often, however, the donor wants to restrict the class of potential appointees. When she does, she creates what has historically been called a **special power.** Thus, a power to appoint "among my children" or "among my descendants" or "among my relatives" is a special power. In the last couple of decades, many scholars have tried to change the traditional terminology, and have called these powers **non-general powers.** Nevertheless, lawyers continue to label these powers "special" at least as often as they refer to them as "non-general." We will call them special powers.

It is generally clear whether the donor has created a special power or a general power. Suppose, however, the donor authorizes the donee to appoint "to anyone except herself or her estate." Is the power general or special? Consider the following Restatement provision:

Restatement (Third) of Property. (Tentative Draft No. 5, 2006).

Section 17.3 General Power; Nongeneral Power

(a) A power of appointment is general to the extent that the power is exercisable in favor of the donee, the donee's estate, or the creditors of either, regardless of whether the power is also exercisable in favor of others.

(2) A power of appointment that is not general is a nongeneral power.

Because general powers of appointment are included in the donee's taxable estate, the donor will sometimes find it useful to create a power that will not be construed as general, but that nevertheless gives the donee broad powers. Hillman v. Hillman, 433 Mass. 590, 744 N.E.2d 1078 (2001) is illustrative. Donor created a trust and gave her son, the donee, a power to appoint among "my said son's spouse, his issue, my issue, or the spouses of any of his issue or of any of my issue." Because the son was among donor's issue, the donee appeared to have the right to appoint to himself, making the power a general power. Donee, however, sought and obtained a judgment declaring that he did not have the power to appoint to himself. The Supreme Judicial Court of Massachusetts, expressing a reluctance to attribute to the donor an intention that would benefit only the taxing authorities, held that donee was not entitled to appoint to himself.

General powers of appointment arise in a variety of other situations. The settlor of a revocable trust holds a general power of appointment over trust principal because the settlor is entitled to appoint the principal to herself by revoking the trust. A trust beneficiary holds a general power of appointment when the beneficiary has power to compel payments to herself. For instance, if a trust instrument gives a beneficiary an unqualified power to invade principal, the beneficiary holds a general power of appointment over that principal.

b. *Exclusive and Non–Exclusive Powers*

Suppose the donor creates a special power of appointment. Must the donee appoint something to every member of the class of permissible appointees? Generally, the answer is no. The donee is free to exclude one or many members of the class of permissible appointees. Because the donee is free to exclude objects of the power, we say that the power is **exclusive** (or, in the terminology recently adopted by the Restatement, **exclusionary**). See generally Restatement (Third) of Property: Wills and Other Donative Transfers, § 17.5. (Tentative Draft No. 5, 2006); Ferrell–French v. Ferrell, 691 So.2d 500 (Fla. Dist. Ct. App. 1997).

If, however, the donor explicitly requires the donee to appoint some assets to each member of the class, we say that the power is **non-exclusive** or **non-exclusionary**; the donee may not exclude any objects of the class. Restatement § 19.1. As the court in Ferrell–French v. Ferrell, supra, explained:

> the problem with a non-exclusive power is how much is the minimum amount that must be left to any member of the class in order for the appointment to be valid?

691 So.2d 500 at 501. For this reason, courts generally construe powers as exclusive in the absence of express language in the instrument creating the power (but see Hargrove v. Rich, 278 Ga. 561, 604 S.E.2d 475 (2004), in which the Georgia Supreme Court held that when the donee held a power to appoint "to her brothers or sisters or her nieces and nephews," the donee could not appoint to only a single niece; the court relied on donor's use of the word "and," while the will otherwise used the word "or").

3. TIME OF APPOINTMENT

If the donor gives the donee a power of appointment that the donee is free to exercise immediately, we call the donee's power **presently exercisable.** See Restatement (Third) of Property: Donative Transfers, § 17.4 (Tentative Draft No. 5, 2006).

Often, however, when donor creates a power of appointment, donor wants the donee to wait before deciding how to appoint the property. Donor may create a **postponed power**—a power exercisable by the donee only after the expiration of a stated time or after the occurrence or nonoccurrence of a specified event. See e.g., N.Y. EPTL 10–3.3(g). Once the time has expired or the condition has occurred, the power becomes **presently exercisable.** If the donor wants the donee to have as full a picture as possible when deciding how to distribute trust property, donor will specify that donee may only exercise the power by will. If the donor requires that the power be exercised by will, donor has created a **testamentary** power of appointment.

> ***Example 2:*** *Donor creates a trust to benefit her two daughters for life, and gives to her surviving daughter a power to appoint, by deed or by will, among donor's descendants. Is the power presently exercisable, postponed, or testamentary?*
>
> ***Solution:*** *The power is neither presently exercisable nor testamentary. It is not presently exercisable because neither daughter currently has the power to exercise it. It is not testamentary because the surviving daughter can exercise the power by deed or by will. The exercise of the power is* ***postponed****, because we will not know who the donee is until one sister dies. At the death of the first sister to die, the power will become presently exercisable; the surviving daughter may exercise immediately by deed if she chooses.*

PROBLEMS

1. John Smith creates a trust, and directs that income from the trust should be paid to his wife and daughter for so long as either remains alive. The trust instrument then provides:

> "I grant to my wife a power to appoint the principal, by will, among any blood relatives of my wife or myself. If the power is not exercised, I direct that, at the death of my wife, the trust principal should be divided as if I survived my wife and then died intestate."

A. The Parties:

1) Who is the donor of the power?

2) Who is the donee of the power?

3) Who are the members of the class of permissible appointees?

4) Who are the takers in default?

B. Scope and Timing:

1) Is the power general or special? Is the wife entitled to appoint in favor of her estate?

2) When will the power become exercisable?

3) Suppose the trust instrument were changed to give the wife a power to appoint "by deed or by will." When would the power become exercisable?

2. Donor's will created a trust to benefit her daughter Alice for life. The will provided that at Alice's death, "My trustee shall distribute any amount of the principal ... to ... any descendants of mine other than my child for whom this trust is created, and any charitable scientific or educational organizations, as such child shall appoint by will." Alice's will exercised the power in favor of her son, Mark. Alice's sister, Beatrice, argued that the power was non-exclusive, and that Alice was required to appoint half of the trust assets to all of Donor's descendants in equal shares and the other half to charity. Should Beatrice prevail? See Estate of Hope, 223 P.3d 119 (Colo. App. 2007).

B. POWERS OF APPOINTMENT AND THE INTERNAL REVENUE CODE

The definition of a power of appointment is different for federal tax purposes than for state law purposes. Because the Code's focus is on figuring out whom to tax, its definition is broader than the one found in state property law. The Code's definition includes not only non-fiduciary powers but also trustees' powers to invade and distribute principal, which are fiduciary in nature.

The Code also defines general powers differently than state law does. Under state law, if a donee can appoint to herself, she has a general power. This is not necessarily the case under the Code. If the donee's power to appoint principal to herself is limited by an ascertainable standard, the power is non-general for tax purposes. I.R.C. §§ 2041(b)(1)(A), 2514(c)(1). The Code suggests that the power to distribute principal for a beneficiary's "health, education, support, or maintenance"—or some combination of those terms—would be an ascertainable standard. The definition matters because property subject to a general power is part of donee's taxable estate, whereas property subject to a non-general (or special) power is not.

PROBLEM

D is the beneficiary of a trust that provides that trust income is payable to her at least annually.

1. If the trust instrument also includes the following provisions, in which cases does D hold a general power of appointment under the Internal Revenue Code? In which of these cases, if any, does the answer depend on whether D is the trustee of the trust?

a. The Trustee shall pay to D so much of the trust principal as D shall request in writing.

b. The Trustee shall pay to D so much of the trust principal as the Trustee deems necessary for D's happiness.

c. The Trustee shall pay to D so much of the principal as the Trustee deems necessary for D's health, education, support and maintenance.

d. The Trustee shall pay such amounts from trust principal to such persons or entities as D shall direct from time to time.

e. The Trustee shall pay such amounts from trust principal to such one or more of the group consisting of D's issue and the spouses of D's issue as D shall direct from time to time.

2. Assume now that the trust instrument gives D only a right to annual income during D's lifetime, and makes the following provisions for the trust principal upon D's death. In which of these cases does D hold a general power of appointment?:

a. On D's death, the Trustee shall distribute the trust estate to such persons or entities, including D's estate, as D shall appoint by will. In default of appointment, the Trustee shall distribute the trust estate to D's issue, by representation.

b. On D's death, the Trustee shall distribute the trust estate to such one or more of the group consisting of D's issue and the spouses of D's issue, as D shall appoint by will. In default of appointment, the Trustee shall distribute the trust estate to D's issue, by representation.

SECTION II. CREATION AND EXERCISE

Now that we have surveyed powers of appointment terminology, we turn to more important questions: why and how does a donor create a power of appointment, and how does a donee exercise the power?

The donor generally creates a power of appointment in conjunction with creation of a trust. What language should the donor use to create the power? Consider what motivated the donor to choose the words he used in the following case:

Estate of Hamilton

New York Appellate Division, Third Department, 1993.
190 A.D.2d 927, 593 N.Y.S.2d 372.

■ CREW, J.:

Appeal from a decree of the Surrogate's Court of Albany County (Marinelli, S.), entered December 13, 1991, which, inter alia, adjudged that Anita G. Hamilton failed to exercise in her last will and testament the general power of appointment which was granted to her by the last will and testament of decedent.

On February 26, 1989 Milton W. Hamilton (hereinafter decedent) died, survived by his spouse, Anita G. Hamilton (hereinafter Hamilton), his daughters, respondents Mary H. McLaughlin, Gwendolyn H. Stevens, and his stepson, respondent John H. Ricketson. Paragraph fourth of decedent's last will and testament, executed on April 5, 1982, directed that the residuary of decedent's estate be divided into two funds, Fund A and Fund B. Fund A was a marital deduction trust and Fund B was a bequest to McLaughlin and Stevens. Paragraph fourth further provided that upon Hamilton's death, the principal remaining in Fund A was to be "paid, transferred or distributed ... in such manner ... as [Hamilton] may by her last Will and Testament direct and appoint"; decedent specified, however, that this power of appointment was "exercisable only by specific reference to said power in [Hamilton's] last Will and Testament". In the event that Hamilton failed to effectively exercise the power of appointment, the assets remaining in Fund A would pass to McLaughlin and Stevens.

Hamilton died 15 days after decedent, leaving a last will and testament dated December 22, 1967. Paragraph second of Hamilton's will provided as follows:

> "By this paragraph of my Last Will and Testament, I do specifically exercise the power of appointment given to me by paragraph 'Sixth' of the Last Will and Testament of my husband ... dated the 26th day of August, 1966, in favor of my son, JOHN HENRY RICKETSON ... or to his issue him surviving, to the extent of seven-eighths (7/8ths) of the fund over which I have the power of appointment, and I give, devise and bequeath to SUE M. RICKETSON, wife of my son, one-eighth (1/8th) of the fund over which I have the power of appointment under the said Last Will and Testament of my husband ... By these provisions, I do specifically exercise the power of appointment given to me by the Will of my said husband" (emphasis supplied).

Decedent's and Hamilton's respective wills were subsequently admitted to probate.

Petitioner thereafter commenced this accounting proceeding seeking, inter alia, a determination as to whether Hamilton had effectively exercised the power of appointment granted her in decedent's 1982 will. Surrogate's Court concluded, inter alia, that although Hamilton had validly exercised the power of appointment given her in decedent's 1966 will, that will was revoked by subsequent wills executed by decedent in 1975 and 1982. Accordingly, Surrogate's Court decreed that Hamilton did not satisfy the "specific reference" requirement contained in decedent's 1982 will and, therefore, the remainder of the trust would pass to McLaughlin and Stevens. This appeal by Ricketson followed.

We affirm. EPTL 10–6.1 sets forth the rules governing the exercise of a power of appointment and provides, in pertinent part, that

> "[i]f the donor has expressly directed that no instrument shall be effective to exercise the power unless it contains a specific reference to the power, an instrument not containing such reference does not validly exercise the power"

(EPTL 10–6.1[b]). This particular provision was derived from Real Property Law former § 147(4), which required a "reference to the specific power" in order for the exercise to be effective (L 1964, ch. 864). With the enactment of EPTL 10–6.1(b), the language was revised slightly to require a "specific reference to the power" (L. 1966, ch. 952, eff. Sept. 1, 1967) and was apparently designed to allow the donor to prevent the blind exercise of the power of appointment by the donee (see generally, *Matter of Carmel*, 118 Misc. 2d 1048, 1050–1051; *Matter of Berard*, 89 Misc. 2d 838, 840).

Here, in order to effectively exercise the power of appointment granted her in decedent's 1982 will, Hamilton had to make "specific reference to said power" in her last will and testament (see, EPTL 10–6.1[b]; Matter of Gilchrist, 95 Misc. 2d 873). This she did not do. The only power referenced by Hamilton in her will was the power of appointment granted her under decedent's 1966 will which, as noted previously, had been revoked by decedent's subsequent execution of a new will in 1975 and again in 1982, in which decedent clearly manifested his intent to revoke all prior wills and codicils (see, EPTL 3–4.1[a][1][A]). Thus, Hamilton's sole reference was to a power that had ceased to exist.

The remaining issues do not merit extended discussion. While it is true that decedent granted a power of appointment to Hamilton in his subsequent wills, we cannot infer from Hamilton's exercise of the appointive power conferred under decedent's 1966 will that she similarly intended to exercise any such power existing under decedent's 1982 will. In any event, Hamilton's intent in this regard is irrelevant for decedent "made it crystal clear" that the power of appointment granted by his 1982 will was exercisable only by Hamilton's specific reference thereto in her last will and testament (see, *Matter of Gilchrist, supra,* at 874; see also, *Matter of Carmel, supra,* at 1049). We similarly reject Ricketson's assertion that Hamilton's exercise of the power of appointment conferred by decedent's 1966 will "reasonably approximates" the manner in which decedent directed the power be exercised under his 1982 will. The parties' remaining arguments have been examined and found to be unpersuasive.

■ MIKOLL, J. P., YESAWICH JR., MAHONEY and HARVEY, JJ., concur.

QUESTIONS

1. Why did Milton Hamilton create a power of appointment at all? Was this a case in which he wanted to maximize his wife's discretion to distribute the property as she saw fit?

2. Did tax objectives drive Milton Hamilton's desire to create this power of appointment? If so, what tax objectives? Note that Milton Hamilton's will was executed in April 1982. In 1981, Congress had amended the estate tax laws to permit QTIP trusts to qualify for the marital deduction. Do you think Milton Hamilton's lawyer was up to date when he drafted the will? How would you advise Milton if he came into your office today?

3. Why did Milton require that the power be "exercisable only by specific reference" to the power? Should Milton's reasons matter? See Matter of Strobel, 149 Ariz. 213, 717 P.2d 892 (1986) (distinguishing cases in which decedent required specific reference "to restrict the wife's interest in the trust as much as possible, in order to gain benefit of the marital deduction and yet control who ultimately would receive the corpus after the wife's death" from cases in which the specific reference requirement was included to prevent inadvertent exercise of the power). See also Smith v. Brannan, 152 Or.App. 505, 954 P.2d 1259 (1998) (reaching same result as Estate of Hamilton with respect to trust created for marital deduction purposes).

If Milton Hamilton had included the specific reference requirement to prevent inadvertent exercise, how would the *Strobel* court have decided the principal case?

4. How would you draft a specific reference clause that would have avoided the litigation in Hamilton if

(1) Milton wanted to require Anita to refer to his 1982 will?

(2) Milton wanted only to be sure that Anita referred to a power of appointment created in Milton's last will, whenever executed?

5. Should a donor, in creating a power, require that the donee make specific reference to the power? The practice of requiring specific reference developed before 1942, when undesirable tax consequences often followed from inadvertent exercise of powers. For powers created after 1942, those consequences have disappeared.

One non-tax reason remains for discouraging inadvertent exercise: in many jurisdictions, as we shall see, creditors of the donee of a general power may reach the appointive property if and only if the donee exercises the power. If, therefore, the donee is insolvent, inadvertent exercise may subject the appointive property to creditor claims. Is this a strong enough reason to include a specific reference clause? See Edward H. Rabin, Blind Exercise of Powers of Appointment, 51 Cornell L. Rev. 1 (1965) (answering "no," and emphasizing that most donees have solvent estates, where blind exercise presents no difficulty).

NOTES

1. Consider the Uniform Probate Code's treatment of the specific reference problem:

Section 2–704. Power of Appointment; Meaning of Specific Reference Requirement.

If a governing instrument creating a power of appointment expressly requires that the power be exercised by a reference, an express reference, or a specific reference, to the power or its source, it is presumed that the donor's intention, in requiring that the donee exercise the power by making reference to the particular power or to the creating instrument, was to prevent an inadvertent exercise of the power.

How would the *Hamilton* case have been decided if the UPC had been in effect?

2. Many states have statutes (like New York's) that explicitly provide that donee's appointment is effective only if donee has complied with donor's specific reference requirement. As the *Hamilton* case illustrates, however, the statutes do not definitively resolve whether particular language by the donee satisfies the requirement the donor has imposed.

The common law rule was similar, requiring the donee to comply with formal requirements imposed by the donor. The Restatement, reflecting more recent case law, takes a somewhat more flexible "substantial compliance" approach. Restatement (Third) of Property: Wills and Other Donative Transfers (Tentative Draft, No. 5, 2006) provides, in relevant part:

> Substantial compliance with formal requirements of an appointment imposed by the donor, including a requirement that the instrument of exercise make reference or specific reference to the power, is sufficient if (i) the evidence establishes that the donee

knew of and intended to exercise the power, and (ii) the donee's manner of attempted exercise did not impair the donor's purpose in imposing the requirement.

Courts often hold that a disposition of all "property to which I may have a power of appointment at the time of my death" constitutes a "specific reference" to a power of appointment. See, e.g., Motes/Henes Trust v. Motes, 297 Ark. 380, 761 S.W.2d 938 (1988); Matter of Strobel, 149 Ariz. 213, 717 P.2d 892 (1986). Indeed, in Carter v. Bank One Trust Co., 760 N.E.2d 1171 (Ind. App. 2002), the court held an appointment effective even though the donor had imposed a specific reference requirement and the donee's will failed to mention the power of appointment at all. The court noted that the will had disposed of the appointive property and concluded that reference to the described property subject to the power was enough to make the exercise effective.

In none of these cases was there evidence that the specific reference requirement was intended to prevent all exercise of the power. Instead, the donor's apparent objective was to prevent only *inadvertent* exercise. See generally Martha A. Cromartie, Powers of Appointment—Does a General Residuary Clause Fulfill a Specific Reference Requirement?, 65 N.C. L. Rev. 1475 (1987).

Will of Block

Surrogate's Court, New York County, 1993.
157 Misc.2d 716, 598 N.Y.S.2d 668.

■ PREMINGER, S.

As an incident to the judicial settlement of two intermediate accounts, the trustees ask the court to determine whether and to what extent a limited testamentary power of appointment was effectively exercised by decedent's son.

Decedent, Dina W. Block, died in 1981, a domiciliary of New York. Her will established a trust of one half of her residuary estate for the benefit of her son Paul, Jr. and his twin sons, Allan and John. The trust terminated upon Paul, Jr.'s death and he was given a limited power to appoint the trust principal by will "unto and among" these two sons in whatever proportion he chose. The twins' older half-brother Cyrus was not a permissible appointee. In default of the exercise of the power, the trust fund was to be divided into separate trusts for the life income benefit of Allan and John. United States Trust Company, Paul, Jr. and his brother William served as trustees under Dina Block's will.

Paul, Jr. died an Ohio domiciliary in 1987. His will, which was executed more than a year after his mother's death, did not refer to his power of appointment under her will. It left his entire residuary estate to a revocable trust he had created in 1974. Under the 1974 trust, after certain payments to his wife (not relevant here), there are separate subtrusts for all three of Paul's sons: 35% each to Allan and John, and 30% to Cyrus.

The trustees seek direction whether Paul's disposition of his residuary estate without reference to the appointive assets, and in partial violation of the limitations Dina imposed, nevertheless effectively exercised his limited power of appointment. It is clear that this question must be answered by referring to the local law of New York rather than Ohio. (EPTL 3–5.1[g][2][A]; *Matter of Acheson*, 28 N.Y.2d 155, 164; *Matter of Bauer*, 14 N.Y.2d 272, 277; *Matter of Deane*, 4 N.Y.2d 326, 331.)

In New York, an effective exercise of a power of appointment need not refer to the power. (EPTL 10–6.1[a],[b].) The Legislature has abrogated the common-law rule still in effect in Ohio which requires that a donee manifest a clear intent to exercise the power (see, *Clinton County Natl. Bank & Trust Co. v. First Natl. Bank*, 62 Ohio St 2d 90, 403 NE2d 968). Under New York law a conventional residuary clause disposing of the testator's remaining assets exercises a power of appointment unless "the intention that the will is not to operate as an execution of the power appears expressly or by necessary implication" (EPTL 10–6.1[a][4]; see, *Lockwood v. Mildeberger*, 159 N.Y. 181).

There is no question that Paul's will did not expressly negate an intention to exercise the power. The more difficult question is whether there is an adequate basis for finding "by necessary implication" that Paul did not intend to exercise the power.

The New York cases and statutes governing the exercise of powers of appointment strongly favor finding a valid exercise, in furtherance of the presumed intention of most power holders. In addition to the presumption of exercise by a residuary disposition discussed above, compliance with specific directions by the donor of a power as to certain formalities of exercise is excused by EPTL 10–6.2. Furthermore, under EPTL 10–6.6 the exercise of a power in favor of some persons who are not permissible appointees is not void, nor need such an over-extensive exercise of a power give rise to a "necessary implication" that the donee did not intend to exercise the power. (See, *Matter of Slocum*, 192 Misc. 1026.)

Courts have also been restrictive in finding a "necessary implication" not to exercise a power. (*Lockwood v. Mildeberger*, 159 N.Y. 181, 186, *supra*; *Matter of Slocum,* 192 Misc. 1026, *supra; Matter of Davis*, 186 Misc. 397.) It has been held that proof of the implied intent not to exercise must be " 'impossible to be otherwise' ", " 'not to be avoided' " and " 'inevitable' ". *(Lockwood v. Mildeberger, supra*, at 186, 53 N.E. 803.) Several cases have required that the intent be demonstrated from an examination of the text of the will and ruled that evidence outside the will must be rejected. (*Matter of Hopkins*, 46 Misc. 2d 273 [Sur. Ct., N.Y. County 1964]; *Matter of Thorne*, 9 Misc. 2d 126 [Sup. Ct., N.Y. County 1957]; *In re Farrell's Will*, 106 N.Y.S.2d 878 [Sur. Ct., Kings County 1951].) In those few cases where the necessary intent not to exercise a power of appointment has been found, the evidence has been overwhelming. (See, e.g., *Guaranty Trust Co. v. Halsted*, 245 N.Y. 447 [exercise would have caused perpetuities invalidity]; *Chase Natl. Bank v. Chicago Tit. & Trust Co.*, 246 App. Div. 201 [involving a written attempt to release the power].)

Nothing in the text of Paul, Jr.'s will gives rise to the "necessary implication". The only possible indicia are: (1) the fact that this is the will of the domiciliary of a jurisdiction which would not deem it to have exercised the power (*Clinton County Natl. Bank & Trust Co. v. First Natl. Bank*, 62 Ohio St 2d 90, 403 NE2d 968, supra); (2) the fact that the presumed exercise of the power was inconsistent with its limitations; and (3) the inference that the donee knew of the existence of the power because he was a trustee of the appointive assets.

None of these factors standing alone has been sufficient to trigger the imposition of the necessary implication. (See, *Lockwood v. Mildeberger, supra*; *Matter of Slocum*, 192 Misc. 1026, *supra*; *Matter of Davis*, 186 Misc. 397, *supra; Matter of Hopkins*, 46 Misc. 2d 273; *Matter of De von der Hallen*, 9 Misc. 2d 927; *In re Farrell's Will*, 106 N.Y.S.2d 878 [Sur Ct, Kings County 1951], *supra; Matter of Thorne, 9* Misc. 2d 126, *supra.)* No different result occurs when they have combined. It is true that dictum in prior cases suggest that actual knowledge of the existence of the power "might be" sufficient to create the implication. *(Lockwood v. Mildeberger, supra, at* 187; *Matter of Davis*, 186 Misc. 397, 401.) But it must be evident that the existence of the power was within the testator's contemplation at the very moment of execution of the will. Nothing in the routine responsibilities of a trustee would establish this level of knowledge. Although Paul's failure to refer to his power of appointment could be interpreted as reliance on the Ohio rule that silence is nonexercise, it is at least as likely that he did not have the power in mind when he signed his will.

It must be remembered that the New York statutory presumption that a power has been exercised goes beyond the actual intent of the donee. It applies, for example, to situations where the power was created after the will was executed. (See, e.g., *Matter of Davis, supra; Matter of Thorne*, 9 Misc. 2d 126, *supra; Hirsch v. Bucki*, 162 App. Div. 659.) This is because the "emphatic command" of the statute (*Matter of Thorne, supra,* at 131, 167 N.Y.S.2d 211) is an example of the long-approved concept that, in the absence of compelling evidence of an intention not to exercise, "the statute steps in and sends the property, subject to the power, in the same direction as that in which the testatrix has sent her own property." (*Lockwood v. Mildeberger, supra,* at 188, 53 N.E. 803.) This is the result effectuated here by holding that Paul has effectively exercised his power of appointment in his will.

Having deemed the power exercised, it is now necessary to determine the extent of its exercise. It is undisputed that the power could not be exercised in favor of Cyrus. The question is what becomes of the 30% share invalidly allocated to him by Paul, Jr.'s will. Was the power of appointment exercised with respect to 70% only or the entire appointive property? Here the court's task is to further the valid portions of the testator's plan where to do so does not disturb his fundamental intention.

There is nothing in the pertinent instruments or in the applicable statutes which warrants the conclusion that the power of appointment was executed only partially. The provisions of Paul's will and trust dispose of property of much greater value than the appointive assets.[1] The court determines that Paul, Jr.'s bequests of 35% each of the residuary estate to Allan and John demonstrate that his testamentary scheme was to benefit his twin sons equally. Consequently, the court concludes that the entire appointive property is to be disposed of for their primary benefit, in equal shares.

The accounts being proper in all respects are settled.

NOTES AND QUESTIONS

1. *The Common Law Rule.* As the Block opinion indicates in discussing Ohio law, the common law rule is that the donee's disposition of his own estate, without any mention of the power of appointment, is not sufficient to constitute an exercise of the power.

2. *The Uniform Probate Code.* The original version of the Uniform Probate Code—enacted as law in a number of states—adopted the common law position, and several other states enacted statutes to the same effect.

The 1990 version of the UPC changed the Code's earlier position with respect to general, but not special, powers. The Code provides:

> **Section 2–608. Exercise of Power of Appointment.**
>
> In the absence of a requirement that a power of appointment be exercised by a reference, or by an express or specific reference, to the power, a general residuary clause in a will, or a will making general disposition of all of the testator's property, expresses an intention to exercise a power of appointment held by the testator only if (i) the power is a general power and the creating instrument does not contain a gift if the power is not exercised or (ii) the testator's will manifests an intention to include the property subject to the power.

Thus, a general residuary clause operates to exercise a general power of appointment if the donor did not make a provision for takers in default. If donor did make a provision for takers in default, or if the power is special, a general residuary clause exercises the power only if the will manifests an intention to exercise the power. How would Estate of Block have been decided if the Uniform Probate Code had been in effect?

The Restatement (Third) of Property: Wills and Other Donative Transfers, § 19.4 (Tentative Draft No. 5, 2006) takes the same position as the UPC. The Restatement also provides that the donee's disposition of the appointive property manifests an intention to exercise the power of appointment. Id., § 19.3

3. *The New York Statute.* EPTL § 10–6.1(a)—the focus of the opinion in Estate of Block—provides that "an effective exercise of a power of

---

1. The main difference between the trusts for Allan and John under Paul, Jr.'s will and those created by his mother's will if he failed to exercise his power of appointment is the greater discretion Paul gave for trustees to invade for the twins.

appointment does not require an express reference to such power," and then requires only a manifestation of the donee's intent to exercise the power. The statute goes on to provide that such a manifestation exists when the donee "[l]eaves a will disposing of all of his property or all of his property of the kind covered by the power, unless the intention that the will is not to operate as an execution of the power appears expressly or by necessary implication." A minority of other states follow the New York rule.

4. ***Why All the Controversy?*** Why do states take such divergent approaches to the problem raised in Estate of Block? In part, at least, because two dramatically different situations recur.

First, in many cases, the donee writes her will without knowing of the power or without thinking about the power. As in all cases in which donor creates a power of appointment, donor has indicated that she wants donee to use her judgment in exercising the power. Donee, if she knew about the power, would most likely exercise the power in favor of the beneficiaries of her own estate. Hence, we can best effectuate intent both of donor and of donee by treating a general residuary clause as an exercise of the power. That is, for cases like these, the New York rule, applied in Estate of Block, makes good sense.

Second, in other cases, the donee writes her will knowing of the power, and does not mention the power expressly because she does not want to exercise the power. In these cases, the New York rule might significantly frustrate donee's estate plan. Estate of Deane, 4 N.Y.2d 326, 151 N.E.2d 184, 175 N.Y.S.2d 21 (1958), is illustrative. Donee had a power of appointment over an $800,000 trust created in New York by her father. The takers in default were donee's son (two-thirds of the corpus) and donee's sister (one-third). Donee's personal estate amounted to between $50,000 and $60,000. Donee's will, drafted in Texas, which followed the common law rule, made no mention of the power of appointment and left her entire estate to her grandson. The New York Court of Appeals held that donee's will exercised the power, so that the entire estate passed to donee's minor grandson—holding inadmissible testimony by donee's Texas lawyer that he had told donee that if she wanted the trust corpus to pass to her son and her sister, it would not be necessary to mention the trust in the will!

Note that the court in Estate of Block grudgingly acknowledged dictum in other New York cases suggesting that the general New York rule should not be applied in this second set of cases—where donee knew of the existence of the power and failed to mention the power in his will. Yet in both Estate of Block and Estate of Deane, the court held that the general residuary clause exercised the power even where donee apparently did know of the existence of the power.

For an illuminating discussion of the issues, see Susan French, Exercise of Power of Appointment: Should Intent to Exercise be Inferred from General Disposition of Property?, 1979 Duke L.J. 747.

5. ***Practice Questions.*** How could donee's lawyer in Estate of Block have avoided the litigation in this case? Suppose you practice in a jurisdiction that requires express reference to a power of appointment in order to exercise that power. If you are drafting a will in which donee wants *not* to exercise the power, how would you draft the will?

6. ***Must the Will be Probated to Exercise the Power?*** When a donor creates a testamentary power of appointment, donor contemplates that the donee will exercise the power in donee's will. Suppose, however, that donee's will is never probated. Is the will nevertheless effective to exercise the power of appointment? Compare Lumbard v. Farmers State Bank, 812 N.E.2d 196 (Ind. App. 2004) (exercise effective) with Scott v. Scott, 77 P.3d 906 (Colo. App. 2003) (exercise ineffective). Does it matter that in *Lumbard*, donee's daughter, acting on advice of counsel, never sought probate of the donee's will, while in Scott, a probate court held that the codicil purporting to exercise the power was not entitled to probate?

7. ***Choice of Law.*** Does it make sense in cases like *Block* and *Deane* to apply New York law to determine whether donee exercised the power? In each case, donee's lawyer was advising donee in a state where donee would have had to mention the power in order to exercise the power. Would you have expected the lawyer to know that the law of New York was different? That the power was created in New York? What lessons do these cases teach you about your obligations as an estate planner?

PROBLEM

Settlor created three irrevocable trusts. Although Settlor was domiciled in Connecticut, the assets of all the trusts consist of intangible personal property located in New York and each of the trusts has a New York trustee. All of the instruments state that they shall be "construed and regulated by the laws of the State of New York." All trusts give Settlor's daughter Mary Wheat an income interest in the trust and the power to appoint the principal, "to such persons as Mary shall appoint by Will or by Instrument of Appointment executed like a Will and dated after Settlor's death."

Mary died in 2007, a domiciliary of Connecticut. Her 2006 will gave the residuary of her estate in equal shares to her children and grandchildren. The will does not expressly refer to the power of appointment. Mary also left a handwritten note dated October 22, 2002, which states, "I am leaving all 3 trusts to my husband Clayton E. Wheat." The note is signed "Mary C. Wheat" and "subscribed and sworn to" before a Connecticut notary public whose signature and stamp are affixed. Mary Chappell Wheat had two prior wills, both of which expressly exercised her powers of appointment.

Did Mary validly exercise the power? Connecticut follows the common law rule with respect to exercise and the New York statute relied on in *Block* is still good law. See Matter of Chappell, 25 Misc.3d 704, 883 N.Y.S.2d 857 (Surr. Ct. 2009).

The Consequences of Non-Exercise: The Agency Theory of Powers of Appointment

PROBLEM

Oscar Zilch creates a trust under the terms of which he gives his son Abner a power to appoint the trust corpus, by will "among Abner's relatives by blood or marriage." The trust instrument names no takers in default. Chloe Zilch, Oscar's daughter and Abner's sister, was the residuary beneficiary of Oscar's estate. Abner's will—executed in a jurisdiction which has adopted UPC § 2–608—makes no mention of the power of appointment, and divides Abner's estate evenly between his only daughter Bertha and the Abner Zilch Foundation, a charitable foundation. At Abner's death, how should the appointive property be distributed?

* * *

The donee of a power of appointment has often been conceptualized as the donor's agent. On this theory, the appointive property belongs to the donor, who has authorized the donee to act on her behalf, usually after the donor has died and is no longer able to act on her own behalf. The donee is merely an agent doing the donor's bidding.

One consequence of this conceptualization (we will see others) arises when donee fails to exercise the power of appointment. Because the donee was only an agent, if donee fails to exercise the power, we look to the donor's wishes, not the donee's, to determine how the appointive property should be distributed. See Melanie B. Leslie, The Case Against Applying the Relation–Back Doctrine to the Exercise of General Powers of Appointment, 14 Cardozo L. Rev. 219, 220 (1992). Of course, if the donor named takers in default, the appointive property passes to the takers in default. What happens, however, if donor did not name takers in default?

If the power of appointment is general, the common law approach has been to pass the appointive property back to the donor, and then, if donor is dead, through the default clause in donor's will. If there is no default clause, the property passes through donor's estate. The Restatement (Third) of Property: Wills and Other Donative Transfers, § 19.22(b) (Tentative Draft No. 5, 2006) takes a different approach. The Restatement provides that unappointed property passes to the donee or the donee's estate unless "the donee released the power or expressly refrained from exercising the power." The theory is that because donor gave the donee the power to appoint to anyone, donor would not object to the property being distributed through donee's estate.

If, however, the power was a special power, the consequences are clear. When donor creates a special power, the donor prevents the donee from appointing in favor of her estate, so distributing the appointive property through the donee's estate in the event of non-exercise would frustrate donor's intent. If the donor has provided for takers in default, the default clause controls. But, if there is no default clause, the property does not automatically pass through donor's estate; if the class of permissible appointees is a clearly defined and limited class, courts generally distribute the property to members of that class. See Restatement (Third) of Property: Wills and Donative Transfers, § 19.23(b) (Tentative Draft No. 5, 2006). That is, if donor gives her husband the power to appoint among the couple's children, and husband makes no appointment, the appointive property would be distributed to the children equally. If donor gives her husband the power to appoint among the husband's "heirs" or "relatives," the property would pass to the distributees of husband's estate as if husband had died intestate—even though donor had given donee power to distribute among relatives who were not distributees. The assumption here is that donor's intent would be better effectuated by distributing the property among the class of permissible appointees than by having the property pass back to the donor's estate. (In addition, having the property pass through the husband's estate could have undesirable tax consequences, and require administration of a long-closed estate). Some courts have conceptualized this result by saying that the special power was a "power in trust" or an "imperative power": donee had an obligation (though not a legal duty) to exercise the power in favor of class members, and if donee did not act on that obligation, the property should be distributed to those people who would have received the property if donee had acted on the obligation created by donor.

If, however, the power is a special power, but one not limited in favor of a defined class—as, for instance, a power to appoint "among my friends" or "to anyone other than donee or donee's estate or donee's creditors," it would be extraordinarily difficult to determine which beneficiaries should take if donee does not exercise the power. As a result, the property will generally pass back to donor, through the default clause in donor's will, or through the donor's estate. See Restatement (Third) of Property: Wills and Other Donative Transfers, § 19.23 (c) (Tentative Draft No. 5, 2006).

SECTION III. SCOPE OF THE POWER

PROBLEM

Anna Smith's will disposed of the residue of her estate into a trust, by the terms of which trust income was to be paid to her husband Ben during his lifetime. Anna's will also gave Ben a power to appoint the corpus, by will, "among our common descendants." Anna died in 1994, survived by Ben and by the couple's two children, Chauncey and Dagmar. The residue of her estate was valued at $1,000,000. A year later, Ben remarried and had another child, Esther.

Ben has approached you for advice. He wants answers to the following questions:

1. Can he make an appointment of one-half of the trust corpus in further trust, with income to be paid to Chauncey for life, and principal

to be distributed, at Chauncey's death, to Chauncey's children? (Examine section ***A***, *infra*).

2. What will happen if Ben appoints one-third of the trust property to his daughter Esther? (Examine section ***C***, *infra*).

3. If Ben exercises the power in favor of Chauncey and Dagmar, will Chauncey and Dagmar be entitled to make gifts from the appointive property to Esther? (Examine section ***C***, *infra*).

4. Suppose Ben contracts with Chauncey, for $100,000 in cash, to exercise Anna's power of appointment in favor of Chauncey. Will Ben later be able to change his mind and exercise the power (at least in part) in favor of Dagmar? If so, will Chauncey have any remedy? If Ben doesn't change his mind, will Dagmar have any remedy? (Examine sections ***C*** and ***D***, *infra*).

5. Suppose Chauncey promises Ben that if Ben exercises Anna's power in Chauncey's favor, Chauncey will give one-half of the money to Esther. What will happen if Ben exercises the power in favor of Chauncey and (a) Chauncey performs the promise or (b) Chauncey reneges on the promise? (Examine sections ***C*** and ***D***, *infra*).

Based on the material in this section, how would you answer Ben's questions?

A. EXERCISING A POWER BY CREATING ANOTHER TRUST

Suppose donee holds a power to appoint property among her children, age 8, 10, and 15. Donee believes that the children will not be ready to manage the trust assets for a considerable period of time. Can donee create three trusts, one for each child, providing that each child should receive income from a trust until the child reaches age 30, with the principal to be distributed to the child upon reaching the age of 30? The modern answer to that question is yes. Consider the following section from the Restatement (Third) of Property: Wills and Other Donative Transfers (Tentative Draft No. 5, 2006):

> **Section 19.14 Nongeneral Power–Permissible Appointments**
>
> Except to the extent that the donor has manifested a contrary intention, the donee of a nongeneral power is authorized to make an appointment, including one in trust and one that creates a power of appointment in another, that solely benefits permissible appointees of the power.

Of course, donee could not create a trust that would pay income to a child for life, and distribute principal to grandchildren at the child's death, because the donor did not make the grandchildren permissible appointees. But so long as the trust benefits only permissible appointees (objects of the power), and so long as the donor has not manifested a contrary intent, donee is free to exercise the appointment by creating another trust or by appointing the property to an existing trust that benefits only permissible appointees. See, e.g. Reisman v. Kaufman, 266 Mich.App. 522, 702 N.W.2d

658 (2005) [upholding appointment to trust that benefited only permissible appointees].

Our hypothetical deals with special powers, but the same rule applies to general powers: the donee may make appointments in trust. With general powers, we do not even have to worry about appointments to non-objects, because donor has not restricted the class of permissible appointees. Indeed, we do not even have to worry about a contrary expression made by donor, because donee could always exercise the power in favor of herself or her estate, and then create a new trust out of the estate residue. See Restatement (Third) of Property: Wills and Other Donative Transfers, § 19.13 (Tentative Draft No. 5, 2006).

Note that section 19.14 of the Restatement (Third) of Property applies unless the donor "manifests a contrary intent." What evidence would be sufficient to establish that a donor intended to preclude an appointment in further trust? Suppose donor's will, in creating the power of appointment, used the following language:

> ... [u]pon the death of my spouse, the entire principal remaining in the trust shall be paid over, conveyed and distributed to such person or persons, but excluding the estate of my spouse, *free of trust,* in such manner and in such proportions as my spouse may designate and appoint in and by my spouse's last will and testament.

If the donee exercises his power by appointing the trust property to the trustee of another trust, would the exercise be valid? See In re Chervitz Trust, 198 S.W.3d 658 (Mo. App. 2006) (holding that the language was not sufficient to preclude appointment in further trust).

One concern should remain for the donee who wants to appoint in further trust: the Rule Against Perpetuities. That is a subject we will take up in Chapter Ten.

B. Exercising a Power by Creating Another Power

Suppose now that the donee of a power not only wants to use the appointive assets to create another trust, but also wants to give one of the trust beneficiaries a further power to appoint the trust property. If the donee's power is a general one, creating a new power presents no difficulties. Again, since the donee could have appointed in favor of herself or her estate, and then created a new trust and a new power, there would be little reason to prevent her from doing directly—creating a power while exercising donor's power—what she could have done indirectly by first appointing in favor of her own estate. See Restatement (Third) of Property: Wills and Other Donative Transfers, § 19.13, cmt. f (Tentative Draft No. 5, 2006).

With special powers, the problem is a bit more complex. Because the donor has limited the class of permissible appointees, donee is clearly not free to appoint by creating a general power of appointment in someone outside the donor's class of permissible appointees. Suppose, however, the donee appoints by giving a general power of appointment to a person who is within the class of permissible appointees. Or suppose the donee appoints by giving to a non-object of the power a special power to appoint among people who are within the class of permissible appointees. In each case the Restatement (Third) of Property: Wills and Other Donative Transfers, § 19.14 (Tentative Draft No. 5, 2006), would hold the appointment effective (see especially cmt. e), but there is also authority to the contrary. Consider the following example:

> ***Example 3:*** *Marla Matriarch, by will, creates a trust, and gives her son, Oscar Offspring, a testamentary power to appoint the principal among Marla's descendants.*
>
> *(1) Can Oscar, in his will, dispose of the trust corpus by creating a trust for the benefit of his sister Susie for life, and giving Susie a general testamentary power of appointment?*
>
> *(2) Can Oscar, in his will, give his wife, Olive, a power to appoint the trust property among Oscar's children (after providing that the property should be held in trust for those children until Olive's death)?*
>
> ***Solution:*** *The Restatement would permit both appointments, for the following reasons:*
>
> *(1) Since Susie is a permissible appointee, Oscar could have given the trust corpus to Susie outright. Susie could then have disposed of the property as she saw fit. Giving Susie a general power of appointment is, in large measure, equivalent to giving her the property outright. Hence, there is no reason to prevent Oscar from giving Susie a general power of appointment.*
>
> *(2) By the terms of Marla's power, Oscar could, himself, have appointed among his children. If Marla trusted Oscar to make the appointments, Marla presumably also trusted Oscar to delegate decisionmaking authority to Olive, so long as Oscar specified that Olive's power was limited to Marla's class of permissible appointees.*

Case law dealing with these issues is relatively sparse, so the drafter might want to be cautious about exercising a power by creating another power. Caution is especially warranted because creation of further powers raises complex Rule Against Perpetuities problems, which we will confront in Chapter Ten.

C. EXCEEDING THE POWER'S SCOPE

1. LIMITS ON THE HOLDER OF A SPECIAL POWER

By definition, the holder of a special power may not make appointments to persons outside the class of permissible appointees. How does form relate to substance? Consider the following case:

Will of Carroll

Court of Appeals of New York, 1937.
274 N.Y. 288, 8 N.E.2d 864.

■ HUBBS, J.

In 1910 William Carroll died leaving a will by the fourth paragraph of which he devised and bequeathed the residue of his estate to his executors in trust to pay the income to his wife during her life. By the fifth paragraph he directed that upon the death of the wife the residuary trust be divided into two equal shares, the proceeds of one to be for the use and benefit of his daughter Elsa during her life, and the proceeds of the other share for the use and benefit of his son Ralph during his life. In the fifth paragraph he gave his daughter power by her last will and testament to dispose of the property so set aside for her use "to and among her children or any other kindred who shall survive her and in such shares and manner as she shall think proper." A similar power of appointment was given to Ralph to dispose of his share "to and among his kindred or wife." With respect to the share set aside for the use of the daughter Elsa, the will provided that in the absence of any valid disposition of the corpus by her, it should pass "to her then surviving child or children, descendant or descendants" and should there be no surviving child or descendant of the daughter, then the share on her decease should pass to the donor's "surviving heirs or next-of-kin, according to the nature of the estate."

Elsa died on June 26, 1933, without leaving any child or descendant her surviving. The mother, Grace Carroll, survived her and was living at the time of the trial, as was also the brother Ralph. Elsa left a will by which she left $5,000 to her brother, and $250,000 to one Paul Curtis, a cousin, such bequest to go to his son if he predeceased her. The remainder of her share of the estate of her father she gave to her executors in trust.

When Elsa's will was drawn, the petitioning executor, Content, as her attorney, prepared the will and attended to its execution and also prepared a letter directed to Elsa by the legatee Paul Curtis, which letter read as follows: "I am informed that by your last will and testament you have given and bequeathed to me the sum of Two Hundred and Fifty Thousand Dollars ($250,000). In the event that you should predecease me and I should receive the bequest before mentioned, I hereby promise and agree, in consideration of the said bequest, that I will pay to your husband, Foster Milliken, Jr., the sum of One Hundred Thousand Dollars ($100,000) out of the said bequest which you have given to me by your said will."

It is not contended by any of the parties to this proceeding that Foster Milliken, Jr., husband of Elsa, was of her kindred, and, therefore, a proper object of the power granted to his wife in her father's will. The question here involved is as to the effect of the attempted provision for her husband upon the bequest to Paul Curtis.

Content testified that he had advised Elsa that she could not lawfully make her husband a beneficiary of any part of her father's estate; that she had drawn a previous will in which she had given the residue of the estate of her father to her brother Ralph with a request that he pay to her husband the sum of $10,000 per annum; that he advised her that that provision could not be enforced; that on October 6, 1931, she told him that she was not satisfied; that she was growing away from her brother and that she wanted to increase the bequest to her cousin Paul Curtis; that she had given Curtis $50,000 in a prior will; that she wanted to leave him $250,000, and that he prepared the will with the prior will before him and on October 13 she and Mrs. Elliott came to his office where she executed the will; that after the will was executed she told him: "Paul would like to do something for Foster. He would like to leave him some of this money I am leaving to him, and Paul is perfectly willing to put this in writing to show his good faith." He then talked with Paul, dictated the letter and had it signed. He was not sure whether the letter was delivered to Elsa or whether he kept it for her. Curtis testified that several days before the will was executed Elsa told him she was going to make a new will; that she knew if her brother Ralph heard about it he would probably start a row with her mother; that she had previously left Curtis $50,000 and his son $50,000, and that she was going to leave him $150,000 and add to it $100,000 which she would like him to give to Mr. Milliken; that he told her if she wanted him to do so, he would sign a paper to that effect; that she said she did not know whether it would be necessary but if she wanted him to she would make a date for him to go down to Mr. Content's office; that she called him upon the day the will was executed and asked him to meet her there; that he was not present when the will was executed but that he went in afterwards and heard the letter dictated and signed it.

The surrogate determined that the promise made by Curtis so vitiated and permeated the bequest to him that the appointment constituted a fraud upon the power and made the bequest to him void.

The Appellate Division, two justices dissenting, decided that the only reasonable interpretation to be placed upon the transaction is that Elsa desired to appoint $150,000 to her cousin and an additional $100,000 to her husband; accordingly, that the lawful appointment of $150,000 to Curtis is separable from the unlawful appointment of $100,000 to him for the benefit of the husband.

It seems to us that the conclusion is inescapable that the testimony of Content, the attorney who drew the instruments, and of Curtis, who was the legatee, do not affect the true intent and purpose of the letter. Stress is laid upon the fact as testified to by Content that the testatrix Elsa did not tell him of the understanding with Curtis until after the will had been executed. Nevertheless, it appears from the testimony of Curtis that she had an understanding with him prior to the execution of the will and the writing constituted only a record of the actual prior agreement. The Surrogate had the benefit of hearing the witnesses testify and of observing their conduct. He found nothing in their testimony to detract from the force of the letter signed by Curtis. Concededly, the attempted bequest for the benefit of the husband was not valid. Curtis alone testified that he was to receive $150,000 and the husband $100,000. Content testified that she told him she wanted to leave Curtis $250,000, and that he did not know until after the will was drawn of the understanding between Curtis and the testatrix. The letter says that the agreement to pay the husband $100,000 is in consideration of a bequest of $250,000. No one can say whether she would have left Curtis $100,000, $150,000 or a lesser or greater sum had it not been for the agreement to take care of her husband. Only by speculation can it be said that she would have left him $150,000 had it not been for that agreement. Had it not been for her continued possession either personally or by her attorney of the promise on the part of Curtis, no one can say but what she might have changed the will. Curtis was a party to the attempted fraud on the power. If the bequest to him be sustained to the extent of $150,000 on his own testimony, he suffers no penalty. It seems to us that on the facts, the conclusion of the Surrogate was correct; that the entire bequest is involved in the intent to defeat the power and that it is impossible to separate and sustain the bequest to Curtis to the extent of $150,000.

* * *

The order of the Appellate Division should be modified in accordance with this opinion and as so modified affirmed, without costs.

QUESTIONS

1. Grandmother gives Mother a power to appoint property among Mother's daughters. Mother appoints equally among her three daughters. The daughters, believing it unfair that their brother has been excluded, each give one-third of their share to the brother. Does anyone have a cause for complaint? How is Will of Carroll different?

2. Why is the entire bequest to Curtis invalid? Would the court have reached the same result if Curtis had promised to pay Foster Milliken $1,000 instead of $100,000?

3. Evaluate the conduct of lawyer Content. What advice would you have given if Elsa Milliken had approached you?

2. CONSEQUENCES OF INEFFECTIVE APPOINTMENTS

We have already discussed the consequences of a donee's *failure* to make an appointment. What happens, however, if donee makes an appointment, but the appointment is *ineffective*? The consequences are not always the same.

General Powers: The Capture Doctrine

Because the donee of a general power has complete discretion in choosing appointees, donee's appointment can never be ineffective for exceeding the power's scope. A donee's appointment can be ineffective, however, if the appointee is dead, or if the appointment violates the Rule Against Perpetuities. What happens to the appointive property if donee makes such an ineffective appointment?

Recall that at common law, when the donee of a general power makes no appointment at all, the appointive property passed through the donor's estate—not the donee's estate. Common law courts, however, treated ineffective exercise differently from non-exercise. Courts assumed that the donee would have preferred to have the appointive property pass to the beneficiaries of donee's own estate rather than having the property pass back to the donor's estate. They therefore held that the donee's ineffective appointment *captures* the appointive property for donee's estate.

> ***Example 4:*** *Peter Patriarch's will creates a trust and gives a general testamentary power of appointment to his daughter, Delilah. Peter names the ASPCA as taker in default. Delilah's will includes a residuary clause which disposes of "all of my property, including the power of appointment granted to me by my father's will." The residuary clause creates a trust to benefit Delilah's descendants, but the trust violates the Rule Against Perpetuities. How should the appointive property be distributed?*
>
> ***Solution:*** *The donee's attempted exercise of the power "captured" the appointive property for her own estate. The property should therefore be distributed to her heirs, by intestate succession, not to the ASPCA.*

In California, the capture doctrine has been embodied in California Probate Code, § 672(b), which provides:

> If the donee of a general power of appointment makes an ineffective appointment, an implied alternative appointment to the donee's estate may be found if the donee has manifested an intent that the appointive property be disposed of as property of the donee rather than as in default of appointment.

Note, however, that the capture doctrine is superfluous in any jurisdiction that adopts the Restatement rule holding that upon failure to exercise a general power, the appointive property passes through the donee's estate rather than the donor's estate. In Restatement jurisdictions, if the power is general, the property will pass through the donee's estate whether or not the donee takes actions that "capture" the power; capture is, therefore, irrelevant.

Note also that the capture doctrine would never apply to special powers. If the power is special, the donor has not authorized donee to appoint the property in favor of her own estate, so it would violate the donor's intent to permit donee to capture the property for her own estate.

Special and General Powers: Allocation of Assets

We have already seen that when the donee of a special power fails to exercise the power, one of three consequences generally follows: (1) the property passes to the takers in default, if the instrument names takers in default; (2) if the instrument does not name takers in default, the property is distributed among the class of permissible appointees, if that class is adequately defined and limited; or (3) if donor has not expressly named takers in default, and if the class of permissible appointees is not adequately defined and limited, the property passes through the donor's estate. Generally, the same consequences follow if the donee exercises the power improperly—in favor of people outside the class of permissible appointees.

Suppose, however, donee's will has blended the appointive assets with donee's own property, and has disposed of both in part to members of the class of permissible appointees, and in part to people outside that class. Can the assets be "allocated" (or "marshalled") to give full effect to donee's will? The answer given by the Restatement (Third) of Property: Wills and Other Donative Transfers, § 19.19 (Tentative Draft No. 5, 2006), is yes: if the donee has blended appointive assets with donee's own assets, the assets should be allocated to maximize the effectiveness of donee's intended dispositions.

> ***Example 5:*** *Dan Donee holds a special testamentary power to appoint among his children. Dan's will disposes of "the residue of my estate, together with any powers of appointment I may hold, as follows: one-half to my wife Edna, and one-half to my daughter Felicity." Dan is survived by Edna, Felicity, and his estranged son Gunther. At Dan's death, the appointive property is valued at $400,000, while his personal estate totals $600,000. How should Dan's estate and the appointive property be distributed?*
>
> ***Solution:*** *Edna and Felicity should each take $500,000. The $400,000 in appointive assets should all be allocated to Felicity, so that Dan will not have appointed to persons outside the class of permissible appointees, and Felicity should also take $100,000 of Dan's own assets, while the other $500,000 of Dan's own assets should be distributed to Edna—thus giving full effect to Dan's estate plan.*

Note that in Example 5, a careful lawyer would have structured Dan's will to avoid any need for allocation of assets. (Every estate planner should provide her client with a checklist which asks, in some form, "Do you have any powers of appointment? Please provide a copy at your earliest convenience.") The allocation of assets doctrine largely saves Dan and his beneficiaries from the effects of lawyer error.

How can we tell whether donee has blended his own assets with appointive assets? In Example 5, the blending is obvious: Dan has disposed of his own assets and the appointive assets in the same clause of his will. Suppose, however, that Dan's will made a general devise of $500,000 to his daughter Felicity, and that the residuary clause left "the residue of my estate, together with any power of appointment I might hold" to his wife Edna. Has Dan sufficiently blended the appointive assets with his own property to permit allocation of assets? [The Restatement's answer is yes; see section 19.19, illus. 5, (Tentative Draft No. 5, 2006)]. Would your answer be different if Dan had made no general devise to Felicity, but had instead made a specific devise to Felicity of "my 5,000 shares of ABC Corp. Stock" (worth $500,000)?

We have so far talked about cases in which the donee of a special power exercises in favor of a non-object of the power. The allocation doctrine also applies—with either a special power or a general power—when donee has made a disposition that would be invalid under the Rule Against Perpetuities with respect to appointive property, but valid with respect to donee's own estate. In that case, too, courts will allocate assets to maximize the effectiveness of donee's intended dispositions.

QUESTION

Reconsider Example 5. Suppose, at Donee's death, the appointive assets had been valued at $600,000, and Donee's own estate had been valued at $400,000. How should Donee's estate, and the appointive property, be distributed?

D. CONTRACTS TO APPOINT AND RELEASES

1. CONTRACTS TO APPOINT

Suppose a mother gives her son a power to appoint property among the son's children. In his old age, the son needs care, and contracts with one of his daughters to exercise the power of appointment in favor of that daughter in return for the daughter's promise to provide lifetime care. Can the daughter enforce the contract against her father, the donee of the power?

Notice the problem. If the contract is enforceable, the donee—who was not entitled to appoint in favor of himself—has now arranged to benefit from his status as donee of the special power. This appears to be contrary to the wishes of the donor, who created the power in the first instance. For this reason, courts typically hold that when a power is special, a donee's contract to appoint is unenforceable, at least so long as the contract benefits a person outside the class of permissible appointees.

Suppose, now, that the donee's power is general, not special. Is a contract to appoint enforceable? Yes—but only if the power is presently exercisable. If the power is not presently exercisable, the assumption is that the donor wanted to permit the donee to retain discretion until some point in the future, when more circumstances relating to the appointment will have unfolded. If the donee were permitted to make a contract that binds him to appoint in a particular way, donee would have the power to relinquish the discretion donor wanted him to have. Hence, for testamentary powers, and for other powers not presently exercisable, contracts to appoint are not enforceable against the donee. See Restatement (Third) of Property: Wills and Other Donative Transfers, § 21.2(b). (Tentative Draft No. 5, 2006); Carmichael v. Heggie, 332 S.C. 624, 506 S.E.2d 308 (1998).

In New York, this doctrine is embodied in EPTL § 10–5.3(a), which provides:

NY EPTL § 10–5.3(a). CONTRACT TO APPOINT; POWER NOT PRESENTLY EXERCISABLE

(a) The donee of a power of appointment which is not presently exercisable, or of a postponed power which has not become exercisable, cannot contract to make an appointment; except that this prohibition shall not apply if the donor and donee are the same person. Such a prohibited contract, if made, cannot be the basis of an action for specific performance or damages, but the promisee can obtain restitution of the value given by him for the promise unless the donee has exercised the power pursuant to the contract.

PROBLEM

By the terms of his mother's will, Carl Contractor received a general testamentary power of appointment over trust assets. Carl then contracted with Flabby Abs Gym to appoint $20,000 in favor of Flabby Abs in return for a lifetime membership at the Gym.

1. If Carl's will exercised his mother's power entirely in favor of Carl's wife, Cecilia, does Flabby Abs have any remedy under the New York statute? If the statute were not in force, how would you argue that Flabby Abs should have no remedy? See Northern Trust Co. v. Porter, 368 Ill. 256, 13 N.E.2d 487 (1938).

2. Suppose Carl's power of appointment had been created not by his mother's will, but by an *inter vivos* trust instrument Carl had himself created. Would Flabby Abs have any remedy for breach by Carl? If so, why?

3. Suppose Carl did appoint $20,000 in favor of Flabby Abs. Would anyone have any remedy against Carl or Flabby Abs? Consider the following opinion:

Benjamin v. Morgan Guaranty Trust Co.

New York Appellate Division, Second Department, 1994.
202 A.D.2d 536, 609 N.Y.S.2d 276.

MEMORANDUM:

In an action seeking, inter alia, to invalidate the exercise of a power of appointment and for an accounting, the plaintiffs appeal from so much of an order of the Surrogate's Court, Suffolk County (Signorelli, S.), dated March 13, 1992, as granted that branch of the defendant's motion which was for summary judgment dismissing so much of the plaintiffs' complaint as sought to invalidate the exercise of the power of appointment by the beneficiary of the marital trust, as set forth in the Will of Henry Rogers Benjamin, and found that defendant trustee, Morgan Guaranty Trust Company of New York, was not liable to the plaintiffs for damages.

ORDERED that the order is affirmed insofar as appealed from, with costs.

The plaintiffs contend, among other things, that the appointments made by Germaine Benjamin Cromwell, the widow of Henry Rogers Benjamin and beneficiary of the marital trust created by his will, of the remainder of the marital trust to the two hospital intervenors, should be declared invalid because these appointments were made pursuant to an agreement with the defendant trustee, and were, therefore, (1) in contravention of the testator's intention when he created the power of appointment, and (2) invalid by reason of EPTL 10–5.3, which prohibits the contracting away of such a power of appointment. We disagree.

The will creating the marital trust also granted a general power of appointment to Mrs. Cromwell upon her death. Although it is true that EPTL 10–5.3(a) proscribes entering into a contract which would limit or direct how a power of appointment may be exercised, and such a contract is unenforceable, any appointment made pursuant to such a contract which otherwise complies with the scope of the power of appointment is not rendered invalid by virtue of the existence of the contract (see, *Matter of Brown*, 33 N.Y.2d 211, 351 N.Y.S.2d 655, 306 N.E.2d 781; *Farmers' Loan & Trust Co. v. Mortimer*, 219 N.Y. 290, 114 N.E. 389; *Matter of Rogers*, 168 Misc. 633, 6 N.Y.S.2d 255). Here, the appointments were within the scope of the power of appointment, and the Surrogate's Court properly declined to declare them invalid.

We have examined the plaintiffs' remaining contentions, and find them to be without merit.

QUESTION

Why would a court hold a contract to appoint unenforceable, yet give effect to an appointment made pursuant to an unenforceable contract?

2. RELEASES

In the preceding section, we discovered that a contract to exercise a power of appointment in favor of a particular person is not enforceable (unless the power is a general, presently exercisable power). Should a donee be able to bind himself—by contract or otherwise—*not* to exercise a power of appointment?

Logic suggests that the answer should be no. All of the reasons for refusing to enforce contracts to appoint—preserving donee's discretion for as long as possible, assuring that donee of a special power does not use the power to benefit people outside the class of permissible appointees—also suggest that donees ought not to be able to bind themselves not to exercise the power.

In this area, however, logic must take a bow to history. In 1942, Congress enacted a tax statute that taxed the exercise or non-exercise of most powers of appointment—but permitted donees to "release" their powers without incurring gift tax. Predictably, beginning in 1943, a majority of the state legislatures enacted statutes permitting donees to release their powers to avoid the impact of the federal tax. Almost all of the favorable tax consequences of release have long been eliminated from the tax code, but the doctrine permitting free release of powers lives on.

What is the effect of a release? Generally, a release assures that the appointive property will pass to the takers in default. If, however, the power is a special power limited in favor of a defined class (a "power in trust"), a release assures that the property will pass to the members of the defined class.

Moreover, in many jurisdictions, the donee of a power may execute a "partial release" of the power—binding herself not to exercise the power in favor of particular people. See Restatement (Third) of Property: Wills and Other Donative Transfers, § 20.1 and cmt. e; § 22.2 and cmt. d (Tentative Draft No. 5, 2006). How does a partial release work?

> ***Example 6.*** *Donee holds a special testamentary power to appoint trust property among her "relatives by blood or marriage." Donee executes a release of the right to appoint the property to anyone but her issue. Donee's partial release prevents her from appointing to her husband, her brother, or anyone other than her issue.*

Suppose after the partial release in Example 6, donee's will fails to exercise the power. How should the appointive property be distributed? That is, has the partial release converted the power into an "imperative" power to distribute among donee's issue, or should the property pass to the takers in default? There is little authority on the issue. What arguments would you make for each position?

Note also that by executing a partial release, a donee may convert a general power into a special power:

> ***Example 7.*** *Donee holds a general testamentary power to appoint trust property. She executes a release of the right to appoint to anyone but her issue. Donee's partial release has converted her general power into a special power.*

Suppose, in Example 7, Donee's motive for executing a partial release is to avoid having the appointive assets taxed in her estate (recall that property subject to a general power is part of donee's taxable estate, while property subject to a special power is not). The Code would thwart this attempt to avoid taxation. Section 2514(b) provides that a partial release of a general power constitutes a transfer of property for tax purposes. In other words, Donee's execution of a partial release will not enable her to avoid estate and gift tax.

Once we give donees the power to execute not merely total releases, but also partial releases of powers of appointment, haven't we undermined the doctrine that a donee may not contract to exercise a special power or a general testamentary power? In particular, if a donee holds a general power, how is a partial release limiting the class of permissible appointees to one person different from a contract to appoint in favor of that person? Moreover, how can we tell whether donee has executed an enforceable release or an unenforceable contract? Consider the following case:

Seidel v. Werner

Supreme Court, New York County, 1975.
81 Misc.2d 220, 364 N.Y.S.2d 963, aff'd on opinion below, 50 A.D.2d 743, 376 N.Y.S.2d 139.

■ SILVERMAN, J.:

* * *

Plaintiffs, trustees of a trust established in 1919 by Abraham L. Werner, sue for a declaratory judgment to determine who is entitled to one half of the principal of the trust fund—the share in which Steven L. Werner, decedent (hereinafter "Steven"), was the life beneficiary and over which he had a testamentary power of appointment. The dispute concerns the manner in which Steven exercised his power of appointment and is between Steven's second wife, Harriet G. Werner (hereinafter "Harriet"), along with their children, Anna G. and Frank S. Werner (hereinafter "Anna" and "Frank") and Steven's third wife, Edith Fisch Werner (hereinafter "Edith").

Anna and Frank claim Steven's entire share of the trust remainder on the basis of a Mexican consent judgment of divorce, obtained by Steven against Harriet on December 9, 1963, which incorporated by reference and approved a separation agreement, entered into between Steven and Harriet on December 1, 1963. That agreement included the following provision:

> "10. The Husband shall make, and hereby promises not to revoke, a will in which he shall exercise his testamentary power of appointment over his share in a trust known as 'Abraham L. Werner Trust No. 1' by establishing with respect to said share a trust for the benefit of the aforesaid Children, for the same purposes and under the same terms and conditions, as the trust provided for in Paragraph '9' of this Agreement, insofar as said terms and conditions are applicable thereto."

Paragraph 9 in relevant part provides for the wife to receive the income of the trust, upon the death of the husband, for the support and maintenance of the children, until they reach 21 years of age, at which time they are to receive the principal in equal shares.

On March 20, 1964, less than four months after entry of the divorce judgment, Steven executed a will in which, instead of exercising his testamentary power of appointment in favor of Anna and Frank, he left everything to his third wife, Edith:

> "First, I give, devise and bequeath all of my property * * * including * * * all property over which I have a power of testamentary disposition, to my wife, Edith Fisch Werner."

Steven died in April, 1971 and his will was admitted to probate by the Surrogate's Court of New York County on July 11, 1973.

1.

Paragraph 10 of the separation agreement is a contract to exercise a testamentary power of appointment not presently exercisable (EPTL 10–3.3) and as such is invalid under EPTL 10–5.3, which provides as follows:

> "(a) The donee of a power of appointment which is not presently exercisable, or of a postponed power which has not become exercisable,

cannot contract to make an appointment. Such a contract, if made cannot be the basis of an action for specific performance or damages, but the promisee can obtain restitution of the value given by him for the promise unless the donee has exercised the power pursuant to the contract."

This is a testamentary power of appointment. The original trust instrument provided in relevant part that:

> "Upon the death of such child [Steven] the principal of such share shall be disposed of as such child shall by its last will direct, and in default of such testamentary disposition then the same shall go to the issue of such child then surviving per stirpes".

It is not disputed that New York law is determinative of the validity of paragraph 10 of the separation agreement; the separation agreement itself provides that New York law shall govern.

The reasoning underlying the refusal to enforce a contract to exercise a testamentary power was stated by Judge Cardozo in the case of *Farmers' Loan and Trust Co. v. Mortimer* (219 N.Y. 290, 293–294):

> "The exercise of the power was to represent the final judgment, the last will, of the donee. Up to the last moment of his life he was to have the power to deal with the share as he thought best * * * To permit him to bargain that right away would be to defeat the purpose of the donor. Her command was that her property should go to her son's issue unless at the end of his life it remained his will that it go elsewhere. It has not remained his will that it go elsewhere; and his earlier contract cannot nullify the expression of his final purpose. 'It is not, I apprehend, to be doubted,' says Rolt, L. J., in Cooper v. Martin (LR [3 Ch. App.] 47, 58) 'that equity * * * will never uphold an act which will defeat what the person creating the power has declared, by expression or necessary implication, to be a material part of his intention.' "

(See also, *Matter of Brown*, 33 N.Y.2d 211.)

* * *

3.

As indicated, the statute makes a promise to exercise a testamentary power in a particular way unenforceable. However, EPTL 10–5.3 (subd [b]) permits a donee of a power to release the power, and that release, if in conformity with EPTL 10–9.2, prevents the donee from then exercising the power thereafter.

Under the terms of the trust instrument, if Steven fails to exercise his power of appointment, Anna and Frank (along with the children of Steven's first marriage) take the remainder, i.e., the property which is the subject of Steven's power of appointment. Therefore, Harriet, Anna and Frank argue that at a minimum Steven's agreement should be construed as a release of his power of appointment, and that Anna and Frank should be permitted to take as on default of appointment.

There is respectable authority—by no means unanimous authority, and none binding on this court—to the effect that a promise to appoint a given sum to persons who would take in default of appointment should, to that extent, be deemed a release of the power of appointment. (See Restatement, Property, § 336 [1940]; Simes and Smith, Law of Future Interests, § 1016 [1956].)

This argument has the appeal that it seems to be consistent with the exception that the release statute EPTL 10–5.3 (subd. [b]) carves out of EPTL 10–5.3 (subd [a]); and is also consistent with the intentions and reasonable expectations of the parties at the time they entered into the agreement to appoint, here in the separation agreement; and that therefore perhaps in these circumstances the difference between what the parties agreed to and a release of the power of appointment is merely one of form. Whatever may be the possible validity or applicability of this argument to other circumstances and situations, I think it is inapplicable to this situation because:

(a) It is clear that the parties did not intend a release of the power of appointment. (Cf. *Matter of Haskell*, 59 Misc. 2d 797.) Indeed, the agreement—unlike a release of a power of appointment—expressly contemplates that something will be done by the donee of the power in the future, and that that something will be an exercise of the power of appointment. Thus, the agreement, in the very language said to be a release of the power of appointment, says (par. 10, supra):

> "The Husband shall make * * * a will in which he shall exercise his testamentary power of appointment." (Emphasis added.)

(b) Nor is the substantial effect of the promised exercise of the power the same as would follow from release of, or failure to exercise the power.

(i) Under the separation agreement, the power is to be exercised so that the entire appointive property shall be for the benefit of Anna and Frank; under the trust instrument, on default of exercise of the power, the property goes to all of Steven's children (Anna, Frank and the two children of Steven's first marriage). Thus the agreement provides for appointment of a greater principal to Anna and Frank than they would get in default of appointment.

(ii) Under the trust instrument, on default of exercise of the power, the property goes to the four children absolutely and in fee. The separation agreement provides that Steven shall create a trust, with income payable to Harriet as trustee, for the support of Anna and Frank until they both reach the age of 21, at which time the principal shall be paid to them or the survivor; and if both fail to attain the age of 21, then the principal shall revert to Steven's estate. Thus, Anna and Frank's interest in the principal would be a defeasible interest if they did not live to be 21; and indeed at Steven's death they were both still under 21 so that their interest was defeasible.

(iii) Finally, under the separation agreement, as just noted, if Anna and Frank failed to qualify to take the principal, either because they both died before Steven or before reaching the age of 21, then the principal would go to Steven's estate. Under the trust instrument, on the other hand, on default of appointment and an inability of Anna and

Frank to take, Steven's share of the principal would not go to Steven's estate, but to his other children, if living, and if not, to the settlor's next of kin.

In these circumstances, I think it is too strained and tortuous to construe the separation agreement provision as the equivalent of a release of the power of appointment. If this is a release then the exception of EPTL 10–5.3 (subd. [b]) has swallowed and destroyed the principal rule of EPTL 10–5.3 (subd. [a]).

I note that in *Wood v. American Security and Trust Co.* (253 F. Supp. 592, 594), the principal case relied upon by Harriet, Anna and Frank on this point, the court said: "The Court finds that it is significant that the disposition resulting from the agreement is in accordance with the wishes of the testator in the event the power should not be exercised."

Furthermore, the language of the instrument in that case was much more consistent with the nonexercise of the powers of appointment than in the case at bar.

Accordingly, I hold that the separation agreement is not the equivalent of a total or partial release of the power of appointment.

4.

Anna and Frank also seek restitution out of the trust fund of the value given by them in exchange for Steven's unfulfilled promise. EPTL 10–5.3 (subd. [a]) provides that although the contract to make an appointment cannot be the basis for an action for specific performance or damages, "the promisee can obtain restitution of the value given by him for the promise unless the donee has exercised the power pursuant to contract."

Anna and Frank's remedy is limited, however, to the claim for restitution that they have (and apparently have asserted) against Steven's estate. They may not seek restitution out of the trust fund, even if their allegation that the estate lacks sufficient assets to meet this claim were factually supported, because the trust fund was not the property of Steven, except to the extent of his life estate, so as to be subject to the equitable remedy of restitution, but was the property of the donor of the power of appointment until it vested in someone else. (*Farmers' Loan & Trust Co. v. Mortimer*, 219 N.Y. 290, 295, *supra*; see *Matter of Rosenthal*, 283 App. Div. 316, 319; see, also, EPTL 10–7.1 and 10–7.4.)

* * *

6.

Accordingly, on the motions for summary judgment I direct judgment declaring that defendant Edith Fisch Werner is entitled to the one-half share of Steven C. Werner in the principal of the Abraham L. Werner trust; to the extent that the counterclaims and cross claims asserted by Harriet, Anna and Frank seek relief other than a declaratory judgment, they are dismissed.

NOTES, QUESTIONS, AND PROBLEMS

1. Does the court in Seidel v. Werner hold that partial releases are unenforceable, or does it hold that Steven Werner's agreement was not a partial release?

2. Suppose you had been representing Harriet Werner in drafting the separation agreement. How would you have drafted the language to assure that Steven exercised the power of appointment in favor of Harriet, Anna, and Frank? Would your language have accomplished its objective?

3. The court holds that Anna and Frank are not entitled to restitution out of the trust fund. Why not? Didn't Steven have the power to appoint in favor of the creditors of his estate (remember that Steven's power was a general power)? If Steven had power to appoint in favor of the creditors of his estate, why shouldn't Anna and Frank, as creditors of the estate, be entitled to share in the trust fund? Reconsider this question in light of the materials in the next section.

4. N.Y. EPTL § 10–5.3(a) provides that a donee may not contract to make an appointment under a power that is not presently exercisable. Section 10–5.3(b), cited in Seidel v. Werner, provides that the prohibition on contracts to appoint does not extend to releases. In 1977, in light of Seidel v. Werner, section 10–5.3(b) was amended, and now reads as follows:

> (b) The provisions of this section shall not abridge the ability of the donee of a power of appointment which is not presently exercisable to release his power pursuant to 10–9.2 or to make the power, after release, an imperative power, except that where the donor designated persons or a class to take in default of the donee's exercise of the power, a release with respect to appointive property must serve to benefit all those so designated as provided by the donor.

What effect does the amended statute have on partial releases in New York? Consider the following problem:

> Oscar Zilch has given his son Abner a general testamentary power to appoint trust property. Oscar has also provided that, in default of exercise, the property should be distributed among those persons who would succeed to Abner's estate by intestate succession.
>
> Which of the following releases by Abner would be enforceable in light of EPTL § 10–5.3?
>
> 1. Abner makes an agreement with his children releasing his power to appoint to his wife.
>
> 2. Abner makes an agreement with his wife and children releasing his power to appoint one-half of the trust corpus.
>
> Suppose Oscar's trust instrument had not provided for takers in default. Would your answer to either question be different?

5. Does the New York experience—Seidel v. Werner and amended EPTL § 10–5.3(b)—represent a triumph of logic over history? See generally

Samuel M. Fetters, Future Interests, 1975 Survey of New York Law, 27 Syracuse L. Rev. 365, 375–76 (1976). Would you recommend similar "reform" elsewhere?

6. How does a donee accomplish an effective release of a power of appointment? Consider the following provision from the Restatement (Third) of Property: Wills and Other Donative Transfers (Tentative Draft No. 5, 2006):

Section 20.3 Methods of Releasing a Releasable Power

The donee of a releasable power can release the power, in whole or in part, by:

(1) delivering a writing declaring the extent to which the power is released to a person who could be adversely affected by an exercise of the power.

(2) joining with some or all of the takers in default in making an otherwise effective transfer of an interest in the property that is subject to the power; the power is released to the extent that an exercise of the power thereafter would defeat the interest transferred.

(3) contracting with a person who could be adversely affected by an exercise of the power not to exercise the power; the power is released to the extent that a subsequent exercise of the power would violate the terms of the contract.

(4) communicating in any other appropriate manner an intent to release the power; the power is released to the extent that a subsequent exercise of the power would be contrary to manifested intent.

(5) utilizing any method authorized by the donor or by applicable statute.

SECTION IV. RIGHTS OF CREDITORS

PROBLEM

I.M. Rich, a person of considerable means, intends to create a spendthrift trust to benefit his profligate son, I. Look Rich, for life. I.M. wants to give I. Look maximum discretion over how the trust principal should be distributed at I. Look's death, but wants to assure that I. Look's creditors will not be able to reach the trust principal. In light of the material that follows, recommend drafting for I.M.'s trust instrument.

* * *

We have already discussed the agency theory of powers of appointment: the donee of a power is the donor's agent for distributing the donor's property. The agency theory suggests that appointive property should not be subject to the claims of the donee's creditors. After all, the appointive property does not belong to the donee.

When donor creates a *special* power of appointment, there is general agreement that the appointive property should not be subject to claims by the donee's creditors. Here, the agency theory is at its most persuasive: donor has explicitly prevented donee from exercising the power in favor of himself, his estate, his creditors, or his estate's creditors. Instead, the donor has sought to assure that the donee will exercise his discretion to benefit some third party. As a result, whether or not the donee exercises the power of appointment, the donee's creditors may not reach the appointive assets. See Restatement (Third) of Property: Wills and Other Donative Transfers, § 22.1 (Tentative Draft No. 5, 2006); Cal. Prob. Code, § 681; N.Y. EPTL § 10–7.1.

When donor creates a *general* power of appointment, the agency theory is considerably less persuasive: donor has given donee the power to appoint in favor of himself, his estate, or his creditors, and it is far less clear why donee, who has power to use the appointive property to pay his debts, should not be compelled to do so. Nevertheless, the authorities are in disarray on this point.

The *equitable assets doctrine* reflects the common law position, and holds that the appointive property is subject to claims by donee's creditors—*but only if the donee actually exercises the power*. If the donee chooses not to exercise the power, permitting the appointive property to pass to the takers in default, then the creditors may not reach the appointive property. The equitable assets doctrine, then, effectively permits the insolvent donee to choose between having the appointive assets pass to his creditors, or to the takers in default. If, as is often the case, the takers in default are the donee's close family members, the choice should not be a difficult one.

The Restatement (Third) of Property: Wills and Other Donative Transfers, § 22.3 (Tentative Draft No. 5, 2006) and the Restatement (Third) of Trusts, § 56, cmt. b (Tentative Draft No. 2, 1999), take a different position. The Restatements would treat property subject to a presently exercisable general power of appointment as the property of donee, available to satisfy claims by the donee's creditors—whether or not the donee actually exercises the power. When property is subject to a general testamentary power of appointment, the Restatements would also make the property available to satisfy claims by the donee's creditors whether or not the power is exercised, but creditors would not be entitled to reach the property until the donee's death.

The position of the Restatements is similar, but not identical, to the position taken, by statute, in California. The difference is that under the California statute, the donee's own property must be used first to satisfy creditor claims, but if the donee's own property (or, in the case of a general testamentary power, the donee's estate) is inadequate, creditors may reach appointive property, whether or not the power is actually exercised. Cal. Prob. Code, § 682.

New York, on the other hand, distinguishes sharply between general powers that are presently exercisable and general testamentary powers. New York treats a general presently exercisable power as the equivalent of absolute ownership in the donee, and hence subjects the appointive property to claims of the donee's creditors. In New York, creditors may reach this property *whether or not the donee exercises the power.* (N.Y. EPTL § 10–7.2). With respect to general testamentary powers, however, the New York statute provides that the donee's creditors may not reach appointive property, whether or not the donee has exercised the power. (N.Y. EPTL § 10–7.4).

Compare the two statutes:

* * *

CALIFORNIA PROBATE CODE

SECTION 682. PROPERTY COVERED BY GENERAL POWER.

(a) To the extent that the property owned by the donee is inadequate to satisfy the claims of the donee's creditors, property subject to a general power of appointment that is presently exercisable is subject to the claims to the same extent that it would be subject to the claims if the property were owned by the donee.

(b) Upon the death of the donee, to the extent that the donee's estate is inadequate to satisfy the claims of creditors of the estate and the expenses of administration of the estate, property subject to a general testamentary power of appointment or to a general power of appointment that was presently exercisable at the time of the donee's death is subject to the claims and expenses to the same extent that it would be subject to the claims and expenses if the property had been owned by the donee.

(c) This section applies whether or not the power of appointment has been exercised.

* * *

NEW YORK EPTL

SECTION 10–7.4. CREDITORS OF THE DONEE; GENERAL POWER NOT PRESENTLY EXERCISABLE

(a) Property covered by a general power of appointment which, when created, is not presently exercisable is subject to the payment of the claims of creditors of the donee, his estate and the expenses of administering his estate, only:

(1) If the power was created by the donee in favor of himself; or

(2) If a postponed power becomes exercisable in accordance with the terms of the creating instrument, except in the case of a testamentary general power.

* * *

Note that the New York statute does permit creditors to reach appointive assets when the donor and the donee are the same person. The Restatement takes the same position. Restatement (Third) of Property: Wills and Other Donative Transfers, § 22.2 (Tentative Draft No. 5, 2006). The rationale for this rule is the same as the rationale for refusing to enforce self-settled spendthrift trusts: a person ought not to be able to insulate his own assets from the claims of his creditors.

PROBLEM

I.M. Rich has created a trust and given his son, I. Look Rich, a general testamentary power of appointment over the trust principal. I.M. Rich has provided that "in default of appointment, I direct that at my son's death, the property should be distributed among my son's children or their issue, per stirpes." I. Look Rich approaches you about drafting his own will. He fears that his own estate may be insolvent. If possible, he would like 75% of the appointive property to pass to his son, and the other 25% to pass to his daughter, who has amassed considerable wealth of her own. What drafting advice would you give I. Look Rich

(1) in a jurisdiction that embraces the common law equitable assets doctrine?

(2) in California?

(3) in New York?

Would a partial release of the power be helpful to I. Look Rich in any jurisdiction?

NOTE ON POWERS IN BANKRUPTCY

Section 541(b)(1) of the Bankruptcy Code of 1978 (11 U.S.C. § 541(b)(1)), provides

> Property of the estate does not include any power that the debtor may exercise solely for the benefit of an entity other than the debtor.

If the donee becomes a bankrupt during his lifetime, which powers become a part of the bankruptcy estate? Only general, presently exercisable powers, because those are the only powers the debtor/donee would be able, during his lifetime, to exercise in favor of himself. If the debtor/donee has a general, presently exercisable power, the bankruptcy code treats that power as the equivalent of absolute ownership of the appointive property, and the appointive property becomes a part of the bankruptcy estate. See generally Note, Powers of Appointment Under the Bankruptcy Code: A Focus on General Testamentary Powers, 72 Iowa L. Rev. 1041 (1987).

SECTION V. POWERS OF APPOINTMENT AS A TAX PLANNING TOOL

A. INTRODUCTION

Powers of appointment are a basic tool for tax planning. Consider a decedent who wants to give a beneficiary extensive control over assets, but wants to avoid having those assets pass through the beneficiary's estate. If the decedent gives the property outright to the beneficiary, the property will be taxed twice: once in the decedent's estate, and then again in the beneficiary's estate. Typically, the decedent wants to avoid that result. Can the decedent avoid taxation in the beneficiary's estate by giving the beneficiary a power of appointment instead of leaving the property outright to the beneficiary?

The answer depends on the type of power the decedent gives the beneficiary. Section 2041(a)(2) of the Internal Revenue Code includes within the donee's gross estate the value of all property over which the donee has a *general* power of appointment. As a result, if decedent gives the beneficiary a life interest in trust together with a general power of appointment, the trust property will pass through the beneficiary's estate, and decedent will not have achieved her estate tax objective.

If, on the other hand, decedent gives the beneficiary a *special* power of appointment over trust property, the property will not be included in the beneficiary's estate, and decedent will have achieved her estate tax objective.

The special power of appointment, then, is attractive for estate planning purposes because the appointive property will not be included in the donee's estate. This makes special powers useful whenever a decedent of means wants to minimize the number of times a given asset is subject to estate taxation.

Before Congress enacted the Generation–Skipping Transfer Tax, the special power of appointment was an incredibly powerful tool for the very rich. Imagine a decedent with $20,000,000 in assets. If decedent left her property outright to her son, who in turn left the same property outright to decedent's grandchildren, decedent's $20,000,000 in assets would have been taxed twice, once in decedent's estate, and a second time in the estate of decedent's son. Suppose, however, the same decedent left all of her property in trust, giving her son a right to all income, together with a limited power to invade principal, and a special power to appoint among decedent's issue. If the son then appointed the property to decedent's grandchildren (or to any other members of the class of permissible appointees), decedent's assets would have been subject to estate tax only once—at decedent's death. Because decedent's son held only a special power of appointment, the son would not have been treated as an owner of the property, and no estate tax on his mother's assets would have been due at the son's death. The mother's "generation-skipping trust" would have saved the family millions of dollars. Not surprisingly, many of the super rich kept their family dynasties intact by generous use of generation-skipping trusts.

The Generation–Skipping Transfer Tax has limited the usefulness of generation-skipping trusts for the super rich, and hence, the usefulness of special powers of appointment. But because the generation-skipping transfer tax includes an exemption for each decedent—equal to the exclusion amount applicable in the year of decedent's death ($5,000,000 in 2011–12)—the generation-skipping trust, and the special power of appointment, remain important planning tools.

PROBLEM

Elbert Elderly, a 90–year old man, wants to leave his $5,000,000 estate in equal shares to his two children, Abner, age 62, and Bertha, age 58. Both

Abner and Bertha are millionaires in their own right, and have begun to engage in their own estate planning. Abner and Bertha each have three children, and both of Elbert's children expect to leave most of their assets to their own children. If Elbert consulted you about drafting his will, how would you advise him about his proposed distribution of assets? Would use of a power of appointment be advantageous for Elbert? How would you explain those advantages to Elbert?

B. WHEN IS PROPERTY SUBJECT TO A POWER INCLUDED IN DONEE'S ESTATE?

In many estates, decedent's goal is to confer on a donee as much power over trust assets as possible without causing those assets to be included within the donee's estate. In other words, decedent's goal is to create a power that is as broad as possible, but not a general power within the meaning of the Internal Revenue Code. What limits does decedent face?

1. THE STATUTE

26 U.S.C. § 2041. POWERS OF APPOINTMENT.

(a) In General. The value of the gross estate shall include the value of all property—

* * *

(2) Powers created after October 21, 1942. To the extent of any property with respect to which the decedent has at the time of his death a general power of appointment created after October 21, 1942, or with respect to which the decedent has at any time exercised or released such a power of appointment by a disposition which is of such nature that if it were a transfer of property owned by the decedent, such property would be includible in the decedent's gross estate under sections 2035 to 2038, inclusive. . . .

(b) Definitions. For purposes of subsection (a)—

(1) General power of appointment. The term "general power of appointment" means a power which is exercisable in favor of the decedent, his estate, his creditors, or the creditors of his estate; except that—

(A) A power to consume, invade, or appropriate property for the benefit of the decedent which is limited by an ascertainable standard relating to the health, education, support, or maintenance of the decedent shall not be deemed a general power of appointment.

* * *

(C) In the case of a power of appointment created after October 21, 1942, which is exercisable by the decedent only in conjunction with another person—

(i) If the power is not exercisable by the decedent except in conjunction with the creator of the power—such power shall not be deemed a general power of appointment.

(ii) If the power is not exercisable by the decedent except in conjunction with a person having a substantial interest in the property, subject to the power, which is adverse to exercise of the power in favor of the decedent—such power shall not be deemed a general power of appointment. For the purposes of this clause a person who, after the death of the decedent, may be possessed of a power of appointment (with respect to the property subject to the decedent's power) which he may exercise in his own favor shall be deemed as having an interest in the property and such interest shall be deemed adverse to such exercise of the decedent's power.

(iii) If (after the application of clauses (i) and (ii)) the power is a general power of appointment and is exercisable in favor of such other person—such power shall be deemed a general power of appointment only in respect of a fractional part of the property subject to such power, such part to be determined by dividing the value of such property by the number of such persons (including the decedent) in favor of whom such power is exercisable.

For purposes of clauses (ii) and (iii), a power shall be deemed to be exercisable in favor of a person if it is exercisable in favor of such person, his estate, his creditors, or the creditors of his estate.

(2) Lapse of power. The lapse of a power of appointment created after October 21, 1942, during the life of the individual possessing the power shall be considered a release of such power. The preceding sentence shall apply with respect to the lapse of powers during any calendar year only to the extent that the property, which could have been appointed by exercise of such lapsed powers, exceeded in value, at the time of such lapse, the greater of the following amounts:

(A) $5,000, or

(B) 5 percent of the aggregate value, at the time of such lapse, of the assets out of which, or the proceeds of which, the exercise of the lapsed powers could have been satisfied.

* * *

Note section 2041(b)(1)'s definition of a general power of appointment—a power "exercisable in favor of the decedent, his estate, his creditors, or the creditors of his estate." So long as the trust settlor assures that a donee of the power cannot exercise the power in her own favor, or in favor of her estate, or her creditors, or the creditors of her estate, the trust principal will not be included in the donee's taxable estate.

Suppose, now, that settlor gives the donee a power to invade the principal of the trust for her own benefit. Has settlor given the donee a general power of appointment within the meaning of the statute? With careful drafting, a trust settlor can give the donee considerable authority over trust principal without subjecting the principal to estate tax in the donee's estate.

2. POWERS OF INVASION OVER THE ENTIRE PRINCIPAL OF THE TRUST

Consider the exception articulated in section 2041(b)(1)(A): when the donee has a power to consume or invade for her own benefit, the power is not a general power *if* the power "is limited by an ascertainable standard relating to the health, education, support, or maintenance of the decedent." On the other hand, if the donee has discretion to consume for any reason, or for reasons unrelated to health, education, support, or maintenance, then she has a general power of appointment, and the trust principal will be included in her taxable estate. The *Best* case, reproduced below, demonstrates that unwanted litigation will result if the lawyer is careless in drafting the trust language.

Alternatively, settlor could appoint someone other than the donee as trustee, and give the trustee power to invade. If settlor takes this course, and does not give the donee power to remove the trustee, settlor need not impose an "ascertainable standard" for invasion of trust principal. At the same time, however, settlor has reduced his donee's control over the estate.

What happens if settlor appoints his donee a co-trustee along with some other person, and gives the trustees unlimited power to invade for the donee's benefit? If the statute did not treat such a power as a general power, most trust settlors would simply find a co-trustee whose primary loyalty is to the donee, and give the trustees power to invade for the donee's benefit. To avoid that result, the statute designates powers exercisable in conjunction with another person as general powers unless the other person has "a substantial interest in the property, subject to the power, which is adverse to exercise of the power in favor of the decedent." I.R.C. § 2041(b)(1)(C)(ii). The meaning of that qualification was at issue in the *Best* case, reproduced below.

PROBLEM

Wanda Wife's only daughter is Deborah Daughter. Wanda has assets valued at $4,000,000; Deborah's assets are valued at $5,000,000. Wanda's will devises her estate to Deborah, as trustee. What tax consequences will follow at the deaths of Wanda and Deborah if Wanda's testamentary trust includes the following dispositive provisions (Assume Wanda dies in 2011 and Deborah in 2012):

a. "I direct that Deborah pay to herself all trust income during her lifetime, and I authorize Deborah, in her uncontrolled discretion, to make such payments as she deems appropriate for her own benefit. At Deborah's death, I direct that the principal be distributed in equal shares to Deborah's three children."

b. "I direct that Deborah pay to herself all trust income during her lifetime, and I authorize Deborah to invade principal as necessary for her support, health, and maintenance. At Deborah's death, I direct that the principal be distributed as my daughter Deborah shall appoint by will."

c. "I direct that Deborah pay to herself all trust income during her lifetime, and I authorize Deborah to invade principal as necessary for her support, health, and maintenance. At Deborah's death, I direct that the principal be distributed as my daughter Deborah shall appoint by will among anyone other than Deborah herself, her estate, her creditors, or the creditors of her estate."

d. "I direct that Deborah pay to herself all trust income during her lifetime. If Deborah obtains the express written consent of my granddaughter Sally, I authorize her to invade principal for any purposes she deems appropriate. At my daughter's death, I direct that the principal be distributed in equal shares to my three grandchildren."

Best v. United States

United States District Court, District of Nebraska, 1995.
902 F.Supp. 1023.

■ SHANAHAN, J.

Before the court is filing no. 25, the "Motion for Summary Judgment" filed by the plaintiff, Kathleen Best ("Best"), Personal Representative of the Estate of Alma Anderson, Deceased. Best claims a refund for federal estate taxes and interest paid pursuant to a deficiency assessment by the Internal Revenue Service ("IRS"). For the refund, Best contends that (1) Alma Anderson did not possess a testamentary general power of appointment, but, instead, held a power limited by an ascertainable standard related to the health, education, support, or maintenance of a decedent, see 26 U.S.C. § 2041(b)(1)(A), and (2) Alma Anderson held the power with her son, John Anderson, who had a substantial interest in the property which was adverse to the exercise of the power granted to Alma Anderson. See 26 U.S.C. § 2041(b)(1)(C)(ii).

BACKGROUND

On February 12, 1959, Alfred Anderson executed his "Last Will and Testament," and on January 19, 1967, died testate. In his will which was admitted to probate, Alfred Anderson appointed Alma Anderson, who was Alfred's surviving spouse, and their son, John Anderson, as trustees of the testamentary trust established by Alfred's will. Generally, the trustees, as empowered by the will, were authorized to distribute assets of the trust to Alma Anderson. Upon Alma's death, the trust corpus was distributable to the Anderson children, Kathleen Best and John Anderson, or to their heirs (filing no. 26). Article IV(e) of the will contains the following:

> I order and empower my Trustees to pay over to my wife, out of the principal of said trust, at any time and from time to time, such sum or sums as my Trustees in their sole and absolute discretion shall

determine [sic] may be *reasonably necessary for her comfort, support and maintenance* [emphasis added].

On June 14, 1972, Alma Anderson and John Anderson qualified as trustees. However, on August 18, 1982, John Anderson died. After Alma Anderson was discharged as trustee on September 1, 1983, the Omaha National Bank was appointed as the successor trustee (filing no. 26). Alma Anderson died on March 26, 1989.

Certain material facts are uncontroverted.

In December 1989, Best, as personal representative of Alma Anderson's estate, paid $242,761 in federal estate taxes (filing no. 7). On November 25, 1992, the IRS notified Best that a deficiency in payment of taxes was assessed against Alma Anderson's estate for $381,007 plus $122,995 in interest (filing no. 7). In calculating this deficiency, the IRS included in Alma Anderson's gross estate the value of the corpus of the Alfred Anderson testamentary trust, namely, shares of stock in Anderson Equipment Company valued at $944,390 (filing no. 7). On October 15, 1992, Best paid the IRS $434,030 which included the deficiency assessment and interest. Subsequently, on November 6, 1992, Best also paid the IRS an additional $69,976 in interest, bringing the total payment to $504,006 concerning the assessed deficiency which was thus satisfied by Best. On February 10, 1992, Best filed a "Claim for Refund and Request for Abatement" with the IRS (filing no. 7). On April 22, 1993, the IRS disallowed Best's claim on the ground that Alma Anderson held a general power of appointment over the trust corpus rather than a power of appointment limited by an ascertainable standard or a power exercisable in conjunction with a person with an adverse interest. The IRS, therefore, reaffirmed its position that the corpus of Alfred Anderson's testamentary trust was an asset included in Alma Anderson's gross estate (filing no. 1; exhibit "D").

For federal estate tax purposes, the gross estate of a decedent includes "any property with respect to which the decedent has at the time of his death a general power of appointment created after October 21, 1942...." 26 U.S.C. § 2041 (a)(2). As expressed in 26 U.S.C. § 2041(b):

> (1) General power of appointment.—The term "general power of appointment" means a power which is exercisable in favor of the decedent, his estate, his creditors, or the creditors of his estate; except that—
>
> (A) A power to consume, invade, or appropriate property for the benefit of the decedent which is limited by an ascertainable standard relating to the health, education, support, or maintenance of the decedent shall not be deemed a general power of appointment.

Treas. Reg. § 20.2041–1(c)(2) states:

> (2) Powers limited by an ascertainable standard. A power to consume, invade, or appropriate income or corpus, or both, for the benefit of the decedent which is limited by an ascertainable standard relating to the health, education, support, or maintenance of the

> decedent is, by reason of section 2041(b)(1)(A), not a general power of appointment. A power is limited by such a standard if the extent of the holder's duty to exercise and not to exercise the power is reasonably measurable in terms of his needs for health, education, or support (or any combination of them). As used in this subparagraph, the words "support" and "maintenance" are synonymous and their meaning is not limited to the bare necessities of life. A power to use property for the comfort, welfare, or happiness of the holder of the power is not limited by the requisite standard. Examples of powers which are limited by the requisite standard are powers exercisable for the holder's "support", "support in reasonable comfort", "maintenance in health and reasonable comfort", "support in his accustomed manner of living", "education, including college and professional education", "health", and "medical, dental, hospital and nursing expenses and expenses of invalidism". In determining whether a power is limited by an ascertainable standard, it is immaterial whether the beneficiary is required to exhaust his other income before the power can be exercised.

Best contends that the testamentary trust under Alfred Anderson's will conferred an invasionary power limited by an ascertainable standard so that the corpus of the testamentary trust estate is excludable from the gross estate of Alma Anderson. On the other hand, the United States contends that Alma Anderson had a general power of appointment over the corpus of the trust; hence, the value of the corpus was includable in Alma Anderson's gross estate.

Thus, the question before the court is whether the Internal Revenue Service properly included the value of the trust corpus in Alma Anderson's gross estate.

ANALYSIS

* * *

Although federal law dictates how a decedent's estate will be taxed, "state law controls in determining the nature of the legal interest which the taxpayer had in the property or income sought to be reached by the statute." Morgan v. Commissioner, 309 U.S. 78, 82, 84 L. Ed. 585, 60 S. Ct. 424 (1940). See also Vissering v. Commissioner of Internal Revenue, 990 F.2d 578, 580 (10th Cir.1993): "We look to state law ... to determine the legal interests and rights created by a trust instrument, but federal law determines the tax consequences of those interests and rights;" Brantingham v. U.S., 631 F.2d 542, 545 (7th Cir.1980): "The determination as to what legal rights and interests are created by a specific instrument is a question of state law." Therefore, Nebraska law determines whether the language in Alfred Anderson's will, namely, "reasonably necessary for [Alma Anderson's] comfort, support and maintenance," creates a general power of appointment, subjecting such power to federal estate taxation.

Also, the court keeps in mind that, for the purpose of federal estate taxation, 26 U.S.C. § 2041(a)(2) pertains to "any property with respect to which the decedent has at the time of his death a general power of appointment." A review of several decisions discloses that both a life estate and an interest in a trust corpus may be "property" for the purposes of § 2041(a)(2). See Brantingham, supra (7th Cir. 1980) (decedent's power to consume a life estate was limited by an ascertainable standard pursuant to 26 U.S.C. § 2041(b)(1)(A)); First Virginia Bank v. U.S., 490 F.2d 532 (4th Cir.1974) (decedent's power to consume life estate was not limited by an ascertainable standard pursuant to 26 U.S.C. § 2041(b)(1)(A)); Vissering, supra (decedent's power to consume trust corpus was limited by an ascertainable standard pursuant to 26 U.S.C. § 2041(b)(1)(A)).

* * *

In relation to the plain language of 26 U.S.C. § 2041(b)(1)(A), namely, "a power to consume, invade, or appropriate property for the benefit of the decedent which is limited by an ascertainable standard relating to the health, education, support, or maintenance of the decedent," the court notes Treas. Reg. § 20.2041–1(c)(2), which states that:

> "Support" and "maintenance" are synonymous and their meaning is not limited to the bare necessities of life. A power to use property for the comfort, welfare, or happiness of the holder of the power is not limited by the requisite standard. Examples of powers which are limited by the requisite standard are powers exercisable for the holder's "support," "support in reasonable comfort," "maintenance in health and reasonable comfort," [and] "support in his accustomed manner of living."

* * *

As directed by Alfred Anderson's words in establishing the testamentary trust, the trustee could not use the trust estate solely for Alma Anderson's comfort, but could use the assets of the trust "reasonably necessary" for her "comfort and support" as well as "comfort and maintenance." Thus, language in the Alfred Anderson testamentary trust has a strikingly and essential similarity to the power to "support in reasonable comfort" and "maintenance in health and reasonable comfort," powers which are explicitly approved in Treas. Reg. § 20.2041–1(c)(2) for excludability from a decedent's gross estate.

Courts have held that use of the word "comfort," when used conjunctively with the other specified purposes permitting excludability from a decedent's gross estate, does not destroy an invasionary power limited by an ascertainable standard in reference to "health, education, support, or maintenance of the decedent" pursuant to 26 U.S.C. § 2041(b)(1)(A). For instance, in Vissering v. Commissioner of Internal Revenue, 990 F.2d 578 (10th Cir.1993), the court examined the testamentary language in a trust which allowed an invasion "required for the continued comfort, support, maintenance, or education of said beneficiary." The trust assets, according to a decision by the United States Tax Court that was under review, were includable in the Estate of Norman Vissering, the deceased beneficiary of the trust. As observed by the Circuit Court in Vissering: "The appeal turns on whether decedent held powers permitting him to invade the principal of the trust for his own benefit unrestrained by an ascertainable standard relating to health, education, support, or maintenance." 990 F.2d at 578. In Vissering, the court also stated:

> The Internal Revenue Service (IRS) and the Tax Court focused on portions of the invasion provision providing that the trust principal could be expended for the "comfort" of decedent, declaring that this statement rendered the power of invasion incapable of limitation by the courts.
>
> ... The instant language states that invasion of principal is permitted to the extent "required for the continued comfort" of the decedent, and is part of a clause referencing the support, maintenance and education of the beneficiary. Invasion of the corpus is not permitted to the extent "determined" or "desired" for the beneficiary's comfort but only to the extent that it is "required." Furthermore, the invasion must be for the beneficiary's "continued" comfort, implying, we believe, more than the minimum necessary for survival, but nevertheless reasonably necessary to maintain the beneficiary in his accustomed manner of living. These words in context state a standard essentially no different from the examples in the Treasury Regulation, in which phrases such as "support in reasonable comfort," "maintenance in health and reasonable comfort," and "support in his accustomed manner of living" are deemed to be limited by an ascertainable standard. Treas. Reg. § 20.2041–1(c)(2).

990 F.2d at 579–81. See, also, Brantingham, supra, at 545 (power to invade life estate if necessary for "maintenance, comfort and happiness" is an invasionary power limited by an ascertainable standard); Hunter v. U.S., 597 F. Supp. 1293 (W.D.Penn. 1984) (trustee's power to invade trust corpus "for the comfortable support and maintenance of any beneficiary therein, or should any emergency arise" is an invasionary power limited by an ascertainable standard); Toledo Trust Co. v. U.S., 1987 U.S. Dist. LEXIS 16111 (N.D. Ohio 1987) (power to invade trust corpus for "care, comfort and support" is an invasionary power limited by an ascertainable standard).

Also, this court believes that the Supreme Court of the State of Nebraska, if presented with this case at hand, would hold that a trust document, permitting invasion of the trust's principal or corpus when "reasonably necessary for [Alma Anderson's] comfort, support and maintenance," does not create a general power of appointment, but does create an invasionary power "limited by an ascertainable standard relating to the health, education, support or maintenance" of Alma Anderson consistent with 26 U.S.C. § 2041(b)(1)(A) and, thus, permits excludability from Alma Anderson's gross estate.

Therefore, the court finds and concludes that Alma Anderson did not have a general power of appointment concerning the assets of the testamentary trust created by Alfred Anderson's will. Consequently, the value of the trust corpus under Alfred Anderson's will is excluded from the gross estate of Alma Anderson, Deceased. For that reason, the plaintiff, Kathleen A. Best, as personal representative of the Estate of Alma Anderson, Deceased, is entitled to a refund of the estate tax and interest paid to the Internal Revenue Service concerning the corpus of the trust included in Alma Anderson's gross estate. Hence, Kathleen A. Best, as personal representative, is entitled to a refund of the estate tax and interest paid pertinent to the trust corpus included in Alma Anderson's gross estate and, thus, is entitled to a refund in the amount of $504,006 which is the principal and interest paid by the Estate of Alma A. Anderson, Deceased, concerning the deficiency assessed by the IRS for federal estate taxes.

Because the court has determined that Alma Anderson held a power of appointment limited by an ascertainable standard, it is unnecessary to decide whether the corpus of the trust included in Alma Anderson's estate should have been excluded pursuant to 26 U.S.C. § 2041(b)(1)(C)(ii).

* * *

QUESTIONS

1. What was wrong with the drafting in Article IV(e) of Alfred Anderson's will? Redraft Article IV(e) in a manner that would have avoided the litigation in this case.

2. Suppose the court had concluded that the power of invasion in the trust instrument was not limited by an ascertainable standard. Would the trust corpus have been excluded pursuant to 26 U.S.C. § 2041(b)(1)(C)(ii)? What is the argument for the IRS? For the estate?

3. According to the treasury regulations quoted in the Best opinion, a trust for the "comfort, welfare, or happiness" of the beneficiary is not limited by an ascertainable standard. See also Forsee v. United States, 76 F. Supp. 2d 1135 (D. Kan. 1999) [discretion to invade for "happiness, health, support, and maintenance" not limited by an ascertainable standard]. By contrast, a trust for the "maintenance in health and reasonable comfort" is limited by an ascertainable standard. As a result, the approved formulation have become the "magic words." But if the "ascertainable standard" rule is designed to include property in the estate when the decedent has unlimited discretion to use the property as his own, does the distinction drawn in the regulations accomplish the statutory goal?

As a legal matter, is the trustee subject to greater constraint when permitted to invade for "maintenance in health and reasonable comfort" than when permitted to invade for "comfort, welfare, or happiness?" Reconsider the support and discretionary trust materials in Chapter Seven.

As a practical matter, are trust beneficiaries likely to challenge the trustee's decision to invade? Consider the situation where the trust instrument gives the trustee-spouse a power to invade for her "maintenance in health and reasonable comfort," together with a special power to appoint among her children. Is any child likely to challenge her mother's invasion of principal? Why not?

For thorough discussions of the ascertainable standard test, see John G. Steinkamp, Estate and Gift Taxation of Powers of Appointment Limited by Ascertainable Standards, 79 Marq. L. Rev. 1996, 236–76 (1995); Amy Morris Hess, The Federal Taxation of Nongeneral Powers of Appointment, 52 Tenn. L. Rev. 395, 409–19 (1985).

3. LIMITED POWERS OF INVASION: LAPSE AND THE $5,000/5% POWER

As we have seen, if a trust settlor gives a donee a power to invade principal for the donee's own benefit, section 2041 treats the power as a general power of appointment, and includes the trust principal in the donee's estate. Moreover, the donee cannot release the power to avoid inclusion in the estate; release would constitute a taxable gift by donee.

Suppose, however, the settlor limits the donee's power to invade principal to a fixed dollar amount each year, or to a fixed percentage of the trust estate. If the donee actually invades principal for her own benefit, the principal, to that extent, will become part of her taxable estate. What if donee does not exercise the power to invade principal?

Consider the problem. Trust settlor might give donee power to withdraw 25% of the initial trust principal each year. Over four years, donee would have the power to make the entire trust principal her own. If she does not exercise the power, what estate tax consequences follow? Section 2041(b)(2) addresses that question, and provides that "lapse" of the power—failure to exercise the power to withdraw 25%—"shall be considered a release" of the power. That is, if settlor gives donee a power to withdraw 25% of the trust principal in year one, and donee does not exercise the power, donee will be treated as having made a taxable gift in that year. The same result would follow in each of the three succeeding years. As a result, a trust settlor would find it extremely unattractive, from a tax perspective, to give a beneficiary a power to withdraw 25% of trust principal each year.

The statute, however, includes an important exception: to the extent that the property "which could have been appointed" by exercise of lapsed powers did not exceed the greater of $5,000 or 5 percent of the aggregate value of the "assets out of which, or the proceeds of which, the exercise of the lapsed powers could have been satisfied," lapse of the power will not be treated as a release, and will not, therefore, create estate or gift tax consequences (See I.R.C. § 2041(b)(2), supra).

Example 8: *Settlor creates a trust and gives his daughter a power, each year, to withdraw 5% of the trust principal's value at the time of withdrawal. Over a five-year period, the daughter withdraws no assets. As each year's power to withdraw 5% lapses, the lapse generates no estate or gift tax consequences.*

Example 9: *Settlor creates a trust and gives his daughter a power, each year, to withdraw 15% of the trust principal's value at the time of withdrawal. Over a five-year period, the daughter withdraws no assets. As each year's power to withdraw 15% lapses, the lapse generates the following consequences. With respect to 5% or $5,000, whichever is* *greater, the lapse generates no estate or gift tax consequences. With respect to the balance over that amount, the daughter has made a taxable gift.*

This does not mean, however, that creation of a power to withdraw 5% or $5,000 will have no estate or gift tax consequences. Consider the following case:

Estate of Kurz v. Commissioner

United States Court of Appeals, Seventh Circuit, 1995.
68 F.3d 1027.

■ EASTERBROOK, J.

Between her husband's death, in 1971, and her own, in 1986, Ethel H. Kurz was the beneficiary of two trusts. Kurz received the income from each. She was entitled to as much of the principal of one (which we call the Marital Trust) as she wanted; all she had to do was notify the trustee in writing. She could take only 5 percent of the other (which we call the Family Trust) in any year, and then only if the Marital Trust was exhausted. When Kurz died, the Marital Trust contained assets worth some $3.5 million, and the Family Trust was worth about $3.4 million. The estate tax return included in the gross estate the whole value of the Marital Trust and none of the value of the Family Trust. The Tax Court held that Kurz held a general power of appointment over 5 percent of the Family Trust, requiring the inclusion of another $170,000 under 26 U.S.C. § 2041(a)(2). 101 T.C. 44 (1993); see also T.C. Memo 1994–221 (computing a tax due of approximately $31,000).

Section 2041(b)(1) defines a general power of appointment as "a power which is exercisable in favor of the decedent, his estate, his creditors, or the creditors of his estate". Kurz had the power to consume or appoint the corpus of the Marital Trust to anyone she pleased whenever she wanted, and the Estate therefore concedes that it belongs in the gross estate. For her part, the Commissioner of Internal Revenue concedes that the 95 percent of the Family Trust that was beyond Kurz's reach even if the Marital Trust had been empty was not subject to a general power of appointment. What of the other 5 percent? None of the Family Trust could be reached while the Marital Trust contained 1¢, and the Estate submits that, until the exhaustion condition was satisfied (which it never was), the power to appoint 5 percent in a given year was not "exercisable", keeping the Family Trust outside the gross estate. To this the Commissioner replies that a power is "exercisable" if a beneficiary has the ability to remove the blocking condition. Suppose, for example, that the Family Trust could not have been touched until Ethel Kurz said "Boo!". Her power to utter the magic word would have been no different from her power, under the Marital Trust, to send written instructions to the trustee.

The Tax Court was troubled by an implication of the Commissioner's argument. Suppose the Family Trust had provided that Kurz could reach 5 percent of the principal if and only if she lost 20 pounds, or achieved a chess rating of 1600, or survived all of her children. She could have gone on a crash diet, or studied the games of Gary Kasparov, or even murdered her children. These are not financial decisions, however, and it would be absurd to have taxes measured by one's ability to lose weight, or lack of moral scruples. Imagine the trial, five years after a person's death, at which friends and relatives troop to the stand to debate whether the decedent was ruthless enough to kill her children, had enough willpower to lay off chocolates, or was smart enough to succeed at chess. The Tax Court accordingly rejected the Commissioner's principal argument, ruling that raw ability to satisfy a condition is insufficient to make a power of appointment "exercisable".

If not the Commissioner's position, then what? The Estate's position, 180 opposed, is that the condition must be actually satisfied before a power can be deemed "exercisable". The Tax Court came down in the middle, writing that a condition may be disregarded when it is "illusory" and lacks any "significant non-tax consequence independent of the decedent's ability to exercise the power." Of course, illusions are in the eye of the beholder, and we are hesitant to adopt a legal rule that incorporates a standard well suited to stage magicians (though some legal drafters can give prestidigitators a run for their money). No one doubts that the Kurz family had good, non-tax reasons for the structure of the trust funds. The only question we need resolve is whether a sequence of withdrawal rights prevents a power of appointment from being "exercisable". Despite the large number of trusts in the United States, many of them arranged as the Kurz trusts were, this appears to be an unresolved issue. Neither side could find another case dealing with stacked trusts, and we came up empty handed after independent research.

For a question of first principles, this one seems remarkably simple. Section 2041 is designed to include in the taxable estate all assets that the decedent possessed or effectively controlled. If only a lever must be pulled to dispense money, then the power is exercisable. The funds are effectively under the control of the beneficiary, which is enough to put them into the gross estate. Whether the lever is a single-clutch or double-clutch mechanism can't matter. Imagine a trust divided into 1,000 equal funds numbered 1 to 1,000, Fund 1 of which may be invaded at any time, and Fund n of which may be reached if and only if Fund n–1 has been exhausted. Suppose the beneficiary depletes Funds 1 through 9 and dies when $10 remains in Fund 10. Under the Kurz Estate's view, only $10 is included in the gross estate, because Funds 11 through 1,000 could not have been touched until that $10 had been withdrawn. But that would be a ridiculously artificial way of looking at things. Tax often is all about form, see Howell v. United States, 775 F.2d 887 (7th Cir.1985), but § 2041 is an anti-formal rule. It looks through the trust to ask how much wealth the decedent actually controlled at death. The decedent's real wealth in our hypothetical is $10 plus the balance of Funds 11 through 1,000; the decedent could have withdrawn and spent the entire amount in a trice. Whether this series of trusts has spendthrift features (as the Kurz trusts did) or is invested in illiquid instruments (as the Kurz trusts were) would not matter. The

Estate does not deny that Kurz had a general power of appointment over the entire Marital Trust, despite these features. If the costs of removing wealth from the trust do not prevent including in the gross estate the entire corpus of the first trust in a sequence (they don't), then the rest of the sequence also is includable.

Wait!, the Estate exclaims. How did first principles get into a tax case? After consulting the statute, a court turns next to the regulations. 26 C.F.R. § 20.2041–3(b) provides:

For purposes of section 2041(a)(2), a power of appointment is considered to exist on the date of a decedent's death even though the exercise of the power is subject to the precedent giving of notice, or even though the exercise of the power takes effect only on the expiration of a stated period after its exercise, whether or not on or before the decedent's death notice has been given or the power has been exercised. However, a power which by its terms is exercisable only upon the occurrence during the decedent's lifetime of an event or a contingency which did not in fact take place or occur during such time is not a power in existence on the date of the decedent's death. For example, if a decedent was given a general power of appointment exercisable only after he reached a certain age, only if he survived another person, or only if he died without descendants, the power would not be in existence on the date of the decedent's death if the condition precedent to its exercise had not occurred.

The Kurz Estate takes heart from the provision that "a power which by its terms is exercisable only upon the occurrence during the decedent's lifetime of an event or a contingency which did not in fact take place or occur during such time is not a power in existence on the date of the decedent's death." Like the Tax Court, however, we do not find in this language the strict sequencing principle the Estate needs.

This is the Commissioner's language, and the Commissioner thinks that it refers only to conditions that could not have been satisfied. Regulation-writers have substantial leeway in their interpretation, see Shalala v. Guernsey Memorial Hospital, 131 L. Ed. 2d 106, 115 S. Ct. 1232, 1236–37 (1995), because the delegation of the power to make substantive regulations is the delegation of a law-creation power, and interpretation is a vital part of the law-creation process. See Homemakers North Shore, Inc. v. Bowen, 832 F.2d 408 (7th Cir.1987). A reading must of course be reasonable—must be an interpretation—else the rulemaker is revising the law without the requisite notice and opportunity for comment. Pettibone Corp. v. United States, 34 F.3d 536, 541–42 (7th Cir.1994). The Commissioner's understanding of the regulation tracks its third sentence, which is designed to illustrate the second. It says: "For example, if a decedent was given a general power of appointment exercisable only after he reached a certain age, only if he survived another person, or only if he died without descendants, the power would not be in existence on the date of the decedent's death if the condition precedent to its exercise had not occurred." All three examples in the third sentence deal with conditions the decedent could not have controlled, at least not in the short run, or lawfully. The rate of chronological aging is outside anyone's control, whether one person survives another does not present an option that may be exercised lawfully, and whether a person has descendants on the date of death is something that depends on the course of an entire life, rather than a single choice made in the administration of one's wealth.

By contrast, the sequence in which a beneficiary withdraws the principal of a series of trusts barely comes within the common understanding of "event or ... contingency". No one could say of a single account: "You cannot withdraw the second dollar from this account until you have withdrawn the first." The existence of this sequence is tautological, but a check for $2 removes that sum without satisfying a contingency in ordinary, or legal, parlance. Zeno's paradox does not apply to financial transactions. Breaking one account into two or more does not make the sequence of withdrawal more of a "contingency"—at least not in the sense that § 20.2041–3(b) uses that term.

No matter how the second sentence of § 20.2041–3(b) should be applied to a contingency like losing 20 pounds or achieving a chess rating of 1600, the regulation does not permit the beneficiary of multiple trusts to exclude all but the first from the estate by the expedient of arranging the trusts in a sequence. No matter how long the sequence, the beneficiary exercises economic dominion over all funds that can be withdrawn at any given moment. The estate tax is a wealth tax, and dominion over property is wealth. Until her death, Ethel Kurz could have withdrawn all of the Marital Trust and 5 percent of the Family Trust by notifying the Trustee of her wish to do so. This case is nicely covered by the first sentence of § 20.2041–3(b), the notice provision, and the judgment of the Tax Court is therefore

AFFIRMED.

QUESTIONS

1. The two-trust scheme employed in the *Kurz* case was quite common before Congress introduced portability into the estate tax law. The "Family Trust" also called the credit shelter trust or bypass trust, was taxed in the husband's estate, while the marital trust took advantage of the marital deduction, and was taxed only in the wife's estate.

How did the lawyer who drafted the *Kurz* trusts go awry? Why, in light of section 2041(b)(2), was there any estate tax due on the Family Trust? Why didn't the court discuss section 2041(b)(2)?

2. Suppose the Marital Trust had permitted Ethel Kurz to withdraw principal only for "support in her customary manner of living." Would 5% of the Family Trust have been included in her taxable estate? If your answer is no, would you recommend such a restriction on withdrawal from the marital trust?

3. Suppose the Family Trust had permitted Ethel Kurz to withdraw 5% of principal only for "support in her customary manner of living." Would 5% of the Family Trust have been included in Kurz's estate?

4. In light of the estate tax consequences in the *Kurz* case, why would the drafter of a trust instrument ever create a 5%/$5,000 withdrawal power rather than simply giving the beneficiary a power to invade principal measured by an ascertainable standard?

5. Although portability reduces the importance of the *Kurz* case in the marital context, the principles enunciated in the opinion remain important when a decedent creates a trust for someone other than a surviving spouse.

CHAPTER NINE

Classification and Construction of Future Interests

Mention of "future interests" conjures up in many students an image of dusty old rules with no relevance to the modern world. Nothing could be further from the truth. Whenever anyone creates an ordinary private express trust, the trust instrument—if it is properly drafted—invariably creates future interests. The trust property has to be distributed to someone when the trust terminates.

If future interests are so ordinary, so common, why, one might ask, do they present problems worthy of special study? Recall the "time gap" problems we discussed in the wills chapter. Testators write wills during their lifetimes, but the wills do not become effective until death. Unanticipated events often occur between will execution and death: in particular, named beneficiaries may die, and other relatives may be born to testator.

Creation of trusts exacerbates the "time gap" problem. Decades may pass between the time settlor creates a trust and the time a future interest may become possessory. Especially when instruments are inartfully drafted, it may be very difficult to determine how settlor would have wanted the trust property distributed had she known what events would actually occur. Consider the following, apparently simple, case:

> ***Case 1:*** *Settlor creates an inter vivos trust, directing that income be distributed to her daughter, D, for life, and directing that at D's death, the trust property be distributed to D's son X.*

Settlor obviously expects that X will survive his mother, D, and that the property will be distributed to X at D's death. But suppose X does not survive. Is X's estate entitled to the property? Or should the property be distributed to X's issue, if any? Or should the property simply revert to Settlor's own estate because the designated beneficiary has died? In Case 1, the uncertainty is about testator's intention if a designated beneficiary happens to die before that beneficiary's interest becomes possessory. In other cases, however, the uncertainty may also include the possible birth of new beneficiaries. Consider the following:

> ***Case 2:*** *Settlor creates the same trust as in Case 1, but directs that at D's death, the trust property be distributed "to D's children." At the time the trust is created, D has three children, E, F, and G. After creation of the trust, J and K are born to D. E dies before D.*

Note the complications. Are J and K entitled to share as "children?" What happens to E's share—should it be divided among the other "children," or should it pass through E's estate or to E's issue?

These questions are principally questions of construction: what meaning should we attach to settlor's words when settlor wrote those words without fully anticipating the events which would actually occur? This chapter explores those construction questions—both because they are important in estates litigation, and because they are critical in establishing good drafting habits. Before we turn to construction issues, however, we need to spend some time on classification of future interests.

Why worry about classification? Lawyers speak (and write) in shorthand. For instance, in Case 1, above, a lawyer or a judge might start her analysis by asking whether X's remainder was contingent or vested. In fact, the lawyer might be asking that question only as an aid in discovering what settlor intended. Nevertheless, so long as lawyers and judges continue to use the shorthand, law students must become familiar with the terminology. And, as we shall see, in some cases—particularly when the Rule Against Perpetuities is involved—the classification of particular interests might determine their validity. For these reasons, it remains important to understand the classification of future interests.

SECTION I. CLASSIFICATION OF FUTURE INTERESTS

A. FUTURE INTERESTS AND PRESENT INTERESTS

Let's start by distinguishing future interests from present interests. A future interest is one that does not become possessory immediately upon its creation. Consider, for instance, a transfer of property to T as trustee, with directions that T should "pay income to B for life, and at B's death, distribute the principal to C." B's interest is a present interest because she is entitled to the immediate beneficial enjoyment of the trust property. C's interest is future because her beneficial enjoyment is delayed until some time in the future; that is, until B's death.

Even if a future interest will not become possessory for a long time, the future interest is a legally recognized and enforceable relationship from the moment it is created. It does not spring into existence for the first time on the future date when the owner of the future interest becomes entitled to enjoyment of the property. The word "present" or "future" immediately preceding the word "interest" refers to the time of beneficial enjoyment, not to the existence of the legal relationship. Thus, if settlor creates a trust, with directions that T should, at B's death, distribute the trust principal to C, C has a future interest the moment settlor creates the trust.

What rights does this future interest give to C? First, C may bring an action against T for any acts by T that would impair C's interest: that is, T may be liable for breach of fiduciary duty if T mismanages or misappropriates the trust property. If the future interest follows a legal life estate in land, the holder of a future interest may bring an action for "waste" if the life estate holder takes actions that impair the value of the future interest. Second, the holder of the future interest, C, may generally sell or otherwise dispose of that future interest even before the interest becomes possessory. Thus, a future interest has a present value to its holder. (Of course, if the likelihood is small that the future interest will become possessory, or if the interest will not become possessory for many years, the value of the future interest may not be great.)

B. THE CATEGORIES OF FUTURE INTERESTS

The elaborate system of classification for future interests emanates from several sources. First, many differentiations are historical hangovers from the rigid, inflexible formalism of the medieval land law. Second, much of the complexity is the product of Property scholars in the 19th and 20th centuries who sought to depict the existing law of future interests as a neat logical package, full of fine distinctions based on minute differences in language.

You may—and you should—become impatient with the refinements and subtleties that supposedly differentiate the various types of future interests. As we study the various types of future interests, ask yourself whether a court is likely to permit disposition of a family's hard-earned wealth to turn on the fine distinctions that underlie the supposed legal categories. Nevertheless, the categories themselves have become a significant part of the legal lore. The most recent Restatement of Property seeks to simplify the classification system, but vestiges of the traditional system remain important, especially in those jurisdictions that continue to apply the common law Rule Against Perpetuities.

1. THE BASIC CLASSIFICATION SYSTEM

The first step in classifying a future interest is to determine who holds the future interest at the moment the future interest is created. The grantor either creates a future interest in himself, or in someone else. Traditionally, future interests held by the grantor were divided into three categories: *(1) the possibility of reverter; (2) the right of entry (sometimes called a "right of re-entry" or a "power of termination"); and (3)the reversion*. The Restatement (Third) of Property collapses all of these interests into a single interest, and calls that interest a reversion. Restatement (Third) of Property (Wills and Other Donative Transfers), § 25.2, cmt. d. For estate planning purposes, the differences among future interests in the grantor are of limited significance.

If the grantor creates a future interest in someone other than himself, the future interest has traditionally been classified as one of two interests: *(1) a remainder or (2) an executory interest.* The reasons for distinguishing between remainders and executory interests have all but disappeared, and the Restatement (along with statutes in some states) has purged the term "executory interest" from the future interest vocabulary. Restatement (Third) of Property (Wills and Other Donative Transfers), § 25.2, cmt. c.

Whenever you confront a future interest—whether under traditional terminology or more modern usage—you should ask yourself first whether the future interest is held by the grantor, or by someone else. In other words, ask whether the future interest has been created in the transferor, or in a transferee.

> ***Example 1:*** *S creates an inter vivos trust, providing that the trustee should pay the income from the trust to A, S's child, for four years, and then should distribute the principal of the trust to S. S has a future interest in the trust property, but that future interest cannot be a remainder (or an executory interest). Why not? Because the future interest is held by S, the grantor of the property.*

> ***Example 2:*** *S creates a similar inter vivos trust, but provides that after four years, the trustee should distribute the principal of the trust to W, S's wife. W has a future interest in the trust property, but that future interest cannot be a reversion. Why not? Because the holder of the future interest, W, is not the grantor of the property. She is not a transferor; she is a transferee.*

2. FUTURE INTERESTS IN THE GRANTOR

Future interests held by the grantor are less important for estate planning purposes than future interests held by third parties. Few people seeking to transmit wealth intentionally create future interests in themselves. Indeed, people planning their estates should almost always avoid creating future interests in themselves. For our purposes, then, there is little value in focusing on any remaining distinctions among future interests in the grantor. We can treat them all as reversions.

3. FUTURE INTERESTS IN PERSONS OTHER THAN THE GRANTOR

a. *Traditional Distinctions Among Remainders*

When future interest problems arise in the estate planning context, the issues generally involve future interests in persons other than the grantor. As we have seen, the most important of those future interests are remainders. Traditional doctrine recognizes four different types of remainders:

Indefeasibly Vested Remainders

Vested Remainders Subject to Open (or Subject to Partial Divestment, or Subject to Partial Defeasance)

Vested Remainders Subject to Complete Divestment (or Subject to Complete Defeasance)

Contingent Remainders

Not all remainders will become possessory estates. Suppose, for instance, T's will devises Blackacre "to A for life, remainder to B if B survives A, and otherwise to C." If B dies before A, B's interest will not become possessory at all. We call B's remainder a *contingent remainder.* How can we tell whether a remainder is contingent? Generally, by asking two questions.

One must first ask whether the remainder is held by some ascertained person? If the answer is no, the remainder is contingent. Consider the following example:

> ***Example 3:*** *T's will devises Blackacre "to my daughter for life, remainder to her children." At the time of T's death, his daughter has no children. No ascertainable person holds a remainder. Since a vested remainder must be vested in someone, the remainder cannot be vested. The remainder in the daughter's children is, therefore, a contingent remainder.*

Second, if the remainder is held by an ascertained person, one must ask whether the remainder is subject to a condition precedent. If the remainder is subject to a condition precedent, it will be classified as a contingent remainder even if it is held by an ascertained person.

A remainder can be classified as "vested" even though it is subject to a condition. As we have seen, if a remainder is subject to a condition precedent, the remainder is contingent. A vested remainder, however, can be subject to a condition subsequent. If it is, we say that the remainder is a *vested remainder subject to complete divestment.* These two remainders—contingent remainders and vested remainders subject to complete divestment—are the hardest to distinguish. In each case, the remainder may never become possessory. Gray offered the following distinction between the two forms of remainder:

> If the conditional element is incorporated into the description of, or into the gift to, the remainder-man, then the remainder is contingent; but if, after words giving a vested interest, a clause is added divesting it, the remainder is vested.

John Chipman Gray, The Rule Against Perpetuities § 108 (4th ed. 1942). Gray's formulation has taken on a life of its own. Let's examine two examples illustrating the formulation:

> ***Example 4:*** *T devises Blackacre "to A for life, remainder to B if B survives A, otherwise to C." According to Gray, B has a contingent remainder because the condition—surviving A—appears in the same clause as the grant to B.*

> ***Example 5:*** *T devises Blackacre "to A for life, remainder to B, but if B fails to survive A, then to C." Gray's formulation would make B's remainder in this case a vested remainder subject to complete divestment. Why? Because in this case, the survivorship condition comes not in the same clause as the grant to B, but in a clause that follows the grant to B. Another way to say that the clause "follows" the grant to B is that the clause "subsequent" to the grant to B. Hence, the condition is called a "condition subsequent." By contrast, if the conditional language had preceded the grant, the condition would generally be called a "condition precedent."*

The distinction between Examples 4 and 5 may appear unduly fine. And, indeed, the principal authority invoked for the sharp distinction is generally confined to secondary authorities like Gray. Courts do not often confront cases in which a lot turns on the placement of the comma, and when they do confront those cases, they do not invariably find the comma determinative. Consider the following case:

Webb v. Underhill

Court of Appeals of Oregon, 1994.
130 Or.App. 352, 882 P.2d 127.

■ ROSSMAN, P.J.

In this action to partition real property, ORS 105.205, plaintiffs appeal from a summary judgment for defendant. We hold that the determinative issue in the case, whether the alternative beneficiaries' remainder interests are contingent or vested, is a question of law that is amenable to resolution on summary judgment, and that the trial court correctly held that those interests are contingent. Accordingly, we affirm.

Ernest Webb, owner of the Buck Hollow Ranch, died in 1972. His will devises all of his property to his wife Agnes for life, or until she remarries, with the remainder of the property to be divided equally among four of Ernest's six children upon Agnes' death or remarriage. If any one of the four named children is deceased at that time, that one-quarter share will go to his or her lineal descendants, if any. Specifically, the will provides:

> "For her use, benefit and enjoyment, for such period of her natural life as she shall remain unmarried, I give to my beloved wife, Agnes Webb, all of my property of every kind and nature, with the provision, however, that if my said wife shall remarry, that said property shall *at the date of the marriage* revert as follows: One Dollar ($1.00) each to Irene Barton and to Vivian Morse [two of Ernest's six children]. The remainder shall be divided equally between [the other four children]:
>
> "Delbert Webb
>
> "Delores Rhodig
>
> "La Velle Underhill
>
> "Wayne L. Webb
>
> "But if one or more of these shall be dead, their share shall go to their lineal descendants, if any. If one or more of the four who live in Oregon and are last mentioned, shall be dead leaving no lineal descendants, the share of the deceased one, dead without lineal descendants, shall go to the survivors of the four who live in Oregon (last mentioned) or to their lineal descendants. The said four being Delbert Webb, Delores Rhodig, La Velle Underhill, and Wayne L. Webb.
>
> "*At the death of my said wife*, if she shall yet be in the use and enjoyment of said property, such as remains shall be divided as follows: One Dollar ($1.00) each to Irene Barton and to Vivian Morse. The remainder shall be divided equally between:

> "Delbert Webb
>
> "Delores Rhodig
>
> "La Velle Underhill
>
> "Wayne L. Webb
>
> "But if one or more of these shall be dead, their share shall go to their lineal descendants, if any. If one or more of the four who live in Oregon and are last mentioned, shall be dead leaving no lineal descendants, the share of the deceased one, dead without lineal descendants, shall go to the survivors of the four who live in Oregon (last mentioned) or to their lineal descendants. The said four being Delbert Webb, Delores Rhodig, La Velle Underhill, and Wayne L. Webb." (Emphasis supplied.)

After Ernest's death, his son Delbert died. Delbert is survived by his wife Carol, who subleases a portion of the ranch, and their three adult children (the grandchildren).

Plaintiffs, who seek to sell the ranch as a single parcel and distribute the proceeds according to their respective interests, are Ernest's wife Agnes, two of Ernest's children (Wayne and Delores), Delbert's wife Carol and the grandchildren. Defendant is Ernest's daughter La Velle.

To maintain an action to partition property, a plaintiff must be a tenant in common, with a vested remainder in the property. ORS 105.205. Agnes, as the sole life estate holder, is not a tenant in common, and Carol is a mere lessee. Therefore, neither of those parties fits within the requirements of the partition statute. Below, plaintiffs argued that the grandchildren's interests vested indefeasibly at the time of Delbert's death. They conceded below that the children's interests are contingent, but, on appeal, their reply brief may be viewed as an attempt to withdraw that concession. Defendant argued that all of the remainder interests are contingent, in that the children or their lineal descendants must survive Agnes' death or remarriage to take under the will.

The trial court ruled that both the children's and grandchildren's interests are contingent and conditioned upon surviving to the date of Agnes' death or remarriage. Having concluded that none of the plaintiffs holds a vested remainder, the court held that they could not maintain this partition action. ORS 105.205. Accordingly, it granted defendant's motion for summary judgment and dismissed the case.

The issues on appeal are whether the children's and grandchildren's interests in the property are vested, and whether resolution of that question involves a factual determination that precludes summary judgment....

We hold that, in this case, the question of whether the remainder interests are contingent or vested is a purely legal one. Although the trial court erroneously segmented its decision into factual "findings" regarding the testator's intent and legal "conclusions" regarding plaintiffs' ability to maintain this partition action, the dispositive legal question to be resolved was and is what type of future interests are possessed by Ernest's four named children and their lineal descendants under the terms of his will. In the emphasized portions of the will, set out above, the testator expressly provides that the triggering event by which all distributions are determined is the death or remarriage of the life tenant. When the language of a will is unambiguous, there is no basis for resorting to extrinsic evidence to ascertain the testator's intent. Scarlett v. Hopper, 110 Or. App. 457, 460, 823 P2d 435 (1992).

We turn to trial court's legal conclusions, beginning with an analysis of the future interests of Ernest's four named children. Plaintiffs acknowledge that the will contains a survivorship requirement that the children must meet, in order for them to personally take, but contend that the children's interests are most aptly described as "vested remainders subject to divestment" should they fail to survive the life tenant. That is incorrect. The devise in this case created *alternative* remainder interests in both the children and the grandchildren. Love v. Lindstedt, 76 Or. 66, 147 P. 935 (1915).[1] When a life estate is followed by two alternative remainder interests, and "the vesting of the second depends upon the failure of the first, and the same contingency decides which one of the two alternative remainders shall take effect in possession," both interests are alternative *contingent* remainders. 76 Or at 72. Here, surviving the death or remarriage of the life tenant is the contingency that decides whether and which of the alternative remainder interests will vest indefeasibly. If one of the children dies before the triggering event, his or her estate—and, accordingly, his or her spouse, if any—will take nothing under the will. Until the triggering event takes place, it cannot be known who will be entitled to take under Ernest's will. See Jerman v. Jerman, 129 Or. 402, 407, 275 P. 915 (1929).

[In an omitted portion of the opinion, the court concluded that testator's grandchildren did not have vested remainders].

In sum, until Agnes' death or remarriage, all of the future interests in this case will remain contingent. There is presently no party who may maintain a partition action.

Affirmed.

NOTES AND QUESTIONS

1. Using Gray's formulation, would the court have concluded that the remainder in the children was vested or contingent? Why?

---

1. There is support in the Restatement for plaintiffs' position that a remainder interest can be vested yet subject to a survivorship requirement, i.e., a survivorship requirement does not necessarily mean that the remainder interest is contingent. However, Love v. Lindstedt, supra, supports the view that a devise "to A for life, remainder to B, but if B predeceases A, then to C" creates alternative remainder interests in B and C. Paulus, J., "Future Interests in Oregon," 15 Will. L. Rev. 151, 159 (1979). Under the facts of this case, "B and C" would represent Ernest's named children and their lineal descendants.

2. How would you redraft Ernest Webb's will to create a vested remainder subject to complete divestment? How would you redraft it to more clearly create a contingent remainder?

3. See generally Edward C. Halbach, Vested and Contingent Remainders: A Premature Requiem for Distinctions Between Conditions Precedent and Subsequent, in Essays for Austin Wakeman Scott (1964).

* * *

Distinguishing between contingent remainders and vested remainders subject to complete defeasance is the most difficult problem in classifying remainders. The other two kinds of vested remainders are easier to identify.

The *indefeasibly vested remainder* is the easiest remainder to understand. Subject to some unimportant qualifications, a remainder is indefeasibly vested when it is certain to become possessory whenever and however the preceding estates end.

> ***Example 6:*** *T's will devises the remainder of her estate to a trustee, and directs that "income be paid to my sister, S, for life, then to my daughter, D." The remainder in D is indefeasibly vested because D's interest is certain to become possessory. If D dies before S, D's interest will pass to D's estate. That is, even if D's remainder does not become possessory in D personally, the interest will nevertheless become possessory in persons of D's choosing, or, if D leaves no will, in D's heirs.*

Note also that there are no events which might act to diminish or divest D's interest, either before or after the interest becomes possessory. This, too, is a characteristic of the indefeasibly vested remainder.

The *vested remainder subject to open* or *subject to partial divestment* is a remainder which, like an indefeasibly vested remainder, is certain to become possessory. But the holder of a vested remainder subject to open, unlike the holder of an indefeasibly vested remainder, may find his share of the property reduced as more beneficiaries become eligible to share the property. Because the class of possible takers is still open, his share may be partially divested by new members of the class.

> ***Example 7:*** *T's will devises the remainder of her estate to a trustee, and directs that "income be paid to my son, Q, for life, then to be distributed among Q's children." At the time of T's death, Q has two children, R and S. R and S have vested remainders subject to open. Their interest is certain to become possessory, but their share of the remainder may diminish if Q has additional children. Thus, if Q has no additional children, R and S will each be entitled to 50% of the remainder; if Q has three more children, each child will be entitled to only 20% of the remainder.*

Note that the devise in Example 7 is a devise to the "class" of Q's children. The class of Q's children remains "open" so long as Q is alive. Why? Because we presume that Q can have additional children so longer as Q is alive [More on that presumption when we discuss the Rule Against Perpetuities]. Vested remainders subject to open are most common when the grantor creates a "class gift," such as a gift "to the children of A" or to the "nephews and nieces of B."

PROBLEM

T's will provides: "I devise $100,000 in trust, and I direct my trustee to distribute income to my daughter until my daughter's death. At my daughter's death, I direct my trustee to distribute the trust principal

a. to my son, S."

b. to my daughter's children, in equal shares."

c. to my nephew, N, if he survives my daughter."

Classify each future interest, assuming that at T's death, his daughter has one living child. Would any of your answers be different if the daughter had not yet had any children?

b. Executory Interests

Now that we have studied remainders, let us turn to executory interests. Executory interests typically arise in two situations.

First, by definition, a remainder cannot cut short, or "divest" a vested remainder in fee simple. If a future interest in someone other than the grantor would operate to cut short a vested remainder in fee, that future interest must be an executory interest. Typically, executory interests follow vested remainders subject to complete divestment. Suppose, for instance, T devises Blackacre "to my daughter, D, for life, remainder to my grandson G, but if G fails to survive D, then the remainder should be distributed to my nephew N." Following Gray's classification system, G has a vested remainder subject to complete divestment (but see Webb v. Underhill, supra). Because G has a vested remainder, N cannot have a remainder. Instead, N has an executory interest.

Second, executory interests arise when there is certain to be a time gap between the end of the prior estate and the time the future interest will become possessory. *For a future interest to be a remainder, the interest must be one that may become possessory immediately upon the natural expiration of a prior estate created in the same instrument.* If the interest cannot become possessory until after a "gap," the interest cannot be a remainder. Suppose, for instance, T devises Blackacre "to my daughter, D, for life, and one year after her death, I direct that Blackacre pass to my grandson G." G's future interest cannot become possessory immediately upon the expiration of D's life estate. By the terms of the grant, there will be a necessary gap between D's death and G's right to possession. As a result, G cannot have a remainder. G has an executory interest.

The difference between a contingent remainder and an executory interest is generally of limited importance today. Indeed, in some states, the distinction has been abolished by statute. See N.Y. EPTL §§ 6–3.2 and 6–4.10. The Restatement, too, has abandoned the distinction.

c. *Restatement Simplification*

The Restatement (Third) of Property (Wills and Other Donative Transfers) attempts to simplify the classification of future interests as follows:

Restatement (Third) of Property (Wills and Other Donative Transfers) Section 25.3

A future interest is either contingent or vested. A future interest is contingent if it might not take effect in possession or enjoyment. A future interest is vested if it is certain to take effect in possession or enjoyment . . . .

That is, the Restatement abolishes the distinctions among contingent remainders, vested remainders subject to complete divestment, vested remainders subject to open, and executory interests. All of those interests now fall within the contingent remainder category. So, for instance, under the Restatement formulation, if O grants a remainder to A for life, remainder to A's children, A's children—even if alive—have a contingent interest for so long as A remains theoretically capable of having children.

For the most part, the Restatement's simplification makes eminent good sense. The real issue facing most estate planners, and most estate litigators, is not classification of future interests, but construction of those interests: what meaning were the grantor's words intended to convey. For example, if testator's will conveys Blackacre "to my wife for life, remainder to my surviving children," what does the word "surviving" mean—those alive at testator's death, or those alive at the wife's death? In resolving that question, however, courts (and lawyers) may discuss the question by asking whether the remainder was vested at testator's death (in all of the children then alive) or whether the interest remained contingent until the wife's death. Resolving that question does not require mastery of the complexities of the common law classification scheme.

On the other hand, the Restatement's simplification does not mesh perfectly with the common law Rule Against Perpetuities (a fact of which the Restatement's drafters were well aware). The Restatement, however, modifies the Rule to mesh with the simplified classification system. But in those jurisdictions that retain the common law Rule, the traditional classification system retains at least some significance.

SECTION II. CONSTRUCTION OF FUTURE INTERESTS: GIFTS TO INDIVIDUALS

All too often, trust instruments do not anticipate the wide variety of events which might occur between the time the settlor creates the trust and the time the trust terminates. In particular, if settlor has directed that the trust principal be distributed to particular beneficiaries, what happens if some or all of those beneficiaries die before the time for distribution?

In many ways, the problem is analogous to the "lapse" problem you have already discovered when you studied wills; in each case, the problem is that a named beneficiary has died before that beneficiary becomes entitled to possession of property. The problems are not, however, identical. Remember that a will typically has no effect until testator's death. The beneficiaries of a will have no property interest in testator's estate until testator's death. By contrast, when settlor has created a trust—and for this purpose it doesn't matter whether the trust was created by will or by *inter vivos* instrument—the remainder beneficiaries of the trust have a property interest (albeit a future interest) from the moment the trust becomes effective.

You should not assume, therefore, that an antilapse statute will save a gift of a future interest to a remainderman who dies before her interest becomes possessory. As a drafter, you should be careful to anticipate, and explicitly provide for, as many contingencies as possible. The drafting will be easier, however, if you first familiarize yourself with rules of construction that courts have developed to deal with unexpected death of beneficiaries.

We will start by examining future interests in named individuals, and then we will move to consider gifts to classes—"children," "issue," and the like.

A. SHOULD WE IMPLY A CONDITION OF SURVIVAL?

Uchtorff v. Hanson

Supreme Court of Iowa, 2005.
693 N.W.2d 790.

■ STREIT, JUSTICE.

H.L. Mencken once said the capacity of human beings to bore one another seems vastly greater than that of any other animal. The subject-matter of this appeal—a medieval interest known as a remainder—proves Mencken's point, although we shall do our best to bring matters to resolution as painlessly and interestingly as possible. Much is at stake.

At issue is a trust fund. After the family patriarch who controlled the trust fund died, his only child, a son, followed him to the grave. Years later the patriarch's wife passed away. The district court ruled the son was not entitled to the trust fund unless he survived his mother. The son's widow appeals. She claims her late husband's interest vested upon his father's death, and therefore she should receive the trust fund because the son left everything to her. We agree with the widow and reverse.

I. Facts and Prior Proceedings

The facts are not disputed. Alfred Uchtorff died in 1979. Alfred's will is a hairy beast almost twenty pages in length. Fortunately, the parties only dispute "Item VI" of the will. In Item VI, Alfred exercised his power of appointment over "Trust A," a trust fund his father established before a majority of the members of this court were born. In relevant part, Item VI provided:

> B. I appoint [the trust fund] property to [a bank] and to my wife Pearl E. Uchtorff, in trust, nevertheless, and to hold as a trust fund for the following uses and purposes, to wit:
>
> 1. During the lifetime of my wife Pearl E. Uchtorff ... the trustees shall pay to her ... the net income from the trust fund.
>
> ....
>
> 3. The provisions of this subdivision 3 shall be effective in any of the following stated events: (i) the event of the death of my said wife before my death; (ii) the event of remarriage of my said wife after my death without renunciation by her; (iii) *the event of the death of my said wife after my death, without renunciation by her and without remarriage by her*; or (iv) the event of incompleteness or insufficiency or failure for any reason of the appointment hereinbefore made for the benefit of my said wife....
>
> In any of the stated events ..., I appoint said [trust fund] ..., in the manner in this subdivision 3 ... provided.
>
> (a) *In the event that my son, Richard E. Uchtorff shall survive me, I appoint the [trust fund] to the said Richard E. Uchtorff, as an indefeasibly vested interest in fee.*
>
> (b) In the event that my son, Richard E. Uchtorff shall not survive me, I appoint the same to [a bank], and to Carolyn Uchtorff, ..., in trust nevertheless and to hold as a trust fund for [a class composed of the representative issue of the marriage of Richard and Carolyn, subject to divestment under certain circumstances.]

(Emphasis added.)

When Alfred died, he was survived by his wife, Pearl Uchtorff, and their son and only child, Richard Uchtorff. Richard was married to Carolyn Uchtorff. Richard and Carolyn had three children, Sally Hanson, Taylor Armstrong–Lucas, and Julie Kurt ("the children"). Richard and Carolyn eventually divorced, and Richard later married Christa Uchtorff.

Richard died in 1988. Richard disinherited his three children in his will, writing:

> I make no provisions in this will for my children for several reasons which I consider sufficient, and generally because of their longstanding and continuous disrespectful conduct to me.

Richard left everything to Christa instead.

Pearl enjoyed the income from the trust fund until her death in 2003. She never renunciated [sic] her beneficiary interest in the trust fund, nor did she ever remarry. Today the trust fund contains hundreds of thousands of dollars.

After Pearl's death, the bank, as surviving co-trustee of the trust fund, petitioned the district court for construction of Alfred's will. Two factions claimed the trust fund as their own. Christa argued Richard's remainder interest in the trust fund vested upon Alfred's death and should now pass, like the rest of Richard's assets, through Richard's will to her. The children rejoined, asserting Christa's claim must fail because Richard did not survive Pearl. The district court ruled Alfred's will was ambiguous and did not specifically state what should happen if Richard predeceased Pearl. The court held Iowa's new trust code therefore mandated the children receive the trust fund. Christa appealed.

* * *

III. The Merits

A. Vested or Contingent Remainder

The first question presented in this appeal is whether Richard had a vested or a contingent remainder in the trust fund once he survived Alfred.[2] Contrary to the district court, we think the plain and unambiguous language of Alfred's will indicates Richard's remainder interest in the trust fund vested at Alfred's death.

1. General Principles

This appeal involves a remainder interest, long one of the law professor's favorite instruments of torture. Stated in its most general terms, a remainder

> is a future interest created in someone other than the transferor that, according to the terms of its creation, will become a present estate (if ever) immediately upon, and no sooner than, the expiration of all prior particular estates created simultaneously with it.

Thomas F. Bergin & Paul G. Haskell, Preface to Estates in Land and Future Interests 62 (1984) [hereinafter Bergin & Haskell]. Alfred's will clearly gave Richard a remainder interest in the trust fund. Richard's interest was a future interest that could become a present estate immediately upon and no sooner than when Pearl's prior interest expired, i.e., when Pearl died, remarried, or renounced her life interest, but only if Richard survived Alfred.

A remainder is either vested or contingent. Moore v. McKinley, 246 Iowa 734, 745, 69 N.W.2d 73, 80 (1955).

> A vested remainder, whereby the estate passes by the conveyance, but the possession and enjoyment are postponed until the particular estate is determined, is where the estate is invariably fixed to remain to certain determinate persons. Contingent remainders are where the estate in remainder is limited to take effect either to a

2. As an aside, we point out Iowa's anti-lapse statute is not involved in this appeal. Lapse only occurs when a beneficiary fails to survive the *testator*. Iowa Code § 633.273(1); cf. In re Estate of Cole, 549 N.W.2d 313, 314 n.2 (Iowa Ct. App. 1996). Nor does the statute apply, in any event, to a will such as this one, which expressly makes survival of the testator a condition of taking under the will. Iowa Code § 633.273(1); see Bankers Trust Co. v. Allen, 257 Iowa 938, 945, 135 N.W.2d 607, 611 (1965).

> dubious or uncertain person or upon a dubious or uncertain event, so that the particular estate may be determined and the remainder never take effect.

Id. at 746–47, 69 N.W.2d at 81. A remainder may be vested even when enjoyment is postponed until the happening of some future condition; it is contingent only if the remainder interest is "dependent on some *dubious circumstance*, through which it may be defeated...." Taylor v. Taylor, 118 Iowa 407, 409, 92 N.W. 71, 71 (1902) (emphasis added). Vested remainders are devisable and alienable. Moore, 246 Iowa at 746, 69 N.W.2d at 80.

2. The Terms of the Will: Richard's Remainder Vested Upon Alfred's Death

To decide the nature of Richard's remainder, the parties direct our attention to Item VI, paragraph 3(a) of the will. That provision states:

> (a) In the event that my son, Richard E. Uchtorff shall survive me, I appoint the [trust fund] to the said Richard E. Uchtorff, as an indefeasibly vested interest in fee.

This provision of the will initially rendered Richard's remainder interest contingent, because appointment of the trust fund to Richard was expressly conditioned upon one uncertain event, i.e., that Richard survive Alfred. Once Richard survived Alfred, this condition, the only uncertain event upon which appointment of the trust fund to Richard was predicated, was fulfilled. Richard's interest in the trust fund vested when Alfred died and needed only to wait until Pearl's interest ended to become an estate in possession. See 28 Am. Jur. 2d Estates § 255, at 273 (2000) ("Upon the happening of the contingency upon which the estate in remainder is limited, the remainder becomes vested in right and awaits only the termination of the precedent particular estate to become an estate in possession.").

Survival to Time of Possession Not Required

It could be argued the express terms of the will state Richard's remainder remained contingent until Pearl's death. The will indicates appointment of the trust fund to Richard in the manner set forth in paragraph 3(a) would occur in "in the event" Pearl renounced the trust fund, remarried, or died. Although it is true this part of Alfred's will places a *condition* upon Richard's *possession* of the trust fund, see Points v. Points, 312 Ky. 348, 227 S.W.2d 913, 915 (Ky. 1950) (equating "in the event" with "if"), this condition does not make Richard's *interest a contingent remainder*. Expiration of Pearl's estate was inevitable. Although Pearl's interest might end earlier through renunciation or remarriage, it was certain to cease at the very latest at her death. See Dickerson, 200 Iowa at 118, 202 N.W. at 603 (pointing out, as evidence of vestedness, that "termination of the precedent estate, is certain to occur[,] if not by the remarriage of the widow, then by her death").

Only when a condition serves to make it dubious or uncertain that the remainder interest will *ever* pass does the condition make the remainder contingent. Moore, 246 Iowa at 746–47, 69 N.W.2d at 81. It does not matter that Richard did not survive Pearl, or even that it could not have been known at any time prior to Richard's death whether Richard would survive Pearl and gain possession of the trust fund. "It is not the certainty of possession or enjoyment which distinguishes the vested remainder, but the certainty of the right to future enjoyment if the remainderman lives until the life tenancy terminates." Lingo v. Smith, 174 Iowa 461, 468, 156 N.W. 402, 405 (1916); accord Dickerson, 200 Iowa at 118, 202 N.W. at 603; cf. Houts, 201 N.W.2d at 470–71 (noting an estate is not rendered contingent because the portion, quantity, or amount of property beneficiary will receive remains uncertain until a future date). This is because

> [a] vested remainder confers a present fixed right to the future enjoyment ..... The fact that the devisee is not to have the enjoyment of possession until the termination of the intermediate estate does not prevent the vesting of the remainder immediately upon the death of the testator.... *No uncertainty of enjoyment will render the remainder contingent.*

Moore, 246 Iowa at 745–46, 69 N.W.2d at 80 (emphasis added, citations omitted). Subdivision three of the will was certain to take effect *sometime*; if Richard had lived long enough, he would have had the right to enjoy the trust fund when Pearl died. Put another way, Richard's remainder vested *in interest* upon Alfred's death, even if it was not secured in enjoyment or possession. "Death of the life tenant merely fixed the time for enjoyment." Clarken v. Brown, 258 Iowa 18, 24, 137 N.W.2d 376, 379 (1965). In this case Pearl's death simply came too late for Richard.

To rule otherwise would have absurd results. "There could be no such thing as a vested remainder" because the very definition of a remainder assumes the existence of a prior estate. Bergin & Haskell at 6. As we stated in Katz,

> Of course [a remainderman] may predecease the termination of the trust. But this does not make the remainder ... contingent for it is an uncertainty which may attach to all remainders, vested or contingent. Certainty of possession and enjoyment by the remainderman is not essential to a vested remainder.

242 Iowa at 652–53, 47 N.W.2d at 808 (citations omitted); see also Dickerson, 200 Iowa at 118, 202 N.W. at 603 ("He may die before coming into the actual possession of the remainder, but that is a contingency attaching to all remainders.").

At the time of Alfred's death it was clear that whatever happened in the future, it was certain Pearl's interest would terminate, and Richard was next in line. Because the trust fund was certain to pass at some time, "the remainder then vested and only the right of possession and enjoyment awaited termination of the trust." Katz, 242 Iowa at 654, 47 N.W.2d at 809. The text of the will states as much: Richard, upon surviving his father, took the trust fund "as an indefeasibly vested interest in fee." This phrase plainly and specifically indicates Richard's interest in the trust fund vested at the moment of his father's death and was not subject to defeasance upon the happening of any subsequent event. Richard was free to devise his vested remainder as he saw fit.[3]

Other Evidence of a Vested Remainder

The structure of the devise in Article VI bears the telltale signs of a vested remainder. First, the remainder was invariably fixed to a determinate person, Richard, whose only impediment to taking possession and enjoyment of the trust corpus was based upon a certain event, at the very latest his mother's death. See Moore, 246 Iowa at 746, 69 N.W.2d at 81. Second, nothing in Article VI states that Richard's interest was contingent upon surviving his mother. Third, the will does not explicitly provide any alternate beneficiaries who should take on the condition that Richard failed to survive his mother. The failure to do so is evidence of a vested remainder. See Dickerson, 200 Iowa at 119, 202 N.W. at 603 ("failure to make provision for the disposition of the remainder, if the son should die before the termination of the trust, is a circumstance entitled to weight as indicating that the condition is not precedent to the vesting of the estate"); Schrader v. Schrader, 158 Iowa 85, 90, 139 N.W. 160, 162 (1912) (same); see also Johnston, 234 Iowa at 205, 12 N.W.2d at 178. Fourth, an alternative arrangement was provided in the will only for the circumstance in which Richard did not survive his father, which, as we have shown previously, was the only uncertain event upon which Richard's interest was predicated. Fifth, Article VI is different than another part of the will. Article IV of Alfred's will stated Richard was entitled to other assets "in the event [he] shall outlive the survivor of myself *and my said wife*." (Emphasis added.) Article VI, on the other hand, simply says "in the event that my son, Richard E. Uchtorff shall survive *me*." (Emphasis added.) Unlike Article VI, Article IV also provided for the disposition of the Article IV property in equal shares to Richard's children should Richard predecease Pearl. Divining testator intent is never an easy task, but looking at the whole of the will in this case it is clear Alfred knew how to make Richard's interest contingent upon Richard surviving Pearl but did not do so with respect to the trust fund. See Elkader Prod. Credit Ass'n v. Eulberg, 251 N.W.2d 234, 237–38 (Iowa 1977) (indicating testamentary instrument must be considered as a whole and each part given meaning and effect if possible).

B. The Iowa Trust Code

1. *Iowa Code § 633.4701*

The children also maintain a provision of the new Iowa Trust Code supersedes our reasoning.... That provision provides:

> *Unless otherwise specifically stated by the terms of the trust*, the interest of each beneficiary is contingent on the beneficiary surviv-

---

3. Likewise Richard was free to convey his vested remainder during his life or borrow against it, as many do. To hold otherwise would wreak havoc upon the settled expectations of many parties to such transactions.

> ing until the date on which the beneficiary becomes entitled to possession or enjoyment of the beneficiary's interest in the trust.

Iowa Code § 633.4701(1) (emphasis added). The children contend Alfred's will is insufficiently specific concerning the nature of Richard's interest in the trust fund. Christa rejoins that the trust code does not apply in this case, and, to the extent it purports to apply retroactively to this case and divest Richard's estate of a vested property right, it is unconstitutional. See Iowa Const. art. I, § 21 ("No . . . law impairing the obligation of contracts shall ever be passed."); see also Iowa R.R. Land Co. v. Soper, 39 Iowa 112, 117 (1874) (recognizing retrospective laws may be declared unconstitutional if they interfere with vested rights). Although the legislature enacted the trust code in 1999, see 1999 Iowa Acts ch. 125, and it did not become effective until 2000, see 1999 Iowa Acts ch. 125, § 109, it purports to apply to *all* trusts past, present, and future, as well as all proceedings concerning trusts commenced on or after July 1, 2000. See Iowa Code § 633.1106; see also Mitchellville Cmty. Ctr., Inc. v. Vos (In re Clement Trust), 679 N.W.2d 31, 37 n.1 (Iowa 2004).

2. Alfred's Will Specifically States Richard's Interest Vested

Alfred's will states with sufficient specificity that Richard's interest vested upon his mother's death. By its terms it states Richard took "an indefeasibly vested interest in fee." It is true Alfred's will does not mimic the statute and state "the interest of each beneficiary is not contingent on the beneficiary surviving until the date on which the beneficiary becomes entitled to possession or enjoyment of the beneficiary's interest in the trust." This is not surprising, however, since Alfred's will was written decades before the new trust code was a glimmer in the legislature's eye. We do not think the statute requires magic words. "We must think things not words, or at least we must constantly translate our words into the facts for which they stand, if we are to keep to the real and the true." Oliver Wendell Holmes, Jr., Law in Science and Science in Law, 12 Harv. L. Rev. 443, 460 (1899). This is not so much a matter of interpretation than it is of translation. Translating the old-fashioned phrase "indefeasibly vested interest in fee" into post-trust code language, we find a specific statement that Richard need not survive Pearl. See In re Estate of Arends, 311 N.W.2d 686, 689 n.2 (Iowa Ct. App. 1981) ("Intention should be determined at the time the will is made, based upon the facts then existing."). This reading of the statute is consistent with the overall framework of the trust code. "The provisions of a trust shall always control and take precedence over any section of this trust code to the contrary." Iowa Code § 633.1105. The provisions of Alfred's will that granted Richard a vested interest therefore trump any provisions in the trust code that would, by default, mandate a different result. Notwithstanding the enactment of the new trust code, the intent of the testator still reigns supreme in this instance.

3. A Little History Helps

Some history will also illuminate matters. As indicated, Alfred referred to Richard's interest as an "indefeasibly vested interest in fee." Given the history of the law in the area, Alfred's use of this phrase is telling. The question has often arisen in the courts as to whether, *in the absence of such a phrase*, one should *imply* a condition of survival of the possessor of the precedent estate. Historically, courts did not do so; for various reasons, remainder interests were usually construed as vested rather than contingent whenever possible. See, e.g., Fulton, 179 Iowa at 951, 162 N.W. at 254; Schrader, 158 Iowa at 88, 139 N.W. at 161. In the context of the case at bar, there was

> a pervasive constructional preference in the property law for vested future interests over contingent future interests and for early vesting over vesting at a later time; this means, in this context, *that there is a constructional preference for there being no condition of survivorship of the life tenant.*

Bergin & Haskell at 127 (emphasis added). Thus in 1916 in Lingo we stated:

> *All estates will be regarded as vested unless a condition precedent thereto is so clearly expressed that it cannot be regarded as vested without doing violence to the language of the will.* To effectuate this rule, words of seeming condition are, if possible, to be construed as postponing the time of enjoyment....
>
> *The law presumes that words of postponement relate to the enjoyment of the remainder rather than the vesting thereof, and the intent to postpone the vesting of the estate must be clear and manifest.*

Lingo, 174 Iowa at 467, 468, 156 N.W. at 404, 405 (emphasis added) ..... Viewed in this historical context, Alfred's use of the phrase "indefeasibly vested interest in fee" is evidence Alfred intended to forestall any implied inference that Richard's interest was contingent upon Richard surviving his mother. Although the new Iowa Trust Code completely reverses the common law preference for vested interests and deems all interests contingent upon survival to the time of possession unless specifically stated otherwise, it is also clear the provisions of the trust must govern. In this case we are constrained to follow the intent of the testator, determined at the time the will is made and based upon the facts then existing, that specifically granted a vested remainder to Richard, which is a specific statement he need not survive Pearl. See Iowa Code § 633.1105; Arends, 311 N.W.2d at 689 n.2.

IV. Disposition

Upon the death of his father, Richard had a vested remainder in the trust fund. He was therefore free to devise it to his wife Christa instead of his children. The district court must be reversed.

REVERSED.

QUESTIONS AND PROBLEMS

1. Why would it be incorrect to characterize the issue in Uchtorff as a "lapse" issue?

2. What steps, if any, could Alfred Uchtorff's lawyer have taken to forestall the litigation in this case? On drafting problems generally, see John L. Garvey, Drafting Wills and Trusts: Anticipating the Birth and Death of Possible Beneficiaries, 71 Or. L. Rev. 47 (1992).

3. Focus on paragraph VI(B)(3)(a) and (b) of Alfred Uchtorff's will. Assume that Alfred's power of appointment was a general power. At common law (before enactment of the Iowa statute discussed in the case), how would the appointive property have been distributed if the paragraph had been drafted as follows:

1. "(a) I appoint the trust fund to my son Richard E. Uchtorff."[no paragraph (b)]

2. (a) is identical to the language in Uchtorff's actual will; (b) is omitted entirely.

3. "(a) In the event that my son, Richard E. Uchtorff shall survive until the happening of the first of the stated events, I appoint the trust fund to my son, Richard E. Uchtorff." [no paragraph (b)]

4. (a) [same as in 3, above]

"(b) In the event that my son, Richard E. Uchtorff shall not survive until the happening of the first of the stated events, I appoint the same to [a bank], and to Carolyn Uchtorff . . ., in trust and to hold as a trust fund for [a class composed of the representative issue of the marriage of Richard and Carolyn]."

How would your answers be different if the Iowa statute were in effect in the jurisdiction?

4. Most often, when a testator or a trust settlor leaves a remainder interest to someone, that someone is a family member. What effect would implying a condition of survivorship have on distribution of property among family members? Consider the following (not atypical) trust: Testator creates a trust to provide income for his wife during her lifetime, and provides at the wife's death that the trust principal shall be divided between Testator's daughter, Debbie, and son, Sam. If Sam dies before the wife, leaving his estate to his children (Testator's grandchildren) George and Greta, how would the Uchtorff court distribute the trust principal when Testator's wife dies? Does this hypothetical suggest why courts have been loathe to imply survivorship conditions?

Change one fact: Sam's will leaves his entire estate to his partner Steve. How would the Uchtorff court distribute the trust principal? Are you confident that the distribution would be consistent with Testator's intent? Cf. Edward C. Halbach, Jr., & Lawrence W. Waggoner, The UPC's New Survivorship and Antilapse Provisions, 55 Alb. L. Rev. 1091, 1133 (1992) [asserting that most transferors prefer to have property pass to descendants of beneficiary or transferor rather than others—spouses and charities—outside the bloodline].

Which of these situations do you think is more likely to arise—the will in favor of George and Greta, or the will in favor of Steve? Does your answer affect your evaluation of the wisdom of the common law rule that does not imply survivorship conditions? That is, should we devise rules (or presumptions) for the more common case, even if applying those presumptions might frustrate the intent of a trust settlor in a less common case?

5. Suppose Richard Uchtorff had died owing $1,000,000 to a collection of creditors, all of whom had filed claims against his estate. At Pearl's death, how would the trust principal have been distributed? How would the principal have been distributed if the court had implied a condition of survivorship? See Jones v. Hill, 267 Va. 708, 594 S.E.2d 913 (2004) [refusing to imply survivorship condition, and permitting creditors to reach vested interest of deceased beneficiary]; Estate of Sinner, 2006 WL 2872978 (Iowa App. 2006) [same].

6. In Uchtorff, the bank, as trustee, sought instructions about how the trust property should be distributed. Suppose, instead, that the bank (or another trustee), had decided on its own (or on advice of counsel) what the trust instrument meant, and had distributed the property accordingly. If one of the beneficiaries then challenged the bank's construction, and was successful, would the trustee be personally liable for that beneficiary's share? See Estate of Silsby, 914 A.2d 703 (Me.2006).

NOTE ON THE PRESUMPTION IN FAVOR OF EARLY VESTING

Common law courts developed a presumption in favor of early vesting for several reasons. See generally Edward H. Rabin, The Law Favors The Vesting of Estates: Why?, 65 Colum. L. Rev. 467 (1965). First, at common law, vested interests were alienable; contingent interests were not. As a result, if an owner of land devised that land "to my wife for life, remainder to my daughter," the wife and daughter could combine to sell the land to an eager party—so long as the daughter's remainder was treated as vested. If, however, the daughter's remainder were treated as contingent (on surviving her mother), then no group of people could have joined together to sell the land—no matter how advantageous a sale would have been to all of the parties involved. In that environment, it is hardly surprising that courts embraced a presumption in favor of early vesting. Today, in the large majority of states (although by no means in all), contingent interests are freely alienable, reducing the pressure for a presumption in favor of early vesting. Moreover, to the extent that, today, most property subject to future interests is property held in trust, with a trustee who enjoys power to sell the property, concerns about alienability provide even less support for the presumption in favor of early vesting.

Second, as we shall see, the Rule Against Perpetuities invalidates future interests if they do not "vest" within the Rule's period. As a result, a presumption in favor of early vesting operated to save some number of future interests from invalidity under the Rule. This reason for the presumption in favor of early vesting still exists today—but only in those cases where there is some prospect that an interest might otherwise be invalid under the Rule.

Third, vested remainders accelerated into possession upon premature termination of preceding estates; contingent remainders did not. See generally Patricia J. Roberts, The Acceleration of Remainders: Manipulating the Identity of the Remaindermen, 42 S.C. L. Rev. 295, 302–03 (1991). As a result, by construing a remainder as vested, courts could avoid the prospect of undisposed of property. For instance, suppose T's will devised property to his sister S for life, remainder at the sister's death to testator's brother, B, if B survived, and otherwise to B's child, C. Suppose S disclaimed her interest. Who would now be entitled to possession? Since B had not yet satisfied the condition precedent, B's remainder could not accelerate into possession. By contrast, if T had created a vested remainder in B, B's interest would accelerate into possession. Today, disclaimer statutes generally deal with this problem by treating the disclaiming beneficiary as if she predeceased testator. See, e.g., Uniform Probate Code § 2–1106(b)(3)(B).

Finally, vested remainders were not subject to the common law rule that contingent remainders were destructible—a rule abolished virtually everywhere.

Even at common law, the presumption in favor of early vesting had one significant cost (other than frequent frustration of testator's intent): early vesting required trust remainders to pass through the deceased beneficiary's estate:

Susan F. French, Imposing a General Survival Requirement on Beneficiaries of Future Interests: Solving the Problems Caused by the Death of a Beneficiary Before the Time Set for Distribution, 27 Ariz. L. Rev. 801, 804–05 (1985).

Although distributing the property to the donee's estate presents many attractive features, it is both cumbersome and costly. It is cumbersome because the probate process itself is cumbersome, and to make matters worse, the beneficiary may die long before the property becomes distributable. Too often, the future interest was not recognized as an asset of the beneficiary's estate, and a probate must be opened or reopened years later to receive and then distribute the property.

The process is costly for several reasons. First, the administrative expense of the probate must be paid. Second, the value of the future interest is taxable as part of the beneficiary's estate. Third, it exposes the property to the claims of the beneficiary's creditors and the claims of forced or pretermitted heirs.

See also Laura E. Cunningham, The Hazards of Tinkering with the Common Law of Future Interests, 48 Hastings L.J. 667, 698–99 (1997); Jesse Dukeminier, The Uniform Probate Code Upends the Law of Remainders, 94 Mich. L. Rev. 148, 161–62 (1995).

"Transmissible" Remainders and the Estate Tax

In creating a presumption in favor of early vesting, one of the factors common law courts did *not* have to worry about—at least until 1916—was the estate tax. For many modern-day testators and their lawyers, however, the estate tax is of critical importance. And the presumption in favor of early vesting can have disastrous tax consequences for testator's family if testator's lawyer isn't careful about the drafting of future interests.

The problem is this: if, at decedent's death, decedent holds a "transmissible" future interest, that future interest will be included in the decedent's estate for federal estate tax purposes, even if decedent never enjoyed use or possession of the property during her lifetime. If, on the other hand, decedent does not hold a "transmissible" future interest, the future interest will not be included in decedent's estate.

How do we determine whether a future interest is transmissible? The question is whether decedent's interest terminated with his death (in which case it is not taxable as an asset of his estate), or whether he can pass it on to others, in which case it will be taxed in his estate.

> ***Example 8:*** *T devises property in trust, income to be paid to his sister S, for life, remainder to his brother B. B dies before S. B's remainder was not conditioned on surviving S. As a result, the remainder is an asset of B's estate, and will pass under the terms of his will, or by intestate succession. Since the remainder was transmissible by B, the remainder would have been included in B's estate.*
>
> ***Example 9:*** *T devises property in trust, income to be paid to his sister S, for life, remainder to his brother B, but if B fails to survive S, then to B's daughter D. B dies before S. Because B's remainder was conditioned on surviving S, B had nothing to transfer at his death. The remainder was not transmissible, so the remainder would not have been included in B's estate.*

Not all remainders classified as vested will be considered transmissible. Some remainders may be vested, but not transmissible. In Example 9, we might say that B's remainder was vested subject to complete divestment—rather than contingent—but even though the remainder was vested, it was not transmissible because it terminated at B's death. Conversely, it is possible for a contingent remainder to be transmissible. Consider the following:

> ***Example 10:*** *T devises property "to A for life, then to B if A survives to age 90." B dies when A is 70 years old. B's remainder is still contingent, but B has something to transfer. The interest is transmissible, and would therefore be included in B's estate. Note, however, that only the present value of the future interest would be included in the estate.*

How much does it matter whether T creates a transmissible remainder? It can matter a lot. Reconsider Examples 9 and 10. In Example 9, the corpus of T's trust will be taxed in T's estate, and the present value of the remainder interest will be taxed again in B's estate at the time of B's death. By contrast, in Example 10, the corpus will only be taxed in T's estate; because B's remainder is not transmissible, it will not be taxed in B's estate. The general drafting lesson, then, is to avoid transmissible remainders whenever possible.

Should this tax planning principle cause courts to abandon the presumption in favor of early vesting? That is, would most testators, if they thought about the matter, prefer to have their wills and trust instruments construed to avoid taxation, or to preserve early vesting? Cf. Edward C. Halbach & Lawrence W. Waggoner, The UPC's New Survivorship and Antilapse Provisions, 55 Alb. L. Rev. 1091, 1133 (1992) [noting tax advantages of UPC provision eliminating early vesting].

For a discussion of the tax issue, see the majority and dissenting opinions of the Pennsylvania Supreme Court in In re Estate of Houston, 414 Pa. 579, 201 A.2d 592 (1964), where millions of dollars in taxation turned on whether the court construed an ambiguous remainder as "vested" or "contingent." By the way, the will in Estate of Houston had been drafted by a prominent Philadelphia law firm. Fortunately for the firm (but not necessarily for the estate!), the Houston case was decided before the modern revolution in legal malpractice.

There is, however, one caveat to the general principle that testators should avoid transmissible remainders: beware the Generation–Skipping Transfer Tax. Because the GST Tax often has a marginal rate even higher than the estate tax, a testator must be careful, while avoiding transmissible remainders, also to avoid creating "skip" transactions in excess of the exemption from the GST Tax. See generally Laura E. Cunningham, The Hazards of Tinkering with The Common Law of Future Interests: The California Experience, 48 Hastings L.J. 667, 687 (1997).

Statutory Modification of the Common Law Rule

Dissatisfaction with the presumption in favor of early vesting—both because of its adverse tax consequences and because of the occasional need for reprobating estates—has led to proposals for change. Iowa Trust Code § 633.4701 (now § 633A.4701), quoted and discussed in Uchtorff v. Hanson, reverses the common law rule against implied conditions of survivorship. The statute provides a rule of construction; it applies "unless otherwise specifically stated by the terms of the trust."

Why didn't the Iowa statute mandate affirmance of the district court's determination in Uchtorff? What language is necessary to overcome the statute's presumption that future interests are contingent on survivorship until the date on which the beneficiary becomes entitled to possession or enjoyment? Reconsider Problem 3 after the Uchtorff opinion. In which circumstances would the statute mandate a departure from the common-law result?

When a well-drafted trust instrument includes an express condition of survivorship, the instrument will generally dictate how the beneficiary's interest should be distributed if the beneficiary does not survive until the date of distribution. But a trust instrument that includes no express condition is not likely to include instructions about how to distribute the property when a beneficiary does not survive until distribution. As a result, if a statute (or a court) implies a condition of survivorship, the statute must set forth principles for distributing property of beneficiaries who do not satisfy survivorship conditions.

Statutes that imply survivorship requirements into gifts of future interests typically assume that the grantor would want issue of a deceased beneficiary to enjoy the property that would have passed to the beneficiary if the beneficiary had survived. In this respect, these statutes resemble antilapse statutes, which deal with will beneficiaries who fail to survive a testator. Iowa Trust Code § 633A.4701(3) is illustrative. It provides:

> If a beneficiary dies prior to becoming entitled to possession or enjoyment of the beneficiary's interest and no alternate beneficiary is named in the trust, and the beneficiary has issue who are living on the date the interest becomes possessory, the issue of the beneficiary who are living on such date shall receive the interest of the beneficiary.

Note that the statute applies only when "no alternate beneficiary is named in the trust." If an alternate beneficiary is named, then the property passes to that alternate beneficiary, not to issue of the deceased beneficiary. The Iowa statute also includes a qualification to the principle that issue of deceased beneficiaries receive their deceased parent's share: the principle does not apply when the beneficiary's interest is subject to an express condition of survivorship. Iowa Trust Code § 633A.4701(8), provides:

> Subsections 2, 3, 4, 5, 6, and 7 do not apply to any interest subject to an express condition of survivorship imposed by the terms of the trust. For the purposes of this section, words of survivorship including, but not limited to, "my surviving children", "if a person survives" a named period, and terms of like import, shall be construed to create an express condition of survivorship. Words of survivorship include language requiring survival to the distribution date or to any earlier or unspecified time, whether those words are expressed in condition precedent, condition subsequent, or any other form.

PROBLEM

T's will devises $100,000 to a trust, and directs the trustee to distribute trust income to T's sister S for so long as S lives. The instrument provides further that when S dies, the trust should terminate, and the trust principal should be distributed

> (Case 1) "to my daughter, D."
>
> (Case 2) "to my daughter, D, if she survives S."
>
> (Case 3) "to my daughter, D, if she survives S, and if she does not, to her issue, per stirpes."

In the residuary clause of T's will, she leaves "the residue of my estate to the Trustees of Williams College."

Suppose D survives T, but dies before S. Suppose further that D's will left all of her property to her husband, E, and that she died survived by E, and by her two children, F and G.

In Cases 1, 2, and 3, how should the $100,000 be distributed (a) at common law; and (b) under the Iowa statute?

Uniform Probate Code § 2–707

Like the Iowa statute, the Uniform Probate Code reverses the common law presumption that a future interest is vested unless the grantor specifies otherwise. Also like the Iowa statute, the UPC permits the share of a deceased beneficiary to pass to the beneficiary's descendants.

The UPC, however, goes beyond making most future interests contingent on survival; it also changes significantly the effect of trust language designed expressly to create a survivorship condition. That is, suppose S's trust instrument provides "to my wife, W, for life, remainder to my cousin C, if she survives W." At common law, C would be entitled to take only if C survived W. Otherwise, the trust property would, at W's death, pass back to S's estate, and ultimately through the residuary clause of S's will, or through intestate succession. The Iowa statute would mandate the same result (see Iowa Trust Code § 633A.4701(8), supra). By contrast, UPC § 2–707 would instead create a substitute gift in favor of C's descendants—even though the language of S's trust instrument expressly requires C to survive W!

At first glance, the statute seems absurd. Many have concluded that even in the final analysis, the statute represents a colossal mistake. See David M. Becker, Eroding the Common Law Paradigm for the Creation of Property Interests and the Hidden Costs of Law Reform, 83 Wash. U. L. Q. 773 (2005); David M. Becker, Uniform Probate Code Section 2–707 and the Experienced Estate Planner: Unexpected Disasters and How to Avoid Them, 47 U.C.L.A. L. Rev. 339 (1999); Jesse Dukeminier, The Uniform Probate Code Upends the Law of Remainders, 94 Mich. L. Rev. 148 (1995). But the statute does have some advantages. In particular, the statute reduces the number of transmissible remainders testators might inadvertently create. See Lawrence W. Waggoner, The Uniform Probate Code Extends Antilapse–Type Protection to Poorly Drafted Trusts, 94 Mich. L. Rev. 2309 (1996); Edward C. Halbach & Lawrence W. Waggoner, The UPC's New Survivorship and Antilapse Provisions, 55 Alb. L. Rev. 1091 (1992). As a result, the statute might reduce the tax bills of estates served by poorly-trained lawyers. To the extent that modern probate reform seeks to remove the premium on hiring a good lawyer, UPC 2–707 makes some sense. But see Laura E. Cunningham, The Hazards of Tinkering with the Common Law of Future Interests: the California Experience, 48 Hastings L.J. 667, 698 (1997) [noting that the statute's primary benefit inures to affluent beneficiaries who have hired sloppy lawyers, while less affluent beneficiaries might be the primary losers]. Might the statute also have the potential to turn currently competent lawyers into incompetents if they don't adjust to the statutory change? See David M. Becker, Uniform

Probate Code § 2–707 and the Experienced Estate Planner: Unexpected Disasters and How to Avoid Them, 47 U.C.L.A. L. Rev. 339, 348, 384–86 (1999).

Navigating through the statute is no easy matter. The statute's most critical provisions are in section 2–707(b). Focus on those provisions in working through the problems that follow the statute. For now, you may skim over 2–707(b)(2), which deals with class gifts. We will return to that section shortly.

* * *

UNIFORM PROBATE CODE

SECTION 2–707. SURVIVORSHIP WITH RESPECT TO FUTURE INTERESTS UNDER TERMS OF TRUST; SUBSTITUTE TAKERS.

(a) [Definitions.] In this section:

(1) "Alternative future interest" means an expressly created future interest that can take effect in possession or enjoyment instead of another future interest on the happening of one or more events, including survival of an event or failure to survive an event, whether an event is expressed in condition-precedent, condition-subsequent, or any other form. A residuary clause in a will does not create an alternative future interest with respect to a future interest created in a nonresiduary devise in the will, whether or not the will specifically provides that lapsed or failed devises are to pass under the residuary clause.

(2) "Beneficiary" means the beneficiary of a future interest and includes a class member if the future interest is in the form of a class gift.

(3) "Class member" includes an individual who fails to survive the distribution date but who would have taken under a future interest in the form of a glass gift had he [or she] survived the distribution date.

(4) "Descendants", in the phrase "surviving descendants" of a deceased beneficiary or class member in subsections (b)(1) and (b)(2), mean the descendants of a deceased beneficiary or class member who would take under a class gift created in the trust.

(5) "Distribution date," with respect to a future interest, means the time when the future interest is to take effect in possession or enjoyment. The distribution date need not occur at the beginning or end of a calendar day, but can occur at a time during the course of a day.

(6) "Future interest" includes an alternative future interest and a future interest in the form of a class gift.

(7) "Future interest under the terms of a trust" means a future interest that was created by a transfer creating a trust or to an existing trust or by an exercise of a power of appointment to an existing trust, directing the continuance of an existing trust, designating a beneficiary of an existing trust, or creating a trust.

(8) "Surviving", in the phrase "surviving beneficiaries" or "surviving descendants", means beneficiaries or a descendants who neither prede-

ceased the distribution date nor are deemed to have predeceased the distribution date under Section 2–702.

(b) [Survivorship Required; Substitute Gift.] A future interest under the terms of a trust is contingent on the beneficiary's surviving the distribution date. If a beneficiary of a future interest under the terms of a trust fails to survive the distribution date, the following apply:

(1) Except as provided in paragraph (4), if the future interest is not in the form of a class gift and the deceased beneficiary leaves surviving descendants, a substitute gift is created in the beneficiary's surviving descendants. They take by representation the property to which the beneficiary would have been entitled had the beneficiary survived the distribution date.

(2) Except as provided in paragraph (4), if the future interest is in the form of a class gift, other than a future interest to "issue," "descendants," "heirs of the body," "heirs," "next of kin," "relatives," or "family," or a class described by language of similar import, a substitute gift is created in the surviving descendants of any deceased beneficiary. The property to which the beneficiaries would have been entitled had all of them survived the distribution date passes to the surviving beneficiaries and the surviving descendants of the deceased beneficiaries. Each surviving beneficiary takes the share to which he [or she] would have been entitled had the deceased beneficiaries survived the distribution date. Each deceased beneficiary's surviving descendants who are substituted for the deceased beneficiary take by representation the share to which the deceased beneficiary would have been entitled had the deceased beneficiary survived the distribution date. For the purposes of this paragraph, "deceased beneficiary" means a class member who failed to survive the distribution date and left one or more surviving descendants.

(3) For the purposes of Section 2–701, words of survivorship attached to a future interest are not, in the absence of additional evidence, a sufficient indication of an intent contrary to the application of this section. Words of survivorship include words of survivorship that relate to the distribution date or to an earlier or an unspecified time, whether those words of survivorship are expressed in condition-precedent, condition-subsequent, or any other form.

(4) If the governing instrument creates an alternative future interest with respect to a future interest for which a substitute gift is created by paragraph (1) or (2), the substitute gift is superseded by the alternative future interest

if:

(A) the alternative future interest is in the form of a class gift and one or more members of the class is entitled to take in possession or enjoyment; or

(B) the alternative future interest is not in the form of a class gift and the expressly designated beneficiary of the alternative future interest is entitled to take in possession or enjoyment.

(c) [More Than One Substitute Gift; Which One Takes.] If, under subsection (b), substitute gifts are created and not superseded with respect to more than one future interest and the future interests are alternative future interests, one to the other, the determination of which of the substitute gifts takes effect is resolved as follows:

(1) Except as provided in paragraph (2), the property passes under the primary substitute gift.

(2) If there is a younger-generation future interest, the property passes under the younger-generation substitute gift and not under the primary substitute gift.

(3) In this subsection:

(A) "Primary future interest" means the future interest that would have taken effect had all the deceased beneficiaries of the alternative future interests who left surviving descendants survived the distribution date.

(B) "Primary substitute gift" means the substitute gift created with respect to the primary future interest.

(C) "Younger-generation future interest" means a future interest that

(i) is to a descendant of a beneficiary of the primary future interest,

(ii) is an alternative future interest with respect to the primary future interest,

(iii) is a future interest for which a substitute gift is created, and

(iv) would have taken effect had all the deceased beneficiaries who left surviving descendants survived the distribution date except the deceased beneficiary or beneficiaries of the primary future interest.

(D) "Younger-generation substitute gift" means the substitute gift created with respect to the younger-generation future interest.

(d) [If No Other Takers, Property Passes Under Residuary Clause or to Transferor's Heirs.] Except as provided in subsection (e), if, after the application of subsections (b) and (c), there is no surviving taker, the property passes in the following order:

(1) if the trust was created in a nonresiduary devise in the transferor's will or in a codicil to the transferor's will, the property passes under the residuary clause in the transferor's will; for purposes of this section, the residuary clause is treated as creating a future interest under the terms of a trust.

(2) if no taker is produced by the application of paragraph (1), the property passes to the transferor's heirs under Section 2–711.

(e) [If No Other Takers and If Future Interest Created by Exercise of Power of Appointment.] If, after the application of subsections (b) and (c), there is no surviving taker and if the future interest was created by the exercise of a power of appointment:

(1) the property passes under the donor's gift-in-default clause, if any, which clause is treated as creating a future interest under the terms of a trust; and

(2) if no taker is produced by the application of paragraph (1), the property passes as provided in subsection (d). For purposes of subsection (d), "transferor" means the donor if the power was a nongeneral power and means the donee if the power was a general power.

* * * * *

NOTES AND QUESTIONS

1. UPC § 2–707 applies only to future interests "under the terms of a trust." It does not apply to future interests that follow legal life estates. Why distinguish between the two situations? The statute's drafters offered the following rationale in the official comment:

> The rationale for restricting this section to future interests under the terms of a trust is that legal life estates in land, followed by indefeasibly vested remainder interests, are still created in some localities, often with respect to farmland. In such cases, the legal life tenant and the person holding the remainder interest can, together, give good title in the sale of the land. If the antilapse idea were injected into this type of situation, the ability of the parties to sell the land would be impaired if not destroyed because the antilapse idea would, in effect, create a contingent substitute remainder interest in the present and future descendants of the person holding the remainder interest.

2. If UPC § 2–707 had been in effect, would the statute have changed the result in Uchtorff v. Hanson?

PROBLEMS

1. Frank Barone's will devises $100,000 in trust, income to be paid to his wife Marie for her life, remainder at Marie's death to his son Raymond. The will leaves the remainder of Frank's estate to the Police Athletic League. Raymond dies before Marie. Under UPC § 2–707, how would the trust principal be distributed at Marie's death if

(a) Raymond died childless, with a will leaving his entire estate to his wife, Debra? [Hint: examine UPC § 2–707(b)]

(b) Raymond died survived by three children, Ally, Michael, and Geoffrey, and a will leaving his entire estate to his wife, Debra? [Hint: examine UPC § 2–707(b)(1)].

Which of your answers would be different, and how, if UPC § 2–707 were not in effect? What do you think Frank would have wanted? Raymond? Do we care what Raymond wanted?

2. Assume the same facts as in Problem 1, except that the will provides that the trust remainder should be paid, at Marie's death, "to my son Raymond, if he survives Marie." [Hint: examine UPC § 2–707(b)(3)].

3. Again, assume the same facts as in Problem 1, except that the remainder is to be paid, at Marie's death, "to my son, Raymond, if he survives Marie, and if he does not, then to my other son, Robert." Assume

(a) Robert survives Marie.

(b) Robert dies before Marie, leaving a child, Carl, and a will disposing of his entire estate to his wife, Amy.

(c) Robert dies before Marie, childless, intestate, and survived by his wife, Amy. [Hint: examine UPC 2–707(b)(4)].

B. Express Conditions of Survival

We have seen that in general, the common law did not, in the absence of language to the contrary, require the holder of a future interest to survive until the interest became possessory. Suppose, however, the testator wanted to require survival. What language would suffice for that purpose? Consider the following case:

Matter of Krooss

Court of Appeals of New York, 1951.
302 N.Y. 424, 99 N.E.2d 222.

■ Fuld, J.

Herman Krooss died in 1932. He was survived by his wife Eliese and his two children, a son, John Krooss, and a married daughter, Florence Maue. By his will, he gave his residuary estate, real and personal, to his wife, "to have and to hold the same for and during the term of her natural life," with the power to use any part of it for her support and maintenance that she deemed necessary; no trust was created. The will further provided:

> "Upon the death of my beloved wife, Eliese Krooss, I then give, devise and bequeath all the rest, residue and remainder of my estate, as well real as personal, and wheresoever situate, to my beloved children, John H. Krooss and Florence Maue, nee Krooss, share and share alike, to and for their own use absolutely and forever.
>
> In the event that either of my children aforesaid should die prior to the death of my beloved wife, Eliese Krooss, leaving descendants, then it is my wish and I so direct that such descendants shall take the share their parent would have taken if then living, share and share alike, to and for their own use absolutely and forever."

Florence Maue died, without having had descendants, in 1947, three years before the life beneficiary Eliese. Some months after Eliese's death, Florence's husband, as executor of his wife's estate, instituted the present proceeding in the Surrogate's Court of Bronx County to compel John Krooss, as executor under Eliese's will and as administrator c.t.a. of Herman Krooss' estate, to render and settle his respective accounts. In order to determine whether the executors of Florence's estate had status to prosecute the proceeding, the surrogate was required, initially, to construe Herman's will. He decided that the interest given to Florence was vested at the testator's death, subject to be divested only in the event of her predeceasing her mother leaving descendants, that it passed under her will, and that her husband, as executor, was entitled to bring the action.[4] The Appellate Division modified that determination. Disagreeing with the surrogate's interpretation, the Appellate Division construed the will as imposing upon each of the remaindermen a condition that he or she survive the life beneficiary; Florence having died without children before Eliese, that condition was not met, and, concluded the court, as to Florence's share in the remainder, Krooss died intestate.

The law has long favored a construction of language in deed and will that accomplishes the vesting of estates; such a result is preferred because, among other things, it enables property to be freely transferred at the earliest possible date. (See, e.g., Matter of Watson, 262 N.Y. 284, 300; Dougherty v. Thompson, 167 N.Y. 472, 483; Connelly v. O'Brien, 166 N.Y. 406, 408; Hersee v. Simpson, 154 N.Y. 496, 502; McArthur v. Scott, 113 U.S. 340, 378.) Accordingly, the courts are intent upon restricting defeating events to the exact circumstances specified.

The will under consideration is simple in language and simple in plan. The testator gave his widow a life estate and a power to use the principal if it proved necessary for her maintenance and support. What remained after her death he gave "absolutely and forever" in equal shares to his two children, Florence and John. Had the will stopped at that point, there would be no question that the remainders were vested. And, since that is so, additional language will not be read as qualifying or cutting down the estate unless that language is as clear and decisive as that which created the vested remainder. (See, e.g., Goodwin v. Coddington, 154 N.Y. 283, 286; Byrnes v. Stilwell, 103 N.Y. 453, 460.) The further language used by the testator in this case demonstrates, not that he was rendering the vesting of the estates in his children conditional upon survival of the life beneficiary, but that he was willing to have those estates divested only upon the combined occurrences of two further events. He explicitly provided, if either of his children died before his wife, "leaving descendants," then "such descendants shall take the share the parent would have taken if then

4. In her will, Florence left her residuary estate in trust to her husband and to her brother John, as trustees, to pay the net income therefrom to the husband for life; on his death, the principal was to be distributed between Florence's two nephews, the children of her brother John, if living, and to their issue per stirpes if either should die before the termination of the trust.

living". If the words used mean what they say, then, divestiture of the remainder estates depended upon the happening of two plainly expressed and stipulated conditions: (1) the child, Florence or John, must die before the life beneficiary, and (2) the child so dying must leave descendants. Only if both of those conditions came to pass was the remainder—by apt and unequivocal language already vested in Florence and John—to be divested and bestowed instead upon the descendants of him or her who might have died.

When a will contains language that has acquired, through judicial decision, a definite and established significance, the testator is taken to have employed that language in that sense and with that meaning in mind. See, e.g., Matter of Wittner, 301 N.Y. 461, 465; Manion v. Peoples Bank of Johnstown, 292 N.Y. 317, 321; Washbon v. Cope, 144 N.Y. 287, 297–298; Keteltas v. Keteltas, 72 N.Y. 312, 314–315; Livingston v. Greene, 52 N.Y. 118, 124; see, also, 2 Page on Wills, § 916, pp. 793–794; 1 Davids, New York Law of Wills, § 492, p. 806. The thought was well expressed by this court in the Keteltas case (supra, 72 N.Y. 312, 314–315):

> "The primary object in construing wills is to ascertain the intention of the testator, and when that has been ascertained, it is to be implicitly obeyed, however informal the language in which such intention has been conveyed. But the intention is not matter of speculation or arbitrary conjecture. It is sought for in the language used; and when language or a certain collocation of words has once received judicial construction, precedents are formed which are followed in later cases. It is a general rule of construction that when a testator uses technical words, he is presumed to employ them in their legal sense, and that words in general are to be taken in their ordinary and grammatical sense unless the context clearly indicates the contrary."

Over the years, the courts have uniformly held that language such as that used by the testator here, or language substantially identical, creates a vested remainder in fee subject to be divested by the remainderman's failing to survive the life beneficiary, if, but only if, such remainderman leaves issue or descendants surviving. (See, e.g., Staples v. Mead, 214 N.Y. 625, affg. 159 App. Div. 922, 152 App. Div. 745, 144 N.Y.S. 1146, 137 N.Y.S. 847; Byrnes v. Stilwell, supra, 103 N.Y. 453; Livingston v. Greene, supra, 52 N.Y. 118; Smiley v. Bailey, 59 Barb. 80; Flanagan v. Staples, 28 App. Div. 319; Gray v. Garman, 2 Hare 268; Matter of Bright's Trust, 21 Beav. 67; Remmers v. Remmers, 280 Ill. 93; see, also, Note, 109 A.L.R. 5.) Staples v. Mead (supra, 214 N.Y. 625, affg. 159 App. Div. 922, 152 App. Div. 745) furnishes a helpful precedent. The testator gave the residue of his estate to executors in trust for the life of his wife, with directions to pay one third of the income to her, one third to her daughter Sarah and one third to grandchildren of testator, living at his death and to the estate of any grandchild who died leaving issue. The will further provided that, upon the death of the wife, the trust was to continue for the life of the daughter, with income payable one half to the daughter and the other half to the grandchildren and the issue of deceased grandchildren. The will then went on to provide that "upon the death of my said daughter I then give, devise and bequeath my entire estate unto my grandchildren and to the issue of any grandchild who may have died *leaving issue* * * * share and share alike." (Emphasis supplied.) A grandchild, John Mead, died during Sarah's lifetime. Just as did Florence in the case before us, John left a will and no issue. Plaintiffs claimed that the grandchild John took a vested remainder, subject to be divested only upon his death leaving issue; accordingly, plaintiffs urged, upon John's death without issue his estate remained vested and passed under his will. It was the defendants' contention that the interest given to John ceased if he died before the termination of the life estate, and, since that did occur, the estate that would otherwise have gone to John went to the other grandchildren who survived the life tenant. The Appellate Division held—and the Court of Appeals affirmed on appeal from both the final judgment (159 App. Div. 922, 144 N.Y.S. 1146) and the interlocutory judgment (152 App. Div. 745, 137 N.Y.S. 847)—that the will bestowed a vested remainder upon the grandchild John and that such remainder was defeated only if he (1) died before his mother and (2) left issue. In the course of its opinion, the court wrote (152 App. Div., at pp. 748–749):

> "It is true that the death of John * * * before his mother, leaving issue, was a contingency upon which his estate might have been divested, and vested in his issue; but this was not an event upon which the vesting in him depended. (Doscher v. Wyckoff, 132 App. Div. 139, 142.) 'It was not a gift limited to take effect upon an uncertain event; it was a gift, which the uncertain event might chance to defeat.' (Stringer v. Young, 191 N.Y. 157, 162.) The event in this case, the death of the donee leaving issue, did not happen, and his gift was not defeated, but remained vested." (Emphasis supplied.)

Leading commentators in the field, after reviewing the cases, have expressed themselves in similar fashion. (See 2 Powell on Real Property [1950], §§ 330–331, pp. 728–737; 2 Redfield on Law of Wills [1866], § 65, pp. 648–649; 3 Restatement, Property, § 254, Comment a, Illustration 1, particularly Example II, pp. 1284–1286.) Thus, Professor Richard R. Powell of Columbia University Law School and Reporter on Property for the American Law Institute, in his recent work on the Law of Real Property, considers the subject at some length and sums up the law in this way (op. cit., § 330, pp. 729–730):

> "Supplanting limitations differ, in that some provide a taker who is to become the substitute whenever the prior taker fails to survive, while others provide a taker who is to become the substitute only under some circumstances. In cases of the second type, the constructional preference for early indefeasibility causes the requirement of survival to be strictly construed, and to operate only under the exact circumstances stipulated. * * * Similarly, in a gift 'to my wife B for life, then to my children and the issue of those of my children who may be dead leaving children,' the interest of a child of the testator who dies without surviving issue is indefeasible."

Turning to the will before us, we find that, at the expiration of the wife's life estate, the testator "then" gave the remainder to his children "absolutely and forever." The use of the word "then" as an "adverb of time" must be, as it long has been, construed to relate solely "to the time of enjoyment of the estate, and not to the time of its vesting in interest." (Staples v. Mead, supra, 152 App. Div. 745, 749, affd. 214 N.Y. 625.) Hence, the sole combination of events which could divest the "absolute" gift to the daughter Florence was her death before her mother, "leaving descendants". Only one of the specified conditions was fulfilled; although Florence did predecease her mother, she did not leave descendants. Consequently, her absolute gift remained vested and was not defeated. Not only the language employed, but the omission of any "words of survivorship" (Byrnes v. Stilwell, supra, 103 N.Y. 453, 459) to indicate an intent that Florence's brother was to take if Florence died without children, illumines the testator's design to give his daughter a vested remainder.

* * *

The order of the Appellate Division should be reversed and the decree of the Surrogate's Court affirmed, with costs in this court and in the Appellate Division to all parties, appearing separately and filing separate briefs, payable out of the estate.

QUESTIONS

1. Suppose, instead of the first paragraph quoted from Herman Krooss's will, Krooss's will had included the following paragraph:

> Upon the death of my beloved wife, Eliese Krooss, I devise the rest of my estate to my beloved children John and Florence, if they survive my wife, share and share alike.

Suppose this paragraph had been followed, verbatim, by the second paragraph the court quotes in its opinion. How would Herman Krooss's estate have been distributed? Why? Do these paragraphs suggest an intent materially different from the intent suggested by Krooss's actual will? Cf. Estate of Corwith, 163 Misc.2d 831, 622 N.Y.S.2d 424 (1995).

2. Do you think the result in Krooss advanced testator's intent? Was the content of Florence's will relevant? Suppose Florence had left her estate to her husband outright, or to her husband's relatives. Are you certain the court would have reached the same construction of Herman's will?

Suppose elsewhere in the will, Herman Krooss had expressed a strong dislike for Florence's husband. Would the court have reached the same result?

3. The court suggests that Herman Krooss's will created a vested remainder subject to complete divestment. How would you argue that the will created a contingent remainder? Does the classification make a difference in this case?

4. Suppose you were hired to draft Herman Krooss's will. How would you have changed the language to preclude litigation, and to make it clear that his children would take only if they survived Herman's wife? To make it clear that his children would take even if they did not survive Herman's wife?

* * *

In Matter of Krooss, the court had to decide whether testator had imposed a survivorship condition at all. In other cases, it is clear that testator intended to require the beneficiary to survive somebody. The question is *who*. Consider the following problems:

PROBLEMS

1. Kate Webb's will provides:

> "I give and devise to my daughter, Ada W. Sacrison, a life estate, with remainder over at the death of the said Ada W. Sacrison, share and share alike, to my grandsons, Francis Marion Browning and Robert Stanley Browning, or, if either of them be dead, then all to the other."

Kate Webb died in 1954. She was survived by her daughter, Ada, and grandchildren Francis and Robert. Francis died in 1972, survived by his wife and no children, and with a will that left his estate to his wife. Ada died in 1975.

Who has claims to the remainder at Ada's death? How should those claims be resolved? What words would you have added to Kate Webb's will to eliminate any ambiguity and to require that each grandson survive Ada Sacrison, the life tenant?

2. Dewey Bowen's will creates a trust for the benefit of his wife for life. The will then provides:

> "Upon the death of my wife, the Trustee shall pay all of the remaining assets in this Trust or otherwise of the estate in equal shares to my sisters-in-law, namely Maybelle Lawson, Kate Hipkins, and Lois Maynard. In the event that Maybelle or Kate is not in life, then it is my will and desire that their share be added to the share of any surviving sister-in-law. In the event that Lois is not in life, it is my desire that her share shall go to my sister, Nelle Newton, and her two daughters, Dorothy Garrett and Nelle Roots, all on a share and share alike basis per capita."

All three sisters-in-law were alive at Dewey's death, but only Maybelle was alive at the death of Dewey's wife. How should the trust principal be divided, assuming Kate Hipkins' will left all of her property to her husband, Jake; Lois Maynard's will left all of her property to Dorothy Garrett; and Nelle Newton had died with a will leaving all of her property to Dorothy Garrett? See Lemmons v. Lawson, 266 Ga. 571, 468 S.E.2d 749 (1996).

3. Ruby Walker's will created a trust, with directions that during the lifetime of her daughter Joan, the trustee distribute to the daughter "all of the net income of the trust for her lifetime." The will then provided

a. if my grandson, Richard, shall have attained the age of 35 at the time of the death of my daughter, my said grandson shall be paid the entire balance of the trust estate.

b. if my grandson should die prior to attaining the age of thirty-five (35) years, the trust estate shall be paid over to his issue, per stirpes, or, if my grandson should die without issue, to the persons who would take my intestate estate if I had then died intestate.

In 1985, Richard died at the age of 36, not survived by a spouse or issue, and with a will leaving his estate to his friend Zack. Joan died without issue in 2001. At that time, Ruby's closest living relative was her grand-niece, Wendy, granddaughter of her sister. How should the trust property be distributed? See Blue Ridge Bank and Trust Co. v. McFall, 207 S.W.3d 149 (Mo. App. 2006).

4. Florence Chavin's trust instrument provided that

> "upon the death of Settlor, Trustee shall pay over, transfer and convey whatever remains of the trust estate, discharged of the trust, to Settlor's son, LESLIE S. CHAVIN, if he shall then be living. If Settlor's son shall then be deceased, to Settlor's then living issue, per stirpes."

Florence died survived by Leslie and by two grandchildren born to her other son, Favel. Leslie was murdered in Brazil before the trustee distributed the trust estate. Leslie's will left his estate to a cousin. How should the trust proceeds be distributed? See Chavin v. PNC Bank, 816 A.2d 781 (Del. 2003).

SECTION III. CONSTRUCTION OF CLASS GIFTS

Oscar Zilch, who has two children, Abner and Beulah, wants to provide for them in his will. He can do so by making specific, general, or residuary devises to Abner and to Beulah. But suppose Oscar believes he may have more children in the future. How can he account for them, without writing a new will upon the birth of each child?

One might answer that requiring Oscar to write a new will upon the birth of each child would not be particularly onerous, and that pretermitted child statutes will protect afterborns in any event. But the problem extends beyond children. Oscar might want to provide for his nieces and nephews, or his grandchildren. Rather than naming each niece and nephew—and thereby risk excluding nieces and nephews born after execution of the will, Oscar might want to make a *class gift*—a gift to all members of a designated group—rather than making separate gifts to individually named members of the group. And he might want to designate a multi-generational class (issue of my brothers and sisters, rather than nieces and nephews).

Class gifts are convenient, but they must be drafted with care. Class gifts invite construction questions. A hypothetical illustrates the problems that might arise:

Oscar Zilch's will devises property, in trust, income to his sister for life, remainder "to my grandchildren." At Oscar's death, his two children, Abner and Beulah are still alive. Abner has had two children, Charlie and Daphne. After Oscar's death, but before the death of Oscar's sister, Beulah has two children, Edith and Frank. Daphne and Edith die in a tragic automobile accident. At the death of Oscar's sister, Abner and his current wife are contemplating starting a new family. At Oscar's sister's death, who is entitled to the trust principal?

Note that the answer to the question depends on the meaning of the words "my grandchildren." Do they include only grandchildren born before Oscar's death, or do they also include grandchildren born after Oscar's death but before the death of his sister? Do they include grandchildren who might be born after the sister's death? What about grandchildren who die before the death of Oscar's sister?

Careful drafting of the class gift would avoid all of these questions. Unfortunately, not all wills and trust instruments are drafted so carefully. Courts have developed principles of construction to deal with wills and trust instruments that are less-than-explicit about the drafter's intent. The constructional principles also provide a useful background for future drafting. In this section, we explore construction issues that surround class gifts.

A. INCREASE IN CLASS MEMBERSHIP

Suppose testator's will devises $20,000 "to be distributed among my grandchildren." First, consider the easy question: should grandchildren born after execution of the will, but before testator's death, be entitled to share? The answer is yes. By using the word "grandchildren" rather than naming individual grandchildren, testator expressed an intention that the devise not be limited to grandchildren living at the time of will execution. Moreover, no good practical reason exists for excluding grandchildren born by the time of testator's death.

Now, consider the harder question: what about grandchildren born *after* testator's death. Those grandchildren will not be entitled to share in the $20,000. Consider why. Suppose we adopted a rule permitting all grandchildren, whenever born, to share in the $20,000. How much could we distribute to those grandchildren alive at testator's death? If each grandchild would be entitled to an equal share, we have to know how many shares there will be before we can make a distribution. But we will not know definitively how many shares there will be until the death of testator's last surviving child—which may occur long after testator's death. Therefore, if we permitted all grandchildren to share, we could make no distribution to grandchildren living at testator's death. Would that result reflect testator's intent? Almost invariably, the answer is no. When testator makes a devise of $20,000 to her grandchildren, she intends that her grandchildren will receive money at that time—not years later when it is no longer physiologically possible for additional grandchildren to be born.

Vested remainder subject to open

Let's now reduce this insight to a general rule: *when a grantor makes a class gift, membership in the class may continue to increase until at least one member of the class becomes entitled to possession of the property that is the subject of the class gift*. Put another way, the class "closes" when one member of the class becomes entitled to take her share of the property. See generally Edward C. Halbach, Issues About Issue: Some Recurrent Class Gift Problems, 48 Mo. L. Rev. 333, 358–59 (1983). This rule is often called the "*class-closing rule*" or the "*rule of convenience*" (because without the rule, it would often be difficult, or inconvenient, to distribute property subject to a class gift). The Restatement (Third) of Property (Wills and Other Donative Transfers) (Tentative Draft No. 4, 2004), expresses the rule as follows:

Section 15.1 When Class Closes—Rule of Convenience

> Unless the language or circumstances indicate that the transferor had a different intention, a class gift that has not yet closed physiologically closes to future entrants on the distribution date if a beneficiary of the class gift is then entitled to distribution.

The rule applies both to present and future interests. Consider some examples:

> ***Example 11:*** *T's will creates a trust, and directs that income be paid to T's wife for life. T also directs that, at his wife's death, the remainder be distributed "to my grandchildren". At T's death, T has two grandchildren, A and B. After T's death, but before his wife's death, another grandchild, C, is born. It appears likely that one of T's children will have more children after T's wife's death. Who is entitled to share in the trust remainder?*
>
> ***Solution:*** *A, B, and C may share, but additional grandchildren may not. A, B, and C, are entitled to possession at the wife's death. The class-closing rule closes the class of grandchildren at that point, because otherwise, it would be impossible to distribute any amount to A, B, and C.*
>
> ***Example 12:*** *O creates an inter vivos trust, and directs that trust income be used for the education of his son, S, until S graduates from college. Upon S's graduation, O directs that the trust should terminate, and the trust principal should be distributed "to my nieces and nephews." O had one niece, X, at the time the trust was created. O died before S graduated from college, but another niece, Y, was born before O's death. A nephew, Z, was born after O's death but before S's graduation. O's brother appears likely to have more children. Who is entitled to share in the trust principal?*
>
> ***Solution:*** *X, Y, and Z may share. No niece or nephew will be entitled to possession until S's graduation, so the class will not close before that time. No subsequently born niece or nephew will be entitled to take, because if we allowed such nieces or nephews to share, we would not be able to distribute anything to X, Y, and Z until the death of O's last surviving sibling.*

The common law recognizes one significant exception to the class-closing rule: if, at the time an interest is intended to become possessory, no member of the class has yet been born, then the class-closing rule will not apply, and we will wait for the class to close naturally.

Example 13: *T's will creates a trust, and directs that income be paid to T's wife for life. T also directs that, at the wife's death, the remainder be distributed "to my grandchildren". At T's wife's death, T has not yet had any grandchildren. Do we distribute the trust remainder to T's first grandchild as soon as that grandchild is born?*

Solution: *No. The class-closing rule does not apply because no member of the class was born when, by the terms of the instrument, the class gift was designed to become possessory. As a result, the remainder will not be distributed until the death of all of T's children, when the class of grandchildren will close "naturally" or "physiologically."*

Sometimes, a will or trust instrument will provide for distribution when one or more members of the class reach a certain age. When does the class close for those gifts? Consider the following case:

In re Evans' Estate

Supreme Court of Wisconsin, 1957.
274 Wis. 459, 80 N.W.2d 408.

[The third clause of decedent's will provided as follows:

" 'Third, I give, devise and bequeath to my grandchildren the sum of Fifty Thousand Dollars ($50,000), said sum to be placed in trust by my executor in a trust company or a bank exercising trust powers, the income from the principal being allowed to accumulate until said grandchildren shall respectively become of age. After each grandchild becomes of age he is to receive the income which accumulates on his share, said income to be paid to him annually until he reaches the age of thirty years. After each grandchild reaches the age of thirty years he is to be paid his full share of the principal sum of this bequest together with the interest which has accumulated thereon. * * * ' "

At the time of his death, decedent left six grandchildren, four of whom were born prior to the execution of the will and two of whom were born after the execution. In the probate proceedings the court entered a final judgment assigning the sum of $50,000 to the six grandchildren by name. Subsequently but before the eldest of the six attained the age of 30, three additional grandchildren were born. The trustee, having been advised of the birth of such additional grandchildren and being concerned as to whether they might be beneficiaries, brought the present proceedings to construe the final judgment and the will. The lower court held that the final judgment was not binding upon the grandchildren born after the death of the testator, because they were not adequately represented in that proceeding, and construed Article Third of the Will to create a gift vested in the six grandchildren living at the time of death of testator subject to being reopened to admit additional grandchildren, the trust to be divided each time a grandchild reaches the age of 30 on the basis of the number of grandchildren then actually living. The trustee appeals.]

■ FAIRCHILD, CHIEF JUSTICE. Before taking up the question of whether or not the judgment entered April 17, 1942, is *res judicata* as to grandchildren born after the date of death of the testator, it seems well to pass upon the nature and inclusiveness of the bequest. If the gift grant in Article Third is to a class, and that class is so fixed by the terms of the bequest that there may be an interval of time during which the class may increase, then the gift is one which vests in the existing number of the class and such other persons as thereafter become members of the class. That interval continues to the point of time or event which is specified and certain. The gift we are considering is to "my grandchildren," and because of the absence of an alternative gift over or reversion in favor of the testator's heirs, it bespeaks an intention of a vested gift. The grandchildren living at the death of the testator are members of the class, but the class is subject to a change by addition of after-born grandchildren who came into being before the coming of the event which closes forever the membership in the class.

The time fixed for closing the class is set in the bequest: "After each grandchild reaches the age of thirty years, he is to be paid his full share of the principal sum of this bequest together with the interest which has accumulated thereon." This controls the increase in membership in the class. The time of the distribution of the *corpus* settles the question of maximum membership. In the absence of words in the will indicating a contrary intent, a testator would naturally desire to include all grandchildren born at the time of the distribution of the *corpus*. In Simes, The Law of Future Interests, we find the following recognition of rules of construction:

> "The maximum membership in the class is determined when the time for distribution has arrived. The class may increase until that time, and persons born thereafter are excluded." Sec. 634, p. 69.
>
> "The time for distribution arrived when the first member of the class attained the designated age." Sec. 644, p. 89.
>
> In 5 American Law of Property, the following rules are recognized:
>
> "When a class gift is postponed until the occurrence of some event, such as the attainment of age twenty-one, the class does not normally close until the first member of the class attains the designated age." Sec. 22.44, p. 372.
>
> "It must be kept in mind that the probable desire of the average transferor, when he describes his transferees by a group designation, is to benefit as many persons who comply with the description as he can, without at the same time causing too much inconvenience." Sec. 22.43, p. 364.

The gift may be so made that the class may either increase or decrease after the death of the testator until the arrival of the fixed point of time or the happening of the specified event. It may be so worded that there may be an interval of time during which the class may increase but during which it cannot decrease. The most common example of this kind of gift is one which vests in the existing members of a class and in such other persons as thereafter become members of the class up to the point of time or event which is specified. Page on Wills, sec. 1052. It is considered that the three grandchildren born after the death of the testator and before the distribution of the *corpus* are members of the class and inherit as such.

* * *

[In the omitted portion of the opinion the court held that the final judgment in the original probate proceedings was not binding on the afterborn grandchildren, because they were not represented therein by either a guardian ad litem or the existing members of the class (grandchildren already born who had antagonistic interests); hence the defense of res judicata was without merit.]

* * *

Inasmuch as and because the trial court erroneously held that membership in the class opened up each time a new grandchild is born, until such time as the entire trust *corpus* was distributed, the order must be modified to correct this error.

We do not continue a discussion of other questions not necessary for a determination of the material issues.

Order modified so as to provide that membership in the class permanently closed when the oldest grandchild arrived at the age of thirty years, and as so modified it is affirmed. Cause remanded for further proceedings according to law.

QUESTIONS

1. When will the class of grandchildren close in the Evans case? Will all grandchildren be entitled to a distribution of principal at that point?

2. Suppose, at the time when the oldest grandchild reaches the age of 32, and the youngest grandchild is 8, another grandchild is born. Will the newborn grandchild ever be entitled to take a share of the trust principal? Why not?

NOTES

1. How would you classify the interest of decedent's oldest grandchild in the Evans case? Suppose decedent's oldest grandchild dies before reaching age 30. Would that grandchild's estate or successors be entitled to share in the principal?

Note that typically, as the court holds in Evans, a devise to a person "to be paid upon reaching the age of 30" or "when she reaches the age of 30" is not construed to require survivorship until the age of 30. Instead, the interest is construed as a vested interest, and if the devisee does not reach the prescribed age, the devise is payable to the devisee's estate. See, e.g., In re Mansur's Will, 98 Vt. 296, 127 A. 297 (1925); Clobberie's Case, 2 Vent. 342, 86 Eng.Rep. 476 (1677).

2. Professor Frederick Schneider reports that at the time the Evans case was decided, Wisconsin had a statutory Rule Against Perpetuities that required interests to vest within lives in being plus 30 years—which explains the particular age contingency used in the Evans will. In jurisdictions that follow the common law Rule Against Perpetuities, it would have been even more important to construe the interests of grandchildren as vested, because if the interest of each grandchild was contingent upon surviving to the age of 30, the entire interest in grandchildren would have been invalid.

3. The class-closing rule applied in the Evans case is a rule of construction. If, in a particular case, the grantor manifests an intent that the class close earlier—or not until the class closes physiologically—the intent of the grantor will control.

Sherrod v. Cooper, 65 N.C.App. 252, 308 S.E.2d 904 (1983), is illustrative. Testator's will provided:

> "I will and bequeath to my granddaughters May McLaughlin Sherrod and Elizabeth Llewellyn Sherrod and any unborn children of my son, Watson N. Sherrod, Jr. my farm ... share and share alike. This bequest to be handled by the children's father, Watson N. Sherrod, Jr. as he thinks best until the oldest child shall have reached the age of thirty years...."

In a proceeding to construe the will, the court embraced the proposition, derived from a 1901 case, that with gifts of real estate, if there is no intervening life estate, the class closes at testator's death unless there is clear language to the contrary. The court concluded that the language of the will was not sufficiently clear to establish that the class should remain open until the oldest granddaughter reached age 30. Do you agree?

PROBLEMS

1. Jessie Trevitte devised a tract of land "to John Trevitte for life, and at his death in fee to his children." After Jessie's death, the real estate was sold, and the proceeds were divided. John was paid the value of his life estate; the rest was placed in trust for John's children. John's two children contend that they have a vested interest in the trust income and principal, and seek the principal now. Are they entitled to the principal? See Trevitte v. Trevitte, 1990 WL 73852 (Tenn. App. 1990).

2. Philomena Lux's will leaves the residue of her estate to her grandchildren, and further provides that any real estate in the residue of her estate "shall be maintained for the benefit of my grandchildren and shall not be sold until the youngest of said grandchildren has reached twenty-one years of age." Philomena's son is alive and now 45 years old. If Philomena currently has grandchildren aged 24, 22, and 17, when should the real estate be sold and the proceeds distributed? See Lux v. Lux, 109 R.I. 592, 288 A.2d 701 (1972).

3. Testator's will devises $100,000 in trust, income to be distributed to her husband, H, for life, remainder at H's death "to my nieces and nephews who reach age 21." At H's death, T's parents are dead. Who is entitled to the trust remainder, and when, if, at H's death:

(a) Testator's only brother, B, is alive, and has two children, F, age 14, and G, age 11; after husband's death, the brother has two additional children, J, born 5 years after the husband's death, and K, born 9 years after the husband's death.

(b) Same as (a), except that F dies in an auto accident at age 19.

(c) B has no children at the husband's death, but later has three children—M, N, and O, born 4, 6, and 9 years, respectively, after H's death.

(d) Same as (c) except that O dies at age 20.

(e) Testator's brother has two children, P, age 24 and Q, age 18, at H's death; B has another child, R, born 3 years after H's death.

B. DECREASE IN CLASS MEMBERSHIP: SURVIVORSHIP AGAIN

Suppose testator's will makes a $100,000 devise, in trust, and directs that income be paid to her husband, H, for life. She directs further that upon her husband's death, the trust principal should be distributed "to my children." At first glance, testator's meaning may seem clear enough. There is no chance (putting aside modern technology) that testator will have more children after her death, so we do not have to worry about a potential increase in the class of children.

What happens, however, if one of testator's children dies before H does? Consider the following problem:

PROBLEM

Testator's will directs that, after her husband's death, trust principal be divided among "my children". Testator had three children, A, B, and C. A died before H, leaving a daughter, D, and a will dividing her estate equally between her husband, E, and Valparaiso University. At H's death, who is entitled to the trust principal?

There are three realistic solutions:

1. "Children" means "children," but we impose no survivorship requirement. In other words, we treat the class gift to children in the same way we would treat a gift to three individual children: the three children have an indefeasibly vested interest as soon as their mother dies. As a result, B and C each take one-third of the trust principal; E and Valparaiso share the final third.

2. "Children" means "children," but we impose a survivorship requirement. Since A did not survive H, she did not qualify to take as a child. B and C share the trust principal.

3. "Children" really means "issue." Therefore, D steps into A's shoes and takes A's share. The trust principal is divided equally among B, C, and D.

The most orthodox approach is the first, but as you will see from the following materials, there is considerable support for the other two approaches as well. The Restatement of Property adheres to the orthodox approach, but only after the ALI narrowly rejected an effort to adopt the third approach. See Restatement (Third) of Property (Wills and Other Donative Transfers), § 15.4 (Tentative Draft No. 4, 2004); see also The ALI Reporter, Fall 2004 (reporting on 57–50 vote to reject the third approach). As we shall see, the Uniform Probate Code would endorse the third approach (UPC § 2–707(b)(2)).

Much depends on context. A lawyer litigating a dispute over the meaning of a class gift should look for indicia of the grantor's intent to "tip" the court in her client's favor. A lawyer drafting a will or trust instrument should never draft a class gift to "children" without explanation or clarification. Reconsider the hypothetical devise. How would you redraft the devise to make it clear that testator's intent was to have the trust principal divided in accordance with solutions (1), (2), and (3), respectively?

The problem is not limited to class gifts to children. Gifts to any single-generation class create the possibility of ambiguity when some members of the class die before their interest becomes possessory. In considering the following case, ask yourself how you would have drafted the will to eliminate any ambiguity.

Usry v. Farr

Supreme Court of Georgia, 2001.
274 Ga. 438, 553 S.E.2d 789.

■ FLETCHER, CH. J.

At issue in this appeal is when title to the remainder interest under the will of Watson Usry vested. On summary judgment, the trial court held that the remainder vested at the time of Usry's death and not at the death of the life tenant. Because Usry's will expressed the intention of providing for those who survive him and all five grandchildren survived him, we affirm.

Watson Usry died in 1967. The relevant clause of Usry's will provided successive life estates in his lands, first to his wife Lucille and then to their children, with the remainder to his grandchildren. Usry had three children, the last of whom died in 2000. There are five appellants: the four children of Usry's son Jack, and Jack's widow, Evelyn. Usry's fifth grandson, Hoyt, died in 1970 leaving three young children, all of whom were alive at the time of Usry's death. Hoyt's three children are the appellees. Appellants claim that the remainder vested upon the death of the last life tenant and not upon the death of Usry. Therefore, because they are the only grandchildren who survived the life tenants, they take all lands under the will. Appellees contend that the remainder vested upon Usry's death, and that Hoyt, who survived Usry, had a vested interest under the will, and therefore his children stand in his shoes and take under the will along with appellants.

1. The construction of a will is a question of law for the court. The cardinal rule for construing wills is to ascertain and give effect to the testator's intent. Item Three of the will provided,

> I will, bequeath and devise all of the land, with improvements thereon, which I may own at my death to my Wife, LUCILLE, to be hers for and during her lifetime, and at her death same is to go to my children who may survive my wife, and to my grandchildren with restrictions as follows: Any of my children taking land under this Item shall have a life interest therein, share and share alike, with any grandchildren who take hereunder taking the part which their father or mother would have taken. Upon the death of my last surviving child title in fee simple to said lands shall vest in my grand-children, per stirpes and not per capita.

The first sentence of Item Three establishes a life estate first in Usry's wife Lucille and then in the children who survive Lucille. This sentence imposes a requirement that the children survive Lucille before taking under Item three. In contrast, no requirement that the grandchildren survive the life tenants is imposed. Therefore, at Usry's death, fee simple title vested in his five grandchildren, who were all alive at that time. The possessory interest vested when Usry's son Ned, the last life tenant, died in April 2000. At that time, the grandchildren were entitled to take possession, with the appellees taking the share that had vested in Hoyt.

The testator's intention that the only survivorship requirement apply to his life appears expressly in Item Eight of the will. In that provision, Usry declared that "my entire plan of disposition is the result of a conscientious effort to provide for the welfare of my loved ones who survive me, and to fairly divide and distribute the worldly goods for which I have worked so hard." Because we must construe the will as a whole, we must consider this clause in construing the remainder of the will. Usry's stated intention of providing for those who survive him is fatal to the claim of appellants who would defer vesting well beyond the death of Usry until the conclusion of the life estates.

The dissent's concern that this construction provides an anomalous result is not well-founded. The testator himself decided to leave successive life estates to his widow and children. Obviously, if his children were to enjoy a life estate that followed their mother's life estate, the children had to survive their mother. Because the testator decided that his children were to enjoy only a life estate, there is nothing unusual about his further providing for title to vest in his loved ones who survive him.

2. Usry's express intention with regard to a survivorship requirement is consistent with the statutory rule in Georgia favoring vesting of title as of the time of the testator's death. Appellants contend that the last sentence of Item Three demonstrates an intention that the remainder vest, not at the testator's death, but at the conclusion of the life estates. However, this Court has repeatedly held that virtually identical language is not sufficient to divest the remainder share from one who survives the testator but predeceases the life tenant. In view of the strong preference in Georgia for early vesting, the language required to render a remainder contingent upon surviving the life tenant must be clear and unambiguous. The last sentence of Item Three fails to meet this standard when considered along with Item Eight. To the extent that this sentence would permit a construction favoring a contingent remainder, it must give way to the construction favoring a vested remainder, where both constructions are possible.

We construe the final sentence of Item Three, and similar language in Item Five, to refer to the time the grandchildren take possession in the land and become entitled to enjoy the title to the remainder, which had vested at Usry's death. This construction is consistent with our case law that recognizes that a vested remainder will have both a vesting of title and a vesting of possession.

Judgment affirmed.

■ CARLEY, J., dissenting.

The law of Georgia favors the early vesting of remainders "in all cases of doubt," but not where "a manifest intention to the contrary shall appear." O.C.G.A. § 44–6–66. "This preference for vested interests is only a presumption and will give way to a clear intent to make the interest subject to a contingency." Verner F. Chaffin, Studies in the Georgia Law of Decedents' Estates and Future Interests, p. 332 (1978). Because the controlling terms of Watson Usry's will leave no doubt of his clear intent that his grandchildren must survive their parents to inherit, their remainders are contingent and the preference for early vesting does not apply in this case. Therefore, I dissent to the majority's affirmance of the trial court's erroneous ruling.

Item Three of Mr. Usry's will creates a life estate in his widow and then in those of their children who survived her. Thus, he clearly intended that his children's interests not vest at his death, but at the death of his wife. With regard to the grandchildren, Item 3 provides: "Upon the death of my last surviving child title in fee simple to said lands shall vest in my grand-children, per stirpes and not per capita." (Emphasis supplied.) A "fee simple" estate " 'is the entire and absolute property in the land; no person can have a greater estate or interest.' [Cit.]" Houston v. Coram, 215 Ga. 101, 102(1) (109 S.E.2d 41) (1959). Thus, Item 3 clearly expresses the testator's intent that his grandchildren would have no interest in the property until such time as the entire and absolute estate passed to them at the death of the last life tenant.

Despite this clear expression of Mr. Usry's intent, the majority concludes that what he really meant was for title to pass to his grandchildren at his death and that only possession be postponed until the death of his last surviving child. This is patently erroneous, as title cannot vest both at the time of the testators' death and then again at the death of the last life tenant. As the majority correctly notes, "there are two vestings of a vested remainder," a vesting of title and a vesting of possession. (Emphasis supplied.) Crawley v. Kendrick, 122 Ga. 183, 184(1) (50 S.E. 41) (1905). However, the issue here is whether the grandchildren's remainders are vested or contingent. O.C.G.A. § 44–6–61. The will does not specify that their interests vest at the testator's death with possession delayed until the last life tenant dies. The instrument unambiguously provides that the grandchildren take no "title" until that time. One can hold title without possession or possession without title. However, fee simple title in the grandchildren vests either at the time of Mr. Usry's death or when his last child dies. The will expressly indicates that his children must survive his widow to take a life estate and, by postponing the vesting of title in his grandchildren, implicitly requires that they survive the life tenants. See Ruth v. First Nat. Bank of Atlanta, 230 Ga. 490, 493 (197 S.E.2d 699) (1973).

The error in the majority's analysis is that it equates the absence of an express requirement for survivorship as conclusive evidence of the testator's intent to create vested, rather than contingent, remainders. However, the law favors the early vesting of remainders only in cases of doubt, and no doubt arises simply because the testator did not specifically provide that the remaindermen must survive to take. A postponement of the vesting of title can be the functional equivalent of a survivorship requirement. See Wells v. Ellis, 184 Ga. 645, 646 (1) (192 S.E. 380) (1937). The applicable rule of construction is to ascertain the testator's intent based upon a consideration of the entire will and the circumstances surrounding its execution. Timberlake v. Munford, 267 Ga. 631, 632 (481 S.E.2d 217) (1997). Contrary to the majority opinion, the testator's will did not provide "for title to vest in his loved ones who survive him." In Item 8 of Mr. Usry's will, he expressed only the general intent "to provide for the welfare of my loved ones who survive me...." However, the relevant inquiry is the construction of the specific provisions of the instrument so as to determine how he intended to provide for them. There is a distinction between the expression of a general testamentary intent to provide for survivors, as in Item 8, and a specific provision for the vesting of title in those who survive, as in Item 3. In Item 3, Mr. Usry created life estates for his widow and children, and provided that his grandchildren would not take title until the death of the last surviving child. Thus, he obviously did not intend to provide for the welfare of all of his survivors, since only those children who outlived his widow were to take life estates. Under the majority's anomalous construction, the remainder to a grandchild who survived Mr. Usry and died before his or her own parent would be vested, but the parent of that grandchild would have no interest unless he or she outlived Mrs. Usry. Based upon the will as a whole, the more reasonable interpretation is that the testator intended all remainders to be contingent upon survival until the time of vesting. Mr. Usry accomplished that intent by expressly providing that his children survive his widow and by specifically providing that title would not pass to his grandchildren until the death of the last life tenant.

The trial court erred in misapplying the preference for early vesting so as to violate the testator's manifest intent to create contingent remainders for his children and grandchildren. Because the majority endorses, rather than corrects that error, I dissent.

QUESTION

How would Chief Justice Fletcher have decided the Problem set out before the case? Justice Carley?

PROBLEMS

1. Uncle Sam's will provides that "the remainder of my estate should be held in trust until the death of my last surviving niece or nephew. When my last surviving niece or nephew dies, I direct that the trust principal be divided among my grandnieces and grandnephews." At the death of the last surviving niece and nephew, Uncle Sam is survived by four living grandnieces and by two children of a deceased grandniece. The deceased grandniece executed a valid will leaving all of her property to her husband. Usry v. Farr has just been decided. How would the majority construe "grandnieces and grandnephews"?

If you were arguing for the children of the deceased grandniece, how would you distinguish Usry? What arguments would you make if you were representing the living grandnieces? Redraft the will to support the position of the children of the deceased grandniece. Then redraft it to support the beneficiaries of the will of the deceased grandniece. Finally, redraft it to support the living grandnieces.

2. Uncle Casey's will creates a trust for the benefit of his daughter for life, and directs that at the daughter's death, the remainder should be distributed "to my nieces and nephews." Uncle Casey's only sister, Sally, had two children, Ralph and Terry. At the time Uncle Casey executed his will, Sally and Ralph were dead. Ralph was survived by his two sons, Whitey and Ford, who were also the beneficiaries of his will. At the death of Uncle Casey's daughter, how should the trust principal be distributed? Cf. In re Kittson's Estate, 177 Minn. 469, 225 N.W. 439 (1929). Redraft Uncle Casey's will to make it clear that Terry should take all. Now redraft the will to make sure that Whitey and Ford will share in the estate.

3. Robert Hartman's will created a trust for the benefit of his daughter Myrtle Schmid. At Myrtle's death, the trust property was to be distributed to Myrtle's son, Robert Schmid. The will provided, however, that "if my grandson Robert Schmid be not living at the time of the termination of the trust, and there should be another child, or children, of my daughter

Myrtle living at that time, then my trustees should distribute the trust to those children in equal shares. If there be no such other children living, the trust principal should be distributed [to five named relatives]." Robert died before Myrtle, and Myrtle had no more children. Are Robert's children entitled to the trust principal? See Will of Hartman, 347 N.W.2d 480 (Minn. 1984).

* * *

Express Survivorship Conditions

One way to make it clear that testator intends to require survival is to include express language to that effect. Unless the language is chosen carefully, however, the will may leave open the possibility of litigation. Suppose, for instance, testator's will creates a trust, and directs that trust income be paid to his brother for life, with the remainder, at the brother's death, to be paid to his brother's "surviving children." If, at the brother's death, the brother is survived by one child and by the issue of a deceased child, how should the trust principal be distributed? Reconsider the following case:

Matter of Marine Midland Bank, N.A.

Court of Appeals of New York, 1989.
74 N.Y.2d 448, 547 N.E.2d 1152, 548 N.Y.S.2d 625.

[Reproduced at p. 326, supra]

NOTES

1. In light of the express survivorship requirement in Carl Gustafson's will, how could the three dissenting judges conclude that Leonard's two children should share in the principal of Carl's trust? Whose argument is more persuasive, the majority's or the dissent's?

2. How would you have drafted Carl Gustafson's will to avoid the ambiguity that led to this litigation? Assume Carl wanted to preclude the children of deceased children from sharing in the trust principal (unless all of Carl's children were dead).

3. The residuary clause of testator's will creates a trust, directs that income should be distributed to her children for life, and then provides that trust principal should be distributed in equal shares to the children who survive me of my sister, Frances S. Bridges, but not to any of the descendants of any of them who do not survive me.

Frances Bridges' only child survives the testator, but dies before Frances, leaving a son who survives Frances. Is Frances' grandson entitled to the trust principal, or should it be distributed by intestate succession? See Estate of Silsby, 914 A.2d 703 (Me. 2006).

Including More Remote Generations: Drafting to Exclude the Beneficiary Who Dies Childless

In Marine Midland, testator included an express survivorship clause, designed (according to the court) to exclude persons from more remote generations. Suppose, however, testator has the opposite goal: testator wants to make a class gift, but to include persons from more remote generations. Suppose, however, that testator does *not* want to create an indefeasibly vested remainder in all members of the class.

Put more concretely, suppose testator wants to create a trust, and to give a life interest in the trust to his sister. Testator wants to divide the principal among his sister's children at the sister's death. Testator wants the issue of any deceased children to take, but does not want deceased children to be entitled to dispose of their interests by will. How should testator's will be drafted? The question may confront you in practice on a regular basis.

Consider the effort of the drafter of Susan Patterson's will. After creating a life estate to her husband, her will provided:

> "I leave all of the rest, residue and remainder of my estate to my nieces and nephews, equally. In the event of the death of any of my nieces or nephews leaving a child or children surviving them, then the surviving child or children of each such deceased nephew or niece shall receive the share to which such deceased nephew would have been entitled, if living."

Turner v. Adams, 855 S.W.2d 735 (Tex. App. 1993). The will makes clear that if a nephew or niece dies before the time for distribution, leaving children, the children take the share of that nephew or niece—not the will beneficiaries of the deceased nephew or niece.

Suppose one of Susan Patterson's nephews dies, survived by a son and by the son of a deceased daughter. Does the son of the deceased daughter share in Susan Patterson's estate? Note the drafting imperfection: Susan Patterson's lawyer used the single-generation term "children" rather than the multi-generation term "issue." Did the lawyer mean to exclude the son of a deceased daughter? How would you correct this drafting imperfection?

Consider now another drafting problem created by Susan Patterson's lawyer—the one that actually generated litigation over Susan Patterson's estate. Suppose one of Susan Patterson's nephews dies *childless*. What happens to his share? Does the will say? This drafting error is all too common. In Turner v. Adams, the court held that the share of the deceased nephew "lapsed" in favor of the other class members, and that the executor of the deceased nephew's estate was not entitled to a share of the trust principal. See also Martino v. Martino, 35 S.W.3d 252 (Tex. App. 2000) [same result on similar facts].

The result in Turner v. Adams is not, however, the invariable result. Consider the will in Estate of Houston, 414 Pa. 579, 201 A.2d 592 (1964). Henry Houston's will created a trust to endure until the death of his last surviving child, and then provided:

> On the death of my last surviving child I direct that the whole of the principal of the trust estate shall be distributed in equal portions to and among my grandchildren, the children of any deceased grand-child taking their deceased parents share.

A divided Pennsylvania Supreme Court, applying the presumption of early vesting, held that the estates of three deceased grandchildren, all of whom had died childless and intestate, were entitled to share in the trust principal. The majority wrote:

> We reach this construction of the will with regret because (a) it gives a share of the principal to descendants long dead, and (b) it would permit strangers to testator's blood (a deceased grandchild's spouse, or his legatees, or his heirs under the intestate laws) to receive a substantial portion of his estate without any express gift and (c) it greatly depletes, by colossal unforeseeable taxation, the property which testator desired and intended to go to his descendants.

Id. at 596, 201 A.2d at 600. Do you understand the court's point about "colossal" taxation?

From a drafter's perspective, the question is not whether the court's construction in Turner v. Adams was superior to the court's construction in Estate of Houston. The question is how to avoid the problem that led to litigation in both cases—and in a number of others as well. Try your hand at redrafting the remainder in Estate of Houston to avoid the problem that confronted the Pennsylvania Supreme Court.

QUESTIONS AND PROBLEMS

1. Classify the future interests created by the grants in Turner v. Adams and Estate of Houston. Do you see how the parties to the disputes might disagree on the appropriate classification? If we truly care about testator's intent, could testator ever have intended to pay a colossal estate tax?

2. Testator's will created a remainder identical to that in In re Houston. Testator had three children, Ann, Barbara, and Charles. Charles survived Ann and Barbara. Ann had a single child, Diana, who was still alive at Charles' death. Barbara had three children, Ethan and Fran, both of whom died childless and intestate before Charles' death (leaving their brother, George, as their only heir), and George, who was alive at Charles' death. Charles' only child, Hilary, survived Charles.

Which of the parties would want to argue that the remainder in grandchildren was contingent? Which would want to argue that the remainder is vested subject to complete divestment only if a grandchild predeceased the last surviving child, *leaving issue?* If Testator's estate amounted to $1,000,000, how much would turn on the dispute?

Would the parties all take the same position if Ethan and Fran had left wills leaving all of their property to their cousin Diana? To the Trustees of Columbia University?

C. UPC § 2–707: A REPRISE

Recall that UPC § 2–707 would revolutionize the law of future interests by creating an implied survivorship requirement in all future interests. See pp. 811–13, *supra*. In its application to class gifts, the statute imposes a survivorship requirement, but then creates, in section 2–707(b)(2), a "substitute gift" in the surviving descendants of deceased class members.

Suppose, for instance, if testator's will creates a trust for the lifetime of testator's husband, and then provides for distribution to "my children." If one of testator's children, A, is alive at the husband's death, and the other, B, has died leaving two children, C and D, the statute creates a substitute gift in C and D. Hence, A will take half of the trust principal, and C and D will share the other half.

In addition, the statute provides that "words of survivorship attached to a future interest are not, in the absence of additional evidence, a sufficient indication of an intent contrary to application of this section." UPC § 2–707(b)(3). As a result, if our hypothetical testator's will had provided for distribution, after her husband's death, "to my surviving children," C and D, the surviving descendants of deceased children, would still share in distribution of the trust principal. To avoid this result, testator would either have to provide for distribution "to my surviving children, and not to descendants of deceased children," or to include substitute takers in the event that one or more children fail to survive.

Re-examine section 2–707 as preparation for the following questions and problems.

PROBLEMS AND QUESTIONS

1. How would Usry v. Farr have been decided if UPC § 2–707 had been in effect? Matter of Marine Midland Bank?

2. G creates an irrevocable *inter vivos* trust, income to be paid to his sister A for life, remainder at A's death "to those of A's children who survive A, and if none survive A, then to my brother B." A had two children, Y and Z. How should the trust principal be distributed if, at A's death,

(a) Y is dead and survived by a son X; Z is dead and survived by a daughter W; B is alive?

(b) Y is alive, Z is dead and survived by W; B is alive?

(c) Y is dead and survived by X; Z is dead and survived by W; B is dead and survived by a daughter V. [Hint: see section 2–707(b)(4)].

* * *

As you might surmise from working through these problems, section 2–707 has been criticized for its undue complexity. See David M. Becker, Uniform Probate Code § 2–707 and the Experienced Estate Planner: Unexpected Disasters and How to Avoid Them, 47 U.C.L.A. L. Rev. 339 (1999); Eric Tucker Kimbrough, Lapsing of Testamentary Gifts, Antilapse Statutes, and the Expansion of Uniform Probate Code Antilapse Protection, 36 Wm. & Mary L. Rev. 269 (1994). We will spare you problems involving the application of section 2–707(c). If you want to work some out, the official comment to the statute includes a number of them.

D. ADOPTED MEMBERS OF THE CLASS

It is well established in most jurisdictions today that a will or trust provision leaving a future interest to a person's children or grandchildren includes that person's adopted children or grandchildren. See, e.g., Uniform Probate Code § 2–705(b). Even when the gift is to "issue," a term not used in the UPC because of its biological connotation, courts typically hold that adopted members of the class are entitled to take on an equal footing with natural-born class members. See, e.g., Bowles v. Bradley, 319 S.C. 377, 461 S.E.2d 811 (1995).

These constructional rules, however, do not apply when language in the will or trust instrument establishes that testator or settlor had a different intention. For instance, in Weissinger v. Simpson, 861 So.2d 984 (Miss. 2003), the court held that a future interest in a nephew's "then living issue" excluded the nephew's adopted children, because elsewhere in the will, testator had used the phrase "children, including adopted children." The court reasoned:

> We find that Brooks used two different terms in his will because he intended different results for each term. When Brooks intended to include adopted children, he used the language "including adopted children." When Brooks intended to exclude adopted children, he used the word "issue" without the words "including adopted children."

Id. at 988.

A more difficult issue arises with old trust instruments drafted at a time when the general understanding was that adoptive children did not qualify as "children" within the meaning of a class gift in a will or trust instrument. Should courts apply the law in effect at the time the will or trust instrument was executed, or should they apply the law in effect at the time the future interest becomes possessory?

Sometimes the same issue arises in reverse. You will recall from the intestate succession materials that, for a time, the legislative trend was to transplant adoptive children entirely into their adoptive families for inheritance purposes, barring all inheritance from and through genetic parents. In more recent years, a number of courts have permitted inheritance from and through genetic parents after an adoption by a relative of one of the natural parents. See, e.g., UPC § 2–119. Suppose a child was adopted by a relative of his or her genetic parent at a time when such adoptions terminated the right to inherit from the genetic family, but the state statute now permits inheritance through the genetic family. That issue arose in the following case:

Newman v. Wells Fargo Bank, N.A.

Supreme Court of California, 1996.
14 Cal.4th 126, 926 P.2d 969, 59 Cal.Rptr.2d 2.

■ BAXTER, J.:

We are asked to decide whether, in looking to the law of intestacy as a guide to a testator's presumed intent when a will provision is ambiguous, a court should consider the law in effect at the time the will or testamentary trust was executed to determine if a child adopted out of a designated ancestor's family is among "issue" and "children" the testator intended to benefit, or should apply the law in effect at the death of the ancestor through whom the child may take. Appellant, minor A., a creditor of Jon E. Newman, claims that even though Newman was adopted by Newman's stepfather in 1946, he remains a "child" of Earl Mitchell, his natural father, within the meaning of the will of Helen Lathrop, Mitchell's sister, and is entitled to share in a testamentary trust created for the benefit of Mitchell who is now deceased, Mitchell's siblings, and their children.

Lathrop executed her will and died in 1972. Appellant relies on a 1985 change in the law of intestate succession which permits "adopted-out" children to take if adopted by a stepparent. Other beneficiaries of the trust contend that the law in effect when Lathrop executed the will and when she died applies, as that law presumably will carry out her intent.

* * *

I—Background

Helen Lathrop, a resident of Belvedere, California, died in December 1972. Her will, dated November 3, 1972, left the residue of her estate to a testamentary trust under which the income was to be paid to her six brothers and sisters, or on the death of any of them to that person's living "issue" by right of representation. On the death of the last of the siblings, the trust estate was to be distributed per capita to the then-living children of the siblings. The will was admitted to probate in the Marin County Superior Court early in 1973, and the residue of the Lathrop estate was ordered distributed to Wells Fargo Bank, as trustee of the testamentary trust, in May 1974. The trust, whose provisions parallel those of Lathrop's will, is administered by the trustee under the supervision of the San Francisco Superior Court.

Jon E. Newman's natural father Earl Mitchell, a brother of Helen Lathrop and an income beneficiary of the trust, died in 1993. Jon E. Newman had been adopted by his stepfather in 1946. In August 1993, the guardian ad litem of minor A. petitioned the superior court for an order attaching 25 percent of Jon E. Newman's share of the income of the Lathrop trust. The petition alleged that Newman was the defendant in an action pending in the State of Washington, that the guardian and Newman had entered into a settlement agreement that had been approved by the court, and that "John [sic] E. Newman has agreed to stipulate to an order of the California court to attach 25% of his share of the income of the

Lathrop Trust." The petition was granted on November 1, 1993, but thereafter Wells Fargo Bank, as trustee, filed a petition for advice and instructions pursuant to Probate Code section 17200. The Wells Fargo petition alleges that Newman had been adopted by his stepfather W. E. Newman in 1946, and asks if Newman was "issue of" Earl Mitchell at the time of Mitchell's death. . . .

* * *

II—Discussion

Former Probate Code section 257 provided from 1955 through 1985 (Stats. 1955, ch. 1478, § 1, p. 2690):

> An adopted child shall be deemed a descendant of one who has adopted him, the same as a natural child, for all purposes of succession by, from or through the adopting parent the same as a natural parent. An adopted child does not succeed to the estate of a natural parent when the relationship between them has been severed by adoption, nor does such natural parent succeed to the estate of such adopted child, nor does such adopted child succeed to the estate of a relative of the natural parent, nor does any relative of the natural parent succeed to the estate of an adopted child.

Effective January 1, 1985, provisions of the former Probate Code, including former section 257 were repealed (Stats. 1983, ch. 842, § 19, p. 3024) and replaced by new provisions, containing former section 6408 (Stats. 1983, ch. 842, § 55, p. 3083). The new section permitted the establishment of a parent-child relationship between an adopted person and the person's natural parent under specified circumstances. Former section 6408, subdivision (a) was amended in 1985 and the provisions governing the parent-child relationship between an adopted person and his or her natural parent were placed in a new section, former section 6408.5, subdivision (a). (Stats. 1985, ch. 982, § 21, pp. 3118–3119.) The code, including former section 6408.5, was repealed in 1990 (Stats. 1990, ch. 79, § 13, p. 463) and a new code, containing a new, substantially similar provision as section 6408 was enacted (Stats. 1990, ch. 79, § 14, p. 721).

At the time Newman's father died in 1993, subdivision (b) of former section 6408 (former section 6408(b)) provided:

> "The relationship of parent and child does not exist between an adopted person and the person's natural parent unless both of the following requirements are satisfied:
>
> "(1) The natural parent and the adopted person lived together at any time as parent and child, or the natural parent was married to, or was cohabiting with, the other natural parent at the time the child was conceived and died before the birth of the child.
>
> "(2) The adoption was by the spouse of either of the natural parents or after the death of either of the natural parents."

* * *

A. The will of Helen M. Lathrop and the circumstances of its execution.

Nothing on the face of the Lathrop will assists in understanding her intent with regard to adopted-out children when she directed that trust income be paid to the issue of a deceased sibling and that on the death of the last sibling the trust corpus be distributed to the then-living children of her siblings.

* * *

Earl Mitchell was a named beneficiary of the trust created by the will. The adoption of his son Jon E. Newman by Jon's stepfather had occurred in 1946, more than 25 years before the will was executed and Lathrop's death. No extrinsic evidence was offered below to establish whether Lathrop was aware of the adoption or whether she intended that children adopted out of the family of a sibling be on an equal footing with the adopted-out child's cousins when either income or remainder distributions from the trust were made. Thus, we find nothing on the face of the will or in the circumstances of its execution to guide us in ascertaining the intent of the testator with respect to the status of Jon E. Newman other than the fact that he had been adopted out at the time the Lathrop will was executed. Also relevant, however, is the fact that Lathrop's will appears to have been prepared by an attorney or other person familiar with the Probate Code. The will is in proper form, includes all standard provisions, uses many technical terms, and one copy in the record bears an "OFFICE COPY" stamp dated on the date the will was executed.

B. Presumptions in aid of construction.

A testator is presumed to be aware of the public policy reflected in the statutory definitions of the terms used in a will at the time the will is executed and to intend that those definitions be followed in construction of the will unless a contrary intent is expressed in the will. This presumption is strongest when an attorney has drafted the will because "where an instrument has been drawn by one skilled in the law, the presence of legal and technical terms is an indication that the legal term of art has been used, and therefore is to be accepted, in accordance with its legal definition. (Estate of Thompson [(1931) 18 Cal. App. 2d 680, 64 P.2d 984]; Maud v. Catherwood (1945) 67 Cal. App. 2d 636, 641, 155 P.2d 111.)" (Wells Fargo Bank v. Huse (1976) 57 Cal. App. 3d 927, 932, 129 Cal. Rptr. 522.)

Three California decisions applying these rules to the inheritance rights of adopted persons stated the law and public policy of which Lathrop was presumably aware at the time she executed her will; two of them were decided only the year before her will was made. The earliest, Estate of Heard (1957) 49 Cal. 2d 514, 319 P.2d 637 (Heard), considered the rights of a child adopted into the testator's family. In Heard, this court looked to former Probate Code section 257 for guidance as to the presumed intent of the testator who left testamentary trust gifts to "issue" of other beneficiaries, and held that a child adopted by the son of the testator after the will was made and the testator had died was the lawful "issue" of the testator's son and entitled to a share of the trust left to such issue. The court explained the relevance of section 257: "We cannot suppose that wills are made in a vacuum; that the status of an adopted child being the same as a biological offspring, which is the public policy of this state, may be completely ignored, or that it was ignored by a testator when making a will any more than he may be said to ignore any other rules of law and public policy. When he has not said anything about 'adopted' children using that word or the equivalent, the court in seeking his intent is in fact endeavoring to ascertain what his wishes would be if adopted children were called particularly to his mind. Lacking that, the court must assume that his will would fit it and be compatible with the general body of the law and public policy. Otherwise the court is left with little if any basis for interpreting the instrument." (49 Cal. 2d at p. 522.)

* * *

More recently in Wells Fargo Bank v. Huse, supra, 57 Cal. App. 3d 927, the court applied the presumption that a testator is aware of the law applicable at the time a will is executed and intends that law to govern construction of the will to a trust which failed to specify whether the term "lawful" issue was restricted to natural born issue or included adopted children. As here, there was no extrinsic evidence bearing on the trustor's intent. The court noted that among the circumstances surrounding the execution of a document which may be considered in interpreting it were "relevant statutes, case law and public policy in effect at the time of the execution of the document which, in the absence of a contrary intent, are deemed to become a part of the testamentary scheme (Estate of Heard (1957) 49 Cal. 2d 514, 521–522, 319 P.2d 637; Estate of Stanford (1957) 49 Cal. 2d 120, 138, 315 P.2d 681.)" (57 Cal. App. 3d at p. 933.)

Contrary to the assumption of appellant, the court is not free to depart from these precedents and presume that the 1985 statutory change under which a child adopted out of a decedent's family by a stepparent may still inherit reflects Lathrop's intent. The Legislature has acknowledged that the law and policy in effect when a person dies is presumed to reflect a decedent's intent with regard to the status of adopted children, including children adopted out of a decedent's family. It did so in section 6414, subdivision (a), which as noted above precludes application of the 1985 change in the law of intestate succession governing the status of adopted-out children to decedents who died before the 1985 change became effective. By creating this limitation on the application of the new policy permitting certain adopted-out children to take by intestate succession, the Legislature gave persons who did not want their estates distributed in accordance with the new policy the opportunity to change their wills or, if they had not made a will, to make one with provisions addressing the status of an adopted-out child. Since the Legislature is aware that the law of intestate succession is often a referent when the court must construe the terms of a will, the court must respect this legislative limitation on retroactive application of the policy governing the status of children adopted by a stepparent.

Section 6414, subdivision (a) and this court's reasoning in Heard therefore compel a conclusion that the law to which the court must look to find the presumed intent of a testator with regard to adopted children is the law in effect when a will is executed. Were we to look to later enacted laws, the result would be inconsistent with the legislative policy reflected in section 6414, subdivision (a) and we would have to assume that a testator who is presumptively aware of the current meaning of the words the testator is using to identify the recipients of his or her bounty in a class gift to children or issue, intends to permit a future Legislature to change the pattern of distribution through a post mortem amendment of the law of intestate succession.

* * *

Relying on out-of-state authority, appellant also argues that a testator should be presumed to know that the law may change after the will is executed and therefore intends to have terms used to identify members of a class construed in light of the law in effect at the time the class closes. (See Solomon v. Central Trust Co. of Northeastern Ohio (1992) 63 Ohio St. 3d 35 [584 N.E.2d 1185]; In re Davidson's Will (1947) 223 Minn. 268 [26 N.W.2d 223]; Carnegie v. First Nat. Bank of Brunswick (1963) 218 Ga. 585 [129 S.E.2d 780]; Merson v. Wood (1961) 202 Va. 485 [117 S.E.2d 661].) That is not, and has not been, the rule in this state with regard to adopted children. The rule is that stated in Heard, Russell and Haneberg. The court will assume that the testator intended the will to be compatible with the law and public policy in effect at the time the will is executed and that, if the testator has a contrary intent, that intent will be made clear in the will. (Heard, supra, 49 Cal. 2d 514, 522.)

We presume as we must that Lathrop knew the meaning of "issue" and "children" as those terms were understood at the time she executed the will. We also presume that she knew that under former Probate Code section 257, a child adopted out of a sibling's family was not "issue" who would inherit through his or her natural father or mother at that time. Lathrop is presumed to have known that adopted-out children such as Newman would no longer be treated as a child of the natural parent in the eyes of the law and would not be included among the children or issue of her siblings to whom she left interests in the testamentary trust.

IV—Disposition

The judgment of the Court of Appeal is reversed.

■ KENNARD, J. [dissenting]:

* * *

The majority asserts that the terms "issue" and "children" are inherently ambiguous whenever a child has been adopted into or out of a family and "the will is not specific with regard to the rights of the adopted child." It takes the position, however, that these asserted ambiguities should be resolved not by examining the circumstances surrounding the will to decide which meaning the evidence best supports but by applying a legal presumption that the testator intended that the meanings of those terms be determined by applying the laws of intestate succession. It then focuses on the question of whether to apply the intestate succession laws as they existed at the time of Mitchell's death or those laws as they existed at the time of the making of the will and the testator's death. The majority chooses the latter approach and concludes that Newman is not the issue of his biological father, Mitchell, because Newman would not have inherited through Mitchell under the intestate succession provisions ... in effect at the time the will was drafted and at the time of the testator's death.

I disagree. In my view, the proper place to begin is by examining the ordinary meanings of the terms "issue" and "children" as they are used in the will. Our statutes as they existed at the time Lathrop's will was drafted and at her death require us to give the terms "issue" and "children" their "ordinary and grammatical sense, unless a clear intention to use them in another sense can be collected, and that other can be ascertained." (Prob. Code, former § 106; see also Estate of Russell, supra, 69 Cal. 2d 200, 210–212.) (This provision continues in substance today as Probate Code section 21122.)

The ordinary and grammatical sense of the term "issue" encompasses the biological, blood relationship of parent and offspring. (Estate of Pierce, supra, 32 Cal. 2d 265, 271 [ordinary meaning of "lawful issue" is "offspring of parentage"]; Webster's Third New Internat. Dict. (1961) p. 1201 [defining "issue" as "offspring, progeny ...: one or more persons descended from a common ancestor"].) Adoption by a stepparent cannot alter or sever this blood relationship.

* * *

Moreover, it is important to keep in mind that a principal reason a testator drafts a will is to escape the intestate succession laws, not to advance them. A decedent wishing to adhere to the policies and distributional scheme of the intestate succession statutes has no need of a will, but can simply let the law take its course. Thus, in the absence of a statutory presumption on the order of former section 108, a court should not conclude that a testator has implicitly and unspokenly adopted the intestate succession statutes as the testator's plan of distribution unless there is evidence that the testator intended to do so. Here there is none.

QUESTIONS

1. Jon E. Newman was 36 years old when Helen Lathrop executed her will. Presumably, Helen knew of his existence and of his adoption—26 years earlier—by his stepfather. What inferences would you draw about Helen's intent in light of her failure to make any explicit provision for Newman?

Would the court in this case have reached a different result if there had been evidence, outside the will itself, that Helen Lathrop cared deeply for Jon Newman and approved of blended families?

2. Suppose you had been Helen Lathrop's lawyer. Should you have known of Newman's situation? In light of the dispositions Lathrop apparently wanted to make in her will, what questions should you have asked while interviewing Lathrop (or put in the questionnaire you ask clients to complete)?

If you had known of Newman's adoption, how would you have drafted the will in this case to avoid litigation? First, redraft the will to assure that Newman would be included. Next, redraft the will to assure that Newman would be excluded. Would you rely on the intestate succession statute's treatment of adoption in choosing language to include in the will? If not, how strong should the presumption be that Lathrop's lawyer drafted with the then-effective intestate succession statute in mind?

3. If Helen Lathrop's lawyer was unlikely to have relied on the intestate succession statute in effect when her will was executed, why prefer the 1972 policy toward adoptees over the 1996 policy? If the legislature now presumes that persons adopted by the spouse of one of their natural parents are generally treated as "family" by the other genetic parent and his relatives, why not apply that presumption even to instruments that predate the new presumption?

4. Suppose Jon Newman had been born to Helen Lathrop's brother in 1970, so that Newman was a cute (or perhaps rambunctious) toddler at the time Lathrop executed her will. Suppose further that Newman's father, Earl Mitchell, was killed in a tragic auto accident in 1975, that Newman's mother remarried, and that her new husband adopted Newman in 1978—seven years before the legislature changed the adoption statute.

Would the California Supreme Court have reached the same result it reached in the principal case? If the hypothetical case arose three years after the principal case, how would you argue the hypothetical case if you represented the adopted-out child?

5. In 1955, Barbara Piel gave birth to an out-of-wedlock child, Elizabeth. Barbara subsequently had two other children. Then, in 1963, Barbara's mother—the heir to the Jello fortune—created two trusts with income to be distributed to her daughter Barbara for life, and the principal to be distributed at Barbara's death into shares "for each then living child of hers." There is no evidence that Barbara's mother knew of Elizabeth. In 1963, adopted-out children were entitled to inherit from their biological parents, but the following year, the legislature amended the statute to permit adopted-out children to inherit only from their adoptive parents. At Barbara's death in 2003, is Elizabeth entitled to a share of trust principal? See Matter of Piel, 10 N.Y.3d 163, 855 N.Y.S.2d 41, 884 N.E.2d 1040 (2008).

NOTES

1. ***Adult Adoptions.*** In most states, adoption is not restricted to minor children; adults may adopt other adults. Suppose inheritance is the motivating factor for an adoption. Should courts permit the adoptee to inherit? The problem has arisen on a number of occasions when wills or trust instruments have created class gifts.

Consider, for instance, the facts in Davis v. Neilson, 871 S.W.2d 35 (Mo. App. 1993). Nielson's grandmother had created a trust to benefit Nielson until he reached age 40, when the trust principal would be distributed to his "issue, per stirpes." The will even defined issue to include adopted children. Nielson had two natural children—both living with his ex-wife, out-of-state. Just before his 40th birthday, Nielson adopted six people—including his secretary, his secretary's adult son, a nephew, and some acquaintances. Several of the adoptees were older than Nielson. When the trustee refused to distribute the trust principal—valued at between $1,000,000 and $2,500,000—to the adopted "children," litigation resulted. The court held that the adult adoptees were not entitled to inherit, citing an article by Professor Rein:

> Common sense tells us that a donor would normally expect anyone partaking of his bounty to be a true family member and not just some willing adult adopted for the purpose of reducing or defeating a gift-over to others.

Jan Ellen Rein, Relatives by Blood, Adoption, and Association: Who Should Get What and Why, 37 Vand. L. Rev. 711, 758 (1984). A number of other courts have reached the same result. The case that engendered the most notoriety involved the Doris Duke Trust, with an estimated value of $170,000,000 at the time of the 1995 litigation. James B. Duke had created a trust for his daughter, Doris, and had provided that at the death of his daughter, two-thirds of the trust income, and ultimately two-thirds of the corpus, would be paid to her lineal descendants. If Doris died without lineal descendants, the trust corpus was to be distributed to a charitable trust. In 1988, at age 75, Doris adopted a 35-year-old woman. When Doris died five years later, her adopted daughter sought, unsuccessfully, to capture the trust income and corpus. Trust of Duke, 305 N.J.Super. 408, 702 A.2d 1008 (1995), aff'd 305 N.J.Super. 407, 702 A.2d 1007 (App. 1997). For other cases reaching the same result, see In re Ellison Grandchildren Trust, 261 S.W.3d 111 (Tex. App. 2008); Trust Agreement of Vander Poel, 396 N.J.Super. 218, 933 A.2d 628 (App. 2007); First National Bank of Dubuque v. Wathen, 338 N.W.2d 361 (Iowa 1983); Cross v. Cross, 177 Ill.App.3d 588, 126 Ill.Dec. 801, 532 N.E.2d 486 (1988). In some states, statutes explicitly construe the word "children" to include children adopted while under the age of 18, but exclude children adopted while over 18. See, e.g., R.I. Gen. Laws § 15-7-16.

In other cases, the right of the adult adoptee to inherit has been upheld. See, e.g., Evans v. McCoy, 291 Md. 562, 436 A.2d 436 (1981). [Woman, age 76, adopts 21-year-old neighbor; three years later, at age 79, she adopts 53-year-old cousin]. Courts are more likely to permit adult adoptees to inherit when the relationship between the "parent" and the "child" appears to track a traditional parent-child relationship, as when a person adopts an adult stepchild. See, e.g., Satterfield v. Bonyhady, 233 Neb. 513, 446 N.W.2d 214 (1989).

2. *Class Gifts and Non–Marital children.* The same sorts of issues that arose in the Newman case can also arise with respect to non-marital children. Shifting mores have been matched by shifts in legislative treatment of those children, and, because trusts can last a long time, cases still arise in which the issue is whether a class gift was intended to include non-marital children. See, e.g., Powers v. Wilkinson, 399 Mass. 650, 506 N.E.2d 842 (1987) [holding non-marital child not entitled to inherit, but concluding that for all instruments executed after date Powers was decided, non-marital children would be entitled to inherit as "children" or "issue"].

Uniform Probate Code § 2–705(a) provides, as with adopted children, that individuals born out-of-wedlock should be treated for purposes of class gifts in the same way they are treated for intestate succession. Section 2–705(b) provides a qualification when the transferor is not the natural parent: "an individual born to the natural parent is not considered the child of that parent unless the individual lived while a minor as a regular member of the household of that natural parent or of that parent's parent, brother, sister, spouse, or surviving spouse." For commentary on the UPC provision, see Patricia G. Roberts, Adopted and Nonmarital Children—Exploring the 1990 Uniform Probate Code's Intestacy and Class Gift Provisions, 32 Real Prop., Prob. & Tr. J. 539 (1998).

E. CLASS GIFTS AND ASSISTED REPRODUCTION

Children in gestation have long been treated as alive for class gift purposes. Because the ordinary biological gestation period is nine months, treating children in gestation as members of a class rarely causes inconvenience. But suppose children are born to deceased parents through the use of frozen sperm or frozen embryos.

UPC 2–705(g) provides:

> The following rules apply for purposes of the class-closing rules:
>
> (1) A child in utero at a particular time is treated as living at that time if the child lives 120 hours after birth.
>
> (2) If a child of assisted reproduction or a gestational child is conceived posthumously and the distribution date is the deceased parent's death, the child is treated as living on the distribution date if the child lives 120 hours after birth and was in utero not later than 36 months after the deceased parent's death or born not later than 45 months after the deceased parent's death.
>
> (3) An individual who is in the process of being adopted when the class closes is treated as adopted when the class closes if the adoption is subsequently granted.

Suppose S creates a trust for the benefit of her son, Abe, for life, with the remainder to be distributed, at Abe's death, "to Abe's children." At the time S created the trust, Abe was 50 years old, and had two children, Carol and Dan, ages 25 and 22. Abe, a widower, subsequently married Barbara. When Abe took ill, Abe, at Barbara's request, froze some of his sperm for potential future use. At Abe's death, the sperm remained frozen. In light of the UPC position, how and when should the trustee distribute the trust proceeds?

F. GIFTS TO "HEIRS"

It is not uncommon for a testator or settlor to direct that, in some circumstance, the trust principal should be distributed "to my heirs." Often the reference to the heirs is simply a default provision; settlor has directed a preferred distribution, but if all of the persons in the preferred class happen to be dead, testator directs distribution "to my heirs." At other times, settlor simply directs that at a specified time, distribution should be made to the heirs. When settlor makes a future gift to "heirs", settlor leaves open an important question: as of what date should the heirs be determined—the date of testator's death, or the date upon which the interest in heirs should become possessory?

This vexing question appears not only when settlor makes an express gift to heirs, but also when all or part of a dispositive instrument proves ineffective, and the court finds it necessary to decide what to do with property the original owner has never validly transferred. Often, the property should pass to testator's "heirs," but the question, again, is heirs *as of what time*?

The following case explores the problem:

Harris Trust and Savings Bank v. Beach

Supreme Court of Illinois, 1987.
118 Ill.2d 1, 112 Ill.Dec. 224, 513 N.E.2d 833.

■ SIMON, J.:

In construing either a trust or a will the challenge is to find the settlor's or testator's intent and, provided that the intention is not against public policy, to give it effect . . .

In this case Harris Trust and Savings Bank, Robert Hixon Glore and William Gray III, trustees of two trusts, sought instructions from the circuit court of Cook County regarding to whom and in what manner the trusts should be distributed. The central controversy is over the proper construction of the remainder over to the heirs following the death of a life tenant: specifically, the question is whether the settlor intended that his heirs be ascertained at his death, or whether he desired that they be determined after the death of his wife, who was the life tenant.

The pertinent facts in this case are as follows: Frank P. Hixon and Alice Green entered into an antenuptial agreement dated March 30, 1921, and following that, they were married. The agreement created a trust consisting of 200 shares of preferred stock of Pioneer Investment Company, a Hixon family holding company. The trust provided that Alice was to receive the net income of the trust for life and that she could "dispose of Fifty Thousand ($50,000) Dollars of said fund in such a manner as she" deemed fit and proper. In exchange for the provisions made for her in the trust, Alice surrendered any interest, including dower, which she might have had in Hixon's estate. If Hixon survived Alice, the trust property was to be reconveyed to him. If Alice survived Hixon, the trust provided that on her death "the balance of said trust fund shall be divided among the heirs of the party of the first part [Hixon], share and share alike."

On May 31, 1926, Hixon created a second trust to provide for Alice. The principal of this trust consisted of 300 shares of stock of Pioneer Investment Company. This trust provided that Alice was to receive the income from the principal for life and upon her death "this trust shall terminate, and the trust fund shall be distributed equally among my [Hixon's] heirs."

In 1930, Hixon executed his will, which was interpreted by our appellate court and is not at issue in this case (Harris Trust & Savings Bank v. Beach (1986), 145 Ill. App. 3d 682), leaving gifts to specific individuals and charities. He divided the residue of his estate equally among his daughters, Ellen Glore and Dorothy Clark and in trust for Alice. Hixon died in 1931, when he was 69 years old. He was survived by Alice, who was then 49, by Dorothy and Ellen, who were then 38 and 36, respectively, and by his grandchildren, Frances Glore Beach, Charles F. Glore, Jr., and Robert Hixon Glore, who were then minors.

Alice lived for 51 more years. Both the 1921 and the 1926 trusts continued for her benefit until she died in February 1982. At that time, Hixon's then living descendants were his grandchildren, Frances Glore Beach and Robert Hixon Glore (the grandchildren), and the children of his deceased grandchild, Charles F. Glore, Jr.—Charles F. Glore III, Sallie Glore Farlow, and Edward R. Glore (the great-grandchildren). The parties agree that both the 1921 and the 1926 trust should be distributed in the same manner.

If Hixon's heirs are those surviving at his death, the trust estates will pass under the wills of his two daughters, Ellen H. Glore and Dorothy H. Clark, who both died in 1973. Ellen had three children. One child, as noted above—Charles F. Glore, Jr.—is deceased and survived by three children, Hixon's great-grandchildren. Ellen's other two children—the grandchildren Robert and Frances—are living and are parties to this suit. Dorothy had no children. The devisees under her will are defendants California Institute of Technology, Santa Barbara Foundation, Santa Barbara Cottage Hospital and the Kansas Endowment Association (collectively the charities), and her husband Alfred. Alfred is deceased and his portion of the assets would be distributed to his devisees, Frederick Acker, as special trustee under the will of Charles F. Glore, Jr., and Robert Hixon Glore. On the other hand, if the heirs are determined at the time of Alice's death, the trust estates will be divided among Hixon's now-living descendants—the two grandchildren and three great-grandchildren.

The four charities assert that the heirs should be those heirs alive at Hixon's death; this determination would include them since they were devisees under Dorothy's will. The grandchildren and the great-grandchildren argue that the heirs should be those who were surviving at Alice's death, but they disagree over whether the trust should be divided *per stirpes* (by each share) or *per capita* (by each head).

I

The word "heirs" refers to "those persons appointed by the law to inherit an estate in case of intestacy." (Le Sourd v. Leinweber (1952), 412 Ill. 100, 105.) When used in its technical sense, the testator's or settlor's heirs are, of course, determined at the time of his or her death. (Hull v. Adams (1948), 399 Ill. 347, 352.) This court, however, has never adopted the technical meaning of the word "heirs" as a rule of law. We have observed that " 'heirs' when used in a will does not necessarily have a fixed meaning. It may mean children or, where there are no children, it may mean some other class of heirs * * * if the context of the entire will *plainly shows* such to have been the intention of the testator." (Emphasis added.) (Stites v. Gray (1954), 4 Ill. 2d 510, 513.) A determination of the class of heirs, therefore, is governed by the settlor's or testator's intention rather than by a fixed rule of law. The rule in Illinois, however, has been that, unless the settlor's intention to the contrary is "plainly shown" in the trust document, courts will rely upon the technical meaning of the term "heirs" by applying it as a rule of construction. (Harris Trust & Savings Bank v. Jackson (1952), 412 Ill. 261, 266.) The charities are, therefore, correct in their observation that presently our rule of construction requires us to determine heirs at the settlor's death unless the trust or will provides clear evidence to the contrary. (See, e.g., Stites v. Gray (1955), 4 Ill. 2d 510, 513; Le Sourd v. Leinweber (1952), 412 Ill. 100, 105; Hull v. Adams (1948), 399 Ill. 347, 352.) The initial question we must address is whether we should continue to adhere to this standard of proof.

The charities contend that this high degree of proof is necessary to rebut the rule of construction because of the policy favoring early vesting of remainders....

.... Early vesting is an axiom which must not get in the way when a contrary intent is demonstrated by a preponderance of the evidence. Requiring clear and convincing evidence or a plain showing to rebut the presumption in favor of the technical meaning of the term "heirs" (see Stites v. Gray (1955), 4 Ill. 2d 510, 513; Le Sourd v. Leinweber (1952), 412 Ill. 100, 105; Hull v. Adams (1948), 399 Ill. 347, 352), has its roots in the maxim favoring early vesting of remainders. Frequently this policy, as is the case here, frustrates what the ordinary settlor would have intended. We hold that because the primary reason for early vesting is no longer as important as it formerly was, proof by the preponderance of the evidence that the settlor, testator, or donor intended to use the term "heirs" in its nontechnical sense is sufficient to delay the vesting of a gift to a time other than at the grantor's death.

The result of delaying a gift to the heirs is not dramatic. The fear that a contingent remainder could be prematurely destroyed no longer exists. Further, should a predeceased member of the class be excluded from the gift, the result is not drastic. If the predeceased "heir" leaves issue, as is the case here, the settlor's own blood still enjoys the gift. If, on the other hand, a predeceased member fails to leave issue, as also occurred here, the gift is prevented from falling into the hands of strangers. In sum, by altering the degree of proof necessary to delay the vesting of a gift to the heirs, we do no harm. Instead, we further the ordinary grantor's intent, which is exactly what a proper rule of construction ought to do. Consequently, in this case we must determine which parties have offered the preponderant proof as to Hixon's intent—the charities or the grandchildren and great-grandchildren.

Hixon's trusts, as the charities stress, do not explicitly state the point at which his heirs should be determined. The 1921 trust provides that the "balance of said trust fund shall be divided among the heirs," and the 1926 trust states that "the trust shall be distributed equally among my [Hixon's] heirs." When the trusts are considered as a whole, however, it becomes apparent that the documents revolve totally around Alice's life and death; Hixon's life and death play only secondary roles. As the grandchildren and great-grandchildren note, the trusts were created for Alice's benefit in exchange for her rights to dower or any other portion of Hixon's estate. The trusts were intended to last throughout her life, and depending upon when she died, the trust principal would either revert to Hixon or be distributed to his heirs. Alice's central role in the trust is indicative of Hixon's intent to make her and not himself the point of reference for determining the heirs. . . .

The circumstances under which Hixon created the trust provide additional evidence of his intent to vest the gift at Alice's death. Hixon was 20 years older than Alice and he would consequently have expected her trusts to last for a considerable time after his own death. During this time, changes in the family through births and deaths would certainly occur. Rather than leave the remainder of the principal to his daughters, as he left the residue of his estate in his will, his use of an indefinite term such as "heirs" covered the inevitable changes in family circumstances that might occur.

* * *

The grandchildren and great-grandchildren also claim that the language in the trusts instructing the trustees to "divide or distribute" the principal "equally among the heirs" invokes the "divide and pay over rule," which would operate to vest the gift at Alice's death. This rule is one of construction to aid courts in determining whether a gift to a class is a vested or contingent remainder. (Hull v. Adams (1948), 399 Ill. 347, 357.) If a gift to a class is vested, it is considered a true legal estate once the trust is executed. On the other hand, if the gift is a contingent, it "is not an estate, but merely the possibility of acquiring one." 399 Ill. 347, 357.

Under the "divide and pay over rule," when a trustee is directed to divide or distribute a gift to a class at a time after the settlor's death, the gift is contingent and possession and enjoyment of that gift are delayed until the time of distribution. The gift is contingent under the rule not only because it is dependent upon the happening of an event—the trustee dividing and distributing the assets—but also because the members of the class who would be alive and able to enjoy the gift would not be ascertained until the trustees performed their duty of distributing the assets. See Hull v. Adams (1948), 399 Ill. 347, 357.

* * *

The provision in the 1921 trust creating a reversion in Hixon should Alice predecease him also advances the grandchildren's and great-grandchildren's argument that Hixon's intention was that the heirs be determined at Alice's death. The reversionary clause conditioned the duration of the trust on Alice's survival. If Alice failed to survive Hixon, the trust would terminate and Hixon's reversion would operate. On the other hand, if Alice survived Hixon, the reversion would not take effect and the principal would be distributed to the heirs. The grandchildren and great-grandchildren persuasively stress that considering the heirs at Hixon's death would lead to nearly the same result as if the reversion had occurred. In both instances the bulk of the principal would pass through the estates of Hixon's two daughters. Hixon's intention that the result was to be different should Alice survive and the reversion fail is an indication that Hixon must have intended that his heirs be determined at Alice's death. Viewing all of these indications with respect to Hixon's intent together, we conclude that the preponderant proof favors the position of the grandchildren and great-grandchildren and Hixon's heirs should therefore be determined at Alice's death.

II

Because we have concluded that it was Hixon's intention that the heirs were to be ascertained at Alice's death, the doctrine of worthier title is not applicable. The doctrine, which was developed in medieval England but abolished there in 1833, voids a gift to the grantor's heirs. It was premised on the notion that it was worthier to take by descent than by devise. (Moynihan, Introduction to the Law of Real Property 152 (1962).) The doctrine was incorporated into American common law, but in Illinois our legislature abolished it in 1955. See Ill. Rev. Stat. 1985, ch. 30, par. 188.

In Illinois, the doctrine applies only where the devisees would take exactly the same estate by devise as they would by descent. (McNeilly v. Wylie (1945), 389 Ill. 391, 393.) It "is not applicable where there is a difference in kind or quality of the estate or property to be passed under the devise from that which would descend under the statute [the laws of descent and distribution]." (389 Ill. 391, 393; accord Darst v. Swearingen (1906), 224 Ill. 229; Boldenweck v. City National Bank & Trust Co. (1951), 343 Ill. App. 569.) Therefore, under Illinois law the doctrine is not likely to operate when the heirs are determined after the termination of a life estate; when vesting is postponed the devisees rarely receive either the same amount or the same estate as they would had their gift taken effect at the testator's death. See McCormick v. Sanford (1925), 318 Ill. 544, 546.

Having already concluded that Hixon's heirs are to be determined at Alice's and not at Hixon's death, those who would take Hixon's estate under the laws of descent and distribution had Hixon died intestate—Alice and the two daughters—are not the same as those who will take after Alice's death—the grandchildren and great-grandchildren. As a result, the doctrine is not relevant and therefore we need not reach the other issues briefed before this court: whether the doctrine is a rule of construction or rule of law and whether the doctrine is an anachronism which should be abandoned in the case of trusts established in Illinois prior to our 1955 statutory abolition of the doctrine.

III

The final question is whether the gift to the grandchildren and great-grandchildren should be distributed per stirpes or per capita. The great-grandchildren contend that because Hixon used the words "share and share alike" and instructed the trustees to distribute the gift "equally," the gift must be divided on a per capita basis. The great-grandchildren accurately observe that, "When the words 'equally,' 'equal among,' 'share and share alike,' or other similar words, are used to indicate an equal division among a class, the persons among whom the division is to be made are usually held to take per capita unless a contrary intention is discoverable from the will." (Dollander v. Dhaemers (1921), 297 Ill. 274, 278.) However, " 'it is worthy of remark that the leading cases which sustain a distribution per capita intimate that a very small indication of intent to the contrary would change the rule.' " (297 Ill. 274, 280, quoting Eyer v. Beck (1888), 70 Mich 179, 181, 38 N.W. 20.) When a testator leaves his estate to his or her heirs, courts generally conclude that the testator intended the gift to be distributed in accordance with laws of descent and distribution which provide for a per stirpes distribution. (Carlin v. Helm (1928), 331 Ill. 213, 221–22; see also Ill. Rev. Stat. 1985, ch. 110 1/2, par. 2.1.) Under these circumstances we have stated that "a gift to issue 'equally' and 'share and share alike' does not require that each of such issue shall have an equal share with the other; that the mandate is satisfied if the issue of equal degree taking per stirpes share equally." Condee v. Trout (1942), 379 Ill. 89, 93.

In the present case, Hixon left the remainder in the trust principal to his heirs. That he provided for his heirs to share equally in that gift fails to rebut the presumption in favor of a per stirpes distribution; the gift to the class of heirs is a sufficient indication that Hixon intended the remainder to be divided in accordance with the laws of descent and distribution. This conclusion is bolstered by the wording of the statute, in effect both at Hixon's death and when he executed the trusts, which used the terms "equally among" and in "equal parts" in describing the per stirpes distribution of estates. That Hixon employed the words "equally" and "share and share alike" in his instructions to the trustees regarding the division of his estate is therefore not inconsistent with an intention that the heirs share equally under a per stirpes distribution. See Ill. Rev. Stat. 1937, ch. 39, par. 1.

* * *

We conclude that the remainder in the heirs should be distributed per stirpes with the three great-grandchildren each taking one-ninth of the estate and the two grandchildren each taking one-third. The judgments of both the circuit and appellate courts are reversed and the case is remanded for a distribution of the trust principal in a manner consistent with this opinion.

Judgments reversed; cause remanded.

NOTES AND QUESTIONS

1. What was at stake in this case? Why did it matter when the heirs were determined?

2. ***The Common Law Rule.*** As the court in Harris Trust indicates, at common law, courts generally held that a future interest in A's "heirs" vested at A's death. As in other areas, there were several reasons for this presumption in favor of early vesting—the need to avoid the doctrine that contingent remainders were "destructible," the desire to make it easier to transfer property (by assuring that the owners of the property were identifiable people—rather than heirs whose identity might not be ascertained for many years), and the desire to avoid invalidity under the Rule Against Perpetuities. The final concern remains of some importance today. The common law rule is far from obsolete. Note that even the court in Harris Trust concludes that the meaning of the word "heirs" is to be determined from the context of the case; the court does not hold that heirs are invariably to be determined as of the time the interest in heirs becomes possessory. For a recent case concluding that a testator's heirs should be determined at the time of testator's death, not the time the interest in heirs becomes possessory, see Stevens v. Radey, 117 Ohio St.3d 65, 881 N.E.2d 855 (2008) [when will created trust for life of testator's father, but made no provision for assets after father's death, property passed to testator's heirs at the time of testator's death, not the time of the father's death]. See generally Patricia J. Roberts, Class Gifts in North Carolina—When Do We "Call the Roll"?, 21 Wake Forest L. Rev. 1, 34–35 (1985).

3. ***Determining "Heirs" for Purposes of Distributing Property Subject to an Ineffective Grant.*** Suppose testator had disposed of the residue of his estate by creating a testamentary trust. The trust provided that income should be paid to his children and their heirs until the death of his last surviving child, then to his grandchildren and their heirs until the death of his last surviving grandchild, at which time the principal was to be distributed to his great-grandchildren. As we shall see (and as you may remember from your first-year Property course), the interest in great-grandchildren is invalid under the Rule Against Perpetuities. Who is entitled to the trust principal upon the death of the last surviving grandchild? If the property would revert to testator because he has made no valid disposition of the property, the property would have to pass to his heirs. (Since the invalid provision was itself made in the residuary clause of testator's will, we cannot distribute the property through the residuary clause; instead, the property must pass by intestate succession to testator's heirs.)

In this situation, should the heirs be determined as of the time of testator's death, or as of the death of the last surviving grandchild? If we determined testator's heirs as of the last grandchild's death, would we have effectively undermined the Rule Against Perpetuities? Hence, when we must determine who takes a future interest invalidly disposed of by testator's will or settlor's *inter vivos* trust instrument, we generally distribute the property to testator's heirs as determined at the time of testator's death; that is, we maintain the presumption in favor of early vesting.

4. ***Tax Consequences.*** If a future interest is held by heirs determined at the time of testator's death, those heirs are likely to hold a vested remainder which will be a "transmissible remainder" for federal estate tax purposes. As we have seen, the transmissible remainder will be taxed and probated in the heir's estate if the heir dies before the interest becomes possessory. By contrast, if the determination of heirs is postponed until the death of the income beneficiary, an heir who dies in the meantime will not hold an interest subject to estate tax. As a result, there are generally—but not always—tax advantages to the construction of "heirs" adopted by the court in Harris Trust. (But see Laura E. Cunningham, The Hazards of Tinkering with the Common Law of Future Interests: the California Experience, 48 Hastings L.J. 696–98 (1997)) [considering the generation-skipping transfer tax aspects of rules postponing vesting of future interests]. As a result, a number of states (and the drafters of the Uniform Probate Code) have promulgated statutes codifying the result in the Harris Trust case:

UNIFORM PROBATE CODE

SECTION 2–711. FUTURE INTERESTS IN "HEIRS" AND LIKE.

If an applicable statute or a governing instrument calls for a present or future distribution to or creates a present or future interest in a designated individual's "heirs," "heirs at law," "relatives," or "family," or language of similar import, the property passes to those persons, including the state under Section 2–105, and in such shares as would succeed to the designated individual's intestate estate under the intestate succession law of the designated individual's domicile if the designated individual died when the disposition is to take effect in possession or enjoyment. If the designated individual's surviving spouse is living but is remarried at the time the disposition is to take effect in possession or enjoyment, the surviving spouse is not an heir of the designated individual.

The Restatement (Third) of Property (Wills and Other Donative Transfers) (Tentative Draft No. 4, 2004) takes the same general approach:

Section 16.1 Class Gift to "Heirs"—Presumptive Meaning

> Unless the language or circumstances indicate that the transferor had a different intention, the term "heirs" (or a like term), in a class gift to the "heirs" (or to a class described by a like term) of a designated person, means the persons who would succeed to the designated person's intestate estate if the designated person died intestate on the distribution date owning only the subject matter of the gift.

5. ***The "Divide and Pay Over" Rule.*** The court in Harris Trust purports to rely on the "divide and pay over rule" to support its construction of the gift to heirs as contingent on survival to the time of distribution. The rule has been applied not only to gifts to heirs, but to all sorts of future interests. Unfortunately, however, the rule is of little help. The rule was first articulated in Matter of Crane, 164 N.Y. 71, 58 N.E. 47, 48 (1900):

> Where the only words of gift are found in the direction to divide or pay over at a future time the gift is future, not immediate; contingent and not vested.

So articulated, the rule simply adopts the preference for construing class gifts to be contingent on survival to the time of distribution. But, as the court in Harris Trust also notes, the rule is said not to apply when distribution is postponed only for the purposes of creating an intervening estate. In virtually every case, however, at least one of the purposes of making the class gift a *future* interest is to permit the life beneficiary to enjoy the property during his or her life. (In Harris Trust, for instance, distribution was postponed to permit Alice to live on the trust income until her death.) Hence, a court could always invoke either the divide and pay over rule, or its exception, to support whatever construction the court preferred. The rule itself is of little utility in construing the class gift.

6. ***Per capita v. Per stirpes Distribution.*** In the Harris Trust case, the grandchildren and great-grandchildren had a dispute among themselves about how the trust principal should have been divided. Do you understand the dispute? What argument did the great-grandchildren advance?

The Doctrine of Worthier Title

In the Harris Trust case, the charities sought to invoke the *Doctrine of Worthier Title* to support their position. At common law, when a grantor made a transfer in the form "to A for life, remainder to my heirs", courts often construed the transfer not to create a remainder in grantor's heirs, but instead to create a reversion in grantor. Why would they distort the grantor's plain language in that way? In the words of the New York Court of Appeals in In re Burchell's Estate, 299 N.Y. 351, 87 N.E.2d 293, 296 (1949):

> The doctrine had its origin in the feudal custom of awarding certain valuable incidents to the overlord upon the descent of property held by a feoffee. These incidents did not accrue if the property was acquired through purchase, and, in order to obviate this means of curtailing the payments of incidents, title by descent was declared to be more worthy

than title by purchase. If a gift over might pass to an heir by descent rather than by gift, he took his title through inheritance.

The doctrine outlived its feudal origins because it continued to have a useful purpose: it promoted alienability of property—particularly land. If grantor's heirs held a remainder in land while grantor was still alive, there was no way for any group of people to agree to reunite all estates in the land into a single fee simple absolute. The heirs, as an unascertained group, were incapable of conveying good title to anyone. The Doctrine of Worthier Title, by substituting a reversion in the grantor for a remainder in the heirs, provided a neat solution to this problem.

Over time, however, it became clear that the doctrine often frustrated the intention of the grantor—who *did* want to create a remainder in his heirs. In Doctor v. Hughes, 225 N.Y. 305, 122 N.E. 221 (1919), the New York Court of Appeals, in an opinion by Judge Cardozo, transformed the doctrine from a rule of law into a rule of construction—the doctrine would now be used as an aid in ascertaining grantor's intent, nothing more.

Today, lawyers invoke the doctrine, with varying success, in a number of areas. In cases like Harris Trust, a lawyer might invoke the doctrine to capture property for the grantor's estate, rather than permitting the property to pass pursuant to an earlier trust instrument. (Ask yourself why the charities would have been better off in Harris Trust if the court had invoked the Doctrine of Worthier Title). In addition, some courts have invoked the Doctrine of Worthier Title to enable the settlor of an irrevocable trust with a remainder in settlor's heirs to modify or revoke the trust so long as she obtained the consent of the life beneficiaries; if the future interest were truly treated as a remainder, rather than a reversion, permitting modification by consent would be more problematic. See Hatch v. Riggs National Bank, 361 F.2d 559 (D.C. Cir. 1966).

Estates lawyers should principally be aware of the doctrine as a tool for their litigation arsenal. If lawyers are careful in drafting future interests in heirs—specifying the time at which heirs are to be determined, the doctrine should not present significant drafting problems.

G. CLASS GIFTS OF INCOME

We have dealt so far with class gifts of principal. Consider, however, a common problem. Testator creates a trust, and directs that income should be divided among her children until the death of the last surviving child. What happens when the first of testator's children dies? Who is entitled to share in the income? Consider the following case:

Dewire v. Haveles

Supreme Judicial Court of Massachusetts, 1989.
404 Mass. 274, 534 N.E.2d 782.

■ WILKINS, J.:

This petition for a declaration of rights seeks answers to questions arising from an artlessly drafted will that, among its many inadequacies, includes a blatant violation of the rule against perpetuities. The case is before us on a reservation and report by a judge of the Probate and Family Court on a statement of agreed facts. The judge listed a large number of issues, but we shall deal with them only to the extent necessary to permit a declaration of the present rights of the parties. We transferred the case here on our own motion.

Thomas A. Dewire died in January, 1941, survived by his widow, his son Thomas, Jr., and three grandchildren (Thomas, III, Paula, and Deborah, all children of Thomas, Jr.). His will placed substantially all his estate in a residuary trust. The income of the trust was payable to his widow for life and, on her death, the income was payable to his son Thomas, Jr., the widow of Thomas, Jr., and Thomas Jr.'s children. After the testator's death, Thomas, Jr., had three more children by a second wife. Thomas, Jr., died on May 28, 1978, a widower, survived by all six of his children. Thomas, III, who had served as trustee since 1978, died on March 19, 1987, leaving a widow and one child, Jennifer. Among the questions presented, and the most important one for present purposes, is to whom the one-sixth share of the trust income, once payable to Thomas, III, is now payable.

In his will, the testator stated: "It is my will, except as hereinabove provided, that my grandchildren, under guidance and discretion of my Trustee, shall share equally in the net income of my said estate." At another point, he referred to the trust income being "divided equally amongst my grandchildren." The rule against perpetuities violation occurred because the will provided for the trust's termination "twenty-one years after the death of the last surviving child of my said son, Thomas A. Dewire, Jr., when the property of the trust shall be equally divided amongst the lineal descendants of my grandchildren."

There is no explicit provision in the will concerning the distribution of income on the death of a grandchild while the gift of income to grandchildren continues, nor is there any statement as to what the trustee should do with trust income between the death of the last grandchild and the date assigned for termination of the trust twenty-one years later.

Our task is to discern the testator's intention concerning the distribution of a grandchild's share of the trust income on his death. As a practical matter, in cases of this sort, where there is no express intention, we must resort to reasonable inferences in the particular circumstances which on occasion shade into rules of construction that are applied when no intention at all can be inferred on the issue. In this case, the reasonable inference as to the testator's intention is that Jennifer should take her father's share in the income.

Certain points are not in serious controversy and are relatively easy to resolve. The gift of net income to the testator's grandchildren, divided equally or to be shared equally, is a class gift. See Smith v. Haynes, 202 Mass. 531, 533 (1909). The class includes all six grandchildren, three of whom were born before and three of whom were born after the testator's death. B.M.C. Durfee Trust Co. v. Taylor, 325 Mass. 201, 204 (1950). Hall v. Hall, 123 Mass. 120, 122 (1877). See Casner, Class Gifts to Others than to "Heirs" or "Next of Kin": Increase in the Class Membership, 51 Harv. L. Rev. 254, 260 (1937). Because there is a gift over at the end of the class gift, the testator intended the class gift to his grandchildren only to be a gift of a life interest in the income of the trust. Rolland v. Hamilton, 314 Mass. 56, 57–59 (1943), and cases cited. The general rule is that, in the absence of a contrary intent expressed in the will or a controlling statute stating otherwise, members of a class are joint tenants with rights of survivorship. Old Colony Trust Co. v. Treadwell, 312 Mass. 214, 218 (1942). Meserve v. Haak, 191 Mass. 220, 223 (1906). See G. L. c. 191, § 22 (1986 ed.) (antilapse statute).

This last stated principle becomes important in deciding whether Jennifer, the child of the deceased grandson, takes her deceased father's share in the trust income or whether the remaining class members, the other five grandchildren, take that income share equally by right of survivorship. Jennifer argues, under the general rule, that the will manifests an intent contrary to a class gift with rights of survivorship. We agree with this conclusion. Thus we need not decide, as Jennifer further argues, whether the rule of construction presuming a right of survivorship in class members should be rejected in the circumstances and replaced by a rule based on principles similar to those expressed in the antilapse statute.

Before we explain why the will expresses an intention that, during the term of the class gift, Jennifer, while living, should take her father's share in the income, we discuss the rule against perpetuities problem. The prospect that interests under this will may vest beyond the permissible limit of the rule against perpetuities is not only theoretically possible, it is actuarially likely. The interests of the grandchildren in the trust income vested at their father's death (if not sooner) and, because he was a life in being at the testator's death, those interests vested within the period of the rule. The gift over at the end of the class gift of income to the grandchildren, however, might not vest seasonably because another grandchild could have been born after the testator's death and could be the surviving grandchild. In this case, in fact, the three youngest grandchildren were born after the death of the testator but they are measuring lives for the term of the class gift. The parties agree that the purported gift of the remainder to the lineal descendants of the testator's grandchildren "twenty-one years after the death of the last surviving" grandchild violates the rule against perpetuities in its traditional form and would be void. See Second Bank–State St. Trust Co. v. Second Bank–State St. Trust Co., 335 Mass. 407, 410–411 (1957). There is no need at this time to decide the question of the proper distribution of trust income or assets at the death of the last grandchild. The question will be acute at the death of the last grandchild, when the class gift of income from the trust will terminate.

The rule against perpetuities problem need not be resolved at this time. It has some bearing, however, on what should be done during the term of the class gift with the one-sixth share of the trust income that is in dispute. We reject the argument that, because of the violation of the rule against perpetuities, the income interests should be treated as being more than life interests. There is no authority for such a proposition. Although the gift over violates the rule against perpetuities in its traditional form and in time may prove to violate it in actual fact, the language providing for such a distribution may properly be considered in determining a testator's intention with respect to other aspects of his will. See J.C. Gray, The Rule Against Perpetuities §§ 629–631, at 599–600 (4th ed. 1942) ("a provision void for remoteness is still to be resorted to for construing the rest of the will"). For the purposes of distribution of assets, a will is to be construed as if a provision violating the rule against perpetuities is not contained in it (Fosdick v. Fosdick, 6 Allen 41, 43 [1863]), but we have never said that the language of a void clause cannot be used to determine the testator's intention as to dispositions that do not violate the rule.

We are now in a position to discuss the question whether the class gift of income to grandchildren calls for the payment of income equally to those grandchildren living from time to time (as joint tenants with rights of survivorship) or whether the issue of any deceased grandchild succeeds by right of representation to his income interest. The latter result better conforms with the testator's intentions.

The testator provided that the trust should terminate twenty-one years after the death of his last grandchild. It is unlikely that the testator intended that trust income should be accumulated for twenty-one years, and we would tend to avoid such a construction. See Meserve v. Haak, 191 Mass. 220, 222 (1906). Certainly, we should not presume that he intended an intestacy as to that twenty-one year period. See Anderson v. Harris, 320 Mass. 101, 104–105 (1946). He must have expected that someone would receive distributions of income during those years. The only logical recipients of that income would be the issue (by right of representation) of deceased grandchildren, the same group of people who would take the trust assets on termination of the trust (assuming no violation of the rule against perpetuities). If these people were intended to receive income during the last twenty-one years of the trust as well as the trust assets on its termination, it is logical that they should also receive income during the term of the class gift if their ancestor (one of the grandchildren) should die. Such a pattern treats each grandchild and his issue equally throughout the intended term of the trust. Where, among other things, every other provision in the will concerning the distribution of trust income and principal (after the death of the testator and his wife) points to equal treatment of the testator's issue per stirpes, there is a sufficient contrary intent shown to overcome the rule of construction that the class gift of income to grandchildren is given to them as joint tenants with the right of survivorship.

* * *

Judgment shall be entered declaring that (1) Jennifer Ann Dewire in her lifetime is entitled to one-sixth of the net income of the trust during the period of the class gift of income, that is, until the death of the last grandchild (and a proportionate share of the income of any grandchild who dies leaving no issue), (2) no declaration shall be made at this time concerning the disposition of trust income or principal on the death of the last grandchild of Thomas A. Dewire. . . .

So ordered.

NOTES AND QUESTIONS

1. As the court points out, the traditional construction of a trust giving "income to my children for so long as one of my children remains alive" would be to treat the children as the equivalent of joint tenants with a right of survivorship: when the first child dies, the other children divide up the share of the deceased child.

Note that in Dewire itself, the court rejected that construction of the will. Why? On what facts did the court rely to conclude that the issue of a deceased grandchild should be entitled to her deceased parent's share of income?

2. Suppose you were drafting a trust instrument for a testator who wants income to be divided among his children for so long as one of the children remain alive, but who also wants the issue of a deceased child to succeed to her parent's share. How would you draft the trust instrument to accomplish that result without the ambiguity that would lead to litigation? Would you be better off creating separate trusts, or would that create unacceptable inefficiencies?

CHAPTER TEN

The Rule Against Perpetuities

Mention of the Rule Against Perpetuities strikes dread into the hearts of many lawyers (not to mention many law students). Consider the California Supreme Court's reaction in the infamous case of Lucas v. Hamm, 56 Cal.2d 583, 364 P.2d 685, 15 Cal.Rptr. 821 (1961), in which the court held that a lawyer was not liable for malpractice when he drafted a will that violated the Rule:

> The complaint, as we have seen, alleges that defendant drafted the will in such a manner that the trust was invalid because it violated the rules relating to perpetuities and restraints on alienation. These closely akin subjects have long perplexed the courts and the bar. Professor Gray, a leading authority in the field, stated: "There is something in the subject which seems to facilitate error. Perhaps it is because the mode of reasoning is unlike that with which lawyers are most familiar.... A long list might be formed of the demonstrable blunders with regard to its questions made by eminent men, blunders which they themselves have been sometimes the first to acknowledge; and there are few lawyers of any practice in drawing wills and settlements who have not at some time either fallen into the net which the Rule spreads for the unwary, or at least shuddered to think how narrowly they have escaped it." (Gray, The Rule Against Perpetuities (4th ed. 1942) p. xi; see also Leach, Perpetuities Legislation (1954) 67 Harv. L.Rev. 1349 [describing the rule as a "technicality-ridden legal nightmare" and a "dangerous instrumentality in the hands of most members of the bar"].) Of the California law on perpetuities and restraints it has been said that few, if any, areas of the law have been fraught with more confusion or concealed more traps for the unwary draftsman; that members of the bar, probate courts, and title insurance companies make errors in these matters ...

Lucas has been widely—and justifiably—assailed as a blot on the profession, and its vitality, even in California, is in some doubt. Nevertheless, the court's opinion illustrates a prevalent attitude toward the Rule. As Professor Susan F. French has put it:

> The victims of the Reign of Terror engendered by the Rule Against Perpetuities are not those whose interests are threatened by unborn widows, fertile octogenarians, and magic gravel pits, but the law students and practitioners laboring in the fields of property law.

Susan F. French, Perpetuities: Three Essays in Honor of My Father, 65 Wash. L. Rev. 323, 325 (1990).

The Rule's legendary intricacy has frustrated many an estate plan, spawned countless litigations, generated volumes of academic commentary, and, in recent years, led to significant law reform. In light of recent reforms, has the Rule become irrelevant? Can a student of Estates and Trusts avoid the subject altogether? In a significant number of states, the answer is probably "yes," but in others, an understanding of the Rule remains critical for the estate planner.

Perpetuities reform is at the cutting edge of the law. A large number of states have abolished the Rule altogether, and others have sharply reduced its bite.

Nevertheless, the common law Rule remains in effect in a number of states, and remains the foundation for perpetuities reform statutes in some other states. An understanding of the Rule, therefore, remains important, both to navigate through the reform legislation and to avoid drafting errors. The drafter of a will or trust instrument has not done her job if the will she drafts generates perpetuities litigation, even if a court ultimately upholds the instrument. Perpetuities litigation represents a needless expense to the estate, and it is the drafter's job to avoid that expense.

Our primary focus will be on the common law Rule Against Perpetuities. Until recently, the various statutory reforms have represented attempts to protect a testator or settlor against the effect of a poorly drafted instrument. Even in states that have enacted these reforms, a drafter should not act in reliance on these "salvage" doctrines; if the drafter avoids violating the common law Rule, the salvage doctrines become irrelevant.

After we explore the common law Rule, we will consider the shape and impact of reform legislation. Two types of reform have predominated in recent years. First, the Uniform Statutory Rule Against Perpetuities (USRAP)—incorporated into sections 2–901 through 2–906 of the Uniform Probate Code—builds on the common law Rule, but saves many grants that would have been invalid at common law. Second, an increasing number of states, in an effort to compete for trust business, have authorized the creation of "dynasty" trusts that avoid the Rule Against Perpetuities altogether. See generally Joel C. Dobris, The Death of the Rule Against Perpetuities, or the RAP Has No Friends, 35 Real Prop, Prob. & Tr. J. 601 (2000).

SECTION I. MAKING SENSE OF THE RULE: A BIT OF POLICY, AND A BIT OF HISTORY

Imagine Fannie Farmer, a wealthy landowner, determined to control the destiny of her family for generations to come. Suppose she writes a will leaving Blackacre—her 1,000 acre farm—as follows:

> 1. To my oldest living child for life, then, in succession, for life, to the oldest living descendant of each previous life tenant.
>
> 2. If any life tenant should die without issue, the property shall pass, for life, to the oldest of my descendants then alive, and

then, in succession to the oldest living descendant of each previous life tenant.

3. Any descendant of mine who marries a Roman Catholic shall be treated, for purposes of this will, as if that descendant died on the date of the marriage.

Would such a devise be problematic?

The answer is yes, for two separate reasons: first, the devise makes Blackacre inalienable; and second, the devise permits Fannie to exercise—from the grave—a degree of control over both the land and her family that many people believe is both inefficient and unfair. Let us examine each of these reasons.

Inalienability. If Fannie's devise were enforceable, Blackacre would effectively be inalienable. Suppose, for instance, Fannie's 25–year–old granddaughter, City Slicker, inherits a life estate upon her father's death. Although Slicker is a lousy farmer, she is a good business person, and needs capital to invest in an industrial plant. Because Slicker holds only a life estate, she will not be able to sell Blackacre to raise funds for her proposed investment. Moreover, she cannot even join with holders of future interests to sell Blackacre because many of the holders of future interests are not yet born.

Why is inalienability bad? Because it frustrates the ability of the current owners and prospective buyers to make a deal that will make them both better off. A good farmer, who could make Blackacre far more productive than Slicker and her kin, cannot acquire the land, while Slicker cannot acquire the investment capital that will make her better off. Moreover, even if Slicker wanted to operate the farm, Slicker would find it difficult to obtain a mortgage to finance improvements to the farm, because at Slicker's death, a lender's security would disappear. No living person benefits from Fannie's restriction; the only beneficiary—Fannie—may long be dead.

Now suppose Fannie had written a slightly different will, leaving Blackacre in trust, with the income to be payable as specified above. Are the concerns about inalienability still important? No, because the trustee is free to sell Blackacre to a better farmer, and to reinvest the proceeds to pay income to Fannie's descendants. There would be no reason to assume that Fannie's devise would reduce Blackacre's productivity—unless you believe trustees, by virtue of their position, are too risk averse and therefore make less productive investments. (We will consider the investment obligations of trustees in Chapter Thirteen.)

Intergenerational Equity. Land is essentially finite in quantity (with apologies to the Dutch). If Fannie's contemporaries followed her lead, all currently living landowners could impose restrictions on land use or ownership that would bind their descendants for generations to come. Members of subsequent generations would never have the same opportunity to control future use and ownership of land. Fannie's generation will have specified—for all time—who will succeed to land "ownership" and when.

This concern about wealthy members of one generation controlling the future disposition and use of wealth applies not only with land, but with other assets as well. Even if Fannie creates a trust, which would enable the trustee to sell the land, the proceeds of any sale would be controlled by the trust's provisions forever. Many people believe it is simply unfair to permit members of the current generation, by tying up property with future interests and trusts, to prevent members of future generations from giving effect to their own preferences about use and disposition of property—or, as in Fannie's devise, about their own marriage.

Are these concerns too fanciful to worry about? Won't people in Fannie's position recognize the inefficiency and inequity of provisions like those in Fannie's will? History provides us with an answer to those questions: if given the chance, many wealthy landowners will take the opportunity to tie up land for generations, regardless of the inefficiencies or inequities their actions create. For centuries, English common law reflected constant struggle between wealthy landowners devising new mechanisms to tie up land, and their successors seeking mechanisms to free land from restrictions imposed by their ancestors. The battle was not limited to courts; Parliament, too, weighed in—on both sides of the dispute.

The Rule Against Perpetuities represents the judicial compromise between those who wanted to tie up their property for generations and those who wanted to escape from restrictions imposed by their ancestors. The Rule began to take shape in the Duke of Norfolk's Case—decided in 1682—in which Lord Nottingham sustained a set of contingent interests created by the Earl of Arundel, but warned that courts would not sanction unlimited use of contingencies to tie up land:

> .... [T]he utmost limitation of a fee upon a fee, is not yet plainly determined, but it will be soon found out, if men shall set their wits on work to contrive by contingencies, to do that which the law has so long labored against, the thing will make itself evident, where it is convenient, and God forbid, but that mischief should be obviated and prevented.

Over time, the Rule crystallized into Gray's classic formulation:

> No interest is good unless it must vest, if at all, not later than twenty-one years after some life in being at the creation of the interest.

John Chipman Gray, Rule Against Perpetuities 191 (4th ed. 1942).

Does the formulation make any practical sense? The premise behind the Rule is that people with property should be permitted to tie up their property for a reasonable period of time—but no longer. The Rule defines reasonableness indirectly, in terms of life events rather than a period of years.

Suppose, for instance, a wealthy decedent knows that one or more of her children have a propensity to squander their money. Should she be able to structure her estate plan to protect her grandchildren (and the children themselves) from financial mismanagement? The Rule's answer is yes: a decedent may always tie up property for the lifetime of any person known to decedent—for the lifetime of any person alive at the time decedent creates that person's interest. Moreover, suppose at the death of the profligate beneficiary, decedent's ultimate beneficiaries—perhaps her grandchildren—are minor children. Shouldn't decedent be able to postpone vesting of their interests until they reach a reasonable age? Again, the Rule's answer is yes: the Rule permits decedent to keep the property in trust, and to avoid distribution to ultimate beneficiaries, until 21 years past the death of people alive when decedent created the interest. In effect, then, the Rule Against Perpetuities permits the wealthy decedent to control the disposition of her property for the lifetime of persons whose propensities she knows or fears, and for 21 years thereafter.

Suppose, however, a wealthy decedent creates a trust, and directs that her property shall remain in trust through the lifetime of her great-grandchildren, whenever born. If any of those great-grandchildren are born after decedent's death, decedent will never have had the opportunity to observe their habits or qualities. She has no reason to know which of the great-grandchildren might need protection from their own imprudence. Under those circumstances, the Rule deems it unreasonable for decedent to impose contingencies on the power of her great-grandchildren to use the property. Again, the Rule acts indirectly—by denying decedent the right to control disposition of property for longer than 21 years after the death of persons alive at the creation of the interest. Whether decedent actually knew of the propensities of any of her beneficiaries is not relevant in determining the validity of a future interest. But the general idea behind the Rule is this: it is unreasonable for a decedent to attempt to control property beyond the period during which decedent might plausibly assert some special knowledge of the propensities of one of her beneficiaries.

We offer this "rationale" for the Rule to show that the Rule's long endurance is partly attributable to the fact that it makes some practical sense. But it would be simplistic to suggest that the Rule developed in its current form because of that rationale. The Rule developed in response to particular cases and its precise shape may be as much the product of accident as of forethought. Could we improve on the Rule? Undoubtedly. And, as we shall see, legislators, scholars, and judges have made numerous attempts to do so. Nevertheless, it is much easier to apply the existing Rule with some idea of the policy that underlies the Rule's compromise.

SECTION II. THE RULE'S OPERATION

A. WHICH INTERESTS ARE SUBJECT TO THE RULE

The Rule Against Perpetuities is a rule against remoteness in vesting. That is, the Rule requires every interest to "vest" (or fail) within the Rule's period: lives in being plus 21 years. The important corollary to this principle is that interests that are vested as soon as they are created never violate the Rule.

As a result, drafters need worry about the Rule only when they create future interests in third parties. As we shall see, present interests and future interests in the grantor are "vested" at creation, and cannot, therefore, violate the Rule.

1. PRESENT INTERESTS

Whenever an instrument creates a present interest, the interest, by definition, is vested, and hence not subject to the Rule Against Perpetuities.

> ***Example 1:*** *T's will leaves Blackacre to A for life, remainder to A's surviving children. A's interest is a present possessory interest, and therefore a vested interest. As a result, A's interest is not subject to the Rule Against Perpetuities.*

Every present interest is vested whether that interest is held outright or in trust.

> ***Example 2:*** *T's will leaves $300,000 to Q Bank as trustee, with directions to pay income to A for life, and then to distribute principal to A's surviving children. A's interest, even though held in trust, is a present interest, and therefore not subject to the Rule Against Perpetuities.*

If, however, a trust beneficiary has no right to trust income or principal until a condition has been satisfied, the interest is not vested. Thus, if the beneficiary's right to income is conditioned on the trustee's exercise of discretion, the beneficiary has no immediate right to possession, and the interest is not vested. This does not mean, however, that the beneficiary's interest is invalid under the Rule; so long as the beneficiary is a person alive when the settlor created the trust, the beneficiary's interest is valid because the condition will be satisfied (or not), and the interest will vest (or not) within the beneficiary's lifetime.

> ***Example 3:*** *T's will leaves $300,000 to Q Bank as trustee, with directions to pay to A for life "so much of the trust income as the trustee, in its uncontrolled discretion, deems advisable." A's interest is not vested until the trustee exercises its discretion. A's interest is valid under the Rule Against Perpetuities because the trustee cannot exercise the discretion to pay income to A after A's death.*

2. FUTURE INTERESTS IN THE GRANTOR

Future interests in the grantor of an interest in property are by definition vested, and hence not subject to the Rule Against Perpetuities. This rule has been the subject of frequent attack, and makes no practical sense.

> ***Example 4:*** *O conveys Blackacre "to my sister S and her heirs for so long as Blackacre is used as a single family residence. If the premises are no longer used as a single family residence, Blackacre shall revert to me or to my estate." O retains a possibility of reverter, which is not subject to the Rule Against Perpetuities. O's*

interest is therefore valid even though O's interest might not become possessory for more than 100 years.

3. FUTURE INTERESTS IN TRANSFEREES

The Rule's principal application is to future interests in transferees.

The Rule as a Rule Against Contingency. The Rule is principally a rule against contingency; a property owner may not create interests that might remain contingent for too long—that is, for longer than the Rule's period. Why focus on contingency? Consider two reasons.

First, as a historical matter, the Rule was designed to promote alienability of land. Contingency inhibits alienability. So long as ownership of a future interest remains in doubt, with several potential claimants, assembling them all to consider a potential transfer is likely to be difficult and expensive. Some of the contingent beneficiaries may not be born, making it effectively impossible to secure their consent to a transfer. Even among the living beneficiaries, there may be disagreement about the likelihood that particular contingencies will occur, causing disagreement about how much of the sale proceeds each contingent beneficiary should receive. As we have seen, however, the concern about inalienability is of less force today, with the increased use of trusts, which permit the trustee to alienate trust property.

Second, contingencies increase the opportunity for a dead property owner to control ownership or use of property from the grave. Once an interest is vested in a particular beneficiary, the dead property owner has lost the opportunity to control the property (or his family). So, to the extent that the Rule Against Perpetuities is rooted in intergenerational equity—in a desire to prevent the dead from controlling the living—a rule that limits contingency also limits dead hand control. Consider, for example, a devise, in trust, "to my son and his heirs for so long as none of them marry a Jew, and if any of them does marry a Jew, then to my daughter and her heirs." By creating a contingent interest, settlor has attempted to control his son's descendants for generations. By limiting the duration of contingency, the Rule Against Perpetuities limits the settlor's ability to control his family from the grave.

Because the Rule is a rule against contingency, it does not affect interests vested when created.

> ***Example 5:*** *T devises Blackacre "to A for life, remainder to A's children until the death of A's last surviving child, then to B." A is a five-year old child at the time of T's death. B's interest is vested under the Rule and therefore valid—even though B's interest might not become possessory for more than 100 years. (We say that the interest in B is certain to become possessory, even though B may be dead at the time the interest actually becomes possessory.)*

Interests vested when created are always valid. By contrast, interests not vested when created are subject to the Rule, and require more careful evaluation. Recall the categories of future interests in transferees:

Indefeasibly Vested Remainders

Vested Remainders Subject to Complete Defeasance

Vested Remainders Subject to Open (or Subject to Partial Defeasance)

Contingent Remainders

Executory Interests

For purposes of the Rule, only the first two categories—indefeasibly vested remainders and vested remainders subject to complete defeasance—are vested interests. *Vested remainders subject to open are not vested for purposes of the Rule.* We will explore that fact in greater detail when we discuss class gifts. How do we determine whether unvested interests will vest within the period of the Rule? That is the question to which we now turn.

B. APPLYING THE RULE: VESTING AND MEASURING LIVES

The Rule requires that for an interest to be valid, we must be able to prove, at the time of the interest's creation, that the interest will vest or fail within the period of "lives in being plus 21 years." To understand the Rule, it is essential to understand what it means for an interest to "vest," what it means for an interest to "fail," and how to determine whether the interest will vest within "lives in being plus 21 years."

1. WHEN WILL AN INTEREST VEST?

As we have seen, if an interest is vested at the time of creation, the interest is valid under the Rule Against Perpetuities. Our concern, then, is with interests that are not vested at the time of creation. Future interests change over time. Interests that are contingent when created often become vested at some later time. Consider the following example:

> ***Example 6:*** *T's will devises property in trust, with directions that income should be distributed "to A for life, then to A's children and their heirs for so long as at least one child of A remains alive," and with a direction that at the death of A's last child, the principal should be distributed "to those of A's grandchildren then living." When will the future interests in A's children and in A's grandchildren vest?*
>
> ***Analysis:*** *T's will creates two future interests: one in A's children, and another in those of A's grandchildren who survive A's last surviving child. Neither of these interests is vested at the time of its creation—T's death. Consider first the interest in A's children. What interest do the children have? If A does not yet have children, the interest is a contingent remainder (because we cannot have a vested remainder in unascertained or unborn persons). If A has children, the interest is a vested remainder subject to open—which is not, for purposes of the Rule, a vested interest. When will the interest in A's children vest indefeasibly? At A's death, when A will become unable to have more children.*

Consider next the interest in A's grandchildren. What interest do the grandchildren have? At the time of T's death, they have a contingent remainder—whether or not any grandchildren of A have yet been born. When will that interest vest? At the death of A's last surviving child. Why? Because by the terms of the will, only those grandchildren of A who are alive at that time are eligible to take the remainder interest.

2. WHAT DOES IT MEAN FOR AN INTEREST TO "FAIL" OR "FAIL TO VEST?"

Not all contingent interests will vest. Indeed, when we say that an interest is contingent, we are conceding that the interest will vest only if a particular (and uncertain) contingency actually occurs. If the contingency does not occur, the interest fails; that is, the interest will never vest and never become possessory.

Reconsider Example 6. Assume that A has no children at the time of the conveyance. If A never has children, the interest in A's children will fail at A's death. If A does have children, the interest in A's children will vest by the time of A's death. Thus, one of two things will definitely happen by A's death: either the interest in A's children will have vested, or the interest will have failed. The interest in A's children cannot remain contingent past the time of A's death.

Note that whether a contingent remainder fails has nothing to do with the Rule Against Perpetuities. Contingent interests fail because the required contingencies do not occur. If you understand that fact, you will understand the following point, and avoid one of the most common confusions about application of the Rule Against Perpetuities: *to say that a contingent interest fails is not equivalent to saying that the interest is invalid under the Rule Against Perpetuities!* Example 6 illustrates the principle. The interest in A's children might fail, but the interest is perfectly valid under the Rule Against Perpetuities. Why? Because we will know whether the interests will vest or fail at A's death—a time within the period of the Rule. That is, the interests of A's children cannot remain contingent past the date of A's death, and, as you already know, the Rule is a rule against contingency.

The lesson is that in evaluating the validity of an interest, the first step is to determine, *by the terms of the instrument itself*, the last moment at which the interest could vest or fail. The Rule Against Perpetuities itself is irrelevant to that determination. Then, once you have determined the last moment at which the interest could vest or fail, you must determine whether that moment is within the period permitted by the Rule. If it is not, vesting will be too remote, and the interest will be invalid under the Rule.

3. INTERESTS CAN VEST BEFORE THEY BECOME POSSESSORY

A future interest can vest before it becomes a possessory interest. Consider the following example:

Example 7: *T's will devises property in trust, with directions that income should be distributed "to A for life, then to A's children and their heirs for so long as at least one child of A remains alive," and with a direction that at the death of A's last child, the principal should be distributed "to those of A's grandchildren alive at A's death." When does the interest in A's grandchildren vest?*

Analysis: *The interest will vest at A's death, because by the terms of the will, only those grandchildren of A who are alive at A's death are eligible to take the remainder interest. If none are alive at that time, the interest would fail altogether, but the interest could not remain contingent after A's death. Grandchildren born later would not share in the remainder. Note, however, that although the grandchildren born at A's death have an indefeasibly vested remainder, they will not have a right to possession until the death of A's last surviving child.*

The Rule Against Perpetuities requires only that an interest vest within the required period; it does not require that the interest become possessory within that period.

PROBLEM

Compare the interest in A's grandchildren created in Example 7 with the interest in A's grandchildren created in Example 6. Is either interest valid under the Rule Against Perpetuities? If yes, which one? Explain why.

4. "LIVES IN BEING": CHOOSING MEASURING LIVES

To be valid, an interest must vest, in Gray's words, "not later than twenty-one years after some life in being at the creation of the interest." The Rule Against Perpetuities is a rule of proof: if you can *prove* that an interest will vest within the period of "twenty-one years after some life in being," you have proven that the interest does not violate the Rule. The trick, then, is to choose a life in being—a so-called "measuring life" (or "validating life")—so that you can guarantee that the interest in question will vest within twenty-one years after the measuring life dies. To make the point more concrete, to establish that an interest does not violate the rule, you must be able, at the time the interest is created, to point to a living person (or to a group of living people), and to guarantee that within 21 years after the death of that person (or the death of the last member of the group), the interest in question will have vested or failed.

Note that the Rule does not require you to be able to point to a single living person and guarantee that the interest in question will vest within the lifetime of that person plus 21 years; an interest is valid under the Rule if you can point to a group of living people and guarantee that the interest in question will vest within 21 years of the death of the last survivor of the members of the group. In other words, *even if the interest is not certain to vest within the lifetime of a single person, the interest is valid if it is certain to vest within the lifetime of a group of people, all of whom are alive at the time of the conveyance.*

> ***Example 8:*** *T's will leaves property in trust, "income to be distributed to my children for their lives, and at the death of my last surviving child, the principal is to be distributed to my youngest grandchild." T is survived by three children, A, B, and C. Who can we use as measuring lives to establish the validity of the interest in T's youngest grandchild?*
>
> ***Analysis:*** *We cannot use A, B, or C individually to establish the validity of the interest, because we do not know, at T's death, which child will live longest. For instance, if we try to use A, B could have a child 30 years after the death of A, and that child might be T's youngest grandchild. On the other hand, if we point to A, B, and C collectively, we know that the youngest grandchild of T will be born by the death of the survivor of A, B, and C. Therefore, we can use A, B, and C together as measuring lives to establish the validity of the interest in T's youngest grandchild.*

One further point: in testing the validity of the interests created by a single instrument, you need not use the same measuring life for each interest. To reiterate, *different measuring lives may be used to establish the validity of different interests in the same instrument.*

Strategies for Choosing Measuring Lives. First, focus on your goal. You want to identify a measuring life (or a group of measuring lives) who satisfies two criteria:

> (1) the interest you are testing must vest within 21 years after the death of that measuring life; and
>
> (2) the measuring life must be a person alive at the time the interest was created.

Note that if you can find even one measuring life who satisfies these two criteria, the interest you are testing is valid under the Rule Against Perpetuities.

> ***Example 9:*** *T devises Blackacre "to A for life, remainder to A's youngest child for life, remainder to B if B survives A's youngest child, otherwise to C." Is B's interest valid under the Rule Against Perpetuities?*
>
> ***Solution:*** *Yes. We can use B as a measuring life. B has a contingent remainder. At B's death, one of two circumstances will have occurred: either (1) A's youngest child will have died, and B's interest will have vested; or (2) A's youngest child will still be alive, and B's interest will have failed. Either way, the remainder will not remain contingent past the time of B's death. As a result, we can be certain that the interest will have vested or failed within B's lifetime. Therefore, B satisfies the first criterion for measuring lives. Since B was a life in being at the creation of the interest, B satisfies the second criterion for measuring lives. B's interest is*

therefore valid even though we cannot use anyone else as a measuring life. A does not satisfy the first criterion, since A's youngest child could survive A by more than 21 years. A's youngest child does not satisfy the second criterion, since A's youngest child could be a person born after T's death.

(Note: this example also illustrates the principle that different measuring lives can be used to validate different interests in the same grant. We can use A's life to validate the interest in A's youngest child, and B's life to validate the interest in B).

Once you understand that your goal is to find a measuring life who satisfies the two criteria, how do you start your search? Start by determining when the interest you are testing will vest. Most contingent interests will vest (a) at a time defined in the instrument creating the interest (b) if a specified contingency has occurred. Both the time of vesting and the contingency generally have some relationship to lifetime events. That is, the interest is likely to vest at the death of a particular person, or at the time a particular person reaches a specified age. The most common contingency is survivorship: the grantor may provide, for instance, that the interest vests in those children of A who survive A. Make a list of all of those people during whose lifetime, or at whose death, or within 21 years of whose death, the interest in question will vest or fail. Some scholars (and some students) find it useful to speak of assembling the lives causally related to vesting. See, e.g., Jesse Dukeminier, Perpetuities: The Measuring Lives, 85 Colum. L. Rev. 1648, 1665–74 (1985).

For instance, consider Example 9. Ask when the interest in B will vest, and what contingencies have to be satisfied for the interest to vest. The interest will vest at the death of A's youngest child, but only if B is then alive. So we know that the interest will vest or fail during the lifetime of (1) A's youngest child; and (2) B. That is, A's youngest child and B both satisfy the first criterion for measuring lives.

Once you have assembled your list of persons who satisfy the first criterion—persons during whose lifetime (or within 21 years of whose death) the interest must vest or fail, you must turn to the second criterion for measuring lives: are the persons on your list certain to be alive at the creation of the interest? Again, consider Example 9. Test the two people who satisfy the first criterion: A's youngest child and B. Can you guarantee that either of them was alive at the creation of the interest, here, T's death? Consider A's youngest child first. So long as A was alive at T's death, A was capable of having another child (as we shall see, the Rule presumes that people—men and women—can have children at any age). Therefore, at the moment of T's death, we do not know that A's youngest child has yet been born. As a result, A's youngest child does not satisfy the second criterion for measuring lives. Does that mean the interest in B is invalid under the Rule? No. It just means we have to test the next life on our list: B. Was B alive at T's death? Yes! (If T made a bequest to someone named "B," or to someone named "Bill Bates," that person must have been alive at T's death. In other words, treat "letters" as living people.)

Therefore, B satisfies *both* criteria for measuring lives, and the interest in B is valid.

To summarize: in testing the validity of an interest under the Rule Against Perpetuities, take the following steps:

(1) Determine when the interest will vest or fail, and upon what contingencies;

(2) List all persons during whose lifetime, or at whose death (or within 21 years of whose death) the contingencies will occur, causing the interest to vest or fail. This list is a list of persons who satisfy the first criterion for measuring lives.

(3) Check to see whether any of the persons on the list were certain to be alive at the creation of the interest. That is, check to see which of the persons on the list satisfy the second criterion for measuring lives. If any of the people on the list satisfy the second criterion, the interest is valid under the Rule Against Perpetuities. If none of the persons on the list satisfy the second criterion, the interest is invalid under the Rule Against Perpetuities.

Now, let us work out some additional examples.

Example 10: *T's will creates a trust, and directs her trustee to pay trust income "to my husband for life, and then to my husband's youngest child for life." The will directs that at the death of the husband's youngest child, the trust principal be distributed "to my youngest grandchild." Which interests, if any, are invalid under the Rule Against Perpetuities?*

Solution: *All interests are valid. Consider first the interest in the husband's youngest child. Step 1. When does that interest vest? At husband's death, when we will know for sure the identity of husband's youngest child. Step 2. During whose lifetime or at whose death will the interest vest? At the death of T's husband. Step 3. Was the husband alive at the creation of the interest? Yes. Therefore, we can use the husband as a measuring life, and the interest in the husband's youngest child is valid.*

Now consider the interest in T's youngest grandchild. Step 1. When does that interest vest? At the death of T's last surviving child, when no more grandchildren can be born to T. Step 2. During whose lifetime or at whose death will the interest vest? At the death of all of T's children. Step 3. Were all of the children alive at the creation of the interest? (Put in other terms, is the class closed?) Yes. T could not have had children after her death. Therefore, we can use T's children as measuring lives, and the interest in T's youngest grandchild is valid. (A closed class of lives will often save an interest).

Example 11: *Same will as Example 10, except that at the death of the husband's youngest child, the trust principal is to be distributed "to T's youngest grandchild then living." Is the interest in the youngest grandchild valid?*

Solution: *No. Step 1. When will the interest vest? At the death of the husband's youngest child. Because T has imposed a survivorship condition, the interest in the youngest child will not necessarily vest by the death of the last of T's children. Step 2. During whose lifetime, or at whose death, will the interest vest? Here, we know that the interest will vest by the death of (1) the husband's youngest child and (2) T's youngest grandchild. Step 3. Can we guarantee that either of these people were lives in being at the creation of the interest? No. The husband could have had a child after T's death, and one of T's children could have had a child after T's death. Therefore the interest in the youngest grandchild is invalid under the Rule Against Perpetuities.*

Note that in Example 10, we assumed that T's husband could not have children after his death. We also assumed that T's children could not have children after their death. Neither statement is technically accurate. Even without the benefit of modern technology, a child could be born to a father for up to nine months after the father's death. For Rule Against Perpetuities purposes, a child is treated as "in being" from the moment of conception. Hence, for purposes of the Rule, all of a parent's children will have been identified by the parent's death.

Frozen embryos, sperm banks, and other modern technologies have spawned numerous Rule Against Perpetuities hypotheticals. To date, however, no court has held an interest invalid under the Rule because of the possibility that a child might be born years after its natural parents' death. The reason is obvious: if contingent interests were to be invalid because of the possibility that children might be born to their parents long after the parents' death, even the most innocuous future interests would be invalid. A devise "to my daughter for life, remainder to my daughter's youngest child" would create an invalid remainder in the grandchild because of the possibility that a grandchild would be born 30 or 40 years after the death of testator's daughter. Nevertheless, the possibilities have generated more interest than one normally associates with the Rule Against Perpetuities.

If you have followed the discussion so far, you should understand that the measuring life need not be a person named in the instrument. Consider the following example:

Example 12: *T devises property "to my maid M and her heirs until the birth of my first grandchild, and upon the birth of my first grandchild, the property should be distributed to that grandchild." At T's death, T leaves one surviving child, C, who is not mentioned in T's will. Is the interest in the grandchild valid, and if so, who can be used as the measuring life?*

Solution: *The interest is valid because we can use C as a measuring life. We can be sure that the interest in the grandchild will vest, or fail, by the time of C's death. Note that we cannot use M or the grandchild—the two people named in the instrument—as measuring lives (Explain which criterion each fails to meet).*

5. TWENTY–ONE YEARS

We have focused almost exclusively on the "lives in being" component of the Rule's period. The Rule's period, however, is "lives in being plus 21 years." What impact does the "21–year" period have on analysis of future interests?

In most circumstances, the 21 years are irrelevant—unless the creator of the interest has expressly postponed vesting by 21 years, or has included a condition requiring survivorship to a specified age. The reason should be apparent. If we cannot guarantee that an interest will vest within a person's lifetime, we will not generally be able to guarantee that the same interest will vest within 21 years of her death—again, unless, the instrument expressly postpones vesting until 21 years after the person's death, or the instrument provides for vesting in those of a person's children who reach age 21.

Reconsider Example 11. We could not use T's children as measuring lives because H's youngest child might survive all of T's children, and the interest in T's youngest grandchild would not vest until the death of H's youngest child. But if H's youngest child could outlive T's children by one day, H's youngest child could also outlive T's children by 25 years. Hence, extending the "lives in being" period by 21 years would not enable us to use T's children as measuring lives, and would not save the grant.

There are of course, situations when the 21–year period is helpful in upholding an interest. Consider the following:

> ***Example 13:*** *T devises property "to my children for life, remainder to the first of my grandchildren to reach age 21." Step 1. When will the interest vest? When T's first grandchild reaches age 21. Step 2. During whose lifetime will the interest vest? During the lifetime of T's grandchildren. Note that the interest might not vest within the lifetime of T's children. If, however, we ask whether the interest will vest within 21 years of the death of T's last surviving child, the answer is yes; any grandchildren born to T's children will reach the age of 21 within 21 years after the death of all of T's children. Step 3. We cannot use T's grandchildren as measuring lives because one or more of them might have been born after T's death. We can use T's children as measuring lives because they were all born by T's death. Hence, the interest in the grandchild is valid—but only because we can add 21 years to the lives of T's children.*

The 21 years may also be used without any measuring life. Thus, if T devises property "to those of my descendants alive 21 years after my death", the devise is valid, because the interests will vest within 21 years of the creation of the interest.

One caution: the 21–year period can be tacked on to the end of a life in being, but it cannot precede a life in being. Thus, T may not direct that trust principal be distributed "to those of my descendants alive at the death of the last survivor of all of my issue born within 21 years after my death."

PROBLEMS

Which of these devises are valid under the Rule Against Perpetuities? For those interests you conclude are valid, identify the measuring life you would use to prove your conclusion.

1. T devises Blackacre "to A for life, remainder to the first child of A who

a. reaches the age of 18."

b. reaches the age of 40."

c. graduates from college."

2. T devises property, in trust, with directions to pay income "to A for life, and then to distribute principal

a. to the first child of mine who reaches age 18."

b. to the first child of mine who finishes college."

3. T devises property, in trust, and directs the trustee to pay income "to my sister for life, then to my sister's children until the death of the last survivor of my sister's children," and then to distribute principal to

a. "my brother's children."

b. "my brother, if he is then alive."

c. "those of my brother's children who are then alive."

d. "my youngest grandchild."

e. "my oldest surviving grandchild."

Would any of your answers change if (1) T's brother were dead at the time of T's death; or (2) T's children were all dead at the time of T's death?

4. T devises real estate in trust, and provides that

> "The above described real estate is given, devised and bequeathed to the said John Warren [T's grandson], and subject to said Trust named above for and during his natural life, and at his death to his then living child or children, or survivors thereof, and in the event there be no descendants of said child or children, then to his sisters, viz: Emma B. Warren and Goldy Maude Warren, for the sole use and benefit forever, share and share alike, subject to the following conditions, viz: That in the event of the death of either of said sisters and leaving no child or children, or descendants of said child or children, then to the survivor, and if neither of said sisters is living, then to my legal heirs at law, as per the laws of descent, share and share alike for their sole use and benefit forever."

See Warren v. Albrecht, 213 Ill.App.3d 55, 157 Ill.Dec. 160, 571 N.E.2d 1179 (1991).

NOTE

The Rule Against Perpetuities has spawned an abundant literature designed to make it easier for students (and lawyers) to understand its operation. Among the most entertaining (and enlightening) efforts are two classic articles by Professor Leach—W. Barton Leach, Perpetuities in a Nutshell, 51 Harv. L. Rev. 638 (1938), and W. Barton Leach, Perpetuities: The Nutshell Revisited, 78 Harv. L. Rev. 973 (1965).

More recent efforts include Melanie B. Leslie & Stewart E. Sterk, Trusts & Estates (Concepts and Insights) (2nd ed. 2011); Maureen E. Markey, Ariadne's Thread: Leading Students Into and Out of the Labyrinth of the Rule Against Perpetuities, 54 Clev. St. L. Rev. 337 (2006);Darryl C. Wilson, Waltzing to R.A.P., 39 Creighton L. Rev. 129 (2005); Roger W. Andersen, Understanding Trusts and Estates 287–317 (3rd ed. 2003); Jesse Dukeminier, A Modern Guide to Perpetuities, 74 Cal. L. Rev. 1867 (1986); Carolyn B. Featheringill, Understanding the Rule Against Perpetuities: A Step by Step Approach, 13 Cumb. L. Rev. 161 (1983).

For suggestions directed at the drafter of wills and trust instruments, see William McGovern, Perpetuities Pitfalls and How Best to Avoid Them, 6 Real Prop., Prob. & Tr. J. 155 (1971).

SECTION III. RECURRING PROBLEMS

A. WHEN DOES THE PERPETUITIES PERIOD START TO RUN?: REVOCABLE AND IRREVOCABLE INTER VIVOS TRUSTS

Future interests must vest within the period of "lives in being plus 21 years" from the creation of the interest. When is an interest created? Generally, the answer is straightforward. If decedent creates a future interest in an instrument designed to take effect immediately, the period starts to run from the date of the instrument. If decedent creates a future interest in a will—which does not become effective until decedent's death—the period starts to run at the moment of decedent's death.

Why does it matter? The principal trap for the drafter is that if a person makes an *inter vivos* transfer, the transferor might have children born after the transfer. As a result, the transferor's children will not meet the second criterion for measuring lives—they might not all be lives in being at the creation of the interest. By contrast, when testator makes a disposition by will, testator's children, as a class, are available as measuring lives because testator can't have any more children.

> ***Example 14:*** *O, during her lifetime conveys property into an irrevocable trust, directing that income be paid "to my children and their heirs for so long as one of my children remains alive" and directing that principal then be paid "to my oldest grandchild alive at the death of my last surviving child." The remainder in the grandchildren is invalid. The interest will vest during the lifetime*

of (a) testator's children and (b) testator's grandchildren, but we cannot be certain that all of testator's grandchildren are alive at the time of the transfer, and we cannot be certain that all of testator's children are alive at the time of the transfer. Hence, neither class can be used as measuring lives.

Example 15: *Same transfer, except the trust is created by will. Now, the interest in the oldest grandchild is valid, because the interest will vest at the death of testator's last surviving child. We can use testator's children as measuring lives because all of testator's children will have been born by testator's death.*

Suppose decedent creates an *inter vivos* trust, but reserves powers to revoke or modify the trust. Consider the following case.

Cook v. Horn

Supreme Court of Georgia, 1958.
214 Ga. 289, 104 S.E.2d 461.

[In 1929 O.J. Massee, Jr., created a revocable inter vivos insurance trust. He transferred to the trustee Bank certain insurance policies made payable to the Bank. The trust instrument provided that the trustee would collect the proceeds of the policies and hold them in trust for certain purposes: the income was payable to the widow for life; on her death (or if she predeceased the settlor, then on his death) the principal was to be divided into as many shares as the settlor had children then living and deceased children whose issue were then living; the income from the share of a living child was payable to him for life, and at his death the principal distributable to his issue, provided that the share of any such issue under 21 should be retained in trust until such issue reached 21; there were detailed gifts over to the other children or their issue if a child died without issue; there was also a provision for distribution, on the death of the widow or settlor, to the issue of a deceased child if the issue had attained 21 and for holding in trust the share of issue of the deceased child not then 21 until the issue reached 21. The trust instrument reserved to the settlor the usual powers, including a power to change beneficiaries of any insurance policy and to amend or revoke the trust agreement in whole or in part.

The children of the settlor petitioned the court to terminate the trust; they contend that remainder interests beyond theirs are void under the Rule. The lower court sustained a demurrer to the petition. The portion of the opinion construing the document and disposing of other contentions is omitted.]

■ WYATT, PRESIDING JUSTICE.

* * * It is next contended that the instrument in question violates the rule against perpetuities, and that since the limitations beyond the petitioners are void, they are entitled to have the property delivered to them. In order to determine this question, it is necessary first to determine when this instrument took effect, whether at the time it was executed and

delivered, or at the death of the settlor. This question is settled by the decision of this court in Wilson v. Fulton National Bank, 188 Ga. 691, 4 S.E.2d 660, where an instrument similar in all material respects to that here under consideration was held to create a valid trust, to convey a present interest, and not to be testamentary in character.

It is contended that, if the trust instrument is effective to convey a present interest at the time it was executed and delivered, as is held above, then the limitations beyond the petitioners are void as violative of the rule against perpetuities, because there was a possibility at that time that the settlor would have additional children born to him thereafter, by whose life the duration of the trust would be limited. This result does not necessarily follow. While there is a scarcity of authority on this question, and none that we have found in Georgia, the prevailing opinion by both the courts of other jurisdictions and recognized text writers is that, when a settlor has the power during his lifetime to revoke or destroy the trust estate for his own exclusive personal benefit, the question whether interests, or any of them, created by an instrument or deed of trust are void because in violation of the rule against perpetuities, is to be determined as of the date of the settlor's death and not as of the date the instrument is executed and delivered. See Ryan v. Ward, 192 Md. 342, 64 A.2d 258, 7 A.L.R.2d 1078; Mifflin's Appeal, 121 Pa. 205, 15 A. 525, 1 L.R.A. 453; Goesele v. Bimeler, 14 How. 589, 14 L.Ed.554; Manufacturers Life Insurance Company v. von Hamm–Young Co., 34 Haw. 288; Pulitzer v. Livingston, 89 Me. 359, 36 A. 635; City Bank Farmers Trust Co. v. Cannon, 291 N.Y. 125, 51 N.E.2d 674, 157 A.L.R. 1424; Equitable Trust Co. v. Pratt, 117 Misc. 708, 193 N.Y.S. 152, affirmed on opinion below 206 App.Div. 704, 199 N.Y.S. 921; Gray, Rule Against Perpetuities, (4th Ed.) 510, par. 524; 45 Harv.L.Rev.896; 51 Harv.L.Rev.638; 86 U. Pa. L.Rev. 221; Restatement of Property, § 373 and comments (c) and (d), and Ryan v. Ward, 192 Md. 342, 64 A.2d 258, 7 A.L.R.2d 1078.

While none of these authorities is binding upon this court, the conclusion reached by them is in accord with the aim of and reason for the rule against perpetuities, which is to prevent the tying up of property for an unreasonable length of time and to prohibit unreasonable restraint upon the alienation of property. So long as the settlor of an inter vivos trust has the absolute right to revoke or terminate the trust for his own exclusive personal benefit, there is no tying up of property and no restraint upon the alienability of the property in the trust fund, and thus no reason to include this time during which the trust is so destructible in determining whether a limitation is violative of the rule against perpetuities. Restatement, Property, sec. 373 states: "The period of time during which an interest is destructible, pursuant to the uncontrolled volition, and for the exclusive personal benefit of the person having such a power of destruction is not included in determining whether the limitation is invalid under the rule against perpetuities." We conclude that this rule is a sound one, which does no violence to the rule against perpetuities, but is in complete accord with its aim and purpose.

In the instant case, the settlor, during his lifetime, had an absolute right to revoke or terminate the trust, to change the beneficiaries in the policies, and to receive any and all benefits under the policies. Therefore, under the rulings above made, the time from which it will be determined whether any of the limitations in the trust agreement are void for remoteness is the date of the settlor's death. When so considered, it is apparent that none of the limitations in the instrument violate the rule against perpetuities, since all limitations under the instrument will end and all interests vest within twenty-one years after the death of the settlor's children plus the usual period of gestation, and, of course, no children can be born to the settlor after his death plus the usual period of gestation. It follows, the limitations over to the issue of the children of the settlor are valid, and the petitioners are not entitled to have the trust terminated for any reason alleged. The judgment of the court below dismissing the petition on general demurrer was therefore not error.

Judgment affirmed.

All the Justices concur.

QUESTIONS

1. Why did it matter in Cook v. Horn whether the Rule's period began to run (a) at the time the trust instrument was executed, or (b) at the date of O.J. Massee's death?

2. In Cook v. Horn, settlor reserved a power to revoke the trust instrument in whole or in part. Suppose, however, settlor had created an *inter vivos* trust, and had delivered $100,000 to the trustee, pursuant to a trust instrument which reserved to the settlor the power to withdraw from the trust "such sums as he may in his absolute discretion see fit, but not in excess of the sum of $5,000 per year." Should the perpetuities period run from the date on which the trust was created, or from the date of decedent's death? See Ryan v. Ward, 192 Md. 342, 64 A.2d 258 (1949) [date of trust creation].

Should it matter whether settlor actually exercised the power to withdraw principal?

3. Why did the children in Cook v. Horn challenge the validity of the trust?

PROBLEMS

1. S creates an irrevocable *inter vivos* trust, and directs that income be paid "to my children until the death of my last surviving child", and then directs that the trust principal be divided equally "among my grandchildren." Is the interest in grandchildren valid under the Rule?

Would the same interest be valid if the trust were revocable? If the trust were a testamentary trust?

2. Consider the following language, taken from the irrevocable trust instrument at issue in Ryan v. Ward, 192 Md. 342, 64 A.2d 258 (1949). The instrument reserved the trust income to the grantor for the grantor's lifetime, and then provided:

> "From and after the death of the Grantor, the Trustee shall pay over the net income . . . unto Frank R. Ward, son of the Grantor, during his lifetime, and upon the death of the Grantor's said son, Frank R. Ward, or from and after the Grantor's death in case his said son should predecease him, the Trustee shall pay the net income derived from the trust fund unto the lineal descendants, per stirpes, from time to time living, of the Grantor's said son until the death of the last surviving child of the Grantor's said son, who shall be living at the time of the Grantor's death, and upon the death of the last surviving child of the Grantor's said son, who shall be living at the time of the death of the Grantor, the trust hereby created shall terminate, and the corpus or principal thereof shall be by the Trustee conveyed . . . in equal and even shares unto the then living children of the Grantor's said son, and unto the issue then living of each then deceased child of the Grantor's said son, so that each then living child of the Grantor's said son shall take and receive, absolutely, one equal share thereof, and the issue then living of each then deceased child of the Grantor's said son shall take and receive, per stirpes and not per capita, one equal share thereof absolutely."

Show why the trust instrument violated the Rule Against Perpetuities, and redraft the instrument to avoid any perpetuities problem. How do you think the drafter made the critical error?

B. REMOTE POSSIBILITIES

Most of the worst perpetuities problems arise from a drafter's failure to contemplate realistically implausible—but theoretically possible—events which might cause future interests to vest beyond the period of the Rule. Remember, the Rule requires that we can prove—to a logical certainty—that an interest will vest within the Rule's period. If an extraordinarily unlikely event could cause an interest to vest beyond the period of the Rule, the common law invalidated the interest from its inception; the common law did not wait to see whether the unlikely event actually occurred. Remote possibilities have so much become part of the lore of the Rule Against Perpetuities, that a number of them have generated their own names, each derived from the unlikely event that has led to perpetuities problems: the fertile octogenarian, the precocious toddler, the unborn widow, and the slothful executor. In this section, we examine the drafting pitfalls associated with each of these remote possibilities.

1. THE FERTILE OCTOGENARIAN

Arguably the most famous perpetuities case of all time is Jee v. Audley, 1 Cox 324, 29 Eng. Rep. 1186, decided by the Court of Chancery in 1787. In *Jee*, testator's will created a life interest in his wife, followed by a future interest which vested within the rule's period, but which could have (but might not have) endured for centuries. When and if that interest expired, the will provided that the property should be "equally divided between the daughters *then* living of my kinsman John Jee and his wife, Elizabeth Jee." At the time of Edward Audley's death, John and Elizabeth Jee were each over 70.

Who could serve as measuring lives for the interest in the Jee daughters? Since the Jee daughters' interest was contingent upon survival of the designated event, the interest would have to vest or fail by the death of the last Jee daughter. Hence, the Jee daughters as a class satisfied the first criterion for measuring lives. The question before the court, then, was whether the Jee daughters satisfied the second criterion for measuring lives: were they all "lives in being" at the time of Edward Audley's death? Counsel for the daughters argued that they were—that because of their parents' age, it was clear that there could be no further Jee daughters. Lord Kenyon's response has become a classic:

> "I am desired to do in this case something which I do not feel myself at liberty to do, namely to suppose it impossible for persons in so advanced an age as John and Elizabeth Jee to have children; but if this can be done in one case it may in another, and it is a very dangerous experiment, and introductive of the greatest inconvenience to give a latitude to such sort of conjecture.... I am of opinion, therefore, though the testator might possibly mean to restrain the limitation to the children who should be living at the time of the death, I cannot, consistently with decided cases, construe it in such restrained sense, but must intend it to take in after-born children."

As a result, Lord Kenyon held the interest in the Jee daughters invalid, and cemented the common law Rule that people—men and women—are capable of having children until the moment they die.

What drafting consequences follow from the rule in Jee v. Audley? When drafting an instrument spanning multiple generations, the drafter must not refer to the "children" of a living person as if it would be impossible for that person to have additional children.

> ***Example 16:*** *T's will devises property in trust, "income payable to my sister's children until the death of my sister's last surviving child, and at that time, the principal should be distributed among my then-living issue, per stirpes." T's sister is 85 years old at T's death. Is the devise to the issue valid?*
>
> ***Solution:*** *No. The interest in issue will vest in issue living at the death of the sister's last surviving child. Consider (1) then-living issue, and (2) the sister's children, as measuring lives. Issue might be born to testator at any point after testator's death, so then-living issue are not lives in being at testator's death. The sister, despite her advanced age, might have more children after testator's death. As a result, her children as a class do not satisfy the second criterion for measuring lives, and the interest in issue is invalid.*

Suppose, in Example 16, testator's will had provided "income to my sister's children Andrea, Brian, and Carla and their heirs until the death of the survivor of Andrea, Brian, and Carla, and at that time, the principal should be distributed among my then-living issue, per stirpes." The interest in then-living issue would be valid. Do you see why?

PROBLEMS

1. S, an 85–year–old settlor of an irrevocable *inter vivos* trust, directs that

> "trust income be distributed to myself for life, then to my children and their heirs until the death of my last surviving child, and at that time, the principal should be distributed among my then-living grandchildren, per capita."

Is the bequest to grandchildren valid under the Rule? Would the bequest be valid if the same provision had been made in settlor's will? Redraft the *inter vivos* trust provision to eliminate any Rule Against Perpetuities problems.

2. T, in her will, creates a trust, and directs that

> "trust income be distributed to my children until the Chicago Cubs win the World Series, and at that time, the principal should be distributed....
>
> a. to my then-living nieces and nephews."
>
> b. to my now-living nieces and nephews."
>
> c. to my now-living nieces and nephews who are also alive when the Cubs win the World Series."

Which distribution of principal would be valid under the Rule Against Perpetuities, assuming T has one living 65–year–old sister (and three deceased brothers)?

NOTES

1. If the common law's presumption that people—especially women—can have children at any age seems absurd, what limits would you suggest? Newspapers occasionally report births to women over the age of 60, and reports of births to octogenarian fathers are common. See, e.g., Gina Kolata, A Record and Big Questions as Woman Gives Birth at 63, N.Y. Times, Apr. 24, 1997, at A1 [reporting on woman who had received donated egg]; Bonnie Miller Rubin & Ronald Kotulak, Never Too Old a Reality for Dads—And Moms, Chi. Trib., Apr. 25, 1997, at 1 [reporting same birth, and birth the previous week of a child to actor Tony Randall, then 77 years old].

Should the common law's presumption be rebutted by evidence of a hysterectomy or other medical procedure that precludes further children?

Does the possibility of adoptive children, together with modern reproductive technology, suggest that the common law position makes sense even in the modern era?

In Demund v. LaPoint, 169 Misc.2d 1020, 647 N.Y.S.2d 662 (N.Y.Sup. Ct.1996), an 80–year–old woman without biological children adopted her 61–year old nephew so that the nephew would qualify as her child and succeed to a remainder interest created by her father's will. The court foiled her effort, relying upon a New York statute indicating that "the person adopted is not deemed the child of the foster parent so as to defeat the rights of remaindermen."

Consider the following discussion of the effect of new reproductive technologies (NRTs) on the Rule Against Perpetuities:

> **Sharona Hoffman & Andrew P. Morriss, Birth After Death: Perpetuities and the New Reproductive Technologies, 38 Ga. L. Rev. 575, 624 (2004):**
>
> First, the NRTs vastly expand the set of interests that fail any version of the Rule that incorporates the common law Rule and does not simply rule out the possibility of posthumously conceived children. The problems of the unborn widow and the fertile octogenarian pale in comparison to the number of interests possibly affected by NRTs. Second, the NRTs vastly expand the set of impermissible class gifts. Third, the NRTs make possible events previously excluded by reformers as sufficiently improbable that they could be dismissed. Fourth, by reducing the set of interests that pass the common law Rule, the NRTs restrict the options for courts seeking to reform interests that fail under the Rule. Finally, the NRTs potentially extend the gestational period of the Rule indefinitely for children conceived but not yet born.

2. New York, by statute, has addressed several remote possibilities. The statute provides that when the validity of an interest depends on the ability of a person to have a child at some future time, it shall be presumed that a female over the age of fifty-five years cannot have children. N.Y. EPTL § 9–1.3(e)(1). The statute also directs that "[i]n the case of a living person, evidence may be given to establish whether he or she is able to have a child at the time in question." 9–1.3(e)(2).The statute also provides expressly that when the validity of an interest depends upon the ability of a person to have a child at some future time, the possibility that the person will have a child by adoption should be disregarded (Section 9–1.3(e)(3)).

2. THE PRECOCIOUS TODDLER

W. Barton Leach, Perpetuities in Perspective: Ending the Rule's Reign of Terror, 65 Harv. L. Rev. 721, 732 (1952).

With the Fertile Octogenarian doctrine on the books and with the cases breeding much more successfully than the octogenarians it was inevitable that sooner or later a will drawn by some hapless lawyer would produce the *Case of the Precocious Toddler* and stumble into raising the question whether babies, too, can have babies in this Never Never Land of the Rule. My attempts to concoct such a gift for classroom purposes seemed labored and farfetched to me and to my students. But the mother country came to my rescue in Re *Gaite's Will Trusts* (1 All Eng. Rep. 459) where the bequest was upon trust "to pay the income to A for life and thereafter to pay the principal to such of A's grandchildren living at my death or born within five years thereafter as shall attain the age of twenty-one." At testator's death A was a widow, sixty-five years old; she had two children living and one grandchild. However, if the widow should remarry and have another child, and that child should marry and have a child, and if all this should happen within five years, the baby who was the product of this impetuous and libidinous episode might reach the age of twenty-one beyond the period of perpetuities.

NOTES

1. In Gaite's Will Trusts, 1 All Eng. Rep. 459 (1949), discussed in the excerpt from Professor Leach, the court held the bequest valid on the ground that under English law, a marriage between persons under the age of 16 would be void, and grandchildren born to such a marriage would therefore be illegitimate and, under then-current law, not entitled to take under the terms of the instrument. Would that ground be available today, when non-marital children are entitled to inherit equally with marital children?

2. N.Y. EPTL § 9–1.3(e)(1) deals with the precocious toddler problem by creating a presumption that a male cannot have a child before the male reaches the age of 14, and that a female cannot have a child before the female reaches the age of 12. Show why the disposition in Gaite's Will Trusts would have been valid had the New York statute been in effect.

3. THE UNBORN WIDOW

The precocious toddler problem may be largely of theoretical interest, but another remote possibility problem—that of the "unborn widow"—has generated a reasonable volume of litigation.

Dickerson v. Union National Bank

Supreme Court of Arkansas, 1980.
268 Ark. 292, 595 S.W.2d 677.

■ GEORGE ROSE SMITH, J.:

The principal question on this appeal is whether a trust created by the holographic will of Nina Martin Dickerson, who died on June 21, 1967, is void under the rule against perpetuities, because it is possible that the interest of the various beneficiaries may not vest within the period allowed by that rule. Cecil H. Dickerson, Jr., one of the testatrix's two sons, attacks the validity of the trust. The chancellor rejected Cecil's attack.... We disagree with the chancellor....

The facts are not in dispute. The testatrix was survived by her two children. Cecil, 50, was single, and Martin, 45, was married. At that time the two sons had a total of seven children, who of course were the testatrix's grandchildren.

The testatrix named the appellee bank as executor and directed that at the close of the administration proceedings the bank transfer to itself as trustee all the assets of the estate. The terms of the trust are long, but we may summarize them as follows:

The trust is to continue until the death of both sons and of Martin's widow, who is not otherwise identified. The income is to be divided equally between the two sons during their lives, except that Cecil's share is to be used in part to provide for a four-year college education for his two minor children, who are named, and for the support and education of any bodily heirs by a later marriage. When the two named minor children finish college, their share of the income is to revert to Cecil. Upon Martin's death his share of the income is to be paid monthly to his widow and children living in the home, but the share of each child terminates and passes to the widow when that child marries or becomes self-supporting. The trustee is given discretionary power to make advance payments of principal in certain cases of emergency or illness. If either son and his wife and all his bodily heirs die before the final distribution of the trust assets, that son's share in the estate and in the income passes to the other son and then to his bodily heirs.

As far as the rule against perpetuities is concerned, the important part of the will is paragraph VIII, from which we quote:

> VIII. This Trust shall continue until the death of both my sons and my son Martin's widow and until the youngest child of either son has reached the age of twenty-five years, then at that time, the Trust shall terminate and the Union National Bank Trustee shall distribute and pay over the entire balance of the Trust Fund in their hands to the bodily heirs of my son, Cecil H. Dickerson, and the bodily heirs of my son William Martin Dickerson, in the same manner and in the same proportions as provided for by the general inheritance laws of Arkansas.

Upon the death of the testatrix in 1967, her will was presented to the Faulkner Probate Court by her son Cecil, who lived in Conway, Arkansas. (The other son, Martin, was living in Indiana.) The probate court entered a routine order reciting that the will had been properly executed, admitting the instrument to probate, and appointing the bank as executor, without bond. On May 31, 1968, the probate court entered another routine order approving the executor's first and final accounting, allowing fees to the executor and its attorneys, discharging the executor, and closing the administration of the estate. That order made no reference to the validity of the trust or to the manner in which the assets of the estate were to be distributed.

. . . On August 11, 1967, about a month after the probate of the will, the bank filed in the Faulkner Chancery Court an ex parte "Declaration of Trust," in which the bank expressed its desire to perform the trust and asked the court to find and decree that it held the property in trust for the beneficiaries of the testamentary trust. * * * On October 4 the chancery court entered an order reciting the appearance of the bank only, finding that the bank had been appointed as administrator of the estate and as trustee of the trust, authorizing the bank to transfer all the real and personal property (except $18,000) to the trust estate, and instructing the trustee as to the proper treatment of capital gains as trust income.

Nothing further appears to have taken place in the case until 1977, when Cecil Dickerson filed in the same proceeding the present complaint against the bank and its trust officer. The complaint, after reciting the background facts, asserts that the trust is void under the rule against perpetuities. The complaint charges the trust officer with violations of his fiduciary duties in failing to deliver all the assets of the estate to the heirs of the testatrix and in failing to ask the probate court to construe the will with respect to violations of the rule against perpetuities. The complaint charges that the trust officer concealed the trust's defects from the court and from the testatrix's two sons. The prayer is for an order restraining the trustee from making further transfers or distributions of the trust funds, for recovery of Cecil's half interest in the estate, for compensatory and punitive damages, and for other proper relief. The charges of negligence and wrongdoing on the part of the bank were later dismissed without prejudice. The other matters were heard upon stipulated facts, culminating in the degree dismissing Cecil's complaint....

... [T]he trust is void because there is a possibility that the estate will not vest within a period measured by a life or lives in being at the testatrix's death, plus 21 years. A bare possibility is enough. "The interest must vest within the time allowed by the rule. If there is any possibility that the contingent event may happen beyond the limits of the rule the transaction is void." Comstock v. Smith, 255 Ark. 564, 501 S.W.2d 617 (1973).

The terms of this trust present an instance of the "unborn widow," a pitfall that is familiar to every student of the rule against perpetuities. This trust is not to terminate until the deaths of Cecil, Martin, and Martin's widow, but the identity of Martin's widow cannot be known until his death. Martin might marry an 18–year–old woman twenty years after his mother's death, have additional children by her, and then die. Cecil also might die. Martin's young widow, however, might live for another 40 or 50 years, after which the interests would finally vest. But since Cecil and Martin would have been the last measuring lives in being at the death of the testatrix, the trust property would not vest until many years past the maximum time allowed by the rule. The rule was formulated to prevent just such a possibility—uncertainty about the title to real or personal property for an unreasonably long time in the future.

The violation of the rule, except for the interposition of a trust, is actually so clear that the appellee does not argue the point. Instead, it insists that the property would vest in Cecil and Martin's bodily heirs at their deaths, with only the right of possession of the property being deferred until the termination of the trust.

This argument overlooks the fact that the words "bodily heirs" were used in the decisive paragraph VIII of the will not as words of limitation, to specify the duration of an estate granted to Cecil and Martin, but as words of purchase, to specify the persons who would take at the termination of the trust. Obviously the identity of those persons cannot be determined until the death of Martin's widow; so the ownership would not vest until that time.

A vested remainder, simply stated, is a present interest that cannot be defeated by any contingency. Such an interest can be transferred by deed, by will, or by inheritance, even though the right of possession may not accrue until some time in the future. The simplest example is a conveyance or devise to A for life, remainder to B. Since A must eventually die, B's remainder is a present vested interest which cannot be defeated by any contingency. As we said in Hurst v. Hilderbrandt, 178 Ark. 337, 10 S.W.2d 491 (1928), in describing a vested remainder: "[T]here is some person in esse known and ascertained, who, by the will or deed creating the estate, is to take and enjoy the estate, and whose right to such remainder no contingency can defeat." To the same effect see Steele v. Robinson, 221 Ark. 58, 251 S.W.2d 1001 (1952); National Bank of Commerce v. Ritter, 181 Ark. 439, 26 S.W.2d 113 (1930); Restatement of Property, § 157, Comment f (1936).

Here the testatrix directed that at the termination of the trust the property be distributed as provided by the general inheritance laws of Arkansas. At the time of the deaths of Cecil and Martin it would be utterly impossible to say who would take, in the case we have supposed, at the death of Martin's young widow 50 years later. Under our law the surviving descendants would then take per capita if they were related to Cecil and Martin in equal degree, but per stirpes if in unequal degree. Ark. Stat. Ann. §§ 61–134 and–135 (Repl. 1971). If there were no surviving descendants of one brother, the entire property would go to the surviving descendants of the other. If there were no surviving descendants of either, the property would revert to the testatrix's estate and go to her collateral heirs. Thus it is really too plain for argument that the interest of every descendant (or "bodily heir") of Cecil or Martin would be contingent upon his surviving the death of Martin's widow, at which time—and only at which time—the title would finally vest.

* * *

Reversed and remanded for further proceedings.

NOTES AND QUESTIONS

1. Cecil Dickerson was a significant beneficiary of his mother's trust. Why did he seek to establish that the trust was invalid?

2. If you had been arguing this case for the bank, could you have argued that when Nina Dickerson referred to "my son Martin's widow" in the trust instrument, she meant "Martin's current wife?" How would you have made that argument in the context of the Dickerson case? Cf. Perkins v.

Iglehart, 183 Md. 520, 39 A.2d 672 (1944) [rejecting argument that term "widow" referred to a particular living person].

Suppose the will had referred to "my son Martin's wife." Would the result in the case have been different?

3. Suppose the trust instrument in Dickerson had referred to "Martin's current wife" instead of "Martin's widow." Can you argue that the interest in "bodily heirs" was still invalid under the Rule Against Perpetuities?

4. T devises property, in trust, "income payable to my daughter for life, remainder to my daughter's widower for life" and directs that at the death of the widower, the remainder should be distributed to:

a. "my daughter's children."

b. "my daughter's then-living children."

In each devise, is the interest in the widower valid? Is the interest in the children valid?

5. N.Y. EPTL § 9–1.3(c) provides that when necessary to save an interest from invalidity under the Rule Against Perpetuities, a reference to a "spouse of another without other identification" shall be treated as "a reference to a person in being on the effective date of the instrument."

4. THE SLOTHFUL EXECUTOR

Suppose testator's will leaves all of her property to "the four officers of Lodge 168 of the Benevolent and Protective Order of Elks who shall be in office at the time my estate is distributed." Does the devise violate the Rule Against Perpetuities? The answer would be no if we could presume that her estate would be distributed within 21 years of her death, or within the lifetime of some existing person. Can we be certain, however, that the estate will be distributed within that period? Consider the following excerpt from In re Campbell's Estate, 28 Cal.App.2d 102, 82 P.2d 22 (1938):

> Cases are not unknown where parties, through ignorance or neglect, have continued to occupy and use for a long period property left by a decedent before resorting to probate. Property in the form of bank deposits has remained unclaimed for years before probate proceedings were commenced. The closing of many estates has been delayed for years both through neglect and by intention, because of circumstances and conditions. A long delay by reason of protracted litigation is a very real possibility. All of these possibilities, not to mention others, might become realities in a particular case, causing a delay beyond the time limited.

The court in Campbell's Estate held the bequest to the Elk officers invalid under the Rule. But see, *contra*, Belfield v. Booth, 63 Conn. 299, 27 A. 585 (1893).

NOTES AND QUESTIONS

1. In each of the following cases, how would you argue that the devise in question is valid under the Rule?

a. "to my issue, payable upon distribution of my estate."

b. "to my daughter, if she survives until my executor distributes my estate assets."

2. New York's EPTL § 9–1.3(d) provides:

> Where the duration or vesting of an estate is contingent upon the probate of a will, the appointment of a fiduciary, the location of a distributee, the payment of debts, the sale of assets, the settlement of an estate, the determination of questions relating to an estate or transfer tax or the occurrence of any specified contingency, it shall be presumed that the creator of such estate intended such contingency to occur, if at all, within twenty-one years from the effective date of the instrument creating such estate.

The New York statute was designed to reverse the result in cases like Campbell's Estate. Can you see why the statute, if read literally, would make *all* interests valid for purposes of the Rule Against Perpetuities? Do you think the drafters intended that result?

C. APPLICATION TO CHARITABLE GIFTS AND TRUSTS

We have focused, so far, on interests created in natural persons (or in private trusts created for the benefit of natural persons). Let us turn now to the Rule's application to charitable beneficiaries. Start by disabusing yourself of the widely held—but incorrect—notion that the Rule Against Perpetuities does not apply to charitable interests.

Suppose testator, a former bank president, devises land to his bank on the following terms:

> For their use as long as the present institution shall continue to exist on the following conditions, viz.:. . . . (2) That when the institutions shall cease to exist the trustees [of the bank] shall convey the whole estate to the then authorized managers of the Home for Aged Women in Roxbury. . . .

Is the interest in the Home for Aged Women valid under the Rule Against Perpetuities? Note that the interest is not vested, and might not vest for hundreds of years, if the bank were to exist for so long. As a result, the gift to the home is invalid under the Rule. Institution for Savings in Roxbury v. Roxbury Home for Aged Women, 244 Mass. 583, 139 N.E. 301 (1923). That is, if a future interest in a charity follows interests in non-charities, the future interest is valid only if it certain to vest (or fail) within the period of the Rule.

Now, suppose testator devises property to her church, and provides that

> if the said Church shall be dissolved, or if its religious sentiments shall be changed and abandoned, then my will is that this real estate shall go to my legatees . . .

Is the interest in the legatees valid or invalid under the Rule? Again, note that the interest might not vest for hundreds of years. As a result, even if the interest in the legatees follows a charitable interest, the interest in the legatees is invalid under the Rule. See Brown v. Independent Baptist Church, 325 Mass. 645, 91 N.E.2d 922 (1950). That is, a future interest in a non-charitable grantee, even if it follows a charitable devise or a charitable trust, is valid only if the future interest is certain to vest (or fail) within the period of the Rule.

What differences are there, then, between the Rule's treatment of charitable interests and its treatment of privately-held interests? There are two. First, charitable trusts and foundations can endure in perpetuity; in jurisdictions that retain the common law Rule Against Perpetuities, private trusts cannot. Since private trusts must have identifiable beneficiaries, the interests of each of those beneficiaries must vest within the period of the Rule. As a result, a private trust cannot last forever. Once all of the beneficiaries whose interests vested within the Rule's period have died, the trust must end because there is no beneficiary to whom the trustee can distribute trust monies. Estate of Keenan, 519 N.W.2d 373 (Iowa 1994), is illustrative. Decedent sought to create a trust establishing a perpetual fund for the purposes of providing scholarships to any blood heirs of decedent or her husband. The Iowa Supreme Court held that the trust violated the Rule Against Perpetuities (although the court also attempted to reform the trust to assure that the entire fund would be used to provide scholarships for decedent's blood relatives). By contrast, because a charitable trust need not have identifiable beneficiaries, the Rule imposes no limit on trust duration. If a testator creates a trust, naming trustees, and directs that the trustee pay the net income from the trust, as a scholarship, "to the highest ranking student in the second-year class at Cardozo Law School," the trust can endure forever.

Second, if the testator or trust settlor creates one charitable interest, and then directs that upon some contingency, the trust shall pass to another charitable beneficiary, the interest in the second charitable beneficiary is valid under the Rule. Suppose, for instance, testator's will devises property to "the Independent Baptist Church of Woburn, but if the church shall be dissolved, to the Home for Aged Women of Roxbury." The interest in the Home for Aged Women is now valid. Why? On the theory that the perpetual use of the property by charities is a benefit that exceeds any harm resulting from the long-term contingency. See Storr's Agricultural School v. Whitney, 54 Conn. 342, 345, 8 A. 141, 143 (1887):

> As one charitable use may be perpetual, the gift to two in succession can be of no longer duration nor of greater evil. The property is taken out of commerce, but it instantly goes into perpetual servitude to charity.

D. CONSEQUENCES OF INVALIDITY

If a will or trust provision violates the Rule Against Perpetuities, what happens to the property subject to the invalid provision? This important question is closely related to another, equally important, question: how does invalidity of one provision in a will or trust instrument affect other provisions in the same instrument? The various provisions of a will or trust instrument generally reflect a scheme on the part of the testator or trust settlor, making it difficult to treat any one provision in isolation. Hence, generalization is dangerous. As the New York Court of Appeals put it in discussing whether a single invalidity in a testamentary trust should invalidate the entire trust:

> This is not strictly law; it is a matter of good judgment, the judgment of men who according to our judicial system must in the last analysis determine the question.

In re Durand's Will, 250 N.Y. 45, 53, 164 N.E. 737, 740 (1928). Nevertheless, a few basic principles have emerged.

In general, if an interest is void under the Rule Against Perpetuities, the void interest is excised, or surgically removed, from the dispositive instrument, leaving the rest of the instrument to take full effect. See 7 American Law of Property, sec. 24.47 (1952). What does this mean? Suppose, for instance, testator's will leaves her estate, in trust, "income to be paid to my children for life, then to my grandchildren for life, principal to be distributed, at the death of my last surviving grandchild, to my great-grandchildren in equal shares." The interest in great-grandchildren is invalid under the Rule. But, by striking out the interest of great-grandchildren, we do not affect the life interests in children or grandchildren. Those interests remain valid. What happens to the trust property at the death of the last grandchild? If the trust was not created in the will's residuary clause, the trust property would fall into the residue, and pass to testator's residuary beneficiaries. If testator devised the entire residue of his estate to the trust, then the invalidity of the devise to great-grandchildren would cause the trust principal to pass by intestate succession. See In re Richardson Trust, 138 N.H. 1, 634 A.2d 1005 (1993).

By contrast, if the invalid interest would operate to divest a prior interest, the effect of invalidity is to make the prior interest absolute. Suppose, for instance, testator devises her home "to my daughter for life, remainder to my daughter's children, but if any of my daughter's children should enter the priesthood, that child's share of the house shall be divided among his siblings." The final interest is invalid under the Rule (do you see why?). As a result, we strike the divesting condition from the instrument, and the daughter's children take a fee simple absolute at the daughter's death. See Proprietors of the Church in Brattle Square v. Grant, 69 Mass. 142, 3 Gray 142 (1855).

These general principles do not apply, however, if a court could give effect to more of testator's dispositive scheme by invalidating a broader range of interests. When it would appear that testator would prefer invalidation of multiple interests, or even the entire will, the doctrine of *infectious invalidity* permits a court to invalidate valid interests as well as invalid ones. Suppose, for instance, testator's will leaves half of his estate to his son outright, and the other half in trust, with income payable to his daughter for life, remainder to those of the daughter's children who reach age 30. The remainder in the daughter's children is invalid under the Rule.

If the court invalidates only that interest, however, the son might take well more than half of the estate—a result testator certainly did not intend. A court might reasonably conclude that testator would prefer to have her entire estate pass by intestacy. The court could apply the doctrine of infectious invalidity to invalidate the entire will. See generally 7 American Law of Property, §§ 24.48–24.52.

PROBLEM

T's will leaves property in trust, with directions that the trustee should "pay income to my brother for life, then to my brother's children and their heirs until the death of my brother's last surviving child, and then distribute the principal among my brother's grandchildren, per capita." At T's death, T's brother is alive, 70 years old, and has two daughters. T is also survived by a sister, but by no lineal descendants. Assume that at T's death the property designated to pass into the trust is worth $200,000. Assume further that the residue of T's estate is worth $300,000. How should a common law court treat the remainder to the brother's grandchildren (and the rest of T's estate) if the residuary clause of T's will directs that the residue be distributed:

a. "to my brother's children in equal shares."

b. "to my sister."

c. "to the American Red Cross."

SECTION IV. CLASS GIFTS

A. THE GENERAL RULE

If the owner of property makes a gift to a class of beneficiaries—to children, grandchildren, nephews and nieces, issue, etc.—the Rule Against Perpetuities invalidates the gift to each member of the class if it would be possible for the gift to vest in any member of the class at a time beyond the Rule's period—lives in being plus 21 years. The same proposition can be stated another way: a vested remainder subject to open is not vested for purposes of the Rule Against Perpetuities. Example 17 illustrates the rule.

> ***Example 17:*** *T devises property, in trust, with directions that income should be paid "to my sister S for life, then to S's children for so long as one of S's children remains alive," and that the principal should then be distributed "to S's grandchildren." At the time of T's death, S, age 75, has two children, ages 51 and 46, and five grandchildren, ages 24, 19, 15, 13, and 10. Does the devise of the principal to grandchildren violate the Rule Against Perpetuities?*
>
> ***Solution:*** *Yes. Note that at T's death, S's grandchildren have a vested remainder subject to open; more grandchildren might be*

born to S, and those grandchildren would be entitled to share the trust principal with the five existing grandchildren. Hence, the interest in S's grandchildren is not now vested within the period of the Rule. When will the interest in S's grandchildren vest indefeasibly? At the death of S's last surviving child. Can we use S's children as measuring lives? No, because S, who is still alive, might have more children; that is, S's children might not all be lives in being at the creation of the interest. Of course, we cannot use S's two existing children because an afterborn child might survive the existing children by more than 21 years. Hence, since the interest in grandchildren could vest in a grandchild born to an afterborn child of S, the interest in all grandchildren—even those alive at T's death—is invalid.

Why have the "all or nothing" rule illustrated in Example 17? In many cases, the rule better effectuates the grantor's intent than a rule that would hold that a vested remainder subject to open is vested for purposes of the Rule. Consider the following variant on Example 17:

Example 18: *The residuary clause of T's will devises property, in trust, with directions that income should be paid "to my sister S for life, then to S's children for so long as one of S's children remains alive," and that the principal should then be distributed "to S's grandchildren." At the time of T's death, S, age 75, has two children, ages 51 and 46, and five grandchildren, ages 24, 19, 15, 13, and 10. After T's death, one of S's children has two more children. All seven grandchildren survive S's last surviving child.*

The all-or-nothing rule invalidates the entire remainder. If S was T's only heir, the remainder will be distributed with the balance of S's estate, and ultimately, it is likely that all of S's grandchildren will share in the remainder (depending on the provisions in the wills written by S and S's children).

By contrast, if the court upheld the interest in the five grandchildren alive at testator's death, only those five grandchildren would share; the other two would be left with nothing. This result would appear less likely to effectuate testator's intent.

The point is not to argue that the all-or-nothing rule always effectuates testator's intent; it frequently does not. The point is to recognize that the all-or-nothing rule sometimes generates rational results.

PROBLEM

Christa Kreuzer's will creates two testamentary trusts. Trust A is for the benefit of children born to or adopted by her daughter Michelle before Michelle's 40th birthday. Trust B is for the benefit of children born to or adopted by Christa's son Keith before Keith's 40th birthday. Christa's will provided that "upon the last beneficiary of each trust attaining the age of 35 years, or sooner dying, the trustees are to distribute to those beneficiaries, then living, the then remaining principal and accumulated income." If all of the beneficiaries of either trust died before reaching age 35, the corpus of the trust was to be distributed to the other trust. Christa died in 1994, survived by Michelle, then age 34, by Keith, then age 31, and by Michelle's daughter Heather, then age 3. Michelle had another daughter, Amber, in 1997.

a. Do either of the trusts violate the Rule Against Perpetuities?

b. If yes, how and when should the trust corpus be distributed?

c. Would your answers be different if N.Y. EPTL § 9–1.2 were in force? That statute provides:

> Where an estate would, except for this section, be invalid because made to depend, for its vesting or its duration, upon any person attaining or failing to attain an age in excess of twenty-one years, the age contingency shall be reduced to twenty-one years as to any or all persons subject to such contingency.

See Estate of Kreuzer, 243 A.D.2d 207, 674 N.Y.S.2d 505 (1998).

B. THE AMELIORATIVE IMPACT OF THE CLASS–CLOSING RULE OF CONVENIENCE

As a matter of construction, courts hold that when one member of a class becomes entitled to distribution of a share of the property in question, the class closes, and subsequently born members of the class do not share in the property. For example, suppose testator's will creates a trust which directs that income be paid to testator's unmarried 50–year–old daughter for life, and that principal be paid, at the daughter's death, "to those of my son's children who reach age 21." If, at the daughter's death, the son has three children, ages 24, 17, and 14, the 24–year–old is entitled to immediate distribution of one-third of the trust principal. The two younger children will be entitled to one-third of the principal if they survive to age 21. If the son has an additional child born after the death of testator's daughter, however, that additional child will not qualify to take under her grandmother's will. We say that the class of eligible takers "closed" when the 24–year–old became entitled to possession. This "Rule of Convenience," or "Class–Closing Rule," makes it possible for the trustee to distribute a share of trust principal to the 24–year–old; if it were not for the Rule of Convenience, trustee would not be safe in distributing any principal to the 24–year–old because, in theory, testator's son could have an infinite number of additional children, each of whom might become entitled to an infinitely small share of the trust principal (For more extensive discussion of the Rule of Convenience, see Chapter Nine, Section III, *supra*).

Although the Rule of Convenience developed for reasons unrelated to the Rule Against Perpetuities, the Rule of Convenience sometimes operates to save class gifts that would otherwise be invalid under the Rule Against Perpetuities. The reason is simple enough: the Rule of Convenience operates to close a class artificially before the class would close "naturally" by the death of the parent of the class members. If we can be sure that the interest in members of the class will vest (or fail) by the time the Rule of Convenience closes the class, the class gift will be valid under the Rule Against Perpetuities even if the class might not close "naturally" until beyond the Rule's period. Consider the following example:

> ***Example 19:*** *T's will creates a trust, directs that the trustee distribute income "to my daughter for life," and directs that the trustee then distribute principal "to my daughter's grandchildren." At T's death, T's daughter has a 3–year–old granddaughter. Is T's devise of principal valid under the Rule Against Perpetuities?*
>
> ***Solution:*** *Yes. At T's death, the daughter's 3–year–old granddaughter has a vested remainder subject to open. When will the remainder vest indefeasibly (or, in other words, when will the class close)? The class of the daughter's grandchildren will not close naturally until the death of the daughter's last surviving child. Since the daughter is still alive, we cannot use the daughter's children as measuring lives. Hence, were it not for the Rule of Convenience, the devise to the daughter's grandchildren would be invalid under the Rule Against Perpetuities. Because of the Rule of Convenience, however, we know that the 3–year–old will be entitled to immediate possession upon the death of the daughter. The Rule of Convenience will therefore close the class of the daughter's grandchildren "artificially" at the daughter's death; none of the daughter's grandchildren who are subsequently born will be entitled to take. Hence, the interest in the daughter's grandchildren will vest indefeasibly at the daughter's death. Since the daughter is a life in being, the interest in her grandchildren is valid under the Rule Against Perpetuities.*

PROBLEM

T's will creates a trust with directions to distribute trust income to his wife for life, and then to distribute trust principal "to my nephews and nieces." Consider whether the Rule invalidates the devise of principal to nephews and nieces if, at T's death,

a. T's parents are dead, and T's only brother is childless.

b. T's mother is alive and 80 years old, and T is her only child.

c. T's parents and brother are dead; T has a 5–year–old niece.

d. T's mother is alive and T's brother has a 5–year–old daughter.

e. T's mother is alive and T's brother has a 35–year–old daughter.

Which of your answers would be different if the devise of principal had been to "those of my nieces and nephews who reach age 20?" To "those of my nieces and nephews who reach age 30?"

SECTION V. POWERS OF APPOINTMENT

As we have seen, powers of appointment are an important estate planning tool. The Rule Against Perpetuities applies to powers of appointment, and creates traps for the careless drafter.

Powers of appointment present two distinct perpetuities problems: first, is the power itself valid under the Rule Against Perpetuities; and second, when the power is exercised, is the exercise valid under the Rule? We now turn to those issues.

A. IS THE POWER VALID?

If a power of appointment is both general *and* exercisable by an *inter vivos* instrument, the power is valid under the Rule Against Perpetuities if the power is certain to become exercisable during the period of the Rule. By contrast, if the power is special, *or* if the power is general and testamentary, the power is valid if there is no possibility that it will actually be exercised beyond the period of the Rule.

What explains this difference in treatment? If a donee has a general power, and if the power has become exercisable immediately, the donee has the equivalent of fee simple ownership; if the donee wants to, the donee can exercise in favor of herself, and eliminate any contingencies in the instrument creating the power. Since the Rule Against Perpetuities is designed to prevent interests from remaining contingent for too long, the Rule's purposes are not frustrated if we can be certain that a donee will be able to exercise the power in favor of herself within the Rule's period.

When a donee holds a special power or a general testamentary power, the donee does not have the equivalent of absolute ownership; the donee will never be able to exercise in favor of herself. For so long as it remains possible for the donee to exercise the power, interests in the appointive property might remain contingent. Hence, the Rule invalidates the power if there is any possibility that the power might be exercised beyond the Rule's period—lives in being plus 21 years.

Note that the Rule Against Perpetuities will never invalidate the most common powers of appointment: powers given by the donor to identified donees whom the donor knows and trusts. If the donor gives a power—even a special testamentary power—to her spouse, or to one of her children, or to a trusted sibling—the power will be exercised within the donee's lifetime. So long as the donee was identified (and therefore alive) at the time the donor created the power, the power cannot possibly be exercised beyond the period of the Rule.

Nevertheless, there are circumstances in which a careless drafter might create a power of appointment invalid under the Rule Against Perpetuities. The risk is greatest when donor creates a discretionary trust, and gives the trustee a power to pay or withhold income to designated beneficiaries.

> ***Example 20:*** *T's will creates a trust, designates a corporate trustee, and directs the trustee to pay income to T's daughter D for D's life. At D's death, the will confers on the corporate trustee discretion to distribute among D's children, each year, as much, or as little, income as the trustee believes appropriate. The will then directs that at the death of D's last surviving child, the principal is to be distributed to the Girl Scouts of America. Does the will create any Rule Against Perpetuities problems?*
>
> ***Analysis:*** *T has conferred upon the corporate trustee a power to appoint trust income among D's children. Since the trustee's power lasts until the death of the last of D's children, and since D's children might not all have been alive at T's death, the trustee might still be exercising the power well beyond the period of lives in being plus 21 years. As a result, the power is invalid under the Rule. (The interest in the Girl Scouts, because vested at creation, is nevertheless valid under the Rule).*

The limited case law generally supports the analysis in Example 20, and invalidates the trustee's power altogether. See, e.g., Arrowsmith v. Mercantile–Safe Deposit & Trust Co., 313 Md. 334, 545 A.2d 674 (1988). One might argue, however, that a court should treat the power as a series of annual powers, and should therefore uphold the trustee's right to exercise discretion for the first 21 years after D's death. See John Chipman Gray, The Rule Against Perpetuities, §§ 410.1–410.5 (4th ed. 1942).

When a drafter creates a power of appointment in a class of people, some of whom might be unborn at the creation of the power, the drafter may also run afoul of the Rule. Consider the following example:

> ***Example 21:*** *S, settlor of an irrevocable inter vivos trust, reserves income to herself during her lifetime, and directs that at her death, the trust principal should be divided into as many shares as S has children. The trustee is then directed to pay income to each child for that child's lifetime, and to distribute principal on each child's share as the child shall direct by will. S has no children at the time she creates the trust (but two children are subsequently born to S).*
>
> ***Analysis:*** *The powers S has created in her children are invalid under the Rule Against Perpetuities. S's children were not lives in being at the time the powers were created, and it is possible that S's children might survive S by more than 21 years. As a result, it is possible that one or more of S's children could exercise the power beyond the period of the Rule. Hence, the powers are invalid.*

Despite Examples 20 and 21, it bears repeating that whenever the donor of a power of appointment creates a power in an identified, living person, the power is valid under the Rule Against Perpetuities.

PROBLEM

Reconsider Example 21. How would S's powers be treated if S had two living children when S created her *inter vivos* trust and

(a) no additional children were born to S after execution of the instrument?

(b) two additional children were born to S after execution of the instrument?

B. HAS THE POWER BEEN VALIDLY EXERCISED?

1. THE SCOPE OF THE RELATION–BACK DOCTRINE

The more difficult perpetuities problems involve not the power's validity, but the power's exercise. When the donee of a power makes outright appointments to identified beneficiaries, exercise of the power raises no perpetuities problems; if the power itself was valid, so is the donee's exercise. The donee has not, by making outright appointments, prolonged the contingency of any interests.

Suppose, however, the donee exercises the power by creating a trust, and suppose further that some of the trust beneficiaries have contingent future interests. How do we determine whether those contingent interests violate the Rule Against Perpetuities? Should we treat those interests as if they were created by the donee, and measure the perpetuities period from the time the donee exercised the power? Or should we instead honor the "agency" theory of powers of appointment, and treat the donee as merely acting on the donor's behalf to "fill in the blanks" in a disposition made by the donor when the donor created the power—that is, should we measure the perpetuities period from the time the donor created the power?

The judicial answer to these questions has varied with the type of power involved. If the donor gives the donee a general power exercisable by an *inter vivos* instrument, courts uniformly hold that the perpetuities period should be measured from the time of exercise. The rationale should be familiar by now: the donor has given the donee the functional equivalent of an absolute interest, so we should treat any appointment just as we would treat any other property disposition made by the donee. The agency theory simply doesn't fit when the donor has given the donee power to exercise in favor of herself during her own lifetime.

Example 22: *T's will creates a trust, giving his wife, W, an income interest for life, and a general power to appoint the principal in favor of herself or anyone else by will or by inter vivos instrument. At T's death, the couple's only son, S, is alive, and childless. W dies 30 years later, outliving S. W's will exercises T's power by creating a trust to pay income to S's only daughter, G, for life, and to distribute principal among G's children at G's death. Does W's exercise violate the Rule Against Perpetuities?*

Analysis: *No. Because the power was general and exercisable by W during her lifetime, the perpetuities period on W's exercise runs from the time of exercise—even though W actually exercised the power by will. G was a life in being at W's death, and all interests will vest within G's lifetime. Hence, all interests are valid under the Rule Against Perpetuities.*

By contrast, if donor creates a special power of appointment, the agency theory of powers of appointment is more plausible. As a result, courts typically apply *the relation-back doctrine*—the doctrine that we should read the donee's appointment back into the instrument in which donor created the power. The relation-back doctrine requires that we measure the perpetuities period from the time the donor created the power.

Example 23: *Same facts as Example 22, except that T has given W a power to appoint "among our descendants." Does W's exercise violate the Rule Against Perpetuities?*

Analysis: *Yes. Because T created a special power, we measure the perpetuities period from the time T created the power—T's death. At T's death, G was not yet born. Hence, G would not qualify as a measuring life. Hence, the remainder interest in G's children is invalid under the Rule.*

If the relation-back doctrine applies to special powers, and not to general powers exercisable by *inter vivos* instrument, how should we treat general testamentary powers? Consider the following case:

Industrial National Bank of Rhode Island v. Barrett

Supreme Court of Rhode Island, 1966.
101 R.I. 89, 220 A.2d 517.

■ PAOLINO, JUSTICE.

This is a bill in equity brought by the Industrial National Bank of Rhode Island, executor and trustee, and Aline C. Lathan, co-executor, under the will of Mary M. Tilley, deceased, for construction of the latter's will and for instructions to the executors and trustee thereunder. The adult respondents have filed an answer to the bill and all minor and contingent interests and those of persons unascertainable or not in being are represented by a guardian ad litem appointed for that purpose by the court. The guardian has filed an answer neither admitting nor denying the bill's allegations and submitting the interests of his respective wards to the court's care and protection.

After the cause was heard in superior court and was ready for hearing on the final decree it was certified to this court for our determination under G.L.1956, § 9–24–28.

* * *

It appears that Arthur H. Tilley, husband of the deceased, died January 28, 1959. Under the eighth clause of his will, admitted to probate

February 5, 1959, he devised the property, which qualified for the full marital deduction, to the Industrial National Bank, in trust, with directions to pay the net income at least quarterly to his wife for life and such amounts of the corpus annually or at more frequent intervals as she should in writing request, for her comfort and support, and without being accountable to any court or remainderman therefor. He also conferred upon her a general testamentary power of appointment over the corpus remaining at her death.

Mary M. Tilley died October 28, 1963. Under the fourth clause of her will, admitted to probate November 7, 1963, she exercised her general testamentary power of appointment to the Industrial National Bank, in trust "to pay over the net income thereof to and for the use and benefit of my granddaughters, Aline C. Lathan and Evelyn M. Barrett * * * equally for and during the term of their natural lives, and upon the death of either of them, to pay over said net income to her issue, *per stirpes* and not *per capita.*" The trustee was also given uncontrolled discretion to pay over to either of said grandchildren, or the issue of any deceased grandchild, for specific purposes, portions of the principal. Finally, the testatrix provided the trust would terminate "twenty one (21) years after the death of the last survivor of the younger grandchild or issue of either grandchild of mine living at my death * * *."

On the date of Arthur H. Tilley's death, Aline C. Lathan and Evelyn M. Barrett and one great-grandchild were in being. On the date of Mary M. Tilley's death the aforesaid respondents plus six additional great-grandchildren were in being. One great-grandchild was born subsequent to her death.

* * *

The complainants contend that Mrs. Tilley's exercise of the power of appointment created under her husband's will does not violate the rule against perpetuities on two alternative grounds.

First, they say, in clause eighth of his will, Arthur H. Tilley manifested a clear intent to bestow upon his wife an unlimited power to consume the trust principal giving her in effect a general power of appointment exercisable during her lifetime.

* * * [The Court held that the power to withdraw, even though broad and even though the trustee was not accountable for such withdrawals, was not equivalent to a general power of appointment.]

* * *

The complainants next contend that even if Mrs. Tilley had only a general testamentary power of appointment, the better-reasoned authorities hold the perpetuity period should be counted from the date of the power's exercise rather than its creation, which would make the gift here vest within the prescribed time.

* * *

It is fundamental law that when the free alienation of a future interest in property is limited, the interest must vest within lives in being plus twenty-one years from the date of the creating instrument. When the persons who will take or the extent of their interests are to be determined by the exercise of a subsequent power of appointment, the rule against perpetuities requires that the vesting time be computed as if the appointment were a part of the instrument creating the limitation, because until it is exercised the limitation is incomplete.

Nevertheless as the primary concern behind the rule is to prevent restraint on alienation, a distinction is made between general and special powers. In the case of a general power of appointment by deed and will, all courts hold that since the donee has absolute disposing power over the property and may bring it into the market place at any time, he has what is tantamount to a fee. Therefore, since whatever estates may be created by one seized in fee may be also created under a general power, the commencement of the limitation is computed from the time of the power's exercise and not its creation.

In the case of a general power of appointment by will, however, the weight of authority counts the perpetuity period from the date of creation on the ground that since the donee cannot freely alienate the property during his life, he is not the practical owner thereof. A minority view disagrees with this position on the theory that the concept of actual ownership clouds the substance of the matter, which is that if the person having the power without the ownership may appoint to whomsoever he pleases at the time he exercises it, he is in the same position *in respect to the perpetuity* as if he were actually the owner. Thorndike, General Powers And Perpetuities, 27 Harv.L.Rev., pp. 705, 717. Also see Northern Trust Co. v. Porter, 368 Ill. 256, 13 N.E.2d 487 (1938), for leading citations on both positions.

Since this is a case of first impression, we have read with interest the authorities supporting the above positions. See Gray, General Testamentary Powers And The Rule Against Perpetuities, 26 Harv.L.Rev., p. 720; Thorndike, General Powers And Perpetuities, supra; Annot., 1 A.L.R. 374; and Northern Trust Co. v. Porter, supra. From this reading it appears that the early English cases in counting the perpetuity period did not distinguish between a general power to appoint by deed and will and a general power to appoint by will only and we think the cases following this position are the more persuasive.

In essence the majority jurisdictions characterize a general power of appointment by will as being in the nature of a special power, and, as such, a part of the creating instrument of the donor. They reach this result solely on the ground that because the donor has tied up ownership of the property until the donee's death, the restraint on alienation is sufficient to count the perpetuity period from the power's creation.

We think that this position misapprehends the fundamental concepts involved here. The law does not prohibit an estate being tied up for the life of any one individual, but prohibits only restraint beyond lives in being plus twenty-one years. See Thorndike, supra. When the donee exercises his power, he is *at that time* the practical owner thereof, *for the purposes of the rule*, as he can appoint to anyone of his choice as well as his own estate. Furthermore when he exercises the power he can create, unlike the case of a special power, estates entirely independent from those created or controlled by the donor, and so, as to the donee, the power is a general one. See Perpetuities In Perspective: Ending The Rule's Reign Of Terror, by W. Barton Leach, 65 Harv.L.Rev. 721.

Consequently, we hold the trust created by clause fourth of Mrs. Tilley's will pursuant to her general testamentary power of appointment is valid. We arrive at this conclusion not only because logic favors its adoption but also because we believe it is in line with the trend to obviate the technical harshness of the rule against perpetuities and decide cases on the substance of things. 6 American Law of Property § 24.45 (1952), p. 118; 3 Restatement, Property § 343 (1940), p. 1913; Union & New Haven Trust Co. v. Taylor, 133 Conn. 221, 50 A.2d 168. For a learned discussion of this problem, see Perpetuities In A Nutshell, 51 Harv.L.Rev. 638, and Perpetuities: The Nutshell Revisited, 78 Harv.L.Rev. 973, both being articles by W. Barton Leach.

NOTES AND QUESTIONS

1. Why would Mary Tilley's exercise have been invalid if the perpetuities period had been measured from her husband's death?

2. Recall that at common law, a donee who disposes of her own estate without mention of any power of appointment is deemed not to have exercised the power. Hence, the appointive property would be distributed through donor's estate. This common law doctrine is, in effect, an application of the relation-back doctrine. Consider now Uniform Probate Code § 2–608, which creates a presumption that a will disposing of all testator's property exercises any general power of appointment testator might hold—even if the will makes no mention of the power. Should the UPC provision, and comparable statutes in other states, be treated as an implicit rejection of the relation-back doctrine, at least with respect to general powers, and an endorsement of the court's approach in the Barrett case? See generally Melanie B. Leslie, The Case Against Applying the Relation–Back Doctrine to the Exercise of General Powers of Appointment, 14 Cardozo L. Rev. 219, 228–30 (1992). Apparently, the drafters of the UPC didn't think so. In section 2–902, and the comments to that section, the Code treats general testamentary powers like special powers, and concludes that the Rule's period should be measured from the time of creation—not the time of exercise. Did the drafters of the UPC miss an opportunity to reduce the risk of Rule violations?

3. For more general discussion of the problem raised in the Barrett case, see Robert L. Fletcher, Perpetuities: Basic Clarity, Muddled Reform, 63 Wash. L. Rev. 791, 815–18 (1988).

4. *Savings Clauses.* We shall soon examine use of perpetuities savings clauses in dispositive instruments as a mechanism to guard against perpetuities violations. Even experienced drafters who take a dim view of savings clauses are more likely to use them to guard against invalidity in case the testator or settlor of a trust should unexpectedly acquire a power of appointment. In light of *Barrett*, can you see why?

2. THE SECOND-LOOK DOCTRINE

As we have seen, for special powers and, in most jurisdictions, for general testamentary powers, the Rule's period is generally measured from the time the power is created, not from the time of exercise. But what facts can we take into account in assessing the validity of an interest? The *second-look doctrine* provides that we can take into account all facts known at the time the donee exercises the power.

Ordinarily, the common law Rule Against Perpetuities focuses on possibilities. If some series of events, however remote, could cause a future interest to vest or fail beyond the Rule's period, the future interest is invalid. For instance, if an 80–year old testator's will were to create a trust for the benefit of her husband for life, then for her grandchildren for life, with the principal to be distributed to great-grandchildren at the death of testator's last grandchild, the interest in great-grandchildren would be invalid if any of testator's children were alive at testator's death. (Make sure you understand why!)

Suppose, now, that testator's will creates a trust for the benefit of her husband for life, and gives the husband a special power to appoint among descendants. The husband then appoints, in further trust, for the benefit of the grandchildren for life, with the principal to be distributed to great-grandchildren at the death of the last grandchild. Suppose further that all of testator's children have died before the husband exercises the power, and that no additional grandchildren were born after testator's death. Is the husband's exercise valid under the Rule Against Perpetuities?

The relation-back doctrine instructs us to measure the Rule's period from the time the wife created the power. At that time, the couple's children were still alive, and could have more children. If we read the husband's appointment back into the wife's will, and ask whether the appointment is valid, taking into account only those facts known at the time of the wife's death, then the husband's appointment would be invalid.

The second-look doctrine rejects this approach, and permits us to take into account all facts known at the time of the husband's death—in particular, the fact that all of testator's grandchildren were actually born at the time of testator's death. Hence, even though the relation-back doctrine requires us to measure the Rule's period from the time of testator's death, we can use testator's grandchildren as measuring lives, and the husband's appointment is valid. Of course, if, at the time of the husband's death, one of testator's children were still alive, the appointment would be invalid, because even if we take into account facts known at the time of the husband's exercise, we still could not be sure that the interest in great-grandchildren would vest within the period of the Rule. (Again, be sure you understand why!)

The second-look doctrine applies only to interests created under powers of appointment. The doctrine is not equivalent to the "wait and see" doctrine adopted in many jurisdictions to salvage interests invalid under the Rule Against Perpetuities.

PROBLEMS

1. T's will creates a trust, with directions to the trustee to distribute income to T's brother, B, during his lifetime, and to distribute the principal "to those of B's descendants as B shall designate by will." B's will appoints the property, in trust, with directions to distribute income "among my children or the survivors of them for so long as one of my children remains alive," and to distribute principal, at the death of the B's last surviving child, "among my grandchildren, per capita." Is B's appointment valid if:

a. B's only two children were alive at T's death?

b. One child of B was alive at T's death, another was born after T's death, and both survived B?

c. Both of B's children were born after T's death, and died (leaving children) before B's death?

2. Arthur Smith, by will, disposes of property "in trust for my children for their lives, and I give to the survivor of them the power to appoint the property by will among my descendants."

Burton Smith, the surviving child, appoints the property, by will, "in trust for my children for their lives, and I give to the survivor of them the power to appoint the property

(a) by will."

(b) by will or by *inter vivos* instrument."

Consider, in each of the following fact situations, whether the power created in Burton's will is valid under the Rule Against Perpetuities:

1. Burton never has children.
2. Burton has two children, neither alive at Arthur's death.
3. Burton has two children, one alive at Arthur's death.
4. Burton has two children, both alive at Arthur's death.

(Note: even if the power created in Burton's will were valid, Burton's child's exercise might be invalid if the child tries to create a further trust. Do you see why?)

C. VALIDITY OF GIFTS IN DEFAULT OF APPOINTMENT

What happens if the donor creates a power of appointment, and the donee chooses not to exercise the power at all? If the donee has made provisions for takers-in-default, how should we determine whether the provision for takers-in-default is valid under the Rule Against Perpetuities? The Rule's period should be measured from the donor's creation of the power, but should the second-look doctrine apply? Consider the following problem in light of the case that follows it:

PROBLEM

Donor, during his lifetime, creates a trust, income to be paid to his wife during her lifetime, and principal to be distributed as the wife shall appoint by will from among donor's descendants. The trust instrument further provides that if the wife shall not exercise the power of appointment, the property should be distributed "in trust, income to be distributed among my children until the death of the last survivor of those children, at which time the principal should be distributed to my grandchildren, in equal shares." If the wife does not exercise the power of appointment, is the gift in default of appointment valid if testator had two living children on the date of execution and

a. no children are born to testator after execution of the trust instrument?

b. one child is born to testator after execution of the trust instrument, but that child dies before the wife's death?

c. one child is born to testator after execution of the trust instrument, that child survives, but no grandchildren are born to testator after execution of the trust instrument?

Sears v. Coolidge

Supreme Judicial Court of Massachusetts, 1952.
329 Mass. 340, 108 N.E.2d 563.

■ WILKINS, JUSTICE.

These two petitions under G.L.(Ter.Ed.) c. 231A seek binding declarations as to the validity of the provisions relating to income and to gifts of principal by way of remainder in a deed of trust executed by Thomas Jefferson Coolidge, late of Manchester, under date of February 12, 1913. The settlor died on November 17, 1920. In each case a decree was entered declaring that the life interests are valid; but that the gifts over of principal are invalid and void, and upon the termination of the trust the personal representatives of the settlor's estate are to receive the principal and any unpaid accumulated income. The petitioners, the trustees, and numerous other persons interested in the trust or in the settlor's estate appealed.

The net income of the trust was payable one third semi-annually to "such of the issue of my deceased son as shall be living at the time of each such semi-annual payment," and two thirds, divided into three parts payable semi-annually, one part each to Marian A. Sargent and to Sarah L. Newbold and after their death to their respective issue, and one to the living issue of Eleonora R. Sears, who were the petitioners Eleonora R. Sears and Frederick R. Sears.

The appeals relating to the life interests have been "waived and withdrawn." We are now concerned only with the decrees in so far as they affect the remainder interests. Whenever we refer to the appellants, we shall mean all or some of those who are seeking to establish the validity of the remainder interests. The facts are undisputed and, for the most part, are embodied in a written stipulation in the Probate Court. The evidence is reported.

The fundamental issue is whether the remainder interests violate the rule against perpetuities. Paragraph 5 of the trust instrument provides that the capital of the trust is to be distributed "in equal shares to and among my issue living" at the time of distribution. Distribution is to take place upon "whichever shall first happen" of two events: (1) "the death of the last survivor of those of my children, grandchildren and great grandchildren who shall be living at my death"; or (2) "the attainment of fifty years by the youngest surviving grandchild of mine who shall be living at my death." The second event first happened. William A. Coolidge, the youngest grandchild living at the settlor's death, attained the age of fifty years on October 21, 1951.

Where a trust instrument contains two alternative conditions, of which the first might be too remote and the second, which actually occurs, is not too remote, the rule is not violated. Jackson v. Phillips, 14 Allen 539, 572–573; Stone v. Bradlee, 183 Mass. 165, 171–172, 66 N.E. 708; Gray v. Whittemore, 192 Mass. 367, 372, 78 N.E. 422, 10 L.R.A., N.S., 1143; Springfield Safe Deposit & Trust Co. v. Ireland, 268 Mass. 62, 67–68, 167 N.E. 261, 64 A.L.R. 1071. Accordingly, the appellants contend that the attainment by the youngest grandchild of the age of fifty years was certain to occur within the period required by the rule, and that as matter of construction the reference in paragraph 5 to "the youngest surviving grandchild of mine who shall be living at my death" must be read as if "grandchild" were qualified by "now living" or similar words. In support are adduced various facts in the settlor's family situation obvious to him when he executed the deed of trust. He was then eighty-one years of age and had been a widower for twelve years. At that time he had two living children, Marian A. Sargent, who was aged fifty-nine and had been a widow for twenty years, and Sarah L. Newbold, who was then fifty-five years of age. During the preceding year there had died two of his children, T. Jefferson Coolidge and Eleonora R. Sears. The settlor then had ten living grandchildren. Four were the minor sons of his deceased son. Two were the children of his deceased daughter, one being the petitioner, Eleonora R. Sears, and the other Frederick R. Sears, the administrator of whose estate is the petitioner Fiduciary Trust Company. One was the child of Marian A. Sargent, and three were the children of Sarah L. Newbold. The oldest grandchild was thirty-five and the youngest was seven. No further grandchildren were born in the settlor's lifetime, but the youngest of the ten died before the settlor.

The appellees argue, on the other hand, that it is not permissible thus to qualify the clause in paragraph 5, and for present purposes we accept their position on this point, and assume that the phrase "the youngest surviving grandchild of mine who shall be living at my death" is not to be interpreted as excluding grandchildren who might be born after the trust instrument was created.

The appellants make the contention that the settlor in the trust deed reserved a power which was at least equivalent to a special power of appointment, and that the validity of the remainders must in any event be determined in the light of the facts existing at his death when it was known that his only grandchildren had been lives in being at the time the trust was created. This has been referred to in the arguments as "a second look."

Paragraph 9 reads: "I reserve to myself power at all times to make any additions to the trust property, to change and alter any or all of the trusts herein set forth and to declare new uses and trusts of the property in any way or manner except such as will vest in myself the trust property or any beneficial interest therein, to name and appoint any other persons than those above specified or hereafter appointed as beneficiaries, whether by way of addition or substitution, and to appoint other trustees instead of or in addition to any or all of those above named. Every such change, alteration, nomination and appointment shall be made by my deed and shall take effect immediately upon the delivery thereof to any person who shall at the time be acting as a trustee under the provisions of these presents."

The point, which, so far as appears, has not been pressed upon an appellate court before, is based upon the analogy of Minot v. Paine, 230 Mass. 514, 120 N.E. 167, 1 A.L.R. 365. The theory is that at the settlor's death the expiration of the power to divert the property from the takers in default was the same in effect as an appointment of the remainders by the settlor's will.

The reserved power is, at the very least, akin to a power of appointment.... And, for present purposes, we treat it as having attributes of a special power to appoint by deed.

* * *

Since it is permissible to make use of the circumstances known when a power, which is special or testamentary, is exercised to determine validity under the rule, it seems reasonable to afford the same opportunity in cases where such a power is not exercised. In the case of the trust instrument under consideration until it became too late for the settlor to exercise the reserved power no one could tell what might be the ultimate disposition of the trust property. As long as there remained a right to change, alter, and make new appointments, no instructions to the trustees or declaratory decree would ordinarily have been given as to the validity of the settlor's limitations. See National Shawmut Bank v. Morey, 320 Mass. 492, 497–500, 70 N.E.2d 316, 174 A.L.R. 871; Young v. Jackson, 321 Mass. 1, 7, 71 N.E.2d

386; Burn v. McAllister, 321 Mass. 660, 662, 75 N.E.2d 114. Upon his death it could be learned for the first time what definitely were to be the terms of the trust. It then could be seen for the first time that there was to be no failure to vest within the period limited by the rule. No further grandchildren had been born. In these precise circumstances there is no compelling decision which prevents taking advantage of facts known at the moment when the power ceased to be exercisable. American Law of Property, § 24.36. We are unwilling to apply the rule so as to invalidate the trust instrument.

The appellees strongly urge that the doctrine of a "second look" has no place in reading the original limitations in default of appointment, which were capable of examination when created, and which should retain the same meaning throughout. They argue that its adoption would be a nullification of the rule "that executory limitations are void unless they take effect ex necessitate and in all possible contingencies" within the prescribed period. Hall v. Hall, 123 Mass. 120, 124. But this rule, while recognized, was assuaged as to the exercise of a power of appointment in Minot v. Paine, 230 Mass. 514, 522, 120 N.E. 167, 1 A.L.R. 365. It was there deemed wise not to apply unmodified a remorseless technical principle to a case which it did not fit. That principle seems equally inappropriate here.

The decrees are reversed and the causes are remanded to the Probate Court for the entry of decrees in accordance with this opinion. Costs and expenses of appeal are to be in the discretion of the Probate Court.

So ordered.

SECTION VI. SAVINGS CLAUSES

Many a law student (and too many lawyers) have been heard to observe "the Rule Against Perpetuities isn't important any more, because a good lawyer always includes a perpetuities savings clause in any instrument she drafts." Perpetuities savings clauses do, indeed, save many interests from invalidity under the Rule, but careless drafting of savings clauses has itself engendered far too much litigation.

Unfortunately, the drafter of an instrument must be well acquainted with the Rule Against Perpetuities to draft an appropriate savings clause. Consider the drafter's goals. Generally, the drafter wants to avoid invalidity of any interests she creates, but also wants to avoid premature termination of any trust she creates. For a variety of reasons, including tax reasons, the creator of the trust often wants to keep the trust in existence for as long as possible. Why shouldn't the drafter simply direct that if any provision of the trust would otherwise be invalid under the Rule Against Perpetuities, the trust should endure "only for so long as permitted by the applicable Rule Against Perpetuities?" That sort of provision, after all, doesn't require the drafter to understand the Rule. The following case, however, explores some of the potential consequences.

Estate of Holt

Supreme Court of Hawaii, 1993.
75 Haw. 224, 857 P.2d 1355.

■ MOON, C.J:

The trustee of a testamentary trust filed a petition for instructions in circuit court to determine the correct termination date of the trust. The circuit court held that in order to avoid violating the Rule Against Perpetuities, the trust must terminate twenty-one years after the death of the last survivor among the testator's eleven children. Because the last survivor died in 1986, the court held that the trust must terminate in the year 2007. The guardian ad litem, appointed by the court to represent the interests of unascertained or yet unborn trust beneficiaries, now appeals to this court, contending that the trust should not terminate until twenty-one years after the death of the last survivor of the testator's grandchildren who were alive at the time of the testator's death. We disagree and affirm the ruling of the circuit court.

I. BACKGROUND

The testamentary trust, which is the subject of this appeal, was created by the 1914 will of George H. Holt (Holt), who died in 1929. The testamentary trust was the subject of a prior appeal decided by this court in *In re Trust Estate of George H. Holt, Deceased*, 42 Haw. 129 (1957) (*Holt I*). Both this court's 1957 decision and the instant appeal focus on the following provision of Holt's will:

> All the rest, residue and remainder of my estate I give, devise and bequeath to my trustees hereinafter named, and their successor or successors in trust: In trust to hold, care for and manage the same for as long a period as is legally possible; determination or ending of said trust to take place when the law requires it under the Statute; and during the pendency of said trust to pay the income from the same to my said wife during her life, or so long as she shall remain a widow, and after her death or future marriage, to stand possessed thereof, in trust as aforesaid, and to pay the income to all of my heirs in equal shares per stirpes, and upon the final ending of the term of said trust, as aforesaid, to divide my trust estate among the persons entitled to the same at that time under the Law per stirpes.

There are currently fifty-three income beneficiaries, twelve of whom are Holt's grandchildren, who were living at the time of Holt's death.

The question confronting this court in Holt I was how to correctly interpret the trust phrase, "and to pay income to all of my heirs in equal share per stirpes."

* * *

We ... stated that the issue presented was whether the word "heirs" was to be limited to Holt's children, or whether "heirs" should "include persons who were his heirs from time to time as the income accrued[.]" *Id.* at 133. We noted that if the word were limited to the children, ... it would ... be possible "that such heir's right to the share of the income would go, after his death, to persons who would not be in the line of descent from the testator." *Id.* at 134. If, however, "heirs" were construed to include "persons who were [Holt's] heirs from time to time as the income accrued," then

> each of the persons who were initially determined to be his heirs would only be entitled to his proportionate share of the income which accrued during his life. Such heir would have no control over the disposition of the share of the income which accrued after his death. The share of income accruing after his death would go to persons who would be testator's heirs and who traced their descent through such heir.

Id. (citation omitted).

We decided that the latter construction was the correct one, reasoning that

> the testator provided that upon the termination of the trust the corpus be divided among "the persons entitled to the same at that time under the law per stirpes." We construe this provision to mean that the corpus is to be distributed, per stirpes, to persons who are testator's heirs at the termination of the trust. If the provision for the payment of the income is considered in connection with the provision for the distribution of the corpus, it is apparent that the testator intended to benefit all persons who were his heirs at any time between the date of the death of the widow and the termination of the trust. There is no indication in the will that the testator intended to benefit only persons who were his heirs at the time of the death of the widow and persons who were his heirs at the termination of the trust and to exclude from its provisions persons who were his heirs at any time during the intervening period.
>
> * * *

Id. at 135.

On January 10, 1991, Bishop Trust Company, Ltd. (trustee), current trustee of the Holt testamentary trust, filed in the circuit court a petition for instructions asking the court to determine the correct termination date of said trust. The trustee stated that twelve of the fifty-three currently living heirs of Holt had been alive on the date of his death in 1929. The trustee further stated that it was "uncertain about the termination date of the Trust ... and whether the 'lives in being' which limit the duration of the Trust under the Rule Against Perpetuities are those of Testator's heirs or Testator's children or some other person(s)." The trustee thus requested that the court decide "whether the Trust terminates twenty-one years after the death of the last survivor of Testator's heirs alive on the date of [his] death, or twenty-one years after the death of the last survivor of [his] children, or twenty-one years after the death of some other person(s), or on some other date." Also on January 10, 1991, the circuit court ordered the appointment of a guardian ad litem (GAL) to represent the interests of any unascertained or not yet born beneficiaries under Holt's will.

On September 17, 1992, following a hearing on the trustee's petition for instructions, the circuit court ruled that the term "heirs" in Holt's will referred to Holt's eleven children alive at the time of both his and his widow's deaths, and that said children were the "measuring lives" applicable in a calculation of the trust's legal duration under the Rule Against Perpetuities (RAP). Implicit in the court's ruling was the conclusion that the "heirs" specifically referred to in the testamentary trust were the proper measuring lives for any RAP calculation. Because the last of Holt's surviving eleven children had died in 1986, the court held that the trust must terminate twenty-one years following that child's death, i.e., in the year 2007.

The GAL appealed, contending that the term "heirs" should also include any of Holt's grandchildren who were alive at his death. Although the GAL essentially agrees with the circuit court that the "heirs" mentioned in the trust are the proper measuring lives for any RAP calculation of the trust's legal duration, the GAL argues that the trust should not terminate until twenty-one years after the death of the last survivor among the twelve current surviving grandchildren.

II. DISCUSSION

Instead of including an explicit termination date for the instant testamentary trust, Holt provided that the trust was to last "for as long a period as is legally possible, determination or ending of said trust to take place when the law requires it." Implicit in the circuit court's order is the conclusion of law that the trust, lacking an explicit termination date, must come to an end within twenty-one years after lives in being at the trust's creation in order to avoid violating the RAP. The circuit court further concluded as a matter of law that said lives in being—the "measuring lives" for RAP purposes—were the "heirs" specifically referred to in the applicable trust provision, and that the term "heirs" must refer to Holt's eleven children alive at the time of both Holt's and his widow's deaths. The GAL has essentially only challenged the last of the foregoing conclusions by the circuit court, arguing that the term "heirs" must also refer to any of Holt's grandchildren alive at the time of his death.

* * *

All of the parties are in agreement with the circuit court's conclusion that the RAP is applicable to the instant testamentary trust. "The [RAP] is said to be part of the English common law and is therefore applicable in Hawaii." *In re Estate of Chun Quan Yee Hop*, 52 Haw. 40, 43, 469 P.2d 183, 185 (1970) (citing *Fitchie v. Brown*, 18 Haw. 52, 69 (1906), *aff'd*, 211 U.S. 321, 53 L. Ed. 202, 29 S. Ct. 106 (1908)). The common law RAP germane to the instant case provides that " '[n]o interest is good unless it must vest, if at all, not later than twenty-one years after some life in being at the creation of the interest.' " Id. 52 Haw. at 42 n.3, 469 P.2d at 185 n.3 (citation omitted).

In the instant case, the circuit court correctly determined that although the testamentary trust and its specific terms were set forth in Holt's will, such trust only became operational at the death of the testator. Therefore, for purposes of the RAP, the specific interests included in the testamentary trust were created at Holt's death. *See* J. Gray, *The Rule Against Perpetuities*§ 231, at 235 (4th ed. 1942); W.B. Leach and O. Tudor, *The Rule Against Perpetuities*§ 24.12(a), at 44 (1957). Accordingly, in order to avoid a violation of the RAP, any interest provided for in the instant trust must vest, if at all, not later than twenty-one years after some lives in being at Holt's death. Such lives in being at the creation at relevant interests are commonly referred to as the "measuring lives" under the RAP. *See* W.B. Leach and O. Tudor, § 24.13, at 47–48.

The circuit court concluded that the proper measuring lives under the Holt trust were those "heirs" specifically referred to in the trust instrument. None of the parties disputes this conclusion. Although the court did not detail its reasoning, such conclusion is in accord with general RAP law:

> Not infrequently a testator directs that property be held in trust "for my children and their descendants, as long as the law allows" or similar verbiage.... Courts have given such wording a practical construction and held that it means for the lives of the prime beneficiaries (the children in the case suggested), and twenty-one years thereafter, and sustained the gift.

Id. at 49 (citation omitted). Courts have generally held that if an explicit termination date is lacking, but specific beneficiaries are named in the trust instrument, then such beneficiaries are the applicable measuring lives for a calculation of legal trust duration under the RAP. See, e.g., *Fitchie v. Brown*, 18 Haw. 52 (1906), *aff'd,* 211 U.S. 321, 53 L. Ed. 202, 29 S. Ct. 106 (1908); *Betchard v. Iverson*, 35 Wash. 2d 344, 212 P.2d 783 (1949); *Stellings v. Autry*, 257 N.C. 303, 126 S.E.2d 140 (1962); *Klugh v. United States*, 588 F.2d 45 (4th Cir.1978).

The single issue in dispute in the present case is whether the term "heirs" in the instant trust—comprising the group of applicable measuring lives—refers only to Holt's eleven children alive at the time of his widow's death or whether the term also includes those of Holt's grandchildren alive at that time. As previously noted, this court in *Holt I* stated unequivocally that "[w]hen a gift is made in a will to heirs of a designated person, the word 'heirs' means persons who succeed to the property of such designated person under the law which governs intestate succession," and that under the applicable law, "[t]estator's heirs on [the date of his widow's death] were his eleven surviving children." 42 Haw. at 132–33. We said nothing about any of Holt's surviving grandchildren being included in the class of "heirs" on the applicable date. Therefore, according to our plain statement in Holt I, it is apparent that the circuit court was "right" in holding that the applicable measuring lives were limited to Holt's eleven surviving children.

However, the GAL argues that this court in Holt I also broadened the category of heirs under the trust to include all persons who were Holt's heirs from time to time as the income accrued and stated that "it is apparent that the testator intended to benefit all persons who were his heirs at any time between the date of the death of his widow and the termination the trust." Id. at 135. The GAL contends that this broadening of the category of Holt's heirs means that any of Holt's grandchildren alive at his widow's death were also "heirs," and that these grandchildren are therefore also measuring lives for any RAP calculation. We disagree.

In *Holt I*, we broadened the category of heirs to include all "persons who were [Holt's] heirs *from time to time as the income accrued*." Id. at 133 (emphasis added). We did *not* extend the meaning of the term "heir" for purposes of the RAP to include those persons "who succeed to the property of [a] designated person under the law which governs intestate succession." *Id.* Neither did we hold that Holt's grandchildren who were alive at the time of his widow's death were among his heirs *at that time.* In other words, we did not rule that Holt's surviving grandchildren, whose parents were still alive, possessed a right to a share of the trust income at the time of Holt's widow's death. On the contrary, those grandchildren whose parents were still alive and any of Holt's grandchildren born after his widow's death would only come to possess such a right to an income share when their "Holt-parent" died, thus transforming them *at that time* into Holt's heirs.

* * *

Therefore, the identity of Holt's heirs at any particular time following his widow's death would necessarily vary, depending on who was alive at that time. A grandchild or a great-grandchild or a great-great-grandchild, whose parent in the Holt line was still living, would be at most a *potential* heir who would himself or herself become an heir only upon the death of his or her Holt-parent. Accordingly, as the circuit court in the instant case correctly determined, at the time of Holt's widow's death, the category of Holt's "heirs," which also comprised the category of applicable measuring lives for RAP purposes, included only Holt's eleven surviving children. Additionally, because the last of Holt's eleven surviving children died in 1986, the circuit court correctly determined that the instant testamentary trust must terminate twenty-one years after 1986—in the year 2007.

III. CONCLUSION

Based on the foregoing, we affirm the September 17, 1992 order of the circuit court holding that the Holt trust must terminate in the year 2007.

NOTES AND QUESTIONS

1. A successful savings clause should specify (1) the time at which the trust will terminate if the dispositive provisions would otherwise violate the Rule Against Perpetuities and (2) the persons entitled to the principal at the time for termination. Was Holt's will clear on either point? Who will become entitled to the principal when the trust terminates in 2007?

Many lawyers are skeptical about the value of savings clauses, in part because the lawyer who is unaware that he has drafted an instrument that violates the Rule Against Perpetuities is not likely to be aware of the problem he is trying to cure. Professor Robert Fletcher, after extensive discussion of the difficulties in drafting savings clauses, concluded as follows:

> The principal lesson in this discussion of savings clauses is to draft Plan A [the client's basic plan—eds.] so that it is free from error. Savings clauses may be useful, but they are potential for trouble. Just hope yours is never put to use.

Robert L. Fletcher, Perpetuities: Basic Clarity, Muddled Reform, 63 Wash. L. Rev. 791, 822 (1988).

2. Holt's will specified that the trust was to endure "for as long a period as is legally possible." Does the court's holding accomplish that result? Redraft Holt's will so that the trust would last beyond 2007.

Note that theoretically, Holt could have created a trust to endure for 21 years past the death of the last survivor of all people alive at the moment of his death. Do you understand why? Do you understand why Holt would not have drafted such a provision, and why a court would be unwilling to enforce it? Cf. In re Leverhulme, 169 L.T.R. 294, 298 (Chancery 1943), in which the court, while upholding a trust on stare decisis grounds, wrote:

> I hope that no draftsman will think that because of my decision today he will necessarily be following a sound course if he adopts the well-known formula referring to the descendants living at the death of the testator of her late Majesty Queen Victoria. When that formula was first adopted there was, not doubt, little difficulty in ascertaining when the last of them died.... I do not at all encourage anyone to use the formula in the case of a testator who dies in the year 1943 or any later date.

3. The abstract formula used by the drafter in Holt is, unfortunately, all too common. Consider the following variations, each of which has engendered recent litigation:

> a. "If any trust created hereunder shall violate any applicable rule against perpetuities, accumulations or any similar rule of law, the Trustees are hereby directed to terminate such trust on the date limited by such rule or law...." Ludwig v. AmSouth Bank of Florida, 686 So.2d 1373 (Fla.App.1997).
>
> b. "Upon the death of [my] last surviving grandchild, the income should be paid to [my] great-grandchildren per stirpes, to continue so long as permitted by the laws of the Commonwealth of Pennsylvania or until the death of such great-grandchildren." Estate of Coates, 438 Pa.Super. 195, 652 A.2d 331 (1994).

4. A savings clause is more likely to be successful if it selects a group of lives in being on the effective date of the instrument, and directs that if the trust would otherwise violate the Rule Against Perpetuities, the trust should terminate 21 years after the death of the last survivor of the group. The drafter must be careful to assure that the lives selected are alive on the effective date of the instrument, which, in the case of an *inter vivos* instrument, will not be the date of testator's death. Consider, for instance, Ryan v. Ward, 192 Md. 342, 64 A.2d 258 (1949), in which the drafter directed termination of an irrevocable *inter vivos* trust upon the death of the last surviving child of the Grantor's son, who shall be living at the time of the death of the Grantor.

What error did the drafter commit?

5. Savings clauses are particularly appropriate to guard against a donee's potentially invalid exercise of a power of appointment. When donee's lawyer drafts donee's will, the lawyer (and, indeed, the donee) may not know the terms of a power of appointment the donee will later receive from one of the donee's relatives. Hence, if the donee's residuary clause creates a trust, and also exercises "any power of appointment I may hold at my death," there is significant potential that donee's exercise of the power will violate the Rule Against Perpetuities (Remember that if the power is a special power, the period will be measured from the donor's creation of the power, not from the donee's exercise). How would you draft a savings clause to deal with this problem?

SECTION VII. PERPETUITIES REFORM: LEGISLATIVE AND JUDICIAL SALVAGE DOCTRINES

To this point, our treatment of the Rule Against Perpetuities has focused on the common law Rule, for two reasons: first, to understand the various perpetuities reforms, one must first understand the common law Rule; second (and in our view, most important), the drafter of a will or trust instrument should never draft an instrument that violates the common law Rule. Modern reform doctrines might save instruments which, by their terms, violate the common law Rule, but saving the instruments could require considerable delay, uncertainty, and litigation expense. In addition, drafting an instrument that violates the Rule would not do much for the lawyer-drafter's professional reputation. To the extent the principal role of the estates lawyer is as drafter—not litigator—the common law Rule remains the foundation for perpetuities learning.

Nevertheless, rigid adherence to the common law Rule has become far less prevalent over the last several decades. Many states have taken steps to revamp the Rule—either by adopting some form of "wait-and-see" doctrine or by adopting constructional rules to ameliorate the harshest results generated by the Rule. Most recently, the Uniform Statutory Rule Against Perpetuities (USRAP) has been incorporated into the Uniform Probate Code. USRAP declares valid all interests that would be valid under the common law Rule, but also validates any interests that actually vest within 90 years. More recently, a number of legislatures have abolished the Rule altogether.

A. CONSTRUCTION AND REFORMATION

In a number of states, statutes mandate construction of instruments to prevent violations of the Rule Against Perpetuities. Tex. Prop. Code Ann., sec. 5.043, is illustrative:

> Within the limits of the rule against perpetuities, a court shall reform or construe an interest in real or personal property that violates the rule to effect the ascertainable general intent of the creator of the interest. A court shall liberally construe and apply this provision to validate an interest to the fullest extent consistent with the creator's intent.

In other states, courts construe wills and trust instruments to avoid the Rule, even without the benefit of statute. See, e.g. Warren v. Albrecht, 213 Ill.App.3d 55, 157 Ill.Dec. 160, 571 N.E.2d 1179 (1991). In New York, as we have already seen, the legislature has enacted a number of constructional rules designed to minimize the impact of remote possibilities. For a discussion of the New York statutory reform, see Frederick R. Schneider, A Rule Against Perpetuities for the Twenty–First Century, 41 Real Prop., Prob. & Tr. J. 743, 774–80 (2007). See also Ira Mark Bloom, Perpetuities Refinement: There is an Alternative, 62 Wash. L. Rev. 23 (1987), advocating rules like those enacted in New York as preferable to wholesale reworking of the Rule Against Perpetuities through the wait-and-see-doctrine or the Uniform Statutory Rule Against Perpetuities. Professor Bloom's research—supported by earlier work done by others—suggests that very few interests (perhaps as few as one per year, nationwide) are actually held invalid under the Rule. Id. at 34–35.

New York has not enacted a general rule requiring construction or reformation to avoid the impact of the Rule Against Perpetuities. See N.Y. EPTL § 9–1.3.

B. WAIT AND SEE

For many years, adoption of the wait-and-see doctrine was the most revolutionary form of perpetuities reform. The Rule Against Perpetuities, in its common law form, invalidates future interests if there is even a remote possibility that the interest will remain contingent for longer than the period of the rule. Proponents of wait-and-see argued that courts should not upset testamentary plans based on a remote possibility that interests would remain contingent for too long; instead, they argued, courts should wait and see whether those interests would actually remain contingent for longer than the Rule's period.

Opponents of wait-and-see countered with two arguments. First, unlike the common law Rule, which enables courts to determine the validity of all interests immediately upon their creation, the wait-and-see doctrine would itself increase contingency by making it impossible to determine—often for years after an interest's creation—whether the interest would be valid under the Rule. If the purpose of the Rule is to reduce contingency, wait-and-see undermines that purpose. Second, many have argued that there is no logical way to determine how long we should wait before determining whether an interest is valid under the Rule. Consider the following example:

> ***Example 24:*** *Testator's will devises property, in trust, "income to be paid to my brother for life, then to my brother's children and their heirs until the death of my brother's last surviving child, remainder to my brother's grandchildren, per stirpes." How long must we wait to determine whether the interest in the brother's grandchildren is valid? Suppose we wait until the brother's death. If the brother has had no more children, then we know that the brother's children can be used as measuring lives to save the devise to the brother's grandchildren. But suppose the brother has another child after testator's death. Is the interest in the brother's grandchildren invalid, or do we wait longer, to see whether the afterborn child survives the before-born children? If the afterborn does survive, do we wait still longer to see whether the afterborn survives the beforeborns by more than 21 years?*

Professor Jesse Dukeminier, the foremost modern proponent of wait-and-see, considered it easy to answer the questions raised in Example 24. Dukeminier suggests that application of wait-and-see starts by assembling the people whose lives are "causally related to vesting." If any of these people are alive at the creation of the interest in question, we wait until the death of the last of these people, and if the interest actually vests within 21 years of the death of the last of these people, the interest is valid. In Dukeminier's words:

> First, we assemble the causally-connected lives, who fix the limits of the perpetuities period. Second, we test each of these lives in search of a validating life. Third, if we do not find a validating life among these causally-related lives, we wait and see whether the interest vests during these lives plus twenty-one years.

Jesse Dukeminier, Perpetuities: The Measuring Lives, 85 Colum. L. Rev. 1648, 1656 (1985). Dukeminier argued that a legislature could easily replace the common law Rule with a one-sentence statement of wait-and-see: "No interest is good unless it vests within twenty-one years after the death of all persons in being when the interest is created who can affect the vesting of the interest." Id. at 1713. For Dukeminier, then, in Example 24 we would wait until the death of testator's brother and any of testator's brother's children or grandchildren who were alive at testator's death. We then wait an additional 21 years. If, at that time, the brother's last surviving child has died, then the interest in the brother's grandchildren is valid under the Rule. Otherwise, the interest is invalid.

Note that Dukeminier's formulation of wait-and-see can leave the validity of an interest uncertain for a very long time; his formulation goes well beyond accounting for "remote possibilities."

Professor Lawrence Waggoner has criticized Dukeminier's version of wait-and-see on another ground: he questions the notion that we can identify a discrete set of "causally-related lives" for dispositions that do not satisfy the common-law Rule:

> ... [A] common law measuring life is a person for whom there is *no* chain of events that *might possibly* arise after the creation of the contingent interest that would allow the interest to remain in existence and still contingent beyond the twenty-first anniversary of the person's death. Only in the case of valid interest will there be such a person. There is no such person in the case of invalid interests. Invalid interests are invalid, not because they might remain in existence and contingent beyond the twenty-first anniversary of the death of a *particular* measuring life, but rather because there is *no* measuring life that makes them valid....
>
> Thus, the common law Rule's central test of validity—the real test, I shall call it—contains no mechanism for marking off a "perpetuity period" in each given case....
>
> Since a wait-and-see rule against perpetuities applies to interests that would be invalid under the common law Rule—that is, interests for which by definition no validating life exists—the common law Rule does not, in my view, identify the lives to be used in measuring off the wait-and-see perpetuity period.

Lawrence W. Waggoner, Perpetuities: A Perspective on Wait-and-See, 85 Colum. L. Rev. 1714, 1715–16 (1985).

C. USRAP

Scholars unhappy with both the common law Rule and wait-and-see developed an alternative—the Uniform Statutory Rule Against Perpetuities (USRAP), which has now been incorporated into the Uniform Probate Code. The drafters of USRAP abandoned the effort to tie a waiting period to "lives in being." Instead, USRAP upholds a contingent future interest if (1) it satisfies the common law Rule against perpetuities *or* (2) the interest actually vests within 90 years from the time of its creation. That is, for an interest not valid under the common law Rule, we wait until 90 years after the interest's creation, and if the interest is still contingent, the interest is invalid. Although USRAP appears simple enough at first glance, the statute is not without its problematic aspects. Most important, however, USRAP is built around the common law Rule, and does not dispense with the need to understand that rule.

Uniform Probate Code

Section 2–901. Statutory Rule Against Perpetuities.

(a) [Validity of Nonvested Property Interest.] A nonvested property interest is invalid unless:

(1) when the interest is created, it is certain to vest or terminate no later than 21 years after the death of an individual then alive; or

(2) the interest either vests or terminates within 90 years after its creation.

(b) [Validity of General Power of Appointment Subject to a Condition Precedent.] A general power of appointment not presently exercisable because of a condition precedent is invalid unless:

(1) when the power is created, the condition precedent is certain to be satisfied or becomes impossible to satisfy no later than 21 years after the death of an individual then alive; or

(2) the condition precedent either is satisfied or becomes impossible to satisfy within 90 years after its creation.

(c) [Validity of Nongeneral or Testamentary Power of Appointment.] A nongeneral power of appointment or a general testamentary power of appointment is invalid unless:

(1) when the power is created, it is certain to be irrevocably exercised or otherwise to terminate no later than 21 years after the death of an individual then alive; or

(2) the power is irrevocably exercised or otherwise terminates within 90 years after its creation.

(d) [Possibility of Post-death Child Disregarded.] In determining whether a nonvested property interest or a power of appointment is valid under subsection (a)(1), (b)(1), or (c)(1), the possibility that a child will be born to an individual after the individual's death is disregarded.

(e) [Effect of Certain "Later-of" Type Language.] If, in measuring a period from the creation of a trust or other property arrangement, language in a governing instrument (i) seeks to disallow the vesting or termination of any interest or trust beyond, (ii) seeks to postpone the vesting or termination of any interest or trust until, or (iii) seeks to operate in effect in any similar fashion upon, the later of (A) the expiration of a period of time not exceeding 21 years after the death of the survivor of specified lives in being at the creation of the trust or other property arrangement or (B) the expiration of a period of time that exceeds or might exceed 21 years after the death of the survivor of lives in being at the creation of the trust or other property arrangement, that language is inoperative to the extent it produces a period of time that exceeds 21 years after the death of the survivor of the specified lives.

Section 2–902. When Nonvested Property Interest or Power of Appointment Created

(a) Except as provided in subsections (b) and (c) and in section 2–905(a), the time of creation of a nonvested property interest or a power of appointment is determined under general principles of property law.

(b) For purposes of Subpart 1 of this Part, if there is a person who alone can exercise a power created by a governing instrument to become the unqualified beneficial owner of (i) a nonvested property interest or (ii) a property interest subject to a power of appointment described in Section 2–901(b) or (c), the nonvested property interest or power of appointment is created when the power to become the unqualified beneficial owner terminates. [For purposes of Subpart 1 of this Part, a joint power with respect to community property or to marital property under the Uniform Marital Property Act held by individuals married to each other is a power exercisable by one person alone.]

(c) For purposes of Subpart 1 of this Part, a nonvested property interest or a power of appointment arising from a transfer of property to a previously funded trust or other existing property arrangement is created when the nonvested property interest or power of appointment in the original contribution was created.

SECTION 2–903. REFORMATION.

Upon the petition of an interested person, a court shall reform a disposition in the manner that most closely approximates the transferor's manifested plan of distribution and is within the 90 years allowed by section 2–901(a)(2), 2–901(b)(2), or 2–901(c)(2) if:

(1) a nonvested property interest or a power of appointment becomes invalid under Section 2–901 (statutory rule against perpetuities);

(2) a class gift is not but might become invalid under Section 2–901 (statutory rule against perpetuities) and the time has arrived when the share of any class member is to take effect in possession or enjoyment; or

(3) a nonvested property interest that is not validated by Section 2–901(a)(1) can vest but not within 90 years after its creation.

SECTION 2–904. EXCLUSIONS FROM STATUTORY RULE AGAINST PERPETUITIES. Section 2–901 (statutory rule against perpetuities) does not apply to:

(1) a nonvested property interest or a power of appointment arising out of a nondonative transfer, except a nonvested property interest or a power of appointment arising out of (I) a premarital or postmarital agreement, (ii) a separation or divorce settlement, (iii) a spouse's election, (iv) a similar arrangement arising out of a prospective, existing, or previous marital relationship between the parties, (v) a contract to make or not to revoke a will or trust, (vi) a contract to exercise or not to exercise a power of appointment, (vii) a transfer in satisfaction of a duty of support, or (viii) a reciprocal transfer;

(2) a fiduciary's power relating to the administration or management of assets, including the power of a fiduciary to sell, lease, or

mortgage property, and the power of a fiduciary to determine principal and income;

(3) a power to appoint a fiduciary;

(4) a discretionary power of a trustee to distribute principal before termination of a trust to a beneficiary having an indefeasibly vested interest in the income and principal;

(5) a nonvested property interest held by a charity, government, or governmental agency or subdivision, if the nonvested property interest is preceded by an interest held by another charity, government, or governmental agency or subdivision;

(6) a nonvested property interest in or a power of appointment with respect to a trust or other property arrangement forming part of a pension, profit-sharing, stock bonus, health, disability, death benefit, income deferral, or other current or deferred benefit plan for one or more employees, independent contractors, or their beneficiaries or spouses, to which contributions are made for the purpose of distributing to or for the benefit of the participants or their beneficiaries or spouses the property, income, or principal in the trust or other property arrangement, except a nonvested property interest or a power of appointment that is created by an election of a participant or a beneficiary or spouse; or

(7) a property interest, power of appointment, or arrangement that was not subject to the common-law rule against perpetuities or is excluded by another statute of this State.

SECTION 2–905. PROSPECTIVE APPLICATION.

(a) Except as extended by subsection (b), Subpart 1 of this part applies to a nonvested property interest or a power of appointment that is created on or after the effective date of Subpart 1 of this Part. For purposes of this section, a nonvested property interest or a power of appointment created by the exercise of a power of appointment is created when the power is irrevocably exercised or when a revocable exercise becomes irrevocable.

(b) If a nonvested property interest or a power of appointment was created before the effective date of Subpart 1 of this Part and is determined in a judicial proceeding, commenced on or after the effective date of Subpart 1 of this Part, to violate this state's rule against perpetuities as that rule existed before the effective date of Subpart 1 of this Part, a court upon the petition of an interested person may reform the disposition in the manner that most closely approximates the transferor's manifested plan of distribution and is within the limits of the rule against perpetuities applicable when the nonvested property interest or power of appointment was created.

What is the rationale for USRAP? Its drafters apparently believed that the wait-and-see doctrine was too complicated. As a result, they chose a fixed period—90 years—during which courts (and beneficiaries) would wait to see whether future interests would vest. Why 90 years? Consider the following excerpt from the "General Comment" to the Statutory Rule Against Perpetuities:

> The philosophy behind the 90–year period is to fix a period of time that approximates the average period of time that would traditionally be allowed by the wait-and-see doctrine. The flat-period-of-years method was not used as a means of increasing permissible dead-hand control by lengthening the permissible vesting period beyond its traditional boundaries. In fact, the 90–year period falls substantially short of the absolute maximum period of time that could theoretically be achieved under the common-law Rule itself, by the so-called "twelve-healthy-babies ploy"—a ploy that would average out to a period of about 115 years. . . .
>
> The framers of the Uniform Statutory Rule derived the 90–year period as follows. The first point recognized was that if actual measuring lives were to have been used, the length of the permissible vesting period would, in the normal course of events, be governed by the life of the youngest measuring life. The second point recognized was that no matter what method is used to identify measuring lives, the youngest measuring life, in standard trusts, is likely to be the transferor's youngest descendant living when the trust was created. The 90–year period was premised on these propositions. Using four hypothetical families deemed to be representative of actual families, the framers of the Uniform Statutory Rule determined that, on average, the transferor's youngest descendant in being at the transferor's death—assuming the transferor's death to occur between ages 60 and 90, which is when 73 percent of the population die—is about 6 years old. . . . The remaining life expectancy of a 6–year–old is about 69 years. The 69 years, plus the 21–year tack-on period, gives a permissible vesting period of 90 years.

Is this rationale persuasive? Is it appropriate to use the twelve-healthy-babies ploy (a practice that violates the spirit but not the letter of the common law Rule) as the basis for formulating a new statutory rule? Would it be better to treat the twelve-healthy-babies ploy as an abuse that should itself serve as the focus for reform? Or is the insight behind USRAP that limitations on the duration of owner control are themselves outmoded? If that is the case, shouldn't states abolish the Rule altogether?

At its peak, USRAP was enacted into law in about half of the 50 states. See, e.g., J. Rodney Johnson, Wills, Trusts and Estates, 34 U. Richmond L. Rev. 1069 (2000); Ronald C. Link & Kimberly A. Licata, Perpetuities Reform in North Carolina: The Uniform Statutory Rule Against Perpetuities, Nondonative Transfers, and Honorary Trusts, 74 N.C. L. Rev. 1783 (1996); Amy Morris Hess, Freeing Property Owners from the RAP Trap: Tennessee Adopts the Uniform Statutory Rule Against Perpetuities, 62 Tenn. L. Rev. 267 (1995); Lawrence W. Waggoner, The Uniform Statutory

Rule Against Perpetuities: Oregon Joins Up, 26 Willamette L. Rev. 259 (1990).

The Mechanics of USRAP

The basics of USRAP are simple: if an interest is valid under the common law Rule, it is also valid under USRAP; if the interest is not valid under the common law Rule, we wait for up to 90 years to see whether the interest does, in fact, vest within that 90 year period. As a result, no trust created today in a USRAP jurisdiction will be held invalid for the next 90 years. Professor Dukeminier has argued that holding the Rule "in abeyance" for 90 years will effectively mark the end of the Rule, because lawyers will, over that period, lose knowledge and understanding of the Rule. See Jesse Dukeminier, The Uniform Statutory Rule Against Perpetuities: Ninety Years in Limbo, 34 UCLA L. Rev. 1023, 1025–27 (1987). Is he right? See David M. Becker, If You Think You No Longer Need to Know Anything about the Rule Against Perpetuities, Then Read This!, 74 Wash. U. L.Q. 713 (1996).

What happens if an interest proves invalid under USRAP? The statute provides for reformation "in the manner that most closely approximates the transferor's manifested plan of distribution and is within the 90 years allowed" by the statute. UPC § 2–903.

No lawyer, however, should want to create an interest whose validity might not be determined for 90 years. Lawyers will generally want to draft instruments whose validity is clear at the time the instrument becomes effective. Under USRAP, for how long can a lawyer postpone vesting of a future interest while still assuring—at the time of creation—that the interest will be valid? Section 2–901(e) gives a complicated answer to that question. Consider the following examples:

> ***Example 25:*** *Settlor's will creates a trust, and provides that the trust shall last for 90 years, and that 90 years after creation, trust principal should be distributed to settlor's then living issue, per stirpes. Is the trust valid under USRAP, and if so, when should the principal be distributed?*
>
> ***Solution:*** *The trust is valid at creation because we know—at creation—that the future interest in trust principal will vest within the statute's 90–year period. The principal will be distributed 90 years after creation. (UPC § 2–901(a)(2)).*
>
> ***Example 26:*** *Settlor's will creates a trust, and provides that the trust shall last until the later of (1) 21 years after the death of settlor's last surviving child; or (2) 90 years; at which time principal should be distributed to settlor's then living issue, per stirpes. Is the trust valid, and if so, when should the principal be distributed?*
>
> ***Solution:*** *The trust is valid at creation because we know—at creation—that both events will occur within the statute's period. But, under section 2–901(e), the trust will terminate, and the*

principal will be distributed, 21 years after the death of testator's last surviving child, ***not*** *at the end of 90 years.*

Does the statutory solution to Examples 25 and 26, taken together, seem compelling? If you think not, consider Example 27:

Example 27: *Settlor's will creates a trust, and provides that the trust shall last until the later of (1) the death of settlor's last surviving child; or (2) 90 years; at which time principal should be distributed to settlor's then living issue, per stirpes. Is the trust valid, and if so, when should the principal be distributed?*

Solution: *The trust is valid, and distribution will be made at the later of the death of settlor's last surviving child or 90 years. Section 2–901(e) does not apply because the trust instrument does not include "a period of time not exceeding 21 years after the death" of a specified life in being. (Consider what would happen if the trust provided that it would terminate upon the later of (1) one week after the death of settlor's last surviving child; or (2) 90 years).*

Even the best of statutes often have glitches. These anomalies in USRAP arose for complicated tax reasons beyond the scope of this course. For further discussion, see Jesse Dukeminier, The Uniform Statutory Rule Against Perpetuities and the GST Tax: New Perils for Practitioners and New Opportunities, 30 Real Prop., Prob. & Tr. J. 185, 189–91 (1995).

PROBLEMS

1. In 2012, settlor creates an *inter vivos* trust, providing that income should be distributed among my issue, per stirpes, "until one year after the death of my last surviving child, or until 50 years have passed, whichever occurs later," and then provides for distribution of principal to "my then-living issue, per stirpes." Testator's last surviving child dies in 2025. Under USRAP, when should principal be distributed?

2. Suppose the same trust was created in settlor's will, and that settlor had died in 2012. When should principal be distributed?

USRAP and Powers of Appointment

It is not quite true that 90 years will pass before USRAP invalidates a trust. If the donee of a power of appointment exercises that power by creating another trust, USRAP might well invalidate that trust before 90 years elapse. By its terms, USRAP applies to all interests created by the exercise of a power of appointment after the statute's effective date. UPC § 2–905(a). Thus, if a trust created a power of appointment in 1950, and the donee exercised the power in a USRAP state in 1996, the exercise of the power is subject to USRAP.

How does USRAP affect powers of appointment? Section 2–902 provides that the time of creation of a power of appointment shall be determined under "general principles of property law." That means that for all special powers, the relation-back doctrine generally applies, and the Rule's period runs from the time of creation of the power. For general testamentary powers, most—but not all—states also apply the relation-back doctrine, and USRAP was presumably not designed to change state law in any state (despite general language in the comment indicating that the relation-back doctrine applies to general testamentary powers).

What this means is that when a donee exercises a special (and, in most states, a general testamentary) power by creating a further trust, future interests created by the trust instrument are valid if either (a) the trust is valid under the common-law rule against perpetuities or (b) all future interests actually vest within 90 years *measured from the time the power was created.*

Example 28: *In 1950, T, by will, creates a trust to endure until the death of T's last surviving child, and gives that child a power to appoint among T's issue. In 1950, T had no living grandchildren. In 1998, A, T's last surviving child exercises the power by creating an additional trust "income to my children until the death of my last surviving child, remainder to my then-living issue." The remainder in issue would be invalid under the common law Rule. Hence, the remainder in issue will only be valid if the last of A's children dies before 2040—90 years after T's creation of the interest.*

Example 28 illustrates that a thorough knowledge of the common law Rule is important—even in USRAP jurisdictions—when one's client holds a power of appointment. In that situation, USRAP may not give the client much margin of safety if the trust instrument creates an interest invalid under the common law Rule.

PROBLEM

Testator, in her 1958 will, created a trust, and provided that income should be distributed to her niece, Nancy, until Nancy's death, and that principal should then be distributed among Nancy's issue as Nancy should appoint by will. Nancy died in 2011 in a USRAP jurisdiction. Will Nancy's appointment be valid if Nancy's will provides:

a. "income to my children until the death of all but one of my children, remainder should then be distributed to the survivor."

b. "income to my children until the death of the last survivor, remainder should then be distributed to my descendants, per stirpes."

Assume that Nancy had three children: Amy, born in 1953, Ben, born in 1955, and Christine, born in 1970. Assume further that Ben will die in 2045, Amy in 2055, and Christine in 2065.

D. ABOLITION OF THE RULE

Not content with the expanded planning opportunities afforded by USRAP, a growing number of state legislatures have gone a step further and made it possible for a settlor to create a perpetual trust. Indeed, some of these states had previously enacted USRAP, and have now repealed it. See, e.g., Ariz. Rev. Stat. § 14–2901; N.J. Stat. § 46:2F–9. Some scholars have supported abolition. See, e.g. G. Graham Waite, Let's Abolish the Rule Against Perpetuities, 21 Real Estate Law Journal 93 (1992).

In a number of these states, however, repeal of the Rule Against Perpetuities has been accompanied by enactment of a statutory rule against unreasonable restraints on alienation. See Frederick R. Schneider, A Rule Against Perpetuities for the Twenty–First Century, 41 Real Prop.,Prob & Tr. J. 1, 49 (2007). Professor Schneider suggests that in these jurisdictions, abolition of the Rule has largely been a matter of form rather than substance:

> [I]n Alaska, Idaho, New Jersey, South Dakota, and Wisconsin, the statutory rules against restraint on alienation of property will function as a surrogate for the Rule. In these states, interests in property that cannot be alienated for longer than the time allowed by the statutes will be void.... The statutory rules maintain the alienability of the property within the same time period allowed by the common law Rule. Because the statutory rules fulfill the general purpose of the Rule, these five states might as well have retained the Rule.

Id. at 52.

The movement to abolish the Rule has largely been tax driven. In the words of Professors Turnier and Harrison:

> [I]n the absence of the RAP, a trust to which assets were transferred with use of the [generations skipping transfer tax] exemption would provide perpetual relief from the estate tax. Focusing on this, and sensing the opportunity to enable local financial institutions and attorneys to harvest a bounty of fees and commissions, a number of states have repealed the RAP. Potential clients are promised that, within a period of years, assets transferred to trusts managed by local financial institutions will blossom into fortunes for the descendents of the transferors that will escape estate taxation forever.

William J. Turnier & Jeffrey L. Harrison, A Malthusian Analysis of the So–Called Dynasty Trust, 28 Va. Tax Rev. 779, 782 (2009); see also Ira Mark Bloom, The GST Tax Tail is Killing The Rule Against Perpetuities, Tax Notes, April 24, 2000, pp. 569–76; Joel C. Dobris, Changes in the Role and the Form of the Trust at the New Millennium, or, We Don't Have to Think of England Anymore, 62 Albany L. Rev. 543, 572, n.135 (1998). But see Joshua C. Tate, Perpetual Trusts and the Settlor's Intent, 53 Kan. L. Rev. 595 (2005) [arguing that concerns about control of property supplement concerns about tax avoidance in motivating trust settlors to create perpetual trusts].

In recent years, a number of states have modified their trust laws to make themselves attractive havens for trust creation. These states saw that if they could advertise the potential for creating perpetual trusts—with the attendant tax savings—they might attract trust dollars from residents of other states. Ira Mark Bloom, The GST Tax Tail is Killing The Rule

Against Perpetuities, Tax Notes, April 24, 2000, pp. 569–76, at 571–73. Although the statutes vary in form, Professor Lynn Foster concludes that "if one asks how many states allow dynasty or perpetual trusts, by whatever means, the answer is twenty-three states and the District of Columbia." Lynn Foster, Fifty–One Flowers: Post–Perpetuities War Law and Arkansas's Adoption of USRAP, 29 U. Ark. Little Rock L. Rev. 411, 430 (2007). Professors Sitkoff and Schanzenbach have studied the movement of trust dollars into states that have abolished the Rule, and have concluded that by 2003, more than $100 billion in trust assets had moved from states that retained the Rule Against Perpetuities to those that had abolished the Rule. Robert H. Sitkoff and Max M. Schanzenbach, Jurisdictional Competition for Trust Funds: An Empirical Analysis of Perpetuities and Taxes, 115 Yale L.J. 356, 404 (2005). Further study of the data reveals that the primary motivation for movement of these assets has been tax avoidance—not the desire to maintain dynastic control of wealth. Max M. Schanzenbach and Robert H. Sitkoff, Perpetuities or Taxes? Explaining the Rise of the Perpetual Trust, 27 Cardozo L. Rev. 2465 (2006). See also Mary Louise Fellows, Why the Generation–Skipping Transfer Tax Sparked Perpetual Trusts, 27 Cardozo L. Rev. 2511 (2006).

Legislation in these states has taken various forms. In some states, the Rule has been abolished only with respect to interests held in trust. Some states have retained rules restricting suspension of the power of alienation; hence, to create a perpetual trust, the settlor must take care to give the trustee, or some other person, the power to sell trust property.

The Sitkoff and Schanzenbach study demonstrates that these states stand to lose billions of trust dollars if settlors believe that they can derive significant tax benefits by creating out-of-state trusts. Because it is so easy for a settlor to create a trust in another state, abolition of the Rule in some states has created significant pressure for abolition in other states—particularly those with highly regarded banking and financial services industries. See Stewart E. Sterk, Jurisdictional Competition to Abolish the Rule Against Perpetuities: R.I.P for the R.A.P., 24 Cardozo L. Rev. 2097, 2104 (2003):

> From the settlor's perspective, using a Delaware or Alaska institution as trustee represents an insignificant constraint. Capital is extraordinarily mobile, so whether the trust property constitutes securities or cash, it will make little difference to the settlor whether legal title is held by a Delaware bank or a New York bank. If the law is more favorable in Delaware, an informed settlor would prefer to transfer assets to Delaware. . . .
>
> Faced . . . with the prospect that Delaware and Alaska would attract trust dollars from local banks and trust companies, other states quickly began to respond by abolishing or significantly curtailing their own Rule Against Perpetuities. Because capital is so mobile, other states had little to gain by clinging to existing law; money would simply flow outward, so that the Rule would apply to less and less property.

See also Jesse Dukeminier & James E. Krier, The Rise of the Perpetual Trust, 50 UCLA L. Rev. 1303 (2003); Joel C. Dobris, The Death of the Rule Against Perpetuities, or the RAP Has No Friends, 35 Real Prop, Prob. & Tr. J. 601 (2000); Angela M. Vallario, Death by a Thousand Cuts: The Rule Against Perpetuities, 25 J. Legis. 141, 162 (1999).

Before leaving the Rule Against Perpetuities, it is worth considering whether abolition of the Rule would be a good thing or a bad one. Consider the following:

Susan F. French, Perpetuities: Three Essays in Honor of My Father, 65 Wash. L. Rev. 323, 352 (1990).

The arguments over the costs and benefits of dead hand control are no easier to assess in trying to determine whether long-term trusts are good or bad for families. The primary effect of the Rule Against Perpetuities is to limit the extent to which the dead hand can control future ownership of property. The Rule requires that ultimate ownership be knowable within 21 years after lives in being. The harm controlled is that of uncertainty. Whether uncertainty is really bad for families is another hard question to answer.

Certainty of ownership is good both for the person who ends up owning the property and for the person who loses it, because it permits both to plan their lives accordingly. On the other hand, certainty of receiving gift property may reduce the incentive to productive labor for the recipient. Certainty of loss may produce a sense of unfairness, and demoralization or worse in the loser, which may lead to unproductivity or even unsocial conduct. Having property tied up in a trust providing a steady stream of economic benefits to a family may provide a solid base from which family members can pursue productive lives without the insecurity and compromises on education and culture that lack of money may bring. Alternatively, it may induce them to arrogance and sloth. If more members of our society had a secure financial base, we might have a healthier, better educated and more creative society. We might end up, however, with a more complacent, boring, and less productive society. Who knows?

CHAPTER ELEVEN

PLANNING FOR INCAPACITY

SECTION I. INTRODUCTION

Because incapacity can come at any age, it presents unique estate planning challenges. Most young and middle-aged adults do not imagine losing capacity until extreme old age, and they often fail to consider how they might mitigate the impact of a loss of capacity. Incapacity raises several concerns, including: the need for disability and/or long-term care insurance, the possible need for someone to manage one's property and financial affairs, the possible need for someone to manage one's health, the need for extra money for health care and domestic services and the need to plan for an orderly and rational death.

Estate planning clients have come to expect lawyers to provide services aimed at solving these problems. Lawyers should be prepared: (1) to provide documents and planning to empower someone chosen by the client to manage the client's *financial* affairs; and (2) to provide documents that communicate the client's wishes regarding *medical* care and death, and that empower an agent or surrogate chosen by the client to manage the client's health care and make the client's health care decisions. Failure to plan adequately will often toss unlucky clients and their families into inefficient, expensive and often destructive default regimes.

SECTION II. MANAGING THE CLIENT'S ASSETS

A. THE DEFAULT REGIME: CONSERVATORSHIP

Suppose Alice discovers that her grandfather hasn't paid his bills in three months, has a stack of uncashed dividend checks, has no joint accounts with anyone, has no power of attorney or revocable trust, and is unwilling to sign a bunch of postdated checks. There is no foolish relative willing to forge Grandpa's signature, nor is there a friendly banker willing to bend the rules. There's often only one solution: a court appointed conservator (also referred to as a "committee" or "guardian") of Grandpa's *property*.

If Alice brings a conservatorship proceeding, she will have to serve Grandpa with the necessary papers. If Grandpa objects, the proceeding may well become an adversarial one. In many states, Alice will have to serve Grandpa's other close relatives, who might object to the guardianship. Because adversarial conservatorship proceedings are expensive, painful and often humiliating to those who may no longer be competent, conservatorship should be viewed as a course of last resort.

Even if Grandpa is in no condition to object and no close relatives object, conservatorship proceedings can be expensive, time consuming and embarrassing. Consider the following excerpt from the UPC conservatorship statute:

UNIFORM PROBATE CODE

SECTION 5–401. PROTECTIVE PROCEEDING.

Upon petition and after notice and hearing, the court may appoint a limited or unlimited conservator or make any other protective order provided in this part in relation to the estate and affairs of:

(1) a minor, if the court determines that the minor owns money or property requiring management or protection that cannot otherwise be provided or has or may have business affairs that may be put at risk or prevented because of the minor's age, or that money is needed for support and education and that protection is necessary or desirable to obtain or provide money; or

(2) any individual, including a minor, if the court determines that, for reasons other than age:

(A) by clear and convincing evidence, the individual is unable to manage property and business affairs because of an impairment in the ability to receive and evaluate information or make decisions, even with the use of appropriate technological assistance, or because the individual is missing, detained, or unable to return to the United States; and

(B) by a preponderance of evidence, the individual has property that will be wasted or dissipated unless management is provided or money is needed for the support, care, education, health, and welfare of the individual or of individuals who are entitled to the individual's support and that protection is necessary or desirable to obtain or provide money.

SECTION 5–408. ORIGINAL PETITION: PROCEDURE AT HEARING.

(a) Unless excused by the court for good cause, a proposed conservator shall attend the hearing. The respondent shall attend and participate in the hearing, unless excused by the court for good cause. The respondent may present evidence and subpoena witnesses and documents, examine witnesses, including any court-appointed physician, psychologist, or other individual qualified to evaluate the alleged impairment ... and otherwise participate in the hearing. The hearing may be held in a location convenient to the respondent and may be closed upon request of the respondent and a showing of good cause.

(b) Any person may request permission to participate in the proceeding. The court may grant the request, with or without hearing, upon determining that the best interest of the respondent will be served. The court may attach appropriate conditions to the participation.

NOTES AND QUESTIONS

1. Suppose the court determines that Grandpa does not understand the nature of the conservatorship proceeding.

a. Should the court recommend appointment of legal counsel for Grandpa?

b. Does the United States Constitution require the court to appoint legal counsel for Grandpa? Does that depend on the powers enjoyed by the conservator? See Matter of Grinker, 77 N.Y.2d 703, 570 N.Y.S.2d 448, 573 N.E.2d 536 (1991); cf. Conservatorship of John L., 48 Cal.4th 131, 105 Cal.Rptr.3d 424, 225 P.3d 554 (2010) [finding no violation of due process when court determined that proposed conservatee had waived right to be present at trial based on court-appointed attorney's statement to that effect].

c. If a lawyer were appointed to represent Grandpa, would the lawyer's appointment increase granddaughter's legal costs?

d. Who has the burden to prove incapacity? What type of evidence might that party present? What type of evidence might Grandpa offer to refute the allegation of incapacity?

2. Suppose that Grandpa truly believes that he is competent to manage his affairs, and he retains a lawyer who is willing to represent him.

a. If the court eventually determines that Grandpa lacks capacity, Grandpa will have spent a great deal of money for no purpose. Is a lawyer under an ethical obligation to decline to represent someone who appears obviously incapacitated?

b. Who is responsible for paying Alice's lawyer? Some courts have held that attorney fees incurred in the good-faith initiation of a conservatorship proceeding constitute necessary expenses for the support or benefit of the protected person, and reasonable attorney fees incurred may be assessed against the protected person's estate. See In re Guardianship of Donley, 262 Neb. 282, 631 N.W.2d 839, 843–46 (2001).

3. Who should be appointed conservator? Consider the following statute:

SECTION 5–413. WHO MAY BE CONSERVATOR: PRIORITIES.

(a) Except as otherwise provided in subsection (d), the court, in appointing a conservator, shall consider persons otherwise qualified in the following order of priority:

(1) a conservator, guardian of the estate, or other like fiduciary appointed or recognized by an appropriate court of any other jurisdiction in which the protected person resides;

(2) a person nominated as conservator by the respondent, including the respondent's most recent nomination made in a durable power

of attorney, if the respondent has attained 14 years of age and at the time of the nomination had sufficient capacity to express a preference;

(3) an agent appointed by the respondent to manage the respondent's property under a durable power of attorney;

(4) the spouse of the respondent;

(5) an adult child of the respondent;

(6) a parent of the respondent; and

(7) an adult with whom the respondent has resided for more than six months before the filing of the petition.

(b) A person having priority under subsection (a)(1), (4), (5), or (6) may designate in writing a substitute to serve instead and thereby transfer the priority to the substitute.

(c) With respect to persons having equal priority, the court shall select the one it considers best qualified. The court, acting in the best interest of the protected person, may decline to appoint a person having priority and appoint a person having a lower priority or no priority.

(d) An owner, operator, or employee of [a long-term care institution] at which the respondent is receiving care may not be appointed as conservator unless related to the respondent by blood, marriage, or adoption.

Notwithstanding statutes like 5–413, it is not uncommon for courts to appoint financial institutions, strangers, or worse, friends of the judge, as conservators.

4. If a conservator is appointed to manage Grandpa's affairs, what powers does she have? She unquestionably has power to meet Grandpa's basic financial needs—paying his bills, preserving his assets, and so on. But what other actions may the conservator take? May the conservator engage in estate planning on Grandpa's behalf? For example, should the conservator have the power to minimize Grandpa's estate taxes by making $13,000 annual gifts to Grandpa's children and grandchildren? Should it matter if the conservator is one of the donees? See, e.g., In re Daly, 142 Misc.2d 85, 536 N.Y.S.2d 393 (Surr. Ct. 1988). Should the fact that Grandpa is unable to form a judgment deprive the family of access to effective tax planning? Consider the following statute:

SECTION 5–411. REQUIRED COURT APPROVAL.

(a) After notice to interested persons and upon express authorization of the court, a conservator may:

(1) make gifts, except as otherwise provided in Section 5–427(b);

(2) convey, release, or disclaim contingent and expectant interests in property, including marital property rights and any right of survivorship incident to joint tenancy or tenancy by the entireties;

(3) exercise or release a power of appointment;

(4) create a revocable or irrevocable trust of property of the estate, whether or not the trust extends beyond the duration of

the conservatorship, or revoke or amend a trust revocable by the protected person;

(5) exercise rights to elect options and change beneficiaries under insurance policies and annuities or surrender the policies and annuities for their cash value;

(6) exercise any right to an elective share in the estate of the protected person's deceased spouse and to renounce or disclaim any interest by testate or intestate succession or by transfer inter vivos; and

(7) make, amend, or revoke the protected person's will.

Section 5–411 also sets forth factors that courts should consider in determining whether to grant the applicant's request. See 5–411(c). For reading see Elizabeth G. Clark, Substituted Judgment: Medical and Financial Decisions by Guardians, 24 Est. Plan. 66 (1997); see also In re Guardianship and Conservatorship of Garcia, 262 Neb. 205, 631 N.W.2d 464 (2001) (reversing lower court determination that allowed conservator to amend, modify or revoke principal's trust agreement, because he could not show that modification or revocation was in the principal's best interest).

5. One might assume that a trusted guardian would be unlikely to take unfair advantage of his or her position. Unfortunately, those assumptions would be naïve, as the following excerpt from a recently conducted Congressional study indicates:

Guardianship: Cases of Financial Exploitation, Neglect, and Abuse of Seniors

GAO REPORTS
Congressional Quarterly (2010)

According to the U.S. Census Bureau, by the year 2025, the number of Americans aged 65 and older will increase by 60 percent. As citizens age, they may become physically or mentally incapable of making or communicating important decisions for themselves, such as those required to handle finances or secure their possessions. Compared to the general population, adults over the age of 65 are more likely to live alone than those of younger ages. Given these statistics, it is important to ensure that systems designed to protect seniors from abuse and neglect function properly.

Courts may appoint a family member, a professional guardian, a nonprofit social service agency, or a local or state agency, to care for an incapacitated person. While many guardians serve the best interests of the incapacitated people they are appointed to protect, others have taken advantage of these vulnerable individuals, . . .

Although we could not determine whether allegations of physical abuse, neglect, and financial exploitation by guardians were widespread, we reviewed hundreds of allegations of abuse occurring nationwide between 1990 and 2010. . . .

Although we continue to receive new allegations from family members and advocacy groups, we could not locate a single Web site, federal agency, state or local entity, or any other organization that compiles comprehensive information on this issue. We attempted to identify entities compiling this information by contacting state courts, federal agencies, advocacy groups, and a professional guardian association. We also searched the Internet. Our research did not identify any public, private, or non-governmental organization that systematically tracks the total number of guardianships or allegations of abuse, neglect, and exploitation by guardians. GAO previously found that many of the courts we surveyed did not track the number of guardianships that they were responsible for monitoring....

We also discovered that information about complaints or disciplinary action taken against guardians may not be publicly available. In addition, we found that state and local enforcement may consist of measures not specific to guardians, such as discipline by a bar association for lawyers or by a regulatory board for Certified Public Accountants. Thus, the exact number of allegations about abuse, neglect or exploitation by guardians remains unknown.

* * *

Examples of potential abuse, neglect, and exploitation appear below:

* Public guardians appointed to care for an 88–year–old California woman with dementia allegedly sold the woman's properties below market value to buyers that included both a relative of the guardian and a city employee. One of the public guardians also moved the ward into various nursing homes without notifying family members, who had to call the police to help them find their relative. The woman developed bed sores during this time that became so serious her leg had to be amputated at the hip.

* In Nevada, a former case manager in the public guardian's office who started her own guardianship business is accused of using her position to take at least $200,000 from her wards' accounts, in part, to support her gambling habit.

* A New York lawyer serving as a court appointed guardian reportedly stole more than $4 million from 23 wards, including seniors suffering from mental and physical impairments as well as children suffering from cerebral palsy due to medical malpractice. Some of the stolen funds were part of a court award intended to pay for the children's medical and developmental needs.

* In Arizona, court-appointed guardians allegedly siphoned off millions of dollars from their wards, including $1 million from a 77–year–old woman whose properties and personal belongings, such as her wedding album, were auctioned at a fraction of their cost.

* A Texas couple, ages 67 and 70, were declared mentally incompetent and placed in a nursing home after the husband broke his hip. Under the care of court—appointed guardians, their house went into foreclosure, their car was repossessed, their electricity was shut off, and their credit was allowed to deteriorate. The couple was allegedly given a $60 monthly allowance and permitted no personal belongings except a television.

* In 2001, a Texas probate judge was appointed a guardian for a 91–year–old woman who displayed signs of senility. She later changed her will for the first time in 40 years, bequeathing $250,000 to the

probate judge, the court appointed guardian, the judge's personal accountant, and the court-appointed attorney associated with her case.

* A 93–year–old Florida woman died after her grandson became her temporary guardian by claiming she had terminal colon cancer. He then moved her to hospice care, where she died 12 days later from the effects of morphine. The woman's condition was later determined to be ulcerative colitis, and the guardian's claims that she had 6 months to live were false. In addition, the guardian is accused of stealing $250,000 from the woman's estate.

* In Michigan, two former public guardians allegedly embezzled $300,000 from at least 50 clients between 1999 and 2009. One of the reported embezzlers used the wards' funds to buy animal feed and other supplies for her farm.

We examined 20 cases in which guardians stole or otherwise improperly obtained more than $5.4 million in assets from 158 incapacitated victims. In some of these cases, the guardians also physically neglected and abused the people they had been appointed to care for.

6. In addition to vulnerability to corruption, what other costs does the conservatorship system create? Professor Leslie Salzman explains:

> When an individual has a diminished ability to meet personal needs or manage property, a court may authorize a guardian to make crucial decisions on the individual's behalf. The guardian may be authorized to make decisions regarding where and with whom the person will live or spend time, what type of medical treatment he or she will receive, and how (or if) the individual will spend his or her money. By limiting an individual's right to make decisions, guardianship not only divests the individual of the important right to self-determination but also marginalizes that person and removes him or her from a host of interactions involved in decision making. In this way, guardianship segregates a person from many critical aspects of social, economic, and civic life.

She argues that guardianship should, in many cases, be replaced by a "supported decision-making" system in place in several other countries:

> Other nations have implemented supported decision-making models, including the judicially appointed "legal mentor" and the privately created "representation agreement."
>
> Described in its most basic and general terms, a legal mentor acts as the individual's agent, with the individual's consent, pursuant to specified powers similar to those that might be given pursuant to a power of attorney. The legal mentor is usually appointed through a simple local court procedure with the consent of the individual needing assistance. In contrast, under the private representation agreement model of supported decision making, an individual who might not be able to demonstrate that she has "legal capacity" in the traditional sense may enter into an agreement with an individual or support network to provide her with

> assistance making or communicating decisions which will then be legally binding.
>
> * * *
>
> In this way, supported decision making is less isolating than guardianship and provides greater opportunities for a person with a disability to interact with others.

Leslie Salzman, Rethinking Guardianship (Again): Substituted Decision Making As A Violation of the Integration Mandate of Title II of the Americans With Disabilities Act, 81 U. Colo. L. Rev. 157 (2010).

For other interesting reading on the conservatorship/guardianship issues, see Symposium, The Uniform Guardianship and Protective Proceedings Act of 1997—Ten Years of Developments, 37 Stetson L. Rev. 1 (2007), with contributions by Professors Rebecca Morgan, Linda S. Whitton, Lawrence Frolik, Sally Balch Hurme, Naomi Karp and Erica Wood, Pamela Teaster, Erica Wood, Susan Lawrence and Winsor C. Schmidt. See also the Second National Guardianship Conference, 31 Stetson L. Rev. 573 (2002) with articles by Mary F. Radford, Joan L. O'Sullivan, Lawrence A. Frolik, Bruce S. Ross, Edward D. Spurgeon, Mary Jane Ciccarello, Sally Balch Hurme, Erica Wood, Alison Barnes, Winsor C. Schmidt, Jr., and Marshall B. Kapp. For a discussion of the development of the notion of incompetence and its practical consequences, see Margaret K. Krasik, The Lights of Science and Experience: Historical Perspectives on Legal Attitudes Toward the Role of Medical Expertise in Guardianship of the Elderly, 33 Am. J. Legal Hist. 201 (1989). For an argument that the current legal system often favors the family's goals for the elderly relative, rather than the individual's desires, see Alison Barnes, The Liberty and Property of Elders: Guardianship and Will Contests as the Same Claim, 11 Elder L. J. 1 (2003). For an exploration of how factors such as race, gender, and income level affect the likelihood that a guardian will be appointed, see Joseph A. Rosenberg, Poverty, Guardianship, and the Vulnerable Elderly: Human Narrative and Statistical Patterns in a Snapshot of Adult Guardianship Cases in New York City, 16 Geo. J. on Poverty L. & Pol'y 315 (2009).

The best way to comprehend the costs of a conservatorship proceeding is to observe a hearing in a contested proceeding. Since we cannot reproduce that for you, consider the following case:

In re Maher

Supreme Court, Appellate Division, 1994.
207 A.D.2d 133, 621 N.Y.S.2d 617.

■ FRIEDMANN, JUSTICE.

On this appeal—which appears to represent a case of first impression at the appellate level—we are asked to consider the propriety of a determination by the Supreme Court, Kings County (Leone, J.), embodied in a judgment entered October 8, 1993, that the respondent, Francis E. Maher, was not incapacitated as that term is defined in the recently enacted Mental Hygiene Law article 81. Based upon this determination, the court dismissed, with prejudice, the petition for a guardian for the respondent's property which had been brought by Francis E. Maher, Jr., the respondent's son. Since the court properly applied the standards and carried out the legislative intent of Mental Hygiene Law article 81, we now affirm.

THE FACTS OF THIS CASE

On December 11, 1992, the respondent, attorney Francis E. Maher, suffered a stroke which left him with right-sided hemiplegia and aphasia. He was admitted to St. Luke's–Roosevelt Hospital where, on December 12, he underwent surgery, inter alia, to evacuate a hematoma from the frontal portion of his brain. For some time after the operation, the respondent remained partially paralyzed and aphasic, although occasionally he was able to speak a few words and to move a bit on his right side.

By order to show cause dated December 17, 1992, the appellant commenced a proceeding pursuant to Mental Hygiene Law article 77 for the appointment of a conservator. On December 17, 1992, the Honorable Sebastian Leone, Justice of the Supreme Court, appointed Ronald M. LaRocca, Esq., as temporary receiver, and Margaret M. Bomba, Esq., as the guardian ad litem, for the respondent. The guardian ad litem filed a report dated January 4, 1993, wherein she stated that due to the respondent's physical condition "he is presently incapable of managing his own business and financial affairs", and she recommended the appointment of a conservator of his property. The guardian ad litem objected to the appointment of Ronald M. LaRocca as conservator because of a "perceived conflict of interest"—due to the fact that LaRocca also represented a hospital that owed the respondent considerable sums in attorneys' fees for services rendered in past litigation. By order dated January 20, 1993, the Supreme Court permitted LaRocca to withdraw as temporary receiver and appointed the appellant and Elizabeth Maher, the respondent's sister and for many years his office manager, as temporary receivers pending the conservatorship hearing, upon the posting of an undertaking in the sum of $1,000,000 with an authorized surety company. LaRocca subsequently became the attorney for the appellant in the instant proceeding.

On March 31, 1993—the day on which the respondent executed a power of attorney naming the appellant as his "attorney-in-fact"—the temporary receivers advised the court that the respondent's condition had "improved dramatically" and that the appellant wished to discontinue the proceeding. The guardian ad litem joined in the application, and the court granted the request orally, directing the parties to settle an order withdrawing the petition.

However, according to the appellant, on the very night of the withdrawal petition, namely March 31, 1993, the respondent's condition abruptly deteriorated, and he began to behave in an irrational and abusive manner. At about this same time, the respondent also declared his intention to marry Ms. Helen Kelly, an attorney formerly associated with his law firm, whom he had been seeing since shortly after the death of his first wife in March of 1992. It was the guardian ad litem's considered opinion that the respondent's agitation was provoked by his sons' attempts to isolate him from Ms. Kelly and other friends, as well as by their refusal to permit him access to funds of any kind.

On May 7, 1993, the appellant announced his intention to go forward with the conservatorship proceeding, based on his allegation that the respondent had become "confused and irrational". On May 19, 1993, the respondent revoked the previously-issued power of attorney in favor of the appellant, and executed a new power of attorney in favor of Irwin F. Simon, an attorney who had done per diem work for the respondent's law firm for many years. The guardian ad litem submitted her interim report dated May 20, 1993, along with a proposed order to withdraw the petition. The appellant promptly opposed the guardian ad litem's motion to dismiss, and requested a hearing to explore the need for the appointment of a conservator. The guardian ad litem submitted a "Supplemental Report" on June 1, 1993, defending herself against the appellant's charges of bias, and again urging the dismissal of the petition.

On June 1, 1993, the respondent disappeared from the home that he had shared with the appellant and another of his sons. On June 17, 1993, the respondent married Ms. Kelly.

At the outset of the hearing, which was held on June 21, 1993, and July 16, 1993, the proceeding was converted, with the consent of all parties, to one for the appointment of a guardian for property management under Mental Hygiene Law article 81. At the hearing, testimony was taken from the respondent's sister, Betty Maher, two of his sons, George and the appellant, his speech pathologist, Susan Sachs, and Dr. Valerie Lanyi, a rehabilitation specialist who had treated the respondent at the Rusk Institute, and who had seen him in consultation as recently as June 10, 1993. Testifying for the respondent were the respondent himself, and his wife, Mrs. Helen Kelly Maher. At the conclusion of the hearing, the court found that the appellant had not carried his burden of proving by the requisite clear and convincing evidence that (1) the respondent was incapacitated, and (2) a guardian was necessary to manage his property and financial affairs. * * *

THE NEW FRAMEWORK ESTABLISHED BY MENTAL HYGIENE LAW ARTICLE 81

* * * [I]n 1992 the New York State Law Revision Commission proposed the creation of a single statute to replace Mental Hygiene Law articles 77 and 78. The projected legislation envisioned "a new type of guardianship proceeding based on the concept of the least restrictive alternative—one that authorizes the appointment of a guardian whose authority is appropriate to satisfy the needs of an incapacitated person, either personal or financial, while at the same time tailored and limited to only those activities for which a person needs assistance. The standard for appointment under this new procedure focuses on the decisional capacity and functional limitations of the person for whom the appointment is sought, rather than on some underlying mental or physical condition of the person. The proposal encouraged the participation of the allegedly incapaci-

tated person in the proceeding to the greatest extent possible" (Koppell and Munnelly, at 17).

As a threshold matter, the new legislation emphasizes that "it is desirable for and beneficial to persons with incapacities to make available to them the least restrictive form of intervention which assists them in meeting their needs", while at the same time permitting them "to exercise the independence and self-determination of which they are capable". Such intervention was therefore to be "tailored to the individual needs of that person", taking into account "the personal wishes, preferences and desires of the person", and affording the person "the greatest amount of independence and self-determination and participation in all the decisions affecting [his] life" (Mental Hygiene Law § 81.01).

In exercising its discretion to appoint a guardian for an individual's property (the focus of the instant proceeding), a court must make a two-pronged determination: first, that the appointment is necessary to manage the property or financial affairs of that person, and, second, that the individual either agrees to the appointment or that the individual is "incapacitated" as defined in Mental Hygiene Law § 81.02(b) (Mental Hygiene Law § 81.02[a]).

As to the first prong, "the court shall consider the report of the court evaluator [heretofore the Guardian ad litem, although with certain significant differences, as laid out in Mental Hygiene Law § 81.09] * * * and the sufficiency and reliability of available resources [e.g., powers of attorney, trusts, representatives and protective payees] * * * to provide for personal needs or property management without the appointment of a guardian" (see, Mental Hygiene Law §§ 81.02[a][2], 81.03[e]).

As to the second prong, a determination of incapacity must be based upon clear and convincing evidence that the person is likely to suffer harm because he is unable to provide for property management and cannot adequately understand and appreciate the nature and consequences of such inability. The burden of proof is on the petitioner (see, Mental Hygiene Law §§ 81.02[b], 81.12[a]). In reaching its determination, the court must give primary consideration to the functional level and functional limitations of the person, including an assessment of the person's ability to manage the activities of daily living related to property management (e.g., mobility, money management, and banking), his understanding and appreciation of the nature and consequences of any inability to manage these activities, his preferences, wishes, and values regarding management of these affairs, and the nature and extent of the person's property and finances, in the context of his ability to manage them (Mental Hygiene Law §§ 81.02[c], 81.03[h]).

Even if all of the elements of incapacity are present, a guardian should be appointed only as a last resort, and should not be imposed if available resources or other alternatives will adequately protect the person (see Law Revision Commission Comments, McKinney's Cons. Laws of N.Y., Book 34A, Mental Hygiene Law § 81.02, 1994 Pocket Part, at 241–242).

ISSUES RAISED ON THIS APPEAL

* * * Contrary to the appellant's contention, the clear and convincing evidence in the hearing record establishes only that the respondent suffers from certain functional limitations in speaking and writing, but not that he is likely to suffer harm because he is unable to provide for the management of his property, or that he is incapable of adequately understanding and appreciating the nature and consequences of his disabilities. Indeed, by granting a power of attorney to Irwin Simon, and by adding his wife as a signatory on certain of his bank accounts, the respondent evidenced that he appreciated his own handicaps to the extent that he effectuated a plan for assistance in managing his financial affairs without the need for a guardian.

Several witnesses testified to the respondent's ability to understand what he was told and to make his wishes known demonstratively. For example, the respondent's sister testified that she believed that her brother understood her when she provided him with information about the office. The appellant himself conceded that he routinely discussed collection and related business matters with the respondent, and that the respondent had regularly indicated his satisfaction with the appellant's management of his law firm's affairs. Dr. Lanyi, the physician in charge of the respondent's rehabilitation, expressed her doubt that at the time of his discharge from the Rusk Institute in mid-March 1993, the respondent could have managed his checkbook as he had formerly done, but opined that he was nonetheless, even at that time, aware of the magnitude of the sums he was spending. Moreover, according to Dr. Lanyi, when she last saw the respondent on June 10, 1993, her patient appeared to understand everything she said to him or asked of him, noting that on that occasion he had consistently responded to her remarks and inquiries in a prompt, calm manner, with appropriate words or gestures. The respondent's speech therapist, too, documented a steady improvement in her patient's ability to comprehend and respond to the tests she administered. Generally, the consensus among all witnesses was that the respondent had made, and was continuing to make, dramatic progress in his ability to comprehend information and to express himself—as well as in his mobility, which seemed essentially restored to normal—since the initial cerebrovascular episode.

Moreover, the court, which was in the best position to observe the respondent throughout the hearing, remarked that he reacted fittingly to the proceedings—even to the point of making it clear to his attorney and the court when he felt that certain questions or answers were objectionable. The court was further persuaded that the respondent knew the correct responses to the questions put to him on the stand, although he was not able verbally to express them.

This case is therefore distinguishable from those relied upon by the appellant, where the respondent had demonstrably ceased to comprehend his practical affairs, as evidenced, inter alia, by a documented dissipation or impending loss of substantial assets * * * No such loss or imminent threat of loss has been even alleged, let alone proven, in the case at bar. It is further worthy of note that two of these cases, Ginsberg and Flowers, were decided under the now-repealed Mental Hygiene Law article 77, where the legal standard for a determination of incapacity—whether the respondent suffered from a substantial impairment of his ability to care for his property and manage his finances—was expressly found wanting by the Legislature in fashioning Mental Hygiene Law article 81* * *.

The instant case more closely resembles those where the allegedly incapacitated person has effectuated a plan for the management of his affairs which obviated the need for a guardian * * *.

* * * [W]e do not find the size of the property involved, standing alone, to be dispositive. Rather, in the matter before us, there has been no showing that the respondent has lost the ability to appreciate his financial circumstances, or that others have taken control of his affairs without his comprehension or rational supervision. There has further been no demonstration of any waste, real or imminent, of the respondent's assets. There is an absence of proof that the respondent's chosen attorney and his wife (who is also an attorney) are incapable of managing the property at issue in accordance with the respondent's wishes.[1] Under such circumstances, the appellant has failed to demonstrate the need for a guardian under the standards enunciated in Mental Hygiene Law article 81. * * *

ORDERED that the judgment is affirmed insofar as appealed from, with costs.

■ O'Brien, J.P., and Joy and Krausman, JJ., concur.

NOTES AND QUESTIONS

1. As evidence that Maher had capacity, the court points out that Maher executed a power of attorney and added his new wife's name to his bank accounts. Why are these acts evidence of capacity?

2. Although there was no evidence of fraud or undue influence in the *Maher* case, an increasing number of children are contesting marriages between their elderly parents and caregivers. For instance, in Estate of Berk, 71 A.D.3d 883, 897 N.Y.S.2d 475 (2010), two sons challenged a trial court's grant of summary judgment in favor of their father's new wife's elective share claim, arguing that there was a triable issue of fact about whether the wife knowingly took unfair advantage of decedent's incapacity by marrying him to obtain his money. Decedent met his wife when she immigrated from China at the age of 40 and was hired to be his home health attendant. Decedent, a successful businessman, was 91 years old, weak and confused. There was evidence that decedent's wife was abusive. Their marriage occurred in secret, and decedent's wife informed his family

1. It is further worthy of note that there has been no serious allegation, let alone demonstration, that either Ms. Kelly or Mr. Simon—two individuals with whom the respondent had long been acquainted (cf., Matter of Ginsberg [Ginsberg], NYLJ, Jan. 3, 1992, at 27, col 6)—used fraud, duress, or undue influence on the respondent in order to bring about either his marriage or his execution of a second power of attorney.

of the marriage after decedent's death, while riding in a car on the way to the funeral home. Decedent left an estate of $5,000,000 and a will that left his property to his children and grandchildren. The appellate court reversed the grant of summary judgment and allowed decedent's sons to contest the wife's right to elect.

3. What impact might contested guardianship proceedings like the one in *Maher* have on the quality of family relationships? For an interesting article exploring how mediation can be a superior alternative to court proceedings for resolving guardianship issues, see Susan N. Gary, Mediation and the Elderly: Using Mediation to Resolve Probate Disputes Over Guardianship and Inheritance, 32 Wake Forest L. Rev. 397 (1997).

B. PLANNING AROUND THE DEFAULT RULES: POWERS OF ATTORNEY

If a property owner and a relative consult you about dealing with problems of incapacity, how would you advise them to avoid the default regime? One option is to create a revocable *inter vivos* trust—a device we have already studied. Suppose, however, the property owner does not want to convey her assets into a trust with someone else as trustee, but instead wants to be able to deal with the property as if it were her own. She merely wants to assure that her relative will also be able to deal with the property, on her behalf, if the need arises. A second option is a durable power of attorney.

With this option, the property owner (the principal) gives the attorney-in-fact, or agent, or power holder, the power to stand in the property owner's shoes and act for him as to property matters. See Gerry W. Beyer, Estate Plans: The Durable Power of Attorney for Property Management, 59 Tex. B.J. 314 (1996). Note that the attorney-in-fact need not be a lawyer; the property owner can give a power of attorney to her son, or her accountant, or her neighbor. In this day and age, virtually every client who asks for a will should be asked if she wants a durable power. This is surely the case for all clients middle-aged or older.

In 2006, the National Conference of Commissioners on Uniform State Laws adopted the Uniform Power of Attorney Act (UPAA). The Act includes a statutory form power of attorney, reproduced below:

[INSERT NAME OF JURISDICTION]
STATUTORY FORM POWER OF ATTORNEY
IMPORTANT INFORMATION

This power of attorney authorizes another person (your agent) to make decisions concerning your property for you (the principal). Your agent will be able to make decisions and act with respect to your property (including your money) whether or not you are able to act for yourself. The meaning of authority over subjects listed on this form is explained in the Uniform Power of Attorney Act [insert citation].

This power of attorney does not authorize the agent to make health-care decisions for you.

You should select someone you trust to serve as your agent. Unless you specify otherwise, generally the agent's authority will continue until you die or revoke the power of attorney or the agent resigns or is unable to act for you.

Your agent is entitled to reasonable compensation unless you state otherwise in the Special Instructions.

This form provides for designation of one agent. If you wish to name more than one agent you may name a coagent in the Special Instructions. Coagents are not required to act together unless you include that requirement in the Special Instructions.

If your agent is unable or unwilling to act for you, your power of attorney will end unless you have named a successor agent. You may also name a second successor agent.

This power of attorney becomes effective immediately unless you state otherwise in the Special Instructions.

If you have questions about the power of attorney or the authority you are granting to your agent, you should seek legal advice before signing this form.

DESIGNATION OF AGENT

I ______________________________ name the following
(Name of Principal)
person as my agent:

Name of Agent: ______________________________ Agent's

Address: ______________________________

Agent's Telephone Number: ______________________________

DESIGNATION OF SUCCESSOR AGENT(S) (OPTIONAL)

If my agent is unable or unwilling to act for me, I name as my successor agent:

Name of Successor Agent: ______________________________

Successor Agent's Address: ______________________________

Successor Agent's Telephone Number: ______________________________

If my successor agent is unable or unwilling to act for me, I name as my second successor agent:

Name of Second Successor Agent: ______________________________

Second Successor Agent's Address: ______________________________

Second Successor Agent's Telephone Number: ______________________________

GRANT OF GENERAL AUTHORITY

I grant my agent and any successor agent general authority to act for me with respect to the following subjects as defined in the Uniform Power of Attorney Act [insert citation]:

(INITIAL each subject you want to include in the agent's general authority. If you wish to grant general authority over all of the subjects you may initial "All Preceding Subjects" instead of initialing each subject.)

(___) Real Property

(___) Tangible Personal Property

(___) Stocks and Bonds

(___) Commodities and Options

(___) Banks and Other Financial Institutions

(___) Operation of Entity or Business

(___) Insurance and Annuities

(___) Estates, Trusts, and Other Beneficial Interests

(___) Claims and Litigation

(___) Personal and Family Maintenance

(___) Benefits from Governmental Programs or Civil or Military Service

(___) Retirement Plans

(___) Taxes

(___) All Preceding Subjects

GRANT OF SPECIFIC AUTHORITY (OPTIONAL)

My agent MAY NOT do any of the following specific acts for me UNLESS I have INITIALED the specific authority listed below:

(CAUTION: Granting any of the following will give your agent the authority to take actions that could significantly reduce your property or change how your property is distributed at your death. INITIAL ONLY the specific authority you WANT to give your agent.)

(___) Create, amend, revoke, or terminate an inter vivos trust

(___) Make a gift, subject to the limitations of the Uniform Power of Attorney Act [insert citation to Section 217 of the act] and any special instructions in this power of attorney

(___) Create or change rights of survivorship

(___) Create or change a beneficiary designation

(___) Authorize another person to exercise the authority granted under this power of attorney

(___) Waive the principal's right to be a beneficiary of a joint and survivor annuity, including a survivor benefit under a retirement plan

(___) Exercise fiduciary powers that the principal has authority to delegate

[(___) Disclaim or refuse an interest in property, including a power of appointment]

LIMITATION ON AGENT'S AUTHORITY

An agent that is not my ancestor, spouse, or descendant MAY NOT use my property to benefit the agent or a person to whom the agent owes an obligation of support unless I have included that authority in the Special Instructions.

SPECIAL INSTRUCTIONS (OPTIONAL)

You may give special instructions on the following lines:

____

____

____

____

____

____

____

EFFECTIVE DATE

This power of attorney is effective immediately unless I have stated otherwise in the Special Instructions.

NOMINATION OF [CONSERVATOR OR GUARDIAN] (OPTIONAL)

If it becomes necessary for a court to appoint a [conservator or guardian] of my estate or [guardian] of my person, I nominate the following person(s) for appointment:

Name of Nominee for [conservator or guardian] of my estate:

____

Nominee's Address: ______________________________

Nominee's Telephone Number: ______________________

Name of Nominee for [guardian] of my person: ____________

Nominee's Address: ______________________________

Nominee's Telephone Number: ______________________

RELIANCE ON THIS POWER OF ATTORNEY

Any person, including my agent, may rely upon the validity of this power of attorney or a copy of it unless that person knows it has terminated or is invalid.

SIGNATURE AND ACKNOWLEDGMENT

______________________________ ______________

Your Signature Date

____
Your Name Printed
____

____
Your Address

____
Your Telephone Number

State of ______________________
[County] of ____________________

This document was acknowledged before me on ______________________,
(Date)

by______________________________.
(Name of Principal)

______________________________ (Seal, if any)
Signature of Notary
My commission expires: __________

[This document prepared by:
____
____]

IMPORTANT INFORMATION FOR AGENT

Agent's Duties

When you accept the authority granted under this power of attorney, a special legal relationship is created between you and the principal. This relationship imposes upon you legal duties that continue until you resign or the power of attorney is terminated or revoked. You must:

(1) do what you know the principal reasonably expects you to do with the principal's property or, if you do not know the principal's expectations, act in the principal's best interest;

(2) act in good faith;

(3) do nothing beyond the authority granted in this power of attorney; and

(4) disclose your identity as an agent whenever you act for the principal by writing or printing the name of the principal and signing your own name as "agent" in the following manner:

(Principal's Name) by (Your Signature) as Agent

Unless the Special Instructions in this power of attorney state otherwise, you must also:

(1) act loyally for the principal's benefit;

(2) avoid conflicts that would impair your ability to act in the principal's best interest;

(3) act with care, competence, and diligence;

(4) keep a record of all receipts, disbursements, and transactions made on behalf of the principal;

(5) cooperate with any person that has authority to make health-care decisions for the principal to do what you know the principal reasonably expects or, if you do not know the principal's expectations, to act in the principal's best interest; and

(6) attempt to preserve the principal's estate plan if you know the plan and preserving the plan is consistent with the principal's best interest.

Termination of Agent's Authority

You must stop acting on behalf of the principal if you learn of any event that terminates this power of attorney or your authority under this power of attorney. Events that terminate a power of attorney or your authority to act under a power of attorney include:

(1) death of the principal;

(2) the principal's revocation of the power of attorney or your authority;

(3) the occurrence of a termination event stated in the power of attorney;

(4) the purpose of the power of attorney is fully accomplished; or

(5) if you are married to the principal, a legal action is filed with a court to end your marriage, or for your legal separation, unless the Special Instructions in this power of attorney state that such an action will not terminate your authority.

Liability of Agent

The meaning of the authority granted to you is defined in the Uniform Power of Attorney Act [insert citation]. If you violate the Uniform Power of Attorney Act [insert citation] or act outside the authority granted, you may be liable for any damages caused by your violation.

If there is anything about this document or your duties that you do not understand, you should seek legal advice.

NOTES AND QUESTIONS

1. Under the power of attorney, who owns the principal's property, the principal or the agent?

2. Under the law of most states, powers expire upon the principal's incapacity unless the power expressly states otherwise. Because most people want powers to continue after incapacity, it is important to make a power *durable*—valid beyond incapacity. The Uniform Power of Attorney Act reverses that long-standing presumption and directs that a power is durable unless the power expressly provides that it is terminated by the incapacity of the principal. UPAA § 104.

Review the Model Form. Where does it establish that the power is durable?

3. ***Formalities.*** In most states, and under the Model Uniform Power of Attorney Act, a power is validly executed if the principal (or another individual directed by the principal in the principal's conscious presence) signs it. UPAA § 105. Section 105 also provides that notarization of the principal's signature creates a presumption that the signature is valid.

4. What obligations does the agent have under the Statutory Form?

5. ***General Grant of Authority v. Specific Grant.*** Suppose the principal initialed the "All Preceding Subjects" line in the "GRANT OF GENERAL AUTHORITY" section, but initialed no other part of the form. Would the agent have the authority to revoke the principal's revocable living trust? Change the beneficiary designation on the principal's insurance policy? Make a will for the principal? Is it good policy to allow agents to make wills for principals? See Ralph C. Brashier, Policy, Perspective and the Proxy Will, 61 S.C. L. Rev. 63 (2009) (critiquing recently enacted statutes that permit proxy will-making by guardians and examining whether agents acting under powers of attorney should be allowed to make wills on behalf of the principal).

6. Can a principal appoint more than one attorney-in-fact? UPAA section 111 authorizes this, and provides that "[u]nless the power of attorney otherwise provides, each coagent may exercise its authority independently." Would you recommend appointing two agents? What are the pros and cons of this course of action?

7. ***Bank Bureaucracy.*** There is one functional drawback to durable powers—not every financial intermediary will honor them. When a bank or broker refuses, usually one of two excuses is offered: (1) "We only take our own form" or (2) "Your power of attorney is stale—it was signed too long ago." When the agent complains, the bureaucrat (or his boss) either gives in or tells the agent to "sue me." What is your explanation for this conservatism on the part of the financial bureaucrats?

To combat this problem, the UPAA creates a statutory cause of action against banks and other financial service vendors who refuse to accept a power of attorney:

> **SECTION 120. LIABILITY FOR REFUSAL TO ACCEPT ACKNOWLEDGED STATUTORY FORM POWER OF ATTORNEY (Alternative B)**
>
> * * *
>
> (b) Except as otherwise provided in subsection (c):
>
> (1) a person shall either accept an acknowledged statutory form power of attorney or request a certification, a translation, or an opinion of counsel under Section 119(d) no later than seven business days after presentation of the power of attorney for acceptance;
>
> (2) if a person requests a certification, a translation, or an opinion of counsel under Section 119(d), the person shall accept the statutory form power of attorney no later than five business days after receipt of the certification, translation, or opinion of counsel; and

(3) a person may not require an additional or different form of power of attorney for authority granted in the statutory form power of attorney presented.

(c) A person is not required to accept an acknowledged statutory form power of attorney if:

(1) the person is not otherwise required to engage in a transaction with the principal in the same circumstances;

(2) engaging in a transaction with the agent or the principal in the same circumstances would be inconsistent with federal law;

(3) the person has actual knowledge of the termination of the agent's authority or of the power of attorney before exercise of the power;

(4) a request for a certification, a translation, or an opinion of counsel under Section 119(d) is refused;

(5) the person in good faith believes that the power is not valid or that the agent does not have the authority to perform the act requested, whether or not a certification, a translation, or an opinion of counsel under Section 119(d) has been requested or provided; or

(6) the person makes, or has actual knowledge that another person has made, a report to the [local adult protective services office] stating a good faith belief that the principal may be subject to physical or financial abuse, neglect, exploitation, or abandonment by the agent or a person acting for or with the agent.

(d) A person that refuses in violation of this section to accept an acknowledged statutory form power of attorney is subject to:

(1) a court order mandating acceptance of the power of attorney; and

(2) liability for reasonable attorney's fees and costs incurred in any action or proceeding that confirms the validity of the power of attorney or mandates acceptance of the power of attorney.

See also Maenhoudt v. Bank, 34 Kan.App.2d 150, 115 P.3d 157 (2005) (reversing lower court grant of summary judgment in favor of bank that refused to honor a power of attorney, and remanding to determine whether the bank 1) compared the signature on the power with the one the bank had on file, 2) obtained proper identification from the agent, 3) determined whether the transaction was within the scope of the agent's authority, and 4) had reason to know that the principal was the victim of fraud).

8. ***Springing Powers of Attorney.*** For clients who want to do something about incapacity, but who don't want to sign a traditional power of attorney, or fund a trust, the law recognizes a so-called "springing" power of attorney. The client signs today, but the power doesn't come into existence until future events cause the power to "spring" into action. The likely event that will cause the springing is the certification by one or two doctors that the principal is no longer competent to manage his own affairs. A more mechanical trigger is the principal's taking up residence in a nursing home. What advantages and disadvantages might that trigger have

over a mental incompetence standard? Springing powers of attorney (and standard ones, as well) can include a power to create and fund a revocable *inter vivos* trust for the principal. Springing powers should not be seen as panaceas, however. They are subject to staleness concerns as well as physician resistance to certification. They are going to work best when the client and her lawyer are well known to the doctors and the financial intermediaries who must act.

9. *Conservator or Agent?* Suppose Donald executed a power of attorney naming his daughter Brenda as his attorney-in-fact. One year later, Donald suffered a stroke and became incapacitated. A court named Brenda and Suzanne, Donald's wife, co-guardians. Chase Bank, the custodian of Donald's IRA account, was served with the power of attorney and the guardianship letters. In the ensuing three years, Brenda withdrew approximately $1,000,000 from Donald's IRA based on her power of attorney. Suzanne confronted Brenda after discovering the withdrawals, and Brenda committed suicide. Suzanne then sued Chase, arguing that the guardianship order rendered the retirement account within the court's control and effectively terminated the power of attorney. Should Chase be held liable for disbursing the funds to Brenda? See Russell v. Chase Investment Services Corp., 212 P.3d 1178 (Ok. 2009) [holding Chase not liable because the power of attorney was valid, the guardian had the right to revoke it, but had failed to do so].

10. Perhaps the most contentious issue presented by powers of attorney involves the extent to which agents can make gifts. Because agents are often related to the principal, gifts to family members may involve a conflict of interest. In the worst case, the agent may want to make gifts to herself. Does the Model Form allow the agent to make gifts of any kind? Would you recommend that your client authorize the agent to make gifts? If so, to whom and under what circumstances?

Consider the following case:

Estate of Huston

Court of Appeal, 1997.
51 Cal.App.4th 1721, 60 Cal.Rptr.2d 217.

OPINION

■ WARD, ASSOCIATE JUSTICE.

Mary Deonne Greene, the niece of decedent Amelia D. Huston and a residuary beneficiary under decedent's will, appeals from an order confirming the gift of a $90,000 annuity from decedent to her attorney-in-fact and financial representative, John. E. Amberg. * * * We conclude the gift was void as having been outside Amberg's authority under his power of attorney. We therefore reverse.

FACTUAL AND PROCEDURAL BACKGROUND

Decedent died at the age of 90 in January 1993, and on March 15, 1993, the court admitted her will to probate and appointed Amberg as executor thereof.

In May 1994, Amberg, acting in his personal capacity, filed a petition for determination of ownership and for order of conveyance and transfer of assets of estate. The petition sought transfer of a $90,000 annuity to himself. Greene, * * * [and two other] residuary beneficiaries under decedent's will, objected to Amberg's petition. Paul Daily, decedent's brother, and Martha Galloway, decedent's niece, affirmatively consented to the transfer; another niece, Dorothy Nobel, did not respond. Paul Daily, Galloway, and Nobel were also residuary beneficiaries under decedent's will.

A hearing on the petition was held in November 1994. At the hearing, Amberg testified that he and his wife had been neighbors and social friends of decedent and her husband since 1975. Decedent's husband died in 1983; before his death, he asked the Ambergs to look after decedent. In 1984, decedent asked Amberg to take charge of her financial affairs. In 1984 and 1985, decedent signed durable powers of attorney prepared by her attorney, Robert Rose, designating Amberg as her attorney-in-fact. Amberg managed decedent's financial affairs until her death. Amberg was first paid $50 an hour, and later, $60 an hour, for his services to decedent.

Argia Montgomery, decedent's long-time friend, assisted decedent in her final years with errands, supervised her household and nursing staff, and acted as her companion. Decedent nominated Montgomery as her agent in a durable power of attorney for health care. Decedent paid Montgomery $500 per month for her services.

In March 1984, decedent executed a will [Lawyer] Rose prepared for her. Under the will, decedent bequeathed her condominium and its furnishings to Montgomery. The residuary assets of the estate were to be distributed by formula to other beneficiaries. In October 1985, decedent executed a codicil to her will, also prepared by Rose, adding specific bequests in favor of Montgomery and Amberg. In August 1986, decedent executed a second codicil to her will, again prepared by Rose, altering its provisions concerning the disposition of her condominium and its contents in the event Montgomery predeceased her.

Martha Galloway, decedent's niece and a residuary beneficiary under the will, testified she visited decedent in 1987. Decedent disclosed that she was leaving her condominium to Montgomery and stated she was concerned about what she should do to treat Montgomery and Amberg equitably, because Montgomery and Amberg were the ones who took care of her. Decedent told Galloway she wanted Montgomery and Amberg "to share in her assets equally."

In 1988, decedent became bedridden and seldom left her home. She ceased accepting visits from most of her friends and acquaintances, but kept in contact with them by correspondence and telephone. However, she continued to receive regular visits from Montgomery and Amberg.

Amberg testified that in late 1989, Amberg visited decedent to review her finances. He told her she had a $100,000 certificate of deposit maturing soon. Decedent told Amberg she wished to purchase an annuity with the proceeds of the certificate of deposit and give it to him. She stated she was giving her condominium, which she believed was worth $90,000 to $100,000, to Montgomery, and she wished Montgomery and Amberg to share alike in the assets of her estate. Amberg told her she should retain the right to the payments made on the annuity during her lifetime, because she would need the income to pay her expenses, and the annuity should pass to him only upon her death. Decedent agreed with this proposal. Amberg further suggested that if he predeceased her, the annuity should pass as a portion of her estate upon her death. Decedent agreed. Decedent and Amberg agreed that $10,000 from the maturing certificate of deposit should be deposited in decedent's checking account to pay her ongoing expenses, and $90,000 would be invested in the annuity.

Amberg testified he visited the bank where decedent maintained her certificate of deposit; he told the branch manager he wished to purchase a $90,000 annuity; that the monthly payments on the annuity were to be payable to decedent during her lifetime; that upon her death, the annuity should be payable to him; and that if he predeceased her, the annuity should pass to her estate. On his suggestion, the branch manager telephoned decedent and confirmed her wish to purchase the annuity in the form described by Amberg.

Amberg testified the branch manager completed the application form for the purchase of the annuity, designating decedent as the owner of the annuity, Amberg as the annuitant, and decedent's estate as the beneficiary. Amberg signed the application form as prepared by the branch manager. When Amberg received the annuity, he informed decedent of his receipt. The first one or two monthly checks issued under the annuity were made payable to Amberg. He endorsed the checks and deposited them in decedent's bank account. He instructed the company that had issued the annuity to issue future annuity checks to decedent. Thereafter, the checks were issued to decedent or her estate. Amberg deposited all the checks during decedent's lifetime into her checking account. * * *

Decedent was mentally alert until her death in 1993. She knew the persons with whom she was dealing and was able to carry on intelligent conversations and make rational decisions concerning her personal affairs.

Amberg testified that after decedent's death, he learned the provisions of the annuity did not conform to decedent's wishes for its disposition following her death. The annuity provided that Amberg was entitled to distribution of the monthly payments during its term, but the principal value would pass to the residuary beneficiaries of the estate upon the maturity of the annuity. Thus, Amberg filed and served a notice of proposed action on the residuary beneficiaries, seeking their consent to the transfer of any interest of the estate in the annuity to himself.

On January 12, 1995, the trial court entered an order holding that decedent's estate held any interest it might have in the annuity as "[t]rustee of a resulting trust for benefit of [Amberg]." The order was supported by detailed findings of fact. Greene has appealed from that order.

DISCUSSION

I. The Gift was Void Because It was Outside the Scope of Amberg's Authority Under the Power of Attorney

Greene contends the gift was void, because under the express terms of the power of attorney, Amberg was forbidden to make a gift to himself. Amberg's power of attorney provided, "you shall not make gifts to yourself." In addition, Probate Code section 4264 states, "A power of attorney may not be construed to grant authority to an attorney-in-fact to perform any of the following acts unless expressly authorized in the power of attorney:

"(c) Make or revoke a gift of the principal's property in trust or otherwise."

"A power of attorney conferring authority to sell, exchange, transfer or convey real property for the benefit of the principal does not authorize a conveyance as a gift or without a substantial consideration * * * and a conveyance without the scope of the power conferred is void."

Here, the trial court found that Amberg had purchased the annuity pursuant to decedent's express instructions, and that a representative of the bank where the annuity was purchased discussed the terms of the annuity with decedent and confirmed her intention that the annuity would pass to Amberg upon her death, unless he predeceased her. Amberg testified that before purchasing the annuity, he discussed the transaction with decedent, and she agreed to the terms of the transaction. At the bank, he told the bank manager, " 'Why don't you call Mrs. Huston and talk with her and double check it,' I said, 'simply because my name is appearing on this document personally and everything I've done has been under the powers to me under the durable power of attorney.' " The bank manager then telephoned decedent and discussed the annuity with her. The trial court, as sole judge of the credibility of witnesses, accepted Amberg's testimony as true. Moreover, Amberg's testimony was corroborated by that of Martha Galloway, decedent's niece, who testified that in a conversation with decedent, decedent expressed her desire to treat Amberg "equally," "fairly," and "equitably" with Montgomery, because Amberg and Montgomery were the ones who took care of decedent. In addition, Mrs. Amberg testified that after Amberg told her about the transaction, she telephoned decedent and thanked her for her generosity, and decedent replied that she was happy to be able to do something for Amberg, that she had wanted to do for a long time. This substantial evidence in the record supports the trial court's findings that the annuity was purchased with the decedent's knowledge, consent, and approval.

A question therefore arises whether decedent's oral assent to the gift served to ratify the transaction and make the gift valid. We conclude that it did not. "A power of attorney is a written authorization to an agent to perform specified acts on behalf of the principal. [Citation.] The rights and liabilities created by the exercise of such authority are centered in the law of agency. [Citation.]" * * * Ratification of an agent's act "can be made only in the manner that would have been necessary to confer an original authority for the act ratified, ..." (Civ.Code, § 2310.) Because a power of attorney must be in writing, any act performed by the agent acting under the power of attorney must therefore be ratified in writing to be valid.

Even though, from the evidence at trial, it is apparent decedent in fact wished to make a gift to Amberg, nonetheless, she failed to comply with the formalities necessary to do so, such as by modifying Amberg's authority under the power of attorney or by executing another codicil to her will. We therefore conclude the gift was void. * * *

DISPOSITION

The judgment is reversed. Each party shall bear its own costs on appeal.

■ HOLLENHORST, ACTING P.J., and MCKINSTER, J., concur.

NOTES AND QUESTIONS

1. Decedent's power of attorney stated "you shall not make gifts to yourself." Had the power not included this language, would the court have validated Amberg's act?

2. How would this case have been decided if Amelia Huston had executed the Model Statutory Durable Power of Attorney and checked the box allowing the agent to make gifts? Consider the following section of the Uniform Statutory Power of Attorney Act:

> **SECTION 217. GIFTS.**
>
> * * *
>
> (b) Unless the power of attorney otherwise provides, language in a power of attorney granting general authority with respect to gifts authorizes the agent only to:
>
> (1) make outright to, or for the benefit of, a person, a gift of any of the principal's property, including by the exercise of a presently exercisable general power of appointment held by the principal, in an amount per donee not to exceed the annual dollar limits of the federal gift tax exclusion under Internal Revenue Code Section 2503(b), 26 U.S.C. Section 2503(b), [as amended,] without regard to whether the federal gift tax exclusion applies to the gift, or if the principal's spouse agrees to consent to a split gift pursuant to Internal Revenue Code Section 2513, 26 U.S.C. 2513, [as amended,] in an amount per donee not to exceed twice the annual federal gift tax exclusion limit; and
>
> (2) consent, pursuant to Internal Revenue Code Section 2513, 26 U.S.C. Section 2513, [as amended,] to the splitting of a gift made by the principal's spouse in an amount per donee not to exceed the aggregate annual gift tax exclusions for both spouses.
>
> (c) An agent may make a gift of the principal's property only as the agent determines is consistent with the principal's objectives if actually

known by the agent and, if unknown, as the agent determines is consistent with the principal's best interest based on all relevant factors, including:

(1) the value and nature of the principal's property;

(2) the principal's foreseeable obligations and need for maintenance;

(3) minimization of taxes, including income, estate, inheritance, generation-skipping transfer, and gift taxes;

(4) eligibility for a benefit, a program, or assistance under a statute or regulation; and

(5) the principal's personal history of making or joining in making gifts.

Does section 217 provide an answer to the question?

3. ***The Risks of a Durable Power: Misuse of Authority.*** Did the decedent want Amberg to receive the annuity? Was Amberg greedy? Did he abuse his trust? In a footnote the court wrote, "We hasten to add that the record does not reflect any dishonesty or bad faith on the part of Amberg. He simply failed to conform to the rules imposed upon a person acting in the fiduciary capacity in which he was placed." 51 Cal.App.4th at 1727 n.1. But other agents are not so honest. As Professor Dessin explains:

> Recently, however, concerns have been voiced that perhaps we have created an instrument of abuse rather than a useful tool. Sometimes the problems are as clear as wrongful misappropriation of the principal's property by the agent. Often, however, problems arise because the standards governing the behavior of agents under durable powers of attorney have never been clearly defined. In many instances, those standards have not even been considered. Legislatures, courts, and commentators have often simply assumed the application of various bodies of law without careful reflection. In light of the popularity of the financial durable power of attorney, it is surprising that there has been no in-depth consideration of the parameters of the agent's duty. There has been only the occasional sentence written, often merely noting the application of general fiduciary principles.

Carolyn L. Dessin, Acting as Agent Under a Financial Durable Power of Attorney: An Unscripted Role, 75 Neb. L. Rev. 574, 575–76 (1996).

A high profile example of a misuse of a power of attorney involves the famous socialite and philanthropist Brook Astor. Astor owned a famous Childe Hassam painting titled "Flags, Fifth Avenue," which she dearly loved. By her friends' account, she had intended to donate the painting at her death to the Metropolitan Museum of Art. Astor had purchased the painting for $172,000. When her son, Anthony, acting with her power of attorney, sold the painting for $10 million dollars, he reported to the IRS that the painting's original purchase price had been $7 million. That meant that the 100–year–old Astor failed to report millions of dollars in capital gains. The alleged deception was discovered when Astor's grandson, Philip Marshall, brought an action accusing his dad of neglecting Astor and taking her money. After Philip Marshall filed suit, a Manhattan judge removed Anthony as his mother's guardian and replaced him with Astor's longtime friend, Annette de la Renta, and the JPMorgan Chase bank. See "Paint Misbehavin"; Astor Son's Tax Error on Art, The New York Post, Sept. 25, 2006.

4. ***The Lawyer's Role.*** Would it be ethical for you to represent a distant heir of the decedent in an attempt to set aside the gift in Amberg, if you believed that it truly represented the decedent's wishes? In framing your answer consider both sides taking into account the following statement of Professor Collett:

> Because of the dissatisfaction with the partisan model, an alternative model is emerging * * * which has most recently been christened 'socially responsible lawyering.' Under the 'socially responsible' model, the impact on third parties, and even society at large, is an independent consideration in the attorney's decisions during representation.

Teresa Stanton Collett, Response to the Conference: The Ethics of Intergenerational Representation, 62 Fordham L. Rev. 1453, 1463–64 (1994). Professor Collett's response appears in the Proceedings of the Conference on Ethical Issues in Representing Older Clients. The symposium includes the following articles of interest, among others: Jan Ellen Rein, Clients With Destructive and Socially Harmful Choices—What's an Attorney to Do?: Within and Beyond the Competency Construct, 62 Fordham L. Rev. 1101 (1994); Burnele V. Powell & Ronald C. Link, The Sense of a Client: Confidentiality Issues in Representing the Elderly, 62 Fordham L. Rev. 1197 (1994); and Jeffrey N. Pennell, Representations Involving Fiduciary Entities: Who is the Client?, 62 Fordham L. Rev. 1319 (1994).

PROBLEM

Mycroft Holmes is an eccentric of great wealth. His doctors tell him that within a year he may be mentally incapacitated. They also tell him he is likely to live for a long time. He comes to you as a client. You are satisfied that he is currently competent. What incapacity planning would you suggest for him?

SECTION III. HEALTH CARE AND DEATH DECISIONS

The Schiavo Autopsy; The Post–Mortem

By Andrew Metz.
Newsday, June 16, 2005.

When Terri Schiavo died, she was blind, massively brain-damaged, unable to eat or drink, and beyond medical redemption, according to the autopsy performed on the Florida woman who ignited a national end-of-life debate.

The post-mortem, released yesterday, bolstered the claims of Schiavo's husband, who fought in court for seven years to disconnect his incapacitated wife's feeding tube over objections by her parents and conservative supporters who included abortion foes, congressional Republicans and President George W. Bush.

Schiavo's parents, Mary and Bob Schindler, hoped the exam would prove their daughter was responsive and could have recovered. Instead, it showed a 41-year-old woman with a brain so debilitated it was half the normal weight.

"This damage was irreversible, and no amount of therapy or treatment would have regenerated the massive loss of neurons," said Jon Thogmartin, the Pinellas–Pasco, Fla., medical examiner who led the autopsy.

Stephen Nelson, a neuropathologist and consultant on the exam, said the findings were also consistent with the diagnosis that Schiavo was in a persistent vegetative state, a condition the Schindlers refused to accept.

The report, however, did not explain why Schiavo collapsed 15 years ago and raised doubts about the long-standing suspicion it was because of an eating disorder. The theory had helped her husband, Michael, win a $1 million malpractice suit that lighted intense intrafamily enmity.

Thogmartin said the underlying cause of Schiavo's collapse may never be known but there was no evidence she was abused, as the family had alleged. He said Schiavo ultimately died of dehydration, 13 days after her feeding tube was removed.

George Felos, Michael Schiavo's lawyer, said his client was relieved at the results. "Mr. Schiavo has received so much criticism throughout this case that I'm certain there's a part of him that was pleased to hear these results and the hard science behind them," Felos said.

The new medical findings, however, did little to divert the family and their allies from a fight that engrossed the nation and prompted extraordinary intervention by Congress and the president.

"We knew all along that Terri was profoundly brain-damaged. We simply wanted to bring her home and care for her," her brother, Bobby Schindler, told The Associated Press yesterday.

David Gibbs, the parents' attorney, yesterday still insisted Schiavo "demonstrated a will to live" before she died March 31. He said the family is reviewing the autopsy and considering legal options.

The autopsy report revealed intimate details about Terri Schiavo's anatomy and end of life. It included 274 external and internal pictures, some of which Felos said will be made public, and it said she was brought into the exam at 112 pounds, clad in a pink and white gown, accompanied by three pillows and a blanket.

It also was a reminder of the supercharged political debate that grew around one family's intractable dispute. House Majority Leader Tom DeLay (R—Texas), who helped engineer legislation seeking to restore the feeding tube, insisted at the time Schiavo "is as alive as you or I." Yesterday, spokesmen for DeLay and Bush, who signed the law, were less outspoken and said their prayers remained with the Schindlers.

Arthur Caplan, director of the Center for Bioethics at the University of Pennsylvania, described the autopsy as "a dagger into the heart" of the campaign to keep Schiavo alive.

"It shows that when you want to see something, you can make yourself believe it," he said. "Or if you come with a big ideological bias, then you are willing to go around saying anything."

As Man Lay in Coma–Like State, His Brain Was Busy Rebuilding

By Karen Kaplan.
Los Angeles Times, July 4, 2006.

Terry Wallis awoke from a coma-like state 19 years after tumbling over a guardrail in a Chevy pickup and falling 25 feet into a dry Ozarks riverbed. Now doctors armed with some of the latest brain-imaging technology think they may know part of the reason.

Although Wallis had showed few outward signs of consciousness, his brain had been methodically rebuilding the white-matter infrastructure necessary for him to interact with the outside world, researchers reported Monday in the Journal of Clinical Investigation.

"I believe it's a very, very slow self-healing process of the brain," said lead author Henning Voss, a physicist at Cornell University's Weill Medical College Citigroup Biomedical Imaging Center in New York.

Wallis emerged in 2003 from a minimally conscious state at the age of 39 and uttered his first word since Ronald Reagan had been in the White House: "Mom." Since then, the onetime mechanic from Big Flat, Ark., has regained the ability to form sentences and has recovered some use of his limbs, though he still can't walk or feed himself.

Using PET scans and an advanced imaging technique called diffusion tensor imaging, the researchers examined Wallis' brain after he regained full consciousness. They found that cells in relatively undamaged areas had formed new axons, the long nerve fibers that transmit messages between neurons.

"In essence, Terry's brain may have been seeking out new pathways to reestablish functional connections to areas involved in speech and motor control to compensate for those lost due to damage," said the study's senior author, Dr. Nicholas Schiff, a neurologist at the Weill Medical College.

Schiff cautioned that Wallis was a "1–in–300–million" case. But Dr. Steven Laureys, a neurologist at the University of Liege in Belgium, said the findings will force doctors to reconsider the way they treat patients who are languishing in minimally conscious and persistent vegetative states.

"It does show there are changes happening" in the brain, said Laureys, who coauthored a commentary that also appears in the journal. "It obliges us to reconsider old dogmas."

In a minimally conscious state, a patient shows intermittent signs of awareness but is generally unable to interact with the outside world. It is a less severe condition than a persistent vegetative state, in which the patient is awake but has no awareness of self or surroundings.

The late Terri Schiavo, the Florida woman at the center of a bitter right-to-die battle, had been in a persistent vegetative state for 15 years when her husband won a court order to have her feeding tube removed last year.

Neurologists believe that the longer a patient remains in a minimally conscious or persistent vegetative state, the lower the chances for recovery. As a result, such patients are often neglected by doctors and insurance companies, and it can be difficult for family members to find facilities that will accept them, Laureys said.

In his last few years at the Stone County Nursing and Rehabilitation Center in Mountain View, Ark., Wallis' family began to notice that Wallis, a Ford enthusiast, would grunt when a Chevrolet commercial came on the television. They said he answered questions by blinking. About two years before he regained full consciousness, doctors started administering the antidepressant Paxil, which they think may have contributed to his recovery.

Within a week of his first utterance, Wallis began speaking in simple sentences. Once paralyzed from the neck down, he can now point with his left hand and move both legs.

The researchers scanned Wallis' brain eight months after his awakening and found strong evidence that axons were making new connections in the cerebellum, the region that controls movement. The activity, which was stronger than in the brains of 20 healthy people scanned for comparison, seemed to correlate with Wallis' physical improvement, Voss said.

When his brain was rescanned 18 months later, signs of growth in the cerebellum had leveled off and other areas of the brain were using more energy.

Wallis' language skills improved during that time—he learned to count to 25 without interruption, and his speech became more intelligible. But when the researchers looked for evidence of increased activity in the language centers of his brain, they found none.

"Maybe we just missed it, or maybe the language areas are unusable because important connections are missing," said Voss, who theorizes that another part of the brain picked up the slack.

Voss and his colleagues also scanned the brain of a car accident victim who is still minimally conscious and found significant axonal regrowth as well. That patient, however, has not shown corresponding clinical improvement, according to the study.

"We have to understand this much better to know how to promote healing in other patients," Voss said.

"We're still a long way from therapies."

NOTES

The families of Terri Schiavo and Terry Wallis faced perhaps the most agonizing decision a loved one may ever be asked to make: whether to end life support or to prolong a seemingly hopeless existence. Some family members may be sure that their incapacitated loved one would have wanted to be kept alive at any cost. Others may be equally sure that she would not have wanted to live in a seriously compromised condition. The issue invokes people's deepest beliefs and attitudes, religious and otherwise, and it can tear families apart.

To complicate matters, financial concerns may play a role. Bottom-line oriented insurers, hospitals short of beds, and families being bankrupted by an illness of a relative might be tempted to end life, or to sustain it to benefit from the incapacitated relative's financial situation.

Both Terri and Terry faced incapacity at a young age, and it is not surprising that neither had documents in place that might have guided family members through the decision making process. But these cases highlight the importance of including health care documents as part of any estate plan a lawyer may create.

A. The Health Care Default Regime

People can be reluctant to consider issues that might arise should they become incapacitated through accident or illness. When a person's incapacity seriously compromises his or her quality of life, how far should the medical establishment go in trying to prolong that life? When the incapacitated person can no longer communicate whether he or she wishes to accept life-sustaining treatment, how can the law determine what the person would have wanted? Should a close relative or friend be able to make that decision for the incapacitated person?

In Cruzan v. Director, Missouri Dept. of Health, 497 U.S. 261, 110 S.Ct. 2841, 111 L.Ed.2d 224 (1990), the parents of Nancy Cruzan, who was in a persistent vegetative state, challenged a Missouri statute requiring them to establish by clear and convincing evidence that Cruzan would not have wanted to continue artificial life sustaining treatment. Although the Supreme Court recognized that a competent adult has a constitutionally protected right to refuse artificial nutrition and hydration, it concluded that the Missouri statute, designed to protect the incompetent, was not an unconstitutional restriction on this right. Many states have adopted the "clear and convincing standard" for this purpose.

The question becomes more difficult when the patient is not unconscious, but is sufficiently incapacitated so as to have no meaningful quality of life. Courts are often reluctant to issue orders permitting family members or guardians to end life-sustaining treatment in these situations. For example, in Wendland v. Wendland, 26 Cal.4th 519, 110 Cal.Rptr.2d 412, 28 P.3d 151 (2001), the California Supreme Court upheld a trial court determination forbidding Rose Wendland, Robert Wendland's wife and conservator, from withholding artificial nutrition and hydration on the ground that she had not established by clear and convincing evidence that removal would have been consistent with Robert's wishes. An automobile accident had rendered Wendland conscious but seriously brain damaged and unable to survive without artificial nutrition and hydration. After two years, Rose refused permission to reinsert Robert's feeding tube. Robert's wife, brother and children believed that this was consistent with his wishes, and they were supported by Robert's treating physician and the hospital ethics committee. Robert's mother and sister objected and intervened, the feeding tube was reinserted pending a court order, and a six-year legal battle began.

At the trial, Robert's treating physician testified that, to the highest degree of medical certainty, Robert would never be able to make medical treatment decisions, walk, talk, feed himself, eat, drink, or control his bowel and bladder functions. Robert's wife, brother and daughter all recounted various statements that Robert had made to the effect that "he wouldn't want to live like a vegetable" or in a "comatose state."

The trial court found the conservator had not met her duty and burden to show by clear and convincing evidence that conservatee Robert Wendland, who is not in a persistent vegetative state nor suffering from a terminal illness would, under the circumstances, want to die. Conservator has likewise not met her burden of establishing that the withdrawal of artificially delivered nutrition and hydration is commensurate with conservatee's best interests ...

* * *

> The testimony adduced focuses upon two pre-accident conversations during which the conservatee allegedly expressed a desire not to live like a 'vegetable.' These two conversations do not establish by clear and convincing evidence that the conservatee would desire to have his life-sustaining medical treatment terminated under the circumstances in which he now finds himself. One of these conversations allegedly occurred when the conservatee was apparently recovering from a night's bout of drinking. The other alleged conversation occurred following the loss of conservatee's father-in-law, with whom he was very close. The court finds that neither of these conversations reflect an exact 'on all-fours' description of conservatee's present medical condition. More explicit direction than just 'I don't want to live like a vegetable' is required in order to justify a surrogate decision-maker terminating the life of ... someone who is not in a PVS [persistent vegetative state].

The Court of Appeals reversed on the ground that the court was obligated to show some deference to the guardian's determination that removal of the feeding tube would be in Robert's best interest. The

California Supreme Court reversed the appellate court and reinstated the trial court's determination, closing with the following remarks:

> We emphasize, however, that the clear and convincing evidence standard does not apply to the vast majority of health care decisions made by conservators ... Only the decision to withdraw life-sustaining treatment, because of its effect on a conscious conservatee's fundamental rights, justifies imposing that high standard of proof. Therefore, our decision today affects only a narrow class of persons: conscious conservatees who have not left formal directions for health care and whose conservators propose to withhold life-sustaining treatment for the purpose of causing their conservatees' deaths. Our conclusion does not affect permanently unconscious patients, including those who are comatose or in a persistent vegetative state [citations omitted] persons who have left legally cognizable instructions for health care, persons who have designated agents or other surrogates for health care, or conservatees for whom conservators have made medical decisions other than those intended to bring about the death of a conscious conservatee.

NOTES AND QUESTIONS

1. What evidence did Rose present regarding Robert's unwillingness to live in a severely compromised state? When a family member is seeking the cessation of extraordinary measures, how likely is it that they will be able to recount formal and detailed discussions about end-of-life issues? Do people routinely discuss whether they would want to be kept alive under a variety of conditions?

According to Rose, Robert was estranged from his mother and sister, and had no meaningful relationship with them. Why did his mother and sister have standing to object to a decision made by Rose, Robert's wife and legal guardian, and supported by his children, hospital doctors, and the hospital ethics committee? Who should have standing to challenge end-of-life decisions?

2. Suppose Robert had been in a persistent vegetative state. Would the court have reached the same result? See Conservatorship of Morrison, 206 Cal.App.3d 304, 253 Cal.Rptr. 530 (1988) (allowing guardian of 90–year–old woman in persistent vegetative state to authorize withdrawal of feeding tube). Some unpublished opinions suggest that in these cases courts should apply a "preponderance of the evidence" standard instead of requiring clear and convincing evidence of the patient's wishes. Why? Given that some coma patients recover, why shouldn't families of unconscious patients also have the same burden of proof?

3. Suppose that Robert would not, in fact, have wanted to continue living in his severely compromised condition. What steps could he have taken to ensure that his wife could have made the decision to withdraw the feeding tube? The following section explores two possibilities: the Durable Health Care Power of Attorney and the "Living Will".

B. Legal Documents: (Attempting to) Draft Around the Default Regime

1. THE DURABLE HEALTH CARE POWER OF ATTORNEY

In executing a durable health care power of attorney, an individual appoints an agent to make any health-care decision that the individual could make if she had capacity. Following is a good example of a durable power of attorney for health care:

DURABLE POWER OF ATTORNEY FOR HEALTH CARE

1. Designation of Health Care Agent.

I, ______ do hereby designate and appoint

____

(name of agent)

____

(address and telephone number of agent)

as my attorney in fact (agent) to make health care decisions for me as authorized in this document. For the purposes of this document, "health care decision" means consent, refusal of consent, or withdrawal of consent to any care, treatment, service, or procedure to maintain, diagnose, or treat an individual's physical or mental condition.

2. Creation of Durable Power of Attorney for Health Care.

By this document I intend to create a durable power of attorney for health care. This power of attorney shall not be affected by my subsequent incapacity.

3. General Statement of Authority Granted.

Subject to any limitations in this document, I hereby grant to my agent full power and authority to make health care decisions for me to the same extent that I could make such decisions for myself if I had the capacity to do so. In exercising this authority, my agent shall make health care decisions that are consistent with my desires as stated in this document or otherwise made known to my agent, including, but not limited to, my desires concerning obtaining or refusing or withdrawing life-prolonging care, treatment, services, and procedures.

4. Statement of Desires, Special Provisions, and Limitations.

In exercising the authority under this durable power of attorney for health care, my agent shall act consistently with my desires as stated below and is subject to the special provisions and limitations stated below:

5. Inspection and Disclosure of Information Relating to My Physical or Mental Health.

Subject to any limitations in this document, my agent has the power and authority to do all of the following:

(a) Request, review, and receive any information, verbal or written, regarding my physical or mental health, including, but not limited to, medical and hospital records.

(b) Execute on my behalf any releases or other documents that may be required in order to obtain this information.

(c) Consent to the disclosure of this information.

(If you want to limit the authority of your agent to receive and disclose information relating to your health, you must state the limitations in paragraph 4.)

6. Signing Documents, Waivers, and Releases.

Where necessary to implement the health care decisions that my agent is authorized by this document to make, my agent has the power and authority to execute on my behalf all of the following:

(a) Documents titled or purporting to be a "Refusal to Permit Treatment" and "Leaving Hospital Against Medical Advice."

(b) Any necessary waiver or release from liability required by a hospital or physician.

7. Autopsy; Anatomical Gifts; Disposition of Remains.

Subject to any limitations in this document, my agent has the power and authority to do all of the following:

(a) Authorize an autopsy.

(b) Make a disposition of a part or parts of my body under the Uniform Anatomical Gift Act.

(c) Direct the disposition of my remains.

8. Duration.

This durable power of attorney for health care expires on ________________

____

(Fill in this space ONLY if you want to limit the duration of this power of attorney)

9. Designation of Alternate Agents.

If the person designated as my agent in paragraph 1 is not available or becomes ineligible to act as my agent to make a health care decision for me or loses the mental capacity to make health care decisions for me, or if I revoke that person's appointment or authority to act as my agent to make health care decisions for me, then I designate and appoint the following persons to serve as my agent to make health care decisions for me as authorized in this document, such persons to serve in the order listed below:

A. First Alternate Agent: ______________________________
(name of first alternate agent)

B. Second Alternate Agent: ______________________________
(name of second alternate agent)

10. Nomination of Conservator of Person.

* * *

If a conservator of the person is to be appointed for me, I nominate the following individual to serve as conservator of the person:

____
(name of person nominated as conservator)

11. Prior Designations Revoked.

I revoke any prior durable power of attorney for health care.

DATE AND SIGNATURE OF PRINCIPAL

I sign my name to this Durable Power of Attorney for Health Care on

______________ at ______________________________, ________________.
(date) *(city)* *(state)*

____
(you sign here)

(THIS POWER OF ATTORNEY WILL NOT BE VALID UNLESS IT IS SIGNED BY *EITHER* A NOTARY PUBLIC *OR* TWO QUALIFIED WITNESSES WHO ARE PRESENT WHEN YOU SIGN OR ACKNOWLEDGE YOUR SIGNATURE.)

NOTES AND QUESTIONS

1. *Enforceability of Durable Powers Regarding Health Care.* A health care durable power of attorney exists because of a statutory authorization in a given state. See, e.g., 755 Ill. Comp. Stat. 45/4–1 et seq. The attorney-in-fact has as much power over her principal's health care decisions as the principal. That power derives from the statute and the principal's decision to sign the power. In theory, when the attorney-in-fact authorizes the appendectomy, it is legally the same as the patient authorizing the operation. In theory, the attorney-in-fact's decision is legally the same as the patient's. Thus, for example, in the Illinois Powers of Attorney for Health Care Law, an individual may delegate, "without limitation, all powers an individual may have to be informed about and to consent to or refuse or withdraw any type of health care for the individual." 755 Ill. Comp. Stat. 45/4–3.

2. *Who Should Serve as Agent?* Some statutes expressly prohibit owners, operators or employees of a residential long-term health-care institution at which the principal is receiving care from serving as agents. See, e.g., Uniform Health Care Decisions Act, Section 2 (b). Prohibiting a class of people with an obvious conflict of interest from making tough decisions makes sense, but whom should the client choose to hold the power? What considerations should the client take into account?

3. *HIPAA.* In 1996, Congress passed the Health Insurance Portability and Accountability Act of 1996 (HIPAA). Title II of HIPAA (known as the "privacy rule"), sets forth detailed rules designed to keep patients' medical records private. In particular, it prohibits third parties, with certain exceptions, from gaining access to patients' medical records without a patient's express authorization. This could pose a dilemma for one seeking to invoke authority to act under a power of attorney designed to take effect only on the principal's incapacity. A thorough exploration of the impact of HIPAA is beyond the scope of this book. It will suffice for now to say that it may be important to authorize, in advance of incompetency, the agent to receive medical information otherwise protected by HIPAA.

---

2. ADVANCE DIRECTIVES OR "LIVING WILLS"

Historically, Advance Health Care Directives (originally referred to as "living wills") were requests that the signer be allowed to die. "Living will" is ultimately a colloquial label that means different things in different states. In a state that has not adopted a living will statute, the term describes a document that is simply an expression of the signer's hopes and philosophy about medical care in the face of death, and which may not be legally binding. In such a state, a law-abiding physician could ignore a living will. However, a court in that state could, in the exercise of its discretion, direct that the terms of the living will be carried out for a particular signer. At that point, for that patient, the living will has become a document that is enforceable.

Many states, however, have enacted "living will" or "advance directive" statutes that turn living wills from requests into directives. These statutes include provisions insulating the care provider against civil or criminal liability and providing for patient transfer to a provider who will respect the terms of the "living will" or "declaration." See, e.g., Ohio Rev. Code Ann. § 2133.11; 755 Ill. Comp. Stat. 35/1 et seq.

In 1993, the Commissioners on Uniform Laws approved the Uniform Health Care Decisions Act. To date, at least eight states have adopted it, and other states have used it as a model for revising their natural death statutes. See, e.g., Wendland v. Wendland, 26 Cal.4th 519, 110 Cal.Rptr.2d 412, 28 P.3d 151 (2001) (stating that California's revised natural death statutes are substantially influenced by the Uniform Health Care Decisions Act). Part One of the Act includes a form health care power of attorney.

Part Two includes a so-called "living will" form, with which an individual may create a legally enforceable document directing whether and to what extent an attending physician should authorize life-extending treatment:

Part 2
Instructions for Health Care

If you are satisfied to allow your agent to determine what is best for you in making end-of-life decisions, you need not fill out this part of the form. If you do fill out this part of the form, you may strike any wording you do not want.

(6) END-OF-LIFE DECISIONS: I direct that my health-care providers and others involved in my care provide, withhold, or withdraw treatment in accordance with the choice that I have marked below:

[ ] (a) Choice Not To Prolong Life

I do not want my life to be prolonged if (i) I have an incurable and irreversible condition that will result in my death within a relatively short time, (ii) I become unconscious and, to a reasonable degree of medical certainty, I will not regain consciousness, or (iii) the likely risks and burdens of treatment would outweigh the expected benefits, OR

[ ] (b) Choice To Prolong Life

I want my life to be prolonged as long as possible within the limits of generally accepted health-care standards.

(7) ARTIFICIAL NUTRITION AND HYDRATION: Artificial nutrition and hydration must be provided, withheld, or withdrawn in accordance with the choice I have made in paragraph (6) unless I mark the following box. If I mark this box [ ], artificial nutrition and hydration must be provided regardless of my condition and regardless of the choice I have made in paragraph (6).

(8) RELIEF FROM PAIN: Except as I state in the following space, I direct that treatment for alleviation of pain or discomfort be provided at all times, even if it hastens my death:

____

____

(9) OTHER WISHES: (If you do not agree with any of the optional choices above and wish to write your own, or if you wish to add to the instructions you have given above, you may do so here.) I direct that:

____

QUESTIONS AND NOTES

1. Should a client execute both a living will *and* a health care power of attorney? If not, which would be preferable? What advantages are there to the durable health care power of attorney? The living will?

Many states, such as California and New Jersey, now offer forms that combine the health care power of attorney with an advance directive.

2. Is it possible to foresee today the nature of the health care alternatives that might face your client 10 to 15 years from now? If not, does limited foresight argue in favor of any one of the three documents? Consider Professor Ray Madoff's insight:

> Although people regularly prepare living wills that state their wishes in the event of difficult circumstances, it is very difficult to imagine these situations honestly and accurately predict how one is going to feel. One of the limitations of the living will is that it presumes that people, when they are young and healthy, are going to be able accurately to assess how they would feel in the face of serious and debilitating illness. The will to live is so strong, that although they may first be discouraged about their situation, most people continue to find meaning in their lives, even if they did not think they could.

Ray D. Madoff, Autonomy and End-of-Life Decision Making: Reflections of a Lawyer and a Daughter, 53 Buff. L. Rev. 963 (2005).

3. Who bears the burden of decision-making when the client executes a durable health care power of attorney? Do you think most clients want to impose such burdens on spouses or other loved ones? How confident would you be that your spouse or "significant other" would "pull the plug" when you want it pulled? Do these problems argue in favor of a living will?

4. Oral changes to living wills are recognized in Florida Statute section 765.304, and oral revocations in the Illinois Living Will Act, 755 Ill. Comp. Stat. 35/5. How do you explain this casualness about oral manifestations of intent when we are so fussy about oral wills, revocations and the like?

5. For an excellent article explaining how to use Mental Health Advance Directives to plan for the future when an individual has been diagnosed with Alzheimer's Disease, see Lisa Brodoff, Planning For Alzheimer's Disease with Mental health Advance Directives, 17 Elder L. J. 239 (2010).

C. PRACTICAL PROBLEMS: PERSUADING THE PHYSICIANS

Physicians have historically treated the appropriateness of life-support measures as medical decisions for physicians to make.

Suppose, however, a patient does not want the physicians to have the last word. Can the patient dictate—on a form likely to be accepted by physicians and hospitals—the patient's desires? Consider the following:

EMERGENCY MEDICAL SERVICES
PREHOSPITAL DO NOT RESUSCITATE (DNR) FORM

An Advance Request to Limit the Scope of Emergency Medical Care

I, ______________________________, request limited emergency care
(print patient's name)
as herein described.

I understand DNR means that if my heart stops beating or if I stop breathing, no medical procedure to restart breathing or heart functioning will be instituted.

I understand this decision will **not** prevent me from obtaining other emergency medical care by prehospital emergency medical care personnel and/or medical care directed by a physician prior to my death.

I understand I may revoke this directive at any time by destroying this form and removing any "DNR" medallions.

I give permission for this information to be given to the prehospital emergency care personnel, doctors, nurses or other health personnel as necessary to implement this directive.

I hereby agree to the "Do Not Resuscitate" (DNR) order.

____
Patient/Surrogate Signature Date

____
Surrogate Relationship to Patient

By signing this form, the surrogate acknowledges that this request to forego resuscitative measures is consistent with the known desires of, and with the best interest of, the individual who is the subject of this form.

I affirm that this patient/surrogate is making an informed decision and that this directive is the expressed wish of the patient/surrogate. A copy of this form is in the patient's permanent medical record.

In the event of cardiac or respiratory arrest, no chest compressions, assisted ventilations, intubation, defibrillation, or cardiotonic medications are to be initiated.

____
Physician Signature Date

____
Print Name, Telephone

THIS FORM WILL NOT BE ACCEPTED IF IT HAS BEEN AMENDED OR ALTERED IN ANY WAY

* * *

QUESTIONS

1. How is this form different from a living will? Why would a physician or hospital be more likely to honor this form?

2. Why might physicians take comfort from dual signatures? What is the purpose of this form? Why, would you guess, is it commonplace advice to families not to call emergency services when Grandma is in extremis and it seems that the end is near? What virtue is there in having the two logos on the form if there is a dispute going on in the ambulance about what is to be done? Why does the form say it is unacceptable "if amended or altered in any way?" Would you guess this form is as useful in another state as it is in California? How useful is it in California if it is entirely handwritten by the patient, using exactly the same terms? What are the arguments in favor of unchangeable, printed forms?

NOTE

When the client is in the hospital, or nursing home, and in extremis, there often will be someone negotiating with a physician for a DNR order. That someone may be a relative or friend and that someone may be holding a living will or durable health care power of attorney. That negotiator will be asking the doctor to exercise her professional judgment and sign the order and that negotiator will be claiming that the papers in hand (or the stories of "what mother always wanted") should both convince the physician to act and constitute the patient/client's consent. In some states the negotiator may be claiming the doctor must add the DNR order to the chart. If the doctor is the family physician, and if the patient has known the doctor for thirty years, and if doctor and patient come from the same community, religion, neighborhood and generation, then all will likely be well. If not, then who knows. As Justice Stevens put it in his concurrence in Washington v. Glucksberg, "[f]or doctors who have long-standing relationships with their patients, who have given their patients advice on alternative treatments, who are attentive to their patient's individualized needs, and who are knowledgeable about pain symptom management and palliative care options, * * * heeding a patient's desire to assist in her suicide would not serve to harm the physician-patient relationship." 521 U.S. 702, 748 (1997) (Stevens, J., concurring).

These issues are extraordinarily complex and both jurisdiction and fact specific. There may be statutes, government and hospital regulations, and expressed rules of medical ethics brought to bear.

The most remarkable fact of all is that a 1995 study of the highest quality, sponsored by the Robert Wood Johnson Foundation, strongly suggests that it is very hard for patients and families to successfully communicate their end of life choices and goals to physicians and that it is just as hard to get physicians to change their ways and reduce futile life-extending procedures. For instance, of the patients who did not want to be resuscitated, doctors understood their wishes only 47% of the time. Of those same patients who did not want to be resuscitated, 49% died without a DNR order ever being entered in their chart. As a result of failures of communication, or perhaps even in defiance of patient wishes, 46% of DNR orders were written within two days of death, suggesting very strongly that up until that time extraordinary measures were being taken to extend life with no practical purpose in view and against the wishes of the patients! Other DNR patterns suggested that the specialty of the physician in charge of the case and the hospital the patient was in were key factors affecting the timing of the DNR order. And a 1997 study suggests that seriously ill patients themselves fail to communicate their wishes to their doctors. Jan C. Hoffman et al., Patient Preferences for Communication with Physicians About End-of-Life Decisions, 127 Annals Internal Med. 1 (1997).

It seems clear that in a hospital setting the most important documentary event is the entering of a DNR order into the patient's chart. The study implies (or we infer) that the best way for that to happen is if there is a very aggressive agent holding a health care power of attorney. At that point it is tempting to ask if just as bankers tend to ignore durable powers, will the same be true of doctors? See The Support Investigators, A Controlled Trial to Improve Care for Seriously Ill Hospitalized Patients: The Study to Understand Prognoses and Preferences for Outcomes and Risk of Treatment (SUPPORT), 274 JAMA 1591 (1995); Council on Ethical and Judicial Affairs, American Medical Association, Guidelines for the Appropriate Use of Do–Not–Resuscitate Orders, 265 JAMA 1868 (1991).

D. Physician-Assisted Suicide

Many people don't want to be kept alive past the point of no return, especially if there is to be a waste of family or social resources, great pain, great loneliness or loss of dignity and life's value. In the 1980s, several studies found that approximately 27% of annual Medicare expenditures were spent on the approximately 6% of Medicare enrollees who die each year. Additionally, 40% of the annual amount was spent in the enrollees' final 30 days of life. See Anne A. Scitovsky, The High Cost of Dying Revisited, 72 Milbank Q. 561 (1994). More recently, however, these statistics have been challenged as somewhat misleading. See Alliance for Aging Research, The Seven Deadly Myths: Uncovering the Facts About the High Cost of the Last Year of Life (1997). If these costs are not insured, they become the equivalent of an estate tax for the middle class. If you don't believe it, read First Healthcare Corp. v. Rettinger, 342 N.C. 886, 467 S.E.2d 243 (1996), noted in 32 Wake Forest L. Rev. 591 (1996). In First Healthcare, the wife was contractually liable for nursing home services for her husband. Her husband suffered from Parkinson's disease, and over time he became bedridden and severely demented. The wife requested the removal of her husband's nutrition and hydration tubes, but the nursing home resisted on the ground that state law, as applied to the case, was unclear. After extensive litigation, a court ordered the nursing home to remove the tubes and the husband died. The nursing home then sued the husband's widow for nursing home services from the date of the first request to remove the tubes to the date of death. The widow resisted, pointing out that the services would not have been necessary if the home had complied with her request instead of litigating. The nursing home won.

Many clients fear "prolonged dying, accompanied by substantial emotional and financial expense. Many Americans today fear they will lose control over their lives if they become critically ill, and their dying will be prolonged and impersonal. This has led to an increasingly visible right-to-die movement.... Many worry about the economic and human cost of providing life sustaining treatment near the end of life." See The Support Investigators, A Controlled Trial to Improve Care for Seriously Ill Hospitalized Patients: The Study to Understand Prognoses and Preferences for Outcomes and Risks of Treatment (SUPPORT), 274 JAMA 1591 (1995).

In recent years, these concerns have focused on physician-assisted suicide, euthanasia and whether there is a constitutionally protected right to die. See, e.g., Cass Sunstein, The Right to Die, 106 Yale L.J. 1123 (1997). Oregon was the first state to enact a "death with dignity" statute, which allows a terminally ill patient who is acting voluntarily and not suffering from depression to request a prescription for medication to end life. ORS §§ 127.800–127.897. The measure was approved by voters on November 8, 1994. A few years later, in Washington v. Glucksberg, 521 U.S. 702, 117 S.Ct. 2258, 138 L.Ed.2d 772 (1997), the Supreme Court rejected a due process challenge to Washington State's prohibition on assisted suicide. The Court stated that the states' interests in regulating assisted suicides were "(1) preserving life; (2) preventing suicide; (3) avoiding the involvement of third parties and use of arbitrary, unfair, or undue influence; (4) protecting family members and loved ones; (5) protecting the integrity of the medical profession; and (6) avoiding future movement toward euthanasia and other abuses. 79 F.3d, at 816–832." 521 U.S. 702, 728 n. 20.

In response to Washington v. Glucksberg, the Oregon state legislature introduced a ballot initiative to repeal the Death With Dignity Act, but the measure was rejected by 60% of voters. On November 6, 2001, Attorney General John Ashcroft published in the Federal Register a declaration that has become known as the "Ashcroft directive." The declaration states that "assisting suicide is not a 'legitimate medical purpose' within the meaning of 21 C.F.R. § 1306.04 (2001)," and that "prescribing, dispensing, or administering federally controlled substances to assist suicide violates the CSA." The directive further suggests that a physician who so prescribes, dispenses, or administers a drug may be subject to suspension or revocation of her license.

After publishing the directive, Ashcroft challenged Oregon's assisted suicide statute in federal court, on the ground that it violated the federal Controlled Substances Act (CSA). The United States Supreme Court held that the statute does not allow the Attorney General to prohibit doctors from prescribing regulated drugs for use in physician-assisted suicide permitted under state law. See Gonzales v. Oregon, 546 U.S. 243, 126 S.Ct. 904, 163 L.Ed.2d 748 (2006). For an important analysis of the federalism issues related to physician-assisted suicide, see Brian H. Bix, Physician Assisted Suicide and Federalism, 17 Notre Dame J.L. Ethics & Pub Pol'y 53 (2003).

In 2008, the voters in the State of Washington passed an assisted suicide law modeled on Oregon's. Then, in 2009, Montana became the third state to legalize physician-assisted suicide. Unlike Oregon and Washington, recognition of assisted suicide came from the state's highest court. See Baxter v. Montana, 354 Mont. 234, 224 P.3d 1211 (2009).

QUESTIONS

1. Which approach is preferable, the prohibition on assisted suicide or the position taken by Montana, Oregon and Washington? If we prohibit assisted suicide, are we favoring the lucky? Will those who happen to die in their sleep and those who know their doctors and how to deal with them get the death they want? See Gina Kolata, "Passive Euthanasia" Is the Norm In Today's Hospitals, N.Y. Times, June 28, 1997, at A1; Gina Kolata, When Morphine Fails to Kill, N.Y. Times, July 23, 1997, at B10. On the other hand, will allowing assisted suicide render the ill and weak among us vulnerable to the influence of others? Will it discourage them from obtaining care to enhance their quality of life?

2. Currently, there is a constitutional right to refuse medicine, hydration, or nutrition, but there is no constitutional right to be prescribed poison or to have a physician assist you in killing yourself. Are you convinced by the distinction?

3. If you are convinced that sophisticated patients, in nuanced conversations with physicians are able to obtain passive euthanasia then, in some sense, the Washington v. Glucksberg Court was being asked to come up with a default rule for people incapable of having those conversations. At that point, is it any surprise that the default rule comes out in favor of life?

4. The Supreme Courts of Alaska and Florida have refused to recognize a state constitutional right to assisted suicide. In so finding, both courts emphasized that the power to legitimize assisted suicide belongs solely to the legislature. See Sampson v. State, 31 P.3d 88 (Alaska 2001); Krischer v. McIver, 697 So.2d 97 (Fla. 1997). For a Constitutional Analysis of assisted suicide laws, see Kevin P. Quinn, Assisted Suicide and Equal Protection: In Defense of the Distinction Between Killing and Letting Die, 13 Issues L. & Med. 145 (1997).

SECTION IV. LONG-TERM CARE AT JOURNEY'S END

Many older people fear dying alone, short of money and in need of care. Medicare does not solve the problems they fear. Long-term custodial care is not a medical problem, and it is not covered by Medicare. Custodial care may be covered by Medicaid, but only for poor people. Middle-class elderly have to rely on savings, family and friends, long-term care insurance and the safety net of becoming poor in order to qualify for Medicaid.

Why doesn't Medicare provide custodial care? The mechanical answer is that the statute doesn't cover it, and the real answer is straightforward—it costs too much money. Focus on the "Medi" not on the "care." Medicare is medical insurance, and custodial care isn't medical care. You have to be in need of hospitalization or skilled nursing home care to get the room, board and bedpans under Medicare, and most folks only need the room and board.

What about savings? You can't be too thin or too rich, as the saying goes. Finding the money to pay for custodial care is not a legitimate concern of truly prosperous people. Excluding medical costs (which can be substantial), average rates for senior care in 2009 were as follows:

The average costs in the United States (in 2009) are:

- $198/day for a semi-private room in a nursing home
- $219/day for a private room in a nursing home
- $3,131/month for care in an Assisted Living Facility (for a one-bedroom unit)
- $21/hour for a Home Health Aide
- $19/hour for a Homemaker services
- $67/day for care in an Adult Day Health Care Center

http://www.longtermcare.gov/LTC/Main_Site/Paying_LTC/Costs_Of_Care/Costs_Of_Care.aspx.

Most nursing home stays are less than three years in duration. Many nursing homes currently take people who can pay for the first year or so, with the understanding they will be allowed to stay on as Medicaid patients after their funds run out. Of course, long terminal illnesses with the patient outside the nursing home can be very costly, too.

Despite the great fear and the horror stories, many middle-class people die leaving inheritances for their survivors and without having spent a decade in the nursing home on welfare.

The problem is the uncertainty. Very few people have large enough families or fortunes to survive worst-case scenarios—"Let's assume that you enter the nursing home at age 71 and that you live to be 115, with an annual inflation rate of 3%, you'll need...."

The obvious solution is insurance. The market for long-term care insurance improves and increases every year. The problems are that not enough people want to buy it early enough, and the insurance companies are still reluctant to provide truly attractive products. This corporate reluctance results from lack of experience with the costs, concerns about predicting inflation over the decades, concerns about having to pay for services families currently provide themselves at no direct cash cost to any one and pricing problems. If young people don't buy the insurance, then the company doesn't get their premiums to invest for forty years, and then older people have to be charged high premiums that scare them away.

Congress has offered some tax relief. This is described in David M. English, New Legislation on Long–Term Care and Other Tax Issues Affecting the Elderly, 23 Est. Plan. 494 (1996). Oversimplifying, the premiums on long-term care insurance can be deductible as medical expenses; in very specific circumstances and with much record-keeping, some long-term care expenditures actually made are deductible as medical expenses, and, to the extent the proceeds of life insurance cashed in before death are income taxable, Congress has set aside those rules, in specific circumstances. For a thoughtful analysis of the various ways that policymakers have sought to address the problem of long-term care, see Joshua M. Weiner, Jane Tilly and Susan M. Goldenson, Federal and State Initiatives to Jump Start the Market for Private Long–Term Care Insurance, 8 Elder L.J. 57 (2000).

The great truth is that long-term custodial care is just another estate tax on the middle class and that long-term care insurance is just a form of inheritance insurance. See Howard J. Saks, Update on Long–Term Care Insurance and Checklist for This Wealth Protection Tool, 23 Est. Plan. 275 (1996). See generally Joel C. Dobris, Medicaid Asset Planning by the Elderly: A Policy View of Expectations, Entitlement and Inheritance, 24 Real Prop., Prob. & Tr. J. 1 (1989). Buying the insurance may allow clients the freedom to make substantial, tax-oriented gifts.

As Professor Leavis warned, we have not heard the last of these issues: " '[T]he advancement of science and technology means a human future of . . . decisions and possible non-decisions so momentous and insidious in their consequences' that humanity will need all the intelligence and spiritual guidance that high culture can provide." David Lehman, His Critical Condition, Wall Street J., June 10, 1997, at A16 (reviewing Ian MacKillop, F.R. Leavis: A Life in Criticism (1995)).

CHAPTER TWELVE

CO-ORDINATING NON-PROBATE ASSETS WITH THE PROBATE ESTATE

SECTION I. INTRODUCTION

With the growth of alternatives to probate, many clients of even modest means hold both probate assets and assets that pass outside of probate, including P.O.D. accounts, revocable trusts, retirement plan assets, and life insurance. Laymen (and all too many lawyers) are not fully aware of the distinction between probate and non-probate assets and often assume that a single document will operate to dispose of all of a decedent's assets. That assumption is frequently untrue. It can lead to needless litigation, which often results in frustration of the client's objectives.

In this chapter, we explore the co-ordination problems presented by the disparate legal rules that govern disposition of assets at a decedent's death.

SECTION II. P.O.D. ACCOUNTS, REVOCABLE TRUSTS, AND WILLS

Chapter Seven explored the growth of bank account trusts, and, later, revocable trusts, as will substitutes. Today, nearly all states recognize the validity of these probate alternatives. Chapter Four also discussed the pour-over will as a device for assuring that all of a decedent's assets pass in accordance with the terms of a single instrument: the revocable trust. Often, however, clients (or their lawyers) are careless, and execute documents with conflicting instructions. Consider the following case:

Araiza v. Younkin

Court of Appeal of California, Second Appellate District, 2010.
188 Cal.App.4th 1120, 116 Cal.Rptr.3d 315.

■ YEGAN, J.

Lori Younkin appeals from the trial court's order confirming ownership of a Bank of America savings account to respondent Ronald A. Araiza, as successor trustee of the Lucia Howery Living Trust, and naming

Gabriella Reeves the beneficiary of that account. Appellant, the stepdaughter of Lucia Howery, contends she is the owner of the savings account.... Respondent contends Howery changed the beneficiary of the savings account in her living trust.... We affirm.

Facts

In 2001, Lucia Howery opened a checking account and a savings account at the Bank of America. Although she named appellant as the beneficiary of the savings account, Howery was the only person authorized to withdraw funds from it.

In August 2005, Howery established the Lucia Howery Living Trust. The declaration of trust states that Howery, as trustor, "declares the establishment of a revocable living trust by delivering to the Trust without consideration all property described in the attached Schedule of Trust Property...." The schedule lists "Savings accounts," as among the categories of personal property delivered to the trust. Howery's declaration of trust further provides that, during her life, the trust will "hold, administer, and distribute all property" allocated to it for Howery's own benefit. At her death, the successor trustee

> "shall make the following distributions:
>
> I give my 2004 Infinity automobile to LORI YOUNKIN. ...
>
> I give the following savings and checking accounts to GABRIELLA REEVES, Bank of America [checking account], contents of my safe deposit box at Bank of America, and Bank of America [savings account]."

At some point, Howery authorized Gabriella Reeves to sign checks written on the Bank of America checking account. She received a single monthly statement for both accounts; the statements were addressed to both Howery and Reeves. Bank of America was unable to locate a signature card for the checking account. It had only one signature card for the savings account; it lists Howery as the account holder and Younkin as the beneficiary.

Howery died on April 29, 2009. At that point, respondent Araiza became the successor trustee. Respondent is the attorney who drafted Howery's living trust. He is also the son of Gabriella Reeves.

After Howery's death, respondent petitioned the trial court for an order allowing him to convey the Bank of America accounts to Reeves. Appellant filed a written objection on the sole ground that she is the owner of the savings account. The trial court found that Howery's living trust changed the beneficiary from appellant to Reeves.

Contentions

Appellant contends she is the sole owner of the savings account because Howery named her as the beneficiary and never changed that designation in a manner authorized by *section 5303*. Respondent contends the living trust documents were sufficient to change the beneficiary.

Discussion

Change in Beneficiary by Trust

The type of savings account Howery established is referred to in the Probate Code as a "Totten trust" account. "The term Totten trust describes a bank account opened by a depositor in his [or her] own name as trustee for another person where the depositor reserves the power to withdraw the funds during his [or her] lifetime. If the depositor has not revoked the trust then, upon his [or her] death, any balance left in the account is payable to the beneficiary." (Estate of Fisher (1988) 198 Cal. App.3d 418, 424 [244 Cal. Rptr. 5]; see also § 80.)

A Totten trust is one form of "multiple-party account" governed by the California Multiple–Party Accounts Law. (§§ 5100–5407.) Section 5302 describes the treatment of funds remaining in a multiple-party account on the death of one of the parties. Subdivisions (a) and (b) of section 5302 describe rights of survivorship in joint accounts (§§ 5130, 5302, subd. (a)), and pay on death or "P.O.D." accounts. (§§ 5130, 5139, 5140.) Where, as here, the multiple-party account is a Totten trust, "On death of the sole trustee ..., (A) any sums remaining on deposit belong to the person or persons named as beneficiaries, if surviving, or to the survivor of them if one or more die before the trustee, unless there is clear and convincing evidence of a different intent...." (§ 5302, subd. (c)(2).) Rights of survivorship, "cannot be changed by will." (§ 5302, subd. (e).)

Section 5303, subdivision (a) provides that the rights of survivorship described in section 5302 "are determined by the form of the account at the death of a party." (§ 5303, subd. (a).) Subdivision (b) lists the methods by which the terms of a multiple-party account may be modified. It provides:

> "Once established, the terms of a multiple-party account can be changed only by any of the following methods:
>
> (1) Closing the account and reopening it under different terms.
>
> (2) Presenting to the financial institution a modification agreement that is signed by all parties with a present right of withdrawal. ...
>
> (3) If the provisions of the terms of the account or deposit agreement provide a method of modification of the terms of the account, complying with those provisions.
>
> (4) As provided in subdivision (c) of Section 5405."[1]

Appellant contends that she remains the sole beneficiary of the savings account because Howery did not use one of the methods listed in section 5303, subdivision (b) to change the beneficiary. This narrow reading of the statute, however, fails to harmonize it with section 5302. Section 5302, subdivision (c)(2) provides that sums remaining on deposit in a Totten trust after the death of the sole trustee belong to the person named as beneficiary, "unless there is clear and convincing evidence of a different

---

1. Section 5405, subdivision (c) provides that the parties to a multiple-party account may give written notice to the financial institution that withdrawals from the account are not permitted except with the signature of more than one party, or more than one survivor.

intent. . . ." Here, although the signature card for the savings account named appellant as the beneficiary, there is clear and convincing evidence that Howery had a "different intent" at the time of her death. She established a living trust that expressly stated her intention to give the savings account to Reeves. The trial court properly relied on the living trust to find that Howery intended to change the beneficiary of her Totten trust from appellant to Reeves. Because the change was made by a living trust rather than by a will, it is not invalidated by section 5302, subdivision (e).

Conclusion

The judgment (order conveying title to personal property) is affirmed. Costs to respondent.

■ GILBERT, P. J., and COFFEE, J., concurred.

NOTES AND QUESTIONS

1. How did the court reconcile its conclusion with section 5303(b) of the California Multiple–Party Accounts Law? Are you persuaded?

Suppose, at the time she created the revocable trust, Lucia Howery's savings account had $5,000 on deposit. One year after she created the revocable trust, Howery deposited $50,000 in the account, and, at the bank's request, signed a new signature card with Lori Younkin's name pre-printed on it. Would the court have reached the same result? See Kostin v. Kent, 278 Mich.App. 47, 748 N.W.2d 583 (2008) (holding that subsequently executed Totten Trust designation supersedes disposition in revocable trust agreement).

2. If the revocable trust had provided "I leave my bank accounts to Gabriella Reeves," would the court have reached the same result? Would it matter whether Howery had other bank accounts?

3. Suppose Lucia Howery had not executed the 2005 revocable trust agreement, but had instead written a will leaving her savings account at Bank of America to Gabriella Reeves. How would the savings account have been distributed at Howery's death? Why would Lori Younkin take the account in that circumstance if she didn't take the account in the actual case?

The California approach with respect to Totten Trusts and wills is not universal. In New York, by statute, an explicit provision in decedent's will overrides a beneficiary designation. N.Y. EPTL § 7–5.2(2). Which approach do you prefer, and why?

4. What if Howery had established the revocable trust in 2000, *before* naming Younkin as the beneficiary of her savings account trust. Then, in 2005, Howery executed a pour-over will directing that all of her property be distributed to the 2000 revocable trust. How would the court have distributed the savings account trust?

5. If Lucia Howery had hired you in 2005 to draft a will or revocable trust agreement, what would you have done to avoid the litigation in this case? How would you know about the bank account trusts? How would you know whether she had other accounts about which she had forgotten? See Kent D. Schenkel, Testamentary Fragmentation and the Diminishing Role of the Will: An Argument for Revival, 41 Creighton L. Rev. 155, 160–62 (2008).

SECTION III. RETIREMENT PLAN ASSETS

Once upon a time, most Americans were covered by what are often called "traditional pension plans," or, in the vocabulary of the Employee Retirement Income Security Act (ERISA), "defined benefit plans." In a defined benefit plan, the employee, upon retirement, receives monthly (or weekly) payments for as long as the employee lives. At death, however, the defined benefit plan has no value to the employee; all of the benefits were paid out during the employee's lifetime, and there is nothing to distribute to the employee's successors (although some plans pay benefits for the life of the surviving spouse). Defined benefit plans, then, present few challenges for drafters of wills and trust instruments.

The last forty years, however, have brought a seismic shift in the way Americans provide for retirement. An ever-increasing number of employers have shifted from defined benefit plans to "defined contribution plans." These defined contribution plans do not guarantee participants any specific weekly or monthly income distribution. Instead, the employer makes payments on a regular basis into an account created for each employee. The employee often matches these payments with contributions of her own, building up a "nest egg" for retirement. Federal income tax rules create incentives for employees to contribute, and make it difficult or disadvantageous for participants to withdraw money from these accounts before reaching retirement age. Then, upon retirement, the participant begins withdrawing money from these accounts to finance her retirement.

The rise of defined contribution plans creates both an opportunity and a problem for estates lawyers. The opportunity exists because clients do not always "use up" the benefits in their defined contribution plans. Indeed, for many clients, the defined contribution plan will dwarf other forms of wealth. The problem is that—unbeknownst to many clients and all too many lawyers—the assets in these accounts do not necessarily pass through the client's probate estate. Instead, they pass in accordance with the payable-on-death designation the client made when the client agreed to participate in the plan. (Moreover, as we shall see, ERISA limits the power of a married client to designate persons other than his or her spouse.)

The problem is not limited to employer-sponsored retirement plans. A similar problem exists with Individual Retirement Accounts (IRAs), tax-advantaged retirement accounts for those who do not participate in employer-sponsored plans. As with employer-sponsored plans, participants make contributions to these plans while they are working, and typically begin withdrawals at retirement. And as with employer-sponsored plans, participants do not always use up their IRA assets before death. IRA assets, like defined contribution plan assets, pass in accordance with the payable-on-death designation in the contract with the entity that holds the assets. IRA assets are not, however, subject to the same ERISA rules.

Imagine, then, a client who walks into a lawyer's office and says "I want a simple will leaving all of my property to my children in equal shares." If the lawyer follows the client's direction, has the lawyer achieved the result the client expected? Consider the following case:

Nunnenman v. Estate of Grubbs

Court of Appeals of Arkansas, 2010.
2010 Ark.App. 75.

■ **PITTMAN, J.**

In 2003, decedent Donald Grubbs transferred his individual retirement account (IRA) to Raymond James and Associates, Inc., naming appellant as the beneficiary to receive the residue in the event of his death. Decedent was hospitalized in May 2005 and died on June 9 of that year. On June 3, 2005, decedent summoned an attorney to the hospital, where decedent made and executed a last will and testament that did not mention the IRA account. This will left decedent's entire estate to his mother, Shervena Grubbs, who was also named as executrix. In that capacity, Shervena Grubbs filed this action for an injunction freezing the assets of the IRA account based on her assertion that a note that she found in decedent's Bible months after his death had the effect of changing the beneficiary designation in the IRA account to make her the beneficiary. The trial court agreed and awarded her the account. Appellant asserts that the trial court clearly erred in so doing. We agree, and we reverse.

This case requires construction of three documents: a will, an IRA, and a handwritten note, which was assertedly found by Shervena Grubbs in a Bible some time after decedent's death. The cardinal rule for the interpretation of wills and other testamentary documents is that the intent of the testator should be ascertained from the instrument itself and effect given to that intent. Rowland v. Faulkenbury, 47 Ark. App. 12, 883 S.W.2d 848 (1994). The purpose of construing a will is to arrive at the testator's intention; however, that intention is not that which existed in his mind, but rather that which is expressed by the language of the instrument. Mills Heirs v. Wylie, 250 Ark. 703, 466 S.W.2d 937 (1971).

An IRA constitutes a contract between the person who establishes the IRA for his or her retirement and the financial institution that acts as the custodian of the IRA. Alexander v. McEwen, 367 Ark. 241, 239 S.W.3d 519 (2006). Like an insurance policy, an IRA includes designation of beneficiaries to receive the residue in the event of the retiree's death. *See id.* The rules pertaining to the construction of contracts are well settled: In construing any contract, we must consider the sense and meaning of the words used by the parties as they are taken and understood in their plain and ordinary meaning. Coleman v. Regions Bank, 364 Ark. 59, 216 S.W.3d 569 (2005). The intention of the parties is to be gathered, not from particular words and phrases, but from the whole context of the agreement. *Id.* When a written contract refers to another instrument and makes the terms of that instrument a part of the contract, the two are construed together as the agreement of the parties. Isbell v. Ed Ball Construction Co., 310 Ark. 81, 833 S.W.2d 370 (1992). When contracting parties express their intention in clear and unambiguous language in a written instrument, we must construe the written agreement according to the plain meaning of the language employed. However, where the meaning of a written contract is ambiguous, parol evidence is admissible to explain the writing. Coble v. Sexton, 71 Ark. App. 122, 27 S.W.3d 759 (2000). Ambiguities can be patent or latent. When, on its face, the reader can tell that something must be added to the written contract to determine the parties' intent, the ambiguity is patent; a latent ambiguity, on the other hand, arises from undisclosed facts or uncertainties of the written instrument. *Id.*

There are no Arkansas cases dealing specifically with attempts to change IRA beneficiaries by will, but the cases involving insurance policy beneficiaries, cited by appellant, are analogous and instructive. It is generally held that, where a life insurance policy reserves to the insured the right to change the beneficiary but specifies the manner in which the change may be made, the change must be made in the manner and mode prescribed by the policy, and according to most courts any attempt to make such change by will is ineffectual. *See generally* Wanda Ellen Wakefield, Annotation, Effectiveness of Change of Named Beneficiary of Life or Accident Insurance Policy by Will, 25 A.L.R. 4th 1164 (1992). However, Arkansas law is contrary to the general rule: Arkansas holds that a change of beneficiary can in fact be accomplished in a will so long as the language of the will is sufficient to identify the insurance policy involved and an intent to change the beneficiary. Pedron v. Olds, 193 Ark. 1026, 105 S.W.2d 70 (1937); see also Allen v. First National Bank, 261 Ark. 230, 547 S.W.2d 118 (1977).

With these principles in mind, we now turn to the documents involved in the present case. Decedent's IRA application and agreement with Raymond James and Associates, Inc., designated appellant as sole beneficiary of his IRA. Appellant was identified by name, social security number, and date of birth. The effect of this designation upon decedent's estate and the method of changing beneficiaries were specified as follows:

> I understand that if I designate "my will" or some variation thereof as my Beneficiary, that the Custodian shall interpret this term as my estate and that if I do not designate any Beneficiary, my Beneficiary shall also be deemed to be my estate. I understand that I may revoke this beneficiary designation at any time by completing and submitting a new beneficiary designation, which shall supercede all prior beneficiary designations. Such replacement designation shall be submitted on either a form provided by the Custodian for this purpose and/or in some other manner deemed acceptable to the Custodian.

Decedent's last will, made and executed with the assistance of an attorney shortly before his death, expressly revoked any prior will and stated:

> I hereby give, devise, and bequeath all of my estate and property, of every kind and nature, and wherever situated, to my mother, Shervena T. Grubbs, should she survive me.

This testamentary provision is unambiguous. As appellant argues, it is also inadequate to effect a change of beneficiary because the language is insufficient to identify the IRA account involved and an intent to change the beneficiary. See Allen v. First National Bank, 261 Ark. 230, 547 S.W.2d 118 (1977). The trial court found, however, that decedent's IRA beneficiary was changed from appellant to appellee by virtue of a note that appellee assertedly found in a Bible in decedent's home after his death. This document, handwritten on a Nations Bank notepad, provided in its entirety as follows:

> May 2005
>
> My Will
>
> I Donnie Grubbs want all of my estate All IRA and any SBC Telco and all other assets and worldly goods to go to my Mother Shervena Grubbs. Being of sound mind.
>
> Donnie Grubbs

The trial judge recognized in his letter opinion that this handwritten note appears dubious. He was right. It was found by appellee, who was the only person who could benefit from its discovery. The plausibility of appellee's account of this fortuitous discovery is not helped by the conflicts in the testimony at trial. Appellee testified that she found the note while at decedent's house in the company of decedent's former coworker, Mr. Tommy Moran, and that she immediately showed the note to Mr. Moran. However, Mr. Moran testified that appellee did not do so, and that he had never seen the document or known of its existence until the day of the trial.

Nevertheless, assuming that the note was authentic, and that it might properly be considered to contradict or vary the unambiguous terms of decedent's IRA beneficiary designation or his last will, the trial court clearly erred in finding that it was an effective change of decedent's IRA beneficiary. As appellant argues, if the note is regarded as a holographic will, it was revoked by the express terms of decedent's last will and by operation of law pursuant to Ark. Code Ann. § 28–25–109(a)(1) (Repl. 2004). If the note is not regarded as a will, then the rule permitting change of beneficiaries in a will has no application to it, and appellee had the burden of proving that decedent intended for the note to be a change of beneficiaries and did everything reasonably possible to effectuate a change of beneficiary. Allen v. First National Bank, supra. In light of the undisputed evidence that decedent could and did summon an attorney to his bedside mere days before his death and thereby execute a valid and unambiguous last will, the trial court could not reasonably find that decedent did everything reasonably possible to change beneficiaries given his failure to employ similar efforts to communicate his intent to do so to the custodian of the IRA.

Reversed and remanded.

■ VAUGHT, C.J., and GLADWIN, GLOVER, and MARSHALL, JJ., agree.

■ HART, J., dissenting.

[T]he issue before us is not whether the note should or should not have been admitted to probate as a holographic will—it was not. As noted previously, it was simply a piece of evidence regarding Grubbs's donative intent. The question, therefore, is whether the trial court properly admitted the document into evidence. The admission of evidence is left to the sound discretion of the trial court, and we will not reverse an evidentiary decision absent an abuse of that discretion. *Metzgar v. Rodgers, 83 Ark. App. 354, 128 S.W.3d 5 (2003).* It is axiomatic that a determination of the authenticity of the note, and subsequently its admissibility, was well within the trial judge's discretion. Finally, to the extent that Nunneman challenges the credibility of the witnesses, it is again axiomatic that appellate courts in Arkansas defer to the trial court's evaluation of the credibility of the witnesses. *O'Fallon v. O'Fallon ex rel. Ngar, 341 Ark. 138, 14 S.W.3d 506 (2000).*

... Nunneman argues that the trial judge erred in finding that the handwritten note and the will, considered together, effected a change in the beneficiary of Mr. Grubbs's account. She cites Arkansas law regarding life insurance policies and asserts that the law created by *Pedron v. Olds, 193 Ark. 1026, 105 S.W.2d 70 (1937)*, and its progeny should control.

Simply stated, we should have declined to apply the law concerning life insurance policies to the case at bar because the thing in question is an IRA, not a life insurance policy. The differences between a life insurance policy and an IRA with a pay-on-death designation are profound. In the first place, with certain exceptions not germane to this discussion, life insurance policies *always* pay money to a designated beneficiary; that is their purpose. Conversely, a pay-on-death designation in an IRA is a contingency that few of us hope will occur. Moreover, life insurance policies are governed by a different statutory scheme than pay-on-death designations.

NOTES AND QUESTIONS

1. Donnie Grubbs' will left all of his property to his mother. Why wasn't the will adequate to ensure that his mother received his IRA account?

2. If Donnie's will left any room for doubt about his intention, why wasn't that doubt erased by the letter signed in May 2005? In light of the conflicting testimony presented at trial, combined with Mrs. Grubbs' financial incentives, the court was undoubtedly suspicious about the origins of the letter. But suppose the court had harbored no suspicions at all. Would Mrs. Grubbs have been entitled to the IRA account? Why or why not?

3. Suppose Donnie's June 2005 will had provided explicitly "I devise my IRA at Raymond James and Associates, Inc., to my mother, Shervena Grubbs." Who would have been entitled to the account, Shervena Grubbs or Chrissey Nunneman?

As the *Nunnenman* opinion concedes, the Arkansas approach represents a minority view, both with respect to IRA accounts and with respect to life insurance. For the more common approach, see, e.g. Banc of America Investment Services, Inc. v. Davis, 2009 WL 277050 (Tenn App. 2009) [Testator's will explicitly leaves 25% of his IRA account to each of four relatives, but court awards account to testator's girlfriend, who had earlier been named as beneficiary on the bank's beneficiary designation form]; Lincoln Life and Annuity Co. v. Caswell, 31 A.D.3d 1, 813 N.Y.S.2d 385 (2006) [Insurance policy passes to contingent beneficiary named on insurance company's beneficiary designation form despite explicit provision in will, executed 15 years later, devising policy proceeds to designated individuals and charities].

New York's approach to insurance policy designations stands in stark contrast to New York's approach to beneficiary designations in bank account trusts, where, by statute, an explicit provision in decedent's will overrides a beneficiary designation. N.Y. EPTL § 7–5.2(2). Is there any reason for the difference in approach?

4. Does Shervena Grubbs have a malpractice claim against Donnie's lawyer? Why or why not?

5. ***Preparing a Checklist.*** How would Donnie Grubbs' lawyer have known that Donnie had an IRA? How would a lawyer know whether a client was the beneficiary of an employer-sponsored retirement plan? To guard against mistakes and omissions, an estates lawyer would be well advised to prepare a checklist of questions to ask a client about the nature of the client's assets. Prominent among questions on the list should be questions about any retirement accounts the client has, and about any life insurance the client might have.

If Donnie Grubbs' lawyer had learned of Donnie's IRA, what steps should the lawyer have taken to make sure that the IRA was distributed in accordance with Donnie's wishes and to avoid litigation over disposition of the IRA?

6. Many people establish IRA accounts early in their careers, when their principal concern is sheltering assets from income taxation. Is it likely that these account holders think seriously about the beneficiaries they name? Is it likely that they will remember, 20 years later, who they named on the bank's beneficiary designation form? If not, why should courts place more weight on that designation than on a decedent's will, written at a time when decedent is focused on succession to his or her estate?

The court in *Grubbs* resolved the disposition of Donnie's IRA as a matter of state law. In the course of its opinion, the court suggested that if Donnie's will had explicitly left his IRA to his mother, the court would have given effect to the will provision. Suppose, however, the dispute had not been over an IRA, but had instead involved disposition of an employer-sponsored defined contribution plan. Could the Arkansas court have given effect to an explicit will provision leaving the plan assets to Donnie's mother? Consider the following case:

Kennedy v. Plan Administrator for DuPont Savings and Investment Plan

Supreme Court of the United States, 2009.
555 U.S. 285, 129 S.Ct. 865, 172 L.Ed.2d 662.

■ JUSTICE SOUTER delivered the opinion of the Court.

The Employee Retirement Income Security Act of 1974 (ERISA), 88 Stat. 829, 29 U.S.C. § 1001 et seq., generally obligates administrators to manage ERISA plans "in accordance with the documents and instruments governing" them. § 1104(a)(1)(D). At a more specific level, the Act requires covered pension benefit plans to "provide that benefits ... under the plan may not be assigned or alienated," § 1056(d)(1), but this bar does not apply to qualified domestic relations orders (QDROs), § 1056(d)(3). The question here is whether the terms of the limitation on assignment or alienation invalidated the act of a divorced spouse, the designated beneficiary under her ex-husband's ERISA pension plan, who purported to waive her entitlement by a federal common law waiver embodied in a divorce decree that was not a QDRO. We hold that such a waiver is not rendered invalid by the text of the antialienation provision, but that the plan administrator properly disregarded the waiver owing to its conflict with the designation made by the former husband in accordance with plan documents.

I

The decedent, William Kennedy, worked for E. I. DuPont de Nemours & Company and was a participant in its savings and investment plan (SIP), with power both to "designate any beneficiary or beneficiaries ... to receive all or part" of the funds upon his death, and to "replace or revoke such designation." App. 48. The plan requires "[a]ll authorizations, designations and requests concerning the Plan [to] be made by employees in the manner prescribed by the [plan administrator]," *id.*, at 52, and provides forms for designating or changing a beneficiary, *id.*, at 34, 56–57. If at the time the participant dies "no surviving spouse exists and no beneficiary designation is in effect, distribution shall be made to, or in accordance with the directions of, the executor or administrator of the decedent's estate." *Id.*, at 48.

The SIP is an ERISA " 'employee pension benefit plan,' " 497 F.3d 426, 427 (5th Cir. 2007); 29 U.S.C. § 1002(2), and the parties do not dispute that the plan satisfies ERISA's antialienation provision, § 1056(d)(1), which requires it to "provide that benefits provided under the plan may not be assigned or alienated." The plan does, however, permit a beneficiary to submit a "qualified disclaimer" of benefits as defined under the Tax Code, see 26 U.S.C. § 2518, which has the effect of switching the beneficiary to an "alternate ... determined according to a valid beneficiary designation made by the deceased." Supp. Record 86–87 (Exh. 15).

In 1971, William married Liv Kennedy, and, in 1974, he signed a form designating her to take benefits under the SIP, but naming no contingent beneficiary to take if she disclaimed her interest. 497 F.3d at 427. William and Liv divorced in 1994, subject to a decree that Liv "is ... divested of all right, title, interest, and claim in and to ... [a]ny and all sums ... the proceeds [from], and any other rights related to any ... retirement plan, pension plan, or like benefit program existing by reason of [William's] past or present or future employment." App. to Pet. for Cert. 64–65. William did not, however, execute any documents removing Liv as the SIP beneficiary, 497 F.3d at 428, even though he did execute a new beneficiary-designation form naming his daughter, Kari Kennedy, as the beneficiary under DuPont's Pension and Retirement Plan, also governed by ERISA.

On William's death in 2001, petitioner Kari Kennedy was named executrix and asked DuPont to distribute the SIP funds to William's Estate. *Ibid.* DuPont, instead, relied on William's designation form and paid the balance of some $400,000 to Liv. *Ibid.* The Estate then sued respondents DuPont and the SIP plan administrator (together, DuPont), claiming that the divorce decree amounted to a waiver of the SIP benefits on Liv's part, and that DuPont had violated ERISA by paying the benefits to William's designee.

So far as it matters here, the District Court entered summary judgment for the Estate, to which it ordered DuPont to pay the value of the SIP benefits. The court relied on Fifth Circuit precedent establishing that a beneficiary can waive his rights to the proceeds of an ERISA plan " 'provided that the waiver is explicit, voluntary, and made in good faith.' " App. to Pet. for Cert. 38.

The Fifth Circuit nonetheless reversed. The Court of Appeals held that Liv's waiver constituted an assignment or alienation of her interest in the SIP benefits to the Estate, and so could not be honored. *Id.,* at 430. The court relied heavily on the ERISA provision for bypassing the antialienation provision when a marriage breaks up: under 29 U.S.C. § 1056(d)(3), a court order that satisfies certain statutory requirements is known as a qualified domestic relations order, which is exempt from the bar on assignment or alienation. Because the Kennedys' divorce decree was not a QDRO, the Fifth Circuit reasoned that it could not give effect to Liv's waiver incorporated in it, given that "ERISA provides a specific mechanism—the QDRO—for addressing the elimination of a spouse's interest in plan benefits, but that mechanism is *not* invoked." 497 F.3d at 431.

We granted certiorari to resolve a split among the Courts of Appeals and State Supreme Courts over a divorced spouse's ability to waive pension plan benefits through a divorce decree not amounting to a QDRO. We subsequently realized that this case implicates the further split over whether a beneficiary's federal common law waiver of plan benefits is effective where that waiver is inconsistent with plan documents, and after oral argument we invited supplemental briefing on that latter issue, upon which the disposition of this case ultimately turns. We now affirm, albeit on reasoning different from the Fifth Circuit's rationale.

II

[The Court held that the wife's waiver of benefits did not constitute an assignment or alienation in violation of the statute].

III

The waiver's escape from inevitable nullity under the express terms of the antialienation clause does not, however, control the decision of this case, and the question remains whether the plan administrator was required to honor Liv's waiver with the consequence of distributing the SIP balance to the Estate. We hold that it was not, and that the plan administrator did its statutory ERISA duty by paying the benefits to Liv in conformity with the plan documents.

ERISA requires "[e]very employee benefit plan [to] be established and maintained pursuant to a written instrument," 29 U.S.C. § 1102(a)(1), "specify[ing] the basis on which payments are made to and from the plan," § 1102(b)(4). The plan administrator is obliged to act "in accordance with the documents and instruments governing the plan insofar as such documents and instruments are consistent with the provisions of [Title I] and [Title IV] of [ERISA]," § 1104(a)(1)(D), and the Act provides no exemption from this duty when it comes time to pay benefits.

The Estate's claim therefore stands or falls by "the terms of the plan," § 1132(a)(1)(B), a straightforward rule of hewing to the directives of the plan documents that lets employers " 'establish a uniform administrative scheme, [with] a set of standard procedures to guide processing of claims and disbursement of benefits.' " Egelhoff v. Egelhoff, 532 U.S. 141, 148 (2001) (quoting Fort Halifax Packing Co. v. Coyne, 482 U.S. 1, 9 (1987)); see also Curtiss–Wright Corp. v. Schoonejongen, 514 U.S. 73, 83 (1995) (ERISA's statutory scheme "is built around reliance on the face of written plan documents"). The point is that by giving a plan participant a clear set of instructions for making his own instructions clear, ERISA forecloses any justification for enquiries into nice expressions of intent, in favor of the virtues of adhering to an uncomplicated rule: "simple administration, avoid[ing] double liability, and ensur[ing] that beneficiaries get what's coming quickly, without the folderol essential under less-certain rules." Fox Valley & Vicinity Constr. Workers Pension Fund v. Brown, 897 F.2d 275, 283 (7th Cir. 1990) (Easterbrook, J., dissenting).

And the cost of less certain rules would be too plain. Plan administrators would be forced "to examine a multitude of external documents that might purport to affect the dispensation of benefits," Altobelli v. IBM Corp., 77 F.3d 78, 82–83 (4th Cir. 1996) (Wilkinson, C. J., dissenting), and be drawn into litigation like this over the meaning and enforceability of purported waivers. The Estate's suggestion that a plan administrator could resolve these sorts of disputes through interpleader actions merely restates the problem with the Estate's position: it would destroy a plan administra-

Newman v Wells Fargo bank p 844

Issue - child was adopted by a relative of his or her genetic parent. at a time when such adoptions terminated the rights to inherit from the genetic family, but the state statute now permits inheritance through the genetic family

2) As trustee of the testamentary trust, Wells Fargo petition alleges that Newman had been adopted by his stepfather W. E Newman, and asks if Newman was "issue of" Carl Mitchell at the time of Mitchells death.

3) In looking at the laws of intestacy as a guide to testator's true intent when a will provision is ambiguous, should a court consider the law in effect at the time the will or testamentary trust was executed to determine if a child adopted out of a designated ancestor's family is among "issue" + "children" the testator intended to benefit, or should apply the law in effect at the death of the ancestor through whom the child may take.

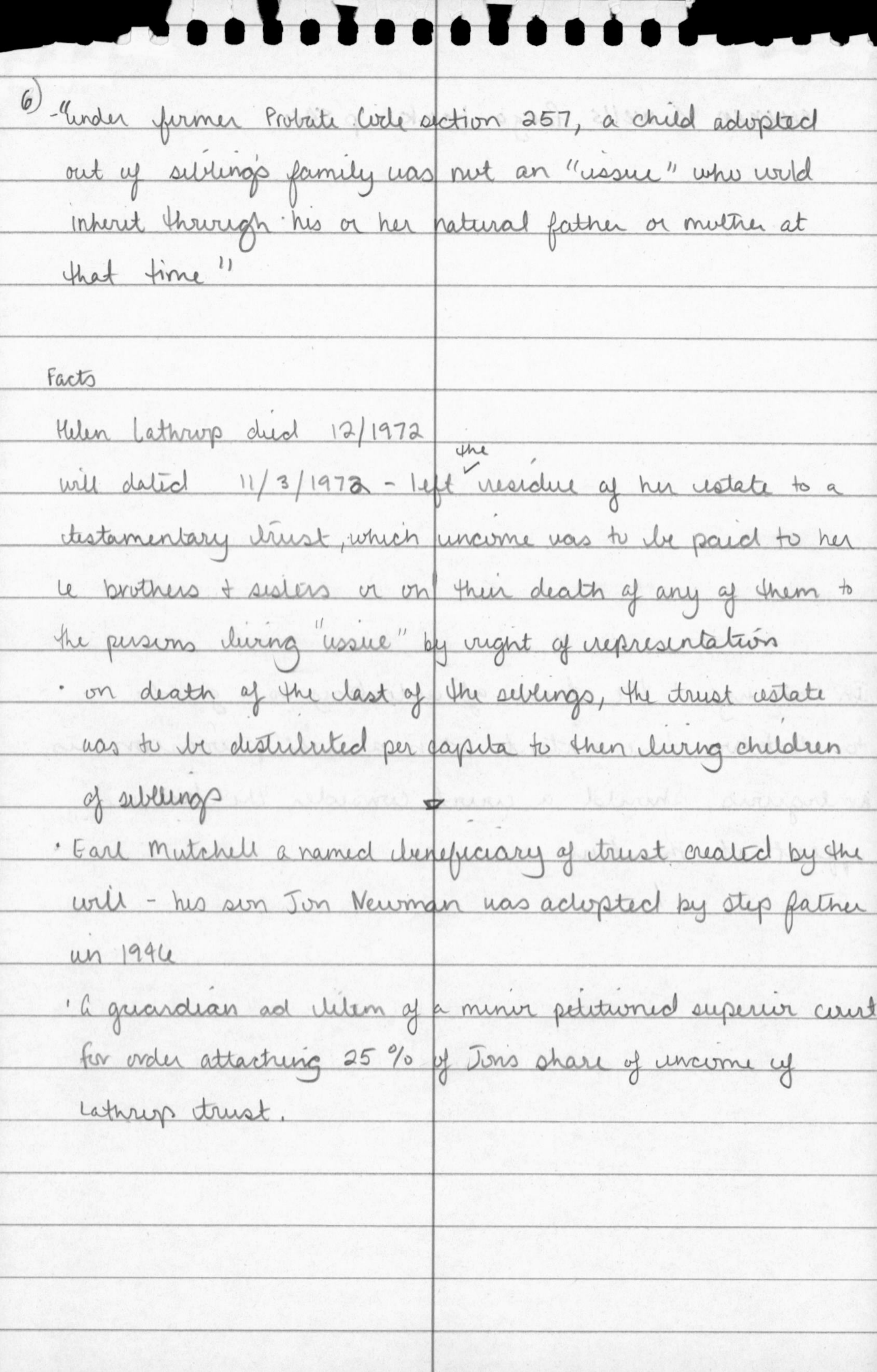

6) -"Under former Probate Code section 257, a child adopted out of sibling's family was not an "issue" who would inherit through his or her natural father or mother at that time"

Facts

Helen Lathrop died 12/1972

will dated 11/3/1972 - left the residue of her estate to a testamentary trust, which income was to be paid to her le brothers + sisters or on their death of any of them to the persons living "issue" by right of representation

- on death of the last of the siblings, the trust estate was to be distributed per capita to then living children of siblings

- Earl Mitchell a named beneficiary of trust created by the will - his son Jon Newman was adopted by step father in 1946

- A guardian ad litem of a minor petitioned superior court for order attaching 25 % of Jon's share of income of Lathrop trust.

tor's ability to look at the plan documents and records conforming to them to get clear distribution instructions, without going into court.

The Estate of course is right that this guarantee of simplicity is not absolute. The very enforce-ability of QDROs means that sometimes a plan administrator must look for the beneficiaries outside plan documents notwithstanding § 1104(a)(1)(D); § 1056(d)(3)(J) provides that a "person who is an alternate payee under a [QDRO] shall be considered for purposes of any provision of [ERISA] a beneficiary under the plan." But this in effect means that a plan administrator who enforces a QDRO must be said to enforce plan documents, not ignore them. In any case, a QDRO enquiry is relatively discrete, given the specific and objective criteria for a domestic relations order that qualifies as a QDRO, see §§ 1056(d)(3)(C), (D), requirements that amount to a statutory checklist working to "spare [an administrator] from litigation-fomenting ambiguities," Metropolitan Life Ins. Co. v. Wheaton, 42 F.3d 1080, 1084 (7th Cir. 1994). This is a far cry from asking a plan administrator to figure out whether a claimed federal common law waiver was knowing and voluntary, whether its language addressed the particular benefits at issue, and so forth, on into factually complex and subjective determinations. See, *e.g.,* Altobelli, supra, at 83 (Wilkinson, C. J., dissenting) ("[W]aiver provisions are often sweeping in their terms, leaving their precise effect on plan benefits unclear"); Mohamed v. Kerr, 53 F.3d 911, 915 (8th Cir. 1995) (making "fact-driven determination" that marriage termination agreement constituted a valid waiver under federal common law).

These are good and sufficient reasons for holding the line, just as we have done in cases of state laws that might blur the bright-line requirement to follow plan documents in distributing benefits. Two recent preemption cases are instructive here. Boggs v. Boggs, 520 U.S. 833, held that ERISA preempted a state law permitting the testamentary transfer of a nonparticipant spouse's community property interest in undistributed pension plan benefits. And in *Egelhoff* we held that ERISA preempted a state law providing that the designation of a spouse as the beneficiary of a nonprobate asset is revoked automatically upon divorce. 532 U.S. at 143. We said the law was at fault for standing in the way of making payments "simply by identifying the beneficiary specified by the plan documents," id., at 148, and thus for purporting to "undermine the congressional goal of 'minimiz[ing] the administrative and financial burden[s]' on plan administrators," id., at 149–150.

What goes for inconsistent state law goes for a federal common law of waiver that might obscure a plan administrator's duty to act "in accordance with the documents and instruments." See Mertens v. Hewitt Associates, 508 U.S. 248, 259 (1993). And this case does as well as any other in pointing out the wisdom of protecting the plan documents rule. Under the terms of the SIP Liv was William's designated beneficiary. The plan provided an easy way for William to change the designation, but for whatever reason he did not. The plan provided a way to disclaim an interest in the SIP account, but Liv did not purport to follow it. The plan administrator therefore did exactly what § 1104(a)(1)(D) required: "the documents control, and those name [the ex-wife]." McMillan v. Parrott, 913 F.2d 310, 312 (6th Cir. 1990).

IV

Although Liv's waiver was not rendered a nullity by the terms of § 1056, the plan administrator properly distributed the SIP benefits to Liv in accordance with the plan documents. The judgment of the Court of Appeals is affirmed on the latter ground.

NOTES AND QUESTIONS

1. In the portion of the Supreme Court's opinion not reproduced above, the Court analogized the interest of a retirement plan beneficiary to the interest of a spendthrift trust beneficiary. The Court reasoned that because a beneficiary is entitled to disclaim an interest in a spendthrift trust (even though the beneficiary may not alienate or assign that interest), a retirement plan beneficiary's waiver of rights should not be treated as alienation or assignment of the beneficiary's interest.

Why should ERISA treat the interest of a beneficiary of a retirement plan the way courts treat the interests of a spendthrift trust beneficiary?

2. Consider the ERISA provision on which the Court relied in holding that DuPont's plan administrator had properly distributed plan benefits to Liv. Who was that provision designed to protect? If a waiver itself is not inconsistent with ERISA, does the Kennedy estate have a claim against Liv? If not, why not?

3. What steps should William Kennedy's divorce lawyer have taken to effectuate the divorce agreement?

4. For most employer-sponsored defined contribution plans, federal law treats the employee's spouse as the beneficiary of funds in the plan account at the time of the employee's death. The employee can designate a different beneficiary only if the spouse consents to the designation.

When the employee retires, however, the employee typically has the option to transfer plan assets—without the spouse's consent—to an IRA. Federal law does not constrain the employee's choice of beneficiary once the funds are in an IRA.

5. Why didn't William Kennedy's divorce operate to revoke the beneficiary designation? Suppose Kennedy's home state had adopted UPC 2–804, which provides that a divorce "revokes any revocable . . . disposition or appointment of property made by a divorced individual to his [or her] former spouse in a governing instrument." Would the Supreme Court have reached a different result? Why or why not? See Egelhoff v. Egelhoff, 532 U.S. 141, 121 S.Ct. 1322, 149 L.Ed.2d 264 (2001).

If William Kennedy's money had been in an IRA, and the beneficiary designation named Liv as the beneficiary, would Liv have been entitled to take? Why or why not? Doesn't the custodian of the assets face precisely the same problems faced by DuPont's plan administrator in the Kennedy case?

NOTE ON CHOOSING PLAN BENEFICIARIES

In both Grubbs and Kennedy, the decedent had designated plan beneficiaries without consulting a lawyer. Moreover, in Grubbs, the lawyer who prepared Donnie Grubbs' will never made any effort to ascertain or change plan beneficiaries. Suppose, however, a lawyer diligently inquires about a client's beneficiary designation forms, and the client has no recollection of whom she has designated as the plan beneficiaries. Once the lawyer tracks down the necessary forms, what recommendations should the lawyer make? (As noted above, if the plan is an employer-sponsored plan, the employee's spouse might have to consent to any designation).

One alternative is to name the client's estate as the beneficiary. That alternative has one significant advantage: it assures that the retirement account and the rest of the client's estate will be administered as an integrated whole even if some future lawyer redrafts the client's will without taking account of beneficiary designations. That advantage, however, will generally be outweighed by significant disadvantages. First, subjecting plan assets to estate administration may generate unnecessary commissions for the estate executor. Second, the income tax advantages associated with retirement plan assets can generally be extended for a longer period if the plan beneficiary is an individual rather than the estate.

The other alternatives are to name individual beneficiaries, or to designate a trust as the beneficiary of the plan assets. (Of course, if the client designates a trust, the client must be sure to create the trust that serves as the beneficiary of plan assets). The choice between individuals and a trust should reflect many of the same concerns the client faces in deciding how to distribute other assets.

SECTION IV. LIFE INSURANCE

A. INTRODUCTION

Many people buy life insurance to assure financial security for their dependents in case of the untimely death of a breadwinner. Parents buy life insurance to assure the funding of their children's college education and working spouses or partners (or higher income spouses) insure themselves to protect "nonworking" (or lower income) spouses or partners, just as nonworking spouses insure themselves to allow for the hiring of domestic help to care for home and hearth. As Professor Smith puts it:

> [T]erm insurance is useful when the need for money in the event of the insured's death is limited to a particular time period. For example, insuring a parent may be a useful application of term insurance if his or her work provides an income stream which would pay for the

> college education of his or her children. Likewise, insuring a business owner for the term of a substantial business loan is another situation in which term insurance may be useful.

Robert B. Smith, Reconsidering the Taxation of Life Insurance Proceeds Through the Lens of Current Estate Planning, 15 Va. Tax Rev. 283, 291 (1995).

Life insurance is available in two basic forms: "term" insurance and "whole life" insurance. Term insurance provides a pure death benefit; the policy has no cash value, and the policy premiums reflect the risk of the insured's death during the term. By contrast, when an insured buys a whole life policy, the insurance company invests much of the premium to generate a cash surrender value for the insured, and to protect the insured against increases in premiums as the insured grows older. For that reason, term insurance sells for a fraction of the cost of whole life insurance. For instance, at age 30, a $100,000 term policy might cost about $200 per year, while the same $200 might buy about $14,000 of whole life. As a result, if the insured's primary concern is protecting the family against lost income, term insurance is a far better investment. Life insurance salesmen love to sell more expensive whole life policies, emphasizing cash surrender value and the fact that, if the policy is not surrendered, the insured will remain insured for life. But for those customers concerned primarily about protecting the family's financial security, a common piece of advice is "buy term and invest the difference."

Buying life insurance can generate advantages beyond protecting financial security. In some jurisdictions, life insurance proceeds are insulated from claims by the insured's creditors. In others, life insurance proceeds are insulated from a spouse's right of election. Consider, for instance, the following Pennsylvania statute:

20 PENNSYLVANIA STATUTES ANNOTATED

SECTION 2203 RIGHT OF ELECTION; RESIDENT DECEDENT

> (a) Property subject to election. When a married person domiciled in this Commonwealth dies, his surviving spouse has a right to an elective share of one-third of the following property:[a broad range of assets] * * *
>
> (b) Property not subject to election. The provisions of subsection (a) shall not be construed to include any of the following * * *
>
> > (2) The proceeds of insurance * * * on the life of the decedent.
>
> Note, however, that the UPC's elective share provisions do not extend the same protection to life insurance proceeds.
>
> Just as an estates lawyer must ask about any retirement plan assets owned by a decedent, the lawyer must also inquire about life insurance policies. Like retirement accounts, life insurance proceeds pass to designated beneficiaries by contract, and therefore pass outside the probate estate. As with retirement accounts, lawyers should take care to assure that beneficiaries are properly designated, because as

the court in Nunnenman indicates, in most states, even a clear provision in the insured's will does not supersede the policy designation. Consider the following excerpt:

Lincoln Life and Annuity Company of New York v. Caswell

Supreme Court of New York, Appellate Division, 2006.
31 A.D.3d 1, 813 N.Y.S.2d 385.

■ FRIEDMAN, J.:

There is no dispute as to the material facts. In April 1985, Aetna Life Insurance and Annuity Company (Aetna) issued Policy No. U1179854, a life insurance policy in the face amount of $200,000 (the '854 policy), to Martha L. Hubbard (hereinafter, the insured). The '854 policy provides that, to change the beneficiary, "[a] signed request must be sent to Aetna. When Aetna gives its written acceptance, the change will take effect as of the date the request was signed."

On two occasions, the insured changed the beneficiary designation in the manner provided by the '854 policy. Her last such change was made by a signed request dated October 9, 1987. That request, made on a printed form Aetna provided for the purpose, designated the insured's son, Robert W. Hubbard, Jr., as primary beneficiary, and defendant Bennie Caswell, Jr. (sued herein as Benjamin Caswell), as contingent beneficiary. Aetna's acceptance of that request is dated October 27, 1987. Since Robert W. Hubbard, Jr. predeceased the insured, giving effect to the October 1987 beneficiary designation would make Caswell the sole beneficiary of the '854 policy.

More than 15 years after she filed the October 1987 beneficiary designation with Aetna, the insured executed a last will and testament, dated June 16, 2003. This will specifically refers to the '854 policy by number, and purports to "devise and bequeath" portions of the proceeds of that policy to various individuals and charities. It appears that the will purports to leave Caswell only $25,000 of the proceeds of the '854 policy. There is no indication that the insured ever took any steps to have the legatees of the '854 policy under the will designated as beneficiaries of the policy in the manner provided by the policy itself.

The insured died on May 17, 2004, and her will of June 2003 has been filed in probate proceedings in Surrogate's Court. In June 2004, Caswell and the nominated executors of the insured's estate, by their respective attorneys, sent letters to the insurance company asserting conflicting claims to the proceeds of the '854 policy.

[T]he dispositive question that emerges in this case is whether the insured's specific testamentary disposition of the '854 policy in her will can be deemed to constitute "substantial compliance" with that policy's requirements for effecting a change of beneficiary. Our answer to this question is "no." Although the will may constitute some evidence of the insured's subjective intentions, the making of the will plainly was not an attempt to comply with the simple change-of-beneficiary procedure set forth in the '854 policy. So far as the record shows, in the 15 years the insured lived after effecting the October 1987 change of beneficiary, she did nothing at all that could be characterized as an attempt to comply with the change-of-beneficiary procedure required by the policy, which, again, was simply to send the insurer a signed request-a procedure the insured herself had followed twice before she executed her will. Nor is there any evidence that the insured was "physically or mentally incapable of attempting to substantially comply with the requirements of the policy" (*McCarthy v. Aetna Life Ins. Co.*, 92 N.Y. 2d 436, at 441–442, 681 N.Y.S. 2d 790, 704 N.E. 2d 557).

In view of the foregoing, Caswell's motion for summary judgment should have been granted to the extent of declaring him the sole beneficiary of the '854 policy.

* * *

B. Some Basic Tax-Oriented Estate Planning With Insurance

If a decedent dies owning an insurance policy on his own life, the full value of the death proceeds will be included in his estate. Most people buy insurance on their own life. Note that one tenet of estate planning is to always try to get future growth out of a client's estate. Further note that insurance is one of the few assets in this world that is guaranteed to go up in value: the policy is always worth more once the insured dies than it is while the insured is alive! As a result, the policy is an asset that is emotionally easy to give away. Giving away an insurance policy can have significant estate tax advantages. If the insured gives the policy away when its value is low, the gift will not generate significant gift tax consequences. Indeed, in many cases, the annual gift tax exclusion or the lifetime estate and gift tax exemption may permit the insured to give away the policy without any adverse tax consequences. By contrast, if the insured dies owning the policy, the estate tax generated by the policy will be more significant, because the policy's value is at its highest at the time of the insured's death. Life insurance proceeds owned by a decedent are included in the decedent's taxable estate. As a result, some people who want insurance for their families do not want to own the insurance themselves; they would prefer that another person, or a family trust that is not in the insured's estate, own the policy. When the insured person dies, the policy proceeds are not in the insured's estate because he never owned it.

Harry and Wilma Childe are married and have one child, Harold. Harry and Wilma are prosperous. Harold earns a meager salary. As long as Harry and Wilma are alive they will continue to provide for Harold's needs beyond his meager salary and act as his safety net. However, they want the psychological assurance that after they are gone Harold will be provided for. Harry and Wilma decide to meet this goal with insurance. They buy a so-called second-to-die (or survivor) policy that only pays at the death of the survivor of Harry and Wilma. The premiums on such policies can be lower than one might think because of the delay in the payout of the proceeds.

If Harry owns any policy on his life it will be subject to estate tax in his estate when he dies. The same would be true as to Wilma if she owned the policy. A tax-oriented solution is obvious—the policy can be bought and owned by Harold; and his parents can give him money to pay the premiums.

What are the tax virtues of this plan? The gifts of cash to pay the insurance premiums would qualify for the annual gift tax exclusion (in 2011 $13,000, or $26,000 if Harry and Wilma both make the gift). When the surviving parent dies the policy will not be included in the survivor's estate because the survivor will have nothing of value vis a vis the policy—no proceeds and no incidents of ownership. Why? Because the policy belonged to Harold all those years! And there will be no generation-skipping transfer tax problems because there will be no taxable skipping of a generation. Thus the value of the insurance policy passes to Harold at virtually no tax cost. Of course, if Harold dies first, the value of the property passes through his estate, but the value will be lower than face value (because his surviving parent has not yet died), and, in any event, Harold may not be fortunate enough to be subject to estate taxation.

PROBLEM

INTERNAL REVENUE CODE SECTION 2042.

PROCEEDS OF LIFE INSURANCE

The value of the gross estate shall include the value of all property

(1) Receivable by the executor. To the extent of the amount receivable by the executor as insurance under policies on the life of the decedent.

(2) Receivable by other beneficiaries. To the extent of the amount receivable by all other beneficiaries as insurance under policies on the life of the decedent with respect to which the decedent possessed at his death any of the incidents of ownership, exercisable either alone or in conjunction with any other person.

* * *

Harry, a 50 year old man, buys a $1 million insurance policy on his life. The annual premium is $13,000 per year. He dies owning the policy, which is payable to his daughter Jill. He has an estate which exceeds the lifetime exemption, so his estate will be taxed at a marginal rate of 35%. How much estate tax, if any, will Harry's estate have to pay on account of the policy?

Assume that Harry had Jill buy the policy when he was age 50, and that each year he gave her $13,000 which she then used to pay the premiums on the policy. Again, he has a taxable estate. How much estate tax, if any, will Harry's estate have to pay on account of the policy?

Assume that Harry had no use for insurance and just kept the premiums in the bank. Assume at his death that Harry had $100,000 in the bank on account of the insurance he never bought. Again, he has a taxable estate. How much estate tax, if any, will Harry's estate have to pay on account of the policy he never bought?

What planning techniques do your answers bring to mind?

The next level of sophistication involves having the policy owned not by an individual (Harold), but rather by an irrevocable trust in which the insureds, Harry and Wilma, have no beneficial interest. When the insured dies, again there will be no tax consequences. In a perfect world the donors, here Harry and Wilma, will give the trust enough money each year to cover the premiums and they will make those premium transfers free of any gift tax consequences. The trust prevents Harold from doing anything "stupid" with the money. (Or maybe Harold has two siblings who can't get along with one another and the trust is there to be sure the premiums get paid and the death proceeds get distributed in equal shares.) See Chawla v. Transamerica Occidental Life Ins. Co., 440 F.3d 639 (4th Cir. 2006) (confirming that a trustee has an insurable interest and thus can buy such insurance).

There is, however, a worm in the apple. Oversimplifying, the gifts of money to the trust will not qualify for the annual exclusion (let's say $13,000) because gifts to a trust are not gifts of a "present interest" under section 2503(b) of the Internal Revenue Code. Therefore, they do not qualify for the gift tax exclusion. The current solution, which the IRS accepts, but does not like, is to draft the trust so that it qualifies as a so-called "Crummey trust." We have discussed Crummey trusts in Chapter Seven. See Crummey v. Commissioner, 397 F.2d 82 (9th Cir.1968).

As a reminder, a Crummey trust gives one or more individuals (usually family members who are beneficiaries under the trust) the power to pull out $13,000 from the trust for a limited period of time. Thus the trust created by Harry and Wilma might give Harold a 30 day window to pull out $13,000. Of course, Harold would not actually withdraw the money, even though there's no formal agreement precluding him from withdrawing the money. Why do you think the Crummey power qualifies for the present interest gift tax exclusion ($13,000 at this writing)? Why do you think Harold will never take out the $13,000? Harold's withdrawal power makes the first $13,000 gift a nontaxable transfer. If Harold has a child then the child, even if a minor, can also have a power to withdraw and the gift tax exclusion is available for another $13,000.

When the trustee receives the insurance proceeds at the death of the insured they are held according to the terms of the trust. If the trust is one that runs afoul of the generation-skipping transfer tax then settlors can assign portions of their GST exemption ($5,000,000 in 2011) to the trust as they donate premium money each year.

The intricacies of this transaction are beyond the scope of this course, but the above should give you a sense of this kind of planning.

CHAPTER THIRTEEN

ESTATE AND TRUST ADMINISTRATION

In this chapter, we explore the responsibilities of two kinds of fiduciaries: the people in charge of probate estates (personal representatives, or administrators or executors) and the people in charge of trusts (trustees). There is meaningful overlap, but they have different jobs and, to one degree or another, different duties. The current wisdom is, however, that they have more in common than not. And there are other fiduciaries such as guardians, conservators, custodians under the Uniform Transfers to Minors Act and the like. They function more like trustees than personal representatives. With that in mind, we will focus on personal representatives and trustees.

In a sentence, personal representatives wind up a decedent's affairs and trustees administer ongoing trusts. Personal representatives are liquidators and trustees manage and dispense portfolios.

Estate and trust administration has earned its reputation for being cumbersome and costly. There are reasons why efforts to streamline the process have met with resistance. First, the interests of fiduciaries and the interests of beneficiaries are not always aligned. The processes surrounding estate and trust administration are designed in part to protect beneficiaries against careless or faithless fiduciaries. Second, the players in the process—lawyers among them—derive significant income from administration, and change threatens that income stream.

As you work through the materials in this chapter, consider whether existing doctrinal rules serve the purposes for which they were designed. Consider also how you would advise your clients—settlors, fiduciaries, or beneficiaries—to work within the existing doctrinal framework.

SECTION I. ESTATE ADMINISTRATION

"I have always understood that it takes about three years to settle an estate. In civilized countries, that is; there are countries here in Europe where it can go on for ten if there is enough money to pay the costs." Robertson Davies, The Manticore 71 (1972).

In today's United States three years may be a reasonable estimate if the executor has to file a federal estate tax return. In a nontaxable estate an energetic executor can hope to be done in a year. Settling an estate is often akin to running, or liquidating, a small business. An executor or an administrator has to collect (or marshal) the decedent's assets, pay his bills and taxes, and deliver the net estate to the devisees or heirs. In this section, we consider the "why" and "how" of estate administration—along with some of the perils and pitfalls.

A. Do We Need to Administer the Estate?

A client, Fran, walks into your office with the following story: My mother has just died. Her will leaves half of her property to my sister Emily, and half to me. She has some jewelry, some furniture, and a coin collection—worth a total of about $30,000. What should we do?

If you were advising Fran, would you suggest probating her mother's will? There are two basic reasons for probating a will, and neither of them is applicable to Fran's mother.

First, probate provides proof of ownership. Indeed, the very word "probate" derives from the same Latin root as the word "prove." Whenever a potential will beneficiary (or intestate heir) will need to prove ownership, probate may be necessary. When an estate includes real property, probate will almost inevitably be necessary. Without probate, the decedent's will beneficiaries won't be able to prove to potential purchasers that they actually own the real property they are trying to sell. Even if the will beneficiaries have no present desire to sell, probate will pave the way for future transfers. Proof may be important even if the decedent owned no real estate. For instance, suppose a decedent owned stocks or bonds, or even had $50,000 in a savings account. If one of decedent's children showed up and asked for the securities or money, would you expect that broker or the bank to transfer the assets or turn over the cash? How would the bank or the broker know that the will left the property to the children, or even that the will was valid? To protect its own interests against other claimants, the bank or broker might insist on probate before transferring the decedent's assets.

Second, probate protects beneficiaries against adverse claims to the estate assets—both by other potential beneficiaries, and by creditors. Probate establishes a short statute of limitations on claims by persons who might challenge the will, and against persons who have claims against the decedent. Suppose, for instance, Fran's mother had been in business, and several clients had been dissatisfied with goods or services she had provided. Fran's mother's estate is liable for any claims against Fran's mother. In the absence of any probate proceeding, those claims would be subject to the ordinary contract statute of limitations. Probate requires notice to creditors. What effect does notice have? Consider the following statute:

Nevada Revised Statutes Annotated

Section 147.040 Claims: Limit on time for filing.

1. A person having a claim, due or to become due, against the decedent must file his claim with the clerk within 90 days after the mailing for those required to be mailed, or 90 days after the first publication of the notice to creditors pursuant to NRS 155.020. * * *

3. If a claim is not filed with the clerk within the time allowed by subsection 1 or 2, the claim is forever barred, but if it is made to appear, by the affidavit of the claimant or by other proof to the satisfaction of the court, that the claimant did not have notice as provided in NRS 155.020 or actual notice of the administration of the estate, the claim may be filed at any time before the filing of the final account.

In light of the statute, do you see why Fran might want to probate her mother's will, even if Fran's mother owned no real estate and her mother's liquid assets were all held in P.O.D. accounts that passed to Fran and her sister outside of probate? [Note that assets in P.O.D. accounts are subject to the claims of the depositor's creditors].

Administration of an estate may be important even when decedent has left no will. Intestate heirs face the same problems as will beneficiaries when they seek to persuade purchasers that their title is bona fide or to persuade banks to release money. Do you see why? Similarly, intestate heirs benefit from a short statute of limitations on creditor claims.

PROBLEMS

1. Grandpa dies intestate with $100,000 in cash and $200,000 in bearer bonds (bonds, the interest of which and principal of which are payable to the bearer and are therefore the equivalent of cash) in a state with no estate tax. Grandpa is survived by two mentally competent adult children. They are his only heirs. They are prepared to split his property equally. Grandpa has no debts and no other property. His funeral and burial were prepaid and he lived in a hotel where his bill is fully paid. Grandpa's two kids come to you and ask if they need to begin an estate administration. What is your response?

2. The facts are the same as in Problem 1, with these exceptions: the $100,000 is in a bank account in Grandpa's name only and the bonds are not bearer bonds, but instead bonds registered in Grandpa's name only. What is your response now?

3. The facts are the same as in Problem 1, with the two following exceptions: first, there is a dubious claim outstanding that Grandpa owes $50,000 to a company that preys on senior citizens using telephone solicitations. Second, there is a skeleton in the family closet: a chap who is the son of a woman who once worked for Grandpa claims to be Grandpa's third child. What is your response now?

4. The facts are the same as in Problem 1, with this exception: Grandpa lived in a condominium in his name that is worth $100,000 and that the two kids want to sell as soon as possible. What is your response now?

5. The facts are the same as in Problem 1, with this exception: the cash is held in two equal Totten trusts, one payable to Child One and the other payable to Child Two. What is your response now?

6. Mike Goode, a sole practitioner of law, has died. He is survived by his wife. He does not have a taxable estate. All of his assets were in joint name with his wife who has collected them all by the time she contacts you. They live in a rented apartment and she has arranged for the orderly transfer of all of Mike's files to Lucy Lawyer, who had the office next door to Mike. Should there be an administration of Mike's estate?

B. Where Do We Administer the Estate—Domiciliary and Ancillary Jurisdiction Over Probate

When decedent's assets are all located in her home state, the decedent will almost certainly offer her will for probate in that state, and most likely in the county where decedent lived. Orders issued by the courts of decedent's home state will be sufficient to persuade local banks and brokers to release assets to the estate executor, and the probated will, entered in the county records, will provide adequate notice with respect to ownership of real property. If decedent owns real property in other counties, filing the will in those other counties might be helpful. Alternatively, the executor could issue a deed to any beneficiary of real property, and that beneficiary could record the deed in the county where the property is situated.

When decedent's assets extend beyond her home state, the situation becomes more complicated. A Connecticut court has no power to transfer land in Florida. Moreover, a Florida bank might be reluctant to transfer assets to a Connecticut executor based on an unfamiliar piece of paper issued by a Connecticut probate court.

To deal with these issues, the executor might seek *ancillary administration* in the county in Florida in which the real property is located. The executor might face an immediate problem: Florida might not permit the Connecticut executor to function within the state. Like a number of states, Florida permits only residents of the state and relatives of the decedent to act as executors. If the decedent's will named a Connecticut bank (or a Connecticut lawyer) as executor, someone else will have to qualify as executor in Florida. What rationale could Florida offer for restricting the power of non-residents to act as executors? Do you think the rationale captures the real reason for the prohibition?

In effect, ancillary administration requires two separate and parallel administration proceedings. If decedent owned property in more than two states, administration might be required in multiple states. Ancillary administration significantly adds to the cost of probate. As a result, an executor is well advised to find out whether financial institutions in sister states will release assets to the executor without ancillary administration.

PROBLEM

William Wealthy, a New York domiciliary, consults you for estate planning advice. Wealthy owns vacation homes in Palm Beach, Florida, Vail, Colorado, and Nantucket, Massachusetts. He intends to leave all three homes to his daughter, Wanda, and he wants to minimize the costs of administering his estate. What suggestions might you offer?

C. How the Executor Probates the Will

After a person dies owning probate property, someone will likely begin a proceeding in the appropriate court. That court might be called the probate court, or the surrogate's court, or the orphans' court, or in some states it might be a court of general jurisdiction. Probate is an intensely local process. Procedures vary considerably from state to state. Typically, however, probate is a judicial proceeding. The proceeding begins when someone, generally the executor named in the will, offers the will for probate. If the named executor is unwilling or unable to proceed, someone else might petition for probate of the will. And if the decedent left no will, an intestate heir (in an order of priority prescribed by statute) will seek administration of the estate.

At this point, the probate process starts to diverge from state to state, and sometimes from estate to estate.

The simplest probate system, sometimes called probate "in common form," is an informal process in which the court admits the will to probate—tentatively—as soon as the proponent offers the will and the court determines that the proponent's petition meets basic procedural requisites. The proceeding itself is an *ex parte* proceeding. Once the court admits the will to probate, the executor provides notice to heirs and creditors. If none of them object, probate becomes final with the passage of time; no formal proceeding will be necessary. Only if a party with standing objects will there ever be a formal proceeding.

In other jurisdictions, the proceeding is formal from day one. This more formal probate, sometimes referred to as probate "in solemn form," is structured more like a litigation. The proponent petitions for admission of the will to probate and serves a copy of her petition on the persons who are financially better off if the will is denied probate—let us say the decedent's intestate successors. The heirs are then required to show cause why the will should not be admitted to probate. If they don't successfully oppose the probate then the will is admitted. Their failure to appear is similar to defaulting in a lawsuit. Or, if they waive their right to oppose the probate petition, that is akin to confessing judgment. The will is not, however, admitted to probate until the conclusion of the proceeding.

Some states have only one kind of probate, while others allow the proponent of the will to choose between the two forms. In some states, the procedures depend on the value of the estate, with more formality required for larger estates. The UPC approach offers a choice of procedures. Informal probates are provided for, beginning at section 3–301 and formal probates are dealt with beginning at section 3–401. Indeed, the UPC allows will beneficiaries to avoid administration altogether if they agree to assume personal responsibility for taxes, debts, and any claims against the estate (including claims by other persons claiming entitlement to inheritance). See

UPC sections 3–312–3–322. For a discussion of the UPC's approach, see Karen J. Sneddon, Beyond the Personal Representative: the Potential of Succession Without Administration, 50 S. Tex. L. Rev. 449 (2009).

If a jurisdiction provides a choice between formal and informal administration, why would you ever advise a client to opt for formal administration?

Under either form of probate, a day arrives, early in the administration of the typical estate, when the court determines that it has jurisdiction and that the instrument before it is the last will and testament of the decedent. At that point, the court formally appoints the executor (or other personal representative), and issues *letters testamentary* or, if there is no will, *letters of administration*. These letters are, if you wish, the rough equivalent of a business license for the estate. For instance, letters testamentary or letters of administration are the documents the executor needs to convince financial institutions to transfer the decedent's assets.

D. ASCERTAINING AND MAXIMIZING THE SIZE OF THE ESTATE: COLLECTING ASSETS AND DISPOSING OF CREDITOR CLAIMS

Once the estate's personal representative obtains authority to act on behalf of the estate, the personal representative's objective is to distribute the estate to the will beneficiaries or intestate heirs as quickly as possible. Achieving that objective is not always as easy as it might seem.

First, the personal representative must collect and protect all of the estate's assets. If all of the decedent's assets were in banks or brokerage accounts, arranging to transfer title to the estate, or to the estate beneficiaries, will not pose significant problems once the personal representative produces letters testamentary. But suppose the decedent owned valuable art or other tangible assets. Artist Andy Warhol's nominated executor wisely made arrangements to guard Warhol's apartment on the date of his death. Relatively recently, a registered list of stolen artworks included 150 Warhols (of the thousands of Warhols extant). The executor of Alfred Nobel's estate literally sat on Nobel's millions as "he rode a horse-drawn cab through Paris ... 'with a revolver at the ready in case of a direct attack or a prearranged collision with another vehicle....' " Lawrence K. Altman, M.D., Alfred Nobel and the Prize that Almost Didn't Happen, N.Y. Times, Sept. 26, 2006, quoting the executor.

At the same time the personal representative worries about marshalling the estate's assets, the personal representative also must deal with creditor claims. Undisputed claims promptly presented to the personal representative—the nursing home bill, decedent's telephone bill, etc.—present no serious difficulties. But suppose claims are disputed or contingent, or suppose the personal representative does not know about the claim. The personal representative now has a problem, because if he or she distributes the estate assets without paying rightful claims, the executor will remain personally liable to unpaid creditors.

In this section, we explore the problems personal representatives face in the course of administering the estate—problems that contribute to the delays associated with estate administration.

1. COLLECTING ASSETS

Suppose decedent had lent money to one or more people who had defaulted on the loans. Or, suppose it is not clear whether decedent's payment of money to some of those people was a loan or a gift. Or, suppose decedent died as a passenger in a car crash, giving rise to a number of claims against the drivers and owners of both the car in which decedent was riding and the car with which that car collided. How should the personal representative deal with these problems? Consider the personal representative's alternatives.

First, the personal representative has power to sue on behalf of the estate. Second, the personal representative has power to act on behalf of the estate in settling or compromising any claims. Be careful to understand what this settlement power entails. Because the personal representative holds legal title to estate assets, the personal representative has power to bind the estate to a settlement with a debtor of the estate; the debtor cannot escape from a settlement by contending that the personal representative lacked power to make the settlement. But the personal representative's settlement power does *not* insulate him or her from claims by the estate beneficiaries that the settlement breached fiduciary duties the personal representative owed to those beneficiaries. Third, the personal representative can seek advance court approval for any prospective settlement. Court approval will almost inevitably insulate the personal representative from claims by disgruntled beneficiaries. Finally, the personal representative can approach the estate beneficiaries, and ask them to approve any compromise of settlement (by waiving any claims they might have against the personal representative for breach of fiduciary duty arising out of settlement of the claim.)

Which of these alternatives the personal representative should choose depends on the facts of the individual case. Consider the following problems:

PROBLEMS

1. After his retirement from an environmental engineering firm, decedent engaged in occasional consulting work for the firm, at an hourly rate of $100 per hour. Two weeks before her death, decedent had billed the firm $6,000 for 60 hours of work on a consulting project, and decedent's records showed that she had worked an additional 20 hours since the last bill. Although she had been in close contact with the firm throughout the project, and had reported many of her findings orally, she had not yet reduced any of those findings to writing. Decedent's executor reports that the engineering firm has offered to pay $2,000 in full settlement of all claims by the estate. The executor seeks your advice. Your experience tells you that litigating decedent's $8,000 claim against the firm would cost a minimum of $5,000. What course of action would you recommend, and why?

2. Two years before his death, decedent sold a house he owned for $800,000. The buyer paid $100,000 in cash, and gave decedent a purchase money mortgage for the other $700,000. A month before decedent's death, the purchaser defaulted on the mortgage. The market value of the house has now declined to $600,000, and the purchaser is insolvent. Decedent's executor reports that the purchaser is willing to convey a deed to the house in lieu of foreclosure on the mortgage loan, so long as the executor releases the purchaser from personal liability on the loan. Again, the executor seeks your advice. What course of action would you recommend, and why?

3. Three years before decedent's death, her son, Don, purchased a condominium apartment. Decedent furnished the $100,000 down payment. For the ensuing three years, Don paid decedent $500 each month in what appeared to be interest on the down payment. Decedent and Don had no formal loan agreement. Decedent died with a will—executed five years before her death—that named her daughter, Ellen, as executor, and that provided for distribution of her estate "to my three children, or their issue, in equal shares." Ellen, as executor, asked Don about the down payment, but Don contends that he made an oral deal with his mother that in return for the down payment, he would pay her $500 per month for the rest of her life. Ellen seeks your advice. What course of action would you recommend, and why?

2. CREDITORS' CLAIMS

Just as the personal representative stands in the decedent's shoes with respect to claims the decedent has against debtors, the personal representative also bears responsibility for dealing with the decedent's creditors. The personal representative has the same power to settle claims against the estate that the representative has for settling claims by the estate.

Creditor claims fall into two distinct categories. For most personal representatives, the most important category involves debts or claims incurred by the decedent before death. But when the decedent was actively engaged in a business enterprise at the time of her death, the personal representative may be shortchanging the beneficiaries if the representative simply stops operation of that enterprise immediately upon death. If the personal representative maintains the enterprise's going concern value by operating the business after decedent's death, the personal representative may also have to confront post-death creditors. This section deals separately with the two categories of claims.

a. Pre–Death Creditors

Creditor claims against the estate enjoy priority over the claims of estate beneficiaries; the beneficiaries of an insolvent decedent have nothing to inherit. When someone dies, the personal representative's job is to pay the debts the decedent incurred during life.

At the same time, the personal representative's primary allegiances are rarely to creditors. A testator chooses an executor who will safeguard the interests of beneficiaries. When a decedent dies intestate, close family members—not creditors—typically enjoy priority as potential administrators. Why, then, do executors pay creditor claims? In part, it is ingrained in the culture. Indeed, many wills start with the provision: "I direct that my executor pay all my just debts as soon as convenient." In part, however, personal representatives pay creditor claims to avoid the prospect of personal liability: if a personal representative distributes estate assets to beneficiaries without satisfying creditor claims, the executor remains "on the hook" to those creditors.

The prospect of personal liability creates just the right incentives with respect to well-established obligations of the decedent: the rent bill, bills for medical or nursing care, and for utilities. These bills arrive in the mail, and the personal representative will promptly pay them (or compromise them, if there are disputed issues).

But the personal representative may not know about all claims against the decedent. Perhaps the decedent infringed a copyright or used defective materials on a construction job. How should the personal representative handle such possibilities? If the victimized author or home purchaser can seek relief at any time until the ordinary statute of limitations expires, the personal representative cannot safely distribute estate assets to beneficiaries until all relevant limitations periods have expired. (Recall that if the personal representative distributes assets without satisfying creditor claims, the personal representative remains personally liable for those claims). The result would be considerable delay in distribution of all estates—because the personal representative can never be sure that an unexpected claim won't "pop up" in the future.

To deal with this problem, a number of states have enacted short statutes of limitations on creditor claims against estates. These statutes promote the interest of efficient and timely winding up of a decedent's affairs.

These so-called nonclaim statutes come in two basic forms. Some statutes impose a special, short, statute of limitations on creditor claims, measured from the date of a decedent's death. For instance, the California statute extinguishes all claims, "whether arising in contract, tort, or otherwise" one year after the date of decedent's death. Cal. Code Civ. Pro. § 366.2. Statutes like these in effect impose on creditors the obligation to learn of the decedent's death, and to process claims accordingly.

The second form of nonclaim statute provides that once a personal representative provides notice to creditors, creditor claims are extinguished within an even shorter period—often as little as 60 days. The Uniform Probate Code combines the two forms of statutes:

UNIFORM PROBATE CODE

SECTION 3–801. NOTICE TO CREDITORS.

(a) Unless notice has already been given under this section, a personal representative upon appointment may publish a notice to creditors once a week for three successive weeks in a newspaper of general circulation in the county announcing the appointment ... notifying creditors of the estate to present their claims within four months after the date of the first publication of the notice or be forever barred.

(b) A personal representative may give written notice by mail or other delivery to a creditor, notifying the creditor to present his [or her] claim within four months after the published notice, if given as provided in subsection (a), or within 60 days after the mailing or other deliver of the notice, whichever is later, or be forever barred.

UNIFORM PROBATE CODE

SECTION 3–803. LIMITATIONS ON PRESENTATION OF CLAIMS.

(a) All claims against a decedent's estate which arose before the death of the decedent, ... are barred against the estate, the personal representative, the heirs and devisees, and any nonprobate transfers of the decedent, unless presented within the earlier of the following:

(1) one year after the decedent's death; or

(2) the time provided by Section 3–801(b) for creditors who are given actual notice, and within the time provided in Section 3–801(a) for all creditors barred by publication.

Does the federal constitution limit the states' power to cut off creditor claims so quickly? Consider the following case:

Tulsa Professional Collection Services, Inc. v. Pope

United States Supreme Court, 1988.
485 U.S. 478, 108 S.Ct. 1340, 99 L.Ed.2d 565.

■ O'CONNOR, J., delivered the opinion of the Court.

This case involves a provision of Oklahoma's probate laws requiring claims "arising upon a contract" generally to be presented to the executor or executrix of the estate within two months of the publication of a notice advising creditors of the commencement of probate proceedings. Okla.Stat., Tit. 58, § 333 (1981). The question presented is whether this provision of notice solely by publication satisfies the Due Process Clause.

I

Oklahoma's Probate Code requires creditors to file claims against an estate within a specified time period, and generally bars untimely claims. Ibid. Such "nonclaim statutes" are almost universally included in state probate codes. See Uniform Probate Code § 3–801, 8 U.L.A. 351 (1983); Falender, Notice to Creditors in Estate Proceedings: What Process is Due?, 63 N.C.L.Rev. 659, 667–668 (1985). Giving creditors a limited time in which to file claims against the estate serves the State's interest in facilitating the administration and expeditious closing of estates. Nonclaim statutes come in two basic forms. Some provide a relatively short time period, generally two to six months, that begins to run after the commencement of probate proceedings. Others call for a longer period, generally one to five years, that runs from the decedent's death. See Falender, supra, at 664–672. Most States include both types of nonclaim statutes in their probate codes, typically providing that if probate proceedings are not commenced and the shorter period therefore never is triggered, then claims nonetheless may be barred by the longer period. * * * Most States also provide that creditors are to be notified of the requirement to file claims imposed by the nonclaim statutes solely by publication. See Uniform Probate Code § 3–801, 8 U.L.A. 351 (1983); Falender, supra, at 660, n. 7 (collecting statutes). Indeed, in most jurisdictions it is the publication of notice that triggers the nonclaim statute. The Uniform Probate Code, for example, provides that creditors have four months from publication in which to file claims. Uniform Probate Code § 3–801, 8 U.L.A. 351 (1983). * * *

The specific nonclaim statute at issue in this case, Okla.Stat., Tit. 58, § 333 (1981), provides for only a short time period and is best considered in the context of Oklahoma probate proceedings as a whole. Under Oklahoma's Probate Code, any party interested in the estate may initiate probate proceedings by petitioning the court to have the will proved. § 22. The court is then required to set a hearing date on the petition, § 25, and to mail notice of the hearing "to all heirs, legatees and devisees, at their places of residence," §§ 25, 26. If no person appears at the hearing to contest the will, the court may admit the will to probate on the testimony of one of the subscribing witnesses to the will. § 30. After the will is admitted to probate, the court must order appointment of an executor or executrix, issuing letters testamentary to the named executor or executrix if that person appears, is competent and qualified, and no objections are made. § 101.

Immediately after appointment, the executor or executrix is required to "give notice to the creditors of the deceased." § 331. * * * This notice is to advise creditors that they must present their claims to the executor or executrix within two months of the date of the first publication. As for the method of notice, the statute requires only publication: * * * A creditor's failure to file a claim within the 2–month period generally bars it forever. § 333. The nonclaim statute does provide certain exceptions, however. If the creditor is out of State, then a claim "may be presented at any time before a decree of distribution is entered." § 333. Mortgages and debts not yet due are also excepted from the 2–month time limit. * * *

II

H. Everett Pope, Jr., was admitted to St. John Medical Center, a hospital in Tulsa, Oklahoma, in November 1978. On April 2, 1979, while still at the hospital, he died testate. His wife, appellee JoAnne Pope, initiated probate proceedings in the District Court of Tulsa County in accordance with the statutory scheme outlined above. * * *

Appellant Tulsa Professional Collection Services, Inc., is a subsidiary of St. John Medical Center and the assignee of a claim for expenses connected with the decedent's long stay at that hospital. Neither appellant, nor its parent company, filed a claim with appellee within the 2–month time period following publication of notice. * * *

Appellant then sought rehearing, arguing for the first time that the nonclaim statute's notice provisions violated due process. In a supplemental opinion on rehearing the Court of Appeals rejected the due process claim on the merits. Id., at 15.

Appellant next sought review in the Supreme Court of Oklahoma. That court granted certiorari and, after review of both the § 594 and due process issues, affirmed the Court of Appeals' judgment. With respect to the federal issue, the court relied on Estate of Busch v. Ferrell–Duncan Clinic, Inc., 700 S.W.2d 86, 88–89 (Mo.1985), to reject appellant's contention that our decisions in Mullane v. Central Hanover Bank & Trust Co., 339 U.S. 306, 70 S.Ct. 652, 94 L.Ed. 865 (1950), and Mennonite Board of Missions v. Adams, 462 U.S. 791, 103 S.Ct. 2706, 77 L.Ed.2d 180 (1983), required more than publication notice. 733 P.2d 396 (1986). The Supreme Court reasoned that the function of notice in probate proceedings was not to " 'make a creditor a party to the proceeding' " but merely to " 'notif[y] him that he may become one if he wishes.' " Id., at 400 (quoting Estate of Busch, supra, at 88). In addition, the court distinguished probate proceedings because they do not directly adjudicate the creditor's claims. 733 P.2d, at 400–401. Finally, the court agreed with *Estate of Busch* that nonclaim statutes were self-executing statutes of limitations, because they "ac[t] to cut off potential claims against the decedent's estate by the passage of time," and accordingly do not require actual notice. 733 P.2d, at 401. This conclusion conflicted with that reached by the Nevada Supreme Court in Continental Insurance Co. v. Moseley, 100 Nev. 337, 683 P.2d 20 (1984), after our decision remanding the case for reconsideration in light of *Mennonite,* supra. 463 U.S. 1202, 103 S.Ct. 3530, 77 L.Ed.2d 1383 (1983). In *Moseley,* the Nevada Supreme Court held that in this context due process required "more than service by publication." 100 Nev., at 338, 683 P.2d, at 21. We noted probable jurisdiction, 484 U.S. 813 (1987), and now reverse and remand.

III

Mullane v. Central Hanover Bank & Trust Co., supra, 339 U.S., at 314, 70 S.Ct., at 657 established that state action affecting property must generally be accompanied by notification of that action: "An elementary and fundamental requirement of due process in any proceeding which is to be accorded finality is notice reasonably calculated, under all the circumstances, to apprise interested parties of the pendency of the action and afford them an opportunity to present their objections." In the years since *Mullane* the Court has adhered to these principles, balancing the "interest of the State" and "the individual interest sought to be protected by the Fourteenth Amendment." Ibid. The focus is on the reasonableness of the balance, and, as *Mullane* itself made clear, whether a particular method of notice is reasonable depends on the particular circumstances.

The Court's most recent decision in this area is *Mennonite,* supra, which involved the sale of real property for delinquent taxes. * * * In *Mennonite,* a mortgagee of property that had been sold and on which the redemption period had run complained that the State's failure to provide it with actual notice of these proceedings violated due process. The Court agreed, holding that "actual notice is a minimum constitutional precondition to a proceeding which will adversely affect the liberty or property interests of *any* party, whether unlettered or well versed in commercial practice, if its name and address are reasonably ascertainable." * * *

Applying these principles to the case at hand leads to a similar result. Appellant's interest is an unsecured claim, a cause of action against the estate for an unpaid bill. Little doubt remains that such an intangible interest is property protected by the Fourteenth Amendment. As we wrote in Logan v. Zimmerman Brush Co., 455 U.S. 422, 428, 102 S.Ct. 1148, 1154, 71 L.Ed.2d 265 (1982), this question "was affirmatively settled by the *Mullane* case itself, where the Court held that a cause of action is a species of property protected by the Fourteenth Amendment's Due Process Clause." * * * Appellant's claim, therefore, is properly considered a protected property interest.

The Fourteenth Amendment protects this interest, however, only from a deprivation by state action. Private use of state-sanctioned private remedies or procedures does not rise to the level of state action. * * * Nor is the State's involvement in the mere running of a general statute of limitations generally sufficient to implicate due process. See Texaco, Inc. v. Short, 454 U.S. 516, 102 S.Ct. 781, 70 L.Ed.2d 738 (1982). * * * But when private parties make use of state procedures with the overt, significant assistance of state officials, state action may be found. * * * The question here is whether the State's involvement with the nonclaim statute is substantial enough to implicate the Due Process Clause.

Appellee argues that it is not, contending that Oklahoma's nonclaim statute is a self-executing statute of limitations. Relying on this characterization, appellee then points to *Short,* supra. Appellee's reading of *Short* is correct—due process does not require that potential plaintiffs be given notice of the impending expiration of a period of limitations—but in our view, appellee's premise is not. Oklahoma's nonclaim statute is not a self-executing statute of limitations.

It is true that nonclaim statutes generally possess some attributes of statutes of limitations. They provide a specific time period within which particular types of claims must be filed and they bar claims presented after expiration of that deadline. Many of the state court decisions upholding nonclaim statutes against due process challenges have relied upon these features and concluded that they are properly viewed as statutes of limitations. * * *

As we noted in *Short,* however, it is the "self-executing feature" of a statute of limitations that makes *Mullane* and *Mennonite* inapposite. See 454 U.S., at 533, 536, 102 S.Ct., at 794, 796. The State's interest in a self-executing statute of limitations is in providing repose for potential defendants and in avoiding stale claims. The State has no role to play beyond enactment of the limitations period. While this enactment obviously is state action, the State's limited involvement in the running of the time period generally falls short of constituting the type of state action required to implicate the protections of the Due Process Clause.

Here, in contrast, there is significant state action. The probate court is intimately involved throughout, and without that involvement the time bar is never activated. The nonclaim statute becomes operative only after probate proceedings have been commenced in state court. The court must appoint the executor or executrix before notice, which triggers the time bar, can be given. Only after this court appointment is made does the statute provide for any notice; § 331 directs the executor or executrix to publish notice "immediately" after appointment. Indeed, in this case, the District Court reinforced the statutory command with an order expressly requiring appellee to "immediately give notice to creditors." The form of the order indicates that such orders are routine. Record 14. Finally, copies of the notice and an affidavit of publication must be filed with the court. § 332. It is only after all of these actions take place that the time period begins to run, and in every one of these actions, the court is intimately involved. This involvement is so pervasive and substantial that it must be considered state action subject to the restrictions of the Fourteenth Amendment.

Where the legal proceedings themselves trigger the time bar, even if those proceedings do not necessarily resolve the claim on its merits, the time bar lacks the self-executing feature that *Short* indicated was necessary to remove any due process problem. Rather, in such circumstances, due process is directly implicated and actual notice generally is required. * * * Our conclusion that the Oklahoma nonclaim statute is not a self-executing statute of limitations makes it unnecessary to consider appellant's argument that a 2–month period is somehow unconstitutionally short. * * * We also have no occasion to consider the proper characterization of nonclaim statutes that run from the date of death, and which generally provide for longer time periods, ranging from one to five years. See Falender, 63 N.C.L.Rev., at 667–669. In sum, the substantial involvement of the probate court throughout the process leaves little doubt that the running of Oklahoma's nonclaim statute is accompanied by sufficient government action to implicate the Due Process Clause.

Nor can there be any doubt that the nonclaim statute may "adversely affect" a protected property interest. * * *

In assessing the propriety of actual notice in this context consideration should be given to the practicalities of the situation and the effect that requiring actual notice may have on important state interests. * * * As the Court noted in *Mullane,* "[c]hance alone brings to the attention of even a local resident an advertisement in small type inserted in the back pages of a newspaper." Id., at 315, 70 S.Ct., at 658. Creditors, who have a strong interest in maintaining the integrity of their relationship with their debtors, are particularly unlikely to benefit from publication notice. As a class, creditors may not be aware of a debtor's death or of the institution of probate proceedings. Moreover, the executor or executrix will often be, as is the case here, a party with a beneficial interest in the estate. This could diminish an executor's or executrix's inclination to call attention to the potential expiration of a creditor's claim. There is thus a substantial practical need for actual notice in this setting.

At the same time, the State undeniably has a legitimate interest in the expeditious resolution of probate proceedings. Death transforms the decedent's legal relationships and a State could reasonably conclude that swift settlement of estates is so important that it calls for very short time deadlines for filing claims. As noted, the almost uniform practice is to establish such short deadlines, and to provide only publication notice. * * * Providing actual notice to known or reasonably ascertainable creditors, however, is not inconsistent with the goals reflected in nonclaim statutes. * * * In addition, *Mullane* disavowed any intent to require "impracticable and extended searches * * * in the name of due process." 339 U.S., at 317–318, 70 S.Ct., at 658–659. As the Court indicated in *Mennonite,* all that the executor or executrix need do is make "reasonably diligent efforts," 462 U.S., at 798, n. 4, 103 S.Ct., at 2711, n. 4 to uncover the identities of creditors. For creditors who are not "reasonably ascertainable," publication notice can suffice. Nor is everyone who may conceivably have a claim properly considered a creditor entitled to actual notice. Here, as in *Mullane,* it is reasonable to dispense with actual notice to those with mere "conjectural" claims. 339 U.S., at 317, 70 S.Ct., at 659.

On balance then, a requirement of actual notice to known or reasonably ascertainable creditors is not so cumbersome as to unduly hinder the dispatch with which probate proceedings are conducted. Notice by mail is already routinely provided at several points in the probate process. * * * Indeed, a few States already provide for actual notice in connection with short nonclaim statutes. * * * We do not believe that requiring adherence to such a standard will be so burdensome or impracticable as to warrant reliance on publication notice alone. * * *

Whether appellant's identity as a creditor was known or reasonably ascertainable by appellee cannot be answered on this record. * * * Appellee of course was aware that her husband endured a long stay at St. John Medical Center, but it is not clear that this awareness translates into a knowledge of appellant's claim. We therefore must remand the case for further proceedings to determine whether "reasonably diligent efforts," *Mennonite,* supra, at 798, n. 4, 103 S.Ct., at 2711, n. 4 would have identified appellant and uncovered its claim. If appellant's identity was known or "reasonably ascertainable," then termination of appellant's claim without actual notice violated due process.

IV

We hold that Oklahoma's nonclaim statute is not a self-executing statute of limitations. Rather, the statute operates in connection with Oklahoma's probate proceedings to "adversely affect" appellant's property interest. Thus, if appellant's identity as a creditor was known or "reasonably ascertainable," then the Due Process Clause requires that appellant be given "[n]otice by mail or other means as certain to ensure actual notice." *Mennonite,* supra, at 800, 103 S.Ct., at 2712. Accordingly, the judgment of the Oklahoma Supreme Court is reversed and the case is remanded for further proceedings not inconsistent with this opinion.

It is so ordered.

■ JUSTICE BLACKMUN concurs in the result.

■ CHIEF JUSTICE REHNQUIST, dissenting. * * *

NOTES AND QUESTIONS

1. Who was the creditor in the Pope case? The most significant creditors of middle-class estates are likely to be hospitals and nursing homes. If the decedent was a Medicaid recipient in a nursing home then the state government might be a significant creditor. To whom would a personal representative send notice if the decedent was a Medicaid recipient? How likely is it that the state would submit a claim within the statutory time limit?

2. In light of Pope, is California's one-year limitation period on creditor claims constitutional? Is UPC 3–803(a) constitutional? See Sarajane Love, Estate Creditors, the Constitution, and the Uniform Probate Code, 30 U. Rich. L. Rev. 411 (1996).

3. What constitutes a "reasonably diligent effort" to identify a claimant? Suppose your jurisdiction has enacted UPC 3–801 and 3–803. The estate's personal representative has investigated, and has provided personal notice to all potential claimants revealed by the investigation. The personal representative has also provided notice by publication. Four months after the first publication of the notice, no claimants have yet filed a claim. Would you advise the personal representative to distribute estate assets? Why or why not?

4. Notice by publication is not free. Legal notices serve as a significant revenue source for many local newspapers. After Pope, would you advise a personal representative to pay to publish a notice to creditors? How much protection would the notice provide? If the personal representative could not rely on the notice, what benefits would the estate derive from paying for the notice?

In some jurisdictions, publication of the notice might be mandatory (perhaps the product of the local newspaper lobby), and if an effective enforcement mechanism were in place, the personal representative would have no choice but to publish the notice.

5. Suppose a creditor knows of the death and of the probate. Is the creditor nevertheless entitled to notice? Courts have split on the issue. Compare In re Estate of Sheridan, 117 P.3d 39 (Colo. Ct. App. 2004), with Estate of Pennington, 16 Kan.App.2d 792, 829 P.2d 618 (1992). How would one prove that the creditor had actual notice?

PROBLEMS

1. Your client is Elena Executor. She plans to provide notice of her father's death by publication. She asks for your legal opinion on whether she has to notify any of the following creditors directly, as individuals who are reasonably ascertainable:

a. Able Creditor, who left a message on the decedent's answering machine asking why his payment is late?

b. Baker Creditor, whose letters demanding payment were found by Elena in Dad's desk?

c. Carlos Creditor, whose name appears on Dad's income tax return for last year as someone to whom Dad was paying substantial interest payments?

2. Decedent was a home builder. He routinely offered customers a five-year guarantee on the homes he sold. At decedent's death, would Pope require his personal representative to send notice to each of the home purchasers, or would notice by publication be sufficient? See U.S. Trust Company of Florida Savings Bank v. Haig, 694 So.2d 769 (Fla. Dist. Ct. App. 1997).

Suppose a home purchaser receives actual notice, or notice by publication. How would you advise the purchaser to respond if the home has not yet shown any signs of defects? Is there any way the home purchaser can protect her rights under the guarantee?

3. Executor sought to give actual notice under Pope by sending the notice to a corporate creditor at its general headquarters. An internal delay at the creditor's headquarters kept the notice from being forwarded to the creditor's legal department in a timely fashion. During that time the nonclaim statute ran. The creditor sought to file a late claim, claiming that it did not receive actual notice until the notice reached its legal department. What result? See Gertner v. Superior Court, 20 Cal.App.4th 927, 25 Cal.Rptr.2d 47 (1993).

3. POST–DEATH CREDITORS

So far, we have dealt with claims by creditors that arose out of actions taken by the decedent. Suppose, instead, that the creditor claims arise out of events that occur after decedent's death, but before estate assets have been distributed to the estate beneficiaries. Suppose, for instance, the personal representative contracts for accounting services, and doesn't pay the accountant. Or suppose the personal representative causes personal injuries while riding a tractor on decedent's farm. These circumstances raise two basic questions: (1) does the creditor, whether a contract creditor or a tort creditor, have recourse against the personal representative, the estate, or both? (2) who should ultimately bear the loss for the injury suffered by the creditor? Consider those questions as you read the following case:

Vance v. Estate of Myers

Supreme Court of Alaska, 1972.
494 P.2d 816.

■ CONNOR, J:

The central question in this case concerns the liability of an estate for the torts of a trustee, executor, or administrator.

Appellant brought a tort action against the administrator of the appellee's estate.

Charles O. Myers died in Fairbanks, Alaska, on May 3, 1969. Shortly thereafter Howard E. Holbert was appointed administrator of the estate. By court order Holbert was allowed to operate the business owned by the decedent, Chuck's Corner Bar, in Nenana, Alaska.

On August 31, 1970, the appellant filed suit against several persons, including Holbert as administrator of the estate of Myers. The complaint alleges that appellant's husband, for whom she is suing as guardian ad litem, was physically injured in an altercation in Chuck's Corner Bar on June 5, 1970. It is alleged that the injuries resulted, in part, from the actions of the administrator and an employee of the administrator in that they served drinks to John Vance, when Vance was already intoxicated. The complaint further alleges that this rendered Vance incapable of caring for his own safety, that the employee assisted in dragging Vance to the street outside the bar after Vance had been beaten by another person in the bar, and that the employee failed to protect Vance from being beaten in the bar while Vance was in a helpless condition.

Under the traditional rule a trustee, executor, or administrator was normally liable for torts committed by him or his servants in the administration of the trust or estate. But such torts did not result in the imposition of direct liability upon the assets of the trust or estate. *Kirchner v. Muller,* 280 N.Y. 23, 19 N.E.2d 665 (1939); *Brown v. Guaranty Estates Corp.,* 239 N.C. 595, 80 S.E.2d 645 (1954); *Barnett v. Schumacher,* 453 S.W.2d 934 (Mo. 1970); A. Scott, "Liabilities Incurred in the Administration of Trusts," 28 Harv.L.Rev. 725 (1915). The orthodox view, still adhered to in a great number of jurisdictions, is that the person to whom the trustee has incurred liability in the administration of the trust must bring an action against the trustee personally, but not in his representative capacity. The claimant may not reach the trust estate directly and apply it to the satisfaction of his claim.

The personal liability of the trustee or executor for torts of his agents is now generally qualified, however, by allowing the executor or trustee to obtain reimbursement from the assets of the estate when he is personally without fault. *Restatement 2d, Trusts, § 247.* If the claim against the trustee is uncollectible, it is generally recognized that the plaintiff may then reach the trust assets to the extent of the trustee's right to reimbursement. *Restatement 2d, Trusts, § 268*; H. Stone, "A Theory of Liability of Trust Estates for the Contracts and Torts of the Trustee," 22 Colum.L.Rev. 527 (1922). In some jurisdictions, when the trustee's right to reimbursement is clear, the courts have allowed suit against the trustee in his representative capacity, thus avoiding circuity of action. *Ewing v. Wm. L. Foley, Inc.,* 115 Tex. 222, 280 S.W. 499 (1926); *Dobbs v. Noble,* 55 Ga.App. 201, 189 S.E. 694 (1937); *Smith v. Coleman,* 100 Fla. 1707, 132 So. 198 (1931).

One of the original principles underlying the basic rule was that the trustee had an obligation to the trust beneficiaries to manage the estate without fault. Trust property should not be impaired or dissipated through wrongdoing of the trustee. This is, of course, a sound principle where the trustee acts outside the scope of his authority. It evolved at a time when the administration of trusts and estates was relatively passive and seldom required active management of a business enterprise. In much of the earlier case law the courts seem to be concerned exclusively with protecting the estate and the beneficiaries from the acts of reckless and improvident fiduciaries. *Parmenter v. Barstow,* 22 R.I. 245, 47 A. 365 (1900); *Birdsong v. Jones,* 222 Mo.App. 768, 8 S.W.2d 98 (1928). Little thought seems to have been given to the plight of the tort victim for harms done to him by the operation of a business enterprise.

Where the trustee's wrongful acts or omissions occur within the general scope of his authority to manage trust assets, and more particularly when the trustee himself has no appreciable assets, the impact of the traditional rule has been perceived as unjust. For this reason the courts have sought mechanisms, described above, by which the claimants in these circumstances could ultimately reach the assets of the estate. Many of the resulting decisions represent only a partial solution to the problem. Circuity of action is still often required, suit being filed first against the trustee, and only when collection against the trustee has been exhausted and proved futile is enforcement allowed against the estate directly. *Kirchner v. Muller, supra*; *Schmidt v. Kellner,* 307 Ill. 331, 138 N.E. 604 (1923). Even that procedure assumes that the trustee has a right to be exonerated out of the estate for the liability he has incurred, which is not always the case even when the trustee's tort was committed within the scope of his authority. Reimbursement may be denied to the trustee when he is personally at fault.

A strained, and we think erroneous, approach to the whole problem is exemplified in such cases as *Fetting v. Winch,* 54 Or. 600, 104 P. 722 (1909). There the executor was in possession of a building which was an asset of the estate, but he was not actively managing it. A suit was brought for death caused by an elevator accident attributable to the negligence of one of the building's janitors, employed by the executor. The court held that the executor could not be found liable individually, as he had not been personally negligent. Neither could the estate be held liable because, not being a legal person, it was incapable of committing a tort. The court refused to impose respondeat superior liability upon the executor because it felt that the doctrine should not be applied in an instance where the executor derived no profit or personal advantage from the enterprise. In other words, the plaintiff would have no avenue of recovery against the business enterprise conducted by means of the building, no matter how clear his cause of action.

The traditional rule and its exceptions have been criticized by recognized scholars and jurists as being inadequate and unfair to the tort creditor. Dean, later Chief Justice, Harlan Fiske Stone pointed out fifty years ago in a salient law review article that the traditional rule was premised upon theories which were untenable. The trustee's right to indemnity should not be the measure of the plaintiff's rights against the assets of the trust, for this leads to uneven results based solely upon the criterion of whether the trustee was or was not personally at fault. The true reason for reaching the assets of the estate should be the policy of casets of the estate loss resulting from the trustee's tort upon the estate, rather than upon the tort victim. This would bring the law of trust liability into harmony with the modern doctrine that an economic enterprise should bear the burden of the losses caused by it, including actionable personal injuries which result from its operations. H. Stone, *op. cit.,* 542–545.

One of the current reasons advanced for perpetuating the traditional rule is that if the tort claimant is allowed to sue the trustee in his representative capacity, the beneficiaries may not be adequately represented. That is, a conflict can exist between the trustee as an individual and the trustee in his official capacity, for often he will be named a party defendant in both those capacities. *Johnston v. Long,* 30 Cal.2d 54, 181 P.2d 645 (1947). But this problem can be minimized by the appointment of a special representative to protect the interests of the estate and beneficiaries when such a conflict between the estate and the fiduciary appears. *In re Estate of Gregory,* 487 P.2d 59, 63 (Alaska 1971).

Other courts have held that the trustee may be sued in his representative capacity in cases such as the one before us. *Miller v. Smythe,* 92 Ga. 154, 18 S.E. 46 (1893); *Smith v. Coleman,* 100 Fla. 1707, 132 So. 198 (1931); *Carey v. Squire,* 63 Ohio App. 476, 27 N.E.2d 175 (1939). We are convinced this is the right result. It should be recognized that in respect to tort liability a trustee acting within the general scope of his authority can subject the estate to liability, in the same manner as could an agent acting on behalf of an ordinary principal. That the estate lacks legal personality is true. But that factor should not be a roadblock to achieving realistic justice. See commentary, *Restatement 2d, Trusts, § 271A, comment a.-c.* at 23.

We hold that an administrator, executor, or trustee may be sued in his representative capacity, and collection may be had from the trust assets, for a tort committed in the course of administration, if it is determined by the court that the tort was a common incident of the kind of business activity in which the administrator, executor, or trustee was properly engaged on behalf of the estate. It follows that appellant's action against appellee was proper.

NOTES AND QUESTIONS

1. Make John Vance a more sympathetic character—an innocent bystander injured during a barroom brawl between patrons who had been served one (or five) too many. Under the traditional common law rule, what remedy would be available to Vance? If Howard Holbert had been insolvent, but the Myers estate was worth millions, would Vance have been entitled to any recovery? What justification would there be for such a result?

2. Suppose Holbert had been solvent, and Vance recovered a $500,000 judgment against Holbert. Under the traditional rule, would Holbert be entitled to indemnification from the estate? If not, why not?

In a jurisdiction that adheres to the traditional approach, what advice would you give to someone in Holbert's position who was contemplating accepting an appointment as personal representative? How could Holbert protect himself?

3. According to the court in the Vance case, who bears the loss if Vance is the innocent victim of a barroom brawl? Note that most jurisdictions have embraced some version of the Vance approach, either by statute or by case law.

UPC § 3–808(b) provides that "[a] personal representative is individually liable for obligations arising from ownership or control of the estate or for torts committed in the course of administration of the estate only if he is personally at fault." UPC § 3–808(c) goes on to provide that claims "on obligations arising from ownership or control of the estate or on torts committed in the course of estate administration may be asserted against the estate by proceeding against the personal representative in his fiduciary capacity, whether or not the personal representative is individually liable therefor." In light of that formulation, if Vance sues Holbert as an individual, how should the court dispose of the case? What course of action should Vance take?

4. Suppose Holbert had been not only the administrator, but also the bartender who served drinks to intoxicated patrons. How would the court have disposed of a claim brought by Vance against Holbert as administrator? How would the UPC dispose of such a case? Who should bear the loss in that case?

5. In Smith v. Rizzuto, 133 Neb. 655, 276 N.W. 406 (1937), an apartment house was devised to the trustee. A tenant was injured three days after the death of the decedent, before the trustee had qualified. The injury was allegedly caused by "negligence" in permitting an accumulation of ice on a porch of the apartment house. Is the trustee personally liable? Would he be liable if he refused the appointment upon hearing of the nomination? How could you protect a trustee in this situation?

6. *Contract Claims.* Under the traditional approach, a fiduciary is personally liable on her contracts, even if she signs those contracts in her fiduciary capacity. If the personal representative properly entered into the contract, she is entitled to indemnification from the estate assets (to the extent those assets remain). In light of the traditional rule, suppose a personal representative sells estate paintings or real property believing that the paintings are genuine and that the real property is entirely suitable for use. What risks does the personal representative take if the personal representative then distributes the proceeds (and the rest of the estate) to estate beneficiaries? How would you advise the personal representative to deal with those risks?

UPC § 3–808(a) rejects the traditional approach, providing instead that "[u]nless otherwise provided in the contract, a personal representative is not individually liable on a contract properly entered into in his fiduciary capacity in the course of administration of the estate unless he fails to reveal his representative capacity and identify the estate in the contract."

7. *Fiduciary Management Powers.* How did administrator Holbert obtain the right to run decedent's bar after decedent's death? Suppose he had not sought a court order. What risks would he have taken in operating the bar?

Consider the facts in Estate of Kurkowski, 487 Pa. 295, 409 A.2d 357 (1979). Decedent owned all of the corporate shares in a business that sold and serviced motorcycles. At his death, the value of the business was $43,000, not including the value of a $76,000 life insurance policy issued on decedent's life and payable to the corporation. His wife was appointed administrator of his estate, and continued to run the business for 20 months after decedent's death. At that point, she closed the business, which no longer had any value. Should the administrator-wife have been held liable to the estate for the loss in value (amounting to $119,000)? The Pennsylvania Supreme Court held her liable, holding that the administrator had breached her common law duty to liquidate the estate for purposes of distribution to decedent's heirs (who included children by a prior marriage).

Is it in the interest of estate beneficiaries to have the personal representative operate the decedent's business? The common law's general answer (as reflected in the Kurkowski case) was no. The fear was that the personal representative was likely to run the business into the ground. As a result, the personal representative's duty was to sell the business as quickly as possible.

Of course, there are circumstances where the beneficiaries will be better off if the personal representative continues to operate the business as a going concern rather than liquidating the business as quickly as possible. In those situations, the common law permitted the personal representative to seek judicial approval. A number of modern statutes give a personal representative limited power to continue an unincorporated business even without a court order. See, e.g., Uniform Probate Code § 3–715(24). As Vance and Kurkowski illustrate, the personal representative's best course of action in that case is to seek judicial approval for the decision to continue operating the business.

When a decedent writes a will, decedent can deal with the problem more directly, by conferring on the executor power to continue operation of decedent's business. Even when decedent does not operate a business, a well-drafted will will confer on the executor a variety of management powers—including the power to borrow money. See, for instance, the Jacqueline Onassis will reproduced in chapter 4, supra. Of course, conferring management powers on the personal representative provides only limited protection to the representative; the representative will still be liable if the decisions she makes do not comply with the duties of care and loyalty outlined in Sections II and III, *infra*.

E. COMPENSATING THE FIDUCIARY (AND THE FIDUCIARY'S LAWYER)

1. HOW SHOULD PERSONAL REPRESENTATIVES BY COMPENSATED?

The estate's personal representative is supposed to act for the benefit of the estate, not for his or her own benefit. Can we expect the personal representative to act with diligence if he or she works for free? Certainly when the personal representative is a trust company, a lawyer, or another professional, it would be unreasonable to expect the representative to work for free. Even family members may be reluctant to assume the time-consuming tasks of marshalling assets and dealing with creditor claims without some compensation for their time.

Who should decide, however, how much compensation is appropriate? The personal representative, who makes most other decisions on behalf of the estate, has a clear conflict of interest on this issue: allowing the personal representative to set her own compensation is not a sensible solution.

Compensation could be set by the testator in the will, but that presents a number of problems. First, that solution doesn't work at all for intestate decedents. Second, many testators die decades after executing their last will; the compensation provided in a 1990 will may not be appropriate in 2015 given changes in the size and complexity of the estate. Third, how will a testator know what compensation is appropriate? Most testators will be ignorant about the work necessary to administer an estate, and will look to their lawyers for guidance. But the decedent's lawyer also has a conflict of interest. If the lawyer recommends generous compensation for the personal representative, will that make the representative more likely to select the lawyer to represent the estate?

As a result of these difficulties, most states regulate compensation of personal representatives by statute. Consider two alternative statutory schemes:

UNIFORM PROBATE CODE

SECTION 3–721. PROCEEDINGS FOR REVIEW OF EMPLOYMENT OF AGENTS AND COMPENSATION OF PERSONAL REPRESENTATIVES AND EMPLOYEES OF ESTATE.

After notice to all interested persons or on petition of an interested person or on appropriate motion if administration is supervised, the propriety of employment of any person by a personal representative including any attorney, auditor, investment advisor or other specialized agent or assistant, the reasonableness of the compensation of any person so employed, or the reasonableness of the compensation determined by the personal representative for his own services, may be reviewed by the Court. Any person who has received excessive compensation from an estate for services rendered may be ordered to make appropriate refunds.

CALIFORNIA PROBATE CODE

SECTION 10800. COMPENSATION FOR ORDINARY SERVICES.

(a) Subject to the provisions of this part, for ordinary services the personal representative shall receive compensation based on the value of the estate accounted for by the personal representative, as follows:

(1) Four percent on the first one hundred thousand dollars ($100,000).

(2) Three percent on the next one hundred thousand dollars ($100,000).

(3) Two percent on the next eight hundred thousand dollars ($800,000).

(4) One percent on the next nine million dollars ($9,000,000).

(5) One-half of one percent on the next fifteen million dollars ($15,000,000).

(6) For all amounts above twenty-five million dollars ($25,000,000), a reasonable amount to be determined by the court.

(b) For the purposes of this section, the value of the estate accounted for by the personal representative is the total amount of the appraisal value of property in the inventory, plus gains over the appraisal value on sales, plus receipts, less losses from the appraisal value on sales, without reference to encumbrances or other obligations on estate property.

CALIFORNIA PROBATE CODE

SECTION 10801. ADDITIONAL COMPENSATION FOR EXTRAORDINARY SERVICES.

(a) Subject to the provisions of this part, in addition to the compensation provided by Section 10800, the court may allow additional compensation for extraordinary services by the personal representative in an amount the court determines is just and reasonable.

(b) The personal representative may also employ or retain tax counsel, tax auditors, accountants, or other tax experts for the performance of any action which such persons, respectively, may lawfully perform in the computation, reporting, or making of tax returns, or in negotiations or litigation which may be necessary for the final determination and payment of taxes, and pay from the funds of the estate for such services.

PROBLEMS

1. Under the California statute, if the decedent's estate has $800,000 in assets and no liabilities, how much can the personal representative collect in commissions? What if the estate has $3,000,000 in assets.

2. Suppose now that decedent's estate has $800,000 in assets and $1,000,000 in liabilities. How much can the personal representative collect in commissions? What problems would you foresee if commissions were based only on the "net" value of the estate?

QUESTIONS

1. Is there any reason to assume that the personal representative of a $10,000,000 estate will have more work to do than the representative of a $7,000,000 estate? What justifications might there be—other than the extra work associated with managing more money—for assessing commissions as a percentage of the assets in the estate?

2. In a jurisdiction that has adopted the UPC, what advice would you give to the executor of an $800,000 estate who asks how much she is entitled to in commissions? Suppose she claims $40,000 in commissions. Who is likely to object? If no one objects, what outcome is likely? Is the result likely to be the same in California?

3. Would you advise a personal representative to keep a record of time spent administering the estate? Does your answer depend on whether the estate is administered in California or in a UPC jurisdiction?

4. Decedent's will names the Faithful Trust Company as executor of her estate. Upon decedent's death, the trust company learns that the estate is worth $1,000,000, and that the beneficiaries (some of whom have received payments from decedent during her lifetime), are at war with one another. Is Faithful Trust obligated to accept an appointment as executor? Do you think it would be easier to persuade Faithful Trust to serve in a UPC jurisdiction or in California? Why?

5. In light of these questions, which commission structure would you think preferable—a fee schedule or a "reasonableness" standard?

6. *Negotiated Fees.* Thomas Testator expects that his estate will be worth $15,000,000 at his death, that he is leaving all of his property to his wife, and that all of his assets are in a single index fund. He approaches you to ask what fees his estate executor will be entitled to collect. How would you respond? If Thomas asks whether he can limit executor fees to $50,000, what advice would you give to him? Would a will provision directing that the executor accept compensation of $50,000 be effective? Consider the following California statute:

CALIFORNIA PROBATE CODE

SECTION 10802. COMPENSATION PROVIDED BY DECEDENT'S WILL.

> (a) Except as otherwise provided in this section, if the decedent's will makes provision for the compensation of the personal representative, the compensation provided by the will shall be the full and only compensation for the services of the personal representative.
>
> (b) The personal representative may petition the court to be relieved from a provision of the will that provides for the compensation of the personal representative.
>
> . . . .
>
> (d) If the court determines that it is to the advantage of the estate and in the best interest of the persons interested in the estate, the court may make an order authorizing compensation for the personal representative in an amount greater than provided in the will.

Would the California statute require the executor to accept appointment and accept the $50,000 commission? If not, why not? What other device could Tom Testator use to insure that an executor accepts appointment at the stated fee?

2. ATTORNEY FEES

Lawyers play a significant role in estate administration. When a will names a family member as an executor, that family member is not likely to understand the scope of his or her responsibilities. Because banks and trust companies are repeat players, they have more familiarity with the process, but they, too need legal advice. How much should they pay for that advice?

Theoretically, of course, the personal representative could shop around for an estate lawyer. As a practical matter, however, the personal representative is likely to start and end the search with the lawyer who drafted the will for testator. For the non-professional executor, choosing the testator's lawyer is a matter of convenience. For the professional executor, there may also be an aspect of "one hand washes the other." After all, the lawyer might have recommended the executor to the testator; if the executor returns the favor, the lawyer is more likely to make similar referrals in the future.

Who, then, will monitor the fees paid by the personal representative to the lawyer for the estate? If the personal representative is also a beneficiary, the personal representative has some incentive to minimize fees, but may have too little expertise to know what constitutes a reasonable fee. And if the personal representative is a professional, the personal representative has fewer incentives to keep fees low.

Historically, many states dealt with this problem by tying lawyer compensation to the compensation of the personal representative. The current California statute (among others) preserves that structure, including a compensation schedule that mirrors the compensation schedule for personal representatives. California Probate Code, § 10810. But the California statute also provides the following exception:

CALIFORNIA PROBATE CODE

SECTION 10811. ADDITIONAL COMPENSATION FOR EXTRAORDINARY SERVICES.

(a) Subject to the provisions of this part, in addition to the compensation provided by Section 10810, the court may allow additional compensation for extraordinary services by the attorney for the personal representative in an amount the court determines is just and reasonable.

(b) Extraordinary services by the attorney for which the court may allow compensation include services by a paralegal performing the extraordinary services under the direction and supervision of an attorney. The petition for compensation shall set forth the hours spent and services performed by the paralegal.

(c) An attorney for the personal representative may agree to perform extraordinary service on a contingent fee basis subject to the following conditions:

(1) The agreement is written and complies with all the requirements of Section 6147 of the Business and Professions Code.

(2) The agreement is approved by the court following a hearing noticed as provided in Section 10812.

(3) The court determines that the compensation provided in the agreement is just and reasonable and the agreement is to the advantage of the estate and in the best interests of the persons who are interested in the estate.

That exception provoked the following litigation:

Estate of Stevenson

Court of Appeal of California, Second Appellate District, 2006.
141 Cal.App.4th 1074, 46 Cal.Rptr.3d 573.

■ MALLANO, J.

Under the Probate Code, an attorney for the administrator of an estate may be paid for extraordinary services under a "contingency fee" agreement if the trial court approves the agreement after a noticed hearing. (Prob. Code, § 10811, subd. (c).) The trial court may dispense with notice for "good cause." (Id., § 1220, subd. (c).)

In this case, the trial court approved an agreement entitling counsel to attorney fees based on hourly rates and the total number of hours worked. The trial court dispensed with notice of the hearing and sealed a portion of the record so that creditors of the estate would not learn about the fee agreement until after they had concluded settlement negotiations with the estate.

Counsel managed to resolve most of the creditors' claims through settlement, reducing about $12 million in original claims to $1.7 million in court-approved settlements. Counsel also obtained about $700,000 in payments, resulting in an estate with a negative net worth of $1 million. Pursuant to the approved agreement, the administrator petitioned the trial court for approximately $1.25 million in attorney fees.

Upon learning of the fee petition, a creditor objected to the agreement on the ground that it left nothing for creditors. The trial court decided not to award fees pursuant to the agreement and instead awarded $200,000.

The administrator appeals the trial court's order, arguing that counsel was entitled to an award under the agreement. We conclude that the trial court did not abuse its discretion because the agreement was not a "contingency fee" agreement within the meaning of the Probate Code, and the trial court erred in dispensing with notice of the hearing. Further, the fee award was just and reasonable under the circumstances. We therefore affirm.

I

BACKGROUND

On August 17, 2001, Dan Stevenson killed himself. On January 2, 2002, appellant Kenneth Petrulis was appointed administrator with will annexed. Letters of administration issued two days later. Petrulis, an attorney, chose the firm of Goodson & Wachtel (Goodson), where he worked, to represent the estate. The trial court approved a stipulation providing that Petrulis would not share in Goodson's attorney fees, and Goodson would not share in Petrulis's commissions.

In the first half of 2002, Petrulis served notice of the proceedings on creditors. Numerous claims, totaling more than $12 million, were filed. Several creditors requested special notice of the proceedings. (See Prob. Code, § 1250; all further statutory references are to the Probate Code unless otherwise indicated.)

On March 15, 2002, Petrulis filed a petition to establish the estate's ownership of property. The petition alleged that Stevenson had been insolvent for the last 20 years of his life; he had borrowed funds from several creditors (lenders), often using the funds from one lender to repay funds borrowed from another lender. Stevenson had purchased one or more life insurance policies naming some of the lenders as beneficiaries, who had received policy proceeds after his death. The payment of those proceeds, according to the petition, had the effect of defrauding other creditors. Petrulis sought to recover the insurance proceeds as well as double damages (see § 859). The petition was served on the lenders.

In April and May 2002, several lenders filed objections to the petition. In June 2002, Petrulis filed a reply to the objections, explaining that the lenders had charged usurious interest on the loans, and some of the lenders had defrauded other creditors through the receipt of life insurance proceeds. Petrulis argued that the lenders, collectively, constituted a single joint venture or partnership.

In subsequent amended petitions, filed in September 2002 and February 2003, Petrulis alleged that the lenders had charged usurious rates and defrauded other creditors by accepting assignments of the life insurance proceeds. He sought to (1) recover usury penalties and specified interest payments, (2) reduce the balance of the loans by the amount of interest paid, and (3) recover property fraudulently transferred to other creditors.

On August 26, 2002, Petrulis filed an ex parte petition, seeking the trial court's approval of three agreements related to Goodson's compensation as counsel for the estate. The petition recited that the estate had no assets to inventory; the estate's primary asset was a claim against the lenders for the recovery of insurance proceeds and a potential recovery of usurious interest; the estate also had a claim against Prudential Insurance Company of America (Prudential) for wrongfully paying proceeds to certain lenders under two life insurance policies and wrongfully withholding proceeds from the estate under a third policy; the lenders' claims against the estate exceeded $12 million; and the estate was without resources to defend itself against the lenders and to pursue its own claims.

Petrulis requested that the trial court dispense with notice of the petition to the lenders, other creditors, and Prudential on the ground that knowledge of the "details and structure" of the agreements would put the estate "at a disadvantage in the litigation." Petrulis also sought to dispense with notice for the sake of expediency in light of an impending trial date in one matter. The petition stated that "[t]he creation of a pool of assets for the Estate will permit those creditors who are owed money to receive some or all of the amounts owed."

The third proposed agreement, the "Lodestar Fee Agreement," stated that Goodson would be paid its normal hourly rates "multiplied by a ... factor of ... two hundred percent" for work on claims involving the lenders, plus reimbursement of costs. The multiplier was said to be appropriate given the "contingent nature of the payment of said fees and the deferral of the payment of said fees, if at all." The Lodestar Fee Agreement further provided: "If the assets of the Estate after payment of all other statutory attorney fees and costs, representative's commissions and any other administrative costs ('Net Assets') are not adequate to pay the Attorney's Fees in full, [Goodson] agrees to reduce its Attorney's Fees to an amount equal to the greater of (1) the Net Assets available in the Estate which are payable to and are paid to [Goodson]; or (2) [Goodson's] normal hourly rates without a [multiplier]."

On September 3, 2002, after a hearing attended by Petrulis and an attorney representing [Stevenson's wife] Barbara, the trial court, dispensed with notice of the petition, approved the three agreements, and ordered the petition to be sealed until all litigation matters had been resolved.

Respondent William Wilks had filed a creditor's claim against the estate, seeking $1.34 million in unpaid loans and interest. He had also requested special notice. After negotiations with the estate, Wilks reduced his claim to $627,725. At the time, he did not know about the existence or approval of the Lodestar Fee Agreement. The estate accepted Wilks's compromise, agreeing not to contest it or seek to increase or decrease the amount. The trial court approved the settlement.

The estate engaged in settlement negotiations with other lenders, working with a forensic accountant in that effort. The estate was successful in negotiating a reduction in the amounts of almost all claims; some lenders agreed that they owed money to the estate. Upon petition by Petrulis, the trial court approved the settlements with these lenders, around 38 in all.

On August 15, 2003, Petrulis filed a petition for the payment of attorney fees pursuant to the Lodestar Fee Agreement. A hearing was scheduled for September 23, 2003. According to the petition, Goodson had spent 2,127.1 hours on the lenders' claims, which had initially totaled about $12.2 million. Through settlement, Goodson had reduced that amount to around $1.7 million. In addition, certain lenders had agreed to pay money to the estate, totaling $698,585. The estate therefore had a negative net worth of about $1 million.

In the petition, Petrulis contended that, based on normal hourly rates, Goodson would be entitled to $627,213 in attorney fees. But using the multiplier set forth in the Lodestar Fee Agreement, Petrulis actually requested fees of $1.25 million, plus $70,870 in costs. Notice of the hearing on the petition was served on, among others, creditors who had requested special notice.

After receipt of the notice, Wilks filed objections to the petition. He pointed out he had never been given notice of the Lodestar Fee Agreement or an opportunity to object to it. He asserted that Goodson had induced him to reduce his $1.3 million claim to around $627,000 by telling him he would probably get "100% on the dollar of his compromised claim." Wilks argued that Goodson's petition, if granted, would leave the estate with no assets for creditors—the same situation that existed before Goodson did any work for the estate. Thus, Goodson's efforts would have generated attorney fees, nothing more.

On February 4, 2005, the trial court issued a minute order, concluding: "[T]he estate cannot be considered to have received a benefit if only attorney's fees and administrative costs are generated. Though the lodestar contract was approved by the Court, we must assess realistically what benefit there was to the estate by settlements reducing claims, and which go unpaid. ... [G]ood faith with creditors would require a substantial payment consistent with the settlement. The estate should not have been 'created' to pay legal fees.... The issue of litigation counsel's fees may be reconsidered on the filing of a final account...." The court awarded $200,000 in fees and $73,144 in costs. A formal order was later entered to the same effect. Petrulis appealed.

II

DISCUSSION

A. Approval of Lodestar Fee Agreement

Petrulis bases his primary challenge to the attorney fee award on section 10811, subdivision (c), which provides in part: "An attorney for the personal representative may agree to perform extraordinary service on a contingent fee basis subject to the following conditions: [¶] (1) The agreement is written and complies with all the requirements of Section 6147 of the Business and Professions Code. [¶] (2) The agreement is approved by the court following a hearing noticed as provided in [Probate Code] Section 10812. . . ." (Italics added; hereafter section 10811(c).)

Petrulis argues that, once the trial court approved the Lodestar Fee Agreement, Goodson was entitled to fees according to the plain terms of the agreement: payment for total hours worked, using Goodson's normal hourly billing rates and a multiplier of 200 percent. We disagree for two reasons. First, the approved fee agreement does not come within section 10811(c). Second, the trial court, at Petrulis's request, erroneously dispensed with notice of the hearing on the proposed agreement.

1. Scope of Section 10811(c)

As stated, section 10811(c) permits an attorney to perform extraordinary services on a contingency fee basis provided the fee agreement is first approved by the court. (§ 10811(c)(2).) Such services include litigation to benefit the estate and the settlement of creditors' claims. (See Estate of Hilton (1996) 44 Cal.App.4th 890, 895, fn. 5 [52 Cal. Rptr. 2d 491]; Estate of Keith (1936) 16 Cal. App. 2d 67, 68–70 [60 P.2d 171]; Cal. Rules of Court, rule 7.703(c), adopted Jan. 1, 2003; 2 Cal. Decedent Estate Practice (Cont.Ed.Bar 2006) § 20.20, pp. 20–36 to 20–37.) The question here is whether the Lodestar Fee Agreement constitutes a "contingency fee" agreement within the meaning of the statute. We conclude it does not.

Under the agreement, Goodson was to be paid for the total number of hours worked based on hourly rates—twice the firm's normal hourly rates if sufficient assets were available after the estate paid administrative expenses (see, e.g., §§ 10800, 10810); otherwise, at normal hourly rates. Barbara was personally obligated to pay up to $250,000 in attorney fees if normal hourly rates were used.

[T]he use of percentages in contingency fee agreements ensures that the client will receive a portion of any recovery. Yet, the Lodestar Fee Agreement gives attorney fees priority over everything but the estate's administrative expenses, potentially leaving nothing for creditors or the sole beneficiary. Indeed, Goodson argues that, under the agreement, it was entitled to fees of more than $1 million notwithstanding that the assets in the estate were worth only about $700,000, and the estate owed the lenders around $1.7 million.

In this case, the Lodestar Fee Agreement did not state that Goodson would receive a percentage or portion of any recovery. Rather, it authorized Goodson to take the entire recovery. And in the petition for the payment of attorney fees, Petrulis claimed, incredibly, that Goodson was entitled to more than the entire recovery. Further, the agreement guaranteed that Goodson would be awarded attorney fees in some amount—based on normal hourly rates if the estate's assets were inadequate to pay double hourly rates. Accordingly, the Lodestar Fee Agreement did not constitute a contingency fee agreement, and section 10811(c) did not apply.

2. Lack of Notice of the Petition

In the alternative, the trial court erred in dispensing with notice of the hearing on the petition to approve the Lodestar Fee Agreement. The trial court approved the agreement by way of an ex parte petition, dispensed with notice of the hearing, and ordered the petition sealed until the estate concluded all litigation. Sections 10811(c)(2) and 1220, subdivision (a)(2), required notice of such a hearing unless there was "good cause" to dispense with it (§ 1220, subd. (c)). As we explain, good cause did not exist.

Petrulis contends the lack of notice was proper because he did not want creditors to learn about his litigation strategy; if they did, he argues, they would have had an unfair advantage in the litigation. Also, expediency supposedly justified the lack of notice because of an approaching trial date.

Notice is the cornerstone of estate proceedings. As a matter of fundamental rights, creditors who are known or reasonably ascertainable must be notified—in a manner reasonably calculated to provide actual notice—that probate proceedings have been instituted. (See Tulsa Professional Collection Services v. Pope (1988) 485 U.S. 478, 487–491 [99 L. Ed. 2d 565, 108 S. Ct. 1340, 1346–1348]; Venturi v. Taylor (1995) 35 Cal.App.4th 16, 20–23 [41 Cal. Rptr. 2d 272].) The presumption is therefore in favor of notice under section 10811(c).

Contrary to Petrulis's concerns, the Lodestar Fee Agreement did not disclose "litigation strategy." It simply described the estate's claims against the lenders, namely, the lenders had charged usurious interest, and some lenders had improperly received life insurance proceeds. The estate's petition to establish ownership of property and its reply to the creditors' objections, both of which were filed before the petition to approve the Lodestar Fee Agreement, disclosed exactly this "litigation strategy." Thus, the fee petition and the Lodestar Fee Agreement did not reveal anything new.

Nor should creditors be kept in the dark about a court-approved method of compensating an estate's attorney. The Lodestar Fee Agreement arguably gave Goodson the right to recover all of its fees out of the estate's assets—at twice the normal hourly rates—before creditors could recover anything. Consequently, the lenders had a significant interest in knowing about Goodson's compensation before negotiating with the estate to reduce the amount of their claims. A court cannot approve an agreement under section 10811(c) unless it finds that the agreement is "in the best interests of the persons who are interested in the estate" (§ 10811(c)(3)), which includes creditors (§ 48, subd. (a)(1)). Here, an entire group of interested persons was excluded from the decision-making process.

Last, expediency did not justify dispensing with notice. The record does not suggest the lenders were at fault for the estate's failure to seek approval of the Lodestar Fee Agreement at an earlier point. And by invoking expediency and keeping the agreement a secret, the estate should have known that it was merely postponing objections by the creditors. Having opted for expediency early on, the estate cannot legitimately complain that Wilks eventually got his day in court. Thus, there was no good cause for dispensing with notice, and the trial court erred in that respect.

In sum, because the Lodestar Fee Agreement was not a contingency fee agreement and was approved without notice, the agreement was not proper under section 10811(c).

E. Priority of Payment of Debts

Under section 11420, administrative expenses, which include attorney fees, must be paid before the estate pays general creditors like the lenders. (§ 11420, subd. (a)(1), (7); Estate of Turino (1970) 8 Cal. App. 3d 642, 647–648 [87 Cal. Rptr. 581].) Petrulis interprets this statute to mean that the trial court had to award Goodson all of its requested fees and that whatever was left, if anything, could go to the lenders or others.

But section 11420 controls only the priority of payment, that is, the order in which various types of expenses are to be paid, not the amount. The statute dictates who gets paid first, second, and on down the line. It does not govern how much anyone is to be paid or how any particular amount is to be calculated. Rather, the trial court first determines the amount of attorney fees by applying criteria specified elsewhere (see pt. II.F., post), and section 11420 then ensures that the attorneys get paid in full before any general creditors are paid.

F. Factors for Determining Fees for Extraordinary Services

"Every [probate] attorney should be fully and fairly paid for his services, having in mind their nature, their difficulty, the value of the estate, and the responsibility thus cast upon the counselor." (Estate of Byrne (1898) 122 Cal. 260, 266 [54 P. 957], italics added.)

The trial court expressly found that Goodson's efforts, though "heroic," had done virtually nothing to benefit the estate. The lenders' claims, though substantially reduced through settlements, still exceeded the estate's assets by about $1 million. The assets were worth about $700,000. At most, according to the trial court, Goodson had created an estate to pay legal fees.

Nevertheless, Petrulis argued that Goodson should be awarded more than $1 million in fees. But from what source was that sum to have been paid? The request appeared incredible on its face. Given that the assets in the estate did not exceed $700,000, we cannot say that a fee award of

$200,000 was an abuse of discretion. That left $427,000 in assets (after the award of costs) and $1.7 million still due the lenders.

Further, the petition to approve the Lodestar Fee Agreement specifically stated, "The creation of a pool of assets for the Estate will permit those creditors who are owed money to receive some or all of the amounts owed." But the petition for payment of attorney fees left nothing for them. The trial court acted within its discretion in rejecting that result. And, as stated by the trial court, "The issue of litigation counsel's fees may be reconsidered on the filing of a final account. . . ."

III

DISPOSITION

The order is affirmed.

NOTES AND QUESTIONS

1. Dan Stevenson's estate was clearly insolvent at the time of his death. Who would have sought appointment of a personal representative of an insolvent estate? Why administer the estate? If Stevenson's will beneficiaries would not receive any assets as a result of administration, to whom did the personal representative owe fiduciary duties?

2. If the Goodson firm had not entered into the Lodestar Fee Agreement with Petrulis, the personal representative, to what would Goodson have been entitled under the California fee statute? Would Goodson have had any incentive to locate assets for the estate? Would you agree to serve as lawyer for an estate with no assets? With more liabilities than assets?

3. Suppose Petrulis had entered into an agreement with the Goodson firm to pay the firm's hourly rate for work done for the estate. Would the agreement have been enforceable under the California statute? Why or why not?

4. The Lodestar agreement entitled Goodson to twice its hourly rates if Goodson recovered funds from the lenders, and to much less, perhaps nothing (except for funds Stevenson's wife had agreed to pay), if the estate had no assets. Why wasn't the agreement a contingent fee agreement within the meaning of the California statute? Why would the California statute permit contingent fee agreements but not agreements like the Goodson lodestar agreement?

Note that the California statute provides for reasonableness review of contingent fee arrangements. Why? Why shouldn't the client be entirely free to shift to the lawyer some of the risk that legal work for the estate will be complicated—while also providing the lawyer an incentive to discover more assets? Is it because the lawyer is in a much better position to evaluate the risks than the client?

5. Why would lawyers and personal representatives be first in line to collect estate assets? Why shouldn't they be treated like other creditors of the estate?

6. Why did the California courts award fees of $200,000 to Goodson? If the agreement was invalid, why shouldn't the Goodson firm have been limited to the fees provided in section 10810 of the California Probate Code (fees equivalent to the fees payable to a personal representative)?

7. Many states do not have statutory schedules for lawyer fees, but provide for "reasonable" fees for lawyers representing estates. In those states, should retainer agreements between personal representatives and lawyers be presumed reasonable?

The executor of Andy Warhol's estate hired an entertainment lawyer with no estates experience to serve as counsel for the estate. The retainer agreement called for a fee of 2% of the estate. The Surrogate's court concluded that the retainer agreement was unenforceable, because the court was obligated to determine the reasonable value of the services performed. The court then concluded that the lawyer was entitled to a fee of $7.2 million—a fee reduced on appeal to $3.5 million.

Suppose, before his death, Warhol had hired a lawyer to handle all of his legal affairs. Would a court have reviewed the fee Warhol agreed to pay? If not, why should a court review the fee the executor agreed to pay? Is there any reason why an executor might agree to pay a lawyer more than necessary to secure competent legal counsel?

Do the fees paid to the estate lawyer come out of the personal representative's pocket? If not, what incentive does the personal representative have to negotiate a low fee? If the personal representative does negotiate a low fee, and the lawyers then do a bad job, might the beneficiaries contend that the personal representative was being penny-wise and pound foolish?

8. *Other Administrative Expenses.* The personal representative is entitled to hire other professionals, including accountants and appraisers, to assist in the administration of the estate, and to treat fees for those services as expenses of the estate. Yet statutes rarely regulate fees for those professional in the way they regulate lawyer fees. Why? Is there any reason to think the potential for abuse is greater when the personal representative hires a lawyer than when the representative hires an accountant?

PROBLEMS

1. Guy Olden is a client of yours. He is a rich widower, famous for his good manners and his orderliness in business affairs. His brood of children are famous for suing each other on what seems to be a fairly regular basis—several local lawyers have made many a house payment on fees from Guy's kids. Guy has always done business with The Bank of GraniteRock and with your firm. It is rather hard to imagine strangers taking over as advisers to Guy and his successors—the start-up cost would be enormous. It's time to do some serious estate planning for Guy. You dread the appointment for fear he will ask you to promise to represent the executor of his estate, come what may, and because you know he will ask your advice on whom to appoint as executor. Representing Guy has been a pleasure. Dealing with his kids is another story. The Bank of GraniteRock has informed you that it reserves its right to refuse to qualify as an executor in any situation. What would induce you, a prosperous lawyer with plenty of other business, to represent Guy's executor, besides a sense of duty and a concern for reputation, and what would induce the Bank to be his executor? In the abstract, what would you do to give Guy the results he wants?

2. Gallatin A. Young is a pop singer of enormous wealth. His financial empire is byzantine in its complexity. His prodigious appetite for life is well-known. He lives on the road in a shadowy world of hangers-on, claimants, possible offspring, contracts, lawsuits and businesses.

If he came to you for estate planning whom would you recommend as his executor(s)? Would you recommend that he negotiate commissions and legal fees? What should the fee structure be? What kind of language, if any, would you put into his will regarding compensation of lawyers? What ethical problems, if any, would this present for you?

"Double-dipping"—when a lawyer is both the fiduciary and the lawyer for the fiduciary

An estate representative is free to hire whomever she wants as her attorney. Indeed, that freedom is such that directions in wills to "hire Lawyer Jones" are against public policy. When the estate representative is the lawyer, the representative is also entitled to serve as her own lawyer.

The only question is whether the lawyer-executor who uses herself as estate lawyer can get paid twice. The answer varies from state to state. It's acceptable in some states and against public policy in other states. And some states split the difference and reduce the compensation so that the lawyer must take less than separate executors and lawyers would get. There is a tendency to approve double-dipping only when the testator has been fully informed, beyond any doubt, that the lawyer-executor will be getting substantial compensation. See N.Y. SCPA section 2307–a.

What honest financial advantage is there in being the nominated fiduciary in a state where double-dipping is forbidden? What selfish advantage lies in a lawyer-fiduciary's power to pick his own lawyer when he has decided not to hire himself? What special risk does the dishonest fiduciary-attorney who hires himself pose to the beneficiaries of the trust or estate?

Most bank trust departments go out of their way to hire the lawyer who wrote the instrument in which they are nominated. Why do you suppose that is? What advantage does that practice offer lawyers who don't want to act as fiduciaries or whose clients don't want lawyer fiduciaries? See generally Paula A. Monopoli, American Probate 35–37 (2003).

Interestingly enough, the standard wisdom among lawyers is to never seek appointment as a fiduciary. The custom is not saintly, it's designed to protect fee income. The belief is that many clients will be offended and will end up going to a new lawyer. So, even if one is not ethical, one is unwise to solicit fiduciary appointments.

SECTION II. THE DUTY OF LOYALTY

Recall the position of the trustee or executor: she holds legal title to property, but she holds that legal title for the benefit of the trust or estate beneficiaries. What incentive does the trustee have to spend time and effort maximizing the interests of the beneficiaries? Of course, most trustees will try to "do the right thing" regardless of legal incentives. And maintaining a positive business reputation may induce many corporate trustees to keep beneficiary interests paramount. At the margins, however, social norms and market pressures may provide inadequate protection against "agency costs" generated by the fact that the trustee's personal benefit is not perfectly correlated with the effort the trustee devotes to managing the trust. But in some cases, social norms and market pressures may be inadequate to protect beneficiaries against slothful, incompetent, or avaricious trustees. See Robert H. Sitkoff, An Agency Cost Theory of Trust Law, 89 Cornell L. Rev. 621, 631 (2004); Melanie B. Leslie, Trusting Trustees: Fiduciary Duties and the Limits of Default Rules, 94 Geo. L.J. 67, 77–94 (2005).

Legal doctrine—in the form of fiduciary duties—operates to supplement the protections provided by moral scruples and market pressures. Of those fiduciary duties, the two most basic are the duty of care and the duty of loyalty. The duty of care (the subject of the next section) requires the trustee to put in the time and effort necessary to safeguard the interests of the beneficiaries. The duty of loyalty, by contrast, operates to ensure that the trustee acts in the interests of trust beneficiaries rather than in self-interest.

The duty of loyalty requires the fiduciary to act only for the benefit of the trust beneficiaries. The fiduciary may not deal with the property so as to personally benefit directly or indirectly. The fiduciary's central concerns must be the carrying out of the testator's or settlor's intent and the welfare of the beneficiaries. An important element of the duty of loyalty is a flat prohibition against any transactions involving self-dealing. Restatement (Third) of Trusts: Prudent Investor Rule § 170 (1992). See Gregory S. Alexander, A Cognitive Theory of Fiduciary Relationships, 85 Cornell L. Rev. 767 (2000).

Why prohibit self-dealing? Suppose it is in the interest of trust beneficiaries to sell an apartment house owned by the trust. Why shouldn't the trustee be able to purchase the house if the trustee is willing to pay as much or more than the highest outside bidder? Consider the problem: if the trustee is willing to pay $200,000 for the house, is the house worth more or less than $200,000 to the trustee? If it were worth less, would the trustee pay $200,000 for the house? If it is worth more, is the trustee benefiting personally from the transaction with the trust? If yes, isn't the trustee breaching his fiduciary duty?

A simple application of the prohibition against self-dealing comes in sales by the fiduciary of her own property to the trust, or the converse, the purchase of estate or trust property by the fiduciary. The beneficiary has the right to disaffirm or avoid such a transaction; of course, if it is to the beneficiary's advantage he or she may affirm it. Proof of good faith or lack of personal profit on the part of the fiduciary is immaterial. It should be apparent that a sale to the fiduciary's spouse or to a third party who conveys back to the fiduciary stands on no better footing.

The prohibition also prevents a trustee from feathering his or her own nest. Samuel P. King & Randall W. Roth, Broken Trust 110 (2006) (A trustee "routinely ordered Bishop Estate staffers to run errands for her— . . . big ones. . . . When the renovation of her beach house needed variances . . . [she] ordered two high level staffers [of the trust] to attend to the matter. . . . [She traveled first class] with an entourage.").

Consider the Uniform Trust Code's formulation:

SECTION 802. DUTY OF LOYALTY.

(a) A trustee shall administer the trust solely in the interests of the beneficiaries.

(b) Subject to the rights of persons dealing with or assisting the trustee as provided in Section 1012, a sale, encumbrance, or other transaction involving the investment or management of trust property entered into by the trustee for the trustee's own personal account or which is otherwise affected by a conflict between the trustee's fiduciary and personal interests is voidable by a beneficiary affected by the transaction unless:

(1) the transaction was authorized by the terms of the trust;

(2) the transaction was approved by the court;

(3) the beneficiary did not commence a judicial proceeding within the time allowed by Section 1005;

(4) the beneficiary consented to the trustee's conduct, ratified the transaction, or released the trustee in compliance with Section 1009; or

(5) the transaction involves a contract entered into or claim acquired by the trustee before the person became or contemplated becoming trustee.

(c) A sale, encumbrance, or other transaction involving the investment or management of trust property is presumed to be affected by a conflict between personal and fiduciary interests if it is entered into by the trustee with:

(1) the trustee's spouse;

(2) the trustee's descendants, siblings, parents, or their spouses;

(3) an agent or attorney of the trustee; or

(4) a corporation or other person or enterprise in which the trustee, or a person that owns a significant interest in the trustee, has an interest that might affect the trustee's best judgment

. . .

The simplest form of self-dealing involves a purchase and sale transaction or a loan transaction with the fiduciary on one side of the transaction and the estate or trust on the other side. Courts have developed a "no further inquiry rule" that permits beneficiaries to rescind these transactions even though the fiduciary may have negotiated a "fair" price for the trust or estate. The fiduciary may not even purchase at a public auction sale, because the fiduciary's self-interest might conflict with her duty to avoid the sale if possible, or to see that the sale is held under conditions that will yield the highest price.

Often, however, self-dealing is less direct. The fiduciary may engage in transactions with a relative, or with a corporation in which the fiduciary has a financial interest. Does the no further inquiry rule extend to such transactions? The UTC and some commentators take the position that there is no flat prohibition on so-called "indirect self-dealing," but the fiduciary has the burden of showing that the transaction was completely fair to the beneficiaries, despite the taint of possible conflict. See John Langbein, Questioning the Trust Law Duty of Loyalty: Sole Interest or Best Interests?, 114 Yale L.J. 929, 980 (2005). Does that position make sense? Professor Leslie argues that the no further inquiry rule, with its advance approval requirement, is the appropriate rule to apply to indirect self-dealing involving professional trustees and their corporate affiliates. See Melanie B. Leslie, Common Law, Common Sense: Fiduciary Standards and Trustee Identity, 27 Cardozo L. Rev. 2713 (2006).

QUESTIONS

1. Re-examine the Uniform Trust Code. If a trustee sells property to his sister, can the beneficiaries invalidate the sale? Suppose the trustee sells to his niece? To a corporate client of his wife's accounting firm? For more discussion of the UTC's duty of loyalty provisions, see Karen E. Boxx, Of Punctilios and Paybacks: The Duty of Loyalty Under the Uniform Trust Code, 67 Mo. L. Rev. 279 (2002).

2. Suppose the trustee's sister is willing to pay more for trust property than anyone else. The trustee has a duty to use reasonable efforts to obtain the highest price possible for the property. How should the trustee structure the transaction to avoid a violation of the duty of loyalty?

As you read the following case, consider how you would have advised the executor to proceed:

Matter of Kinzler

Supreme Court, Appellate Division, 1993.
195 A.D.2d 464, 600 N.Y.S.2d 126.

■ MEMORANDUM BY THE COURT.

In a proceeding for the judicial settlement of the account of the executor of a decedent's estate, the executor appeals, * * * from stated portions of a decree of the Surrogate's Court * * * which, inter alia, (1) awarded the objectants' attorney $7,000 as and for legal fees, payable by the estate, (2) held that the sale of the decedent's residence to one of the beneficiaries, who was also a testamentary trustee under the will, was tainted with a conflict of interest and self-dealing, (3) held the payment by the executor to himself of advance legal fees, without prior court order, to be improper and ordered him to refund $11,595.15, plus interest in the amount of $16,398.68, for a total of $27,993.83, and (4) fixed the legal fees of the executor in amounts less than requested.

ORDERED that the decree is affirmed insofar as appealed from, without costs or disbursements.

The decedent Pauline Kinzler died on February 26, 1986. She was survived by three daughters: Gloria Zweibon, Louise Kinzler, and the respondent Beatrice Hornstein. Her will was drafted by her son-in-law, Bertram Zweibon, the appellant herein, whom she also nominated as the Executor.

The will divided her estate into three parts, to be distributed one-third outright to Louise Kinzler, one-third outright to Gloria Zweibon, and one-third in trust for the benefit of Beatrice Hornstein, as the income beneficiary, and the remainder to Hornstein's children, Jay, Joseph and Eric. Louise Kinzler and Gloria Zweibon were appointed cotrustees of the testamentary trust by the will.

In October 1987 Beatrice Hornstein and two of her children, Joseph and Eric, brought the instant proceeding. Bertram Zweibon, the executor, opposed the petition on various grounds. However, the Surrogate directed the executor to submit an account.

After the executor submitted the account and filed a petition for final judicial settlement thereof, the respondents filed various objections to the account. The executor appeals * * *.

"The general rule is that, where legal services have been rendered for the benefit of the estate as a whole, resulting in the enlargement of all the shares of all the estate beneficiaries, reasonable compensation should be granted from the funds of the estate" * * *

At bar, the efforts of the respondents' attorney resulted in a directive that the attorney-fiduciary refund over $11,000 to the estate, plus interest in the amount of over $16,000, for a total of almost $28,000. Thus, clearly the distributive shares of all the beneficiaries of the estate were substantially enlarged by the efforts of the respondents' attorney. The test for awarding legal fees payable by the estate was, therefore, satisfied. Consequently, neither the directive that the estate pay the respondents' attorneys' fees, nor the amount awarded, was unreasonable.

The Surrogate's finding that the sale of the decedent's house to Louise Kinzler was tainted by conflict of interest and self-dealing is also supported by the record. The executor sold an asset of the estate, in which the testamentary trust had a one-third interest, to a cotrustee. Thus, the self-dealing is the purchase by the testamentary cotrustee of an asset in which the trust had a one-third interest. A person "standing in the relation of a fiduciary capacity, cannot deal with or purchase the property, in reference to which he holds that relation" * * *.

Moreover, the executor was aware of the hostility between the daughters. Yet, his administration of the estate was clearly marked by a lack of impartiality. Up until the commencement of the litigation, he refused to pay income to the respondent Beatrice Hornstein, claiming that income was needed to pay estate taxes.

Moreover, upon the sale of the decedent's house, the appellant made a cash distribution of approximately $50,000 (1/3 of the purchase price) to his wife, and only assigned the purchase money mortgage for the property to the trust. "An executor must at all times discharge his fiduciary duties so that all legatees are treated in like manner and without prejudice or discrimination" * * *. Here, it is evident that the executor failed this test.

The executor also violated SCPA 2111 when he paid himself compensation in advance for legal services rendered, without obtaining prior court approval. "[T]he court cannot condone and must admonish counsel for his failure to comply with SCPA 2111 in that he, as a sole fiduciary, paid himself compensation in advance for legal services rendered without obtaining prior court approval. Even though those who benefit from this estate [might have] consented to the unauthorized advance payment of legal fees, the court cannot ignore the violation of the aforesaid statute by a member of the Bar" * * *. Accordingly, the Surrogate properly surcharged interest on the unauthorized advance payment of the appellant's legal fees. Nor did the court improvidently exercise its discretion in fixing the legal fees at $10,000. SCPA 2110 states that it is ultimately the court's responsibility to decide what constitutes reasonable compensation * * *. In determining what constitutes just and reasonable compensation for an attorney's services, the court should "consider the time spent, the difficulties involved in the matters in which the services were rendered, the nature of the services, the amount involved, the professional standing of the counsel, and the results obtained" * * *. The court may also consider whether the attorney was also the executor entitled to commissions * * *.

At bar, the court considered all these factors. It also concluded that the quality of services rendered by the appellant was "considerably less than satisfactory". In view of the court's observations, as well as the fact that the appellant also received commissions in the amount of $21,791.02, the court did not improvidently exercise its discretion in limiting his entire legal fees, including services rendered in connection with the accounting proceeding, to $10,000.

We have considered the appellant's remaining contentions and find them to be meritless.

QUESTIONS AND NOTES

1. Executor Zweibon sold decedent's house to his sister-in-law, Louise Kinzler. Who breached the duty of loyalty with respect to that transaction? Why? How would the Uniform Trust Code resolve the issue?

Pauline Kinzler's home was a valuable estate asset. Empty, it generated no return for any of the estate beneficiaries. If executor Zweibon had asked for your advice about how to proceed with the house, what advice would you have given him? Suppose Louise had been eager to buy the house. What advice would you have given her?

2. Suppose Zweibon had sought an appraisal before selling the property to his sister-in-law. Would the appraisal have insulated the sale from attack? Why or why not? Does it matter who conducted the appraisal, and how? Cf. Estate of Talty, 376 Ill.App.3d 1082, 315 Ill.Dec. 866, 877 N.E.2d 1195 (2007) (appraisal conducted by CPA employed by corporation controlled by trustee).

3. What remedies were available to the Hornsteins as a result of the breach of fiduciary duty? What remedies would have been available if Louise Kinzler had sold the home for $300,000 two months after buying it for $150,000? Would it matter if, after the sale, the market price increased to $500,000? Dropped to $200,000?

4. What did executor Zweibon do with the proceeds of the sale to Louise Kinzler? Did that constitute a breach of the duty of loyalty? Why?

5. ***Conflicts of Interest.*** As the husband of an estate beneficiary, executor Zweibon was in a conflict of interest position: actions that were good for some of the estate beneficiaries might not have been good for his wife, and vice versa. Should courts allow executors to serve when they are in a conflict of interest position? Why or why not?

6. Should the decedent in Kinzler have picked a different trustee? One outside the family? Who? How realistic is the search in a modest estate? On the difference between professional and non-professional trustees, see Melanie B. Leslie, Common Law, Common Sense: Fiduciary Standards and Trustee Identity, 27 Cardozo L. Rev. 2713 (2006).

Matter of Estate of Rothko

Court of Appeals of New York, 1977.
43 N.Y.2d 305, 401 N.Y.S.2d 449, 372 N.E.2d 291.

■ COOKE, JUDGE.

Mark Rothko, * * * [a famous] abstract expressionist painter * * *, died testate on February 25, 1970. The principal asset of his estate consisted of 798 paintings of tremendous value, and the dispute underlying this appeal involves the conduct of his three executors in their disposition of these works of art. In sum, that conduct as portrayed in the record and sketched in the opinions was manifestly wrongful and indeed shocking.

Rothko's will was admitted to probate on April 27, 1970 and letters testamentary were issued to Bernard J. Reis, Theodoros Stamos and Morton Levine. Hastily and within a period of only about three weeks and by virtue of two contracts each dated May 21, 1970, the executors dealt with all 798 paintings.

By a contract of sale, the estate executors agreed to sell to Marlborough A.G., a Liechtenstein corporation (hereinafter MAG), 100 Rothko paintings as listed for $1,800,000, $200,000 to be paid on execution of the agreement and the balance of $1,600,000 in 12 equal interest-free installments over a 12–year period. Under the second agreement, the executors consigned to Marlborough Gallery, Inc., a domestic corporation (hereinafter MNY), "approximately 700 paintings listed on a Schedule to be prepared", the consignee to be responsible for costs covering items such as insurance, storage restoration and promotion. By its provisos, MNY could sell up to 35 paintings a year from each of two groups, pre–1947 and post–1947, for 12 years at the best price obtainable but not less than the appraised estate value, and it would receive a 50% commission on each painting sold, except for a commission of 40% on those sold to or through other dealers.

Petitioner Kate Rothko, decedent's daughter[,] and [the guardian of the decedent's son, Christopher Rothko, both] * * * entitled to share in his estate by virtue of an election under EPTL 5–3.3, instituted this proceeding to remove the executors, to enjoin MNY and MAG from disposing of the paintings, to rescind the aforesaid agreements between the executors and said corporations, for a return of the paintings still in possession of those corporations, and for damages. * * * The Attorney–General of the State, as the representative of the ultimate beneficiaries of the Mark Rothko Foundation, Inc., a charitable corporation and the residuary legatee under decedent's will, joined in requesting relief substantially similar to that prayed for by petitioner. On June 26, 1972 the Surrogate issued a temporary restraining order and on September 26, 1972 a preliminary injunction enjoining MAG, MNY, and the three executors from selling or otherwise disposing of the paintings referred to in the agreements dated May 21, 1970, except for sales or dispositions made with court permission. * * *

Following a nonjury trial covering 89 days and in a thorough opinion, the Surrogate found: that Reis was a director, secretary and treasurer of MNY, the consignee art gallery, in addition to being a coexecutor of the estate; that the testator had a 1969 *inter vivos* contract with MNY to sell Rothko's work at a commission of only 10% and whether that agreement survived testator's death was a problem that a fiduciary in a dual position could not have impartially faced; that Reis was in a position of serious conflict of interest with respect to the contracts of May 21, 1970 and that his dual role and planned purpose benefited the Marlborough interests to the detriment of the estate; that it was to the advantage of coexecutor Stamos as a "not-too-successful artist, financially", to curry favor with

Marlborough and that the contract made by him with MNY within months after signing the estate contracts placed him in a position where his personal interests conflicted with those of the estate, especially leading to lax contract enforcement efforts by Stamos; that Stamos acted negligently and improvidently in view of his own knowledge of the conflict of interest of Reis; [and] that the third coexecutor, Levine, while not acting in self-interest or with bad faith, nonetheless failed to exercise ordinary prudence in the performance of his assumed fiduciary obligations since he was aware of Reis' divided loyalty, believed that Stamos was also seeking personal advantage, possessed personal opinions as to the value of the paintings and yet followed the leadership of his coexecutors without investigation of essential facts or consultation with competent and disinterested appraisers, and that the business transactions of the two Marlborough corporations were admittedly controlled and directed by Francis K. Lloyd. It was concluded that the acts and failures of the three executors were clearly improper to such a substantial extent as to mandate their removal under SCPA 711 as estate fiduciaries. The Surrogate also found that MNY, MAG and Lloyd were guilty of contempt in shipping, disposing of and selling 57 paintings in violation of the temporary restraining order dated June 26, 1972 and of the injunction dated September 26, 1972; that the contracts for sale and consignment of paintings between the executors and MNY and MAG provided inadequate value to the estate, amounting to a lack of mutuality and fairness resulting from conflicts on the part of Reis and Stamos and improvidence on the part of all executors; that said contracts were voidable and were set aside by reason of violation of the duty of loyalty and improvidence of the executors, knowingly participated in and induced by MNY and MAG * * *. The Surrogate held that the present value at the time of trial of the paintings sold is the proper measure of damages as to MNY, MAG, Lloyd, Reis and Stamos. He imposed a civil fine of $3,332,000 upon MNY, MAG and Lloyd, same being the appreciated value at the time of trial of the 57 paintings sold in violation of the temporary restraining order and injunction. It was held that Levine was liable for $6,464,880 in damages, as he was not in a dual position acting for his own interest and was thus liable only for the actual value of paintings sold MNY and MAG as of the dates of sale, and that Reis, Stamos, MNY and MAG, apart from being jointly and severally liable for the same damages as Levine for negligence, were liable for the greater sum of $9,252,000 "as appreciation damages less amounts previously paid to the estate with regard to sales of paintings." * * *

The Appellate Division * * * modified [the Surrogate's opinion] * * *. [T]he majority affirmed on the opinion of Surrogate Midonick, with additional comments. Among others, it was stated that the entire court agreed that executors Reis and Stamos had a conflict of interest and divided loyalty in view of their nexus to MNY * * * The majority agreed with the Surrogate's analysis awarding "appreciation damages" * * *.

* * *

In seeking a reversal, it is urged that an improper legal standard was applied in voiding the estate contracts of May, 1970, that the "no further inquiry" rule applies only to self-dealing and that in case of a conflict of interest, absent self-dealing, a challenged transaction must be shown to be unfair. The subject of fairness of the contracts is intertwined with the issue of whether Reis and Stamos were guilty of conflicts of interest. Scott is quoted to the effect that "[a] trustee does not necessarily incur liability merely because he has an individual interest in the transaction * * * In Bullivant v. First Nat. Bank [246 Mass. 324, 141 N.E. 41] it was held that * * * the fact that the bank was also a creditor of the corporation did not make its assent invalid, *if it acted in good faith and the plan was fair*" (2 Scott, Trusts, § 170.24, p. 1384 [emphasis added]) * * *.

* * * First, a review of the opinions of the Surrogate and the Appellate Division manifests that they did not rely solely on a "no further inquiry rule", and secondly, there is more than an adequate basis to conclude that the agreements between the Marlborough corporations and the estate were neither fair nor in the best interests of the estate. * * * The opinions under review demonstrate that neither the Surrogate nor the Appellate Division set aside the contracts by merely applying the no further inquiry rule without regard to fairness. Rather they determined, quite properly indeed, that these agreements were neither fair nor in the best interests of the estate.

To be sure, the assertions that there were no conflicts of interest on the part of Reis or Stamos indulge in sheer fantasy. Besides being a director and officer of MNY, for which there was financial remuneration, however slight, Reis, as noted by the Surrogate, had different inducements to favor the Marlborough interests, including his own aggrandizement of status and financial advantage through sales of almost one million dollars for items from his own and his family's extensive private art collection by the Marlborough interests * * *. Similarly, Stamos benefited as an artist under contract with Marlborough and, interestingly, Marlborough purchased a Stamos painting from a third party for $4,000 during the week in May, 1970 when the estate contract negotiations were pending * * *. The conflicts are manifest. Further, as noted in Bogert, Trusts and Trustees (2d ed.), "The duty of loyalty imposed on the fiduciary prevents him from accepting employment from a third party who is entering into a business transaction with the trust" (§ 543, subd. [S], p. 573). "While he [a trustee] is administering the trust he must refrain from placing himself in a position where his personal interest or that of a third person does or may conflict with the interest of the beneficiaries" * * * Here, Reis was employed and Stamos benefited in a manner contemplated by Bogert (see, also, Meinhard v. Salmon, 249 N.Y. 458, 464, 466–467, 164 N.E. 545, 547–548 * * *). In short, one must strain the law rather than follow it to reach the result suggested on behalf of Reis and Stamos.

Levine contends that, having acted prudently and upon the advice of counsel, a complete defense was established. Suffice it to say, an executor who knows that his coexecutor is committing breaches of trust and not only fails to exert efforts directed towards prevention but accedes to them is legally accountable even though he was acting on the advice of counsel * * *. When confronted with the question of whether to enter into the Marlborough contracts, Levine was acting in a business capacity, not a legal one, in which he was required as an executor primarily to employ such diligence and prudence to the care and management of the estate assets and affairs as would prudent persons of discretion and intelligence (King v. Talbot, 40 N.Y. 76, 85–86), accented by "[n]ot honesty alone, but the punctilio of an honor the most sensitive" (Meinhard v. Salmon, 249 N.Y. 458, 464, 164 N.E. 545, 546, supra). Alleged good faith on the part of a fiduciary forgetful of his duty is not enough * * *. He could not close his eyes, remain passive or move with unconcern in the face of the obvious loss to be visited upon the estate by participation in those business arrangements and then shelter himself behind the claimed counsel of an attorney * * *.

Further, there is no merit to the argument that MNY and MAG lacked notice of the breach of trust. The record amply supports the determination that they are chargeable with notice of the executors' breach of duty.

The measure of damages was the issue that divided the Appellate Division (see 56 A.D.2d, at p. 500, 392 N.Y.S.2d at p. 872). The contention of Reis, Stamos, MNY and MAG, that the award of appreciation damages was legally erroneous and impermissible, is based on a principle that an executor authorized to sell is not liable for an increase in value if the breach consists only in selling for a figure less than that for which the executor should have sold. For example, Scott states:

> "The beneficiaries are not entitled to the value of the property at the time of the decree if it was not the duty of the trustee to retain the property in the trust and the breach of trust consisted *merely* in selling the property for too low a price" (3 Scott, Trusts [3d ed.], § 208.3, p. 1687 [emphasis added]).
>
> "If the trustee is guilty of a breach of trust in selling trust property for an inadequate price, he is liable for the difference between the amount he should have received and the amount which he did receive. He is not liable, however, for any subsequent rise in value of the property sold". (Id., '208.6, pp. 1689–1690.)

A recitation of similar import appears in Comment *d* under Restatement, Trusts 2d (§ 205): "*d.* Sale for less than value. If the trustee is authorized to sell trust property, but in breach of trust he sells it for less than he should receive, he is liable for the value of the property at the time of the sale less the amount which he received. If the breach of trust consists *only* in selling it for too little, he is not chargeable with the amount of any subsequent increase in value of the property under the rule stated in Clause (c), as he would be if he were not authorized to sell the property. See § 208." (Emphasis added.) However, employment of "merely" and "only" as limiting words suggests that where the breach consists of some misfeasance, other than solely for selling "for too low a price" or "for too little", appreciation damages may be appropriate. Under Scott (§ 208.3, pp.

1686–1687) and the Restatement (§ 208), the trustee may be held liable for appreciation damages if it was his or her duty to retain the property, the theory being that the beneficiaries are entitled to be placed in the same position they would have been in had the breach not consisted of a sale of property that should have been retained. The same rule should apply where the breach of trust consists of a serious conflict of interest—which is more than merely selling for too little.

The reason for allowing appreciation damages, where there is a duty to retain, and only date of sale damages, where there is authorization to sell, is policy oriented. If a trustee authorized to sell were subjected to a greater measure of damages he might be reluctant to sell (in which event he might run a risk if depreciation ensued). On the other hand, if there is a duty to retain and the trustee sells there is no policy reason to protect the trustee; he has not simply acted imprudently, he has violated an integral condition of the trust.

* * *

[Omitted is the Court's discussion of the computation of appreciation damages in light of the difficulties in valuing works of art, and the trial record of evidence to support the computation.]

Accordingly, the order of the Appellate Division should be affirmed * * *.

QUESTIONS AND NOTES

1. Describe the "sins" of each executor in *Rothko*.

2. The Rothko estate needed large amounts of cash for a variety of purposes including paying estate taxes on the assets not going to charity. Where would the executors likely get the money to pay these bills? What problems would this create for them? Why did the executors arrange for sales over a number of years?

3. Suppose executor Stamos (a "not-too-successful artist, financially") had consulted you when the famous Marlborough Gallery took an interest in his paintings and his collection? What advice would you have given him?

4. Suppose executor Levine had consulted you, concerned that Reis and Stamos were acting in self-interest rather than the interest of the Rothko estate. What advice would you have given him?

Section 39 of the Restatement (Third) of Trusts provides that "if there are three or more trustees their powers may be exercised by a majority." Section 703 of the Uniform Trust Code takes the same position, although it also provides expressly that a co-trustee "must participate in the performance of a trustee's function" unless unavailable due to temporary incapacity or absence. By contrast, the common law rule, embodied in section 194 of the Restatement (Second) of Trusts, required trustees to act unanimously. Would the advice you would offer to Levine differ depending on the rule in effect?

5. Suppose Mark Rothko had wanted to insulate his executors from liability for breach of the duty of loyalty. Consider two provisions he could have included in his will:

> a. I direct that none of my executors shall be held liable to my estate for any breach of the duty of loyalty.
>
> b. I direct that none of my executors shall be held liable to my estate for disloyalty in selling estate paintings to the Marlborough Galleries.

Would either of these provisions be enforceable? To what extent should the duty of loyalty be treated as a "default rule," freely modifiable by the testator or the settlor to suit individual circumstances? Compare John H. Langbein, Mandatory Rules in the Law of Trusts, 98 Nw. U. L. Rev. 1105, 1121–25 (2004) with Melanie B. Leslie, Trusting Trustees: Fiduciary Duties and the Limits of Default Rules, 94 Geo. L.J. 68, 112–119 (2005).

Suppose Rothko had included clause (b) in his will. Would the clause have insulated his executors from liability on the facts of the Rothko case?

6. Would the duty of loyalty extend to an attorney of the fiduciary, so as to bar the attorney from purchasing estate or trust assets from the fiduciary? See In re Bond & Mtge. Guar. Co., 303 N.Y. 423, 103 N.E.2d 721 (1952). For an analysis of such agency costs, see Robert H. Sitkoff, An Agency Costs Theory of Trust Law, 89 Cornell L. Rev. 621 (2004).

7. Could the fiduciary sell to an employee, such as her secretary? Cf. Noonan's Estate, 361 Pa. 26, 63 A.2d 80 (1949).

8. ***Corporate Trustees.*** Suppose a corporate trustee—the trust department of a major bank—seeks to invest trust assets. May the trustee invest in mutual funds managed by the bank—funds that generate revenue for the bank? Or would such investments constitute impermissible self-dealing? Statutes in most states explicitly authorize trustee banks to invest in their proprietary mutual funds. The Uniform Trust Code takes the position that such investments do not create a presumption of conflict, but requires disclosure to beneficiaries, in an annual report, of the compensation earned by the trustee on those investments. See Uniform Trust Code, § 802(f). For criticism of the UTC's position, see Melanie B. Leslie, In Defense of the No Further Inquiry Rule,: A Response to Professor Langbein, 47 Wm. & Mary L. Rev. 541, 570–80 (2005).

9. ***Lawyers.*** As we have seen, a trustee or executor who also happens to be a lawyer can, in most states, recover fees for legal work he or she does for the trust or the estate. Isn't this clear self-dealing? Who will police the fees charged by the lawyer, or the hours billed, or the quality of the trustee-lawyer's work? See generally George Gleason Bogert & George Taylor Bogert, The Law of Trusts and Trustees 543(M), at 362 (rev. 2d ed. 1993). Nevertheless, courts and legislatures have authorized the practice (although some states prohibit the lawyer from collecting both fees and commissions). Professor Langbein supports the practice, reasoning that

> Integration promotes economies of scale and other synergies. The sheer informational advantage possessed by a trustee or executor who has already mastered the affairs of the trust or estate for purposes of routine administration often makes that person better suited than a newcomer to provide legal, accounting, real estate brokerage, or other needed services.

John H. Langbein, Questioning the Trust Law Duty of Loyalty: Sole Interest or Best Interest, 114 Yale L.J. 929, 978 (2005).

10. *Appreciation Damages*. When a fiduciary breaches a duty by selling a trust asset at too low a price, the trustee is generally liable for the difference between the price the trustee should have received on the date of sale and the price the trustee actually received. Whether the value of the property increases or decreases after that date is irrelevant, because the trust beneficiaries were not entitled to have the trustee retain the property; the trustee was free to sell (and sometimes required to sell), and breached only by selling at too low a price.

In Rothko, by contrast, the court awarded appreciation damages to the estate beneficiaries—that is, the court held that the executors were liable for the difference between the value of the paintings *at the time of trial* and the price paid to the estate. Because Rothko paintings increased significantly in value after Rothko's death, this measure resulted in significantly higher damages. Why did the court award appreciation damages? Would it have awarded those damages if the executors had not violated the terms of the preliminary injunction issued on September 26, 1972?

Note also that when the trust beneficiaries have a right to invalidate a sale (as they generally do when an executor or trustee engages in self-dealing), they are entitled to the equivalent of appreciation damages: if they can undo the transfer, they recover the appreciated property. But if the property finds its way into the hands of a bona fide purchaser, the beneficiaries can no longer undo the transfer. See, e.g., Uniform Trust Code § 1012 (protecting bona fide purchasers). Appreciation damages put the beneficiaries in the same position they would have been in if the self-dealing trustee had retained the property for himself rather than transferring it to a bona fide purchaser.

SECTION III. THE DUTY OF CARE

The modern fiduciary's job is to manage estate or trust property. How much care must the fiduciary take in performing that job? It is not enough for the fiduciary to take the care most of us take with our own finances: the "reasonably prudent person" familiar from tort law often pays too much for goods, falls behind in paying bills, makes risky investments (including buying lottery tickets), and often leaves others—parents, spouses, etc.—to pick up the pieces.

Fiduciaries must do better. Common law courts invented a somewhat different character—the "prudent person"—to serve as a model for fiduciary behavior. The behavior of a trustee or executor must measure up to the prudent person standard. That is, a trustee who avoids ordinary negligence nevertheless breaches her duty of care if she acts imprudently. In this section, we examine the various components of the duty of care.

A. The Duty of Care in General

Allard v. Pacific National Bank

Supreme Court of Washington, 1983.
99 Wash.2d 394, 663 P.2d 104.

■ Dolliver, Justice.

Plaintiffs Freeman Allard and Evelyn Orkney are beneficiaries of trusts established by their parents, J.T. and Georgiana Stone. Defendant Pacific National Bank (Pacific Bank) is the trustee of the Stone trusts. Plaintiffs appeal a King County Superior Court decision dismissing their action against Pacific Bank for breach of its fiduciary duties as trustee of the Stone trusts. Plaintiffs also appeal the decision of the court denying their demand for a jury trial, refusing to allow their expert testimony regarding ordinary standards of trust administration, and awarding attorney fees and costs to Pacific Bank.

We agree with the Superior Court that plaintiffs' claims are primarily equitable in nature and we affirm its decision that plaintiffs have no right to jury trial. We conclude, however, that Pacific Bank breached its fiduciary duties regarding management of the Stone trusts. We also find the Superior Court incorrectly awarded attorney fees and costs to Pacific Bank. We need not and do not reach the issue of whether the trial court improperly excluded plaintiffs' expert witnesses on the issue of generally accepted trust practices.

J.T. and Georgiana Stone, both deceased, established trusts in their wills conveying their property upon their deaths to Pacific Bank to be held for their children and the issue of their children. The Stones' children, Evelyn Orkney and Freeman Allard, are life income beneficiaries of the Stone trusts. Upon the death of either life income beneficiary, the trustee is to pay the income from the trust to the issue of the deceased beneficiary. When all the children of the deceased beneficiary reach the age of 21 years, the trusts direct the trustee to distribute the trust corpus equally among the issue of that beneficiary.

In 1978 the sole asset of the Stone trusts was a fee interest in a quarter block located on the northwest corner of Third Avenue and Columbia Street in downtown Seattle. The trust provisions of the wills gave Pacific Bank "full power to * * * manage, improve, sell, lease, mortgage, pledge, encumber, and exchange the whole or any part of the assets of [the] trust estate" and required Pacific Bank to exercise the judgment and care under the circumstances then prevailing, which prudent men exercise in the management of their own affairs, not in regard to speculation but in regard to the permanent disposition of their funds, considering the probable income as well as the probable safety of their capital.

The Third and Columbia property was subject to a 99–year lease, entered into by the Stones in 1952 with Seattle–First National Bank (Seafirst Bank). The lease contained no rental escalation provision and the rental rate was to remain the same for the entire 99–year term of the lease. The right of first refusal to purchase the lessor's interest in the property was given to the lessee. The lease also contained several restrictive provisions. One paragraph required any repair, reconstruction, or replacement of buildings on the property by the lessee to be completed within 8 months from the date the original building was damaged or destroyed "from any cause whatsoever". Another paragraph provided that, upon termination of lease, the lessee had the option either to surrender possession of all improvements or to remove the improvements. The lease prohibited, without the lessor's consent, any encumbrance which would have priority over the lessor in case of the lessee's insolvency.

In June 1977 Seafirst Bank assigned its leasehold interest in the Third and Columbia property to the City Credit Union of Seattle (Credit Union). Eight months later, on February 14, 1978, Credit Union offered to purchase the property from Pacific Bank for $139,900. On April 25, 1978, Pacific Bank informed Credit Union it was interested in selling the property, but demanded at least $200,000. In early June 1978, Credit Union offered $200,000 for the Third and Columbia property. Pacific Bank accepted Credit Union's offer, and deeded the property to Credit Union on August 17, 1978. On September 26, 1978, Pacific Bank informed Freeman Allard and Evelyn Orkney of the sale to Credit Union.

On May 1, 1979, plaintiffs commenced the present action against Pacific Bank for breach of its fiduciary duties regarding management of the Stone trusts, against Credit Union and Seafirst Bank for participation in the alleged breach, and against Credit Union for conversion. Plaintiffs' complaint requested money damages from Pacific Bank, Credit Union, and Seafirst Bank. The complaint also requested the imposition of a constructive trust on the Third and Columbia property and the removal of Pacific Bank as trustee. On March 18, 1980, plaintiffs filed their demand for a trial by jury under Const. art. 1, § 21.

Based on its determination plaintiffs' cause of action was primarily equitable in nature, the trial court struck their demand for trial by jury. The trial court also granted motions by Credit Union and Seafirst Bank for a partial summary judgment dismissing them from the case. Plaintiffs did not appeal the summary judgments dismissing Credit Union and Seafirst Bank.

At trial, the primary dispute was over the degree of care owed by Pacific Bank to the Stone trusts and to the Stone trust beneficiaries. Plaintiffs attempted to call expert witnesses to testify Pacific Bank failed to comply with the ordinary standards of trust administration when it sold the Third and Columbia property. Plaintiffs' first expert witness, Edmond R. Davis, was former manager of the trust department legal division of

Security First National Bank, now Security Pacific National Bank, in California. Plaintiffs presented an offer of proof Edmond Davis would testify Pacific Bank failed to comply with ordinary standards of trust practice in making its decision to sell the Third and Columbia property and in the steps it took to sell the property. Plaintiffs' other excluded expert witness, McLain Davis, was former manager of the trust department probate division of the National Bank of Commerce, now Rainier Bank. Plaintiffs' offers of proof regarding the testimony of McLain Davis indicated the witness would testify a bank trustee, acting in accordance with ordinary standards of trust practice, would not be excused from obtaining an appraisal by lack of funds in the trust account. Furthermore, according to plaintiffs, McLain Davis would have testified a trustee would not be acting in accordance with ordinary trust practices if the trustee dispensed with obtaining an outside appraisal or other prospective purchasers where its own internal appraisal indicated the sale was for an amount in excess of the property's fair market value.

At trial it was unquestioned that both witnesses were qualified as experts in trust administration. Rather, the trial court sustained defendant's objections to the testimony of plaintiffs' expert witnesses on the grounds the witnesses would testify as to legal opinions, inadmissible under ER 702, 704. The exclusion of plaintiffs' proffered expert witnesses left plaintiffs with no direct testimony regarding ordinary standards of trust administration.

At the culmination of the trial, the court entered judgment dismissing plaintiffs' action against Pacific Bank. It determined Pacific Bank acted in good faith and in conformance with its duties under the Stone trust instruments. The court concluded Pacific Bank neither had a duty to inform the trust beneficiaries prior to sale of the Third and Columbia property nor a duty to obtain an independent appraisal of the property or to place the property on the open market. Finally, the trial court awarded Pacific Bank $51,507.07 attorney fees and costs from the income and principal of the Stone trusts. From this judgment plaintiffs bring appeal.

I

* * *

[In the omitted portion of the opinion, the Court noted that distinctions between actions at law and equity proceedings are based upon nature rather than form and that when beneficiaries sue a trustee to restore funds to the trust the proceeding is equitable, the trial court having wide discretion in the determination.]

The beneficiaries of the Stone trusts essentially allege Pacific Bank improperly depleted the trust assets by selling the Third and Columbia property for less than its fair market value. The trial court properly determined plaintiffs' action against Pacific Bank was equitable in nature. The denial of plaintiffs' demand for a jury trial was proper. None of the beneficiaries have a present right to receive distribution of the trust corpus.

Their only remedy for depletion of the trust corpus is restoration of the value of the corpus by the trustee, often referred to as a "surcharge" on the trustee. * * * Since the trustee is under no duty to pay money besides the trust income to the beneficiaries, they have no action at law for breach of the trust agreement.

II

We now consider the crux of the case before us. Defendant contends it had full authority under the trust instrument to exercise its own judgment and impartial discretion in deciding how to invest the trust assets and a duty to use reasonable care and skill to make the trust property productive. See findings of fact 12–14. It further contends the sale of the property was conducted in good faith and with honest judgment. Finding of fact 19. Plaintiffs assert this discretion was limited by its fiduciary duties and that defendant in its management of the trusts breached its fiduciary duty.

Plaintiffs' argument regarding Pacific Bank's alleged breach of its fiduciary duties is twofold. First, Pacific Bank had a duty to inform them of the sale of the Third and Columbia property. Second, Pacific Bank breached its fiduciary duties by failing either to obtain an independent appraisal of the Third and Columbia property or to place the property on the open market prior to selling it to Seattle Credit Union. We agree with plaintiffs' position in both instances and hold defendant breached its fiduciary duty in its management of the trusts.

A

Initially, plaintiffs and amicus curiae the Attorney General of the State of Washington contend Pacific Bank should be held to a higher standard of care than the ordinary, prudent investor standard provided in RCW 30.24.020. Plaintiffs and amicus curiae argue the ordinary, prudent investor standard is inappropriate where the trustee represents that it has greater skill than that of a nonprofessional trustee. They fail to mention, however, the terms of the Stone trust agreements which specifically adopt the prudent investor standard of care provided in RCW 30.24.020.

RCW 30.24.020 provides:

> In acquiring, investing, reinvesting, exchanging, selling and managing property for the benefit of another, a fiduciary shall exercise the judgment and care under the circumstances then prevailing, which men of prudence, discretion and intelligence exercise in the management of their own affairs, not in regard to speculation but in regard to the permanent disposition of their funds, considering the probable income as well as the probable safety of their capital.

Under the trust agreements, Pacific Bank is required as trustee to

> exercise the judgment and care under the circumstances then prevailing, which prudent men exercise in the management of their own affairs, not in regard to speculation but in regard to the permanent disposition of their funds, considering the probable income as well as the probable safety of their capital.

Significantly, the statute recognizes the standard of care required of a trustee is "subject to any express provisions or limitations contained in any particular trust instrument". RCW 30.24.020. Furthermore, the terms of the trust instrument control as to the investments made by a trustee. RCW 30.24.070. Except where impossible, illegal, or where a change of circumstances occurs which would impair the purposes of the trust, the nature and extent of the duties and powers of a trustee are determined by the trust agreement. * * * Although in some future case we may be called upon to determine if a corporate professional trustee should be held to a higher standard because of the language in the trust instruments, this issue need not be decided here. Cf. Restatement (Second) of Trusts § 227, comment d (1959).

B

The Stone trusts gave Pacific Bank "full power to * * * manage, improve, sell, lease, mortgage, pledge, encumber, and exchange the whole or any part of the assets of [the] trust estate". Under such an agreement, the trustee is not required to secure the consent of trust beneficiaries before selling trust assets. 3 A. Scott, Trusts § 190.5 (3d ed. 1967). * * * The trustee owes to the beneficiaries, however, the highest degree of good faith, care, loyalty, and integrity. * * *

Pacific Bank claims it was obligated to sell the property to Credit Union since Credit Union, as assignee of the lease agreement with Seafirst Bank, had a right of first refusal to purchase the property. Since it did not need to obtain the consent of the beneficiaries before selling trust assets, Pacific Bank argues it also was not required to inform the beneficiaries of the sale. We disagree. The beneficiaries could have offered to purchase the property at a higher price than the offer by Credit Union, thereby forcing Credit Union to pay a higher price to exercise its right of first refusal as assignee of the lease agreement. Furthermore, letters from the beneficiaries to Pacific Bank indicated their desire to retain the Third and Columbia property. While the beneficiaries could not have prevented Pacific Bank from selling the property, they presumably could have outbid Credit Union for the property. This opportunity should have been afforded to them.

On a previous occasion, we ruled the trustee's fiduciary duty includes the responsibility to inform the beneficiaries fully of all facts which would aid them in protecting their interests. * * * We adhere to the view expressed in Esmieu. That the settlor has created a trust and thus required the beneficiaries to enjoy their property interests indirectly does not imply the beneficiaries are to be kept in ignorance of the trust, the nature of the trust property, and the details of its administration. G. Bogert, Trusts and Trustees § 961 (2d ed. 1962). If the beneficiaries are able to hold the trustee to proper standards of care and honesty and procure the benefits to which they are entitled, they must know of what the trust property consists and how it is being managed. G. Bogert, Trusts and Trustees, supra.

The duty to provide information is often performed by corporate trustees by rendering periodic statements to the beneficiaries, usually in the form of copies of the ledger sheets concerning the trust. * * * For example, such condensed explanations of recent transactions may be mailed to the beneficiaries annually, semiannually, or quarterly. G. Bogert, Trusts, supra. Ordinarily, periodic statements are sufficient to satisfy a trustee's duty to beneficiaries of transactions affecting the trust property. The trust provisions here, for example, provide the trustee

> shall furnish on or before February 15 of each year to each person described in Section 1 of Article IV who is then a beneficiary * * * a statement showing how the respective trust assets are invested and all transactions relating thereto for the preceding calendar year.

The trustee must inform beneficiaries, however, of all material facts in connection with a nonroutine transaction which significantly affects the trust estate and the interests of the beneficiaries prior to the transaction taking place. The duty to inform is particularly required in this case where the only asset of the trusts was the property on the corner of Third and Columbia. Under the circumstances found in this case failure to inform was an egregious breach of fiduciary duty and defies the course of conduct any reasonable person would take, much less a prudent investor.

C

We also conclude Pacific Bank breached its fiduciary duties regarding management of the Stone trusts by failing to obtain the best possible price for the Third and Columbia property. Pacific Bank made no attempt to obtain a more favorable price for the property from Credit Union by, for example, negotiating to cancel the restrictive provisions in the lease originally negotiated with Seafirst Bank. Cf. Hatcher v. United States Nat'l Bank, 56 Or.App. 643, 643 P.2d 359 (1982) (trustee had not fulfilled its fiduciary duties by merely examining offer to purchase and altering the terms slightly). The bank neither offered the property for sale on the open market, see Rippey v. Denver United States Nat'l Bank, 273 F.Supp. 718 (D.Colo.1967), nor did it obtain an independent, outside appraisal of the Third and Columbia property to determine its fair market value. * * *

Washington courts have not yet considered the nature of a trustee's duty of care regarding the sale of trust assets. Other courts, however, generally require that a trustee when selling trust assets try to obtain the maximum price for the asset. * * * The Oregon Court of Appeals required a trustee to determine the fair market value of trust property prior to selling the property by obtaining an appraisal or by "testing the market" to determine what a willing buyer would pay. * * * Some courts specifically require trustees to obtain an independent appraisal of the property. * * * Other courts merely require that a trustee determine fair market value by placing the property on the open market. * * *

We agree with the Oregon Court of Appeals in *Hatcher* that a trustee may determine the best possible price for trust property either by obtaining an independent appraisal of the property or by "testing the market" to determine what a willing buyer would pay. The record discloses none of these actions were taken by the defendant. By its failure to obtain the best possible price for the Third and Columbia property, defendant breached its fiduciary duty as the prudent manager of the trusts.

On the issue of the exclusion by the trial court of the testimony regarding ordinary standards of trust administration, we need not express an opinion. The admission of such evidence is at the discretion of the trial court. * * * Although arguably it was an abuse of discretion and the evidence might properly have been admitted, because of our disposition of the case it is unnecessary to reach that issue and we decline to do so.

* * *

We affirm the trial court's refusal to grant plaintiffs a jury trial. We hold defendant breached its fiduciary duty and reverse the trial court on this issue. The award of attorney fees to Pacific Bank is reversed. The case is remanded for a determination of the damages caused to plaintiffs by defendant's breach of its fiduciary duties as trustee of the Stone trusts and a determination of the amount of attorney fees to be awarded plaintiffs from the trustee individually.

QUESTIONS

1. Does the court in this case hold that a trustee must always inform trust beneficiaries before selling trust assets? If not, how is this case different? Why was it particularly important to inform the trust beneficiaries of the proposed sale? What might they have done differently, and why, if they had known of the sale?

2. The court holds that the trustee—Pacific National Bank—breached its fiduciary duty by failing to offer the property for sale on the open market, and by failing to obtain an appraisal. Suppose the trustee in this case had been the Stones' cousin, Mick, who had little financial expertise. If Mick had taken the same steps taken by Pacific National, would the court have held Mick liable for breach of fiduciary duty?

Should a fiduciary who has special skills—particularly a commercial fiduciary—be held to a higher standard? See Estate of Lychos, 323 Pa.Super. 74, 470 A.2d 136 (1983); UTC § 806; Restatement (Third) of Trusts § 77(2) (In essence, if you have special skills you better use 'em). Suppose you were representing an individual trustee charged with breach. Would you defend the trustee by pleading lack of ability? If not, how would you defend your client?

3. Suppose your client wanted to make it more difficult for trust beneficiaries to sue the trustee for breach of fiduciary duty. Could you include exculpatory language? Consider the following two provisions:

a. "I direct that my executor and trustee shall not be liable except for loss caused by willful neglect or default."

b. "I direct that my executor and trustee shall not be liable for any loss caused by their conduct."

If provision (a) had been included in the trust instruments in the Allard case, would the court have reached a different result? Provision (b)? Can you see why most courts would be entirely unwilling to enforce clauses like provision (b)? If provision (b) were enforceable, what would prevent the trustee from taking the trust proceeds to Tahiti and retiring? See UTC § 1008.

B. DELEGATION OF FIDUCIARY OBLIGATIONS

Every successful manager delegates dozens of decisions daily. Not every trustee is an expert at every aspect of trust administration. Suppose, for instance, settlor chooses her brother as a trustee because her brother has a particularly good feel for the needs of the trust beneficiaries—settlor's children. The brother, however, has no investment expertise. Can the brother delegate investment decisions to an investment advisor? If the investment advisor does a competent job, of course, no one will complain. But what happens if the investment advisor proves unfaithful, or incompetent? Consider the following case:

Shriners Hospitals for Crippled Children v. Gardiner

Supreme Court of Arizona, 1987.
152 Ariz. 527, 733 P.2d 1110.

■ HAYS, JUSTICE (RETIRED).

Laurabel Gardiner established a trust to provide income to her daughter, Mary Jane Gardiner; her two grandchildren, Charles Gardiner and Robert Gardiner; and a now-deceased daughter-in-law, Jean Gardiner. The remainder of the estate passes to Shriners Hospitals for Crippled Children (Shriners) upon the death of the life income beneficiaries. In re Estate of Gardiner, 5 Ariz.App. 239, 240, 425 P.2d 427, 428 (1967). Laurabel appointed Mary Jane as trustee, Charles as first alternate trustee, and Robert as second alternate trustee. Mary Jane was not an experienced investor, and she placed the trust assets with Dean Witter Reynolds, a brokerage house. Charles, an investment counselor and stockbroker, made all investment decisions concerning the trust assets. At some point in time, Charles embezzled $317,234.36 from the trust. Shriners brought a petition to surcharge Mary Jane for the full $317,234.36. The trial court denied the petition, but a divided court of appeals reversed. Shriners Hospitals for Crippled Children v. Gardiner, 152 Ariz. 519, 733 P.2d 1102 (Ct.App.1986).

We granted review on three issues:

1) Whether Mary Jane's delegation of investment power to Charles was a breach of Mary Jane's fiduciary duty.

2) Whether Mary Jane's delegation to Charles of investment power was the proximate cause of the loss of $317,234.36.

3) Whether Robert can properly continue to act as successor trustee and as guardian and conservator for the predecessor trustee Mary Jane.
* * *

1. BREACH OF FIDUCIARY DUTY

In Arizona, a trustee has the duty to "observe the standard in dealing with the trust assets that would be observed by a prudent man dealing with the property of another." A.R.S. § 14–7302. If the trustee breaches that responsibility, he is personally liable for any resulting loss to the trust assets. Restatement (Second) of Trusts §§ 201, 205(a). A trustee breaches the prudent man standard when he delegates responsibilities that he reasonably can be expected personally to perform. Restatement (Second) of Trusts § 171.

We believe that Mary Jane breached the prudent man standard when she transferred investment power to Charles. Mary Jane argues, and we agree, that a trustee lacking investment experience must seek out expert advice. Although a trustee must seek out expert advice, "he is not ordinarily justified in relying on such advice, but must exercise his own judgment." Restatement (Second) of Trusts § 227. In re Will of Newhoff, 107 Misc.2d 589, 595, 435 N.Y.S.2d 632, 637 (1980) (a trustee must not only obtain information concerning investment possibilities but also is "under a duty to use a reasonable degree of skill in selecting an investment"). Mary Jane, though, did not evaluate Charles' advice and then make her own decisions. Charles managed the trust fund, not Mary Jane. A prudent investor would certainly participate, to some degree, in investment decisions.

The dissent in the court of appeals stated that "there is nothing to indicate the trustee 'gave up her trusteeship' or 'delegated' the 'complete management' of trust assets to Charles." Shriners Hospitals for Crippled Children, 152 Ariz. at 525, 733 P.2d at 1108 (Froeb, C.J., dissenting). While we agree that the record on appeal is meager, Mary Jane unquestionably transferred trustee discretion to Charles.

Mary Jane's second accounting of the Gardiner trust states:

> From time to time the Trustee made investments ("investments") in the money market and also in the purchase and sale of shares of stock listed on the New York Stock Exchange, the American Stock Exchange and the Over-the-Counter Markets. * * * *All of said investments were made on behalf of the Trust Estate by a person qualified in that business,* [Charles] *who was selected by and in whom the Trustee justifiably had the utmost trust and confidence.*

(emphasis added)

Most damning, however, are the admissions of Mary Jane's own attorney.

> Now, we can show, if the Court pleases, by way of evidence if counsel will not accept my avowal, we can show that Charles Gardiner for the past many years, including several years prior to and since these assets were placed in his hands for investment, was in the business of a

> consultant and in the business of investing and selecting investments in the stock market, and this he did. And it was only natural that Mary Jane would turn to him to make that selection, to invest those funds and to account in an appropriate proceeding if, as and when required. So the prudent man rule has been adhered to here. She got a man who is capable and fortunately he was a man who was designated as an alternate trustee *and for all practical purposes really served as trustee.*

(emphasis added)

Together, the accounting and admissions establish that Charles was functioning as a surrogate trustee. Mary Jane was not exercising any control over the selection of investments. She clearly breached her duties to act prudently and to personally perform her duties as a trustee. In re Kohler's Estate, 348 Pa. 55, 33 A.2d 920 (1943) (fiduciary may not delegate to another the performance of a duty involving discretion and judgment).

Even on appeal, Mary Jane does not argue that she, in fact, exercised any discretionary investment power. Instead, she argues that her lack of investment experience made it prudent for her to delegate her investment power. She relies on the Restatement (Second) of Torts [*sic*] § 171.

> § 171. Duty Not to Delegate
>
> The trustee is under a duty to the beneficiary not to delegate to others the doing of acts which the trustee can reasonably be required personally to perform.

Mary Jane asserts that her lack of investment experience prevented her from personally exercising investment power and consequently permitted delegation of that power. The standard of care required, however, is measured objectively. In re Mild's Estate, 25 N.J. 467, 480–81, 136 A.2d 875, 882 (1957) (the standard of care required of a trustee does not take into account the "differing degrees of education or intellect possessed by a fiduciary"). The trustee must be *reasonable* in her delegation. A delegation of investment authority is unreasonable and therefore Mary Jane's delegation is a breach of trust. See Estate of Baldwin, 442 A.2d 529 (Me.1982) (bank trustee liable for losses incurred when it failed to monitor management of grocery store despite bank's lack of expertise in grocery store management).

It is of no import that Charles was named as alternate trustee. A trustee is not permitted to delegate his responsibilities to a co-trustee. Restatement (Second) of Trusts § 224(2)(b); see also id., comment a (improper for co-trustee A to direct co-trustee B to invest trust funds without consulting A). Certainly, then, a trustee is subject to liability when she improperly delegates her investment responsibility to an alternate trustee. Bumbaugh v. Burns, 635 S.W.2d 518, 521 (Tenn.App.1982) (impermissible for trustee to delegate discretion as to investment of funds to co-trustee).

Mary Jane also argues that broad language in the trust document permitted her to delegate her investment authority to Charles. A trust document may allow a trustee to delegate powers ordinarily non-delegable.

The Gardiner Trust permits the trustee "to employ and compensate attorneys, accountants, agents and brokers." This language does not bear on Mary Jane's delegation of investment authority. Mary Jane did not simply employ Charles; she allowed him to serve as surrogate trustee. We view this language as merely an express recognition of the trustee's obligation to obtain expert advice, not as a license to remove herself from her role as a trustee.

* * *

* * * [In the portion of the opinion omitted, the Court held Mary Jane would not be liable for the loss unless her improper delegation proximately caused the embezzlement. The causal connection would require findings of fact by the Trial Court. The Court also held that if the Trial Court found Mary Jane liable, Robert would have to be removed as her successor trustee since, as her guardian and conservator, his interest would conflict with his fiduciary duty as trustee to enforce the surcharge against Mary Jane as his predecessor.] * * *

The decision of the court of appeals is vacated, and the case is remanded for further proceedings consistent with this opinion.

QUESTIONS

1. What did Mary Jane Gardiner do wrong in this case? The trust instrument authorized her to employ "attorneys, accountants, agents and brokers." If she was entitled to employ a broker, why wasn't she entitled to entrust investment decisions to the broker?

Suppose, for instance, Ms. Gardiner had approached a broker and asked for advice about trust investments. The broker makes recommendations, and gives reasons for the recommendations. Mary says "That's all gobbledygook to me, but you're the expert. Do what you think best." Has Mary breached her fiduciary duty? If the Shriners Hospital court would answer yes, what is Mary supposed to do?

2. Suppose Mary, as executor of her father's estate, had hired a lawyer to help probate the estate. The lawyer informs her that her father's medical practice should be sold immediately, and recommends that they bypass a statutory requirement that court approval be obtained before selling the practice. With the lawyer's help, Mary sells the practice, but the purchaser never pays the purchase price, and then declares bankruptcy. If the estate beneficiaries bring an action against Mary for breach of fiduciary duty, who should win? Can Mary defend the action by asserting that she relied on the advice of counsel? See Estate of Spirtos, 34 Cal.App.3d 479, 109 Cal.Rptr. 919 (1973) (holding fiduciary liable, despite reliance on advice of counsel). Is it reasonable to expect that Mary—a non-lawyer—will know enough to reject the lawyer's advice?

3. After Gardiner, suppose you represent an Arizona trustee who is determined to deal with an investment advisor. What advice would you give her?

NOTE ON DELEGATION

The Restatement (Second) of Trusts, cited in the Shriners Hospital case, reflected the common law rule that a trustee was not entitled to delegate trust functions. Of course, the trustee could solicit advice, but remained responsible for making the ultimate decisions about investment, distribution, and other critical matters.

Note how the court in the Shriners Hospital case applied that rule: Mary Jane Gardiner was responsible for losses to the trust only if her delegation proximately caused the embezzlement that led to the losses. If she had delegated, and the delegate had made prudent investment decisions that nevertheless generated losses because of a general decline in the stock market, Mary Jane would not have been liable for the losses suffered by trust beneficiaries.

The Restatement (Third) of Trusts and the Uniform Prudent Investor Act, both promulgated in the 1990s, reversed the common law rule, and authorized trustees to delegate essential investment functions. Consider the following explanation of the change:

John H. Langbein, The Uniform Prudent Investor Act and the Future of Trust Investing, 81 Iowa L. Rev. 641, 650–53 (1996)

As the investment function has grown ever more complex, there is ever less reason to believe that nonspecialists are fit to conduct it. Especially when family members or other amateurs serve as trustees, the need for outside investment expertise is often acute. The old nondelegation rule permitted such trustees to take advice from outside specialists, but required the trustees to go through the motions of appearing to evaluate the advice and to form an independent judgment about whether or not to follow it. Often enough, this resulted in de facto delegation. "When the investment advisor recommends and the trustee routinely decides to follow the advice, the trustee in reality is delegating the selection of investments."

* * *

The 1992 Restatement achieves a major reform of the nondelegation rule. Nominally, the Restatement leaves the general nondelegation principle intact, but effectively reduces it to a subrule of the duty of prudent administration and makes it easy to overcome. The new rule reads: "A trustee has a duty personally to perform the responsibilities of the trusteeship except as a prudent person might delegate those responsibilities to others." Applying that norm to the investment function, the new Restatement not only empowers the trustee to delegate investment and management powers, it provides that the trustee "may sometimes have a duty ... to delegate (investment) functions ... in such manner as a prudent investor would delegate under the circumstances."

The Uniform Act follows the Restatement in crafting a delegation regime. Section 9(a) empowers the trustee to "delegate investment and management functions that a prudent trustee of comparable skills could properly delegate under the circumstances." As replacement safeguards, the Act imposes duties of care, skill, and caution on trustees in selecting agents, in formulating the terms of the delegation, and in reviewing "the agent's performance and compliance with the terms of the delegation." The Act provides that the trustee who complies with these standards "is not liable ... for the decisions or actions of the agent to whom the function was delegated." Instead, an aggrieved beneficiary must look exclusively to the agent, who "owes a duty to the trust to exercise reasonable care to comply with the terms of the delegation."

QUESTIONS

1. Suppose Mary Jane Gardiner had given all of the trust proceeds to Bernard Madoff's investment firm to invest. Madoff's firm had established an enviable track record of producing admirable returns for investors, but ultimately, the firm collapsed and it became clear that Madoff had been engaged in a massive Ponzi scheme—using funds advanced by new investors to generate returns for old investors. If the trust's funds were lost as a result of the investment with Madoff, who would bear the loss if the common law rule were in effect? Who would bear the loss under the Uniform Prudent Investor Act? Which result do you prefer?

2. Suppose the trustee had been not Mary Jane Gardiner, but a local bank. Who would bear the loss under the common law rule? Under the Uniform Prudent Investor Act? Which result do you prefer?

* * *

The approach taken by the Uniform Prudent Investor Act and the Restatement (Third) is not without its critics. Professor Melanie Leslie argues that a rule holding a professional trustee liable for the action of its delegates "is probably the rule the settlor would have agreed to if he had thought about the issue during the drafting process." Melanie B. Leslie, Common Law, Common Sense: Fiduciary Standards and Trustee Identity, 27 Cardozo L. Rev. 2713, 2736 (2006). She emphasizes that, when a professional trustee is involved, the "settlor chose the trustee largely because of its expertise in trust management." Consider also the following argument:

Stewart E. Sterk, Rethinking Trust Law Reform: How Prudent is Modern Prudent Investor Doctrine?, 95 Cornell L. Rev. 851, 902 (2010)

Consider first the argument that the "modern" rule embraced by the Restatement (Third) and the UPIA provides appropriate incentives for trustees to employ investment advisors with greater expertise. Freedom from liability for the advisor's wrongdoing is not necessary to provide that incentive. Even if the trustee who hires an investment advisor remained liable for the advisor's wrongdoing, the trustee would still hire the advisor if the trustee believed the advisor's assistance would reduce the trustee's own expected liability. That is,

> where the trustee is unsure of his or her own investment prowess and is fearful to make errors that could cause losses to the trust that subject him or her to liability, the trustee has personal incentives to seek advice that reduces that liability. So long as the trustee is free to pay for the advisor's services out of the proceeds of the trust, the trustee has every reason to hire the advisor.
>
> Moreover, freeing the trustee from liability encourages trustees who do have investment expertise to delegate investment responsibilities. By delegating, the trustee shifts liability risk to the delegate—and, in the case of the delegate's insolvency, to the trust beneficiaries—without losing the right to collect commissions. That is, under the Restatement (Third) and the UPIA, there is every reason for even a professional trustee to delegate investment responsibility to the detriment of trust beneficiaries.

C. PORTFOLIO MANAGEMENT

Suppose decedent's will creates a testamentary trust for the benefit of her husband for life, with a remainder to her children. She names her sister—or her lawyer—as trustee. At the time of decedent's death, the property that will fund the trust includes 10,000 shares of ExxonMobil stock. What investment obligations does the trustee have with respect to the stock? Can the trustee retain the stock? If not, what investments are "prudent"? Consider that question as you read the following materials.

A Bit of History

Courts have historically assumed that the trust settlor wanted, first, to preserve the corpus of the trust intact for the ultimate remainder beneficiary, and second, to generate as much income as possible consistent with safety of the corpus. Remember that early trusts typically consisted of land—where the corpus was safe from destruction, and where the trustee had no significant investment decisions to make. See John H. Langbein, The Contractarian Basis of the Law of Trusts, 105 Yale L.J. 625, 632–43 (1995). Courts tended to assume that settlors who created trusts in assets other than land generally wanted to accomplish the same objectives: "safety" first, income second. The trustee had no obligation to increase the size of the trust corpus—note, again, that with land, there was no possibility of increasing the size of the corpus; any profits to be derived from the land were "income" to be distributed to the trust's income beneficiaries.

To implement this preference for safety, courts articulated the prudent person rule set out in Harvard College v. Amory, 26 Mass. (9 Pick.) 446, 461 (1830):

> All that can be required of a trustee to invest, is, that he shall conduct himself faithfully and exercise a sound discretion. He is to observe how men of prudence, discretion and intelligence manage their own affairs, not in regard to speculation, but in regard to the permanent disposition of their funds, considering the probable income, as well as the probable safety of the capital to be invested.

In a number of states, the prudent person rule evolved into a flat prohibition against certain assets—sometimes including common stocks—

deemed too speculative for trust investments. Statutes and cases created laundry lists—often very short lists—of permissible trust investments.

These constraints were not disastrous in a time of no, or low, inflation. "Safe" investments in real estate mortgages or bonds—where the trust received a promise to pay interest and a promise to return the money at the end of the term—would prevent loss of the corpus, and would generate market returns for the income beneficiary. However, as inflation became a fact of economic life, statutory and common law restrictions on investments guaranteed only that the corpus would shrink over time—a result certainly not intended by the trust settlor. Most states liberalized their fiduciary investment rules, at least to some extent, to make it possible for the trustee to protect the trust corpus. To one degree or another, it became possible to make more modern investments, to buy more stock. Remember, these are default rules. A settlor could broaden, or narrow, the investment authority of her trustee.

Not until the 1990s, however, did Modern Portfolio Theory (MPT) turn the world of fiduciary investing upside down. Modern Portfolio Theory rejects the notion that risky investments are imprudent investments. Instead, Modern Portfolio Theory emphasizes that any asset, if bought at the right price, and if properly placed in a portfolio, with an understanding of diversification and risk, can be a wise investment. Diversification is key: investors should reduce risk by holding many different investments rather than by assuring that each investment is "safe." That is, investors should think in portfolio terms, not in terms of individual investments.

The Restatement (Third) of Trusts and the Uniform Prudent Investor Act incorporated Modern Portfolio Theory into trust law: no longer are stocks in any way suspect as "risky" investments for trustees. Even highly speculative stocks become appropriate if purchased as part of a properly diversified portfolio. How can the trustee, especially the individual trustee, assure that the trust assets are adequately diversified? Often, by purchasing one or more mutual funds that themselves reflect investments in many different companies. Often, the easiest and most successful strategy is to purchase an "index" fund, like the Standard & Poor's 500 Index, which requires no active management by anyone, yet historically outperforms most actively managed mutual funds. As to speculation, see Joel C. Dobris, Speculations on the Idea of 'Speculation,' in Trust Investing: An Essay, 39 Real Prop., Prob. & Tr. J. 439 (2004).

In light of Modern Portfolio Theory, consider the following case. Note that the trustee's actions in the Janes case were taken before New York enacted the Prudent Investor Act. Do you think the statute nevertheless had an impact on the court's decision?

In re Estate of Janes

Court of Appeals of New York, 1997.
90 N.Y.2d 41, 681 N.E.2d 332, 659 N.Y.S.2d 165.

■ LEVINE, JUDGE.:

Former State Senator and businessman Rodney B. Janes (testator) died on May 26, 1973, survived solely by his wife, Cynthia W. Janes, who was then 72 years of age. Testator's $3,500,000 estate consisted of a $2,500,000 stock portfolio, approximately 71% of which consisted of 13,232 shares of common stock of the Eastman Kodak Company. The Kodak stock had a date-of-death value of $1,786,733, or approximately $135 per share.

Testator's 1963 will and a 1969 codicil bequeathed most of his estate to three trusts. First, the testator created a marital deduction trust consisting of approximately 50% of the estate's assets, the income of which was to be paid to Mrs. Janes for her life. In addition, it contained a generous provision for invasion of the principal for Mrs. Janes's benefit and gave her testamentary power of appointment over the remaining principal. The testator also established a charitable trust of approximately 25% of the estate's assets which directed annual distributions to selected charities. A third trust comprised the balance of the estate's assets and directed that the income therefrom be paid to Mrs. Janes for her life, with the remainder pouring over into the charitable trust upon her death.

On June 6, 1973, the testator's will and codicil were admitted to probate. Letters testamentary issued to petitioner's predecessor, Lincoln Rochester Trust Company, and Mrs. Janes, as coexecutors, on July 3, 1973. Letters of trusteeship issued to petitioner alone. By early August 1973, petitioner's trust and estate officers, Richard Young and Ellison Patterson, had ascertained the estate's assets and the amount of cash needed for taxes, commissions, attorneys' fees, and specific bequests.

In an August 9, 1973 memorandum, Patterson recommended raising the necessary cash for the foregoing administrative expenses by selling certain assets, including 800 shares of Kodak stock, and holding "the remaining issues until the [t]rusts [were] funded." The memorandum did not otherwise address investment strategy in light of the evident primary objective of the testator to provide for his widow during her lifetime. In a September 5, 1973 meeting with Patterson and Young, Mrs. Janes, who had a high school education, no business training or experience, and who had never been employed, consented to the sale of some 1,200 additional shares of Kodak stock. Although Mrs. Janes was informed at the meeting that petitioner intended to retain the balance of the Kodak shares, none of the factors that would lead to an informed investment decision was discussed. At that time, the Kodak stock traded for about $139 per share; thus, the estate's 13,232 shares of the stock were worth almost $1,840,000. The September 5 meeting was the only occasion where retention of the Kodak stock or any other investment issues were taken up with Mrs. Janes.

By the end of 1973, the price of Kodak stock had fallen to about $109 per share. One year later, it had fallen to about $63 per share and, by the end of 1977, to about $51 per share. In March 1978, the price had dropped even further, to about $40 per share. When petitioner filed its initial accounting in February 1980, the remaining 11,320 shares were worth approximately $530,000, or about $47 per share. Most of the shares were used to fund the trusts in 1986 and 1987.

In addition to its initial accounting in 1980, petitioner filed a series of supplemental accountings that together covered the period from July 1973 through June 1994. In August 1981, petitioner sought judicial settlement of its account. Objections to the accounts were originally filed by Mrs. Janes in 1982, and subsequently by the Attorney General on behalf of the charitable beneficiaries (collectively, "objectants"). In seeking to surcharge petitioner for losses incurred by the estate due to petitioner's imprudent retention of a high concentration of Kodak stock in the estate from July 1973 to February 1980, during which time the value of the stock had dropped to about one-third of its date-of-death value, objectants asserted that petitioner's conduct violated EPTL 11–2.2(a)(1), the so-called "prudent person rule" of investment. When Mrs. Janes died in 1986, the personal representative of her estate was substituted as an objectant.

Following a trial on the objections, the Surrogate found that petitioner, under the circumstances, had acted imprudently and should have divested the estate of the high concentration of Kodak stock by August 9, 1973. The court imposed a $6,080,269 surcharge against petitioner and ordered petitioner to forfeit its commissions and attorneys' fees. In calculating the amount of the surcharge, the court adopted a "lost profits" or "market index" measure of damages espoused by objectants' expert—what the proceeds of the Kodak stock would have yielded, up to the time of trial, had they been invested in petitioner's own diversified equity fund on August 9, 1973.

The Appellate Division modified solely as to damages, holding that "the Surrogate properly found petitioner liable for its negligent failure to diversify and for its inattentiveness, inaction, and lack of disclosure, but that the Surrogate adopted an improper measure of damages" (223 A.D.2d 20, 23). In a comprehensive opinion by Presiding Justice M. Dolores Denman, the Court held that the Surrogate's finding of imprudence, as well as its selection of August 9, 1973 as the date by which petitioner should have divested the estate of its concentration of Kodak stock, were "well supported" by the record. The Court rejected the Surrogate's "lost profits" or "market index" measure of damages, however, holding that the proper measure of damages was "the value of the capital that was lost"—the difference between the value of the stock at the time it should have been sold and its value when ultimately sold. Applying this measure, the Court reduced the surcharge to $4,065,029. We granted petitioner and objectants leave to appeal, and now affirm.

I. Petitioner's Liability

Petitioner argues that New York law does not permit a fiduciary to be surcharged for imprudent management of a trust for failure to diversify in the absence of additional elements of hazard, and that it relied upon, and complied with, this rule in administering the estate. Relying on Matter of Balfe (152 Misc. 739, 749, mod 245 App.Div. 22), petitioner claims that elements of hazard can be capsulized into deficiencies in the following investment quality factors: "(i) the capital structure of the company; (ii) the competency of its management; (iii) whether the company is a seasoned issuer of stock with a history of profitability; (iv) whether the company has a history of paying dividends; (v) whether the company is an industry leader, (vi) the expected future direction of the company's business; and (vii) the opinion of investment bankers and analysts who follow the company's stock." Evaluated under these criteria, petitioner asserts, the concentration of Kodak stock at issue in this case, that is, of an acknowledged "blue chip" security popular with investment advisors and many mutual funds, cannot be found an imprudent investment on August 9, 1973 as a matter of law. In our view, a fiduciary's duty of investment prudence in holding a concentration of one security may not be so rigidly limited.

New York followed the prudent person rule of investment during the period of petitioner's administration of the instant estate. This rule provides that "[a] fiduciary holding funds for investment may invest the same in such securities as would be acquired by prudent [persons] of discretion and intelligence in such matters who are seeking a reasonable income and the preservation of their capital" (EPTL 11–2.2[a][1]).[1] Codified in 1970 (see, L 1970, ch 321), the prudent person rule's New York common law antecedents can be traced to King v. Talbot (40 N.Y. 76), wherein this Court stated:

> [T]he trustee is bound to employ such diligence and such prudence in the care and management [of the trust], as in general, prudent men of discretion and intelligence in such matters, employ in their own affairs.
>
> This necessarily excludes all speculation, all investments for an uncertain and doubtful rise in the market, and of course, everything that does not take into view the nature and object of the trust, and the consequences of a mistake in the selection of the investment made. * * *
>
> [T]he preservation of the fund, and the procurement of a just income therefrom, are primary objects of the creation of the trust itself, and are to be primarily regarded (id., at 85–86 [emphasis supplied]).

No precise formula exists for determining whether the prudent person standard has been violated in a particular situation; rather, the determination depends on an examination of the facts and circumstances of each case * * *. In undertaking this inquiry, the court should engage in "a balanced and perceptive analysis of [the fiduciary's] consideration and action in light of the history of each individual investment, viewed at the time of its action or its omission to act" (Matter of Donner, 82 N.Y.2d 574, 585 [quoting Matter of Bank of N.Y., 35 N.Y.2d 512, 519]). And, while a court should not view each act or omission aided or enlightened by hindsight (see, Matter of Bank of N.Y., supra, at 519 * * *, a court may, nevertheless, examine the

1. The recently-enacted Prudent Investor Act requires a trustee "to diversify assets unless the trustee reasonably determines that it is in the interests of the beneficiaries not to diversify, taking into account the purposes and terms and provisions of the governing instrument" (EPTL 11–2.3[b][3][C]). The Act applies to investments "made or held" by a trustee on or after January 1, 1995 and, thus, does not apply to the matter before us.

fiduciary's conduct over the entire course of the investment in determining whether it has acted prudently * * *.)

As the foregoing demonstrates, the very nature of the prudent person standard dictates against any absolute rule that a fiduciary's failure to diversify, in and of itself, constitutes imprudence, as well as against a rule invariably immunizing a fiduciary from its failure to diversify in the absence of some selective list of elements of hazard, such as those identified by petitioner. Indeed, in various cases, courts have determined that a fiduciary's retention of a high concentration of one asset in a trust or estate was imprudent without reference to those elements of hazard. * * * The inquiry is simply whether, under all the facts and circumstances of the particular case, the fiduciary violated the prudent person standard in maintaining a concentration of a particular stock in the estate's portfolio of investments.

Moreover, no court has stated that the limited elements of hazard outlined by petitioner are the only factors that may be considered in determining whether a fiduciary has acted prudently in maintaining a concentrated portfolio. Again, as commentators have noted, one of the primary virtues of the prudent person rule "lies in its lack of specificity, as this permits the propriety of the trustee's investment decisions to be measured in light of the business and economic circumstances existing at the time they were made" (Laurino, Investment Responsibility of Professional Trustees, 51 St. John's L. Rev. 717, 723 [1977] [emphasis supplied]).

Petitioner's restrictive list of hazards omits such additional factors to be considered under the prudent person rule by a trustee in weighing the propriety of any investment decision, as: "the amount of the trust estate, the situation of the beneficiaries, the trend of prices and the cost of living, the prospect of inflation and deflation" (Restatement [Second] of Trusts § 227, comment [e]). Other pertinent factors are the marketability of the investment and possible tax consequences (id., comment [o]). The trustee must weigh all of these investment factors as they affect the principal objects of the testator's or settlor's bounty, as between income beneficiaries and remainder persons, including decisions regarding "whether to apportion the investments between high-yield or high growth securities" (Turano & Radigan, N.Y. Estate Administration § 14–P, at 409 [1986]).

Moreover, and especially relevant to the instant case, the various factors affecting the prudence of any particular investment must be considered in the light of the "circumstances of the trust itself rather than [merely] the integrity of the individual investment" (6 Rohan, N.Y. Civ Prac–EPTL & 11–2.2[5], at 11–513, n 106 [1996]). As stated in a leading treatise:

> [t]he trustee should take into consideration the circumstances of the particular trust that he is administering, both as to the size of the trust estate and the requirements of the beneficiaries. He should consider each investment not as an isolated transaction but in its relation to the whole of the trust estate (3 Scott, Trusts § 227.12, at 477 [4th ed.]).

Our case law is entirely consistent with the foregoing authorities. Thus, in Matter of Bank of N.Y. (35 N.Y.2d 512), although we held that a trustee remains responsible for imprudence as to each individual investment in a trust portfolio, we stated:

> The record of any individual investment is not to be viewed exclusively, of course, as though it were in its own water-tight compartment, since to some extent individual investment decisions may properly be affected by considerations of the performance of the fund as an entity, as in the instance, for example, of individual security decisions based in part on considerations of diversification of the fund or of capital transactions to achieve sound tax planning for the fund as a whole. The focus of inquiry, however, is nonetheless on the individual security as such and factors relating to the entire portfolio are to be weighed only along with others in reviewing the prudence of the particular investment decisions (35 N.Y.2d, at 517, supra [emphasis supplied]).

Thus, the elements of hazard petitioner relies upon as demonstrating that, as a matter of law, it had no duty to diversify, suffer from two major deficiencies under the prudent person rule. First, petitioner's risk elements too narrowly and strictly define the scope of a fiduciary's responsibility in making any individual investment decision, and the factors a fiduciary must consider in determining the propriety of a given investment.

A second deficiency in petitioner's elements of hazard list is that all of the factors relied upon by petitioner go to the propriety of an individual investment "exclusively * * * as though it were in its own water-tight compartment" (Matter of Bank of N.Y., supra, at 517), which would encourage a fiduciary to treat each investment as an isolated transaction rather than "in relation to the whole of the trust estate" (3 Scott, op. cit., at 477). Thus, petitioner's criteria for elements of hazard would apply irrespective of the concentration of the investment security under consideration in the portfolio. That is, the existence of any of the elements of risk specified by petitioner in a given corporate security would militate against the investment even in a diversified portfolio, obviating any need to consider concentration as a reason to divest or refrain from investing. This ignores the market reality that, with respect to some investment vehicles, concentration itself may create or add to risk, and essentially takes lack of diversification out of the prudent person equation altogether.

Likewise, contrary to petitioner's alternative attack on the decisions below, neither the Surrogate nor the Appellate Division based their respective rulings holding petitioner liable on any absolute duty of a fiduciary to diversify. Rather, those courts determined that a surcharge was appropriate because maintaining a concentration in Kodak stock, under the circumstances presented, violated certain critical obligations of a fiduciary in making investment decisions under the prudent person rule. First, petitioner failed to consider the investment in Kodak stock in relation to the entire portfolio of the estate (see, Matter of Bank of N.Y., supra, at 517; 3 Scott, op. cit.), i.e., whether the Kodak concentration itself created or added to investment risk. The objectants' experts testified that even high quality growth stocks, such as Kodak, possess some degree of volatility because their market value is tied so closely to earnings projections (cf., Turano & Radigan, op. cit., at 409). They further opined that the investment risk arising from that volatility is significantly exacerbated when a portfolio is heavily concentrated in one such growth stock. * * *

Lastly, there was evidence in the record to support the findings below that, in managing the estate's investments, petitioner failed to exercise due care and the skill it held itself out as possessing as a corporate fiduciary (see, Matter of Donner, 82 N.Y.2d, at 578, supra; Restatement [Second] of Trusts, '227, Comment on Clause [a]). Notably, there was proof that petitioner (1) failed initially to undertake a formal analysis of the estate and establish an investment plan consistent with the testator's primary objectives; (2) failed to follow petitioner's own internal trustee review protocol during the administration of the estate, which advised special caution and attention in cases of portfolio concentration of as little as 20%; and (3) failed to conduct more than routine reviews of the Kodak holdings in this estate, without considering alternative investment choices, over a seven-year period of steady decline in the value of the stock.

Since, thus, there was evidence in the record to support the foregoing affirmed findings of imprudence on the part of petitioner, the determination of liability must be affirmed * * *.

II. Date of Divestiture

As we have noted, in determining whether a fiduciary has acted prudently, a court may examine a fiduciary's conduct throughout the entire period during which the investment at issue was held * * *. The court may then determine, within that period, the "reasonable time" within which divestiture of the imprudently held investment should have occurred * * *. What constitutes a reasonable time will vary from case to case and is not fixed or arbitrary * * *. The test remains "the diligence and prudence of prudent and intelligent [persons] in the management of their own affairs" (id., at 511 [citations omitted]).

* * *

Again, there is evidentiary support in the record for the trial court's finding, affirmed by the Appellate Division, that a prudent fiduciary would have divested the estate's stock portfolio of its high concentration of Kodak stock by August 9, 1973, thereby exhausting our review powers on this issue. Petitioner's own internal documents and correspondence, as well as the testimony of Patterson, Young, and objectants' experts, establish that by that date, petitioner had all the information a prudent investor would have needed to conclude that the percentage of Kodak stock in the estate's stock portfolio was excessive and should have been reduced significantly, particularly in light of the estate's overall investment portfolio and the financial requirements of Mrs. Janes and the charitable beneficiaries.

III. Damages

Finally, as to the calculation of the surcharge, we conclude that the Appellate Division correctly rejected the Surrogate's "lost profits" or "market index" measure of damages. Where, as here, a fiduciary's imprudence consists solely of negligent retention of assets it should have sold, the measure of damages is the value of the lost capital * * *. Thus, the Surrogate's reliance on Matter of Rothko in imposing a "lost profit" measure of damages is inapposite, since in that case the fiduciary's misconduct consisted of deliberate self-dealing and faithless transfers of trust property * * *.

In imposing liability upon a fiduciary on the basis of the capital lost, the court should determine the value of the stock on the date it should have been sold, and subtract from that figure the proceeds from the sale of the stock or, if the stock is still retained by the estate, the value of the stock at the time of the accounting * * *. Whether interest is awarded, and at what rate, is a matter within the discretion of the trial court * * *. Dividends and other income attributable to the retained assets should offset any interest awarded * * *.

Here, uncontradicted expert testimony established that application of this measure of damages resulted in a figure of $4,065,029, which includes prejudgment interest at the legal rate, compounded from August 9, 1973 to October 1, 1994. * * *

Accordingly, the order of the Appellate Division should be affirmed, without costs.

■ KAYE and TITONE, BELLACOSA, SMITH, CIPARICK and WESLEY, JJ., concur.

NOTES AND QUESTIONS

1. Who did the settlor choose to make investment decisions for his family? If those investment decisions had increased the value of the trust portfolio, who would have benefited from the increase? Does trust law doctrine enable the trust beneficiaries to have their cake and eat it too: if the trust investments increase in value, they enjoy the benefit, while if those investments decline, the trustee bears liability for breach of fiduciary duty?

If courts are too willing to impose liability for breach of fiduciary duty, what will that do to the fees trustees charge for their services? Might that explain the general judicial reluctance to impose liability on trustees for their investment decisions?

2. Why should legislators and judges decide what constitutes prudent investment practice? Aren't trustees as a class more knowledgeable about investment alternatives and in a better position to decide what risks are worth taking? Moreover, won't the market discipline trustee investment behavior: if a particular trust company underperforms, won't settlers abandon it for trust companies with a more successful investment track record?

Professors Leslie and Sitkoff have suggested that market forces are unlikely to discipline trustee behavior to the same extent that the market disciplines corporate officials. See Melanie B. Leslie, Trusting Trustees: Fiduciary Duties and the Limits of Default Rules, 94 Geo. L.J. 67, 83

(2005); Robert H. Sitkoff, Trust Law, Corporate Law, and Capital Market Efficiency, 28 J. Corp. L. 565, 571 (2003). Moreover, if trust settlers do look to a trustee's track record, they are likely to focus on past returns, but will they focus on the risks the trustee took to get those returns? See Stewart E. Sterk, Rethinking Trust Law Reform: How Prudent is Modern Prudent Investor Doctrine?, 95 Cornell L. Rev. 851, 882 (2010).

3. In light of the Prudent Investor Act (adopted in New York after the trustee made the disputed decisions in the Janes case), what should a trustee do if an estate executor turns over $3,000,000 in assets, half of which is invested in Microsoft stock? How much Microsoft stock should the trustee sell, and what should the trustee do with it?

Suppose the trustee sold all of the Microsoft stock and invested it all in United States government bonds. Would that be good for the trust beneficiaries? Would investment in government bonds pose any risk for the trustee?

4. Perhaps the easiest way for a trustee to diversify stock investments is to purchase mutual funds. A mutual fund invests in an array of different stocks, so that the mutual fund investor obtains the benefits of diversification while buying a single investment. As discussed above, among the most diversified mutual funds are "index" funds, which purchase all of the stocks in a particular index, and attempt to duplicate the results of that index. Index funds minimize management costs; because the funds buy *all* of the stocks in the index, they eliminate the need for so-called stock "experts" to research and pick the "best" stocks. Many experts question the ability of "experts" to outperform the market over the long run.

Suppose a trustee invests the trust portfolio entirely in an S & P 500 index fund. Has the trustee protected itself against claims of imprudence? Although purchasing a stock index fund may protect the trust against diversifiable risk, not all risk is diversifiable. In particular, the risk that the entire market will decline—as it did in 2000–02 and again in 2007–09—is not a diversifiable risk. In its discussion of the Prudent Investor Rule, the Restatement cautions that

> Decisions concerning a prudent or suitable level of market risk for a particular trust can be reached only after thoughtful consideration of its purposes and all of the relevant trust and beneficiary circumstances. This process includes, for example, balancing the trust's return requirements with its tolerance for volatility.

Restatement (Third) of Trusts, § 90, cmt. e(1). The Restatement goes on to suggest that a trustee might reduce risk "by mixing a moderately risky portfolio with essentially 'riskless' assets (such as short-term federal obligations) rather than by developing a low-risk portfolio for the entire trust estate." Id., cmt. h(1).

5. In light of the Restatement formulation, what advice could you provide to a trustee about how much of the trust portfolio it should invest in equities and how much in fixed-income investments if the trustee wants to minimize its liability? What advice would you provide to a beneficiary who asks whether it is worth bringing an action for breach of fiduciary duty when the trustee has invested 80% of the trust in equities, which have declined in value by 40% over an 18–month period? Would trustees be better off with clearer rules than those articulated in the Restatement and the Uniform Prudent Investor Act? Would beneficiaries be better off? See generally Stewart E. Sterk, Rethinking Trust Law Reform: How Prudent is Modern Prudent Investor Doctrine?, 95 Cornell L. Rev. 851, 889–92 (2010).

6. A diversification strategy can be summarized as "Don't put all your eggs in one basket." Suppose a trustee prefers a different strategy, summarized as "Put all your eggs in one basket and watch the basket." That is, suppose a trustee learns a lot about a small number of companies, and invests only in those companies. Has the trustee acted imprudently? The Restatement (Third) of Trusts authorizes "active" investment strategies (those where the trustee chooses individual investments) as well as "passive" investment strategies (think index funds). Restatement (Third) of Trusts § 90, cmt. h. But how many active investments must the trustee make to comply with the diversification requirement?

7. ***Executor Investments.*** Unlike a trustee, whose investment time horizon generally extends for a considerable period of time, an executor's responsibility is to wind up the estate as quickly as possible. In a substantial or complicated estate, however, more than a year is likely to pass before the executor can distribute estate assets. Does the executor have a responsibility to diversify estate assets during that year? May the executor liquidate all securities and hold cash during that period?

Consider In re Duffy, 25 Misc.3d 901, 885 N.Y.S.2d 401 (Surr. Ct. 2009), aff'd 79 A.D.3d 1732, 913 N.Y.S.2d 627 (2010). Decedent died on July 19, 2001, survived by a husband 38 years her junior and an estate with an investment portfolio of $619,417.96. The executor retained all of decedent's investments (75% of which was concentrated in six stocks), and transferred the portfolio to the husband on October 7, 2002. By that time, the portfolio had lost more than a third of its value. Should the executor have been held liable for failing to diversify?

The court held that the executor was not liable, indicating that there was "a critical line between (a) deciding upon retention after considering all facts and circumstances according to the statute, and (b) merely doing *nothing* with respect to the assets at issue." In part, however, the court emphasized that during the relevant period, the stock market generally had declined just as much as the estate portfolio, so that even if the executor's action constituted breach, the beneficiary had not established that the breach caused the loss. Finally, the court rejected the notion that the executor had an obligation to liquidate the estate portfolio and to hold all cash during the period of administration.

8. ***Inception Assets More Generally.*** In Janes, the settlor died with an undiversified portfolio. How much time did the court give Janes to transform the portfolio into one that complies with the prudent investor rule (or, at the time of the Janes case, the prudent person rule)? Note that generally, the trustee must sell improper investments with reasonable diligence, and what's reasonable depends on factors such as current and expected market prices, and tax considerations. See Robert H. Jeffrey, Tax–Efficient Investing Is Easier Said Than Done, 4 J. Wealth Mg't (Summer 2001). If Mark Rothko's estate's art works were to be sold, it might not be a good idea to sell them all the first day the executors took office. Do you see why?

In Janes, the trust settlor might have been quite happy to have the trustee retain his concentration of Kodak stock. If Janes and the trustee were both happy to have the trustee retain the Kodak stock, what advice would you have given them about how to arrange that?

Suppose the will authorized the trustee to:

> "hold and retain any ... securities ... held or owned by me at my death, if in their discretion they shall deem it prudent and for the best interest of my estate so to do, notwithstanding the fact that the retention of such investments might, except for this express direction, be in violation of the laws of this State governing trust investment."

Would that language have insulated the trustee from liability for failure to diversify? See Matter of Peter Martin Wege Trust, 2008 WL 2439904 (Mich.App.) (holding that quoted provision exempted the trustee from obligation to diversify).

Why should the trust settlor be entitled to override otherwise applicable fiduciary rules? See generally Rob Atkinson, Obedience as the Foundation of Fiduciary Duty, 34 Iowa J. Corp. L. 43, 64–78 (2008) (noting the tripartite nature of trust law, and the trustee's dual responsibilities to settlor and beneficiaries).

9. ***Shares in Closely Held Corporations.*** When a decedent's primary asset is her share of a family business, diversification becomes complicated. First, there may be a very thin market for decedent's shares; often, non-family members will have no interest in becoming enmeshed in a family business, and family members may not have the cash to buy out part of the decedent's interest. Second, the decedent may want to keep the business in the family, even if that leaves his beneficiaries with undiversified interests. Of course, if decedent places shares of a closely held corporation in trust, decedent can include express language in the trust instrument authorizing the trustee to retain those shares, essentially overriding the diversification requirement of the prudent investor rule. Suppose, however, the trust settlor is silent. May the trustee retain the shares? See, e.g. Trust of Hyde, 44 A.D.3d 1195, 845 N.Y.S.2d 833 (Surr. Ct. 2007) (holding that trustee was entitled to retain stock in closely held corporation, despite diversification requirement, where there was indication that settlers "wanted the ownership of Finch Pruyn to remain in the family and the trusts were used as vehicles to achieve such a result.").

10. ***Socially Responsible Investing.*** Suppose a trustee decides to invest trust assets only in "socially responsible" companies. If excluding other alternatives reduces the expected return to trust beneficiaries, has the trustee breached its fiduciary duty? See generally Joel C. Dobris, SRI—

Shibboleth or Canard (Socially Responsible Investing, That Is), 42 Real Prop., Prob. & Trust J. 755 (2008).

PROBLEM

Mary is a trustee of a trust created by her mother for the benefit of Mary's sister Andrea, and ultimately, Andrea's children. Andrea and her husband are poor academics, and her mother wanted to assure the family's welfare. The trust assets—valued at $300,000—are currently invested in tax-exempt, municipal bonds, an investment often favored by older investors, which Mary's mother had held because of their tax advantages, advantages that are worth much less to Andrea.

Mary has just learned of an investment "opportunity." Her brother-in-law, Tom, is selling shares in a corporation which intends to buy a Pacific island to set up an enormous disposal site for nuclear wastes. Tom intends to persuade various foreign governments to dispose of their wastes on the island. If he is successful, the enterprise will generate enormous returns for the shareholders; Tom estimates that each share will quadruple in value within the next seven years. Tom cautions, however, that there is a significant risk of failure, in which case the shares will be wholly worthless. Tom cannot accurately estimate the risk of failure, but he hazards a guess that the enterprise has a 50% chance of success.

Mary consults you for legal advice. She informs you that she believes in Tom; in the past, every enterprise he has pursued has turned to gold. She also tells you that she has invested all of her own liquid assets—$100,000—in Tom's enterprise. She does not want to see Andrea and her family shut out of the enterprise, and would like to invest the trust's funds in Tom's enterprise. She wants to know whether she would be breaching her fiduciary duty by investing all, or part, of the trust's funds in the enterprise. How would you advise Mary?

Suppose Mary invested the entire trust corpus in Tom's enterprise. If the enterprise succeeds, who reaps the benefit of Mary's investment? If the enterprise fails, who should bear the loss?

On the prudence of one form of "esoteric" investment, see Robert J. Aalberts & Percy S. Poon, Derivatives and the Modern Prudent Investor Rule: Too Risky or Too Necessary?, 67 Ohio St. L.J. 525 (2006).

* * *

The investment duties embodied in the prudent investor rule are largely "default" rules that can be overcome when the settlor and the trustee agree on different investment strategies. What documentation suffices to overcome the prudent investor rule? Consider the following case:

McGinley v. Bank of America, N.A.

Supreme Court of Kansas, 2005.
279 Kan. 426, 109 P.3d 1146.

■ NUSS, J:

This case requires us to review a revocable trust instrument and a subsequent letter from the grantor to the trustee. Seven months after

Marie McGinley established her trust with Bank of America, N.A., (Bank) as trustee, she signed a letter directing the Bank to retain Enron stock held in the trust. The letter also stated that McGinley agreed to exonerate the Bank from any loss it sustained for continuing to retain the stock and that she relieved the Bank from any responsibility for analyzing and monitoring that stock.

Years later when the value of the Enron stock decreased significantly, McGinley sued the Bank for the amount of lost value. She alleged nine counts including, among others, breach of fiduciary duty.

[T]he core issue is whether the language in McGinley's trust instrument and subsequent letter shield the trustee Bank from liability. We hold the Bank is shielded and affirm the district court.

FACTS

The material facts, including those expressly determined by the district court as its findings of fact, are undisputed. On November 9, 1990, 79–year–old Marie McGinley established the Marie McGinley Revocable Trust (the trust), with Bank of America, N.A., serving as trustee. McGinley signed the instrument as grantor, the Bank signed as trustee, and her husband Francis signed expressing his consent to its provisions. The trust instrument, as well as a revocable trust instrument for Francis, were drafted by the McGinleys' legal counsel.

The trust was revocable at Marie McGinley's sole discretion. Article III, Revocability, states in relevant part:

"During the lifetime of Grantor this trust shall be and remain revocable, with Grantor hereby reserving the right and power, at Grantor's discretion, to revoke, alter, amend, modify or change this trust indenture, in whole or in part, at any time and from time to time, without the consent of the Trustee, any beneficiary or any other person or persons by written notification to Trustee." (Emphasis added.)

The trust was for McGinley's benefit, with funds to be provided to her at her request.

The trust provided the Bank, as trustee, with certain discretionary powers. Article VIII, Powers of the Trustee, states in relevant part:

"In addition to the powers conferred by common law, by statute, and by other provisions hereof, the Trustee and all Successor Trustees of all the trusts created hereunder, without application to or approval by any Court, *shall have the following discretionary powers and authority.*

> "A. *To manage, care for and protect the entire trust estate in accordance with its best judgment and discretion and to collect the income and profits therefrom, and to hold and retain any of the property coming into its hands hereunder* in the same form of investment as that in which it is received by it, although it may not be of the character of investments otherwise permitted by law to Trustees. *It*

> *shall also have full power and authority to insure against loss, improve, sell, lease, mortgage or exchange the whole or any part of such property, whether real or personal, on such terms and conditions as to it deems advisable, and to invest and reinvest any of the trust corpus held hereunder, in such amounts as it sees fit, in such property, real or personal, as it deems advisable* although the same may not be of the character permitted for Trustees' investment by the ordinary rules of law." (Emphasis added.)

These trustee discretionary powers contained some restrictions, however, as Article VIII. A went on to reserve to McGinley the exclusive power to control all purchases and sales of trust assets. It states that:

> "provided, however, that during the lifetime of Grantor, *she shall be consulted by the Trustee as to any purchase or sale, and the Trustee shall abide by the Grantor's decision* unless, in the sole opinion of the Trustee, the Grantor is incapable of managing [her] affairs, in which event the decision of the Trustee as to all investment matters shall be final and conclusive." (Emphasis added.)

Later, shares of Enron stock previously purchased by McGinley were transferred into the trust with other assets. Approximately 7 months after the trust instrument was signed, a form letter bearing the signature "Marie M. McGinley" and dated June 21, 1991, was apparently delivered to the Bank by her husband. Titled "Direction by Powerholder to Retain Securities," the letter was addressed to the Bank. The district court made a finding of fact, which McGinley does not dispute on appeal, that the letter was issued in accordance with Article VIII of the trust. In language the parties characterize as "directive" the letter stated:

> "I hereby direct you to continue to retain the following securities as assets of the above referenced account:
>
> "Shares or Par Value Security Name
>
> "1,541 shares Enron Corp."
>
> In language McGinley characterizes as "exculpatory" the letter went on to state:
>
> "I understand that you do not monitor these securities, and I hereby agree to exonerate, indemnify and hold the Bank harmless from any and all loss, damage and expense sustained or incurred by the Bank for continuing to retain these securities as assets of this account. I also relieve the Bank from any responsibility for analyzing or monitoring these securities in any way. I hereby bind all beneficiaries of the designated account, my heirs, my executors, and my assigns to the terms of this letter. This release and indemnification will remain in force and effect until my death, my disability (as determined in accordance with the trust agreement) or my written revocation of this letter." (Emphasis added.)

The value of the Enron stock substantially increased from 1991 through 2000. All increases in the number of Enron shares were the result of stock splits, as the Bank never purchased Enron stock for the trust. At the apparent height in value, December 29, 2000, the trust contained 9,500 shares of Enron stock valued at $789,687.50 and representing approximately 77% of the total market value of the trust.

Because of declines in Enron stock value, by March 30, 2001, the shares amounted to approximately 66% of the total market value of the trust; by June 29, 2001, approximately 64%; by September 28, 2001, approximately 50%; and by December 31, 2001, approximately 2%. By the latter date, the trust contained 8,000 shares of Enron stock valued at only $4,800.

McGinley never revoked the June 21 letter, nor did she ever advise the Bank to continue to hold the Enron stock in her trust. At all relevant times, she was capable of managing her own affairs. The Bank continues to act as trustee of her trust and as trustee of Francis' trust, of which McGinley is a beneficiary.

On January 3, 2003, after the continued substantial decline in Enron stock value, McGinley sued the Bank. On March 22, 2004, the district court granted summary judgment to the Bank.

ANALYSIS

McGinley's First Argument: *The letter and its exculpatory provision were invalid because the Bank failed to adequately communicate and explain them to McGinley. Specifically, the letter is ineffective as a trust amendment, i.e., there is no clear and convincing evidence that McGinley intended so because it was written by the Bank on its own initiative and because of the Bank's other conduct.*

It is clear from the specific language used in Section VIII. A of the trust that McGinley intended to carve out, from the general discretionary powers granted to the Bank as trustee, an exclusive authority for herself regarding all purchases and sales of trust assets. That section states the Grantor "shall be consulted by the Trustee as to any purchase or sale, and the Trustee shall abide by the Grantor's decision."

Other trust provisions reveal McGinley also intended to retain a great deal of overall power. In Article III, she retained exclusive authority to revoke, alter, amend, modify, or change the trust instrument, in whole or in part, at any time without the consent of the trustee or any other entity or person. In Article V, she retained exclusive authority to direct the trustee to make payments for her benefit, not only from income but also principal.

We therefore hold that through the express provisions of Article VIII. A, as drafted by McGinley's own counsel, she reduced the Bank's responsibilities contained in the prudent investor rule, an alteration which is clearly authorized by the statutes previously discussed. The alteration required the Bank to abide by her decisions on buying and selling trust assets.

Pursuant to McGinley's retained authority to control buying and selling trust assets under Article VIII. A, she also signed the June 21, 1991, "Direction by Powerholder to Retain Securities" which directed the Bank to continue to retain the Enron stock. There, she expressly agreed to exonerate, indemnify and hold the Bank harmless from any and all loss, damage and expense sustained or incurred by the Bank for continuing to retain the Enron stock. Moreover, McGinley also expressly acknowledged that the Bank does not, and would not, monitor the Enron stock. She not only specifically relieved the Bank from any responsibility to *monitor* the stock, but also from any responsibility to *analyze* it.

Her June 21 letter essentially told the Bank: "Do not sell my Enron stock until I say otherwise in writing, or die or become disabled. There is no need to bother me with asking my permission to sell it and therefore no need to monitor or analyze it. *I* will let you know." The letter was merely one manifestation of her right, reserved under the trust, to control the Bank's sale of trust assets.

McGinley argues that the Bank's conduct evidences that the letter was an ineffective amendment. On this issue, the district court held:

"Finally, Plaintiff contends that Defendant rendered the Directive legally ineffective by selling some Enron stock. Through this argument, Plaintiff seems to indicate that Defendant could release itself from its obligations to retain the Enron stock by simply selling some of the stock. This argument also fails since the language of the Directive clearly provides that it is to remain in effect until Plaintiff's death, disability, or written revocation. It is undisputed that none of the events required to render the document legally ineffective have occurred. Thus, Plaintiff has failed to show that Defendant's action of selling some of the stock rendered the disclaimer ineffective."

We agree. The same holds true for McGinley's argument that internal Bank documents state there was "no investment directive on file" and "no investment restrictions." Regardless of how the Bank described the trust in its internal documents, the legal effect of the express and unambiguous terms of the trust instrument control. See Guy Pine, Inc. v. Chrysler Motors Corp., 201 Kan. 371, 376, 440 P.2d 595 (1968) ("One party to a contract cannot unilaterally change the terms of the contract.").

The essence of McGinley's argument is that the Bank's actions operate as parol evidence to aid in this court's interpretation of the trust instrument and the June 21 letter. The problem with this argument is that the trust instrument, and its resultant letter, are clear and unambiguous on their faces. Accordingly, there is no need to resort to parol evidence, *i.e.*, conduct of a party which might aid in interpretation of those documents.

McGinley's Second Argument: *The exculpatory provision is invalid because of the Bank's failure to adequately communicate its contents and effect to McGinley.*

We acknowledge that the June 21 letter contains language concerning a release of liability which could therefore suggest McGinley "was fully aware that there were risks associated with the disclaimer." We further acknowledge the Bank's argument, based upon analogizing the letter to a contract, that a person who signs such a document is bound by its terms regardless of his or her failure to understand them, in the absence of fraud, undue influence or mutual mistake as to the contract's contents. Rosenbaum v. Texas Energies, Inc., 241 Kan. 295, 299, 736 P.2d 888 (1987). Nevertheless, these acknowledgments do not fully address McGinley's allegation on appeal, *i.e.,* that the trustee Bank abused its fiduciary relationship with its beneficiary (McGinley) because some evidence reveals that instead of fully and affirmatively communicating the contents and effect of the letter to McGinley personally, it merely obtained her signature through her husband. See Brown v. Foulks, 232 Kan. 424, 657 P.2d 501 (1983) ("fiduciary relation" has reference to any relationship of blood, business, friendship, or association in which one of the parties reposes special trust and confidence in the other who is in a position to have and exercise influence over the first party).

However, McGinley provides no relevant authority for her argument that the letter's exculpatory provision is invalid because of the Bank's abuse of the fiduciary relationship. Her references to the Restatement (Second) of Trusts, § 222 (1959) and K.S.A. 2002 Supp. 58a–1008 are inapplicable primarily because they concern invalidation due to a fiduciary's placement of exculpatory provisions in *trust instruments*, not the grantor's subsequent letters to the trustee. See English, *The Kansas Uniform Trust Code*, 51 Kan. L. Rev. 311, 344 (2003). These authorities certainly do not concern letters issued in accordance with trust provisions that had been drafted by a grantor's own legal counsel.

Similarly unpersuasive is her only other cited authority, the opinion of her expert witness, Steve Ramirez. Specifically, he opines that the letter was not an effective disclaimer of the Bank's duties because the Bank failed to disclose the risks of the exculpatory provision and failed to disclose that while the provision was intended to protect the interests of the Bank, there was little or no likelihood that it would protect the assets of the trust. He cites no legal authority for this specific opinion, however.

Clearly the better practice for the Bank would have been to have communicated to McGinley the letter's contents and effect before she signed it, and to have notified her of evolving circumstances, *e.g.*, steady decreases in Enron's value which reduced the investment portfolio's overall worth, or steady increases, though desirable, which unbalanced the portfolio. However, McGinley fails to direct this court to any relevant authority showing the Bank had a legal obligation to do so under the facts of this case.

McGinley's Third Argument: *Even if the exculpatory provision is valid, the Bank's failure to recommend portfolio diversification lacked good faith and was indifferent to McGinley's best interest which places its conduct beyond the reach of the provision. Specifically, when the Bank failed to disclose to McGinley its evaluation of her trust being overconcentrated and failed to recommend diversification, the Bank was reckless and indifferent to McGinley's best interest. Additionally, McGinley specifically asked the Bank for its professional advice as to which stocks to sell and which stocks to keep in 2000, and the Bank failed to disclose that in its professional opinion the Enron investment should be lowered to less than 15% of the value of the trust.*

In effect, McGinley argues that when circumstances evolve, the trustee should override the decisions of the grantor, *i.e.*, protect her from herself. Overriding would be inconsistent with the Kansas statutes previously discussed because the trustee is only protected when following written instructions from the grantor or when relying upon the express provisions of the trust instrument, not when directly contradicting them.

McGinley references only Rajala v. Allied Corp., 919 F.2d 610, 614 (10th Cir. 1990), for her proposition, "The duty to disclose arises under Kansas law when there is a fiduciary relationship which may be created by contract or may arise from the relationship of the parties." Although the court in *Rajala* discusses Kansas fiduciary duty law, it does not mention a duty to disclose, particularly after the trustee has received a written directive from the grantor to retain the stock and to not analyze or monitor it.

As for McGinley's argument regarding the failure of the Bank to disclose in its professional opinion the Enron investments should be lowered to less than 15% of the value of the trust, she cites no authority other than her expert witness, *i.e.,* "Ramirez believes it was a breach of the Bank's fiduciary duties." Her record references, however, do not support this assertion. While one reference expresses that the Bank has some general fiduciary duties as a professional trustee, the others primarily concern the Bank's alleged conflict of interest because of its national involvement in Enron. This issue was argued to the district court but abandoned on appeal.

We have thoroughly reviewed other arguments suggested by McGinley scattered throughout her brief and conclude they have no merit.

Affirmed.

NOTES AND QUESTIONS

1. When Mrs. McGinley established the trust with Bank of America, do you think she agreed to pay a fee to the bank? In light of the language of the trust instrument and the court's opinion, what services did she buy? Was she entitled to the bank's investment expertise, and did she get that expertise?

2. Did the trust instrument relieve Bank of America of all responsibility for investments in Mrs. McGinley's trust portfolio? If Mrs. McGinley took no role in investment decisions, and did not respond to communications from the bank, would the bank have had a responsibility to invest trust funds prudently? Would the bank have been liable for imprudence in this case?

3. Who drafted the letter relieving Bank of America of the responsibility for monitoring Enron securities? At the time the letter was drafted, did Bank of America owe a fiduciary duty to McGinley? Why didn't that duty preclude Bank of America from writing a letter advancing its own interest at the expense of the interest of the trust beneficiary?

4. The court emphasizes that the trust instrument (by contrast to the letter) was drafted by Mrs. McGinley's lawyer. Why did the lawyer draft a trust instrument authorizing the bank to invest in securities not otherwise authorized by law? Why would such language be in Mrs. McGinley's interest?

Would it ever be in a trust beneficiary's interest to include a broad clause exculpating the trustee from all liability for investment decisions? Why would the lawyer for a trust settlor ever include an exculpatory clause in a trust instrument? Professor Leslie offers two possible explanations: (1) the trust company insists on the exculpatory clause and settlor's lawyer may be interested in currying favor with the trust company, or (2) the settlor is worried that particular beneficiaries may tend to be overly litigious. Melanie B. Leslie, Common Law, Common Sense: Fiduciary Standards and Trustee Identity, 27 Cardozo L. Rev. 2713, 2744–47 (2006). Which explanation do you find more plausible?

By contrast, Professor Leslie emphasizes that there are often good reasons for a settlor's lawyer to include transaction-specific exculpatory clauses. Id. at 2744. For instance, the settlor might want to authorize the trustee to make investments in which the trustee has an interest, or might want to authorize the trustee to hold a portfolio that is not adequately diversified.

UNIFORM TRUST CODE

SECTION 1008. EXCULPATION OF TRUSTEE.

(a) A term of a trust relieving a trustee of liability for breach of trust is unenforceable to the extent that it:

(1) relieves the trustee of liability for breach of trust committed in bad faith or with reckless indifference to the purposes of the trust or the interests of the beneficiaries; or

(2) was inserted as the result of an abuse by the trustee of a fiduciary or confidential relationship to the settlor.

(b) An exculpatory term drafted or caused to be drafted by the trustee is invalid as an abuse of a fiduciary or confidential relationship unless the trustee proves that the exculpatory term is fair under the circumstances and that its existence and contents were adequately communicated to the settlor.

The comment to section 1008 goes on to provide that "[t]he requirements of subsection (b) are satisfied if the settlor was represented by independent counsel. If the settlor was represented by independent counsel, the settlor's attorney is considered the drafter of the instrument even if the attorney used the trustee's form. Because the settlor's attorney is an agent of the settlor, disclosure of an exculpatory term to the settlor's attorney is disclosure to the settlor."

QUESTIONS

1. Why didn't the court in McGinley apply section 1008(b) to the letter, exculpating the trustee from liability for holding Enron stock?

2. In light of the comment, do you think section 1008 provides adequate protection against abuse by the trustee? Does it provide protection to settlors represented by inadequate counsel?

D. SAFEGUARDING PROPERTY—THE DUTY NOT TO COMMINGLE

UNIFORM TRUST CODE

SECTION 810. RECORDKEEPING AND IDENTIFICATION OF TRUST PROPERTY.

(a) A trustee shall keep adequate records of the administration of the trust.

(b) A trustee shall keep trust property separate from the trustee's own property.

(c) Except as otherwise provided in subsection (d), a trustee shall cause the trust property to be designated so that the interest of the trust, to the extent feasible, appears in records maintained by a party other than a trustee or beneficiary

(d) If the trustee maintains records clearly indicating the respective interests, a trustee may invest as a whole the property of two or more separate trusts.

QUESTIONS

1. A trustee keeps his own funds in one brokerage account and trust funds in a separate brokerage account, with a different broker. Both accounts are in the trustee's name. Has the trustee improperly commingled assets? Has the trustee complied with Section 810?

Why require the trustee to "earmark" trust assets? Earmarking requires the trustee to identify assets as belonging to the trust rather than to the trustee personally. Suppose the trustee dies. How will the trust beneficiary (or the trustee's heirs) prove which account belongs to the trust and which to the estate? Moreover, suppose one account suffers investment losses. If a dishonest trustee contends that the trust account suffered the losses, how will the trust beneficiaries establish that the losses were suffered by the trustee's personal account?

2. Suppose the trustee holds bearer bonds—bonds payable to the holder of the bonds, without identification. Has the trustee violated the duty to earmark? Would it be "feasible" within the meaning of section 810(c) to earmark bearer bonds?

SECTION IV. DUTIES TO MULTIPLE BENEFICIARIES: PRINCIPAL AND INCOME

A. FRAMING THE PROBLEM

Generally, when settlor creates a trust, the trust has more than one beneficiary. Someone may have a right to income (perhaps for life), while someone else may become entitled to the corpus at the death of the income beneficiary. When the trustee makes investments, the trustee has to consider the interests of all beneficiaries. In practice, this creates a potential for conflict.

Suppose, for instance, that in a time of high inflation, the trustee has the opportunity to invest in a real estate mortgage at a very high interest rate—say 11%. The mortgagor promises to pay 11% interest each year, and to repay the principal amount to the trust in ten years. Because of inflation, when the trust principal is repaid ten years from now, the principal will be worth, in constant dollars, a fraction of its current value. If the trustee invests in the mortgage, and pays all 11% to the income beneficiary, the trustee will advantage the income beneficiary at the expense of the remainder beneficiary.

By contrast, suppose the trustee were to purchase corporate stock in a firm that pays few, or no, dividends and plows most of its earnings back into the company, generating higher stock prices. If the trustee were to pay the income beneficiary only the paltry dividends, and to give the shares of stock to the remainder beneficiary at the termination of the trust, the trustee will advantage the remainder beneficiary at the expense of the income beneficiary.

Modern Portfolio Theory (MPT) teaches that an investor should strive to maximize overall return, regardless of form. Traditional treatment of income and principal, however, presented a difficult dilemma for the trustee: an investment that might look like an attractive investment overall does not appear to be attractive for one or more of the trust beneficiaries, because the form of return generated by the investment would not benefit all beneficiaries proportionately.

Besides the global investment dilemma, the trustee faces another set of practical problems that often create controversy among beneficiaries: what constitutes principal, and what constitutes income?

Suppose, for instance, the trust has two principal assets: a stock portfolio and an apartment building. If one of the corporations in the stock portfolio declares a stock dividend, distributing one share of stock to every holder of 100 shares, is the dividend income or principal? And suppose the corporation offers shareholders the option of taking the dividend in stock or in cash. Does that change the answer?

Now turn to the apartment building. The rent that comes in from tenants generally counts as income. But what about payments the trustee made to a broker to find those tenants? Do those payments reduce the income payable to the income beneficiary? And suppose the building needs a new furnace or a new roof. Do those expenditures come out of income or out of principal? Especially when the income beneficiary and the remaindermen are not on good terms (think second wife and children by the first marriage), these questions might provide fertile ground for family battles that benefit no one.

B. Solving the Problem by Drafting: The Unitrust

How might the settlor resolve these problems? A modern approach is to eschew distinctions between "income" and "principal" altogether, and to create a "unitrust." Oversimplifying, a unitrust might provide:

> During the life of income beneficiary the Trustee shall make payments from the Unitrust as follows: Each year the Trustee shall pay to or apply for the benefit of the income beneficiary in equal installments during the year, a sum equal to four percent of the market value of the Unitrust as constituted on the first day of the year. On the death of the income beneficiary, the Trustee shall pay the entire unitrust to the remainder.

Consider how the unitrust "solves" the problem of income and principal. First, examine the global dilemma. If the 11% mortgage will provide the best overall expected return for the trust, do the remaindermen have any reason to object? If, on the other hand, the growth stock offers the highest expected return, does the income beneficiary have any reason to object?

Now consider the practical classification problems. With a unitrust in place, does the trustee have to worry about whether the stock dividend is income or principal? About whether the roof repairs should come out of income or principal? (Of course, the unitrust might require an annual appraisal of the *value* of the apartment building—an expense not necessary with a traditional trust).

QUESTION

How should the settlor choose the percentage of market value payable to the income beneficiary? Should the amount be the same in times of low inflation as in times of high inflation? Is there a way for the settlor to account for variable economic conditions? See generally Joel C. Dobris, Why-five? The Strange, Magnetic and Mesmerizing Affect of the Five Percent Unitrust and Spending Rate on Settlors, Their Advisors, and Retirees, 40 Real Prop., Prob. & Tr. J. 39 (2005).

C. Statutorily Authorized Conversions to Unitrusts

What if settlor has created a traditional trust requiring the trustee to pay the trust income to designated beneficiaries. What is the trustee to do in light of the prudent investor rule, which arguably requires the trustee to focus on total return in making investment decisions? A majority of states have given trustees the option to convert the trust into a unitrust.

Should a trust beneficiary be entitled to prevent conversion to a unitrust? Suppose the trustee is himself a trust beneficiary who would benefit from conversion to a unitrust. For instance, in Matter of Heller, 6 N.Y.3d 649, 816 N.Y.S.2d 403, 849 N.E.2d 262 (2006), settlor's will created a trust leaving his wife the greater of $40,000 per year or the trust income for life. Two of settlor's children by a prior marriage were named as trustees (as well as remainder beneficiaries) of the trust. The trust, which was invested in income-producing commercial real estate, generated about $190,000 in income, while a unitrust election would reduce the wife's annual income to about $70,000. The Court of Appeals held that the unitrust statute did not prevent a trustee who is also a remainder beneficiary from converting the trust to a unitrust (although the court held that the Surrogate should review any such election for fairness).

By contrast, the California statute (among others) requires that a trustee must provide notice to beneficiaries before converting a trust to a unitrust, and gives the beneficiaries the option to object to conversion. Cal. Prob. Code § 16336.4. Suppose the California statute had been in effect. How would you expect the 95–year old wife in Heller to respond to a notice from the trustee indicating his intention to convert the trust to a unitrust? Would a statute requiring affirmative consent from the beneficiaries be an improvement?

D. A STATUTORY SOLUTION: THE UNIFORM PRINCIPAL AND INCOME ACT

The Revised Uniform Principal and Income Act, promulgated in 1997 by the National Conference of Commissioners on Uniform State Laws, attacks the principal and interest problem for those trusts in which the settlor has not resolved principal and interest questions with express language in the trust instrument. The Uniform Principal and Income Act integrates Modern Portfolio Theory into fiduciary law by giving the trustee a modest power to adjust payments to the various beneficiaries when the nominal return is skewed too far towards income or towards principal.

In other words, if an otherwise perfect fiduciary investment portfolio earns a splendid return, but nothing we ordinarily call "income," the statute permits the fiduciary to make payments to the income beneficiary from principal via an adjustment. See Alyssa A. DiRusso & Kathleen M. Sablone, Statutory Techniques for Balancing the Financial Interests of Trust Beneficiaries, 39 U.S.F. L. Rev. 261 (2005); Mark B. Gillett & Kathleen R. Guzman, Managing Assets: The Oklahoma Uniform Principal and Income Act, 56 Okla. L. Rev. 1 (2003); Terry L. Turnipseed, Tools for Better Balancing the Interests of Income Beneficiaries and Remaindermen, 28 Tax Mgmt. Est. Gifts & Tr. J. 244 (2003).

The adjustment power is codified in section 104 of the Act:

UNIFORM PRINCIPAL AND INCOME ACT

SECTION 104. TRUSTEE'S POWER TO ADJUST.

(a) A trustee may adjust between principal and income to the extent the trustee considers necessary if the trustee invests and manages trust assets as a prudent investor, the terms of the trust describe the amount that may or must be distributed to a beneficiary by referring to the trust's income, and the trustee determines, after applying the rules in Section 103(a), that the trustee is unable to comply with Section 103(b).

(b) In deciding whether and to what extent to exercise the power conferred by subsection (a), a trustee shall consider all factors relevant to the trust and its beneficiaries, including the following factors to the extent they are relevant:

(1) the nature, purpose, and expected duration of the trust;

(2) the intent of the settlor;

(3) the identity and circumstances of the beneficiaries;

(4) the needs for liquidity, regularity of income, and preservation and appreciation of capital;

(5) the assets held in the trust; the extent to which they consist of financial assets, interests in closely held enterprises, tangible and intangible personal property, or real property; the extent to which an asset is used by a beneficiary; and whether an asset was purchased by the trustee or received from the settlor;

(6) the net amount allocated to income under the other sections of this [Act] and the increase or decrease in the value of the principal assets, which the trustee may estimate as to assets for which market values are not readily available;

(7) whether and to what extent the terms of the trust give the trustee the power to invade principal or accumulate income or prohibit the trustee from invading principal or accumulating income, and the extent to which the trustee has exercised a power from time to time to invade principal or accumulate income;

(8) the actual and anticipated effect of economic conditions on principal and income and effects of inflation and deflation; and

(9) the anticipated tax consequences of an adjustment.

(c) A trustee may not make an adjustment [in certain other situations]:

* * *

Of course, the scope of the Uniform Principal and Income Act extends far beyond the adjustment power; the statute attempts to classify most payments made to the trustee as either principal or income, and attempts to classify expenditures made by the trustee as those that should be allocated to income or principal.

QUESTIONS

1. In light of the Uniform Principal and Income Act, would you advise a settlor to create a unitrust? Are there advantages of a unitrust that the UP & IA does not duplicate? Are there advantages of the UP & IA that a unitrust does not capture?

2. Does section 104 of the UP & IA give the trustee a power to adjust when the settlor has created a unitrust? Should it give the trustee such a power?

3. Would you prefer to serve as trustee of a unitrust or as trustee of a trust governed by section 104 of the UP & IA? Why?

PROBLEMS

In each of the following problems, assume that the trust created by the settlor makes the settlor's second husband the beneficiary for the duration of his life, and provides that at the husband's death, the trust property should be distributed to settlor's two children by her first marriage. In each problem, consider what advice you would give to the trustee about how much to pay the husband, and from what pot of money, if (a) the trust is a 4% unitrust governed by the provision reproduced on p. 1089, supra, or (b) the trust, which provides that all income should be distributed to the husband, is governed by section 104 of the UP & IA.

1. The trust's only asset is a minority interest in a family business owned jointly by the trust and settlor's two sisters. The business, which is incorporated, has generally paid dividends of $10 per share (which is roughly 5% of the appraised value of each share). The company has a bad year and declares no dividends.

2. The trust holds a diversified portfolio of mutual funds. The last three years have been marked by a 7% annual inflation rate. The value of the portfolio has increased, in dollar terms, by 5% per year, and the portfolio has also generated cash dividends amounting to 5% of the portfolio's value.

3. The trust holds the same diversified portfolio, but the economy is mired in a recession. The portfolio has declined in value by 7% a year for each of the last three years, and is generating dividend income amounting to 2% of the portfolio's value.

SECTION V. ACCOUNTINGS AND THE DUTY TO INFORM TRUST BENEFICIARIES

Trustees and personal representatives have a duty to report to trust beneficiaries on information relevant to the trust or estate. Without information, the beneficiaries would be in a poor position to monitor the trustee's performance and to protect their own interests. When and how should a fiduciary provide information to beneficiaries? That depends both on the jurisdiction and the circumstances. Section 813 of the Uniform

Trust Code imposes several different reporting requirements: the trustee must report at least annually, but also at the termination of the trust and upon any vacancy in a trusteeship. At each of those times, the UTC requires "a report of the trust property, liabilities, receipts, and disbursements, including the source and amount of the trustee's compensation, a listing of the trust assets and, if feasible, their respective market values." Sometimes, the trustee must provide additional information; as the *Allard* case illustrates, the trustee may also have an obligation to inform beneficiaries about prospective sales of trust property (at least when the property is not publicly traded), to enable the beneficiaries to bid for that property.

Historically, the reports prepared by the trustee have been called "accountings." Some states require judicial accountings in estates and testamentary trusts. Others do not. If these accounts are approved by the court after hearing they are res judicata on all issues which might be raised on the basis of the facts disclosed. Trustees of *inter vivos* trusts are usually not required to account unless the beneficiaries, the estate of a deceased trustee or a successor trustee demand it.

Even when not required to do so by statute or judicial decree, trustees of *inter vivos* trusts normally account to the beneficiaries at appropriate, often regular, intervals. In both testamentary and *inter* vivos trusts, trustees often petition for court or beneficiary approval of their accounts. They do so, in part, out of self-interest. Even without judicial approval, if the beneficiaries approve the trustee's account and give the trustee a release of liability, the trustee may be protected from future claims for breach of fiduciary duty. Even if approval is not obtained, the beneficiaries may be barred after a lapse of time by the equitable doctrine of laches.

Suppose, however, the beneficiaries waive any right to an accounting from the trustee. Or suppose the settlor purports to relieve the trustee of responsibility for reporting to the beneficiaries—or seeks actively to *prohibit* the trustee from making disclosure to the beneficiaries. What effect do such waivers or instructions have? With respect to beneficiary waivers, consider the following case:

In re Freihofer

Surrogate's Court, Albany County, 1997.
172 Misc.2d 260, 658 N.Y.S.2d 811.

■ RAYMOND E. MARINELLI, SURROGATE.

Charles Freihofer died a testate resident of Albany County on January 11, 1981, survived by his spouse, Phoebe Freihofer, and two sons, Andrew and Stephen Freihofer. By the terms of the decedent's Last Will and Testament, duly admitted to probate on January 21, 1981, the entire estate passed to his wife, Phoebe.

However, under renunciation filed in this Court on March 4, 1981 by Phoebe Freihofer, a portion of the decedent's estate made up of properties affiliated with the Charles Freihofer Baking Company, Inc. passed into testamentary trusts for the benefit of the decedent's two sons, Andrew and Stephen Freihofer.

Pursuant to the terms of the Last Will and Testament, Alan E. Steiner, Charles C. Freihofer III and Phoebe B. Freihofer, the widow, were appointed executors on January 21, 1981; letters of trusteeship for the benefit of Andrew and Stephen were issued to Alan Steiner, the sole trustee, on April 3, 1981.

An examination of the Court records in this estate reveals that a New York estate tax proceeding was filed and an Order Fixing Taxes entered on November 14, 1983. The record further indicates that the gross New York estate was valued at $1,405,201.65. There are no receipts or releases in the file, no accounting has been made to the Court, and a report filed on March 25, 1983, pursuant to 22 NYCRR former 1940.15, executed solely by co-executor/attorney Alan E. Steiner shows that at the time the fiduciaries were still holding at least $417,446.00 in estate assets.

On August 30, 1996, Andrew G. Freihofer filed a petition with this Court seeking an Order to Compel Alan E. Steiner, as Trustee of the testamentary trust of Charles F. Freihofer to account. Citation was issued returnable on September 10, 1996, at which time the respondent Executor filed an answer seeking dismissal of the within petition to compel accounting. Thereafter, respondent brought on a motion to dismiss the within petition and in the alternative for summary judgment based upon the following arguments:

1. release of claim
2. documentary evidence * * *

Movant has asserted as a basis for dismissal and/or summary judgment the existence of a release of claim and a receipt, release and waiver signed by the trust beneficiary and petitioner herein, Andrew Freihofer. It is significant that the original release, receipt and waiver was never filed with the Court, and has yet to be submitted for filing, even though its existence is being relied on in the within motion. Further, it is noted that the photocopy of the release submitted is not in a form acceptable for filing in the Surrogate Court, and fails to recite the actual consideration received. The petitioner has stated in his affidavit in response to the motion that at the time the purported release was signed discharging attorney-trustee Steiner, Mr. Steiner was representing the petitioner, and had, in fact, drafted an inter vivos trust agreement into which the testamentary trust assets would pour over, Andrew Freihofer being the grantor, and Alan Steiner, attorney-draftsman, being the sole trustee. It is further alleged, and uncontroverted by the movant, that the testamentary trust chiefly contained assets of the Freihofer Baking Company, and that the trustee, who was acting simultaneously as the petitioner's personal attorney, corporate attorney for Freihofer Baking, trustee and executor under several trusts and wills of Freihofer family members, particularly the Charles Freihofer testamentary trust FBO Andrew Freihofer, and, unbeknown at the time to the petitioner, a member of the Board of Directors of Freihofer

Baking, had a personal interest in the assets held by the testamentary trust that may have been in conflict with the trust beneficiary's best interest.

The failure of the trustee-attorney Alan Steiner to fully disclose the many and potentially conflicting roles he played in the sale of Freihofer Baking, the stock of which constituted the testamentary trust assets now in question, voids any receipt release and waiver he may have obtained from his beneficiary, particularly since he sought his own discharge from liability to that beneficiary while at the same time representing that beneficiary individually.

This Court again looks at the dicta of Matter of Stalbe, 130 Misc.2d 725, 497 N.Y.S.2d 237 (Queens Surrogate's Court, 1985), holding an attorney-fiduciary to a higher standard than a lay fiduciary. Further, Mr. Steiner's legal representation of Andrew Freihofer individually as sole residuary beneficiary of a trust of which Mr. Steiner was sole trustee is an apparent violation of DR 5–101(A) of the Code of Professional Responsibility, which prohibits a lawyer, except with the client's consent after full disclosure [emphasis added], to accept employment if the exercise of his professional judgment on behalf of the client will or may reasonably be affected by the lawyer's own financial or personal interests. See Chang v. Chang, 190 A.D.2d 311, 317, 597 N.Y.S.2d 692.

There can be no more an egregious example of an attorney's judgment being affected than by his seeking discharge of financial liability as a fiduciary from his own client.

The attorney-fiduciary has a duty to provide full disclosure of his stewardship to the beneficiary. Here, the attorney-trustee, who also represented the sole beneficiary individually, has chosen to use none of the mechanisms under Article 22 of the SCPA to disclose, render or settle his accounts. This, despite the fact that he had knowledge of a disgruntled beneficiary, acted simultaneously as that beneficiary's legal counsel, knew the large monetary value of the trust assets and the controversial nature in which they were liquidated, and was aware of his professional duty to discharge himself as against the beneficiary. Under the circumstances, the Court finds as a matter of law that no valid release and discharge has taken place, and the movant cannot now rely upon either documentary evidence or release to avoid judicial settlement of his accounts as trustee. * * *

SCPA § 2205, subd. 1 provides that the Court may grant an order compelling a formal accounting when it appears to be in the best interest of the estate. It appears from the records submitted that the attorney-trustee may have been paid commissions and/or attorney fees prior to judicial settlement of accounts and without consent of the beneficiary. See Matter of Crippen, 32 Misc.2d 1019, 224 N.Y.S.2d 116 (Surr.Ct. New York Co., 1961); Matter of Ross, 33 Misc. 163, 68 N.Y.S. 373 (Surr.Ct., New York Co., 1900). Under authority of these statutes and cases, together with Matter of Stortecky v. Mazzone, 84 N.Y.2d 802, 617 N.Y.S.2d 136, 641 N.E.2d 157 (1994) it appears to be in best interest of the trust for the Trustee to render and judicially settle his accounts as such. The motion is denied in its entirety, and petition granted.

QUESTIONS AND NOTES

1. Freihofer was allowed to demand an account, even after he seemingly signed away that right. Would Freihofer have been able to so set aside his receipt and release if Steiner wasn't his lawyer?

2. You can see that often no one insists on an accounting except an interested party. Andrew Freihofer didn't choose to complain for a long time. If he never complained there would never be an accounting. Every fiduciary who chooses not to account takes the risk that there will be later complaints.

3. Should a trust settlor also be entitled to demand an accounting? Absent language in the trust instrument, the general answer is no. Professor Frances Foster argues that trust beneficiaries are "less likely to understand, demand, and act on trust information" than trust settlors. Frances H. Foster, American Trust Law in a Chinese Mirror, 94 Minn. L. Rev. 602, 640 (2010). Does that mean that a trustee should be obligated to provide information to the trust settlor? Does it suggest that the settlor should have a right to enforce fiduciary duties?

Suppose the settlor, rather than a beneficiary, attempts to relieve the trustee of a duty to account. Consider the following case:

Johnson v. Johnson

Court of Special Appeals of Maryland, 2009.
184 Md.App. 643, 967 A.2d 274.

■ MATRICCIANI, J.:

This case arises from a dispute between a trust beneficiary and its trustee. Appellant, Catherine A. Moreland Johnson (Catherine), is trustee and stepmother to appellee and trust beneficiary, James Michael Johnson (James). Unsuccessful in his efforts to obtain an accounting of the trust from Catherine, James filed a Petition for Court Assumption of Jurisdiction of Trust Estate and Related Relief in the Circuit Court for Calvert County. Catherine opposed the petition, asserting that James lacked a cognizable interest in the trust. After a hearing on the matter, the circuit court ordered Catherine to provide an accounting of the trust at issue, the Johnson Family Trust (the "Trust"), to James by April 25, 2008. In response, Catherine noted this timely appeal.

FACTS AND PROCEEDINGS

Catherine and the late Edward R. Johnson (the "Johnsons") were married on January 9, 1988. On August 25, 2004, the Johnsons established an inter vivos trust known as the Johnson Family Trust. The Trust made the Johnsons Trustors and the first Co–Trustees. Edward died on February 14, 2006. Following Edward's death, his son, James, twice requested an accounting of the Trust. When the requests went unanswered, he filed a Petition for Court Assumption of Jurisdiction of a Trust and Related Relief on October 11, 2007. He asked the court to order his stepmother, Catherine, to file a complete and accurate accounting of her tenure as Trustee. Catherine replied on January 14, 2008, asking the court to deny the requested accounting. The circuit court held a hearing on the matter on January 31, 2008, and it filed an opinion and order on February 12, 2008. The court ordered Catherine to provide an accounting of the Trust to James by April 25, 2008. Catherine noted this timely appeal on March 5, 2008. Relevant excerpts of the Trust and additional facts will be provided throughout the discussion.

DISCUSSION

Under the terms of the Trust, only Catherine held a present interest, entitling her to the Trust income at least quarter-annually. Trust, Article IV. Thus, James's interest, which depends upon his surviving his stepmother, is at best a future interest, contingent upon his survivorship. It is a property interest properly deemed a "remainder interest."

The Right to an Accounting

Having determined that James possesses a future interest in the Trust, we must consider the trial court's decision that his interest gives rise to a right to an accounting.

Because James has a future interest in the Trust, despite the uncertainty of his actually benefitting from that future interest, we hold that he is entitled to an accounting from the Trustee. Maryland Code (1974, 2001 Repl. Vol.), § 14–405(j)(1) of the Estates and Trust Article ("ET") lists several categories of people who are permitted to request an accounting of trust property and transactions. The relevant parties included in the list are "The beneficiary or the beneficiary's legal representative." ET § 14–405(j)(1)(ii). In response, "(2)The trustee shall provide a written accounting of all trust property and trust transactions for the previous year, or for a longer period if needed for tax purposes, upon request by and at reasonable times to a person authorized in paragraph (1) of this subsection." ET § 14–405 (j)(2). In In re Clarke's Will, 198 Md. 266, 81 A.2d 640 (1951), the Court of Appeals expounded on who was permitted to request an accounting. The Court stated that, [HN7] "[i]f the petitioner has any interest at all he is entitled to invoke the court's protection." Id. at 273 (citations omitted). The Court continued by explaining that "[t]he mere fact that future interests are involved will not defeat the power to declare rights...." Id.

The Limitations in the Trust

Catherine contends that the circuit court's order to provide an accounting contravenes the explicit terms of the Trust, making it contrary to Maryland case law that states that the settlor's intent is controlling. James asserts that Maryland law requires a trustee to provide an accounting upon a beneficiary's request.

Catherine argues that three express provisions of the Trust show the settlor's specific intent that no trustee have an obligation to provide an accounting: first, the section that states: "The TRUSTEE shall not be required at any time to file any account in any court, nor shall the TRUSTEE be required to have any account judicially settled." Trust, Article X(C); second, the language that states the Trustors' express intent to create a private trust; and, third, the Trust language that states: "TRUSTORS direct that only the information concerning the benefits held for or distributable to any particular beneficiary be revealed to such beneficiary and that no person shall be entitled to information concerning benefits held for or distributable to any other person." Trust, Article XVI(P). These three provisions, Catherine contends, override James's legal right to request an accounting. She argues that Trustors have the ability to modify their legal obligation to provide an accounting by explicitly eliminating it in the Trust's provisions.

This Court encountered a similar issue in Jacob v. Davis, 128 Md. App. at 450–51. In that case, appellees argued that a section of the contested will relieved the trustee of accounting to the beneficiaries. Id. at 446. We stated that, "[t]o our knowledge, no Maryland appellate decision ha[d] addressed the extent to which a decedent or testator [could] limit the common law duty of a trustee to account in a court of equity." Id. at 450. We further stated that there were not statutes or rules addressing this issue. Id. at 450. Thus, we turned to a recognized authority on Trusts, Bogert's, The Law of Trusts and Trustees. The Jacob Court quoted, but did not expressly adopt, Bogert's explanation of the role of a trustee and the reasons why a Trustor should not be permitted to avoid his duty to account. Id. at 450–51. Bogert's statement reads as follows:

> A [testator] who attempts to create a trust without any accountability in the trustee is contradicting himself. A trust necessarily grants rights to the beneficiary that are enforceable in equity. If the trustee cannot be called to account, the beneficiary cannot force the trustee to any particular line of conduct with regard to the trust property or sue for breach of trust. The trustee may do as he likes with the property, and the beneficiary is without remedy. If the court finds that the settlor really intended a trust, it would seem that accountability in chancery or other court must inevitably follow as an incident. Without an account the beneficiary must be in the dark as to whether there has been a breach of trust and so is prevented as a practical matter from holding the trustee liable for a breach.

The Law of Trusts and Trustees, § 973 at 467.

The Restatement of Trusts also outlines the fiduciary duties of a trustee, explaining:

> [F]iduciary principles include (i) the general duty to act, reasonably informed, with impartiality among the various beneficiaries and interests and (ii) the duty to provide the beneficiaries with information concerning the trust and its administration. This combination of duties entitles the beneficiaries (and also the court) not only to accounting information but also to relevant, general information concerning the bases upon which the trustee's discretionary judgments have been or will be made.

Restatement, § 50 cmt. b at 260 (2003) (internal references omitted). It continues: "It is contrary to sound policy, and a contradiction in terms, to permit the settlor to relieve a "trustee" of all accountability." Id. at cmt. c at 262. We now adopt this reasoning and conclude that a trustor cannot, by including limitations in the Trust instrument, circumscribe the trustee's duty to account to beneficiaries.

This conclusion is in line with recognized Maryland law regarding trusts and accountings. In In re Clarke's Will, 198 Md. 266, 81 A.2d 640, the Court of Appeals liberally interpreted the class of beneficiaries who would be permitted to request an accounting. By broadly construing who was entitled to an accounting, the Court of Appeals recognized the importance of accountings for maintaining the integrity of trusts. See also Ehlen v. Ehlen, 63 Md. 267 (1885) (responding to interested party's petition, court affirmed the order for trustee to bring into court the securities and money held in trust after it was shown that property was in danger).

Permitting a trustor to eliminate the duty to account to beneficiaries would be contrary to the Court of Appeals' decisions regarding who is entitled to an accounting. We conclude that, despite the language in the Trust attempting to eliminate Catherine's duty to account, James is entitled to request an accounting and Catherine is required to provide it.

JUDGMENT AFFIRMED.

NOTES AND QUESTIONS

1. Could Catherine and Edward Johnson have left James without any interest in the trust property at all? That is, could they have provided that, at the first to die, all property in the trust would pass to the survivor? If Catherine and Edward had no obligation to leave James any of the trust property, why would the court hold that they had an obligation to provide James with information about the trust?

2. Suppose the trust instrument had entitled James to an accounting, but only at trust termination. Would the court have upheld that provision? Wouldn't the prospect of an accounting at trust termination be adequate to discipline the trustee? Cf. Matter of Shore, 19 Misc.3d 663, 854 N.Y.S.2d 293 (Surr. Ct., 2008) (holding such a provision invalid because "there is no one in a position to protect the beneficiaries' interests during the existence of the trust."). In Shore, the trustee herself drafted the provision limiting the right to an accounting, and did so on behalf of a trust settlor who had acquired the proceeds in settlement of a personal injury action.

3. Why would a settlor include a provision dispensing with the need for accountings or limiting the beneficiaries' right to an accounting? Should courts honor such a provision?

4. Suppose the settlor names herself as trustee of an inter vivos trust. Would a court enforce a provision excusing her from the obligation to account? Should the answer turn on whether the trust is revocable or irrevocable?

Trust Privacy

A trustee typically has the duty to inform trust beneficiaries about the existence and terms of the trust. See, e.g., Uniform Trust Code, § 813(b). A number of wealthy settlors want to keep trust beneficiaries in the dark about the size and terms of the trust, in part because they do not want those beneficiaries to become slothful or complacent in the knowledge that all of their financial needs have been provided for. Lawyers for these settlors have, in a number of states, successfully lobbied for legislation that permits a trust settlor to override the duty to provide information by including express language to that effect in the trust instrument, and convinced the drafters of the Uniform Trust Code to "bracket" the provisions making the duty to inform mandatory, so that states could adopt much of the code while still giving settlors the option to override the duty to provide information. See generally T.P. Gallanis, The Trustee's Duty to Inform, 85 N.C. L. Rev. 1595, 1604–10 (2007). Most states that have adopted the UTC have watered down the Code's notification provisions in one way or another. Ohio, for instance, permits a settlor to appoint a surrogate to receive information in place of the trust beneficiaries. Ohio Rev. Code Ann. § 5801.04(C). Do you think surrogate notification is an adequate substitute for beneficiary notification? Why or why not?

Professor Frances Foster has catalogued some of the worst financial abuses trustees have inflicted on uninformed trustees. She is critical of the move to permit settlors to keep trusts private:

> "[U]nder recent reforms to promote trust privacy, some states have removed even the most basic protection for beneficiaries—knowledge that a trust exists. These states have left to the settlor's discretion whether current and future beneficiaries are entitled to any notice whatsoever. Trust privacy thus can leave beneficiaries at the mercy of trustees by insulating trustees from any outside supervision or accountability."

Frances H. Foster, Trust Privacy, 93 Cornell L. Rev. 555, 608 (2008).

Information and Revocable Trusts

What information should a trustee provide to beneficiaries of a revocable living trust? If a settlor creates a revocable living trust, naming herself as trustee, does she have an obligation to inform trust beneficiaries of their interest? Must she provide annual reports or accountings? Must she inform the beneficiaries if she modifies or revokes the trust? Are the answers different if the settlor has named someone else as trustee, while retaining the power to revoke?

The Uniform Trust Code addresses these issues in section 603(a), which provides that "[w]hile a trust is revocable [and the settlor has capacity to revoke the trust], rights of the beneficiaries are subject to the control of, and the duties of the trustee are owed exclusively to, the settlor." See also Restatement (Third) of Trusts, § 74, cmt. e (2007).

Against that background, consider J.P. Morgan Chase Bank, N.A. v. Longmeyer, 275 S.W.3d 697 (Ky. 2009). Settlor had created a revocable living trust naming certain charities as beneficiaries. When settlor revoked the trust, creating a new trust with different beneficiaries, the trustee suspected undue influence, and informed the charities of the revocation. The charities then challenged the revocation and the new trust, ultimately obtaining a substantial sum in settlement of the litigation. The trustee of the new trust then brought an action against the trustee of the original revocable living trust, contending that notification of the charitable beneficiaries was a breach of fiduciary duty.

The Kentucky Supreme Court held that the trustee of the original trust had not breached any fiduciary duty, and went so far as to indicate that the trustee had an obligation to inform the remainder beneficiaries of their removal. Is the Longmeyer decision consistent with the Uniform Trust Code (which has not been enacted in Kentucky)? Does Longmeyer represent good policy? Why or why not?

If you were practicing in Kentucky, and a client wanted to create a revocable living trust, what advice would you give the client if she wanted to avoid having the trustee provide information to anyone but the settlor?

SECTION VI. RESIGNATION AND REMOVAL OF TRUSTEES

A. RESIGNATION

Can the trustee of a trust simply say, "it isn't worth it any more. I quit"? What happens to the assets the trustee was managing if the trustee simply quits? No one else has legal title to trust assets, or the power to deal with them. If the trustee could walk away from fiduciary obligations, those assets (and the interests of the beneficiaries) would be in serious jeopardy. Placing trust interests in serious jeopardy is entirely inconsistent with the trustee's fiduciary duty.

At common law, a trustee could not resign his or her position without judicial permission. If the trustee stopped taking care of trust assets without judicial permission, the trustee would be liable for any resulting damage to the trust beneficiaries.

Section 36 of the Restatement (Third) of Trusts provides:

A trustee who has accepted the trust can properly resign:

(a) in accordance with the terms of the trust;

(b) with the consent of all beneficiaries; or

(c) upon terms approved by a proper court.

In other words, if the trust instrument includes provisions permitting the trustee to resign (and presumably also includes provisions for selecting a successor trustee), those provisions are enforceable. In addition, even if the trust instrument is silent, the trustee may resign if the trustee obtains the consent of all trust beneficiaries.

The Uniform Trust Code goes one step further, and permits a trustee to resign upon providing 30 days notice to the beneficiaries, the settlor (if living), and all co-trustees. Uniform Trust Code, § 705. Does the UTC provision make sense? Suppose a trust settlor establishes a trust for the benefit of three financially challenged siblings. After the settlor's death, the trustee sends the siblings a notice tendering its resignation, effective in 30 days. How would you expect the siblings to respond? If the siblings do nothing, what happens? As a practical matter, what does the resigning trustee do with the assets the trustee is holding?

Who would be in favor of the UTC approach, and why?

B. REMOVAL

Suppose the trustee or personal representative wants to continue in office, but the settlor or beneficiaries want to remove the fiduciary. Unless the will or trust instrument authorizes the beneficiaries to remove the trustee, the dissatisfied settlor or beneficiares will have to petition for judicial removal of the trustee. As the following case illustrates, removal is far from automatic:

Kappus v. Kappus

Supreme Court of Texas, 2009.
284 S.W.3d 831.

■ JUSTICE WILLETT delivered the opinion of the Court.

This appeal concerns whether an independent executor's alleged conflict of interest-here, a good-faith dispute over the executor's percentage ownership of estate assets-requires his removal as a matter of law. Probate Code section 149C lists several grounds for removing an executor, but "conflict of interest" (either actual or potential) is not among them, and we refuse to engraft such a test onto the statute. Accordingly, as none of the conditions for removal under section 149C were met in this case, we reverse the court of appeals' judgment and reinstate the trial court's order denying the motion to remove.

I. Background

In the 1980s, James Kappus, his brother John, and their father Walter formed a partnership called Kappus Farms, which purchased 49.482 acres of land in Anderson County. In 1991, James married Sandra, and they had two children. Walter Kappus died in 2001, which led to the unofficial dissolving of the Kappus Farms partnership. After Walter's will was probated, James and John owned the Anderson County land 50/50 as co-tenants. Throughout the time they owned the land, several improvements were added to the property: some by James alone, some by James and Sandra, and some by John alone.

In 2004, James and Sandra divorced. As part of the divorce proceedings, Sandra was given an equitable lien on the real estate for her half of the community improvements made to the land. After the divorce was final, James executed a new will that named John as independent executor (an appointment that nobody challenged) and Sandra's brother as alternative independent executor. The will also set up a testamentary trust with James's children as beneficiaries and John as trustee.

James died in 2005 after a long illness. John initiated probate proceedings, qualified as independent executor, and was issued letters testamentary. As part of the administration of the estate, John intended to pay off James's debts by selling the Anderson County property with the improvements and splitting the proceeds 50/50 between the estate and himself. A buyer offered $110,000 in cash and also agreed to assume a $7,000 debt on a double-wide mobile home, which was one of the improvements on the property.

Sandra, on behalf of her children, opposed the proposed distribution from the property sale, contending the estate was owed more than 50% of the proceeds due to several improvements James had made to the property, and she obtained an injunction preventing the sale from closing. Sandra also sought to remove John as independent executor and trustee of the testamentary trust, alleging that he had a conflict of interest, wasted estate assets, refused to allow the children access to the Anderson County land, and incurred significant expenses in probating the will. After a hearing, the trial court issued an order and accompanying findings of fact and conclusions of law that refused to remove John and found that the Anderson County property should be divided 58.59% for the estate and 41.41% for John.

On appeal, Sandra claimed that the evidence was both legally and factually insufficient to support the trial court's property division and that the estate was owed at least 63.45% of the proceeds. Sandra also claimed the trial court erred as a matter of law in not removing John as both independent executor and trustee. The court of appeals affirmed the trial court's division of the property, but reversed the trial court's decision on removal. Citing Probate Code section 149C(5), the court held that John's shared ownership of the property created a conflict of interest. "Under these circumstances," the court of appeals concluded, "the trial court had no alternative but to remove John as" executor. John appealed his removal to this Court, and we now reverse.

II. Removal as Independent Executor

Since as early as 1848, a Texas testator has been able to opt for the independent administration of his estate including the right to pick his own independent executor. While this power is "well fixed in the Texas law," the testator's chosen executor can be removed under Probate Code section 149C(a), which states, "The county court ... may remove an independent executor when ..." and then lists six specific grounds for removal.[2]

To begin, the grounds to *remove* an independent executor *post*-appointment are different from those to *disqualify* an executor *pre*-appointment. Probate Code section 78 sets out five different bases for disqualification of a would-be executor, including "[a] person whom the court finds unsuitable." In contrast to this catch-all standard that confers broad trial-court discretion, section 149C lists six specific grounds for removal, none quite as expansive as unsuitability. Sandra claims that by being a co-owner of an estate asset, John had a conflict of interest. And when John attempted to sell the land and split the proceeds evenly, despite the estate being owed more than half the proceeds, that potential conflict became an actual conflict and harmed the estate. While no subsection specifically covers "conflict of interest" in those express terms, Sandra argues that such a conflict can justify removal under subsections (2), (5), and (6) of section 149C. We consider each of these subsections in turn.

A. Subsection (2)—"Misapplied or Embezzled"

Sandra's first allegation is that John misapplied or embezzled part of the property committed to his care. She claims that when John attempted to split the proceeds from the potential sale of the Anderson County land 50/50, he improperly tried to divert part of the proceeds to himself since it was ultimately decided that the estate was owed 58.59% of the proceeds.

The evidence here shows that this dispute was, at bottom, a good-faith disagreement between John and Sandra as to how to split the value of the improvements between John and the estate. The record contains no evidence of dishonesty or misappropriation on John's part, much less enough evidence to conclude that Sandra proved misapplication or embezzlement as a matter of law. Accordingly, the trial court did not abuse its discretion in failing to remove John as independent executor on this basis.

---

2. The grounds for removal are:

(1) the independent executor fails to return within ninety days after qualification, unless such time is extended by order of the court, an inventory of the property of the estate and list of claims that have come to the independent executor's knowledge;

(2) sufficient grounds appear to support belief that the independent executor has misapplied or embezzled, or that the independent executor is about to misapply or embezzle, all or any part of the property committed to the independent executor's care;

(3) the independent executor fails to make an accounting which is required by law to be made;

(4) the independent executor fails to timely file the affidavit or certificate required by Section 128A of this code;

(5) the independent executor is proved to have been guilty of gross misconduct or gross mismanagement in the performance of the independent executor's duties; or

(6) the independent executor becomes an incapacitated person, or is sentenced to the penitentiary, or from any other cause becomes legally incapacitated from properly performing the independent executor's fiduciary duties.

TEX. PROB.CODE § 149C(a)(1)–(6).

B. Subsection (5)—"Gross Misconduct or Gross Mismanagement"

Sandra's second allegation is that John committed gross misconduct or gross mismanagement vis-a-vis his actual conflict of interest The use of the adjective "gross" indicates that something beyond ordinary misconduct and ordinary mismanagement is required to remove an independent executor. Gross is defined as "[g]laringly obvious; flagrant." The question then we face today is whether a potential conflict of interest constitutes gross misconduct or gross mismanagement.

The Legislature has provided that creditors of the deceased can be granted letters of administration. Such creditors, by their very nature, have a conflict of interest by virtue of a claim against estate assets. Similarly, it is common for testators in Texas to name spouses (or business partners) as independent executors. If we judicially amended section 149C by declaring a per se removal rule for "conflict of interest" whenever spouse-executors have a shared interest in community property, and issues arise over the separate or community character of estate assets, the surviving spouse could be ousted. While Sandra contends removal would only be justified when the executor has actually asserted a claim adverse to the estate, it seems under her theory that once a beneficiary objects to an executor's proposed valuation and distribution of property, the executor's defense would constitute a conflict of interest that mandates removal. Such a rule, besides having no statutory anchor in the text of section 149C, would undermine the ability of Texas testators to name their own independent executor and also weaken the ability of an executor "free of judicial supervision, to effect the distribution of an estate with a minimum of cost and delay." And it would impose this extra-statutory restriction even if the testator was fully aware of the potential conflict when the executor was chosen.

A good-faith disagreement over the executor's ownership share in the estate is not enough, standing alone, to require removal under section 149C. The statute speaks of affirmative malfeasance, and an executor's mere assertion of a claim to estate property, or difference of opinion over the value of such property, does not warrant removal. A potential conflict does not equal actual misconduct. The court of appeals here did not list any instances of John's misconduct or mismanagement, let alone any that could be labeled "gross," a modifier that implies serious and willful wrongdoing.

We recognize there may be scenarios where an executor's conflict of interest is so absolute as to constitute what the statute terms "gross misconduct or gross mismanagement." In deciding whether an executor's conflict amounts to "gross misconduct or gross mismanagement," trial courts should take into consideration several factors, including the size of the estate, the degree of actual harm to the estate, the executor's good faith in asserting a claim for estate property, the testator's knowledge of the conflict, and the executor's disclosure of the conflict.

In this case, these factors cut squarely in John's favor: the estate was small; there was no actual harm to the estate since the trial court resolved the percentage-of-ownership issue; John asserted his claim in good faith;

and James knew that his brother's co-ownership of estate property might later pose allocation/valuation issues when he named John independent executor. As such, we cannot say that the trial court abused its discretion in failing to remove John as independent executor for gross misconduct or gross mismanagement.

C. Subsection (6)—"Legally Incapacitated"

Sandra's third allegation is that John is legally incapacitated from performing as independent executor. This subsection, as we construe it, is inapplicable to an alleged conflict of interest. An incapacitated person is "[a] person who is impaired by an intoxicant, by mental illness or deficiency, or by physical illness or disability to the extent that personal decision-making is impossible." A conflict of interest does not make it impossible for someone to make decisions. Nor was John under any other legal incapacity that prevented him from carrying out his duties. Accordingly, the trial court did not abuse its discretion in failing to remove John as independent executor on this basis.

III. Removal as Trustee

The second issue is whether the trial court erred in failing to remove John as trustee of the testamentary trust. The removal of a trustee is governed by Trust Code section 113.082. This section gives the trial court more leeway on removal than does the Probate Code, as its four grounds are not as narrow. In fact, in one subsection, the statute allows that "a court may, in its discretion, remove a trustee ... if ... the court finds other cause for removal." While the statute for removal of an independent executor is different from the statute for removal of a trustee, the fiduciary duties owed by both are similar. Given the similarities in the type of duties owed and the level of discretion given a trial court by the statute, we cannot say the trial court abused its discretion in not removing John as trustee when, viewing the same conduct, it was not error to keep him as independent executor.

IV. Conclusion

A good-faith disagreement between an executor and the estate over the percentage division and valuation of estate assets is not grounds for removal as a matter of law. Such a development would (1) depart from the specific grounds for removal listed in the statute, (2) frustrate the testator's choice of executor (particularly the common practice of appointing spouse-executors), and (3) impede the broader goal of supporting the independent administration of estates with minimal costs and court supervision. Accordingly, we reverse the court of appeals' judgment and reinstate the trial court's order denying the motion to remove John Kappus as independent executor and trustee.

NOTES AND QUESTIONS

1. A standard formulation is that "misconduct, not conflict of interest, merits removal of a fiduciary." Matter of Foss, 282 A.D. 509, 513, 125

N.Y.S.2d 105, 110 (1953). Why should that be? Why put beneficiaries at the mercy of a trustee or executor who has a personal interest in treating them unfavorably?

2. Did John Kappus breach any fiduciary duty? If he had, would that have been enough to warrant his removal? Should every breach of fiduciary duty mandate dismissal of the fiduciary? Consider the following:

a. The fiduciary fails to provide the trust beneficiaries with statutorily required annual reports or accountings. See Trust of Baird, 349 Mont. 501, 204 P.3d 703 (2009) (no removal).

b. Testator's will names his daughter as executor, and gives the daughter a life interest in his house on condition that she pay for maintenance, taxes, and insurance. The daughter-executor uses estate funds to pay for repairing a roof, replacing a porch, and paying taxes. Did the executor breach her fiduciary duty? Did the breach warrant removal? See Saccu's Appeal, 97 Conn.App. 710, 905 A.2d 1285 (2006) (no removal).

c. Mother created a revocable living trust, with the property to be distributed among her children at her death. At death, two of the children became successor co-trustees. The third child sought to remove his siblings because they had not distributed the trust property and planned to wait three years to make sure there were no claims against the estate. Should the trustees be removed? Does the answer depend on whether there was any evidence of claims against the estate? Should the answer depend on whether the trustees were taking fees, or running up expenses? See Estate of Socha, 18 Neb.App. 471, 783 N.W.2d 800 (2010) (trustee removed where there was no evidence of claims and where trustees had been paying various family members for services).

Why should some breaches of fiduciary duty result in removal, while others do not? Which breaches should lead to removal?

3. ***Friction Between Trustee and Beneficiaries.*** Should a court remove a trustee when the trustee and the beneficiaries are constantly at loggerheads, even though the trustee has not committed any breach of fiduciary duty? Although courts sometimes say that a fiduciary is subject to removal if its conduct causes mutual animosity, most courts refuse to remove trustees based on friction with the beneficiaries. See, e.g. Symmons v. O'Keeffe, 644 N.E.2d 631 (Mass. 1995).

If courts were willing to remove trustees merely because of friction with the beneficiaries, would that create an incentive for beneficiaries to quarrel with the trustee?

4. ***Standard of Review.*** In Kappus, the trial court had refused to remove the trustee. What role did that fact play in the court's decision? Should it have played any role? Many courts hold that trial court decisions on removal should be reviewed only for abuse of discretion. See, e.g. Estate of Baird, 349 Mont. 501, 204 P.3d 703 (2009).

SECTION VII. FIDUCIARY LITIGATION: WHO PAYS?

Consider the position of Sandra Kappus before she instituted the litigation in the Kappus case. She walks into your office contemplating litigation against her ex-brother-in-law, both to compel him to pay more than half of the property value to the trust, and to seek his removal as trustee. But she wants to know—as many clients do—who pays for the litigation. She understands that the ordinary American rule in civil litigation is that each party pays its own attorney fees. But she doesn't understand whether that rule applies to trust litigation, and if it does, how it applies.

For instance, suppose the American rule applies, and the trustee bears his own litigation costs. Does the trustee bear those costs personally, or can the trustee obtain reimbursement from the trust? Obviously, the answer to that question would be important to Sandra, because if the trustee can obtain reimbursement, she and her children (as beneficiaries of the trust) will in effect be paying for the attorney fees on both sides of the litigation. She may also want to know whether there is any way she can obtain reimbursement of her own attorney fees from the trust—on the theory that her litigation increased the value of the trust. (Of course, if she and her children are the only trust beneficiaries, it may not matter to her whether fees come from her own pocket or from the trust, but if there are other trust beneficiaries, it may matter a lot). And she may also ask whether there is any risk that the trustee will be able to recover the trust's attorney fees from Sandra.

Consider how you would advise Sandra in light of the following materials:

Rudnick v. Rudnick

Court of Appeals of California, Fifth Appellate District, 2009.
179 Cal.App.4th 1328, 102 Cal.Rptr.3d 493.

■ LEVY, ACTING P. J.

Appellants, Philip Rudnick, Robert Rudnick, and Milton Rudnick, are three of the beneficiaries of the Rudnick Estates Trust (RET) and hold a minority interest. Respondent, Oscar Rudnick, is the trustee of the RET. After the majority of the RET beneficiaries approved the sale of the RET's principal asset, the Onyx Ranch, respondent petitioned the probate court for instructions requesting approval of both the sale and the proposed distribution. Appellants opposed this petition.

The probate court concluded that appellants' opposition was primarily for the purpose of causing unnecessary delay in the sale and was in bad faith. The court then awarded approximately $226,000 in attorney fees and costs to respondent and ordered these fees charged against appellants' future trust distributions.

Appellants contend the probate court's order should be reversed because the court had neither equitable nor statutory authority to make this award. However, contrary to appellants' position, the probate court, as a court sitting in equity, had the authority to charge the awarded fees against appellants' trust interests. Accordingly, the order will be affirmed.

BACKGROUND

[In preparation for the trust's termination, the trustee set about liquidating the trust's assets. The trust instrument provided that no sale of assets would become effective until it was approved by a majority of trust beneficiaries. In 2007, the trustee provided the beneficiaries with drafts of an agreement selling the 68,000 acre Onyx Ranch—the trust's major asset—to CIM Group for $48 million. Although 60% of the beneficiaries voted to approve the sale, appellants Philip, Robert and Milton Rudnick opposed the sale, and sought appointment of a temporary trustee, together with an injunction against the sale.—eds.]

On February 21, 2008, respondent filed a petition in the probate court to obtain instructions to consummate the Onyx Ranch sale to CIM as required by the purchase and sales agreement and to approve a distribution of proceeds in accordance with the Ashe accounting. The purchase and sales agreement provided that if it was not approved by the court on or before May 4, 2008, the agreement would terminate. The hearing on this petition was set for April 3, 2008. However, appellants filed an ex parte application to vacate the April 3 date.

On April 17, 2008, appellants filed objections to the petition for instructions. According to appellants, the RET assets were worth substantially in excess of $48 million, the transaction violated respondent's fiduciary duty, and the transaction violated the terms of the RET.

The hearing on the objections commenced on April 21 and took over eight days. On May 2, 2008, the court ruled in respondent's favor and instructed him to consummate the sale.

Thereafter, respondent filed a motion to recover the attorney fees and costs incurred in connection with the petition for instructions and to charge that amount to appellants' future distributions from the RET based on appellants' bad faith conduct in opposing the petition. The probate court granted respondent's motion in the amount of $226,295.16 and ordered these fees charged to appellants' future trust distributions as requested.

The court concluded that appellants' opposition to the petition was not made in good faith. Rather, appellants' primary motivation in opposing the petition was to disrupt the sale by preventing respondent from closing by the due date. The court found that appellants created unnecessary delays and asserted disingenuous arguments causing the RET to incur significant legal expenses. Under these circumstances, the court concluded that it was not fair to burden the majority beneficiaries, who approved the sale of the Onyx Ranch to CIM in accordance with the terms of the RET, with the payment of these fees. The court noted that it appeared that appellants were either unwilling or incapable of understanding that they did not own the RET assets to the exclusion of the other beneficiaries. Appellants were partial owners who agreed many years ago that, in liquidating the RET assets, the majority of the beneficiaries would determine the conditions of such liquidation. Accordingly, appellants' "refusal to follow the protocol they agreed to cannot result in detriment to the other beneficiaries without consequences."

DISCUSSION

Appellants contend the probate court could not award attorney fees as costs or sanctions absent statutory authority or contract and thus the award was prohibited as a matter of law. Appellants rely on Bauguess v. Paine (1978) 22 Cal.3d 626 [150 Cal. Rptr. 461, 586 P.2d 942], wherein the California Supreme Court held that, apart from situations authorized by statute, attorney fees may not be awarded as a sanction under the trial court's supervisory power. This inherent supervisory power permits a court to take appropriate action to secure compliance with its orders, to punish contempt, and to control its proceedings. (Id. at p. 637.) The court reaffirmed this rule in Olmstead v. Arthur J. Gallagher & Co. (2004) 32 Cal.4th 804, 809 [11 Cal. Rptr. 3d 298, 86 P.3d 354].

However, this award was not made under the probate court's supervisory power. Rather, it was made under the broad equitable powers that a probate court maintains over the trusts within its jurisdiction. (Hollaway v. Edwards (1998) 68 Cal.App.4th 94, 99 [80 Cal. Rptr. 2d 166].)

It should first be noted that the attorneys hired by a trustee to aid the trust are entitled to reasonable fees paid from the trust assets. (Kasperbauer v. Fairfield (2009) 171 Cal.App.4th 229, 235 [88 Cal. Rptr. 3d 494].) This includes attorney fees incidental to litigation that benefits the trust. (Thomas v. Gustafson (2006) 141 Cal.App.4th 34, 44 [45 Cal. Rptr. 3d 639].) Further, the RET agreement itself provides that all expenses incurred by the trustee in administering or protecting the trust shall be a charge upon the trust estate. Thus, the attorney fees and costs incurred by the trustee in defending the petition for instructions are chargeable to trust assets.

Appellants do not dispute that the subject attorney fees and costs are payable from the trust. Appellants' objection is to the fact that this burden has been shifted entirely to their share of the trust estate.

The probate court charged the attorney fees to appellants' future trust distributions rather than the trust as a whole because it concluded that it would be unfair to burden the majority beneficiaries with the payment of the fees that were incurred in responding to appellants' bad faith opposition to the Onyx Ranch sale. Contrary to appellants' position, such an order is authorized by the probate court's equitable powers and authority over the administration of the trust. (Estate of Ivey (1994) 22 Cal.App.4th 873, 884 [28 Cal. Rptr. 2d 16].)

This rule was succinctly stated by the court in Conley v. Waite (1933) 134 Cal.App. 505 [25 P.2d 496]. "[W]hen an unfounded suit is brought against [the trustee] by the cestui que trust, attorney's fees may be allowed him in defending the action and may be made a charge against the interest in the estate of the party causing the litigation." (Id. at p. 506.) The court in Estate of Ivey followed Conley v. Waite and further noted, "That a probate court has equitable power to charge one beneficiary's share of a trust for frivolous litigation against the trust is supported by treatises." (Estate of Ivey, supra, 22 Cal.App.4th at p. 883.) As examples, the Ivey court quoted Bogert, Trusts and Trustees (rev. 2d ed. 1981) and Fratcher, Scott on Trusts (4th ed. 1988) as follows:

> " 'Courts having jurisdiction over trust administration have the power to allocate the burden of certain trust expenses to the income or principal account and not infrequently do so in connection with accountings or suits relating to the administration of the trust. Sometimes this authority is stated in statutory form, but it exists as part of the inherent jurisdiction of equity to enforce trusts, secure impartial treatment among the beneficiaries, and to carry out the express or implied intent of the settlor.' [Citation.] 'Where the expense of litigation is caused by the unsuccessful attempt of one of the beneficiaries to obtain a greater share of the trust property, the expense may properly be chargeable to that beneficiary's share.' [Citations.]"

(Estate of Ivey, supra, 22 Cal.App.4th at p. 883, italics added.) Thus, under established law, the probate court's order charging attorney fees to appellants' future trust distributions was permissible pursuant to its equitable supervision of the RET.[1]

The order is affirmed. Costs on appeal are awarded to respondent.

■ KANE, J., and POOCHIGIAN, J., concurred.

NOTES AND QUESTIONS

1. Who would have opposed allowing the trustee to recover its litigation expenses from the trust proceeds? Why?

2. In *Rudnick*, the trust was large enough that the court could assess the trust's costs against the share of the disgruntled beneficiaries. But suppose their share was smaller than the trust's legal costs. Would a court hold the beneficiaries personally liable for the trust's legal costs?

Suppose the trust had been a spendthrift trust. Could a court assess the trust's legal fees against the share of spendthrift trust beneficiaries? In Chatard v. Oveross, 179 Cal.App.4th 1098, 101 Cal.Rptr.3d 883 (2009),

---

1. Similarly, based on the probate court's equitable powers alone, it has been held that beneficiaries who have incurred attorney fees, either to vindicate their position as beneficiaries (Wells Fargo Bank v. Marshall (1993) 20 Cal.App.4th 447, 458 [24 Cal. Rptr. 2d 507]) or for the benefit of the trust (Estate of Reade (1948) 31 Cal.2d 669, 672 [191 P.2d 745]), are entitled to have those fees paid by the trust.

several trust beneficiaries established that the trustee, who was also a trust beneficiary, had breached her fiduciary duty. The court held that even though the trust included a spendthrift provision, the trustee-beneficiary's interest was reachable to satisfy a claim for breach of fiduciary duty. The court relied on the settlor's presumed intent. Would the analysis justify assessing legal fees against a beneficiary who brought frivolous litigation against the trustee?

3. Suppose the disgruntled beneficiaries had established that the Onyx Ranch was in fact worth $80 million, leading the court to hold that the trustee had breached its fiduciary duty in arranging a sale for $48 million. If the disgruntled beneficiaries had successfully enjoined the sale and persuaded the court to appoint a substitute trustee, who would have paid the trustee's litigation costs? The beneficiary's litigation costs? Consider the following excerpt from Matter of Kinzler, 195 A.D.2d 464, 465–66, 600 N.Y.S.2d 126 (1993).

> "The general rule is that, where legal services have been rendered [by a beneficiary's lawyer] for the benefit of the estate as a whole, resulting in the enlargement of all the shares of all the estate beneficiaries, reasonable compensation should be granted from the funds of the estate"(*Matter of Burns,* 126 A.D.2d 809, 812; *see also,* SCPA 2110). However, in such case, the services rendered must be substantial, and must be directed toward a bona fide issue, and may not be merely nominal in overcoming an obvious erroneous claim by the fiduciary (*see, Matter of Bellinger,* 55 A.D.2d 448, 451; *Matter of Lounsberry,* 226 App Div 291; *Matter of Graves,* 197 Misc. 638).
>
> At bar, the efforts of the respondents' attorney resulted in a directive that the attorney-fiduciary refund over $11,000 to the estate, plus interest in the amount of over $16,000, for a total of almost $28,000. Thus, clearly the distributive shares of all the beneficiaries of the estate were substantially enlarged by the efforts of the respondents' attorney.

4. Suppose now that the beneficiaries had been unsuccessful in their claim for breach of fiduciary duty, but the court had concluded that their claim was made in good faith to protect the trust. Who would have paid the trustee's litigation costs? The beneficiary's litigaton costs? See Capaldi v. Richards, 870 A.2d 493 (Del. 2005) (holding that in case of good faith unsuccessful claim designed to maximize value of trust, both beneficiaries and trustee can recover litigation costs from the trust itself).

5. Suppose a trust beneficiary brings an action to construe a trust instrument. Another beneficiary responds, disputing the plaintiff-beneficiary's construction of the trust instrument. Can the trustee appear, and recover its litigation expenses from the trust? Cf. Mears v. Addonizio, 336 N.J.Super. 474, 765 A.2d 260 (2001) (holding that when trustee takes no position in dispute between beneficiary and party who allegedly committed undue influence over trust settlor, trustee could not recover $20,000 in legal fees in connection with the litigation).

6. How much discretion should courts have in determining who should bear litigation costs? What reasons, if any, are there to treat fiduciary litigation differently from ordinary civil litigation?

INDEX

References are to Pages

ABATEMENT
Generally, 283–290.
Special rules concerning allocation of taxes, 291–293.

ACCOUNTING
See also Fiduciaries; Principal and Income.
Concepts of principal and income, 1088–1092.
Duty of fiduciary to account, 1092–1101.

ACCUMULATION OF INCOME
Charitable trusts, 698–737.

ACTS OF INDEPENDENT SIGNIFICANCE
See Facts of Independent Significance.

ADEMPTION
Extinction, by, 293–305.
Satisfaction, by, 305.

ADMINISTRATION OF TRUSTS
See also Fiduciaries.
Appointment, qualification and removal of fiduciary, 62, 81–82, 524, 1009, 1102–1107.
Contract liability, 1026.
Duties of fiduciary, 1041–11101.
Income and principal allocation, 1088–1093.
Portfolio management, 1067–1086.
Tort liability, 1021–1025.

ADMINISTRATORS AND EXECUTORS
See also Decedents' Estate Administration; Fiduciaries.
Appointment of, 1009.
Function of, 1006–1007.

ADOPTED PERSONS
Adult adoption, 116, 852–853.
Class gift, inclusion in, 845–854.
Equitable adoption, 120–121.
Intestate succession, 109.
Same-sex couples, 504–507.

ADVANCE DIRECTIVES
See also Health Care.
Generally, 974.

ADVANCEMENTS
Presumption, 165.
Requirement of a Writing, 165–166.
UPC, 165.

AFTER-BORN-CHILDREN
See Children; Future Interests.

ANCILLARY PROBATE
Generally, 1008.

ANTE-MORTEM PROBATE
Generally, 490–491.

ANTILAPSE STATUTES
Generally, 308–310.
Uniform Probate Code provision, 316–319.

ASSET PROTECTION TRUSTS
Generally, 618–639.

ATTESTATION
See Witnesses; Wills.

ATTORNEYS
See Legal Profession.

AVOIDING PROBATE
See also Will Substitutes.
Avoiding administration after death, 45–47, 60–64, 1006–1007.

BANK ACCOUNTS
Deposit in trust for another (Totten Trusts), 567–568,984–988.
Joint accounts, 57–58, 569–570.
POD accounts, 58–59, 569, 984.

BENEFICIARIES
Charity as, 698–710.
Class as. *See* Class Gifts.
Disclaimer (Renunciation), 154–164.
Pets as, 528–530.
Trust,
Failure to designate, 526.
Nature of interest, 519.
Power to terminate trust, 688–696.

CAPACITY
To make a trust, 533–534.
To make a will, 413–442.

CHARITABLE CORPORATIONS
Non-profit corporation as charitable, 705.

CHARITABLE GIFTS
Application of Rule Against Perpetuities, 898–899.
Tax advantages, 697.

CHARITABLE TRUSTS
Application of Rule Against Perpetuities, 898–899.
Cy pres doctrine, 710–736.
Discriminatory provisions, 726–736.
Enforcement, 707.
Purposes, 698–706.
Tax advantages, 697.

CHILDREN
Adoption, 109–120.
Non-marital children, 130–142.
Pretermitted child statutes, 213–220.
Reproductive technology, 142–147.
Same-sex couples, 115.

CLAIMS AGAINST DECEDENT'S ESTATE
See also Creditors' Rights.
Procedure and problems, 1013–1014.

CLASS GIFTS
Adopted members of the class, 845–854.
Application of anti-lapse statute to, 310–311.
Class-closing,
Assisted reproduction, 854–855.
Rule of convenience, 830–835.
Construction of, 828–868.
Decrease of class, 835–840.
Gifts of income, 865–868.
Increase in class membership, 829–834.
Lapse, 310–311.
Non-marital children, 854.
Rule Against Perpetuities applied to, 901–904.
Vested remainders subject to open, 796, 800.

CODICILS
See also Revocation of Wills.
Integration of wills, 262–268.
Republication by, 382.
Revocation by, 368.
Revocation of, 383.

COMMUNITY PROPERTY
Classification of property, 100–106, 212–213.
Generally, 100–106.

COMPENSATION OF ATTORNEY
See Fees.

COMPENSATION OF FIDUCIARY
Basis for determining, 1027–1030.

CONFLICTS OF INTEREST
Fiduciary conflicts, 1028, 1041–1054.
Lawyer representing both spouses, 34–35.

CONSERVATORSHIPS
Generally, 938–951.
Powers of the conservator, 941.
Procedure to appoint conservator, 939–940.

CONSTRUCTION OF WILLS
Abatement, 283–291.
Accessions during testator's lifetime, 304.
Ademption, 293–305.
Ambiguities, 333–3352.
Latent, 344–345.
Patent, 344–345.
Class gifts, 310–311.
Death of beneficiary before testator (lapse), 306.
Death without issue, 307.
Effect of failure of interest, 311.
Exoneration, 291.
Extrinsic evidence, 332–333.
Gift "to children," 310.
Integration, 262–263.
Survivorship express or implied, 803, 822.
Residue of a residue, 308.

CONSTRUCTIVE TRUST
Fraudulent conduct in execution of will, 471–472.
Generally, 548.
Nature and concept, 548.

CONTEST OF WILLS
See also Contest of Trusts, Probate.
Ante-mortem probate, 490.
Constructive trust, 548.
Grounds,
Fraud, 469–472.
Lack of testamentary formalities, 227–243.
Mistake, 353.
Testamentary incapacity, 413–442.
Undue influence, 442–469.
No-contest clauses, 486–487.
Standing to contest, 426.

CONTINGENT REMAINDERS
See Future Interests.

CONTINUATION OF DECEDENT'S BUSINESS
Generally, 1026–1027.

CONTRACTS
Agreement to make or not to revoke will, 389–405.
Fiduciary liability on, 1026.
Mutual wills, 397.
Power to appoint property, 763–765.
To make wills, 404–405.

CREDITORS' RIGHTS
Claims against,
Decedent's estate, 1012–1026.
Donee of power of appointment, 772–775.
Trust beneficiary, 600–656.
Continuation of decedent's business, 1026–1027.

CREDITORS' RIGHTS—Cont'd
Homestead exemption, 203.
Nonclaim statutes, 1014.
Notice, 1014–1021.
Standing of heir's creditor to contest will, 426.
Statutes of limitations, 1014.
Trust over which settlor retains control, 617–656.

CURTESY
See Spouse.

CUSTODIAL TRUSTS
See Trusts.

CY PRES DOCTRINE
Application to charitable gift, 710–736.

DEATH WITHOUT ISSUE
Class gifts, 842.
General principles, 802–803.

DECEDENT'S ESTATE ADMINISTRATION
See also Personal Representatives; Probate.
Acquisition of estate, 1006–1012.
Ancillary administration, 1008.
Claims against estate, 1010–1027.
Creditors' claims,
Post-death creditors, 1021–1027.
Pre-death creditors, 1010–1020.
Jurisdiction, 1008.
Letters testamentary, 1010.
Marshalling estate assets, 1010–10111.
Notice, 1014.
Operating business, 1027.
Procedure in general, 1009.
Reasons for administering, 1006.
Safeguarding property, 1010.

DEPENDENT RELATIVE REVOCATION ("DRR")
See also Revocation of Wills.
Generally, 384–389.

DESCENT
See also Intestate Succession.
Modern law, 68.
Table of consanguinity, 71.

DEVIATION FROM TRUST TERMS
See Trusts.
DISCLAIMER (Renunciation)
Expectancy, of, 154–164.
Bankruptcy, 159.
Elective share, 178–203.
General nature, 154.
Mechanics of, 161.
Public assistance, 160.
Tax consequences of, 160.
UPC, 161.

DISCRETIONARY TRUSTS
Generally, 550–556.

DISINHERITANCE
Children, 224.
Negative, 282.
Spouse, 170.

DIVIDENDS
See Principal and Income.

DIVORCE
Effect on will, 378–380.
Effect on trust, 592–593.

DOWER
See Spouse.

DURABLE POWERS OF ATTORNEY
See Powers of Attorney.

ELDERLY
See also Powers of Attorney.
Advance directives, 974.
Asset transfers, 641–656.
Health care decisions, 965–971.
Long-term care insurance, 982.
Medicaid, 982.
Medicare, 982.
Physician-assisted suicide, 980.

ELECTIVE SHARE
Augmented estate under UPC, 169, 180.
General nature of system, 167–170.
Nonprobate assets as subject to, 170–180.
Operation of statutes, 176–178.
UPC, 180–188.
Waiver, 196–203.

ESCHEAT
Generally, 72, 99.

ESTATE ADMINISTRATION
See Decedents' Estate Administration.

ESTATE TAX
See Taxation.

ETHICS
See also Legal Profession.
Drafting will devising property to lawyer, 457.
Lawyer as trustee, 565–566.
Marketing revocable trusts, 593–600.
Naming self as fiduciary for estate, 1040.
Naming self as lawyer for estate, 1040, 1052–1053.
Representation of both spouses, 34–35.
Safekeeping will for client, 242.
Witnessing will, 242.

EUTHANASIA
Generally, 969.

EXCULPATORY CLAUSES
Validity and construction, 566, 1086.

EXECUTORS
See Fiduciaries; Decedents' Estate Administration.

EXECUTION OF WILLS
See Wills.

EXONERATION
Intent to exonerate liens, 291.

EXPECTANCY OF HEIR
Assignment of, 164.
Disclaimer of, 154.

EXPENSES
See Principal and Income.

EXTRINSIC EVIDENCE
See Construction of Wills.

FACTS OF INDEPENDENT SIGNIFICANCE
Generally, 276.

FEDERAL TAXES
See Taxation.

FEES
See also Fiduciaries; Principal and Income.
Attorney,
As fiduciary, 1052.
As fiduciary's lawyer, 1030–1039.
Double-dipping, 1040.

FIDUCIARIES
See also Accounting; Decedents' Estate Administration; Administration of Trusts; Principal and Income.
Attorney for, 1064.
Care and skill required, 1054–1087.
Compensation, 1027–1030.
Conflict of interest, 1041–1053, 1102–1107.
Delegation of functions, 1061–1067.
Duties,
Accounting, 1092–1101.
Care, of, 1054–1087.
Informing Beneficiaries, 1100–1101.
Investing, 1067–10798.
Loyalty, 1041–1053.
Management, 1053–1060.
Removal, 1102–1107
Resignation, 1001
Safeguarding property, 1010.
Earmarking estate property, 1087.
Liability,
Exculpatory clauses, 566, 1079–1086.
For creditors' claims, 1012–1027.
Litigation costs, 1108–112.
Powers,
Continuation of decedent's business, 1026.
Distribution, 1010.
Invasion of principal, 779.
Investments (Portfolio Management), 1067–1079.
Management, 1053–1060.
Standard of Care, 1053–1054.

FRAUD
Effect on will, 472.
In the inducement, 469.
Remedy for, 471.

FUTURE INTERESTS
Classification, 793.
Construction of class gifts, 828–831.
"Divide and pay over" rule, 863.
Express conditions of survival, 803, 822–828.
Interests in transferees,
Contingent remainders, 795, 796, 802.
Executory interests, 801–802.
Indefeasibly vested remainder, 795–796, 800, 802.
Vested remainder subject to complete divestment (or defeasance), 796–800, 802.
Vested remainder subject to open, 795–796, 800–802.
Reversionary interests,
Possibility of reverter, 794.
Reversion, 794.
Right of entry, 794.
Survivorship,
Decrease in class membership, 835–840.
Express conditions of, 822–828.
UPC, 818–821.
Transferability,
Tax consequences, 764.
Vesting,
Presumption in favor of early, 812–813.
Worthier Title, Doctrine of, 864.

GAY COUPLES
See Same–Sex Couples.

GENERATION-SKIPPING TRANSFER TAX (GST)
See Taxation.

GIFTS
Advancement in intestate estate, 164–165.
Causa mortis, 52.
Effect upon devise or bequest, 305.
"Heirs," gifts to, 855.
Inter vivos, 47–52.
Requirements for, 47–52.

GUARDIANSHIPS
For incompetent adults, 938.
Person and property, 938.
Trust as way to avoid necessity for, 951.

HEALTH CARE
See also Physician–Assisted Suicide.
Advance directives, 974.
Do-not-resuscitate orders, 979.
Durable power of attorney, for, 972.
Living will. *See* Advance directives.
Long-term care insurance, 983.
Planning for incapacity, 938.
Surrogate decisionmaker, 951.

HEALTH CARE, DURABLE POWER OF ATTORNEY FOR
See Health Care; Powers of Attorney.

HEIRS
Defined, 67.
Gifts to heirs of grantor, 855.
Pretermitted, 213.
Testamentary gift to testator's heirs, 855.

HOLOGRAPHIC WILLS
See also Wills.
Requirements for, 250–259.

HOMESTEAD
Rights of family, 203–205.

HOMICIDE
Murderer's right to take under will or intestacy, 16–24.
UPC, 25–26.

HOMOSEXUAL COUPLES
See Same–Sex Couples.

INCAPACITY
Estate planning for, 938.

INCOME TAXATION
See Taxation.

INCORPORATION BY REFERENCE
Nature and requirements, 262, 269–275.
Pour over trusts, 576.

INHERITANCE
See Intestate Succession.

INSANE DELUSION
Effect on validity of will, 428–437.
Lucid intervals, 424.

INSURANCE
Estate planning, 999–1000.
Rights of surviving spouse in, 193.
Tax advantages of, 1002–1004.

INSURANCE TRUSTS
Nature and validity, 1004.

INTEGRATION OF WILLS
See Wills.

INTERPRETATION AND CONSTRUCTION OF WILLS
See Construction of Wills; Wills.

INTER VIVOS TRUSTS
See Trusts.

INTESTATE SUCCESSION
Adopted persons, 109.
Advancements, 164–166.
Collateral relatives, 69, 92–100.
Community property, 100–106, 212–213.
Degrees of kinship, 69–71.
Disclaimer, 154–164.
Distribution,
  Per capita, 88.
  Per stirpes, 86–87.
  Representation, by, 88–90.
Escheat, 72, 99.
Expectancy, assignment and release of, 164.

INTESTATE SUCCESSION—Cont'd
Halfbloods, 107–108.
Homestead and exemption statutes, 203–205.
Homicide, 16.
Issue, 69.
Non-marital children, 130–135.
Offenses barring succession, 16, 91–92.
Renunciation. *See* Disclaimer.
Reproductive technology, 142–147.
Simultaneous death, 147–154.
Surviving spouse, 72–85.
Table of consanguinity, 71.
Theories underlying statutes, 65.
Uniform Parentage Act, 132–135, 140.

INVESTMENTS
See Portfolio Management.

ISSUE
Death without, 803.
Defined, 68.

JOINT TENANCY
  Generally, 53.
Right of survivorship, 571.

JOINT WILLS
Contractual nature and effect, 389–405.

JURISDICTION OF PROBATE COURTS
Ancillary, 1008.
Estate or trust involving several states, 1008.
Probate of wills and will contests, 1009–1010.

KILLER OF DECEDENT
Right to take under will or intestate law, 16.

LAPSE
Anti-lapse statute applications, 306–324.
Class gifts, 310.

LEGACIES, DEVISES AND BEQUESTS
Demonstrative, 290.
General, 288.
Residuary, 288.
Specific, 288.

LEGAL PROFESSION
Duty of competence, 35.
Ethics,
  Drafting will devising property to lawyer, 466.
  Drafting will favoring another client, 443.
Lawyer as trustee, 566.
Malpractice, 35.
Marketing revocable trusts, 593–600.
Naming self as fiduciary for estate, 566, 1040.
Naming self as lawyer for estate, 1041.
Representation of both spouses, 34–35.
Safekeeping will for client, 242.
Witnessing will, 236.

LESBIAN COUPLES
See Same–Sex Couples.

LETTERS TESTAMENTARY
See Decedents' Estate Administration.

LIFE INSURANCE
Estate planning, 1002–1004.
Forms,
  Term life, 1000.
  Whole life, 1000.
Life insurance trusts, 1005.
Tax consequences, 1003.

LIMITATIONS, STATUTE OF
See Creditors' Rights.

LIVING PROBATE
See Ante-mortem Probate.

LIVING TRUSTS
See Trusts.

LIVING WILLS
See Advance Directives.

LONG-TERM CARE INSURANCE
See Health Care.

LOST OR DESTROYED WILLS
See Wills.

LOYALTY, DUTY OF
See Fiduciaries.

MALPRACTICE
See Legal Profession.

MARITAL DEDUCTION
See Taxation.

MARRIAGE
Partnership theory of, 167, 168–169, 179.

MARSHALLING ASSETS
See Decedents' Estate Administration.

MERGER
Legal and equitable interest in trust, 524–525.

MINORS
Use of trusts to provide for, 548–549.

MISTAKE
Construction of will to remedy, 353.
Modification of trust to correct, 689–696.
Will resulting from mistake, 353.

MODERN PORTFOLIO THEORY
See Portfolio Management.

MODIFICATION OF TRUSTS
See Trusts.

MURDER OF ANCESTOR
Murderer's right to take under will or intestacy, 16.

MUTUAL WILLS
See Contracts.

NO-CONTEST CLAUSES
See Contest of Wills.

NONCLAIM STATUTES
See Creditors' Rights.

NON-MARITAL CHILDREN
Inclusion in class gift, 854.
Intestate succession, 130.

NONTESTAMENTARY ACTS
See Facts of Independent Significance; Gifts.

NOTICE
  See also Creditors' Rights.
Creditors of decedent, 1014–1021.
Heirs on probate, 1009–1010.

OMITTED CHILDREN
See Children; Heirs.

OMITTED SPOUSE
See Spouse.

OFFSHORE TRUSTS
Generally, 619–629.

PAYABLE-ON-DEATH ACCOUNTS
Generally, 58.

PERPETUITIES, RULE AGAINST
See Rule Against Perpetuities.

PERSONAL REPRESENTATIVES
  See also Administration of Trusts; Decedents' Estate Administration; Fiduciaries; Probate.
Accounting, 1093–1099.
Ancillary administration, 1008.
Appointment, 81–82.
Compensation, 1027–1030.
Delegation, 1061–1066.
Function, 1010–1012.
Investment duty, 1066–1079.
Liability in contract and tort, 1025–1026.
Litigation costs, 1108–1112.
Operating a business, 1026–1027.

PHYSICIAN-ASSISTED SUICIDE
Legislation concerning, 979–980.

POD ACCOUNTS
See Payable-on-Death Accounts.

PORTFOLIO MANAGEMENT
Common stocks, 1067.
Continuation of business, 1026.
Diversification, 1076–1077.
Fiduciary duties, 1067–1077.
Modern Portfolio Theory, 1067, 1088–1089.
Prudent investor rule, 1067.
Retention, 1077.
Social investing, 1078–1079.
Standard of care, 1067.

POUR-OVER TRUSTS
Validity and effect, 576.

POWERS OF APPOINTMENT
Agency theory, 753.
Allocation of assets, 761–762.

POWERS OF APPOINTMENT—Cont'd
Appointment in trust, 754–755.
Bankruptcy, 775.
Benefit to non-object of special power, 757–763.
Choice of law, 752.
Classification,
General, 739.
Capture doctrine, 761.
Special, 739.
Limits on the holder of, 762.
Contracts,
To appoint, 763.
To release, 765.
Creation of new powers and future interests, 757.
Creditors of the donee, 772–775.
Exclusive or non-exclusive nature, 740.
Exceeding the power's scope, 757.
Exercise by residuary clause, 750–751.
Failure to exercise effectively, 760–762.
Intent to exercise, 747.
Perpetuities, Rule Against, 905–913.
Release of, 765–772.
Scope, 739.
Tax factors,
Generally, 742.
Powers of invasion,
Limited, 786.
Over entire principal, 779.
Property included in power holder's estate, 777.
Terminology, 738–741.
Theory at common law, 753.
Time of appointment, 740.

POWERS OF ATTORNEY
Durable powers generally, 951.
Fiduciary duty of attorney, 955.
Funding revocable trust by, 963.
Health care application, 972.
Risks associated with use of, 964.
Springing, 958.
Use in planning for incapacity, 951.

PRECATORY LANGUAGE
Generally, 534.

PRENUPTIAL AGREEMENTS
Validity, 196–201.
Waiver of elective share, 202.

PRETERMITTED HEIRS
See Children; Heirs.

PRETERMITTED SPOUSE
See Spouse.

PRINCIPAL AND INCOME
Conflict between income and remainder beneficiaries, 1088.
Modern Portfolio Theory (MPT), 1088.
Uniform Principal and Income Act (1997), 1091.
Unitrust, 1089.

PROBATE
See also Contest of Wills; Decedents' Estate Administration.
Avoidance of judicial proceedings, 45, 58.
Contest of will,
Effect of no-contest clause, 486–487.
Grounds for, 413.
Standing to, 426.
Effect of decree, 1010.
Interested parties, 1009–1010.
Lost or destroyed wills. *See* Wills.
Need for, 1006.

PROFESSIONAL RESPONSIBILITY
See Legal Profession.

PROTECTIVE TRUSTS
Nature and freedom from claims of creditors of beneficiary, 617–639.

PRUDENT INVESTOR RULE
See Portfolio Management.

PURCHASE MONEY RESULTING TRUST
Trust arising from payment, 547–548.

RELEASE OF EXPECTANCY
Heirs release to ancestor, 154.

REMAINDERS
See also Future Interests.
Classification of, 795–797.

RENUNCIATION
See Disclaimer.

REPUBLICATION
Codicil republishing will, 382.

RESULTING TRUSTS
Express trust with no beneficiary named, 548.
General nature, 548.

RETIREMENT PLANS
Choosing beneficiaries, 999.
Defined benefit plans, 988.
Defined contribution plans, 988.
IRAs, 988–989.

REVIVAL OF REVOKED WILLS
See also Dependent Relative Revocation.
By revocation of revoking will, 382.
Codicil, by, 383.

REVOCABLE TRUSTS
See Trusts.

REVOCATION OF TRUSTS
See Trusts.

REVOCATION OF WILLS
Acts directed to instrument, 369.
Codicil, by, 368.
Dependent relative revocation, 384–389.
Destruction of copy, 376.
Lost or destroyed wills, 375.

REVOCATION OF WILLS—Cont'd
Age, 413.
Mistake, 353.
Operation of law, by, 378.
Partial revocation, 376–377.
Physical act, by, 369.
Revalidation of revoked will, 382–383.
Revival by revocation of revoking will, 382.
Subsequent instrument, by, 367.

RULE AGAINST PERPETUITIES
Application to revocable trusts, 885.
Charitable gifts and trusts, 898.
Class gifts, 901.
Consequences of invalidity, 899.
Gift in default of appointment, 913.
History, 870.
Interests subject to, 873–876.
Measuring life, 878–879.
Modern reform, 924.
Policy behind, 870–873.
Powers of appointment,
  Validity of exercise of,
    Relation-back doctrine, 907.
    Second-look doctrine, 913.
  Validity of,
      Generally, 905.
    Gifts in default of appointment, 914.
Reform, 924.
Remote possibilities,
  Fertile octogenarian, 889.
  Precocious toddler, 892.
  Slothful executor, 897.
  Unborn widow, 893.
Savings clauses, 917.
USRAP, 927.
Vesting, 876.
Wait-and-see doctrine, 926.

SAME–SEX COUPLES
Adoption, 115.
Adult adoption, 504–507.
AIDS, 492.
Charitable remainder trusts, 503.
Estate planning strategies for, 502–504.
Intestate succession, 84–85
Undue influence, 493.

SIGNATURE
Placement of, in will, 236.

SIMULTANEOUS DEATH ACT
Operation of statute, 152–153.

SPECIMEN INSTRUMENTS
Codicil, 368.
Revocable Trust, 571.
Will, 405.

SPENDTHRIFT TRUST
Claim for alimony, 614.
Nature and effectiveness, 607.

SPOUSE
Allowance during administration, 205.
Community property, 100,212.
Curtesy, 169.

SPOUSE—Cont'd
Dower, 169.
Effects of election on other testamentary gifts, 169.
Election against will, 169.
Forced share, 169.
Homestead, 203.
Marriage after execution of will, 206.
Pretermitted, 381.
Rights in account deposited in trust for another, 569.
Rights in ERISA plans, 998.
Rights in insurance proceeds and life insurance trust, 193.
Rights in intestate estate, 72.
Rights in property subject to general power of appointment, 167–170.
Rights in revocable living trust, 592.
Social and legal developments in protection of, 168–169.
Unintentional disinheritance of, 206.

STATUTE OF FRAUDS
Compliance with in creating trusts, 545.

STATUTE OF USES
Generally, 525.

SUBSTANTIAL COMPLIANCE
See Wills

SURVIVORSHIP
  See also Simultaneous Death Act.
Class gifts, 828.
Express and implied conditions of, 803, 822.

TAXATION
Charitable gifts, 518.
Creation of trusts to minimize taxes, 656–671.
Estate and inheritance taxes,
  Mechanics of, 511.
  Estate planning to reduce, 656–657.
  Generation-skipping tax, 510, 776.
Gift tax,
  Annual gift exclusion, 512.
  Gifts between spouses, 518.
  Impact of taxes on testamentary gifts, 515.
Integration of estate and gift tax, 514.
Marital deduction, 517.
Power of appointment, 742.
Qualified terminable interest trust (QTIP), 667.
Stepped-up basis, 514.
Unified credit, 511.

TENTATIVE TRUSTS
See Totten Trusts.

TERMINATION OF TRUSTS
  See also Trusts.
Generally, 672–696.

TESTAMENTARY CAPACITY
Age, 413.
Justifications for, 425.
Lucid intervals, 424.
Mental capacity in general, 413.

TOD ACCOUNTS
See Transfer-on-Death Accounts.

TORTS
Fiduciary liability for, 1021–1025.

TOTTEN (TENTATIVE) TRUSTS
See also Trusts.
Effect of Will Provisions on, 984.
Special problems concerning, 568.
Trust intent, 568.

TRANSFER-ON-DEATH ACCOUNTS
Generally, 59.

TRANSGENDERED TESTATORS
Generally, 85, 491.

TRUSTEES
See also Fiduciaries, Portfolio Management.
Attorney as, 566.
Beneficiary as, 524.
Capacity to serve, 524.
Compensation, 1027–1028.
Delegation of duties, 1061.
Duty to safeguard property, 1088.
Failure to name, 524.
Liability,
Contract and tort, 1026, 1027.
Litigation costs, 1109.
Merger doctrine, 525.
Powers,
Invasion of principal, 779.
Termination of trust, 672.
Qualification, 524.
Removal, 1102.
Resignation, 1101.
Settlor as, 524.

TRUSTS
See also Beneficiaries; Constructive Trusts; Portfolio Management; Resulting Trusts; Termination of Trusts; Totten Trusts; Trustees.
Active and passive trusts, 525.
Active duties of trustee, 525.
Animals as beneficiaries, 529–530.
Asset protection 619–631.
Beneficiary,
Determined in future, 671.
Nature of interest, 525.
Necessity of, 526.
Who can be, 526–527.
Capacity to make, 533.
Charitable trust, 697.
Creation of,
By will, 519.
Inter vivos, 519.
Creditors' rights against, 617.
Crummey trust, 658.

TRUSTS—Cont'd
Discretionary, 550, 600.
Durable power of attorney as alternative to, 951.
Formalities, 533, 540–548.
Generation-skipping trust, 670.
Government benefits, 641.
Intent, 534.
Life insurance trust, 1004.
Living trust. *See* Revocable trusts.
Marital deduction trust, 664.
Merger doctrine, 524.
Modification of trust,
Generally, 672.
Reasons for,
Impracticability of trust purposes, 695.
Mistake, 689.
Provision for needy beneficiaries, 695–696.
No-contest clauses, 575.
Offshore trusts, 619–631.
Passive, 525.
Pets, 528–529.
Precatory language, 534.
Property, 532.
Qualified terminable interest trust (QTIP), 667.
Reasons for creating living trusts, 588.
Requisites, 522.
Res. *See* Property.
Revocable trusts, 570.
Revocation, 671.
Settlor,
As trustee, 524.
Spendthrift trust,
Alimony and support claims against, 614–615.
Generally, 607.
Spray or sprinkle trust, 565.
Standby trust, 533.
Supplemental needs trust, 646.
Support trust, 550, 600.
Tax factors in creating,
Income, 664.
Generation-skipping, 670.
Gift, estate and inheritance, 664.
Termination, 671.
Trustee,
Beneficiary as, 524.
Selection of, 524.
Terminology and function, 520.

UNDUE INFLUENCE
See also Contest of Wills.
Effect on validity of will, 442.
Nature of confidential relationship,
Attorney-client, 466.
Nursing home operators, 467.
Spiritual advisors, 467.
Presumptions, 454.

WIDOWS' AND WIDOWERS' RIGHTS
See Spouse.

WILL SUBSTITUTES
Joint tenancy, 53.
Life insurance, 999.
POD accounts, 58–59, 567, 984.
Retirement plan assets, 988.
Revocable trusts, 571.

WILLS
See also Probate; Revocation of Wills.
Attestation, 236.
Beneficiary as witness, 238.
Capacity to execute, 413.
Classification of legacies, devises and bequests, 288, 290.
Codicil, 368.
Construction to rectify mistake, 353.
Contracts, 404.
Dependent relative revocation (DRR), 384–389.
Electronic wills, 260.
Execution of,
Attestation by witness, 236.
Attestation clause, 240.
Formalities, 227, 229–230.
Intention to attest, 234.
Presence, 230.
Procedure recommended, 241.
Request to witnesses, 241.
Self-proving affidavit, 241.
Sequence of signing, 242.
Signature, 235.
Extrinsic evidence, 332.
Facts of independent significance, 276.
Holographic wills, 250.
Incorporation by reference, 262.
Integration, 262.
Joint wills, 389.
Limitations on testamentary power, 8–16.
Living wills. *See* Advance directives.
Lost or destroyed wills, 375.
Mistake,

WILLS—Cont'd
Mistake—Cont'd
In the inducement, 354.
Of fact, 355.
Presence requirement, 230.
Pretermitted heirs. *See* Children; Heirs.
Pretermitted spouse. *See* Spouse.
Reasons for formalities, 228.
Renunciation (disclaimer) by devisee or legatee, 154.
Republication by codicil, 382.
Restrictions on testation, 8–16.
Revocation. *See* Revocation of Wills.
Revival by revocation of revoking will, 382.
Safekeeping of, 242.
Sample will, 405.
Self-proving affidavit, 240.
Signature of testator,
Location, 236.
Nature of, 235.
Necessity, 235.
Signature of witness, 234.
Statute of Frauds, 227.
Statute of Wills, 228.
Statutory and form wills, 259.
Substantial compliance, 243, 248.
Tortious interference, 473.
Witnesses,
Beneficiary as witness, 238.
Competence, 238.
Interested, 238.
Number, 236

WITNESSES
See also Wills.
Competence, 236.
Interested, 238.
Number, 236.

WORTHIER TITLE, DOCTRINE OF
See also Future Interests.
Gifts to heirs of grantor, 864.

†